UNIBANCO
GUIDES

BRAZIL

ABOUT THIS GUIDEBOOK

The hotels, restaurants, attractions, agencies, guides, and other establishments and services listed in the *Brazil Guide* were selected by a team of specialized reporters. No compensation of any kind was accepted from the establishments mentioned. Sponsor Unibanco exercised no control over the content of this guide.

Restaurant price categories were established by calculating the price for the most popular choice plus a 10% service fee. Hotel prices are based on the daily rate for a double occupancy room.

Addresses, telephone numbers, business hours, and prices were supplied by the establishments and verified and updated by the *Guide's* researchers. However, the *Guide* cannot be responsible for any inaccuracies or changes after the publication date (May 2008). Please note that business hours and service prices are subject to constant changes due to fluctuations in demand between high and low seasons for tourism and should be confirmed in advance whenever possible.

Before traveling, visitors are advised to consult the Highway Patrol (see Useful Information, page 568) for information regarding road conditions and toll fees along the proposed route.

Collaborators

André Corrêa do Lago, Daniel Mason, José Hamilton Ribeiro, Liz Calder, Marcos Caetano, Marcos Sá Corrêa, Nelson Motta, Niède Guidon, Ricardo Legorreta, Sebastião Salgado, Thomaz Souto Corrêa, and Valentino

Sponsor

⬡ UNIBANCO

2008

BEÍ
Rua Dr. Renato Paes de Barros, 717, 4º and
CEP 04530-001 Itaim-Bibi São Paulo SI
Tel.: (11) 3089-8855 Fax: (11) 3089-8899
www.bei.com.br bei@bei.com.br

UNIBANCO
GUIDES

BRAZIL

BEĨ

Concept, editorial coordination, editing,
cover, graphic design, and layout
BEĨ

Editing
BEĨ

Desktop Publishing
BEĨ

Project Consultant and Editor
Ben Harder

Associate Editors
Jenny Pegg and Gwen Glazer

Translation
Alison Entrekin and Lynne Reay Pereira

Proofreading
Arlete Sousa and Ben Harder

Fact Checking
Juliana Raddatz Macedo

Maps and Illustrations
Luiz Fernando Martini,
Ronaldo Lopes Teixeira, and
Sírio José Braz Cançado

BEĨ Team
EDITORIAL DIRECTORS:
Marisa Moreira Salles and Tomas Alvim
SENIOR EDITORS: Francesca Angiolillo, Laura
Aguiar, Marcelo Pen, and Ricardo Ditchun
REPORTING: Andressa Paiva, Fernanda
Quinta, and Laura Folgueira
DESIGN AND LAYOUT: Alexandre Costa,
Américo Freiria, and Yumi Saneshigue
DESIGN ASSISTANTS: Paulo Albergaria and
Rosilene de Andrade
TRAINEE: William Rabelo
GRAPHIC PRODUCTION: Luis Alvim
MARKETING: Adriana Domingues
ADMINISTRATIVE STAFF: Ana Paula Guerra
and Gercilio Corrêa
PRESS AND PUBLIC RELATIONS:
Laura Folgueira
SALES: Fernanda Gomensoro and
Tatiane de Oliveira Lopes

Printing and Bound
Ipsis

Dados Internacionais de Catalogação na Publicação (CIP)
(Câmara Brasileira do Livro, SP, Brasil)

Unibanco Guides Brazil / [conception, editorial coordination, editing,
cover, graphic design and layout Bei; translation Alison Entrekin and Lynne
Reay Pereira ; maps and illustrations Luiz Fernando Martini ... et al.]. – 2. ed
rev. – São Paulo: Bei Comunicação, 2008. – (Brazil Unibanco Guides)

Título original: Guia Unibanco Brasil
Vários colaboradores. Vários ilustradores.
ISBN 978-85-7850-001-6

1. Brasil - Descrição e viagens - Guias 2. Turismo - Brasil I. Martini, Luiz
Fernando. II. Série.

08-05761   CDD-918.1

Índice para catálogo sistemático:
1. Brasil : Guias turísticos   918.1

TABLE OF CONTENTS

How to Use This Guidebook   9

Portuguese Glossary and
  Phrasebook   11

Introduction

History   17
The Brazilian People   26
Cuisine   29
  The Quest for Perfect Feijoada,
    by Thomaz Souto Corrêa   34
Carnival   36
Folk Art   39
Visual Arts   43
Design and Fashion   47
  Brazil Lights up the Runways,
    by Valentino   50
Architecture   53
  Modern Architecture in Brazil,
    by André Corrêa do Lago   56
Cinema   58
Popular Music   61
  Brazilian Music,
    by Nelson Motta   66
Football   69
  Brazilian Football,
    by Marcos Caetano   70
Adventure and Ecotravel   73
Flora and Fauna   77

THE SOUTHEAST   88

Rio de Janeiro   89
The City of Rio de Janeiro   90
  Historical Center   90
  Cinelândia and Environs   98
  Lapa   103
  Santa Teresa   105
  Glória and Catete   107
  Cosme Velho, Maracanã,
    and São Cristóvão   108
  Flamengo, Botafogo, and Urca   109
    Panoramic Views and
      Fashionable Beaches   110
  Copacabana   112
  Casual Dining   114
  Ipanema and Leblon   115

Outdoor Rio   121
  Lagoa Rodrigo de Freitas
    and Jardim Botânico   123
  Gávea and São Conrado   126
  Barra da Tijuca and Recreio
    dos Bandeirantes   128
  Carnival   130
The City of Niterói   132
Mountains and Inland   134
  Petrópolis   134
  Parque Nacional da Serra
    dos Órgãos   138
  Teresópolis   139
  Vassouras   139
  Visconde de Mauá   140
  Parque Nacional do Itatiaia   142
The South Coast   143
  Angra dos Reis   143
  Ilha Grande   145
  Paraty   147
    A Literary Paradise,
      by Liz Calder   150
The North Coast   152
  Búzios   152
  Cabo Frio   155
  Arraial do Cabo   156

São Paulo   159
City of São Paulo   160
  Praça da Sé and Environs   160
  Praça da República
    and Environs   163
  Luz and Environs   165
  Mercado Municipal
    de São Paulo   168
  Liberdade   170
  Higienópolis   171
  Avenida Paulista   173
  Parque do Ibirapuera   176
  Jardins   179
  Pinheiros   182
  Vila Madalena   183
  Morumbi   184
  Other Museums and
    Outdoor Trips   186
  Cultural Activities   188
  Nightlife   189

Mountain Ranges	190
Campos do Jordão	190
Santo Antônio do Pinhal	191
Cunha	192
The North Coast	193
São Sebastião	193
Ilhabela	194
Ubatuba	196
Best Beaches	198
Historical Cities	200
Santos	200
Santana de Parnaíba	202
Bananal	203
The Countryside and the Coast	204
Brotas	204
Serra da Bocaina	205
Juréia	206

■ MINAS GERAIS	207
Belo Horizonte	208
Around Belo Horizonte	211
Sabará	212
Parque Natural do Caraça	213
Ouro Preto	214
Ouro Preto's Historical Center	215
Other Attractions	220
Ouro Preto, my Fantasy Land by Ricardo Legorreta	221
Mariana	222
Congonhas	223
Tiradentes	226
Historical Center	226
Other Attractions	227
São João del-Rei	229
Diamantina	230
Estrada Real	232

■ ESPÍRITO SANTO	233
Vitória	234
Historical Center	234
Vila Velha	237
Guarapari	238
Serra Capixaba	239
Domingos Martins	239
Itaúnas	241

■ THE NORTHEAST	242
■ BAHIA	243
Salvador	244
Pelourinho	244
Cidade Baixa	250
From the Historical Center to Barra	251
Bonfim and Environs	252
Carnival in Salvador	253
Syncretism and Candomblé Temples in Bahia	255
Beaches	256
Baía de Todos os Santos	258
Recôncavo Baiano	259
The North Coast	260
Estrada do Coco	260
Linha Verde	262
Morro de São Paulo	263
Ilha de Boipeba	265
Península de Maraú and Baía de Camamu	266
Itacaré	268
Ilhéus	269
Porto Seguro	272
Arraial d'Ajuda	274
Trancoso	275
Cumuruxatiba and Ponta do Corumbau	277
Abrolhos	278
Chapada Diamantina	279
Mucugê	281
Parque Nacional da Chapada Diamantina	282
Andaraí and Igatu	284

■ SERGIPE	285
Aracaju	286
São Cristóvão	288

■ ALAGOAS	289
Maceió	290
North Coast	292
Barra de Santo Antônio	292
São Miguel dos Milagres	293
Japaratinga	294
Maragogi	294
South Coast	295

Mouth of the São Francisco River 296
   Penedo 296
   Piaçabuçu 298
   Piranhas 298

■ PERNAMBUCO 299
Recife 300
   Beaches 300
   Historical Center 300
   Santo Antônio, São José,
     and Boa Vista 303
   Environs of Recife 307
Olinda 309
Ilha de Itamaracá 313
The South Coast 314
   Porto de Galinhas and Tamandaré 314
Fernando de Noronha 316
Zona da Mata 319
   Tracunhaém 319
The Agreste Region 320
   Caruaru 320
   Bezerros 321
   A Journey into the Backlands,
     by Daniel Mason 322
Sertão 324
   Petrolina 324
   Triunfo 324

■ PARAÍBA 325
João Pessoa 326
The Coast 327

■ RIO GRANDE DO NORTE 329
Natal 330
   Environs of Natal 332
The South Coast 334
   Pipa 336
The North Coast 338

■ CEARÁ 339
Fortaleza 340
   Beaches 340
   Historical Center 341
   Other Attractions 342
   Around Fortaleza 343
The East Coast 344
   Cascavel 344
   Beberibe 345
   Canoa Quebrada 345

The West Coast 346
   Jericoacoara 346
   Camocim 347
Sertão 348
   Juazeiro do Norte 348

■ PIAUÍ 349
Serra da Capivara 350
   São Raimundo Nonato 350
   Parque Nacional Serra da Capivara 351
   The Long Tale of Prehistoric Man,
     by Niède Guidon 352
Parque Nacional de Sete Cidades 354

■ MARANHÃO 355
São Luís 356
   Historical Center 356
Alcântara 359
Lençóis Maranhenses 360
The Parnaíba Delta 363

▌ THE NORTH 364

■ AMAZONAS 365
Manaus 366
   Cultural Circuit 366
   Traveling by Boat
     in the Amazon Region 368
   Jungle Hotels 369
   From Manaus to the
     Caribbean by Road 371
   The Amazon Rainforest: Brazil's
     Greatest Treasure,
     by Sebastião Salgado 372
   The Contagious Merriment of the
     Parintins Folk Festival 374

■ PARÁ 375
Belém 376
   Núcleo Cultural Feliz Lusitânia 377
   Cultural Circuit 378
   Estação das Docas 379
Ilha de Marajó 380
Santarém 382

■ TOCANTINS 383
Jalapão 384
   Highlights 384
   How to Get Around 385

THE CENTRAL WEST 386

▪ DISTRITO FEDERAL AND GOIÁS 387
Brasília 388
  Architectural Tour 390
  Pirenópolis 394
  Waterfalls and Rocks 394
  The Feast of the Holy Spirit 395
Chapada dos Veadeiros 396
  Alto Paraíso de Goiás and São Jorge 397
  Parque Nacional da Chapada
    dos Veadeiros 397
  Around the Park 398
City of Goiás 400

▪ MATO GROSSO AND
MATO GROSSO DO SUL 403
Northern Pantanal 404
  Cáceres 404
  Land of Water and Animals 405
  Rodovia Transpantaneira 406
  Parque Nacional do Pantanal
    Mato-Grossense 407
Chapada dos Guimarães 408
Nobres 410
Southern Pantanal 411
Ranches in the Pantanal 412
Bonito 414
  Three Reports from the Pantanal,
    by José Hamilton Ribeiro 418

THE SOUTH 420

▪ PARANÁ 421
Curitiba 422
  Historical Center 422
  Cultural Circuit 423
  The Serra do Mar by Train 425
Guartelá 426
Lapa 426
Foz do Iguaçu 427
  Parque Nacional do Iguaçu 428
  Around the Park 429
  The Argentinean Side 430

▪ SANTA CATARINA 431
Florianópolis 432
  The North Coast 433
  Beaches in the East 433
  The South 433
  Beaches in Florianópolis 434
  Lagoa and the Central Region 436
  A Boat Ride 437
  Sports 438
The North Coast 439
  Bombinhas 439
  São Francisco do Sul 442
The South Coast 443
  Guarda do Embaú 443
  Garopaba 444
  Praia do Rosa 445
  Laguna 446
Mountain Ranges 446

▪ RIO GRANDE DO SUL 449
Porto Alegre 450
  Cultural Circuit 450
Mountain Ranges 454
  Gramado and Canela 454
  Canela's Nature Reserves 455
  Vineyard Tours in Bento Gonçalves
    and Garibaldi 456
  Wandering in the Gaucho Mountains,
    by Marcos Sá Corrêa 458
  The Southern Canyons 460
Missões 461

HOTELS, RESTAURANTS,
AND SERVICES 462

USEFUL INFORMATION 568

ACKNOWLEDGMENTS
AND PHOTO CREDITS 576

How to Use This Guidebook

The *Brazil Guide* was created to introduce you to the best of Brazil and at the same time provide local historical, cultural and nature information. It has been organized in the following format:

The **introduction** discusses fundamental aspects of the country: history, ethnic makeup, cuisine, folk art, visual arts, fashion and design, architecture, motion pictures, music, football, Carnival, adventure sports and environment. Articles written by professionals and renowned personalities complement the information.

The guidebook is divided in geographical regions, according to Brazil's official political boundaries. Different **destinations** or arrival points are suggested for each region. We have indicated 22 unforgettable destinations – in most cases cities equipped with airports and complete infrastructure. In some cases, however, we have suggested local destinations of great interest that are removed from the large centers. These locations can be reached by highways or roadways from the **major cities**, which are easily accessible and offer good lodging options.

The **itineraries** for each destination are trips of a few days duration. The itineraries include short, one day excursions where we have indicated the most interesting attractions.

Maps and illustrations help you plan trips or excursions. In various cities we have indicated walking tours, directed by simple maps with point to point indications; the important cultural and architectural buildings are indicated by numbers and described in detail. However, the map numbering system, while highlighting the attractions that should be visited, does not necessarily follow a sequential route.

Sidebars with additional information about the local culture are found throughout the guidebook. Hotels, inns and restaurants that are especially pleasant or interesting have been highlighted in the sidebars indicated as **Our Recommendation**. Addresses and telephone numbers for the restaurants are found along with the description in the sidebar. Hotel telephone numbers are included in the listing at the end of the guidebook along with other complementary information.

In the section, **Hotels, Restaurants and Services**, at the end of the guidebook, color coded regional alphabetical listings of all cities are included for easy reference. The listing is not intended as a complete account of all establishments but rather to indicate those that we considered most interesting, pointing out their advantages and disadvantages.

Please note that the guide abides by the official Brazilian geographical divisions, but the itineraries were planned for practicability and touristic appeal. For example, the city of São Cristovão in Sergipe, is found under the destination of Salvador, Bahia with an itinerary beginning in the capital city of Bahia, Salvador. Likewise for the city of João Pessoa in Paraíba, with an itinerary beginning in the city of Recife.

The organized and practical layout of the *Brazil Guide* makes it a valuable travel companion, able to suggest and advise – a guidebook in the widest sense of the word.

Portuguese Glossary and Phrasebook

Pronunciation

Brazilian Portuguese may use familiar characters, but that fact belies its foreignness. A little practice with the language will help you request directions and will ease other attempts to communicate. Many letters are pronounced in ways that seem strange or counterintuitive to native English speakers. For example, double *r*'s and *r*'s that begin words sound similar to an *h*. Certain other consonants behave somewhat unpredictably. In addition, crowned vowels *(ã)* and those followed by an *n* or *m* are nasalized, a sound difficult for many foreigners to make. (To say "são", sound out the first three-and-a-half letters of *sound*.) When not nasal, vowels sound like:

a: "ah" or "uh"
e: "e" as in *Meg*, or almost silent
i: "ee"
o: "au" as in *caught*, "o" as in *or*, or "ou" as in *you*
u: by itself, "ou," but "w" when followed by another vowel

Directions

Direita [jee-RAY-ta] – Right
Esquerda [esh-CARE-dah] – Left
Reto [REH-to] – Straight
Vire [VEER-ee] – Turn
Norte [NOR-chee] – North
Sul [SOOL] – South
Leste [LES-chee] – East
Oeste [oo-ES-chee] – West
Aberto [ah-BEAR-too] – Open
Fechado [feh-SHA-doo] – Closed

Transportation

Aeroporto [er-oo-POUR-too] – Airport
Barco [BAHR-koo] – Boat
Bilhete [bil-YEH-chee] – Ticket (for transportation)
Carro [CA-hoo] – Car
Estação [es-ta-SAOW] – Station
Horário [oh-RA-ree-oo] – Schedule
Ônibus [OH-knee-boos] – Bus
Rodoviária (Rod.) [ho-do-vee-AH-ri-a] – Bus station
Trem [TRAYM] – Train

Practicalities

Banco [BAHN-koo] – Bank
Caixa automático [KAI-sha oh-toe-MA-chee-ko] – ATM
Câmbio [KAHM-bee-oo] – Currency exchange
Correio [koh-HAY-oh] – Post office
Drogaria [droh-gah-REE-ah], Farmácia [far-MAH-see-ah] – Pharmacy
Hospital [os-pee-TAW] – Hospital
Livraria [leev-rah-REE-ah] – Bookstore
Loja [LOH-zha] – Store
Médico [MEH-dee-koo] – Doctor
Polícia [poh-LEE-see-ah] – Police
Real [hay-OW] – The Brazilian currency (plural: reais [hay-EYES])
Troco [TROH-koo] – Change

Around Town

Avenida (Av.) [ah-veh-KNEE-da] – Avenue
Bairro [BYE-hoe] – District/suburb
Capela [ca-PEH-la] – Chapel
Casa [KAH-za] – House

Catedral [cah-teh-DROW] – Cathedral

Centro [SEN-chroo] – Center; downtown

Edifício [eh-dee-FEE-see-oo] – Building

Feira [FAY-ra] – Fair

Igreja (Ig.) [ee-GRAY-jah] – Church

Jardim (Jd.) [zhar-DEEM] – Garden

Largo (Lgo.) [LAR-goo] – Plaza

Mercado [mer-KAH-doo] – Market

Museu [moo-SEH-OO] – Museum

Parque [PAR-key] – Park

Ponte [PAHN-chee] – Bridge

Praça (Pça.) [PRAH-shah] – Square

Praia [PRY-ah] – Beach

Rua (R.) [HOO-ah] – Street

In Nature

Cachoeira [ka-show-AY-rah] – Waterfall

Caverna [kah-VARE-nah] – Cave

Estrada [ess-TRA-dah] – Road

Fazenda [fa-ZEN-dah] – Farm

Floresta [flo-RES-tah] – Forest

Garganta [gar-GAHN-ta] – Gorge

Gruta [GREW-ta] – Cave

Ilha [EEL-ya] – Island

Lagoa [lah-GO-ah] – Lake

Lago [LAH-goo] – Lake

Mata [MAH-ta] – Forest

Mirante [me-RAHN-chee] – Lookout

Morro [MOE-hoo] – Hill

Parque – Park (Pq. Est. denotes an estadual or state park; Pq. Fl. a florestal or forest park)

Pico [PEE-koo] – Peak

Ribeirão [hee-bay-RAOW] – Brook

Rio [HEE-oo] – River

Rodovia (Rod.) [hoe-doe-VEE-ah] – Highway

Serra [SEH-ha] – Mountain range or continuous hills

Trilha [TREAL-ya] – Trail

Vale [VAH-leh] – Valley

Via [VEE-ah] – Highway

Accommodations

Albergue [all-BEAR-ge] – Hostel

Banheiro [bahn-YAY-roo] – Bathroom

Cama [KAH-ma] – Bed

Hotel [oh-TELL] – Hotel

Pousada [poo-ZAH-da] – Guesthouse

Quarto [KWAR-too] – Room

Food and Drink

Água [AH-gwa] – Water

Bebida [beh-BEE-dah] – Drink

Bife [BEE-fee] – Steak

Cachaça [ka-SHAH-sah] – Traditional Brazilian white rum, made from sugarcane

Café-da-manhã [kah-FAY da mon-YA] – Breakfast

Caipirinha [kay-pee-REEN-ya] – The most famous Brazilian cocktail, made of cachaça, lime, sugar, and ice. Try one with "cachaça envelhecida" (aged cachaça).

Camarão [kah-ma-RAOW] – Shrimp

Cardápio [car-DAH-pee-oo] – Menu

Carne [CAR-knee] – Meat

Carne de porco [CAR-knee jee POUR-koo] – Pork

Cerveja [sare-VAY-ja], chopp [SHOP] – Beer

Churrascaria [chew-hoss-ka-REE-ah] – Barbeque restaurant

Comida [koo-MEE-dah] – Food

Conta [CONE-tah] – Bill

Frango [FRAN-goo] – Chicken

Lanchonete [lawn-choh-NEH-chee] – Lunch counter, snack bar

Massas [MAH-sauce] – Pasta

Pão [POW] – Bread

Peixe [PAY-shee] – Fish

Prato [PRAH-too] – Plate

Queijo [KAY-jew] – Cheese

Refrigerante [he-free-jer-ON-chee] – Soft drink

Restaurante [hess-tow-RAHN-chee] – Restaurant

Sobremesa [soh-bray-MAY-za] –
Dessert
Sorvete [sore-VEH-chee] –
Ice cream
Suco [SOO-koo] –
Juice

NIGHTLIFE

Bar – Bar
Barraca [ba-HA-ka] – Beach snack bar
Boate [BWA-chee] – Nightclub
Cinema [SEE-nay-ma] – Cinema
Teatro [tay-AHT-roo] – Theater

KEY WORDS AND PHRASES

Hello – Oi, Olá (informal)
[OY, oh-LAH]
Good morning – Bom dia
[bome JEE-ah]
Good afternoon – Boa tarde
[bwa TAR-jee]
Good evening – Boa noite
[bwa NOY-chee]
Goodbye – Tchau [CHOW]
Please – Por favor [pour fah-VOAR]
Thank you (very much) – (Muito) obri-
gado [MOO-EE-toh oh-bree-GAH-
doe] is what men say. Women say:
(Muito) obrigada
Yes – Sim [SEEM]
No – Não [NOW]
Today – Hoje [OH-jee]
Tomorrow – Amanhã [ah-mahn-YA]
My name is… – Meu nome é…
[may-oo KNOW-me EH]
What's your name? – Qual é seu nome?
[k-wow EH say-oo KNOW-me]
I'm sick/hurt – Estou doente/com dor
[ess-TOH doe-EN-chee/comb
DOOR]
Where is….? – Onde fica….?
[OWN-jee FEE-ka]
I need help – Preciso de ajuda
[preh-SEE-zoo jee ah-JEW-dah]
I don't speak Portuguese – Não falo
português. [NOW FAH-loo pour-
chew-GAYss]
How much (is this)? – Quanto custa?
[KWAN-too KOOS-tah]
I'd like… – Gostaria…
[goes-ta-REE-ia]
Help – Ajuda [ah-JEW-dah]

NUMBERS

0: zero [say-roo]
1: um [OOM]
2: dois [DOYCE]
3: três [TRACE]
4: quatro [KWAH-troo]
5: cinco [SEEN-koo]
6: seis [SAYS]
7: sete [SHE-chee]
8: oito [OY-two]
9: nove [NOH-vee]
10: dez [DAYS]
20: vinte [VEEN-chee]
30: trinta [TREEN-ta]
40: quarenta [kwah-REN-ta]
50: cinqüenta [seen-KWAIN-ta]
100: cem [SAME]
200: duzentos [du-ZEN-toos]
500: quinhentos [keen-YAYN-toos]
1000: mil [MEW]

DAYS

Monday – Segunda-feira (Seg.)
[seh-GOON-dah FAY-rah]
Tuesday – Terça-feira (Ter.)
[TARE-sah]
Wednesday – Quarta-feira (Qua.)
[KWAR-tah]
Thursday – Quinta-feira (Qui.)
[KEEN-tah]
Friday – Sexta-feira (Sex.)
[SAYSH-tah]
Saturday – Sábado (Sáb.)
[SAH-ba-doo]
Sunday – Domingo (Dom.)
[doh-MEAN-goo]

HISTORY

In the five centuries that separate pre-Columbian Pindorama from modern-day Brazil, the country has evolved from colony to empire, monarchy to republic, and dictatorship to democracy. The nation's self-reinvention shows no sign of slowing.

In all the history books, the story of Brazil begins at the same point – Porto Seguro in Bahia. It was there that a fleet led by Pedro Álvares Cabral anchored on April 22, 1500. The Portuguese stayed for ten days while gathering information and exchanging gifts with the Indians. However, the discoverers found evidence of neither the spices nor the precious metals they sought and, having no idea of the size of the land they'd found, departed what they called "Santa Cruz Island".

The land that the Indians called *Pindorama* – "land of the palm trees" – was luxuriant but oriented toward subsistence. The only item that could offer economic return in trade was the pigment-containing brazilwood that covered vast areas. Within a short time, the red dye from this plentiful wood was supplying the textile industries of England and Holland. It was the Indians who logged the forests of what was now called "Land of the Santa Cruz". This wood gave the new territory its lasting name. "Brazil" comes from the French *brésil*, derived from the Tuscan *verzino*, which was the name of the reddish wood from Asia previously used for dye in Europe. Within thirty years of the land's discovery, this term had supplanted other official names for the region.

The Portuguese realized that their trading posts could not maintain control of the new land, which other foreigner powers also coveted for its brazilwood. In the first decades of the 16th century, the Portuguese Crown sent Martim Afonso de Sousa to establish a colony, starting with the construction of the two villages of São Vicente and Santo André da Borda do Campo, later São Paulo. In 1494, the Tordesilhas Treaty between Portugal and Spain divided the world in two hemispheres, separated by an imaginary line, with the lands to the west being Spanish and those to the east Portuguese. The land between Brazil's coast and the boundary established by that treaty was

A hand-drawn 16th-century map, Arquivo Ultramarino de Lisboa collection divided from north to south in fifteen large tracts called *capitanias* and granted to noblemen called *donatários*. The system proved a fiasco. The only three to prosper were Pernambuco, Bahia and São Vicente.

THE SUGAR ECONOMY

With the failure of the hereditary system of *capitanias*, the Portuguese Crown decided to take a new approach to their administration of the colony. In 1549 Tomé de Sousa was appointed Governor General of Brazil, and founded the first capital – the city of Salvador in Bahia. The new administrator authorized the exploitation of brazilwood and established sugarcane mills.

Sugar production sustained the Portuguese administration and determined the organization of social and economic life for most of the colony. Its legacy lasted for centuries: export-oriented economic monoculture, based on large rural properties and dependent on African slave labor. The sugar baron lived in the "*big house*", while slaves resided in separate quarters. The divide between the "*big house*" and slave quarters, and between barons and slaves, echoed through all aspects of colonial Brazilian society.

There were, however, also some poor freemen, who formed a group of respected, specialized workers. They lived on plantations in the shadow of the sugar baron or settled in the towns.

Moagem da cana-de-açúcar, a drawing by Rugendas published in 1853

THE NATIVE INHABITANTS

To establish the sugarcane crops, the Portuguese colonizers took over land formerly inhabited by native Indians. Prior to the rise of African slave labour, it was the Indians, principally the Tupi-Guarani peoples, who cleared the land. The Tupi-Guarani around two thousand years ago had started large-scale migrations from the Amazon basin to the South and to the North and Northeastern coastline, driving their enemies into the interior of the country. Their history is fragmentary, having been surmised from the discovery of material remains and artifacts. The people left no written records.

Throughout Brazilian history the Portuguese, French, Dutch and Spanish exploited disputes between different indigenous peoples. At other times they encouraged the local native tribes to join forces to fight off invaders. Between 1555 and 1567, the Tamoios Confederation challenged Portuguese dominion over a portion of the coast that extended from Bertioga, in São Paulo, to Espírito Santo. From 1683 to 1710 the Janduís Confederation led an Indian uprising in Ceará and Rio Grande do Norte. Led by Chief Ajuricaba, the Manáos Indians from the Rio Negro, in the Amazon basin, resisted being captured as slaves during the first quarter of the 18th century. In 1767, the Guarani living in Jesuit missions, which were created to convert the natives, resisted being relocated to the Spanish side until they were defeated by Portuguese and Spanish troops.

The history of the Brazilian Indian is one of resistance – and extermination. The indigenous population was an estimated 2 to 5 million at the time of European discovery. This number has been reduced to roughly 700,000 today.

EUROPEAN INVASIONS

The Dutch were a constant threat to Portuguese dominion. First they tried to invade Bahia, where they were defeated in 1625. In 1630 they tried again, this time in Pernambuco, the world's largest sugar producer. Brazilian Holland, led by Count Maurice of Nassau, peacefully absorbed the local Portuguese inhabitants. Artists such as Frans Post and Albert Eckhout portrayed scenes of a prosperous and organized Dutch colony. When expelled in 1654, the Dutch took sugarcane seedlings with them to the Antilles. Portugal would retain the Brazilian territory, but would never again dominate the world sugar market.

The Dutch and the Indians weren't the only challenges to Portuguese dominion. English pirates prowled the South American coastline. And from the beginning, brazilwood attracted French merchants, who established trading posts on the coast in 1504, and in 1555 founded the *França Antártica* colony. In the course of Portuguese efforts to dislodge the French, Estácio de Sá founded Rio de Janeiro in 1565. The French were eventually expelled in 1567, but they returned in 1594 to Maranhão, which they left, except for the town of São Luís, in 1615. The final French attempts to invade Brazil were in 1710 and 1711.

EXPANDING THE FRONTIERS

Brute force defined the borders of Brazil. During the first decades of occupation, Portuguese settlements stayed close to the coast. The interior was covered by dense forests and inhabited by threatening savages – and in the vivid medieval imaginations of the conquerors, perhaps even monsters and ghosts. In 1616, the Portuguese discovered the mouth of the Amazon river, where they constructed the Presépio fort, the origin of Belém. The frontier expanded to encompass territory that, by the Tordesilhas Treaty, belonged to Spain. The same process occurred in the South. Expeditions organized and funded by the Portuguese Crown *(entradas)* and by private individuals *(bandeiras)* left São Paulo and penetrated far inland in search of gold, precious stones and prospective slaves. The *bandeirantes* went as far west as the Paraguay river, where they even assaulted Jesuit missions in pursuit of Indians as slaves, and they also invaded missionary villages on Spanish territory. The Portuguese headed south from Rio de Janeiro and founded the colony of Sacramento on the opposite bank of the Prata river. During the 18th century, a series of treaties expanded the area of the colony from the original 2.5 million km^2 (1 million sq. mi.) to more than 8 million km^2 (3 million sq. mi.).

THE GOLD RUSH

Toward the end of the 17th century, *bandeirantes* discovered the first gold and precious stone deposits in Minas Gerais, Goiás and Mato Grosso. The discovery moved the colony's focus from the sugar-producing coastal regions to the newly discovered gold-mining areas, which attracted intense interest from both sides of the ocean.

A population explosion was just one consequence of the gold rush. Gold also fostered an urbanization boom and generated a flow of trade to supply the mining towns with basic necessities. The Portuguese Crown quickly implemented strategies to control the exploitation of wealth. All gold was to be sent to official foundries for weighing and

Inhabitants of Minas Gerais portrayed in an 1853 drawing by Rugendas

casting, and one fifth of all gold was retained for the Portuguese treasury. Heavy taxation and rigid controls generated growing resentment among miners, which peaked in 1789 with the rebellion known as the *Inconfidência Mineira*. The government violently suppressed the movement and exiled most sympathizers. A second lieutenant named Tiradentes was hanged. Only years later did the Republic recognize Tiradentes as a martyr, a symbol of the struggle for freedom.

While significant, the *Inconfidência* was by no means the first rebellion in the colony. During the 16th and 17th centuries, Portugal faced a series of local uprisings, including some among African slaves. The 18th century brought others, growing larger and developing an anti-outsider bent. Through these conflicts, a new identity emerged: the Brazilian, a person born in Brazil or who had immigrated, and no longer felt Portuguese.

BRAZIL, SEAT OF AN EMPIRE

In 1808, the Portuguese royal family took refuge in Brazil, fleeing the threat of the invasion of Lisbon by Napoleon's troops. In 1815, the colony became the official seat of the Portuguese Empire. The Royal Court's arrival transformed Rio de Janeiro, which had been Brazil's capital since 1763. Dom João VI opened Brazilian ports for trade with friendly nations – especially England – and encouraged visits by European scientists and artists. In 1816, after the fall of Napoleon, a group of French artists immigrated to Brazil. Known as the French Mission, this group included the artist Jean-Baptiste De-bret and the architect Grandjean de Montigny, and they proved to have great influence on their adopted nation's visual arts. In 1821, Dom João VI returned to Portugal, leaving his son Pedro as the prince regent. The Brazil that he departed had been changed forever from the one where he had come to stay.

INDEPENDENCE

The conflicting economic interests of Portugal and the Brazilians drove the separatist movement that culminated in Dom Pedro's re-fusal to obey orders to return to Portugal. On September 7, 1822, on the banks of Ipiranga creek in São Paulo, the prince regent declared the country's independence. Proclaimed Emperor Dom Pedro I, he approved Brazil's first Constitution in 1824. In 1831 he returned to Portugal, relinquishing the throne to his son, who was then only five years old.

THE REIGN OF PEDRO II

In the early 1830s, Brazil was an independent empire with a child emperor. The government therefore entered a period of regency, dur-ing which successive rebellions threatened to tear the young coun-try apart. A strategic decision to lower the age of majority for Pedro II, which allowed him to ascend to the throne in 1840, eased the cri-sis. The new emperor put down local rebellions and led Brazil into its largest war to date, which began in 1865 and resulted in the thor-ough defeat of Paraguay in 1870.

During the long reign of Pedro II, coffee became Brazil's dominant export commodity. Coffee plantations first arose in the state of Rio de Janeiro, in the region of the Paraíba Valley, and then expanded to-ward São Paulo. Later, plantations spread to the western regions of São Paulo state. In the beginning, the plantations relied on slave labor. By the middle of the century, however, plantation owners began to bring over European immigrants to work as farm laborers. Mass immigra-tion of Europeans and Asians lasted until 1930 and played an impor-tant role in the development of Brazilian society and culture.

THE END OF THE EMPIRE

Starting in the 1870s, a series of political crises weakened the sta-tus of Pedro II. Controversy over proposals to abolish slavery pitted slave owners against supporters of economic modernization. In 1871, approved on the wings of a strong popular campaign, the *Ventre Livre* (Free Womb) Law mandated that the children of slave women were born free. In 1888, the struggle over slavery, and slavery itself, ended with Princess Isabel signing the *Áurea* Law.

The princess, however, did not enjoy the prestige that her father had, and at the time of Abolition the country was already concerned about succession. A disaffected military un-

Dom João VI, by Debret

dermined whatever authority the government still retained. On November 15, 1889, Marshal Deodoro da Fonseca proclaimed the country a Republic, with the support of the Republican Party. The Empire bequeathed to the Republic a country of continental proportions. Though relatively unmodernized, agrarian and deep in debt, Brazil was, unlike Spanish America after its own independence, united.

THE FIRST REPUBLIC

The first Republican Constitution (1891) separated Church and State and established a centralized federal regime with a powerful president. São Paulo, the new center of economical power, dominated the political scene. Starting in 1894, politicians from São Paulo and Minas Gerais, the most populated state, alternated in administering the government. The political agreement behind this compromise was known as *café-com-leite*, or "coffee with milk", with São Paulo representing the coffee and Minas Gerais the milk. The elections excluded the illiterate, who formed the majority of the population.

A economic crisis in 1929 degenerated into a political crisis between the states of São Paulo and Minas Gerais. A coup d'état in 1930, which put the southern native *(gaúcho)* Getúlio Vargas in power, settled the issue. Vargas increased government intervention in the economy, centralized power and created a lasting framework of labor rights, including paid vacations, fixed working hours and a minimum wage. His legacy influences policies to the present day. In 1937, Vargas consolidated his control into a dictatorship, the "*Estado Novo*" (New State), which was overthrown by a wave of democracy in 1945.

DEMOCRATIC EXPERIMENTATION

For better or worse, democratic governments and regular elections followed until 1964. But economic crises and inflationary surges, the bane of the nation since the Empire, continued, with various factions manipulating nationalism and populism. In 1951, Getúlio Vargas returned to the presidency, this time by popular vote. In 1954, during an intense power struggle, he committed suicide.

Between 1956 and 1960, Juscelino Kubitschek promoted industrialization, stimulated the expansion of the country's automotive industry and constructed a new capital city, Brasília. The downside of this spurt of modernization was a deepening of the national debt and soaring inflation. Kubitschek's successor, Jânio Quadros, stepped down in 1961, and vice-president João Goulart, considered a leftist by the military, assumed the Presidency. This laid the groundwork for a 1964 coup that propelled Brazil into a long military dictatorship.

DICTATORSHIP IN BRAZIL

In twenty-one years of dictatorship, the Generals eliminated rights, suppressed political parties, imposed press censorship, battled guerrillas and tortured political prisoners. During the first few years of the regime, nevertheless, economic policies limited inflation caused by rising deficits, which brought about a surge of prosperity that modernized industrial and service sectors. The so-called "economic miracle" started to collapse in the 70s during the international oil crisis, and it gave way to an inflationary spiral marked by monetary correction and indebtedness in foreign currencies.

Toward the end of the 70s, civil society gradually resurrected itself. Under pressure, the government granted amnesty to former militants. In the industrial region of São Paulo, strikes by metalworkers helped forge a new generation of defiant leaders. Lacking political legitimacy and weakened by a serious economic recession, the military government in 1984 faced a campaign for direct presidential elections that brought millions of people into the streets. That protest, the largest popular movement in the history of the country, and a move by Congress to permit direct elections forced the military to make concessions. The subsequent indirect election in January of 1985 installed a civilian, Tancredo Neves, but he became ill just before his inauguration and died in April. In his place Vice President José Sarney, Chairman of the official party of the military regime, assumed the Presidency. Sarney nevertheless governed in relative normalcy through 1989, one year after the enactment of the new Constitution.

DIRECT ELECTIONS

In 1989, in a climate of euphoria, the country finally chose its
president by direct vote. The win-
ner was Fernando Collor de Mello, who upon assuming power in
1990 began to implement an ambitious economical plan that included opening the country up to
foreign investment and privatizing
public companies. However, a
spate of serious accusations once
again brought the multitudes into
the streets. Accused of corruption,
Collor was impeached and removed from office in 1992, and

Crowds in São Paulo demanding direct elections

Vice President Itamar Franco took the country's helm. Finance Minister Fernando Henrique Cardoso introduced the *Plano Real* in 1994,
which finally brought an end to runaway inflation.

Buoyed by its success, Cardoso was elected president in 1994 and
reelected in 1998. He implemented economical reforms such as the
end of government monopolies over telecommunications and oil and
the privatization of state-owned companies.

In 2002 former metal worker Luiz Inácio Lula da Silva was elected
president. To the relief of some and frustration of others, Lula did not
break radically with the policies of the previous government, despite
his broad base of popular support from the left. Moreover, under Lula, corruption scandals involving high-ranking government officials
and the Brazilian National Congress loomed over politics in 2005 and
2006. Legal investigations yielded unsatisfactory results: many indicted
parliamentarians were saved from expulsion by their peers.

Yet despite the bumpy road, the economy has remained stable under Lula, who Lula was re-elected president in 2006. Even subsequent
scandals in 2007 and 2008 could not put a damper on his popularity.
He continues to poll strongly, especially among the poor, thanks to
his popular appeal and the success of his economic program.

Today, as it consolidates its democratic institutions, Brazil faces several challenges. Perhaps the most urgent of these is to raise the average income. A mature country yet a young nation, Brazil continues
to build on its history as rising to meet these challenges.

THE BRAZILIAN PEOPLE

The Brazilian population is a product of intermixing among indigenous, African and European peoples. The Portuguese language, the country's unifying factor, weaves together an ethnic and social mosaic of disparate regions and cultures.

Brazil is a nation of many faces and names, a child of the collision of Indians, Blacks and Portuguese, and subsequent waves of immigrants from every corner of the planet. It is said that a Brazilian passport is a highly sought item on the foreign black market, because any person – regardless of color or name – can pass for Brazilian. Diversity defines the country's population.

That being the case, it may seem impossible to talk about the "Brazilian people" as anything more than an abstraction. But there is unity in this heterogeneous mass.

Recognizing it requires seeing eye-to-eye with the Brazilian understanding of the word *people*. The traditional concept of people as an ethnic or national group was dear to the authoritarian tradition, and it has been used throughout the country's history to numb the perception of social inequalities and deflate political tensions. In this way, the military regime of 1964 took advantage of the nation's euphoria after Brazil's outstanding performance in the 1970 World Football Championship, presenting it as a victory for a patriotic, disciplined and courageous population. An earlier dictatorship under Getúlio Vargas instituted a farcical nativist policy that included parades of uniformed students chanting anthems in the Tupi-Guarani language.

Ironically, Brazil's long history of separatist movements has been instrumental in forging a sense of national history common to all Brazilians. For example, the leaders of the *Inconfidência Mineira*, or Minas Gerais Conspiracy, called for the creation of the "Nation of Minas". In 1798, rebellions in Salvador represented the "Bahian people"; in 1817, an uprising in Recife called for a "Pernambucan Republic". The *Farroupilhas* from Rio Grande do Sul did

THE BRAZILIAN POPULATION ACCORDING TO THE 2000 CENSUS	
169,590,693 Inhabitants	
White	53.8%
Mulatto	39.1%
Black	6.2%
Asian	0.5%
Indigenous	0.4%

not see themselves as Brazilians, but as gauchos or cowboys. The persistence of a Brazilian nation in spite of these divisive movements is a source of national pride.

This tension have presented a challenge to a long line of historians, scholars and writers. From Afonso Celso to Sérgio Buarque, from Euclides da Cunha to Jorge Amado, many have tried to define Brazil and Brazilians, scouring all this diversity in search of something that might be unique and specific to this varied and unusual population.

Gilberto Freyre, one of the most original "interpreters", suggested that intermixing was the source of Brazilian "racial democracy". But the 2000 Census, which found that 64% of poor Brazilians and 69% of indigent people are Negros, belies his romantic notion. More than half a century after Freyre, the anthropologist Darcy Ribeiro rejected the idea of racial democracy, but confirmed that Brazilians are a distinct people, with unique characteristics, originating from a confluence of races.

The concept of the Brazilian people developed gradually and only coalesced in the 19th century, with the creation of the Republic. But this people exists. Traveling across the country one discovers many cultures, each with their distinctive regional and local traits. There is an underlying unity and common culture, expressed through the Portuguese language, in a country bounded by Spanish speaking countries.

Detail of *Operários*, by Tarsila do Amaral. Oil on canvas, Palácio Boa Vista collection

CUISINE

Brazil's cuisine is the best embodiment of its culture.
A wealth of traditional dishes and regional specialities
combines ingredients from across the country with influences
from throughout the world. It's only a small stretch to claim
that all the diversity and creativity of Brazilian culture
can be tasted in each bite of many dishes.

Culinary scholars insist on a distinction between gastronomy and cooking. The former, say specialists, is art; the latter is practice. Gastronomy demands a refined palate; while even the best cooking takes aim, at least in part, at the more modest goal of satisfying hunger. For those who accept this distinction, Brazil's cooking scores high marks, but in the realm of gastronomy, the country is still taking its first steps. Most of the head chefs in Brazil's leading restaurants are either foreign or follow the classical European canon. Only the younger generation has begun to examine how they can best deploy genuinely Brazilian ingredients in the kitchen and on the table. These concepts, however, matter little to the visitor who is simply curious to taste what people cook and eat in Brazil. A trip through the country is bound to result in discovery of new flavours, aromas and combinations. Depending on one's appetite, disposition and pocketbook, the traveler may frequently go to the gastronomical temples of Rio de Janeiro and São Paulo or concentrate instead on restaurants specializing in regional cuisines throughout the country. Choose dishes from the finest European culinary traditions, or wander through street markets choosing from delicacies – such as *cupuaçu*, *cajá*, *caju* and other unusual fruits – on display.

A TASTEFUL GEOGRAPHY

More challenging than tracing the rise of the nation's culinary tradition is mapping this fragmented cuisine. Each region finds its own way to combine its natural resources and cultural influences. In the North, recipes call for freshwater fish from Amazonian rivers and seafood. These get combined with manioc – a root also known in the USA as tapioca – the staple food of the indigenous populations, now found throughout the country in different forms.

Feijoada accompanied by rice, fried banana, sliced orange, vinaigrette and pork crackling

Pão de queijo (cheese bread), an icon of Minas Gerais cuisine

In Recôncavo Baiano (the Bahia region), African influence is evident in the use of *azeite-de-dendê* (dendê palm oil), coconut milk, and hot peppers used to season dishes. Specialties include *vatapá,* in which shrimp is mixed with bread crumbs, cashews, peanuts and dendê oil, and *abará,* a purée of beans stuffed into shrimp and steamed in banana leaves.

In São Paulo and rural Minas Gerais, popular recipes such as cracklings, beef jerky, and beans mixed with manioc flour date back to the days of the muleteers and are designed to replenish the energy of travelers. The Center West region follows the same tradition, with the addition of signature recipes that take advantage of the abundance of freshwater fish.

In São Paulo and Rio de Janeiro, many codfish dishes reflect Portuguese traditions and tastes. São Paulo also dines on traditional Italian dishes, particularly pizza, as well as Japanese, Syrian and Lebanese recipes, all brought by immigrants.

Visitors heading to the South will discover in Paraná *barreado,* meat cooked in pans sealed with manioc flour, and in Santa Catarina the shrimp recipes inherited from the Azorean colonization. In the rural areas of Rio Grande do Sul, small communities preserve the 19th-century culinary traditions of European immigrants, as well as the famous *churrascos* (barbecues). The country has, of course, much more to offer: sweets, preserves, breads, cookies and crackers, farmers' markets throughout the rural communities, cheeses from Minas Gerais, cold cuts from São Paulo, wines from the South, the ever-present *cachaça* (a rumlike spirit distilled from sugarcane) and *caipirinhas* (*cachaça* mixed with sugar and limes or other fruit). Cities also offer the international flavors of sandwiches and fast food. The list of dining possibilities and flavors waiting to be discovered could by itself justify a journey.

FRUITS OF THE EARTH

The *caju* (cashew apple) is the tropical version of the forbidden fruit. It has a very real legacy of danger and passion. North American poet Elizabeth Bishop suffered a severe allergic reaction to one of these fruits in 1955, during her first trip to Brazil. As fate had it, she fell in love with the Brazilian Lota Macedo Soares, who had cared for her throughout the crisis, and ended up staying in Brazil. The country subsequently served as the setting of many of her poems.

Travelers not looking to relive the poet's harrowing experience will find many other Brazilian fruits. There are those naturally associated with the tropics – bananas, coconuts, pineapples and mangos – and those of Europe ancestry that have adapted to the mild climate of Brazil's South and Southeast, including apples, strawberries, peaches and pears. Another group includes fruits native or long ago imported to Brazilian shores. Oranges, papaya, guava, passion fruit, *pitomba* (p. 33), and *jabuticaba* (p. 33) have all become part of Brazil's heritage. There are also hundreds of regional fruits that rarely make it farther than local markets. However, in the past few years, many of them have been commercialized and are becoming popular throughout the country, either fresh as frozen pulp. A short list starts with *açaí* and includes names such as guarana, *graviola* (cherimoya fruit), *cupuaçu*, bilimbi and *pequi* (souari nut). The last has a succulent pulp that hides seeds full of thorns. Perhaps it will figure in the next plot of a visitor who faces unexpected danger – and passion.

OF BEANS AND MYTHS

Any thoughts of Brazilian cuisine bring to mind its most popular dish. Elevated to the status of a national symbol, *feijoada* has a mythical origin. It is often said that the dish originated in the slave quarters, where slaves took animal parts that were not fit for the tables of the "big house" and cooked them in a pot with beans. In truth, the tradition of stewed dishes containing grains and meat comes from Portugal and other European countries. Arriving in Brazil, the Portuguese adapted their version of the stew to the ingredients that were readily available. In fact, slaves generally didn't receive so much as the tails, ears or feet that were left over from the master's table. The legend is just one more seasoning added to *feijoada*.

Bakuri

Sweetsop

Tamarind

Yellow strawberry guava

Acerola

Cherimoya

Guarana

Pitomba

Cashew fruit

Mango

Jabuticaba

Jenipapo

Hog plum

THE QUEST FOR PERFECT FEIJOADA

And so it was that *feijoada* was derived from the great Portuguese stew. I am a fanatical glutton when it comes to these two dishes. It was with the master Câmara Cascudo that I discovered the relationship between them. The Portuguese brought their stews to our country. Here they found beans cultivated by the Indians. So they started cooking beef jerky in the bean broth, adding their favorite pork cuts – sausage, back bacon, spareribs and pork loin – and so invented the almost perfect *feijoada*.

There are those who consider what is described above as perfect, just requiring the finishing touches of seasoning like garlic, bay leaf and onion. But for us, the *feijoada* fanatics, the delicacy is never complete without what the untutored call "the inferior pork cuts". As if, brave reader, the pig were not constituted entirely of prime cuts, in its serene mission to deliver itself up completely for our gluttony. According

to some historians the Africans added these cuts, including the ears, feet and tail. Blessed be those who insist on the snout.

And speaking of ignorance, we bristle at the mention of the nonsense to which the misguided give the name "light *feijoada*". How is it possible, wise reader, for anyone to entertain even for an instant the idea of a "diet *feijoada*"? Of a "low-cal *feijoada*"? It's as if one could desire a "fat lettuce". Or a "succulent cauliflower".

It is impossible to have a light course of small items – a shot of *cachaça*, a sip of *caipirinha*, a little beer, some cracklings, and a few small fried sausages – unless it is just an appetizer for the hefty main course. We expect sumptuous black beans, the crock of steaming meat, the finely chopped collard greens with bits of crisp bacon, and the manioc meal, and only the last should be light. The signature pepper is essential, it must be *picante* enough to bring our taste buds to that final understanding between all the ingredients and give us the supreme satisfaction that is always found in good beans.

Feijoada cannot be hurried; it is not "fast". A complete *feijoada* is the one that has no time limit. An acceptable invitation for *feijoada* comes with the promise of good conversation first. The dish requires an unhurried appreciation of appetizers. We heavyweight fanatics think that it is necessary to eat a lot of pork fat cracklings as appetizers exactly because the *feijoada* is still to come. Using the same gluttonous reasoning, the fried sausage should be savoured long before the beans are served.

Nothing to do with *feijoada* can be diminutive. To eat "just a little bit" is gastronomically irresponsible. The just price is hunger and scorn.

A good *feijoada* makes time pass slowly, the hours drag on, people never feel full, the alcohol loosens up the conversation, and the palate is only satisfied when drowsiness arrives. And then one must submit to it. If there is anything better than *feijoada*, it is the post *feijoada* nap…

Never accept an invitation for a *feijoada* as if it were a normal meal. Remember that the concoction draws on three cultures: Indian, Portuguese, and African. And never forget that the incomplete *feijoada* is the worst of all. But then, on second thought, all good *feijoada* ends up being incomplete.

Thomaz Souto Corrêa,
journalist and glutton

THE BRAZILIAN MENU

The following is an abbreviated list of some typical dishes served in different regions of Brazil. However, it does not comprehensively cover the eating habits of Brazilians nor does it address more recent creations that have been incorporated into day-to-day urban life. These include the *pastel*, or deep fried pastry pocket, which is eaten in the street markets, preferably accompanied by sugarcane juice; the "*por quilo*" self-service buffet restaurants where customers pay according to the weight of the food on their plates; the "*prato feito*" (known everywhere as "PF"), a complete dish for one person that arrives on a plate filled in the kitchens of simple pubs. Equally unique are the *rodízios*, restaurants that offer all you can eat – generally meat – at a fixed price. Also absent from the list, but present everywhere in the country, is Brazil's staple dish of rice and beans, served with meat, salad and perhaps French fries. Nothing is simpler, and nothing better.

Southeast
Tutu de feijão (beans and manioc flour)
Torresmo (cracklings)
Vaca atolada (braised short ribs
in manioc paste)
Camarão ensopado com chuchu
(shrimp and chayote stew)
Cuscuz (couscous)
Quibebe (pumpkin purée)
Doce de leite (milk-based caramel dessert)
Goiabada (sweetened guava paste)

Northeast
Cuxá (dried shrimp, sesame seeds,
fish steaks, amaranth and rice)
Galinha de cabidela (stewed chicken,
tomato and onion)
Moqueca (stewed fish, tomato and onion)
Sarapatel (stewed pork liver, heart and lungs)
Caruru (okra with shrimp, cashews,
peanuts and dendê oil)
Acarajé (beans fritters fried in dendê
oil with shrimp sauce)
Arroz de hauçá (rice, beef jerky, dried shrimp,
bacon, coconut milk, dendê oil)
Bolo Souza Leão (manioc cake)
Bolo-de-rolo (roll cake)
Quindim (egg yolk and coconut based pudding)

North
Pato no tucupi (stewed duck served on
a bed of toasted manioc meal)
Tacacá (shrimp stewed in manioc broth)
Maniçoba (stewed manioc greens, beef jerky,
sausage, pork loin, tail and ears)
Pirarucu de casaca (baked fresh water fish with
banana, grapes, prunes, eggs, olives and tomato)
Frito marajoara (fried buffalo meat)
Torta de cupuaçu (cupuaçu pie)

Center West
Arroz com pequi (rice and souari nuts)
Caldo de piranha (Piranha broth)
Pamonha salgada (corn meal paste
served in corn husks like tamales)
Alfenins (sweets made from raw sugar)
Furrundum (sweet papaya purée flavored
with ginger and cinnamon)

South
Barreado (beef cooked in pans sealed
with manioc meal)
Arroz de carreteiro (rice, beef jerky,
tomato and onion)
Churrasco (Brazilian barbecue)
Caldo de camarão (shrimp broth)
Ambrosia (milk and egg based pudding)

CARNIVAL

A festival of European origins, Carnival has been
transformed over the centuries by Brazil's Black
population. Today, it's the most magnificent
mass celebration in the world.

Other countries celebrate Carnival, but Brazil is the country of
Carnival. Throughout the country, the four-day spectacle lures
frolicking masses to the streets, attracts legions of tourists, and drives
the economy. It's fair to criticize the commercialization and the
prices of admission tickets and costumes, and to dismiss the naïve
idea that social hierarchies temporarily disappear. Nevertheless, for
most Brazilians, Carnival is a ritual celebration of life, full of untamed, authentic energy that transcends the demands of the market,
the ogling tourists and the television broadcasters.

FROM *ENTRUDO* TO PARADES

The Portuguese precursor to Carnival was called *entrudo*. These pre-
Lent festivities, which arrived in Brazil in the 16th century,
consisted of pranks involving invasions of homes and play fighting in
the streets using mud, flour, egg and water as ammunition.
Those traditions changed gradually over centuries. "*Limõezinhos de
cheiro*", small wax balls filled with perfumed water, replaced the dirty
water once thrown at passers-by. In 1840, a hotel in Rio de Janeiro
introduced the country to the word *Carnival* when it organized a ball
inspired by the elite costume balls of Venice. But the *entrudo* didn't
disappear. In 1850 the architect Grandjean de Montigny, a member of
the French Mission, died of respiratory complications from a cold that
he caught in Rio after receiving a "soaking". During the Carnival of
1907, the daughters of President Afonso Pena drove along the avenue
in a convertible. That began the tradition of the "*corso*", a procession
of decorated cars that gathered multitudes along the streets.

While the rich paraded down the streets in cars and enjoyed themselves at the balls to the sound of polkas, the people in the suburbs
of Rio de Janeiro transformed the *entrudo*. They organized groups
that paraded in the streets and played the novel rhythms of sambas
and *marchinhas* (Carnival songs). These groups, called *ranchos*, *cordões*
and *blocos*, were the beginnings of the samba schools.

Thousands dance until dawn at the Marquês de Sapucaí parades in Rio

In 1932 the first competitive parade between the samba schools was held in Rio de Janeiro. The municipal administration, recognizing its potential appeal to tourists, began to support the parades in 1935. (It was also at this time that Carnival became one with the *jogo do bicho*, an illegal lottery that involves animal symbols and is akin to the numbers game in Harlem.) To the present day it is one of the largest financial sponsors of the samba schools. The professionalization of the festival had continued throughout the century, particularly in the 1960s with the introduction of television.

CARNIVAL, CARNIVALS

Rio de Janeiro's innovations of balls, parades and floats spread to other Brazilian cities, where the *entrudo* got replaced with the new Rio trend. However, each region added its traditions and music, creating in the festival the regional variations that persist to this day. Today, São Paulo and most other large cities reproduce the Rio Carnival with minor adaptations, while smaller rural towns, as well as Recife and Olinda in the state of Pernambuco, and Salvador in Bahia, forgo the celebration.

In Rio the parades have become so large that they have been assigned a special stadium, the Sambódromo, since 1984. The competition between samba schools attracts celebrities and tourists from all over the world. It is an expensive extravaganza, organized by professionals. The music used today is a narrative samba that interprets the theme of the school's parade. The *marchinhas* persist in the dance parties and in the *blocos* that still pass through the city.

In Pernambuco, Carnival is a street festival. Here, *frevo* emerged from the combination of European traditions and African rhythms. Along with this music, the Carnival in Pernambuco also maintains various local traditions, including dances called *maracatus*, which slaves created to display religious and historical symbols and set to percussion instruments, *caboclinhos,* and *ursos*. In Salvador, the *trios elétricos*, which are trucks equipped with sound systems and stages for bands to perform on, dominate the festivities. Created in the 1950s, the *trios* lead multitudes of people through the city streets, playing everything from *frevo* to *axé*, a musical style popular since the early 1980s. Recife, Salvador and various other Brazilian cities also organize off-season Carnivals, called *micaretas*. Although they lack the long tradition of Carnival, they give visitors a taste of the real thing – and generate welcome income for residents.

A European tradition infused with African flavors, Carnival has survived as part spontaneous celebration, part tourist-driven spectacle. A festival for all classes, it is the strongest proof of the Brazilian gift for joy and happiness.

Carnival-goers make merry day and night at Recife's freeform street carnival

FOLK ART

Produced through techniques handed down from generation to generation, Brazil's handicrafts reflect the culture, ingenuity and identity of various communities. Look closely, and see their similarities and nuance contradictions as well.

They are objects handled carelessly in the course of everyday life – coffee pots, bowls, hammocks, blankets – or displayed as household or personal decorations – lace, towels and figurines. Nevertheless, handicrafts also contain history and reflect heritage and identity. While each is unique because it is handmade by one individual, all are part of a long lineage that gives them common meaning and sentimental value. Handicrafts are a form of expression as well as a set of tools for living.

Ceramic made of clay, Pernambuco

Sometimes, too, they are merely tools for making a living in a world of modern economic realities: a visitor walking along the streets of any of Brazil's better-known centers for folk art will see large numbers of identical articles made specifically to appeal to the tastes of tourists.

CLAY FROM THE EARTH

Mining clay, shaping it, and firing it seem to have been almost innate in Brazil. The people of Marajó Island in the modern state of Pará

Marajoara pottery, Pará

were working with ceramics around three thousand years ago. The ceramic vases, urns and amphoras they created are all that remains of the Tapajônica civilization that originated west of the island, along the Amazonian tributary known as Tapajós River. Today the location is home to many stores offering replicas of the Marajoara and Tapajônica pieces. The best pieces are those that recreate originals through faithfully reproduction of traditional designs, whether the stylized and geometric forms in Marajoara, or the elaborate and embossed detailing in Tapajônica. Quality products also use dyes made from seeds, roots and fruits.

Ceramics spread far and wide early in Brazil's prehistory. Indians throughout the country still produce pieces decorated with traditional motifs. In remote areas of the Northeast, figurines molded by the followers of master Vitalino, the most famous artisan in the region, are easily found in street markets in places like Caruaru in the state of Pernambuco. Communities of women from Espírito Santo make pans known for their beauty and durability. Artisans from the Jequitinhonha Valley in

Representation of Mestre Vitalino, Pernambuco

Minas Gerais and Paraíba Valley in São Paulo recreate their environment through a visual repertoire of saints, traditional characters, animals and folkloric figures.

A Vast and Varied Universe

Brazilian handicrafts are very diversified. In the South you may stumble upon articles such as European embroidery and handpainted, Ukrainian eggs created by immigrants that settled in the interior of Paraná and Rio Grande do Sul. Along the coastline from Ceará to Santa Catarina, lacemakers continue the European tradition, brought to Brazil in the colonial days, of working cloth and thread into decorative articles. Also, along the coast, widely admired glass bottles contain landscapes created using colored sand. And in the remote interior of Brazil, along with the clay figurines, there is a cornucopia of articles made from leather, feathers, beads, seeds, stones and fibers. There, too, is a variety of indigenous basketry made from woven fibers such as bamboo, burity palm, sisal, maranta, rushes, as well as wood engravings that decorate volumes of *cordel* literature. Last but not least, a whole range of toys, bowls, figurines and decorations are carved from the

Jequitinhonha Valley pottery, Minas Gerais

same wooden material used to make *carrancas*, the grotesque figures once mounted on the bow of the ships on the São Francisco River to scare off the evil spirits that threatened the voyage.

FROM THE LAND TO THE MARKET

On the banks of the Tocantins River, in Jalapão State Park, grows a golden-hued grass. Used to make purses, bags and hats, it has moved from the landscape of the dunes and rivers to conquer the large

Viola-de-cocho, Pantanal

cities of the Southeast, and it has leapt from there into fashion magazines worldwide. Buyers approve, the community works and the money

circulates. However, older institutions and artisans have announced the imminent extinction of the golden grass if the region maintains the accelerated pace of production that has developed to meet demand.

Far from the savannah, on the beaches of the North coast of São Paulo, long-time inhabitants sculpt boats out of a single tree trunk, without joints, just like in the olden days. But in the past few years conflicts between organizations that support these artisans and those formed to protect the environment have been increasing. The trees used for the canoes are of valuable and rare species, and like the grass from Tocantins, they are threatened with extinction. And so, popular culture bears the weight of its own impacts.

Votive offerings,
Ilha do Ferro, Alagoas

Animal figures carved by Meinaco Indians

Casal, by Ismael Nery, c. 1928

VISUAL ARTS

From the beginning, colonial Brazil's untamed landscapes and cultures attracted the imaginations of European artists. Over time, the country grew out of this objectification and developed its own artistic tradition that drew on European influences but also cast an eye farther afield.

The first landscapes of the Americas painted by a renowned European artist are of Brazil. Maurice of Nassau brought artists Frans Post and Albert Eckhout to Brazil during the Dutch occupation of Recife (1630–1654), where they spent seven years painting scenes of the New World. Many foreign artists came to Brazil for extended stays, attracted by the country's energy and promise of adventure. They brought art forms created in the Old World, but these traditions fermented in the minds of Brazilian-born artists. By the beginning of the 20th century, the modernists coined an expression to describe what happens to art in Brazil: anthropophagy or self-consuming and self-renewing creativity.

Even the baroque style brought to Brazil by the Catholic Church was adorned with new excesses, colors, ornaments and materials in the Northeast and in Minas Gerais, where Aleijadinho wielded his talent. Portuguese art that arrived here had already absorbed the influences of the Crown's colonies in India and China. In 1808, the Portuguese Royal Court relocated to Rio de Janeiro. Intent on developing the city, King João VI invited a group of French artists to establish the Royal School of Sciences, Arts and Trades, which later became the Imperial Academy of Fine Arts.

In 1816, this French Mission arrived in Brazil – bringing with them the neoclassic style, that would serve as a model for Brazilian art and architecture throughout the following years. Members of the French Mission included the artists Nicolas Antoine Taunay and Jean-Baptiste Debret, among others. Taunay left an important series of landscapes of Rio de Janeiro and its surroundings. The vast works of Debret captured people, places, and scenes of everyday life.

In the second half of the 19th century, romanticism became deeply rooted in the country. Having finally gained independence from Portugal, the country began to construct its identity. Artists such as Pedro Américo and Victor Meireles created epic paintings of patriotic heroes and historic scenes. Almeida Júnior, born in rural São Paulo, portrayed scenes of Brazilian farm life.

In the early 1920s, São Paulo's Modern Art Week revolutionized the course of art in Brazil. Young artists, led by Oswald and Mário de Andrade, caused an uproar when they broke with the established canon. The modernists declared national art and culture anthropophagic. The top names of modernism at the time were Anita Malfatti, Di Cavalcanti, Tarsila do Amaral, Victor Brecheret and Lasar Segall. Their work reverberated through the following decades in the aesthetics of various artists such as Cândido Portinari, Ismael Nery, Flávio de Carvalho, Alfredo Volpi, Alberto da Veiga Guignard and Cícero Dias, as well as the sculptors Maria Martins, Bruno Giorgi and Alfredo Ceschiatti.

In 1951, São Paulo hosted the 1st Biennial Visual Arts Exhibition, which put Brazil on the map of the international art scene. Today, that event is considered one of the greatest of its kind. At its advent, however, abstractionism and concretism were just gaining popularity in the country, and influenced the work of Lygia Pape, Amílcar de Castro, and Lygia Clark. In the 1960s, Lygia Clark would produce an important body of work of avant-gardism and experimentialism, a field that also featured Hélio Oiticica, the creator of the famous *parangolés* – a type of fabric cape. Pop art soon incorporated the culture of the masses, often leaving the canvas behind in favor of installation pieces, using many mediums such as text, video and photography. The "happenings" emerged, events that investigated new languages and directions as well as politically engaged art. Great names of this period include Antônio Dias, Luis Paulo Baravelli and Wesley Duke Lee. In the 1980s, Sergio Fingermann, Leda Catunda, Daniel Senise, Leonilson, and their ilk led a comeback in the popularity of painting.

In the final years of the 20th century and the beginning of the 21st, a new artistic generation has emerged. The likes of Nuno Ramos, Vik Muniz, Adriana Varejão, Beatriz Milhazes, Waltercio Caldas, and Cildo Meireles are gaining international acclaim, and their names regularly appear in the catalogues of leading museums worldwide. The sculptor Frans Krajcberg, a native of Poland who immigrated to Brazil in 1948, is also enjoying international acclaim from his works using charred trees.

While Brazil is making its presence felt internationally, the internal market is ebullient as a result of the new SP Arte. This international fair, to be staged for the forth time in 2008, brings together gallery owners, art dealers, and auctioneers, and has proved a great success in sales. Its objective is to become the largest fair of its kind in South America.

Escultura, by Amílcar de Castro, *c.* 1980

Zona operária, by Cícero Dias, 1928

Design and Fashion

Thanks to Brazil's industrial modernization and the emergence of new talents, Brazilian products — with their distinctive styles, materials, colors and creativity — are spreading around the world.

Foreigners who arrived in Brazil the early half of the 20th century, fresh out of the new European design schools, quickly recognized the valuable raw material they encountered. They eagerly applied their training to the materials, tones and forms that they discovered in Brazil. The Swiss John Graz, the Italian Lina Bo Bardi and the German Karl Heinz Bergmiller were pioneers in producing furniture with a distinctive Brazilian design. The greatest name of this era is Joaquim Tenreiro, a native of Portugal who descended from a long line of cabinet makers. Tenreiro arrived in Rio in the 1920s and criticized the "provincialism of a society that only saw value in imported items and denied its own epoch". He defended simplicity against ostentation. It was no accident that the esteemed architect Oscar Niemeyer invited Tenreiro to design the furniture for his houses. Tenreiro knew how to handle the warm climate of the country. His pieces used the diversity of Brazilian woods and reeds instead of the velvets that had been used extensively until then.

International recognition came quickly. Sergio Rodrigues received first prize in the International Furniture Competition in Cantù, Italy, in 1961 for his design of the Mole (soft) armchair. The 80s and 90s saw the rise of a new generation. The creative furniture of the brothers Fernando and Humberto Campana has been displayed in the New York Museum of Modern Art and is praised by foreign design magazines. Along with the Campana brothers, other noteworthy names from this period are Carlos Motta, Marcelo Ferraz, Francisco Fanucci, Claudia Moreira Salles, Maurício Azeredo, Fernando Jaeger and the team of Gerson de Oliveira and Luciana Martins. The use of Brazilian wood and an increasing awareness of environmental responsibility characterize the creations of these artists.

The Legacy, Embraer's executive jet

A similar process occurred in the fashion world. Years before, only imported items were appreciated and Brazilian fashion had to copy American and European patterns. The explosion of Brazilian models on the international runways awakened the interest of the fashion world in the country. But years before supermodel Gisele Bündchen's sensual strides conquered the runways of fashion shows, many Brazilian designers had already managed to present and sell their collections in Paris and New York. Brazilian design began to win over the international market without offering a uniform style, but rather by incorporating themes from Brazil's diversity.

With the movement to internationalize the appeal of Brazilian styles, large investments were made to modernize the textile industry and to support Brazilian design. Brazil was the first Latin American country to establish a serious fashion calendar.

Havaianas (flip-flops) have achieved worldwide fame, and some cost a small fortune in fashionable stores in Tokyo, Milan and Paris, where the quintessential Brazilian brand of plastic sandals, Melissa, is also in high demand. Even high-tech projects have not been too intimidating from Brazilian designers: Embraer airplanes have gained significant worldwide market share.

Balanço, Puzzle, and Fold rings, by Antonio Bernardo

The jewelry sector also received recognition. In 2000, Cecília Rodrigues was rated as one of the top fourteen jewelers in the world by Christie's. In Germany, Antonio Bernardo received one of the most important international design awards – the Red Dot Award (for his Expand ring in 2004) – as well as the iF Design Award (for his Fold ring in 2005, and his Puzzle and Balanço rings in 2006). Excellence of design and the precision of technique have proven basic elements of Brazil's contribution to the world's beauty.

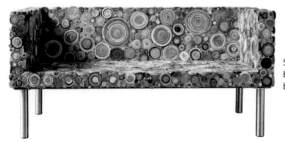

Sushi sofa, by the Campana brothers

Gift box for Sagatiba cachaça, by Claudia Moreira Salles

Three-legged chair, by Joaquim Tenreiro

Girafa stackable stools, by Lina Bo Bardi, Marcelo Ferraz, and Marcelo Suzuki

Havaianas, by São Paulo Alpargatas

Brazil Lights up the Runways

My fascination with Brazil started long before I first set foot in this enchanting country. I have always been fascinated by movies and I still have vivid images in my mind of *Flying Down To Rio*, with Fred Astaire. Entering the realm of the fashion world, one cannot think of Rio without envisioning Carmen Miranda and her incredible costumes propelled by Walt Disney World.

My first trip to Brazil was in the summer of 1962, when I was invited to the 5th Fenit (Brazilian Textile Industry Show) in São Paulo. It was a fair where six Italian couturiers were invited to show creations using Brazilian fabrics. The power of this metropolis, even then, was astounding; you could really feel the heart of the Brazilian economy throbbing.

After the São Paulo show, I took a two week vacation to visit Rio de Janeiro and Salvador. Both cities, so different from Brazil's biggest city, enchanted me with their tropical seduction. Rio de Janeiro, the *"cidade maravilhosa"* is really one of the marvels of the world, and every time I meet one of the many Brazilian friends I still have from this first trip it reminds me of the emotions of that first visit. I was staying at the Copacabana Palace Hotel and fell in love with the swing of people walking down the street – the innately gracious and harmonious moves of Brazilian beauties that have always been the greatest contingent of my catwalk shows.

Dress used by Marisa Berenson for her wedding

With its deep African roots, Salvador was a completely different picture. Its delicious food and folklore transported me to a world so different from what I had experienced until then. Years later, in 1977, I had a whole collection dedicated to Bahia and it was certainly one of my big hits. The show took place in Paris, at the Pavillon Gabriel. It started with a platform coming up from below, with thirty girls and boys all dressed in white cotton and piqué, dancing to an enthusiastic samba rhythm. Marisa Berenson chose to wear one of the finale dresses of the collection for her wedding in Los Angeles, where I was one of her best men.

The second time I went to Brazil, I was already quite famous there and I had the joy of experiencing Carnival. It was one of the most fantastic shows that I ever saw: Samba schools parading in the Avenida with their colourful and frenzied costumes. I recall two sleepless nights watching school after school passing by…

Nowadays I am in constant contact with my Brazilian friends and there are so many models gracing my shows that it is like I am always dreaming of Brazil. For many years the muse of my collections was Dalma Callado, who was awarded model of the 80s, a Paulista girl with perfect measures and a great personality. She was an inexhaustible source of inspiration. She made the finale of my shows so many times, and whatever dress she wore was guaranteed to become a bestseller of the collection.

Some years later, another beauty appeared on the catwalks: Gisele Bündchen. She is considered one of the most beautiful women in the world, and perfectly combines some very German features with a heart, a soul and a rhythm that are sensually and unmistakable Brazilian.

Bahia Tribute Collection

Mario Testino, one of the best fashion photographers of today, and certainly a man with a fascination for Brazil, regularly returns to Europe from Brazil with planes full of beauties that embody the incredible mix of races and moods that make Brazilian men and women so special.

Sometimes during my fashion shows you can have the feeling that I work for the Brazilian Tourism Office in partnership with the Brazilian embassy: on the catwalk you see Gisele, Isabelli Fontana, Carolina Ribeiro, Raquel Zimmermann, Ana Beatriz… while in the first rows sit Brazilian friends and clients of many years.

Last but not least, Brazilian music has been part of my shows: Caetano Veloso, Gilberto Gil and Gal Costa are among my favorites, and I can never forget João Gilberto and Tom Jobim and their fabulous bossa nova.

Valentino,
Italian Fashion Designer

Brazilian National Congress, Brasília, c. 1962, photo by Marcel Gautherot

ARCHITECTURE

Brazil's architectural heritage is by nature more freeform than that of its Spanish-speaking neighbors. Flexibility has enabled the country's leading architects to tap multiple creative influences and fruitfully improvise a rich, uniquely Brazilian style.

In a famous passage in his book *Raízes do Brasil (Roots of Brazil)*, historian Sérgio Buarque de Holanda compared the Portuguese and Spanish, respectively, to sowers of seeds and layers of ceramic tiles. He noted that Portuguese cities in South America grew haphazardly, as if from seeds scattered on the ground, whereas the Spanish brought to the colonies the same organized and measured urban planning that defined their metropolitan cities back home.

Consequently, the narrow, winding streets of Brazilian cities contrast with the perpendicular lines so common in other Latin American cities. Brazil bears the mark of this willful surrender to chance, this addiction to improvisation that's visible in countless cul-de-sacs, irregular intersections and labyrinthine alleyways. Through five hundred years of history, Brazilian architects and urban planners have tried to impose rationalism and order on this tradition of chaos, with various degrees of success. Brasília reflects perhaps their only unequivocally triumph over the heritage of the sowers of seeds.

However, long before the plans for Brazil's capital city left the drawing boards of Oscar Niemeyer and Lúcio Costa, the Portuguese introduced their sense of colonial architecture. It was rapidly absorbed into the Brazilian way of doing things. The lack of traditional Iberian building materials, an abundance of local materials that were unknown in Europe, and climatic differences encouraged local builders to be creative and resourceful. They readily adapted styles based loosely on models brought from the Old World.

Today their adaptability is evident in many of the country's historical centers. An excursion through Salvador, the capital city of Bahia, for example, is a tour of a diversity of architectural styles. There you will find churches with austere façades and luxurious interiors, adorned with gold and Brazilian woods. This apparent contradiction exists thanks to the historical shortage of stones used for the Portuguese church façades, and the surfeit of quality woods. Resource-

Igreja de Nossa Senhora do Carmo and Igreja São Francisco de Assis, in Mariana, Minas Gerais

ful Portuguese artisans simply carved the hardwoods using techniques that they'd previously applied to stone. Ever since a successful revitalization project in Salvador transformed the Pelourinho area into a tourist magnet, other cities have been following suit. Many have restored long-hidden beauty to old row houses.

In the 18th century, the gold rush shifted the colony's economic center to Minas Gerais and led to magnificent, baroque constructions in cities like Ouro Preto and Tiradentes. Antônio Francisco Lisboa, an architect and sculptor known as Aleijadinho, built beautiful churches and sculpted extraordinary soapstone figures. The immigration to Brazil of the Portuguese royal family caused another construction boom at the beginning of the 19th century, as Rio de Janeiro replaced Lisbon as the seat of the Empire. Rio de Janeiro maintained the title of capital city after independence and during the first seventy years of the Republic, and its distinction as the center of the political, economical and cultural scenes continued to be reflected in its streets.

At the beginning of the 20th century, the city received new, wide avenues and luxurious neoclassic buildings such as the National Library, the National Museum of Fine Arts and the Municipal Theater, the last of which was inspired by the Opera House in Paris. Various architectural trends of that era, including art nouveau and art deco, distinguish the city's remarkable buildings.

Industrial growth put São Paulo on the map of modernity in the first decades of the 20th century. In the 1920s and 30s, the works of Gregori Warchavchik and Flávio de Carvalho brought some of the country's first modernist buildings to the city of São Paulo. But it was Rio that would serve as the international launching point for this Brazilian movement. In the mid-1930s, the architect Le Corbusier helped to design the new offices of the Brazilian Ministry of Education, and the resulting building became a worldwide icon of modernism. Other architects involved in the project included a who's who of Brazil's most influential of the century: Lúcio Costa, Oscar Niemeyer, Affonso Reidy, Jorge Moreira, Carlos Leão and Ernani Vasconcelos.

Over the following two decades Brazil became a worldwide trendsetter in architecture. Modern buildings such as the Pampulha complex in Belo Horizonte, the Museum of Modern Art in Rio and the entirety of the country's new capital city, Brasília, reflect this movement. Between 1940 and 1960, Brazilian architecture acquired a modern and avant-garde image throughout the world – a surprising development for a country on the periphery of geopolitics. The vitality of this period was driven by names such as Lina Bo Bardi, Vilanova Artigas, Rino Levi, João Filgueiras Lima ("Lelé"), and Paulo Mendes da Rocha – who, in 2006, won the Pritzker, considered the world's most important architecture prize. At the end of the 1970s, a slump in public construction diverted innovative architectural energies toward designs for houses, stores, hotels and restaurants. Today, architects such as Aurelio Martinez Flores, Isay Weinfeld, Márcio Kogan, Roberto Loeb, Marcelo Ferraz, Severiano Porto, Roberto Montezuma, Acássio Gil Borsoi, Sylvio de Podestá, Álvaro Hardy, Flávio Kiefer, Júlio Collares, Carlos Maximiliano Fayet, James Laurence Vianna, Mauro Neves Nogueira, João Walter Toscano, Marcos Acayaba and Marcelo Moretim continue the tradition of quality in Brazilian architecture.

São Paulo State Art Gallery

MODERN ARCHITECTURE IN BRAZIL

During the past century, Brazil created and refined an architectural style that is one of the few globally recognized as being distinctly "national". Though comprising several separate creative impulses, which makes it difficult to define precisely, this evolving style is quintessentially Brazilian. In the 1940s, revolutionary buildings rose up around Brazil, and in the following decade, the country established itself as a global center of modern architeture. Three projects are perhaps enough to encapsulate Brazil's contribution to 20th century architecture: the Ministry of Health and Education in Rio de Janeiro (built 1936-1942), the city of Brasília (1957-1960) and the São Paulo Art Museum (1956-1968).

MINISTRY OF HEALTH AND EDUCATION

Few could have imagined, in the 1930s, the international impact that the Ministry of Health and Education project would have on the architectural community. A glass building of that size had never before been built anywhere in the world, and it was the first time that a government had officially adopted an avant-garde design. The Ministry building, now called Gustavo Capanema Palace, and known for a time as the Ministry of Culture and Education, combined so many innovations that it was almost an experimental project. The office building, supported by tall pillars, allows pedestrians to circulate freely in its shadow, and the rest of the building structure incorporates space for public activities such as theater and exhibitions. Exposure to sunlight could be controlled by the brise-soleil. Ceramic tiles, paintings by Portinari and gardens by Burle Marx reinforce the perception that the goal was to create a complete work of art.

The project arose out of the cooperation of a group of young Brazilian architects – Affonso Reidy, Carlos Leão, Ernani Vasconcelos, Jorge Moreira and Oscar Niemeyer – under the coordination of Lúcio Costa with Le Corbusier as a consultant. Le Corbusier was so enthusiastic about the result that he counted the Ministry among his most important projects. But could Le Corbusier really claim the project as his own, or was it a creation of the Brazilians? During the following decade, the Brazilian architects demonstrated that they could create world-class modernist architecture without consulting the master.

BRASÍLIA

A British magazine once defined Brasília as both the pinnacle and the tomb of modernist ideals. On one hand, the city would swiftly become the definitive reference of 20th century urbanism. On the other, its utopian urbanism is on a scale neither attempted nor reproduced elsewhere. In Europe, the utopian urban planning of the early 20th century focused on low-income areas. In Brasília, by contrast, it was universally applied to official palaces, administrative, commercial and office buildings, and housing for various income levels. Unlike the Ministry of Education building, Brasília does not captivate followers all over the world. But like the Ministry building, it showed that Brazil could construct on a monumental scale what Europe had done on only a limited scale.

In addition to the urban planning by Lúcio Costa, who landed the assignment by winning a national competition in 1956, Brasília is a landmark for its challenging architectural innovations. One example is the Alvorada Palace built in 1958: previously, palaces had classical columns and were designed to project solidity and formality. In Alvorada, Niemeyer created a new paradigm of monumentality that is transparent, light and almost fragile. Many criticize Brasília without understanding what it symbolizes more than any other city in the world. Brasília demonstrates that a group of Brazilians – from the President to the laborer – planned and executed the idealized form of an architectural era.

THE SÃO PAULO ART MUSEUM

Perplexed were the guests at the 1968 opening of the São Paulo Art Museum, or MASP. They encountered the finest collection of Western art south of the equator – without any form of hierarchy or emphasis. All the pieces were set out in an immense rectangular room on glass stands, with the descriptions located behind the pieces, forcing the visitor to examine the piece first without any other outside reference. That was Lina Bo Bardi's unusual approach to exhibiting the paintings.

MASP is one of the world's greatest examples of what's called brutalist architecture. Structural elements define the form of the building. Four external pillars suspend the exhibit halls and eliminate the need for internal structural elements. The ground floor, completely open, resembles a large covered public square. The main material used in the construction is exposed concrete, which creates a vivid contrast with the fragility of the exhibited artworks and eliminates the distractions of art's typical neoclassical settings. The project by Lina Bo Bardi, officially named the Assis Chateaubriand Museum after the businessman who assembled its collection, has been an inspiration to architects all over the world. A visit to MASP, in spite of some recent internal alterations, shows how Brazil absorbed and creatively recast a most diverse range of cultures.

The three examples include one instance in which Brazilians worked under the influence of a European, another in which Brazilians created their own utopian capital, and a third in which a European took inspiration from Brazil itself. Together, they demonstrate the caliber of modern Brazilian architecture, in all of its complexity and diversity.

André Corrêa do Lago,
diplomat, architectural critic, and member of the Architectural
and Design Committee of the New York Museum of Modern Art (MoMA)

CINEMA

Brazil's motion-picture industry has combined technical savvy with artistic grace, launching a renaissance that, overseas, is making cinema one of the country's best recognized areas of cultural excellence.

At the turn of this century, something new appeared in Brazil's cultural panorama: a cinematic explosion. At the beginning of the 1990s there had been only two or three feature-length movies being made each year. By 2003 the figure had leapt to forty. And the appeal of this new crop of films is not limited to domestic audiences. Cinema-goers from half the world have been moved by the raw emotion of, for example, *Central do Brasil (Central Station)* or *Cidade de Deus (City of God)*, whose directors, Walter Salles and Fernando Meirelles, respectively, are developing promising international careers.

However, Brazilian cinema took time to reach the limelight. The first signs of life developed in the 1920s and 30s, with the works of Humberto Mauro and Mário Peixoto. The following decades saw the slapstick comedies of Atlântida and the melodramas of Vera Cruz, pioneering studios in terms of movie-industry professionalism. At the end of the 1950s the Cinema Novo movement emerged, led by such prestigious directors as Nelson Pereira dos Santos, Ruy Guerra, and Glauber Rocha, giving Brazilian productions international exposure for the first time. In 1962, Anselmo Duarte was awarded the Palme d'Or at the Cannes Festival for *O pagador de promessas (The Given Word)*. After that came movies from directors such as Cacá Diegues, Bruno Barreto, Arnaldo Jabor, Suzana Amaral, and Hector Babenco.

Despite all this talent, however, the industry almost ground to a halt at the beginning of the 1990s due to the withdrawal of public financing during the Collor government. The turnaround, triggered by a new fiscal incentive law, began in 1994. Carla Camurati's frugal production, *Carlota Joaquina, Princess of Brazil*, attracted a big audience with minimal advertising.

If the rudimentary techniques of the Cinema Novo were part of an aesthetic and political project, the goal of the new cinema is artistic perfection. The presence of Brazilians at the Oscars is the best proof of its accomplishments. In the last years, many Brazilian movies have received Oscar nominations.

Meanwhile, *Diários de motocicleta (The Motorcycle Diaries)*, directed by Walter Salles, shown at the official selection of the Cannes Festival, embodies Brazilian film's new internationalism. Robert Redford, an American, produced that picture; the leading roles were played by Mexican and Argentinean actors; the screenplay was written by a Puerto Rican; and it was filmed in several neighboring countries. The movie continues in the tradition of Hector Babenco's *O beijo da mulher aranha (Kiss of the Spider Woman)*, for which William Hurt received the Oscar for best actor.

If we take critical acclaim as a measure of success, the results are equally impressive, with Brazilian productions being selected for the world's most important film festivals. In 2008, two Brazilian films were screened at the Cannes Film Festival: Walter Salles and Daniela Thomas's *Linha de Passe* (at press time, still unnamed in English) and Fernando Meirelles's *Blindness* – the latter, based on José Saramago's novel *Ensaio Sobre a Cegueira (Blindness)*, was chosen to open the festival.

Documentaries are also enjoying a revival. Productions such as *Ônibus 174 (Bus 174)* by José Padilha, *Nelson Freire* by João Moreira Salles and *Edifício Master (Master: A Building in Copacabana)* by Eduardo Coutinho have all achieved strong audience responses. In fact,

Linha de Passe, by Walter Salles, 2008

Blindness, by Fernando Meirelles, 2008

box-office success is becoming the norm. Several films, such as *O auto da compadecida (The Dog's Will),* by Guel Arraes, have surpassed the 2-million-viewer mark. Four million people have watched Hector Babenco's *Carandiru,* and the 2005 film *2 filhos de Francisco (Two Sons of Francisco),* by Breno Silveira, set new box-office records in Brazil's now-flourishing film industry, with 5.3 million viewers.

Successes have paved the way, and the subjects treated in films have subsequently diversified. Urban violence is a frequent theme, and documentaries like Caíto Ortiz's *Motoboys (Motoboys: Crazy Life)* portray the vibrant life of big cities. But films such as *Baile perfumado (Perfumed Ball),* by Lírio Ferreira and Paulo Caldas, are set in the wilderness of the *sertão.*

In recent years movie-theater multiplexes have sprung up Brazil's larger cities, setting new standards for comfort, as well as projection and sound quality. The new theaters are not only a welcome sign of the modernization of the country's film industry, but also evidence of the public's higher expectations. Nevertheless, Brazil still has only 1,600 cinemas nationwide, and all of these are concentrated in just 8% of the cities

Popular Music

Brazil's rich musical traditions merge influences
from all continents. Waves of innovation from foreign
shores have been sculpted to the nation's tastes and,
in turn, have shaped musical tastes around the world.

In the first years of Portuguese colonization, the Jesuits adapted religious hymns to tribal dances to help convert Indians to Chris-
tianity. This is but one example of music being used in Brazil for enticement or seduction. A few years later, Africans reached Brazil, and
their percussion instruments were incorporated into the national arsenal – *conga* drums, *cuícas* (friction drum), *ganzá* shakers
and *marimbas* (similar to a xylophone) that accompanied slaves' evening sing-alongs. Perhaps those
weary slaves were the first to recast, through music, even the most oppressive of circumstances into a festive atmosphere.

Cuíca

Enticement, seduction, lament and celebration
are the tangled roots of the tree of Brazilian Popular Music, or MPB. Its branches reflect an extensive array of styles and rhythms.

Different groups' musical styles began to merge when slave celebrations gained a degree of acceptance in the "big house". The *umbi-
gada* (navel to navel contact) and African beats took on Iberian
influences and became the *lundu* dance. The sinuous movements of
that style were often seen as lascivious, but in spite or perhaps because of this, it was welcome at the masters' balls. With the rising
numbers of Africans among the Brazilian popula-
tion, the inevitable Africanization of music pro-
ceeded in spite of critics' protestations. By the
end of the 18th century, the *lundu* was well established in the local culture. So, too, was the
modinha, which are European folk songs that
crossed the ocean and got set to Brazilian themes and
rhythms. The *modinha* remained popular with all social classes throughout the 19th century. At the turn of the 20th century, another European rhythm, the polka, became a national rage. The polka influenced *maxixe* dance, which arose in the backyards of Rio de

Afoxê

Janeiro's peripheral ghettos. It was assimilated, with some reservations, by the elites. In 1914, Nair de Teffé, the wife of President Hermes da Fonseca, shocked conservatives at a soirée by singing the risqué *maxixe Corta-jaca*, by Chiquinha Gonzaga. The same mixture that produced *maxixe* in Rio created the *frevo* in Pernambuco. Today, the latter form is one of the most popular rhythms in Brazil and the signature music of Carnival in the Northeast.

Cavaquinho

THE BEGINNINGS OF SAMBA

In 1917, the recording of the song *Pelo telefone* by Donga marked the birth of samba, an offshoot of *maxixe*. Both musical styles originated in working class districts of Rio de Janeiro, at the parties of African immigrants who had moved here from Bahia. In the following decades, the genre matured and gained popularity. During the same period, recordings and radio became important means of mass communication. Already distinct from *maxixe* and inextricably linked to Carnival, the samba quickly swept beyond the city limits and through the social classes. By the 1930s, it was no longer the music of poor blacks in Rio but a national art form. In that short time it assumed the position that it still holds today as one

Ganzá

of the pillars of national identity. The definitive form of samba was established over the 1930s and 40s by great artists such as Sinhô, Noel Rosa, Ismael Silva, Ary Barroso, Lamartine Babo and Cartola.

BEYOND SAMBA

During the maturation of samba, Brazil's musical melting pot continued producing other styles. Donga, the creator of the first samba, played in a jazz band alongside the legendary master Pixinguinha. Pixinguinha wrote magnificent *choros*. That type of music, which became popular at the end of the 19th century among Rio's working class, features European polkas, waltzes and mazurkas by a trio playing a flute, a ukulele-like *cavaquinho* and a guitar. These *choros* later had a powerful influence on composer Heitor Villa-Lobos, who was a pioneer in the use of popular traditions in concert music. Clas-

Tamborim

sical music has a long history in Brazil. Classical and popular music have followed parallel paths, so at many points the two have shared influences.

Caixa

By the 1940s the musical industry discovered the traditional rhythms of the rural Northeast. For example, Dorival Caymmi incorporated the accent and themes from Bahia into the Rio samba. On the radio, the sounds of Luís Gonzaga and his accordion were at the top of the charts. Known as the "king of *baião*", after that Country and Western-like musical style, he also played *xote*, *xaxado* (folkdances) and other sounds that were popular at country dances. By the end of the 1940s, a new and slower version of samba, known as the *samba-canção*, emerged to challenge the rural dance styles. That new form of samba created great radio idols, singers who touched legions of fans. In the post-war period, with North American influence in Brazil ascendant, the *samba-canção* bred with jazz, and bossa nova was born.

THE SOUND OF THE NEW BRAZIL

Like samba, bossa nova has a birth certificate. In 1958, the release of João Gilberto's first album marked its appearance. Young university students, gathered in apartments of Rio's upscale Zona Sul, created bossa nova to contrast with the grandiloquent and dramatic style that then dominated popular music. The new sound was intimate, with quiet vocals accompanied by innovative and sophisticated guitar rhythms. The soundtrack for modern Brazil, bossa nova shared the euphoria of industrialization and growth. Stirred into the pot with jazz and the samba were the classical approach of Tom Jobim and the lyrics of Vinicius de Moraes. In the mid-1960s, Frank Sinatra recorded bossa, opening the way for the traffic in artists and musical styles between the two countries.

A few years after its emergence, bossa nova fragmented as a musical movement. Some factions argued for a return to the "roots", while others were captivated by the potential of electric guitars. In 1964, the military dictatorship exacerbated these differences. In an environment of increasing restrictions on political liberties, televi-

Agogô

Pandeiro

sion stations organized university music festivals that served to express different cultural currents. This permitted the rise of artists whose influence would carry through the century, including Chico Buarque, Caetano Veloso and Gilberto Gil. Songs of protest that challenged the censure imposed by the regime also rose up from these festivals.

In 1968, Caetano, Gil and Tom Zé launched tropicalism, a movement that explicitly proclaimed the anthropophagic character – the assimilation and transformation of foreign influences – of Brazilian music. Tropicalism discussed the concepts of good and bad taste, of national and foreign. It mixed the influences of the Beatles, the traits of music considered tacky, and the great popular Brazilian tradition. The bands Mutantes and Secos e Molhados brought this potent brew of influences to the masses. At the same time, American easy-listening and commercial rock became Brazil's Jovem Guarda or New Guard. Artists such as Roberto and Erasmo Carlos popularized that youth movement. In the 1970s, in another development, Paulinho da Viola renovated and revitalized classic samba. At the same time, composers and vocalists such as Milton Nascimento and Elis Regina made names for themselves.

Berimbau

THE "ANTHROPOPHAGIC" TRADITION

The movement of absorption and recreation of international musical influences continued throughout the last years of the 20th century. In the 1980s, Brazilian rock reached the hit parade, finally achieving success in one of the few areas where foreign music had always outdone its homegrown competition.

Emerging Brazilian "rock stars" included Cazuza and Lobão, and bands such as Legião Urbana, Paralamas do Sucesso and Titãs. Yet international influences continue to arrive and take on a local flavor. In Maranhão, dancers turned reggae into a romantic ballroom style. In Rio, the funk beat of Miami Bass

Flute

acquired a strong dose of eroticism, while in São Paulo, the rap lyrics of Racionais MCs became a channel for protest against violence and racism.

In Recife, the heirs of Chico Science mixed the traditional *maracatu* (a Brazilian dance of African origin) with electronic rhythms and punk in a movement known as the *mangue* beat. Electronica fuses with samba in the music of Marcelo D2, with funk in the music of DJ Marlboro, and with bossa nova in the music of Bebel Gilberto. Meanwhile, Marisa Monte, Céu, and Moska continue the tradition of Brazilian Popular Music, but bring it closer to international pop. In Rio, Seu Jorge is revitalizing samba, while Los Hermanos mix rock with the *samba-canção*. Rio is also home to O Rappa's reggae. Proof of Brazilian music's intentional unorthodoxy can be heard in the work of the Orquestra Imperial. Composed of musicians of different sensibilities, such as Moreno Veloso, Rodrigo Amarante, Nina Becker, and Nelson Jacobina, the group offers an irreverent take on the big bands of old. Moving between the old and the new, the vulgar and the sophisticated, Brazilian music continues to reinvent itself – and to redefine international expectations – every day.

Atabaque

TO HEAR THE MASTER

The Reserva Técnica Musical do Instituto Moreira Salles maintains much of the tradition of Popular Brazilian Music, or MPB. The Institute is home to the Centro Petrobras de Referência da Música Brasileira which holds roughly 13,000 recordings made between 1902 and 1964, including those of Noel Rosa and Chiquinha Gonzaga. Researcher Humberto Fransceschi painstakingly obtained, restored and catalogued the collection, starting with 78 rpm records, over a fifty-year period. Visitors can learn about and listen to the recordings at no charge at the Institute's access terminals, and research rooms are open to the public. There are also occasional lectures and exhibitions *(Rua Marquês de São Vicente, 476, Gávea, Rio de Janeiro, tel. (21) 3284-7474)*. The collection may be accessed at the website *www.ims.com.br*.

Brazilian Music

When people talk or think of Brazil, before even the classic images of the sun, the beaches, the suntanned girls, or Carnival, or football, the first thing that comes to mind is the sound, the rhythm. It could be a swinging samba or a cool and elegant bossa nova. Music may well be Brazil's greatest contribution to beauty and joy in the world. Brazilian music has become our finest, most widely consumed and most desired export product – with the exception, of course, of Gisele Bündchen. Above all else, it has such an intense and intimate place in Brazilians' lives that one can tell the history of modern Brazil through nothing more than the history of its popular music. Melodies and lyrics throughout time have witnessed every crisis, each moment in the past, and shows precisely how the Brazilian nation felt at the time. So, popular music tells a story about the feelings of Brazilians.

An analysis of the rich and glorious history of our music, the most powerful cultural production we have, combines the miseries and downfalls of our social and political tradition, and can help any foreigner, and ourselves, to better understand us. Popular music has a presence and importance in the daily lives of Brazilians that is matched in few countries.

Music, like football, both demands and gives pride, talent and national passion: the passion to dribble and sidestep, the love of dance and of joy. We can acknowledge that we are politically, socially and scientifically underdeveloped. But the music we produce is very modern, globalized, competitive, diversified and increasingly respected and in demand in the most demanding markets. Like no other form of national expression, Brazilian popular music tells the story of our dreams and passions, our fears and frustrations. It embodies our imagination. Heard by rich and poor, young and old, men and women of all races, it talks, it sings about all of them. Americans know this well: it is impossible to understand the United States without movies and popular music. In Brazilian culture, movies are less culturally prominent than the *novelas*, or nighttime soap operas. So, the quality art of Brazil's musicians and lyricists, their popular music, assumes the task of registering our feelings, of capturing important moments, and of recording our personal and collective history.

Since the explosion of bossa nova in the 1960s, popular music has become Brazil's greatest contribution to international pop culture. Bossa's strong and contagious beats, and its soft melodies and sweet words, inspired musicians, writers and filmmakers, and became the imagined sound track for the lives of millions of people. It receives respect and fosters friendship everywhere that music is loved.

Everyone knows, well, on second thought they likely don't know, that we have very talented writers. There are a few translations of Jorge Amado, Machado de Assis and Guimarães Rosa, but one cannot speak of a "Brazilian literature". We have world-class poets such as João Cabral de Melo Neto and Carlos

Drummond de Andrade, but they write in Portuguese and there isn't anything that you could call a "Brazilian poetry".

Celebrated movies like *Central do Brasil* (*Central Station*) or *Deus e o Diabo na Terra do Sol* (*Black God, White Devil*) are expressions of the talent of Walter Salles Jr. and Glauber Rocha, but unlike the Iranians we do not have anything that could be called "Brazilian cinema".

Of course, besides the physical beauty of our young men and women, we have a number of great athletes. They play not only football but also volleyball, tennis, Formula 1, yachting and Olympic gymnastics. Still, we are far from being a world power in sports.

We have been blessed with the occasional first-rate actress, like Fernanda Montenegro and Marília Pêra, and an extraordinary playwright or two, including Nelson Rodrigues. But we cannot talk about a "Brazilian theater".

However, in any place in the world, when the subject is music, we feel like the French talking about wine or an American talking about business. The music of Antonio Carlos Jobim and João Gilberto not only enchanted the world but also influenced American jazz and inspired geniuses such as Miles Davis and Stevie Wonder. Since bossa nova, the sounds of Sergio Mendes, Caetano Veloso, Milton Nascimento, Gilberto Gil, Hermeto Paschoal, Ivan Lins and more recently Marisa Monte, Daniela Mercury, Bebel Gilberto and many others continue to bring happiness, elegance and sophistication to international pop music. Brazilian beats make people dream and dance. Above all else, with its diversity of rhythms, beats, styles, and endless recombinations, Brazilian Popular Music expresses the country's ethnic and cultural diversity, the richness of our melting pot, and shows the best that we have to offer as people and as artists. Welcome to the *Brazilian Melting Pop*.

BASIC ALBUM COLLECTION

Chega de Saudade – João Gilberto
O Amor, o Sorriso
e a Flor – João Gilberto
Terra Brasilis – Antonio Carlos Jobim
A Tábua de Esmeraldas – Jorge Ben
Minas – Milton Nascimento
Tropicália – Caetano Veloso, Gilberto Gil, Os Mutantes, Tom Zé
Acabou Chorare – Novos Baianos
Maria Fumaça – Banda Black Rio
Amoroso – João Gilberto
Gal Canta Caymmi – Gal Costa

Brasil – João Gilberto, Caetano Veloso, Gilberto Gil e Maria Bethânia
Falso Brilhante – Elis Regina
Tim Maia Disco Club – Tim Maia
Charme do Mundo – Marina Lima
O Último Romântico – Lulu Santos
MM – Marisa Monte
Ao Vivo – Cássia Eller
Orchestra Klaxon – Max de Castro
Tribalistas – Arnaldo Antunes, Carlinhos Brown, Marisa Monte
À Procura da Batida Perfeita – Marcelo D2

Nelson Motta,
writer, journalist and music producer

Ronaldinho Gaúcho, Brazil vs. Wales, 2006

FOOTBALL

In Brazil, football is more than just a
popular sport. It was key in forging the national
identity, and it still plays a crucial role in the
country's economy, culture and social life.

A passion for football, or what North Americans call soccer, is not exclusive to Brazilians. Many other nationalities exhibit the same enthusiasm, and even fanaticism, of the fans who flock to stadiums in São Paulo or Rio de Janeiro. But for Brazilians, football is more than just a sport or a game. It is part of the identity, an expression of the culture, a metaphor for the potential of the people and nation.

According to the CBF (Brazilian Football Confederation) there are 800 professional clubs in Brazil, 13,000 amateur ones and over 300 stadiums. It is estimated that more than 30 million people play the game, and it supports a US$32-billion a year business. Brazilian Portuguese has even absorbed several idioms from football jargon. Even people who have never been to a match use such familiar expressions as "*pendurar a chuteira*" (literally "to hang up one's boots", to retire), "*pisar na bola*" ("step on the ball", to make a mistake) or "*tirar o time de campo*" ("withdraw the team from the field", to beg off or quit).

Football provides an effective conversational ice-breaker. If you find yourself among strangers in a bar or a taxi, or at a party, you can easily start a conversation by commenting on the performance of a player or a team.

However, the game's greatest attribute is something else – it is a truly democratic sport. Social background is of no importance and it can be played by anyone, regardless of their physique; you don't have to have an athletic build or be of a particular height to dominate the ball. For children from underprivileged backgrounds, the sport has become a dream ticket to fame and fortune, but very few actually make it – according to the CBF, the vast majority of professional players only earn around R$500 a month. But in the end, what really matters is that football allows Brazilians to dream. Life in Brazil is hard, sometimes very hard, but all it takes is a little boy and a ball to conjure up the possibility of triumph and glory.

Brazilian Football

If a recently arrived visitor were to make a list of the five greatest tragedies in Brazil's history – tragedies being understood as events so traumatic that people gather in the streets to sit on the curb and cry on each other's shoulders – he would discover that no less than three of them have to do with sports. The first occurred in 1950 at Rio's Maracanã Stadium; just weeks after it opened, when the Brazilians fell to Uruguay in the final of the 1950 World Cup. The event subsequently became known as the *Maracanazo* (the Maracanã fiasco). Second was the elimination of the unforgettable 1982 team of Zico, Sócrates, Júnior, Cerezo and Falcão in the quarter-finals of the World Cup against Italy, an episode that became known as the *tragédia do Sarriá* (the Sarriá tragedy). And third, the tragic death of Ayrton Senna on the Tamburello curve of the Ímola grand-prix circuit on Labor Day in 1994. (Only two national tragedies are political: the suicide of the so-called "people's president", Getúlio Vargas, in 1954, and the death of Tancredo Neves, the first civilian president after more than twenty years of military rule, just a few days before his inauguration in 1985.)

If the same visitor were also to list the country's five most glorious moments, the result would be even more oriented toward sports. The achievements that fill every Brazilian with pride are not represented by any of the several stars on our flag, but by those five little stars embroidered above the crest of the national football team, representing the country's World Cup victories in the 1958, 1962, 1970, 1994 and 2002. At first glance, this might appear somewhat insubstantial, to say the least, but in a world where football is increasingly becoming a symbol for the unity of peoples and the identity of nations, and where FIFA (the sport's governing body) has more members than the UN, the perspective is a little different. Many Europeans would willingly trade their respective countries' military and scientific exploits for the right to display those five stars on the shirts of their national sides.

After this brief survey of Brazil's triumphs and failures, our visitor would certainly conclude that the country lacks great generals, revolutionary leaders, space-travel pioneers and almost every other type of traditional heroic figure. Our Alamo was the Sarriá, our Waterloo the *Maracanazo* and our great heroes are not historical giants like Henry V, Lincoln or Gagarin. Nevertheless, even though they have won no wars, led no revolutions and never journeyed through space, Brazil's heroes are just as famous as those of the great nations. The country's distinctly unmilitary idols need only one name each: Didi, Garrincha, Tostão, Gérson, Romário and Ronaldo. Surnames, military ranks, and noble titles are superfluous. Only one title exists as an exception to that rule, and it too belongs to a football hero: *o Rei* (the King), conferred on Pelé in recognition of his peerless footballing genius, became a title accepted nearly worldwide without the need to fire a single shot.

A visit to a football stadium offers valuable insight into local customs. This experience is imperative. To return home from Brazil without having been to a game is as serious a cultural omission as going to Athens and not visiting the Parthenon. Brazil's stadiums fall short of European and North American ones in terms of comfort and safety, but with a few simple precautions you can enjoy an unforgettable experience and, at the same time, capture the true essence of the Brazilian character. And there is a wide choice, from the simple Vila Belmiro in Santos, the home ground of Pelé, the greatest of them all, to the majestic Maracanã in Rio and Morumbi in São Paulo, not to mention Brinco de Ouro da Princesa and Moisés Lucarelli, the grounds of Campinas arch-rivals Guarani and Ponte Preta, both with a 30,000 capacity and a mere 300 meters (328 yards) apart. The Estádio Zerão, in the city of Macapá in the Amazon region, is located exactly on the equator, so the line at midfield also divides the world. Nowhere else can people attend a game where one goal is in the northern hemisphere and the other in the southern hemisphere.

Brazilians will put up with people who change their vocation, their political party, their religion and even their sex, but they will not, under any circumstances, tolerate a fan who switches teams. So, as a visitor, think very carefully about which side you intend to support to avoid being branded as a turncoat later. Keep in mind, every Brazilian has a favorite team, and turning your back on theirs is a sin almost as mortal as suggesting that Maradona was better than Pelé. (Warning: maintaining that Maradona was better than Garrincha is also considered a serious breach of good manners.)

Taking these few precautions, visitors will discover that everything about Brazilian football is pure delight. The game is slower here, and best players have time to show off their skills, relishing their domination of the ball with a series of swerves, feints and dribbles. The rhythmic play of the ball dictates the tone of the game. The fans are spirited but extremely demanding – referee, players and authorities are routinely booed. As Nelson Rodrigues, one of the country's acclaimed sports columnists, once wrote: "Brazilians don't even respect a minute of silence". It is no coincidence that Rodrigues was also the country's best playwright, because here drama and football are inseparable. Football imitates art; art imitates life; life imitates football. And so, regardless of politics, the economic situation, or international crises, as long as the Brazilian shirt is yellow, that yellow that turns gold with the sweat of the players, and emblazoned with the stars of the country's footballing triumphs, Brazil will be a united, peaceful and happy nation.

Marcos Caetano,
sports columnist

ADVENTURE AND ECOTRAVEL

Opportunities for ecotourism and adventure exist all over Brazil. Some areas welcome guests with fully modern services, while others offer more rudimentary facilities in the midst of magnificent and nearly untouched wilderness.

Adventure tourism and adventure sports aren't entirely one, according to specialists, but there's plenty of room for both in Brazil. Adventure sports such as mountain biking and rafting demand training, discipline and a high level of physical fitness. Adventure tourism broadly refers to both these demanding sports and other adventure-related activities, such as rappelling and snorkeling, which can be undertaken with a minimum of preparation. Rappelling can be done in various situations, and snorkeling is a leisure activity that does not require previous training.

Since nature and adventure sports go hand in hand, it's easy to see why Brazil has become an important ecotourism destination. The country's size and its diverse landscapes make it irresistible both for those seeking to peacefully contemplate beauty and for those looking for thrills, excitement and the "adrenaline" that adventurers talk about so much. The natural richness and abundance is unparalleled – and unfortunately not always matched by organization and infrastructure, even in officially designated Conservation Areas such as national parks, environmentally protected areas and privately owned reserves. The traveler is therefore best off thoroughly investigating his or her destination in advance, through tourist information centers, travel agencies, sports magazines and experienced tourists and adventurers – as well as, of course, this volume.

A COUNTRY OF INFINITE POSSIBILITIES

Which destinations should be recommended to an ecotourist willing to brave Brazil? There's almost nowhere one can go wrong. One place to start might be the city of Brotas, in the center of São Paulo state, with its many rivers and a unique geological structure that is the source of some 30 waterfalls. Thanks to these unique natural features, the city has become one of the most popular and well estab-

Rappelling, Anhumas Abyss, in Bonito, Mato Grosso do Sul

lished centers of adventure tourism in Brazil, with a range of sports including rafting, *bóia-cross* (going down a river on an inflatable inner tube), rappelling, horseback riding, trekking, mountain biking and canopy tree climbing. If the adventurer wants to combine sports with big-city attractions, the best place to head to is Rio de Janeiro, which has managed a rare feat: preserving a magnificent forest reserve – Parque Nacional da Tijuca – in the heart of the large city. The reserve is well designed to address the needs of visitors, and myriad trails leading to waterfalls and caves, as well as to Pedra Bonita, a popular jump point for hang gliding. Mountain climbers can climb Pão de Açúcar and many of the city's other landmark mountains.

Chapada Diamantina, an oasis of crystal clear waters and gentle hills in the backlands of Bahia, offers opportunities for mountain climbing, trekking, biking and snorkeling. Caves, lagoons, rivers and waterfalls compose a landscape that many describe as the most beautiful in Brazil.

In the state of Mato Grosso do Sul, in the Central West region, is another favorite destination – the town of Bonito – a paradise for hiking, snorkeling, diving and rafting. The nearby Pantanal offers many options for trails and horseback riding in one of the country's largest ecological sanctuaries. The region is also one of the country's most popular locations for sport fishing.

Jalapão, in Tocantins, offers one of Brazil's best locations for rafting in an almost untouched region, perfect for those willing to trade comfort for the pleasure of being surrounded by wild nature. Far to the south, Florianópolis, in the state of Santa Catarina, combines trails and coastline that is ideal for surfing and diving.

Countless opportunities for water sports line Brazil's vast coastline. There are the favorite diving destinations such as Fernando de Noronha in Pernambuco, Abrolhos in Bahia, Arraial do Cabo in Rio de Janeiro, and Bombinhas in Santa Catarina. For sailing the best areas include Ilhabela in São Paulo, Angra dos Reis in Rio de Janeiro, Jericoacoara in Ceará, and Imbituba in Santa Catarina.

This list hardly scratches the surface of what the country has to offer the adventurous traveler. There are also the mountain ranges in the south, the mountains and high peaks in the Southeast, the wild beaches in the Northeast, and the rich and lush Amazon Rainforest. A wide range of amazing possibilities await those seeking adventure or tranquility, physically demanding challenges or serene and timeless beauty.

Diving

Sailing

Rafting

Off-road

Surfing

Canopy climbing

FLORA AND FAUNA

The huge expanse of Brazilian territory offers a diversity of environments. Each ecosystem is a universe: travel through them and experience the sense of enchantment and wonder that must have enveloped Brazil's first visitors.

Throughout the 19th century, many European researchers criss-crossed Brazil to inventory its riches. Coming from France, England, Germany and the Netherlands, these naturalists – a term describing botanists, zoologists, geologists and other natural history experts – not only catalogued an host of Brazilian animal and plant species, but also classified the territory itself for the first time, broadly delineating what scientists would eventually call ecosystems. Currently, IBAMA (Brazilian Institute of the Environment and Renewable Natural Resources) distinguishes seven broad ecological regions in the country – a classification that does not differ greatly from that proposed by the pioneering studies of the naturalists.

THE AMAZON RAINFOREST

When considering Brazilian plants and animals, it is impossible to not mention the immense green patch that spreads over the northwestern part of the country. Brazil contains roughly 3.5 million km² (1.35 million sq. mi.) of the Amazon's total 7 million square kilometers (2.7 million sq. mi.). The Amazon River and its tributaries form a complex network of waterways that sustain an incredible biodiversity.

The variety of forest environments accounts for this diversity. There are regions of aquatic forests (*igapó*) that are constantly flooded, meadows that are periodically flooded and upland forests that are spared direct contact with running water. Patches of savannah landscapes and a type of dry scrub vegetation called *campinarana* by the locals are nestled in the heart of the forest. Each area has distinct animal and plant life. There is a considerable variety, including tree species like mahogany (threatened by illegal logging), cabbage-bark, cedar, palm, Brazil nut, silk-cotton, sapodillas, *pau-mulato*, mauriti palms, Guiana chestnut and Brazilian spiny club palms. There is also an immense variety of herbs and grasses, as well as the Amazon's sig-

High waters in Nhecolândia (MS), one of the most remote areas of the Pantanal

Royal water lily, the Amazon

nature flower, the royal water lily that floats on rivers and inlets displaying flowers on top of large circular leaves. The list of birds includes macaws, toucans, woodpeckers, hoatzins, wrens (the *uirapuru*, whose song, according to legend, is so sweet that other birds stop to listen), cock-of-the-rocks and manakins. Reptiles include Brazilian land turtles, turtles, lizards, anacondas, boa constrictors, bushmasters and dozens of other snake species. The list of mammals includes bats, grisons, coatis and anteaters, as well as the whitelipped peccary, the three-toed sloth, the spotted cavy and the Brazilian tapir. There are various primate species such as ouakari monkeys, capuchin monkeys and howling monkeys. The cat family includes jaguars and cougars. There are also roughly 3,000 species of fish swimming in the rivers, as well as aquatic mammals like manatees and Amazon porpoises.

THE CERRADO (SAVANNAH)

The Cerrado has a distinct landscape: large tracts of level land scattered with sparse vegetation and gnarled tree trunks with thick bark. The savannah's dry winters leave the fields yellowish and the trees bare. In the summer, the green returns along with the rain.

A dense forest of tall trees flourishes along the riverbanks which divide the plateau. Outlining the marshes, long lines of mauriti palms form pathways – and throughout centuries, these palm trees guided muleteers, indicating from afar the location of water for the cattle. The Brazilian savannah has 10,000 plant species. Trees found here include tecomas, golden spoon fruit trees, rosewoods and copals, as well as shrubs such as vellozia. Flowers include strawflowers; fruit trees include souari nuts, the fruit of which is used extensively in local cuisine.

These ecosystems are also the habitat of hundreds of different animal species. Among the birds are ostriches, crested seriemas, owls, macaws, parrots and parakeets. In the fields roam animals such as anteaters, deer, armadillos, jaguars, cougars, bush dogs and maned wolves. There are also snakes like the boa constrictor, the Brazilian dragon aroid and the tropical rattlesnake, as well as lizards and a large number of insects that are far from being completely identified.

THE PANTANAL

The waterways flowing down from the Andes and the central Brazilian plateau join with those from the Paraguay basin to form the Pantanal. This large region of lowlands in the hearts of the states of Mato Grosso and Mato Grosso do Sul extends to the west toward Bolivia and Paraguay, covering an area of 250,000 km^2 (96,500 sq. mi.) – larger than the United Kingdom. It is a vast system made up of more than 100 rivers. It is a universe unto itself, split into two seasons: the rainy season that the locals call winter that extends from November to March and is characterized by extensive flooding. The dry season or summer runs from April to October, when the water levels

Hyacinth macaw, the Pantanal

Baby iguana, Cerrado savannah

White woodpecker, the Pantanal

Hairy saki monkey, the Amazon

Brazilian pine, the South

Capybaras, the Pantanal

Caraguatá bromeliad, the Pantanal

Margay tiger cat, the Pampas

Quipá cactus, Caatinga

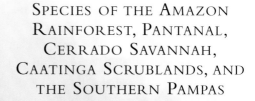

Species of the Amazon Rainforest, Pantanal, Cerrado Savannah, Caatinga Scrublands, and the Southern Pampas

Armadillo, Caatinga scrublands

Pacu (top) and curimba fish, the Pantanal

Great anteater, Cerrado savannah

Alligators, the Pantanal

Maned wolf, Cerrado savannah

Buriti palm swamp, Cerrado savannah

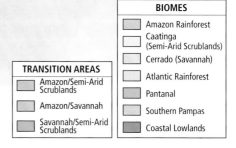

TRANSITION AREAS	
	Amazon/Semi-Arid Scrublands
	Amazon/Savannah
	Savannah/Semi-Arid Scrublands

BIOMES	
	Amazon Rainforest
	Caatinga (Semi-Arid Scrublands)
	Cerrado (Savannah)
	Atlantic Rainforest
	Pantanal
	Southern Pampas
	Coastal Lowlands

slowly drop and leave behind a nutritious loam that enables the proliferation of life on the lowlands. The floodplain becomes an expanse of grassland with a few scattered trees, ideal for cattle grazing. It is not a co-incidence that cattle ranching is one of the pillars of the Pantanal economy.

This unique environment is a meeting point for plants and animals from many different regions. This is what distinguishes the Pantanal – not the existence of exclusive species, but the huge numbers and variety of species. Plants and animals typically found in the Amazon, the Savannah and the central plateau are also found here.

Bird species include red and blue macaws, toucans, hummingbirds, spoonbilled ducks, hawks, jabiru storks, kingfishers and cormorants. Mammals include capybaras, jaguars, anteaters, deer, otters and Brazilian otters. The region also has an abundance of anacondas, boa constrictors, adder snakes, alligators and lizards such as the teju lizard and iguanas, as well as frogs and toads of all sizes and colors. The Pantanal waters contain more than 200 different species of fish (including dourados, speckled catfish and piranhas) that attract fishermen from all over the world. Fishing is prohibited during the spawning season, when the schools of fish swim upstream to lay their eggs. The vegetation of the Pantanal varies in accordance with its own ecological niches. There are palm trees from the Savannah and others such as yellow and purple tecomas. The dry hilltops are home to cacti, as well as bromeliads.

Cougar, Caatinga scrublands

Centuries-old fig tree, the Pantanal

The other extreme of the Pantanal has rich aquatic vegetation that is fundamental for the development of animal life in the rivers. These plants often group together and form floating green "islands" on the rivers. In the hidden waters of the Pantanal, it is even possible to find the quintessentially Amazonian royal water lily.

THE CAATINGA (SEMI-ARID SCRUBLANDS)

Life can actually thrive in the parched vastness of the Caatinga. There are roughly 700,000 km² (270,000 sq. mi.) identified by rugged ground and a hot, dry climate.

The semi-arid climate of the Caatinga is characterized by two seasons: the rainy summer season and the dry winter season. During the drought, the rivers dry up, the plants shed their leaves and the soil cracks. When rain starts to fall, green foliage spreads once again.

In the Caatinga, regions dotted with shrubs, cacti and thorny plants alternate with sparse forests consisting of small trees and bushes. There, visitors will find cacti like the Peru cereus (whose flower, according to the locals, is a sign of the rainy season), the xique-xique cactus, the palm cactus and the floral wreath cactus. There are also shrubs and trees such as the castorbean plant, aveloz, acacia, piassava palm, angico, tecoma and nettlespurge. Some regions boast fruit trees such as the yellow mombin and cashew, as well as the hardwoods brauna, the tonka-bean tree and the Chinese date tree. The region's animals include bats, cavies, three-banded armadillos, brockets and lizards, as well as snakes like the tropical rattle snake, the false coral snake and the boa constrictor. The most common birds are caiques, doves, picazuro pigeons (known as the *asa-branca*, it is the symbol of the *sertão* or backlands of the Northeast, thanks to the song by Luís Gonzaga of the same name) and the laughing hawk, a small hawk whose call is considered an omen of doom.

THE ATLANTIC RAINFOREST

When the Portuguese arrived in Brazil, the Atlantic Rainforest covered more than 1 million square kilometers (400 thousand sq. mi.). Today, only 7 percent of this area remains. Even so, it is still one of the world's most diversified ecosystems.

Extending from the states of Rio Grande do Norte to Rio Grande do Sul, the rainforest covers coastal and inland areas in a strip of land of varying width (on average 200 kilometers, or 124 mil.). In the Northeast it is a narrow strip along the coast, widening in the south of Bahia and continuing southward in an irregular pattern until it reaches Paraná and Santa Catarina where it extends far inland. Moisture carried by the winds blowing off the ocean is a common factor among all regions.

The forest, fragmented by human devastation, contains an immense biodiversity. As well as huge variety of invertebrate fauna (many still unknown) and fish, amphibians, snakes and other reptiles, there are 25 species of primates, many exclusive to the regions. These include the golden lion tamarin in the south of Bahia, the saki monkey in the regions between Espírito Santo and Minas Gerais and the spider monkey in the Southeastern region. Throughout the entire forest, there are large cats like the margay tiger cat, the leopard and the jaguar. The forest is also home to anteaters, hairy six-banded armadillos and three-toed sloths. Birds include the Brazilian tanager that inhabits the coastal region and the seven-colored tanager that lives in Alagoas and Pernambuco. Toucans, white herons and parrots are also found throughout the forest. Typical plant species are ferns, bromeliads and orchids, as well as flowering trees such as the manaca rain tree, princess flower and the ringworm shrub. The forest also boasts palm trees – such as the one from which açaí is extracted –, silverleaf pumpwood trees, pink shower trees, Paraná pines, sibipirunas and albarco jequitibas that can reach a height of 50 meters (164 feet). The brazilwood tree that gave Brazil its name, now almost extinct, is also native to the Atlantic Rainforest.

THE SOUTHERN PAMPAS

The Southern part of the country contains a large area of open plains. Vegetation is thicker between Santa Catarina and Rio Grande do Sul, especially in the more mountainous areas. Heading further south, the land becomes flatter and more homogenous, forming an immense green carpet called the Pampas that extends beyond the border of Rio Grande do Sul to Uruguay and Argentina. The grassy plains are dotted with fig, trumpet and other trees. Typical animals include the Pampas fox (or grison), the Pampas cat, deers, jaguars and raccoons. Closer to the coast, the fields encounter wetland ecosystems with aquatic plants like water lilies and rushes. The area is inhabited by mammals such as rice rats, capybaras and gophers, reptiles such as the broad-nosed cayman and birds such as the great white shouldered tanager, the black-necked swan and teal ducks from Patagonia. The region also hosts many fish, including the cichlid.

COASTAL LOWLANDS

Brazil's long coastline features a wide array of natural formations: sea cliffs, beaches, dunes, remote rocky stretches, coastal lowlands and forests. But the mangrove swamps deserve special attention. These swamps are found from Amapá to Santa Catarina in bays and estuaries where the rivers flow into the ocean. The currents of water deposit sediment and organic material on the loamy bottom where the mangroves trees grow.

These trees vary in height. Their roots protrude from the ground and coexist with the swamp animal life: shrimp, crabs, oysters and mussels, as well as salt-water fish like snook fish, catfish and mullet. Sea otters, coatis, raccoons also reside in the lowlands; birds like the scarlet ibis, bittern and heron also seek out the habitat to reproduce.

For many years, the mangrove swamps – dark areas full of mud and insects – were associated with unhealthiness and backwardness, and as a result, many were filled in or used as garbage dumps. Their importance to the equilibrium of marine life was only recognized a few decades ago, and today many of them are legally protected. Despite many recurring problems such as pollution, smuggling and deforestation, the country has matured, and the swamps still offer the same sensation of enchantment and wonder that the ancient explorers experienced.

Mangrove swamp, coastal lowlands

SPECIES OF THE ATLANTIC RAINFOREST AND COASTAL LOWLANDS

Booby, coastal lowlands

Crab, coastal lowlands

Bromeliad, Atlantic forest

Golden trumpet, Atlantic forest

Butterflies, Atlantic forest

Saffron toucanet, Atlantic forest

Woolly spider monkey, Atlantic forest

Orchid, Atlantic forest

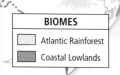

BIOMES

Atlantic Rainforest

Coastal Lowlands

THE SOUTHEAST

The Southeast region of Brazil is comprised of the states of Rio de Janeiro, São Paulo, Minas Gerais, and Espírito Santo. Rio de Janeiro is one of the most beautiful and vibrant state capitals in the country. São Paulo has established itself as the business, shopping, and culinary heart of Latin America. Belo Horizonte, the capital of Minas Gerais, is steeped in cultural traditions, and Vitória, in Espírito Santo, offers a surprising amount of peace and quiet considering its urban setting. The southeast's attractions aren't limited to big cities, however. On Rio de Janeiro's state coastline you'll find idyllic retreats like Paraty, a jewel of Brazilian colonial architecture. Many small mountain towns are historic and fun to explore. The coast of São Paulo state has a fabulous string of beaches, while the state's interior is a mecca for adventure sports enthusiasts, as well as those just seeking relaxation in the mild mountain climate. Minas Gerais has magnificent historical towns, most built at the height of the gold rush, now guardians of a rich cultural heritage. Espírito Santo draws visitors with a little bit of everything: a lovely coastline, mountains, and historical cities.

RIO DE JANEIRO

MINAS GERAIS

N

1 cm = 30 km
1 inch = 47.3 mi.

Belo
Horizonte

Feira de
Santana

BR
040

ROD. WASHINGTON LUÍS

Rio Paraíba do Sul

RIO DE
JANEIRO

Macaé

P. N. de
Itatiaia

Visconde
de Mauá

BR
393

Penedo

Resende

Vassouras

Petrópolis

Teresópolis

P. N. da
Serra dos
Órgãos

RJ
106

São
Paulo

SÃO
PAULO

DUTRA

BR
116

RIO-SANTOS

Guanabara
Bay

BR
101

Búzios

Cabo Frio

P. N. da
Serra da
Bocaina

BR
101

Sepetiba
Bay

Niterói

Lagoa de
Araruama

Arraial
do Cabo

Paraty
Bay

Angra
dos Reis

P. N. da
Barra da
Tijuca

Rio de
Janeiro

Saquarema

Paraty

Ilha
Grande

Ubatuba

ATLANTIC OCEAN

HIGHLIGHTS

- The rich historic, cultural, and architectural heritage of **Rio de Janeiro.**
- Lively **Copacabana, Ipanema,** and **Leblon** beaches.
- Outdoor activities in **Rio,** including trails, climbing, paragliding, hang-gliding, diving, running, and cycling.
- The magnificent coastal views of **Paraty,** **Angra dos Reis,** and **Ilha Grande,** on the south coast.
- The beautiful beaches near **Búzios, Cabo Frio,** and **Arraial do Cabo,** on the north coast.
- The fresh mountain air of historical towns like **Petrópolis, Teresópolis, Vassouras, Visconde de Mauá,** and **Itatiaia.**

WHEN TO GO

- In **summer** to enjoy the beaches that dot the state's beautiful coastline. Keep in mind, however, that prices are high this time of year, and hotels and restaurants are generally crowded.
- During **Carnival** to celebrate in the streets of Rio with traditional *blocos* and to see the dazzling samba school parades.
- During the **winter** months, when mild temperatures make a relaxing stay in the mountains even more inviting.

THE CITY OF RIO DE JANEIRO

HISTORICAL CITY CENTER

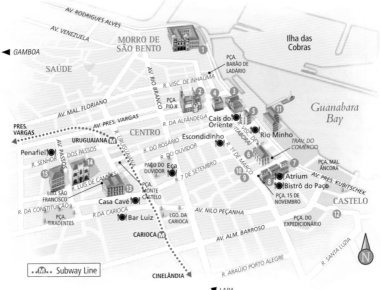

AV. RODRIGUES ALVES

AV. VENEZUELA

◄ GAMBOA

MORRO DE
SÃO BENTO

Ilha das
Cobras

PÇA.
BARÃO DE
LADÁRIO

SAÚDE

AV. RIO BRANCO

R. VISC. DE INHAÚMA

PÇA.
PIO X

Guanabara
Bay

AV. MAL. FLORIANO

PRES.
VARGAS

AV. PRES. VARGAS

R. DA ALFÂNDEGA

Cais do
Oriente

R. VISC. DE ITABORAI

Rio Minho

TRAV. DO
COMÉRCIO

AV. PASSOS

URUGUAIANA Ⓜ

CENTRO

R. DO ROSÁRIO

Escondidinho

R. 1º DE MARÇO

R. DOS PASSOS

R. SENHOR

Penafiel

R. DO OUVIDOR

PAÇO DO
OUVIDOR

Eça

R. 7 DE SETEMBRO

PÇA. MAL.
ÂNCORA

AV. PRES. KUBITSCHEK

LGO. SÃO
FRANCISCO

R. LUÍS DE CAMÕES

PÇA.
MONTE
CASTELO

Atrium

Bistrô do Paço

CASTELO

R. DA CONSTITUIÇÃO

Casa Cavé

PÇA. 15 DE
NOVEMBRO

PÇA.
TIRADENTES

R. DA CARIOCA

LGO. DA
CARIOCA

AV. NILO PEÇANHA

PÇA. DO
EXPEDICIONÁRIO

Bar Luiz

CARIOCA Ⓜ

AV. ALM. BARROSO

..Ⓜ.. Subway Line

CINELÂNDIA ◄

R. ARAÚJO PORTO ALEGRE

R. SANTA LUZIA

N

▼ LAPA

❶ Igreja do Mosteiro de São Bento
❷ Igreja Nossa Senhora da Candelária
❸ Casa França–Brasil
❹ Centro Cultural Banco do Brasil (CCBB)
❺ Centro Cultural Correios
❻ Igreja Nossa Senhora da Lapa dos Mercadores
❼ Praça Quinze and Estação das Barcas
❽ Paço Imperial

❾ Igreja Nossa Senhora do Carmo da Antiga Sé
❿ Igreja da Ordem Terceira do Carmo
⓫ Espaço Cultural da Marinha
⓬ Igreja Nossa Senhora do Bonsucesso
⓭ Igreja de São Francisco de Paula
⓮ Real Gabinete Português de Leitura
⓯ Centro de Arte Hélio Oiticica

The walking tour outlined here is best enjoyed during weekday business hours, when Rio's streets are alive with the energy and pulse of the city. Evenings and weekends are hit-or-miss, as some churches may be closed to casual visitors, fewer taxis are available, and the police presence is significantly reduced. On weekends visitors can attend mass and enjoy festivals, plays, and other performances at cultural centers, but the streets are not as safe as they are on weekdays.

The baroque architecture of a monastery church

① IGREJA DO MOSTEIRO DE SÃO BENTO

Rio's greatest baroque monument is São Bento Monastery Church. The church was constructed between 1633 and 1690. Its austere façade belies a rich interior with sumptuous gilt woodcarvings. The eight magnificent side altars are decorated with 17th- and 18th-century statues. Note the delicate angels throughout the church, and, in the sacristy, the representation of Christ in *Senhor dos martírios*, a panel painted in 1690 by Friar Ricardo do Pilar, who is also responsible for four other paintings in the monastery. On Sundays at 10am the monks sing Gregorian chants – arrive early if you want to hear them. *Rua Dom Gerardo, 68, Centro, tel. (21) 2291-7122. Daily, 7am – 11am and 2:30pm – 6pm. Guided visits, Mon – Sat, 8am – 4pm.*

② IGREJA NOSSA SENHORA DA CANDELÁRIA

Church construction began in 1775 but was not completed until 1898. The "new" building replaced an older chapel that was built here in the late 16th century. The church interior is lined with marble. Its ceiling panels, painted by Zeferino da Costa in 1880, tell the story of the church's early days. The beautiful bronze doors were created in 1901 by Portuguese sculptor Antônio Teixeira Lopes. The sculpture known as the *Mulher com ânfora (Woman with Amphora)* was sculpted by Humberto Cozzo in 1934 and presently stands in front of the church. *Praça Pio X, Centro, tel. (21) 2233-2324. Mon – Fri, 7:30am – 4pm; Sat, 8am – noon; Sun, 9am – 1pm.*

③ CASA FRANÇA–BRASIL

The France-Brazil House was Rio's first neoclassical building. Its design is the

Igreja Nossa Senhora da Candelária

work of French architect Grandjean de Montigny, who came to Brazil in 1816 with the French Mission *(see box on page 100)*. The house has played many roles in the history of Rio; its first, in 1820, was as the city stock exchange. It has since been a customs house, a bank archive, and a court of law. Today, restored and renovated, it houses a cultural center. The center hosts exhibitions throughout the year *(program details are available online: www.casafrancabrasil.rj.gov.br)*. It is worth taking a moment to admire the 24 Doric columns under the large central dome and skylight. They are made of wood but painted with a technique called *trompe l'oeil* to look like marble. There is a small bookshop, café, and cinema. The **Arte Temperada Bistrô e Buffet** *(tel. (21) 2253-2589; daily, noon – 7pm)*, at the back of the building, serves French and Brazilian dishes daily. *Rua Visconde de Itaboraí, 78, Centro, tel. (21) 2253-5366. Daily, 8:30am – 8:30pm.*

A view of downtown Rio de Janeiro; the bridge that leads to Niterói is visible at the top

❹ CENTRO CULTURAL BANCO DO BRASIL (CCBB)

The Bank of Brazil Cultural Center's building was designed in the neoclassical style by Francisco Joaquim Bethencourt da Silva, a disciple of Grandjean de Montigny. Construction began in 1880 and was finished in 1906. It was built to house the stock exchange and became the property of Banco do Brasil in the 1920s. The bank's cultural center has called it home since 1989. Nowadays it hosts some of Rio's chicest events, including fine art exhibitions, concerts, and plays. It is also a popular spot to relax with friends and enjoy a drink after work. The architecture is lovely, particularly the columns, the ornamental details, and the design of the central hall. The center has a cinema, library, and restaurant.

Rua Primeiro de Março, 66, Centro, tel. (21) 3808-2020. Tue – Sun, 10am – 9pm.

❺ CENTRO CULTURAL CORREIOS

What is today the Correios Cultural Center was originally intended to serve as a venue for professional courses taught by the Lloyd Brasileiro steamship company. Construction of the neoclassical building began around 1920, but the Brazilian postal service acquired it before construction was completed and continued to use it until the 1980s. After a series of renovations it became a cultural center in 1993. It still retains a few of its original features, including a tiny elevator with room for just three passengers and an operator. The auditorium, which seats 200, hosts films, plays, concerts, and other performances. The ground floor has a small art gallery, a very pleasant café, and a working post office. There are occasionally open-air events in the adjacent square, **Praça dos Correios.**

Rua Visconde de Itaboraí, 20, Centro, tel. (21) 2253-1580. Tue – Sun, noon – 7pm.

6 IGREJA NOSSA SENHORA DA LAPA DOS MERCADORES

A modest church on Rua do Ouvidor, Nossa Senhora da Lapa dos Mercadores is considered by many the loveliest house of worship in the city. The interior is carved of wood and lit by a skylight in the sacristy. Built by street vendors in 1750, it was renovated extensively in the 19th century. During the Revolta da Armada (Naval Revolt) of 1893, cannon fire aimed at Itamaraty Palace hit the bell tower and knocked down a marble statue of the Madonna. The statue survived unscathed and the cannonball now sits in the sacristy. When you step out of the chapel, take a moment to admire the ornate façades of nearby buildings and the

---

THE OLD DOWNTOWN TAVERNS

The narrow streets of the historical city center overflow with *botecos* (bars) and restaurants, most of which are Portuguese. Traditional, congenial **Rio Minho** first opened its doors in 1884. They serve appetizing snacks at the bar and are famed for dishes like the Sopa Leão Veloso, a seafood stew *(Rua do Ouvidor, 10, tel. (21) 2509-2338; Mon – Fri, 11am – 4pm)*. A little farther away is **Bar Luiz**, a local institution. It was opened in 1887 by Adolf Rumjaneck, a German immigrant, and has been at the same address since 1927. Bar Luiz serves well-chilled *chope* (draft beer) and German dishes, including wurst, cold cuts, and a variety of cooked meat dishes *(Rua da Carioca, 39, tel. (21) 2262-6900; Mon – Sat, 11am – 11:30pm)*. The bar is one of the stops on the walking tour of Cinelândia and surroundings *(see page 98)*. Simple **Penafiel** has been drawing lunchtime customers back since 1913. It serves generous portions of traditional Portuguese dishes, including squid and fish with rice, *mocotó à portuguesa* (calf's foot), tripe, and codfish with rice and broccoli *(Rua Senhor dos Passos, 121, tel. (21) 2224-6870; Mon – Fri, 11am – 3:30pm)*.

Paço Imperial: from royal residence to cultural center

cobblestones beneath your feet.
*Rua do Ouvidor, 35, Centro, tel. (21)
2509-2339. Mon – Fri, 8am – 2pm.*

**❼ PRAÇA QUINZE AND ESTAÇÃO
DAS BARCAS**
Quinze de Novembro Square is home
to many historic treasures, including
Paço Imperial *(pictured above)* and the
Chafariz do Mestre Valentim, a
pyramid-shaped, marble-and-gneiss
fountain built in 1789 to replace the
original, which was built in 1750. From
the square, you can see the **Arco do
Teles,** a small and arched passage
constructed by the Teles de Meneses
family in the 19th century. The Cais
Pharoux quays once served as an
important gateway to the city. They
were built in the 19th century to
connect Rio and Niterói by ferry.
Today the quays are used by **Estação
das Barcas** and boats run between Rio,
Niterói, and Paquetá 24 hours a day at
regular intervals *(timetable available – in
Portuguese – at www.barcas-sa.com.br, or*

tel. (21) 2533-7792). **Monumento ao
General Osório,** a bronze statue of
General Osório, also stands in the
square. The monument was sculpted by
Rodolfo Bernardeli over the course of
six years, reaching completion in 1894.

❽ PAÇO IMPERIAL
The colonial-style Imperial Palace was
built in 1743 and served as the
residence of two viceroys. In 1808,
with the arrival of Dom João and his
court, it became the Portuguese seat of
government. In 1815 the colony of
Brazil became part of the United
Kingdom of Portugal, Brazil, and the
Algarve. Finally, in 1822, the palace
became the Imperial seat of
government. The building is a national
heritage site, and rightly so; many
important historic events have taken
place within its walls. It was here that
Dom João VI was proclaimed King of
Portugal, here that Pedro I defied
orders to return to Portugal, and here
that slavery was abolished in 1888.

After Brazil became a republic, the building served as headquarters for the national post and telegraph service. It was restored in 1985 and now houses a cultural center with a good contemporary art program *(program details available at www.pacoimperial.com.br)*. There is also a music store called **Arlequim** *(tel. (21) 2220-8471; Mon – Fri, 9am – 8pm; Sat, 10am – 6pm)*, a café, **Bistrô do Paço** *(tel. (21) 2262-3613; Mon – Fri, 11:30am – 7:30pm; Sat, Sun, and holidays, noon – 7pm)*, and a cinema. *Praça 15 de Novembro, 48, Centro, tel. (21) 2533-4491. Tue – Sun, noon – 6pm.*

⑨ Igreja Nossa Senhora do Carmo da Antiga Sé

The church's rococo interior carvings are the work of master sculptor Inácio Ferreira Pinto. It has other noteworthy features, as well: a marble font, majestic ceiling paints, and a high altar ornamented with silver. Quite a few historic Catholic ceremonies were held here, including Pedro I's coronation Mass and a number of royal baptisms and weddings. Unfortunately, the church's façade has been heavily modified and very few of the features that were present when it was built in 1761 remain. *Rua 7 de Setembro, 14, corner of Rua Primeiro de Março, Centro, tel. (21) 2242-7766. Mon and Fri, 10am – 5pm; Tue – Thu, 9am – 5pm; Sat, 11am – 5pm.*

⑩ Igreja da Ordem Terceira do Carmo

Ordem Terceira do Carmo Church opened its doors for Mass in 1770. It is one of the only churches in Rio with a façade made completely of stone. In the chapel stand six altars representing scenes from the Passion of Christ. The marble font in the sacristy is the work of master sculptor Valentim da Fonseca e Silva, also known as Mestre Valentim. The high altar is

The six altars of Igreja da Ordem Terceira do Carmo depict the Passion of Christ

decorated with a rare statue of Saint Emerentiana (said to be Jesus' great-grandmother) and her daughter, Saint Anne (the Virgin Mary's mother, Jesus' grandmother).

Rua Primeiro de Março, no #, Centro, tel. (21) 2242-4828. Mon – Fri, 8am – 4pm.

⑪ ESPAÇO CULTURAL DA MARINHA

The Navy Cultural Center has its own museum ship, the *Bauru*, as well as a submarine, the *Riachuel*. It also exhibits navigational instruments, items salvaged from shipwrecks, and a small rowing galley built in 1808 and used by the Imperial family. The center leads guided trips to **Ilha Fiscal,** an island with interesting neo-gothic buildings. The last royal ball was held on Fiscal in the days before Brazil was proclaimed a republic.

Avenida Alfredo Agache, no #, Centro, tel. (21) 2104-6025. Tue – Sun, noon – 5pm. Trips to Ilha Fiscal: Thu – Sun, 1pm, 2:30pm, and 4pm.

⑫ IGREJA NOSSA SENHORA DO BONSUCESSO

Casa de Misericórdia Hospital was founded in the 16th century and a small adobe chapel was built on the grounds shortly thereafter. The church, also known as Nossa Senhora da Misericórdia e Santa Isabel, has been renovated many times since. It was given its current name after one such renovation in the 19th century. The façade, cupola, and main chapel are also products of 19th century restoration work. The church is home to 17th-century altarpieces, the oldest in the city. The altarpieces and the pulpit were taken from the old Jesuit College on Morro do Castelo when it was demolished in 1922.

Largo da Misericórdia, no #, Centro, tel. (21) 2220-3001. Mon – Fri, 8am – 3:30pm.

⑬ IGREJA DE SÃO FRANCISCO DE PAULA

The chapel was founded in 1759, but its inaugural ceremony wasn't held

Ilha Fiscal; guided tours start from the Espaço Cultural da Marinha

The spectacular reading room in the Real Gabinete Português de Leitura

until 1865. The façade has a curvilinear stone frontispiece and a number of baroque features. Though the church is small, dilapidated, and surrounded by street vendors, it's worth visiting because its best features are found inside. The church has stained-glass windows from Munich, ornamental work by master sculptor Mestre Valentim in the main chapel, carvings by Antônio de Pádua Castro, and paintings by Vítor Meireles.
Largo de São Francisco, no #, Centro, tel. (21) 2509-0070. Mon – Fri, 11am – 12:30pm.

⑭ REAL GABINETE PORTUGUÊS DE LEITURA

The library, with a collection of over 350,000 books, is the most impressive Portuguese-language library outside Portugal. It is housed in a Manueline-style building that was constructed in 1837. Readers sit at jacaranda tables in the grand reading room under beautiful tall ceilings and an iron and stained-glass skylight. The library has a collection of rare books, some of which date back to the early 16th century.
Rua Luís de Camões, 30, Centro, tel. (21) 2221-3138. Mon – Fri, 9am – 6pm.

⑮ CENTRO DE ARTE HÉLIO OITICICA

Hélio Oiticica's imposing 19th century neoclassical home was a music conservatory before it became an art center. Hélio was one of the most avant-garde artists in Brazil in the 1960s and 70s. He created *parangolés*, multi-colored works of art that can be worn like capes. The center's six galleries hold temporary exhibitions of work by famous artists, as well as Oiticica's own creations.
Rua Luís de Camões, 68, Centro, tel. (21) 2242-1213. Tue – Fri, 11am – 6pm; Sat, Sun, and holidays, 11am – 5pm.

CINELÂNDIA AND ENVIRONS

① Palácio Gustavo Capanema
② Biblioteca Nacional
③ Museu Nacional de Belas-Artes
④ Teatro Municipal
⑤ Igreja e Convento de Santo Antônio
⑥ Igreja da Ordem Terceira de São Francisco da Penitência
⑦ Confeitaria Colombo
⑧ Museu Histórico Nacional

At the dawn of the 20th century the area around Avenida Central (now Avenida Rio Branco), in Cinelândia, was the haunt of politicians, artists, intellectuals, and anyone looking for a good, unhurried chat. The city's first cinemas appeared here. These days most of them have been made into Protestant churches. The avenue, however, remains a cultural hotspot. A number of eclectic, vaguely neoclassical buildings are concentrated nearby: the **Teatro Municipal,** the **Biblioteca Nacional,** the **Museu Nacional de Belas-Artes,** and a restored building that houses the **Cine Odeon** BR. All of these, with the exception of the cinema, were built under the watchful eye of Mayor Pereira Passos in the early 20th century. Houses and slums were demolished to make way for the avenue, which cut through the quays to Flamengo Beach, changing the city's landscape forever.

① PALÁCIO GUSTAVO CAPANEMA
Built between 1937 and 1943, Gustavo Capanema palace was the first example of "modernist" architecture in Brazil. French-Swiss architect Le Corbusier served as a consultant to the Brazilian design team, which included Lúcio Costa, Oscar Niemeyer, and Afonso Eduardo Reidy, among others. The palace sits on pillars ten meters high, allowing air to circulate beneath the building and granting easy access to the street. The palace was originally built to house the Brazilian Ministry of Education and Culture. Today it is still a public administration building, so access is largely restricted to government employees. However,

visitors are welcome to roam the lovely garden, which was designed by Burle Marx, and to appreciate the tiled murals by Cândido Portinari and the sculptures by Bruno Giorgi.
Rua da Imprensa, 16, Centro, tel. (21) 2220-1490. Mon – Fri, 9am – noon and 3pm – 5pm.

❷ BIBLIOTECA NACIONAL

The National Library's architecture combines art nouveau and neoclassical elements. The building, completed in 1910, was designed by General Francisco Marcelino de Sousa Aguiar. It creates an immediate first impression in visitors as they stand at the base of the majestic staircase leading to the first floor. As you enter, note the bronze sculpture to the right. It was created by the sculptor Correia Lima and represents intelligence. To the left is a sculpture by Rodolfo Bernardelli that symbolizes learning. The library owns over 3 million books and other documents. Its collection includes letters belonging to the Brazilian imperial family, two first editions (1572) of *Os Lusíadas (The Lusiads),* two copies of the Mazarin Bible (also known as the Gutenberg Bible, printed on parchment in 1462), and an 11th-century Greek gospel. None of these treasures are on display, however; they're kept carefully tucked away in safes. Guided tours *(Mon – Fri, 11am – 3pm)* wind their way through the 1st, 2nd, and 3rd floors, with stops at the reading and research rooms and at two panels painted by Rodolfo Amoedo *(A memória* and *A reflexão).*
Avenida Rio Branco, 219, Centro, tel. (21) 2220-9608. Mon – Fri, 9am – 8pm; Sat, 9am – 3pm.

❸ MUSEU NACIONAL DE BELAS-ARTES

The National Museum of Fine Art was founded in 1937. It occupies a neoclassical building that was designed by members of the French Mission in

Biblioteca Nacional, built in 1910, has largely neoclassical architectural features

Teatro Municipal, on the left

(1876), by Nicolau Facchinetti. There are some 16,000 pieces in the museum collection, with many famous artists well-represented, including Frans Post, Cândido Portinari, Anita Malfatti, Lasar Segall, Alfredo Volpi, and Auguste Rodin. Since 2006, parts of the museum have been closed to visitors for restoration work.
Avenida Rio Branco, 199, Centro, tel. (21) 2240-0068. Tue – Fri, 10am – 6pm.

❹ TEATRO MUNICIPAL
Inspired by the Paris Opera, the municipal theater was designed by Francisco Oliveira Passos, son of then-mayor Francisco Pereira Passos, in collaboration with Frenchman Albert Guilbert. Guided tours of the theater include opportunities to appreciate its marble staircases, onyx handrails, bronze sculptures by Rodolfo Bernardelli, paintings by Eliseu Visconti, and foyer panels by Rodolfo Amoedo. It's a good idea to reserve your tour tickets in advance *(tel. (21) 2299-1667)*. The building was opened in 1909 to seat 2,400. It was built facing Avenida Rio Branco to take advantage of the view of Guanabara Bay and the Arcos de Lapa aqueduct; unfortunately the city's skyscrapers now obscure the vista. The theater's season runs March through December. Concerts are held on Sundays at 11am. Tickets can be purchased at the theater starting at 9am. *Praça Floriano, no #, Centro, tel. (21) 2299-1667. Mon – Fri, 1pm – 4pm.*

1816 at the behest of Dom João VI *(see the following box)*. The museum has a very important collection of some 5,000 works of 19th-century Brazilian art. Highlights include *Primeira missa no Brasil* (1860), by Vítor Meireles, *Batalha do Avaí* (1877), by Pedro Américo, and *São Tomé das Letras*

❺ IGREJA E CONVENTO DE SANTO ANTÔNIO
The church and monastery were built between 1607 and 1616 for a community of Franciscan friars. The paintings, sculptures, and tiles inside the monastery are almost perfectly preserved. The church, on the other

---

THE FRENCH MISSION

The French Mission arrived in Brazil in March 1816. It brought with it many artists, including the painters Jean-Baptiste Debret and Nicolas Taunay, and architect Grandjean de Montigny, who designed the Casa França–Brasil. It is thought that Dom João VI supported the mission because he wanted to encourage a national arts program and establish an academy of arts and crafts in Brazil. Lebreton brought a small collection of paintings with him; these formed the beginning of the collection on display at the Museu Nacional de Belas-Artes.

---

hand, has been extensively modified, but still retains a few of its original features, including a neocolonial frontispiece (1822), a sacristy chest made by Manuel Setúba (1749), and tiled panels depicting the life of Saint Anthony. The church and monastery's strategic position made it a refuge during the French invasion of 1711. Monastery visits must be booked a week in advance, but the church is open to the public seven days a week. *Largo da Carioca, no #, Centro, tel. (21) 2262-0129. Mon – Fri, 8am – 6pm; Sat, 8am – 11am and 2pm – 4pm; Sun, 9am – 11am.*

⑥ IGREJA DA ORDEM TERCEIRA DE SÃO FRANCISCO DA PENITÊNCIA
Few colonial buildings in the city can rival the church's dazzling, opulent gilt carvings. Church construction began in 1657 but wasn't completed for 115 years – the final thirty years were dedicated entirely to gilding. Recently, restoration work closed the church for twelve years, but it reopened in 2000 and today welcomes visitors to appreciate works from its extensive collection of religious art. While there, take a leisurely look at the pulpit and its carved figures, which are covered in gold leaf. There are particularly fine paintings by Caetano da Costa Coelho on the main chapel ceiling depicting the glorification of Saint Francis. The church also has carvings by Portuguese sculptor Manuel de Brito and an elevated statue of Christ on the high altar that represents the vision Saint Francis had when he received the stigmata. Caretaker Dona Maria Desidéria will happily share tales of the church's history with those who stop for a chat. *Largo da Carioca, 5, Centro, tel. (21) 2262-0197. Tue – Fri, 9am – noon and 1pm – 4pm.*

⑦ CONFEITARIA COLOMBO
To visit this old confectioner's is to step back in time. The Belgian mirrors, jacaranda furniture, Portuguese floors, and Italian marble all date back to the day the doors first opened in 1894. The menu pays homage to illustrious patrons of old: there is *chá Virginia Lane* (tea

The 17ᵗʰ-century complex: Igreja e Convento de Santo Antônio

named after a starlet), *filé-mignon à gaúcha* (in honor of President Getúlio Vargas), and *sopa creme de palmito* (cream of palm heart soup, musician Chiquinha Gonzaga's favorite). Writers Olavo Bilac and Machado de Assis also frequented Confeitaria Colombo back in the day. The confectioner's makes dozens of sweet pastries and desserts. Some, like *pastel de nata* (custard tartlet), *trouxinha de ovos*, and *ovos moles* (both sweet egg custards), are made from very old recipes. You can also buy famous Leques Gaufrettes wafer biscuits, an in-house specialty made here since 1920. The biscuits are great with ice cream. **Espaço Memória,** upstairs, sells replica china, crystal, and menus. A pianist plays popular and classical music during lunchtime and happy hour.
Rua Gonçalves Dias, 32, Centro, tel. (21) 2505-1500. Mon – Fri, 9am – 8pm; Sat, 9:30am – 5pm. Closed on Sundays.

❽ Museu Histórico Nacional
The National History Museum encompasses Forte de Santiago, a fortress dating from 1603, Casa do Trem Bélico and its collection of weapons (1762), and Arsenal de Guerra (1764). The museum collection is comprised of more than 287,000 historical artifacts related to Brazilian colonial history. Highlights include items from the Imperial Pharmácia (imperial pharmacy), some of which date to 1847; the largest coin collection in Latin America; the painting *Batalha naval do Riachuelo* (Naval Battle of Riachuelo), by Vítor Meireles; and the Senate Throne where Dom Pedro II sat during legislative assemblies.
Praça Marechal Âncora, no #, Centro, tel. (21) 2550-9260. Tue – Fri, 10am – 5:30pm; Sat, Sun, and holidays, 2pm – 6pm.

A look inside Confeitaria Colombo, which first opened its doors in 1894

The 42 arches of the 270-meter-long Aqueduto da Carioca have graced this spot since 1750

LAPA

The birthplace of many of Rio's rogues and the 1930s haunt of bohemians like composer Noel Rosa and drag-artist Madame Satã, Lapa owes its name to its mid-18th-century church, Igreja Nossa Senhora do Carmo da Lapa do Desterro. After a period of decline, the neighborhood has made a comeback. Its streets are full of historic nooks and crannies and its music venues, bars, and taverns entertain a variety of customers with the sounds of samba, *chorinho*, and *MPB* (popular Brazilian music). Lapa is accessible by bus, car, or taxi via Avenida Mem de Sá, Avenida República do Paraguai, or Avenida Augusto Severo.

ARCOS DA LAPA AND PASSEIO PÚBLICO

Aqueduto da Carioca *(Largo da Lapa, no #)* is a 270-meter-long (886-foot) aqueduct with 42 arches. The aquaduct segments are also known as the **Arcos da Lapa** (Lapa Arches). It was built in 1750 under the direction of mayor Conde de Bobadela to carry water from the Carioca River to Praça Carioca square. It no longer diverts water, but it's interesting to look at. In 1788 the city constructed **Passeio Público** park *(Rua do Passeio Público, no #)*. It has an old gate by Mestre Valentim and a lead sculpture of a boy by an unknown artist.

CULTURAL ATTRACTIONS

Sala Cecília Meireles is one of the best chamber music recital venues in the city *(Largo da Lapa, 47, tel. (21) 2224-4291; Mon – Fri, 9am – 6pm; box office: Mon – Fri, 1pm – 6pm; Sat, Sun, holidays, and concert days, 1pm – 6pm)*. The **Escola de Música da** UFRJ hosts classical music concerts *(Rua do Passeio Público, 98, tel. (21) 2240-1391; Mon – Fri, 8am – 8pm)*. **Feira Rio Antigo** is a fair held on the first

Rio Scenarium: late nights in Lapa

Saturday of each month. Vendors sell furniture, paintings, and rugs *(Rua do Lavradio, tel. (21) 2224-6693, 10am – 7pm)*. **Museu da Imagem e do Som** is a museum of image and sound that houses important collections like photographs of old Rio by Augusto Malta *(Praça Rui Barbosa, 1, tel. (21) 2262-0309; Mon – Fri, 11am – 5pm; it is essential to arrange research visits in advance)*.

Lapa Nightlife
Samba and *choro* buffs will love Lapa's live music scene. Avenida Mem de Sá is home to popular venues like **Estrela da Lapa** *(#69, tel. (21) 2507-6686; Tue – Sat, 9pm until the last customer leaves)*, **Carioca da Gema** *(#79, tel. (21) 2221-0043; Mon – Thu, 6pm – 1am; Fri, 6pm – 3am)*, **Café Cultural Sacrilégio** *(#81, tel. (21) 3970-1461, 2222-7345; Tue – Sat, 7pm – 3am)*, and **Nova Capela**, a bar-restaurant hybrid *(#96, tel. (21) 2252-6228; daily, 11am – 5am)*.

Nearby, unpretentious **Clube dos Democráticos** spins an excellent variety of music *(Rua Riachuelo, 91, tel. (21) 2252-4611; Wed – Sat, 10pm – 4am; Sun, 8pm – midnight)*. Beautiful, popular **Rio Scenarium** is an antique store by day, club by night *(Rua do Lavradio, 20, tel. (21) 3852-5516, 2233-3239; Tue – Sat, 7pm until the last customer leaves)*. Under the Arcos da Lapa, **Comuna do Semente** draws top musicians *(Rua Joaquim Silva, 138, tel. (21) 9781-2451; Sat, 2pm – 2am; Sun – Thu, 8pm – 10pm)*. Reopened in 2004, **Circo Voador** has revived some of the events held during its golden era in the 1980s and 90s, including the Domingueira Voadora dance and its show program *(Rua dos Arcos, no #, tel. (21) 2533-5873, 2533-0354; box office: midnight – 6pm; show days, from 10pm)*. Next door, **Fundição Progresso** plays electronica, samba, *forró*, and rock'n'roll. During Carnival, Monobloco rehearsals are held here *(Rua Arcos da Lapa, 24, tel. (21) 2220-507; daily, 9am – 10pm; shows: 10pm – 5am)*.

Gamboa Nightlife
The port neighborhood of Gamboa, officially known as Saúde, has several good music venues. **Trapiche da Gamboa** is a local samba institution in a beautiful historic building (1867). It draws a variety of people to its samba and *choro* sessions *(Rua Sacadura Cabral, 155, Saúde, tel. (21) 2516-0868; Tue – Thu, 6:30pm – 1am; Fri, 6:30pm – 3am; Sat, 8:30pm – 3am)*. Eccentric **Cabaret Kalesa** sits among the *inferninhos*, or "hellholes" (as the brothels and gaming dens typically found in port areas are called). It draws a modern, alternative crowd to dance to the rhythms of MPB, samba, and electronic music *(Rua Sacadura Cabral, 61, Saúde, tel. (21) 2516-8332; Mon – Sat, 11pm – 5am)*.

SANTA TERESA

Sitting on a hilltop, the old, garden-covered Santa Teresa neighborhood owes its name to 18th-century Santa Teresa convent. The area acquired a bohemian atmosphere thanks to the artists who had studios here. José Bechara, Marcos Chaves, and Raul Mourão all lived in Santa Teresa. The artistic crowd earned the neighborhood an affectionate nickname: "the Montmartre of Rio." You can drive up Santa Teresa's steep streets on your own or take a streetcar, instead *(Estação de Bondes Carioca: Rua Lélio Gama, no #, Petrobrás building, adjacent to the Aqueduto da Carioca, near the Catedral Metropolitana, Centro, tel. (21) 2215-8559; daily, 6:40am – 8:40pm, streetcars depart every 20 minutes).*

MUSEU CHÁCARA DO CÉU
The Chácara do Céu art museum typically exhibits a selection of pieces from its Raymundo Castro Maya (1894-1968) collection, including works by Europeans, like Debret, as well as modern Brazilian artists, like Guignard, Di Cavalcanti, Antônio Bandeira, and Portinari. The museum has a lovely garden designed by landscape architect Burle Marx.
*Rua Murtinho Nobre, 93,
tel. (21) 2224-8981, 2224-8524.
Wed – Mon, noon – 5pm.*

PARQUE DAS RUÍNAS
Ruínas Park is all that remains of a mansion that once belonged to patron of the arts Laurinda Santos Lobo. The park hosts the *Vertentes Cariocas* concert series *(first and last Sunday of each month, 6pm)*, shows for children *(first Sunday of each month, 11am)*, and temporary art exhibits. Ruínas has a dazzling view of the city.
Rua Murtinho Nobre, 169, tel. (21) 2252-1039. Tue – Sun, 8am – 8pm.

A streetcar leaves the city center on its way to Santa Teresa

Portuguese sweets, prepared by Alda Maria, in Santa Teresa

STUDIOS AND GALLERIES

In July, dozens of artists from Santa Teresa open their doors to tourists and visitors during the **Arte de Portas Abertas** (Art with Open Doors) festival. Information about the festival is available from the Santa Teresa Artists' Association *(Chave Mestra – Associação dos Artistas de Santa Teresa, tel. (21) 2507-5352, 2509-5037)*. **Galeria Mauá** exhibits work by local artists *(Rua Monte Alegre, 277, tel. (21) 2507-5352, 2509-5037; Mon – Fri, 2pm – 6pm)*. **Getúlio Damado** makes colorful streetcars from recycled trash. His delightful studio is inside a streetcar *(Rua Leopoldo Fróes, 15, tel. (21) 2531-9066; Mon – Sat, 9am – 8pm; Sun, 9am – 4pm)*. **Ateliê Zé Andrade** sells ceramic dolls, including likenesses of famous people *(Rua Leopoldo Fróes, 83-A, tel. (21) 2242-1415, 8166-9698; visits must be arranged in advance)*. **La Vereda** sells furniture, light fixtures, and decorative items *(Rua Almirante Alexandrino, 428, tel. (21) 2507-0317; daily, 10am – 8pm)*. **Ateliê Balaio de Gato** teaches classes and runs a showroom for jewelry *(Rua Almirante Alexandrino, 2750, apartment 201, tel. (21) 9609-4710, 8758-6390; Sat and Sun, 10am – 5pm)*.

EATING AND DRINKING IN SANTA TERESA

On Rua Pascoal Carlos Magno, **Bar do Mineiro** makes great *cachaças (#99, tel. (21) 2221-9227; Tue – Sun, and holidays, 11am – 1am)*. **Simplesmente** hosts samba jam sessions *(#115, tel. (21) 2221-0337; Mon – Sat, 7pm – 3am)*. **Jasmim Manga**, a bar, bookstore, and cybercafé, sells delicious sweets *(#143, tel. (21) 2242-2605; daily, 9am – 10pm)*. On Rua Almirante Alexandrino, you will find **Espírito Santa**, which sells dishware from the state of Pará *(#264, tel. (21) 2508-7095; Mon – Wed, noon – 6pm; Thu, Fri, and Sat, noon – midnight; Sun, noon – 10pm)*. **Adega do Pimenta** serves German food *(#296, tel. (21) 2224-7554; Mon – Fri, noon – 10pm; Sat, noon – 8pm; Sun, noon – 6pm)*. **Bar do Arnaudo** specializes in northeastern cuisine *(#316-B, tel. (21) 2210-0817, 2222-9476; Mon, noon – 6pm; Tue – Fri, noon – 11pm; Sat and Sun, noon – 8:30pm)*. As you continue down Rua Almirante Alexandrino, you will find tasty seafood at **Sobrenatural** *(#432, tel. (21) 2224-1003; daily, noon – midnight)*, delicious Portuguese sweets at **Alda Maria's house** *(#1116, tel. (21) 2232-1320; Tue – Sun, 2pm – 7pm)*, and German food paired with Brazilian and imported beers at **Mike's Haus** *(#1,458, store #A, tel. (21) 2509-5248; Mon – Thu and Sun, noon – 1am; Fri and Sat, noon – 2am)*.

GLÓRIA AND CATETE

Sloping toward the sea, the Glória neighborhood takes its name from an opulent 18th-century church, Igreja de Nossa Senhora da Glória. The neighborhood is home to **Marina da Glória**, one of Brazil's major nautical centers *(Avenida Infante Dom Henrique, no #, tel. (21) 2205-6716; daily, 8am – 6pm)*, **Hotel Glória**, a charming old hotel *(Rua do Russel, 632, tel. (21) 2555-7272; daily, 24 hours)*, and **Chafariz da Glória**, a fountain built in 1772 *(Rua da Glória, 156)*.

IGREJA NOSSA SENHORA DA GLÓRIA DO OUTEIRO

Igreja Nossa Senhora da Glória was favored by the Brazilian royal family. The church was completed in 1739. It replaced a smaller chapel built in 1670. There is a medallion of the Virgin Mary over the central portal, and the interior has beautiful 18th-century tiled panels. Behind the church is a museum that exhibits religious artifacts, including silver and paintings *(Tue – Fri, 9am – noon and 1pm – 5pm; Sat and Sun, 9am – 1pm). Ladeira da Glória, 135, Glória, tel. (21) 2557-4600. Mon – Fri, 9am – noon and 1pm – 5pm; Sat and Sun, 9am – noon.*

MUSEU DA REPÚBLICA

Now a national museum, neoclassical Catete Palace was once one of the most opulent palaces in Brazil. It served as the seat of Republican government from 1897 to 1960. The palace became the Museum of the Republic when the nation's capital moved to Brasília. The room where President Getúlio Vargas shot himself is on the third floor; the somewhat morbid display includes his revolver and bullet-riddled pajamas. The museum collection encompasses books, documents, and artifacts, including the palace's original furniture. *Rua do Catete, 153, Catete, tel. (21) 3235-2650. Tue, Thu, and Fri, noon – 5pm; Wed, 2pm – 5pm; Sat, Sun, and holidays, 2pm – 6pm.*

Igreja Nossa Senhora da Glória do Outeiro, where members of the Brazilian royal family were baptized

COSME VELHO, MARACANÃ, AND SÃO CRISTÓVÃO

CORCOVADO

The Christ the Redeemer statue atop Morro do Corcovado is one of the best-known landmarks in Brazil, and it is one of the new Marvels of the World. The site offers the highest, most all-encompassing view of Rio. The most interesting and enjoyable way to the top is by train from Cosme Velho Station. Trains run every half-hour, and provide dazzling views of the city's South Zone, two beaches, and Rodrigo de Freitas Lake. Once at the top, a system of escalators and a panoramic lift allow visitors to bypass climbing the 220 steps up to the Christ statue.

Rua Cosme Velho, 513, Cosme Velho, tel. (21) 2492-2252. Daily, 8:30am – 6:30pm.

MUSEU INTERNACIONAL DE ARTE NAÏF DO BRASIL

Near Corcovado, the Brazilian International Naïf Art Museum houses 6,000 paintings. It is considered one of the world's most comprehensive naïf art collections. More than 100 countries are represented in its holdings.

Rua Cosme Velho, 561, Cosme Velho, tel. (21) 2205-8612. Visits must be arranged in advance.

QUINTA DA BOA VISTA, JARDIM ZOOLÓGICO, AND MUSEU NACIONAL

Leafy **Quinta da Boa Vista** park is home to the **Museu Nacional** (National Museum), which was established by Dom João VI in 1818. The palace was the Imperial family's residence from 1822 to 1889. Today it exhibits prehistoric animal skeletons, Egyptian sarcophagi, mummies, and indigenous weapons. The park also has a zoo, the **Jardim Zoológico,** which was opened in 1945. Three hundred fifty species are represented, and more than 2,100 animals live here. **Quinta da Boa Vista** restaurant serves an ox-tail entrée and a seafood stew called *caldeirada* at open-air tables *(tel. (21) 2589-6551, 2589-4279; Mon – Thu, 9am – 4pm; Fri, 9am – 10pm; Sat and Sun, 9am – 6pm).* Be aware that the park is not well-maintained and the surrounding area is dangerous despite the presence of security guards in the park itself.

Avenida Pedro II, no #, São Cristóvão, Quinta da Boa Vista and Museu Nacional: tel. (21) 2568-8262. Tue – Sun, 10am – 4pm; Zoo: tel. (21) 3878-4200. Tue – Sun, 9am – 4pm.

MARACANÃ

The Maracanã stadium was built to host the 1950 World Cup. Unfortunately, the home team lost to Uruguay. Nevertheless, it was an impressive achievement, the largest stadium of its kind in Brazil. Renovations in 2007 for the PanAmerican Games expanded the stadium seating to 95,000. A hall of fame displays historic photographs of great players and the ball with which Pelé scored his thousandth goal. Guided tours cover areas normally off-limits to the casual sports fan, including the VIP seating area, dressing rooms, and the tunnel to the field, where speakers simulate the roar of the crowd during a game. Tours must be booked in advance. If you have time, it's worth catching a game; Be a Local *(tel. (21) 9643-0366, 7816-9581, 9582)* will buy your tickets and provide transportation from your hotel to the game.

Rua Professor Eurico Rabelo, no #, Maracanã, tel. (21) 2299-2941. Daily, 9am – 5pm (Nov – Feb, 9am – 6pm). On game days, visits must be completed four or five hours before kick-off.

FLAMENGO, BOTAFOGO, AND URCA

PARQUE DO FLAMENGO (BRIGADEIRO EDUARDO GOMES)

Flamengo Park was built in the 1960s. It has a modern art museum (Museu de Arte Moderna), sports facilities, bike paths, a children's park, a puppet theater, and areas for model airplane flying and skateboarding. On Sundays and holidays a stretch of Avenida Infante Dom Henrique is closed to traffic and opened to pedestrians. The park, now a national heritage site, was designed by Lota (Maria Carlota) Macedo Soares. Landscape artist Burle Marx conceptualized the outdoor spaces, and architect Afonso Eduardo Reidy designed the buildings.
Avenida Infante Dom Henrique, no #, Flamengo.

MUSEU DE ARTE MODERNA

Rio's Museum of Modern Art, which opened in 1958, is local architect Afonso Eduardo Reidy's masterpiece. Tragically, in 1978 a huge fire destroyed part of the collection and the museum was closed for more than a decade. Today, the museum has 11,000 works of modern and contemporary art from around the world. It also owns the Gilberto Chateaubriand collection of works by the first Brazilian modernists. Visitors can view *Number 16*, by Jackson Pollock, and *O fantasma*, an installation by Antônio Manuel.
Avenida Infante Dom Henrique, 85, Parque do Flamengo, tel. (21) 2240-4944. Tue – Fri, noon – 6pm; Sat, Sun, and holidays, noon – 7pm.

MUSEU DO ÍNDIO

The Indian Museum was established in 1953 by anthropologist Darcy Ribeiro. The museum has one of the largest indigenous collections in Brazil: 14,000 artifacts and other indigenous pieces, 16,000 national and international indigenous ethnology publications, 50,000 pictures, and more than 200 audio recordings.
Rua das Palmeiras, 55, Botafogo, tel. (21) 2286-8899. Mon – Fri, 9am – 5pm; Sat, Sun, and holidays, 1pm – 5pm.

PÃO DE AÇÚCAR

The world-famous cable cars of Pão de Açúcar (Sugarloaf Mountain) have been one of Rio's most popular tourist attractions for decades. The cars leave every 30 minutes from Praia Vermelha, in Urca. The first ride takes you to the top of Morro da Urca (224 meters, 735 feet, above sea level), which has a view of Botafogo Beach and Guanabara Bay. The next stage takes you to the top of Sugarloaf (396 meters, 1,300 feet), where a jaw-dropping view of Rio, Niterói, and Fiscal Island awaits. We recommend you go up on a sunny day to guarantee a clear view, or in the evening to enjoy the sunset. You'll find souvenir shops, jewelry stores, ice-cream parlors, and snack bars at the top.
Avenida Pasteur, 520, Urca, tel. (21) 2546-8400. Daily, 8am – 7:50pm.

A cable car ascends Pão de Açúcar

PANORAMIC VIEWS AND FASHIONABLE BEACHES

← São Paulo

GUADALUPE

COSTA
BARROS

ACARI

DEODORO
TURIAÇU

VILA
MILITAR

MARECHAL
HERMES

CASCADURA

JARDIM
SULACAP

ABOLIÇÃO

ÁGUA
SANTA

SERRA DO NOGUEIRA

TAQUARA

JACAREZINH

Projac

JACAREPAGUÁ

SERRA DOS PRETOS FORROS

MÉIER

BENFICA

CIDADE
DE DEUS

FREGUESIA

Autódromo
Nelson Piquet

LINHA AMARELA

GARDÊNIA
AZUL

ANIL

GRAJAÚ

Morro da
Panela

SERRA DOS TRÊS RIOS

ANDARAÍ

Lagoa da
Tijuca

Pedra da
Gávea
842 m

Pedra
Bonita
696 m

ALTO DA
BOA VISTA

Floresta da Tijuca

USINA

MUDA

👀 The roads to
Tijuca National Park
offer beautiful views of Rio

ESTRADA DAS FURNAS

Mesa do
Imperador
483 m

Parque das
Paineiras 👀

Marina
Barra
Grande

The view from Gávea Rock and
São Conrado Beach. Hang-gliding
and paragliding flights

Morro do
Cochrane

ESTRADA DA VISTA CHINESA

BARRA DA
TIJUCA

Vista
Chinesa
413 m

Parque Nacional da Tijuca

JOÁ

From the Estrada da Canoa road,
one can see São Conrado
and part of the coast
looking toward Guaratiba

Vista Chinesa and Mesa do
Imperador offer views of the
forest as well as the urban area
bordering Rodrigo de Freitas Lake.
To get there, take Estrada Dona
Castorina in Jardim Botânico

JARDIM
BOTÂNI

Cabo da
Gávea

Ponta do
Mourisco

São Conrado

SÃO CONRADO

Favela da
Rocinha

Jardim
Botânico

Jóquei Clube
Brasileiro

Lagoa
Rodrigo de
Freitas

Ilha do
Meio

Gruta da
Imprensa

VIDIGAL

Morro Dois
Irmãos

GÁVEA

AV. BORGES DE MEDE

AV. NIEMEYER

LEBLON

Waterski

Cabo Dois
Irmãos

AV. DELFIM MOREIRA

12 Baixo
Bebê

IPANE

This map shows Rio's best vantage points
and its most fashionable beaches – Leme,
Copacabana, Ipanema, and Leblon. The meeting
points for different groups – tourists, young
people, the elderly, and children – are the twelve
postos (lifeguard stations), dotted along the shore,
from (Posto 1) to Leblon (Posto 12) at intervals
of a kilometer or less. Along this almost 10
kilometers (6 miles) stretch, beachgoers play
beach football, volleyball, gymnastics, and beach
tennis, and go rollerskating, surfing, biking,
running, and walking.

Leblon

11

Ipanema

Volleyball

10

9

Football
footvolley
and volleyball

Gay me

Bodyboardi

👀 Viewpoint

■ Lifeguard Station

7

Ilha das
Palmas

Ilha
Cagarra

Ilha
Comprida

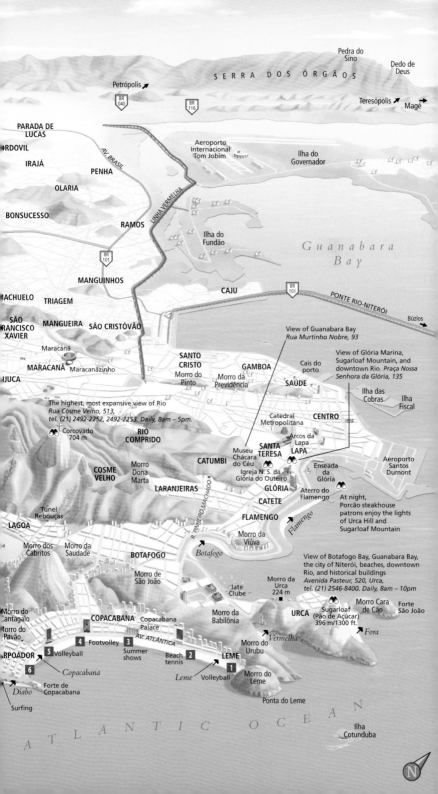

Copacabana Beach with a view of Leme; this stretch of sand teems with life night and day

COPACABANA

Rio natives are known as *cariocas*, and the *carioca* spirit flows freely on the 4 kilometer (2.5 mile) stretch of beach between Leme and Forte de Copacabana. One of the city's most populous neighborhoods, Copacabana never sleeps. It seems people are always swarming the beach kiosks, walking on the crowded promenade, biking along the cycle lane, or playing volleyball or soccer. It's also the beach of choice for elderly locals, who come here to walk and exercise. Unfortunately, with the decline of the middle class and the arrival of prostitution and sex tourism, the neighborhood has lost some of its poetry, but it is still home to the glamorous **Copacabana Palace Hotel.** Every year, thousands of people come here to celebrate the New Year and watch the seafront fireworks display.

EATING

There are a number of good restaurants and bars in Copacabana, from neighborhood watering holes to upscale eateries. Generous servings of *bacalhau à patuscada* (a codfish dish) draw devotees back to cozy **Alfaia** *(Rua Inhangá, 30, store #B, tel. (21) 2236-1222; Mon – Sat, noon – midnight; Sun, noon – 11pm)*. The house specialty at **A Marisqueira** *(Rua Barata Ribeiro, 232, tel. (21) 2547-3920; daily, 11am – midnight)* is the delicious *caldeirada de frutos do mar*, a kind of seafood stew. **Cais da Ribeira** *(Avenida Atlântica, 2964, tel. (21) 2548-6332; daily, noon – 11:30pm)* overlooks Copacabana Beach and serves wonderful Portuguese food. The irresistible creations of Roland Villard, one of the city's most talented chefs, top the menu at **Le Pré Catelan** *(Avenida Atlântica, 4240, Hotel Sofitel, tel. (21) 2525-1160; Mon – Sat, 7:30pm – 11pm)*, which specializes in French cuisine. Tiny, unpretentious **Shirley** *(Rua Gustavo Sampaio, 610, store #A, Leme, tel. (21) 2275-1398; daily, noon – 12:30am)* has been serving simple, generous Spanish dishes for 50 years. Menu mainstays include shrimp with squid and *polvo à espanhola* (octopus). If you can't tear yourself away from the beach, there are several popular kiosks in convenient locations. **Bar Luiz** serves German food and **Caroline Café** serves sandwiches,

exotic drinks, and snacks. Both are located between Posto 2 and Posto 3. In front of the Copacabana Palace Hotel are two more popular hangouts: **Quiosque 35,** which is open 24 hours a day, and lively **Rainbow,** a popular spot for the beach's GLBT community.

COPACABANA PALACE

Copacabana's first hotel and a Rio landmark, the Copacabana Palace was built in 1923. The grand old building helped make the neighborhood internationally famous. It is the city's most charming hotel, the destination of presidents, kings, and Hollywood stars past and present. The 1933 film *Flying Down to Rio* was made here. Fred Astaire and Ginger Rogers danced together for the first time in the movie. Playboy Jorginho Guinle, who dated such beauties as Marilyn Monroe and Rita Hayworth, was born here and insisted on dying in one of the rooms in 2004. It has two restaurants: the **Pérgola,** which overlooks the pool, and the **Cipriani,** one of Rio's most sophisticated dining venues.
Avenida Atlântica, 1702, tel. (21) 2548-7070.

FORTE DE COPACABANA

Copacabana Fort was built in the early 20th century on the place where Igreja de Nossa Senhora de Copacabana once stood. (This is the church that gave the neighborhood its name.) It was from here, in 1922, that a group of mutinous officers set out to face government troops in the middle of Avenida Atlântica, an episode that went down in history as "Os 18 do Forte" (The Fort 18). Mutineers long gone, the complex now houses only the **Museu Histórico do Exército** (Army History Museum) and **Café do Forte** *(Tue – Sun, 10am – 9pm)*. The café is owned by the proprietors of the famous Confeitaria Colombo restaurant, in downtown Rio, which has a dazzling view of Copacabana Beach. Café do Forte serves breakfast and afternoon tea at open-air tables with umbrellas, a lovely view, and refreshing sea breezes. The panoramic view can be appreciated from other places around the fort, as well.
Praça Coronel Eugênio Franco, 1, posto 6, tel. (21) 2521-1032, 2522-4460. Tue – Sun, 10am – 9pm.

Graviola

Papaya

Mangaba

Pitanga

CASUAL DINING

Given that temperatures in Rio typically hover between 30 and 40 degrees Celsius (that's 86 to 104 degrees Fahrenheit) most locals don't bother dressing up when they go out to eat. They value the kind of simple, local dive that serves tasty food in generous portions. Bars, juice bars, and ice-cream parlors fitting this description stretch from Leme to Leblon. Rio social life orbits around its bars, where profession, social class, and surname are forgotten. **Jobi** is a local favorite that has been serving beer into the wee hours for more than fifty years *(Avenida Ataulfo de Paiva, 1166, Leblon, tel. (21) 2274-0547, 2274-5055; daily, 11am – 4am).* **Bracarense** is famous for its savory snacks, like *bobozinhos* (deep-fried shrimp balls) and *bolinhos de camarão com catupiry* (deep-fried shrimp and cream cheese balls) *(Rua José Linhares, 85-B, Leblon, tel. (21) 2294-3549; Mon – Sat, 7am – midnight; Sun, 9am – 10pm).* Another worthwhile destination is **Cervantes**, which serves tasty sandwiches like the *Cervantes especial*, a combination of fillet steak, pâté, and pineapple *(Avenida Prado Júnior, 335-B, Copacabana, tel. (21) 2275-6147; Tue – Thu, noon – 4am; Fri and Sat, noon – 6am; Sun, noon – 4am).* **Bar Lagoa** has served savory snacks and German dishes, like their highly-praised sausage and pork knuckles, for decades. Patrons enjoy a lovely view of Lagoa Rodrigo de Freitas from the bar's veranda *(Avenida Epitácio Pessoa, 1674, Lagoa, tel. (21) 2523-1135; Mon – Thu, 6pm – 2am; Fri – Sun, noon – 2am).* The traditional draft beer at **Devassa** is a local favorite. Devassa has branches in other neighborhoods *(Avenida General San Martin, 1241,* *Leblon, tel. (21) 2540-6087; daily, 5pm until the last customer leaves).* In Flamengo, **Belmonte** also fills with locals, who come for the savory snacks and *cachaças*. Belmonte has branches in Copacabana, Leblon, Ipanema, and Lapa *(Praia do Flamengo, 300, tel. (21) 2552-334; daily, 8am – 3am).* Meanwhile, **Barril 1800** is an ideal spot for a bite to eat after a day at the beach. They serve snacks, pizza, draft beer, and a variety of entrees *(Avenida Vieira Souto, 110, Ipanema, tel. (21) 2523-0085, 2523-3375; daily, 11am until the last client leaves).* Juice bars are another local institution. **Bibi Sucos** serves more than thirty different kinds of juice. They have branches in several neighborhoods *(Rua Miguel Lemos, 31, store #A, Copacabana, tel. (21) 2513-6000; Sun – Thu, 8:30 am – 1:45am; Fri and Sat, 8:30am – 3am).* **Balada Sumos** serves dozens of flavors and makes some pretty unusual juice combination drinks *(Avenida Ataulfo de Paiva, 620, store #A, Leblon, tel. (21) 2239-2699; Sun – Thu, 7am – 2am; Fri and Sat, 7am – 3am).* In Ipanema, **Polis Sucos** has been at the same address for thirty years *(Rua Maria Quitéria, 70-A, Ipanema, tel. (21) 2247-2518; Sun – Wed, 7am – midnight; Thu, Fri, and Sat, 7am – 2am).* **Mil Frutas** ice cream parlor has branches in Jardim Botânico and São Conrado. They serve ice creams made from a variety of Brazilian fruits (including *mangaba, pitanga,* and banana). We recommend the unusual but delicious guava and cheese ice cream *(Rua Garcia d'Ávila, 134, store #A, Ipanema, tel. (21) 2521-1384, 2247-2148; Mon – Fri, 10:30am – midnight; Sat, 9:30am – 1:30am; Sun, 9:30am – 12:30am).*

IPANEMA AND LEBLON

It was here, on the most upscale stretch of beach in Rio, that Tom Jobim and Vinícius de Morais played the opening bars of *Garota de Ipanema (The Girl from Ipanema)*. The song immortalized Ipanema. The beach and surrounding area have something for everyone, no matter what your taste, palate, or pocketbook. Ipanema begins at Arpoador and meets Leblon at Jardim de Alah Canal, which connects Rodrigo de Freitas Lake to the sea. The 6 kilometers (nearly 4 miles) of beach that comprise Ipanema and Leblon are busy night and day. The sidewalks quake with energy, the same vitality present in the volleyball schools, the ladies' footvolley games, the soccer matches, the spontaneous bursts of applause at sunset around Posto 9, and the lively conversations at the gay meeting area between Posto 8 and Posto 9. There is even a beach area for children called **Baixo Bebê,** which sits opposite Rua Venâncio Flores in Leblon. It has diaper changing facilities and a playground.

DINING OUT

Countless bars and restaurants line **Avenida Vieira Souto** (the Ipanema beachfront), **Avenida Delfim Moreira** (the Leblon beachfront), **Rua Prudente de Morais**, **Rua Visconde de Pirajá**, and **Rua Barão da Torre** (in Ipanema), as well as **Avenida Ataulfo de Paiva** and **Rua Dias Ferreira** (in Leblon). Some serve haute cuisine, others simple fare. Friendly beach kiosks are also abundant. Most serve meat, pasta, seafood, and traditional Portuguese entrees. **Margutta** specializes in seafood and Italian cuisine *(Avenida Henrique Dumont, 62, Ipanema, tel. (21) 2259-3718; Mon – Fri, 7pm – 1am; Sat, Sun, and holidays, noon – midnight)*. The Ipanema branch of the steakhouse chain **Porcão** serves *prix fixé* meals that cater to meat lovers *(Rua Barão da Torre, 218, tel. (21) 3202-9155; Sun – Thu, 11:30am – midnight; Fri and Sat, 11:30am – 12:30am)*. For delicious pizza, head to lively **Capricciosa** *(Rua Vinícius de Morais, 134, tel. (21) 2523-3394; daily, 6pm – 2am)*. Popular **Gula**

Ipanema begins at Arpoador and divides Leblon from the Jardim de Alah Canal

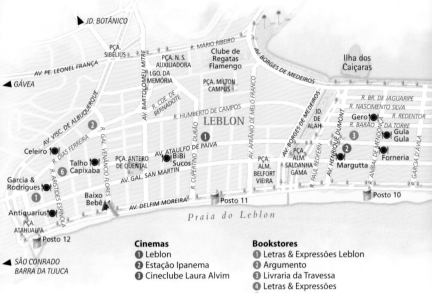

Cinemas
1. Leblon
2. Estação Ipanema
3. Cineclube Laura Alvim

Bookstores
1. Letras & Expressões Leblon
2. Argumento
3. Livraria da Travessa
4. Letras & Expressões
5. Toca do Vinícius
6. Beco das Virtudes

Gula serves salads, grill fare, and light snacks (*Avenida Henrique Dumont, 57, Ipanema, tel. (21) 2259-3084; Sun – Thu, noon – midnight; Fri and Sat, noon – 1am*). **Forneria** makes top quality sandwiches and excellent pasta. The menu is by chef Salvatore Loi (*Rua Aníbal de Mendonça, 112, Ipanema, tel. (21) 2540-8045; Sun – Wed, noon – 1am; Thu – Sat, noon – 2am*). Diners seeking a more sophisticated experience might want to try dinner at the excellent **Antiquarius**. Portuguese food is the house specialty but the menu goes far beyond the usual codfish dishes. The *arroz de pato* (duck with rice) and seafood *açorda* are superb. After your meal you can browse in the antiques store on the mezzanine floor (*Rua Aristides Espínola, 19, Leblon, tel. (21) 2294-1049, 2294-1496; Mon – Wed, noon – 1:30am; Thu – Sun, noon – 2am*). Some say that **Talho Capixaba** makes the best bread in Rio. They also serve great sandwiches (*Avenida Ataulfo de Paiva, 1022, stores #A and #B, Leblon, tel. (21) 2512-8760; Mon – Sat, 7am – 10pm; Sun, 8am – 9pm*). French restaurant and confection shop **Garcia & Rodrigues** is run by chef Christophe Lidy (*Avenida Ataulfo de Paiva, 1251, stores #A and #B, Leblon, tel. (21) 3206-4100; Mon – Fri, 8am – midnight; Sat and Sun, noon – 1am*). **Celeiro** is a favorite haunt for artists and intellectuals. They serve a variety of salads as well as meat, pasta, and vegetarian options (*Rua Dias Ferreira, 199, stores #A, #B, and #C, Leblon, tel. (21) 2274-7843; Mon – Sat, 10am – 6pm*).

FASHION

Ipanema is Rio's fashion department. Here you'll find famous beachwear brands and accessories that are exported worldwide. Shops and boutiques are concentrated in the rectangle formed by **Rua Barão da Torre**, **Rua Garcia d'Ávila**, **Rua Visconde de Pirajá**, and **Rua Aníbal de Mendonça**. Best of all, it's easy to explore them on foot. The pleasant, busy streets are flat and leafy, full of magazine stands and flower stalls. **Galeria Ipanema 2000** is a shopping arcade famous for its bikini stores (*Rua Visconde de Pirajá, 547*). **Salinas** (*stores*

Galleries

1. Laura Marsiaj
   Arte Contemporânea
2. Silvia Cintra Galeria de Arte
3. Bolsa de Arte
4. Jean Boghici
5. Márcia Barrozo do Amaral
   Galeria de Arte
6. Athena Galeria de Arte
7. Arte 21

#204 and 205, tel. (21) 2274-064;Mon – Fri, 9am – 8pm; Sat, 10am – 5pm) and **Totem** (store #F, tel. (21) 2540-0661; Mon – Fri, 9am – 8pm; Sat, 10am – 7pm; Sun, 11am – 5pm) sell swimwear and charming, colorful dresses and shirts. Nearby, **Maria Bonita Extra** sells sophisticated women's labels (Rua Aníbal de Mendonça, 135, stores #C and #D, Ipanema, tel. (21) 2540-5354; Mon – Fri, 9:30am – 8pm; Sat, 9:30am – 5pm). Not far away on Rua Barão da Torre you will find famous designer label **Forum** (#422, Ipanema, tel. (21) 2521-7415; Mon – Fri, 10am – 8pm; Sat, 10am – 6pm).

Jewelry

The best jewelry stores in Ipanema are **Antonio Bernardo** (Rua Garcia d'Ávila, 121, Ipanema, tel. (21) 2512-7204; Mon – Fri, 10am – 8pm; Sat, 10am – 4pm) and **H Stern** (Rua Garcia d'Ávila, 113, Ipanema, tel. (21) 2106-0000, extension 1465, group tours: Mon – Fri, 9am – 7pm; Sat, 9am – 5pm; Sun, 2pm – 6pm). The latter runs guided tours that allow visitors to see gems being cut and polished. The store also has a free shuttle service that picks customers up at their hotels. Reservations are required for shuttle service.

HANDICRAFT MARKET

The **Feira Hippie de Ipanema** (Ipanema Hippie Fair) has livened **Praça General Osório** square, one

---

Toca do Vinicius

Charming **Espaço Cultural Toca do Vinicius** is a record store, book store, and cultural center all in one. They specialize in MPB (popular Brazilian music), bossa nova, samba, and *choro* records. The tiny first-floor museum exhibits newspaper articles, photographs, and lyrics related to local legends Baden Powell, Edu Lobo, Toquinho, Tom Jobim, and Miúcha, as well as personal effects belonging to the poet Vinicius de Moraes. On Sundays there are shows and talks on the sidewalk in front of the store. Sometimes a piano appears there, as well. *Rua Vinicius de Moraes, 129, Ipanema, tel. (21) 2247-5227. Daily, 9am – 10pm.*

block from Ipanema Beach, for 35 years. Hundreds of vendors sell handcrafts at the market, including jewelry and clothes.

BOOKSTORES

Rio's Zona Sul is not just about beaches, boutiques, and galleries. The area has great bookstores, too, where readers can peruse the latest titles and enjoy coffee, draft beer, or a meal. The largest branch of the **Livraria da Travessa** chain has a remarkable collection of books about Rio. There are so many, in fact, that the store rivals the library as a Rio resource. **B!**, a restaurant on the mezzanine floor, serves delicious meals and snacks *(Rua Visconde de Pirajá, 572, Ipanema, tel. (21) 3205-9002; Mon – Sat, 9am – midnight; Sun, 11am – midnight).* **Livraria Argumento** is considered by many the best bookstore in Leblon. They have excellent customer service

Livraria da Travessa has a good books on offer

and the shelves are well-organized, making it easy to find what you're looking for. The bookstore also has its own café, **Café Severino** *(Rua Dias Ferreira, 417, Leblon, tel. (21) 2239-5294; daily, 9am – midnight).* On Friday and Saturday nights, intellectuals and night owls gather at **Letras & Expressões.** The store has three floors, a bar, a huge collection of magazines, and a café, **Café Ubaldo,** that is famous for its cappuccinos *(Rua Visconde de Pirajá, 276, Ipanema, tel. (21) 2247-8737; daily, 8am – midnight).* The Leblon branch has a café with an identical menu, **Café Antônio Torres** *(Avenida Ataulfo de Paiva, 1292, Leblon, tel. (21) 2511-5085; daily, 24 hours).* Tiny **Beco das Virtudes** specializes in the arts. It is both a gallery and a second-hand bookstore. They sell contemporary works, new titles, and rare books that relate to the visual arts, cinema, and theater *(Avenida Ataulfo de Paiva, 1174, store #3, Leblon, tel. (21) 2249-9525; Mon – Fri, 11am – 12:20pm and 3pm – 7pm; Sat, 10am – 3pm).*

CINEMAS

After a day at the beach you might consider enjoying a movie at one of Ipanema's cinemas. **Estação Laura Alvim**, on the beach avenue in Ipanema, has three screens *(Avenida Vieira Souto, 176, tel. (21) 2267-1647),* while **Estação Ipanema** has two *(Rua Visconde de Pirajá, 680, tel. (21) 2279-4603),* as does **Cine Leblon** *(Avenida Ataulfo de Paiva, 391, tel. (21) 2461-2461).*

ART GALLERIES

Rio de Janeiro was the capital of Brazil for many decades. As such, it played a central role in the development of the arts in Brazil. One of the first painting academies in the

Inside Galeria de Marcia Barrozo do Amaral, in Copacabana

Americas was established here in the 19th century. You may want to begin your exploration of the Rio art circuit with contemporary galleries like **Laura Marsiaj Arte Contemporânea**, which shows works by Hildebrando de Castro and Rosângela Rennó *(Rua Teixeira de Melo, 31, store #C, Ipanema, tel. (21) 2513-207, Tue – Fri, 10am – 7pm; Sat, 3pm – 8pm)*, and **Silvia Cintra Galeria de Arte**, which displays the art of Antônio Dias and Daniel Senise, among others *(Rua Teixeira de Melo, 53, store #D, Ipanema, tel. (21) 2267-9401; Mon – Fri, 10am – 7pm; Sat, noon – 4pm)*. **Bolsa de Arte** holds auctions at the Copacabana Palace four times a year. The Bolsa de Arte auctions set the standard for the Brazilian art market. Items can be viewed before the auctions begin *(Rua Prudente de Morais, 326, Ipanema, tel. (21) 2522-1544; Mon – Fri, 9am –*

7pm). Art dealer Jean Boghici owns **Galeria Jean Boghici**. He has many years of experience and sells a variety of excellent works by artists like Portinari and Wesley Duke Lee *(Rua Joana Angélica, 180, Ipanema, tel. (21) 2522-4660, 2547-1972; visits must be arranged in advance)*. Another art establishment mainstay is **Marcia Barrozo do Amaral Galeria de Arte**, which shows works by Frans Krajcberg, Anna Letycia, and Eduardo Sued *(Avenida Atlântica, 4240, basement, store #129, Shopping Cassino Atlântico, Copacabana, tel. (21) 2267-3747; Mon – Fri, 10am – 7pm)*. Next door, **Athena Galeria de Arte**, run by Liecil Oliveira, specializes in Brazilian modernists *(Avenida Atlântica, 4240, basement, store #120, Shopping Cassino Atlântico, tel. (21) 2523-8621, 3813-2222; Mon – Fri, 3pm – 8pm)*. **Arte 21** works with contemporary artists like

The Ipanema promenade at Posto 9, a popular hangout for Rio's gay community

Emmanuel Nassar and Carlos Vergara *(Avenida Atlântica, 4240, basement, store #123, Shopping Cassino Atlântico, tel. (21) 2227-7280, 2227-7267; Mon – Fri, 10am – 7pm; Sat, noon – 6pm).* There are other good galleries in Botafogo, Laranjeiras, Leblon, and Jardim Botânico. The collection at **Lurixs Arte Contemporânea** includes works by famous and lesser-known artists and photographers *(Rua Paulo Barreto, 77, Botafogo, tel. (21) 2541-4935; Mon – Fri, 2pm – 7pm).* Heloísa Amaral Peixoto's charming **H.A.P. Galeria** alternates between exhibiting the gallery's own collection and hosting shows by individual contemporary Brazilian artists *(Rua Abreu Fialho, 11, Jardim Botânico, tel. (21) 3874-2830, 3874-2726; Mon – Fri, 10am – 7pm).* In Barra da Tijuca, the **Anita Schwartz Galeria** works with contemporary artists *(Rua José Roberto Macedo Soares, 30, Gávea, tel. (21) 21/2540-6446, 2274-3873; Mon – Fri, 10am – 7pm).* **Pé de Boi** specializes in folk art from almost every state in the country. Their collection includes ceramic dolls from the Jequitinhonha Valley *(Rua Ipiranga, 55, Laranjeiras, tel. (21) 2285-4395, 2285-5833; Mon – Fri, 10am – 7pm; Sat, 9am – 1pm).*

The GLBT Circuit

The area between Posto 8 and Posto 9, on Ipanema Beach opposite Rua Farme de Amoedo, is the most popular gathering place for gay beachgoers in Rio. After enjoying the sand and sun people tend to flock to bars on Rua Farme, between Rua Visconde de Pirajá and Rua Barão da Torre. **Bofetada** always draws a big crowd *(Rua Farme de Amoedo, 87-A, Ipanema, tel. (21) 2227-1675; daily, 8am until the last customer leaves).* Nearby, but closer to Lagoa Rodrigo de Freitas, is **Dama de Ferro**, a bar and nightclub *(Rua Vinícius de Morais, 288, Ipanema, tel. (21) 2247-2330; Wed – Sat, 11pm until the last customer leaves).* Traditional **Le Boy** nightclub is in Copacabana *(Rua Raul Pompéia, 102, posto 6, tel. (21) 2513-4993; Tue – Sun, from 11pm).* **Fundição Progresso**, in Lapa, holds lively GLBT parties. You should call in advance if you'd like to attend one *(Rua dos Arcos, 24, tel. (21) 2220-5070; Mon – Fri, 10am – 10pm; Sat, 9am – 9pm; check out the program schedule on www.fundicao.org).*

OUTDOOR RIO

TRAILS

One of the most pleasant walks in Rio is the **Pista Cláudio Coutinho**, a trail near Morro da Urca and Sugarloaf Mountain. If you're lucky you may even see monkeys. There are other nice trails in and around the city, like **Pedra do Conde**, **Pico da Tijuca**, and **Pico do Bico do Papagaio** in the Tijuca Forest. The **Pedra da Gávea** trail requires experienced guides. There are also paths along relatively deserted beaches, including **Praia do Inferno, Praia Funda, Praia do Meio**, and **Praia do Perigosinho**.

Contact: Companhia da Escalada, tel. (21) 2567-7105, 9113-5712, 9393-5060; Rio Hiking, tel. (21) 2552-9204, 9721-0594; Trilharte, tel. (21) 2525-2426, 2205-0654; Trilhas do Rio, tel. (21) 2424-5455, 9207-1360; Aribira, tel. (21) 2235-3716, 9505-7631, 9540-3505.

MARATHONS

Rio hosts two important street racing events. The lively **Meia Maratona Internacional do Rio** half marathon *(www.meiamaratonadoriodejaneiro.com.br)* takes place during the second half of the year. Approximately 12,000 competitors complete the 21.1-kilometer (approximately 13-mile) shoreline course from São Conrado Beach to the finish at Largo do Machado, just beyond Flamengo Beach. The city marathon, **Maratona da Cidade do Rio de Janeiro** *(information: tel. (21) 2223-2773)* traverses 42.2 kilometers (just over 26 miles). Nearly 3,000 runners toe the starting line on the last Sunday in June. They start in Praça do Pontal do Recreio, in Recreio dos Bandeirantes, run along the beachfront to the Aterro do Flamengo, and finish on Rua Cruz Lima.

HELICOPTER FLIGHTS

A helicopter ride over Rio quickly reveals why the city is called the *cidade maravilhosa* (marvelous city). People who take these flights swear they will never again climb to the Cristo Redentor statue – Rio's highest

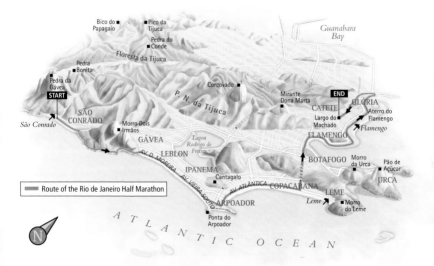

Route of the Rio de Janeiro Half Marathon

lookout point – because the view from the air is unbeatable. The main heliports are in the **Lagoa** neighborhood, on **Morro da Urca**, at the **Mirante do Morro Dona Marta**, and at **Jacarepaguá airport.**
Contact: Helisight, tel. (21) 2511-2141, 2542-7895, 2259-6995; Cruzeiro Táxi-Aéreo, tel. (21) 3325-6500, 9808-2828.

CLIMBING

Rio de Janeiro is the largest urban climbing center in the world. Its many mountains and hills offer dazzling views and climbing routes for all abilities. Sugarloaf Mountain alone has more than 40 such routes. Once at the top you can descend by cable car. Some climbers prefer to take the K2 on **Corcovado,** where those who summit are rewarded with breathtaking views. **Pedra da Gávea**, **Morro Dois Irmãos**, **Cantagalo**, and the mountains on the other side of Guanabara Bay are also of interest to climbers. Most of the climbing agencies offer climbing classes, as well.

Note that some routes require previous climbing experience.
Contact: Companhia da Escalada, tel. (21) 2567-7105, 9113-5712, 9393-5060; Rio Hiking, tel. (21) 2552-9204, 9721-0594; Aribira, tel. (21) 2235-3716, 9221-8741; Trilhas do Rio, tel. (21) 2424-5455, 9207-1360.

PARAGLIDING AND HANG-GLIDING

Praia do Pepino, a beach in São Conrado, is overrun by hang- and paragliders on weekends. A number of pilots offer tandem instructor-student flights from the take-off ramp, **Rampa da Pedra Bonita.** Films and photos are frequently available for purchase if you'd like to document your adventure. When winds are not suitable at São Conrado, gliders head to an alternative hang-gliding ramp at Parque da Cidade, in Niterói.
Contact: Superfly, tel. (21) 9887-6084; Just Fly, tel. (21) 2523-1372, 9985-7540; Hilton Fly Rio Hang Gliding Center, tel. (21) 7840-6325, 9964-2607.

Tandem hang-gliding flights offer a beautiful view the city from the air

Lagoa Rodrigo de Freitas draws vacationers who enjoy water sports

LAGOA RODRIGO DE FREITAS AND JARDIM BOTÂNICO

Walking, running, or cycling on the paths around **Lagoa Rodrigo de Freitas** is one the greatest pleasures Rio has to offer. The lake shore is dotted with clubs, parks, sports facilities, and pedal boats. There's a half-pipe for skateboarding, a heliport, and a roller-skating rink. Kiosks sell coconut water, soda, and beer. At night you can enjoy live music at the kiosks, which also serve a variety of food, including Japanese, Italian, and Arab cuisine. The best stands are in Parque dos Patins and Corte do Cantagalo. Finding a table during the summer months requires patience.
Avenida Epitácio Pessoa and Avenida Borges de Medeiros.

FUNDAÇÃO EVA KLABIN RAPAPORT
The one-time residence of art collector Eva Klabin was opened to the public in 1995 to exhibit her personal collection of more than 2,600 items. The house was constructed in 1931, one of the first to appear on the shores of Lagoa Rodrigo de Freitas. Klabin purchased it in 1952 and renovated, adding a palatial air to the home. Her collection, which is displayed in 10 different rooms, includes ancient Egyptian and Roman art, Renaissance paintings, 17th-century Flemish works, 18th-century English portraits, a collection of Tang dynasty terracotta pieces, bronzes from early Chinese dynasties, and an important collection of decorative items (English silver and oriental rugs, to name two). The foundation organizes quality contemporary art exhibitions. Guided tours are available.
Avenida Epitácio Pessoa, 2480, Lagoa, tel. (21) 3202-8550. Wed – Sun, 2pm – 6pm.

JARDIM BOTÂNICO
The Jardim Botanical Garden's collection of over 8,000 species of plants makes it one of the most important botanical gardens in the world. The 137-hectare (338-acre) garden was created by Dom João Vl in 1808. It was designated a biosphere reserve by Unesco in 1992. Highlights include the **Museu Casa dos**

More than 8,000 species grow in Rio's world-famous Jardim Botânico

Pilões and the **orquidário** (orchid garden), which houses around 1,000 species, many of them exotic. There is a lovely frontispiece on the former **Escola de Belas-Artes** (School of Fine Arts). In addition, the garden has two sculptures by master sculptor Mestre Valentim: *Eco* and *Narciso*. They are among the first of his works to be cast in Brazil. Behind **Café Botânico** is a **cactário** (cactus garden) that grows imported and Brazilian cacti alike. The **Caminho da Mata Atlântica** (Atlantic Forest Trail) was recently restored. **Espaço Tom Jobim** is a cultural center

dedicated to musician Tom Jobim, a great admirer of the Jardim Botânico. It houses his digital and audiovisual collections. Twice a month, on Saturdays around 5pm, the garden hosts **sábados musicais** (musical Saturdays) in the on-site theater. The series promotes a variety of musical traditions, including jazz, traditional samba, and MPB (popular Brazilian music). Gardeners inspired by the botanical center can purchase seedlings at Avenida Pacheco Leão, 2,040, adjacent to the gardens. Bringing plants or seeds home with you might violate customs regulations, however, so it's a good idea to check, first. While on Avenida Pacheco Leão you can also stop to admire the cottages in the workers' village. Contemporary artists Gabriela Machado, Adriana Varejão, and Beatriz Milhazes have studios here, and the village itself is a national heritage site. *Rua Jardim Botânico, 1008, Jardim Botânico, tel. (21) 3874-1808. Daily, 8am – 5pm.*

CULTURAL CENTERS

The **Cavalariças** exhibition space is near Jardim Botânico, inside **Parque Lage**. Here, artists display their work against a backdrop of old buildings. The gallery is right next to the **Escola de Artes Visuais do Parque Lage** (School of Visual Arts), where a new generation of art students is learning their craft *(Rua Jardim Botânico, 414, Jardim Botânico, tel. (21) 2538-1091, 2538-1879; Mon – Thu, 9am – 9pm; 9am – 6pm; Sat, 10am – 1pm).*

FLORESTA DA TIJUCA

The Tijuca Forest blankets a mountain range of the same name. Logging almost wiped the forest off the map in the 19th century. The timber fueled sugar processing plants, brick factories, and expanding coffee plantations. The ecological disaster that resulted from such gross mismanagement of natural resources nearly left the city without water. In 1861, Dom Pedro II ordered that reforestation efforts begin immediately to aid the recovery of the native woods. Over 3,300 hectares (80,000 acres) were planted or rehabilitated. Over time, nature has largely reclaimed what was once entirely her own. Today Tijuca is one of the world's largest "urban" forests. Its rich, diverse flora and fauna thrive once more. *Ipês-amarelos, angicos*, and *jequitibás* trees are home to capuchin monkeys, coatis, armadillos, and anteaters, as well as a profusion of birds. The park's trails lead to the heart of the forest, where hikers are rewarded with lookout points and crystal-clear waterfalls. Such walks make excellent, refreshing summer outings. A number of easy trails start at **Largo do Bom Retiro,** the park's central point, but we recommend you to hire a guide as they are not well sign-posted. The Centro de Visitantes (Visitors' Center) provides athletic, adventuresome visitors with information on the park's more challenging trails. Agencies offer scenic trips in open vehicles for people who prefer to simply sit back and enjoy the view.

Praça Afonso Viseu, Tijuca, tel. (21) 2492-5407. Daily, 8am – 5pm.
Contact: *Jeep Tour, tel. (21) 2108-5800.*

MUSEU DO AÇUDE

Sophisticated Açude Museum occupies an immense 15-hectare (37-acre) area in the middle of the Floresta da Tijuca. Part of its fine art collection is exhibited outdoors against the exuberant greens of the forest. Visitors walk among works by Hélio Oiticica, Lygia Pape, Iole de Freitas, and Nuno Ramos. The main building houses many more works of art, including 18th- and 19th-century Portuguese tile panels and Portuguese-Brazilian furniture. The property once belonged to art collector Raymundo Castro Maya. His collection of oriental art, including iron sculptures and ceramics, is exhibited here, as well.

Estrada do Açude, 764, Alto da Boa Vista, tel. (21) 2492-2119, 2492-5219. Wed – Mon, 11am – 5pm.

Museu do Açude: sophistication and fine art in a forest glade

Instituto Moreira Salles: modernist design by Olavo Redig de Campos

GÁVEA AND SÃO CONRADO

PLANETÁRIO

The two-domed planetarium is considered one of the most modern in Latin America. One dome contains the **Universarium** VIII, which has a viewing area 23 meters (75 feet) in diameter and can display 9,000 projected stars. The other dome is 12.5 meters (41 feet) in diameter and houses the **Spacemaster,** which is capable of simulating the movement of 6,500 stars at any latitude. The Spacemaster shows the sky as it would look with no atmospheric pollution. The complex also has a museum, the **Museu do Universo**, which visitors pass through before the planetarium sessions. There are more than forty interactive displays, including a kinetic sculpture of the solar system. *Rua Vice-Governador Rubens Berardo, 100, Gávea, tel. (21) 2274-0046. Starwatching: Tue and Wed, 6:30pm – 8:30pm. Dome sessions: Sat, Sun, and holidays, 4pm – 5:30pm (children) and 7pm (adults).*

INSTITUTO MOREIRA SALLES (IMS)

The renowned Moreira Salles Institute has been comfortably ensconced in its fine modernist home since 1999. The building was designed by architect Olavo Redig de Campos, and the surrounding landscaping was done by Burle Marx. The Institute has a cinema, exhibition rooms, a café, an art store, a studio, and a considerable photography and music collection. The Reserva Técnica Musical documents and preserves MPB (popular Brazilian music). It has a collection of over 100,000 recordings dating back to 1902, all of which are digitized and available to listen to for free. Highlights include the music of Noel Rosa, Orlando Silva, and Ernesto Nazaré. There is also a collection dedicated to composer and instrumentalist Pixinguinha. Musical history isn't the IMS' only strength, however. The Reserva Técnica Fotográfica has more than 450,000 photographs, mainly from the

19th and 20th centuries, by artists like Marc Ferrez and Marcel Gautherot. Visits to the photo collection must be arranged in advance.
Rua Marquês de São Vicente, 476, Gávea, tel. (21) 3284-7400. Tue – Sun, 1pm – 8pm.

GALLERIES

There are two galleries in Gávea that will please contemporary art buffs. **Mercedes Viegas Arte Contemporânea** *(Rua João Borges, 86, tel. (21) 2294-4305; Mon – Fri, 1pm – 7pm; Sat, 4pm – 8pm)* and **Galeria Anna Maria Niemeyer** *(Rua Marquês de São Vicente, 52, store #205, Shopping da Gávea, tel. (21) 2239-9144; Mon – Sat, 10am – 10pm)* both show works by renowned artists. **Galeria 90 Arte Contemporânea** promotes new talents *(Rua Marquês de São Vicente, 90, Vila 90, stores #101-102, tel. (21) 2529-6588, 2513-7144; Mon – Fri, 2pm – 7pm; Sat, noon – 5pm).*

FAVELA DA ROCINHA

Thanks to its spectacular views of the Rio coastline, the Rocinha *favela* is becoming a tourist attraction in its own right. Because it has become so urban, Rocinha is trying to obtain the status of "neighborhood." Its 170,000 residents have their own bank, hotel, motorcycle-taxi company, and a cable TV channel devoted to local issues. The area's up-and-coming status does not mean it's safe for you to walk around the streets and alleys, however. Visitors should *always* be accompanied by guides. This is the safest way to get to know the area, which is often the scene of violent clashes between police and drug-dealers. Check out the situation before arranging a visit.
Contact: *Favela Tour, tel. (21) 3322-2727, 9989-0074, 9772-1133.*

CASA NIEMEYER

Also known as Casa das Canoas, Oscar Niemeyer himself built this home at the beginning of the 1950s for his family. It is a superb example of modern Brazilian architecture, its curved features blend harmoniously with the natural surroundings. The house is open to the public.
Estrada das Canoas, 2310, São Conrado, tel. (21) 3322-3581. Tue – Fri, 1pm – 5pm; Sat and Sun, 9am – noon.

Casa das Canoas was Oscar Niemeyer's residence in the 1950s

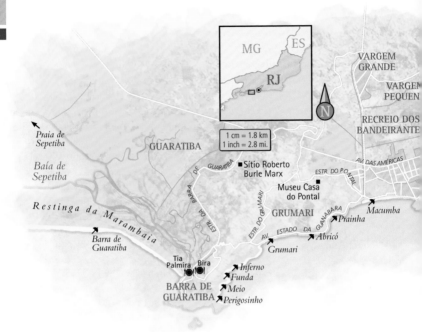

BARRA DA TIJUCA AND RECREIO DOS BANDEIRANTES

Despite belonging to the city's West Zone, Barra da Tijuca has always been considered part of the South Zone. Tijuca has none of the bakeries, juice bars, or corner pubs so typical of the rest of Rio. The neighborhood does have a few wide avenues, a lot of condominiums, and dozens of shopping malls. There are also quite a few cinemas, theaters, cultural centers, bars, and places to dance. Its natural surroundings are lovely; the beaches have strong waves and old stretches of *restinga* vegetation. The West Zone coastline has five main beaches: **Barra da Tijuca**, **Recreio dos Bandeirantes**, **Macumba**, **Prainha**, and **Grumari** (the last two are almost outside the city).

BEACHES

Praia da Barra is 18 kilometers (11 miles) long, making it the longest beach in Rio. It's also the busiest. Barra has kiosks, a cycle path, bathrooms, and showers. The rough but unpolluted waters and strong winds attract surfers, windsurfers, and body boarders. Sand volleyball courts, football posts, and surf schools are scattered up and down the beach. The most crowded spot is **Praia do Pepê**, a 300-meter (984-foot) stretch between Praia da Barra's Posto 1 and Posto 2. Thanks to its coarse sand, strong winds, and high waves, Pepê draws artists, footballers, fitness fanatics, volleyball players, kite surfers, and windsurfers. Though Praia da Barra is suitable for swimming, the water just offshore becomes deep very quickly as you approach **Praia do Recreio**. Recreio is also a good place for surfing because it has strong waves. Its short strip of coarse, dark sand has beach volleyball facilities and lessons are available. Though less popular than Barra, it has reasonable facilities and is ideal for cycling and walking. Strong winds make **Macumba**, at the far end of Praia do Recreio, another favorite

among surfers. Tiny, charming **Prainha**, one of Rio's cleanest beaches, usually has high, long-lasting waves. **Grumari**, a long beach whose strong waves break near shore, is famous for its crystal waters, the cleanest on the entire shoreline. Like Prainha, Grumari is a protected area surrounded by mountains and *restinga* vegetation. **Abricó**, a tiny patch of sand just beyond Grumari, is a nudist beach. There is no bus service to these beaches, but they teem with people on weekends nonetheless. During the workweek the sands are considerably less crowded. **Barra de Guaratiba** is surrounded by trees and mountains. It is a small beach, with compact sand and calm, green waters that draw crowds in summer months. Guaratiba

is close to **Restinga de Marambaia** – a stretch of Atlantic forest in a military area, comprising 42 kilometers (26 miles) of wild, deserted beaches – and gets very crowded in summer. If you're visiting Barra de Guaratiba we recommend lunch at **Tia Palmira**, which serves generous portions of seafood and dishes from Bahia *(Caminho do Sousa, 18, tel. (21) 2410-8169; Tue – Fri, 11:30am – 5pm; Sat, Sun, and holidays, 11:30am – 6pm)*. **Bira**, a restaurant run by Palmira's nephew, serves the same specialties *(Estrada da Vendinha, 68-A, tel. (21) 2410-8304; Thu and Fri, noon – 6pm; Sat, Sun, and holidays, noon – 8pm)*. We recommend tarrying at Guaratiba long enough to enjoy one of its wonderful sunsets.

CASA DO PONTAL AND SÍTIO BURLE MARX

The **Museu Casa do Pontal** houses the largest collection of folk art in Brazil. The museum exhibits late 20th-century art by more than 200 Brazilian artisans. The collection is the legacy of French collector and designer Jacques Van de Beuque. Permanent exhibits are organized by theme (e.g., festive, everyday, imaginary, and religious) *(Estrada do Pontal, 3295, tel. (21) 2490-3278; Tue – Sun, 9am – 5pm)*. Five kilometers (3 miles) from Casa do Pontal is **Sítio Roberto Burle Marx**, the former home of painter and landscape artist Burle Marx. Visits must be arranged in advance by phone. Marx lived here from 1949 to 1994, the year he died. His 36.5 hectare (90 acre) estate is home to 3,500 species of native and exotic plants. The museum in the main house, Museu-Casa, displays memorabilia, furniture, and personal items belonging to the artist. Sítio Roberto Burle Marx is particularly lovely in the springtime when the flowers are in bloom *(Estrada da Barra de Guaratiba, 2019, tel. (21) 2410-1412; Tue – Sat, 9:30am and 1:30pm)*.

CARNIVAL

Few festivals equal Rio's Carnival in size, significance, or sheer extravagance. In addition to the official samba school parade in the Sambódromo (Carnival area), Rio's lively traditional street groups, the *blocos de rua,* have been taking the party to its neighborhoods since 1984. The groups are especially popular in Ipanema, Leblon, and Santa Teresa. Along Avenida Marquês de Sapucaí in the Sambódromo the ground quakes with the energy of thousands of revelers driven by the beat of music and drums. Wild, colorful floats carry performers in equally unforgettable costumes. Even the dourest spectator will find himself entranced. Though the holiday is only four days long, the samba school and *bloco* rehearsals start well beforehand. Rehearsal tickets are affordable. Don't, however, expect much by way of service. Warm beer, suffocating heat, and a queue for the bathroom are part and parcel of your opportunity to experience the inevitable chills that accompany the deafening drum

beat heralding the beginning rehearsal. Nobody is unmoved by the power of these drums. Rehearsals for the **Mangueira** and **Salgueiro** blocos are slightly more formal. Some of the street bands, like **Carmelitas**, **Banda de Ipanema**, and **Escravos da Mauá**, don't charge for rehearsals. Others, like **Simpatia é Quase Amor**, **Suvaco do Cristo**, and **Monobloco**, usually require you buy a ticket. Anyone who intends to join the Carnival samba school parade should plan well in advance. Buy your costume beforehand (some sell out, and prices always shoot up as Carnival approaches) and make sure you know what time your school enters the parade avenue. Tickets must be bought in advance, too. If you don't you are fully at the mercy of ticket-scalpers. During the parades metro service *(Line 1, get off at Praça Onze station)* runs 24 hours a day.

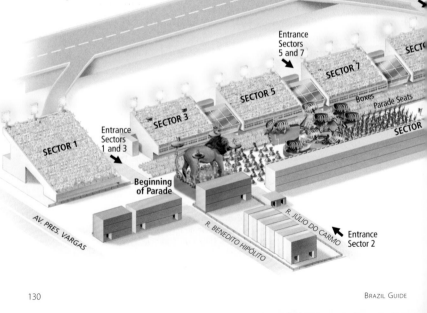

Beginning in August, the two most sought-after rehearsals take place at the **Mangueira** and **Salgueiro** *quadras* (headquarters). Both are ten minutes from the Centro district, and both have good facilities, including parking and box seats. Rehearsals are held on Saturdays starting at 10pm. Mangueira's *quadra*, the Palácio do Samba, sits at the foot of Morro da Mangueira. It's an egalitarian place popular with locals, young people, and scores of tourists. Beginning in January the competition for *quadras* tickets heats up. We recommend you arrive *well* before the rehearsals are supposed to begin. If you want a table you'll need to reserve one in advance by telephone. Salgueiro's *quadra*, in the North Zone's Andaraí

neighborhood, is a popular destination for the younger crowd. Farther from the Rio city center, in the North Zone's Madureira neighborhood, are the traditional *quadras* of **Portela** *(rehearsals begin in September: Wed, 8pm; Fri, 10pm)* and **Império Serrano** *(rehearsals begin in August: Sat, 10pm).*
Contact: *Carioca Tropical Tour Operator, tel. (21) 2547-6327. Mangueira: Rua Visconde de Niterói, 1071, Mangueira, tel. (21) 3872-6787; Salgueiro: Rua Silva Teles, 104, Andaraí, tel. (21) 2238-9226, 2268-0548; Portela: Rua Clara Nunes, 81, Madureira, tel. (21) 2489-6440; Império Serrano: Avenida Ministro Edgar Romero, 114, Madureira, tel. (21) 2489-8722/5696. Samba School League (Liga das Escolas de Samba): www.liesa.globo.com*

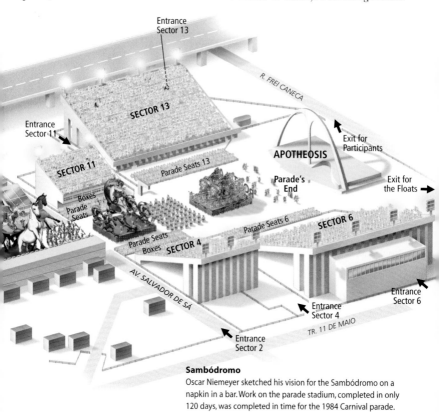

Sambódromo
Oscar Niemeyer sketched his vision for the Sambódromo on a napkin in a bar. Work on the parade stadium, completed in only 120 days, was completed in time for the 1984 Carnival parade.
R. Marquês de Sapucaí, pça. Onze, Cidade Nova.

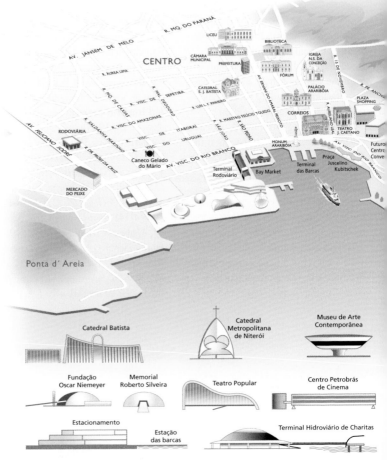

CENTRO

R. MQ. DO PARANÁ
LICEU
BIBLIOTECA
AV. JANSEM DE MELO
CÂMARA MUNICIPAL
PREFEITURA
IGREJA N.S. DA CONCEIÇÃO
R. 15 DE NOVEMBRO
FÓRUM
R. AURELA LIMA
CATEDRAL S. J. BATISTA
PALÁCIO ARARIBÓIA
R. PE. ANCHIETA
PLAZA SHOPPING
R. MAL. SEPETIBA
R. VISC. DE DEODORO
R. LUIS L. PINHEIRO
CORREIOS
R. MQ DE CAXIAS
R. SALDANHA MARINHO
R. VISC. DO AMAZONAS
AV. ERNANI DO AMARAL PEIXOTO
R. MAESTRO FELICIO TOLEDO
R. AURELIO LEAL
TEATRO J. CAETANO
AV. FELICIANO SODRÉ
RODOVIÁRIA
R. VISC. DE ITABORAÍ
R. SÃO JOÃO
R. SÃO PEDRO
MONUM ARARIBÓIA
AV. VISC. DO RIO BRANCO
Futuro Centro Conve
R. DR. PROSPERA CRUZ
Caneco Gelado do Mário
R. VISC. DO URUGUAI
AV. VISC. DO RIO BRANCO
Praça Juscelino Kubitschek
MERCADO DO PEIXE
Terminal Rodoviário
Bay Market
Terminal das Barcas
Ponta d´Areia

Niterói will be the site of a large building complex designed by Oscar Niemeyer

THE CITY OF NITERÓI

Niterói, 17 kilometers (10.5 miles) from Rio, is accessible by boat from Praça Quinze (20 minutes), or by car via the Rio–Niterói Bridge. The city's fortresses still overlook the entrance to Guanabara Bay. Niterói has innate natural beauty and lovely beaches (**Itacoatiara, Piratininga, Camboinhas,** and **Itaipu**). It also has sensational views of Rio. The **Museu de Arte Contemporânea** (MAC), a museum of contemporary art, is in a circular building designed by Oscar Niemeyer. It

opened in 1996. Its windows are strategically placed so that visitor's eyes fall on views of the bay in addition to works of art. Glass encircles the center of the building, and each step reveals a work of art outside – perhaps the Pão de Açúcar, seen from an unusual angle, for example. The museum houses the João Sattamini collection, which includes works produced in the 1980s by approximately 80 important Brazilian artists *(Mirante da Boa Viagem, no #, tel. (21) 2620-2400; Tue – Sun,*

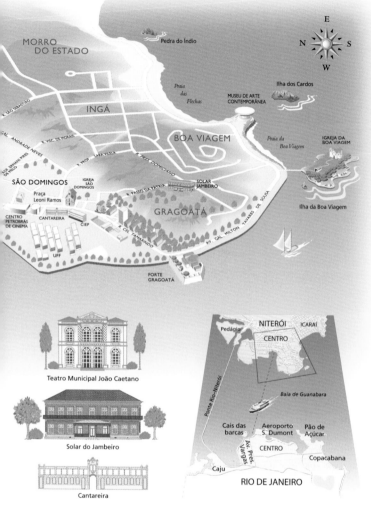

Teatro Municipal João Caetano

Solar do Jambeiro

Cantareira

10am – 6pm). The MAC is the first building on the **Caminho Niemeyer**, a route complex lined by nine Niemeyer buildings and a plaza. After Brasília, no city has more of his buildings than Niterói. Not all of them are complete, however. While Praça Juscelino Kubitschek and Memorial Roberto Silveira are finished, others – like the Fundação Oscar Niemeyer, which will house Niemeyer's collection – are still under construction. Most will be completed in 2008. We also recommend visiting the **Museu Antônio Parreiras**,

which exhibits works by painter Antônio Parreiras. The museum is in a 19th-century house *(Rua Tiradentes, 47, Ingá, tel. (21) 2299-9578, 2719-8728; Tue – Fri, 11am – 5pm; Sat, Sun, and holidays, 2pm – 5pm).* **Solar do Jambeiro** was built in 1872. It's a good example of 19th-century urban residential architecture *(Rua Presidente Domiciano, 195, São Domingos, tel. (21) 2109-2222; Tue – Fri, 1pm – 6pm; Sat and Sun, 10am – 6pm).* The ruins of **Forte da Boa Viagem**, on Boa Viagem beach, are also fun to visit.

MOUNTAINS AND INLAND

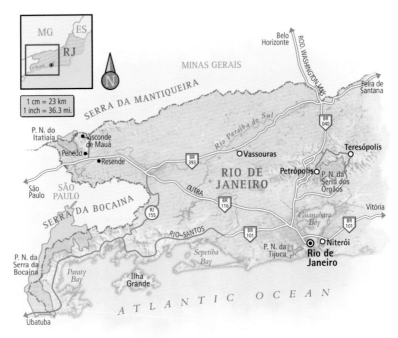

MG
ES
RJ

MINAS GERAIS

Belo Horizonte
ROD. WASHINGTON LUIS

Feira de Santana

1 cm = 23 km
1 inch = 36.3 mi.

SERRA DA MANTIQUEIRA

BR 040

P. N. do Itatiaia
Visconde de Mauá
Penedo
Resende

Rio Paraíba do Sul

Vassouras

Teresópolis

Petrópolis

P. N. da Serra dos Órgãos

São Paulo
SÃO PAULO

BR 393

RIO DE JANEIRO

DUTRA

BR 116

Vitória

SERRA DA BOCAINA

RJ 155

RIO-SANTOS

BR 101

Guanabara Bay

BR 101

P. N. da Serra da Bocaina

Panaty Bay

Ilha Grande

Sepetiba Bay

BR 101

P. N. da Tijuca

Niterói
Rio de Janeiro

A T L A N T I C   O C E A N

Ubatuba

PETRÓPOLIS

Petrópolis' mild climate and green mountains covered in vegetation made it the Brazilian imperial family's favorite summer resort in the 19th-century – and the family had remarkably good taste. Emperor Dom Pedro I acquired land in the area to build a summer palace; his son, Dom Pedro II, ultimately fulfilled his father's idea when he founded the city of Petrópolis in 1843. Today, celebrities and common folk alike enjoy the beauty of the city, which is nestled 800 meters (2,600 feet) above sea level in the Serra dos Órgãos. The mountain range lies 65 kilometers (40 miles) from Rio on Rodovia BR-040 highway. Engineer Júlio Frederico Koeler pioneered the style of many of the German immigrants' houses, and one of the city's most beautiful streets is named after him. Petrópolis retained its glamour even after Brazil was proclaimed a republic. For example, take in the kitsch splendor of **Palácio Quitandinha**, where a casino operated in the 1940s. Several excellent restaurants recently opened in the region, earning it the nickname "Gourmet Valley."

CATEDRAL DE SÃO PEDRO DE ALCÂNTARA

This imposing cathedral, built in the French neo-Gothic style, dates from 1939. The 70-meter (230-foot) steeple houses five bronze bells that were cast in Germany and weigh nine tons. On the right-hand side of the nave – built from marble, onyx, and bronze – is the **Capela Imperial**, which houses a mausoleum containing the remains of Dom Pedro II, his wife Dona Teresa Cristina, Princess Isabel, and her husband, Count d'Eu. The altar contains relics from three saints brought from Rome (saints Magnus, Aurelia, and Tecla). The stained glass windows are inscribed with poems Dom Pedro II wrote during his exile.

Rua São Pedro de Alcântara, 60, Centro, tel. (24) 2242-4300. Mon, 8am – noon; Tue – Sat, 8am – 6pm; Sun, 8am – 1pm and 3pm – 6pm.

MUSEU IMPERIAL

This pink, neoclassical palace offers a glimpse of the imperial family's everyday life. A former summer residence, the palace is exquisitely decorated, from the entrance's white Carrara and black Belgian marble to the dining hall's mahogany furniture. Highlights include the jacaranda hardwood of the music room, where Dom Pedro II held soirées and recitals; Princess Isabel and Leopoldina's room; the paintings and objects in the Emperor's study; and the decor of Empress Teresa Cristina's drawing room. The displayed artifacts include jewelry, crowns, paintings, and personal effects. Visitors must wear felt slippers when touring the museum. French landscape artist Jean Baptiste Binot designed the gardens, which sport imposing imperial palms and 100 species of exotic plants and trees, such as the Portuguese Cypress. The gardens are also the setting for the *Som e Luz* show, a choreographed display of light and shadow on the building's façade.

Rua da Imperatriz, 220, Centro, tel. (24) 2237-8000. Tue – Sun, 11am – 5:30pm. Show: Thu – Sat, 8pm.

CASA DA PRINCESA ISABEL

Another pink, neoclassical building – this one was the home of Princess Isabel and her husband, Count d'Eu, until 1889. It is now the headquarters for the real estate firm Cia, Imobiliária

de Petrópolis, and the antique shop **Antiquário da Princesa**. Descendents of the royal family own the companies. The property firm controls the regional map of the subdivisions that gave rise to the city. Only the gardens are open to visitors.

Avenida Koeler, 42, Centro, tel. (24) 2242-4706. Daily, 11am – 5pm.

PALÁCIO DE CRISTAL

The Crystal Palace represents a type of building popular in Europe after the Industrial Revolution, and its metal and glass parts were manufactured in 1879 in Saint-Saveur-les-Arras, France. Princess Isabel funded its construction for the Petrópolis Horticultural Association, which was run by her husband. In 1888, four years after the palace opened, the princess held a spectacular party where she granted freedom to several slaves, almost as a prelude to her signing the Lei Áurea, the law that officially abolished slavery in Brazil. The building currently hosts occasional exhibits, as well as plays and concerts. *Chorinho*, MPB, and classical music are performed at 6 pm on Saturdays. To check the program, call the city's tourism service *(0800-241516).*

Rua Alfredo Pachá, no #, Centro, tel. (24) 2247-3721. Tue – Sun, 9am – 5:30pm.

CASA DE SANTOS DUMONT

Santos Dumont made history in 1906, when he completed the world's first observed heavier-than-air powered flight in his 14 Bis biplane. He designed this fine three-story house in 1918 and lived there sporadically. The building contains several curiosities popular with children, such as the alcohol-heated shower and the first step of the staircase, which is built so that a visitor must start climbing with their right foot. Dumont, who was an

Palácio Rio Negro was the seat of Rio de Janeiro's state government in the early 20th century

amateur astronomer, installed a telescope on top of the house. *Rua do Encanto, 22, Centro, tel. (24) 2247-3158. Tue – Sun, 9:30am – 5pm.*

Palácio Rio Negro

This neoclassical building was constructed in 1889, just before the declaration of the Republic. It was named after its first owner, the wealthy coffee baron Barão do Rio Negro. It also served as the seat of Rio de Janeiro's state government from 1894 to 1902, when Petrópolis was the state capital; although it is not frequently occupied, it became Brazil's official presidential summer residence in 1903 and is still used today. The furnishings reflect the taste of the many presidents who stayed there. Getúlio Vargas converted the wine cellar into a Roman-style bathhouse, and Juscelino Kubitschek had built-in closets installed. It was closed to visitors in February 2008, with no scheduled reopening. *Avenida Koeler, 255, Centro.*

Palácio Quitandinha

This impressive building once housed the largest casino in Latin America, but it only operated as such for two years before gambling was banned in Brazil

---

in 1946. Now, it is a convention center. The building looks like an austere Norman palace from the outside, but its interior resembles the set of a 1940s Hollywood melodrama. Interior decorator Dorothy Draper designed its garish pink, red, green, and turquoise walls. Celebrities such as Marlene Dietrich, Lana Turner, and Orson Welles visited the palace. Everything is on a grand scale: the dome of the **Salão Mauá** is 13 meters (100 feet) high and 50 meters (165 feet) wide. The mechanized theater has three revolving stages and seats 2,000 people; the whole building can hold 10,000. In the lake, created in the shape of Brazil, a lighthouse stands on the spot that corresponds to Marajó Island.

Avenida Joaquim Rola, 2, Quitandinha, tel. (24) 2104-4495. Tue – Sun, 9am – 5pm.

THE SURROUNDING AREA

The Petrópolis region is known for the variety and quality of its cuisine, which attracts gourmets from around the world – who may wind up wishing they could settle in permanently at one of the charming, fireplace-equipped guesthouses. To indulge the taste buds, take the Estrada União-Indústria road from the town center to **Correias**, **Araras**, and **Itaipava**. In Correias, visit the **Pousada da Alcobaça** *(Rua Agostinho Goulão, 298, Correias, tel. (24) 2221-1240; daily, 8am – noon and 1:30pm – 10pm)*, a Norman-style riverside guesthouse with charming gardens, a small waterfall, and a vegetable garden that supplies the in-house restaurant. **Locanda Della Mimosa** *(Alameda das Mimosas, 30, Vale Florido, Fazenda Inglesa, access at Km 72 of Rodovia BR-040, tel. (24) 2233-5405; Fri and Sat, noon – 4pm and 8pm – midnight)*

is one of Araras' most popular restaurnts. Its chef, Danilo Braga, has won several awards for his delicious homemade Italian pasta dishes. Wine lovers will appreciate **Fazenda das Videiras** *(Estrada Paulo Meira, 6000, access from Estrada Araras–Vale das Videiras, tel. (24) 2225-8090)*, a European-style guesthouse that has a cellar stocked with some of the finest wines in the world. In Itaipava (which has a bustling nightlife), don't miss **Castelo do Barão de Itaipava**, a Renaissance-style building constructed in the 1920s. World-famous architect and modernist urban planner Lúcio Costa created the structure. He and his partner Fernando Valentim are also responsible for designing the capital, Brasília. The **Tamboatá** *(Estrada União-Indústria, 12,360, Itaipava, tel. (24) 2222-5007, 2222-5221; Fri and Sat, 10pm until the last customer leaves)* is the place to eat good pizza and watch well-known musicians perform. The region is also brimming with antique stores and pottery workshops and factories, such as the traditional **Luiz Salvador** *(Estrada União–Indústria, 10588, Itaipava, tel. (24) 2222-2712). For more information on restaurants in Petrópolis, see page 520.*

OUR RECOMMENDATION

🍴 After driving up the mountainside just outside of Petrópolis, stop for snacks and sweets at the traditional **Casa do Alemão**, which specializes in German food. Since 1945, it has been selling its own line of products. The most famous are its delicious croquettes and sausage sandwich, as well as white and red sausages and butter cookies *(Avenida Ayrton Senna, 927, Quitandinha, tel. (24) 2242-3442; daily, 7am – 9:30pm).*

Additional information on page 462.

The city of Teresópolis, surrounded by the natural beauty of the Serra dos Órgãos

Parque Nacional da Serra dos Órgãos

Created in 1939, Serra dos Órgãos National Park spans almost 12,000 hectares of mountainous countryside and encompasses the municipalities of Petrópolis, Guapimirim, Majé, and Teresópolis. Most of it is covered in typical Atlantic forest vegetation, but the higher elevations give way to the highlands' scrubby plants. **Dedo de Deus** – a mountain peak rising to 1,692 meters (5,550 feet) – is the park's best-known landmark, although its highest point is **Pedra do Sino** at 2,263 meters (7,425 feet). The park is a paradise for lovers of adventure sports, and its trails offer spectacular views. On clear days, visitors can see Rio de Janeiro and glimpse Guanabara Bay through the foliage. There are two ways to enter: from Petrópolis *(access from Estrada do Bonfim, Km 18)* or Teresópolis, where the park's headquarters are *(access from Avenida Rotariana)*. The public can use the park for short trips Tuesday through Sunday, from 8am to 5pm. The rest of the time, only climbers who have bought tickets in advance can enter. The best period for hiking is from May to October; swimming in the river is most tolerable between November and February. Beware of summer storms, however, because head water levels tend to rise rapidly and flow down, abruptly increasing river currents and creating flash floods that sweep away everything in their path. The Soberbo, the park's major river, provides wonderful waterfalls for swimming and serves as the terminus for the most accessible trails. The easiest trails, like **Primavera** and **Mozart Catão**, take less than an hour. It takes less than two hours to reach the **Véu de Noiva** waterfall in Bonfim Valley, which is a good place for canyoning and rappelling. The 2,232-meter (7,323-foot) hike to the top of **Pedra do Açu** takes about five and a half hours. The best trek is the four-day hike across the mountains on the 42-kilometer (26-mile) trail from Petrópolis to Teresópolis. Hiring a guide is recommended. Accredited professionals can be hired from two travel agencies: **Avitur** *(Travessa Ranulfo Feo, 41, Várzea, tel. (21) 2742-5770)* and **Vila Nova** *(Rua Dr. Francisco Sá, 179A, store #32, Várzea, tel. (21) 2643-1543).*

TERESÓPOLIS

Teresópolis was named after Dona Teresa, Dom Pedro II's wife. Around the end of the 19th-century, she fell under the spell of the region's climate and natural beauty. It follows, then, that the area is best known for its outdoor activities and its role as a base for highland excursions, while nearby Petrópolis recalls the glorious days of the Empire and boasts palaces and historical collections. Teresópolis is located 87 kilometers (54 miles) from Rio on Rodovia BR-040 highway and then BR-116. It is the highest town in Rio de Janeiro, nestled in the Órgãos mountain range at 910 meters (3,000 feet) above sea level and surrounded by a breathtaking landscape of the mountains, rivers, waterfalls, and a rich diversity of flora and fauna. It also contains the headquarters of **Parque Nacional da Serra dos Órgãos**, with a camping site, rock pools, and trails leading to the peaks. The **Dedo de Deus peak**, an icon in local mountaineering circles, is also located in the park and was first climbed by Brazilians in 1912. During the settling of Teresópolis, many farms were established, such as the one that belonged to George March. He was a Portuguese man of English descent who raised cattle, horses, and mules and grew vegetables to supply the state capital. Other people from Rio followed him

and founded a small village, where they offered lodging to merchants from Minas Gerais en route to the port of Estrela, in Guanabara Bay. Tourism really began to take off in 1908, when the railroad came through and hotels, guesthouses, and restaurants sprung up in its wake. The town became a favorite mountain destination after the road to Rio opened in 1959. The Brazilian Football Confederation runs a quiet training center, **Granja Comari**, in the city.

OUR RECOMMENDATION

🍽 Be prepared for a banquet at **Dona Irene**, a Russian restaurant worthy of the tsars. The portions are enormous – and accompanied by plenty of homemade vodka. Try the *varenik*, a kind of ravioli with potatoes, scaloppini, herbs, and crispy onions. Reservations are required *(Rua Tenente Luís Meireles, 1800, Bom Retiro, tel. (21) 2742-2901; Wed – Sat, noon – midnight; Sun, noon – 6pm; opens Mon and Tue on advance request).*

🏨 **Rosa dos Ventos Hotel** and farm are located in a private park in the middle of the mountains. The ample leisure facilities make the complex feel like a resort. It is the only Brazilian hotel in the Relais & Chateaux chain, which guarantees charm and comfort *(Estrada Teresópolis–Nova Friburgo, Km 22.5, Campanha, tel. (21) 2644-9900, 2532-1197).*

Additional information on page 462.

VASSOURAS

In the middle of the 19th century, Vassouras – in the Paraíba Valley, 111 kilometers (69 miles) from Rio on Rodovia BR-116 highway and then RJ-127 – was the country's top coffee-producing region. Coffee was the main industry during the imperial era, and successful growers rapidly grew rich.

They built imposing manors with dozens of rooms on their plantations and brought furnishings from Europe to decorate their mansions. They also planted imperial palms and fig trees along the streets. Within a few decades, however, the soil became impoverished and the abolition of slavery led to the economic decline of the labor-intensive plantations. The town has not grown since those times, a fact that has helped preserve its historical heritage.

HISTORICAL CENTER

The main square, Praça Barão de Campo Belo, is lined with the city's largest buildings: a beautiful neoclassical church, **Igreja Nossa Senhora da Conceição**, dating from 1846; the **Prefeitura** (City Hall), housed in an 1849 mansion; and the **Casa da Cultura** building, constructed in 1844 and containing a beautiful stone fountain. The colonial-style **Casa da Hera** museum, built in 1830, has a rich collection of 19th-century crystal, silverware, porcelain, candlesticks, lamps, clothing, and furniture *(tel. (24) 2471-2266; Wed – Sun, 11am – 5pm).*

IMPERIAL ESTATES

Fifteen estates from the imperial era have been restored and opened to visitors. Book a trip organized by one of the hotels, because some sites can only be seen by appointment. Most offer an afternoon snack or "colonial tea," with a selection of sweets and pastries. One of the oldest estates is **Cachoeira Grande**, dating from 1825, which belonged to the Baron of Vassouras. A chair that belonged to Dom Pedro II, an 1830 piano, and a phonograph are among the artifacts on display. Ask to see the family's antique car collection in advance; some of the vehicles date back to 1910 *(tel. (24) 2471-1264).*

VISCONDE DE MAUÁ

A hippie enclave in the 1970s and 80s, Visconde de Mauá is about 200 kilometers (125 miles) from Rio. It retains some of the charm but none of the shortcomings of many alternative communities. With excellent hotels and some of the nicest hotels in the region, it is one of the state's most

Rappelling at Santa Clara Waterfall in the village of Maromba: a 20-meter cliff face

romantic and picturesque destinations. Coming from Rio, take the Rodovia Presidente Dutra highway to Km 304 in Resende, then the RJ-163. Coming from São Paulo, 305 kilometers (190 miles) away, take the same highway to Km 311. The low winter temperatures, especially in July, are perfect for a romantic evening and a glass of wine by the fireplace. Most guesthouses cater to couples, serving breakfast until noon, and do not allow children to stay. From December through March, the summer temperatures are mild and conditions are ideal at the many nearby waterfalls. Adventure sports have become popular in the region in recent years. Located on the border of Rio de Janeiro state and Minas Gerais to the north, the community actually consists of three villages: **Visconde de Mauá**, where most of the locals live; **Maromba**, home to the **Escorrega** and **Santa Clara** waterfalls; and **Maringá**, the most attractive village, divided into Maringá Rio and Maringá Minas Gerais by the Preto River. The narrow streets, many of which contain craft shops operating out of little wooden houses, make it hard to get around Maringá village center by car. Visitors should rent horses, motorbikes or four-wheelers. A 14-minute drive along the bumpy, winding RJ-163 takes travelers from Rodovia Presidente Dutra highway to Visconde de Mauá. Be careful: landslides can damage the roads when it rains, so it's a good idea to call some of guesthouses to check on conditions before leaving. Drive slowly to ensure a safe journey while enjoying the view. Visconde de Mauá was named after the Baron – later the Viscount – of Mauá (1813-1889), a banker and industrialist who owned most of the land in the region. At the end of the 19th century, his son established a European colony with government support and divided the land into more than 200 lots. Visconde de Mauá's current economy is based on tourism, and its good restaurants specialize in trout.

VALE DO ACANTILADO

Visconde de Mauá abounds with beautiful scenery and waterfalls. Walking the trail to the 20-meter (66-foot) **Cachoeira do Acantilado** takes about an hour and a half one way. One particular waterfall is the valley's main attraction, as well as the tallest in the region, but the trail also goes by another eight stunning falls. The photogenic Acantilado waterfall can be seen from the start of the trail, nestled in the mountain, and the magnificent view helps encourage tired feet. A lookout area offers a beautiful view before the top. Less energetic visitors can still appreciate the first three waterfalls, which offer wonderful swimming just 10 minutes away from the parking lot. The valley is located on a private property, and an entrance fee is required.
Sítio Cachoeira do Acantilado, Estrada Mauá–Mirantão, Km 3, tel. (24) 9967-6766. Daily, 8am – 6pm.

VIEW FROM PEDRA SELADA

Many tourists, sports enthusiasts, and adventure-seekers visit Visconde de Mauá with the sole intent of climbing to the peak of **Pedra Selada**. The 1.7-kilometer (1-mile) hike to the summit takes about two and a half hours and has some very steep stretches through dense forest. But it's worth it: The view of Paraíba Valley from the top is breathtaking.

Parque Nacional do Itatiaia, the oldest in Brazil

PARQUE NACIONAL DO ITATIAIA

Brazil's first national park was created in 1937. Situated on the border of Minas Gerais, São Paulo, and Rio de Janeiro, 167 kilometers (104 miles) from Rio and 265 kilometers (165 miles) from São Paulo, it is made up of 30,000 hectares of beautiful scenery. The lower part, which can be reached through **Itatiaia** *(Rodovia Presidente Dutra, Km 316)*, is clad in dense Atlantic forest vegetation. It has several guesthouses and numerous waterfalls, including the 40-meter **Véu da Noiva** that splashes into a natural pool. The rugged, rocky landscape of the highlands, accessible from the same highway from exit Km 330, is a different story. Itatiaia, which means "spiky rocks," is the name of the park's two most famous peaks: **Agulhas Negras** and **Prateleiras**. In the lower part of the park, guides are required for climbing or embarking on extensive treks. Before leaving the park, stop at the **Mirante do Último Adeus**, a magnificent vantage point two kilometers (1.3 miles) from the lower entrance.

EATING OUT IN PENEDO
This former Finnish colony is 12 kilometers (7.5 miles) from the town center, and although most of Itatiaia's hotels offer full board, it's worth having a meal in **Penedo**. **Koskenkorva** serves excellent Finnish cuisine and is located in a lush green environment *(Estrada das Três Cachoeiras, 3,955, tel. (24) 3351-2532; daily, noon - midnight)*. The more casual **Rei das Trutas** specializes in trout dishes *(Avenida das Mangueiras, no #, tel. (24) 3351-1387; daily, 11am – 11pm)*, while **Zur Sonne** serves delicious German cuisine. The last restaurant is located in the Alambari Mountains, 15 kilometers (9.5 miles) from Penedo, four kilometers (2.5 miles) of which are unpaved *(Serrinha do Alambari, Km 4, tel. (24) 3381-7108; daily, noon – 6pm and 7pm – 9pm; opens at night subject to prior bookings)*.

THE SOUTH COAST

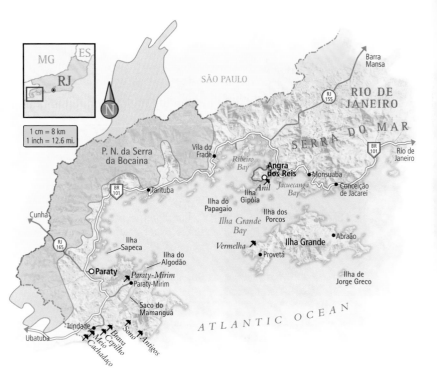

ANGRA DOS REIS

The bay of Angra dos Reis is one of the most beautiful destinations in Southeast Brazil. It owes its beauty to the see, with crystal-clear waters, dozens of beaches, and enough islands and islets that it would take a year to visit each for a day. Its name means "Bay of Kings." It was named after Epiphany Day, or the Day of the Three Kings – the day it was discovered, Jan. 6, 1502. Guests can go swimming and snorkeling on sea excursions. In the town center, the Boat Owners' Association (*Associação dos Barqueiros: tel. (24) 3365-3165)* rents out boats of varying size and cost, but nearly all the hotels offer boat services and some even include

them in their rates. The schooner trip to the islands of **Cataguases**, **Botinas**, **Jipóia**, and **Francisco** is highly recommended. Angra dos Reis is located 168 kilometers (105 miles) south of Rio on the Rodovia Rio–Santos highway (BR-101). From this direction, the small town center looks disappointing, and the beaches are not nearly as attractive as the ones further down the road. Head straight for one of the region's resorts. Five-star hotels and charming guesthouses offer beautiful views, secluded beaches, and modern amenities. Many Brazilian celebrities have houses in or near Angra dos Reis,

The clear waters around Ilha Botinas

and it's a popular place to usher in the New Year. One of the highlights of New Year's Day is a flotilla of brightly decorated boats. The beach **Praia do Anil** is also the departure point for trips to nearby Ilha Grande (see page 145), which is famous for its natural beauty.

GIPÓIA

The region's second-largest island, **Gipóia**, is known for its magnificent beaches and inviting spots for snorkeling. It is just a 30-minute boat trip from the Santa Luzia docks in downtown Angra dos Reis. If you like hustle and bustle, head for **Praia da Jurubaíba** or **Praia do Dentista**, where floating bars deliver snacks and drinks to the boats that swarm the area. **Praia da Juruba**, sheltered by hills, a rocky shoreline, and native vegetation, is more peaceful and

secluded. It can only be reached by canoe; fishermen cast nets and set up traps near the beach. **Praia do Norte** is small and beautiful, with fine white sand. Almost-deserted **Praia Sururu** has gold sand and strong waves that crash against the reefs. **Praia Oeste** is wilder, with warm, shallow waters.

DIVING SITES

Angra is ideal for diving because of its calm, crystal-clear waters, good visibility for most of the year, and average temperature of 23 degrees Celsius (73.4 degrees Fahrenheit). *Parcéis*, or rock pathways, run between four and 12 meters (13 and 40 feet) off the islands of **Ilha de Búzios** and **Ilha das Cobras**. The waters off the rocky shores of **Brandão**, **Josefa**, **Redonda**, and **Papagaio** islands abound with sponges, coral, and colorful fish. The coasts of **Laje Zatim**, **Ilha Imboassica**, and **Ilhas Queimadas** (**Grande** and **Pequena**) are very similar, while the waters off of **Ilha Botinas** and **Ilha dos Porcos** are so clear and full of fish that their enormous shoals are visible even from the boat. Off **Laje Preta**, however, the sea is also four to 12 meters (13 to 40 feet) deep but the water becomes darker farther from the shore.

OUR RECOMMENDATION

Pestana Angra Beach Bangalôs offers private, romantic surroundings. The 27 bungalows, each with a view of the sea and surrounded by vegetation, boast comfortable, spacious rooms with access to a sauna and a jacuzzi on the veranda. It also has a heliport and a restaurant with a panoramic view *(Estrada Vereador Benedito Adelino, 3700, Retiro, tel. (24) 3364-2005)*.

Additional information on page 462.

WRECK DIVING

The wreck of the Panamanian freighter *Pinguino*, which sank in **Enseada do Sítio Forte** inlet in 1967, created a great diving site. At a depth of 15 to 20 meters (50 to 60 feet), divers can explore the freighter's hold, engine room, and captain's cabin. The *Califórnia*, a Brazilian vessel that sank in 1866, rests at the bottom of the inlet of **Enseada de Araçatiba**, near Praia Vermelha beach on Ilha Grande island. A helicopter sank to seven meters (22 feet) to the bottom of **Laje Mataríz**, and even snorklers can see the wreck on clear days. The wreck

of the *Bezerra de Menezes*, a steam-powered freighter that sank in 1860, sits off of one of the bay's headlands.

ILHA GRANDE

Ilha Grande, the largest island in the region, belongs to the municipality of Angra dos Reis. It is one and a half hour away by boat from the mainland. The island has more than 100 beaches, some of them reachable as one-day excursions. One of those beaches – the splendid **Lopes Mendes** – has strong waves that make it ideal for surfing. But it's worth setting aside several days to explore majestic Ilha Grande and hike

Lopes Mendes Beach on Ilha Grande, one of the region's most beautiful spots

its trails, visit its hidden beaches, and scuba dive off its shores. Lush vegetation covers its 192 square kilometers (74 square miles), which are situated within the **Tamoios (APA) Environmental Protection Area**. It also falls within the boundaries of three other conservation reserves: **Parque Estadual Marinho do Aventureiro**, **Parque Estadual da Ilha Grande**, and **Reserva Biológica da Praia do Sul**. Because cars are forbidden, the natural surroundings remain largely untouched despite the increasing presence of visitors. Nearly all the restaurants, shops, and travel agencies that offer trips are concentrated in the small **Vila do Abraão**, where arriving boats dock. The best hotels, however, are scattered elsewhere around the island and are a bit more difficult to reach. Lively *forró* music and dance parties take place on the weekends in the village, where tourists and locals meet to have fun. Boats dock for the night in the calm waters of **Saco do Céu**, a small inlet that is one of the island's most charming spots. On clear evenings, the flat sea becomes a mirror to reflect the stars – an unforgettable sight. The island's past contrasts with its paradisiacal atmosphere: In 1940, it was home to the Cândido Mendes Prison, which became known as Ilha Grande Prison. Most of the maximum-security prison was demolished in 1994.

TREKKING ON THE ISLAND

At least 16 trails run the gamut of difficulty, from easy to very tough. They lead to peaks and **Gruta do Acaiá** grotto, as well as the many waterfalls, beaches, and mussel-breeding farms. The most interesting trek is quite demanding and requires a whole week. It circles the island and has camping sites along the way. The view at the top of 990-meter (0.6-mile) **Pico do Papagaio** is worth the hike. The best times of the year for trekking are May through July and October and November, when temperatures are mild and rainfall is negligible. It's a good idea to hire a guide, because some of the trails can be dangerous even though they are well marked. A good local agency is **Sudoeste SW Turismo** *(tel. (24) 3361-5516)*.

BOAT TRIPS

The schooner excursion to **Freguesia de Santana** offers a marvelous view of the Angra dos Reis coast. (Freguesia's most important historical building is **Igreja de Santana**, a church dating from 1796.) The trip takes visitors to beautiful beaches and snorkeling spots in **Lagoa Azul**. The small lagoon is surrounded by tiny islets and full of brightly colored tropical fish. Boat trips also pass through **Saco do Céu** and **Japariz**, where the sea is calm and ideal for jet skiing in an area close to the mangrove swamps. **Palmas** is another interesting destination; that trip includes a one-hour hike to **Lopes Mendes** and stops at **Ilha do Morcego** island and **Praia do Abraãozinho** beach. If the boat is appropriate and the weather cooperates, add on a trip to the open sea. Rent a seaworthy vessel at the Ilha Grande Boat Owners' Association, where the boats are safe, registered with the Port Authority, and piloted by a qualified crew *(Associação dos Barqueiros de Ilha Grande: tel. (24) 3361-5920)*.

Paraty's rich colonial architecture, facing the bay

PARATY

Paraty (also spelled Parati) is one of the most charming places on the southeast coast of Brazil, as well as a gateway to the past. The town was founded in the mid-17th century, and its historical center, where cars are prohibited, preserves numerous architectural treasures from the 18th century. Paraty became a Unesco World Heritage site in 1966. Its streets are paved with the original, irregular cobblestones, and at high tide, they become canals that allow the ocean to flow in and out. The small colonial center has an artistic vibe: on every corner, someone is playing music, making crafts, or performing a puppet show. A busy cultural program offers culinary, musical, and folklore events, including the beautiful **Festa do Divino**. In mid-2003, the city hosted the first **Flip**, an annual international literary festival promoted by British publisher – and contributor to this book – Liz Calder. Calder loves the town and keeps a home there. Paraty is also synonymous with *cachaça*, the local sugarcane liquor, thanks to the premium brands the nearby distilleries turn out. The Serra da Bocaina mountains surround the town, and dozens of small islands dot its bay. Excellent snorkeling spots and many beautiful beaches, some of them nearly deserted, border the ocean. The town's location at the foot of the mountains makes it a logical starting point for trekking tours in the highlands and visits to the waterfalls. Paraty lies 248 kilometers (154 miles) from Rio and 350 kilometers (218 miles) from São Paulo, on Rodovia BR-101 highway.

HISTORICAL CENTER
Set aside an afternoon for strolling around the narrow streets of Paraty's colonial center. The **Casa da Cultura** occupies a magnificent 1754 mansion, hosts periodic cultural events and houses a good permanent exhibition on local history and culture *(Rua Dona Geralda, 177, tel. (24) 3371-2325; Wed – Mon, 10am –*

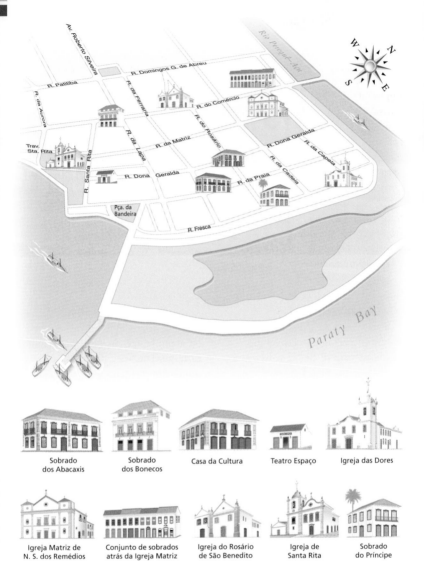

Sobrado
dos Abacaxis

Sobrado
dos Bonecos

Casa da Cultura

Teatro Espaço

Igreja das Dores

Igreja Matriz de
N. S. dos Remédios

Conjunto de sobrados
atrás da Igreja Matriz

Igreja do Rosário
de São Benedito

Igreja de
Santa Rita

Sobrado
do Príncipe

6:30pm). The **Teatro Espaço**, home of the world-famous traditional Puppet Theater, is on the same street. The town's churches are a big draw. The oldest church, **Igreja de Santa Rita** in Largo Santa Rita, dates from 1722 and houses the **Museu de Arte Sacra**, a museum of religious art. The 1725 **Igreja do Rosário** in Largo do

Rosário was the slaves' church. It was decorated in a simple way, except for the altars' gold leaf, which was added in the early 20th century. **Igreja Matriz de Nossa Senhora dos Remédios** is also worth a visit. Construction on the church began in 1787, but the cost of the ambitious project meant it took almost 100 years to complete it. In the main square, Praça da Matriz, an outdoor market displays many of Paraty's arts and crafts. The fair is open daily and always has music and puppet shows. Built at the turn of the century, **Igreja Nossa Senhora das Dores** displays typical 18th-century style – note the delicate tracery of the balconies and the crystal chandelier over the choir stalls. The aristocracy used the church during the imperial era. Don't forget to admire the architecture of the **Sobrado dos Bonecos**, **Sobrado dos Abacaxis**, and the **Sobrado do Príncipe** – the latter belongs to the Orleans e Bragança royal family.

BOAT TRIPS

Schooners, small fishing boats, and trawlers can all be rented at the quay. Various routes stop at three or four beaches. Diving is permitted – amid spectacular scenery – off the islands of **Ilha do Algodão** and **Ilha Sapeca**. The stunning **Saco do Mamanguá**, a green bay flanked by steep cliffs, is an unforgettable destination; visitors can reach it by boat from **Praia de Paraty-Mirim** beach.

A TRIP TO CUNHA

A winding, unpaved, bumpy road that narrows to a single lane at sharp curves leads to the historical town of **Cunha**. The spot offers breathtaking views of the bay and the beauty of the forest, but only 4×4 vehicles can safely reach it during the rainy season. *(For more information on Cunha, see page 192)*.

SURFING AND DIVING IN TRINDADE

Trindade – a former fishing village and one-time hippie enclave that now thrives on tourism – is a memorable destination just 25 kilometers from Paraty and seven kilometers (four miles) from the Rodovia Rio-Santos highway. It's reachable on a paved, well-marked road. The dirt roads within the town are packed on holidays, but even during the high season, it never loses its rustic charm. It also boasts excellent beaches for surfing, such as **Praia do Cepilho** and **Praia Brava**, and others with calm waters and rock pools, like **Praia do Meio** and **Praia do Cachadaço**. The latter has a huge natural stone pool, ideal for snorkeling and watching fish, and it is only a 20-minute walk from Praia do Meio. Alternatively, visitors can hire boats at the beach, which can get to Praia do Cachadaço in just five minutes. Adventurous travelers can head to the more distant beaches of **Praia do Sono** (a one-hour walk from Vila Oratório) and **Praia dos Antigos** (an additional 40-minute walk from Praia do Sono). Both are seaside paradises untouched by tourism.

The colonial Sobrado dos Abacaxis

A LITERARY PARADISE

Paraty took hold of my imagination long before I ever went there. During my 20s I lived in São Paulo for four years. This was in the 60s, and Brazil and its enchanting music, art, literature and film held me in thrall. We and our friends partied all night and danced to the music of the young Chico Buarque and Gilberto Gil. It was "heaven itself".

Every so often people would mention a mysterious place on the coast between São Paulo and Rio, a place that could be reached only by sea or mule. Artists, bohemians, and gays, so I was told, lived blissfully alongside the local fishermen in this secret place of wonderful architecture and natural beauty. Paraty – the very name was romantic, and I longed to go. But it was never possible at that time.

In 1992 I finally made it there. By then, a road had been built, and Paraty had become a national monument and a favourite holiday place for *paulistas*. It was Carnival, and Paraty's historical centre was gearing up for a party – everyone milling around in the colourful streets filled with dancing, music and children in fancy dress.

The town was just as I had imagined it. Intimate, gay, sometimes melancholy, throbbing with street life at times, quiet as a grave at others. Tucked into that narrow strip of flat land between the protecting mountains and the calm sea, it looks out from its prime spot in the bowl of the bay, decorated by the most ravishing rain forest. It welcomes visitors to share its bounty. And it sighs with relief when they all go away again… Its unique charm is a confluence of this unrivalled natural beauty and the grace of its 18th-century colonial buildings, funded first by gold from Minas Gerais and then by coffee.

As I reminisce, I have in front of me a postcard that I sent my husband Louis Baum in London during that trip in 1992. The card shows the classic view of Paraty: the Santa Rita church and the quays taken from the sea, and on it I wrote: "Here is where we are going to live. Start packing now!" How ever did I know?

In 1999 we returned to this side of the bay to look at a property that was for sale. It was terribly neglected and overgrown, and the land that dropped steeply down to the sea had just a small house on it. Protected by the island of Araújo, its steep banks have been softened by terracing, zigzagging pathways and Mauro Munhoz' inspired architecture. Munhoz is a visionary architect from São Paulo who has worked for many years on a project to reclaim the Paraty waterfront, which has become silted up.

How, then, did Paraty acquire a literary festival – and an international one at that? From way back when we first met Mauro, we have dreamed of ways to bring Paraty's riches to the attention of more people. Not all people, of course – just those in the know. For much of the year there is a tranquility about the place that is precious to the people who live there. In the holidays it fills up with visitors, and the shops and restaurants and *pousadas* (inns) do their business.

We wondered, "What might help the town to prosper during the off-season?" The beauty and intimacy of the 18th century historic center, the existence of so many *pousadas*, well over 100, and of so many charming bars, restaurants, shops and art galleries, all make it an ideal location for festivals, and Paraty is blessed with many of these, both religious and cultural. But since Louis and I are both book people, we began to wonder if a literary festival had any possibility here. A strong motivating factor was our belief that the riches of Brazil's art and literature – not to mention its natural beauty – are not sufficiently appreciated in the rest of the world: how better to raise their international profile than by inviting leading international writers to meet their Brazilian counterparts in such a beautiful and intimate setting?

The first FLIP (Festa Literária Internacional de Paraty), in 2003, was an amazing success. I say amazing because none of us expected such a huge response, from the media, from the authors, from the people of Paraty, and from the public. More than 6,000 people visited Paraty for the four days of the festival. We were able to bring to Paraty the Federal Minister of Culture, Gilberto Gil, on his first visit to the town. We were able to bring Chico Buarque and Adriana Calcanhoto, international literary stars like Don DeLillo, Julian Barnes and Hanif Kureishi, one of the world's leading historians, Eric Hobsbawm, and several leading Brazilian writers.

The success of the literary festival demonstrates a way forward for the town. For all its beauty – *because* of its beauty – Paraty is at a crossroads. Unlike nearby Angra dos Reis, which offers a stark and depressing warning to all beauty resorts with dreams of growing, Paraty has preserved its isolation to a degree. But since the building of the Rio–Santos road and the development of international transport and communications, its tourism has increased. This has brought great benefits to the town, but also dangers. Traditional communities in some outlying settlements are losing inhabitants to the town. And the subtle ties that have held the town and its surroundings together, and made it the jewel it is, are being threatened. Yes, Paraty needs more tourists, but they should be tourists who are sensitive not only to its beauty but also to the fragility of that beauty.

Paraty also, we believe, needs state and federal support for its infrastructure, to enable it to cope with growing numbers of tourists without damage to the natural and urban environment. Should that be allowed to occur, the very things that make Paraty one of the world's most beautiful coastal towns would be under threat.

*Liz Calder, director of Bloomsbury Publishing
and president of Festa Literária Internacional de Paraty*

Búzios: urban sophistication with a fishing-village backdrop

THE NORTH COAST

BÚZIOS

Búzios is an idyllic, eight-kilometer (five-mile) peninsula surrounded by clear green water. It is also a global village, with streets and beaches full of visitors from all over the world. The town has come a long way since the 1950s, when it was a secluded beach retreat that was extremely difficult to reach. In the following decade, actress Brigitte Bardot discovered Búzios; her attention helped transform it into a fashionable international destination. Today it has comfortable, first-class accommodations, cozy bars, sophisticated restaurants, elegant stores, and even a movie theater named after the French actress. With more than 200 hotels and guesthouses, it has lost much of the fishing-village atmosphere and glamour it once had, but its high-end services complement the informality of its beaches. The peninsula is 192 kilometers (120 miles)

east of Rio, on Rodovia BR-101 highway, followed by the RJ-124 and RJ-106. Take a fun day trip to **Barra de São João**, a small village 30 kilometers (19 miles) from Búzios. It was once the home of Brazilian poet Casimiro de Abreu, who celebrated it in his verses, and some of the town's houses have been standing at the edge of the mangrove-lined São João River since the 17th century.

RUA DAS PEDRAS
The heart of Búzios is Rua das Pedras (Street of Stones). It's actually a 400-meter (quarter-mile) stretch of Avenida Bento Ribeiro Dantas, which bisects the town. This town earned its nickname because of its streets' rough-cut paving stones, which deter drivers and invite people to roam on foot. Visitors will find famous designer boutiques, sophisticated restaurants,

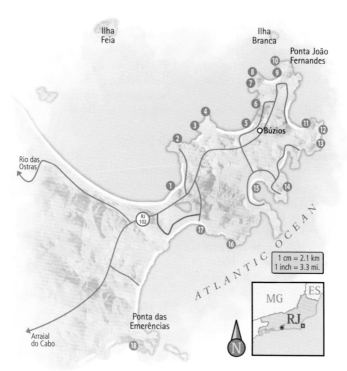

nightclubs, ice-cream parlors, *crêperies*, and street artists. The scene begins to heat up at sunset; hang out in town and mingle with people from all over the world and all walks of life.

THE BEACHES

Armação de Búzios is a winding peninsula dotted with beautiful bays. Its beaches have waters to suit every taste – with or without waves, deep or shallow, cold or mild, crowded or deserted. The town is also a sailor's paradise: it has four yacht clubs and hosts more than a dozen events and competitions – such as the Búzios Sailing Week, which usually takes place in April – every year. Boat tours of the peninsula depart frequently from Praia da Armação, and most serve *caipirinhas*, mineral water, soft drinks, and fruit on board.

❶ MANGUINHOS

Calm waters and steady winds make this beach ideal for windsurfing, as is the neighboring bay of **Baía Formosa**. It faces **Ilha Feia**, a perfect spot for scuba diving.

❷ TARTARUGA

This popular beach is known for its rock pools, unspoiled vegetation, and multicolored pebbles. Divers can also enjoy the coral reefs.

❸ PRAIA DAS VIRGENS

Another deserted beach. It is accessible along the rocks or by sea from Praia dos Amores, but only at low tide — make sure to keep an eye on its level.

❹ PRAIA DOS AMORES

Swimming conditions are ideal in the calm waters at this deserted, untouched beach. Nudity is allowed, albeit informally. The beach is accessible by sea or by scrambling along the rocky coastline.

⑤ Praia do Canto and Praia da Armação

Although **Praia do Canto** is dotted with colonial houses and fishing boats, both of these urban beaches are unfit for swimming.

⑥ Praia dos Ossos

This small inlet is one of the most famous in Búzios. Many international sailing and windsurfing competitions are held there. Visitors can take trips in schooners and glass-bottomed boats to observe the marine life. A flight of stairs leads to **Igreja de Sant'Ana**, a church dating from 1740.

⑦ Azeda

This beach is only accessible on foot, by way of Praia dos Ossos. It has delightful scenery and calm waters, which make it ideal for diving.

⑧ Azedinha

Like Azeda, this beach is an environmental reserve and is also an excellent diving spot. It has a breathtaking bay with green waters.

⑨ João Fernandes

Crowded and vibrant, this beach has many rocky outcroppings. Its many kiosks serve lobster and local fish.

⑩ João Fernandinho

This beach is almost deserted, despite its beautiful rock pools, and accessible only from Praia João Fernandes. Both beaches are good for fishing and diving.

⑪ Brava

This large beach is dotted with lookout points, and its huge waves make it a surfers' paradise. Beware of the current near Laje do Criminoso.

⑫ Olho-de-boi

Some people go nude on this beach, because it is so deserted. Access it on foot from Praia Brava.

⑬ Forno

This is tiny, enchanting inlet with calm waters, moderate winds, and several rock pools. It's ideal for divers and anyone who wants to escape from civilization.

⑭ Foca

Accessible by sea or down a trail, this beach has a narrow strip of sand and heavy breakers.

⑮ Ferradura

This placid bay dotted with kiosks and beach houses is perfect for diving and sailing, as well as for families with small children. It also offers access to **Ponta da Lagoinha**, which has a stunning sunset.

⑯ Ferradurinha

Calm, crystal-clear waters set off a sandy beach with a natural rock pool. It is ideal for diving and accessible from Portal da Ferradura by car or Praia de Geribá on foot.

⑰ Geribá

This fashionable beach, which is four kilometers (2.5 miles) long, is very popular with the younger generation. Visitors must pay to sit in the shade of a parasol, but the beach's many bars and restaurants will pamper you if you do. Powerful breakers hit certain stretches.

⑱ José Gonçalves

Located on a nature reserve, this still-pristine beach has a friendly kiosk on the sand.

Praia das Conchas, ideal for fishing

CABO FRIO

Cabo Frio is much more crowded than Búzios; in fact, it is the biggest and most developed town in the Região dos Lagos region. It is two hours and 148 kilometers (92 miles) by car from Rio de Janeiro on Rodovia BR-101 highway, followed by RJ-124 and RJ-140. Cabo Frio has cold, clear water, lots of sunshine, and a temperate climate all year. The constant northeasterly wind sculpts the fine white sand into dunes. For safety's sake, explore the dunes during the day. Cabo Frio's windmills reveal that the town is one of Brazil's major salt producers

BIKINI STREET

This street's real name is **Rua Gamboa**, but it's better known as Rua dos Biquínis: Bikini Street. During summer, more than 3,500 people daily flock to its 200 stores to buy everything they need for the beach – shorts, t-shirts, sarongs, sandals, and, of course, bikinis. In fact, visitors can put together a complete summer wardrobe on the street.

BEACHES

Praia do Forte is the most famous and crowded beach in Cabo Frio. The Fortress of São Mateus was built there in 1620; now, spontaneous music performances pop up on the esplanade. Even though it's almost impossible to find a spot to sunbathe in the summer, it is an excellent spot for sailors and surfers. Walk along the beach to get to the dunes, but be careful: **Dama Branca**, the highest one, is not safe. Also in this direction is **Praia do Foguete**, which is lined with summer houses. Powerful breakers make this beach ideal for surfing and fishing. Keep going north to reach **Praia Brava**, which is also popular with surfers because of its powerful waves. A little farther in the same direction is the tiny **Praia das Conchas**, a good fishing spot where visitors can rent horses. From there, keep going to find the spectacular dunes of **Praia do Peró**. Shorefront kiosks offer food and drinks.

ARRAIAL DO CABO

The ocean is Arraial do Cabo's main attraction. The town resembles a fishing village. Its white dunes, sandbanks, lagoons, unspoiled beaches, and beautiful headlands are surrounded by hills. From one headland, **Pontal do Atalaia**, visitors can admire a glorious coastal sunset. Arraial is part of colonial history: It was originally the land of the Tupinambá Indians and the finest pau-brasil, or brazilwood, after which the country was named. It was also the scene of Dutch timber smuggling, piracy, and dozens of shipwrecks – there are said to be at least 88 in the area. Now, however, the town is quieter than its more fashionable neighbors. At **Praia Grande**, a beach that stretches as far as the horizon in the direction of the traditional surfing beach **Praia de Saquarema**, people

Arraial do Cabo: stunning coastline

can go drift-net fishing and indulge in the late-afternoon drink and a snack in one of the bars or kiosks. More energetic visitors can go scuba diving and explore the many trails, such as the one to the old lighthouse. The boat trips are also unforgettable, especially the one to **Gruta Azul** grotto that stops at Pontal do Atalaia. Arraial do Cabo is known as the country's scuba-diving capital, and its unique geographical characteristics make it very different from other diving spots in Brazil. The coastal current changes direction there, veering from north-south to west-east and forcing deep waters flowing from the Antarctic up to the surface. As a result, the area is exceptionally rich in marine life, which can be appreciated by underwater sports enthusiasts. Always go diving with an instructor. To reach Arraial do Cabo from Rio city, take Rodovia BR-101 highway, followed by RJ-124, RJ-106, and RJ-140. The trip is 158 kilometers (99 miles) by car.

ILHA DE CABO FRIO

The island of Cabo Frio – just off the tip of Arraial do Cabo and a 14-minute boat trip from Praia dos Anjos – is magnificent walking country, but visitors need the Navy's permission to spend the day there. The Brazilian National Institute of Space Research declared tiny **Praia do Forte**, with its typical sandbank vegetation, fine white sand, and cold, clear, blue water, the most perfect beach in the country. (Who would have thought planetary scientists were experts on beaches?) Praia do Forte offers breathtaking sights, such as the rock formation **Racha de Nossa Senhora**, the hill on the Pontal

Cabo
Frio

Saco do
Cherne **1**

2 Ponta da
Jararaca

Ilha dos
Porcos **3** Ilha dos Porcos
(outside)

Cardeiros **5**

4 Ilha dos Porcos
(inside)

8 Anequim

Arraial
do Cabo

Dona
Paula **13**

Pedra
Vermelha **7**

9 Ponta
Leste

Maramutá **6**

Ilha do
Cabo Frio

1 cm = 2.5 km
1 inch = 3.9 mi.

Harlinger **12**

MG   ES

RJ

N

Gruta Azul
and Thetis **11**

10 Gruta da
Camarinha

do Atalaia headland, **Ilha dos Porcos**, and **Prainha**. A one-and-a-half-hour trail leads to a lighthouse, the ruins of an old one built in 1833, and the lighthouse keeper's home at the peak of the headland. From there, the entire Região dos Lagos region is visible. The thick fog lends a mysterious atmosphere to the place. The waters around the island are excellent for diving, have good visibility, and are home to about 60 species of fish and coral.

1 SACO DO CHERNE
A coral-covered seabed makes this an ideal spot for shallow diving.

2 TEIXEIRINHA
At Ponta da Jararaca, visitors can find huge rocks encrusted with marine creatures. Remains of the *Teixeirinha*, a ship that sank in 1923, are scattered at different depths.

3 PORCOS (OFF THE EAST SHORE)
Inexperienced divers should avoid this site, which has depths up to 40 meters (130 feet) close to the rocks.

4 PORCOS (OFF THE SOUTH SHORE)
A 15-meter (50-foot) dive features lots of sea fans (known as *gorgônias*), seahorses, and the occasional turtles.

5 CARDEIROS
Shallow diving from 6 to 10 meters (20 to 33 feet) in quiet seas reveals green sponges, seahorses, and pink coral.

6 MARAMUTÁ AND
7 PEDRA VERMELHA
Ibama, Brazil's environmental agency, has banned diving in these spots. They

were once popular places for diving schools to introduce people to new waters, but they are now used only for research.

⑧ ANEQUIM
Divers will find forests of sea fans and the wreck of the *Wizard*, which sank in 1839. Anequim's depths are between 10 and 15 meters (33 and 50 feet).

⑨ PONTA LESTE
This site is exceptionally rich in marine life, including sting rays, turtles, barracuda, yellowtail, and mackerel.

⑩ CAMARINHA
Only experienced divers should visit this spot, and only when the sea is calm and visibility is good. For safety reasons, never dive alone.

⑪ GRUTA AZUL
The walls of this underwater grotto, a long-established tourist destination, turn different shades of blue depending on the strength of incoming sunlight. Do not venture inside its underwater cave unless the sea is calm and visibility is excellent.

⑫ HARLINGER
The seabed off Atalaia Headland is strewn with the wreck of the Dutch vessel *Harlinger*, which sank in 1906. The 18- to 25-meter (60- to 80-foot) dive in open waters requires extreme caution.

⑬ DONA PAULA
The Brazilian Navy warship *Dona Paula* floundered here in 1827 while pursuing an Argentinean corsair. The dive is between five and 15 meters (16 and 50 feet).

The crystal-clear waters around Ilha de Cabo Frio are home to over 60 species of fish and coral

SÃO PAULO

MINAS GERAIS

São José do Rio Preto

Belo Horizonte

Rio Mogi-Guaçu

FERNÃO DIAS

SP 310

Brotas

Rio Claro

BR 381

P. N. de Itatiaia

Visconde de Maúa

RIO DE JANEIRO

Rio Tietê

Campinas

Campos do Jordão

Guaratinguetá

SP 068

Rio de Janeiro

Itaguaí

SÃO PAULO

SP 348

São José dos Campos

BR 116

P. N. da Serra da Bocaina

Bananal

SP 171

Angra dos Reis

São Paulo

SP 070

SP 099

DUTRA

Cunha

Paraty

Ilha Grande

TAMOIOS

Ubatuba

SP 098

AYRTON SENNA

RIO–SANTOS

São Sebastião

SP 055

SP 160

SP 150

Santos

Bertioga

Ilhabela

RÉGIS BITTENCOURT

Guarujá

MOGI– BERTIOGA

BR 116

1 cm = 50 km
1 inch = 78.9 mi.

Peruíbe

Curitiba

ATLANTIC OCEAN

MG

SP

PR

RJ

N

HIGHLIGHTS

- The huge variety of culture, entertainment, food, and shopping options in the city of **São Paulo**.
- The cool climate and natural beauty of the mountains around **Campos do Jordão**, **Santo Antônio do Pinhal**, and **Cunha**.
- The enchanting beaches on the **north**

coast of São Paulo.
- The historical buildings in **Santos**, **Santana de Parnaíba**, and **Bananal**.
- Adventure sports in **Brotas** and the **Serra da Bocaina** region, ecotourism in the Atlantic forest in **Juréia**, and caves in **Petar**.

WHEN TO GO

- **All year long** for São Paulo. The city's hotels are usually cheaper on weekends.
- **Campos do Jordão** in **July** for the Festival de Inverno.
- In the **summer** to enjoy the beaches,

although prices are at their highest and hotels and restaurants at their most crowded.
- **Brotas** during the **summer**, when the river is swollen and better for rafting.

THE CITY OF SÃO PAULO

In Brazil's wealthiest city, the population of almost 11 million (18 million in greater São Paulo) enjoys the country's liveliest nightlife and culture scene, along with a wide variety of dining and shopping options. Visitors unfazed by the city's sheer size and apparent standoffishness will find a multifaceted place that pulses with energy. We recommend the metro and the many available taxis to get around the city.

PRAÇA DA SÉ AND ENVIRONS

São Paulo has changed dramatically since its was founded in 1554, but the historical center retains some traces of the past. Anhangabaú Valley divides the old downtown area (known as Centro Velho, which contains the famous square Praça da Sé) from the new downtown area (known as Centro Novo, around Praça da República) *(see page 163)*. The best way to reach the center is by taxi or metro (from the blue line, get off at Sé or São Bento stations; from the red line, exit at República and Anhangabaú). Avoid these areas at night, when the streets are relatively empty.

① LARGO SÃO FRANCISCO

The law school **Faculdade de Direito** is the highlight of this square. In 1828, it moved into an old convent dating from

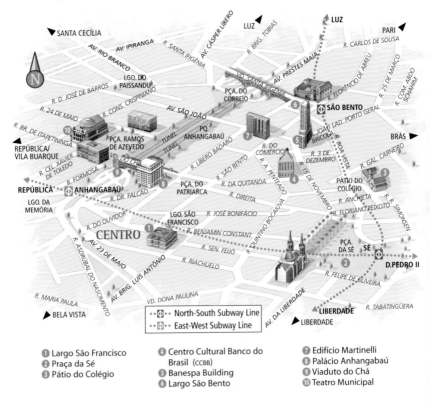

| North-South Subway Line |
| East-West Subway Line |

① Largo São Francisco
② Praça da Sé
③ Pátio do Colégio
④ Centro Cultural Banco do Brasil (CCBB)
⑤ Banespa Building
⑥ Largo São Bento
⑦ Edifício Martinelli
⑧ Palácio Anhangabaú
⑨ Viaduto do Chá
⑩ Teatro Municipal

1645, but the current building was constructed in 1934. Illustrious former students include writers José de Alencar and Monteiro Lobato and former Brazilian president Washington Luís. The first floor houses a museum with portraits of famous alumni and a library that is open to the public *(Largo São Francisco, 95, tel. (11) 3111-4063; Mon – Fri, 8am – 9:45pm)*. **Igreja de São Francisco de Assis**, a church built in 1642, is next door. Its façade was remodeled in the late 19th century, and the interior is home to a beautiful 17th-century statue of Saint Francis *(Largo São Francisco, 133, tel. (11) 3291-2400; daily, 7am – 8pm)*. Another church, **Igreja das Chagas do Seráfico Pai São Francisco**, also stands in the square. It was built in 1676 and considerably extended in 1787; now, it contains 18th-century statues and paintings *(Largo São Francisco, 173, tel. (11) 3106-5297; Mon – Fri, 8am – 5pm)*.

❷ PRAÇA DA SÉ

Every day, thousands of people pass through this square, which marks the center of the city. It was here that 300,000 people gathered in 1984 to demand direct elections. The highlight of the square is **Catedral da Sé**, an imposing building that unites Brazilian elements with Gothic style. Fruit and animals such as armadillos and toucans are carved into its column capitals. The cathedral can seat 8,000 people, and its attractions include an Italian organ with 12,000 pipes. Construction began to replace a 17th-century church in 1912, but it had to be inaugurated, still unfinished, in 1954. The 14 towers laid out in the original design were added between 1999 and 2002. Guided tours are available *(daily except Tue, 9:30am – 4:30pm)*.
Praça da Sé, no #, Centro, tel. (11) 3107-6832. Daily, 8am – 5pm.

❸ PÁTIO DO COLÉGIO

It was here that the Jesuits, led by José de Anchieta and Manuel da Nóbrega, built a college in the 16th century to convert native Indians. This was the beginning of the city of São Paulo. The **Museu Anchieta** now occupies the site. The modest collection boasts some original items, such as a 16th-century granite baptismal font. One wattle-and-daub wall, which can be seen in a garden area with a café, is all that remains of the original building.
Praça Pátio do Colégio, 2, Centro, tel. (11) 3105-6899. Tue – Sun, 9am – 5pm.

❹ CENTRO CULTURAL BANCO DO BRASIL (CCBB)

Film, plays, and art and photography exhibits are all on offer in this lovely 1901 building, which now houses a cultural center. It was the site of the first Banco do Brasil branch in the city, and the bank bought the building and renovated it in 1920. Original details like an enamel mosaic floor, fresco paintings, chandeliers, and stained-glass windows can still remain. Performances of various kinds of music, such as samba and *choro,* are held every Tuesday *(1pm and 7:30pm; tickets available at the center).*
Rua Álvares Penteado, 112, Centro, tel. (11) 3113-3651. Tue – Sun, 10am – 9pm.

❺ BANESPA BUILDING

New York's Empire State Building inspired the Edifício Altino Arantes, better known as the Banespa Building, which was inaugurated in 1947. At 161 meters (528 feet) high, it is still one of the tallest buildings in São Paulo, and the 35th floor offers an impressive view of the city. Guided tours are free. *Rua João Brícola, 24, Centro, tel. (11) 3249-7466. Mon – Fri, 10am – 5pm.*

Vale do Anhangabaú separates the new and old downtown areas

⑥ LARGO SÃO BENTO

This square is the site of São Bento School, dating from 1903, and the rebuilt Monastery and Basilica. Explorer Fernão Dias sponsored 1,650 renovations of the Monastery and Basilica, which were originally built in 1598. The monastery crypt contains the remains of Dias and his wife. The complex was demolished in 1911; its rebuilding lasted until 1922, when the basilica emerged in a German eclectic style. This church holds masses with Gregorian chants, accompanied by a German organ built in 1954 *(Mon – Fri, 7am; Sat, 6am; Sun, 10am)*. Sunday is the church's busiest day, and after mass, the congregation stands in line in the annexed store to buy delicacies made by the monks. Those treats include *pão São Bento*, bread made from a kind of parsnip called *mandioquinha,* and *bolo Santa Escolástica*, cake made with apple and walnuts *(Largo São Bento, no #, Centro, tel. (11) 3328-8799; Mon – Wed and Fri, 6am – 6pm; Thu, 6am – 8am and 4pm – 6pm; Sat, 6am – noon; Sun, 6am – noon and 4pm – 6pm)*. It's worth stopping at

Café Girondino *(Rua Boa Vista, 365, Centro, tel. (11) 3229-4574; Mon – Thu, 7:30am – 11pm; Fri, 7:30am – midnight; Sat and holidays, 8am – 8pm)*.

⑦ EDIFÍCIO MARTINELLI

Italian entrepreneur Giuseppe Martinelli constructed this skyscraper in 1929. Standing at 130 meters (426 feet), this building was the city's tallest skyscraper until the Banespa building was erected in 1947. The terrace, formerly the Martinelli residence, is open to visitors and affords a lovely view of downtown São Paulo. The building was restored in the late 1970s and now houses government offices.
Rua Líbero Badaró, 504, Centro. Mon – Fri, 7:30am – 7:30pm.

⑧ PALÁCIO ANHANGABAÚ

The old Edifício Matarazzo retains the same elegance as when it was inaugurated in 1939. Italian architect Marcello Piacentini designed the building, which currently houses the city hall. It is not open to the public, but visitors can admire the Italian marble façade and enter the lobby. *Viaduto do Chá, 15, Centro, tel. (11) 3113-8000. Mon – Fri, 8am – 8pm.*

❾ VIADUTO DO CHÁ

São Paulo's first viaduct was designed by Frenchman Jules Martin around 1877, and built from metal imported from Germany. It was founded in 1892 near a region of market gardens and small farms, and it doubled in size in 1938. The elegant "Tea Viaduct" overlooking the Anhangabaú Valley is a good vantage point from which to observe the busy city.

❿ TEATRO MUNICIPAL

Cláudio and Domiziano Rossi designed this eclectic-style theater, which was inspired by the Paris Opera and inaugurated in 1911. Ramos de Azevedo later rebuilt it. The architecture and décor – such as the Venetian mosaics and Florentine sculptures – reflects the splendor sought by São Paulo's coffee barons and industrialists in the early 20th century. Orquestra Sinfônica Municipal (Municipal Symphony Orchestra) and the Balé da Cidade (City Ballet) are among the groups that regularly perform in the theater. It seats 1585 and offers free guided tours, which must be booked in advance *(tel. (11) 3223-3022; Tue – Fri, 1pm; Sat, 9:30am and 10:30am; arrange in advance) Praça Ramos de Azevedo, no #, Centro, tel. (11) 3222-8698. Box office: Mon – Fri, 10am – 7pm; Sat and Sun, 2pm – 5pm.*

PRAÇA DA REPÚBLICA AND ENVIRONS

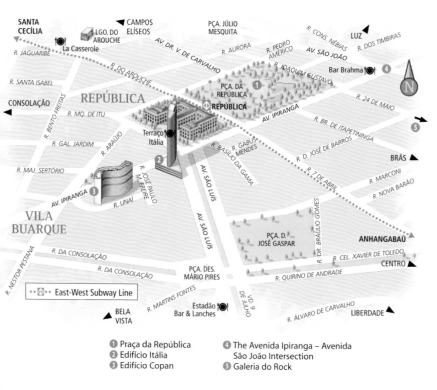

❶ Praça da República
❷ Edifício Itália
❸ Edifício Copan
❹ The Avenida Ipiranga – Avenida São João Intersection
❺ Galeria do Rock

The oval Edifício Itália (foreground), next to curving Edifício Copan, near Praça da República

① Praça da República

Until the end of the 19th century, the former Praça 7 de Abril was no more than a modest square locally known as Praça dos Curros. It was renamed in 1889 in honor of the recently proclaimed Republic. The Caetano de Campos School was inaugurated there in 1894; now, it is the State Department of Education. The square was remodeled at the beginning of the 20th century, acquiring fountains and bandstands. Modernist buildings from the 1930s were also added. The square hosts an art and antique fair on Sundays.

② Edifício Itália

The Circolo Italiano club constructed this imposing oval-shaped building. At 151 meters (495 feet) tall, it is one of the city's tallest buildings. Adolf Franz Heep designed the building, which was constructed between 1956 and 1965. The biggest attraction of this recently restored national-heritage site is the Terraço Itália restaurant on the top floor *(tel. (11) 2189-2929; Mon – Fri, noon –* *midnight; Sat, noon – 1am; Sun, noon – 11pm; holidays, noon – 4am; piano bar: Mon – Thu, 3pm – midnight; Fri and Sat, 3pm – 1am; Sun, noon – 11pm).* The restaurant terrace offers a wonderful view of the city center, several major avenues, the Cantareira Mountains, and Jaraguá Peak. *Avenida Ipiranga, 344, Centro, tel. (11) 2189-2929. Terrace: daily, noon – 8pm.*

③ Edifício Copan

This Oscar Niemeyer building is the most important example of modernist

Our Recommendation

🍴 **Bar Brahma**, founded in 1948, used to be a regular haunt for intellectuals and politicians. After the decline of downtown area in the 1970s and 80s, the house has reclaimed its privileged position, offering samba and *choro* shows and *feijoada* (pork with black beans and traditional accompaniments) on Saturdays *(Avenida São João, 677, Centro, tel. (11) 3333-0855; Mon, 11:30am – 1am; Tue and Wed, 11:30am – 2am; Thu – Sat, 11:30am – 3am; Sun, 11:30am – 11pm).*

Additional information on page 462.

architecture in São Paulo. It was inaugurated in 1966, 15 years after it was first designed, and the building is distinguished by its sinuous S-shaped structure and the horizontal lines of its sun baffles. The building has 38 floors and stands 115 meters (377 feet) high; about 5000 people live in its 1,160 apartments, and the ground floor houses 72 stores and restaurants. The penthouse is very large, extending the full length of the S-curve, and no parapet walls block the view the way they do at Edifício Itália.

Avenida Ipiranga, 200, Centro, tel. (11) 3259-5917. Mon – Fri, 9am – 10:30am and 2:30pm – 4am.

❹ THE AVENIDA IPIRANGA – AVENIDA SÃO JOÃO INTERSECTION

The intersection of Avenida Ipiranga and Avenida São João served as a meeting point for local bohemians for years. It became a symbol of the city after Caetano Veloso immortalized it in his song *Sampa* (an affectionate nickname for the city) in 1978. Both avenues had previously been the subjects of other local composers as well: Paulo Vanzolini and Adoniran Barbosa.

❺ GALERIA DO ROCK

This 1963 building with a wavy façade delights music-lovers of all ages: More than 200 stores sell CDs, LPs, clothes, accessories, and posters. The storekeepers are all rock fans, and they are enthusiastic about helping customers. The basement contains a cluster of hair salon and stores selling skateboarding fashions.

Rua 24 de Maio, 62, or Avenida São João, 439, Centro, tel. (11) 3223-8402. Mon – Sat, 10am – 6pm.

PIZZA, A SÃO PAULO INSTITUTION

Thin or thick crust, traditional or innovative ingredients – whatever you prefer, locals assert that their pizza is the best in the country. Some excellent suggestions: **Castelões** *(Rua Jairo Góes, 126, Brás, tel. (11) 3229-0542; Mon – Fri, noon – 3pm and 6:30pm – midnight; Sat and Sun, noon – 4pm and 6:30pm – midnight)*, **Bráz** *(Rua Vupabuçu, 271, Pinheiros, tel. (11) 3037-7975; Sun – Thu, 6:30pm – 12:30 am; Fri and Sat, 6:30pm – 1am; also in Moema and Higienópolis)*, and **Speranza** *(Rua 13 de Maio, 1004, Bela Vista, tel. (11) 3288-8502, 3288-3512; Mon – Fri, 6pm – 1:30am; Sat, 6pm – 2am; Sun, 6pm – 1am; also in Moema)*.

LUZ AND ENVIRONS

Luz was an elegant neighborhood until it went downhill in the early 20th century, and there are now some rather unsavory areas. A revitalization process started in the 1990s, however, and a good cultural attractions have sprung up. Get to the area by metro from the Luz station (blue line) or by car via Avenida Tiradentes.

❶ SALA SÃO PAULO

Designed by architect Nelson Dupré, the home of the Orquestra Sinfônica de São Paulo can seat 1,501 people and has impeccable acoustics. The ceiling is made of adjustable wooden panels that can be positioned according to the music being played, and it is the only one of its kind in the world. The concert hall occupies the old Júlio Prestes Railway Station building, which was restored and reopened in 1999. Architect Christiano Stockler das Neves designed the building to house the headquarters of the Sorocabana Railroad Company and the old railway station. It was built between 1926 and 1938. During guided tours, visitors learn about the history of the railway and coffee production in São

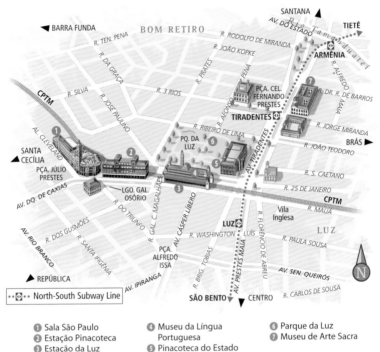

① Sala São Paulo
② Estação Pinacoteca
③ Estação da Luz
④ Museu da Língua Portuguesa
⑤ Pinacoteca do Estado
⑥ Parque da Luz
⑦ Museu de Arte Sacra

Paulo. Concert tickets should be bought in advance.

Praça Júlio Prestes, no #, Luz, tel. (11) 3367-9500. Mon – Fri, 10am – 6pm (or until curtain-up); Sat, 10am – 4:30pm (or until curtain-up); Sun, when there is a concert, from two hours before curtain-up.

② ESTAÇÃO PINACOTECA

Built in 1914 as a storehouse for the Sorocabana Railway, this building used to be the Department of Political and Social Order, a repressive arm of Brazil's military dictatorship. Ramos de Azevedo designed it. Once it was restored, it became an extension of the Pinacoteca State Art Museum in 2003. It holds temporary art exhibits, some of the José and Paulina Nemirovsky collection, and works by Picasso, Chagall, and Léger.

Largo General Osório, 66, Luz, tel. (11) 3337-0185. Tue – Sun and holidays, 10am – 6pm.

③ ESTAÇÃO DA LUZ

English architect Charles Henry Driver designed this sumptuous eclectic–style station, and all of its materials were imported from England. It was inaugurated in 1901 and remodeled in 2004; now, it functions as a railway station and houses the Museu da Língua Portuguesa.

Praça da Luz, 1, tel. 0800-550121. Daily, 4am – midnight.

④ MUSEU DA LÍNGUA PORTUGUESA

The Portuguese Language Museum inside Estação da Luz is the only museum fully devoted to the preservation and study of Portuguese. The attractions are fun, and the interactive areas are impressive. Admission is free on Saturdays. Guided tours are available.

Praça da Luz, no #, Luz, tel. (11) 3326-0775. Tue – Sun and holidays, 10am – 6pm.

⑤ PINACOTECA DO ESTADO

This state art gallery hosts some of the country's best temporary art exhibits. The permanent collection, with some 6,000 works, includes icons of 19th- and 20th-century Brazilian painting such as Vítor Meireles and Cândido Portinari, as well as sculptures by Vítor Brecheret and Auguste Rodin. Ramos de Azevedo designed the eclectic-style building in 1896, and architect Paulo Mendes da Rocha restored it between 1993 and 1998 . The ground floor has a charming café/restaurant.
Praça da Luz, 2, Luz, tel. (11) 3224-1000. Tue – Sun and holidays, 10am – 6pm.

⑥ PARQUE DA LUZ

Opened in 1835 as a botanical garden, the oldest park in the state was a leisure area for local high society until the early 20th century. It has been undergoing restoration work since 2000. The park is home to 70 kinds of birds and 130 plant species. Visit the park in the morning and steer clear of isolated areas.
Praça da Luz, no #, Luz, tel. (11) 3227-3545. Tue – Sun, 9am – 6pm.

⑦ MUSEU DE ARTE SACRA

Of the 5,000 pieces of religious art in this museum's collection, about 900 are on permanent exhibition. Highlights

Pinacoteca do Estado: a precious art collection

include the *Nossa Senhora da Luz* statue, dating from 1579, as well as sculptures and carvings from the 17th and 18th centuries. Some of them are attributed to Aleijadinho, the great baroque sculptor from Minas Gerais. Another highlight is the collection of nativity scenes; take a special look at the one called Napolitano, which has 1,620 pieces.
Avenida Tiradentes, 676, Luz, tel. (11) 3326-1373. Tue – Sun and holidays, 11am – 7pm.

BEXIGA, THE ITALIAN DISTRICT

Officially called Bela Vista, the Bexiga district welcomed many immigrants in the late 19th century – most of all, Italians. The neighborhood now has an air of neglect, but some good trattorias and pizzerias are still going strong. **Capuano** has been serving Italian dishes like fusilli since 1901 *(Rua Conselheiro Carrão, 416, tel. (11) 3288-1460; Tue – Fri, 11:30am – 3pm and 7pm – 11pm; Sat, 11:30am – 4:30pm and 7pm – 12:30am; Sun, 11:30am – 5pm).* **Roperto** offers pasta, beef Parmigiana, and roast kid, as well as live music *(Rua 13 de Maio, 634, tel. (11) 3288-2573, 3284-2987; daily, 11am – 1am).* Bread is another neighborhood attraction at bakeries such as **Basilicata** *(Rua 13 de Maio, 614, tel. (11) 3289-311; Mon – Sat, 7am – 8pm; Sun and holidays, 7am – 2pm),* **São Domingos** *(Rua São Domingos, 330, tel. (11) 3104-7600, 3242-3677; Mon – Sat, 7am – 8pm; Sun and holidays, 7am – 2pm),* and **Italianinha** *(Rua Rui Barbosa, 121, tel. (11) 3289-2838, 3141-4166; Mon, 2pm – 8pm; Tue – Sat, 7am – 8pm; Sun and holidays, 7am – 3pm).* Many of the city's best theaters can also be found in Bexiga *(see page 188).*

MERCADO MUNICIPAL DE SÃO PAULO

An enormous variety of aromas and sounds fill the air in this covered market, which is nicknamed Mercadão. Ramos de Azevedo designed the eclectic-style building; Felisberto Ranzini designed its columns and façades and Russian

Conrado Sorgenicht Filho (of the famous Casa Conrado) did the stained-glass windows. The market began as the general headquarters of the São Paulo troops during the Constitutionalist Movement of 1932

① Casa Irmãos Borges

The stall on Rua B sells mainly codfish and olives, while those on Rua A specialize in chocolate and dried fruit.
Rua A, boxes 11 and 15.
Rua B, box 3.

② Banca do Ramon

This business has five renovated stalls and specializes in codfish.
Rua B, boxes 7 and 20.
Rua H, boxes 21 and 23.
Rua E, box 7.

③ Baldaracci & Bons Amigos

This stall offers the market's best shrimp. Its seafood comes from Santa Catarina, Ubatuba, and Juréia.
Rua B, boxes 30 to 36.

④ Queijos Roni

People in the know insist the ricotta cheese from this modest stall is the best in the market.
Rua D, box 2.

⑤ Rei do Bacalhau

Portuguese produce is the specialty here, including codfish, wine, olive oil, olives, and cheese.
Rua D, box 12.
Rua H, box 32.

⑥ Levi Queijos

This stall is dedicated to cheese. The most popular varieties are Parmesan, Emental, Gouda, and *meia-cura* (semi-matured).
Rua D, box 9.

⑦ Bar do Mané

Giant mortadella sandwiches made a name for this stall, which has been operating since 1933.
Rua E, box 14.

and inaugurated as a market the following year. Remodeling work in 2004 restored the façade and stained-glass windows, and it gave the building new facilities like its mezzanine, which houses eight restaurants. A thousand tons of produce are sold daily from the market's 291 stalls, called "boxes."

Visitors will need patience for the long lines but will be rewarded with the beauty of the surroundings, the liveliness of the atmosphere, and the quality and variety of the food.

Rua da Cantareira, 306, Centro, tel. (11) 3228-9332. Mon – Sat, 6am – 6pm; Sun, 6am – 4pm.

❽ Cruzília
Although it is best known for its Cruzília cheeses produced in the state of Minas Gerais, this stall also sells codfish.
Rua E, box 16.

❾ Porco Feliz
This butcher's stall sells exotic meats: ostrich, kid, capybara, peccary, rhea, alligator, warthog, and turtle. It offers home delivery.
Rua E, box 26.

❿ Santa Teresa Jamoneria
A Spaniard runs this stall, and everything on sale is from Spain. Spanish ham is the best-selling item.
Rua F, box 19.

⓫ G. Frederico Ervas
This stall looks like a cabin lined with sachets of herbs. It sells seasonings, herbs, and spices.
Rua F, box 21.

⓬ Empório Chiappetta
The biggest and most sophisticated stall in the market sells wine, codfish, and dried fruit.
Rua G, box 8.
Rua H, box 11.

⓭ Empório Sta. Therezinha
Highlights here include wine and *cachaças* (sugar-cane rum) at prices to suit every pocketbook.
Rua H, box 10.

⓮ Barraca do Juca
This still sells local and imported fresh fruit and offers home delivery.
Rua H, box 24.

⓯ Tio Ali
This stall, which opened in December 2005, sells olives, dried fruit, and Syrian bread and desserts.
Rua H, box 25.

⓰ Geração Saúde
This health-food stall carries sugar-cane juice, coconut water, fruit, frozen fruit pulp, the new "miracle fruit" *açaí*, and different types of chili peppers.
Rua L, box 30.

⓱ Mortadela Brasil
A new addition to the mezzanine, this stall sells Marba mortadella sandwiches. (The rest of Mercadão sells another brand, Ceratti.)
Mezzanine, box 4.

⓲ Hocca Bar
In operation since 1952, this bar gained fame for its tasty *pastel de bacalhau* (deep-fried codfish pastry). Be prepared: The lines are enormous.
Mezzanine, box 5.
Rua G, box 7.

⓳ Brasileirinho
This restaurant serves Brazilian food and cocktails in unusual combinations, such as passion fruit with lime or coconut with strawberry, peach or guava.
Mezzanine, stall 6.

LIBERDADE

Several waves of immigrants have come to this neighborhood, which was an execution site for condemned prisoners until the mid-19th century. Japanese immigrants started to arrive in 1912, and Liberdade became the Asian district of São Paulo when Chinese and Korean people came after the Second World War. A trip around the area could begin at Praça da Liberdade, which is easily reached on the blue line of the metro (exit at Liberdade station), or by car via Avenida Liberdade or Avenida 23 de Maio. On Sundays, this square is home to a lively fair selling Asian food and other items. Explore the shops on **Rua Galvão Bueno**, **Rua dos Estudantes**, and **Rua da Glória**, which sell items from kimonos to decorative objects. You can find Asian food and drinks in supermarkets like **Comercial Marukai** *(Rua Galvão Bueno, 34, tel. (11) 3341-3350; daily, 8am – 8pm)*. Try something sweet – such as the *ichigo daifuku*, a combination of rice, beans, and strawberries – from **Bakery Itiriki** *(Rua dos Estudantes, 24, tel. (11) 3277-4939; daily, 8am – 7pm)*. **Fonomag** bookstore sells Japanese magazines and books *(Rua Glória, 242, tel. (11) 3104-3329, 3104-3399; Mon – Fri, 8:30am*

Japanese products in the district of Liberdade

– 6:30pm; Sat, 8:30pm – 5pm). Nearby, around Praça João Mendes, visitors will find second-hand bookstores like **Sebo do Messias**, which boasts a vast collection of national and international curiosities, including books, LPs, and games *(Praça João Mendes, 166, tel. (11) 3104-7111, 3106-9596; Mon – Fri, 9am – 7pm; Sat, 9am – 5pm)*.

ASIAN CUISINE

Liberdade has Japanese, Korean, and Chinese restaurants, all offering an array of culinary choices. **Sushi Yassu** is the place to try good sushi and hot dishes like grilled eel *(Rua Tomás Gonzaga, 98, tel. (11) 3209-6622; Tue – Sat, 11:30am –* 3pm and 6pm – 11pm; Sun, noon – 10pm)*. **Korea House** has been serving traditional Korean food and some Chinese dishes for almost 40 years *(Rua Galvão Bueno, 43, tel. (11) 3208-3052; Mon, Tue, Thu, and Fri, 11am – 2:30pm and 6pm – 10pm;* Sat, Sun, and holidays, 11am – 10pm)*. **Chi-Fu** offers traditional Chinese cuisine such as Peking duck *(Praça Carlos Gomes, 168, tel. (11) 3104-2750; daily, 11am – 4pm and 6pm – 10pm)*.
Additional information on page 462.

HIGIENÓPOLIS

◀ PERDIZES

HIGIENÓPOLIS

SANTA
CECÍLIA ▲

R. DR. ALBUQUERQUE LINS

AV. PACAEMBU

R. ENG. EDGAR E. DE SOUSA

R. RIO DE JANEIRO

R. MARANHÃO

R. DR. VEIGA FILHO

AV. HIGIENÓPOLIS

R. JAGUARIBE

R. DR. MARTINICO PRADO

R. ARACAJU

Jardim di Napoli

R. ITATIARA

Padaria Barcelona

AV. ANGÉLICA

R. BAHIA

PÇA. BUENOS AIRES

R. PIAUÍ

R. ALAGOAS

R. SABARÁ

R. ITAMBÉ

BELA VISTA ▶

R. SERGIPE

JD. PAULISTA ▼

CONSOLAÇÃO

Highlights
1. Instituto Moreira Salles
2. Faculdade de Arquitetura e Urbanismo
3. Fundação Armando Álvares Penteado (Faap) and Museu de Arte Brasileira
4. Praça Villaboim
5. Estádio do Pacaembu

Architecture
1. Edifício Piauí
2. Edifício Cinderela
3. Edifício Lausanne
4. Edifício Prudência
5. Edifício Parque das Hortênsias
6. Edifício Bretagne
7. Edifício Louveira
8. Edifício Arper

Higienópolis, with its wide, tree-lined streets, is one of the city's oldest neighborhoods. It grew out of an area of buildings started in 1895 and received the name Higienópolis (Hygiene City) later. The nickname probably came about because of its elevated location, which spared it from the floods and epidemics at the end of the 19th century.

❶ INSTITUTO MOREIRA SALLES
Architect Celso da Costa Carvalho Vidigal designed this cultural institute, which was built in 1980. It holds art exhibits, musical presentations, courses, and lectures. Guided tours are available and should be arranged in advance. Services for researchers interested in the collection of photographs are also available. Check the program schedule at www.ims.com.br.

Rua Piauí, 844, 1ª floor, Higienópolis, tel. (11) 3825-2560. Tue – Fri, 1pm – 7pm; Sat, Sun and holidays, 1pm – 6pm.

❷ FACULDADE DE ARQUITETURA E URBANISMO DA USP
One of the city's few remaining examples of art nouveau style, this building was designed in 1902 by Swedish architect Carlos Eckman to be the home of Conde Antônio Álvares Penteado. Now it houses the post-graduate department of the University of São Paulo's School of Architecture. Paintings by Oscar Pereira da Silva and Carlos de Servi hang in the central lobby. The library is open to the public *(tel. (11) 3256-7341, extension 21; Mon – Fri, 8am – 5pm). Rua Maranhão, 88, Higienópolis, tel. (11) 3257-7688. Mon – Fri, 8am – noon and 1pm – 5pm.*

Praça Charles Miller and Estádio do Pacaembu

and 1970. The **Museu de Arte Brasileira** holds acclaimed international annual exhibits and boasts a collection of around 2500 works, mostly by modernist and contemporary artists. *Rua Alagoas, 903, Higienópolis, tel. (11) 3662-7000. Museum: Tue – Fri, 10am – 8pm; Sat and Sun, 10am – 5pm.*

❹ PRAÇA VILLABOIM
This tiny, leafy square is surrounded by stores and restaurants. Its charm attracts children and adults alike. Don't miss the nearby bakery **Barcelona Doces & Pães** *(Rua Armando Penteado, 33, Higienópolis, tel. (11) 3826-4911; daily, 6am – 10:30pm).*

❸ FAAP AND MUSEU DE ARTE BRASILEIRA
The Fundação Armando Álvares Penteado (Faap) houses a theater, museum, and university. The foundation is named after the count who first conceived of it and designed the main building, which was built between 1947

❺ ESTÁDIO DO PACAEMBU
Built in 1940, the elegant Paulo Machado de Carvalho Stadium is better known as Estádio do Pacaembu. Guided tours of the art deco building include historical photographs and a visit to the stadium facilities, such as the TV and radio broadcasting booths. *Praça Charles Miller, no #, Pacaembu, tel. (11) 3661-9111.*

MODERNIST BUILDINGS

In 2000, *Wallpaper* magazine reported that Higienópolis has one of the world's highest concentrations of modernist buildings built between 1930 and 1960. Architect Artacho Jurado's work – such as **Edifício Piauí**, dating from 1949 – stands out. That building bears typical hallmarks of his work: sinuous ramps cross the garden and lead to the glass-walled façade of the lobby *(Rua Piauí, 428, on the corner of Rua Sabará)*. Another of his designs is **Edifício Cinderela**, built in 1956 with distinctive pink, beige, and blue tiles, winding shapes, verandas, and

columns *(Rua Maranhão, 163, on the corner of Rua Sabará)*. Adolf Franz Heep designed the **Lausanne**, which was built in the late 1950s; it features pilotis, metal sun baffles, and colorful shutters *(Avenida Higienópolis, 101)*. **Prudência**, the work of Rino Levi and Roberto Cerqueira César, was constructed between 1944 and 1948 and boasts a ceramic mosaic façade and enamel tiles *(Avenida Higienópolis, 265)*. The enormous **Bretagne**, considered Artacho Jurado's masterpiece, broke new ground when it was built in 1952. It has multiple commu-

nal areas, a bar, a pool, and gardens. The same architect was responsible for the 1957 **Edifício Parque das Hortênsias**, which sports black, brown, and yellow tiles *(Avenida Angélica, 1106)*. In 1946, Vilanova Artigas and Carlos Cascaldi designed **Louveira**, which is now a national heritage site. It features yellow metal windows, access ramps, and pilotis *(Rua Piauí, 1081)*. **Edifício Arper**, by David Libeskind, was built in 1959. It still has its original façade, enormous verandas, and pebble-dash in the areas connecting blocks *(Rua Pernambuco, 15)*.

AVENIDA PAULISTA

- ❶ Conjunto Nacional
- ❷ Espaço Cultural do Banco Central
- ❸ Parque Trianon
- ❹ Museu de Arte de São Paulo
- ❺ Fiesp
- ❻ Instituto Itaú Cultural
- ❼ Casa das Rosas

Avenida Paulista is a symbol of São Paulo's opulence. In 1891, the Joaquim Eugênio de Lima engineering team designed the avenue, which is almost three kilometers long. In the first half of the 20th century, mansions belonging to coffee barons and industrialists lined the avenue. Most of them were demolished between the 1950s and 70s to make way for large buildings when the area began to establish itself as a financial and cultural center. This avenue is also frequently the site of protests and celebrations. Avenida Paulista is at its busiest during the day. It is served by various bus lines and the metro (Paraíso, Brigadeiro, Trianon-Masp and Consolação stations on the green line).

❶ CONJUNTO NACIONAL

This multi-purpose building, a landmark of Avenida Paulista, was designed by architect David Libeskind and inaugurated in 1958 by then-president Juscelino Kubitschek. The building occupies an entire block; its corridors, lined with art exhibits, serve as passageways for local residents and workers. The ground floor has a cinema, restaurants, and stores (**Livraria Cultura** deserves a special mention). The upper floors are offices, and there is also a residential wing.
Avenida Paulista, 2073, Cerqueira César, tel. (11) 3179-0000. Mon – Sat, 6am – 10pm; Sun and holidays, 10am – 6pm.

❷ ESPAÇO CULTURAL DO BANCO CENTRAL

This cultural center, opened in 1990, holds free exhibitions to make the work of unknown Brazilian artists available to a public audience. In the ground-floor **Museu de Valores**, the collection of

The box-like Masp stands out on Avenida Paulista

notes and coins from several countries explains the history of money.
Avenida Paulista, 1804, Bela Vista, tel. (11) 3491-6122. Mon – Fri, 10am – 4pm.

❸ PARQUE TRIANON (TENENTE SIQUEIRA CAMPOS)

This park was a meeting place for local high society in the early 20th century. It was designed by French landscape artist Paul Villon and opened in 1892. Landscape artist Burle Marx and architect Clóvis Olga remodeled it in 1968. It contains two children's parks, a small aviary for domestic birds, fountains, and sculptures – most notably *Aretusa* (1920) by Francisco Leopoldo da Silva and the lovely *Fauno* (1924) by Vítor Brecheret.
Rua Peixoto Gomide, 949, Cerqueira César, tel. (11) 3289-2160. Daily, 6am – 6pm.

❹ MUSEU DE ARTE DE SÃO PAULO

The São Paulo Museum of Art, or Masp, as it is usually called, is the brainchild of journalist Assis Chateaubriand and art critic Pietro Maria Bardi. It also houses

the greatest permanent collection of Western painting in Latin America, as well as important temporary exhibits. About 500 of its 7,000 works are on permanent display, including paintings from Renaissance artists (Botticelli, Raphael, and Titian), Impressionists (Monet, Manet, and Renoir), and Brazilian modernists (Anita Malfatti and Cândido Portinari). In addition, the collection has works from foreign artists like Frans Post, Eckhout, Debret, and Taunay that depicts life in their respective countries. There are also several bronze Degas sculptures. The building was designed by Lina Bo Bardi and inaugurated in 1968. Four pillars support its box-like shape, which creates a striking 74-meter (243-foot) open space. An antique fair is held there on Sundays.
Avenida Paulista, 1578, Bela Vista, tel. (11) 3251-5644. Tue – Sun, 11am – 6pm.

❺ FIESP

Luís Roberto de Carvalho Franco and Roberto Cerqueira César designed the

CINEMAS

There are several excellent movie theaters on and around Avenida Paulista. The Conjunto Nacional houses the highly praised **Cine Bombril**, where movie-goers can buy tickets for specific seats (*Avenida Paulista, 2073, Bela Vista, tel. (11) 3285-3696)*. HSBC **Belas Artes** boasts six screens (*Rua da Consolação, 2423, Cerqueira César, tel. (11) 3258-4092)*. **Bristol Playarte** in Shopping Center 3 has seven modern screens (*Avenida Paulista, 2064, Bela Vista, tel. (11) 3289-0509)*. **Reserva Cultural** has a restaurant, a bar, a sweetshop, and a bookstore in addition to its four screens (*Avenida Paulista, 900, Bela Vista, tel. (11) 3287-3529)*. **Espaço Unibanco de Cinema** has five screens, a bookstore, and three cafés (*Rua Augusta, 1475, Consolação, tel. (11) 3288-6780)*. In the Jardins area, **Cinesesc** (*Rua Augusta, 2075, Cerqueira César, tel. (11) 3064-1668)* and **Museu da Imagem e do Som** (*Avenida Europa, 158, Jardim Europa, tel. (11) 3062-9197)* both hold special showings. **Unibanco Arteplex** has nine screens (*Rua Frei Caneca, 569, Shopping Frei Caneca, Consolação, tel. (11) 3472-2365)*. All these theaters participate in festivals, including São Paulo's international film festival, **Mostra Internacional de Cinema** in late October or early November.

sloping façade of this building in 1969. It belongs to the São Paulo State Federation of Industries (Fiesp) and houses the **Centro Cultural Fiesp**. After the building was renovated by Paulo Mendes da Rocha, the complex now includes the **Galeria de Arte do Sesi**, a gallery for art and photography exhibits (*Mon, 11am – 8pm; Tue – Sat, 10am – 8pm; Sun, 10am – 7pm)* and the **Teatro do Sesi**, which stages free or reasonably priced plays and musical events. *Avenida Paulista, 1313, Cerqueira César, tel. (11) 3549-4499.*

❻ INSTITUTO ITAÚ CULTURAL
Created in 1988, this cultural center is an important research hub for Brazilian culture. The Centro de Documentação e Referência houses reference material on the visual arts, music, theater, literature, cinema, and video, all of which can be accessed by the public. The **Itaú Numismática – Museu Herculano Pires** has a collection of about 6,000 coins and medals depicting Brazil's history. The center also hosts talks and exhibits. For details, visit *www.itaucultural.com.br. Avenida Paulista, 179, Cerqueira César, tel. (11) 2168-1700. Tue – Fri, 10am - 9pm; Sat and Sun, 10am – 7pm.*

❼ CASA DAS ROSAS
Designed by Ramos de Azevedo in the 1930s and now a national heritage site, this house stands in front of a rose garden inspired by the Palace of Versailles. This lovely garden is a shortcut for anyone going from Avenida Paulista to Alameda Santos. **Espaço Haroldo de Campos de Poesia e Literatura**, a cultural center inside the house, hosts exhibits, courses, recitals, and plays. The library specializes in poetry; it contains a collection of about 30,000 volumes, all donated by the family of poet, translator, and writer Haroldo de Campos. *Avenida Paulista, 37, Cerqueira César, tel. (11) 3285-6986, 3288-9447. Tue – Sun, 10am – 6pm.*

BOOKSTORES

Avenida Paulista has great bookstores. **Livraria Cultura**, in the Conjunto Nacional, offers a vast catalogue and excellent customer service (*#2073, tel. (11) 3170-4033)*. **Fnac** sells books, magazines, CDs, DVDs, televisions, and many other products (*#901, tel. (11) 2123-2000)*. Most of the books sold at **Martins Fontes** are published by the store itself (*#509, stores 17 and 22, tel. (11) 3266-4603)*.

PARQUE DO IBIRAPUERA

MOEMA ▲

- Running track
- Bike track

GATE 7A

GATE 6

PÇA. DO PORQUINHO

AV. IBIRAPUERA

AV. SAGRES

GATE 5

AV. IV CENTENÁRIO

Centro de Convivência ■

Lanchonete

PARQUE INFANTIL

Administração/CEA ■

PÇA. DO LEÃO

GATE 4

Guarda Civil Metropolitana ■

■ Pça. de Jogos

GATE 3

AV. RUBEM BERTA

AV. PEDRO ÁLVARES CABRAL

Restaurante do MAM

PÇA. DA PAZ

Jardins das Esculturas ■

R. ANTÔNIO DE QUEIROGA

COMPLEX

PRODAM

Restaurante

AV. 23 DE MAIO

GATE 1 E 2

Obelisco

PÇA. DA MARINHA

Pavilhão Manoel da Nóbrega

Lanchon

TÚNEL AYRTON SENNA

R. ANTÔNIO DE QUEIRO

PÇA. ESCOTEIRO ALDO CHIORATTO

GATE 10

Homenagem a Ped Álvares Cabral

PÇA. TÚLIO FONTOURA

AV. PEDRO ÁLVARES CABRAL

R. MANU

Highlights
1. Pavilhão da Bienal de Artes
2. Museu de Arte Contemporânea
3. Museu de Arte Moderna
4. Oca
5. Auditório Ibirapuera
6. Museu Afro Brasil
7. Pavilhão Japonês
8. Planetário do Ibirapuera

VILA MARIANA ▲

1. Cycle path
2. Jogging path
3. Bicycle rentals
4. Roller-skating and skateboarding

The city's most popular park was opened in 1954, with architecture by Oscar Niemeyer and landscaping by Roberto Burle Marx. Around 400,000 people use its 1.5 million square meters (371 acres) on the weekends, enjoying the lakes, sports facilities, cycle path, bicycle rentals, and open-air concerts. It also has museums and exhibits. The park has 12 gates, but cars can only enter through gates 3 and 7. The huge *Monumento às bandeiras*, standing in front of gate 9, was designed by Vítor Brecheret as a tribute to the early pioneers and explorers. Italian Galileo Emendabili created the *Mausoléu ao soldado constitucionalista de 1932*, also called the "Ibirapuera obelisk," which now stands in front of gates 1 and 2. *Avenida Pedro Álvares Cabral, no #, Ibirapuera, tel. (11) 5574-5177. Daily, 5am – midnight.*

1 PAVILHÃO DA BIENAL DE ARTES
Oscar Niemeyer designed this building, which has hosted the São

❷ MUSEU DE ARTE CONTEMPORÂNEA

This modern art museum, known as MAC Ibirapuera, has occupied the third floor of the Pavilhão da Bienal since 1963. It holds temporary exhibits and houses a collection of almost 10,000 pieces, among which are works by Anita Malfatti, Di Cavalcanti, Picasso, and Modigliani. MAC has two other buildings in the Cidade Universitária district *(see page 186).*

Parque do Ibirapuera, gate #3, tel. (11) 5573-9932. Tue – Sun, 10am – 7pm.

❸ MUSEU DE ARTE MODERNA

This museum was the first in Latin America to be dedicated to modern and contemporary art. It was founded in 1948 in a building designed by Lina Bo Bardi. The huge *Spider*, a sculpture by Louise Bourgeois, sits in a glass enclosure that can be seen from outside the museum. Pieces from Alfredo Volpi and Mira Schendel are part of the collection of 4,500 works. The museum also holds seminars, national and international exhibits and choral music concerts. The outdoor area includes the Jardim das Esculturas, with 30 sculptures by artists such as Amílcar de Castro and Carlos Fajardo. Guided tours are available.

Parque do Ibirapuera, gate #3, tel. (11) 5549-9688. Tue – Sun, 10am – 6pm.

❹ OCA

Designed by Oscar Niemeyer, this pavilion holds important art exhibits and temporary events. Its official name is Pavilhão Lucas Nogueira Garcez, but its enormous white dome gave rise to its popular name: Oca, after similarly shaped indigenous dwellings. Paulo Mendes da Rocha renovated the building in 1999.

Parque do Ibirapuera, gate #2, tel. (11) 5574-5177.

Paulo Biennial Art Exhibition since 1957. This festival puts around 12,000 national and international works of art on display every other year between October and November. The rectangular building has ample interior space, with curved marquises and ceilings almost eight meters (26 feet) high. The pavilion also hosts events like the Architecture Biennial and São Paulo Fashion Week.

Parque do Ibirapuera, gate #3, tel. (11) 5576-7600. Mon – Fri, 8am – 6pm.

Auditório do Ibirapuera: designed by Oscar Niemeyer and built in 2005

⑤ Auditório Ibirapuera

This modern auditorium is used exclusively for Concerts. Oscar Niemeyer designed and built the wedge-shaped building in 2005. The wall behind the stage has a large door which opens to allow the park's landscape to become a backdrop for the performance.

Parque do Ibirapuera, gate #2, tel. (11) 5908-4290. Box office: Tue – Thu, 9am – 6pm; Fri and Sat, 9am – 9pm; Sun, 9am – 6pm.

⑥ Museu Afro Brasil

This museum is housed in a pavilion designed by Oscar Niemeyer and built in 1953. It displays various facets of African culture and the African diaspora, which began in the 16th century and is still active. The collection contains about 4,000 items, and the museum also holds temporary exhibits. Guided tours are available.

Parque do Ibirapuera, gate #10, tel. (11) 5579-0593. Tue – Sun, 10am – 6pm (entry allowed up to 5pm). Library: Tue – Fri, 10am – 5pm; Sat, 10am – 2pm.

⑦ Pavilhão Japonês

This pavilion is a replica of Kyoto's Katsura Palace. Japanese gardens surround it, and it displays items from Japanese culture such as samurai armor. Sutemi Horiguti, a professor at the University of Tokyo, designed the building; it was constructed in Japan, dismantled, and shipped to Brazil in 1954.

Parque do Ibirapuera, gate #10, tel. (11) 5573-6453. Wed, Sat, Sun, and holidays, 10am – noon and 1pm – 5pm.

⑧ Planetário do Ibirapuera

Latin America's first planetarium opened in 1957. After being closed for seven years, it reopened in 2006 and now boasts modern equipment that allows visitors to see the sky projected from any point in the universe. The planetarium, which is housed in a heritage-listed building, offers 30-minute sessions, but arrive an hour early.

Avenida Pedro Álvares Cabral, no #, gate #10, Parque do Ibirapuera, tel. (11) 5575-5206. Sat and Sun, 3pm, 5pm, and 7pm.

JARDINS

Locals use the name "Jardins" for the area enclosed by **Avenida Paulista**, **Rua Estados Unidos**, **Avenida Rebouças**, and **Avenida Nove de Julho**. It contains art galleries, world-class hotels and restaurants, and the most sophisticated shopping areas in the country. The leafy streets offer an invitation for a stroll. Several bus lines serve the area, and there are metro stations nearby – Brigadeiro, Trianon-Masp, and Consolação – on the green line. Also nearby are the four real Jardins neighborhoods: Jardim Paulista, Jardim América, Jardim Europa, and Jardim Paulistano.

JARDINS STREETS

Rua Augusta, Rua Oscar Freire, Alameda Lorena, Rua Dr. Melo Alves, Rua Bela Cintra, Rua Haddock Lobo, and Rua da Consolação are the most important streets. The famous **Rua Oscar Freire** exemplifies cosmopolitan, refined São Paulo. Visitors will find stores like **Diesel** and **Patachou**, as well as the stores of famous designers like **Fause Haten** *(#1102, tel. (11) 3081-8685)* and young **Andrea Saletto** *(#1072 A, tel. (11) 3082-0149)*. There's no shortage of beachwear stores, such as **Jo de Mer** *(#329, tel. (11) 3081-4232)*. **Luisa Strina,** an art gallery representing famous contemporary artists and launching new talent, is also on the street. **Rua Bela Cintra** is home to the **Antonio Bernardo** jewelry store *(#2063, tel. 3083-5622)* and designer boutiques **Reinaldo Lourenço** *(#2167, tel. (11) 3085-8150)* and **Gloria Coelho** *(# 2173, tel. (11) 3083-1079)*. **Rua Haddock Lobo** is the place for **Emporio Armani** *(#1550, tel. (11) 3897-9090)* and designer **Alexandre Herchcovitch** *(#1151, tel. (11) 3063-2888)*. Find **Fernando Pires** shoes on **Rua da Consolação** *(#3534, tel. (11) 3068-8177)*. **Jacaré do Brasil,** on **Rua Doutor Melo Alves**, offers

---

THE BEST PLACES TO EAT

Frevo, on Rua Oscar Freire, is known for serving the best *beirute* (pita sandwiches) in São Paulo *(#603, tel. (11) 3082-3434; Sun – Wed, 10:30am – 1am; Thu and Fri, 10:30am – 2am; Sat, 10:30am – 3am)*. **Neuhaus**' Belgian chocolates come in 80 varieties *(Alameda Lorena, 1898, tel. (11) 3088-711; Mon – Sat, 10am – 7pm; Sun, noon – 6pm)*. The Portuguese restaurant **Antiquarius**, a branch of the original Rio de Janeiro establishment, serves splendid codfish dishes and duck rice *(Alameda Lorena, 1884, tel. (11) 3082-3015; Mon, 6pm – 1am; Tue – Thu, noon – 3pm and 7pm – 1am; Fri, noon – 3pm and 7pm – 2am; Sat, noon –*

2am; Sun, noon – 6pm). Nearby is **A Bela Sintra**, another place to try classic Portuguese dishes *(Rua Bela Cintra, 2325, tel. (11) 3891-0740, 3891-1090; Mon – Thu, noon – 3:30pm and 7pm – 1am; Fri, noon – 3:30pm and 7pm – 2am; Sat, noon – 1am; Sun, noon – 11:30pm)*. Rua Haddock Lobo is home to **Arábia,** a restaurant specializing in Arab cuisine *(#1397, tel. (11) 3061-2341; Mon – Thu, noon – 3:30pm and 7pm – midnight; Fri, noon – 3:30pm and 7pm – 1am; Sat, noon – 1am; Sun, noon - midnight)*; **Rodeio**, which serves top-quality meat and is famous for its manioc bread and cheese from Minas Gerais *(#1498, tel. (11) 3474-1333; Mon – Thu,*

11:30am – 3:30pm and 6:30pm – 1am; Fri and Sat, 11:30am – 1am; Sun, 11:30am – midnight); and the wonderful **A Figueira Rubaiyat**, which offers Mediterranean-style food *(#1738, tel. (11) 3063-3888; Mon – Thu, 12:30pm – 11pm; Fri and Sat, 12:30pm – 1am; Sun, 12:30pm – midnight)*. Hotel Fasano houses the **Fasano** restaurant and **Baretto** bar *(Rua Vitório Fasano, 88, tel. (11) 3062-4000; Mon – Sat, 7:30pm – 1am)*. Chef Alex Atala shows off his culinary skills at **D.O.M.** on Rua Barão de Capanema *(#549, tel. (11) 3088-0761; Mon – Thu, noon – 3pm and 7pm – midnight; Fri, noon – 3pm and 7pm – 1am; Sat, 7pm – 1am)*.

---

handmade decorative items from all over the country *(#555, tel. (11) 3081-6109)*. **Alameda Loren** is home to art dealer **Paulo Kuczynski**, who sells works by masters of Brazilian modernism *(#1661, tel. (11) 3064-5355)*. **Augôsto Augusta Cultural**, on **Rua Augusta**, is a mixture of bookstore and gallery *(#2161, tel. (11) 3082-1830)*. Antiques dealer **Renée Behar** has a valuable array of furniture and European objects *(Rua Peixoto Gomide, 2088, tel. (11) 3085-3622)*. NK **Store** sells its own brand of women's clothing as well as international labels *(Rua Sarandi, 34, tel. (11) 3897-2600)*. The **Havana Club** bar in the Hotel Renaissance sells cigars and offers a special smoking room for cigar fans. The bar also has a dance floor *(Alameda Santos, 2233, tel. (11) 3069-2233)*.

ALAMEDA GABRIEL MONTEIRO DA SILVA AND ENVIRONS

Décor, furniture, and design stores are clustered on this street. **Etel Interiores** produces exclusive pieces from ecologically certified wood *(#1834, tel. (11) 3064-1266)*. **Firma Casa** sells creations by renowned designers like the Campana brothers *(#1487, tel. (11) 3068-0377)*. **La Lampe** sells its own light fittings as well as those made by Italian manufacturers Artemide and Fontana Arte *(#1258, tel. (11) 3069-3949)*. **House Garden** offers furniture for the office, garden, and patio *(#1218, tel. (11) 3087-7777)*. **Casamatriz**, formerly Tecer, sells national and international rugs and furniture such as the Italian Cappellini *(#679, tel. (11) 3064-6050)*. **Benedixt** has a mix of design items and furniture in classic to contemporary styles *(#663, tel. (11) 3088-1045)*. **Montenapoleone** offers a fine selection of Italian, Scandinavian, and Spanish designs *(#1572, tel. (11) 3083-2200)*. Near Gabriel Monteiro da Silva, **Esther Giobbi Arte & Interiores'** showroom deals in items from all over the world *(Avenida Brasil, 1246, tel. 3085-9666, Jardim América)*. **Asian Elements** sells artifacts from

Benedixt, on Alameda Gabriel Monteiro da Silva, offers classical and contemporary furniture

Indonesia *(Avenida Cidade Jardim, 983, Jardim Paulistano, tel. 3071-2599)*. **Esencial**, in the Itaim Bibi neighborhood, offers Asian and Brazilian items *(Rua Araçari, 246, Itaim Bibi, tel. (11) 3168-5601)*.

Shopping Iguatemi

This mall, opened in 1966, is the oldest and most sophisticated in the country. It has more than 300 stores, including the best Brazil has to offer and international names such as **Tiffany & Co.**, **Louis Vuitton**, **Burberry**, **Emporio Armani**, and **Dolce & Gabanna**. The mall also has charming restaurants like **Gero Caffè**, **Armani Caffè**, and **Café Suplicy**.
Avenida Brigadeiro Faria Lima, 2232, Jardim Paulistano, tel. (11) 3816-6116. Mon – Sat, 10am – 10pm; Sun, 2pm – 8pm.

Museu da Casa Brasileira

Renata Crespi and Fábio da Silva Prado, the mayor of São Paulo from 1934 to 1938, once lived in this 1940s neoclassical building. Now, as a museum, the building displays a collection of 200 exhibits – mostly Brazilian furniture from the 18th and 19th centuries. It hosts concerts on Sundays. Guided tours are available, and a very pleasant restaurant serves lunch.
Avenida Brigadeiro Faria Lima, 2705, Jardim Paulistano, tel. (11) 3032-3727. Tue – Sun, 10am – 6pm.

MuBE and Mis

The **Museu Brasileiro da Escultura** (**MuBE**) opened in 1995, and for some people, the building itself is more of an attraction than its mediocre collection of sculptures.
The museum was designed by Paulo Mendes da Rocha, with landscaping by Burle Marx. The best works on display are *Outono silencioso*, by

Outdoor sculptures are the highlight of MuBE

Arcangelo Ianelli; *Coluna da primavera*, by Francisco Brennand; *Heads*, by Ivaldo Granato; and *Coluna Infinita*, by Kcho *(Avenida Europa, 218, Jardim Europa, tel. (11) 3081-8611; Tue – Sun, 10am – 7pm)*. The **Museu da Imagem e do Som** (**MIS**) displays a collection of photographs and negatives, magnetic tape recordings, documentaries, and science fiction films on celluloid and video *(for program details, visit www.mis.sp.gov.br)*.
Avenida Europa, 158, Jardim Europa, tel. (11) 3062-9197; Tue – Sun, 10am – 6pm.

Daslu

Moving away from the Jardins district, this four-story department store-boutique in the Vila Olímpia neighborhood exemplifies luxury. Daslu sells a range of famous designer clothes, jewelry, perfume, and antiques. It also houses a branch of **Livraria Laselva**, a beauty salon, a spa, and three restaurants *(Avenida Chedid Jafet, 131, Vila Olímpia, tel. (11) 3841-4000; Mon, Thu - Sat, 10am – 8pm; Tue, 10am – 10pm)*.

PINHEIROS

This neighborhood offers a variety of art galleries, bars, stores selling books, furniture, music, and decorations, and top restaurants offering Spanish, Italian, and Japanese cuisine. Avenida Faria Lima, Avenida Henrique Schaumann, and Rua Teodoro Sampaio are the main streets. The area is served by several bus routes and metro stations (Clínicas, Sumaré, and Vila Madalena, on the green line).

PRAÇA BENEDITO CALIXTO

On Saturdays, check out the craft, clothing, and antique fair in this lively square. It attracts artists, decorators, families, young people, and members of the gay community. Be sure to visit the décor stores that line the square. People line up until 4 pm for the hearty meals at the **Consulado Mineiro** restaurant *(tel. (11) 3064-3882; Tue – Thu and Sun,*

OUR RECOMMENDATION

🍽️ Japanese chef **Jun Sakamoto** runs the impeccable restaurant that bears his name. Book in advance if you want to sit at the counter and experience the creativity of one of his taster menus *(Rua Lisboa, 55, tel. (11) 3088-6019; Mon – Thu, 6:30pm – 12:30am; Fri and Sat, 7pm – 1am).*

Additional information on page 462.

noon – midnight; Fri and Sat, noon – 1am). Praça Benedito Calixto, no #, Pinheiros. Sat, 8am – 7pm.

GALLERIES

Brasiliana specializes in folk art *(Rua Artur de Azevedo, 520, tel. (11) 3086-4273; Mon – Fri, 10am – 6pm; Sat, 10am – 5pm)*, as does **Galeria Estação** *(Rua Ferreira de Araújo, 625, tel. (11) 3813-7253; Mon –Fri, 11am – 6pm; Sat, 11am – 3pm)*. **Amoa Konoya** sells indigenous art *(Rua João Moura, 1002, tel. (11) 3061-0639; Mon – Sat, 9am – 6pm)*. Contemporary artists show their work at **Gabinete de Arte Raquel Arnaud** *(Rua Artur de Azevedo, 401, tel. (11) 3083-6322; Mon – Fri, 10am – 7pm; Sat, 11am – 2pm)*. **Choque Cultural** sells street artists' work *(Rua João Moura, 997, tel. (11) 3061-4051; Mon – Sat, noon – 7pm)*.

BOOKSTORES

The five floors of **Fnac** house a cyber café, and the store hosts events that include book launches and lectures *(Praça dos Omaguás, 31, Pinheiros, tel. (11) 3579-2000; daily, 10am – 10pm)*. **Letra Viva** specializes in Spanish-language books *(Avenida Rebouças, 1986, Pinheiros, tel. (11) 3088-7992, 3088-7832, 3088-7780; Mon – Fri, 9am – 6pm; Sat, 9am – 1pm)*.

Market in Praça Benedito Calixto

Gustavo and Otávio Pandolfo exhibition, at Galeria Fortes Vilaça

VILA MADALENA

Tucked inside the Pinheiros neighborhood, Vila Madalena is the liveliest spot in the city's West Zone. The action is concentrated in and around **Rua Aspicuelta**, on **Rua Mourato Coelho**, **Rua Fradique Coutinho**, **Rua Inácio Pereira da Rocha**, **Rua Fidalga**, **Rua Girassol**, and **Rua Harmonia**. The area can be explored on foot or by car. Vila Madalena, on the green line, is the nearest metro station. During the day, visitors can shop at charming clothing stores – including several second-hand shops – as well as stores selling decorative objects, furniture, and educational toys. **Rua Fradique Coutinho** is the street with most of the art galleries, such as **Galeria Fortes Vilaça** and **Galeria Millan Antonio**, which are among the best in Latin America. The former displays work by contemporary artists like Beatriz Milhazes and Adriana Varejão *(#1500, tel. (11) 3032-7066; Tue – Fri, 10am – 7pm; Sat, 10am – 5pm)*. The latter exhibits work by renowned artists like Mira Schendel and Tunga, as well as

photographer Miguel Rio Branco *(#1360, tel. (11) 3031-6007; Mon – Fri, 10am – 7pm; Sat, 11am – 3pm)*. **Galeria Gravura Brasileira** represents names such as Claudio Mubarac and Renina Katz *(#953, tel. (11) 3097-0301; Mon – Fri, 10am – 6pm; Sat, 11am – 2pm)*. At night, the streets of Vila Madalena take on a bohemian air, keeping up a tradition going back to the 1970s, when students, intellectuals, and artists used to gather in local bars. One bar from that era is **Mercearia São Pedro**, which opened in 1968 and continues to attract the alternative clientele that made it famous. It also operates as a mini-market *(Rua Rodésia, 34, tel. (11) 3815-7200; Mon – Sat, 9am – 1am; Sun, noon – 6pm)*. The stretch of Rua Aspicuelta that leads from Rua Mourato Coelho to Rua Fidalga is home to several bars, including **Posto 6**, a combination bar and Japanese restaurant *(Rua Aspicuelta, 644, tel. (11) 3812-7831; Mon – Fri, 6pm – 2am; Sat, 2pm – 2am; Sun and holidays, noon – midnight)*.

MORUMBI

This residential neighborhood, which began to form in the late 1940s, sports luxurious residential condominiums and areas of greenery. Visitors will need their own cars or hired taxis to get around.

ESTÁDIO DO MORUMBI
Inaugurated in 1960, Cícero Pompeu de Toledo Stadium is São Paulo Football Club's home turf. Vilanova Artigas and Carlos Cascaldi designed the stadium, which can hold up to 80,000 spectators. Guided tours are available, and trophies and photographs are on display in a memorial hall.
Praça Roberto Gomes Pedrosa no #, Morumbi, tel. (11) 3749-8000, 3749-8071. Mon – Fri, 10am – 4:30pm; Sat, Sun, and holidays, noon – 4:30pm.

FUNDAÇÃO MARIA LUÍSA E OSCAR AMERICANO
Landscape artist Otávio Augusto Teixeira Mendes designed this house to be surrounded by woods. It is also the work of architect Oswaldo Arthur Bratke, who created this former residence of Maria Luísa and Oscar Americano. The foundation now houses 18th-century paintings, including works by Frans Post, period pieces from Brazil's imperial era, and paintings from 20th-century masters like Di Cavalcanti. The lovely *salão de chá* (tearoom) serves cakes and juice. Every other Sunday, classical concerts are held in the auditorium. (Tickets can be purchased an hour in advance.)
Avenida Morumbi, 4077, Morumbi, tel. (11) 3742-0077; collection: Tue – Fri, 11am – 4:30pm; Sat and Sun, 10am – 5pm; park and tearoom: Tue – Sun, 11:30am – 6pm.

PALÁCIO DOS BANDEIRANTES
In 1954, Francisco da Nova Monteiro designed this building to house a university that was never inaugurated). It became the state government headquarters and the official governor's residence in 1970. Be sure to look at Portinari's striking 1955 painting, *A tempestade acalmada*, hanging in the

Fundação Maria Luísa e Oscar Americano: art and afternoon tea in a green oasis main entrance. The staterooms and galleries boast works by Aleijadinho, Tarsila do Amaral, and Rubem Valentim, among others. On weekends, visitors can go into the Salão de Despacho, which has paintings by Benedito Calixto, Pedro Américo, and Oscar Pereira da Silva. *Avenida Morumbi, 4500, Morumbi, tel. (11) 2193-8282, 2193-8212. Mon – Fri, 10am – 5pm; Sat, Sun, and holidays, 11am – 4pm.*

CASA DA FAZENDA DO MORUMBI
Imperial Regent Antônio Feijó (1784-1843) built this classically decorated house in 1813. Now, it is home to the Academia Brasileira de Arte, Cultura e História (Brazilian Academy of Art, Culture, and History). It holds temporary exhibits of decorative art, which is usually for sale. The gardens abound with fruit trees, including jabuticaba, mango, *ipês,* and jacaranda. Original walls still stand in the old slave quarters. The restaurant serves traditional farm food and afternoon tea. In addition, the center offers classes in art, ceramics, and design. In addition to the main building, Centro Cultural Apsen sells paintings and sculptures; next door, visitors can buy costume jewelry, bags, and miniatures at Oca das Artes. *Avenida Morumbi, 5594, Morumbi, tel. (11) 3742-2810. Tue – Sun, 11am – 5pm.*

PINAKOTHEKE SÃO PAULO
This gallery's forte is modernist Brazilian works by such artists as Portinari and Guignard. Art dealer Max Perlingeiro runs the place, and for four months a year (with no fixed date), he opens his doors to sell to the public. The rest of the year, arrange a visit by phone. *Rua Ministro Nelson Hungria, 200, Morumbi, tel. (11) 3758-5202. Mon – Fri, 10am – 8pm; Sat (during exhibits), 10am – 4pm.*

Galeria Pinakotheke in Morumbi

INSTITUTO LINA BO E P. M. BARDI
Lina Bo designed and finished this house in 1951, and she lived there herself with Pietro Maria Bardi. It has glass walls overlooking 7,000 square meters (75,000 square feet) of Atlantic forest. The property, which is a national heritage site, houses the Instituto Lina Bo e P. M. Bardi, a cultural center that holds exhibits and events related to the country. Inside, visitors can see furniture designed by Bo and Le Corbusier, among others. Visits must be arranged in advance. *Rua Bandeirante Sampaio Soares, 420, Morumbi, tel. (11) 3744-9902, 3744-9830. Mon – Fri, 9:30am – 5pm.*

PARQUE BURLE MARX
This park is made up of 138 square meters (1,485 square feet) of dense Atlantic forest foliage, gardens, and lakes. Many of the different plants have identifying plaques. Roberto Burle Marx designed the park in the 1940s to be a place of contemplation. *Rua Dona Helena Pereira de Morais, 200, Morumbi, tel. (11) 3746-7631. Daily, 7am – 7pm.*

OTHER MUSEUMS AND OUTDOOR TRIPS

CIDADE UNIVERSITÁRIA

The University of São Paulo's main campus, Cidade Universitária (Campus Armando de Salles Oliveira), opened in 1968. Its 4 million square meters (988 acres) contain 19 separate teaching and research units, museums, and cultural centers. The **Instituto de Estudos Brasileiros** (IEB) holds the personal collections of intellectuals like Mário de Andrade and Guimarães Rosa; call in advance to arrange visits. The institute also has an exhibit of works from the 1922 Semana de Arte Moderna (Modern Art Week) *(Avenida Professor Melo Morais, Travessa 8140, tel. (11) 3091-3199; Mon – Fri, 9am – 6pm).* Works by Miró, Picasso, Alfredo Volpi, Anita Malfatti, Modigliani, Braque, and others are on display in the main building of the **Museu de Arte Contemporânea** (MAC) *(Rua da Reitoria, 160, Favo 4, tel. (11) 3091-3039; Tue – Fri, 10am – 6pm; Sat, Sun, and holidays, 10am – 4pm).* The **Museu de Arqueologia e Etnologia** (MAE) exhibits objects from indigenous,

African, and European cultures *(Avenida Professor Almeida Prado, 1466, tel. (11) 3091-4905; Tue – Fri, 9am – 5pm).* Be careful walking around the campus at night, because there isn't much security. Access for people who are not connected to the university is permitted between Monday and Friday from 5am to 2pm.
Visitor's Center (Centro de Visitantes): Praça Professor Reinaldo Porchat, 110, tel. (11) 3091-3121; Mon – Fri, 8am – 8pm.

INSTITUTO BUTANTÃ

This destination makes a very pleasant outing for children and adults alike because of its location in an extensive park. The Institute is important center for biomedical research responsible for 80% of the serums and vaccines in Brazil. The highlight here is the **Museu Biológico**, with terrariums containing snakes, spiders, and lizards. An outdoor snake pit features lanceheads, boa constrictors, rattlesnakes, and false corals. *Avenida Vital Brasil, 1500, Butantã, tel. (11) 3726-7222. Museums: Tue – Sun, 9am – 4:30pm; park and library: Tue – Sun, 8am – 5pm.*

Instituto Butantã: an outing for all age

MEMORIAL DA AMÉRICA LATINA

Many people find this complex – nine buildings that make up a stark 85 square meter (914 square foot) expanse of concrete – one of Oscar Niemeyer's less inspiring works. It opened in 1989. The most distinctive section is the **Pavilhão da Criatividade Darcy Ribeiro**, a pavilion that houses examples of Latin American folk art. Anthropologist Darcy Ribeiro collected some of them.
Avenida Auro Soares de Moura Andrade, 664, Barra Funda, tel. (11) 3823-4600. Tue – Sun, 9am – 6pm. Tickets: tel. (11) 3038-6698. Mon – Sat, 9am – 8pm.

MUSEU PAULISTA (IPIRANGA)

Tommaso Gaudenzio Bezzi designed this neo-renaissance palace, inaugurated in 1890, to commemorate the site where Brazil's independence was declared. Better known as the Museu do Ipiranga, the museum boasts a collection of around 125,000 paintings, objects, sculptures, and photographs. It includes the famous 1888 painting *Independência ou morte*, by Pedro Américo. The imperial chapel, which contains the mortal remains of Empress Leopoldina and Dom Pedro I, stands in front of the museum.

Praça da Independência, no #, Ipiranga, tel. (11) 6165-8000, 6165-8100. Tue – Sun, 9am – 5pm.

JARDIM BOTÂNICO

The Botanical Gardens are home to 380 tree species used for research and conservation spread over 360,000 square meters (almost an acre) of Atlantic forest. Naturalist Frederico Carlos Hoehne designed the area, which opened in 1930. It boasts gardens, greenhouses, and an orchidarium. Howler monkeys, red-breasted toucans, and other animals also inhabit this lovely place.

Avenida Miguel Stéfano, 3031, Água Funda, tel. (11) 5073-6300. Wed – Sun, 9am – 5pm.

Sculptures in the Jardim Botânico

JARDIM ZOOLÓGICO AND ZÔO SAFÁRI

The **Jardim Zoológico** is a good destination for families. More than 300 animals representing 400 species, including the white rhinoceros and snow leopard, live at this zoo. Interesting evening tours are offered on Fridays at 7pm, but they must be booked in advance *(Avenida Miguel Stéfano, 4241, Água Funda, tel. (11) 5073-0811; Tue – Sun and holidays, 9am – 5pm)*. Nearby, visitors can tour a safari site – **Zôo Safári** – in vans or their own cars to observe the 26 animal species, most of which are allowed to roam freely *(Avenida do Cursino, 6338, Vila Morais, tel. (11) 6336-2131, 6336-2132; Tue – Sun, 9:30am – 5pm)*.

MEMORIAL DO IMIGRANTE

The former Hospedaria de Imigrantes was built between 1886 and 1888 to house immigrant workers coming to São Paulo, but it ceased to operate as a hostel in 1978. Now, themed rooms show photographs of daily life in the hostel, old tools, and the history of coffee. Activities include train trips, tram rides, and multimedia terminals that allow visitors to find the names of immigrants who spent time in the hostel.

Rua Visconde de Parnaíba, 1316, Mooca, tel. (11) 6692-1866. Tue – Sun, 10am – 5pm. Train and tram rides: Sun and holidays, 10am – 5pm.

CULTURAL ACTIVITIES

São Paulo offers a wide range of theater, music, and dance performances from Brazil and abroad. The city's main newspapers publish weekly schedules every Friday.

THEATER
The modern **Teatro Abril** puts on grand productions, such as adaptations of Broadway musicals *(Avenida Brigadeiro Luís Antônio, 411, Bela Vista, tel. (11) 6846-6060; Mon – Fri, noon – 8pm; from 8pm onwards, only tickets for that day; www.teatroabril.com.br).*
Cultura Artística offers a wide-ranging program of top-quality music, theater, and dance *(Rua Nestor Pestana, 196, Consolação, tel. (11) 3256-0223, 3258-3616, 3258-3344; Mon – Sat, noon – 7pm; Sun, noon – 5pm; www.culturaartistca.com.br).* **Teatro Oficina** opened in 1960 as the headquarters of an avant-garde theater company, and director José Celso Martinez Corrêa still runs it *(Rua Jaceguai, 520, Bela Vista, tel. (11) 3106-2818, 3106-5300, 3104-0678; Mon – Fri, 9am – 6pm; Sat and Sun, by arrangement; or when there is a performance).* **Teatro Sérgio Cardoso** is home to two orchestras, the Banda Sinfônica do Estado de São Paulo and

the Orquestra Jazz Sinfônica do Estado de São Paulo *(Rua Rui Barbosa, 153, Bela Vista, tel. (11) 3288-0136; advance ticket sales: Wed – Sun, 3pm – 7pm; on the day of the performance: 7pm – 9pm; www.teatrosergiocardoso.sp.gov.br).* The **Teatro Municipal** showcases two orchestras, the Orquestra Sinfônica Municipal and the Orquestra Experimental de Repertório; two choirs, the Coral Lírico and the Coral Paulistano; a string quartet, the Quarteto de Cordas; and the city ballet company, the Balé da Cidade *(Praça Ramos de Azevedo, no #, Centro, tel. (11) 3222-8698; box office: Mon – Fri, 10am – 7pm; Sat and Sun, 2pm – 5pm).*

SHOWS AND CONCERTS
Credicard Hall, the city's largest venue for shows, can seat up to 5,000 people *(Avenida das Nações Unidas, 17955, Santo Amaro, tel. (11) 6846-6010; box office: daily, noon – 8pm; on show days, until curtain-up; www.credicardhall.com.br).* The highly praised **Sala São Paulo,** home of the Orquestra Sinfônica do Estado de São Paulo, boasts impeccable acoustics *(Praça Júlio Prestes, no # , Centro, tel. (11) 3337-5414; Mon – Fri, 10am – 6pm; Sat, 10am – 4:30pm or until curtain-up).* **Teatro Alfa** offers a good view of the stage from any spot in the auditorium, and it holds a variety of shows *(Rua Bento Branco de Andrade Filho, 722, Santo Amaro, tel. (11) 5693-4000; box office: Mon – Fri, 11am – 7pm; Sat and Sun, 11am – 5pm; www.teatroalfa.com.br).* Tiny **Tom Jazz** is great for performances of jazz and Brazilian music *(Avenida Angélica, 2331, Higienópolis, tel. (11) 3255-0084, 3255-3635; Tue – Sat, from 8pm; www.tomjazz.com.br).*

SESC
Sesc's city branches offer an intensive, top-notch sports and cultural schedule for free or at accessible prices. Classes, art exhibits, and performances of theater, music, dance are held in designated rooms, corridors, and open spaces where visitors can move about freely. Visitors can visit several very pleasant branches – including Pompéia, Pinheiros, Vila Mariana, Consolação, and Santana – even if only for a coffee break. *(For details, visit www.sescsp.org.br.)*

NIGHTLIFE

Check the listings in newspapers and magazines before sampling the city's nightlife, because venues are constantly opening and closing.

VILA OLÍMPIA AND ENVIRONS

This area attracts a sophisticated crowd. For electronic music, check out **Lov.e Club & Lounge** *(Rua Pequetita, 189, Vila Olímpia, tel. (11) 3044-1613; Tue – Sat, midnight – until the last customer leaves; Sun, 11pm – 5am)* and chic **Lotus SP** *(Avenida das Nações Unidas, 12551, WTC [World Trade Center], 2ⁿᵈ floor, Brooklin, tel. (11) 3078-3644, 3078-6828; Wed, Fri and Sat, midnight – until the last customer leaves).* **Asia 70** plays old classics *(Praça Procópio Ferreira, no #, Brooklin Novo, tel. (11) 5506-4903; Wed – Sat, 10pm – 5am; restaurant: Thu – Sat, 7:30pm – 12:30am).* For Latin rhythms, try the **Buena Vista Club** *(Rua Professor Atílio Inocenti, 780, Vila Olímpia, tel. (11) 3045-5245; Mon, Tue, Thu, and Fri, 8pm until the last customer leaves; Sat, 9pm until the last customer leaves; Sun, 7pm until the last customer leaves).*

VILA MADALENA

Vila Madalena swings to several rhythms. Spacious **Dolores** plays R&B and hip-hop *(Rua Fradique Coutinho, 1007, Vila Madalena, tel. (11) 3812-6519, 3031-3604; Fri and Sat, 10pm –*

Buena Vista Club in Vila Olímpia

6am). **Grazie a Dio!** plays everything from samba-rock to soul *(Rua Girassol, 67, Vila Madalena, tel. (11) 3031-6568; daily, 8pm until the last customer leaves).*

JARDINS AND ITAIM BIBI

Syndikat Jazz Club Bar showcases new musical talent *(Rua Moacir Piza, 64, Cerqueira César, tel. (11) 3086-3037; Tue – Fri, 8pm until the last customer leaves; Sat, 9pm until the last customer leaves).* In Itaim Bibi, try **Na Mata Café** for dinner, shows, and dancing *(Rua da Mata, 70, Itaim Bibi, tel. (11) 3079-0300; Mon – Sat, noon – 3pm and 7:30pm until the last customer leaves; Sat, 7:30pm until the last customer leaves; Sun, noon – 3:30pm).*

CONSOLAÇÃO

Funhouse grooves to the sound of rock, punk, and electronic music *(Rua Bela Cintra, 567, Consolação, tel. (11) 3259-3793; Tue, 10pm – 5am; Wed – Sat, 11pm – 5am).* DJs and jazz and soul bands play at **Geni** *(Rua Bela Cintra, 539, Consolação, tel. (11) 3129-9638, 3129-9952; Tue – Sun, 6pm until the last customer leaves).*

THE GAY SCENE

Most of São Paulo's gay and lesbian meeting spots are clustered around Consolação. One of the most famous places for dancing is **A Lôca**, an underground club that plays electronic music, rock, and oldies *(Rua Frei Caneca, 916, Bela Vista, tel. (11) 3159-8889; Tue – Thu, midnight – 6am; Fri and Sat, midnight – 10am; Sun, 7pm – 5am).*

MOUNTAIN RANGES

CAMPOS DO JORDÃO

Alps-style architecture and a big winter music festival make Campos do Jordão a popular destination during the winter months. Located 167 kilometers (104 miles) from the city of São Paulo, the town hosts the **Festival de Inverno** every July. Its main focus is classical music; it is one of the biggest festivals in the country, and it brings together acclaimed Brazilian and international musicians and orchestras. Prominent stores and restaurants set up shop temporarily in the winter, especially in the neighborhood of Capivari, hoping to attract young and famous visitors, who come to enjoy the chilly air of the Mantiqueira Range.

The town is also pleasant in the summer, with an array of good restaurants, quality services, and adventure tourism opportunities. Many climbing routes of varying degrees of difficulty can be found at **Pedra do Baú**, a 1,950-meter (6,400-foot) rock, and the neighboring **Pedra do Bauzinho** and **Pedra da Ana Chata**. Visitors can also try a hang-gliding launch ramp and mountain bike excursions *(Altus Turismo Ecológico, tel. (12) 3663-4122)*.

A more laid-back option is the **Horto Florestal**, which has hiking trails through araucaria forest *(Avenida Pedro Paulo, no #, 12 kilometers, 7.4 miles from the center of town; tel. (12) 3663-3762; daily, 8am – 5pm)*. Another of the town's attractions is **Palácio Boa Vista**, the state governor's official winter residence, which houses works by Brazilian artists such as Tarsila do Amaral, and Di Cavalcanti *(Avenida Ademar de Barros, 3001, Alto da Boa Vista, tel. (12) 3662-1122; Wed – Sun, 10am – noon and 2pm –5pm)*. Visitors can also see the **Baden Baden beer factory**, founded in 1999, which offers guided tours that include beer-tasting and a crash course in making beer *(Avenida Mateus da Costa Pinto, 1653, Vila Santa Cruz; tel. (12) 3664-2004, 3664-2033; Mon – Fri, 10am – 4pm; Sat, 10am –5pm; Sun, 10am – 2pm; book visits in advance)*. To get to Campos do Jordão from São Paulo, take Rodovia Presidente Dutra highway (BR-116) or Rodovia Ayrton Senna-Carvalho Pinto highway (SP-070) and Rodovia Floriano Rodrigues Pinheiro highway (SP-123).

An araucaria pine typical of Campos do Jordão, with Pedra do Baú in the background

Hang-gliding from Pico Agudo in Santo Antônio do Pinhal

SANTO ANTÔNIO DO PINHAL

Visitors don't need to go to Campos do Jordão to find entertainment: Santo Antônio do Pinhal is just 26 kilometers (16 miles) away, and it's a good alternative for people who want to escape the hustle and bustle of its famous neighbor. This tiny town, 177 kilometers (110 miles) from São Paulo, is set amid the verdant Mantiqueira Range, approximately 1,000 meters (3,281 feet) above sea level. Its many guesthouses offer panoramic views surrounded by greenery – an invitation to relax. The main avenue, Avenida Ministro Nélson Hungria, is home to most of the town's restaurants, the majority of which specialize in trout dishes. Two main attractions are reachable by car: the waterfall **Cachoeira do Lageado** (with a 15-meter [49-foot] drop), just 8 kilometers (5 miles) from the center of town; and the 1,700-meter (5,577-foot) **Pico Agudo**, a peak nine kilometers (5.5 miles) out of town that offers views of Baú Rock and the Paraíba Valley and acts as a takeoff point for paragliding and hang-gliding flights *(Mariano Turismo, tel. (12) 3666-1334; Xênios Ecoturismo, tel.*

(12) 3666-1815). For adventures closer to the ground, there is **Arvorismo da Xênios**, an 11-stage canopy-climbing course suspended 15 meters (50 feet) above the ground *(Rodovia SP-46, 2600; tel. (12) 3666-1815; daily, 8am – 6pm).* For a more tranquil outing, check out **Igreja Matriz de Santo Antônio do Pinhal**, a neo-Roman church built in 1836 *(Praça Monsenhor José Azevedo, 50, Centro; tel. (12) 3666-1127; daily, 8am – 8pm).* The town is home to a number of orchid growers and the **Jardim dos Pinhais**, park one kilometer from the center, which has several thematic gardens *(Rodovia SP-046, 2600; tel. (12) 3666-2021; daily, 9:30am – 6pm).* Travel to Santo Antônio do Pinhal from São Paulo by taking Rodovia Presidente Dutra highway (BR-116) or Rodovia Ayrton Senna–Carvalho Pinto highway (SP-070) and Floriano Rodrigues Pinheiro highway (SP-123) to the SP-046 turnoff. Nearby is an old railway station, where visitors can find delicious *bolinho de bacalhau* (cod fritters) and enjoy the view from the **Nossa Senhora Auxiliadora lookout**.

Cunha pottery, one of the town's main attractions

CUNHA

Cunha is flanked by the Mar, Bocaina, and Quebra-Cangalha mountain ranges – the mountains are visible from the town center. It is located 1,100 meters (3,609 feet) above sea level, 220 kilometers (137 miles) from São Paulo, and it can be reached on Rodovia Presidente Dutra highway (BR-116) and Rodovia SP-171 highway. The **Núcleo Cunha–Indaiá** of the **Parque Estadual da Serra do Mar** is 30 kilometers (19 miles) away, 20 kilometers of which are on a dirt road. It has three hiking trails that lead to rivers and waterfalls. The shortest, 1.7 kilometers (1 mile) long, is easy and can be undertaken without guides, but the other two, 7.5 and 14.5 kilometers (4.5 and 9 miles) long, can only be hiked in the company park monitors on weekends and must be booked in advance *(Estrada Municipal do Paraibuna, exit Km 56 on Rodovia Cunha–Paraty; tel. (12) 3111-2353; daily, 8am – 5pm).* Eco-tourists will also enjoy **Pedra da Macela**, a rock with an altitude of 1,840 meters (6,037 feet). Visitors who hike up the two-kilometer (1.2-mile) paved trail will be rewarded with a breathtaking landscape view that stretches as far as the coastal town of

Paraty *(Rodovia Cunha–Paraty, Km 65, plus another five kilometers on a dirt road to the start of the trail).*

POTTERS' WORKSHOPS

Several workshops produce high-temperature ceramics in Japanese wood-fired *noborigama* kilns. The pieces are fired twice to glaze and strengthen them *(Luiz Toledo, Alameda Lavapés, 555, tel. (12) 3111-3281; daily, 10am – 6pm; Mieko Ukeseki and Mário Konishi, Rua Jerônimo Mariano Leite, 510, tel. (12) 3111-1468; daily, 9am – 5pm; Suenaga e Jardineiro, Rua Dr. Paulo Jarbas da Silva, 150, tel. (12) 3111-1530; daily, 9am – 6pm).* Other workshops use different kilns such as raku pottery, which has special glazes that give the pieces a cracked appearance *(Zahiro and Gitika, Rodovia Cunha-Paraty, Km 61.5, tel. (12) 3111-3099; daily, 10am – 5pm; Sandra Bernardini, Estrada Municipal do Paraibuna, Km 9, on the way to Serra do Mar Park, tel. (12) 3111-1946; Mon – Fri with prior bookings; Sat, Sun, and holidays, 1pm – 6pm).* Some workshops receive visitors in the kiln openings, when the pottery is removed. In the raku kiln, which is opened at night, the pieces glow.

THE NORTH COAST

Some of the state's most beautiful beaches lie between São Sebastião and Ubatuba on the north coast of São Paulo. From the Rodovia **Rio–Santos** highway (BR-101/SP-055), which hugs the coast, travelers can see a sequence of long, narrow beaches with rich Atlantic forest spilling down the mountains behind them. The sinuous highway, however, requires drivers' full attention – especially at night and on weekends and holidays, when traffic is heavy. From the city of São Paulo, the best way to reach the northern beaches is on Rodovia Presidente Dutra (BR-116) or Rodovia Ayrton Senna (SP-150), followed by Rodovia dos Tamoios (SP-099). To get to the beaches south of São Sebastião, take the Rodovia Anchieta–Imigrantes highway system (SP-150/SP-160) or Rodovia Mogi–Bertioga highway (SP-098).

SÃO SEBASTIÃO

With 100 kilometers (62 miles) of coastline, the municipality of São Sebastião has beaches to suit all tastes: calm or with strong waves, short or long, semi-deserted or very busy. Its city center is 220 kilometers (137 miles) from São Paulo city. **Maresias**, **Camburi**, and **Juqueí** – all of which have their own village centers – are some of the most famous beaches. On weekends, they are overrun by young people in search of surf, sun, and nightlife. In the summer, fashionable São Paulo bars and stores set up seaside locations. Founded at the end of the 17th century, the municipality has a heritage-listed town center with 17th- to 19th-century colonial buildings. **Barra do Una** is the departure point for diving excursions, kayaking on the Una River, and motorboat trips to neighboring islands *(Green Way, tel. (12) 3891-1075)*.

The famous Maresias Beach in São Sebastião

OUR RECOMMENDATION

🍽 Tucked away in a quiet alley, the **Manacá** offers an intimate atmosphere in its three charming kiosks built up on piles. It is one of the best restaurants on the north coast,; the house specialty is fish, accompanied by an excellent selection of wines. Leave cars in a parking lot and take a van to the restaurant. Reservations are recommended *(Rua do Manacá, 102, Camburizinho, tel. (12) 3865-1566; Thu, 6pm – 11pm; Fri and Sat, 1pm – 11pm; Sun, 1pm – 9pm)*.

Additional information on page 462.

ILHABELA

Beautiful beaches and a laid-back atmosphere await visitors on Ilhabela, the country's largest maritime island. It's located about 20 minutes away from the São Sebastião ferry terminal, and cruise ships also stop there in the summer. Lively **Vila**, which is full of bars and restaurants, faces the continent on the west side of the island. This side of the island also has the most accessible (and therefore the busiest) beaches, such as tiny **Praia do Viana** and popular **Praia do Curral**. A long, narrow road cuts across the island on this side and traffic jams are common, especially during the high season. Beaches on the east side, such as **Praia do Bonete** and **Praia dos Castelhanos**, are harder to reach, but they are still wild and more beautiful. **Praia da Fome**, **Praia de Jabaquara**, and **Praia do Poço** are good places for snorkeling and watching fish, and the many shipwrecks around the island attract diving enthusiasts. Adventure sports and trekking are also popular on Ilhabela. More than 300 waterfalls are scattered through the forest; 85 percent of the island, approximately 33.5 hectares (83 acres), is part of the **Parque Estadual de Ilhabela** state park. Insect repellent is a must, especially on the east side. On weekends and holidays, people often have to line up for the ferry that runs between the island and the continent.

EAST SIDE

The only way to get to the east side of the island, where the most beautiful beaches are, is by boat, 4×4 vehicle, or hiking trail. To reach **Praia do Bonete** – a quiet fishing village in the southeast part of the island that's popular among surfers – visitors must take a boat or hike for four hours from **Borrifos**. Boat trips are cancelled in bad weather if the ocean is too rough. Visitors also must take a boat or a 4×4 vehicle to get to the

Ilhabela's Jabaquara Beach, a good place for snorkeling

The long Castelhanos Beach is hard to reach, but rewarding

long **Praia dos Castelhanos**, an excellent surfing spot and one of the most beautiful beaches on Ilhabela. The shortest boat trip and the one least affected by poor weather is the schooner trip to **Praia da Fome** in the north. Lucky passengers might see dolphins along the way.

"SAILING CAPITAL"

Ilhabela has excellent conditions for sailing. The **Semana Internacional da Vela**, one of the world's most important yachting competitions, takes place in July. Visitors and competitors from all over the world flock to the island to watch or participate in the regattas. During the week, in addition to the races, Vila and the Ilhabela Yacht Club host different cultural activities like dance and theater performances, film screenings, music shows, and exhibits. People can even rent boats to see the competitions up close *(Bl3 Escola de Iatismo, tel. (12) 3896-5885; Maremar Turismo, tel. (12) 3896-1418, 3896-*

2443, 3896-3679). Information on the event is available from the Department of Tourism *(Secretaria de Turismo: tel. (12) 3896-6657)*, the Department of Sports *(Secretaria de Esportes: tel. (12) 3896-1765)*, or the Ilhabela Yacht Club *(Yacht Clube de Ilhabela: tel. (12) 3896-2300).*

OUR RECOMMENDATION

🍽 **Ponto das Letras**, the only bookstore in town, offers a nice coffee shop with tasty desserts and savory snacks. Sit at one of the small tables and leaf through books on sailing, most of which are imported *(Rua Dr. Carvalho, 146, Centro, tel. (12) 3896-2104; high season: daily, 9:30am – midnight; low season: Mon – Thu, 10am – 8pm; Fri, 10am – 11:30pm; Sat, 10am – midnight; Sun, 10am – 10:30pm).*

The owners of the charming **Porto Pacuíba Hotel** are of German descent, and it's apparent in the restaurant, which also serves homemade cakes and bread. It's located on tiny Viana Beach *(Avenida Leonardo Reale, 2392, Viana, tel. (12) 3896-2466).*

Additional information on page 462.

The view of Ubatuba's beautiful landscape from Saco da Ribeira

UBATUBA

Ubatuba is home to the most beautiful stretches of São Paulo's coastline. It is situated 235 kilometers (146 miles) from São Paulo, on the border of the state of Rio de Janeiro, and its 100-kilometer (62-mile) bay has more than 70 separate beaches. Some have strong waves and are popular with surfers, like **Itamambuca**; others, like **Figueira**, are practically deserted. They all sit between an island-speckled sea and the Atlantic forest, sprinkled with waterfalls. Ubatuba is also the **Núcleo Picinguaba** base of the **Parque Estadual da Serra do Mar**, the only part of this state park that meets the ocean. It sports several hiking trails and **Ilha Anchieta**, an island with an old prison.

VIEWS TO TAKE YOUR BREATH AWAY

The Rodovia Rio–Santos highway has look-out points at four beaches – **Saco da Ribeira, Praia da Enseada, Praia das Toninhas**, and **Praia do Félix** – where visitors can park cars safely and enjoy or photograph the beautiful Ubatuba coastline.

BEACHES IN FRONT OF UBATUBA

Praia Itaguá stands in front of the beach promenade. Its ocean is not good for swimming, but the view of the mountains is breathtaking. **Praia do Tenório** has white sand and a sea with strong currents. Surfers are drawn to the strong waves of **Praia Vermelha do Norte**, a beach with coarse, reddish sand.

BEACHES SOUTH OF UBATUBA

Approximately 15 kilometers (9 miles) south of downtown Ubatuba is the tiny **Praia da Sununga**, which has strong waves and a fun atmosphere. It is also the location of the legendary **Gruta que Chora** (Crying Cave), whose walls seem to "cry" water. The next beach, **Praia do Lázaro**, has calm seas and is popular with families. A passage between two high walls in its right-hand corner leads to **Domingas Dias**, a small bay with soft sand. Car access to the bay runs through a private area and are not terribly easy.

BEACHES NORTH OF UBATUBA

Praia Itamambuca, 12 kilometers (7 miles) north of downtown Ubatuba, is

OUR RECOMMENDATION

🍽 A refined, creative menu and a simple atmosphere make the restaurant **Terra Papagalli** on Itaguá Beach a good option for a seafood lunch or dinner. The kitchen turns out a wide variety of dishes made with the freshest fish of the day. Reservations are recommended, especially on weekends *(Rua Xavantes, 537-B, Itaguá, tel. (12) 3832-1488. Mon, Wed and Thu, 6pm – 11pm; Fri and Sat, noon – midnight; Sun, noon – 10pm. Closed on Tuesdays).*

Additional information on page 462.

the ultimate surfing beach, with perfect waves and surfing championships all year. **Praia do Félix**, another good spot for surfing and scuba diving, is home to one of the most beautiful sights on the north coast: a mountain that practically tumbles into the water. The lovely **Praia de Prumirim** is about 18 kilometers (11 miles) away, and nearby is a waterfall of the same name, Cachoeira do Prumirim, which can be accessed from the Rodovia Rio-Santos highway. **Praia Puruba** is a strip of sand, where there are no houses, between the ocean and a river. Further along is **Praia de Picinguaba**, which has a fishing village and faces the island of Ilha Comprida.

PARQUE ESTADUAL DA SERRA DO MAR

The **Núcleo Picinguaba**, on Praia da Fazenda beach, is the only section of the Serra do Mar State Park that touches the coast. Its span encompasses mangroves, rocky coastlines, and native *restinga* vegetation. Visitors can take guided hikes – which should be booked in advance – along trails that include lovely views of waterfalls and landscapes. The visitors' center has a video room, public bathrooms, and a photo exhibit of local ecosystems. *Rodovia Rio–Santos, Km 10, tel. (12) 3832-9011. Daily, 9am – 5pm.*

SCHOONER TRIPS

The most traditional schooner trips go to **Ilha do Prumirim** and **Ilha Anchieta** islands. Prumirim, facing the beach of the same name, has diving sites and deserted beaches. On Anchieta, which was once known as the "Isle of Pigs", visitors can see the ruins of an old prison. It was closed down three years after a violent rebellion in 1952. The island is lovely, with beaches, diving sites, and trails. Get a guide for the trail that leads to Praia do Sul beach. *Contact: Mykonos Turismo, tel. (12) 3842-0329, 3842-1388, in Saco da Ribeira.*

Parts of Ubatuba's beachfront are practically deserted

BEST BEACHES

❶ Barra do Una

The Una River flows into the sea in this beach's left-hand corner, and a sandbar separates the fresh water from the seawater. It has areas of both strong waves and calm waters.

❷ Juqueí

Good facilities, calm water, and light-colored sand make this beach popular with families.

❸ Barra do Saí

This beach is shaped like a half-moon, with calm water and light-colored sand, and the mouth of the Saí River can be found in its left-hand corner. The village is quiet and appropriate for families.

❹ Baleia

A long, straight strip of sand is an invitation to take a stroll on this beach, where the waters are calm. Visitors can reach Baleia from Camburi or Barra do Saí.

❺ Camburi and Camburizinho

Camburi is a meeting place for surfers and has light-colored sand. Camburizinho is quieter; most local attractions, such as bars, hotels, and nightclubs, are concentrated on a single dirt road.

❻ Maresias

A meeting place for the young and famous, Maresias is also popular for its surfing championships and shows. All the activity, however, also brings traffic and queues – along the beach's five kilometers (three miles) of light-colored sand.

❼ Paúba

This beach has soft sand and hills covered in lush vegetation.

❽ Toque-Toque Pequeno, Calhetas and Toque-Toque Grande

Although they have no facilities, these three small beaches deserve a visit. It is hard to reach beautiful Calhetas, which faces the sea on two sides.

❾ Guaecá

This straight beach with white sand and calm waves is good for swimming. The right-hand corner attracts surfers.

❿ Figueira

This nearly wild beach can be reached only on trails. It faces Tamanduá Island.

⓫ Grande do Bonete

Calm waters grace this beach, which faces Mar Virado Island. It is a one-hour hike there from Praia da Fortaleza, which is also calm and good for swimming, and attracts scuba divers.

⓬ Domingas Dias

A passage in the right-hand corner of Praia do Lázaro leads to this bay's tranquil waters and soft sand. A private condominium makes car access difficult.

⓭ Sununga

A young crowd is drawn to this beach, which has strong waves. It is also the location of Gruta que Chora (Crying Cave), whose walls seem to "cry" water.

⓮ Tenório

This popular beach has white sand and strong ocean currents.

⓯ Itaguá

This beach in front of the Ubatuba beach promenade is not good for swimming, but the view of the mountains is breathtaking.

⓰ Vermelha do Norte

Popular among surfers because of its strong waves, this beach has coarse, reddish sand.

⓱ Itamambuca

This is one of the best surfing beaches in the region, with good waves all year long and championships in July. It is also surrounded by nature.

⓲ Félix

A good spot for surfing and diving, this beach is one of the most beautiful on São Paulo's north coast.

18 **19** **20** **21** **22**

Paraty

Taubaté

17

SP
125

16

Ubatuba

15

14

das Toninhas

Ilha das
Palmas

12

13

Ilha
Anchieta

Maranduba

11

Ilha do
Mar Virado

ATLANTIC OCEAN

SP
055

Galhetas

10

Massaguaçu

Ilha do
Tamanduá

SP
99

Martim de Sá

Caraguatatuba

Indaiá

Palmeiras

MAR

Enseada

Cigarras

SP
131

Ilhabela

São Sebastião

7

Pitangueiras

Castelhanos

9

Barequeçaba

8

1

Ilhabela
(Ilha de São Sebastião)

Bonete

Borrifos

SERRA DO MAR

MS   MG

SP

PR

N

1 cm = 5 km
1 inch = 7.9 mi.

---

⑲ Prumirim

This lovely, quiet beach has controlled access through a private condominium. It faces Prumirim Island, which offers good diving spots; a waterfall with the same name is nearby.

⑳ Puruba

This wild beach, a short distance before Ubatumirim, is merely a strip of sand between the ocean and a river, with no houses.

㉑ Brava da Almada

Located at the end of a trail, this residential beach has strong waves and a beautiful view of the coast. On the road from the Rodovia Rio–Santos highway is Mirante da Chica bar, with a spectacular view of the mountains and the north coast of Ubatuba.

㉒ Picinguaba

This quiet fishing village offers calm waters and diving off nearby islands.

The belle époque coffee exchange building – Bolsa do Café – in Santos

HISTORICAL CITIES

SANTOS

The port city of Santos, some 70 kilometers (44 miles) east of the city of São Paulo, can be reached on the Anchieta-Imigrantes Highway System (Rodovia SP-150/SP-160). Founded in 1546, it was one of Brazil's first settlements and had its heyday during the coffee boom. Its economy developed around its port, which is the largest in Latin America. It has a good beachfront and a busy nightlife. The city beaches lack in charm, but the famous gardens at the beachfront are impeccably kept.

HISTORICAL CENTER

Start with the **Paço Municipal**, a Louis XVI-style palace that now serves as the town's city hall *(Praça Mauá, no #, Centro, tel. (13) 3201-5000; Sat, Sun, and holidays, 11am – 6pm)*. Nearby, in Barão do Rio Branco Square, is **Igreja do Carmo**. Construction began in 1599 on this church – which is now

heritage-listed – and its adjoining chapel was built in 1760. Highlights include the church's gilded altars in and carved wooden altars in the chapel *(Praça Barão do Rio Branco, no #, tel. (13) 3234-5566; Mon – Fri, 8am – 6pm; Sat and Sun, no fixed hours)*. A walk along Rua 15 de Novembro, leads to the **Bolsa Oficial do Café**, the old coffee exchange building founded in 1922. Local artist Benedito Calixto (1853-1927) contributed paintings and stained-glass windows; the building also still has its original furniture and a 40-meter tall clock tower. Visitors can enjoy some of Brazil's best coffee in its coffee shop *(Rua 15 de Novembro, 95, Centro, tel. (13) 3219-5585; Tue – Sat, 9am – 5pm; Sun, 10am –5pm; admission until 4:15pm)*. Continuing down the same street, turn right on Rua do Comércio and find the beautiful **Casa da Frontaria Azulejada**, an 1865 building with a façade covered in hand-painted Portuguese tiles *(Rua do Comércio, 98, Centro, tel. (13) 3223-7009)*. A few more blocks away is a large square, Largo Marquês de Monte Alegre. Facing it is **Igreja Santo Antônio do Valongo**, a church dating from 1640 that boasts a baroque façade, painted-tile panels, and lovely frescos on both sides of the altar *(Largo Marquês de Monte Alegre, no #, Centro, tel. (13) 3219-1481; Tue – Sun, 8:30am – 5pm)*. The square also borders the state's first train station, **Estação São Paulo Railway**. This Victorian-style building was inaugurated in 1867 and restored in 2004; it currently houses the Department of Tourism *(Secretaria de Turismo: Largo Marquês de Monte Alegre, no #, Centro, tel. (13) 3201-8000)*.

BEACHFRONT ATTRACTIONS

The **Jardim da Praia**, also called Jardim da Orla, is one of the world's biggest beachfront gardens – about 22 hectares (54 acres) and 5.3 kilometers (3.3 miles) long. It has at least 1,700 trees, including palm and tropical almond, and 77 kinds of flowers. The **Museu de Pesca** fishing museum boasts a 23-meter long whale skeleton *(Avenida Bartolomeu de Gusmão, 192, Ponta da Praia, tel. (13) 3261-5260; Wed – Sun, 10am – 6pm)*. Architect João Artacho Jurado designed a large freestanding marquee that provides shade for public benches in front of the intersection of Avenida Conselheiro Nébias and the beach avenue. A few buildings down from the intersection is the **Pinacoteca Benedito Calixto**. This art nouveau mansion, which dates from 1900, is one of the former coffee barons' last remaining seafront residences. It is now a state art gallery, with works by local artist Benedito Calixto (1853-1927), temporary

exhibits, and beautiful gardens *(Avenida Bartolomeu de Gusmão, 15, Boqueirão, tel. (13) 3288-2260; Tue – Sun, 2pm –7pm)*. **Morro de José Menino**, a large hill between Santos and the neighboring city of São Vicente, offers lovely views and ramps for hang-gliding. Going around the bay, reaching São Vicente, visitors will find causeway leading to the tiny Ilha Porchat. At the top of the island is the **Mirante dos 500 anos**, a lookout point designed by Oscar Niemeyer that offers panoramic views of Santos and São Vicente *(Alameda Paulo Gonçalves, no #)*.

VILA BELMIRO

This stadium belongs to the Santos Futebol Clube, where soccer legend Pelé's career took off. Visitors can take guided tours through the stadium and the **Memorial das Conquistas**, which displays posters, old photographs, films, and the club's trophies. (It's not open on match days.)
Rua Princesa Isabel, 77, Vila Belmiro, tel. (13) 3257-4000. High season: daily, 9am – 7pm; low season: Mon, 1pm – 7pm; Tue – Sun, 9am – 7pm. Guided tours every hour: Mon, 1pm – 5pm; Tue – Sun, 9am – 5pm.

DIVING AT LAJE DE SANTOS

This large island of rock, 500 meters long, has a shape reminiscent of a sperm whale. The trip to Laje de Santos takes about an hour and a half by motorboat; it is 45 kilometers (28 miles) out to sea. Visitors aren't actually allowed on the island, but the visibility (up to 20 meters on sunny days) delights nearby divers, who can watch sea turtles and dolphins in the surrounding waters. The trip departs from São Vicente and lasts about seven hours.
Contact: Agência Cachalote, tel. (13) 3239-7213.

SANTANA DE PARNAÍBA

One of the state's oldest towns, Santana de Parnaíba, stands on the banks of the Tietê River. Prospectors settled the region in the 16th century, when they wanted to use the river to explore the state interior in search of precious metals. Located 41 kilometers (25 miles) from the city of São Paulo, it became an important departure point for pioneering expeditions. The town itself was founded in 1580; its historical center has 17th- to 19th-century heritage-listed buildings with restored façades. It is worth exploring on foot. Largo da Matriz is home to **Museu Casa do Anhangüera**, the town's oldest mansion, a 17th-century heritage-listed that has been transformed into a museum. The wattle-and-daub and lath-and-plaster building is believed to have been the home of pioneer Bartolomeu Bueno da Silva (1672-1740). On display at the museum are utensils and furniture (including the typical colonial trundle bed) from the colonial period, as well as indigenous artifacts *(Largo da Matriz,* *9, tel. (11) 4154-1874; Tue – Fri, 8am – 5pm; Sat and Sun, 9am – 5pm).* During **Carnival**, carnival bands take over the downtown streets and play to about 30,000 revelers a day. The group Grito da Noite throws a traditional *samba de bumbo* party on Carnival Friday, accompanied by the sound of *zabumbas*, drums, and rattles and the sight of giant dolls. The streets are strewn with sawdust on the **Corpus Christi** holiday. **São Paulo Antigo,** near the square Largo da Matriz, is one of the town's best restaurants. Housed in an 18th-century mansion, it has a buffet of country-style food. Tables sit next to large windows on the first floor, with views of the town and hills *(Rua Á lvaro Luís do Vale, 66, tel. (11) 4154-2726; Mon – Fri, noon – 3pm; Sat and Sun, noon – 4pm).* Stop at a fishing lake or a distillery in the outskirts of town after a visit to the historical center. The main routes from São Paulo city are Rodovia Castelo Branco highway (SP-280) and Rodovia dos Romeiros highway (SP-312).

View of Santana de Parnaíba; the 1882 church is one highlight

Resgate was the wealthiest farm in Bananal during the coffee boom

BANANAL

The city in the Bocaina Range, 330 kilometers (205 miles) from São Paulo, thrived economically at the beginning of the coffee boom before going into decline. It's worth exploring the alleys, lined with 19th-century mansions. The **Igreja da Matriz** dates from 1811 *(Praça Pedro Ramos, no #, Centro, tel. (12) 3116-5153; Tue – Sun, 8am – 11am and 1pm – 5pm)*, and **Pharmacia Popular**, Brazil's oldest working pharmacy, is preserved to look the way it did when it opened in 1830 *(Rua Manuel de Aguiar, 156, Centro, tel. (12) 9111-0286; Mon – Sat, 9am – 6pm; Sun, 9am – noon)*. Old **coffee plantations** can be visited on the outskirts of town. **Fazenda dos Coqueiros**, dating from 1855, displays period furniture and instruments used to torture slaves *(Rodovia dos Tropeiros, SP-068, five kilometers, three miles, from Bananal, tel. (12) 3116-1358; daily, 9:30am – 4:30pm)*. On the 19th-century **Fazenda Resgate**, visitors will find Spanish artist Villaronga's beautiful murals. Book visits in advance *(Rodovia SP-064/SP-068, Km 324, 10 km from the center of town, tel. (12) 3116-1577; Tue 7am – 11am; Wed – Fri, 7am – 11am and noon – 4pm)*. Visitors can tour old slave quarters, a manor house, and coffee processing equipment at **Pau d'Alho**, which dates from 1817 and is now heritage-listed. Book visits in advance *(Rodovia dos Tropeiros, SP-068, Km 265, tel. (12) 3117-1310; Wed – Sun, 9am – 5pm)*. The farm is located in the nearby municipality of São José do Barreiro (45 kilometers, 28 miles, from Bananal), and it is the main departure point for exploring the Bocaina Range *(see more information on page 205)*.

SÃO LUÍS DO PARAITINGA

In addition to its many heritage-listed 18th- and 19th-century mansions and churches, São Luís do Paraitinga is also known for keeping Paraíba Valley folk traditions alive. It's located 171 kilometers (106 miles) from São Paulo. During **Carnival**, enormous paper mâché dolls parade through the streets. Exhibitions of horseback riding and the African-derived *moçambique* and *congada* dances take place during May and June at the **Festa do Divino Espírito Santo** festivities. Summer is the ideal time for rafting on the **Rio Paraibuna** *(Contact: Paraitinga Turismo, tel. (12) 3671-2691)*. São Luís' accommodations are modest *(tourist information center: tel. (12) 3671-2080)*. Take the opportunity to visit the neighboring town of Cunha, about 80 kilometers (50 miles) away, which is famous for its pottery workshops *(see more information on page 192)*.

A waterfall in Brotas, where adventure sports and encounters with nature await

THE COUNTRYSIDE AND THE COAST

BROTAS

Brotas is the state of São Paulo's main center for ecotourism and adventure sports: **rafting**, **canopy climbing**, **canyoning**, **ultralight trekking**, **hiking**, and more. It attracts hundreds of people on public holidays and weekends. The town became famous for rafting, which draws people of different ages and experience levels to the Jacaré-Pepira River, especially from December to February. Children must be taller than 120cm (four feet) to go rafting with adults, but smaller children can float in tires (known as *bóia-cross*) along the calmer stretches of the river *(Contact: Alaya Expedições, tel. (14) 3653-5656; Brotas Aventura/Canoar, tel. (14) 3653-4463; EcoAção, tel. (14) 3653-8040)*. Another popular attraction is the **Verticália** canopy climbing circuit, with five treetop stretches and six flying foxes. It's one of the largest facilities of its kind in Brazil, run exclusively by Alaya Expedições, and only 3 kilometers (2 miles) from the center of town. But people don't need to be athletes to have fun in these parts:

There are beautiful waterfalls that are easy to reach, and most of the town's activities and services are concentrated on the two main streets – Avenida Mário Pinoti and Avenida Rodolfo Guimarães – lined with old mansions built by coffee barons of times past. Brotas has quality accommodations and at least 16 different agencies offering a range of excursions. At night, young people turn this quiet country town into a livelier place. On public holidays, book trips in advance. One of the most pleasant eateries is the **Malagueta**, which serves grilled dishes and homemade pasta in a dimly lit, calm setting *(Avenida Mário Pinoti, 243, tel. (14) 3653-5491; Thu, 7pm – midnight; Fri, Sat, and Sun, noon – midnight)*. Brotas is 242 kilometers (150 miles) from São Paulo on Rodovia dos Bandeirantes highway; drivers can also take Rodovia Anhangüera highway (SP-330) or Rodovia Bandeirantes highway (SP-348) to Rodovia Washington Luís highway (SP-310), followed by Rodovia Engenheiro Paulo Nilo Romano highway (SP-225).

SERRA DA BOCAINA

Set in a stretch of the Atlantic forest that once covered Brazil's entire coast, **Parque Nacional da Serra da Bocaina** has dozens of waterfalls and rich wildlife, from jaguars to woolly spider monkeys. This 104,000-hectare (257,000-acre) national park is hard to reach, but the restricted access ensures solitude. There is only one guesthouse, a camping ground, and local homes. Take Estrada da Bocaina (Rodovia Estadual da Bocaina highway, SP-221) from the town of **São José do Barreiro** – located 280 kilometers (174 miles) from São Paulo on Rodovia Presidente Dutra highway (BR-116) and Rodovia SP-068 – to a 27-kilometer (17-mile) dirt road that leads to the park gate. Vehicles that don't go off-road can have a hard time getting to the park, and only 4×4 vehicles can get through in rainy weather. The best idea is to hire an appropriate vehicle in São José do Barreiro. Located halfway between the cities of São Paulo and Rio de Janeiro, the park encompasses the whole Bocaina Range and goes as far as Paraty. The **Trilha do Ouro** (the old "Gold Trail" that connected the state of Minas Gerais

with the coast during the gold boom) passes through it, and only people hiking the trail are allowed to sleep in the park – with prior authorization from the park headquarters *(tel. (12) 3117-1225, 3117-2183)*. Permission is not required for one-day trips to visit only the waterfalls near the entrance. Information can be obtained from the headquarters at the beginning of the road to the park, but it doesn't provide much logistical support.

THREE DAYS ON TRILHA DO OURO
The old **Trilha do Ouro**, a path once used to smuggle gold out of Brazil in the 18th century, is a three-day hike. Several waterfalls, such as the lovely **Cachoeira do Veado** (100 meters in two drops), line the path leaving the park gate. Hikers should hire a guide to accompany them on the trail. Although park natives will put guests up in their homes, it is imperative to take tents and food. The trail ends on Mambucaba Beach, between Paraty and Angra do Reis. When hiring a guide, make sure to ask about transportation back.
Contact: MW Trekking, tel. (12) 3117-1220.

Serra da Bocaina, a region of Atlantic forest replete with waterfalls and fauna

Água Suja Cave, in Alto Ribeira State Park, southern São Paulo State

JURÉIA

The town of **Peruíbe** on the south coast is the point of departure for the **Estação Ecológica Juréia-Itatins**, a wildlife sanctuary 158 kilometers (98 miles) from the city of São Paulo. (Access it from the Anchieta-Imigrantes highway system (SP-150/SP-160), followed by the SP-055.) Only 5 percent of the park's 80,000-hectare (197,700-acre) area is open to visitors. This region of Atlantic forest is home to many ecosystems and endangered animals. Guides are not mandatory, but travel agencies offer interesting excursions, such as trekking, jeep trips to deserted beaches, visits to waterfalls, and canoeing. Canoe trips on the Guaraú River mean three hours (round trip) of rowing, but it's worth the effort: the landscape is spectacular, and splashing in the **Cachoeira Secreta** is divine *(Contact: Eco Adventure, tel. (13) 3457-9170, 3457-9390).* To get to Juréia, go through the center of Peruíbe toward the neighborhood of Guaraú (six kilometers on a paved, winding road to the neighborhood), then take a dirt road to Barra do Una.

CAVES IN PARQUE ESTADUAL TURÍSTICO DO ALTO RIBEIRA (PETAR)

The Ribeira Valley, some 350 kilometers (218 miles) south of the city of São Paulo, is home to the **Alto Ribeira State Park** (Petar). The park has about 250 caves protected by an Atlantic forest reserve, but they are hard to get to and can only be visited with a guide. The park has four parts. **Núcleo Santana** – the most visited and the one with the shortest trails – has **Caverna de Santana**. It's the main cave in the park, and the tour through it lasts about an hour and a half. The best-preserved cave, **Caverna de Caboclos**, is hard to reach. One highlight is **Caverna Temimina**, the only cave in Brazil that contains vegetation, thanks to a natural skylight in the ceiling. A small hotel puts up researchers and students at the **Núcleo Ouro Grosso** division. In the **Núcleo Casa de Pedra** division, the cave of the same name has the world's largest portico (215 meters [705 feet] high), but people are not allowed inside. The neighboring towns of Apiaí and Iporanga offer simple meals and accommodations. People who want to camp should book in advance with the park office. *Tourist information center: tel. (15) 3552-1717. Daily, 8am – 5pm. Park office: tel. (15) 3552-1875.*

MINAS GERAIS

MINAS GERAIS

1 cm = 54 km
1 inch = 85.2 mi.

HIGHLIGHTS

- The Pampulha Complex in **Belo Horizonte**, as well as the city's lively culture and nightlife.
- The pleasant trails of **Parque Natural do Caraça**, and the neo-gothic church that sits within its boundaries.
- The Chinese influence seen in the ornamentation of Igreja de Nossa Senhora do Ó, in **Sabará**.
- The steep streets of **Ouro Preto**, and

the city's collection of works by master sculptor Aleijadinho and master painter Ataíde.
- In **Congonhas**, the 12 prophets in the Basílica do Senhor do Bom Jesus de Matozinhos.
- The cobbled streets, gourmet cuisine, and crafts of **Tiradentes**.
- The lovely colonial architecture in and around **Diamantina**.

WHEN TO GO

- In **winter**, when Belo Horizonte's festival and performance season is in full swing.
- **May through October** for Saturday *vesperata* performances in Diamantina.
- At **Carnival**, during **Holy Week**, or on other holidays to see Ouro Preto at its

liveliest. (Keep in mind, however, that lodgings can fill up to a year in advance. Plan ahead!)
- In **August** for the Festival Internacional de Cultura e Gastronomia in Tiradentes.

BELO HORIZONTE

Belo Horizonte, founded in 1897, was one of the first planned capitals in Brazil. Today it is home to 2.3 million inhabitants. Many visitors come to enjoy the city's wealth of artistic and cultural offerings – particularly dance, theater, and music – as well as its great cafés, shops, and bookstores. The local climate is pleasant and mild, ideal for late evenings socializing at lively outdoor *botecos* (bars). Visitors also come here to see the modernist Pampulha Complex, designed by the famous Brazilian architect Oscar Niemeyer. The complex was considered revolutionary in the 1940s, and its bold lines remain unique to this day.

PAMPULHA COMPLEX

Oscar Niemeyer brought modernism to Minas Gerais in the 1940s when he designed and built the Pampulha Complex on the shores of an artificial lake 15 kilometers (9 miles) from downtown Belo Horizonte. The complex was commissioned by then-mayor Juscelino Kubitschek, who wanted to encourage development of the area as a new suburb. Kubitschek later became Brazil's president. All the buildings along Avenida Otacílio Negrão de Lima are Niemeyer designs. Burle Marx, a well-known Brazilian landscape artist, is responsible for most of the landscaping. There are several notable buildings along the avenue: **Igreja de São Francisco de Assis** *(no #, Pampulha, tel. (31) 3427-1644; Tue – Sat, 9am – 5pm; Sun, 9am – 1pm; Mass: 10:30am and 11:30am)*, **Museu de Arte da Pampulha** *(#16585, tel. (31) 3277-7946; Tue – Sun, 9am – 9pm)*, the ballroom known as the **Casa do Baile** *(#751, tel. (31) 3277-7443; Tue – Sun, 9am – 7pm)*, and a yacht and tennis club, **Iate Tênis**

Casa do Baile

Clube *(#1350, tel. (31) 3490-8400; Tue and Thu, 7am – 11pm; Wed and Fri, 7am – 6pm; Sat and Sun, 7am – 7pm)*. The church was built in 1943. One of the outer walls is covered in tiles painted by the artist Portinari. The tiles depict the life of Saint Francis of Assisi. The church was not consecrated until 1959 because the Catholic Church was wary of architecture so different from that of traditional religious buildings. The **Fundação Zoobotânica**, a zoo and botanical foundation, occupies a building originally designed by Niemeyer to serve as a golf course clubhouse. The complex also has two athletic stadiums, **Mineirão** and **Mineirinho**.

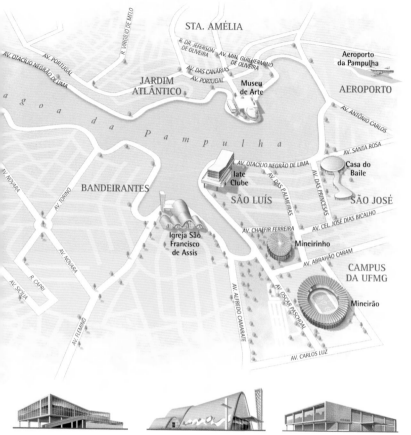

| late Clube | Igreja São Francisco de Assis | Museu de Arte |

SAVASSI AND ENVIRONS

Whether it's lunchtime, happy hour, dinner, or a lazy evening, the bars, restaurants, cafés, and bookstores of **Savassi** attract a diverse crowd. The district encompasses the Funcionários neighborhood and extends almost all the way to Praça da Liberdade, its epicenter is **Praça da Savassi**, a historic square where you will find the bustling, delightful **Livraria Travessa** bookstore and its café *(Avenida Getúlio Vargas, 1405, tel. (31) 3223-8092; Mon – Fri, 8am – 9pm; Sat, 8am – 6pm)*. Patrons soak in radio-era décor at **Dalva Botequim Musical**, which serves traditional Falke Bier. Live *chorinho* music plays on

Saturdays at 4pm *(Rua Ceará, 1568, tel. (31) 3282-2343; Mon – Fri, 5pm – 12:30am; Sat, 1pm – 1:30am)*. Bohemians and artists gather in the studios, art stores, and bars along Rua Congonhas in the **Santo Antônio** neighborhood. Lively **Utópica Marcenaria**, in the **Santa Lúcia** district, is a cultural center, bar, and studio all in one. The center also hosts live music performances *(Avenida Raja Gabáglia, 4700, tel. (31) 3296-2868; Thu – Sat, 9pm – 3am; Sun, 7pm – 2:30am)*.

CULTURE AND HISTORY

The **Mercado Central** market, built in 1929, is a riot of colors, smells, and sounds. Vendors at over 400 stalls hawk

Edifício Niemeyer, a textbook example of modern architecture in Belo Horizonte

OUR RECOMMENDATION

🍽 **Xapuri** is a highly praised restaurant run by chef Nelsa Trombino, who has developed a uniquely modern take on traditional regional cuisine. Don't miss her *frango preguento do Bento*, chicken served with rice, beans, chayote, corn mash, okra, and collard greens. Also, save room for dessert *(Rua Mandacaru, 260, Pampulha, tel. (31) 3496-6198; Tue and Wed, noon – 11pm; Thu – Sat, noon – 2am; Sun, noon – 6pm).*

Additional information on page 462.

medicinal herbs, arts and crafts and other wares. Tired shoppers can rest weary feet at the market's bars *(Avenida Augusto de Lima, 744, Centro, tel. (31) 3274-9434; Mon – Sat, 7am – 6pm; Sun and holidays, 7am – 1pm).* Within walking distance of the market, the historic 19th- century buildings surrounding **Praça da Liberdade** square recall the city's beginnings. The **Palácio da Liberdade**, seat of state government, receives visitors on the last Sunday of each month, from

---

BOTECOS, A LOCAL INSTITUTION

The people of Belo Horizonte love cozy taverns, which they call *botecos*. There are around 8,000 in the city, and they are great places to eat, drink, and chat with friends. The best are found in the Lourdes, Funcionários, and Santo Antônio neighborhoods. Happy hour is particularly popular at **Maria de Lourdes Botequim** *(Rua Bárbara Heliodora, 141, Lourdes, tel. (31) 3292-6905; Mon – Fri, 6pm – 1am; Sat, noon – 1am; Sun, 4pm – 1am).* **Mercearia Lili** *(Rua São João Evangelista,* 696, Santo Antônio, tel. (31) 3296-1951; Mon – Fri, 5pm – midnight; Sat and holidays, 10am – 5:30pm)* has a warehouse-like atmosphere and its tables spill onto the sidewalk. **Graças a Deus** *(Rua Padre Odorico, 68, São Pedro, tel. (31) 3282-6318; Tue – Fri, 7pm – 2am; Sat and Sun, 6pm – 3am)* is a popular destination for singles and serves 30 different beers. **Bar do Salomão** *(Rua do Ouro, 895, Serra, tel. (31) 3221-5677; Mon – Fri, 5pm – until the last customer leaves; Sat and Sun, noon – until the last* customer leaves) is the de-facto hangout for Atlético Mineiro soccer fans, and is therefore a good place to watch games. **Bar do Careca** *(Rua Simão Tann, 395, Cachoeirinha, tel. (31) 3421-3655; Tue – Fri, 6pm until the last customer leaves; Sat, 11am until the last customer leaves; Sun and holidays, noon – until the last customer leaves)* is quite a hike but has good food. Every year the **Comida di Buteco** competition crowns the tastiest *boteco* food in Belo Horizonte *(www.comidadibuteco.com.br).*

8am to 1pm *(Praça da Liberdade, no #, Funcionários)*. While in the square you can view the imposing **Edifício Niemeyer**, built in 1955. As the name suggests, it is the work of the architect Oscar Niemeyer. It is a residential building, however, so visitors are not allowed inside *(Praça da Liberdade, 153)*. The **Museu Histórico Abílio Barreto** houses the Mariquinhas locomotive, which helped move materials used to build the city *(Avenida Prudente de Morais, 202, Cidade Jardim, tel. (31) 3277-8572; Tue – Sun, 10am – 5pm; Thu, 10am – 9pm)*. The **Palácio das Artes,** another Niemeyer building, is the city's largest arts complex. Its substantial artistic offerings are listed online in Portuguese at *www.palaciodasartes.com.br (Avenida Afonso Pena, 1537, tel. (31) 3237-7399; Mon – Sat, 9am – 9pm; Sun, 4pm – 10pm)*.

THE ARTS

Belo Horizonte is home to many renowned dance and music groups. **Grupo Corpo,** a contemporary dance company founded in 1975, has become internationally famous for its fusion of folk music and classical ballet *(www.grupocorpo.com.br)*. **Companhia Primeiro Ato,** established in 1982, marries elements of theater and dance *(www.primeiroato.com.br)*. **Uakti** produces avant-garde music with instruments created by Marco Antônio Magalhães *(www.uakti.com.br)*. **Grupo Galpão** performs classic works in traveling-theater style *(www.grupogalpao.com.br)*. **Giramundo** has performed puppet theater since the 1970s. They display 600 marionettes in a museum *(Rua Varginha, 235, Floresta, tel. (31) 3446-0686; Tue – Sat, 9:30am – 5pm; www.giramundo.org.br)*.

AROUND BELO HORIZONTE

A variety of day trips are located less than 50 kilometers (31 miles) from the city. The state of Minas Gerais has an extensive network of paved roads, though they are often dotted with potholes. In the rainy season the roads can be hazardous. Before driving anywhere, check with the highway patrol for information on current road conditions.

SANTA LUZIA

Santa Luzia is 23 kilometers (14 miles) from Belo Horizonte on Rodovia MG-020 highway. **Igreja Matriz Santuário de Santa Luzia,** a church built between 1744 and 1778, has a beautiful high altar that depicts the Holy Trinity; it was sculpted by a famous Brazilian master artist known as Aleijadinho *(Rua Direita, no #, tel. (31) 3641-4662; Mon – Wed, 8am – 8pm; Thu and Fri, 8am – 5pm; Sat and Sun, 8am – noon and 2pm – 8pm)*. The **Mosteiro de Macaúbas,** an 18th-century convent, was the first girls' school in Minas Gerais. Today, a cloistered community of nuns from the Order of the Immaculate Conception lives here. They sell honey cakes, liqueurs, and other homemade delicacies. Visits are restricted to the outer area, chapel, and snack bar *(Rodovia MG-020, Estrada Santa Luzia – Jaboticatubas, Km 36, tel. (31) 3684-2096; daily, 8am – 11am and 3pm – 5pm)*.

OUR RECOMMENDATION

🍽 Patrons of **La Victoria** have a choice between 20 different poultry, fish, seafood, and other meat dishes, all cooked on an enormous barbecue grill. We recommend the Uruguayan lamb cutlets, and perhaps a glass of wine. The wine list has 160 labels *(Rua Hudson, 675, Jardim Canadá, tel. (31) 3581-3200; Wed – Fri, 6pm until the last customer leaves; Sat, noon – until the last customer leaves; Sun, noon – 6pm)*.

Additional information on page 462.

NOVA LIMA

Nova Lima, 27 kilometers (17 miles) from Belo Horizonte, at the intersection of Rodovias MG-40 and MG-030 highways, grew out of the gold mining boom in Morro Velho. Today, many of its mining-era homes stand as reminders of an English company that sought gold here. **Igreja Matriz de Nossa Senhora do Pilar,** a heritage-listed church, has sculptures by the artist Aleijadinho *(Praça Bernardino de Lima, no #, Centro, tel. (31)* 3541-7444; Mon, 7am – 4pm; Tue – Fri, 7am – 7:30pm; Sat, 8am – noon and Mass at 7:30pm; Sun, Mass only: 7am, 9am, and 6pm). The **District of São Sebastião das Águas Claras**, known as **Macacos**, is a green oasis full of trails and streams. Motorcyclists, 4×4 enthusiasts, and cyclists enjoy coming here on weekends. Sports lovers meet for early drinks in two bars, **Bar do Engenho** and **Bar do Marcinho.** The district also has some nice restaurants.

SABARÁ

Sabará is just 25 kilometers (15 miles) from Belo Horizonte, via Rodovia BR-262 highway. The town, founded in 1674, was one of the first settlements produced by the gold rush. It sits in a majestic valley at the confluence of the **Rio das Velhas** and the **Rio Sabará. Rua D. Pedro II,** formerly Rua Direita, is worth exploring on foot. The town has preserved the baroque art and architecture of its churches, most of which are now national heritage sites. Sabará's crown jewel is the 18th-century **Igreja Nossa Senhora do Ó**. The church's façade has a single central tower and simple, oriental-style ornamentation. The simplicity of the exterior creates a marked contrast with the wealth inside. Rich red, gold, and blue paints depict scenes from the life of Mary and the birth of Jesus on the nave and ceiling panels. Chinese motifs of birds and trees can be seen in the chancel arch and on the panels to the side of the high altar. They are thought to have been inspired by porcelain brought from the Portuguese colony of Macau *(Largo Nossa Senhora do Ó, no #, Siderúrgica, tel. (31) 3671-1724; Mon – Fri, 9am – 5pm; Sat and Sun, 9am – noon and 2pm – 5pm).* **Matriz de Nossa Senhora da Conceição** is considered by some scholars the oldest parish church in Minas Gerais. It was built between 1701 and 1710. The church's interior is lavishly adorned with gilt carvings from the baroque period. A large statue of Our Lady of the Immaculate Conception, brought from Portugal around 1750, sits on the high altar *(Praça Getúlio Vargas, no #, Siderúrgica, tel. (31) 3671-1724; Mon – Fri, 9am – 5pm; Sat and Sun, 9am – noon and 2pm – 5pm).* **Igreja da Ordem Terceira de Nossa Senhora do Carmo** is worth a visit because it is the only church in Sabará with works by the artist Aleijadinho *(Rua do Carmo, no #, Centro, tel. (31) 3671-2417; Tue – Sat, 9am – 11:30am and 1pm – 5pm; Sun, 1pm – 5pm).* The **Museu do Ouro** exhibits more than 300 objects, including works of art, furniture, and tools used in the mining industry. The museum resides in a building that originally served as a gold-weighing and smelting house *(Rua da Intendência, no #, Centro, tel. (31) 3671-1848; Tue – Sat, noon – 5pm).* Finally, Sabará hosts two splendid food festivals: the **Festival Ora-Pró-Nobis**, which takes place in the Pompéu neighborhood in May, and the **Festival da Jabuticaba**, which is held in late October and early November. In either case, there is no shortage of food.

PARQUE NATURAL DO CARAÇA

In the municipality of Catas Altas, 110 kilometers (68 miles) from Belo Horizonte, lies a private nature reserve, Parque Natural do Caraça. Framed by mountains, the preserve's Atlantic forest and Cerrado savannah spread over 11,000 hectares (27,181 acres). The park's name was inspired by the shape of a local mountain peak, said to resemble a recumbent giant with a "big face" (*caraça*). **Santuário Nossa Senhora Mãe dos Homens** sits within the park's boundaries; it was a seminary and college until 1911. The lovely church, built in 1883, was the first neo-gothic house of worship in Brazil. The church collection includes a depiction of *Santa Ceia* (The Last Supper) painted by the artist Ataíde. It is also the last resting place of the embalmed body of Saint Pius the Martyr. Every night around 8pm, at least one member of a local family of maned wolves makes an appearance to be fed by the priests, closely watched by visitors. The complex's museum has a bed used by Dom Pedro II, the last emperor of Brazil *(Mass: Mon – Sat, 8pm; Sun, 11am and 8pm)*. Nearby, trails lead to waterfalls and lookout points. An easy 6-kilometer

The neo-gothic church of Caraça Natural Park

(4.5 mile) trail leads to **Cascatona,** a 70-meter (230-foot), multi-level waterfall. The **Cascatinha** falls are only two kilometers away and have a pool suitable for bathing. The average annual temperature is around 15 degrees Celsius (59 degrees Fahrenheit) so take a warm jacket. One wing of the college has been converted into a simple guesthouse, but anyone looking for something more

---

PARQUE NACIONAL DA SERRA DO CIPÓ

One hundred kilometers (62 miles) from Belo Horizonte, Serra do Cipó National Park straddles the municipalities of Jaboticatubas and Santana do Riacho. Its 33,800 hectares (83 acres) are dazzling, with flowers in bloom year round, beautiful waterfalls, and scenic trails. **Cachoeira da Farofa** is one of the loveliest waterfalls in the park. Despite the distance (7 kilometers, 4.5 miles), the trail to the falls is child-friendly. Worthwhile, but not so easily accessed, is **Cânion das Bandeirinhas,** a three-hour, 12-kilometer (7.5-mile) walk. Only the lower section of the park can be seen without a guide. There are tourist facilities near the park entrance, including toilets, showers, and a visitor's center, as well as bicycle and horse rental agencies. We recommend you bring light snacks with you. The park is best visited in the winter and spring when there is little risk of rain and mud. To access the park, take Rodovia MG-424 highway toward Vespasiano, or, from Lagoa Santa, take Rodovia MG-010 highway to the exit at Km 94. *Tel. (31) 3718-7237. Daily, 8am – 6pm (but no entry after 2pm).*

comfortable can stay in neighboring Santa Barbara. The park can be enjoyed year-round, but summer is best for swimming in the waterfall pools.

Rodovia Padre Jerônimo (MG-436), access by BR-381, between Barão de Cocais and Santa Bárbara, tel. (31) 3837-2698. Daily, 7am – 5pm.

OURO PRETO

Ouro Preto, formerly known as Vila Rica, was once the capital of Minas Gerais. Fueled by the gold rush, the colonial town prospered in the 17th and 18th centuries. Its cobbled streets, austere mansions, and historic churches stand in picturesque relief against the dark mountains beyond. Vila Rica grew substantially in 1711 when two separate settlements – Antônio Dias and Ouro Preto – merged. A sense of rivalry between the two never completely disappeared. It's not by chance that the town has two parish churches. A high point of local cultural and religious life is the yearly Holy Week Procession. In even-numbered years, the procession begins at Matriz do Pilar, in odd-numbered years, at Matriz de Antônio Dias. Two artistic geniuses, the sculptor Aleijadinho (1730-1814) and the painter Manuel da Costa Ataíde (1762-1830), made important contributions to Ouro Preto. The town was also the scene of one of Brazil's great

HISTORICAL TOWNS

The historical towns of Minas Gerais rose from the gold fever that left its mark on the Portuguese colony in the 18th and early 19th centuries. Nearly 30,000 people were drawn to remote parts of Minas Gerais by the promise of wealth. The first settlements appeared around chapels built near the mines. Those cities can be divided into two groups: gold-boom towns, like **Ouro Preto**, **Mariana**, **São João del-Rei**, and **Tiradentes**, and diamond-boom towns, as embodied by **Diamantina**. The rich architectural and artistic heritage of the period is plainly visible in the houses, churches, streets, and alleys. The natural scenery surrounding the towns is often just as dazzling.

A view of Ouro Preto, with Igreja Nossa Senhora do Carmo at the top

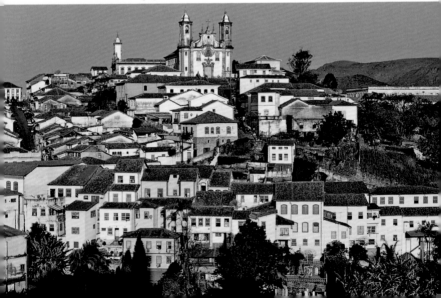

independence movements, the Inconfidência Mineira. In 1897, Belo Horizonte, 99 kilometers (61 miles) to the northwest, became the capital. Ouro Preto fell into oblivion. Nearly 80 years later, the town frozen in time found consolation in its designation as a world heritage site by Unesco. A recent increase in population and traffic now threatens its historical legacy, but can't detract from the splendor of its churches and fountains. Visitors also come to Ouro Preto to experience its lively street Carnival and Holy Week celebrations. We recommend you explore the town on foot whenever possible. Wear comfortable shoes, as the streets are lovely but steep.

OURO PRETO'S HISTORICAL CENTER

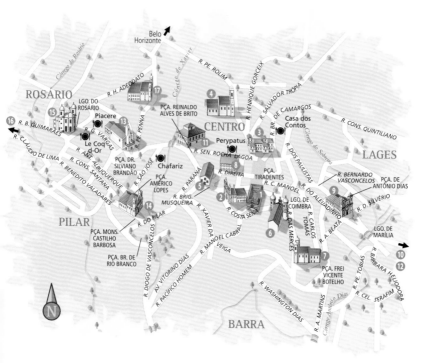

❶ MUSEU DA INCONFIDÊNCIA

The museum, once a council chamber and prison, is a great example of 18th-century architecture in Minas Gerais. Built in 1784 and renovated in 1854, its collection includes the remains of the independence movement conspirators, 18th- and 19th-century furniture, and works by the artists Aleijadinho and Ataíde. The museum was remodeled in 2006.

Praça Tiradentes, 139, Centro, tel. (31) 3551-1121. Tue – Sun, noon – 5:30pm.

❷ IGREJA DE NOSSA SENHORA DO CARMO

This lovely church dates from 1776. It heralded the beginning of the rococo style in Ouro Preto and is the only church in Minas Gerais with decorative Portuguese tiles. The soapstone font and side altars are the

work of the sculptor Aleijadinho, while the sacristy paintings are by Ataíde. Next to the church, in the Casa do Noviciado, is the **Museu do Oratório**, which has 162 shrines and 300 religious items spanning the 17th, 18th, 19th, and 20th centuries. Aleijadinho spent his last years here.
Rua Brigadeiro Musqueira, no #, Centro. Church: tel. (31) 3551-2601. Tue – Sat, 9am – 11am and 1pm – 4:45pm; Sun, 10am – 4:45pm. Museum: tel. (31) 3551-5369. Daily, 9:30am – 5:30pm.

❸ **MUSEU DE CIÊNCIA E TÉCNICA DA ESCOLA DE MINAS**
Built in 1742 to serve as the governor's palace, the building was converted into a school, the Escola de Minas, after the town lost its status as capital. Today it houses the Museum of Science and Technology. The astronomical observatory is open on Saturday nights from 8pm to 10pm. The building has a lovely chapel and its interior fountain is the handiwork of Aleijadinho.

CHURCHES AND RELIGIOUS SOCIETIES

Religion was the seed from which culture in Minas Gerais grew. Towns sprung up around chapels, and brotherhoods, "third" orders (lay people associated with formal Catholic orders), and religious societies became increasingly popular. Since people of the same social group and status tended to come together in the same brotherhoods – for example, brotherhoods of the black community, people of mixed race, high society, and the working class – these groups naturally reflected the rigid social hierarchies of the era. One thing each had in common, however, was a desire to construct places of worship more beautiful and impressive than any other. Such competition is in no small part responsible for the magnificent architectural heritage Brazilian towns enjoy today.

Praça Tiradentes, 20, Centro, tel. (31) 3559-1597. Tue – Sun, noon – 5pm.

❹ **IGREJA DE NOSSA SENHORA DAS MERCÊS E MISERICÓRDIA (MERCÊS DE CIMA)**
Though it opened its doors in 1774, the church's design continued the traditions of earlier 18th-century buildings. Later renovations altered the façade, most notably adding a tower in the center. The soapstone medallion above the door shows the Virgin Mary wrapping her cloak around slaves captured by the Moors.
Rua Padre Rolim, no #, Centro, tel. (31) 3551-4736. Tue – Sun, usually open approximately noon – 4pm (opening times vary).

❺ **CASA DA ÓPERA (TEATRO MUNICIPAL)**
The Municipal Theater was built in 1769 and is the oldest operating theater in Brazil. It has a triangular façade crowned with a lyre and perfect acoustics inside
(Rua Brigadeiro Musqueira, no #, Centro, tel. (31) 3559-3224.

❻ **IGREJA DE SÃO FRANCISCO DE ASSIS**
The Church of Saint Francis of Assisi stands testament to the skill of the artist Aleijadinho, who designed the high altar, pulpits, frontispiece, and interior sculptures. Construction began in 1767 and took decades to complete. The church is a pitch-perfect example of Brazilian colonial architecture. Several decorative details are worth taking a moment to admire: the Cross of Lorraine flanked by two balls of fire, the cylindrical towers, and the carvings on the medallion and portal. Ataíde painted

The ceiling painting in Capela do Padre Faria is one of the oldest in Minas Gerais

the depiction of Our Lady of the Angels of Porciúncula on the ceiling, giving her his own common-law wife's features.

Largo de Coimbra, no #, Centro, tel. (31) 3551-4661. Tue – Sun, 8:30am – noon and 1:30pm – 5pm.

❼ Igreja de Nossa Senhora das Mercês e Perdões (Mercês de Baixo)

Legend has it that a chapel once stood on this spot, built by the wife of a man convicted of killing his own daughter. The present-day church was built in 1772. While there is documented evidence that the event took place, its connection to the chapel is probably apocryphal. The church houses a rich collection of statues and religious items.

Rua das Mercês, no #, Centro, tel. (31) 3551-3282. The church is closed for restoration, with no set date for reopening. We recommend you call ahead to check its status.

❽ Museu Casa Guignard

The painter Alberto da Veiga Guignard (1896-1962) was born in Rio de Janeiro but spent many years in Minas Gerais. He settled in Ouro Preto toward the end of his life and the town appears regularly in his works. There are nearly 1,000 items in the Guignard Museum's collection, including personal items, paintings, documents, and photographs of the artist. The museum is inside an 18th-century house.

Rua Conde de Bobadela (Rua Direita), 110, Centro, tel. (31) 3551-5155. Tue – Fri, noon – 6pm; Sat and Sun, 9am – noon and 1pm – 6pm.

❾ Igreja Matriz de Nossa Senhora da Conceição de Antônio Dias

The façade of the church is very similar to that of the Matriz do Pilar. However, the similarities end at the door. The Matriz de Nossa Senhora has eight sumptuously-appointed altars and carved soapstone pillars. The artist Aleijadinho and his father, Manuel Francisco Lisboa, are buried here. A small museum, **Museu Aleijadinho**, is housed in the sacristy. Note the unusually threatening gaze of the museum's sculpture of Saint Francis.

The church was built in 1727.

Praça Antônio Dias, no #, Antônio Dias, tel. (31) 3551-4661. Tue – Sat, 8:30am – noon and 1:30pm – 5pm; Sun, noon – 5pm.

⑩ CAPELA DO PADRE FARIA

Padre Faria chapel, built in the early 18th century, is also known as **Nossa Senhora do Rosário dos Brancos**. It replaced the makeshift chapel in which Father João de Faria Fialho said Ouro Preto's first Mass in 1699. It's worth taking a few extra moments to appreciate the triple-branched cross in the churchyard,

The igreja Matriz de Nossa Senhora do Pilar altar

the gilt carvings on the main and side altars, and the ceiling paintings, which are among the oldest in the state. Against the Crown's orders, this church alone tolled its funeral bell on April 21, 1792, the day Tiradentes, Brazil's martyr of independence, was executed.

Rua Nossa Senhora do Parto, no #, Padre Faria. Tue – Sun, 8am – 4:30pm.

⑪ CASA DOS CONTOS

Construction of the Contos house began in 1782 and was completed two years later. The residence became a prison for a number of conspirators of the 1789 uprising. One of them, the poet Cláudio Manuel da Costa, died here. There are slave quarters at the back, as was customary at the time. Later, the building was occupied by the Intendência do Ouro gold inspection agency. Today it exhibits 18th- and 19th-century furniture and functions as a library and research center for people who wish to study the gold boom.

Rua São José, 12, Centro, tel. (31) 3551-1444. Mon, 2pm – 6pm; Tue – Sat, 10am – 6pm; Sun and holidays, 10am – 4pm.

⑫ IGREJA DE NOSSA SENHORA DO ROSÁRIO DOS PRETOS (SANTA IFIGÊNIA)

Tradition has it that the church was built at the behest of Chico Rei, a freed slave who became the owner of a gold mine. There is an outstanding sculpture by Aleijadinho of Our Lady of the Rosary on the façade. Inside, the woodcarvings evoke African scenes. The tower clock has been there since 1762 and still keeps time. Note the stone font at the entrance; slaves smuggled gold from the mines by hiding

it in their hair, which they would then wash out in the font for use by the church.
Rua Santa Ifigênia, 396, Alto da Cruz, tel. (31) 3551-5047. Tue – Sun, 8:30am – 4:30pm.

⓭ Igreja de São José

Construction of San Jose church began in 1752, replacing a chapel that had stood on the spot since 1730. The church was finished in 1811. Aleijadinho designed the altarpiece and the tower. The church is under renovation, but it's still possible to take a good look at the central tower balcony, which has a soapstone balustrade.
Rua Teixeira Amaral, no #, Centro. No fixed opening times.

⓮ Igreja Matriz de Nossa Senhora do Pilar

Workers began labor on the present-day church in 1723, replacing an earlier chapel structure. The finishing touches on the façade weren't completed until 1848. The church was inaugurated in 1733, however, with a procession called the Triunfo Eucarístico, which marked the return of the Holy Sacrament to the grounds from its temporary home at the Igreja de Nossa Senhora do Rosário dos Pretos. The church's rich interior was decorated with more than 400 kilos of gold. Every detail speaks the language of extraordinary opulence. The 100 sculpted flowers covered in gold leaf on the central arch are a case in point. An outstanding carving by Francisco Xavier de Brito is located in the main chapel. The **Museu de Arte Sacra,** in the cellar, exhibits historic items from the 16th through 19th centuries, including statues, gold-embroidered cloths, and silverware.

Praça Monsenhor João Castilho Barbosa, no #, Pilar, tel. (31) 3551-4736 (museum). Tue – Fri and Sun, 9am – 10:45am and noon – 4:45pm; Sat, 9am – 4:45pm.

⓯ Igreja Nossa Senhora do Rosário

The church's circular design is similar to that of some churches in Northern Europe. It was built between 1733 and 1785 by a religious order of slaves, replacing an earlier chapel. The church has unique altars dedicated to black saints.
Largo do Rosário, no #, Rosário, tel. (31) 3551-4736. Tue – Sun, 1:30pm – 4:45pm.

⓰ Igreja do Bom Jesus de Matosinhos

This church dates from the late 18th and early 19th centuries. The magnificent soapstone entrance by Aleijadinho depicts the Archangel Michael above the fires of hell. The high altar and nave ceilings have been restored to reveal parts of original paintings by Ataíde.
Rua Alvarenga Peixoto, no #, Cabeças, tel. (31) 3551-4736. Mass: Sat, 6am and 7am; Sun, 9am and 10am.

⓱ Igreja São Francisco de Paula

The newest church in Ouro Preto was begun in 1804 but remained unfinished until 1898. Specialists attribute the lovely statue of Saint Francis on the high altar to Aleijadinho. There's a stunning view of the surrounding area from the churchyard.
Rua Padre Marcos Pena, no #, Centro, tel. (31) 3551-4736. Tue – Sat, 9am – 11:15am and 1:30pm – 4:45pm; Sun, 1:30pm – 4:45pm.

OTHER ATTRACTIONS

MINA DE CHICO REI

One of the oldest historical mines open to visitors, Chico Rei Mine once belonged to Chico Rei, a freed slave said to have been an African king before his capture. With his wealth he obtained freedom for other slaves and built Igreja Santa Ifigênia. There are 360 meters (1,181 feet) of tunnels open to visitors. Marks from the original tools are still visible. A few such tools are on display in the reception area, which also has a gift shop and restaurant.

Rua Dom Silvério, 108, Antônio Dias, tel. (31) 3552-2866. Daily, 8am – 5pm.

PARQUE ESTADUAL DO PICO DO ITACOLOMI

Itacolomi Peak is 1,772 meters (5,814 feet) high. The name means "stone-child" in the indigenous Tupi-Guarani language. Explorers used it as a landmark when they came seeking gold in the backwoods of Minas Gerais toward the end of the 17th century. The Itacolomi Range, part of the larger Espinhaço Range, became a 7,543-hectare (18,640-acre) state park in 1967. Here, Atlantic forest gives way to Cerrado savannah. The park is home to anteaters, coatis, and otters. There are also historic sites to visit, like **Casa Bandeirista,** a home built between 1706 and 1708. Visitors can also enjoy the park trail system, which includes three easy trails between 400 and 1,200 meters (1,300 and 4,000 feet) in length. The park is well organized and has parking facilities, a visitor's center, toilets, and a snack bar. Three guided expeditions are available but must be booked in advance. The expeditions, which are 8 to 16 kilometers (5 to 10 miles) round-trip, are not very difficult and participants enjoy beautiful views of the region.

Rodovia MG-356 (Rodovia dos Inconfidentes), hospital intersection, about 5 kilometers from the center of Ouro Preto, tel. (31) 8835-7260. Tue – Sun, 8am – 5pm.

Pico do Itacolomi, in the background, became a reference point for gold prospectors

OURO PRETO, MY FANTASY LAND

Many years ago I visited Brazil as a typical tourist and I realized what a great country it is. However, I left with the impression that there was a hazy line that separated the country I knew from the real Brazil. I designed a house in Barra do Una and was involved in the construction of a fascinating complex in the state of São Paulo, and had the privilege of meeting some extraordinary Brazilians who honored me with their friendship. Through them I'm getting to know the country and, of course, Ouro Preto was one of the first places I went to.

Some towns have a "soul" that embraces and wins us over, and makes us part of them. From the day I arrived in Ouro Preto I realized that it was one of these towns. The topography and vegetation are powerful and the town respects both in an impressive manner. The streets follow the natural contour of the land and the buildings adapt to the terrain in such a way that their walls and roofs create an urban sculpture. The churches, located in strategic points, become icons within the landscape but do not overpower the scenery. Colors and textures add a final touch to this fascinating town.

Walking along the streets, sitting in the squares and churches I pondered the true values of life, dreamed of romantic and mysterious stories, and created an imaginary world, something that our contemporary lifestyle no longer allows us to do.

The colonial and baroque architecture of Ouro Preto deserves special mention. Almost completely unknown abroad, it is undoubtedly one of the most interesting styles in the Americas. The churches designed by Aleijadinho, with their exceptional proportions, are remarkable. One of their unique features is the contrast between the large flat surfaces and the elaborate stonework, as well as the incredible sculptures integrated into the façades, plazas and staircases. This concept has almost been forgotten by modern architecture, and it should continue to be contemplated by architects. The same can be said of the symmetry of the scale and design of the exteriors and interiors of these churches; their luxurious details emphasize their spirituality. This type of architecture teaches us many concepts and invites us to consider and appreciate its excellence.

I was fortunate enough to be in Ouro Preto during the Holy Week and watch the incredible ceremonies and processions that carried me back in time. These ceremonies, with their local color, demonstrate the spirituality of this very special town.

The people who live here are elegant, peaceful and humane, and have a complement lifestyle. Hotels, restaurants and public areas reflect this way of life, and make the town a consistent and fascinating place. For those who appreciate beauty, elegance and a deeply emotional way of life, Ouro Preto is a mandatory destination.

Ricardo Legorreta,
Mexican architect

Igreja São Francisco de Assis (left) and Igreja Nossa Senhora do Carmo, in Mariana

MARIANA

The town of Mariana is a baroque treasure. It has a population of 51,000 and lies 15 kilometers (9 miles) from Ouro Preto. It was the first administrative center of Minas Gerais and the first planned town in the state. The town's colonial architecture lines the wide streets, particularly **Rua Direita**.

PRAÇA MINAS GERAIS
A replica of the town's old whipping post sits in the square, as does the lovely **Igreja de São Francisco de Assis**, which was built between 1763 and 1794. Note the imposing portal; its soapstone medallion was carved by Aleijadinho. Ataíde the painter is

buried here *(daily, 8am – 5pm)*. Next door is the **Igreja de Nossa Senhora do Carmo**. The church was built between 1784 and 1835, and partially destroyed by fire in 1999. It has beautiful carvings on the side altars, high altar, and altarpieces *(Tue – Sun, 9am – 5pm)*. The **Casa de Câmara e Cadeia**, which dates from 1798, currently serves as the Town Council Chamber *(tel. (31) 3557-2747; daily, 7am – 6pm)*.

CATEDRAL BASÍLICA DE NOSSA SENHORA DA ASSUNÇÃO (SÉ)
A fine example of the first baroque phase in Minas Gerais, this 1750 church also has a beautiful

German Arp-Schitger organ. The organ was already 52 years old when it was presented to the church as a gift from Dom Pedro V in 1753. Three hundred years after its construction it retains most of its original components and is used for concerts.

Praça Cláudio Manoel, no #, tel. (31) 3557-1216, 3558-2785. Tue – Sun, 8am – 6pm. Concerts: Fri, 11am; Sun, 12:15pm.

MINA DE OURO DA PASSAGEM

From Ouro Preto, the mine is 4 kilometers before the Mariana exit. It began operating in the early 18th century and didn't close until 1985. Small trolleys ferry visitors down the narrow tunnels into the mines 120 meters (394 feet) below. A crystal-clear lake sits at the bottom.

Rua Eugênio Eduardo Rapallo, 192, Passagem de Mariana. Mon and Tue, 9am – 5pm; Wed – Sun, 9am – 5:30pm.

CONGONHAS

Congonhas retains little of its past splendor as a gold rush town. Its expansion with the arrival of iron-ore mining destroyed many old buildings. One 18th-century treasure remains, however: the **Santuário do Bom Jesus de Matosinhos** complex, a Unesco world heritage site. The complex is considered an extraordinary example of Brazilian baroque architecture. **Basílica do Bom Jesus de Matosinhos**, was finished in 1817 after sixty years of labor. The church's highlights can all be seen from the outside. The churchyard contains 12 soapstone prophets

sculpted by Aleijadinho and his disciples between 1800 and 1805. They also carved the 66 lovely, life-sized cedar figures representing the Passion of Christ found in the six small shrines in front of the sanctuary. Visitors cannot enter the shrines, but can view the sculptures from outside *(Praça da Basílica, no #, tel. (31) 3731-1590; Tue – Sun, 6am – 6pm).*

The Last Supper shrine

The Road to Calvary shrine

ALEIJADINHO

Aleijadinho was born in Vila Rica (today known as Ouro Preto) in 1730. He was the son of a Portuguese construction foreman, Manuel Lisboa, and his slave, Isabel. His works are scattered around Ouro Preto and other historical towns. As an adult he was afflicted by a disease that crippled him. Aleijadinho means "little cripple" in Portuguese but the diminutive "inho" makes the name more affectionate than it sounds in English. He and his disciples worked in Congonhas from 1796 to 1805, when was already badly affected by physical difficulties. He died in 1814.

THE PROPHETS

❶ Isaiah
The statue of Isaiah stands at the entrance to the stairs. It is thought to be the work of both Aleijadinho and his helpers. Made from two blocks of stone joined at the shoulder, there are errors in the proportions of the torso, but the magnificent head is the master's work alone.

❷ Jeremiah
To Isaiah's left sits a statue of Jeremiah. Aleijadinho sculpted only the head, giving Jeremiah an expression of serene dignity.

❸ Baruch
Considered one of the least significant works in the group, the statue of Baruch has several anatomical errors. The turban seen on this and other statues reveals the influence of European engravings of the period, where biblical figures were frequently represented in "Turkish" apparel.

❹ Ezekiel
The sculpture of Ezekiel manages to create a sense of movement and fluidity, and the expression on Ezekiel's face is arresting. Aleijadinho is believed to be solely responsible for this magnificent work.

❺ Daniel
Daniel, sculpted from one stone block, is considered the finest of the group. Not surprisingly, Aleijadinho is credited with this statue. The body is anatomically perfect, and the face is spectacularly expressive. The prostrate lion at Daniel's feet creates a feeling of power.

❻ Hosea
Opposite Daniel stands a statue of Hosea. Given the statue's noble lines and correct proportions, Hosea was probably Aleijadinho's work, with little or no help from his assistants.

❼ Joel
Head turned to the side, the prophet Joel seems to be looking out over the landscape of Monte do Maranhão. Aleijadinho probably sculpted this statue, as well.

❽ Jonah
Jonah stands opposite Joel, his face turned to heaven, lips parted, a rapturous expression upon his face. The folds of his tunic are interspersed with jets of water coming from the whale at his feet. Jonah was created by Aleijadinho.

❾ Amos
While the other prophets maintain eternally grave expressions, Amos, dressed in simple shepherd's clothing, appears calm and smiling. The sculpture shows some imperfections on the right side. The intent may have been that he would be viewed from the left side only.

❿ Obadiah
Since Obadiah occupies such a prominent position in the churchyard, it received special attention by Aleijadinho, with amazing results. The prophet's raised arm matches the vertical line of the basilica and seems to be invoking divine justice.

⓫ Habakuk
Standing opposite Obadiah, Habakuk raises his arm to heaven in a gesture of strength. Like Obadiah, this is an important figure, and therefore most likely the work of Aleijadinho with minimal help from his assistants.

⓬ Nahum
There are significant errors of proportion and alignment in the statue of Nahum. In addition, the folds of his garments are less skillfully done than those of the other prophets. Scholars believe this one is the work of Aleijadinho's apprentices.

THE SIX PASSION OF CHRIST SHRINES

❶ The Last Supper
Fifteen figures are present in this representation of Christ's last supper. Here, Jesus tells the apostles that one of them will betray him, and they react violently. It is believed that Aleijadinho himself worked on the exceptionally crafted figures.

❷ The Agony in the Garden
Jesus prays in the Garden of Gethsemane while the apostles sleep. High above, an angel offers him a cup of gall. This scene is wholly the work of Aleijadinho.

❸ Jesus is Arrested
Roman soldiers, brandishing lances and torches, approach Jesus to arrest him. The figures of Jesus and Saint Peter are by Aleijadinho, while the soldiers, mere caricatures, are the work of his assistants.

❹ The Scourging and the Crown of Thorns
These two scenes share the same small shrine. In the first scene, Jesus is tied to a low column and seems to be bearing the whip with fortitude. In the second, he looks dejected, a crown of thorns upon his head. Only the two figures of Christ are attributed to Aleijadinho.

❺ The Road to Calvary
Aleijadinho's famous masterpiece, a figure of Christ bearing the cross, is housed in this shrine. His wrinkled hands and expression of pain lend the scene extraordinary drama.

❻ The Crucifixion
In the crucifixion shrine we see Christ nailed to the cross, the very embodiment of desolation and pain. Both Jesus and the figure of the Bad Thief (on Jesus' right) are attributed to the master, who probably helped with Mary Magdalene and the Centurion, as well. This Roman soldier wears a turban similar to those seen on a number of soapstone prophets in the churchyard.

TIRADENTES

In the shadow of the **Serra de São José** sits tiny, well-preserved Tiradentes, a gem among the historical towns of Minas Gerais. Its colonial houses appear frozen in time, and the town has many charming restaurants. Sophisticated visitors come here in search of peace and quiet, and for its cultural events. Tiradentes was named after Independence movement co-conspirator Joaquim José da Silva Xavier, whose nickname, Tiradentes, means "tooth-puller." A martyr of the abortive Inconfidência Mineira revolt, he was born on Pombal Farm on the outskirts of town. Tiradentes lay forgotten after the decline in gold mining in the 19th century. Despite the fact it has been a national heritage site since 1938, it remained isolated until the 1970s, when intellectuals from Rio de Janeiro and São Paulo rediscovered it. Today the town depends on tourism; its guesthouses and hotels can accommodate up to 8,000 people, even though the town's population hovers around only 6,000. Tiradente's cobblestones demand comfortable footwear, as Tiradentes is best explored on foot.

HISTORICAL CENTER

LARGO DAS FORRAS
Former slaves gathered here in 1888 to celebrate the abolition of slavery. The square was remodeled in 1989 by landscape artist Burle Marx. Today it is the heart of town, overflowing with stores, restaurants, and guesthouses. Tiradente's **Prefeitura** (City Hall) occupies a three-story colonial building.

IGREJA MATRIZ DE SANTO ANTÔNIO
Work on the town's most important church began in 1710 and took 40 years to complete. Half a ton of gold was used for the carvings on the seven altars and the choir is decorated with gilded flower garlands gilt with the precious metal. Another highlight is the organ brought from Portuguese organ, brought here in

A stone-paved street in front of Igreja Matriz de Santo Antônio

1788, with the exterior casing, designed in Brazil, covered in rococo carvings and paintings. The sundial in the churchyard dates to 1785; it is one of the oldest historic artifacts in town. The façade was remodeled in 1810 using a design by the sculptor Aleijadinho.
Rua da Câmara, no #, Centro, tel. (32) 3355-1238. Daily, 9am – 5pm. Sound and light show: Sat, 8:30pm; Fri and Sun, 8pm.

IGREJA NOSSA SENHORA DO ROSÁRIO DOS PRETOS

This church is the town's oldest. It was built to replace a simple chapel in 1708. Inside, three altars are adorned with statues of black saints. According to legend, slaves built the church and decorated it with gold smuggled from the mines under their fingernails.
Praça Padre Lourival Salvo Rios, no #, Centro. Parish House (Casa Paroquial): tel. (32) 3355-1238. Tue – Sun, 9am – 5pm.

CHAFARIZ DE SÃO JOSÉ

The Chafariz São José, also known as the *chafariz azul* (blue fountain), is considered the most beautiful fountain in the gold region. A statue of São José de Botas graces the center, and three carved stone faces deliver drinking water that originates in the Mãe-de-Água woods at the foot of the São José Range. The Chafariz São José was built in 1749.
Rua do Chafariz, no #, Centro.

OTHER ATTRACTIONS

EVENTS

Tiradentes has a lively cultural calendar. In January the town hosts the **Mostra de Cinema** film festival. In June the streets are filled with motorcyclists attending the **Encontro de Harley Davidson**. In August the **Festival Internacional de Cultura e Gastronomia** takes center stage, bringing together chefs from Brazil and abroad for a lively celebration of food. The festival's calendar is packed with cooking shows, demonstrations, and classes. Religious and folk celebrations and processions such as **Carnival**, **Holy Week**, and **Corpus Christi** also draw significant crowds.

TRAIN RIDE

A 35 minute, 12-kilometer (7.4-mile) trip from Tiradentes on the charming *maria-fumaça*, or steam train, takes visitors to neighboring **São João del-Rei**. The train was inaugerated by Dom Pedro II in 1881. Its winding route passes through vegetation similar to Atlantic forest. In April the landscape is dotted with colorful wild flowers.
São João del-Rei Train Station (Estação Ferroviária), tel. (32) 3371-8485. Trains leave Tiradentes Fri – Sun and holidays at 9am and 5pm, and São João del Rei at 10am and 3pm.

ART AND CRAFTS

Tiradentes, with its abundance of stores and studios, is a dream come true for craft, visual art, and antique furniture aficionados. **Cuia Brasil** sells items from the heartlands of Minas Gerais (*Rua da Câmara, 83, Centro, tel. (32) 3355-1521; Sun, Mon, Wed, and Thu, 9am – 6pm; Sat, 9am – 8pm*). The studio run by **Paula Spivak** sells shawls, blankets, and rugs (*Rua Francisco Pereira de Morais, 89, Centro, tel. (32) 3355-1537; daily, 9am – 11:30am and 12:30pm – 6pm*). Detailed information about local arts and crafts can be obtained from the **Tiradentes Craft Association**, which also sells local work (*Associação dos Artesãos de Tiradentes: Largo das Forras, 120, Centro,*

A craft store in Bichinho, near Tiradentes

tel. *(32) 3355-1878; Mon – Wed, 9am – 6pm; Thu, 9am – 7pm; Fri and Sat, 9am – 8pm; Sun, 9am – 5pm)*. Antique-shoppers might want to try **Nobre Decadência**, which sells 18th- and 19th-century items from Minas Gerais, Bahia, and São Paulo *(Rua da Câmara, 78, Centro, tel. (32) 3355-1300; Mon – Fri, 9am – noon and 1:30pm – 6pm; Sat and Sun, 9am – 3pm)*. **Francisco Rodriguez** sells restored antique furniture *(Rua Direita, 166, Centro, tel. (32) 3355-1334; Mon, Wed, and Thu, 10am – 6pm; Fri and Sat, 10am – 5pm)*. For a taste of the town's artistic talent,

visit **Ballantyne's Galeria** *(Rua Direita, 26, Centro, tel. (32) 3355-2423; Mon – Wed, 10am – 1pm and 2pm – 5pm; Thu – Sat, 10am – 10pm; Sun, 10am – 2pm)*. Prices are more reasonable in neighboring towns and districts, and in some places visitors can watch artisans at work. **Bichinho**, 7 kilometers (4 miles) from Tiradentes, is home to artist Toty's workshop, **Oficina de Agosto** *(Rua São Bento, 419, tel. (32) 3353-7080; Mon – Fri, 7am – 5pm; Sat, 10am – 5pm; Sun and holidays, 10am – 3pm)*. Here, members of the local community receive artistic training. In **Prados**, 35 kilometers (22 miles) from Tiradentes, wooden animals (particularly monkeys, lions, and turtles) made by the Julião family have become a town symbol. In **Resende Costa**, also 35 kilometers (22 miles) from Tiradentes, women fuel the local economy with their hand-woven blankets, bedcovers, and tablecloths, all of which can be found in the stores on the main street.

OUR RECOMMENDATION

|O| **Tragaluz** serves traditional regional cuisine with contemporary flare. We recommend the classic *picadinho de filé* (beef in wine sauce), and the delicious guava and cream cheese dessert *(Rua Direita, 52, Centro, tel. (32) 3355-1424; Mon and Wed – Fri, 7pm – 10:30pm; Sat and Sun, 12:30pm – 4pm and 7:30pm – 12:30am)*.

Additional information on page 462.

São João del-Rei

Founded at the end of the 17th century, this town was named in honor of the king of Portugal, Dom João V. A mixture of modern and colonial architecture, São João del Rei has a very pleasant historical town center whose colonial buildings can be seen on foot.

Churches

The opulence of the baroque-style **Matriz de Nossa Senhora do Pilar** is visible in its gilt altars and the gem-encrusted statue of Saint Michael. The church was built in 1721 (*Rua Getúlio Vargas, no #, Centro tel. (32) 3371-2568; Mon, 6am – 10:30am; Tue – Sat, 8am – 10:30am and 1:30pm – 8pm; Sun, 6am – noon*). **Nossa Senhora do Carmo**, built between 1732 and 1785, has octagonal towers (*Largo do Carmo, no #, Centro, tel. (32) 3371-7996; daily, 1pm – 7pm*). In **Nossa Senhora do Rosário** a statue of the patron saint, Our Lady of the Rosary, sits on a richly carved throne. The churche was built in 1709 (*Praça Embaixador Gastão da Cunha, Largo do Rosário, no #, tel. (32) 3371-4789; Tue – Sun, 8am – 11am*). The most interesting church in town is the rococo-style **Igreja de São Francisco de Assis**. Its construction began in 1774. The lovely stone carving on the façade is the work of the sculptor Aleijadinho. Inside the church, take a moment to appreciate the Baccarat crystal chandelier that illuminates the main chapel (*Praça Frei Orlando, no #, Centro, tel. (32) 3372-3110; Mon – Sat, 8am – 5:30pm; Sun, 7am – 4pm*).

Museums

Baldwin steam engines, carriages, mechanical parts, and related photographs are exhibited at the **Museu Ferroviário**. The steam train to Tiradentes departs from here at 10am and 3pm on weekends and holidays. The oldest factory in town is the John Somers Pewter Factory; São João del-Rei was at one time a significant producer of pewter (*Avenida Hermílio Alves, 366, Centro, tel. (32) 3371-8485; Tue – Sun, 9am – 11am and 1pm – 5pm*). The **Museu do Estanho** exhibits pewter items from all over Brazil and Europe, as well as items from 17th-century shipwrecks off the Brazilian coast (*Avenida Leite de Castro, 1150, Fábricas, tel. (32) 3372-7338; Mon – Sat, 9am – 6pm; Sun, 9am – 4pm*).

A view of São João del-Rei

Our Recommendation

🍴 While in the historical town center, we recommend a stop at the **Monte Bianco** ice cream parlor (*Rua Maria Teresa, 22, tel. (32) 3371-4462; daily, 10:30am – 9pm*). The shop offers unique flavors, such as *queijo-minas* (a famous local cheese), guava, and *romeu-e-julieta*, a combination of the two.

Additional information on page 462.

Diamantina, gateway to the Jequitinhonha Valley, is known for its beautiful architecture

DIAMANTINA

For more than a century Diamantina was a major producer of diamonds. The town, located 280 kilometers (174 miles) from Belo Horizonte, is now a Unesco world heritage site. Though it is not as opulent as Ouro Preto, Diamantina is considered the best preserved and most tranquil of the historical towns of Minas Gerais.

HISTORICAL CENTER

Some of Diamantina's streets still retain their original rough stone paving. One of the best examples of this is **Beco do Mota**, a street lined by countless bars and studios. **Rua do Burgalhau**, where most of the town's oldest buildings are concentrated, is near the **Mercado Municipal** market *(Praça Barão de Guaicuí, 451, Centro; daily, 6am – 10pm).* Between 1763 and 1771, the **Casa de Chica da Silva** was the residence of Chica da Silva, a famous freed slave who became the most powerful woman in the city *(Praça Lobo de Mesquita, 266, tel. (38) 3531-2491; Tue – Sat, noon – 5pm; Sun and holidays, 8am – noon).* The **Casa de Juscelino** is far more modest. This is where former president Juscelino Kubitschek, a native of Diamantina, spent his childhood. It is an 18th-century wattle and daub building that today houses a museum with photographs and personal items belonging to him *(Rua São Francisco, 241, tel. (38) 3531-3607; Tue – Sat, 8am – 5pm; Sun, 8am – 1pm)*. The **Passadiço da Glória** is one of Diamantina's best-known landmarks. The passage connects a convent school's two buildings, one dating from colonial times, the other a more recent 19th-century addition. It is said that it was built in 1876 to protect the privacy of pupils as they crossed from one wing to another *(Rua da Glória, 297 and 298, tel. (38) 3531-1394; daily, 8am – 6pm)*.

Churches

Diamantina's most sumptuous church is **Nossa Senhora do Carmo**. Inside are beautiful ceiling paintings by Portuguese painter and Inspector General José Soares de Araújo. Local lore has it that the tower is located at the back rather than the front because the slave Chica da Silva – mistress to Crown Contractor João Fernandes de Oliveira – did not want to be disturbed by the church bells *(Rua do Carmo, no #, Centro; Tue – Sat, 8am – noon and 2pm – 6pm; Sun, 8am – noon)*. **Igreja Nossa Senhora do Rosário** has interesting leaning walls.

Inside, the ceiling paintings in the main chapel are by José Soares de Araújo *(Praça Dom Joaquim Silvério de Souza, no #, Centro, tel. (38) 9953-7409; Tue – Sat, 8am – noon and 2pm – 5:30pm; Sun, 8am – noon)*. Outside the town center, the 19th-century, neo-gothic **Basílica do Sagrado Coração de Jesus** has fine French stained-glass windows *(Praça do Sagrado Coração, 11, Largo Dom João, tel. (38) 3531-2455; Mon, 7am – 5pm; Tue – Thu, Sat and Sun, 7am – 8pm)*. **Catedral Metropolitana,** which marks the city center and stands in Praça da Matriz, was built in 1930. Its architecture clashes with that of nearby buildings.

Arts and Crafts

Several stores in Diamantina sell ceramic goods from the Jequitinhonha Valley. Many items are decorated with dried flowers, particularly *sempre-vivas* (strawflowers). Equally well-known are the *arraiolo* rugs, made in traditional Portuguese fashion from sheep's wool with jute backing. The **Cooperativa Artesanal Regional Diamantina**, a coop of approximately 100 artisans, is a good place to buy the rugs *(Rua das Bicas, 115, Serrano, tel. (38) 3531-1100; daily, 8am – 5pm)*.

SERRO

Serro, formerly known as Serro do Frio, was founded in 1702. The town became rich and powerful during the diamond boom but fell into oblivion when the mines dried up. Its rapid decline helped preserve the colonial architecture and verdant natural surroundings. Streets here are steep, so comfortable shoes are a good idea. The historical town center and Itambé Peak can be seen from the **Capela de Santa Rita**, which stands at the top of a huge stone stairway *(Praça João Pinheiro, no #, Centro)*. Lovely **Igreja Matriz de Nossa Senhora da Conceição** dates to 1776. It houses a solid silver chandelier and a large relief depicting the Holy Trinity surrounded by angles and cherubs *(Largo do Pelourinho, no #, Centro)*. Most of the churches open only for Mass, which tend to be held at irregular hours. The town's Department of Tourism (Secretaria de Turismo) can arrange visits and recommend local guides *(tel. (38) 3541-2754)*. Serro prides itself on its unique soft, white cheese, considered one of the best in Minas Gerais.

ESTRADA REAL

During the 17th-century age of explorers, a long byway was built between Paraty and the gold-mining settlements to expedite the transport of gold. The road – later known as the Caminho Real (Royal Road) – began at Vila Rica (Ouro Preto) and crossed the Serra da Mantiqueira mountain range, eventually entering a ravine that led down to Paraty. From there, the gold was transported to Rio de Janeiro, where it was loaded on ships and sent to Portugal. The journey took up to three months. In 1698 explorer Garcia Rodrigues obtained permission from the Portuguese Crown to open a new, shorter route, the Caminho Novo (New Road), which ran between Vila Rica and Rio de Janeiro via Juiz de Fora. This journey could be completed in only 25 days. The routes were both given the generic designation **Estrada Real** (Royal Highway). To encourage tourism, the **Instituto Estrada Real** *(www.estradareal.org.br)* has partnered with the government of Minas Gerais to restore the two original routes as well as a later addition known as the Rota de Diamante, which ran between Ouro Preto and Diamantina. To explore the Estrada Real is to discover the essence of Minas Gerais. As the trails wind their way through mountains, plateaus, palm-fringed waterways, rapids, and Cerrado savannah, travelers enjoy the best of the region's colonial architecture, baroque art, and adventure sports. Nearly 200 of the towns that line the highway's 1,400 kilometers (870 miles) are participating in the restoration project. Many regional paths branch off from the Estrada Real, such as the Trilha Inconfidentes, which connects 16 towns around Tiradentes, and the Circuito das Vilas e Fazendas, which connects rural accommodations around Congonhas. One extension of the Estrada Real, the Caminho de Sabarabuçu (named after the settlement that became Sabará), served as an alternative to the road that linked the Caminho Velho to the Rota do Diamante. This 180-kilometer (112-mile) route forms a loop between Ouro Preto, Sabará, and Cocais, and passes several settled areas.

ESPÍRITO SANTO

1 cm = 38 km
1 inch = 60 mi.

BAHIA — Itabuna

ESPÍRITO SANTO

Rio São Mateus

Itaúnas

Conceição da Barra

São Mateus

MINAS GERAIS

P. N. dos Pontões Capixabas

Rio Doce

Linhares

BR 101

Regência

Belo Horizonte

Santa Teresa

ES 010

Santa Maria de Jetibá

Nova Almeida

Jacaraípe

Manguinhos

Domingos Martins

Serra

Vitória

BR 262

Venda Nova do Imigrante

Vila Velha

P. N. do Caparaó

ES 060

Cachoeiro de Itapemirim

Guarapari

Anchieta

BR 101

RIO DE JANEIRO — Rio de Janeiro

ATLANTIC OCEAN

N

HIGHLIGHTS

- The beaches in and around **Vitória**.
- Surfing and diving on the beach in **Guarapari**.
- The trails and farms of the **Serra Capixaba** mountain range.
- The *forró* music in **Itaúnas** and the dunes just outside it.

WHEN TO GO

- In **November** for *Vital*, Vitória's out-of-season Carnival.
- **Mid-January through the end of March** for diving in Guarapari.
- In the **summer** for rafting on the Jucu River in the mountains around Domingos Martins.
- In **July** for *forró* music festivals in Itaúnas, or **January through March** to witness sea turtles hatching on the town's beaches.

Sunset over the bay in Vitória, a city comprised of 34 islands and part of the mainland

VITÓRIA

Vitória is the capital of and largest island in Espírito Santo state. Created in 1551, it is comprised of 34 islands in all, as well as a mainland area. The city's historic buildings are concentrated in **Cidade Alta** (Upper City). Immediately outside the city are numerous beaches, mangrove swamps, Atlantic forest reserves, and two important ports: **Tubarão** and **Vitória**. Water sports, especially blue marlin fishing, draw many visitors. **Vital**, a lively out-of-season Carnival enjoyed by thousands, takes place in November.

HISTORICAL CENTER

The historical town center is easily explored on foot. We suggest you begin at **Palácio Anchieta**, a 16th-century Jesuit college that became the seat of state government in 1760 *(Praça João Clímaco, no #, tel. (27) 3321-3608)*. Behind the palace is the **symbolic tomb of José de Anchieta**, a famous Jesuit priest who spent his final years in Anchieta, Espírito Santo. In front of the palace is the neo-classical **Escadaria Bárbara Lindemberg**. The staircase is one of many linking Cidade Baixa (Lower City) to Cidade Alta (Upper City). **Igreja de São Gonçalo** is a baroque-style church built between 1707 and 1715. The sanctuary has limestone baptismal fonts and statues from the 18th and 19th centuries *(Rua Cosme Rolim, no #, tel. (27) 3233-2856; Tue – Sun, 9am – 5pm)*. Rua São Gonçalo is the most direct route from the palace to the church. Go back a little until Rua Muniz Freire, which leads to **Capela Santa Luzia** *(no #, tel. (27) 3222-3219)*, on Rua José Marcelino. The chapel, one of the oldest buildings in Vitória, was built in the 1500s. Its frontispiece was partially altered in the 18th century, and the altar was modified in the 19th century. Santa Luzia closed for restorations in March 2008 and it is not clear when it will reopen. On the same street, at number 203, stand a fine pair of **19th-century townhouses.** Nearby in Praça Dom Luís Scortegagna square stands the neo-gothic **Catedral Metropolitana**

① Palácio Anchieta
② Igreja de São Gonçalo
③ Capela Santa Luzia
④ Catedral Metropolitana
⑤ Teatro Carlos Gomes

(tel. (27) 3223-0590; daily, 8am – 7pm).
Construction of the cathedral began in 1920 and wasn't completed until 1970. From the square, stroll down **Escadaria São Diogo**, then turn on **Praça Costa Pereira**. Here you will find **Teatro Carlos Gomes** *(tel. (27) 3132-8396; daily, 7am – 6pm; visits must be arranged in advance).* The theater, built in 1927, was inspired by the famous La Scala opera house in Milan.

BEACHES AND MANGROVES

Vitória's most peaceful beaches are **Praia das Castanheiras**, on Ilha do Frade island, and **Praia da Direita** and **Praia da Esquerda**, on Ilha do Boi island. Back on the mainland, **Praia Camburi** has kiosks and sports facilities for beachgoers. **Praia do Canto** is also a popular destination for water sports enthusiasts. Nearby **Praça dos Namorados** hosts a crafts fair on

---

PRAIA DE MANGUINHOS AND ENVIRONS

Rodovia do Sol connects Vitória to several towns and villages to the north. Manguinhos, Jacaraípe, and Nova Almeida are all approximately 30 kilometers (19 miles) from the city. Manguinhos is known for its white sands and gentle waves. Visitors can enjoy seafood in the gardens of the **Estação Primeira de Manguinhos** restaurant *(Avenida Atapuã, no #, tel. (27) 3243-2687; Nov – Mar and Jul: Tue – Sun, 10am – 5pm; reservations are required for evening meals).* Jacaraípe has a beach, but it's built up and very busy. Artist Neuso Ribeiro exhibits sculptures made from tree roots and other wood at **Casa de Pedra** *(Rua Nossa Senhora de Lourdes, no #, tel. (27) 3252-6029; daily, 8am – 6pm).* Twelve kilometers farther north, in Nova Almeida, there is a 16th-century Jesuit complex that looks much the same today as it did over 400 years ago. The complex, **Igreja e Residência dos Reis Magos**, houses a wooden altarpiece with carvings of plants and animals that was made in India. There is also a painting of the Magi thought to be the oldest oil-on-wood painting in the country *(Praça dos Reis Magos, no #, tel. (27) 3253-1842; Tue – Sun, 9am – 5pm).*

Saturday and Sunday evenings starting at 5pm. There are a number of bars and restaurants on **Praça dos Desejos**, and **Praça da Ciência** has exhibits that demonstrate a number of scientific principles *(Avenida Américo Buaiz, no #, tel. (27) 3345-0882; Tue – Sat and holidays, 8am – noon and 2pm – 6pm; Sun, 2pm – 6pm)*. At night, city youth flock to **Curva da Jurema** for music and dancing. In addition to its beaches, Vitória has an area teeming with marine fauna and flora, an 892-hectare (2,204-acre) mangrove swamp that can be visited during a schooner trip. The two-hour excursion begins at the **Cais do Hidroavião** *(Avenida Dario Lourenço de Sousa, no #, Santo Antônio)* and takes in the marine life reserve **Estação Ecológica Ilha do Lameirão**, the island **Ilha das Caieiras**, the **Santo Antônio** neighborhood, and the mouth of the **Rio Jucu**.
Contact: Agência Náutica Cores do Mar, tel. (27) 3222-3810. Departures Wed – Sun, 10am and 3pm.

THE PANELEIRAS

The local seafood stew known as *moqueca capixaba*, unlike a similar dish served in Bahia, is not made with *dendê* oil. Here it is cooked in traditional clay pots *(panelas)* that are sold by women *(paneleiras)* from the **Associação das Paneleiras de Goiabeiras**. The *paneleiras* continue a 400-year-old cultural tradition. In a large shed on the edge of the mangrove swamp, they prepare the clay, model the cooking vessels, and fire them. They then apply tannin, a dye made from tree bark, which gives the pots their characteristic black color.
Rua das Paneleiras, 55, Goiabeiras, tel. (27) 3327-0519. Mon – Sat and holidays, 8:30am – 6:30pm.

OCEAN FISHING

The coast between Vitória and Guarapari is one of the best places in the world to catch billfish. These waters have also produced two world sport-fishing records: a 636-kilo (1,402-pound) blue marlin and an 82.5-kilo (182-pound) white marlin. Boats with crew and equipment are available for hire. *Contact: Dolphin Pesca Oceânica, tel. (27) 3345-9455; Espírito Santo Yacht Club (Iate Clube do Espírito Santo), tel. (27) 3225-0422.*

Aerial view of the mouth of the Rio Jucu, in Vila Velha

Vila Velha, connected to the state capital by Terceira Ponte bridge

VILA VELHA

Vila Velha lies across the Terceira Ponte bridge, 3.3 kilometers (2 miles) from Vitória. The village has several old buildings and a number of nice beaches. On **Praia da Costa** beach there is a promenade and a path for cyclists. **Praia de Itapuã** is nearby. Both get very crowded in the summer. **Barra do Jucu** is long, good for surfing, and famous for its congo drums. The drums are a local folk tradition. If you long for peace and quiet, however, **Ponta da Fruta** is your best bet.

CONVENTO DA PENHA

The convent enjoys a panoramic view of Vitória from its vantage point atop a 154-meter (505-foot) hill. It was founded in 1558, but the current structure was built in the mid-18th century. The church is home to *Nossa Senhora das Alegrias*, one of the oldest paintings of the Virgin in the Americas. Four early 20th-century works by São Paulo painter Benedito Calixto hang in one of the aisles.
Access from Rua Vasco Coutinho, no #, tel. (27) 3329-0420. Daily, 5:30am – 5pm.

PRAINHA AND ENVIRONS

Parque da Prainha stands at the foot of the hill below Convento da Penha. From the park you can see 16th-century **Igreja Nossa Senhora do Rosário**. The church is the oldest in the state. Its walls, windows, and doors are the originals. The frontispiece, on the other hand, is a product of the 18th century *(Praça da Bandeira, no #, tel. (27) 3239-3113; Mon – Fri, 7am – 11am and 2pm – 5pm, advance notice required; Sat, 8am – 11am; Mass: Sat, 8am and 5:30pm; first Friday of the month, 7pm).* **Forte de São Francisco Xavier**, an early 16th-century fort, has also been modified over time *(Parque da Prainha, no #, tel. (27) 3229-3838; Mon – Fri, 8am – noon and 1:30pm – 4pm; Sat, Sun, and holidays, 8am – noon).* **Farol de Santa Luzia**, a 12-meter (40-foot) lighthouse at Ponta de Santa Luzia, has guided ships into port since 1870 *(Rua Santa Luzia, 2, Praia da Costa, tel. (27) 3139-9980; Sat, Sun, and holidays, 9am – 4:30pm; advance bookings required).*

Guarapari: good diving amid much beach-front development

GUARAPARI

From Vitória, the beach resort town of Guarapari is a 59-kilometer (37-mile) drive south on Rodovia do Sol. The emerald-green waters of popular beaches like **Praia das Castanheiras**, **Praia dos Namorados**, and **Praia da Areia Preta** are a beautiful sight despite the wall of buildings lining the shore. Farther south is **Praia de Meaípe**, a popular nightspot. To the north, many beaches have yet to encounter commercial development and noise. Surfers tend to head to **Três Praias** and **Setiba Pina**. **Praia dos Padres**, to

the south of the aforementioned beaches, is framed by large boulders and almond trees. A 2.4-kilometer (1.4-mile) trail leads from **Parque Paulo César Pinha** to Lagoa de Caraís, a lake with unappealing brown water that is nonetheless good for swimming *(Rodovia do Sol, Km 37.5, Setiba, tel. (27) 3242-3665; daily, 8:30am – 5pm).*

DIVING

The sea around Guarapari is rich with marine life, and is therefore a great spot

ANCHIETA

The beaches of Anchieta are generally serene. **Ubu** and **Parati** are two such stretches. **Iriri** has slightly more traffic. Anchieta is also home to the **Santuário e Museu de Anchieta** church and museum *(Praça da Matriz, no #, tel. (28) 3536-1103; daily, 9am – 5pm).* The church, built in 1569, was altered by Franciscans in the 18th century, but work completed in

1997 restored it to its original form. An on-site archaeological dig has revealed the ruins of a residence built around the same time as the original church. The residence had oyster lime walling that was mixed coral rock. The cell where Jesuit priest José de Anchieta spent his final years now houses a piece of his tibia. The church museum displays religious art and

documents related to the priest. Anchieta is honored with a four day pilgrimage every June known as the **Passos de Anchieta** *(tel. (27) 3227-2661, www.trilhaum.com.br).* The pilgrimage is a 100-kilometer (62-mile) walk along the coast between Vitória and Anchieta that traces the route Anchieta regularly walked in the 16th century.

for scuba diving. Shoals of angelfish, butterfly fish, sea horses, spider crabs, octopus, moray eels, coral, and sponges create a vibrant underwater world. The most popular island diving spots are **Ilha Escalvada**, **Ilha Rasas**, and **Três Ilhas**. There are also two dive sites around sunken ships: the *Beluccia*, shipwrecked in 1903, and the *Victory 8B*, which was intentionally sunk in 2003 to create an artificial reef. The best time to visit is between mid-January and late April, when average visibility is 15 to 20 meters.

OUR RECOMMENDATION

🍽 Meaípe is home to one of the best places to experience regional cuisine. Simple, unpretentious **Cantinho do Curuca** restaurant serves traditional *moqueca* fish stew with rice, *pirão* (thickened sauce), and plantains *(Avenida Santana, 96, tel. (27) 3272-2009; daily, 11am – 10pm).*

Additional information on page 462.

Contact: Atlantes, tel. (27) 3361-0405, www.atlantes.com.br; Acquasub (in Vitória), tel. (27) 3325-0036, www.acquasub.com.br.

SERRA CAPIXABA

DOMINGOS MARTINS

Just 50 kilometers (31 miles) from the sun-and-sand atmosphere of Vitória is the Serra Capixaba mountain range, an adventure sports destination. The area is home to descendents of German and Italian immigrants. Some of these individuals still produce the cheese and sausages of their ancestors. Rodovia BR-262 highway leads to the town of Domingos Martins, where you will find

Igreja Luterana, a Lutheran church that is part of the legacy of German colonization *(Praça Artur Gerhardt, no #, tel. (27) 3268-1177; services: Sun, 9am; other visits must be arranged in advance).* The town's restaurants and stores are concentrated along Rua João Batista Wernersback, which is called **Rua de Lazer** ("leisure street"). Flower lovers won't want to miss a visit to **Reserva e**

European architectural influences in Domingos Martins

Orquidário Kautsky. The best time to see the reserve's orchids is October. It's easy to get to the orchidarium, but the private reserve can only be accessed in a 4×4 vehicle *(Rua Roberto Carlos Kautsky, 234, tel. (27) 3268-1209; Mon – Fri, 7am – 10am and 2pm – 5pm).*

Parque Estadual da Pedra Azul

Pedra Azul (Blue Rock), the 1,822-meter-high (5,978-foot) massif that gives the park its name, is located in the Aracê district. The park has three trails. Two of them – Trilha do Lagarto and Trilha da Pedra Azul – are easy, half mile strolls. The third is approximately 2 kilometers (1 mile) round-trip and requires ropes to navigate past one stretch of the trail. It passes natural rock pools and a profusion of orchids and bromeliads. On clear days it's possible to see the Serra do Caparaó mountain range on the Minas Gerais State border. *Rodovia BR-262, Km 89, Aracê, tel. (27) 3136-3470. Walks: Wed and Sun, 9am and 1:30pm, in two groups of up to 25 people. Visits must be arranged in advance.*

Adventures in the Mountains

The **Rio Jucu** and its rapids are excellent for rafting. During the summer the rapids can reach a level 4 designation. Special outings on moonlit nights are available. Along quiet stretches you can try *bóia-cross* (floating downriver in a tube), and children can try rafting. Agencies offer hiking and rappelling trips to places like **Cascata do Galo** (a 55-meter waterfall) and the 'railway track' (a free descent of approximately 40 meters).
Contact: Emoções Radicais, tel. (27) 3268-2165, www.emocoesradicais.com.br; Rio da Montanha (rafting and rappelling), tel. (27) 3268-1765, 9983-7902, www.riodamontanha.com.br.

Venda Nova do Imigrante

Venda Nova do Imigrante is a food- and craft-loving tourist's dream come true. Here vendors sell tasty cheeses, coffee, jellies, *cachaças*, and *socol* (pork sausage), as well as flowers and crafts made from bamboo, wood, and coffee. The town is 68 kilometers (42 miles) from Domingos Martins and 107 kilometers (66 miles) from Vitória. Many of its citizens are descendents of Italian immigrants who settled here in the late 19th century. Some accommodate visitors on their rural properties along the Rodovia Pedro Cola. In town, the **Agrotur** store sells regional products *(Avenida Evandi Américo Comarela, no #, Centro, tel. (28) 3546-2317; daily, 8am – 5pm).* The mountain scenery around Venda Nova do Imigrante invites leisurely walks. One trail leads to **Cachoeira do Caxixe**, a 60-meter (197-foot) waterfall. It also provides a beautiful view of Pedra Azul.

ECOLOGICAL RESERVE IN LINHARES

To visit **Reserva Natural da Vale do Rio Doce** is to fully appreciate the beauty of the Atlantic forest. The reserve is located in Linhares, 137 kilometers (85 miles) north of Vitória. The reserve encompasses 22,000 hectares (54 acres) of forest, but only 1% of this is affected by research and visitors. Two guided walks, each lasting an hour, explore the region's diversity. A third walking tour demonstrates how seedlings are produced, but it only runs when there is a group of ten or more people who express interest. Coatis and capuchin monkeys are often seen during the walks. The visitor's center has a gift shop, cafeteria, and an exhibition on the Atlantic forest. *Rodovia BR-101, Km 120, Linhares, tel. (27) 3371-9700. Tue – Sun, 7:30am – 3:30pm. Guided walks, limited to twenty people, leave at regular intervals.*

Itaúnas: nature, folk festivals, and plenty of forró music

ITAÚNAS

The modest homes and guesthouses of Itaúnas, 270 kilometers (168 miles) north of Vitória, contribute to its image as a sleepy village. Itaúnas is very popular with university students, however, who flock here during the summer. Visitors can dance *forró*, unwind with a stroll along a beach, or explore the dunes and *restinga* vegetation of the **Parque Estadual de Itaúnas** nature reserve. Most folk festivals take place in January, including Ticumbi, which honors Saint Benedict. In January, February, and March baby turtles hatch on the beaches, a nocturnal event overseen by the **Projeto Tamar** turtle protection organization *(tel. (27) 3762-5196)*. January is also when the town hosts several *forró* music festivals, including the **Festival Nacional do Forró**. Dancing generally begins at midnight and continues through sunup. To reach Itaúnas from Vitória, follow Rodovia BR-101 highway northbound to São Mateus, then turn on Rodovia ES-421 highway. After 14 kilometers, turn onto Rodovia ES-010 highway. The village is a 23-kilometer (15-mile) drive on dirt road. It has no bank or gas station, so fill up in Conceição da Barra, at the end of Rodovia ES-421 highway.

PARQUE ESTADUAL DE ITAÚNAS
If you cross the bridge over the Rio Itaúnas at the far end of the village you will find yourself in Itaúnas State Park. The park protects almost 3,700 hectares (9,143 acres) of dunes, beaches, mangroves, and wetlands. The gentle **Rio Itaúnas** and its tributary, the **Rio Angelim**, are excellent spots for canoeing or kayaking. The park's trails pass through lush vegetation and skirt the ruins of the old village of Itaúnas, which was buried by shifting dunes in the 1970s. A dune buggy is available to take visitors to the cliffs at **Praia de Costa Dourada**, in Bahia. It's also fun to go horseback riding along the beach between Itaúnas and deserted **Praia de Riacho Doce** beach. *Visitor's Center (Centro de Visitantes): Avenida José Basílio (formerly Bento Daher), no #, tel. (27) 3762-5196. Daily, 8am – 5:30pm. Jan – Mar and Jul, open till 9pm.* **Contact:** *Casinha de Aventuras, Avenida José Basílio, no #, tel. (27) 3762-5081.*

THE NORTHEAST

Brazil's Northeast, best known for its stunning beaches, is comprised of the states of Bahia, Paraíba, Sergipe, Alagoas, Rio Grande do Norte, Pernambuco, Ceará, Piauí, and Maranhão. The federal highway system connects the region's coastal capitals and traverses stretches of spectacular natural beauty. Sophisticated hotels and restaurants rub shoulders with simple guesthouses and untamed wilderness areas. On the coast, tiny fishing villages attract tourists and city dwellers alike, enchanting them with natural simplicity and the beauty of dunes, cliffs, and the sea. Inland, the town of Lençóis serves as a starting point for exploration of the Chapada Diamantina plateau and its waterfalls, caves, and canyons. The Northeast, however, offers more than beautiful scenery. Its towns hold a wealth of historical, cultural, and architectural heritage. The arid, storied inland region, known as the *sertão*, has a vibrant, unique culture that embraces Brazil's dynamic heritage. It is home to huge folk festivals, extraordinary arts and crafts, remarkable architecture, and a rich culinary tradition.

BAHIA

- Trips to the architectural and cultural attractions of Pelourinho, **Salvador**.
- The cosmopolitan beaches of **Morro de São Paulo, Trancoso,** and **Itacaré**.

- The unspoiled sands of **Maraú, Ilha de Boipeba**, and **Caraíva**.
- Walks, caves, and waterfalls in **Chapada Diamantina**.
- Diving and whale watching in **Abrolhos**.

WHEN TO GO

- Beaches are beautiful **year-round**. In the summer (December to February), however, the towns are crowded and prices high.
- During **Carnival** for fun among the lively crowds.

- In **January** for Salvador's festivities in honor of Senhor do Bonfim.
- **May through September** for diving in Abrolhos, where visibility can reach 20 meters (65 feet).

SALVADOR

Capital of Bahia and home to 2.6 million residents, the city of Salvador is the epicenter of Afro-Brazilian culture. The city's largely Afro-Brazilian population maintains their religious and cultural traditions, including the largest street carnival in Brazil. Salvador was founded in 1549, and was the nation's first capital. In the 18th century it was the largest city in South America. Since then, from the top of the two 70-meter (230-foot) bluffs that divide the upper and lower sides of the city, it has watched over the ships in **Baía de Todos os Santos** (All Saints Bay). The city's main tourist attractions are clustered in the **Bonfim** and **Barra** neighborhoods. **Pelourinho**, with its charming old buildings and churches, is in Cidade Alta (Upper City). Cidade Baixa (Lower City) has 30 kilometers (19 miles) of city beaches. Note that it's not safe to walk around Cidade Baixa or any poorly lit area at night.

PELOURINHO

Pelourinho, in the heart of Cidade Alta, was home to Salvador's 18th-century upper class. By the 19th century, however, high society abandoned the area and Pelourinho became the haunt of criminals and prostitutes. Today Pelourinho is once more on the up and up, embracing its role as Salvador's cultural center and overflowing with stores, bars, and restaurants. With nearly eight hundred 18th- and 19th- century buildings still standing, it's no wonder the district is a Unesco World Heritage site. One day is hardly enough time to explore **Largo do Pelourinho**, the old district center, where the whipping post (*pelourinho*) that inspired Pelourinho's name stood until the 19th century. We recommend a leisurely stroll through the neighborhood's steep, stone-paved side

Part of Brazil's history is preserved in Pelourinho's historic buildings

Map labels:
PILAR
R. DA NORUEGA
LGO. DO CAIS DO OURO
R. DA ESPANHA
LD. DO CARMO
AV. DR. JOSÉ JOAQUIM SEABRA
R. MQ. DE BARBACENA
PEDRO JULIO BARBUDA
LGO. DO PELOURINHO
R. DA SAÚDE
SAÚDE
PÇA. CONDE DOS ARCOS
R. ALFREDO DE BRITO
R. DO FERRÃO
R. G. DE MATOS
R. DO GENIPAPEIRO
PELOURINHO
Uauá
R. DA FRANÇA
AV. DA FRANÇA
R. MIGUEL CALMON
R. CONS. LAFAYETE
Jardim das Delícias
R. DAS LARANJEIRAS
R. FONTE NOVA DO DESTERRO
TERREIRO DE JESUS
R. DA ORDEM
R. DE S. FRANCISCO
LD. DA ORDEM 3ª
LD. DE S. FRANCISCO
LD. DA PRATA
PÇA. INGLATERRA
AV. ESTADOS UNIDOS
LG. CRUZEIRO DE S. FRANCISCO
Maria Mata Mouro
R. S. FRANCISCO
AV. DR. J. J. SEABRA
LD. DE SANTANA
LD. DO DESTERRO
R. DO GRAVATÁ
COMÉRCIO
R. CORPO SANTO
R. BÉLGICA
PÇA. TOMÉ DE SOUZA
LD. DA PRAÇA
PÇA. DOS VETERANOS
R. DO GRAVATÁ
R. DO TINGUI
PÇA. VISC. DE CAIRU
R. TIRA CHAPEU
R. DA PALMA
R. DA INDEPENDÊNCIA
AV. DAS NAUS
AV. CONTORNO
R. CONCEIÇÃO DA PRAIA
R. DA MONTANHA
R. DA MISERICÓRDIA
R. JOSÉ GONÇALVES
R. DA AJUDA
R. DO TESOURO
R. RUI BARBOSA
TR. ENG. ALIONE
LD. DO BANGALA
R. F. DO GRAVATÁ
N

CIDADE ALTA (UPPER CITY)

1. Igreja and Convento de São Francisco
2. Igreja da Ordem Terceira de São Francisco
3. Igreja da Ordem Terceira de São Domingos de Gusmão
4. Catedral Basílica
5. Museu Afro-Brasileiro and Museu de Arqueologia e Etnologia
6. Museu Udo Knoff de Azulejaria e Cerâmica
7. Museu Tempostal
8. Museu Abelardo Rodrigues
9. Museu da Cidade
10. Fundação Casa de Jorge Amado
11. Igreja Nossa Senhora do Rosário dos Pretos
12. Igreja da Ordem Terceira do Carmo

CIDADE BAIXA (LOWER CITY)

13. Mercado Modelo
14. Igreja Nossa Senhora da Conceição da Praia
15. Solar do Unhão
16. Elevador Lacerda

---

streets. Keep an eye on your belongings, however. Despite the significant police presence, Pelourinho attracts pickpockets.

1 IGREJA AND CONVENTO DE SÃO FRANCISCO

São Francisco Church and Convent is one of the world's most extraordinary baroque monuments. It is also the most lavishly gilded church in Brazil. Eight hundred kilos (1,756 pounds) of gold were used to gild its woodcarvings, and beautiful blue tiles depict scenes from the life of Saint Francis of Assisi. A statue of São Pedro de Alcântara graces one of the side altars, the work of a talented local sculptor, Manoel Inácio da Costa. The tile murals on the ground floor of the cloisters were inspired by Flemish drawings. The Latin inscriptions are from the works of Horace, a rare example of secular classical influence in a Catholic church.

Construction of the complex, which began in 1686, took 64 years to complete. *Largo do Cruzeiro de São Francisco, no #, Pelourinho, tel. (71) 3322-6430. Mon and Wed – Sun, 8am – 11am and noon – 4pm. Mass: Tue, 7am, 8am, 3pm, 4pm, 5pm, 6pm.*

Several of the tile murals in the Convento de São Francisco depict Lisbon before the earthquake of 1755

❷ IGREJA DA ORDEM TERCEIRA DE SÃO FRANCISCO

Ordem Terceira de São Francisco first opened its doors in 1703. The church and nearby São Francisco Church and Convent make an impressive architectural ensemble. The lime and sandstone façade was constructed in the ornate, "plateresque" baroque style of the Spanish colonies. It is the only one of its kind in Brazil. Most of the church's tile murals depict scenes of Lisbon before the 1755 earthquake, including scenes from the wedding celebrations of Dom José, son of Dom João V.

Rua da Ordem Terceira (formerly Rua Inácio Accioli), no #, Pelourinho, tel. (71) 3321-6968. Daily, 8am – 5pm.

❸ IGREJA DA ORDEM TERCEIRA DE SÃO DOMINGOS DE GUSMÃO

Many visitors come to the church to view the allegorical depiction of São Domingos' entry into heaven on the ave ceiling. Artist José Joaquim da Rocha painted it in 1781. He is also responsible for the murals in the main room. Church construction began in 1731 and the façade still retains its rococo lines. The

carvings that originally graced the interior, on the other hand, have been replaced by neoclassical works.

Praça 15 de Novembro, no #, Terreiro de Jesus, Pelourinho, tel. (71) 3242-4185. Mon – Thu, 9am – noon and 2pm – 6pm; Sun, 8am – 10am.

❹ CATEDRAL BASÍLICA

Colégio de Jesus church, where Brazil's 17th-century foremost literary figure Padre Antônio Vieira gave important political sermons, was built by the Jesuits between 1657 and 1672 to replace a pre-existing 16th-century wattle-and-daub church. The basilica's distinctive white limestone walls came to Brazil as ballast aboard Portuguese ships. The twin-tower Portuguese façade is a blend of the Jesuit architectural tradition and unique spiral scrollwork, while the interior combines baroque and rococo styles. It is well worth taking a close look at the jacaranda chest encrusted with ivory, bone, and tortoiseshell, the paintings on copper in the sacristy, and the reliquary busts on the altar, which are dedicated to Saint Ursula.

Praça 15 de Novembro, no #, Terreiro de Jesus, Pelourinho, tel. (71) 3321-4573.

Mon – Sat, 8:30am – 11:30am and
1:30pm – 5:30pm; Sun, 9am and 6pm.

**❺ MUSEU AFRO-BRASILEIRO E MUSEU
DE ARQUEOLOGIA E ETNOLOGIA**
The Afro-Brazilian Museum and the
Museum of Archeology and Ethnology
share a building that housed Brazil's first
medical school in 1833. The Afro-
Brazilian Museum collection includes
maps of routes taken by the first slave
ships, a beautiful collection of African
orixá statues, and 27 cedar panels
depicting Candomblé rituals and deities
carved by Carybé (1911-97). The
Museum of Archeology and Ethnology
displays artifacts from archaeological sites
in Bahia, as well as objects and
photographs connected to the local
indigenous population.
*Praça 15 de Novembro, no # , Terreiro de Jesus,
Pelourinho, tel. (71) 3321-2013. Mon – Fri,
9am – 6pm; Sat and Sun, 10am – 5pm.*

**❻ MUSEU UDO KNOFF DE
AZULEJARIA E CERÂMICA**
The Udo Knoff ceramics museum
displays sections of Brazilian and European
mansion façades. Some date to the 16th
century. The collection, unique in Latin
America, includes the work of its founder,
the German ceramic artist Udo Knoff.
The museum offers ceramics workshops.
*Rua Frei Vicente, 3, Pelourinho, tel. (71)
3117-6388. Tue – Fri, 10am – 6pm; Sat
and Sun, 1pm – 5pm.*

❼ MUSEU TEMPOSTAL
The *tempostal* ("postcard temple")
houses over 35,000 postcards and
photographs from Brazil and other
countries. It was created by Antônio
Marcelino do Nascimento in the 1940s
and later became the property of the
state of Bahia. Today, the collection
bears witness to the historical
transformations experienced by
Salvador and other Brazilian cities.
*Rua Gregório de Matos, 33, Pelourinho, tel.
(71) 3117-6383. Tue – Fri, 10am – 6pm;
Sat and Sun, 1pm – 6pm.*

❽ MUSEU ABELARDO RODRIGUES
The Abelardo Rodrigues museum houses
one of the most valuable collections of
sacred art in the country, the bequest

The sacristy of the Catedral Basílica, whose interior blends baroque and rococo styles

of Abelardo Rorigues (1908-71). The museum's building, the Solar do Ferrão, was originally an 18th-century Jesuit seminary. Statues, engravings, and precious metal objects are on display. *Rua Gregório de Matos, 45, Pelourinho, tel. (71) 3117-6381. Tue – Fri, 10am – 6pm; Sat and Sun 1pm – 6pm.*

⑨ MUSEU DA CIDADE

The city museum's eclectic collection includes statues, votive offerings, paintings, tapestries, and sculptures by local artists, as well as items related to the Candomblé religious tradition, including papier-mâché Candomblé deities by Alecy Azevedo. One room is dedicated to the poet Castro Alves, another to traditional *bruxas de pano* (rag witch dolls).

OUR RECOMMENDATION

🍽 The **Convento do Carmo,** which served as a barracks for the Dutch military in 1624, is now one of the largest luxury hotels in Brazil. The hotel is run by the Pousadas de Portugal guesthouse chain, which has seen to it that the building's 17th- and 18th-century architectural features remain intact. Restaurante Conventual welcomes guests and non-guests alike, allowing the latter an opportunity to admire the decorative adornments of the main lobby *(Rua do Carmo, 1, Santo Antônio, tel. (71) 3327-8400).*

Additional information on page 462.

Largo do Pelourinho, no #, Pelourinho, tel. (71) 3321-1967. Mon – Fri, noon – 6pm.

⑩ FUNDAÇÃO CASA DE JORGE AMADO

Admirers of famed writer Jorge Amado (1912-2001) will enjoy a visit to the Jorge Amado Foundation center, which sells his work and hosts exhibitions, classes, and cultural events. The foundation's collection contains videos, photographs, and awards Amado received during his career. Foreign editions of his books, which have been translated into 50 languages, decorate the walls of the center's cafe, Café Teatro Zélia Gattai. *Largo do Pelourinho, no #, Pelourinho, tel. (71) 3321-0070. Mon – Sat, 10am – 6pm.*

⑪ IGREJA NOSSA SENHORA DO ROSÁRIO DOS PRETOS

Every Tuesday at 6pm a different kind of Mass draws worshipers to Largo do Pelourinho square. Hymns fill the church, but with African rhythms supplied by percussion instruments. The church is a true expression of Bahia's syncretism, the fusion of two distinct cultural traditions. Senhora do Rosário dos Pretos was the patron saint of slaves, and the church was built by a brotherhood of men of African descent. It took almost the entire 18th century to complete the church, since slaves could only work on the building during rare hours off.

ICE CREAM TO BATTLE THE HEAT

The oldest ice cream parlor in Salvador, **A Cubana,** first opened its doors in 1940. They serve regional fruit flavors like *graviola* and *cupuaçu* paired with a small chocolate nut cake. There are two branches *(Rua Alfredo de Brito, 12, Pelourinho, tel. (71) 3321-6162; Sun – Thu, 9am – 10pm; Fri and Sat, 9am – midnight;* *Praça Tomé de Souza, 1, upper part of Elevador Lacerda, tel. (71) 3322-7000; Mon and Wed, 8am – 10:20pm; Tue and Thu – Sun, 8am – midnight).* Le Glacier **Laporte** has forty flavors to choose from, including pepper with nutmeg *(Largo do Cruzeiro de São Francisco, 21, Pelourinho, tel. (71) 3266-3649; daily, 10am – 9pm).* Enjoy the sunset on the Ponta do Humaitá bridge that much more with ice cream from **Sorveteria da Ribeira,** which has stood on the beach of the same name since 1931. The fifty flavors include tapioca and fruits like *mangaba* and *cajá (Rua Belo Horizonte, 102, Jardim Brasil, tel. (71) 3264-6552; daily, 7am – 10:30pm).*

CAPOEIRA

Capoeira is a culturally significant, uniquely Brazilian sport, a blend of martial arts, dance, and ritual brought to Brazil by African slaves. Capoeira movements are particularly popular in Bahia, Rio de Janeiro, and Pernambuco. *Ginga* is the fundamental capoeira movement. It is comprised of evasive ducks, offensive strikes, counter blows, and flourishes. The movements are accompanied by instruments, including the *berimbau, pandeiro,* and *atabaque* and by litanies or laments in a four verse structure. The verses can be prayers, warnings, thanks, challenges, or homages. Over the course of the 19th century, *capoeira*, then less acrobatic and more physical fell from favor and was banned in 1890. It survived in secret nonetheless. In 1932, Manuel dos Reis Machado (1900-74), more popularly known as Mestre Bimba, founded the Centro de Cultura Física (Center for Physical Culture) in Salvador. His clever choice of a name circumvented the capoeira ban, and under his direction "physical culture" flourished, further developing *capoeira* by incorporating new techniques and movements from other martial art forms. In 1937, he gave a performance for President Getúlio Vargas. Legend has it that it was this experience that led the president to revoke the ban. In 1942 the Centro Esportivo de Capoeira Angola (Angola Sports and Capoeira Center) was created under the leadership of Vicente Ferreira Pastinha (1889-1981), also known as Mestre Pastinha. His style, characterized by a relatively slow speed and movements closer to the ground, was similar to the capoeira tradition originally practiced by slaves. Today both styles are popular, and new generations are carrying the sport forward. Bimba's son, Mestre Nenel, founded the **Fundação Mestre Bimba**, which supports the **Escola de Capoeira Filhos de Bimba** school. Open performances (which allow visiting *capoeira* enthusiasts to participate) are held at 11am every Saturday *(Rua Gregório de Matos, 51, basement, Pelourinho, tel. (71) 3322-5082).* The **Associação de Capoeira Mestre Bimba** hosts exhibitions every Tuesday, Friday, and Saturday at 7pm, as well as open performances on Thursdays at 8pm *(Rua das Laranjeiras, 1, 1st floor and ground floor, Pelourinho, tel. (71) 3322-0639).* Two of Pastinha's former apprentices, Mestre João Pequeno and Mestre Morais, have converted Forte Santo Antônio Além do Carmo fort into an Angolan-style *capoeira* center, the **Centro Esportivo de Capoeira Angola.** The center hosts exhibitions every Tuesday, Thursday, and Saturday at 7:30pm, and every Sunday at 5pm. In addition, the **Grupo de Capoeira Angola Pelourinho** (GCAP) hosts exhibitions on Sundays at 7pm *(Forte da Capoeira, Largo de Santo Antônio, Além do Carmo, no #, Santo Antônio, tel. (71) 3243-3518).*

Praça José de Alencar, no #, Pelourinho, tel. (71) 3326-9701. Daily, 8:30am – 6pm.

⑫ IGREJA DA ORDEM TERCEIRA DO CARMO

A steep side street leads to Ordem Terceira do Carmo church. The structure was rebuilt in the rococo style in the 19th century after a fire damaged the original building in 1786. Although it is currently in a poor state of repair, the church is worth a visit if only to see the magnificent cedar statue known as the *Senhor morto* (Dead Lord). The figure was carved in 1730 by a slave named Francisco Xavier Chagas. Small rubies were used to create the effect of streaming blood, a relatively common technique in 18th- and 19th- century Portuguese-Brazilian statuary. The church is part of an architectural ensemble that includes another church, the Igreja de Nossa Senhora do Carmo, and a convent, now a hotel.

Largo do Carmo, no #, Carmo. Mon – Sat, 8am – noon and 2pm – 6pm; Mass: Sun, 9am.

CIDADE BAIXA (LOWER CITY)

⑬ MERCADO MODELO

Busy Modelo Market is a popular destination for tourists seeking arts and crafts and other regional products. Unfortunately, the market has seen better days but it's worth a visit just to see the building, formerly the Customs House. Mercado Modelo is located in the center of Cidade Baixa, near the Elevador Lacerda. *Capoeira* exhibitions are held behind the market.

Praça Visconde de Cairu, 250, Comércio, tel. (71) 3241-2893. Mon – Sat, 9am – 7pm; Sun and holidays, 9am – 2pm.

⑭ IGREJA NOSSA SENHORA DA CONCEIÇÃO DA PRAIA

Spacious and naturally well lit, Igreja Nossa Senhora da Conceição da Praia church was built in the second half of the 18th century on the site of the first chapel in Salvador (1549). The limestone blocks used to construct the church were shipped from Alentejo, Portugal. The painting on the nave ceiling dates to 1774. It is a masterpiece by José Joaquim da Rocha, one of the great names of the Brazilian baroque era.

Rua da Conceição da Praia, no #, Comércio, tel. (71) 3242-0545. Mon, 7am – noon and 2pm – 5pm; Tue – Fri, 7am – 5pm; Sat and Sun, 7am – noon.

⑮ SOLAR DO UNHÃO

It's worth setting aside an entire afternoon to visit this lovely mansion

---

ELEVADOR LACERDA AND PLANO INCLINADO

One of Salvador's most distinctive landmarks, the 74-meter (243 foot)-high **Elevador Lacerda** has linked Praça Tomé de Souza, in Cidade Alta (Upper City), to Praça Visconde de Cairu, in Cidade Baixa (Lower City), since 1873. A 1930 makeover gave the elevator its art deco appearance *(tel. (71) 3243-4030, 3322-7049; daily, 24 hours).* The **Plano Inclinado Gonçalves** is a funicular railway located behind the Basílica. A trip on the railway affords passengers a panoramic view of the bay. It runs between Praça Ramos de Queirós in Cidade Alta, and Rua Guindaste dos Padres, in Cidade Baixa *(tel. (71) 3322-6894; Mon – Fri, 7am – 7pm; Sat, 7am – 1pm; closed on holidays).* Restored and reopened in 2006, the **Plano Inclinado do Pilar**, a funicular system built in 1897, climbs 112 meters (367 feet) in approximately two minutes. The railway links Rua do Carmo, in front of Cruz do Redentor, in Cidade Alta, to Rua do Pilar, in Cidade Baixa *(daily, 7am – 7pm).*

Cidade Baixa with the Elevador Lacerda (left) and Igreja Nossa Senhora da Conceição da Praia (right)

overlooking Todos os Santos Bay. Built in the 17th century for Judge Pedro Unhão Castelo Branco, and later used for commercial purposes, it was restored in 1962 by architect Lina Bo Bardi. Today it houses the **Museu de Arte Moderna** (Museum of Modern Art, or "MAM"), which exhibits works by Tarsila do Amaral and Di Cavalcanti.

The mansion's garden, **Parque das Esculturas**, is a sculpture park with pieces by Carybé and Mário Cravo. There is a bar on the pier with outdoor tables and live music; many come here to enjoy the magnificent sunsets.
Avenida do Contorno, no #, Comércio, tel. (71) 3117-6139. Tue − Fri and Sun, 1pm − 7pm; Sat, 1pm − 9pm.

From the Historical Center to Barra

Museu de Arte Sacra da Bahia

Located in an old convent and church, the Sacred Art Museum has two highlights: a 17th-century ivory figure of Christ nailed to a delicately carved jacaranda cross, and an 18th-century silver altar. Visitors should be aware that Ladeira da Preguiça, one of the roads by which the museum can be accessed, is not safe. It's better to use Largo 2 de Julho.
Rua do Sodré, 276, Dois de Julho, tel. (71) 3283-5600. Mon − Fri, 11:30am − 5:30pm.

Mosteiro de São Bento

Founded in 1582, the Sao Bento monastery was one of the first in the Americas. The building has been modified since that time, but thirty or so

monks still live a cloistered life here. Their Gregorian chants can be heard during Sunday Mass in the monastery church. The church museum houses more than 2,000 pieces of religious art, furniture, and precious metalwork, including works

Our Recommendation

Restaurant **Paraíso Tropical** serves light, delicate versions of traditional Brazilian dishes, replacing *dendê* palm oil with *dendê* fruit juice, and substituting coconut pulp and milk for creamed coconut. In the simple dining area, tables are at the level of the treetops and the décor is reminiscent of a farm *(Rua Edgar Loureiro, 98-B, Cabula, tel. (71) 3384-7464; Mon − Sat, noon − 11pm; Sun, noon − 10pm).*

Additional information on page 462.

by Brother Agostinho da Piedade and painter José Joaquim da Rocha. There is also a library of more than 3,000 books and documents.
Largo de São Bento, 1, Centro, tel. (71) 2106-5200. Mon – Fri, 9am – 11am and 2:30pm – 5:30pm (visits must be authorized); Mass: Mon – Fri, 7am and 6:20pm; Sat, 7am; Sun, 10am (with Gregorian chants).

MUSEU CARLOS COSTA PINTO

The Carlos Costa Pinto museum's historical collection of over 3,000 decorative pieces documents the lifestyle of the Brazilian elite beginning in the 1600s and continuing through the 20th century. Highlights include 19th-century Brazilian paintings and a collection of gold and silver trinkets worn by slave girls.
Avenida 7 de Setembro, 2490, Corredor da Vitória, tel. (71) 3336-6081. Mon and Wed – Sat, 2:30pm – 7pm.

DIQUE DO TORORÓ

Park visitors can take advantage of a number of different facilities, including jogging paths, rowing lanes, fishing decks, a playground, and a performance space. Eight statues of *orixás* (native gods) by sculptor Tati Moreno dot the perimeter of the lake. In the early hours of the 2nd of February, before Iemanjá festivities in the beach of Rio Vermelho begin, followers of Candomblé come to the lake to make offerings to Oxum, the goddess of fresh water.
Avenida Vasco da Gama, no #, tel. (71) 3382-0847.

OTHER MUSEUMS

The highlight of a visit to **Museu Henriqueta Catharino** is a chance to see the dress worn by Princess Isabel for the ceremony at which she became Brazilian Regent. The building is a 1930s mansion. It holds a collection of more than 15,000 items, including furniture, porcelain, and miniature church altars *(Rua Monsenhor Flaviano, 2, Politeama de Cima, tel. (71) 3329-5522; Tue – Fri, 10am – noon and 1pm – 6pm; Sat, 2pm – 6pm).* The **Museu de Arte da Bahia** houses works by José Joaquim da Rocha, José Teófilo de Jesus, and Rodrigues Nunes, all masters of the Bahia school of painting *(Avenida 7 de Setembro, 2340, Corredor da Vitória, tel. (71) 3117-6902; Tue – Fri, 2pm – 7pm; Sat and Sun, 2:30pm – 6:30pm).* Fans of Portuguese and Brazilian literature flock to the **Gabinete Português de Leitura**, a library founded in 1863. It has been at its current address since 1917. There are 22,000 volumes in the collection *(Praça da Piedade, no #, Piedade, tel. (71) 3329-5758; Mon – Fri, 9am – noon and 2pm – 5:30pm).*

BONFIM AND ENVIRONS

BASÍLICA DE NOSSO SENHOR DO BONFIM

Basílica de Nosso Senhor do Bonfim holds a position of distinction in Salvador. It is sacred to both Catholics and followers of Candomblé, who identify Christ with *Oxalá*, the Candomblé god of creation. Construction was completed in 1772. The church's rococo façade is covered with 19th-century Portuguese tiles.

Interior highlights include a room of votive offerings and an 18th-century Portuguese statue of Christ on the high altar. Outside, you can buy ribbons known as *fitinhas do Senhor do Bonfim*, which are said to make wishes come true when time and nature untie them. On the second Thursday after Epiphany (January 6), the church is the final destination of the Festa de Nosso Senhor do Bonfim procession. Hundreds of local

CARNIVAL IN SALVADOR

Two million people crowd the city of Salvador during Carnival. A total of 25 kilometers (16 miles) of streets overflow with revelers dancing behind *trios elétricos* – trucks fitted with huge amplifiers and small stages carrying popular music groups. The musicians electrify the masses with *axé* music, a mixture of *frevo* music and pop. The *trios elétricos* have three routes: **Avenida**, which runs from Campo Grande to Praça Castro Alves square, then to the end of Rua Carlos Gomes road; **Barra/Ondina**, which begins at the Farol da Barra lighthouse and ends at Praia de Ondina beach and **Batatinha**, which cuts through Pelourinho. In the early hours of Ash Wednesday morning, the great meeting of the *trios elétricos* occur in Praça Castro Alves square and in Barra, near the lighthouse. To participate in Carnival celebrations you must be prepared for significant pushing and shoving, and busy public toilets. The best way to enjoy the parades is from the safety of roped-off areas open only to ticket-holders. Ticket packages include a tabard-style t-shirt known as an *abadá*, which uniquely identifies each group.

Heaving crowds outside these areas can be dangerous. The most sought-after *abadás* sell out very quickly, usually the first day tickets go on sale, on Ash Wednesday of the previous year *(to make a reservation for the Camaleão, Araketu, Daniela Mercury, or Timbalada abadás, call **Central do Carnaval**, tel. (71) 3535-3000 or www.centraldocarnaval.com.br; for the Ivete Sangalo abadá, call **Axemix**, tel. (71) 3281-0400, 3281-0401 or www.axemix.com.br).* Salvador's carnival groups, known as *blocos*, energize the city with performances throughout the year. **Filhos de Gandhy** holds rehearsals at 6pm on Sundays, beginning in August and concluding with Carnival *(Rua Gregório de Matos, 53, Pelourinho, tel. (71) 3321-7073).* **Olodum** gives shows at 8pm on Tuesdays in Praça Teresa Batista square. They also hold rehearsals at 6pm on Sundays *(Rua Gregório de Matos, 22, Pelourinho, tel. (71) 3321-5010).* **Ilê Aiyê** holds rehearsals at 10pm beginning in September and concluding with Carnival. The rehearsals are held at their cultural center, **Centro Cultural Senzala do Barro Preto** *(Rua do Curuzu, 228, Liberdade, tel. (71) 3256-8800).*

Dressed in white and blue, Filhos de Gandhy honor the orixás

The altar of the Basílica do Bonfim

women, carrying jugs of scented water and accompanied by a huge crowd, set out from the **Igreja de Nossa Senhora da Conceição da Praia** church headed for Bonfim. Upon arrival, the steps of the Igreja do Bonfim's staircase are washed with the scented water.
Largo do Bonfim, no #, tel. (71) 3316-2196. Tue – Sun, 6am – 11:30am and 1:30pm – 6pm.

FEIRA DE SÃO JOAQUIM
None of the forty or so open markets in Salvador can match São Joaquim's authenticity or the diversity of its wares. In the labyrinth of stalls, amid the shouts of 7,000 vendors, you'll find live hens, dried shrimp, herbal medicine, spices, Candomblé objects, fruits and vegetables, and much more. It's an amazing experience, even more so if you go in the morning.
Avenida Oscar Pontes, no #, Calçada. Daily, 5am until the last customer leaves.

FORTE DO MONTE SERRAT
Monte Serrat fort is one of the nicest-looking military buildings in Brazil. The fort's harmonious architectural lines form an irregular-polygon-shaped perimeter. Its huge circular towers kept guard over the north side of the city in colonial times. Built between 1583 and 1587, the fort complemented the protection afforded by **Forte de Santo Antônio da Barra** *(see page 256)*, which stands to the south. Unfortunately, the combined cannon firepower of the forts could not hold off the Dutch in 1624 and 1625. It was only after the expulsion of the invaders that the majority of the city's fifteen forts were built.
Rua da Boa Viagem, no #, Boa Viagem, tel. (71) 3313-7339. Daily, 9am – 5pm.

SHOPPING

The best place to purchase authentic arts and crafts is the **Instituto Mauá**. Maintained by the government, it sells pieces from handicraft communities around the state, including ceramics from Maragogipinho and basketwork from Massarandupió. There are two stores, one in Porto da Barra (*Praça Azevedo Fernandes,* 2, *tel. (71) 3116-6196; Mon – Fri, 9am – 6pm; Sat, 9am – 1pm*) and another in Pelourinho (*Rua Gregório de Matos,* 27, *tel. (71) 3116-6712; Mon – Fri, 9am – 6pm; Sat, 9am – 1pm*). **Galeria Fundação Pierre Verger** displays photographs and sells books and posters related to anthropologist and photographer Pierre Verger, a Frenchman who made Bahia his home (*Rua da Misericórdia, 9, Pelourinho, tel. (71) 3321-2341; Mon – Sat, 8am – 5pm*). **Tabacaria Rosa do Prado Cigar Shop** is also in Pelourinho. They sell only local cigars (*Rua da Ordem Terceira, formerly Inácio Accioli, 5, Pelourinho, tel. (71) 3322-1258; daily, 9:30am – 7pm*).

Exu

Ogum

Xangô

Logunedé

Iemanjá

Syncretism and Candomblé Temples in Bahia

Religious tradition in Bahia is syncretic, a mixture of Christian traditions and African Candomblé rituals. Though forced to convert to Catholicism, slaves continued to worship their own gods – the *orixás*, which represented the forces of nature – by associating them with Catholic saints. Iemanjá, queen of the sea, was identified with Nossa Senhora da Conceição (Our Lady of the Immaculate Conception); Oxalá, god of creation, was associated with Jesus, and so on. Syncretism thus gave slaves a way to maintain their culture. The worship of *orixás* takes place in Candomblé temples known as *terreiros*. Led by priestesses, called *mães-de-santo* or *ialorixás, terreiros* are attended by initiated members, though some are open to the public. One of the most famous ones is **Gantois**. Vis-

Oxumaré

its are allowed Sunday nights between the end of September and the end of November *(Gantois: Rua Alto do Gantois, 23, Federação, tel. (71) 3331-9231)*. **Ilê Axé Opô Afonjá**, a temple on the outskirts of the city, is actually a complex of buildings. Some are dedicated to a particular *orixás*, others house a museum, library, municipal school, textile workshop, and the residences of the *ialorixá*. This *terreiro* is open to the public on Wednesdays beginning at noon from September to November *(Rua Direita de São Gonçalo do Retiro, 557, Cabula, tel. (71) 3384-6800)*. **Terreiro da Casa Branca**, built in 1830, is the oldest *terreiro* in the country. The main building is the *Casa Branca* (White House), where rituals are held *(Avenida Vasco da Gama, 463, Vasco da Gama, tel. (71) 3334-3100)*.

Euá

Oxaguiã

Omolu

Oxalufã

Oxum

Nanã Buruku

Iansã

Obá

Ossain

Oxóssi

BEACHES

**BARRA, ONDINA, AND RIO VERMELHO
Praia da Barra**, 5 kilometers (3 miles) from the city center, is Salvador's busiest spot during the day and the best point of departure for exploring Salvador's beaches. The promenade is very pleasant at sunset. **Forte de Santo Antônio da Barra**, Brazil's first fort, built in 1534, protects the **Farol da Barra**, a functioning lighthouse that has stood on this spot since 1698. The lighthouse is not open to the public. Nearby, **Museu Náutico** welcomes visitors to view its collection of maps, navigational tools, and model ships *(Praia Almirante Tamandaré, no #, Largo do Farol da Barra, tel. (71) 3331-8039; Mon, 8:30am – noon; Tue – Sun, 8:30am – 7pm)*. An extension of Barra, **Praia de Ondina** beach and its natural pools border both rough and calm seas. **Rio Vermelho's** beaches are unsuitable for bathing, but they are a popular nightlife hotspot.

PIATÃ AND ITAPUÃ
From tranquil **Praia de Piatã** (25 kilometers, 15 miles, from the center) onwards, the beaches are dotted with

Bonfim
Bonfim's church here is famous for its stair-washing ceremony, the Lavagem do Bonfim. Five hundred local women in traditional costume perform this ritual of religious syncretism every January.

Cabula
The Cabula neighborhood, situated on the city outskirts on the way to the airport, is home to the city's most significant Candomblé terreiros (temples).

Pelourinho
The cultural heart of the city, Pelourinho serves as a stage for musical performances and capoeira exhibitions. It even has its own Carnival trio elétrico, Batatinha.

Tororó
One of the city's main parks, Dique Tororó, has public leisure facilities. Next door is Fonte Nova stadium, home turf for the Bahia Futebol Clube soccer club.

Campo Grande
Home to Praça Dois de Julho square, where the Independence of Bahia is commemorated.

Barra
The liveliest tourist spot on the coast, Barra has a beach, a fort, a lighthouse, and a shopping center. At Carnival, this is the starting point for the trio elétrico de Dodô parade.

Ondina
An extension of Praia da Barra beach. During Carnival it serves as the finishing point for the trio elétrico de Dodô parade.

Rio Vermelho
Nightlife is the Rio Vermelho neighborhood's forte. In the evening its streets flow with locals and tourists alike. Rio Vermelho is also home to a popular market where you can try delicious acarajé – savory cakes stuffed with shrimp.

barracas (kiosks) with good tourist facilities. This is particularly true in **Itapuã** (27 kilometers, 17 miles, from the center), a fashionable spot with white sand and coconut palms. A national sea turtle protection project, Projeto Tamar, has a base here. Lovely **Farol de Itapuã** lighthouse is not open to the public, but it complements the ocean view. Nearby, the dark waters of **Lagoa do Abaeté** lagoon contrast with white dunes and colorful vegetation.

STELLA MARIS, FLAMENGO AND ALELUIA
Reefs produce large waves at high tide and rock pools at low tide on **Praia de Stella Maris**, making it a popular destination for surfers and bathers alike. In summer, some of the *barracas* are open at night. **Praia do Flamengo**, 3 kilometers further on, is still unspoiled. **Aleluia** beach is known for its strong waves and is a perennial favorite with the younger crowd. It's home to the famous Barraca do Lôro beach kiosk *(Rua Tales de Azevedo, no #, tel. (71) 3374-7509; daily, 8am – 4:30pm)*, which has another *barraca* on **Praia de Catussaba** *(Rua do Camping, no #, tel. (71) 3374-0767; daily, 8am – 6pm)*.

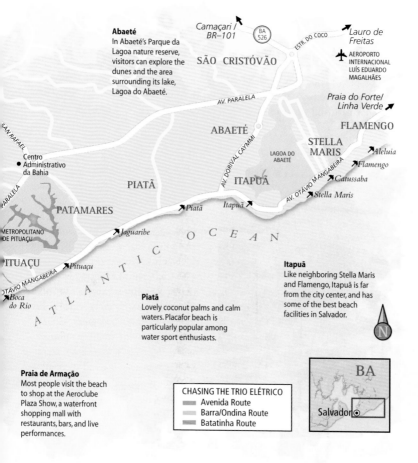

Abaeté
In Abaeté's Parque da Lagoa nature reserve, visitors can explore the dunes and the area surrounding its lake, Lagoa do Abaeté.

Piatã
Lovely coconut palms and calm waters. Placafor beach is particularly popular among water sport enthusiasts.

Itapuã
Like neighboring Stella Maris and Flamengo, Itapuã is far from the city center, and has some of the best beach facilities in Salvador.

Praia de Armação
Most people visit the beach to shop at the Aeroclube Plaza Show, a waterfront shopping mall with restaurants, bars, and live performances.

CHASING THE TRIO ELÉTRICO
▬ Avenida Route
▬ Barra/Ondina Route
▬ Batatinha Route

THE QUEENS OF ACARAJÉ

Acarajé is a small savory cake made with a paste of cooked black-eyed peas, stuffed with *vatapá* (shrimp and fish mixed with bread crumbs, peanuts, and cashews) and dried shrimp, fried in *dendê* palm oil, and seasoned with pepper. The women who sell them on the street are unmistakable in their all-white traditional full skirts, blouses, and turbans. Their necklaces and bracelets honor *orixás*, the Candomblé deities, while the turban reflects North African influences.

Both the women and the *acarajé*, as well as other traditional dishes like *vatapá* and *carurú*, were declared important elements of Brazilian national heritage in 2004. Rio Vermelho is where you will find the most famous *acarajé* makers in the city: **Regina** *(Largo de Santana, no #, Rio Vermelho, tel. (71) 3232-7542; Mon – Fri, 3pm – 10pm; Sat, Sun, and holidays, 10am – 9pm)* and **Dinha** *(Largo de*

Santana, no #, Rio Vermelho, tel. (71) 3334-1703, 3334-0525, 3334-9715; Mon – Fri, 4pm – midnight; Sat and Sun, 11am – midnight). Another famous *acarajé* maker, **Cira**, sells her wares in two locations, one in Largo da Mariquita, and another in Itapuã, her home base *(Rua Aristides Milton, no #, Itapuã, opposite Bar Posto 12, tel. (71) 3249-4170, 9998-9851; daily, 10:30am – 11pm).*

BAÍA DE TODOS OS SANTOS

Todos os Santos Bay is the largest bay in Brazil, and visitors can enjoy any number of boat trips between the mainland and the bay's 39 islands. **Ilha de Itaparica** island, once a favorite destination for sophisticates and other

Salvador's Cidade Baixa, with access to Baía de Todos os Santos

members of Brazilian high society, is still a tranquil place of natural beauty that affords its visitors a lovely view of the city. Itaparica is accessed by public catamaran or ferry boat, both of which depart from the São Joaquim ferry terminal *(next to São Joaquim market, Avenida Oscar Pontes, 1051, Água de Meninos, tel. (71) 3254-1020; ferry boat: daily, 5am – 11:30pm; catamaran: daily, 8am – 6pm).* Tour agencies *(All Tour, tel. (71) 3113-2830; LR Turismo, tel. (71) 3241-1526, 3242-6972)* also organize trips to the island, which depart from the Centro Náutico *(tel. (71) 3242-4366)*, in front of Mercado Modelo market. The bay is excellent for **diving**: the average water temperature is 26 degrees Celsius (79 degrees Fahrenheit), with visibility up to 20 meters (65 feet). The reefs are teeming with rich marine life and there are about forty sunken ships in the area, including the Portuguese command vessel *Sacramento*, which sank in 1668. **Contact:** *Dive Bahia, tel. (71) 3264-3820; Bahia Scuba, tel. (71) 3321-0156, 9975-3839.*

São Félix as seen from Cachoeira, in the Recôncavo Baiano region

RECÔNCAVO BAIANO

CACHOEIRA

The Recôncavo Baiano region is comprised of 33 municipalities from the area surrounding Todos os Santos Bay. One of the loveliest of these towns is **Cachoeira**, 119 kilometers (72 miles) from Salvador, whose distinctive baroque colonial architecture graces the banks of the Rio Paraguaçu river. In Praça **da Aclamação**, Cachoeira's main square, stands the **Museu do Iphan**, which houses a collection of 18th- and 19th-century furniture and historical city documents. The building itself has stood here since 1723 *(tel. (75) 3425-1123; Mon – Fri, 8am – noon and 2pm – 5pm; Sat and Sun, 8am – noon)*. Nearby stands the **Casa de Câmara e Cadeia**, once home to the city council and a prison. The house was built between 1698 and 1712, and today houses the small **Museu dos Escravos** *(Slave Museum, tel. (75) 3425-1018; daily, 8am – 5pm)*. The **Fundação Hansen Bahia**, which occupies a town house built in 1830, is home to works by the German artist Karl Heinz *(Rua 13 de Maio, 13, tel. (75) 3425-1453; Mon – Fri, 9am – 5pm; Sat, 9am – 1pm)*. His house in neighboring São Félix is also a museum. The **Igreja da Ordem Terceira do Carmo** church is one of the town's treasures. The church was built in 1778 and restored in 2006, when it also became home to the **Museu de Arte Sacra do Recôncavo**. The museum's collection of regional religious pieces includes 18th-century wooden statues with oriental details that were made in Macau, near Hong Kong *(Rua Inocêncio Boaventura, no #, tel. (75) 3425-3179; Mon – Fri, 9am – 5pm; Sat and Sun, 9am – 1pm)*. Cachoeira's **Festa de Nossa Senhora da Boa Morte** takes place August 13th, 14th, and 15th, and celebrations include a parade and *capoeira* performances. Most of the festivities take place in a building occupied by **Irmandade da Boa Morte**, a sisterhood created 240 years ago by freed female slaves. They have a memorial to Our Lady and an exhibition room *(Rua 13 de Maio, 32, tel. (75) 3425-1468, 9965-6195. Tue – Sat, 10am – 6pm)*.

SÃO FÉLIX

Across the Rio Paraguaçu river, on the other side of the **Ponte Dom Pedro II** bridge (1885), sits charming São Félix. The town's biggest attraction is the **Fábrica de Charutos Dannemann**. Here you can watch cigars being made, a job traditionally considered women's work. The **Centro Cultural Dannemann**, the factory's cultural center, offers workshops and exhibitions, and hosts two arts festivals, the **Bienal de Artes do Recôncavo** (a biennial arts festival held from November of each even-numbered year through the following January) and the **Festival de Filarmônicas** (a music festival that is also held every other year, in November and the first week of December) *(Avenida Salvador Pinto, 29, Centro, tel. (75) 3425-2208; Tue – Sat, 8am – 5pm; Sun, 1pm – 5pm, Cultural Center only).*

THE NORTH COAST

The North Coast brings to mind a series of beautiful images: charming villages, beaches cut by small streams, and coconut palms swaying in the breeze. This gorgeous stretch of coastline runs from Salvador to Mangue Seco, near Sergipe. The well-maintained Rodovia BA-099 state highway runs the length of the coast. The first 84-kilometer (52-mile) stretch from Salvador to Praia do Forte is called the **Estrada do Coco** (Coconut Highway). The next 146 kilometers (91 miles) are called the **Linha Verde** (Green Line) in recognition of the highway's environmentally friendly construction. Many residents of Salvador have elegant summer homes in this region.

ESTRADA DO COCO

AREMPEBE

Forty kilometers (25 miles) from Salvador, Arempebe beach was a favorite among "alternative" travelers of the 1970s. Today a small community of approximately still embraces its hippie roots, continuing to live in thatched houses with no electricity. Caetano Veloso, Janis Joplin, and Mick Jagger all spent time here. There is a **Projeto Tamar** base at the village entrance. **Barra do Jacuípe**, 10 kilometers (6 miles) further north, draws water sports enthusiasts, and **Itacimirim**, 26 kilometers (16 miles) from Arembepe, offers calm seas with natural pools at low tide.

PRAIA DO FORTE

The town of Praia do Forte is the most popular destination on Bahia's north

Barra do Jacuípe, on the Estrada do Coco highway

Castelo Garcia d'Ávila, one of the oldest stone buildings in Brazil

coast. Ninety-one kilometers (57 miles) from Salvador, it is famous for the **Praia do Forte Eco Resort**, where guests enjoy splendid swimming pools and relaxing spa treatments *(Avenida do Farol, no #, tel. (71) 3676-4000)*. There is much more to Praia do Forte than just the resort, however. Age-old fishing village traditions exist here alongside sophisticated craft and clothing stores. Cars are not allowed in the town center. The nearby coastline offers 14 kilometers (9 miles) of calm waters. **Projeto Tamar**, a turtle conservation group, is based here, and maintains a visitor's center, aquariums, and turtle areas. There is also a store, a bar, and a restaurant *(Avenida Farol Garcia d'Ávila, no #, tel. (71) 3676-*

1045; daily, 9am – 6pm). Between December and February the Tamar team organizes night trips to observe turtles laying eggs in the sand. Turtles are not the only ecological attraction, however. Between July and October biologists from the **Instituto Baleia Jubarte** (Humpback Whale Institute) supervise whale-watching trips organized by Centrotour *(tel. (71) 3676-1091)*. The **Reserva de Preservação Ambiental Sapiranga** natural reserve has several trails that can be enjoyed on foot, by bicycle, on horseback, or by quadricycle. The reserve is home to several endangered animal species, including the marmoset and the three-toed sloth *(Estrada do Coco, Km 52, tel. (71) 3676-1133, 3676-1144; daily, 9am – 5pm)*. The ruins of **Castelo Garcia d'Ávila** castle rise from the top of a small hill. Built between 1551 and 1564, the castle was one of the first stone constructions in Brazil and the only Portuguese building with the characteristics of a mediaeval military fortress *(Rua do Castelo, no #; drive for 2 kilometers along a dirt road to the Praia do Forte exit; tel. (71) 3676-1073; Tue – Sun, 9am – 6pm)*.

OUR RECOMMENDATION

🔳 **Mar Aberto** restaurant, in the center of Arembepe, sits on an airy beachfront terrace. Patrons enjoy fish and fresh lobster *(Largo de São Francisco, 43, tel. (71) 3624-1257, 3624-1623; Mon – Thu, 11:30am – 9:30pm; Fri and Sat, 11:30am – midnight; Sun, noon – 7pm)*.

Additional information on page 462.

LINHA VERDE

IMBASSAÍ

Here, 75 kilometers (47 miles) north of Salvador, is the point where the Barroso River meets the sea. Bridges span the river and provide access to the beach, where beachgoers visit *barracas* and lounge in beach chairs. Imbassaí is a simple village with charming guesthouses, some of which have their own bridges across the river. From the town, it's not far to **Cachoeira de Dona Zilda** waterfall. Visitors can also take a boat trip on the river. Neighboring **Praia de Santo Antônio** beach offers wind-carved dunes, natural pools, and small streams winding their way to the sea.

COSTA DO SAUÍPE

While the beach leaves a lot to be desired, visitors flock to Costa do Sauípe's resorts nonetheless. The hotels (five resorts and six guesthouses) all have swimming pools and leisure facilities. One of them, the Costa do Sauípe resort, is the largest resort in the Northeast. It sits 105 kilometers (65 miles) north of Salvador. The 172-hectare (425 acre) complex has a golf course and tennis courts. Guests also enjoy horseback riding and sailing. Minibuses transport guests around the grounds and bicycle rentals are also available. The leisure facilities are open to non-guests who pay a day use fee.

MASSARANDUPIÓ

Dunes and coconut palms shelter the Massarandupió nudist beach, which lies 123 kilometers (76 miles) from Salvador. A bumpy 10-kilometer (6-mile) dirt road turns off for the beach at the beginning of the highway called Linha Verde. Unaccompanied men are not allowed on the beach.

SÍTIO DO CONDE

A tourist base, Sítio do Conde is almost 202 kilometers (126 miles) Salvador, to the north of Costa do Sauípe. The Itariri and Itapicuru rivers bookend its best beaches. Visitors to **Barra do Itariri**, 13 kilometers (8 miles) to the south, have a tough time choosing between a dip in the fresh water river or a swim in the salty sea. This dilemma repeats itself further north, amid the dunes and powdery sand of **Barra do Itapicuru**, whose waters can also be explored by boat. Nearby, thrill-seekers slide down a 30-meter (100-foot) dune called the **Cavalo Ruço**, located just outside the fishing village of **Siribinha**, 16 kilometers (10 miles) from Sítio do Conde. The dune is reached by a boat trip along the Piranji river.

PROJETO TAMAR

Sea turtles, an endangered species, are protected by law. The renowned **Projeto Tamar** has been working since 1980 to protect Brazilian species with the cooperation of local communities. The project has 21 bases in nine states which, during the egg-laying season (September – March), monitor a total of 1,100 kilometers (680 miles) of coastal habitat. Islands are also monitored January through June. The project has released seven million baby

turtles into the wild since its creation (*www.tamar.org.br*).

MANGUE SECO

Jorge Amado's book, *Tieta do agreste* (Tieta is its English title), was made into a movie and a soap opera. Both productions shot scenes on-location in Mangue Seco, on the banks of the Real river. The town is the last stop on the Linha Verde Highway, 246 kilometers (153 miles) from Salvador. It's a tranquil place, where dunes rise 30 meters (100 feet) toward the sky above a pleasant beach. Dune-buggy trips explore the river mouth, with additional stops at **Coqueiro village** and **Praia da Costa Azul**. Mangue Seco is accessed through Sergipe. From Sergipe, take Rodovia SE-318 highway as far as Pontal, then catch the 15-minute boat ride to Mangue.

MORRO DE SÃO PAULO

Morro de São Paulo is Bahia's premier South Coast destination. The town, first settled in the 16th century, was a sleepy fishing village until the 1980s. Today it is the most famous spot on the **Costa do Dendê**, a region of *dendê* palms stretching from Valença to Itacaré. The town's simple atmosphere, colonial buildings, and sophisticated bars and stores draw visitors from far and wide. The area's natural beauty is also noteworthy: Atlantic forest, *restinga* vegetation, dunes, mangrove swamps, and beautiful beaches with cliffs and tide pools. A ban on cars helps keep the town and its surrounds pristine; jeeps and tractors are used as transportation to more remote destinations. Morro de São Paulo is as much a destination for young people in search of lively nightlife as it is for couples in search of a quiet oasis. Morro de São Paulo is on **Ilha de Tinharé** island. Tinharé, along with **Ilha de Boipeba** and 21 other islands, comprises **Cairu**, the only archipelago municipality in Brazil.

Primeira Praia, the smallest beach in Morro de São Paulo, and its lighthouse

The island is accessed from Valença, where you can park your car in a rented space at the port and take a boat (two hours) or air-taxi (30 minutes) across.

HISTORICAL TOWN CENTER

A steep street sloping up from the docks takes visitors to the **Portaló**, a 16th-century stone archway at the town entrance. **Igreja de Nossa Senhora da Luz** church, built in 1855, stands nearby. The main square, **Praça Aureliano de Lima**, sits at the end of **Rua Caminho da Praia**, a thoroughfare buzzing with shoppers, restaurants, guesthouses, and travel agencies. The **Fonte Grande**, a fountain on the street of the same name, was built in 1746. Fonte Grande street leads to the sleepy village of **Gamboa** and the calm waters of deserted **Praia da Ponta da Pedra**. The path to the **Farol do Morro de São Paulo** lighthouse starts near the Igreja de Nossa Senhora da Luz. The lighthouse was built in 1835 and the 10 minutes it takes to climb to the top are well compensated by the view. Visitors looking for another kind of high can try the "flying fox," a 340-meter (1,115-foot) slide from an elevation of 57 meters (187 feet) down to the beach called Primeira Praia *(tel. (75) 3652-1219, 8805-9796; daily, 10am – 6pm)*. **Fortaleza do Tapirandu** fort is not far from the bottom of the slide. The fort was built in 1630 but lies in ruins today. The fortified walls, built in 1728, were 678 meters (2,224 feet) long.

BEACHES

Most of Morro de São Paulo's beaches are identified by numbers. The first one, **Primeira Praia**, is 500 meters long, heavily developed, and the only beach suitable for surfing. Trendy **Segunda** has rock pools at low tide and a number of popular bars and performance venues that come alive at night. Guesthouses dot

Terceira, a quiet and peaceful stretch of sand with inviting coral reefs ideal for divers just off shore. **Quarta** also promises a quiet atmosphere and guesthouse accommodation. The mangroves at **Quinta**, also known as **Praia do Encanto**, make the water cloudier and the sand disappears at high tide. Deserted **Praia do Pontal** lies to the extreme south, and has 17 kilometers (10.5 miles) of coconut groves. **Gamboa,** a small village with waters suitable for snorkeling, faces Valença from across the water.

BOAT TRIPS

A boat trip is a good way to see more of Morro and the surrounding area than is possible on foot. Tours are generally day-long and leave from Terceira Praia. Most stop at the natural pools in Garapuá village, followed by **Ilha de Boipeba** and its beaches: **Praia de Tassimirim** and **Praia de Cueira**. There's a longer stop in **Boca da Barra** for lunch, then a trip along the **Rio do Inferno** toward Cairu to see the **Igreja and Convento de Santo Antônio**. The complex was built in 1654 and is today a national heritage site. The church and convent are decorated with baroque Portuguese tiles. Please note that swimwear is not allowed inside. During the high season, tours also visit Ilha de Manguinhos and the tide pools of Praia de Moreré. *Contact: Itha do Mar, tel. (75) 3652-1104, 3652-1225.*

OUR RECOMMENDATION

Gardens and palm-covered walkways link the communal areas at the **Porto do Zimbo Small Resort**, which sits adjacent to the natural pools of Quarta Praia. Rooms are comfortable and equipped with air-conditioning and a mini-bar. Some of them have jacuzzis *(Quarto Praia, no #, tel. (75) 3652-2030)*.

Additional information on page 462.

ILHA DE BOIPEBA

Mangroves, dunes, *restinga* vegetation, and coral reefs are protected by the Ilha de Boipeba nature reserve. It is less sophisticated than famous Morro de São Paulo to the north, but Velha Boipeba village does have simple tourist facilities. **Praça Santo Antônio** is home to the unpretentious **Igreja do Divino Espírito Santo**, a 17th-century church. In early June, the village comes alive with *forró* bands during the **Festa do Glorioso Divino Espírito Santo** festival, which honors the Holy Spirit, the island's patron and protector. A three-day stay is ample time to see all the attractions. The best way to reach the island is by motorboat from the village of Torrinhas, in Cairu. The trip takes about 30 minutes. There are also boats from Valença (four hours by sailboat, one hour by motorboat) and Morro de São Paulo (two hours by motorboat). Lastly, direct, half-hour-long flights run between Ilha de Boipeba and Salvador.

BEACHES

Boipeba has almost 20 kilometers (12 miles) of beaches, most of which have calm waters. The most popular is **Boca da Barra**, where kiosks selling snacks capitalize on the crowds. A 30-minute walk south will take you to **Tassimirim**, a beach framed by *restinga* vegetation and coconut groves, with good snorkeling. Even further south is deserted **Praia de Cueira**, where coral reefs alternate with stretches good for surfing. Across the river is **Moreré**, a small fishing village that has good snorkeling just offshore. Walk further still and you will come upon **Bainema**, good for dragnet fishing, and the cliffs at **Ponta dos Castelhanos**. It takes about three and a half hours to walk from Boca da Barra to Ponta dos Castelhanos.

OUR RECOMMENDATION

🍽 Pleasant, simple, **Restaurante Mar e Coco**, on Praia de Moreré, serves delicious shrimp *moqueca* with plantains. Hammocks are available for a post-lunch nap *(tel. (75) 3653-6013; daily, 10am – 5pm; in the low season it's best to call in advance)*.

Additional information on page 462.

Moreré, seen with Bainema in the background

Península de Maraú and Baía de Camamu

The Maraú Peninsula, which extends into Camamu Bay, is uniquely beautiful. Lagoons, seas of dunes, sparkling rivers, and mangroves ornament its face, and most of the beaches offer panoramic views of the islands across the water. It's a good destination for anyone in search of peace and quiet as there are few visitors. The best, though longest, way to reach the peninsula is by sailboat or motorboat from **Camamu**, 335 kilometers (208 miles) from Salvador, to **Barra Grande**, at the tip of the peninsula. The land route to Maraú is accessible only to 4×4 vehicles, coming from Itacaré or Ubaitaba, which are 56 and 90 kilometers (35 and 56 miles) respectively from Barra Grande. *Jardineiras* (all-terrain-adapted pickup trucks) are the best way to get around the peninsula by automobile. They make it possible to visit lovely, largely deserted beaches like **Taipus de Fora** and the remarkable dark waters of **Lagoa do Cassange**, where colors of the sand and sea contrast beautifully. These quiet, island beaches can be visited by boat, too, which also make trips to picturesques villages on the bay, like **Cajaíba**, where lucky visitors may have a chance to watch boats being made in the traditional way.

Contact: Camamu Adventure, tel. (73) 3255-21318, 3258-6236; Natur e Mar, tel. (73) 3258-6361.

Our Recommendation

The décor at **Kiaroa Eco-Luxury Resort** is a blend of tropical and Asian touches. There are 16 suites and eight bungalows. The latter have DVD players and private pools. The beach in front of the resort, Praia de Bombaça, is a practically exclusive stretch of sand. Children under fourteen may not stay at the resort *(Praia da Bombaça, Loteamento Barreta dos Três Coqueiros, Quadra 3, tel. (73) 3258-6215, 3258-6213).*

Additional information on page 462.

❶ Três Coqueiros
Três Coqueiros beach is located near Ponta do Mutá, where the waters of the Maraú River meet the sea. It is accessible from Barra Grande, and known for its strong waves.

❷ Praia de Taipus de Fora
Snorkeling in Praia de Taipus de Fora's tide pools on the coral reefs at low tide is an experience not to be missed.

❸ Lagoa do Cassange
The Cassange lagoon's beach is peaceful and deserted. The lagoon itself is a nice place to swim, and areas good for water sports are not far away. From the Morro da Bela Vista (also known as "Morro do Celular") you can appreciate a scenic view of the lagoon and ocean below.

❹ Morro do Farol de Taipu
From the top of Morro do Farol de Taipu, hikers are rewarded with a panoramic view of the entire peninsula and, in the evening, a beautiful sunset.

❺ Ilha da Pedra Furada
On Pedra Furada Island, beaches are surrounded by forests and mangroves. The island has a good view of Ponta do Mutá (Perforated Rock), thus named for the hole in the middle of one of its stones, the patient work of erosion.

❻ Ilha do Sapinho
Ilha do Sapinho is home to Restaurante do Jorge, well worth a visit for the lobster and *moqueca* stews prepared in the family kitchen.

❼ Ilha do Goió
Goió is best known for its relatively empty beaches.

❽ Ilha do Campinho
The abandoned pier on Campinho Island is a good spot for fishing or an afternoon dive.

❾ Vila de Cajaíba
At the Cajaíba boatyards you can learn about the boat-building tradition of the fishermen.

❿ Saquaíra e Algodões
Summer houses and fishing villages dot the palm-fringed beaches of Saquaíra and Algodões.

⓫ Cachoeira do Tremembé
Tremembé is a waterfall about 30 meters wide.

ITACARÉ

Itacaré's fifteen beaches hug a rugged coastline and forested hills, a landscape different from what predominates in the Northeast. Located 440 kilometers (273 miles) from Salvador, the fishing village stands at the mouth of the Rio Contas river. It was a relatively isolated place until surfers discovered it in the 1970s. July is the best time to surf. Guesthouses and bars are concentrated in the village center, where the sounds of *forró* spill onto the streets. In 1998 the paved **Estrada-Parque** highway opened, making access to Itacaré easy. From Ilhéus, Itacaré is 72 kilometers (45 miles) on Rodovia BA-001 highway.

BEACHES AND ADVENTURE SPORTS

The beaches near the city are the most crowded. The so-called "praias de fora" (out-of-town beaches) are further to the south. They are accessed by trails, some of which pass through private property, where you have to pay a fee. **Prainha**, **São José**, and **Jeribucaçu** beaches are good for surfing. **Engenhoca** and **Havaizinho** are the next two. The former is usually empty; take water and snacks. The latter has good surf and a viewpoint. **Itacarezinho** is the only one with seafront bars and restaurants. Ten minutes away is **Cachoeira do Tijuípe**, a 4-meter (13-feet) waterfall that forms natural pools at its base. Itacaré also has something to offer adventure sports enthusiasts. Visitors can go **rafting** on the Rio Contas river, canyoning, and **canopy climbing**. A **canoe trip** through the mangroves is a more relaxing option. There are also **off-road** trails that lead to the Península de Maraú.
Contact: Eco Trip, tel. (73) 3251-2191; Itacaré Ecoturismo, tel. (73) 3251-3666.

OUR RECOMMENDATION

🍽 **Dedo de Moça** restaurant serves delicately prepared dishes such as beef medallions in red wine. The atmosphere is pleasant, and there's a good variety of wines *(Rua Plínio Soares, 26, Centro, tel. (73) 3251-3372; high season: daily, 4pm – midnight; low season: daily, 7pm – midnight).*

Additional information on page 462.

Itacaré: surfing, adventure sports, and deserted beaches

ILHÉUS

Ilhéus is the largest city on the **Costa do Cacau** (Cacao Coast), which stretches between Itacaré and Canavieiras. It had a more modest beginning, however, as a sugar-cane production settlement during the first years of the colony. By the early 20th century the region became the world's primary producer of cacao, the raw material from which chocolate is made. Writer Jorge Amado (1912-2001) was born here, and it was here that he set his most famous novels. The city has many historic buildings, inviting beaches, and beautiful Atlantic forest

nearby. Most of the buildings in the historical center date from the days of the cacao boom at the dawn of the 20th century. Ilhéus is 462 kilometers (287 miles) from Salvador.

HISTORICAL CENTER

A walk around the Ilhéus city center is an introduction to the life and works of Jorge Amado, as well as the locations of one Amado novel in particular, *Gabriela cravo e canela (Gabriela, Clove, and Cinnamon)*. **Vesúvio Bar**, which opened its doors in 1920, is mentioned several times in the book. Patrons

1. Vesúvio Bar
2. Teatro Municipal
3. Casa de Cultura Jorge Amado
4. Casa dos Artistas
5. Associação Comercial
6. Palácio Paranaguá
7. Rua Antônio Lavigne
8. Igreja matriz de São Jorge dos Ilhéus
9. Palacete de Misael Tavares
10. Casa de Tonico Bastos
11. Catedral de São Sebastião
12. Ilhéus Hotel
13. Antigo porto
14. Bataclan

Ilhéus: beautiful beaches surrounded by the Atlantic forest

lounge around its sidewalk tables and enjoy chilled beer. Nearby stands the **Teatro Municipal** (Municipal Theater), formerly Cine-Theatro de Ilhéus. The theater, built in 1932, was also one of Amado's haunts. The **Casa de Cultura Jorge Amado** resides in the mansion built in the 1920s by Jorge's father using money from a lucky lottery ticket. Guided tours let visitors see the room where the writer slept, photographs, and other personal objects *(Rua Jorge Amado, 21, tel. (73) 3634-8986; Mon – Fri, 9am – noon and 2pm – 6pm; Sat, 9am – 1pm).* The late19 [th]- century **Casa dos Artistas**

arts center, the **Associação Comercial** building, and the **Palácio Paranaguá**, all date from the golden age of cacao. **Rua Antônio Lavigne** was specially paved with English stone for the wedding of the daughter of powerful local cacao baron Misael Tavares. His house, **Palacete de Misael Tavares**, was built in 1922, and sits on the same street, which also leads to **Igreja Matriz de São Jorge dos Ilhéus**, a 16th-century church. The **Casa de Tonico Bastos** house, named for a womanizing character from Jorge Amado's stories, is close to **Catedral de São Sebastião**, a church of truly eclectic design constructed between 1930 and 1967.

JORGE AMADO

Jorge Amado, Brazil's most popular writer, was born in 1912 on Fazenda Auricídia, a farm in Itabuna, near Ilhéus. He grew up on a cacao plantation and the conflicts he witnessed between planters and exporters later became a central theme in his work. Amado was a militant Communist, and was arrested four times and eventually exiled. His 25 novels and other works have been translated into 50 languages. The author received many domestic and international honors before his death on August 6, 2001 in Salvador.

OUR RECOMMENDATION

Transamérica Ilha de Comandatuba resort, south of Ilhéus but north of Canavieiras, is blanketed with gardens and mangroves. Guests have at their disposal a recreation staff, a golf course, and a spa run by the French chain L'Occitane. Water sports are also a popular activity *(Ilha de Comandatuba, no #, tel. (73) 3686-1122, or toll-free 0800-126-060).*

Additional information on page 462.

The **Ilhéus Hotel** was one of the first buildings in the Northeast to install an elevator. A tour of the city center is complete with a stop at the **Antigo Porto** (old port) and the **Bataclan** nightclub, once the haunt of the wealthy and powerful.

VISITING THE CACAO PLANTATIONS

Cacao needs the shade of other trees to thrive. For this reason, cacao plantations also cultivate the tallest species of Atlantic forest trees, making a plantation visit a particularly pleasant experience. Several local plantations welcome visitors. You can watch the production process and try cacao nuts and juice at **Fazenda Primavera** *(Rodovia BR-415, Ilhéus-Itabuna highway, Km 20, tel. (73) 3613-7817, 9983-7627; Mon – Fri, 8am – 4pm; Sat, 8am – noon; book in advance)* and at **Fazenda Yrerê** *(Rodovia BR-415, Ilhéus-Itabuna highway, Km 11, tel. (73) 3656-5054, 9971-7796; Mon – Sat, 9am – 4pm).*

BEACHES IN THE SOUTH

Once a favorite among cacao barons **Praia dos Milionários**, with its kiosks and freshwater showers, is the most popular beach. The next beach, **Cururupe**, has strong waves and mangroves. Surfers, however, usually head for the Olivença district, 16 kilometers (10 miles) from Ilhéus, where the surf is up at **Praia de Back Door** and neighboring **Batuba**. Next come the large hotels on **Canabrava** beach. The road then veers toward the mountains, making access to the quiet coconut palm-fringed beaches like **Acuípe** and **Itapororoca** more difficult.

ECOPARQUE DO UNA

Ecoparque do Una is a private Atlantic forest reserve 45 kilometers (28 miles) from Ilhéus. Its 383 hectares (946 acres) are home to centuries-old trees and several animal species. Bridges suspended 100 meters (328 feet) above ground run through the treetops, allowing lucky visitors a chance to see arboreal golden-lion tamarins, the park's symbol, or yellow-breasted capuchin monkeys. The park's rubber plantation demonstrates rubber tapping.
Rodovia BA-001, Km 45, tel. (73) 3633-1121; Thu – Sat, 9am – 4pm; high season: Tue – Sat, 9am – 4pm (reservations required).

CANAVIEIRAS

Surrounded by mangroves and beaches, Canavieiras is home to a wealth of marine life. One of the town's main attractions is nearby **Ilha de Atalaia**, which is linked to Canavieiras by a bridge. Mud-dwelling crabs known as *aratus* live here. Oddly enough, they are attracted by whistling, and are thus not difficult for locals to find and catch with bamboo sticks. The most popular local beaches are **Praia da Costa** and **Praia de Atalaia**, which both have calm waters. Vendors take advantage of the crowds and set up kiosks selling snacks. To the south, **Barra de Atalaia** beach, at the mouth of the Rio Pardo, is almost always deserted, as is **Praia da Costa Norte**. The sandbanks of **Barra do Albino**, at the mouth of the Rio Patipe, make for a pleasant walk. Barra do Albino is accessed by boat or a 12-kilometer (7-mile) dirt road that turns off near the bridge. Sixteen kilometers (10 miles) north of Canavieiras along Rodovia BA-001 highway lies **Barra Velha**, a quiet, empty beach. Patches of black mud, which locals claim possess aphrodisiac properties, appear at low tide. We recommend you take water and snacks on any of these trips. Canavieiras is also a great place for blue marlin fishing; between November and March the region plays host to enthusiasts from all over the world. Canavieiras is 113 kilometers (70 miles) from Ilhéus and 505 kilometers (313 miles) from Salvador.
Contact: Marina Canes, tel. (73) 3284-3735 (boat trips); Artmarina, tel. (73) 3284-1262 (fishing).

Colonial houses in Porto Seguro, a 16th-century port

PORTO SEGURO

Porto Seguro, founded in 1526, sits on the so-called **Costa do Descobrimento** (Discovery Coast), 723 kilometers (455 miles) of Salvador. It was here that the Portuguese first set foot on the land that would become Brazil. Today it is a popular vacation destination with a solid tourism infrastructure, including an airport, banks, and hotels. Its beaches inevitably become crowded. *Barracas* (beach kiosks) with *axé* and *forró* music blaring spring up everywhere during the high season. Crowds also throng the **Passarela do Álcool**, a street lined with restaurants and stores.

HISTORICAL CENTER

Two hours is all you'll need to see Brazil's first colonial buildings. A tour of the historical center begins with the oldest monument in Brazil, the **Marco da Posse**, brought over from Portugal in 1503. The marble block is engraved with the seal of the Portuguese Crown. Simple **Igreja de Nossa Senhora da Peña** church stands in **Praça Pero de Campos Tourinho** square. The church was built in 1535 and was last renovated in the 18th century. It houses the oldest statue of Saint Francis of Assisi in the country (*no #, tel. (73) 3288-6363; daily, 9am – noon and 2pm – 5pm*). The **Museu de Porto**

PEACEFULNESS IN SANTO ANDRÉ AND BELMONTE

Sparsely populated **Santo André** is 3 kilometers from Santa Cruz Cabrália, north of Porto Seguro. To reach the village you will need to take a car ferry to cross the João de Tiba River. Its coconut groves and flat coastline are an ideal destination for anyone seeking peace and quiet. **Praia de** Guaiú is popular with surfers. Bar Lamarão, in Mojiquiçaba village, serves absolutely delicious crab *pastéis* (deep fried pasties). Sleepy **Belmonte**, 56 kilometers (35 miles) north of Santo Andre, used to be a big cacao production center. Its charming, wide streets are dotted with squares and band-stands and lined with houses with elegant façades. The town has its own lighthouse built in 1800. The sea is brownish in color due to the confluence of several rivers that empty into the ocean here. One of these is the **Jequitinhonha**, which is particularly beautiful at sunset.

Seguro, which was formerly the town council's chambers and prison building, stands in the same square. The museum exhibits indigenous crafts *(no #, tel. (73) 3288-5182; daily, 9am – 5pm)*. The oldest church in Brazil, **Igreja de Nossa Senhora da Misericórdia**, was built in 1526 and today houses a museum of sacred art, the **Museu de Arte Sacra**. Museum highlights include a ruby-encrusted statue of Jesus carrying the cross and a life-size statue of Christ crucified. Both statues date to the late 16th century *(Praça da Misericórdia, no #, tel. (73) 3288-0828; daily, except Wednesdays, 9:30am – 4pm)*. Next to the ruins of the Colégio dos Jesuítas (Jesuit College), built in 1551, is the **Igreja de São Benedito** church, which was probably built in 1549 *(Rua Doutor Antônio Ricaldi, no #)*.

BEACHES

The *barracas* (kiosks) on Porto Seguro's city beaches have become entertainment complexes. Most of them offer dance classes (lambada and *lambaeróbica* – a combination of lambada and aerobics), music shows (*axé* and *forró*), and Internet access, and rent water sports equipment. Check them out if you like lots of action,

crowded beaches and the convenience of seaside services. On **Praia de Taperapuã** the trendiest *barracas* are **Axé Moi, Tôa-Toa**, and **Gaúcho**, on Praia de Rio dos Mangues the place to be is **Barramares**. Beaches further away from the city center, between **Praia de Curuípe** and **Praia do Mutá**, are the quietest. On **Curuípe** beach the **Memorial da Epopéia do Descobrimento** maintains a replica of Pedro Álvares Cabral's flagship. A look around the cabin and the holds demonstrates just how fragile the original vessel was *(Rodovia BR-367, Km 63, Praia do Itacimirim, tel. (73) 3268-2586; high season: daily, 8:30am – 6pm; low season: Mon – Sat, 8:30am – 12:30pm and 1:30pm – 5pm)*.

COROA VERMELHA

On April 26th, 1500, the first Mass on Brazilian soil was celebrated on the tiny island of Coroa Vermelha, between Porto Seguro and Santa Cruz Cabrália. An enormous, solitary steel cross marks the spot where the Portuguese first met the native inhabitants, whose way of life has been endangered ever since. The event is commemorated every year in an open-air amphitheater here.

Coroa Vermelha, where the first Mass on Brazilian soil was celebrated

ARRAIAL D'AJUDA

Arraial d'Ajuda's narrow streets, often lit by candles at night, pulse with crowds who come to enjoy the stores, cafés, and studios. The busiest thoroughfare is **Estrada de Mucugê**. Culinary diversity and the big nightlife scene create a cosmopolitan atmosphere that reaches a fevered pitch among the luaus and raves of the beach *barracas* (kiosks). The same energy can be found in the bars on **Rua da Broadway**. Those looking for more reflective moments may find them at **Igreja Matriz de Nossa Senhora da Ajuda** church, which was built in 1551. It stands in the square called **Largo da Ajuda**. To reach Arraial d'Ajuda from Porto Seguro, you can take a 10-minute car ferry ride, or drive 60 kilometers (37 miles) on Rodovia BA-001 highway.

BEACHES
Arraial has both quiet and lively beaches. **Apaga-fogo** and **Araçaípe** have been taken over by hotels and guesthouses, most of which rent water sport gear. Some stretches of the beach have tide pools. **Mucugê** has strong waves breaking near the beach, but rock pools appear at low tide. You can rent windsurfing equipment and kayaks at **Praia do Parracho**, which has the best luaus. **Pitinga** has a few *barracas* and a number of charming guesthouses. The beach's south end is reserved for nudist bathers, as is the entirety of isolated **Taípe**, with its huge cliffs and strong waves. An hour before low tide is a good time to walk along the 12 kilometer (7 mile) stretch of beach between Mucugê and Trancoso.

WATER PARK
Water slides, a wave pool, and an artificial river entertain adults and children alike at the **Arraial d'Ajuda Eco Parque**. This water park sits in the middle of a swath of Atlantic forest on Praia d'Ajuda beach, which is also known as Praia de Coqueiros, Praia do Delegado, and Praia dos Pescadores.
Estrada do Arraial d'Ajuda, Km 4.5, tel. (73) 3575-8600. Opening days and times vary throughout the year.

In Arraial, the serenity of everyday life contrasts with the lively nightlife and cosmopolitan cuisine

Praia do Espelho reflects the morning sky; in the afternoon, colorful fish fill the waters

TRANCOSO

Trancoso is a name synonymous with sophistication and originality. The village became popular with hippies in the 1970s, and today juxtaposes designer label stores with modest, unadorned buildings. The heart of the village is Quadrado square, which is surrounded by historic, well-homes that have found a second calling as restaurants, bars, furniture stores, craft stores, studios, and guesthouses. Foreigners and locals crowd the streets day and at night. In the evening, candles from the bars shed their flickering light onto starlit streets.

Quadrado has no public lighting. Music spills out the doors and onto the streets. Taste varies widely and includes MPB, jazz, blues, and a little *forró*. Despite its modern indulgences, history continues to make its presence felt in Trancoso. **Igreja de São João Batista** was built in the 18th century on the site of a ruined Jesuit convent. An old bell tower remains, as do pink limestone holy water fonts, a wooden staircase, and a pulpit inside. Every year on January 20 the town overflows for faithful celebrants of the Festa de São Sebastião (Festival of Saint Sebastian).

OUR RECOMMENDATION

On the water's edge, near the Trancoso River, **Pousada Estrela d'Água** offers a choice between spacious rooms and chalets built in its gardens. The pool and communal areas have ocean views *(Estrada Arraial d'Ajuda, no #, 1.5 Km from Trancoso, tel. (73) 3668-1030).*

Additional information on page 462.

BEACHES AND OUTDOOR ACTIVITIES

Beaches with extensive stretches of sand, protected by mangroves and the Trancoso River, are accessible on foot, on horseback, or by bicycle or boat. **Praia dos Nativos**, near the town center, has coarse sand, calm seas, and deserted stretches popular with nudist bathers. The gentle waves of **Praia dos**

Monte Pascoal: The Atlantic forest here was Portuguese explorer Cabral's first view of Brazil

Coqueiros serve as a departure point for boat trips. The stretch of coastline to the south, from Praia de Taípe to Caraíva, is ideal for outdoor activities, including walks, horseback riding, cycling, 4×4 trips, quadricycling, river kayaking, diving, and schooner or motorboat trips. The region's rich natural beauty and diverse animal life are in abundance in the **Vale dos Búfalos** valley, a lush flood plain that is home to numerous bird species and some 4,000 buffalo. Similar beauty can be appreciated from the **Estrada dos Macacos** road, which crosses rivers and farmland and cuts through Atlantic forest inhabited by monkeys. **Estrada**

da Sapiara road is lined with manioc flour mills and coconut plantations. Tours are available through agencies in Porto Seguro, Arraial, and Trancoso. *Contact: Trancoso Receptivo, tel. (71) 3668-1333, 3668-1183.*

CURUÍPE AND ESPELHO
Separated by a small creek, **Praia do Curuípe** and **Praia do Espelho** are part of one of the loveliest stretches of coastline in Bahia. Charming restaurants and guesthouses sit in a postcard perfect landscape of cliffs, rivers, coconut palms, and tide pools. Hammocks and loungers are scattered on the sand. "Praia do Espelho" is an appropriate name. *Espelho* means 'mirror,' and at low tide the water looks like a huge mirror reflecting the blue of the sky. Access to the area by car from Trancoso is controlled by a gate at Condomínio Outeiro das Brisas. The beaches can also be reached by boat or motorboat from Trancoso or Caraíva. It's worth visiting tiny, unsophisticated **Praia dos Amores**, north of Curuípe, at low tide to see its tide pools surrounded by cliffs. The beach is very popular with couples on their honeymoon.

GOLF BY THE SEA

Terravista Golf Course, between Praia de Taípe and Rio da Barra, offers golf lovers one of the best courses in the Northeast. The 18-hole course has four holes on the cliff tops overlooking the sea. Terravista has its own instructors and equipment rental is available. The course even has its own landing strip. *Estrada Municipal de Trancoso, Km 18, Fazenda Itaípe, tel. (73) 2105-2104. Mon – Sat, 8am – 5pm.*

CARAÍVA

Simple and remote, the village of **Caraíva** combines natural beauty with local hospitality. It's the ideal spot for visitors in search of rest and relaxation. There are no paved streets, just sandy tracks, and no electricity, just generators that are switched off at 10pm. Cars are not allowed; carts are the only means of transport. Most come to spend sunny days on deserted beaches with coconut palms and offshore coral reefs. The Rio Caraíva flows through the village and canoe trips are available from local canoe owners and fishermen. A lazy afternoon in the gardens of the **Pousada da Lagoa** restaurant is time well spent. At night musicians play live *forró* music on Rua do Ouriço and Rua do Pelé. One reason the village remains off the beaten track is that it is so difficult to access. At the height of summer, it can be reached by motorboat from Trancoso. Normally, however, visitors take a dirt road off Rodovia BR-101 highway (drive through the village of Monte Pascoal, at Km 753 on Rodovia BR-101), and then cross the Rio Caraíva river by canoe. The **Reserva Indígena de Barra Velha** reservation, home to the Pataxó Indians, is near Monte Pascoal, as well. The Pataxó perform dances and songs for visitors and sell native crafts (necklaces and basket ware). Local tourist agencies organize visits. **Monte Pascoal**, the first Brazilian landform sighted by explorer Pedro Álvares Cabral, is also nearby. Making it to the top requires significant stamina.

CUMURUXATIBA AND PONTA DO CORUMBAU

Anyone looking for isolation but still keen on electricity and running water need look no farther than **Cumuruxatiba**. Cumuru, as it's more commonly known, has colorful cliffs, rivers, extensive beaches, and small, rocky islands ideal for reef diving. The village is accessible by land or sea, whether coming from Porto Seguro in the north (along the Rodovia BR-101 highway) or from Prado and Caravelas in the south. North of Cumuru there are several relatively empty beaches, such as **Barra do Caí** and lovely **Ponta do Corumbau.** The latter is one kilometer long and surrounded by mangroves and sophisticated beach hotels. It has one beach kiosk, Sol e Vida, which sells food and offers fishing trips. Corumbau can be

Ponta do Corumbau, an isolated stretch of sand surrounded by mangroves

reached by motorboat, or in a 4×4 (take Rodovia BR-489 highway, followed by dirt road trek to Vila Corumbau). Other off-road experiences are available through tour agencies, which provide interesting horseback riding and hiking trips, some of which last a few days.

Contact: Aquamar, tel. (73) 3573-1360; guide Hélio Nativa, tel. (73) 8802-8371 (treks).

BOAT TRIPS AND WHALE WATCHING

Most boat trips include a stop at Ponta do Corumbau, where visitors can snorkel in the Carapeba reefs. Trips to observe **humpback whales** are available July through November. There are also motorboat excursions to Caraíva, Praia do Espelho, and Praia de Curuípe.

Contact: Aquamar, tel. (73) 3573-1360; Mestre Antônio Carlos, tel. (73) 3573-1127.

PRADO AND BECO DAS GARRAFAS

Prado, between Caraíva and Caravelas, has a few more tourist facilities than its neighbors. **Beco das Garrafas**, a small street with good restaurants, is in the colorful town center. The brownish sea is not very inviting, but one of the region's star attractions is the lovely, mangrove-fringed Jucuruçu River.

ABROLHOS

The **Arquipélago de Abrolhos**, inside Parque Nacional Marinho de Abrolhos, is a small paradise in the middle of the ocean. The archipelago's five islands – Redonda, Guarita, Sueste, Santa Bárbara, and Siriba – can only be accessed by a guided boat, docking at Siriba. Visibility reaches 20 meters (68 feet) between May and September. You won't be the first to appreciate the variety of coral, fish, turtles, and birds. Charles Darwin visited in 1830. Humpback whales, which can grow up to 16 meters (52 feet) in length and weigh 40 tons, visit the region between July and November to calve and suckle.

Abrolhos offers waters teeming with marine life and ideal for diving

Hawsksbill sea turtle, found in all of the tranquil Abrolhos coastline

Trips to Abrolhos normally stop at Siriba (docking is not allowed at the other islands) and last one or two days; two day trips include an overnight stay on your boat. During the high season trips need to be booked in advance. The best time to see the whales is in September or October, as trips are often canceled in July and August due to bad weather. The archipelago is about 70 kilometers (44 miles) off the coast of Caravelas.
Contact: Abrolhos Embarcações, tel. (73) 3297-1172.

CARAVELAS

Caravelas is the gateway to the Abrolhos, and tour agencies and hotels are not hard to find. The town also has a few architectural landmarks; in particular, **Rua Barão do Rio Branco** and **Rua Sete de Setembro** are lined with colonial homes decorated with Portuguese tiles. The **Centro de Visitantes do Ibama**, run by the Brazilian Institute for the Environment and Renewable Natural Resources (Ibama), has a life-size model of a humpback whale. They also have a collection of photographs and a library *(Praia do Quitongo, no #, tel. (73) 3297-1111; daily, 8am – 8pm)*. Whale lovers might also enjoy the **Instituto Baleia Jubarte**, which monitors humpback whales and supplies the guides that accompany trips to the Abrolhos marine park *(Rua Barão do Rio Branco, 26, Centro, tel. (73) 3297-1320; Mon – Fri, 8am – noon and 2pm – 6pm; Sat, 8:30am – 11:30am)*.

CHAPADA DIAMANTINA

Chapada Diamantina's landscape is an impressive pastiche of caves, waterfalls, canyons, and natural pools. Diamond miners flocked here in the 19th century to make their fortunes, but mining was banned in 1985. Today the region attracts nature lovers. Unfortunately, the road to Chapada Diamantina, Rodovia BR-242 highway is poorly maintained and demands the driver's full concentration. The region can be explored from **Lençóis**, **Vale do Capão (Caeté-Açu)**, **Andaraí**, **Igatu**, and **Mucugê**. There are daily flights to Lençóis airport from Salvador and São Paulo. Most hikes are challenging and

Vale do Paty, in Chapada Diamantina, is an unspoiled example of Bahia's sertão

adventure sports enthusiasts seeking even edgier activities won't be disappointed. It's well worth it to work with an agency for trips and guides. If you hire guides independently, you'll need your own transportation.

Contact: Associação dos Condutores de Visitantes de Andaraí *(ACVA), tel. (75) 3335-2255; Associação dos Condutores de Visitantes de Lençóis (ACVL), tel. (75) 3334-1425; Associação dos Condutores de Visitantes do Vale do Capão (ACVVC), tel. (75) 3344-1087; Pé no Mato, tel. (75) 3344-1105; Terra Chapada Expedições, tel. (75) 3334-1428.*

TORRINHA, PRATINHA AND LAPA DOCE

Eighty-two kilometers (51 miles) north of Lençóis is the **Iraquara** region, best known for its caves. **Gruta de Torrinha** cave has rare aragonite "flower" rock formations. **Gruta da Pratinha** has an underground stream suitable for snorkeling (if you wear a life vest). The sunlight reflected in the waters of **Gruta Azul** creates a beautiful show of dancing colors. **Lapa Doce** has a spacious cavern that rises, 40 meters (131 feet) high, with stalactites and stalagmites.

LENÇÓIS AND VALE DO CAPÃO (CAETÉ-AÇU)

Lençóis, 425 kilometers (264 miles) from Salvador, is the gateway to the Chapada. It's a charming place, with pink stone sidewalks and colonial buildings. The **Vale do Capão** valley is 70 kilometers (43 miles) from away, connected to the town by the Estrada Palmeiras-Caeté-Açu. The **Cachoeira da Fumaça** trail is just off the same road.

MORRO DO PAI INÁCIO

Legend has it that Pai Inácio was a runaway slave who climbed the mountain and jumped to safety with the aid of an umbrella. A thirty minute hike will take you to the top, an altitude of 1,170 meters (3,840 feet).

SALÃO DE AREIAS AND WATERFALLS

The stretch of the Lençóis River known as the Serrano is home to the **Salão de Areias**, whose sandstone rock is mined and ground back into sand by local artisans who use it to make colorful scenes in bottles. The area's waterfalls are well worth seeing. An 8-kilometer trail

leads south from Lençóis to **Cachoeira do Sossego,** a 15 meter waterfall.

GRUTA DO LAPÃO

The Lapão cave is one of the largest quartzite caves in the country. Its entrance is 50 meters (164 feet) wide, and extends one kilometer into the earth. Visitors should plan on setting aside about four and a half hours for the round trip.

CACHOEIRA DA FUMAÇA

This waterfall takes your breath away twice: once on the steep stretches of the 6-kilometer trail up to the canyon rim, and again when you see the waterfall itself. Water cascades from a height of almost 340 meters (1,115 feet), and dissipates long before it hits the ground, creating a smoke-like effect.

MUCUGÊ

Mucugê, 150 kilometers (93 miles) from Lençóis, owes its agreeable climate and mild average temperature (19 degrees Celsius; 66 degrees Fahrenheit) to its high altitude (1,000 meters; 3,280 feet). The historic town center is a national heritage site and home to a number of 19th-century landmarks, including **Igreja Matriz de Santa Isabel, Prefeitura** (City Hall), and the impressive **Cemitério Bizantino** cemetery. Researchers at the **Parque Municipal de Mucugê** study the preservation and cultivation of the rare *sempre-viva* (everlasting) flower.

The park has trails leading to three waterfalls, **Piabinhas** (10 meters), **Tiburtino** (a sequence of falls dropping 200 meters), and **Andorinhas** (10 meters). The longest trail leads to Andorinhas and takes an hour each way *(Rodovia BA-142, Km 96, toward Andaraí, 4 km from Mucugê, tel. (75) 3338-2156; daily, 8am – 6pm).* **Ibiocora,** 56 kilometers (35 miles) south of Mucugê, has two waterfalls, **Cachoeira do Buracão** (85 meters), ahalf hour hike, and **Cachoeira da Fumacinha** (100 meters), an eight hour hike.

PARQUE NACIONAL DA CHAPADA DIAMANTINA

Chapada Diamantina national park is a dazzling island of wilderness offering plenty of **trails** and **adventure sports**. The park has no main gate and the only paved road that crosses it is Rodovia BA-142 highway; the rest of it is rivers, mountains, and forests. Its 152,000 hectares (375,600 acres) encompass Lençóis, Andaraí, Mucugê, and Palmeiras. Chapada Diamantina is often seen as synonymous with the Serra do Sincorá mountain range.

TRAILS

Morro do Pai Inácio–Capão

From the top of Pai Inácio, you can see Morro do Camelo to the north, and a string of valleys and fields stretching toward the foot of Morrão in the south. The top of Pai Inácio is also where the trail to Vale do Capão begins. It is an excellent hike of medium difficulty that traverses breathtaking scenery. The trek is about 30 kilometers (19 miles) long, 25 of which are done by car, and the remaining 5 on foot. The trip requires a full day, unless instead of going straight to Capão you go to Conceição dos Gatos, and from there by car to the valley, in which case it takes about five hours.

Lençóis–Capão

This is a medium-level hike of about five hours. The trail passes by the foot of Morrão and winds along rivers with good spots for swimming.

Morrão

Morrão can be reached any one of several ways from Lençóis, Morro do Pai Inácio, Vale do Capão, or Povoado de Conceição dos Gatos. Once at the foot of the mountain, it takes an hour and a half to get to the top. It's a steep ascent – at several points you'll need to climb rather than walk – but the view makes the effort worthwhile.

Igatu–Andaraí

This is an easy, four hour hike with impressive scenery. Setting out from the central square, continue past Igreja de São Sebastião and the cemetery and walk along the left bank of the Xique-Xique River. The trail climbs steeply, but soon levels out. Throughout the hike you'll be struck by the ways in which the landscape of the Chapada has been changed by mining. There is also a striking panoramic view from the mountains, which overlook the xique-xique (a type of cactus) and the beaches of the Paraguaçu River on the plains below.

Vale do Paty

Getting to Vale do Paty path takes a very long, demanding walk. For precisely this reason there are several rest points along the way. Beautiful hills and majestic walls surround the long, deep valley in the heart of the Sincora Range. You can choose the starting points. The most commonly traveled routes begin in Capão to the north, Guiné to the west, or Andaraí to the east. There is also a less popular path from Mucugê.

Lençóis–Cachoeira da Fumaça

You need to be in good shape to reach the top of the breathtaking Cachoeira da Fumaça falls. There are two ways to get there. One is to start at the bottom of the waterfall and hike to the top – a three-day endeavor that begins in Lençóis and ends in the Vale de Capão. Alternatively, you can head straight to the Vale de Capão, a 50 kilometers (31 miles) journey on paved road followed by 22 kilometers (14 miles) on dirt road and an arduous, six kilometer ascent to the top of the waterfall. While difficult, the latter makes it possible to return to Capão the same day.

ADVENTURE SPORTS

Trekking is not the only exciting way to experience Chapada Diamantina. Agencies and guides in Lençóis are happy to help you set up a climbing, rappelling, and/or canyoning adventure on **Morro do Camelo** (250 meters, 850 feet) or **Pai Inácio** (150 meters, 490 feet). They can also set up trips to **Cachoeira do Mosquito** (two falls, 35 and 50 meters), near the **Morro do Chapéu**, 350 kilometers (217 miles) from Lençóis. Some agencies cover the Ibicoara region, 230 kilometers (143 miles) from Lençóis. These trips include transportation and stop at **Gruta dos Brejões** (123 meters, 404 feet deep), **Serra dos Brejões** (170 meters, 560 feet), or **Cachoeira do Bu-** **racão** (100 meters, 330 feet). Closer to Lençóis, visitors to **Gruta do Lapão** (55 meters, 180 feet) may choose to go bungee or cave-jumping; that is to say, bungee-jumping into a cave.

Contact: Nativos da Chapada, tel. (75) 3334-1314; Adrenalina, tel. (75) 3334-1261; Rony Aleixo (mountain bikes), tel. (75) 3334-1700.

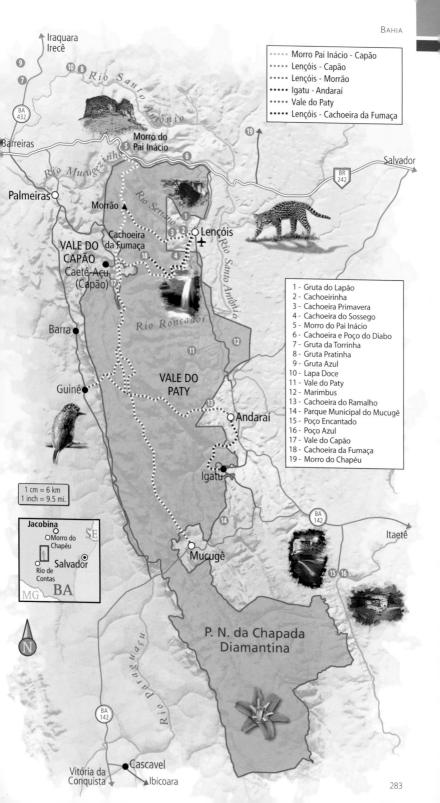

Legenda:
- Morro Pai Inácio - Capão
- Lençóis - Capão
- Lençóis - Morrão
- Igatu - Andaraí
- Vale do Paty
- Lençóis - Cachoeira da Fumaça

1 - Gruta do Lapão
2 - Cachoeirinha
3 - Cachoeira Primavera
4 - Cachoeira do Sossego
5 - Morro do Pai Inácio
6 - Cachoeira e Poço do Diabo
7 - Gruta da Torrinha
8 - Gruta Pratinha
9 - Gruta Azul
10 - Lapa Doce
11 - Vale do Paty
12 - Marimbus
13 - Cachoeira do Ramalho
14 - Parque Municipal do Mucugê
15 - Poço Encantado
16 - Poço Azul
17 - Vale do Capão
18 - Cachoeira da Fumaça
19 - Morro do Chapéu

1 cm = 6 km
1 inch = 9.5 mi.

Lugares:
- Iraquara / Irecê
- Barreiras
- Palmeiras
- Morrão
- VALE DO CAPÃO
- Caeté-Açu (Capão)
- Barra
- Guiné
- Morro do Pai Inácio
- Lençóis
- VALE DO PATY
- Andaraí
- Igatu
- Mucugê
- Itaeté
- Salvador
- P. N. da Chapada Diamantina
- Cascavel
- Vitória da Conquista
- Ibicoara

Rio Santo Antônio
Rio Mucugezinho
Rio Serrano
Rio Roncador
Rio Paraguaçu

Jacobina
Morro do Chapéu
Salvador
Rio de Contas
SE
BA
MG

BA 432
BR 242
BA 142

N

ANDARAÍ AND IGATU

The old diamond-mining town of **Andaraí**, 100 kilometers (62 miles) from Lençóis on Rodovia BA-142 highway, seems frozen in time. It sits on the eastern edge of the Sincora Range, and is a good base for exploring the **Vale do Paty** and **Marimbus**. The charming **Igatu** district, formerly known as Xique-Xique, has a population of about 350. Houses sit abandoned, remnants of the diamond boom. **Galeria Arte & Memória** hosts art and photography exhibitions and displays objects found in the old mines *(Rua Luís dos Santos, no #, tel. (75) 3335-2510; Tue – Sun, 9am – 6pm)*. To reach Igatut take Rodovia BA-142 highway and exit onto the dirt road at Km 52, or Km 82. The town is six kilometers down this road.

The impressive visual effects of Poço Encantado

MARIMBUS

The Santo Antônio River cascades from the heights of the Sincora Mountain Range in Andaraí and eventually spreads out, creating a flooded lowland region known as the Marimbus, or Chapada, Wetlands. The wetlands are home to a diverse population of birds and fish. Anacondas and alligators slide between Victoria waterlilies, and tapirs rustle through the undergrowth.

RAMPA DO CAIM

The 10-kilometer Rampa do Caim trail leads to a lookout point with a splendid view of Chapada Diamantina. Guides usually take visitors to two different viewpoints. One looks out on Cânion **do Paraguaçu** canyon, the other provides a vista of the valley named **Vale do Paty**. It's a two and a half hour trip up, and a slightly shorter journey back.

POÇO ENCANTADO AND POÇO AZUL

The blue shades of Poço Encantado pool are extraordinary. Encantado is located in Itaetê, about 160 kilometers (100 miles) from Lençóis. The area's geologic composition is largely carbonate rock, which is prone to water infiltration and the formation of caves and tunnels. Poço Encantado began as one such tunnel. Between April and September, sunlight strikes the water in such a way as to create an enchanting (hence the name *encantado*) play of color. The pool is accessed by climbing down a 90-meter (290-foot) descent comprised of steps and steep trails. A smaller pool, **Poço Azul**, is located in Nova Redenção, 67 kilometers (42 miles) from Andaraí. The best time to visit Poço Azul is between February and October. Swimming is forbidden in both pools.

SERGIPE

Highlights

- Atalaia Beach, **Aracaju**'s most fashionable.
- The historical city center and sacred art museum in **São Cristóvão**.
- The lovely late 16th-century architecture of **Laranjeiras**.
- Boat trips through the São Francisco River canyon, departing from **Canindé**.

When to Go

- Avoid the rainy season (April through July) to enjoy the beaches and trips on the São Francisco River.
- In January, for the folk performances at Laranjeiras's Encontro cultural festival.
- In June, for the Forró Caju festival – especially on June 24 for St. John's Day festivities.

ARACAJU

Founded in 1855, Aracaju replaced São Cristóvão as the then-province's capital of the then-province. It sits on the banks of the Sergipe River and attracts visitors to about 30 kilometers (19 miles) of beachfront and warm, calm waters. The major historical monuments are concentrated in the city center, with **Praça Fausto Cardoso** square at its heart. **Palácio Olímpio Campos** palace (1863), the old government seat, is another major monument. While in town, make time to climb to the top of

Colina de Santo Antônio hill, which offers a view of most of the capital. The 13-day **Forró Caju** festival, held in **Praça Hilton Lopes**, draws thousands to square in June. The state's best beaches are only a day trip from Aracaju.

BEACHES

Aracaju is really a single beach that changes its name at several points. The trendiest stretch is **Praia de Atalaia**, where an attractive, built-up shoreline offers a promenade shaded by coconut

LARANJEIRAS

Laranjeiras, located 23 kilometers (14 miles) from Aracaju, was founded in 1594. In 1701, the Jesuits built **Capela de Santo Antônio** and the first residence of the order, known as the **Retiro** (Retreat), which is now national heritage listed *(Fazenda Brandão, no #, Zona Rural, tel. (79) 3280-1172; arrange visits with Maísse Gama)*. **Igreja de Nossa Senhora da Con-**

ceição de **Comandaroba**, a 1743 church with rich stone carvings at its entrance, may be the last Jesuit building in Sergipe; the Order of Jesus was expelled from the colony in 1759 *(Rua da Comandaroba, no #, Zona Rural, one kilometer from the town center)*. To visit the church, contact the Department of Tourism to arrange a guided tour *(Secretaria de Turismo: tel. (79) 3281-1332)*.

Collections at the **Museu Afro-Brasileiro** offer information about the history of Brazilian black culture, sugarcane farming and slavery *(Rua José do Prado Franco, 70, Centro, tel. (79) 3281-2418; Tue – Sun, 10am – 5pm)*. Laranjeiras is famous for its folk festivals. For 30 years, it has staged the most important folk art event in the state: the **Encontro Cultural**, which takes place in January.

trees, a bike path, sports facilities and a playground. **Praia de Aruana** has the ever-lively **Passarela do Caranguejo**, a row of kiosks and restaurants specializing in freshwater crab. On the same beach, visitors can see turtles and fish at the **Oceanário de Aracaju**, an aquarium maintained by Projeto Tamar, a group devoted to the protection of sea turtles *(Avenida Santos Dumont, no #, Atalaia beachfront, tel. (79) 3243-3214, 3243-6126; Tue – Fri, 2pm – 8pm; Sat, Sun, and holidays, 9am – 9pm; in January, daily, 9am – 10pm).*

MEMORY AND HISTORY

The 6,000 items on display at the **Memorial de Sergipe** illustrate Sergipe's social and cultural history. Don't miss the possessions belonging to legendary outlaw Lampião and his men, as well as the weapons police used to kill him in 1938 at Grota do Angico, in Sergipe's interior *(Avenida Beira-Mar, 626, 13 de Julho, tel. (79) 3211-3579; Mon, 2pm – 6pm; Tue – Sat, 9am – 6pm).* The **Museu do Homem Sergipano** offers exhibits of archeological objects, documents and photographs in an early 20th-century building *(Rua Estância,* 228, Centro, tel. (79) 3211-5798; Mon – Fri, 8am – noon and 2pm – 5:30pm).

ART AND CRAFT MARKETS

Sergipe's artisans produce a wide variety of traditional arts and crafts. **Museu do Artesanato** displays works in clay and wood, and its stores sell bedspreads, tablecloths and women's clothing *(Praça Olímpio Campos, formerly Rua 24 Horas, no #, Centro, tel. (79) 3214-6834; museum: Mon – Fri, 7am – 6pm; Sat and Sun, 8am – 2pm; stores: daily, 9am – 6pm).* At the **Mercado Municipal Antônio Franco**, visitors will find crafts from all over the state *(Rua José do Prado Franco, no #; Mon – Sat, 7am – 6pm).* **Centro de Arte e Cultura de Sergipe** houses more sophisticated art. The cultural center's collection of fine regional work is all for sale. Top billing is given to the work of José Roberto de Freitas, who goes by the nickname "Beto Pezão" (Bigfoot Beto) and creates clay figurines with enormous feet. Also prominent are the miniature works of Cícero Alves dos Santos, nicknamed "Véio" (Old Guy) *(Avenida Santos Dumont, no #, Atalaia beachfront, tel. (79) 3255-1413; Mon – Sat, 10am – 10pm; Sun and holidays, 2pm – 10pm).*

Pirambu Beach, north of Aracaju, hosts the turtle-conservation headquarters of Projeto Tamar

Igreja e Convento de São Francisco, now the Museu de Arte Sacra de São Cristóvão

SÃO CRISTÓVÃO

Sergipe's former capital was founded in 1590, and its well-preserved town center is worth roaming on foot. Opposite this square is the **Museu de Arte Sacra** *(no #, tel. (79) 9191-6920; Tue and Thu, 9am – 5pm; Wed, Sat and Sun, 1pm – 5pm).* This sacred art museum has a collection of about 500 pieces and is one of the most important of its kind in Brazil. Construction on the Franciscan convent that now houses the museum began in 1657, but it was not finished until 1726. The **Museu Histórico de Sergipe**, located in the same square, displays furniture, decorative items and clothes *(no #, tel. (79) 3261-1435).* The national-heritage-listed church **Matriz de Nossa Senhora da Vitória** dates from the first half of the 17th century and has been extensively restored *(Praça da Matriz, no #, tel. (79) 3261-1152; Tue – Fri, 8am – 11am and 2pm – 4:30pm; Sat, 3pm – 4pm).* Work began on the architectural complex made up of the **Igreja de Nossa Senhora do Carmo** and **Igreja da Ordem Terceira** and the **Convento** in the late 17th century, but its construction took nearly a century to finish *(Praça do Senhor dos Passos, no #, tel. (79) 3261-1605; Tue – Fri, 7am –*

11am and 3pm – 4pm). Dutch invaders reportedly built the **Igreja Nossa Senhora do Amparo**. An old black brotherhood called the Irmandade de Amparo dos Homens Pardos once maintained the structure *(Travessa do Amparo, no #, formerly Rua das Flores; Tue – Fri, 8am – 11:30am and 2pm – 5pm).* In Praça da Matriz, the square in front of the main church, **Casa da Queijada** sells delicious *queijadinhas* (coconut cheesecakes). São Cristóvão is 23 kilometers (14 miles) from Aracaju on Rodovia SE-004 highway (Rodovia João Bebe Água).

CANINDÉ DO SÃO FRANCISCO

This town lies 198 kilometers (123 miles) from Aracaju at the border of Sergipe, Alagoas and Bahia. It serves as the main departure point for boat trips through the majestic **Cânion do São Francisco,** the world's most easily navigated river canyon *(MS-TUR, tel. (79) 9972-1320, (82) 9986-2038).* **Museu Arqueológico**, with its prehistoric human skeletons, is worth a visit *(Rodovia Canindé-Piranhas, Km 2, tel. (79) 2105-6448; Wed – Sun, 9:30am – 4:30pm).* **Grota do Angico**, the cave where police officers killed the outlaw Lampião, is also in Canindé *(Contact: Xingó Parque Hotel, tel. (79) 3346-1245).*

ALAGOAS

HIGHLIGHTS

- Raft trips to the natural pools in **Pajuçara** and schooner trips to the islands in Maceió's **Lagoa Mundaú** and **Lagoa Manguaba** lagoons.
- The blouses, skirts, tablecloths and other items made by the lace makers of **Pontal da Barra**, a village at the entrance to Maceió.
- The **Rota Ecológica**, a route linking Barra do Camaragibe and Japaratinga.
- The architecture of **Penedo**, including its 18th-century churches.

WHEN TO GO

- In **summer** (December to February) for optimal weather, although it is sunny all year round.
- In the **second weekend of January** for the Festival de Tradições Populares folk festival and the Bom Jesus de Penedo procession.
- In **June** for the lively São João festivities in Maceió.
- In **November**, for the Maceió Fest, a very popular out-of-season Carnival.

MACEIÓ

The Alagoas state capital occupies a narrow strip between **Lagoa Mundaú** and the Atlantic, where the sea looks like a watercolor in shades of green. The native Tupi-Guarani people called this region *maayó* or *maçaio-k*, which means "covering the marsh." Maceió became a town in 1815 and state capital in 1839. Today, its population of 880,000 enjoys a lovely coastline and beaches. At night the action is on the beachfront – Pajuçara, Jatiúca and Ponta Negra – and in the neighborhood of Stella Maris. The city also serves as a base for day trips to the coast, but beach-bound traffic causes heavy congestion on holidays.

CITY BEACHES

The most famous beach is **Praia de Pajuçara**, two kilometers (just over 1 mile) from the center. It boasts calm seas, a jogging path, a bicycle lane, and showers. Sailing rafts called *jangadas* leave here for trips to the natural pools that form at low tide (check local papers for the tides). The popular, coconut palm-covered **Praia de Ponta Verde** has a lot of hotels, restaurants, and kiosks with live music, and is 4 kilometers (2.5 miles) from the town center. **Praia de Jatiúca**, 6 kilometers (almost 4 miles) away, holds surfing championships and is the location of Lampião, a bar famous for its *forró* dances. Another popular surfer beach is **Praia de Cruz das Almas**. To the south is **Pontal da Barra**, where you can find simple restaurants serving fresh seafood or take a four-hour boat trip to nine of the 32 lagoon islands in **Lagoa Mundaú** and **Manguaba**.

Contact: Edvantur, tel. (82) 3372-2058, 9981-0738.

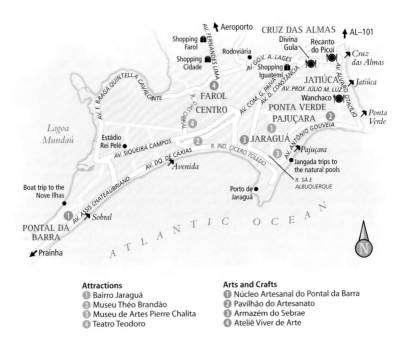

Attractions
1. Bairro Jaraguá
2. Museu Théo Brandão
3. Museu de Artes Pierre Chalita
4. Teatro Teodoro

Arts and Crafts
1. Núcleo Artesanal do Pontal da Barra
2. Pavilhão do Artesanato
3. Armazém do Sebrae
4. Ateliê Viver de Arte

Catamaran Trips to Paripueira

Brazil's longest coral reef starts at Praia de Paripueira, a beach 32 kilometers (20 miles) from Maceió, and extends up to Porto de Galinhas, in Pernambuco state. A catamaran trip to the reef lasts about two hours, including a stop at some natural pools. At low tide you can walk about a kilometer out to sea, where the water is only knee-deep.
Contact: Mar e Cia, tel. (82) 3293-1983, 3293-2031.

Jaraguá Neighborhood

A revitalization project that began in 1995 has breathed life back into this neighborhood, which used to be the heart of the city. Jaraguá began to develop in the 1500s and in the second half of the 19th century it was an important commercial center, but fell into decline with the passage of time. Today it is a national heritage site, and some of its preserved old townhouses and warehouses are now bars. Jaraguá's landmark buildings include the **Associação Comercial**, dating from 1926, and the **Museu da Imagem e do Som**, which dates from 1869 and used to be the Customs House, although it is now an image and sound museum. Lace makers sell their wares at the museum entrance.

Islands like this one dot Lagoa Manguaba

Other Attractions

The collection at the **Museu Théo Brandão**, a museum exhibiting items connected to folk culture, was donated to Alagoas Federal University by local doctor and folklorist Théo Brandão (1907-81). Highlights include anthropomorphic clay jugs made by Júlio Rufino and the ceramics of two masters, Vitalino and Nô Caboclo. There are traditional folklore performances on Thursday nights at 8pm *(Avenida da Paz, 1490, Jaraguá, tel. (82) 3221-2651; Tue – Fri, 9am – 5pm; Sat, 2pm – 5pm)*. You can see

---

Zumbi dos Palmares

Alagoas was the site of Brazil's greatest slave revolt, the União dos Palmares, a confederation of slaves led by Zumbi. Of Angolan descent, Zumbi was born in Palmares – about 70 kilometers (43 miles) from Maceió – in 1655. Baptized Francisco and raised by Father Antônio Melo, he learned Latin and was an altar boy as a youngster. At age 15, he ran away and adopted the name Zumbi. Back in Palmares he joined a community made of up several quilombos, or settlements of escaped slaves, that eventually numbered 30,000. For decades, Palmares held back troops supported by the Portuguese Crown, but in 1694 Zumbi was wounded and Palmares was destroyed. A year later Zumbi returned as leader, but he was subsequently betrayed by one of his commanders, captured and later executed in the Serra Dois Irmãos mountain range, in Viçosa. November 26, the date of is execution in 1695, is now Brazil's Dia da Consciência Negra (Black Awareness Day).

silverware, 19th and 20th-century furniture, and paintings at the **Museu de Artes Pierre Chalita** *(Praça Marechal Floriano Peixoto, 44, Centro, tel. (82) 3223-4298; Mon – Fri, 8am – noon and 2pm – 5pm).* The **Teatro Deodoro** is a theater that has been a center for the region's culture since its inauguration in 1910 *(Praça Marechal Deodoro, no #, Centro, tel. (82) 3315-5651; Mon – Fri, 8am – 2pm; box office: 8am – 10pm).*

Colorful baskets from Alagoas

LACE MAKERS AND OTHER ARTISTS
If you visit just one artisans' place in town, make it the **Armazém do Sebrae**, where you will find wonderful lace, embroidery, sculptures, mats, and bedcovers *(Avenida da Paz, 878, tel. (82) 3223-8200; Mon – Fri, 9am – 6pm; Sat, 9am – 2pm).* The **Mercado de Artesanato da Pajuçara**, a craft market,

showcases the varied work of folk artists in Maceió *(Rua Melo Morais, 617, Levada; Mon – Fri, 8am – 6pm; Sat, 8am – noon).* The **Núcleo Artesanal do Pontal da Barra** features more than 250 stores and studios. The best of them sell lace, especially in the delicate *file* style. The **Pavilhão do Artesanato**, which also sells items from other states in the Northeast, looks like a shopping mall, with some 150 stores and a food court *(Avenida Sílvio Viana, formerly Doutor Antônio Gouveia, 1447, Ponta Verde, tel. (82) 3231-3901; daily, 10am – 10pm).* The **Ateliê Viver de Arte** is a studio run by sisters Rosa Maria and Ana Maria Piatti, who produce painted ceramics, bags and home furnishings *(Avenida Álvaro Otacílio, 4515, Passeio Stella Maris III, store #3, Praia de Jatiúca, tel. (82) 3235-1109, 3235-3887; Mon – Sat, 9am – 9pm).*

THE NORTH COAST

BARRA DE SANTO ANTÔNIO

44 kilometers (27 miles) from Maceió, Barra de Santo Antônio grew out of a 17th-century Dutch settlement and has lovely historical buildings, such as the **Igreja de Nossa Senhora da Conceição**. Divided by the Santo Antônio River, this cheerful town is famous for its lively Carnival and other festivities, such as those held in January to honor its patron saint, São Sebastião.

ILHA DA CROA
Speckled with natural pools and defined by a line of reefs, this so-called island is actually a peninsula that lies about five minutes by boat (or car ferry) from the town's historical center.

CARRO QUEBRADO
To visit the town's best-known beach, cross the Santo Antônio River to Ilha da Croa. From there, you need to follow 6 kilometers (almost 4 miles) of unsigned dirt road, so hiring a guide is recommended. Weather and tide permitting, it's worth extending the trip to two deserted beaches, **Praia do Morro** and **Praia da Pedra do Cebola**.

PRAIA DE TABUBA
Natural pools with crystal-clear waters await visitors to Tabuba, which lies 4 kilometers (2.5 miles) from Barra de Santo Antônio, at the mouth of the Rio Sapucaí. On clear days you can take a *jangada* (raft) trip off the beach.

SÃO MIGUEL DOS MILAGRES

Once, it is said, a fisherman here found a statue of Saint Michael the Archangel, which cured him of a serious illness. True or not, the area's old settlement of Nossa Senhora,

OUR RECOMMENDATION

Everything about **Pousada Aldeia Beijupirá**, from the lobby to the exterior, reflects the good taste of owners Joaquim dos Santos, from Portugal, and Adriana, from the state of Pernambuco. The couple also owns the restaurant of the same name in Porto de Galinhas, Pernambuco. White dominates the color scheme and décor of this guesthouse on Lage Beach, north of São Miguel dos Milagres. The well-equipped bungalows, each having a bedroom and sitting room, afford either a sea or garden view *(Sítio Roteio, no #, Praia da Lage, tel. (82) 3298-6520, 3289-6549).*

Additional information on page 462.

originally a center of anti-Dutch resistance, took the name of this patron saint when it became a town at the beginning of the 19th century. Today, the town – 108 kilometers (67 miles) from Maceió – balances its intrinsically sleepy pace with the needs of travelers in search of its calm, clear waters, where *jangadas* glide by in scenes of unbroken tranquility. **Praia de Porto de Pedras**, a beach with a mangrove swamp near the Manguaba River, lies 15 kilometers (9 miles) from the center. Three other beaches also worth a visit are **Tatuamunha**, deserted and with clear waters, **Patacho**, with calm seas and reefs, and largely unvisited **Lages**, which has coarse sand, coconut palms and reefs.

The Rio Manguaba at Praia de Porto de Pedras, in São Miguel dos Milagres

JAPARATINGA

Near Maragogi, 115 kilometers (71 miles) from Maceió, Japaratinga boasts spectacular beaches like **Praia de Barreiras do Boqueirão**, the last beach on the Rota Ecológica.

Barreiras do Boqueirão is fringed by lovely coconut palms, and fresh water springs line its access road, which explains its other name, Praia das Bicas (Spring Beach).

ROTA ECOLÓGICA AND THE COSTA DOS CORAIS PROTECTED AREA

The Rota Ecológica, the unofficial name for a 35-kilometer (22-mile) ecologically remarkable coastal route between Barra do Camaragibe and Japaratinga, runs past picturesque villages and a good variety of guesthouses along the stunning beaches. (Seven of these 35 kilometers of the Rodovia Costa dos Corais (AL-101 highway) are along dirt roads.)

You can get to it via paved road from **São Luis do Quitunde** by taking the Rodovia AL-435 highway to Barra do Camaragibe. This route skirts part of the **Área de Proteção Ambiental (APA) da Costa dos Corais**, an environmentally protected area that extends for 135 kilometers (84 miles), reaching from the Formoso River, in Tamandaré, Pernam-

buco, to the Meirim River, in Paripueira, Alagoas. The APA, Brazil's largest marine conservation area, was set up in 1997 to protect the local coral reefs, beaches, mangroves, and marine life-including manatees-from extinction. A management plan is currently being developed by a project known as Projeto Recifes Costeiros *(www.recifescosteiros.org.br)*.

MARAGOGI

Halfway between Recife and Maceió, Maragogi is 130 killometers (81 miles) from both and is the most popular tourist destination in Alagoas, after Maceió itself. It boasts colorful beaches, coconut palms and coral reefs, and it's named after the river that borders it.

BEACHES

Praia de Maragogi bustles with hotels, guesthouses, bars, restaurants, and craft stores. Visitors make the most of the natural beauty and boat tours. **Praia de São Bento**, 4 kilometers (2.5 miles) away, is more suitable for those seeking peace and quiet. It's the first beach you see after the bridge over the Rio Salgado, which separates Japaratinga from Maragogi. The village of the same name is well known for its *bolo de goma* (cornstarch cookies), which are similar to the famed

sequilhos eaten in southern Brazil. Lovely, tranquil **Peroba**, 12 kilometers (7 miles) from the center of Maragogi, on the border with Pernambuco, offers coconut palms, natural pools, and intensely blue waters. This beach doesn't have good bar or restaurant facilities, but the number of guesthouses is growing.

TRIPS TO THE GALÉS (POOLS)

Alagoas's signature natural pools are called *galés* in Maragogi and are 6 kilometers from the coast. Visitors can get the site by launch or catamaran. They are known for their huge size, crystal-clear waters and coral-speckled white sand. The teeming fish can only be fed with food approved by Ibama (the Brazilian Institute for Environment and Renewable Natural Resources), which young boys sell on the beach.

SOUTH COAST

MARECHAL DEODORO

This town, once an old settlement known as Santa Maria Madalena da Lagoa do Sul, was the provincial capital of Alagoas until 1839. That honor now belongs to Maceió, 28 kilometers (17 miles) away. This town's current name is that of its most illustrious son, Manuel Deodoro da Fonseca (1827-92), who proclaimed the republic in 1889. The **Casa do Marechal Deodoro**, the house in which he lived, is now a museum *(Rua Marechal Deodoro, no #, Centro, tel. (82) 3263-2608, 3263-1255 – Secretaria de Cultura e Turismo; daily, 7:30am – 5pm)*. Two further attractions are the **Igreja de Santa Maria Madalena** and the **Convento Franciscano**, a church and convent built between 1684 and 1723. This complex houses the **Museu de Arte Sacra do Estado**, whose collection boasts the 17th-century crown belonging to the city's patron saint and protector Nossa Senhora da Conceição. City Hall guides lead tours through the sacred art museum, but as of late 2007, it was closed for restoration *(Praça João XXIII, no #, Centro, tel. (82) 3263-2608, 32631255 – Secretaria de Cultura e Turismo)*.

PRAIA DO FRANCÊS

20 kilometers (12.5 miles) from Maceió, this white-sand beach has plenty of bars and restaurants looking out over its blue-green waters. A naturally calm area of water is perfect for sailing, jet skiing, or banana boat rides, while rougher stretches are popular with surfers.

BARRA DE SÃO MIGUEL

The liveliest seaside spot in Alagoas is here, 33 kilometers (20.5 miles) from Maceió. Reasonable hotel facilities about two beaches – **Niquim**, with calm, reef-protected waters, and **Barra de São Miguel**, popular with surfers. The famous **Praia do Gunga**, 3 kilometers (almost 2 miles) from the center, is a stretch of white sand with the sea on one side and a lagoon on the other. It can be reached by boat from the quays at Barra de São Miguel. The white sands and crystal-clear waters of **Barra do Jequiá** are at the mouth of Rio Jequiá, 35 kilometers (22 miles) from Barra de São Miguel. A raft trip across the river takes you to the **Dunas de Marapé** tourist complex, which has a restaurant and a guesthouse *(tel. (82) 3035-3852, 9302-9525)*.

Barra de São Miguel, south of Maceió, is the liveliest seaside spot in Alagoas

The scenery around the mouth of the Rio São Francisco invites boat and dune buggy tours

MOUTH OF THE SÃO FRANCISCO RIVER

PENEDO

One of the oldest cities in Alagoas, Penedo lies on the banks of the Rio São Francisco. The city is home to 18th-century churches and 19th-century buildings such as the neo-classical **Theatro Sete de Setembro**, and during the second weekend in January it hosts two enjoyable folk celebrations, the **Festival de Tradições Populares** and the **Festa do Bom Jesus**. Local groups show off folklore such as *pastoreio* and *reisado*, and bands play popular music such as *axé* and *forró*. Processions of Bom Jesus, by both river and land, take place on the Sunday. To get to Penedo from Maceió, 168 kilometers (104 miles) away, take the Rodovia AL-101 highway. It can also be reached from Aracajú, 165 kilometers away. Take Rodovia BR-101 highway for about 70 kilometers (43 miles) as far as the highway patrol station. Then take the road to Neópolis, where you can take a ferry across the river.

CHURCHES

The **Igreja de Nossa Senhora da Corrente**, a masterpiece of Brazilian rococo style, was begun in 1764 and finished in the late 19th century. The simple façade belies its rich interior. The high altar is adorned with gold leaf and beautifully carved marble in shades of blue and pink. Both sides of the nave are covered with Portuguese tiles. Equally impressive are the pulpit carvings, nave ceiling paintings and the 19th-century English floor tiles (*Praça 12 de Abril, no #, Centro; Tue – Sun, 8am – 5pm*). Built by the Franciscans between the 17th and 18th centuries, the complex comprising the **Igreja de Nossa Senhora dos Anjos** and the **Convento de São Francisco** is one of the most important architectural treasures in Alagoas. The sober exterior contrasts with the rich rococo carving inside the church.

Look for the optical illusion in the ceiling painting by Libório Lazdro Lial Afes, an artist from Pernambuco (*Praça Frei Camilo de Lellis, 218, Centro, tel. (82) 3551-2279; Tue – Fri, 8am – 11:50am and 2pm – 5pm; Sat and Sun, 8am – 11:30am*). The **Igreja de São Gonçalo Garcia dos Homens Pardos** opened its doors in 1759, just a year after construction began. Its neo-gothic bell towers date from the 19th century (*Avenida Floriano Peixoto, no #, Centro; Tue – Sun, 8am – 5pm*). Construction on the **Catedral de Nossa Senhora do Rosário** began in 1690. The original façade was demolished in 1815, and replaced by the current one, which has beautiful stained glass windows (*Praça Barão de Penedo, no #, Centro, tel. (82) 3551-2686; Tue – Sun, 8am – 5:30pm*).

MUSEUMS

The **Casa do Penedo** museum exhibits photographs, craftwork, and items that belonged to illustrious local families (*Rua João Pessoa, 126, Centro, tel. (82) 3551-2008; Tue – Sun,* 8am – noon and 2pm – 5pm). The **Museu do Paço Imperial** has pieces from the 18th and 19th centuries, including sacred art, furniture, and decorative objects. The 19th-century building that houses the museum has been informally called the Imperial Palace since 1859, when it hosted Emperor Dom Pedro II. Head up to the second floor to enjoy a wonderful view of the São Francisco River (*Praça 12 de Abril, no #, Centro, tel. (82) 3551-2498; Tue – Sat, 11am – 5pm; Sun, 8am-noon*).

MARITUBA

This city, 20 kilometers (12 miles) from Penedo, is a good place for a one-hour canoe trip along navigable canals. Local guides can help you hire a canoeist. Other local attractions are straw craftwork that's sold outside the craftsmen's houses and the Casa da Farinha, a traditional mill where manioc is ground and toasted to make flour. You can also visit the city's many flour mills and a candy factory.
Contact: Secretaria de Cultura e Turismo, tel. (82) 3551-2727.

PIAÇABUÇU

The most popular thing to do in Piaçabuçu is to take a boat or dune buggy to the point where Velho Chico (Old Chico), an affectionate name for the São Francisco River, meets the sea. You can hire a boat for the last 13 kilometers of the river at the roadside bars on the way to Piaçabuçu or at the town quays. Boats stop near the river mouth to let passengers walk to the meeting of the waters. A trip lasts about two and a half hours, depending on how long visitors want to spend looking at the wonderful landscape of marshland, islands, and dunes. A 21-kilometer buggy tour takes about three hours; it goes to the dunes via Pontal do Peba beach, and from there on foot. The more adventurous can take a 200-meter parasailing ride. **Praia do Pontal do Peba**, a beach of fine sand, is famous for shrimp fishing. Piaçabuçu is 138 kilometers (86 miles) from Maceió, most of it along the Rodovia AL-101 highway to Penedo, and from there 26 kilometers (16 miles) along a good road. *Contact: Delta 1, tel. (82) 3552-1226, 9916-2259.*

PIRANHAS

Brightly colored old houses line the banks of the São Francisco River in this charming colonial town. They enchanted Dom Pedro II – as did, according to some, a local noblewoman. Three hundred kilometers (186 miles) from Maceió and near **Canindé do São Francisco**, in Sergipe, Piranhas had an important role in *cangaço* (backland banditry). The bandit king Lampião never attacked the town, but troops set out from here to capture him. Eleven decapitated heads were displayed in the public square, including those of Lampião and his wife, Maria Bonita. A historic photo of the event, taken here, was later sold to newspapers all over the country. Some of Lampião's personal possessions and posters from the 1930s offering a reward for his capture can be seen in the interesting **Museu do Sertão**, which also exhibits items related to navigation on the São Francisco River. The museum, set in the old railway station, was closed for restoration in late 2007 but scheduled to reopen in April 2008 *(daily, 8am – 5:30pm, tel. (82) 3686-3013).*

RIO SÃO FRANCISCO

The São Francisco River rises in the Serra da Canastra mountain range in Minas Gerais, and it waters the otherwise arid lands of four Northeastern states (Bahia, Pernambuco, Sergipe, and Alagoas). Running for about 3,000 kilometers in all, "Old Chico," as the river's known, slakes the thirst of almost 500 municipalities before reaching the sea. Cities not lucky enough to be situated on its banks have campaigned since 1847 to have its course diverted to cure the water shortages so common in the almost rainless interior. Such projects have always caused controversy. The mysticism attached to the river is evident in the famous *carrancas* – grotesque gargoyles placed on boat bows to ward off evil spirits. Brazil's first hydroelectric plant, Angiquinho, was built on Old Chico in 1913. Today the river is dammed at Sobradinho, Paulo Afonso (in Bahia state) and, further ahead in Xingó (in Alagoas). The river's potential as a draw for tourists is only well exploited in Canindé do São Francisco, in Sergipe, and in the cities of Piranhas and Penedo, near the river mouth in Alagoas.

PERNAMBUCO

HIGHLIGHTS

- The culture and architecture in the historical cities of **Recife** and **Olinda**.
- The natural beauty of the coast at **Cabo de Santo Agostinho** and **Tamandaré**.
- The fauna and flora of the island

Fernando de Noronha.
- The handicrafts in **Tracunhaém**.
- The June festivities in **Caruaru** and the backlands culture in **Petrolina** and **Triunfo**.

WHEN TO GO

- **Any time of year** for the beaches and Fernando de Noronha, but summer means the biggest crowds and the highest prices.
- Between **February** and **March** during Carnival for fun and folklore.
- In **June** for the São João festivities in country towns like **Caruaru**.

RECIFE

Situated at the mouth of two rivers, the Capibaribe and the Beberibe, the capital of Pernambuco is crisscrossed by canals and graced with beautiful beaches. Recife was founded around the quays near 1537, and it and used to be surrounded by sugar plantations. Today, with a population of 1.5 million, the city has modern buildings standing next to a vast historical heritage, revealing influences from the Dutch occupation (1630-54) tucked into the bustling commercial streets. Nightlife is concentrated in the neighborhoods of Recife Antigo and Boa Viagem, as well as the nearby city of Olinda. For a glimpse of what's going on in the city, consult the *Agenda cultural*, a small pamphlet available from the Tourist Information Center *(Praça Ministro Salgado Filho, no #, tel. (81) 3232-3594; daily, 24 hours)*.

BEACHES

Praia do Pina and **Praia de Boa Viagem**, and neighboring **Piedade** and **Candeias** in Jaboatão dos Guararapes, offer kiosks and vendors selling fresh pineapple and *caldinho de feijão* (bean broth). Boa Viagem has the best facilities. Young people gather in front of the Acaiaca building, between Rua Félix de Brito and Rua Antônio Falcão. Pay attention to signs on the beaches indicating where shark attacks occur. Enjoy the sea only at low tide and never cross the barrier reef. Surfing is prohibited.

FORTS

Forte do Brum, a wattle and daub fort that the Portuguese built in 1629, was taken by the Dutch a year later. After their expulsion, it was rebuilt in stone *(Praça Comunidade Luso-Brasileira, no #, Recife Antigo, tel. (81) 3224-4620; Tue – Fri, 9am – 4:30pm; Sat and Sun, 2pm – 5pm)*. The Dutch built **Forte de São Tiago das Cinco Pontas** in 1630. After the Portuguese victory in 1654, a new stone fort was erected with only four bastions. That fort is where visitors will find the **Museu da Cidade**, a museum displaying photographs and old maps *(Praça Cinco Pontas, no #, São José, tel. (81) 3232-2812; Tue – Fri, 9am – 5pm; Sat and Sun, 1pm – 5pm)*.

HISTORICAL CENTER

The historical center, also known as the neighborhood of Recife or Recife Antigo, lies between the Capibaribe River and the ocean. Evidence of the Dutch presence *(read more on page 308)* and developments from the beginning of the 20th century give this part of the city a European ambiance. Like the neighboring Santo Antônio, São José and Boa Vista, the cobbled streets and Portuguese stone sidewalks of the city center are best explored on foot. Visitors will stumble across an array of ice-cream parlors and hole-in-the-wall cafes where they can sample fruit juice or coconut water. Seeing the city from a catamaran cruising its canals is another way to enjoy its sights. *Catamarã Tours, tel. (81) 3424-2845, 9973-4077.*

**1 MARCO ZERO AND
2 PARQUE DAS ESCULTURAS**
Marco Zero (Ground Zero), a square with the official name " Praça Barão do Rio Branco," marks the start of three major avenues. Local artist Cícero Dias

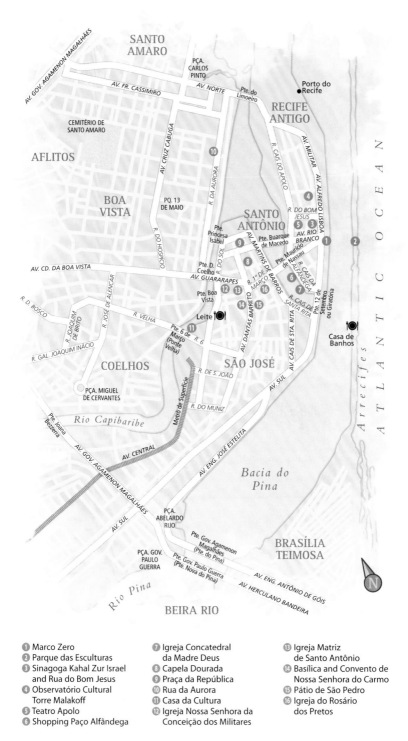

1 Marco Zero
2 Parque das Esculturas
3 Sinagoga Kahal Zur Israel
  and Rua do Bom Jesus
4 Observatório Cultural
  Torre Malakoff
5 Teatro Apolo
6 Shopping Paço Alfândega

7 Igreja Concatedral
  da Madre Deus
8 Capela Dourada
9 Praça da República
10 Rua da Aurora
11 Casa da Cultura
12 Igreja Nossa Senhora da
   Conceição dos Militares

13 Igreja Matriz
   de Santo Antônio
14 Basílica and Convento de
   Nossa Senhora do Carmo
15 Pátio de São Pedro
16 Igreja do Rosário
   dos Pretos

The Parque das Esculturas exhibits works by Francisco Brennand

(1907-2003) created the central floor mosaic of a wind rose. Highlights around the square include the **Instituto Cultural Bandepe**, a cultural center built in 1914; the **Associação Comercial do Recife**, built in 1915; and the **Bolsa de Valores**, the 1912 stock exchange building. **Parque das Esculturas,** a sculpture park built on a reef opposite Marco Zero, was inaugurated in 2000 and exhibits works by local artist Francisco Brennand. Get there by boat from Marco Zero or by car from the Brasília Teimosa neighborhood.

❸ SINAGOGA KAHAL ZUR ISRAEL AND RUA DO BOM JESUS
Because many Jews emigrated from Europe to Recife around the time of the Dutch invasion, the first synagogue in the Americas appeared here around 1636. When the Portuguese returned in 1654, the Jews were forced to leave the country (23 of them went to New Amsterdam in the United States, probably the first Jews in that city). The synagogue closed in 1654, but it was restored and reopened in 2002 *(Rua do Bom Jesus, 197 and 203, tel. (81) 3224-*

2128. Tue – Fri, 9am – 5pm; Sat, 3pm – 7pm). The street where the synagogue stands, Rua de Bom Jesus, boasts well-preserved colorful buildings, some housing bars and restaurants, and it hosts a craft fair on Sunday afternoons.

❹ OBSERVATÓRIO CULTURAL TORRE MALAKOFF
This tower, built in 1855 as a lookout to protect the port, is a good spot to visit at night. The name alludes to a Russian fort that gained fame in the Crimean War (1853-56). The 42-meter (138-foot) tower houses a cultural center, with temporary exhibits. The top provides a lovely view of the surroundings, and in good weather, observers can look at the sky through a telescope.
Praça do Arsenal, no #, Recife Antigo, tel. (81) 3424-8704. Tue – Sun, 4pm – 8pm.

❺ TEATRO APOLO
This theater, a 19th-century architectural treasure, opened in 1846. It features limestone carvings from Portugal on the façade, triangular lintels and curved balconies. Newly restored, it houses a cinema and show

venue as well as another theater, the Teatro Hermilo Borba Filho. Visits must be arranged in advance.
Rua do Apolo, 121, Recife Antigo, tel. (81) 3232-2028. Mon – Fri, 8am – noon and 2pm – 6pm.

❻ SHOPPING PAÇO ALFÂNDEGA
Originally built to house Recife's Oratorian monks, this building eventually became the Pernambuco Customs House in 1826 and is now on the national heritage list. It was restored and reopened as a shopping mall in 2003, with stores featuring labels like **Fause Haten** and **Herchcovitch**. The **Ana Paes** store sells clothes trimmed with lace and *fuxico*

(appliqué flowers made from leftover scraps of material), and **Espaço Cultural Banco do Brasil** holds film festivals and regular screenings.
Rua da Alfândega, 35, Recife Antigo, tel. (81) 3419-7500. Mon – Sat, 10am – 10pm; Sun, noon – 8pm.

❼ IGREJA CONCATEDRAL DA MADRE DEUS
This national heritage site was completed in 1720, but the original design dates from 1679. An Estremoz marble font graces the sacristy.
Rua da Madre de Deus, no #, Recife Antigo, tel. (81) 3224-5587. Tue – Fri, 8am – noon and 1pm – 4:30pm.

SANTO ANTÔNIO, SÃO JOSÉ, AND BOA VISTA

❽ CAPELA DOURADA
This chapel's carved altar, walls and ceiling – all adorned with gold leaf – are the most vibrant expression of baroque art in Recife. Built between 1696 and 1724, the building belongs to the **Convento Franciscano** complex. It includes the **Igreja de Santo Antônio**

church and the old Hospital dos Terceiros Franciscanos. The nearby **Museu Franciscano de Arte Sacra** displays religious art from the 18th century.
Rua do Imperador Dom Pedro II, no #, Santo Antônio, tel. (81) 3224-0530. Mon – Fri, 8am – 11:30am and 2pm – 5pm; Sat, 8am – 11:30am.

Capela Dourada: Gilded carvings showcase the chapel's baroque features

The imposing Teatro Santa Isabel, built in imperial times

⑨ Praça da República

This square is a park of 23,000 square meters (250,000 square feet) in the Santo Antônio neighborhood, located on the site where Count John Maurice of Nassau kept his gardens. Buildings around the square include the **Palácio do Campo das Princesas** (1840), a neoclassical palace that houses the state government; the **Palácio da Justiça** (1928), with eclectic architecture; and the **Liceu de Artes e Ofícios** (1880), inspired by French classicism, with gardens that Frenchman Emile Bérenger designed in 1875 Roberto Burle Marx remodeled in 1936. A huge African baobab tree stands in the square, and when it was planted is unknown. Fire destroyed the heritage-listed **Teatro Santa Isabel** (1850) in 1869, but its façade was restored along with its interior columns and iron parapets – making it one of the loveliest theaters from the imperial period *(tel. (81) 3232-2939; daily, 2pm – 5pm).*

⑩ Rua da Aurora

Facing east and running along the left bank of the Rio Capibaribe, this street gets its name from the first rays of the rising sun that bathe it at dawn. Its colorful, neoclassical buildings dating from the 19th century include the **Secretaria de Segurança Pública** (1842), formerly the residence of the Conde da Boa Vista; the **Ginásio Pernambucano** (1885), the oldest operating school in state; and the **Museu de Arte Moderna Aloísio Magalhães (Mamam)**, a gallery housing exhibits of contemporary national art. Its 900-piece collection includes work by Alex Flemming and João Câmara *(#265, Boa Vista, tel. (81) 3232-1694; Tue and Thu, 1pm – 7pm; Wed, 9am – 7pm; Sun, 1pm – 7pm).* **Cine São Luiz**, the city's oldest cinema, was inaugurated in 1952 and contains 1,200 seats between the stalls

---

Our Recommendation

🍽 **Leite**, which opened in 1882, serves sophisticated international dishes with a strong Portuguese influence. It's a favorite haunt of politicians and entrepreneurs, and it is rumored to serve Recife's best *cartola* (fried banana and cheese, sprinkled with sugar and cinnamon).
Praça Joaquim Nabuco, 147, Santo Antônio, tel. (81) 3224-7977. Sun – Fri, 11am – 4pm.

Additional information on page 462.

and balcony. Stained glass panels of flowers flood the auditorium with light at the end of screening sessions, and seeing a film here in the 1960s was an occasion for evening dress *(# 175, Boa Vista, tel. (81) 3421-7870)*.

⑪ CASA DA CULTURA

The 156 cells of Recife's old prison, built in 1867 and decommissioned in 1973, have been turned into craft stores selling a little bit of everything, including ceramics from Caruaru and embroidery from Passira.
Rua Floriano Peixoto, no #, São José, tel. (81) 3224-2850. Mon – Fri, 9am – 7pm; Sat, 9am – 6pm; Sun, 9am – 2pm.

⑫ IGREJA NOSSA SENHORA DA CONCEIÇÃO DOS MILITARES

Tucked away on a busy street, this church conceals the architectural riches in its interior. The high altar, altarpiece and central arch feature extravagant rococo carvings in white and gold.

Paintings of the Virgin Mary, one of which shows her pregnant, grace the ceilings. The church (now a national heritage site and closed for renovations) was built in the 18th century by a local military brotherhood, the Irmandade dos Sargentos e Soldados do Terço da Infantaria da Guarnição do Recife. Restoration work began in 2007 with no set date for reopening.
Rua Nova, 309, Santo Antônio, tel. (81) 3224-3106.

⑬ IGREJA MATRIZ DE SANTO ANTÔNIO (SANTÍSSIMO SACRAMENTO)

This church, built between 1753 and 1790, mixes baroque and other styles introduced during renovations. Take note of Sebastião da Silva Tavares' ceiling paintings from the 19th century.
Praça da Independência, no #, Santo Antônio, tel. (81) 3224-5076, 3224-9494. Mon – Fri, 7am – noon and 2pm – 6pm; Sat, 4:30pm – 6:30pm; Sun, 7am – noon and 4:30pm – 6:30pm.

CARNIVAL IN RECIFE

Recife's street Carnival is one of Brazil's most diverse festivals. It buzzes with different rhythms, but first place is reserved for *frevo* and *maracatu*. *Frevo* was born at the end of the 19th century and is characterized by marching-style music and frenzied choreography. *Maracatu* involves groups dancing to music made by drums, rattles and *gongués*, which are similar to cowbells. Performers follow the *calunga*, a doll mounted on a pole. Festivities begin a week before Carnival, with *frevo* and *maracatu* groups rehearsing at dance venues, in clubs and on the streets. The **Bloco da Saudade** group has been breathing new life into old traditions with its

women's choir, woodwind and string orchestra and famous Carnival ball. Percussionist **Naná Vasconcelos** rehearses the Carnival's opening ceremony for a whole week before it begins. The ceremony takes place on Carnival Friday and includes more than 400 *maracatu* groups, called *nações* ("nations"). Saturday morning brings **Galo da Madrugada**, when the Santo Antônio, São José and Boa Vista neighborhoods are flooded by more than 2,000 milion revelers, forming the largest Carnival group in the world. Starting on Saturday afternoon, Recife has two main Carnival centers. **Pátio de São Pedro** holds dance performances in its court-

yard, featuring *coco de roda*, *afoxé, ciranda* and *frevo*. The quays at the **Cais da Alfândega** form the stage for **Rec Beat**, a festival of rock and electronic music featuring *mangue beat*, an unlikely blend of soul, funk, hip-hop and *maracatu*. **Avenida Guararapes** is the best place for samba school parades. On Monday night, **Pátio do Terço** hosts the **Noite dos Tambores Silenciosos**: Throngs pay tribute to the black people who died in slavery. **Praça do Arsenal** is the starting point for *frevo* orchestras and *maracatu* and *caboclinho* groups. A list of Carnival events is available from tourist information centers and advertised in the local media.

⑭ BASÍLICA AND CONVENTO DE NOSSA SENHORA DO CARMO

This 18th-century architectural complex – made up of the Basílica and Convento de Nossa Senhora do Carmo, and **Igreja de Santa Teresa da Ordem Terceira do Carmo** – was built on the site where the Palácio Boa Vista, the residence of Count John Maurice of Nassau, once stood. The Basilica's highlights include the blue and gold main chapel ceiling finished in 1767, the rococo altar carvings and the ornately framed balcony paintings. The ceiling of the Igreja de Santa Teresa church is composed of 40 gilded square panels depicting the life of Saint Teresa. This church was inaugurated in 1710, but its rococo frontispiece dates from 1803. *Avenida Dantas Barreto, no #, Santo Antônio, tel. (81) 3224-3341. Mon, 6am – 5pm; Tue – Fri, 6am – 7pm; Sat, 6am – 1pm; Sun, 8am – 1pm and 6pm – 8pm.*

⑮ PÁTIO DE SÃO PEDRO

Rows of colorful, turreted houses transformed into bars and restaurants line this square courtyard, one of the few to preserve the irregular cobblestones so common in colonial Brazil. Now a national heritage site, the courtyard once belonged to the Irmandade dos Clérigos, a brotherhood that financed the construction of the imposing **Concatedral de São Pedro dos Clérigos**. Another attraction in the square is **Buraquinho,** a restaurant serving traditional Northeastern dishes *(#28, tel. (81) 3224-6431; Mon – Sat, 11am until the last customer leaves).* On Tuesday nights, Pátio de São Pedro hosts **Terça-Feira Negra**, a musical performance promoting Afro-Brazilian culture.

⑯ IGREJA DO ROSÁRIO DOS PRETOS

Built between 1739 and 1777 as place of worship for slaves, this church is predominantly rococo in style. Its façade is decorated with stone carvings of exceptional quality. Now a national heritage site, the church is the departure point for the *Cortejo do Rei do Congo*, a ritual slaves brought from Africa and the origin of Recife's *maracatu* tradition. *Rua Estreita do Rosário, no #, Santo Antônio, tel. (81) 3224-3929. Mon – Fri, 9am – 5pm; Sun, 7:30am – 9am.*

The carved stone façade of Concatedral de São Pedro dos Clérigos

Works by Francisco Brennand on display in his ceramic workshop, which was once a sugar mill

ENVIRONS OF RECIFE

The neighborhoods farther from the center and coast of Recife developed from old sugar plantations, and they still have an air of the countryside about them.

OFICINA DE CERÂMICA FRANCISCO BRENNAND

The former site of a sugar plantation became the workshop of award-winning artist Francisco Brennand in 1971. His ceramic sculptures, many of them huge, are scattered around nearby streets, gardens and lakeshores. The Accademia space displays the artist's paintings and drawings. Visitors can spend an entire afternoon here – there's a lot to see, including a café and a small store. *Propriedade Santos Cosme e Damião, no #, access via Avenida Caxangá, Várzea, tel. (81) 3271-2466. Mon – Thu, 8am – 5pm; Fri, 8am – 4pm.*

INSTITUTO RICARDO BRENNAND

Art collector Ricardo Brennand, Francisco Brennand's cousin, opened this institute. It is composed of a Castelo (castle), Pinacoteca (art gallery) and Biblioteca (library), as well as a great café. The collection includes rare paintings, maps, manuscripts and coins from the Dutch occupation. Among the highlights are 17 canvasses by Dutch painter Frans Post – the world's biggest collection of this artist's work – with examples of each phase of his artistic life. The collection of arms and armor is another high point. *Alameda Antônio Brennand, no #, Várzea, tel. (81) 2121-0352. Tue – Sun, 1pm – 5pm.*

MUSEU DO HOMEM DO NORDESTE

This museum is an excellent place to learn about the culture of the Northeast. Each of its three sections showcases elements used in regional construction, such as tiles and objects related to sugarcane cultivation, as well as folklore and artistic displays. The museum underwent restoration work in 2006. *Avenida 17 de Agosto, 2187, Casa Forte, tel. (81) 3073-6332. Mon – Fri, 8am – noon and 2pm – 6pm; Sat and Sun, 1pm – 5pm.*

FUNDAÇÃO GILBERTO FREYRE

Anthropologist Gilberto Freyre (1900-87) lived in this house, where visitors will find a library and Portuguese tiled murals. In his many books – including

Frans Post's *Engenho*, oil on wood, Instituto Ricardo Brennand collection

the 1933 classic *Casa-grande e senzala*, published in English as *The Masters and the Slaves* – Freyre tried to explain Brazilian and Northeastern Brazilian society in a provocative, intelligent way. *Rua Dois Irmãos, 320, Apipucos, tel. (81) 3441-1733. Mon – Fri, 9am – 4:30pm*

MUSEU DO ESTADO
This 19th-century mansion, formerly owned by the Baron of Beberibe's family, was restored in 2006. The **Espaço Cícero Dias** annex displays some of the museum's collection: 17th- and 18th-century furniture, porcelain and paintings by Telles Júnior, among other local artists.

OUR RECOMMENDATION

🍽 **Casa dos Frios**, Recife's oldest delicatessen, has been serving its acclaimed cakes, *bolo de rolo* (jelly roll) and *bolo Sousa Leão* (coconut cake), since it opened its doors in 1957. *Avenida Rui Barbosa, 412, Graças, tel. (81) 2125-0220. Mon – Sat, 8am – 8pm; Sun, 8am – 1pm.*

Additional information on page 462.

Avenida Rui Barbosa, 960, Graças, tel. (81) 3427-9322. Tue – Fri, 10am – 5pm; Sat and Sun, 2pm – 5pm.

ESPAÇO PASÁRGADA
The house where writer and poet Manuel Bandeira (1886-1968) spent his childhood now displays his personal possessions. *Rua da União, 263, Boa Vista, tel. (81) 3131-3013. Mon – Fri, 8am – 4pm.*

SCIENCE AND ART IN DUTCH BRAZIL

The Dutch invaded Pernambuco in 1630. John Maurice of Nassau landed in Recife in 1637 with an entourage that included 46 scholars, and their work resulted in a historical and scientific record that was unprecedented at that time. Among these scholars were two naturalists: doctor Willem Piso and astronomer Georg Marcgrave, who complied several works on the fauna and flora of the new continent. Also with Nassau were painters Frans Post (1612-80) and Albert Eckhout (1610-65), who recorded Pernambuco's scenery, fauna and inhabitants in minute detail.

OLINDA

Located seven kilometers (four miles) from Recife is historical Olinda, a city of friars and nuns, artists, wild merry-makers and fast-talking junior guides. The tops of the steep streets serve as lookout points over the sea – the best spots are **Igreja de Nossa Senhora da Misericórdia** and **Alto da Sé**. Olinda was founded in 1535, destroyed by the Dutch in 1631 and rebuilt after the return of the Portuguese in 1654. There are two parts to the city: the *cidade baixa* (Lower City), which doesn't have many attractions, and the *cidade alta* (Upper City), a world heritage site since 1982. Despite this accolade, however, the upper city suffers from the effects of unregulated urban sprawl. Walking the steep streets of Olinda demands stamina and patience; street vendors often hassle visitors. **Rua do Amparo** is an old street that deserves an afternoon stroll to see its bars, stores, museums and artists' studios.

MUSEU DE ARTE SACRA DE PERNAMBUCO

This museum of 16th-century religious art was once a council headquarters, a bishop's official residence, a college, military barracks and a home for nuns. The museum's collection includes colonial paintings made by Indians in studios run by Jesuits in colonial South American cities such as Bogotá, Cuzco, La Paz and Quito.
Rua Bispo Coutinho, 726, Alto da Sé, tel. (81) 3429-0032. Mon – Fri, 9am – 12:30pm.

OUR RECOMMENDATION

🍽 Friendly **Oficina do Sabor** is living proof that *jerimum* (pumpkin) and shrimp go well together. Try the pumpkin stuffed with shrimp in *pitanga* fruit or mango sauce. *Rua do Amparo, 335, Cidade Alta, tel. (81) 3429-3331. Tue – Sat, noon – 4pm and 6pm – midnight; Sun, noon – 5pm.*

Additional information on page 462.

Historical Olinda, founded in 1535, with Recife in the background

Mass and Gregorian chants fill the Igreja e Mosteiro de São Bento on Sundays

CATEDRAL DA SÉ

Olinda's main church, also called São Salvador do Mundo, has undergone many modifications, from its founding in 1540 to restoration work in the 20th century, which reinstated its 16th-century form. Artistic highlights inside the church include 17th-century tiled panels. The tomb of Dom Hélder Câmara (1909-99), the former archbishop of Olinda, is located near the high altar. Outside the church, visitors will find one of the loveliest views in the region.

Ladeira da Sé, no #, Carmo, tel. (81) 3271-4270 (main office). Tue – Sun, 9am – noon and 2pm – 5pm.

IGREJA AND MOSTEIRO DE SÃO BENTO

This is one of Olinda's most elaborate churches. Highlights include the gilded cedar carvings that grace the high altar, the sandstone choir columns and the finely carved pulpits. The predominantly baroque complex – made up of the church and a monastery – was built at the end of the 16th century, damaged by

---

THE OLINDA ART CIRCUIT

There's no shortage of artists' studios in Olinda. Visit the workspaces of **Iza do Amparo,** who does acrylic paintwork on tablecloths, bedcovers and canvasses *(Rua do Amparo, 159, Amparo, tel. (81) 3429-2357; daily, 10am – 10pm),* or **Tereza Costa Rego,** who creates wood panels depicting local scenes from the past *(Rua do Amparo, 242, Amparo, tel. (81) 3429-2008; arrange visits in advance).* Watercolorist **Guita Charifker**

also has a studio in Olinda *(Rua Saldanha Marinho, 206, tel. (81) 3429-1758; arrange visits in advance),* as do **João Câmara,** a painter from Paraíba and a master of magic realism *(Rua das Pernambucanas, 420, tel. (81) 3222-1563; arrange visits in advance)* and **J. Calazans,** who describes his paintings as "neoprimitive" partly because of their heavy strokes and strong colors *(Ladeira da Misericórdia, 155, 1º floor, Alto da Sé, tel. (81)*

3439-7756, 9192-3793; daily, 9am – 8pm). **Gilvan Samico** is one of Brazil's most famous names in woodcut prints *(tel. (81) 9113-3998; arrange visits with Joseane).* During the **Olinda Arte em Toda Parte** arts festival, which takes place over 10 days in the end of November, artists receive visitors in person in their studios and guesthouses *(Information: Ladeira da Misericórdia, 86, Carmo, tel. (81) 3429-1750).*

fire in 1631 and restored in 1761. Ten o'clock mass on Sunday features Gregorian chants.

Rua de São Bento, no #, Varadouro, tel. (81) 3429-3288. Daily, 8am – 11am and 2pm – 5pm. Monastery: Mon – Sat, 8am – 11:45am and 2pm – 6pm.

IGREJA DE NOSSA SENHORA DA MISERICÓRDIA

This church is also called Igreja de Nossa Senhora da Luz, and it dates from 1540. It was burned down during the Dutch invasion and later restored. Highlights include the Dom João V carvings on the pulpit and altar, the ceiling panels and the Portuguese stone baptismal font. Benedictine nuns sing at 6pm mass, and the courtyard offers a lovely view of Olinda.

Largo da Misericórdia, no #, Alto da Sé. Mon – Fri, 8am – 11am and 2pm – 5pm; Sat, 2pm – 5pm.

IGREJA NOSSA SENHORA DA GRAÇA AND SEMINÁRIO DE OLINDA

The original 1552 chapel was given to the Jesuits for them to build the Real Colégio de Olinda (Olinda Royal College), the "Coimbra of the Americas," which was completed in 1575. The Dutch burned down the church, but restoration work began in 1660. Distinguished preacher Father Antônio Vieira taught at the Seminary, which is still operational. Despite all the reconstruction work, the church and seminary are still a rare example of 16th-century architecture.

Rua Bispo Coutinho, no #, Alto da Sé, tel. (81) 3493-1080. Mon – Fri, 2:30pm – 4pm. Visits Feb – June and Aug – Nov only.

CONVENTO DE SÃO FRANCISCO

This architectural complex was founded in 1585, damaged during the Dutch invasion and renovated in the 17th century. The chapter room in the convent cloisters – the only room remaining from the original building – is worth a look for its blue, yellow and red Portuguese tiles. Inside the church, which is dedicated to Our Lady of the Snows, take a look at the impressive

Igreja de Nossa Senhora das Neves, part of the Convento de São Francisco complex, in Olinda

paneled ceiling with 18th-century paintings depicting the holy family.
Rua São Francisco, 280, Carmo, tel. (81) 3429-0517. Mon – Fri, 7am – noon and 2pm – 5pm; Sat, 7am – noon.

IGREJA E CONVENTO DE NOSSA SENHORA DA CONCEIÇÃO

This treasure, now in the care of the Sisters of Saint Dorothy, was a homeless women's shelter in the 16th century. First opened in 1585, the church was burned down and rebuilt in 1675, and then turned into a convent. Note the ceiling paintings and the baroque gilded statue of Our Lady of the Immaculate Conception, which wears a silver crown.
Rua Bispo Coutinho, no #, Alto da Sé, tel. (81) 3429-3108. Mon, Tue, and Thu – Sat, 6:30am; Wed, 5pm; Sun, 9:30am (during mass).

IGREJA DE NOSSA SENHORA DO MONTE

This church, which dates from 1540, did not suffer greatly during the Dutch invasion. The stone arch over the entrance's doorway is particularly fine. Inside, a statue of São Bento (Saint Benedict) stands on an austere altar. Thirty Benedictine nuns live currently live in the complex. They sing at 5pm mass and sell their famous *bricelets* (wafer-thin puff pastry biscuits) at the side door.
Praça Nossa Senhora do Monte, no #, Bultrins, tel. (81) 3429-0317; daily, 8:30am – 11am and 2:30pm – 5pm.

CASA DA RABECA DO BRASIL

Mestre Salustiano, who oversees the traditional meeting of *maracatu* groups during Carnival, has his workshop here. Casa da Rabeca is also a show venue, especially for the style of *forró* known as *pé-de-serra* and the

---

CARNIVAL ON THE STEEP STREETS OF OLINDA

Various Carnival groups – including samba schools, dancers carrying huge dolls, folkloric characters such as *caboclinhos, maracatus*, bear costumes, and African drum schools – draw 2 million revelers to the steep, narrow streets of Olinda's cidade alta during the annual festival. Each of the 350 groups has its own music, themes, colors and parade day and time; the program is available in hotels, restaurants and other public places. Some of the oldest Carnival groups are **Elefante, Lenhadores** and **Enquanto Isso na Sala de Justiça**. Monday is the day the *maracatu* groups meet. They start out from the Cidade Tabajara neighborhood en route to Olinda, wearing their colorful costumes and masks. The giant dolls are an attraction unto themselves. One of them, **Homem da Meia-Noite** (Midnight Man), created in 1932, opens the festivities at midnight on Saturday. Tuesday brings the **Encontro de Bonecos** – the celebration when other giant dolls, such as **Mulher do Meio-Dia** (Midday Woman), created in 1967, dance to the music of *frevo* orchestras. Although they're not as competitive as they once were, the *maracatu* groups (and to a lesser degree, the *frevo* groups) cultivate a healthy rivalry that leads to a "fight" when they meet in the narrow streets. The group that plays the drums the quietest must give way to the other, but newer groups tend to cede territory to older ones. On Ash Wednesday, the **Bacalhau do Batata** parade marks the end of Carnival.

---

improvised verses of *repentista* musicians. *Rua Curupira, 340-B, Cidade Tabajara, tel. (81) 3371-8246. Opening hours vary according to the program.*

MASKS AND DOLLS

Mestre Julião's brightly colored paper mâché masks depict animals, devils and human faces with exaggerated features. Although he died in 1990, his family continues to make masks in his studio, **Ateliê Julião das Máscaras**, to be used during Carnival or as decoration in private homes *(Avenida Joaquim Nabuco,*

1102, Varadouro, tel. (81) 3439-5439; Mon and Tue, 2pm – 8pm; Wed – Sun, 10am – 8pm). The traditional giant Carnival dolls made by **Sílvio Botelho** are 3.6 meters (almost 12 feet) tall and weigh up to 50 kilos (110 pounds) on average. His studio is closed, but he will make dolls to order *(Rua do Amparo, 45, Carmo, tel. (81) 3439-2443, 9966-3344).* The **Museu do Mamulengo**, near Ribeira Market, houses a collection of more than 700 dolls *(Rua São Bento, 344, Varadouro, tel. (81) 3439-2753; Tue – Sun, 10am – 5pm).*

ILHA DE ITAMARACÁ

Itamaracá, an island 50 kilometers (31 miles) north of Recife on the Rodovias BR-101 and PE-035 highways, offers several daylong trips. A motorboat shuttles visitors to tiny **Coroa do Avião**, an island formed by a sandbank, where kiosks sell snacks. Choose the complete trip, with boats that can be hired on the spot to go to natural pools at low tide, an old ceramic workshop and a mangrove swamp. (Don't forget to take bug repellent.) The Dutch built **Forte Orange** in 1631, but the Portuguese – who are responsible for the fort's current incarnation – renamed it Fortaleza de Santa Cruz de Itamaracá by the Portuguese *(Sítio Histórico Forte Orange,*

no #, Forte Orange, tel. (81) 3544-1622; Mon – Sat, 10am – 5pm; Sun and holidays, 9am – 5pm). There are some basic restaurants near the fort. Visitors can see nine manatees at **Ecoparque Peixe-Boi & Cia** in the rehabilitation unit of Ibama's manatee rescue project, **Projeto Peixe-Boi**. The center has a gift shop and snack bar *(Estrada do Forte Orange, no #, Forte Orange, tel. (81) 3544-1056; Tue – Sun, 10am – 4pm).* The **Estrela de Lia** cultural center on Jaguaribe beach offers presentations of *ciranda* dancing *(Rua Benigno Cordeiro Galvão, units 15 and 16, tel. (81) 9657-5167, 9914-5224; Sat, 9pm; call ahead to confirm that there will be a show).*

IGARASSU

Tiny Igarassu, a national heritage site about 30 kilometers (19 miles) from Recife, is home to preserved buildings from the 18th and 19th centuries. The 18th-century **Pinacoteca do Convento Franciscano Santo Antônio de Igarassu** boasts a valuable collection of 17th- and 18th-century oil paintings on

wood panels depicting religious figures and scenes from history *(Rua Barbosa Lima, no #, tel. (81) 3543-0258; Mon – Fri, 7:30am – noon and 1pm – 5pm; Sat, 9am – 5pm).* People said the epidemic passed over Igarassu thanks to the protection of its patron saints, Cosmas and Damian. **Igreja de São Cosme**

e São Damião church, dating from 1535, was destroyed by the Dutch and rebuilt in 1654. Its baroque features were added in the 18th century, but its interior wall paintings are almost entirely gone *(Rua Frei Caneca, no #, Centro, tel. (81) 3543-0518; Mon – Fri, 8am – noon and 2pm – 5pm; Sat, 8am – noon; Sun, 6am – noon).*

THE SOUTH COAST

The stretch of coast, known as **Costa dos Arrecifes** (Reef Coast) because of the many reefs found there, extends from **Cabo de Santo Agostinho**. It is starts 33 kilometers (21 miles) from Recife – the spot where Spanish navigator Vicente Pinzón supposedly landed three months before the arrival of Cabral in Bahia – to **Tamandaré**, 113 kilometers away (70 miles). The Rodovia PE-060 highway provides access, alternating between busy and peaceful spots. Visitors can make day trips from Recife, but some locations, like **Porto de Galinhas**, have good accommodations.

PORTO DE GALINHAS AND TAMANDARÉ

Clearly marked roads make it easy to get to Porto de Galinhas, 60 kilometers (37 miles) south of Recife. The town is very popular, though, and its crowds can be off-putting for visitors looking for a bit of peace and quiet. Choose a *jangada* raft trip to the natural pools, coral reefs and mangrove swamps, or go to Ilha de Santo Aleixo via boat *(Barco Topázio, tel. (81) 3552-1111)* or dune buggy *(Associação de Bugueiros, tel. (81) 3552-1930)*. Night time fun (in the form of *forró* and raves) is guaranteed on lively **Rua da Esperança** and in **Praça das Piscinas Naturais**. **Tamandaré**, 60 kilometers (37 miles) south of Porto de Galinhas on the Rodovias PE-060 and PE-076 highways is a quieter option. This village's 16 kilometers (10 miles) of beach and blue sea are less crowded and offer fewer amenities. Try the still-unspoiled **Praia de Carneiros**, one of the most beautiful beaches in the country, with about five kilometers of coconut palms, white sand and imposing cliffs.

Porto de Galinhas: visitors ride jangada rafts to natural pools

BEST BEACHES

1 Pedra do Xaréu
A fishing village with rocks and a nice beach, a blue sea with few waves and simple barracas. The road from Calhetas leads to the village.

2 Gaibu
This beach offers white sand and dangerous waters. It has hotels, bars, restaurants and houses, and the rocks on the south side afford a lovely view.

3 Calhetas
Frequented by surfers and divers, this beach is hard to reach. Visitors must clamber over the rocks at Gaibu and then climb a steep trail.

4 Gamboa
At the mouth of the Ipojuca River, this beach has calm waters and mangroves. Gain access from the dirt road from Porto de Galinhas.

5 Muro Alto
Cliffs and a coral reef barrier create an enormous natural pool. They are also responsible for the beach's name, "High Wall." Its calm waters are good for sailing and other water sports.

6 Praia do Cupe
Surrounded by coconut groves and Atlantic forest, this beach has strong waves, especially between March and December. In its left corner, the ocean is calmer and creates natural pools.

7 Porto de Galinhas
This beach near the town is very fashionable and extremely crowded in the summer. It is a departure point for jangada raft trips to the natural pools.

8 Maracaípe
Good waves make this beach ideal for surfing. The nightlife centers around the bars and restaurants clustered on the sandy streets of Vila de Todos os Santos.

9 Carneiros
About 5 kilometers (3 miles) of coconut groves, pale sand and reef walls make up this beach near the mouth of the Formoso River.

1 cm = 5.2 km
1 inch = 8.2 mi.

FERNANDO DE NORONHA

This archipelago of 21 islands can boast some of the country's most beautiful beaches. Located 350 kilometers (220 miles) from Natal and 550 (340 miles) from Recife, it never fails to dazzle visitors, whether they're adventurers, surfers, divers or honeymooning couples. Because of its isolation, the biggest island – Fernando de Noronha – was home to a prison in the 18th century. In 1988, 85 percent of the island was turned into a national marine park; in 2001, along with Atol das Rocas, it was declared a world heritage site, and it is now a sanctuary for birds, turtles and dolphins. The number of visitors is limited and they must pay an environmental preservation tax, calculated according to the length of their stay. Flights are available from Recife and Natal, and cruise ships also stop here. Accommodations range from simple to sophisticated. **Vila dos Remédios**, the main center, grew up around the **Igreja de Nossa Senhora dos Remédios**, built between 1737 and 1772. The island sports stores, cafés, bars and only one bank. The main road, Rodovia BR-363 highway, is only 6.8 kilometers long – Brazil's smallest federal highway. Travelers who

want to explore the island can rent a buggy or motorbike or take a bus that runs every half an hour.

BEACHES

The beaches are made up of tiny pieces of coral, shell particles or dark volcanic pepples. The sea in front of the part of the island facing the mainland is referred to as *mar de dentro* (inner sea), and its beaches have calm waters that are ideal for snorkeling. Check out **Baía do Sancho**, where sea turtles lay their eggs. Its intensely green waters are among the loveliest on the island. At **Baía dos Porcos**, reefs form pools that teem with fish. Kiosks at **Praia do Cachorro** and **Praia do Meio** both serve tasty snacks. Good tube waves for surfing form between November and April, especially on **Praia do Boldró** and **Cacimba do Padre**. On the other side of the island, which faces Africa, the ocean is called *mar de fora* (outer sea). This part of the ocean contains **Praia do Atalaia**, which only allows 100 people per day. At low tide, groups of 25 can dive for 20 minutes at a time to see the many colorful fish. **Praia do Leão**, a bird sanctuary and a site for turtles to lay their eggs, is another popular beach. Rocks make swimming dangerous at high tide. Turtles also visit **Baía do Sueste**, where visitors can see the ruins of Forte de São Joaquim, can be reached by paved road.

BOAT AND KAYAK TRIPS

In the early mornings and afternoons, boats leave from **Praia do Porto** for three-hour trips around the *mar de dentro* side of the island. Apart from the particularly beautiful beaches, visitors can go to **Baía dos**

OUR RECOMMENDATION

🍽 The **Museu dos Tubarões** offers exhibits of shark jawbones and huge dorsal fins, and its store sells cuddly toy sharks. Try a snack of *tubalhau*, similar to salted codfish cakes, in the restaurant. According to the owner, fishing engineer Leonardo Veras, the shark served here are caught from the mainland and are not endangered *(Avenida Joaquim Ferreira Gomes, 40, Vila do Porto, tel. (81) 3619-1365; Mon – Sat, 8:30am – 6:30pm; Sun, noon – 6pm).*

Additional information on page 462.

1 cm = 2.8 km
1 inch = 4.4 mi.

RN
PB
PE
●Recife

Pontal do Norte
Cordilheiras   Macaxeira
Cabeço das Cordas
Buraco do
Inferno
Cação
Cagarras
Funda
Cagarras   Ilha da
Rasa   Rata

N

Ressurreta   Buraco das
Cabras

Ilha do
Meio
Ilha do
Meio
Ilha Sela Gineta   Sela Gineta

INNER
SEA

Ilha
Rasa
Ilha São José   Ponta de Santo Antônio
Ilha Cuscuz   (Air France)
Ilha da Viuvinha   Pedras
5 Buraco da Raquel   Secas I
Porto de Santo Antônio   Pedras
Naufrágio do Porto   Cabeço da Caieira   Secas II
de Santo Antônio (Porto)
Enseada da Caieira

Pontinha

Cachorro   Morro do
Morro de Fora   Francês
Morro de Fora   Vila dos   Vila do
Remédios   Trinta   Ponta da
Meio   Pedra Alta
Conceição
BR   Ilha do Frade
363   Ilha do Frade
Morro
Boldró   do Pico   Atalaia
4   Morro do
Aeroporto   Espinhaço
do Americano   Ponta do Espinhaço
do Bode   Ilha dos
Quixaba   Ovos   Ilha Trinta Réis
Cacimba do Padre   Ilha dos Ovos
Laje Dois Irmãos
Morro Dois Irmãos   Morro
Baía dos Porcos   7   Boa Vista   Baía do
Baía do Sancho   Sueste   Ilha Cabeluda
1   Ilha Chapéu de Sueste
Corveta   Ilha de Fernando   Cabeço Submarino
Ipiranga V17   de Noronha   Ponta das Caracas
3   Iuias
Baía dos   Ponta das Caracas
Golfinhos   2   6   Leão
Morro   Naufrágio do Leão
da Viúva   Morro
do Leão   OUTER
SEA

Cavernas da
Sapata
Ponta Capim
Cabeço da   Açu
Sapata
Ponta do Barro
Ponta da   Vermelho
Sapata

Praia do Leão, a bird sanctuary and the place where turtles lay their eggs on Fernando de Noronha

Golfinhos (Dolphin Bay) to see spinner dolphins up close. Some of them swim alongside the boats *(Barco Naonda, tel. (81) 3619-1307; Associação de Barcos de Turismo, tel. (81) 3619-1360, 3619-1977)*. Two-person guided kayak trips with motor boat support (to tow the kayaks back) last two hours. They run from Praia do Porto to **Cacimba do Padre**, where people can see the famous **Morro Dois Irmãos hill** *(Remos da Ilha, tel. (81) 3619-1914)*.

Hiking Trails

Trails leading to beaches and lookout points reveal more of Fernando de Noronha's beauty. At about 10 kilometers, **Capim-Açu** is the longest of the most popular trails, running from Quixaba to Praia do Leão. It's somewhat difficult, so hikers should be fairly fit and take a guide along. A guide is also necessary for **Trilha Pontinha–Pedra Alta**, a 4.2-kilometer trail that runs through stunning scenery and rock formations, which the guides use to explain the island's geography. The hike ends with a 15-minute supervised dive at Praia do Atalaia. The trail to **Mirante dos Golfinhos** is very popular. It begins at the Sancho parking lot; its two kilometers take hikers to the 70-meter-high (230-foot) lookout point, which affords a view of dolphins at rest and play. The best time to see them is between morning and mid-afternoon, when they return from the open sea to feed. This trail is usually climbed without a guide, but anyone wanting to go there before 8am must be accompanied by a guide. Check the tides before setting out on these walks. (TV Golfino, the local channel, provides this kind of information.)
Ibama, tel. (81) 3619-1210.

Projeto Tamar

The Tamar Project, which is a successful endeavor to protect sea turtles, is a hidden gem. Every night at 9pm, members of the team give free talks on environmental conservation at the **Centro de Visitantes do Projeto Tamar/Ibama**.
Alameda Boldró, no #, Boldró, tel. (81) 3619-1174, 3619-117; daily, 9am – 10pm.

Snorkeling and Diving

A mask and snorkel are indispensable in Noronha. Don't miss the chance to try the "planasub," which was invented on the island. It is a transparent acrylic board that helps amateur divers enjoy underwater delights, wearing a mask and snorkel while being pulled along by a motorboat *(Museu dos Tubarões e Embarcação Golfinho, tel. (81) 3619-* *1365)*. Noronha is a must for diving enthusiasts because of its vibrant marine life – fish, sharks, rays and moray eels darting in and out of the coral. There are 16 diving spots, with underwater visibility up to 50 meters (165 feet) *(Águas Claras, tel. (81) 3619-1225; Atlantis Divers, tel. (81) 3619-1371, 3619-1488; Noronha Divers, tel. (81) 3619-1112)*.

ZONA DA MATA

TRACUNHAÉM

Tracunhaém, population 13,000, is one of Brazil's major centers for ceramics. It is located in the Zona da Mata region, 63 kilometers (39 miles) from Recife on the Rodovias BR-232 and BR-408 highways. Tracunhaém's artisans work in studios that used to be pottery centers. Although Manuel Borges da Silva, known as **Nuca**, stopped working a few years ago due to poor health, his children continue to produce his famous creations, such as lions with curly manes and a doll figure known as Dondoca *(Rua Manoel Pereira de Morais, 118)*. **Zezinho** also runs a well-known studio, where he creates life-sized statues of saints *(Avenida Desembargador Carlos Vaz, 85, Centro, tel. (81) 3646-1215; daily, 7am – 6pm)*. Saints are also the specialty at **Ateliê Maria Amélia** *(Praça Costa Azevedo, 76, Centro, tel. (81) 3646-1778; daily, 7am – 5pm)*. The **Centro de Produção Artesanal** brings together 45 artisans and apprentices and offers arts and crafts courses *(Praça Costa Azevedo, no #, Centro; Mon – Fri, 9am – 6pm)*.

Folk dancing at the Festa Junina celebrations in Caruaru, the longest June festivities in Brazil

THE AGRESTE REGION

CARUARU

Set in the heart of the *agreste* region, Caruaru – 134 kilometers (82 miles) from Recife on Rodovia BR-232 highway) – is most famous for its lively **Festa de São João** festivities and its clay folk art. The **Feira de Caruaru** is the biggest open-air market in the Northeast. Visitors can find arts and crafts, faith healers, herbal medicines, regional food and even electronics in the 150,000 square meters (1,615,000 square feet) of the **Parque 18 de Maio**. Saturday is its busiest day. The clothes fair **Feira da Sulanca** sets up early Tuesday mornings *(Parque 18 de Maio, no #, Centro; Wed – Mon, 8am – 5pm; Tue, 5am – 5pm)*. More

arts and crafts are plentiful in the studios of the **Alto do Moura** neighborhood, 7 kilometers (4 miles) from the center of Caruaru. Artist **Vitalino Pereira da Silva** (1909-63) built his home, now known as **Casa do Mestre Vitalino**, here in 1959. It is now a museum, displaying his work and personal items *(Rua Mestre Vitalino, no #, tel. (81) 3725-080; Mon – Sat, 8am – noon and 2pm – 5pm; Sun, 8am – noon)*. Other artists have studios on the same street: **Luiz Galdino** *(#455, tel. (81) 3722-0369; daily, 8am – 5pm)* and **Família Zé Caboclo** *(#66; Mon – Fri, 8am – noon and 2pm – 6pm; Sat and Sun, 8am – 1pm)*.

COOL WEATHER IN THE AGRESTE REGION

Gravatá, 80 kilometers (50 miles) from Recife on Rodovia BR-232 highway, enjoys a European climate in the *agreste* region. At an altitude of 447 meters (1,470 feet), it has an average annual temperature of 21 degrees Celsius (70 degrees Fahrenheit). In August, the **Festa da Estação** – with work-shops, talks and musical per-formances – marks the end of **Circuito do Frio**, a winter fes-tival that also involves the municipalities of Garanhuns, Triunfo, and Taquaritinga *(Pátio de Eventos Chucre Mussa Zazar, Avenida Joaquim Didier, no #, Centro)*. **Garanhuns**, further away at 230 kilometers (143 miles) from Recife, also boasts an annual temperature of 21 degrees Celsius (70 degrees Fahrenheit). It hosts the **Festival de Inverno**, a 10-day winter celebration in July, with the-ater, music, literature, work-shops and fashion shows held throughout the municipality *(Fundarpe, tel. (81) 3134-3000)*.

MUSEU DO BARRO AND MUSEU DO FORRÓ

On the first floor, block B of **Espaço Cultural Tancredo Neves,** visitors will find the **Museu do Barro Zé Caboclo**. It is one of the most important institutions of its kind in Brazil, with 2,300 clay folk-art pieces from all over the Northeast. On the ground floor is the **Museu do Forró Luiz Gonzaga**, which houses a collection of pieces connected to musician Luiz Gonzaga.
Praça Colonel José Vasconcellos, 100, bloco B, Centro, tel. (81) 3701-1533. Tue – Sat, 8am – 5pm.

FESTA DE SÃO JOÃO

The **Festa de São João** celebrations begin the first weekend of June and continue for the entire month. They take place in Vila do Forró, which resembles a typical country village, in the **Pátio de Eventos Luiz Gonzaga** in Espaço Cultural Tancredo Neves' outdoor area. The streets are taken over by *quadrilha* dancers, *repentistas* (improvisational musical poets) and *bacamarteiros*, who owe their name to the wide-barreled firearms (*bacamartes*) they carry. They march to the beat of *xaxado* music played by bands of accordions, triangles, *zabumba* drums and *pífano* flutes.

BEZERROS

Caruaru's neighbor Bezerros, 27 kilometers (17 miles) away on Rodovia BR-232 highway, is famous for its woodcut prints and *papangus*, a kind of paper *mâché* mask. Woodcut printing is a technique using a carved wooden block to stamp images on paper. Its popularity in the region is associated with *cordel* literature, especially the work of José Francisco Borges, known as **J. Borges**. His studio can be found at **Memorial J. Borges** *(Avenida Major Aprígio da Fonseca, 420, Centro, tel. (81) 3728-0364; Mon – Fri, 8am – 11am and 1pm – 5pm).* Papangus (meaning "those who eat *angu*") – Carnival merry-makers who wear colorful masks made from newspaper – earned their names because they are given *angu* (cornmeal mash) to eat when they visit local homes. Masks made by **Lula Vassoureiro** are the most famous. **Casa de Cultura Popular Lula Vassoureiro** has a museum, store and snack bar *(Rua Otávia Bezerra Vila Nova, 64, Santo Amaro 1, tel. (81) 9102-0665; daily, 8am – noon and 1pm – 5pm).* The

Centro de Artesanato de Pernambuco, made up of a museum, a store and workshops, rivals other establishments in large Northeastern cities, with items from all over Pernambuco *(Avenida Major Aprígio da Fonseca, 770, Km 107 marker on Rodovia BR-232, tel. (81) 3728-2094; Tue – Sat, 9am – 6pm; Sun, 9am – 1pm).* The **Pólo Cultural de Serra Negra** is one of the best spots to buy pieces made in Bezerros *(Rua Vigário Manuel Clemente, 123, Centro, tel. (81) 3728-6713; Mon – Fri, 7am – 5pm).*

THE PASSION OF CHRIST

Fazenda Nova, 187 kilometers (116 miles) from Recife, is home to the world's biggest open-air theater. Every year since 1968, 500 actors – some of them famous – stage the two-and-a-half-hour **Passion of Christ** in the Nova Jerusalém, a theater complex of 100,000 square meters (one million square feet) with nine giant stages. From the day before Palm Sunday to Holy Saturday, an audience of around 8,000 watches the event and often joins in the interactive performance.

A JOURNEY INTO THE BACKLANDS

My first introduction to the Brazilian backlands known as the *sertão* was literary: a tattered, used copy of Mario Vargas Llosa's *War at the End of the World*, and then, five minutes after its last page its inspiration: the classic *Os Sertões (Rebellion in the Backlands)* by Euclides da Cunha. Perhaps a fitting introduction. Although few travelers physically visit the *sertão*, there is hardly a Brazilian who has not dreamed of it, read *Grandes Sertões: Veredas (The Devil to Pay in the Backlands)*, seen or read *Vidas Secas (Barren Lives)*, watched *Deus e o Diabo na Terra do Sol (Black God White Devil)*. Indeed, I continue to be struck by the role of the *sertão* in the Brazilian imagination. I was surprised, then, on my first visit to Brazil, to learn how few Brazil: visit the *sertão*, a pity, as during my travels, I have found few places that are as remarkable.

The *sertão's* beauty lies not in its immediate attractions. It has natural beauty, in the canyons of the Rio São Francisco, and the rich thornscrub ecosystem called caatinga in the Raso de Catarina, the Serra do Araripe, or the Borborema mountains. It has unique food, from a surprisingly good stew of viscera called *sarapatel* to the ubiquitous sun-dried beef known as *carne-de-sol*. It is the birthplace of music like *forró* and *xaxado*. And yet, the greatest beauty of the *sertão* lies in something less palpable, a spirit of the place, of history, of the people who live there.

It is impossible to travel anywhere in the *sertão*, and not be reminded that so many of Brazil's great stories come from here. One can visit Canudos or Monte Santo and pass through the towns that grace the pages of *Os Sertões*, meet old men and women whose grandparents or even parents were alive at the time of Antônio Conselheiro. Although the town of Canudos has been moved and the Rio Vasa Barris dammed, when the water in the dam is low enough, the churches towers can still be seen, and the days of the revolt easily remembered.

One can follow the footsteps of Lampião, starting in his birthplace outside of Serra Talhada, recently turned into a fascinating and picturesque museum by a dedicated researcher who leads tours to the site. Or the site of his first great robbery, in Casa Branca, Alagoas, or Mossoró, Natal, where he made a miscalculated attack and was turned back. Or one can hire a fishing boat to Angicos, Sergipe, a painted town which clings to the Rio São Francisco, and take the same path along which, nearly 65 years ago,

volantes flying columns of the police slipped silently downstream to attack the band of *cangaceiros* camped in the shade and silence of a dry river bed, and with rain of bullets began the end of the long rule of *cangaço* banditry. In Juazeiro do Norte, one can see the true faith of backlanders who have traveled for days to pay homage to Padre Cícero Romero.

Besides the famous historical sites of the *sertão* are others, which continue to live. Not two hours from Recife lies Caruaru, where a raucous free market explodes once a week with crowds that have come from the neighboring towns. There, watchmakers and traditional healers set up shop alongside of mountains of fruit and bags of rice, children dance before heavy speakers blasting the newest *forró* from bands with names like The

Cat's Tail (Rabo do Gato), or Snake's Armpit (Sovaco da Cobra), and salesmen hawk copies of popular poems called *literatura de cordel* ("string literature"; it is often sold dangling from string like pieces of laundry) with names like *Caruaru Today and Yesterday (Caruaru Hoje e Ontem)*, and *The Girl who Turned into a Snake (A Moça que Virou uma Cobra)*. The fair runs all week, and is worth visiting any day, although it is on Saturday that one really sees the true role that it plays in the life of the *sertão*.

Other sites in the *sertão* are similarly famous: the pilgrimages of Juazeiro, the waters of the Rio São Francisco, the moutains of the Serra do Araripe. And there are other, less famous, but equally fascinating spots: the Catimbau National Park near Boique, Pernambuco, the workshop of the great cordel illustrator, J. Borges, in Bezerros, Pernambuco, the religious colony of Santa Brigada, outside Paulo Affonso, Bahia.

In the *sertão*, I often found myself alone. But the loneliness of the place is softened by the kindness of its inhabitants. Indeed it is hard to go for a walk, without being offered a wicker chair and a cup of coffee. The great histories of popular saints and bandits are surrounded by thousands of other stories, shared by the old folk who lived through the droughts and continue to work in the fields.

My two favorite spots in the *sertão* are the towns of Triunfo, in central Pernambuco, and Piranhas, Alagoas. A small town perched in the Borborema mountains, Triunfo is blessed with cool weather, beautiful walks to local waterfalls, a fine museum on the history of the *cangaço*, cobbled streets, and some of the kindest people I have ever met. It is part of Pernambuco's "cold circuit" *(circuito do frio)*, a series of mountain-top cities which have festivals celebrating the cold of winter. It is close to Serra Talhada, from which Lampião's birthplace can be visited, as well as other sites of historical interest such as Princesa Isabel, Paraíba, where the independent República Princesa was once declared.

Piranhas lies in a steep valley along the banks of the São Francisco. Its houses wear a rainbow's array of colors, a flowering against the backdrop of unscarred Caatinga. Restaurants line the river. There is a museum in the railway station. It has two lovely little hotels; otherwise visitors can stay across the river at the Xingo resort. Trips are easy to arrange into the canyons above the Xingo dam, or downstream, to Angicos, Sergipe, where Lampião spent his final night.

If the living history or the kindness of the backlanders is not enough to get one to visit the *sertão*, there is a final reason. While the days can be hot and dry and the shuttered windows of the little towns leave the streets silent, as soon as the sun begins its descent, a tremendous change takes over the *sertão*. There is nothing like this light, which turns the Caatinga an exquisite yellow, and drapes the whitewashed walls gold. Then, from the shuttered houses, children swarm into the streets to play, teenagers gather around music, old men set up on the porch steps in rocking chairs. A single evening makes the long journey worthwhile.

Daniel Mason,
American physician and writer, author of The Piano Tuner

SERTÃO

PETROLINA

Petrolina, 767 kilometers (477 miles) from Recife on the banks of the São Francisco River, boasts a bevy of attractions. **Espaço Cultural Ana das Carrancas** displays expressive clay figures made by Ana Leopoldina dos Santos *(Rodovia BR-407, 500, Cohab Massangano, tel. (87) 3031-4399; daily, 8am – 6pm; call before 1pm to schedule a visit)*. The **Museu do Sertão** houses pre-historic fossils and items belonging to the legendary backlands bandit Lampião *(Rua Esmelinda Brandão, no #, Centro, tel. (87) 3862-1943; Mon and Wed – Fri, 10am – 5:30pm; Tue, 1pm – 6pm; Sat and Sun, 8am – noon and 2pm – 5pm)*. The **Bodódromo** is a cluster of restaurants that developed from the idea of serving only *bode* (goat) meat, although mutton is on its current menu *(Avenida São Francisco, no #, Areia Branca; daily, from 11am)*. Travelers can get to Petrolina from Recife via Rodovia BR-232 highway, but it can be unsafe – especially the section at Salgueiro. It is better to leave from Juazeiro in Bahia. Petrolina airport has flights from Recife and São Paulo.

WINE FROM THE PETROLINA REGION

In the São Francisco Valley, the combination of hot sun, north-eastern soil and river water results in a rare phenomenon: two grape harvests per year. This region sitting on parallel 8 and encompassing Petrolina and Juazeiro, has become a famous wine-producing area, and some of its wines are among the country's best. **Botticelli** has been operating for 23 years in Milano, 90 kilometers (56 miles) from Petrolina. It is open to the public, but visits should be arranged in advance *(Rodovia PE-574, Rodovia da Uva e do Vinho, Km 36, Santa Maria da Boa Vista, tel. (87) 3860-1536; Sat, 8am – noon and 2pm – 5pm; Sun, 8am – noon)*. A pre-arranged visit to **Garziera**, which was founded by a family from the South, starts with the vines and ends with tasting their wines, juices and cheeses *(Vinícola Lagoa Grande, no #, Distrito de Vermelho, Lagoa Grande, tel. (87) 3869-9212; daily, 8am – 5pm)*. At **Vinibrasil**, on the banks of the Rio São Francisco, a wine expert will be your guide. Depending on the month, visitors can watch the pruning or help with harvesting the grapes. The vineyard's own **Rio Sol** wines are served in its restaurant, **Espaço Maria Bonita**, where Portuguese cuisine is the specialty *(Avenida São Francisco, 276-B, Areia Branca, tel. (87) 3864-042. Wed – Sat, lunch subject to reservations; dinner: 7pm until the last customer leaves; wine cellar: 8am until the last customer leaves)*.

TRIUNFO

Triunfo, called the "capital of *rapadura*", is home to the old sugar mills that produce the brown sugar tablets known as *rapadura* between July and December. It is located 450 kilometers (280 miles) from Recife on Rodovias BR-232 and PE-365 highways. **São Pedro** does traditional, hand-made production all year round *(Sítio Bela Vista, Zona Rural, 500 meters from the center, next to Pousada Baixo Verde,* tel. (87) 3846-1229; daily, 8am – 4pm)*. **Biscoitos São Nicolau** – biscuits made with honey, cinnamon and cloves made from a recipe brought by German nuns in 1939 – are very traditional in this region. Triunfo also boasts the highest point in Pernambuco: **Pico do Papagaio**, which reaches 1,260 meters (4,130 feet). The town's tourist board can recommend local guides *(tel. (87) 3846-1256, 3846-1631)*.

PARAÍBA

1 cm = 53 km
1 inch = 84.1 mi.

RIO GRANDE
DO NORTE

Fortaleza

PARAÍBA

CEARÁ

Salgueiro

Souza
Cajazeiras
Pombal
Patos
Natal
Caicó

Mamanguape
Areia
Campina
Grande
Sapê
Santa Rita
Ingá
Conde
Cabaceiras

Natal
Baía da
Traição
Cabedelo
João
Pessoa
Jacumã
Pitimbu

Recife
Recife

PERNAMBUCO

Caruaru

Arcoverde

BAHIA

ALAGOAS

ATLANTIC OCEAN

N

HIGHLIGHTS

- The urban beaches and historical buildings of **João Pessoa**.
- The easternmost point in South America – the **Cabo Branco**

- Lighthouse at **Ponta do Seixas**, in João Pessoa.
- The beaches at the Unesco Biosphere Reserve, **Barra de Mamanguape**.

WHEN TO GO

- The busy **summer** (December through February) or the low season, to relax in João Pessoa when it's quieter.
- **Any time of year** for the coast, except during the rainy season

- (May through July).
- During **Carnival**, visit a lively place like Jacumã on the south coast.
- In **June**, sample some of Brazil's wildest festivities in Campina Grande.

João Pessoa

This city has been given several names since it was founded on the banks of the Paraíba River in 1585. In 1930, the assassination of the governor sparked so much national fervor that the city was renamed for him in its final iteration. Paraíba's capital, with a population of 660,000, has plentiful trees and beaches with calm waters that are good for swimming. Lively **Tambaú**'s wide strip of sand is lined with hotels, bars and kiosks. In summer, the ocean retreats to reveal coral formations called *picãozinhos* (little peaks). To the south, the Farol do Cabo Branco lighthouse offers magnificent views of the city at **Ponta do Seixas**, the easternmost tip of South America. Kiosks on the city beaches offer local specialties such as crab, fried *agulhinha* fish and *arrumadinho* (string beans and beef jerky).

HISTORICAL BUILDINGS
Construction began in 1589 on **Centro Cultural de São Francisco**, an important baroque architectural complex. First built was the convent, which has functioned as a cultural center since 1990. It houses three museums: the Galeria de Pedra, which displays fragments of rocks from different eras discovered during the church's restoration; a second museum that features sacred art; and a third dedicated to folk art. In 1602, construction began on **Igreja de São Francisco**. Its unforgettable interior includes the nave, surrounded by a tiled mural depicting the story of Saint Joseph in Egypt, and its beautifully carved pulpit. To the left of the church is the Capela Dourada, a chapel with a statue of Saint Anthony and other gilded figures *(Praça de São Francisco, no #, Centro, tel. (83) 3218-450; Tue – Sun, 9am – noon and 2pm – 5pm)*. The imposing neo-classical **Teatro Santa Rosa**, dating from 1889, took 36 years to build. The interior of the theater made of German pine *(Praça Pedro Américo, no #, Centro, tel. (83) 3218-4383; daily, 1pm – 6pm; no fixed times on performance days)*.

LITERARY MUSEUMS
Two of the greatest craftsmen of regional Brazilian literature, José Lins do Rego (1901-57) and José Américo de Almeida (1887-1980), started out in Paraíba. The

João Pessoa's calm, clean beaches are excellent for sports

Fundação Casa de José Américo de Almeida operates out of the house where the writer and politician, who governed Paraíba in 1950, lived from 1953 until his death *(Avenida Cabo Branco, 3336, Praia do Cabo Branco, tel. (83) 3214-8506; Mon – Fri, 8am – 5:30pm)*. The **Centro de Convenções do Espaço Cultural José Lins do Rego** is a cultural center that houses a cinema, theater, exhibition spaces and a museum with exhibits of manuscripts, books and a typewriter that belonged to the novelist *(Rua Abdias Gomes de Almeida, 800, Tambauzinho, tel. (83) 3211-6210; Mon – Fri, noon – 6pm)*.

CHURCHES

Igreja de São Frei Pedro Gonçalves was built on the site of a 17th-century chapel that was demolished in 1843. The church's current features date from 1916; visitors can see its first foundations *(Largo São Frei Pedro Gonçalves, no #, Varadouro; Mon – Fri, 9am – noon and 2pm – 5pm)*. The national-heritage-listed **Igreja de São Bento** was built in the early 18th century and has retained its baroque façade *(Rua General Osório, 36, Centro, tel. (83) 3241-7009; Thu, 9am – 5pm; on other days, during 7am mass)*. Another baroque

---

ARTS AND CRAFTS

The Brazilian Agricultural Research Corporation developed cotton which naturally grows in shades of beige, and produces it in the Campina Grande region The raw material is used to make clothes and other items sold at **Algodão de Cor** *(Avenida Nego, 548, Tambaú, tel. (83) 3247-6723; Mon – Sat, 9am – 7:30pm)*. artisans in Gurinhém, in the interior of the state, produce items made from hand-woven cotton, sisal, wicker and coconut fiber that are sold at **Terra do Sol** *(Rua Coração de Jesus, 145, Tambaú, tel. (83) 3226-1940; Mon – Sat, 9am – 7pm)*.

---

church, **Igreja de Nossa Senhora do Carmo**, is an annex of the beautiful **Capela de Santa Teresa d'Ávila** *(Praça Dom Adauto, no #, Centro, tel. (83) 3221-7817; Tue – Sat, 9am – 11am; Mon – Sat, 2pm – 5pm; Sun, mass at 10am)*. The 16th-century **Igreja da Misericórdia** still has the emblem of the Portuguese crown on the arch above the high altar *(Rua Duque de Caxias, no #, Centro; no fixed hours)*. **Matriz de Nossa Senhora das Neves**, built in the 19th century, now stands on the site of the city's first chapel, inaugurated in 1585 *(Praça Dom Ulrico, no #, Centro, tel. (83) 3221-2503; Mon – Fri, 2pm – 6pm; Sat, 4pm – 7pm; Sun, 6am – 10:30am and 4pm – 7pm)*.

THE COAST

SOUTHERN BEACHES

Travelers heading south on Rodovia PB-008 highway will come to **Jacumã**, a busy tourist destination and home to a lively Carnival. Thirty-five kilometers (22 miles) from João Pessoa, it serves as a base to reach neighboring beaches. **Coqueirinho** is one of the region's most beautiful and peaceful seashores, with freshwater springs, majestic cliffs, light-colored sands and gentle waves. **Tambaba** is an official nude beach, and men are only allowed in accompanied by women. People wearing clothes are denied access, but there is one stretch reserved for those who prefer to remain dressed.

NORTHERN BEACHES

Paraíba's north coast is quieter than its south coast. **Praia de Camboinha**, located just in front of Cabedelo, offers boat trips to a sandbank called **Areia Vermelha**, which appears at low tide and is surrounded by coral and reefs.

Traição Bay preserves both natural and native cultural riches

Cabedelo, 18 kilometers (11 miles) from João Pessoa, is home to the **Fortaleza de Santa Catarina**, a fort built in 1589. Check out **Praia Fluvial de Jacaré**, where Jurandy Félix, known as **Jurandy do Sax**, plays Ravel's *Bolero* on the banks of the river every day at sunset. **Barra de Mamanguape** is a Unesco Biosphere Reserve located 48 kilometers (30 miles) from the capital. Surfers like **Praia Campina** and **Praia do Oiteiro** because of their strong waves; both beaches are lined with cliffs and coconut palms. In Mamanguape, **Projeto Peixe-Boi** – a project from Ibama, the Brazilian Institute for the Environment and Renewable Natural Resources – plays a fundamental role in the protection of the manatee *(Estrada da Barra de Mamanguape, no #, Rio Tinto, tel. (83) 9316-6976; daily, 8am – 4pm)*. Further north, **Baía da Traição** (Betrayal Bay) boasts a pristine landscape with yellow sand and a Potiguar Indian reserve.

CAMPINA GRANDE

Sitting 125 kilometers (78 miles) from João Pessoa, Campina Grande is the home of the original *forró* dance called *pé-de-serra*. The town's **São João festivities** are the most visited celebrations in the country. In June, about a million people show up for the festivities. **Parque do Povo**, in the center of town, admits 80,000 people to watch square dancing on the night of June 23 alone. During weekends in June and July, a train called the **Trem For-**roviário takes a "traveling dance" 12 kilometers (seven miles) to the district of Galante *(Praça Coronel Antônio Pessoa, 124, Centro, tel. (83) 3342-0300; departure at 10am)*. The historical importance of cotton farming in the town, which now produces colored cotton, is on display at the **Museu do Algodão** *(Rua Benjamin Constant, Largo da Estação Velha, no #, Centro, public phone (83) 3341-0603; daily, 7am – 11am and noon – 5pm)*. The **Museu Histórico de Campina Grande** is a history museum featuring a collection of maps and photographs *(Avenida Marechal Floriano Peixoto, 825, Centro, tel. (83) 3310-6182; Mon – Fri, 8am – noon and 2pm – 5pm; Sat, 8am – 5pm)*. Works by renowned artists such as Pedro Américo and Di Cavalcanti can be seen at the **Museu de Arte Assis Chateaubriand** *(Parque Evaldo Cruz, no #, Centro, tel. (83) 3310-9733; Mon – Fri, 8am – 11am and 2pm – 5pm)*.

Rio Grande do Norte

The Mãe Luiza lighthouse offers an unrivaled view of Natal

NATAL

Rio Grande do Norte's sunny capital, which folklorist Luís da Câmara Cascudo called "The Sun's Bride," is the gateway for exploring the state's coast by buggy. But the city has its own attractions, too. The best accommodation is to be found along **Via Costeira**, the coastal avenue that links the city center to busy **Praia de Ponta Negra** beach. The city's out-of-season Carnival, **Carnatal**, takes place at the beginning of December.

FORTE DOS REIS MAGOS

This star-shaped fort stands at the point where the Potengi River meets the sea and affords a panoramic view of Natal's shoreline. Construction began on the Feast of the Epiphany in 1598 – hence the name "Fort of the Magi" – and was undertaken to protect the city against a possible French invasion. Stone blocks replaced the fort's original wattle and daub construction in 1628.

The well-preserved fort houses the Marco de Touros, a limestone block dating to 1501 and inscribed with the king of Portugal's cross-and-shield insignia. Originally located where São Miguel do Gostoso village stands today, it signified Portuguese possession of the surrounding lands. By 1962, when it became a national heritage site and was relocated to Natal, it had become an object of cult worship and was considered to have miraculous powers. Locals used to take shavings of the stone to make a healing tea for the sick.

Avenida Café Filho, no #, Praça do Forte, tel. (84) 3202-9006. Daily, 8am – 5pm.

OUR RECOMMENDATION

Craftwork from Northeast Brazil and other countries inspired the décor at **Manary Praia Hotel**. Its cozy rooms have hammocks on the balconies, and the restaurant is particularly good *(Rua Francisco Gurgel, 9067, Ponta Negra, tel. (84) 3204-2900)*.

Additional information on page 462.

FAROL DA MÃE LUIZA AND PARQUE DAS DUNAS

One hundred fifty spiraling steps lead to the top of this lighthouse, also called Farol de Natal. Built in 1951, it reaches 37 meters above the underlying sand dune and stands 87 meters above sea level *(Rua Camaragibe, no #, Mãe Luiza, tel. (84) 3201-0477. Visits subject to prior arrangement)*. The view, naturally, is stunning, taking in parts of the **Parque Estadual Dunas de Natal** (also called Parque das Dunas). This park boasts a jogging track, picnic area, and guided hiking trails that range from 800 to 4,400 meters (2.5 miles) in length *(Avenida Alexandrino de Alencar, no #, Morro Branco, tel. (84) 3201-3985; Tue – Sun, 8am – 6pm; guided walks at 8:30am and 2:30pm)*.

CENTRO DE TURISMO

This tourist complex occupies a 19th-century building that served at various times as a shelter for the poor, an orphanage, and a prison. Its stores now sell souvenirs like embroidery, items made from sisal fibers, and *carnaúba* palm straw boxes. In Cell #2, the **Cooperativa de Produtores Artesanais do Rio Grande do Norte** sells craftwork from several parts of the state *(tel. (84) 3222-3802)*. There is a *forró* dance performance on Thursdays starting at 10pm.

Rua Aderbal de Figueiredo, 980, Petrópolis, tel. (84) 3211-6149. Daily, 8am – 6pm.

CIDADE ALTA AND RIBEIRA

Cidade Alta, the upper part of the city, and the Ribeira neighborhood are home to the city's oldest buildings. The neo-classical **Instituto Histórico e Geográfico do Rio Grande do Norte** houses a collection of rare books and an old baptismal font.
The entrance is marked by **Coluna Capitolina**, a gift from Benito Mussolini as a thank you to Natal for the warm welcome given to two Italian pilots who landed there in 1928 *(Rua da Conceição, 622, Ribeira, tel. (84) 3232-9728; Mon – Fri, 8am – noon and 2pm – 5pm)*. The tiny **Museu Café Filho** houses a collection of personal items and books belonging to João Café Filho, who was president from 1954 to 1955, following the suicide of his predecessor, Getúlio Vargas. The museum occupies an early 19th-century house called "bridal veil" because of its steeply sloped white roof *(Rua da Conceição, 601, Ribeira; Tue – Sun, 8:30am – 5pm)*. The **Teatro Alberto Maranhão**, founded in 1904, is a theater that boasts a Belgian-tile floor and crystal mirrors *(Praça Augusto Severo, Ribeira, tel. (84) 3222-3669; Mon – Fri, 9am – 5pm, no fixed times on performance*

FOLKLORIST CÂMARA CASCUDO

Folklorist, historian, and ethnographer Luís da Câmara Cascudo (1898-1986) was born in what is now the Tirol neighborhood. He is commemorated at two sites in his hometown. In the **Casa de Câmara Cascudo** museum, where he lived for forty years, you can see his table, desk, and typewriter as he used them, covered by a Peruvian cloth. Restoration work began on the museum in 2007 and there is no set date for reopening *(Avenida Câmara Cascudo, 377, Ribeira, tel. (84) 3222-3293; hours prior to restoration: Mon – Fri, 8am – 5pm)*. The **Memorial Câmara Cascudo** houses a library, personal items, such as an agate basin where he was first bathed, and the cigars he smoked compulsively *(Praça André de Albuquerque, 30, Cidade Alta, tel. (84) 3201-6425; Tue – Sun, 8am – 5pm)*. Note that the small natural history museum known as the **Museu Câmara Cascudo** has no connection with him.

Praia de Ponta Negra, in Natal, and the famous sandy strip of Morro do Careca

days). The best way to see historical **Ribeira**, in the lower city, is by walking along lovely, cobblestone **Rua Chile**, whose nightclubs attract a youthful crowd. The **Pedra do Rosário**, also called **Paço da Pátria**, which lies along the bank of the Potengi River, is an ideal spot to enjoy the sunset. It also houses a statue of the Virgin Mary, which, according to legend washed up on the site in a box in 1753. The day it washed up, November 21ˢᵗ, is the feast day of Nossa Senhora da Apresentação (Our Lady of the Presentation), who thus became patroness and protector of Natal. The original statue stands in the city's cathedral; the one by the river is a replica.

BEACHES

Like Ribeira, **Praia de Ponta Negra** is busy at night, and its stores, restaurants and bars with live music stay open into the wee hours. Next to this beach, which has areas for surfing, is **Morro do Careca**, a dune that's currently off limits to forestall erosion. Next comes a series of beaches, such as **Barreira d'Água** and **Areia Preta**, behind which runs **Via Costeira** and its 13 kilometers of hotels, where guests can choose between swimming in the ocean or splashing in the hotel pools. After this hotel-and-beach strip come such beaches as **Praia dos Artistas**, a meeting place for surfers, and **Praia do Meio** and **Praia do Forte**, which both feature calm, shallow waters.

ENVIRONS OF NATAL

GENIPABU

One of Natal's main attractions, Genipabu's famously picturesque dunes are a popular destination for dune buggy tours. The dunes lie 25 kilometers (16 miles) north of Natal, in the municipality of Extremoz. You can get there on Rodovias RN-302 and 304 highways or by a 20-minute ferry ride from Natal. The dromedary

camels at **Dromedunas** come originally from the Canary Islands, and are now used to transport tourists *(Praia de Genipabu, tel. (84) 3225-2053, 3225-2324, 9991-9690; daily, 9am – 5pm).* Despite being a state-protected environmental area, the beach is cluttered with holiday homes, dune buggies, and bars. Beyond Genipabu are the dunes and lakes of **Pitangui** and **Jacumã**. You get down to Jacumã Lake by riding in a cloth chair rigged to a system of ropes and pulleys. A rope-pulled cart on tracks will take you back up.

CABO DE SÃO ROQUE

This cape is the second-closest point in Brazil to Africa, after Ponta do Seixas, in Paraíba. Here you will find the lighthouse called Farol de São Roque and the "árvore do amor" (love tree) – the interlacing branches of two trees that form a heart. The beach in this "corner of Brazil", as it is known, is not suitable for bathing or swimming.

MARACAJAÚ

Sixty kilometers (37 miles) north of Natal, Maracajaú village has coral reefs known locally as *parrachos*. They lie 7 kilometers (4 miles) out to sea and occupy an area of 13 by 2.5 kilometers (8 by 1.5 miles). At low tide, boats take passengers to the reefs to dive and see a variety of fish,

stingrays, and with any luck, lobster and shrimp. A cluster of restaurants surrounds the **Farol Teresa Pança** lighthouse. From June to August, rains make the road conditions extremely poor, and hiring a guide is recommended. You can also cross the sand by dune buggy, tides permitting.

> ### BUGGY TRIPS ON THE DUNES
>
> A buggy trip across the dunes is unforgettable, especially if it's conducted, as drivers like to say, "with emotion" (read, "with radical maneuvers"). But these trips are by no means guaranteed to be accident-free; choose only drivers accredited by **Setur**, Natal's official tourism office *(Secretaria de Turismo de Natal, Rua Mossoró, 359, Tirol, tel. (84) 3232-2498; Mon – Fri, 8am – 5:30pm)*. The driver should have an accreditation card, and a sticker clearly displayed on the vehicle, which should have red license plates. Good hotels can recommend agencies and drivers. The longest route goes from Natal to Fortaleza (one-way only), and takes four days.

Genipabu, perfect for touring by dune buggy

Cajueiro de Pirangi: a giant cashew tree, which canopy covers 8,400 square meters

THE SOUTH COAST

Rio Grande do Sul's south coast is dotted with dunes, lakes, coconut groves, and cliffs. Coral reefs off shore form sheltered natural pools at low tide. Get there by taking the Rota do Sol (Rodovia RN-063 state highway) to Barra do Tabatinga, followed by the Rodovia BR-101 highway; this is the best route for going straight to **Praia da Pipa.**

PIRANGI DO NORTE

The **Cajueiro de Pirangi,** a giant cashew tree said to be 110 years old stands on this beach. The top of the tree covers an area of 8,400 meters (90,420 square feet) and is still growing. It produces between 70,000 and 80,000 cashew fruits each year between November and January *(Avenida Deputado Márcio Marinho, or Praça do Cajueiro, no #, tel. (84) 3278-2684, 3238-2341; daily, 7:30am – 5:30pm).* The nearby artist's studio **Inhepoan** sells ceramic items and local rum *(Rua do Cajueiro, 100, tel. (84) 3238-2958; daily, 7am – 6pm).* A tour option is a two-and-a-half-hour schooner trip that stops at the **Parrachos de Pirangi** reefs for snorkeling *(Contact: Marina Badauê, tel. (84) 3238-2066).*

NÍSIA FLORESTA

This municipality, 43 kilometers (27 miles) from Natal, is famed for its craftwork. The **Associação de Labirinteiras de Campo de Santana** is a group of lace makers who produce *labirinto,* a famous style of northeastern lace made on wooden frames using traditional techniques *(Rua Deoclécio Anselmo, 11, Campo de Santana, tel. (84) 9967-8824; Mon – Sat, 8am – 5pm).* The **Associação de Rendeiras de Alcaçuz** is an association of women who make *renda de bilro,* a kind of bobbin lace *(Rua Projetada, no #, Alcaçuz, tel. (84) 9421-3562; Mon – Sat, 8am – 5pm).* **Arlindo** and **Maria Barbosa** sell baskets, *covos* (shrimp traps), and *samburás* (fish baskets) made from liana and *dendê* palm straw from a stall outside their house *(Rua Tororomba, no #, Tororomba, public phone (84) 8816-8423; daily, 6am – 5pm).* You can buy and taste *cachaça,* a clear liquor, at the Fazenda Brasileira Augusta store, **Cachaça Artesanal de Alambique Papary,** and also visit the stills *(Rodovia RN-063, no #, Timbo, 7 km from Nísia Floresta, tel. (84) 3277-7011; Mon – Fri, 7am – 4pm; Sat and Sun, 10am – 4pm).*

❶ Pirangi do Norte and Pirangi do Sul
These built-up beaches are packed with bars, restaurants, homes, and small apartment buildings. Reefs protect and calm their waters.

❷ Búzios
Long and beautiful, with vacation homes scattered among the dunes. Rough seas and an uneven ocean floor make it unsafe for swimming.

❸ Barra de Tabatinga
Calm, reef-studded waters framed by cliffs alternate with rougher stretches that are ideal for surfing. The lookout point gives a good view of Búzios.

❹ Guaraíras, also know as Malebar
Deserted and untouched, the beach of Guaraíras is difficult to get to, but its white, fine sand faces the open sea. The calmer waters near Guaraíras Lagoon are good for kayaking. To get there, take the ferry boat that leaves from Tibau and crosses Guaraíras lagoon.

❺ Tibau do Sul
Imposing cliffs shelter this beach, also known as Praia do Giz or Cacimbinha. You can take a kayak trip around the mangrove swamp. The lookout point offers a great view of the sunset.

❻ Praia do Madeiro
Tucked between 30-meter (98-foot) red cliffs, this is one of the region's most beautiful beaches. The walk to Baía dos Golfinhos starts here.

❼ Praia do Curral
Surrounded by cliffs, turtles lay their eggs on these white, powdery sands. Rocky terrain makes for a difficult walk to this beach.

❽ Pipa
The main beach in the Pipa district is very easy to reach and has good tourist facilities. Children enjoy the natural pools that form at low tide.

❾ Barra de Cunhaú
Encircled by the Catu and Curimataú rivers and dotted with vacation homes, this bearch has calm waters, ideal for fishing.

❿ Baía Formosa
A charming cove of fishermen's houses, cliffs, and swimmable waters. Near Mata Estrela, an important Atlantic forest reserve.

1 cm = 4.7 km
1 inch = 7.4 mi.

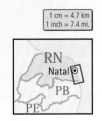

The heart-shaped beach known as Praia do Amor, in Tibau do Sul

Pipa

Beautiful, imposing red cliffs and clear seas, augmented by busy restaurants, bars, cafés, stores, and guesthouses, make Pipa a popular holiday destination. It's an ideal spot for anyone looking for gorgeous beaches and varied nightlife. This old fishing village in the district of Tibau do Sul, 82 kilometers (51 miles) from Natal, wakes up late (the shops only open after 11am), eats well and retires late, too. Crowded beaches suit those who like hustle and bustle, and deserted stretches satisfy anyone in search of peace and quiet.

Our Recommendation

🍽 There is no menu at **Camamo**, a restaurant in Tibau do Sul. Customers must simply trust the creativity of chef-owner Tadeu Lubambo, who selects each day's six dinner dishes. Book ahead – at least a month in advance during the high season – because no more than eight people can enjoy the food, candle-lit atmosphere, and jazz music at a time *(Fazenda Pernambuquinho, no #, Pernambuquinho, Tibau do Sul, tel. (84) 3246-4195; daily, 8pm until the last customer leaves).*

Additional information on page 462.

Beaches

Of the beaches, central **Praia da Pipa** offers the best facilities, but usually gets crowded in the high season. Large, warm, natural pools appear among the reefs at low tide. To the south and surrounded by cliffs, small **Praia do Amor** got its name, Love Beach, because of its heart shape. Here, and in nearby **Praia do Moleque**, shallow pools appear at low tide, when you can observe fish, octopus, and crustaceans; at high tide there are good stretches for surfing. Visitors can get to these beaches either by the steps embedded in the cliffs or by walking from Praia da Pipa. Not many people frequent **Praia das Minas**, which is also surrounded by high cliffs. It has wild landscape and rough seas, and can only be reached by taking a rather precarious set of steps.

Santuário Ecológico de Pipa

Set on 120 hectares (297 acres) of private Atlantic forest, this ecological sanctuary has twelve short, well-marked trails of varying difficulty. Along the way you can see cashew and *murici* trees, as well as other

varieties with labels identifying the species. Among the most difficult of the trails, the **Caminhos dos Piratas** has a descent via wooden steps to Praia do Madeiro; you need to leave the beach before 4pm as the Sanctuary closes at 5pm. The **Passeio da Peroba** walk skirts the cliffs of Ponta do Madeiro and leads to the Mirante das Tartarugas. From this lookout point, you can look to the right and see Baía dos Golfinhos – with its gray tucuxi dolphins (*Sotalia fluviatilis*) – and to the left, Enseada do Madeiro cove. You'll need insect repellent on these walks.
Estrada Goianinha–Pipa, Km 23, Praia de Pipa, tel. (84) 3201-2007. Daily, 9am – 5pm.

DUNE-BUGGY TOURS TO PARAÍBA

A dune buggy trip from Pipa to Praia do Sagi, a beach on the state border with Paraíba, makes for an interesting excursion and lasts about six hours. The route begins in the center of Pipa and the first stop is **Chapadão**, on top of the cliff. From there, buggies head for **Praia de Sibaúma**, a large beach fronted by calm seas. After crossing a small river by ferry, visitors arrive at another beach, pretty **Praia de Barra de Cunhaú**. A further ferry takes you to a large, white beach full of coconut palms and caressed by calm seas. Then comes **Baía Formosa**, which also has calm seas protected by reefs, as well as a lookout point and a rougher stretch suitable for surfing. This bay is the gateway to **Mata Estrela**, the largest remaining expanse of Atlantic forest in Rio Grande do Norte, with 2,039 hectares (5,040 acres) of brazilwood, *restinga* vegetation, and dunes. If also has numerous lake, including one so dark it's known as **Lagoa Coca-Cola**. Nearby, you can swim among the mangroves in the dark waters of the **Rio Sagi**. Baía da Traição, in Paraíba, is on the other side of the river.
Contact: Pipatour, tel. (84) 3246-2234.

Madeiro, in Tibau do Sul, is one of the south coast's most beautiful beaches

THE NORTH COAST

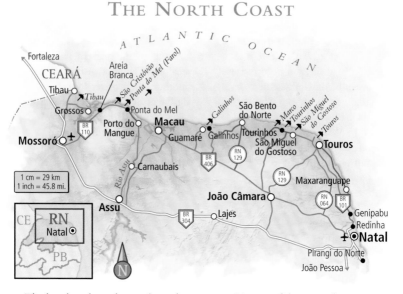

ATLANTIC OCEAN

Fortaleza
CEARÁ
Tibau
Areia Branca
São Cristovão
Ponta do Mel (Farol)
Grossos
Ponta do Mel
Porto do Mangue
Macau
Guamaré
Galinhos
Galinhos
São Bento do Norte
Marco
Tourinhos
São Miguel do Gostoso
Tourinhos
São Miguel do Gostoso
Touros
Touros
Mossoró
BR 110
Carnaubais
Rio Assu
BR 406
RN 129
Maxaranguape
RN 129
João Câmara
RN 064
BR 101
Genipabu
Redinha
Assu
Lajes
BR 304
Natal
Pirangi do Norte
João Pessoa

1 cm = 29 km
1 inch = 45.8 mi.

CE
RN
Natal
PB

N

The beaches along the state's north coast are still relatively unknown to tourists, so visitors to the area will find a 250-kilometer (155-mile) stretch of coastline with a series of fishing villages, semi-deserted beaches, dunes, cliffs, and seas dotted with *jangadas* (sailing rafts) and other boats. A one- or two-day trip, preferable by buggy or in a 4×4 vehicle, is recommended. For safety reasons, it's better not to travel at night. **Touros**, 85 kilometers (53 miles) from Natal, is home to the 1943 lighthouse **Farol do Calcanhar**, the tallest in the country at 65 meters (213 feet). It and its 298 steps are open to visitors on Sundays. Touros is one of the northern-most destinations on the Rodovia BR-101 highway, which runs along the Brazilian coast to the city of Rio Grande, in the state of Rio Grande do Sul. You can snorkel among the reefs at **Praia de Perobas** *(Contact: Pólo das Águas, tel. (84) 3693-3000, 9907-9675)*. About 25 kilometers (15 miles) further on, sleepy **São Miguel do Gostoso** maintains its routine of fishing and *labirinto* lace making. August to January is the flour-making season, you

can visit one of the more than twenty *casas de farinha* (manioc flour mills) to see how manioc is turned into flour. To get to São Miguel, 105 kilometers (65 miles) from Natal, take the Rodovias BR-101 and RN-221 highways. **Galinhos**, 75 kilometers (109 miles) from Natal along the Rodovias BR-406 and RN-402 highways, is for the more adventurous. Cars are not allowed in this village, so you'll need to leave your vehicle on the other side of the Rio Pratagi and cross by boat. Carts are the only transport on the sandy streets and the TV in the public square is on all evening. **Ponta do Mel**, almost in Ceará, is on the Costa do Sal (Salt Coast), or Pólo Costa Branca (White Coast Center), so named for its saltworks. Visitors to this area can see a lighthouse with a view over the dunes, cliffs, and stretches of *caatinga* vegetation. You can reach Ponta do Mel by ordinary car on the Rodovia BR-110 highway, or in a 4×4 vehicle on the Rodovia BR-304 highway (which has neither signs nor gas stations) to Porto do Mangue, and from there across the dunes.

CEARÁ

1 cm = 55 km
1 inch = 86.8 mi.

HIGHLIGHTS

- The historical and cultural attractions of **Fortaleza**.
- Unspoiled **Canoa Quebrada**, the jewel of the east coast.
- Beautiful **Jericoacoara Beach** and **Jijoca de Jericoacoara**

village, popular destinations that retain their traditional east-coast simplicity.
- **Juazeiro do Norte**, in the backlands of Ceará, the site of the largest pilgrimages in the Northeast.

WHEN TO GO

- From **July** to **December** to enjoy the beaches. Crowds and prices peak between **January** and **March**.
- Between **December** and **May**, in the hot, rainy season, to enjoy the lakes, dunes, and beaches.

- During the three pilgrimages honoring Father Cícero in Juazeiro do Norte: **September 15**, **October 30** to **November 2**, and **January 30** to **February 2**.

FORTALEZA

It would be a mistake to think that the capital of Ceará, population 2.3 million, is nothing more than 25 kilometers (16 miles) of city beaches or a base for exploring the coast. Sunny Fortaleza, built in the 17th century, boasts a limited but interesting architectural heritage, modern cultural centers and a buzzing nightlife. In July, there's nonstop dancing in the streets during **Fortal**, the city's out-of-season Carnival.

BEACHES

IRACEMA, MEIRELES AND MUCURIPE
Iracema's beach and neighborhood are named for the novel by Ceará-born writer José de Alencar (1829-77). One busy sidewalk even has a statue of Iracema, the Tabajara Indian woman who is the book's main character. The sea is unsuitable for swimming, but visitors and residents alike can enjoy the sunset from two lookout points: **Ponte Metálica**, a pier built in 1906, and nearby **Ponte dos Ingleses**, built in 1923. On Monday nights, check out the *forró* music at **Bar do Pirata** (*Rua dos Tabajaras, 325, tel. (85) 4011-6161; Mon, 8pm – 3am*). The next beach, **Praia do Meireles**, is home to the most

SEASIDE PLEASURES

Inviting businesses along the shore offer ice cream and cool drinks. **Ponto do Guaraná** makes famous Amazonian *guaraná* juice mixed with plums or peanuts and cashews (*On the promenade in front of Restaurante Geppo's, no #, Meireles; daily, 7am – 10pm*). **X da Xica** serves the famous Xiquito Cearense, a sun-dried beef and clarified butter sandwich served with cheese, lettuce, tomato and mayonnaise (*Rua Antônio Justa, 3455, Meireles, tel. (85) 3242-8514; Sun – Thu, 5pm – midnight; Fri and Sat, 5pm – 6am*). Try the tapioca ice cream or tropical fruit flavors like *murici* and *cajá* at **Sorveteria 50 Sabores** (*Avenida Beira-Mar, 4690, Mucuripe; daily, 9am – 11pm*).

traditional craft market in Fortaleza, open daily from 6pm, with around 600 stalls. Next is **Praia de Mucuripe**, home to Fortaleza's fishing community. Its fish market, **Mercado de Peixe**, contains 30 stalls selling savory seafood.

PRAIA DO FUTURO

This is the prettiest, cleanest city beach in Fortaleza. From 4pm onward – especially on Tuesdays, Thursdays and weekends – the promenade has live music and comedy shows. Visitors can eat very well on the beach; the most popular kiosks on Avenida Zezé Diogo include **Chico do Caranguejo**, which specializes in crab dishes *(#4930, tel. (85) 3262-0108; Fri – Wed, 8am – 6pm; Thu, 8am – 2am)*; **Cuca Legal**, which attracts a young crowd *(#3005, tel. (85) 3265-1648; Mon – Wed, 7am – 6pm; Thu, 7am – midnight)*; and **Itapariká**, which offers facilities for children *(#6801, tel. (85) 3265-1195; Fri – Wed, 8am – 5pm; Thu, 8am – 5pm and 6pm – midnight)*.

HISTORICAL CENTER

MUSEU DO CEARÁ

This museum exhibits around 7,000 items relating to the state's geography and belonging to the famous 19th-century priest Padre Cícero. It also has artifacts from the slave emancipation movement in 1884 – four years before the law that abolished slavery, the Lei Áurea. *Rua São Paulo, 51, Centro, tel. (85) 3101-2610. Tue – Sat, 9am – 5pm.*

PRAÇA DO FERREIRA

This is the city's main square, where visitors will find **Cine São Luís**, a cinema built in a style that combines neoclassical and art deco. The building, finished in 1958, contains a fine Carrara marble staircase and three Czech crystal chandeliers *(tel. (85) 3226-8739)*. **Farmácia Osvaldo Cruz** has operated as a pharmacy since 1932 in an 1890 building. The **Palacete Ceará**, built in 1914, used to be the headquarters of the Club Iracema, an old meeting point for high society.

CENTRO DRAGÃO DO MAR DE ARTE E CULTURA

Fortaleza's main cultural center opened in 1998, and it is located in a well-designed space of 30,000 square meters (322,917 square feet). Travelers will find cinemas, auditoriums, a library, a café, exhibits and a planetarium that holds three shows every day except Mondays. The center also houses the **Museu de Arte Contemporânea do Ceará**, a contemporary art museum displaying works by Brazilian and foreign artists, and the **Memorial da Cultura Cearense**, where visitors can learn about daily life in different parts of the state, such as the backlands of Cariri. The center is named after Dragão do Mar, or Dragon of the Sea – the nickname given to the raftsman Francisco José do Nascimento, an icon of Ceará's abolitionist movement. *Rua Dragão do Mar, 81, Iracema, tel. (85) 3488-8600. Tue – Thu, 9am – 6:30pm; Fri – Sun, 2pm – 8:30pm.*

OUR RECOMMENDATION

🍽 Homey and simple **Colher de Pau** serves regional food such as fried banana, tender sun-dried beef with manioc fried in clarified butter, *baião-de-dois* (rice with beans and meat), *paoca* (beef jerky ground with manioc flour). It also offers mutton, fish and seafood. Fortaleza has two other branches. *Rua Frederico Borges, 206, Varjota, tel. (85) 3267-3773; daily, 11am – midnight.*

Additional information on page 462.

The dazzling art nouveau stained glass windows of the Theatro José de Alencar

THEATRO JOSÉ DE ALENCAR
This theater, the most important architectural landmark in the city, opened in 1910. Constructed of metal, it boasts art nouveau stained glass windows, a movable stage and a side garden designed by landscape artist Roberto Burle Marx. Each theater box bears the name of a work by José de Alencar. The theater offers guided tours in English and Spanish.
Praça José de Alencar, no #, Centro, tel. (85) 3101-2583. Mon – Fri, 8am – 11am and 1pm – 4pm; Sat and Sun, 1pm – 4pm.

OTHER ATTRACTIONS

CASA JOSÉ DE ALENCAR
Part of the 19th-century house where famous Brazilian writer José de Alencar was born and lived has been preserved. Although it could be better maintained, the lovely old farm (which also houses the ruins of a sugar mill) is well worth a visit.
Avenida Washington Soares, 6055, Alagadiço Novo, tel. (85) 3229-1898. Mon – Fri, 8am – 5pm; Sat, 8am – noon.

ARTS AND CRAFTS
In addition to the street fair on Meireles' beachfront, regional crafts can be purchased at the 99 stores in the **Centro de Turismo**. The building also houses two modest museums, the **Museu de Arte e Cultura Popular** and the **Museu dos Minerais** *(Rua Senador Pompeu, 350, Centro, tel. (85) 3101-5508; Mon – Fri, 8am – 4:30pm; Sat, Sun, and holidays, 8am – 11am).*
Stores in the **Centro de Artesanato do Ceará (Ceart)** sell all kinds of handicrafts, such as *labirinto* lace and pieces made from liana straw. Branches are located at Pinto Martins airport, Shopping Iguatemi and the Centro Dragão do Mar, but the main store is

on Avenida Santos Dumont
*(#1589, Aldeota, tel. (85) 3101-1645;
daily, 9am – 6pm).* The **Mercado
Central** also sells regional crafts *(Avenida
Alberto Nepomuceno, 199, Centro, tel. (85)
3454-8586. Mon – Fri, 8am – 6pm; Sat,
8am – 4pm; Sun, 8am – noon).*

TAPIOCA

On the way to the east-coast beaches,
try tapioca with a variety of toppings
at the **Centro das Tapioqueiras,** at the
10 km mark of the Rodovia CE-040
highway *(Avenida Washington Soares,
10215, Messejana, tel. (85) 3474-1326;
daily, 6am – midnight).* On the same

road, at the intersection with **Rua
Barão de Aquiraz**, other tapioca-
makers serve their dishes right from
their front porches.

DUNE BUGGY TRIPS

Buggy drivers can be found near the
Clube Náutico on Meireles Beach.
They offer trips for single days or
longer, such as two-day trips to
Jericoacoara or four-day trips to Natal.
Trips of more than 300 kilometers (190
miles) can be made in 4×4 vehicles.
*Cooperativa de Buggy de Fortaleza,
tel. (85) 9904-7187; Dunnas Expedições,
tel. (85) 3264-2514.*

AROUND FORTALEZA

CUMBUCO

Surrounded by dunes and lagoons, this
fishing village is just 30 kilometers (19
miles) east of Fortaleza on the
Rodovia CE-085 highway. A thrilling
dune-buggy trip in Cumbuco is a
must for any visitor to Fortaleza
*(Cooperativa Cearense dos Proprietários e
Condutores de Veículos de Passeios, tel.
(85) 3318-7309).* The traditional one-
hour trip includes stops at **Lagoa do
Parnamirim** lagoon, **Parque das
Dunas** and **Morro da Barriga** hill.
Thirty-minute *jangada* trips for up to
six people are also available *(Velas do
Cumbuco, tel. (85) 3318-7555; Aldeia
Brasil, tel. (85) 3318-7541).*

AQUIRAZ

Beach Park is Aquiraz's big attraction,
32 kilometers (20 miles) east of
Fortaleza. It is an amusement park
with 18 water rides, such as wave
pools and water slides. The most
thrilling ride, "Insano" ("Insane"), is a
slide 41 meters (134 feet) high. There
is no entrance fee to the complex,
which also contains stores and

restaurants *(Rua Porto das Dunas, 2734,
Porto das Dunas, tel. (85) 4012-3000;
daily during the high season, 11am –
5pm; low season: Fri – Tue, 11am – 5pm,
but confirm in advance by phone or on the
Web site, www.beachpark.com.br).* Aquiraz
also sells *bilro* (bobbin) and *labirinto*
lace at the **Centros de rendeiras da
Prainha** *(Rua Damião Tavares, no #,
Prainha; public phone (85) 3361-5015;
daily, 9am – 8:30pm)* and the **Centros
de rendeiras do Iguape** *(Avenida da
Praia, no #, Iguape, tel. (85) 3361-6447;
daily, 9am – 6pm).*

MARANGUAPE

Visitors with a taste for the white sugar-
cane rum known as *cachaça* or *pinga* will
enjoy the **Museu da Cachaça**, 25 kilometers (16 miles) southwest of Fortaleza
in Maranguape, on the Rodovia CE-065
highway. The museum's main building is
Fazenda Ypióca's farmhouse, built in
1846. The old mill displays machinery,
photos, bottles and huge vats. Visitors can
taste the *cachaça* in the gift shop and bar.
*Fazenda Ypióca, no #, Ypióca, tel. (85) 3341-
0407. Tue – Sun, 8:30am – 5pm.*

The famous Morro Branco, in Beberibe, is a popular destination

THE EAST COAST

The stretch of coast between Aquiraz and the Rio Grande do Norte border is known as **Costa do Sol Nascente** (Sunrise Coast). Set against a beautiful landscape of sun and sand dunes, the region offers a glimpse of rich regional culture. Because the beaches along the Rodovia CE-040 highway are fairly close together, visitors can enjoy pleasurable day trips without too much travel.

CASCAVEL

Lovely beaches and intricate crafts are the twin attractions of **Cascavel,** 64 kilometers (40 miles) from Fortaleza on the Rodovia CE-040 highway. The area features sugar mills, where visitors can watch the production of *rapadura* (hard tablets of brownsugar), regular brown sugar, light molasses and *cachaça*. One mill, **Casa Grande**, boasts the biggest *rapadura* in the world *(Rodovia CE-040, Km 37, tel. (85) 9602-0048; Mon – Fri, 7am – 7pm)*. At the entrance to the town is **Pólo Artesanal**, which sells Indian- and Portuguese-influenced ceramics, as well as furniture and other items made from liana straw *(Rodovia CE-040, Km 56, tel. (85) 3334-0559; Mon – Fri, 8am – 5pm; Sat and Sun, 8:30am – 2pm)*.

JANGADA BOATS

The *jangada*, a kind of raft, is one of the most common types of boat in Ceará and Rio Grande do Norte. It is responsible for the survival of the region's fishing tradition, but its origins are unclear. Its name is said to come from *janga*, a boat made of strips of wood bound together with natural fibers that the Portuguese had seen in Asia and believed to be similar to the boats they saw Indians using in Brazil. Initially, *jangadas* didn't have its current features, which developed gradually. The first records of a *jangada* sail date from the 17th century. *Jangadas* are highly suited to navigating the waters of the Northeast, because the boats can stand up to the waves that breaking on the shore and can be easily beached by fishermen. *Jangadas* are also cheap to maintain and can be produced by the fishing communities.

BEBERIBE

Beberibe, 20 kilometers (12 miles) from Cascavel, boasts two of the most famous beaches on the east coast. **Morro Branco**, with its many bars and restaurants, is very popular with tourists; **Praia das Fontes** has calm seas and red cliffs. Morro Branco also gives visitors a chance to see local crafts up close: artists create *bilro* and *labirinto* lace or make brightly colored sand into art inside tiny bottles, depicting outdoor scenes like the blue sea dotted with *jangadas*. A walk through the natural cliff maze of **Labirinto das Falésias** is another local activity.

CANOA QUEBRADA

Hippies discovered this fishing village perched on the red cliff tops in the 1970s. Located 161 kilometers (100 miles) from Fortaleza, in the municipality of Aracati, the beach is the most famous on Ceará's east coast – and the good tourist facilities draw visitors to its dunes and calm sea. The bars on lively **Broadway** are hopping until the early-morning hours. During the day, dune-buggy trips take visitors to the beaches of **Porto Canoa**, **Majorlândia**, **Quixaba**, **Lagoa do Mato**, **Fontainha**, **Retirinho** and **Retiro Grande**, and then end with a spectacular sunset at **Ponta Grossa**. This trip is more than three hours long, so visitors should go in the afternoon to escape the scorching sun. The one-hour trip from **Porto Canoa** to **Quixaba** is a shorter option. Make sure to check that drivers are registered with the Ceará Tourism Department *(tel. (85) 3101-4672, www.turismo.ce.gov.br)*.

palms and cliffs. The colored sand used to create scenes inside tiny bottles was first collected here. The white cliffs and pale, powdery sand of tranquil **Quixaba** and the quiet waters of **Lagoa do Mato** can be reached on foot or by dune buggy. **Fontainha** is not recommended for swimming, but the sight of the colored dunes is worth the trip. **Retirinho** is a small beach with a barrier reef, gentle waves and fine sand. Last but not least is **Retiro Grande**, a village tucked into the cliffs near a seaweed-covered sea.

The fishing village of Canoa Quebrada, in Aracati

BEACHES

Porto Canoa offers a view of red cliffs and *jangadas* beached on the sand. Travelers can get there on foot from Canoa Quebrada. **Majorlândia** is a good swimming spot, and it also features bars, restaurants and guesthouses surrounded by coconut

Boats on the beach at Jericoacoara

THE WEST COAST

Ceará's west coast, **Costa do Sol Poente** (Sunset Coast), boasts everything from rarely visited beaches to one of the most popular destinations in the Northeast. Every west-coast place has one thing in common, thought: the hospitality extended to visitors. The Rodovia Estruturante highway (CE-085) is the best way to reach the beaches from Fortaleza.

JERICOACOARA

Considered one of Brazil's most beautiful beaches, Jericoacoara draws people from all over the world. It still retains its unlit dirt streets, and it is relatively isolated – only jeeps and dune buggies manage to cross the dunes surrounding it. In 2002, the village and its surroundings were declared a national park, the **Parque Nacional de Jericoacoara**, with no restrictions on visits. Jijoca de Jericoacoara, 280 kilometers (174 miles) provides access to Jericoacoara from Fortaleza, but it's still another 23 bumpy kilometers by dune buggy, truck or *jardineira*, a modified pick-up truck, to get to "Jeri" (as it is known by locals and tourists alike). Take at least four days to fully enjoy everything the region has to offer. A half-hour's walk at low tide will take you to **Pedra Furada**, Jericoacoara's landmark rock, with a natural hole carved out in the center. At high tide, visitors must climb two steep dunes, but it can also be reached by dune buggy with a stop at **Lagoa da Jijoca** lake.

JIJOCA DE JERICOACOARA

The municipal center of Jericoacoara is Jijoca de Jericoacoara, 23 kilometers (14 miles) from the village. Among its attractions are two lagoons, **Lagoa Azul** and **Lagoa do Paraíso**. Both offer green waters surrounded by dunes and good conditions for diving and sailing. (Motorized equipment is forbidden). The best time to visit is the rainy season, between March and May, when water levels are at their highest. Windsurfing is best between July and November, when the winds are strongest.

Buggies will also take people to the region around Jeri. One trip goes to Camocim, taking in lovely beaches. A highlight of that trip is **Duna Encantada**, a dune more than 30-meter (98-feet) high *(Associação de Bugueiros, tel. (88) 3669-2284, 9955-6046)*. The **Duna do Pôr-do-Sol**, 40 meters (130 feet) high, is very popular around 5pm as a viewing spot for the famous Jeri sunset. The **Bar do Forró**, formerly Forró do Raimundo, has been entertaining people for 25 years. It was remodeled in 2007 and has a new owner, but it kept its spacious covered area and dance floor *(Rua do Forró, no #, tel. (88) 3669-2212, 3669-2235; Low season: Tue, Wed, and Sat; High season: Mon – Sat, from 11pm)*.

CAMOCIM

The beach where the Coreaú River meets the sea is a tableau of hundreds of boats and canoes. It is the loveliest sight in Camocim. On the Rodovias CE-085 and BR-402 highways, it is 380 kilometers (236 miles) from Fortaleza. By dirt road, it is 100 kilometers (62 miles) from Jericoacoara; across the beaches, it is 75 kilometers (47 miles). Dune buggy is the best way to go, although some of the stops are the same as those on trips from Jeri. A one-day

---

SOBRAL AND GRUTA DE UBAJARA

Sobral – at the foot of the Serra de Meruoca mountain range, on the banks of the Acaraú River – became the north's major commercial center when the railroad linking it to Camocim was built in 1882. Townhouses and churches from that period have been preserved. Highlights include squares such as **Praça São João, Praça José Sabóia** and **Praça da Sé**. Sobral is 235 kilometers (146 miles) from Fortaleza and can be reached on the Rodovia BR-222 highway. In **Ubajara**, 81 kilometers (50 miles) from Sobral, visitors will find the **Parque Nacional de Ubajara** and the cave that is its major attraction. The Gruta de Ubajara spans 1,120 meters (3675 feet), but only 420 meters (1,380 feet) are accessible. Formations include fine stalactites, curtains and cascades. Visitors reach the mouth of the cave by a trail, which takes three hours, or by chair lift in three minutes.
Estrada do Teleférico, Km 4, tel. (88) 3634-1388. Tue – Sun, 8am – 5pm.

trip through the mangroves of **Praia da Moréia** and **Duna Encantada**, in Nova Tatajuba, can be extended as far as **Guriú** and **Jijoca de Jericoacoara** *(Jegue Tur, tel. (88) 3621-7023)*. Another one-day trip from Camocim leads to **Bitupitá**, on the border with Piauí, where local fishermen use traps made

from tree trunks covered by nets on the sea floor. Fish enter the traps and cannot find their way out. Visitors can savor fresh, fried fish at the beach kiosks. Bitupitá is 40 kilometers (25 miles) from Camocim. Take the Rodovia BR-402 highway to Barroquinha and then a dirt road that only 4×4 vehicles can drive.

SERTÃO

JUAZEIRO DO NORTE

Juazeiro do Norte, the largest town in the Ceará backlands, is 495 kilometers (308 miles) from Fortaleza on the Rodovia BR-116 highway. Father Cícero Romão Batista founded the settlement in 1911. The myth surrounding this priest has turned Juazeiro do Norte into a center for three great pilgrimages: September 15, October 30 to November 2, and January 30 to February 2. The faithful also visit on July 20, the anniversary of his death. During each pilgrimage, 300,000 devoted followers sing hymns in his honor. Some even dress in straw hats and black cassocks, as he did. A 25-meter (82-foot) statue of **Father Cícero** sits on

A clay statue of Padre Cícero

top of **Colina do Horto** hill. The house where he lived is now the **Memorial Padre Cícero,** and it displays some of his personal possessions *(Rua São José, 242, Centro, tel. (88) 3511-2876; Mon – Sat, 8am – 11am and 1pm – 5pm; Sun, 9am –*

11am and 1pm – 5pm). The **Capela de Nossa Senhora do Perpétuo Socorro** is the chapel that houses Father Cícero's tomb *(Praça do Cinqüentenário, no #, Socorro)*. The **Museu Vivo Padre Cícero** is full of votive offerings and books dedicated to him *(Colina do Horto, 8 km (5 mi) from the city center, tel. (88) 3511-7006; daily, 8am – noon and 2pm – 5pm)*. Juazeiro also boasts rich wood and plaster crafts that can be found in the **Centro de Cultura Popular Mestre Noza** *(Rua São Luís, no #, Centro, tel. (88) 3511-3133; Mon – Fri, 8am – 12:30pm and 1pm – 6pm; Sat, 8am – 2pm)*. The **Gráfica de Literatura de Cordel Lira Nordestina** is a print shop that houses old typesetters and machinery, as well as a collection of *cordel* literature for sale *(Avenida Castelo Branco, 150, Rumerão, tel. (88) 3102-1150, 9201-1143; Mon – Fri, 7:30am – 11:30am and 1:30pm – 5:30pm; Sat, 7:30am – noon)*.

PADRE CÍCERO

Cícero Romão Batista was born in the town of Crato, in the Ceará backlands, on March 24, 1844. In 1872, two years after his ordination, he supposedly had a dream in which Jesus asked him to look after the poor in Juazeiro. The first miracle was reported soon after his arrival. During the communion of a devout woman, the consecrated wafer turned into blood. Some parishioners claimed that their own wounds and illnesses had been cured. The news spread throughout the backlands and the. He died in 1934 at the age of 90.

PIAUÍ

ATLANTIC OCEAN

Delta do Parnaíba

Parnaíba ○ ● **Luís Correia**

Camocim

BR 343

P. N. de Sete Cidades

BR 343

Fortaleza

São Luís

Piripiri ○

CEARÁ

MARANHÃO

BR 316

BR 343

● **Teresina**

BR 343

BR 316

Floriano ○ BR 230 ○ **Oeiras**

Picos

PI 140

BR 020

PIAUÍ

Canto do Buriti ○

P. N. Serra da Capivara

BR 316 **Recife**

PERNAMBUCO

Cristino Castro ○ BR 324

São Raimundo Nonato ○ Cel. José Dias

BR 135

BAHIA

TOCANTINS

○ Corrente

Barreiras

1 cm = 111 km
1 inch = 176.2 mi.

N

HIGHLIGHTS

- **Parque Nacional Serra da Capivara**, a reserve contains the world's largest collection of rock paintings.

- The wind-carved rocks in the **Parque Nacional de Sete Cidades** reserve.

WHEN TO GO

- The national parks are at their greenest between **December** and **May**, although rain can make the hiking trails more difficult. From **May** to **November**, the foliage thins around the Caatinga vegetation and animals are easier to observe.

SERRA DA CAPIVARA

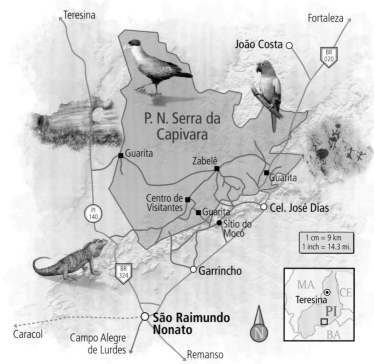

Teresina

Fortaleza

João Costa

BR 020

P. N. Serra da Capivara

Guarita

Zabelê

Guarita

Centro de Visitantes

Guarita

Cel. José Dias

Sítio do Mocó

1 cm = 9 km
1 inch = 14.3 mi.

PI 140

BR 324

Garrincho

MA

CE

Teresina

PI

BA

Caracol

São Raimundo Nonato

Campo Alegre de Lurdes

Remanso

N

SUPPORT TOWN: TERESINA

The capital of Piauí is 200 kilometers (124 miles) from Parque Nacional de Sete Cidades and 540 kilometers (336 miles) from São Raimundo Nonato. It can also be reached from Petrolina, in the state of Pernambuco, 300 kilometers (186 miles) away. Although Teresina is 350 kilometers (217 miles) from the coast, its two rivers – the **Poti** and the **Parnaíba** – provide much-needed cool breezes. Founded in the 18th century, flat Teresina has a simple grid of streets, more than 30 parks and a lively nightlife.

Hotels and restaurants start on page 462.

SÃO RAIMUNDO NONATO

São Raimundo Nonato is a gateway to **Parque Nacional Serra da Capivara**. The town is also home to the **Museu do Homem Americano**, an archaeological museum with pannels, photographs, and rock samples that show research done in the region over the past 30 years. Highlights include the funeral urns and human fossils, especially Zuzu, a skeleton estimated to be around 10,000 years old *(Centro Cultural Sérgio Motta, no #,*

Campestre, tel. (89) 3582-1612; Tue – Sun, 9am – 5pm). Getting to the city isn't easy: it is 540 kilometers (336 miles) south of Teresina on Rodovias BR-316, BR-343, PI-140, and BR-324 highways. If traveling from Petrolina, in Pernambuco, take the Rodovia BR-235 highway west to Remanso and then the Rodovia BR-324 highway north. Some stretches of this 300-kilometer (186-mile) portion of Rodovia BR-324 highway are in poor condition.

Parque Nacional Serra da Capivara

The world's largest collection of rock paintings is on permanent display in the 129,140 hectares (319,100 acres) of the Serra da Capivara National Park. Declared a Unesco World Heritage Site in 1991, the park has more than 800 archaeological sites. About 120 of them are open to visitors, and the park has good facilities. Archaeologist Niède Guidon, who runs the park, claims to have discovered signs of a settlement that could be up to 100,000 years old, although that contradicts the prevailing theory that humans arrived in the Americas about 20,000 years ago via the Bering Strait. Controversy aside, the park is absolutely breathtaking, with rough, hilly land and huge rocks on every side. It's possible to explore the whole park by car, but visitors who want to hike through it can choose from trails of varying difficulty levels. A guide must accompany hikers through the park.

Contact: Trilhas da Capivara, tel. (89) 3582-1294, 9975-9322.

Baixão da Pedra Furada

Toca do Boqueirão da Pedra Furada is the highlight of Pedra Furada Valley, which can be reached by car. The most important archaeological site in the range has hundreds of rock paintings on a wall that can be visited during day or at night, when the walls are lit up. At this site, archaeologists discovered remains of a prehistoric bonfire that, according to Niède Guidon's team, proves that humans lived in the region 100,000 years ago. The geological monument Pedra Furada is nearby. To get there, take Rodovia BR-020 highway to the eastern entrance to the park closest to São Raimundo Nonato, near the visitor's center.

Desfiladeiro da Capivara Trail

This trail can be reached from the gate on Rodovia BR-020 highway, just past the town of Coronel José Dias. It boasts many archaeological sites, some quite close to the highway. Others are a short hike away (1,000 meters at the most), such as **Veadinhos Azuis**, a collection of blue rock paintings – the first in the world to be discovered in this color.

Baixão das Andorinhas and Baixão do Perna Trail

Thousands of swallows flood the canyon of **Baixão das Andorinhas** every afternoon around 5:30pm. It makes a pleasant late-afternoon outing on a trail from the Serra Vermelha gatehouse on Rodovia PI-140 highway. Further down the road, is **Baixão do Perna**, a valley with four archaeological sites. One of these sites has the park's most famous rock painting, which depicts an orgy.

Trilha Interpretativa Hombu

This trail is 9 kilometers (6 miles) long and passes through places where hikers can see *lagartixas-da-serra* (a lizard species endemic to the region), robust and blond-crested woodpeckers and at least 15 sites with rock paintings.

Alto dos Canoas and Caldeirão dos Rodrigues

From the Toca do Arame do Sansão excavation sites at the bottom of Baixão da Pedra Furada, an 800-meter (half-mile) trail leads to a set of stone steps. These stairs go to the top of the plateau and the rock paintings at the **Sítio dos Canoas** site. From the plateau, descend another set of iron stairs to **Caldeirão dos Rodrigues** II in the bottom of the valley, where several rock paintings depict scenes from prehistoric life.

THE LONG TALE OF PREHISTORIC MAN

In 1963, when I was an archeologist at the Museu Paulista, the municipal government of São Raimundo Nonato showed me pictures of prehistoric rock drawings from the region. I immediately detected the differences between them and all that was known in the world in terms of rock drawings. That same year I arranged a trip to the region. I arrived in Casa Nova, in Bahia, but the rains had washed out a bridge and I wasn't able to continue on.

Other circumstances took me to live in France, and for many years those images were imprinted in my memory. I managed to come back in 1970, and local inhabitants showed me the first sites with paintings. At that time, everything was quite different. The local communities lived in complete isolation from the rest of the state. The only road leading to Teresina, the capital city, crossed a long stretch of sand along the Capivara gorge. Today, this stretch is a bustling tourist destination visited by over 400 people per day at times. But then we only had two choices: either get stuck in the sand or drive through at dangerously high speeds, skidding around and almost sliding off the side of the road. There was no electricity or running water in the city.

After 34 years in the region, we are able to retrace its cultural evolution, protect it and present it. The rock paintings represent the most abundant, conspicuous and astonishing manifestation left by prehistoric populations living in the area of the Parque Nacional da Serra da Capivara in remote times.

We took core samples and carried out excavations to date these paintings and situate them in their precise sociocultural context. This led the researchers to accelerate and expand the excavations to collect more data and document this discovery, which revolutionized theories of the peopling of the Americas.

Therefore, we know that men already lived in the area of the park 60,000 years ago. The human presence had been continuous until the arrival of white colonizers. The oldest sites in the area are rock-covered shelters (*tocas* in the regional language), formed by erosion that removed the low part of the rock walls, resulting in an outcropping overhead that serves as a roof.

Prehistoric men used these protected shelters as campsites, burial grounds and place where they could paint aspects of their oral tradition. These peo-

Trails lead to the park's rock paintings

ple lived from hunting, gathering and fishing. The rock paintings portray in detail the sociocultural evolution over at least 15,000 years and is thus one of the most comprehensive and important archives on humanity currently available anywhere in the world.

These prehistoric societies lived in equilibrium with the environment, using it in different ways without ever depleting it. The economic model that we can infer from studies carried out in the area indicate that in the beginning, humans occupied an empty space, with no competitors. The first groups exploited certain limited areas, because there was plenty to hunt and they did not need to make great efforts. The raw materials used for their stone tools were always those located close at hand.

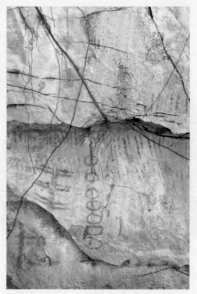

Rock paintings: history written in stone

Over the last 8,000 years, pressured by climatic changes and a drop in production of ecosystems – probably caused by the disappearance of large game – humans underwent a process of adaptation, and developed a wide range of techniques for using all natural resources. They started to be more selective in terms of the raw materials used, at times bringing materials from far away in pursuit of greater quality, enabling improved efficiency in production of tools.

Starting 3,500 to 3,000 years ago, we find the first traces of an agricultural society. From 3,000 to 1,600 years ago, there is evidence of peoples who lived in round villages formed by ten to eleven elliptical houses, built around a central square. They occupied either the wide valleys in the peripheral low plains, or the top of the *chapada* (plateau) on sedimentary formations. Their burial ceremonies were very elaborate. They held secondary burials in urns or graves in the ground.

Archeological data provides a wealth and variety of information on these groups. All the original peoples of the Parque Nacional Serra da Capivara were exterminated by white settlers. Today, all that is left from them is what archeology is able to discover. This legacy has helped us develop this extremely poor region, and offer visitors a structure where the rest points or destinations of the many trails are archeological sites. The Museu do Homem Americano presents a summary of more than thirty years of research amidst a very pleasant setting.

Nième Guidon,
Prehistorian and director of the Fundação Museu do Homem Americano

Rocks that look like twisted cannons at Primeira Cidade

Parque Nacional de Sete Cidades

Sete Cidades National Park, near the town of **Piripiri** and 200 kilometers (124 miles) north of Teresina, has been a national park since 1961. Its 6,221 hectares (15,270 acres) are home to Sete Cidades (Seven Cities), seven clusters of sandstone carved by time and weather. From the **Segunda Cidade lookout point**, visitors can make out shapes that look like roofs, chimneys, castles, forts and houses, as well as animal and human figures. It is also a good place from which to appreciate the landscape. The curiously shaped rocks bear **rock paintings** ranging from 5,000 to 10,000 years old. The area

has many springs, and it straddles the Cerrado and Caatinga landscapes. Their flora and fauna reflect the transitional zone in which they're located. Visitors can drive through all 12 kilometers (seven miles) of the park in three hours or spend three to six hours exploring a smaller area on foot. Another option is to rent bicycles in the park. Explore the park early in the day, before the sun gets too hot, and take snacks and water. Visitors must be accompanied by guides accredited by Ibama, the Brazilian Institute for the Environment and Renewable Natural Resources. Reach the park from Teresina by taking Rodovias BR-343 north to the BR-222 and then the PI-111 highways, which can be followed to the south gate. The park's north gate can be reached from Parnaíba by taking Rodovia BR-343 highway through the town of Piracuruca, which is 140 kilometers (87 miles) south of Parnaíba. The park has a visitors' center and a hotel nearby.

Information: Ibama, tel. (86) 3343-1342. Daily, 8am – noon and 1:30pm – 5pm.

Delta do Parnaíba

Between the coasts of Piauí and Maranhão, the Parnaíba River meets the ocean to form the only open-sea **delta** in the Americas. It is the third largest in the world, after Egypt's Nile River delta and the Mekong in Vietnam. It is a tourist attraction in both states, and it is home to **Ilha do Caju**, an island 50 kilometers (31 miles) from the town of **Parnaíba** in Piauí *(see more information on page 363).*

MARANHÃO

HIGHLIGHTS

- The old side of **São Luís**, with its Portuguese-tiled façades.
- The ruins, churches and the more than three hundred buildings that make up the architectural heritage of **Alcântara**.

- Trips to the lakes and Preguiças River in **Barreirinhas**.
- The desert dotted with lakes amidst the dunes, some 50-meter high, in the **Lençóis Maranhenses National Park** reserve.

WHEN TO GO

- In **May**, for the beautiful Festa do Divino Espírito Santo festivities held in Alcântara.
- In **June**, for the São João festivities in São Luís, especially the 23rd at the height of the *bumba-meu-boi*, the biggest folk festival in Maranhão.
- In **July** and **August**, when the rainy season ends and the lakes are

full in Lençóis Maranhenses.
- From **August** to **December**, when the sun reigns supreme in São Luís (but be prepared for the strong winds).
- Any time is good for a visit to the Parnaíba Delta, but boat trip options are most abundant from **December** to **March**.

SÃO LUÍS

The only Brazilian state capital to have been founded by the French, São Luís was established in 1612 and named Saint Louis in honor of King Louis XIII. The Portuguese took it over in 1615, and their presence can be seen in the architecture, above all in the tiles that cover the buildings in the city's **Historical Center**, which is a Unesco World Heritage Site. Since the 1970s the city has undergone restoration under the "Reviver" project. São Luís stands on an island of the same name, and it's crisscrossed by rivers and bridges linking the **lado antigo (old side)** to the **lado novo (new side)**, where you will find luxury hotels and city beaches like **Praia do Calhau**, which is famed for its sunsets. **Reggae** can be heard on the streets year round, thanks to the *radiolas*, a kind of mobile DJ studio.

HISTORICAL CENTER

Most museums, restaurants, and shops in the historical center can be found near Mercado Praia Grande, a market that stands between the old roads named **Rua do Trapiche**, **Rua do Giz**, **Rua da Estrela** and **Rua Portugal**. At night the bars and cafés on Rua Portugal, with its two blocks full of tiled colonial buildings, exude a bohemian atmosphere.

① Palácio dos Leões
② Casa do Maranhão
③ Casa de Nhozinho
④ Museu de Artes Visuais
⑤ Mercado Praia Grande
⑥ Cafua das Mercês
⑦ Centro Histórico Solar dos Vasconcelos
⑧ Convento das Mercês
⑨ Centro de Cultura Popular Domingos Vieira Filho
⑩ Catedral da Sé
⑪ Edifício São Luís
⑫ Teatro Arthur de Azevedo
⑬ Fonte do Ribeirão
⑭ Museu Artístico e Histórico do Maranhão
⑮ Museu de Arte Sacra

❶ PALÁCIO DOS LEÕES

Leões Palace, the current seat of the
state government, houses a collection
of oil paintings and engravings, with
important canvases by Vítor Meireles
(1832-1903), and 18th-century
furniture. The French built the palace
in 1612 and named it Fort Saint
Louis. Of the original construction,
only the São Cosme and São Damião
bastions remain.
*Avenida Dom Pedro II, no #, Centro,
tel. (98) 3214-8638. Mon, Wed, and Fri,
2pm – 5:30pm.*

❷ CASA DO MARANHÃO

This building, formerly the Customs
House, dates to 1873 and is now a
museum that's home to a colorful
permanent exhibition depicting the
roots of *bumba-meu-boi* and its
many rhythms.
*Rua do Trapiche, no #, Praia Grande,
tel. (98) 3218-9924. Tue – Sun,
9am – 7pm.*

❸ CASA DE NHOZINHO

Occupying a three-story house, this
museum depicts the world of the
indigenous people, and daily life in
Maranhão's countryside and coastal
region. One area is devoted to the work
of Antônio Bruno Pinto Nogueira
(1904-74), known as Nhozinho, who
became famous for the toys he created.
*Rua Portugal, 185, Praia Grande, tel. (98)
3218-9953. Tue – Sun, 9am – 7pm.*

❹ MUSEU DE ARTES VISUAIS

A visit to the Visual Arts Museum
provides a lesson on European tiles,
which are the hallmark of the city
center's architecture. Works by artists
such as Cícero Dias and Alfredo Volpi
can also be seen.
*Rua Portugal, 273, Praia Grande, tel. (98)
3231-6766. Tue – Sun, 9am – 6pm.*

❺ MERCADO PRAIA GRANDE

Praia Grande Market, dating from 1820,
is situated in the Casa das Tulhas.
Elderly men meet here to play cards
and dominoes amid shops selling
grains, spices, and typical products.
*Rua da Estrela, no #, Praia Grande.
Daily, 9am – 8pm.*

❻ CAFUA DAS MERCÊS

The old slave market was turned into
this museum, also known as Museu do
Negro, which is dedicated to preserving
Afro-Brazilian culture. Exhibits include
musical instruments and ritual costumes.
*Rua Jacinto Maia, no #, Desterro. Tue –
Fri, 9am – 6pm.*

❼ CENTRO HISTÓRICO SOLAR DOS VASCONCELOS

The Solar dos Vasconcelos Historical
Center tells the history of São Luís
through illustrated panels, photos, and
historical objects.
*Rua da Estrela, 562, Praia Grande,
tel. (98) 3231-9075. Mon – Fri, 8am –
6:30pm; Sat and Sun, noon – 6pm.*

❽ CONVENTO DAS MERCÊS

Father Antônio Vieira inaugurated
Mercês Convent in 1654 to house
members of the Mercedarian Order.
Today it is home to the Fundação da
Memória Republicana (Memory
of the Republic Foundation), which
includes various institutions like the
Memorial José Sarney, a collection of

A TASTE OF MARANHÃO

The most famous dish in Maranhão is **ar-
roz-de-cuxá**: the rice is cooked with *cuxá*,
a sauce or paste made from sorrel (called
vinagreira or *azedinha* in southern Brazil),
dried shrimp, sesame seeds, and manioc
flour. Also try **guaraná Jesus**, a pink, cin-
namon-flavored soda.

São Luis boasts a rich architectural heritage

documents and objects belonging to Brazil's former president.
Rua da Palma, 506, Centro, tel. (98) 3231-0641. Mon – Fri, 8am – 6pm; Sat, 8am – 2pm.

⑨ CENTRO DE CULTURA POPULAR DOMINGOS VIEIRA FILHO
The Domingos Vieira Filho Cultural Center, also known as Casa da Festa, houses material related to folk rites and traditions, such as the *Tambor-de-Mina* (a religion of African origin) and the Festa do Divino festivities.
Rua do Giz, 205, Praia Grande, tel. (98) 3218-9924. Tue – Sun, 9am – 7pm.

⑩ CATEDRAL DA SÉ
The Jesuit-built Sé Cathedral was inaugurated as Nossa Senhora da Vitória Church in 1699. The current façade dates from 1922, but the high altar's altarpiece dates back to the end of the 18th century. The alterpiece, restored in 1990 and listed as part of the national heritage, is a fine example of baroque, with detailed gilt carvings.
Praça Dom Pedro II, no #, Centro, tel. (98) 3222-7380. Daily, 8am – noon and 2pm – 5:30pm.

⑪ EDIFÍCIO SÃO LUÍS
This three-story corner building is said to be the largest tiled colonial building in Brazil. Built in the 19th century, its interior was destroyed by fire in 1969. It was restored in 1976 and today houses a branch of the bank Caixa Econômica Federal.
Rua de Nazaré, at the intersection with Rua do Egito.

⑫ TEATRO ARTHUR DE AZEVEDO
This theater opened in 1817 under the name Teatro União. It was later renamed Teatro de São Luís, and then, in 1920, Teatro de Arthur de Azevedo. It closed in the 1960s and fell into disrepair until 1991, when renovation

---

BUMBA-MEU-BOI

Maranhão celebrates *bumba-meu-boi* with gusto. This tradition, part of the *festa junina* festivities held in June, mixes African, Portuguese and indigenous influences in a ritual of theater, music, and dance. The celebrations tell the story of Catarina, a pregnant slave who has a craving for the tongue of her master's favorite bull. She convinces her husband – called Pai Francisco, Nego Chico, or Preto Velho – to slay the animal, which he does. Caught by his master, he is ordered to revive the bull or die. A *pajé* (medicine man) helps him, shouting: "Get up, bull, dance, bull," which the animal eventually does. On June 23rd, the eve of Saint John's feast day, the bull is baptized by a priest, outside the church. Dancing commences with the presentation of the bull's hide, decorated with vel-vet, satin, beads and sequins. The festivities have many "accents" or rhythms, such as *matraca* (of indigenous origin), *zabumba* (African inspiration) and *orquestra* (European influence). Among other folklore presentations worth a mention are the Festa do Divino Espírito Santo festivities, the *tambor-de-crioula, dança-do-coco, dança-do-caroço,* and *dança-de-são-gonçalo.*

work restored its original splendor.
Rua do Sol, no #, Centro, tel. (98) 3218-9900. Tue – Fri, from 3pm.

⑬ FONTE DO RIBEIRÃO
This fountain, built in 1796, has five jets of water springing from the mouths of gargoyles and other figures. It faces a stone-paved courtyard, and the water comes from a spring beneath the Historical Center.
Largo do Ribeirão, no #, Centro.

⑭ MUSEU HISTÓRICO E ARTÍSTICO DO MARANHÃO
Dating from 1836, Solar Gomes de Sousa became the Maranhão History and Art Museum in 1973. Inside are recreations of 19th-century residence interiors.
Rua do Sol, 302, Centro, tel. (98) 3218-9920, 3218-9922. Tue – Sun, 9am – 7pm.

⑮ MUSEU DE ARTE SACRA
Occupying a 19th-century townhouse, the Sacred Art Museum exhibits items that European missionaries used in religious plays that were intended to convert indigenous people.
Rua 13 de Maio, 500, Centro, tel. (98) 3218-9920. Tue – Sun, 9am – 7pm.

ALCÂNTARA

Time seems to pass slowly in Alcântara. Founded in the 17th century, the city used to be one of the richest in Brazil, but it declined after the abolition of slavery in 1888. Many of its buildings fell into ruin, but it still has more than three hundred structures from the 17th and 18th centuries. Anyone staying in São Luís, 22 kilometers away, would be well advised to spend a day here. Boats depart from the river terminal in São Luís and the trip takes 15 minutes. There are some lovely buildings around the main square, Praça Matriz: in the **Museu Histórico**, an old house that belonged to the Viveiros family and is now the history museum, one attraction is an iron bed intended for use by the emperor Dom Pedro II *(Tue – Sun, 9am – 4pm)*. The **Casa Histórica do Iphan** is a museum that exhibits tiles, furniture and porcelain *(Mon – Fri, 10am – 1:45pm)*. Also in the square are the ruins of **Igreja de São Matias**, a church whose construction began in 1648. It was used until 1884, but was never completed. The restored interior of another church, **Igreja de Nossa Senhora do Carmo**, dating from 1665, is worth visiting for the exuberantly rococo decorations of the high altar, sacristy, pulpit, tribune, and balconies *(Largo do Carmo, Rua Grande, Centro; daily, 9am – 3pm)*. Alcântara is also well known for its **Festa do Divino Espírito Santo** festivities, which mobilize the entire population for two weeks in May. The **Centro de Lançamento de Alcântara**, a rocket-launching station 7 kilometers from the city, is not open to visitors.

BURITI PALM STRAW CRAFTWORK

Every bit of the *buriti* palm, which is so abundant in Maranhão, is put to good use: Starch is extracted from the core. Its fruit pulp is used to make oil, ice cream, and candy. The leaves are used to thatch roofs. The shoots produce heart of palm, a popular food. And the fiber is used to make bags, such as those sold in Barreirinhas *(see page 360)*, on the ferries that cross the Rio Preguiça and in the lake-side kiosks of Lagoa Bonita.

LENÇÓIS MARANHENSES

One of the unique and wonderful surprises on the northeast coast is this desert dotted with lakes. Its sand dunes can rise up to 50 meters (165 feet) above the waters, giving the area the appearance of a series of sheets drying in the sun. The dunes stretch along 100 kilometers (62 miles) of coast and spread 50 kilometers (31 miles) inland. The coastal beaches are wide and long. Inland, *morrarias*, dunes dotted with lakes, predominate. In the first half of the year, the rains fill the lakes. Later, they gradually dry out, so the months of July and August are the best for visiting the area. In September many of the lakes disappear or shrink in volume, but this is when there are fewer tourists and the attractions are less crowded. At the end of the year only the perennial lakes remain. The dunes span two desert areas: Grandes Lençóis, west of the Preguiças River, and Pequenos Lençóis, to the east. The region houses the **Parque Nacional dos Lençóis Maranhenses**, a 155,000-hectare (383,000-acre) reserve inaugurated in 1981. **Barreirinhas**, 260 kilometers (162 miles) from São Luís, offers the best tourist facilities. To get there, take the Rodovia MA-403 highway, known as the Rodovia Translitorânea. The drive takes about three hours.

The **Instituto Chico Mendes de Conservação da Diversidade** is a conservation organization that gives talks and information on the rules and necessary precautions to take in the park *(Avenida Paulista, no #, Boa Vista, tel. (98)3349-1155; Mon – Fri, 8am – noon and 2pm – 6pm).*

Contact: *Rota das Trilhas, tel. (98)*

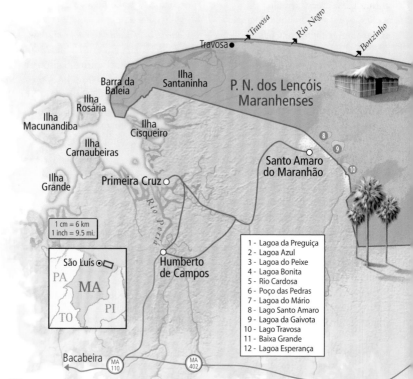

3349-0372; Tropical Adventure, tel. (98) 3349-1987; Eco-Dunas, tel. (98) 3349-0545, 8839-0578.

PREGUIÇAS RIVER CRUISE

The Rio Preguiças provides the best means of visiting the park and its villages, which can be reached by waterborne launch or by *voadeira* – a speedboat with an outboard engine. The first attractions are the 40-meter (130-foot) dunes in **Vassouras**, a village 45 minutes from Barreirinhas, where you can swim in the river or walk along **Praia de Pequenos Lençóis** beach. Next stop is **Mandacaru**, after passing **Espadarte**, **Morro do Boi** and **Moitas**. The view of this village with its lighthouse, **Farol Preguiças**, in the background is one of the loveliest on the trip. While there, be sure to climb the 165 steps to the top of the lighthouse for a panoramic view. After leaving the village, boat tours stop for lunch in **Caburé**, near the river mouth.

JEEP TRIP TO THE LAKES

The main lakes of **Parque Nacional dos Lençóis Maranhenses** form a kaleidoscope of blue and green hues, but they can only be reached in a 4×4 vehicle. After crossing the Preguiça River by ferry, it's a 40-minutes jeep trip to a spot where you proceed on foot. It's a 5-minute walk to the first lake, the turquoise **Lagoa da Preguiça**; another 10 minutes leads to the lovely, popular **Lagoa Azul**. A further 10-minute walk takes you to green-hued **Lagoa do Peixe**. This is one of the few lakes that don't dry up in the summer – Lagoa Azul simply disappears at the end of the year. Another trip, one hour by road, takes you to **Lagoa Bonita**, which is surrounded by dunes towering up to 40 meters (130 feet) high.

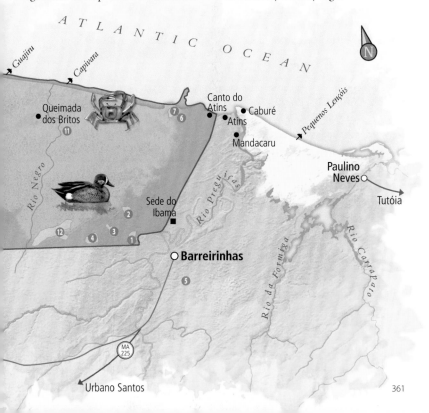

ATINS

This fishing village is where the Preguiças River empties into the sea. Electricity came to Atins just a few years ago and there is still just one public telephone, and no cars. Geography reinforces the remote atmosphere: the village sits between the river and the sea, beside the dunes, with a beach that has both freshwater and tidal salt-water pools. A pool called **Poço das pedras** and a lake, **Lagoa do Mário**, are two of the local attractions.

OTHER WAYS TO SEE THE PARK

Lençóis can also be viewed from above, on 30-minute flights in a twin-engine plane. Flights depart from Barreirinhas and afford panoramic views of the region up to the mouth of the Preguiças River. Another option is to go downriver by kayak or *bóia-cross* (inner tube) on the Cardosa River, which is about one and a half hours by car from Barreirinhas. The descent takes about two hours. Don't forget to take a diving mask to see the fish. *Contact: Eco-Dunas, tel. (98) 3349-0545, 8839-0578.*

Cool lakes nestle amid the vast dunes of Lençóis Maranhenses

Where it meets the ocean, the Paraíba River forms the world's third largest delta.

THE PARNAÍBA DELTA

At the Maranhão-Piauí state border, the Parnaíba River branches out in five directions as it meets the Atlantic, forming the biggest open-sea delta in the Americas, and the third largest in the world after the Nile and Mekong deltas. A succession of beaches, dunes, *igarapés* (channels), and mangroves encircle about 80 islands in an area of approximately 2,700 square kilometers (1,040 square miles). Although 65% of the delta belongs to Maranhão, the main gateway is **Parnaíba**, in Piauí, 354 kilometers (220 miles) from Teresina. There are two boat tours available to visitors intent on seeing the delta's labyrinthine mangroves. One lasts eight hours (lunch and fruit included) and uses large boats for groups of seventy or so people. The boat stops at **Baía das Canárias**, which teems with carnauba palms, and **Ilha de Poldros**, an island of dunes popular among kitesurfers. Another option is to explore the river in a *chalana* (flat-bottomed boat) or a *voadeira*, a simple boat with an outboard motor. Either can accommodated groups of four to eight people. The four-hour trip takes in *igarapés*, Ilha de Poldros and **Baía do Feijão Bravo**, a mangrove-fringed bay where salt-water lakes form at low tide. ***Contact:*** *Eco Adventure Tour, tel. (86) 3323-9595; Natur Turismo, tel. (86) 3323-0426, 9971-5143.*

ILHA DO CAJU

In 1847, an Englishman, James Frederick Clark, headed into the Parnaíba Delta region to exploit its valuable carnauba wood. He eventually settled on this 100-square-kilometer (39-square-mile) island, where he banned hunting and deforestation. Today, Ilha do Caju, 50 kilometers (31 miles) from Parnaíba, belongs to the Maranhão municipality of Araioses and protects 18 kilometers (11 miles) of beaches, four types of marshland, floodlands, lakes, dunes, and forests. Animals such as coatis, armadillos and ocelots, along with the *guará*, a red ibis that is the symbol of the delta, find their home here. To visit the island, you must make a reservation at the **Refúgio Ecológico Ilha do Caju** *(tel. 86-3321-3044)*, the island's only guesthouse, which will furnish boats and guides for trips on foot, horseback or by jeep. We recommend taking rubber boots, long-sleeved clothing, sunscreen and insect repellent.

THE NORTH

Indigenous influence is strong in the remote northern part of Brazil. It is made up largely of the Amazonia region, the most extensive area of continuous forest on the planet, and crisscrossed by a network of rivers that converge at the mighty Amazon. The "river-sea" is the world's biggest in volume and length. Traveling through the region requires perseverance and enthusiasm: transportation difficulties, as well as the heat and humidity, make journeys a challenge even for the most experienced travelers. Long boat crossings are the only alternative to taking on the region's scarce highways. From Manaus, the capital of Amazonas State, visitors can take boats to jungle hotels and go on excursions through the forest. Parintins – which is further down the Amazon River, almost on the Pará State border – is the site of the Festival de Parintins, one of Brazil's biggest folk festivals. A three-hour boat trip from Belém (the capital of Pará, which has old, well-preserved architecture) passes through floodlands and takes visitors to the fluvial island of Marajó, which is famous for its prehistoric mounds and indigenous pottery. The capital of Tocantins State, in the Cerrado savannah, serves as a base for people who want to explore the surprising wilderness of Jalapão State Park.

VENEZUELA   GUIANA   GUIANA FRANCESA   ATLANTIC OCEAN

COLÔMBIA   SURINAME   AMAPÁ

Boa Vista
BR 432
RORAIMA

Macapá
Ilha de Marajó
Belém
BR 174   BR 010

Manaus   Santarém

AMAZONAS   PARÁ   MARANHÃO
BR 319

ACRE   BR 364   Porto Velho   PIAUÍ

Rio Branco   BR 153

PERU   RONDÔNIA   Palmas
Jalapão

MATO GROSSO   TOCANTINS   BAHIA

BOLÍVIA   GOIÁS

D.F.

AMAZONAS

RORAIMA

PARÁ

AM

Boa Vista

P. N. do Jaú

Rio Negro

Presidente
Figueiredo

Anavilhanas

Guanavenas
Jungle Lodge

Reserva de
Mamirauá

Jungle Othon Palace

Manaus

Parintins

Ariaú Amazon Towers

Tefé

Lago
Salvador

Tiwa Amazonas
Eco Resort

Itacoatiara

Encontro
das águas

Rio Solimões

Rio Purus

Rio Madeira

Rio Amazonas

AMAZONAS

1 cm = 93 km
1 inch = 146.8 mi.

BR 174

HIGHLIGHTS

- Jungle hotels **around Manaus**.
- The Anavilhanas archipelago, in **Novo Airão**.
- The Mamirauá Sustainable Development Reserve in **Tefé**.
- The **Manaus** cultural circuit.
- **Parintins** Folk Festival.

WHEN TO GO

- From **July** to **November**, when it rains less, and in the last week of **June** to see the Parintins Folk Festival.

MANAUS

At first sight, Manaus might disappoint visitors who expect immediate contact with nature – the state capital is a hot, steamy metropolis with a population of 1.5 million. The city, however, is rich in architecture and culture, and it deserves a visit. Its historical buildings date from the late 19th and early 20th centuries, when the state capital of Amazonas experienced a boom from the rubber industry and amassed wealth quickly. Most of the historical sites have been restored, which adds to the city's charm. The best idea is to visit the main attractions – one or two are enough – and then head off to the rivers. Aboard a small boat, that "city sensation" disappears completely. After all, the city is practically a concrete island in the middle of the jungle. The classic trip to see the famous meeting of the Negro and Solimões rivers begins right in front of the city. Those who want to enjoy an experience in the forest can stay in a jungle hotel or go on a river trip. Manaus used to be very popular for shopping because of its duty-free zone (Zona Franca), but ever since Brazil opened up to imports in the 1990s, the prices don't hold the same attraction. Nightlife is concentrated around Ponta Negra beach, which has bars and restaurants. On Rodovia BR-174 highway, 2,200 paved kilometers of road connect the city to the Caribbean coast of Venezuela. The road starts in Manaus and runs through beautiful natural scenery.

CULTURAL CIRCUIT

TEATRO AMAZONAS

This theater, inaugurated in 1896, is one of the most impressive examples of neoclassical architecture in Brazil. Everything in the building was imported from Europe except the jacaranda and *macacaúba*, both native Brazilian woods that were used for the seats and part of the floor. It's a superb building: the great hall's parquet floor is made up of 12,000 pieces of inlaid wood. Signed paintings by Domenico de Angelis, inspired by the Amazon landscape, adorn the walls and ceiling. The crystal chandeliers came from Murano. The outside of the dome is covered in 36,000 enamel tiles in the yellow, green, and blue of the Brazilian flag, and the stage curtains depict the meeting of the Negro and Solimões rivers. The annual opera festival takes place between April and May.
Praça São Sebastião, no #, Centro, tel. (92) 3622-1880, 3232-1768. Mon – Sat, 9am – 5pm.

LARGO DE SÃO SEBASTIÃO

São Sebastião Square stands near the Teatro Amazonas. After it was restored in 2004, it became the city's busiest meeting point. The square is reminiscent of the days of the rubber boom, with houses that have been completely restored and carriages with drivers dressed in period costume. From Thursday to Sunday *(6pm – 9pm)*, it serves as the stage for regional music shows, serenades, screenings of old films, children's games and orchestral concerts given by the **Orquestra Amazonas Filarmônica**. Craft stores and good bars complete the picture. Try the **Café do Largo**, which offers a menu of regional and contemporary fast food *(Rua Costa Azevedo, 290, tel. (92) 3234-9641; Tue – Sun, 5pm – 11pm)*, or **Bar do Armando**, a haunt for local artists and intellectuals in search of chilled beer and a snack of roasted pork *(Rua 10 de Julho, no #, tel. (92) 3232-1195; Mon –*

Sat, 2pm – 3am). Also in the square is **Casa J. G. Araújo**, which displays wooden carvings *(Rua Costa Azevedo, 198, tel. (92) 3637-7327, 3622-0767; Mon – Fri, 8am – 5pm; Sun, 5pm – 9pm),* and the **Galeria das Artes**, which displays work by contemporary artists *(Rua Costa Azevedo, 290, tel. (92) 3622-0618; daily, 4pm – 9pm).*

MUSEU DE CIÊNCIAS NATURAIS DA AMAZÔNIA

Although the Amazonian Natural History Museum is far from the center of Manaus and the signs pointing the way are not very helpful, it's worth a visit for anyone interested in biology. The collection includes preserved and stuffed mammals, birds, and insects found in the Amazon region. It also has

aquariums with live specimens of *pirarucu* (giant arapaima), *tambaqui* (red pacu), and other regional fish. *Estrada Belém, no #, Colônia Cachoeira Grande, Aleixo, tel. (92) 3644-2799. Mon – Sat, 9am – noon and 2pm – 5pm.*

MERCADO MUNICIPAL ADOLPHO LISBOA

This reconstruction of the old Parisian market Les Halles was built facing the Negro River. Since it opened in 1882, it has been the main trading center for Manaus' regional products. Restoration work has been in progress since 2006, but it should be finished in 2009. Meanwhile, take a leisurely look at the stalls that have been moved outside around the building. Keep an eye out for interesting items like *jarina*, a seed known as "Amazon ivory" that is

The neoclassical Teatro Amazonas was built with Europe's finest materials

used for crafts and costume jewelry. The most interesting attractions are the medicinal herb stalls, which supposedly sell cures for every ailment. *Rua dos Barés, 46, Centro.*

CENTRO CULTURAL PALÁCIO RIO NEGRO

Originally a rubber baron's residence, this building was acquired by the state in 1918 and served as the seat of state government until 1995. It was turned into a cultural center two years later, after a period of renovation work. Since then, it has housed the Museu da Imagem e Som do Amazonas (image and sound museum), the Cine-Teatro Guarany (cinema), and the Museu de Numismática Bernardo Ramos (coin museum). It also contains the state art gallery, Pinacoteca do Estado, which has a collection of more than 1,000 works, about 300 of which are on display. The Bernardo Ramos Numismatic Museum and the Pinacoteca do Estado are scheduled to be transferred to the Palacete Provincial (*Praça da Polícia, no #, Centro*) some time in 2008. Built in the eclectic style, the palace includes several rooms for temporary and permanent exhibits, including some of the Pinacoteca do Estado collection. Highlights of the palace include a wooden staircase that is over 100 years old and the *acapu* and *pau-amarelo* wood floor, which is similar to the one in the Palácio da Justiça.
Avenida 7 de Setembro, 1546, Centro, tel. (92) 3232-4450, 3633-2850. Mon – Fri, 9am – 5pm.

TRAVELING BY BOAT IN THE AMAZON REGION

Anyone who wants to visit the Amazon forest should make sure to travel by boat. Seeing the **meeting of the waters** is a must. Near Manaus, the dark waters of the Negro River merge with the muddy waters of the Solimões River (**Contact:** *Amazon Explorers, tel. (92) 3613-3558; Selvatur, tel. (92) 3622-2577*). The trips usually last a whole day and include an option to visit the

The beauty of the Amazon region unfolds on a trip along its rivers

On the banks of the Negro River, the Tiwa Amazonas Eco Resort offers wooden chalets with verandas

Reserva Ecológica do Lago de Janauari, where visitors can see river dolphins and alligators and eat lunch at a floating restaurant. Although the trip is beautiful, some people may be frustrated because they think it's too touristy. To escape the crowded boats, hire a private motorboat *(Fontur, tel. (92) 3658-3052; Associação dos Canoeiros Marina do David Fátima, tel. (92) 3658-6159)*. Several options exist for people who want to head farther afield. Tour agencies can organize trips in fully equipped boats with cabins. They can go to fantastic places such as the **Arquipélago Anavilhanas**, an archipelago in the municipality of Novo Airão with more than 400 islands *(**Contact:** Amazon Explorers, tel. (92) 3613-3558; Selvatur, tel. (92) 3622-2577)*,

and the **Parque Nacional do Jaú**, a national park of more than 2 million hectares *(**Contact:** Amazonas Clipper, tel. (92) 3656-1253)*. A good way to get to know the local people and their way of life is to travel on the *navios de recreio* or *gaiolas*, large boats with two or three decks and with hammocks or cabins for sleeping during the journey. These *gaiolas*, which serve as the local "bus service", can transport people to the most distant locations in the region. Going downriver is much quicker than going upriver: a trip from Manaus to Belém takes four to five days, but traveling the other way takes an average of five or six days depending on the type of boat *(Manaus Boat Station – Estação Hidroviária de Manaus, tel. (92) 3621-431, 3621-4316)*.

JUNGLE HOTELS

Staying in a jungle hotel is one way to visit the forest without sacrificing comfort. They all have excellent facilities and offer walks, piranha fishing, nighttime alligator watching, canoeing through the fluvial canals, and visiting riverside communities. These hotels generally include tourist transfers from Manaus by land, air, or river. Some of them rent rooms on a day-by-day basis.

TIWA AMAZONAS ECO RESORT
Facing Manaus on the opposite bank of the Negro River, this

MAMIRAUÁ

Tefé, 663 kilometers (410 miles) from Manaus, is the Amazon region's largest area of protected river plains. The Instituto de Desenvolvimento Sustentável Mamirauá (Mamirauá Institute for Sustainable Development) manages the Mamirauá Reserve and the **Pousada Uacari**, a guesthouse offering three-night packages that include the one-and-a-half-hour river journey between Tefé and the reserve *(tel. (97) 3343-4160)*. There are regular flights between Manaus and Tefé. During a stay at Mamirauá, visitors can take trips to watch birds, monkeys, and river dolphins, paddle canoes, see local communities, and attend talks on the research conducted by the Institute.

ARIAÚ AMAZON TOWERS

This tourist complex, the most famous jungle hotel in the Amazon, is made up of eight suspended towers connected by 8 kilometers (5 miles) of walkways at treetop height – a necessity because of the constant flooding. The stunning view from the top of the two 41-meter (134-foot) towers helps explain why the Amazon is so fascinating. Lodgings range from simple rooms with cold showers to rooms built in the treetops that have jacuzzis and Internet access.
Tel. (92) 2121-5000; reservations: tel. 0800-7025005.

AMAZON JUNGLE PALACE

This hotel is 50 kilometers (31 miles) from Manaus, and it is a good choice for visitors who want to be close to the water. Located in a steel barge anchored in a canal of the Negro River, the hotel rocks in harmony with the tide. It has been closed since

hotel offers comfortable wooden chalets with verandas overlooking the water. It opened in 2003 and is managed by a Dutch group that specializes in outdoor activities. Tiwa also offers adventure sports such as rappelling and flying fox.
Tel. (91) 9995-7892, 9982-3939.

Ariaú Amazon Towers, a hotel made up of eight suspended towers and 8 kilometers of walkways

the beginning of 2008 for refurbishments, but its reopening is scheduled for January 2009. *Tel. (91) 3658-8120.*

GUANAVENAS JUNGLE LODGE
Guanavenas is the perfect spot to get away from civilization for a few days. It is located in Silves, 350 kilometers (217 miles) from Manaus. The hotel, very well-organized, guarantees the guest a comfortable stay in the middle of the forest. It has a 30-meter (98-foot) observation tower. The surrounding fruit trees are home to countless bird species.
Tel. (91) 3656-1500.
More information on jungle hotels on page 509.

Passionflower

Annato

FROM MANAUS TO THE CARIBBEAN BY ROAD

To get to the Caribbean coast of Venezuela, visitors will need to travel for 32 hours and drive 2,200 kilometers (1,370 miles) on paved road in a reasonable condition. Bus service is also available. About 120 kilometers (75 miles) after Manaus sits **Presidente Figueiredo**, a town famous for its many waterfalls and very popular with locals. On the border with the state of Roraima, the road crosses the Território Indígena Waimiri-Atroari indigenous reserve. (Traffic is permitted only during the day.) Next comes **Boa Vista**, Roraima's state capital, where the landscape changes completely and jungle gives way to Cerrado savannah, called *lavrado*. The *tepuis* plateaus, part of the **Canaima National Park**, appear on the horizon on the Venezuelan side as the border nears. The park includes **Monte Roraima**, although some of

the mountain is technically in Brazil, and the **Salto Angel**, the highest waterfall in the world with a drop of 979 meters (3,212 feet). The road runs through **Santa Elena de Uyarén**, a town in Venezuela that serves as a base for visitors to the falls. At the Caribbean coast in **Puerto La Cruz**, a two-and-a-quarter-hour ocean crossing leads to **Isla Margarita**. Brazilians who want to make this journey need their passports, and foreigners should be aware of entry visa requirements between Venezuela and their home countries. The **Eucatur** bus company runs a daily service from Manaus to Puerto La Cruz *(tel. (92) 3648-1524)*. Make sure to get information before leaving, because some services can be suspended at certain times. Traveling by car demands careful planning because of the long distances between gas stations on the Brazilian side.

The Amazon Rainforest:
Brazil's Greatest Treasure

The Amazon is a world apart, the largest green reserve in the world. In the midst of this extraordinary biodiversity, it is one of the last places on Earth where tribal peoples still live much as they have since the Stone Age. Tribes live here that have virtually no history of contact with Western society and preserve pure habits developed during millennia of cultural isolation. The Amazon also is home to the largest reserve of fresh water in the world, and nowhere else in the world is there such a wealth of rivers. The Negro river alone has an average depth of 70 meters (230 feet), which means it could entirely submerge a 20-story building. The number of lakes and floodplains abound, and they are full of hundreds of species of plants, fish and other animals.

We are in the so-called "millennium of water," dedicated to that resource that is becoming dangerously scarce throughout the world. Consequently, the Amazon protects and represents a critical human resource. Those who have water have the oil of the future. Yet incredible as it seems, we are destroying this wealth. From any boat, along the shore of a river, you can easily see the momentum of deforestation caused by cattle ranching and other activities. Species vital to the area are being removed and destroyed and no one can guarantee that they will ever return to grow again.

In these times of deep divide between much of humanity and so much of nature, we must remember that we are part of both. We are killing something we are part of. That's why an increasing number of Brazilians consider it essential to develop controlled ecotourism, to become sufficiently acquainted with the Amazon to respect and protect this greatest of natural treasures.

To begin to understand this unique world, take a boat trip from Belém to Manaus. Take note of the sudden changes in the weather, three or four times throughout the day. Observe the density of light, the many variations of the sun, and the marvelous cloud formations. At times the sky turns lead-grey, creating a fantastic contrast with the green forest. Travel in a small boat so you can explore the inlets that appear along the river banks. You'll pass through various "lakes" that are actually flooded areas of the river. To discover the enchantment of the Amazon, travel leisurely without the rush of conventional tourism. Also at a leisurely pace, discover the lovely small towns of the region.

Make a note in your agenda, and underline it, that it is an absolute must to be in Parintins at the end of June. This is not another Carnival, as the press in the South of Brazil likes to call it, but rather a sensational 3-act opera, with remarkable costumes and decorations. I was so moved by the first representation I saw that I cried. It is a *bumba-meu-boi* with a distinct, traditional indigenous dance, without the usual African or Latin body movements of other popular rhythms. The entire pageant is portrayed and created by an incredible number of talented local artists.

A great civilization lives in the Amazon. I have had the opportunity to spend time with various Indian nations like the *ianomâmis*, *marubos* and *macuxis*. They have a profound knowledge of their forest. From plants, roots and sap of trees, they make natural medicines that correspond to, but have advantages over, antibiotics, anti-inflammatories, and other modern drugs. Large foreign laboratories are trying to patent these formulas, in an attempt to lay claim to ancient wisdom.

The Indians also have practical knowledge of soil fertility, and also know when to rotate their crops and how long the land should remain fallow in order to restore its vitality. These semi-nomadic peoples have an admirable "control" of the forest. There is a great deal of communication between the tribes and interaction among the villages.

This same mastery of the fruits of the land and resources of the region underpins the incredibly rich regional cuisine. The dishes include sophisticated combinations. A grilled *tambaqui* (red pacu) and *surubim* (catfish) are truly delicious. You'll also encounter – and enjoy – a large variety of fish with completely foreign identities. Another exceptional treat for the palate is to go to an ice cream parlor in Manaus or Belém. Take note of the various aromas and tastes. Good parlors offer at least 25 flavors of fruit sherbet, most of which even Brazilians from other regions have never heard of. Many of these fruits simply do not travel. Some have flavors so strong one has to develop a taste for them. But there are others known to make even unromantic visitors believe in love at first taste.

Despite the vast number of unique attractions found there, there are some things that cannot be found here, in spite of rumors. In Brazilian imaginations, the Amazon forest hides the dangerous *caipora*, or hobglobin, and the *mula-sem-cabeça*, a mythical priest's mistress who becomes a headless mule on Fridays and runs about frightening people. I hope that Brazilians overcome their fear of these myths, because it is essential to make Brazilians more aware of the importance of the Amazon. The region offers tourism opportunities for all pocketbooks and budgets. Ecotourism needs to be encouraged with responsibility. I hope that every Brazilian that visits the Amazon will become an activist, a defender of the preservation of Brazil's greatest heritage – the green of our flag.

Sebastião Salgado,
photographer

THE CONTAGIOUS MERRIMENT OF THE PARINTINS FOLK FESTIVAL

In the Amazon, the last week of June is as Carnival time in Rio de Janeiro, because it's time for the **Festival Folclórico de Parintins**. It is the most famous folk festival in the North, and it has been held on Tupinambarana Island in Parintins since 1966. The festival is a variation on the *bumba-meu-boi* festivities, and it includes performances by two groups – the Boi Caprichoso and the Boi Garantido – whose origins go back to the arrival of settlers in the region in the late 19th and early 20th centuries. The spectacle reenacts a local legend about a bull *(boi)*; it takes place in an arena, with dancing, floats, and sumptuous costumes. The dominant colors are blue for the Caprichoso group and red for the Garantido group. Red and blue also show up in the clothes worn by fervent fans, who are something of a sideshow themselves. During the festival, each Boi group gives three different performances – one per night – that last two hours apiece. Reserve a ticket for one of the 35,000 seats in advance. The same goes for lodgings, because beds in Parintins are scarce and the town's population of 100,000 doubles during the festival. Tickets are for sale at the Boi groups' headquarters, although it's easier and safer to use the services of Manaus' tour agencies that can supply tickets, transport, and accommodations. People can watch weekly open rehearsals from April onward in the so-called *currais* (rehearsal areas), which are equivalent to the samba school *quadras*. Access to Parintins is by air on regular flights from Manaus, or by river on the regular boat service, which takes 16 hours from Manaus. Visitors can also take yachts from Manaus, which offer excursions to the festival, including on-board accommodation.

Information: Amazonas State Cultural Department (Secretaria de Estado da Cultura do Amazonas), tel. (92) 3633-2850; Boi Garantido headquarters, tel. (92) 9139-4639; Boi Caprichoso headquarters, tel. (92) 3533-4676.

A Boi Garantido performance in the Bumbódromo in Parintins, Amazonas

PARÁ

HIGHLIGHTS

- Núcleo Cultural Feliz Lusitânia and **Círio de Nazaré**.
- Estação das Docas in **Belém**.
- Buffalo farms and indigenous pottery on **Marajó Island**.
- The beaches at Alter do Chão in **Santarém**.

WHEN TO GO

- From **May** to **November** to visit the capital with less risk of rain.
- The **second weekend of October** for the Círio de Nazaré festivities.
- From **February** to **June** to see the flooded wetlands around Ilha de Marajó.
- From **November** to **July**, when the waters recede and the white beaches of Alter do Chão are more pristine.

BELÉM

1 Mercado Ver-o-Peso
2 Mangal das Garças
3 Museu Forte do Presépio
4 Museu de Arte Sacra

5 Espaço Cultural Casa das
Onze Janelas
6 Theatro da Paz
7 Museu Paraense Emílio Goeldi

Belém was the site of disputes between the Dutch and the English, but it wasn't colonized until the Portuguese seized the area in the 17th century. Right in the center of the city is **Forte do Presépio**, a fort built by Francisco Caldeira Castelo Branco with the help of Tupinambá Indians in 1616. Pará, the state

capital, is strategically located at the head of the Amazon Basin on the shores of Guajará Bay. Its rich architecture includes buildings dating from the colonial period and the rubber boom, all of which are very well-preserved. Despite recent restoration work, however, the city leaves something to be desired when it comes to cleanliness. Still, the huge, ancient mangrove swamps in the central region – and in much of the city – make the atmosphere more pleasant and alleviate the extreme heat of this metropolis, which has a population of almost 1.5 million.

1 MERCADO VER-O-PESO
Visitors looking to get a feel for local culture and the biodiversity of the Amazon region should head for the Ver-o-Peso Market, which has been operating since Belém's early

---

BOAT TRIPS AROUND BAÍA DE GUAJARÁ AND RIO GUAMÁ

These tours are a must for visitors who want to get to know the Amazon region. Visitors can see the lights of Belém at night; some trips allow passengers to get off the boat at certain points to walk along trails in the middle of the forest and see birds like macaws and small mammals like the agouti. **Valeverde Turismo** offers eight different trips, lasting from one-and-a-half hours to seven hours *(tel. (91) 3212-3388)*.

days. It used to be a customs house where merchandise was weighed, hence its name; *ver o peso* means "see the weight". The colors, aromas, and general atmosphere of the market make a visit worthwhile.

The market's 2,000 stalls sell mouth-watering delicacies, including fruits such as *muruci, bacuri, ingá,* and *taperebá* and interesting items like medicinal herbs to cure all ailments. Stay alert – even though the city maintains a police presence inside the market, pickpockets are still active.

Avenida Bulevar Castilho de França, no #, Centro. Daily, 8am – 6pm.

② MANGAL DAS GARÇAS

This interesting 40,000-square-meter (15,440-square-mile) park has landscaping that recreates the Amazon's ecosystems: dry-land forests, flood-land forests, and fields. The park opened in January 2005, and it boasts an aviary, a butterfly vivarium, artificial lakes, a lookout point, and a small navigation museum. Its excellent restaurant, the **Manjar das Garças**, serves sophisticated dishes with regional touches.

Passagem Carneiro da Rocha, no #, Cidade Velha, tel. (91) 3242-5052. Tue – Sun, 10am – 6pm; restaurant: Tue – Sun, noon – midnight.

NÚCLEO CULTURAL FELIZ LUSITÂNIA

The city's cultural hub is concentrated around Praça Frei Caetano Brandão and can be visited on foot. It was fully restored in 2002, and it includes two museums (the **Museu Forte do Presépio** and the **Museu de Arte Sacra**), the **Espaço Cultural Casa das Onze Janelas** cultural center, the **Igreja de Santo Alexandre**, and the **colonial buildings on Rua Padre Champagnat**.

③ MUSEU FORTE DO PRESÉPIO

This museum is the center point of the city. It was built in 1616, and it is known locally as Forte do Castelo. Fragments of cannons, swords, and porcelain were found during its restoration; now, they are displayed in

Formerly the customs house, Mercado Ver-o-Peso overlooks Baía de Guajará

the **Museu do Encontro**, which explains the history of the Portuguese colonization of the Amazon region. The museum also displays pieces of indigenous Tapajó and Marajoara pottery found at various archaeological sites in the Amazon.
Praça Frei Caetano Brandão, no #, Cidade Velha, tel. (91) 4009-8828. Tue – Sun, 10am – 6pm.

④ MUSEU DE ARTE SACRA
The former Palácio Episcopal (Bishop's Palace), built in 1883, houses a collection of 340 religious objects. Most of them are 18th-century wooden sculptures of saints. The museum is in the Igreja de Santo Alexandre annex.
Praça Frei Caetano Brandão, no #, Cidade Velha, tel. (91) 4009-8802. Tue – Sun, 10am – 6pm.

⑤ ESPAÇO CULTURAL CASA DAS ONZE JANELAS
This 18th-centruy building once housed the Royal Hospital. Now, it is a cultural center with a permanent exhibit of modern and contemporary art and a room dedicated to photography. The center's popular bar, **Boteco das Onze** *(Mon, 6pm until the last customer leaves; Tue – Sun, noon until the last customer leaves)*, offers a panoramic view of Guajará Bay and live music every night.
Praça Frei Caetano Brandão, no #, Cidade Velha, tel. (91) 4009-8821, 4009-8823. Tue – Sun, 10am – 6pm.

CULTURAL CIRCUIT

⑥ THEATRO DA PAZ
Built at the height of the Amazon rubber boom in 1878, this theater was restored and reopened in 2002. It regained all the splendor of its original architecture, which was inspired by La Scala in Milan. Note the mirrors, the crystal light fixtures, and the *pau-amarelo* parquet floor in the great hall. Italian Domenico de Angelis created the ceiling painting in the auditorium, which depicts the Greek god Apollo entering Amazonia pulled by horses. The theater holds plays and concerts, and the opera season is between July and August.
Rua da Paz, no #, Centro, tel. (91) 4009-8750. Tue – Fri, 9am – 5pm; Sat, 9am – 1pm (guided tours are offered every hour).

⑦ MUSEU PARAENSE EMÍLIO GOELDI
Opened in 1866, this museum is internationally renowned for its examination of the fauna, flora and customs of the Amazon region. Its 5.2 hectares (13 acres) house the **Parque Zoobotânico**, a zoo and aquarium with a rich collection of regional animals, as well as about 800 species of large trees. One

Theatro da Paz, built at the height of the rubber boom

interesting facet of the zoo: some of the animals are allowed to roam loose. Archaeology enthusiasts shouldn't miss the collection of at least 81,000 items, including fragments of pottery and stone from archaeological sites around the region. *Avenida Magalhães Barata, 376, São Brás, tel. (91) 3219-3369. Tue – Sun, 9am – 5pm.*

ESTAÇÃO DAS DOCAS

The port area is a small-scale version of the Puerto Madero in Buenos Aires, Argentina. It was somewhat rundown until it was restored in 2000, when it became one of Belém's most fashionable tourist spots. The four prefabricated iron warehouses that were imported from England in the early 20th century have been restored. Its 26 units include stores, bars, restaurants, and a movie theater. Visitors can find a great meal at **Lá em Casa**, a branch of the city restaurant that specializes

---

CÍRIO DE NAZARÉ: FAITH'S ULTIMATE EXPRESSION

On the second Sunday of October, more than a million people throng the city's streets in a demonstration of faith that takes over the streets of Belém. The procession honoring Nossa Senhora de Nazaré (Our Lady of Nazareth) is one of Brazil's most popular religious celebrations. The saint supposedly performed miracles after a statue bearing her image was found on the banks of the Murutucu *igarapé* (canal), the current site of the **Basílica de Nazaré** *(Praça Justo Chermont, no #, tel. (91) 4009-8400).* Pilgrims have been journeying to the site since 1793 and they now come from every corner of the state and country to follow the procession from the Igreja da Sé to the basilica. En route, the carriage that carries the statue is protected by a 400-meter rope barrier, which the faithful try to hold onto for the almost five-kilometer (three-mile) route. The religious fervor reaches its peak when followers kneel by the thousands to celebrate the arrival of Our Lady of Nazareth at the basilica.

in regional cuisine. Beer-lovers or anyone who wants to try something new should stop by **Amazon Beer**, which brews its own beer flavored with exotic *bacuri*, a regional fruit. It's also a good spot to see the sunset on **Baía de Guajará**, and it is the place to be at night, when live bands play on two suspended stages that move along two of the warehouses. Amazon Beer also hosts temporary

and permanent art and cultural exhibits, film events, and theater and folk performances on weekends. The complex has a boat terminal, which is the departure point for trips around the region.
Avenida Bulevar Castilho França, no #, Centro, tel. (91) 3212-5525. Sun – Tue, noon – midnight; Wed, noon – 1am; Thu – Sat, noon – 3am. Check the program schedule on: www.estacaodasdocas.com.br.

ILHA DE MARAJÓ

Marajó Island is the largest river island in the world. At 49,000 square kilometers (19,000 square miles), it is bigger than Switzerland or the entire state of Rio de Janeiro. This island is a world apart in the Amazon region. The east side is the most visited; it is overrun with buffalo ranches and dominated by wetlands, similar to the Pantanal in Mato Grosso, with a huge variety of visible birds and.

The coast has wild beaches. It takes about three hours by boat to get from Belém to Vamará, the island's main port. From there, a paved road (the only one on the island) leads to **Soure** and **Salvaterra**, where the island's tourist facilities are concentrated. The area's best accommodations are at **Pousada dos Guarás**, in Salvaterra *(Avenida Beira-Mar, no #, Praia Grande, tel. (91) 3765-1149)*. Make sure to visit the ruins of a Jesuit church built on Joanes Beach in the 18th century. Highlights in Soure – which is known as "the capital of Marajó" – include the buffalo ranches and the studios that produce Marajó ceramics, thus preserving the valuable heritage left by the island's ancestors. Beaches include coconut-palm-fringed **Praia do Pesqueiro.** One interesting note: The police who patrol Soure are mounted on buffalo. Don't miss the presentations of *carimbó* and *lundu*, two very sensual folk dances.
Boats to the port of Câmara leave from the passenger terminal at Belém, Avenida Marechal Hermes, no #, tel. (91) 9601-5312. Ferries depart from the Henvil Company port, in Icoaraci, Rua Siqueira

---

POROROCA, THE GREAT WAVE OF THE NORTH

The *pororoca* is one of the Amazon's most fascinating river phenomena. The "big roar" – the definition of *pororoca* in Tupi-Guarani – is a tidal current that occurs when the rivers are invaded by the sea during tidal floods to create huge waves. The sea swell is more intense between March and April. The waves are up to 3.5 meters (11 feet) high in places like the Capim River, which flows through the municipality of São Domingos do Capim, 130 kilometers (981 miles) from Belém. Since 1999, this town has hosted Pará's portion of the National Pororoca Surfing Championship. Surfers can also enjoy strong *pororocas* in the Canal do Perigoso between two islands, Ilha Mexiana and Ilha Caviana, and on the Araguari River in the state of Amapá.

Mendes, no #, beside the municipal waterfront warehouse, tel. (91) 3249-3400.

THE WEST AND NORTH SIDES

Most of Marajó's western side is forested. The main base in this region is **Breves**, the island's largest town, with boat access from Belém *(The Bom Jesus Company, Avenida Bernardo Sayão, 2000, tel. (91) 3272-1423)*. In the network of islets and channels called **Estreito de Breves**, visitors can come into contact with the Amazon jungle, which is exceptionally lush in this spot. **Afuá**, a whole town built almost entirely on stilts, is also located on the western side near the state of Amapá. To the north of Marajó, **Ilha Mexiana** offers accommodations in the jungle at the **Marajó Park Resort** with can be accessed by plane from Belém *(tel. (91) 3244-4613, www.marajoparkresort.com.br)*. This hotel organizes *pirarucu* (giant arapaima) fishing trips.

Buffalo ranch on Ilha de Marajó

BOAT TRIPS

Anyone who wants to explore the *furos* – branches of the river where the wetlands fauna are clearly visible – should go to the ports of Soure or Salvaterra to rent a *rabeta* (a boat that seats seven). The **Furo do Miguelão** on the Paracauari River is an excellent spot to observe animals. Make sure the boat operator belongs to the *rabeta* owners' association.

BUFFALO RANCHES

Several of Marajó's buffalo ranches are open to the public. Visitors can learn more about this Asian animal, as well as enjoy the wetlands scenery. **Fazenda Bom Jesus**, 12 kilometers (seven miles) from Soure, offers an educational program in which proprietor Eva Abufaiad, an agronomist and vet, explains how to take care of the animals and encourages visitors to ride them *(tel. (91) 3741-1243)*. **Fazenda Araruna**, two kilometers from the center of Soure, offers accommodations in the ranch house and boasts a river beach that is good for swimming *(tel. (91) 3741-1474, 9605-8674)*. Araruna is a great place to see flocks of scarlet ibis. **Fazenda São Jerônimo**, which served as the set for the Rede Globo TV program *No Limite*, also has *igarapés* and a private beach *(tel. (91) 3741-2093)*.

HISTORIC POTTERY

The ceramic traditions of the Marajoara Indians (who created stylized representations of animals) and the Tapajó Indians (who produced zoomorphic sculptures) are kept alive in several craft studios in Marajó and Icoaraci, a district of Belém. The locations are home to artists who both remain true to tradition and invent new everyday items with designs loosely based on ancestral patterns. Potter **Carlos Amaral**, whose studio is in Soure, is one artist who faithfully

A Tapajó vase

reproduces the ancient art of the Marajoaras. He has organized a small exhibit of original pieces on which he bases his work *(Travessa 20, 903, tel. (91) 3741-1172)*. Another respected craftsman, **Mestre Cardoso**, works in his pottery studio in his home in Icoaraci *(Rua 8 de Maio, passagem São Vicente de Paula, 1, tel. (91) 3247-0598)*.

SANTARÉM

With a population of nearly 300,000 inhabitants, Santarém is Pará's second largest city. It sits halfway between Manaus and Belém. Right in front of the city, at the intersection of the Tapajós River's dark green waters and the muddy Amazon, there is a spectacle similar to the famous "meeting of the waters" in Manaus. Santarém is a busy port where visitors have contact with local culture, as well as a good place to buy clothes and accessories made from *buriti* palm, banana tree straw, jute, *tucum* palm, and mallow *(malva sylvestris)* at **Dica Frazão's studio**. She even made handkerchiefs for Pope John Paul II *(Rua Floriano Peixoto, 281, tel. (93) 3522-1026; daily, 7am – 6pm)*. The best village in the area is **Alter do Chão**, which boasts beautiful river beaches. Visitors can also take a trip along the Tapajós River and its tributaries *(Santarém Tur, tel. (93) 3522-4847)*. It is best to come by boat or plane from Manaus or Belém. Rodovia BR-163 highway, which links the city to Cuiabá, is almost entirely dirt road and can be impassable during the rainy season from December to May.

RIVER BEACHES

The crystal-clear waters of the Tapajós River have earned the beaches around Alter do Chão the nickname "the Amazon Caribbean." Many of these beaches, which are 32 kilometers (20 miles) from Santarém, can be reached on foot: **Cururu**, **Ponta de Pedras**, and **Ilha do Amor**. Ilha do Amor is a sandbank in the middle of the river that only appears in the dry season between July and November, when the beaches are generally much more pleasant.

COMMUNITY TOURISM

One original way to explore the Amazon is to take one of a community ecological tourism trip organized by the NGO Projeto Saúde Alegria. It has been operating since 1987 on the Tapajós River, in conjunction with the riverside community. Groups leave Santarém in boats and spend a few days in communities served by the NGO. They interact with residents of the villages, and stay in local residents' houses and learn about their training courses, medical assistance, and cultural programs. At the same time, visitors can enjoy the region's forest and beach scenery.
Information: tel. (93) 3067-8000 or www.saudeealegria.org.br.

TOCANTINS

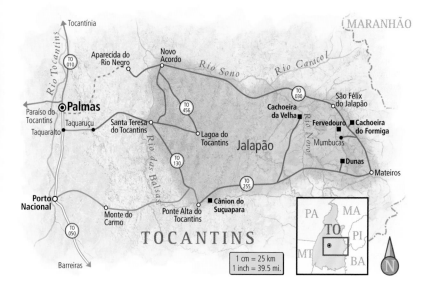

SUPPORT TOWN: PALMAS

Palmas, a planned city, is Brazil's youngest state capital. Construction began in 1988, the year Goiás was carved up to create the state of Tocantins. Palmas became the capital two years later. There's not much to see in the city itself; most people are only here to spend the night on their way to other places, like Jalapão, the region's most popular tourist destination. **Pousada dos Girassóis** *(103 Sul, conjunto 3, lote 44, tel. (63) 3219-4500)* is a good place to stay. The best restaurant in town is **Cabana do Lago** *(103 Sul, Rua SO, 9, lote 5, tel. (63) 3215-4989)*, which serves a very tasty *galinha de cabidela* (chicken stew enriched with blood). Thirty-two kilometers (20 miles) from Palmas are the waterfalls of the Taquaruçu district, a scenic area in the Serrra do Lajeado mountain range. It's worth visiting **Cachoeira do Roncador**, the largest of the region's 50 falls, which drops a stunning 50 meters (164 feet). The road to Taquaruçu is paved.
Additional information on hotels and restaurants on page 462.

HIGHLIGHTS

- The dunes of the Serra do Espírito Santo, and rafting on the Rio Novo, in **Jalapão**.

- The waterfalls of the **Serra do Lajeado**, near Palmas.

WHEN TO GO

- Between **May and September**, the dry season, for rafting on the Rio Novo, in Jalapão.
- During the rainy season (**October through April**), for those who seek adventure, because the poor state of the

roads in Jalapão make driving a challenging experience.
- In **January and February**, the height of the rainy season, for the best wildlife viewing and to witness the Cerrado savanna in all its splendor.

The emerald pool at the base of Cachoeira da Formiga waterfall, near Fervedouro

Jalapão

Jalapão is a vast wilderness in the northernmost reaches of the Brazilian Cerrado savannah. The name "Jalapão" comes from *jalapa*, an abundant local plant used to treat stomach ailments. The region is 34,000 square kilometers (8.5 million acres) in size, only slightly smaller than the state of Rio de Janeiro, and has a population density of less than one person per square kilometer. The area's countless rivers, lakes, waterfalls, dune fields, and plateaus make the state of Tocantins one of the most popular eco-tourism destinations in Brazil. Jalapão rewards visitors with unique experiences in wild places, but demands patience and a willingness to 'rough it' a bit. The state capital, Palmas, is a departure point for the towns of Ponte Alta do Tocantins and Mateiros, which many travelers use as bases for excursions into Jalapão. The 200-kilometer (124-mile) drive from Palmas to Ponte Alta is paved and therefore relatively easy. From Ponte Alta onward, however, it's a bumpy ride on dirt roads interrupted by enormous sand deposits. During the rainy season (October through April) a 4×4 vehicle is absolutely necessary.

Highlights

Though it is far from the most popular natural attractions, Ponte Alta has the best facilities in Jalapão. The only sight nearby, **Gruta do Suçuapara**, is an 18-kilometer (11-mile) drive from the town center. Gruta do Suçuapara is a 15-meter (49-foot) canyon-like crevice in the earth. Once inside, natural spray cools you from the rock walls above. Most of the region's other attractions are near the town of Mateiros, 155 kilometers (96 miles) from Ponte Alta, but Mateiros has only modest accommodations and few food options. The road from Ponte Alta to

Mateiros crosses the region's largest river, the **Rio Novo**, where, from May to September, local guides organize three-day rafting trips with riverside camping. The rapids are relatively gentle and don't require much experience. **Cachoeira da Velha**, on the Rio Novo, is the highest waterfall in Jalapão and marks the end of the rafting trip. Shaped like a horseshoe, it is 25 meters (82 feet) high and almost 100 meters (328 feet) wide. Its waters fall into a deep pool with a river beach suitable for bathing nearby. The

waterfall can also be accessed on foot. Near Mateiros, a dazzling sea of orange dunes contrasts with the Serra do Espírito Santo mountain range beyond. The scene is particularly beautiful at sunset. Some of the dunes reach heights of 40 meters (131 feet). **Fervedouro**, a crystal-clear pool fed by an underground spring, is a fabulous place to swim. The water gushes upward with significant force, keeping swimmers afloat. Not far from Fervedouro is **Cachoeira do Formiga**, a waterfall with an emerald pool.

HOW TO GET AROUND

Given the significant challenges posed by the region's minimalist infrastructure and active sands, the easiest way to explore Jalapão's natural beauty is with the help of a tour agency. **Korubo Expedições** organizes trips in comfortable truck-bus hybrids with panoramic windows and hatches in the vehicle roofs that enable visitors to fully enjoy the landscape. Korubo also provides its clients with accommodation at Safári Camp, a "luxury campsite" on the banks of the Rio Novo. The camp has comfortable tents, a kitchen, and chemical toilets *(tel. (11) 3582-6968; www.korubo.com.br).* Rafting trips are organized by **4 Elementos**. The company supplies

transportation in 4×4 vehicles, as well as all the equipment needed for rafting and camping. Rafting trips are best taken during the dry season (May through September), when torrential rains do not swell the rivers and muddy the roads *(tel. (45) 3529-6040 or www.4elementos.tur.br).* Should you wish to visit Jalapão on your own, two things are indispensable: a 4×4 vehicle and a local guide. Without these you will soon find yourself stuck in the sand or lost. Guides can be hired at **Pousada Planalto**, in Ponte Alta *(tel. (63) 3378-1141).* You can also rent a car, driver, and guide from **Jalapão Tour**, in Palmas *(tel. (63) 3214-6137, 9978-3695).*

CAPIM DOURADO

Before it became famous for crafts made from *capim dourado* (golden grass), the village of **Mumbucas**, near Mateiros, seemed lost to time and space. Its emergence from utter obscurity is largely the effort of a single woman: Dona Miúda. Dona is the matriarch of a community of indi-

viduals descended from slaves. It was she who taught the locals to weave the golden grass, which must be carefully gathered in September to preserve its characteristic color. Although the craft has spread beyond Mumbucas, the most beautiful baskets, bags, belts, bracelets, and sandals in Jala-

pão are those made and sold in the village. Nowadays they can also be purchased from stores in São Paulo and Rio de Janeiro.

Brazil's Central West region doesn't border the ocean, nor does it need to. Visitors come here to enjoy its wealth of cultural and natural attractions, particularly the architectural riches of Brasília, the diverse wildlife of the Pantanal region, and the eco-tourist mecca of Bonito, in Mato Grosso do Sul, where crystal-clear rivers teem with fish. The Pantanal region straddles two states, Mato Grosso and Mato Grosso do Sul. Cuiabá, state capital of Mato Grosso do Sul, is the gateway to the Chapada dos Guimarães mountains and the northern section of the Pantanal. The southern reaches of the Pantanal are best accessed through Campo Grande, capital of Mato Grosso. The capital city is also a good base for visitors en-route to Bonito. From Brasília and Goiânia, it's an easy drive to the historic cities of Pirenópolis and Goiás (where folk traditions are fiercely maintained), as well as the trails, waterfalls, and famous rock formations of the Chapada dos Veadeiros.

DISTRITO FEDERAL AND GOIÁS

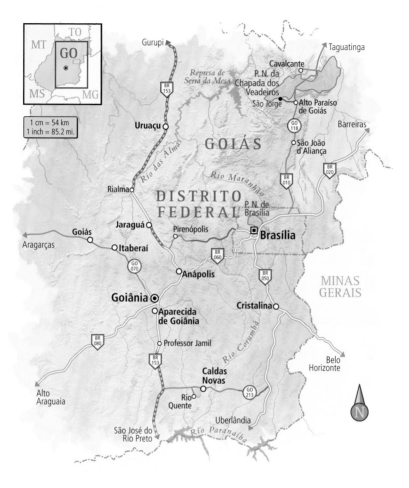

Gurupi

Taguatinga

Represa de
Serra da Mesa

Cavalcante

P. N. da
Chapada dos
Veadeiros

São Jorge

Alto Paraíso
de Goiás

Barreiras

Uruaçu

GOIÁS

GO
118

São João
d'Aliança

Rio das Almas

Rio Maranhão

Rialma

DISTRITO
FEDERAL

BR
010

P. N. de
Brasília

Jaraguá

Pirenópolis

Brasília

Goiás

Itaberaí

BR
060

Aragarças

GO
070

Anápolis

BR
050

MINAS
GERAIS

Goiânia

Aparecida
de Goiânia

Cristalina

BR
080

Professor Jamil

Rio Corumbá

BR
153

Caldas
Novas

Belo
Horizonte

Alto
Araguaia

Rio
Quente

GO
213

São José do
Rio Preto

Uberlândia

Rio Paranaíba

N

HIGHLIGHTS

- The works of Niemeyer (architecture), Lúcio Costa (urban planning), and Burle Marx (landscaping) in **Brasília**.
- The historic streets and religious festivals of **Pirenópolis** and **Goiás**.
- The waterfalls and Cerrado savannah of the **Chapada dos Veadeiros**.
- The hot springs of **Caldas Novas** and **Rio Quente**.

WHEN TO GO

- Between **April** and **July**, before the weather gets too dry in Brasília and Pirenópolis.
- Between **May** and **September** to avoid muddy trails in the Chapada dos Veadeiros.
- At **Easter** to see the Procissão do Fogaréu procession in Goiás.
- In **May** or **June** to enjoy the Festa do Divino Espírito Santo festival in Pirenópolis.

BRASÍLIA

Brasília, the nation's capital, impresses visitors before they've even had a chance to step off the plane. The aerial view afforded by a window seat and a clear day provides a bird's-eye view of the *plano piloto* (city layout) from above. The city is one of the largest planned urban spaces in the world. Its street grid, which itself looks like a plane, was designed by city planner Lúcio Costa. Brasília was inaugurated in 1960 and declared a Unesco world heritage site in 1987. Eixo Monumental Avenue is the city's central east-west axis, while Eixo Rodoviário is the main north-south thoroughfare. To the east (in the airplane's 'cockpit') is the center of national government and it is here that most of the buildings by the architect Oscar Niemeyer are clustered. Brasília is flanked to the northeast, east, and southeast by an artificial lake, Lago do Paranoá. The city itself is divided into sectors, including hotel, residential, and commercial areas. A car is a necessity; almost nobody walks to his or her destination because most places are too spread out. Thankfully, Brasília's roads are quite good compared to those of most Brazilian cities. Because the air is so dry (in winter the humidity dips below 30%) most public buildings are surrounded by ornamental ponds, which are also a welcome relief in the summer when temperatures climb to over 30 degrees Celsius (86 degrees Fahrenheit). The city is home to many works by great 20th-century Brazilian artists, including Athos Bulcão, Bruno Giorgi, Di Cavalcanti, and Portinari. With its population now approaching 2.5 million, the federal capital has quickly become a metropolis. Even so, there are extensive green areas.

Palácio da Alvorada

Palácio da Justiça

Teatro Nacional

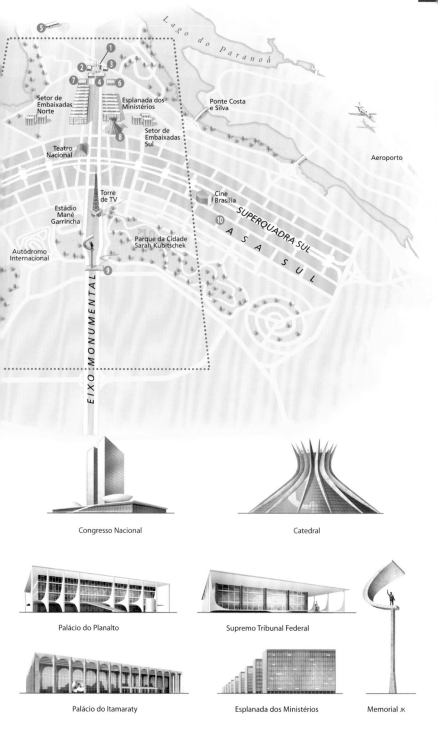

Lago do Paranoá

Setor de
Embaixadas
Norte

Esplanada dos
Ministérios

Ponte Costa
e Silva

Setor de
Embaixadas
Sul

Aeroporto

Teatro
Nacional

Torre
de TV

Cine
Brasília

Estádio
Mané
Garrincha

SUPERQUADRA SUL

Autódromo
Internacional

Parque da Cidade
Sarah Kubitschek

A S A   S U L

EIXO MONUMENTAL

Congresso Nacional

Catedral

Palácio do Planalto

Supremo Tribunal Federal

Palácio do Itamaraty

Esplanada dos Ministérios

Memorial JK

Congresso Nacional: the House of Representatives (foreground), the Senate

ARCHITECTURAL TOUR

❶ PRAÇA DOS TRÊS PODERES
From the center of Três Poderes Square it's an easy walk to Palácio do Planalto palace, the Congresso Nacional building, and the Supremo Tribunal Federal building. From here you can also see the famous *Os guerreiros (Candangos)* sculpture by Bruno Giorgi and the two parallel lines of ministry buildings that comprise the Esplanada dos Ministérios. It's a good idea to stop by the **Espaço Lúcio Costa** space, in the square's underground area, to see the enormous model of the original city plan *(tel. (61) 3325-6163; daily, 9am – 6pm).*

❷ PALÁCIO DO PLANALTO
Planalto Palace, the presidential office building, is the seat of Brazilian executive power. It is open to the public on Sundays when the president is not there. The thirty-minute tour includes a stop in the presidential office, which is viewed through an acrylic panel. Tours are limited to 25 people and generally form quickly. You can watch the changing of the guard (either the Presidential Guard or the

Independência Dragoons) every two hours, from 8am to 6pm.
Praça dos Três Poderes, no #, tel. (61) 3411-2317. Sun, 9:30am – 2:30pm. www.presidencia.gov.br

❸ SUPREMO TRIBUNAL FEDERAL (STF)
The Brazilian Supreme Federal Court offers curious visitors a half-hour guided tour of the courthouse. Exhibits in the judicial museum explore the court's storied history; the museum even houses a historic, full-scale assembly room, which was brought from Rio de Janeiro and reconstructed here in 1978. At the front of the building stands a famous granite statue known as *A justiça (Justice)*. It was sculpted by Alfredo Ceschiatti in 1961.
Praça dos Três Poderes, no #, tel. (61) 3217-4038. Sat, Sun, and holidays, 10am – 5:30pm. www.stf.gov.br

❹ CONGRESSO NACIONAL
One of Brasília's most distinctive landmarks is the National Congress building. The Congresso Nacional has two unique domes, one convex, the

other concave. It houses the national Senate, which is comprised of 81 senators (three from each of Brazil's 27 states), and the House of Representatives (Câmara dos Deputados), which is comprised of 513 state-elected representatives. Sessions of the Senate are convened under the convex dome, while House sessions take place under the concave one. When legislators are in session the Brazilian flag is hoisted in front of the corresponding dome. Guided tours of the complex are available and take about an hour. The building's halls are lined by works of art by Athos Bulcão, Di Cavalcanti, and other Brazilian artists.

Praça dos Três Poderes, no #, tel. (61) 3216-1771. Daily, 9:30am – 5pm. www.camara.gov.br e www.senado.gov.br

⑤ PALÁCIO DA ALVORADA

Alvorada Palace is the official presidential residence. It was designed by the architect Oscar Niemeyer. Like all his works, the palace has many unique features, including a marble and glass façade supported by white columns. The building was renovated in 2005. Visitors should set aside thirty minutes to see the staterooms (the Salão Nobre and the Salão de Estado), the library, and the banquet hall.

Via Presidencial, no #, tel. (61) 3411-2317. Wed, 3pm – 5:30pm.

⑥ PALÁCIO ITAMARATY

The Ministry of Foreign Relations is one of Niemeyer's loveliest buildings. It is better known as Itamaraty, its name before the capital moved from Rio to Brasília. One of its walkways arches over ornamental ponds with islands of tropical plants, then passes through one of the largest public art collections in Brazil. On the ground floor Niemeyer created an impressive 220-square-meter

(2,400-square-foot) hall with no support columns, as well as an equally impressive 8-foot-wide spiral staircase with no handrail. Athos Bulcão is the talented artist behind the relief images on the ministry's marble walls. The garden with plants from the Amazon region was designed by Burle Marx, and the *Meteoro* sculpture, made in 1967 from a single 4-ton block of Carrera marble, is the work of Bruno Giorgi. The palace also houses sculptures by Maria Martins, Vítor Brecheret, and Alfredo Ceschiatti, and paintings by Portinari, Manabu Mabe, and Alfredo Volpi, as well as foreign artists like Frans Post and Debret. On the upper level visitors can see the desk on which Princess Isabel signed the Lei Áurea, the law that abolished slavery, in 1888. Visits need to be arranged in advance.

Esplanada dos Ministérios, tel. (61) 3411-8051 (during visiting hours). Mon – Wed, 2pm – 4:30pm, every 50 minutes; Thu and Fri, 2pm – 4:30pm, every 25 minutes; Sat, Sun, and holidays, 10am – 3:30pm, every 30 minutes. www.mre.gov.br

⑦ PALÁCIO DA JUSTIÇA

The Ministry of Justice was constructed in the same style as Itamaraty, its neighbor across the street.

The spiral staircase in Itamaraty

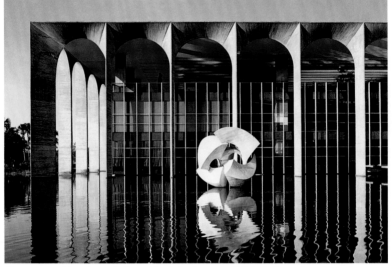

Meteoro, a marble sculpture by Bruno Giorgi, dominates the Palácio do Itamaraty water garden

The ministry has its own unique features, however, including a cascading water garden designed by landscape architect Burle Marx. The library has a desk and chair that belonged to José Bonifácio de Andrada e Silva, advisor to Dom Pedro I and father of Brazilian Independence. In the auditoriums film reviewers determine ratings classifications for movies that will be released around the country. Thirty-minute guided tours are available and must be arranged in advance by phone or e-mail. In the same building, **Salão Negro** hosts rotating exhibitions whose themes generally relate to citizenship and human rights. *Unfortunately, the palace is currently closed to the public, and it is not clear when it will re-open. We recommend you call for the latest news. Esplanada dos Ministérios, bloco T, tel. (61) 3429-3216. cerimonial@mj.gov.br*

❽ Catedral Metropolitana

Metropolitan Cathedral is a Brasília icon. Its architecture diverges wildly from that of most churches. The building, designed by Niemeyer, has a distinctive circular shape, with white supports that curve inward and meet at the top like a crown. Inside, light filters through colorful stained-glass windows by Marianne Peretti. Paintings by Di Cavalcanti depict the Holy Way. Alfredo Ceschiatti sculpted the four bronze apostles in front of the building and the three suspended angels inside it. One of the interior panels was painted by Athos Bulcão. *Esplanada dos Ministérios, no #, tel. (61) 3224-4073. Mon – Sat, 8am – 5pm; Tue – Fri and Sun, 8am – 6pm. www.catedral.org.br*

❾ Memorial JK

The JK Memorial is a splendid tribute to the city's founder, former Brazilian President Juscelino Kubitschek. The white, marble, pyramid-shaped building was inaugurated in 1981, five years after the former president perished in a car accident on Rodovia Presidente Dutra highway in São Paulo. A 28-meter-tall statue of Kubitschek stands in front. The Memorial houses his private library, personal items, and a display containing the papers and objects he had with him when he died. The president's burial chamber is on the upper floor.

Eixo Monumental Oeste, Praça do Cruzeiro, no #, tel. (61) 3225-9451. Tue – Sun, 9am – 6pm (open daily Jan, Feb, and July). www.memorialjk.com.br

⑩ **IGREJINHA NOSSA SENHORA DE FÁTIMA**

Tiny, beautiful Nossa Senhora de Fátima church was constructed in 1958, the first house of worship in Brasília. The Kubitschek family built it to fulfill a vow of thanks when their daughter Márcia was cured of a disease. From the outside, the church looks like a tile-covered nun's coif. It was designed by Athos Bulcão, and its stylized figures represent the Holy Spirit and the Star of the Nativity.

EQS 307/308, tel. (61) 3242-0149. Mon, 9am – 8pm; Tue – Sun, 6:30am – 8pm.

LEISURE

Parque Sarah Kubitschek, better known as **Parque da Cidade,** is Brasília's largest recreation area, 400 hectares (988 acres) of green space landscaped by Burle Marx. The park has numerous restaurants, a go-kart track, horseback riding, bicycle paths, and an amusement park *(Eixo Monumental Oeste, tel. (61) 3325-1092)*. Arts and crafts aficionados may enjoy a visit to **Feira da Torre** fair, which is held on Saturdays and Sundays near the **Torre de Televisão**. The top of the television tower is 75 meters (246 feet) up, providing great views of the city *(Eixo Monumental Sul, tel. (61) 3321-7944; Tue – Sun, 9am – 5:45pm; Mon, 2pm – 5:45pm)*. For a truly bird's eye perspective, try a **panoramic helicopter flight** with Esat Aerotáxi. Their 12-minute flights pass over Lago do Paranoá, Palácio da Alvorada, Parque da Cidade, the Memorial JK, Nelson Piquet autodrome, and Mané Garrincha stadium.

Contact: Esat Aerotáxi, tel. (61) 3323-8777.

CULTURE

Museu de Valores, located in the Banco Central headquarters, exhibits coins from Brazil and abroad, as well as the biggest gold nugget ever found in Brazil, a 60,820 kilo (134,000 pound) monster *(SBS, quadra 3, bloco B, 1^0 subsolo, tel. (61) 3414-2093; Tue – Fri, 9:30am – 5:30pm; Sat and Sun, 2pm – 6pm. www.bcb.gov.br)*. Shows, plays, films, and exhibitions are hosted by cultural centers around the city. **Centro Cultural Banco do Brasil** is one such center. The building was designed by Niemeyer and is now a national heritage site *(SCES, trecho 2, lote 22, tel. (61) 3310-7087; Tue – Sun, 9am; check the program schedule on their site: www.bb.com.br/cultura)*. At least twice a year film lovers flock to Brasília to celebrate cinema. The **Festival de Brasília de Cinema Brasileiro** is held every November. It screens new movies and awards honors to the best Brazilian feature films *(www.sc.df.gov.br)* . Up to 20,000 people arrive in Brasília every July for the **Festival Internacional de Cinema – FIC Brasília**. The festival features independent films from Brazil and around the world *(www.ficBrasília.com.br)*.

THE CANDANGOS

Construction of Brazil's new capital Brasília required many thousands of workers, most of whom came from the Northeast and settled in Brasília's satellite cities. These workers came to be known as "*candangos*," a derogatory term formerly used by Africans to refer to the Portuguese. To-day, the word no longer carries a pejorative connotation, and is instead used to describe city residents or natives.

PIRENÓPOLIS

Charming Pirenópolis is a popular weekend destination for Brasília residents. The town is 140 kilometers (87 miles) from Brasília and 125 kilometers (78 miles) from Goiânia *(see page 401)*. During the week its streets are quiet – many restaurants don't even bother to open – but on Saturdays and Sundays its narrow lanes and bars fill to overflowing. The weekend arts and crafts fair in the town center is a popular place to find hand-woven items and silver and wood jewelry. The streets of the center are paved with quartz cobblestones and are best explored on foot. **Rua Direita** is particularly charming, as it was here that the first mansions were built in the 18th century. Pirenópolis' history dates back to the gold rush, when pioneers found gold in the Almas River at the foot of the Serra dos Pireneus. These prospectors founded the town in 1727. **Igreja Matriz Nossa Senhora do Rosário**, an early 17th-century church, was damaged by fire in 2002 but has been restored *(Praça da Matriz, no #)*. Built in only four years beginning in 1750, **Igreja do Bonfim** still has its original altar. It also has an imposing cedar statue of Senhor do Bonfim. According to legend, 250 slaves carried the statue on foot from Bahia *(Rua do Bonfim, no #)*. While in Pirenópolis, you might want to pass by **Cine Pireneus** to admire its 1936 art deco façade. The theater also sells sweets and *castanha de baru*, popular regional nuts *(Rua Direita, no #)*.

WATERFALLS AND ROCKS

Don't risk getting lost on solo trips into the surrounding wilderness. We recommend you hire a guide from the **Tourist Information Center**, where you can also obtain information on agencies specializing in adventure sports *(CAT – Centro de Apoio ao Turista, Rua do Bonfim, 14, tel. (62) 3331-2633)*.

WATERFALL TOUR
Reserva Ecológica de Vargem Grande nature reserve has parking facilities, well sign-posted trails, toilets, and a bar. Trails to the park's waterfalls are short: it's only 500 meters (less than half a mile) to Cachoeira Santa Maria and only 1,800 meters (1 mile) to Cachoeira do Lázaro. To reach the reserve, you have to drive on a largely unpaved road 11 kilometers (7 miles) to the **Parque Estadual da Serra dos Pireneus**, 20 kilometers (12 miles) from Pirenópolis. The park's highest peak is 1,385 meters (4,544 feet) and offers a great view from the top. Four natural pools, the Pocinhos do Sonrisal, are nearby. There are eight waterfalls in the reserve's **Várzea do Lobo** region, known collectively as the Cachoeiras dos Dragões and varying in height from 3 to 70 meters (10 to 230 feet). A trail that leads past the falls takes four hours, but it's necessary to set aside a whole day due to the poor state of the 43-kilometer (28-mile) road.

CIDADE DE PEDRA
Dozens of sandstone and quartz rock formations in the shape of towers and natural amphitheaters form the Cidade de Pedra (City of Rock). Tourist facilities are nowhere to be found, and tourists may not enter the area without a guide. The "city" sits 51 kilometers (32 miles) from Pirenópolis, a two hour journey by car on unpaved road.

THE FEAST OF THE HOLY SPIRIT

Pirenópolis is famous for its festival in honor of the Holy Spirit. The festival, known as Festa do Divino Espírito Santo, is held fifty days after Easter. It is one of the oldest religious events in the country, though it is not native to Brazil. The festival actually originated in the Middle Ages, and was brought to Brazil by the Portuguese. Pirenópolis celebrated the holiday for the first time in 1826, and the town's unique folkloric and theatrical contributions ensure that festivities here are different from those held elsewhere. Locals begin preparations 20 days in advance by asking for donations from local farms. Many churches hold a daily Mass and novena, watched over by a banner of the Holy Spirit. Then, on Pentecost Sunday, the 'reigning Emperor of the Holy Spirit' leads a celebratory procession and a new emperor is chosen. During these days of fevered excitement, the sacred and profane join together in processions, firework displays, masked parades, medieval dramatic presentations, dances, and simulated cavalry battles known as *cavalhadas*. The *cavalhadas* are held in the town football stadium. There are three days of simulated cavalry battles between Christian warriors, led by Charlemagne (who was crowned emperor by Pope Leo II in 800), and the Moors, who controlled the Iberian Peninsula and tried to impose Islam on the region. On the first day, the Christians, dressed in blue, enter the stadium from the west, while the Moors, dressed in red, enter from the east. A Moorish spy has infiltrated the Christian ranks but is caught and killed, which provokes a battle. In the second day, the Moors are defeated by the Christians and baptized by a priest. Finally, Christians and Moors enter from the west and take part in friendly competitions to celebrate the conversion of the Moors. A museum dedicated to the *cavalhadas* exhibits costumes and implements used in the festivities *(Rua Direita, 39, tel. (62) 3331-1166. Daily, 10am – noon and 2pm – 6pm).*

CHAPADA DOS VEADEIROS

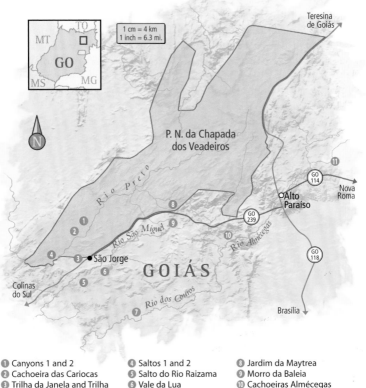

1 cm = 4 km
1 inch = 6.3 mi.

Teresina de Goiás

P. N. da Chapada dos Veadeiros

Rio Preto

Rio São Miguel

São Jorge

GOIÁS

Colinas do Sul

Rio dos Couros

Alto Paraíso

Nova Roma

Rio Almécegas

Brasília

① Canyons 1 and 2
② Cachoeira das Cariocas
③ Trilha da Janela and Trilha do Abismo
④ Saltos 1 and 2
⑤ Salto do Rio Raizama
⑥ Vale da Lua
⑦ Cataratas dos Couros
⑧ Jardim da Maytrea
⑨ Morro da Baleia
⑩ Cachoeiras Almécegas
⑪ Cachoeira do Vale do Rio Macaco

The highest of Brazil's plateaus, Chapada dos Veadeiros, was named for the deer hunts (*veado*) that used to take place here. The plateau stands at the same latitude as Machu Picchu, in Peru, and rises to an altitude of 1,200 meters (3,900 feet). Several of the region's rivers have headwaters here. Because of its location and its abundance of quartz crystal, toward the end of the 20th century the area drew people interested in mysticism. It has lost some of its "mystic" appeal, but what remains is nature at its most beautiful. The Cerrado savannah provides habitat for pampas deer, maned wolves, rheas, and jaguars. One of the most popular destinations is **Parque Nacional da Chapada dos Veadeiros**, but there's plenty to see outside its boundaries. We recommend renting a guide and a 4×4 vehicle. The best time to visit is during the dry season (May - September).

OUR RECOMMENDATION

Casa Rosa Pousada das Cerejeiras, in Alto Paraíso, is formerly a private residence, that was renovated and now has four large rooms with bathrooms as well as eight comfortable chalets for up to five people. The beauty of this guesthouse is complemented by its attentive service *(Rua Gumercindo Barbosa, 233, Centro, tel. (62) 3446-1319)*.

Additional information on page 462.

ALTO PARAÍSO DE GOIÁS AND SÃO JORGE

Alto Paraíso de Goiás and São Jorge are good places to stay if you want to explore the plateau. Alto Paraíso is 230 kilometers from Brasília, on Rodovia GO-118 highway. It is the "mystic" capital of the Planalto Central. Incense and new age music are part of daily life for the locals, who are dependent on eco-tourism. Though tourist facilities are limited, they are still the best the area has to offer. One of the most popular local activities is to admire the sunset from the "**airport**," a landing strip built for UFOs that has been abandoned. You can hire guides and pick up information on adventure sports excursions at the Tourist Information Center (*Centro de*

Apoio ao Turista, Avenida Ari Ribeiro Valadão Filho, 1100, Centro, tel. (62) 3446-1159). A further 36 kilometers (22 miles) on Rodovia GO-239 highway will take you to the quiet village of **São Jorge** and the entrance to Chapada dos Veadeiros National Park. The village has only had electricity for a decade and tourist facilities are minimal. Park guides tend to be former prospectors who know the region well – ask your guesthouse to recommend one, since there is no tourist information center in São Jorge. A guide is recommended or obligatory for all the attractions listed in the pages to follow, with the exception of Jardim de Maytrea.

PARQUE NACIONAL DA CHAPADA DOS VEADEIROS

Chapada dos Veadeiros National Park was created in 1961. The park spans 65,000 hectares (161,000 acres) at an altitude of 1,400 to 1,700 meters (4,600 to 5,600 feet). Spring is a

particularly colorful season here, as orchids, bromeliads, and meadows full of *buriti* palms and straw flowers burst into bloom. The Visitors' Center has drinking water and bathrooms,

Cachoeira das Cariocas, a waterfall in Parque Nacional da Chapada dos Veadeiros

including one for the disabled. There is
no restaurant, however, so we
recommend you bring snacks and
water bottles. Two trails leave from the
center. The first is 6.7 kilometers
(4 miles) long and leads to **Cachoeira
das Cariocas**, a waterfall with a
10-meter (32-foot) drop, as well as
Preto River **Canyons 1 and 2**. Access
to Canyon 1, which extends back
1.5 kilometers (1 mile), is not possible
between November and July because
of the rains. The second canyon trail is
4.5 kilometers (3 miles) long and its
grade is steeper. It skirts rapids and
leads to the **Rio Preto waterfalls**. One
of the falls, Salto 1, is 80 meters (262
feet) high and has natural pools at the
bottom. Salto 2 is 120 meters (393
feet) high. From the top you can enjoy
a fantastic view of the valley. These
trips are not for children under five,
but small children can go on a 400-
meter trail that leads to a river close to
the Visitors' Center. The park is located
at the end of a 1-kilometer stretch of
dirt road from São Jorge. Park visitors
must be accompanied by a guide. You

Salto 1 waterfall, with its 80-meter drop

can hire one in Alto Paraíso or São
Jorge. Guides are also sometimes
available at the park Visitors' Center if
you arrive early enough in the day.
*Tel. (62) 3455-1116. Tue – Sun, 8am –
6pm; entry not allowed after noon.*

AROUND THE PARK

VALE DA LUA
The rather surprising groups
of rock formations known as the Vale
da Lua are bisected by the São
Miguel River. They look like the
surface of the moon, and 'Vale da
Lua' is in fact Portuguese for 'Moon
Valley.' There are rock pools suitable
for bathing. We recommend you
wear shoes with non-slip soles,
as the rocks are very slippery.
The trail to the formations is easy
and short, less than a mile round-trip.
You'll find the turn-off 35 kilometers
(22 miles) from Alto Paraíso, on the
road to São Jorge.

TRILHA DA JANELA E DO ABISMO
Janela e do Abismo trail leads to the
Cachoeira do Abismo waterfall and
promises hikers a spectacular view of
the waterfalls known as Saltos 1 and 2.
In the winter Cachoeira do Abismo
disappears. Be forewarned: the steep
5.5-kilometer (3-mile) trek leaves even
the guides (you must have one)
gasping for breath. The trailhead is
1 kilometer from São Jorge.

CATARATAS DOS COUROS
After a 3-kilometer trek visitors are
rewarded with wonderful rock faces,
plunging waterfalls, and the rapids and

natural pools of the Rio dos Couros. The falls are 52 kilometers (32 miles) from Alto Paraíso. They are also known as the Cachoeiras de São Vicente.

VALE DO RIO MACACO

The waterfalls and canyons along the pleasant Macaco River can be appreciated by car and on foot. Guides lead day-trips that generally include 52 kilometers (32 miles) in a 4×4 vehicle and a steep walk at the end. Rappelling and canyoning are popular activities during the dry season (May to October).

MORE WATERFALLS
AND LOOKOUT POINTS

The region certainly isn't experiencing a waterfall shortage. **Almécegas 1 and 2**, located on Fazenda São Bento farm, are both impressive. The former has a particularly grand 50-meter (164-foot) drop. The trail to the falls begins 12 kilometers (7 miles) from Alto

OUR RECOMMENDATION

🍽 Halfway between Alto Paraíso de Goiás and São Jorge, **Rancho do Waldomiro** restaurant serves *matula*, also known as Cerrado *feijoada*. A typical cattleman's dish, it contains sun-dried beef, sausage, pork offal, white beans, and manioc flour. Because *matula* is a time-intensive recipe we recommend stopping by early to order the dish, then returning later to enjoy it (*Estrada Alto Paraíso–São Jorge, Km 18*).

Additional information on page 462.

Paraíso; three kilometers of this distance is dirt road. It's then a 1,600-meter (1-mile) walk to Almécegas 1 and a further 300 meters or so to Almécegas 2. There are also a number of places between Alto Paraíso and São Jorge where drivers can stop to admire the area's natural beauty. One such place, at Km 20 on the road to São Jorge, is **Jardim de Maytrea,** which has groves of *buriti* palms and postcard-perfect views.

In the Chapada dos Veadeiros region, springs feed the many rivers

CITY OF GOIÁS

Goiás Velho, as everyone calls the city of Goiás, enchants its visitors and its native population (of some 27,000 residents) alike. The charming streets and 18th-century colonial buildings cast a spell over Unesco inspectors, as well. They declared it a world heritage site in 2001. The town is 141 kilometers (88 miles) from Goiânia *(see page 401)* and 320 kilometers (199 miles) from Brasília on Rodovia GO-070 highway. It was founded in 1727 by explorer Bartolomeu Bueno da Silva Filho, also known as Anhangüera. The town grew in a haphazard manner during the gold rush, and the uneven, poorly-planned streets wreak havoc with traffic in the Historical Center to this day. The best spot for a bird's eye view of the tangle of roadways is the Alto de Santana lookout point in front of **Igreja de Santa Bárbara**. One hundred steps lead up to the church *(Rua Passo da Pátria)*. Goiás was the state capital until 1937. Every year, to commemorate its July 25 birthday, it becomes the capital once again from July 24 to July 26. Two

other significant events held annually in Goiás are the **Procissão do Fogaréu,** a Holy Week procession, and **Fica,** the International Environmental Film Festival, in June.

CASA DE CORA CORALINA

The city's main attraction is the home of local poet Cora Coralina. The small house on the banks of the Vermelho River was built in 1770. The house was where Cora, her mother, and her grandfather were raised. She lived in Goiás until she was 22, then moved to São Paulo. She returned when she was 66 and lived here until she died. Although Cora had only three years

OUR RECOMMENDATION

🍽️ **Paróchia** serves delicious, sauce-covered dishes, like *filé ao conde d'arcos*, filet mignon in mustard and caper sauce. We recommend the *empadão goiano*, a traditional savory pie *(Praça Doutor Tasso de Camargo, 18, Centro, tel. (62) 3371-3291).*

Additional information on page 462.

CALDAS NOVAS AND RIO QUENTE

The thermal pools of **Caldas Novas,** Goiás's most popular tourist destination, entertain and rejuvenate over 1 million visitors a year. The pools, fed by underground hot springs, can reach temperatures of up to 57 degrees Celsius (135 degrees Fahrenheit). Caldas Novas is 160 kilometers (99 miles) from Goiânia *(see page 401)* and 295 kilometers (183 miles) from Brasília. Neighboring **Rio Quente** is 30 kilometers (19 miles) away and has hot springs, as well. Tourist facilities are plentiful and include an airport, hotels that cater to families, and several water parks. At the end of the school year hordes of students come here to celebrate graduation. This can be more than a little disturbing for anyone seeking peace and quiet. The Rio Quente Resorts complex provides employment for nearly all of the town's 2,000 inhabitants. The resort owns **Hot Park**, a water park with slides and pools with currents *(tel. (64) 3452-8000;* *Tue, Wed, and Fri – Sun, 9:30am – 5pm).* Since the park is open to guests and non-guests alike, anyone wishing to stay in a more conventional hotel can stay at the Parque das Primaveras, in Caldas Novas, and still take advantage of Hot Park's facilities. If you can tear yourself away from the warm pools, you might want to think about exploring the waterfalls of **Parque Estadual da Serra de Caldas Novas** *(tel. (64) 3453-5805; daily, 8am – 3pm),* as well.

Igreja do Rosário (background), a Unesco world heritage site located in Goiás Velho

of schooling, reading was her passion. She published her first book at the age of 75, with two more published before her death in 1985, at age 95. A further six books were published posthumously. Her bedroom, kitchen, and the room where she wrote about simple, everyday life have been kept exactly as she left them. The house was flooded by river water at the end of 2001, but the entire collection of documents was saved and the house was reopened in 2002.

Rua Dom Cândido Penso, 20, Centro, tel. (62) 3371-1990. Tue – Sat, 9am – 4:45pm; Sun, 9am – 1pm.

IGREJA DE SÃO FRANCISCO DE PAULA

Goiás's third church was built in 1761. It has a beautiful staircase leading to an atrium. Paintings on the chapel ceilings and the main body of the church depict scenes from the life of Saint Francis. They were painted in 1869 by André Antônio da Conceição.

Praça Zaqueu Alves de Castro, no #, Centro.

MUSEU DAS BANDEIRAS

The Bandeiras Museum building was constructed in 1766. Up until 1937, when the capital was moved to Goiânia, it contained the municipal government headquarters on the upper floor and a jail on the lower floor. Declared a national heritage site in 1950, it is now a museum. The museum exhibits three hundred 18th-

---

GOIÂNIA

Goiás, the leafy, well-planned state capital, is 210 kilometers (130 miles) from Brasília. It serves as a base for anyone visiting Goiás Velho (141 kilometers, or 88 miles, away) or Caldas Novas (172 kilometers, or 142 miles, away). **Castro's Park** is among the city's more sophisticated hotels *(Avenida República do Líbano, 1520, setor Oeste, tel. (62) 3096-2000).* For something to eat, try **Chão Nativo 1**. The restaurant's self-service buffet offers regional food, 40 hot dishes kept warm on a wood-burning stove, and a variety of salads, liqueurs, and desserts *(Avenida República do Líbano, 1890, setor Oeste, tel. (62) 3223-5396; Mon – Fri, 11am – 3:30pm; Sat, Sun, and holidays, 11am – 4pm).*

---

and 19th-century artifacts related to the history of the occupation of the Central West and the formation of Goiás' society. The most interesting exhibit is the "*enxovia*," a dank dungeon where prisoners were kept and accessed directly from the courthouse by means of a trap door. If a defendant found guilty, the trap door would open and he would be sent straightaway to the dungeon. Museum restoration work was completed in 2006.
Praça Brasil Ramos Caiado, no #, Centro, tel. (62) 3371-1087. Tue – Sat, 9am – 5pm; Sun, 9am – 1pm.

PALÁCIO CONDE D'ARCOS

Built in 1755, the palace was once the seat of state government. It

regains this status every year between July 24 and 26, when Goiás celebrates its birthday. Ninety-eight governors from the imperial, colonial, and republican eras lived here. Accordingly, the palace furniture collection spans the 18th, 19th, and 20th centuries. Today, the palace serves as a cultural center, hosting exhibitions, book launches, and talks.
Praça Doutor Tasso de Camargo, 1, Centro, tel. (62) 3371-1200. Tue – Sat and holidays, 8am – 5pm; Sun, 9am – 1pm.

SERRA DOURADA

The lovely mountain range flanking Goiás Velho contains a state park and a biological reserve, that can only be visited with a guide. The park has no tourist facilities. Guides familiar with the region are available for hire *(tel. (62) 9651-4979)*. Visitors should be prepared for a 47-kilometer (29-mile) drive into the park, some of it on dirt road. At 1,050 meters (3,445 feet), the views from nearby escarpments are gorgeous, and the area has many beautiful streams and rock formations.

OUR RECOMMENDATION

Charming is the only word that best describes the two-hundred-year-old farmhouse **Pousada Dona Sinhá**. The tiny inn has colonial-style décor, eight guest rooms, and a comfortable, home-like atmosphere *(Rua Padre Arnaldo, 13, Centro, tel. (62) 3371-1667)*.

Additional information on page 462.

PROCISSÃO DO FOGARÉU, A UNIQUE SPECTACLE

Nearly 10,000 people fill the streets of **Goiás Velho** during Easter to watch the Procissão do Fogaréu, the only spectacle of its kind in Brazil. As has been done for the past 200 years, all the lights in the city are turned off or quenched at midnight on Wednesday of Holy Week. Forty hooded men light flares in front of Igreja da Boa Morte *(Rua Luís do Couto, no #)*, pictured to the

right, and walk through the town center to the beat of drums. They represent the Pharisees, who persecuted Jesus and encouraged his arrest. A crowd carrying candles joins the group on the way to the Igreja do Rosário, where a table is prepared for a symbolic Last Supper *(Largo do Rosário, no #)*. Afterward, the procession heads for Igreja de São Francisco de Paula, which represents the

Garden of Gethsemane *(Praça Zaqueu Alves de Castro, no #)*. Here, the hooded figures encounter Jesus, represented by an elegant banner. The banner is a replica of the original, which was painted by José Joaquim da Veiga Vale (1806-74), an important local artist. When the banner is lowered, trumpets sound, the bishop delivers a sermon, and Jesus is symbolically arrested and crucified.

MATO GROSSO AND MATO GROSSO DO SUL

AMAZONAS

PARÁ

RONDÔNIA

TOCANTINS

Porto
Velho

BR
174

Alta Floresta

Colíder

Sinop

Sorriso

MATO
GROSSO

Comodoro

Nobres

Nova Mutum

P. N. da Chapada
dos Guimarães

BR
163

Pontes e
Lacerda

Cuiabá

Chapada dos
Guimarães

D. F.

Cáceres

Poconé

Barão de
Melgaço

GOIÁS

BOLÍVIA

PANTANAL
NORTE

Porto
Jofre

BR
364

Goiânia

P. N. do Pantanal
Mato-grossense

PANTANAL
SUL

MATO
GROSSO
DO SUL

MINAS
GERAIS

N

Puerto
Suárez

Corumbá

Aquidauana

Miranda

Campo
Grande

BR
262

Bodoquena

Anastácio

São Paulo

P. N. da Serra
da Bodoquena

Bonito

SÃO PAULO

Ourinhos

PARAGUAI

SÃO PAULO

1 cm = 175 km
1 inch = 276 mi.

PARANÁ

Cascavel

HIGHLIGHTS

- The **Transpantaneira Highway**, a highway in Northern Pantanal.
- **Acorizal Reserve**, at the confluence of the Rio Cuiabá and the Rio Paraguai.
- Cidade de Pedra in **Chapada dos Guimarães**.

- Pousada Recanto Barra Mansa and Fazenda Rio Negro in **Southern Pantanal**.
- Gruta do Lago Azul and Abismo Anhumas in **Bonito**.
- River floating in **Bonito** and **Nobres**.

WHEN TO GO

- From **March** to **October** to fish.
- From **June** to **October** to see the animals.
- From **December** to **February** for the waterfalls in the Chapada dos Guimarães although torrential rains mean this time of year is not good for walking.
- From **January** to **April** to see the floodplains, although this period can be too hot for some people.
- From **May** to **September** to go river floating in Bonito and Nobres, when the rivers are clearest, although some waterfalls dry up completely during this period.

Northern Pantanal

Northern Pantanal corresponds to the section of the floodplain in the state of Mato Grosso. Paved access roads from the state capital, Cuiabá provide access to two frequent tourist destinations: Cáceres and Poconé. The former, located on the banks of the Paraguai River, is famous for fishing. Cáceres is located at the beginning of the Rodovia Transpantaneira, a 145-kilometer (90-mile) dirt road with several ranches, guesthouses, and abundant wildlife. At the end of the Transpantaneira, visitors can take a boat to the Pantanal National Park and the NGO Ecotrópica's nature reserves in the Serrra do Amolar mountain range, which offers dazzling scenery.

Cuiabá

Cuiabá has the region's only airport, as well as several tourist agencies and road connections to the Northern Pantanal's main attractions. Once a prospecting settlement, Cuiabá grew on the banks of the river that gave the city its name. Now, it is a thriving metropolis with half a million inhabitants, although it still retains its cultural traditions. One of the most popular and pleasant things to do in Cuiabá is eat at a *peixaria*, a restaurant that serves freshwater fish. Two recommendations: **Peixaria Popular** *(Avenida São Sebastião, 2324, Goiabeiras, tel. (65) 3322-5471; Mon – Sat, 11:30am – 4pm and 7:30pm until the last customer leaves; Sun, 11am – 4pm)* and **Porto da Conceição** *(Passagem da Conceição, no # (the road to the ferry), Várzea Grande, tel. (65) 3625-3802; Thu – Sat, 11am – 10pm; Sun, 11am – 4pm)*. For local culture, visit **Sesc Casa do Artesão**, a store selling crafts and everyday objects from the Pantanal. A museum in its basement displays works from all over the state *(Rua 13 de Junho, 315, Porto, tel. (65) 3322-3220, 3322-2047; Mon – Fri, 9am – 6pm; Sat, 9am – 2pm)*. Also worth a visit is **Sesc Arsenal**, the best cultural center in Cuiabá, which offers a wide program of events *(Rua 13 de Junho, no #, Porto, tel. (65) 3616-6900, 3616-6914; Mon, 8am – 6pm; Tue – Fri, 8am – 11pm; Sat and Sun, 4pm – 8pm. Bar (Choperia): Tue – Sun, 5pm – 11pm)*.

Cáceres

After the Paraguai River flows flowing down the Serra das Araras mountains, it meets the extreme north of the floodplain at Cáceres, 215 kilometers (134 miles) from Cuiabá. This charming city, with a population of 85,000, preserved its buildings from the 19th century, when it was the region's major port. Now, it is the starting point for trips on the Paraguai River – mainly fishing trips on boat-hotels *(for more information on this kind of transportation, see page 406)* – from March to October, when fishing is allowed. Visitors can have a pleasant meal on the floating restaurants that serve fish or alligator meat from accredited breeders. Try **Kaskata** *(Rua Coronel José Dulce, no #, Beira Rio, tel. (65) 3223-2916, 3223-1107; daily, 11am – 11pm)*. Every year, the town hosts the **Festival Internacional de Pesca**, an international fishing festival with hotly disputed competitions that brings crowds to Cáceres in September.

Land of Water and Animals

Despite its name, which means swamp in Portuguese, the Pantanal is a floodplain that becomes waterlogged at certain times of the year and extends over Brazilian, Paraguayan, and Bolivian territory. The ebb and flow of the waters rule all kinds of life in this vast region. In November, when the torrential rains begin, the Paraguai River and its tributaries flood the surrounding area; in March, when the rains subside, the rivers shrink back to their normal routes. Life buzzes in every season. Visitors can see alligators, peccary, otters, capybaras, deer, and monkeys, and with a little luck, maybe even rarer animals such as jaguars and tapirs. About 650 recorded species of birds fly in flocks or gather in the trees, and the clamor of macaws, jabirus, spoonbills, cormorants, wattled jacanas, and others heralds the beginning and end of each day. The birds' mating season, between July and November, is the best time to see them. The Pantanal is also the kingdom of the mosquito, so don't forget to bring bug repellent and wear pants and long-sleeved shirts. Pack a hat, boots, binoculars, and a flashlight. This unique geography bred an unusual environment, which resulted from the mixing of many cultures and integrated perfectly with nature. Traces of Indian, Paraguayan, São Paulo, Minas Gerais, and Southern culture are evident in many ways: the local cattlemen's daily lives, the Hispanic sound of local guitars, the folk festivities, local food, and the custom of drinking yerba maté tea. This world soaks up external influences and their impacts, but it stays true to its origins and essence.

The forested banks of the Correntoso, in Southern Pantanal

PARAGUAI RIVER BOAT TRIPS

Sailing down the Paraguai River from Cáceres is takes visitors on a journey through the Pantanal's geography and history. At the beginning of the trip, the mountain range follows the meanderings of the river, which widens as it gets farther from Cáceres. The scene eventually opens up as the river spreads out in bays and islands. There are semi-abandoned ranches and old buildings from when the area produced beef jerky for export, as well as archaeological sites containing indigenous burial grounds. The best places to stay are **Pantanal Três Rios** *(tel. (65) 3223-9500)* and **Baiazinha** *(tel. (65) 3291-1036)*. Both guesthouses offer trips for fishing or just enjoying the river, and charming Baiazinha organizes horseback riding or walking tours to see the panoramic views of the Pantanal. **Estação Ecológica Taiamã** is about 160 kilometers (99 miles) from Cáceres or three to four hours in a powerful motorboat along the river *(tourist information: tel. (65) 3222-3455)*. This area of 11,200 hectares (27,676 acres) is situated on a large island, but people are not allowed to fish or get off boats in order to preserve the wildlife. After five days on a boat-hotel, visitors will pass through the outer limits of the Pantanal Mato-Grossense National Park and arrive at Corumbá in Mato Gross do Sul.

RODOVIA TRANSPANTANEIRA

The 126 famous bridges, mostly in a poor state of repair, lend an air of adventure to the 145 kilometers (90 miles) of the unpaved Rodovia Transpantaneira highway. It begins in the prospecting town of Poconé, 96 kilometers (60 miles) from Cuiabá. Small artificial lakes have sprung up in the areas where earth was removed to construct the road, which was started in 1972. Some of the lakes are perennial, attracting birds,

The Rodovia Transpantaneira: adventure and beautiful wilderness

FISHING

Long before the Pantanal attracted eco-tourists, it was a fishing paradise. The number of species found here – about 260 – is modest when compared to the 1,800 in the Amazon area, but the abundance of *pintado* (speckled catfish), *dourados* (dorados), and carp, among others, is truly impressive. It decreased appreciably over the past few years, however, because of predatory fishing, the silting up of the rivers, and the amount of pesticides washed downstream. Today, fishing enthusiasts must observe rigid rules intended to reduce pressure on diminishing fish stocks. During the breeding season from November to February, fishing is banned in the Pantanal. To fish in other months, people need a license from the environmental authorities. They also must respect minimum sizes, which vary according to the species. The following sites have information on regulations: *www.sema.mt.gov.br* and *www.sema.ms.gov.br*.

capybaras, and other creatures. Groups of giant otters can be spotted on the first half of the road, between Poconé and the Pixaim River, and the area's cattle ranches almost become islands in the flood season. Visitors can spend the day there but cannot stay overnight. The second half of the road is almost unexplored, with forest spilling into the road in some places. Near the end, the lovely Campo do Jofre is comes into view – an open plain where visitors can observe capybaras, deer, alligators, and hosts of birds. The journey ends at Porto Jofre, on the banks of the Cuiabá River, which is very popular with fishing enthusiasts. Travel in a 4×4 vehicle in the rainy season.

OUR RECOMMENDATION

The **Araras Eco Lodge** stands out from the rest of the hotels and farmhouses along the Rodovia Transpantaneira highway. Visitors will find plenty of creatures around the guesthouse, mainly hyacinth macaws, thanks to the owner's conservation work. Three lookout points are accessible by walkways over the wetlands *(Rodovia Transpantaneira, Km 32, tel. (65) 3682-2800).*

Leaving the Rodovia Transpantaneira highway – 25 minutes by boat from Porto Jofre on the right bank of the Cuiabá River – sits the sophisticated, isolated **Refúgio Ilha do Caracará**, which is very popular among fishing buffs. A boat-hotel takes visitors to fish in far-off areas and stays out overnight on the Cuiabá River. It also rents out 100-HP motorboats and offers trips to the Pantanal Mato-Grossense National Park *(no #, tel. (31) 2126-5656, 2126-5570).*

Additional information on page 462.

PARQUE NACIONAL DO PANTANAL MATO-GROSSENSE

The Serra do Amolar mountain range stands at the intersection of the Cuiabá and Paraguai rivers. The range is a series of rocky escarpments with high peaks, and a network of channels and bays at the foot of the range makes up the 135,000-hectare (333,592-acre) Pantanal Mato-Grossense National Park. Created in 1981, the park is not yet open to the public, but visitors can get in by obtaining authorization from Ibama, Brazil's environmental institute. Wildlife can be observed much more easily than in other parts of the region: 259 bird species and 56 mammal species have been recorded, and clusters of Victoria water lilies add to the landscape. The only accommodations available are in the

Reserva do Acorizal, a private reserve that belongs to the Ecotrópica NGO. (Three more Ecotrópica reserves are located in the area around the national park.) This reserve includes the slopes and mountains of the Serra do Amolar. The guesthouse is simple and the service is friendly but somewhat improvised; however, the spectacular location makes up for the lack of amenities.

Information: Parque Nacional do Pantanal Mato-Grossense, tel. (65) 3648-9100; Ecotrópica, tel. (65) 3052-6615. How to get there: Charter a motor boat in Porto Jofre, at the end of the Rodovia Transpantaneira highway. The trip along the Cuiabá River takes three hours. Boats can be hired at Refúgio Ilha do Caracará Hotel. Visitors can also take an air taxi from Cuiabá; there's a landing strip near the Reserva do Acorizal.

CHAPADA DOS GUIMARÃES

Huge sandstone rock faces mark the place where the central plateau meets the floodplains in Chapada dos Guimarães, 62 kilometers (39 miles) from Cuiabá. The rivers that rise in the plateau tumble down in waterfalls, helping to create the Pantanal. Those waterfalls and rock faces are the region's main attractions. With a population of 15,000, the town of Chapada dos Guimarães has good hotels and restaurants. It serves as a base for visitors, and large-scale, disorganized tourism has taken away a bit of the area's famous mysticism. Because Chapada stands in the center of the South American continent and is crossed by latitude 15° South, which supposedly brings positive energy, some people believe it is a good spot to make contact with other dimensions. Whether you are looking for extra-sensory vibrations or just want to enjoy nature, avoid weekends, which are usually crowded. Local agencies organize trips throughout the region.

Contact: Atmã Turismo Ecológico e Venturas, tel. (65) 3301-3391.

CAVERNA AROE JARI AND GRUTA DA LAGOA AZUL

Aroe Jari, extending for 1400 meters (almost 1 mile) in the direction of the national park, is one of Brazil's biggest sandstone caves. It looks like a tunnel and the ground is flat, and it has no mineral formations. In the dry season, the cave can be explored from one end to the other without any difficulty. In the wet season, however, water springs from fissures in the rocks. The lake **Gruta da Lagoa Azul** is near one of the tunnel mouths, and the midday sun brings out the blue color of the water when it strikes the surface. Swimming is not allowed. The caves are 42 kilometers (26 miles) from the town of Chapada dos Guimarães (32 kilometers on dirt road), and the trip includes an eight-kilometer (five-mile) walk there and back. Buy an entrance ticket in advance at one of the town's travel agencies.

PARQUE NACIONAL DA CHAPADA DOS GUIMARÃES

Created in 1989, Chapada dos Guimarães National Park takes up 33,000 hectares (82,000 acres) and is home to most of the region's attractions. The main building has a restaurant, snack bar, craft store, and visitors' center, which displays aerial pictures, maps

Sandstone rock faces in the Parque Nacional da Chapada dos Guimarães, in Mato Grosso

and photos of the local fauna and flora. The park is also home to animals such as the giant anteater, the pampas deer, and the maned wolf, as well as typical regional plants. A five-minute walk from the parking lot leads to a lookout point of Chapada's picture-postcard view: the **Cachoeira Véu da Noiva**, a waterfall with an 86-meter (282-foot) drop. Other trails, such as the one that leads to the lower section of Véu da Noiva, are longer and poorly marked. It's very easy to get lost at the many forks along the trails, so hire a guide in town. Two trails begin near the main building. The **Circuito das Cachoeiras** takes four hours and runs past several waterfalls along the Independência River. The **Morro de São Jerônimo** trail takes the whole day and leads to the region's highest point at 836 meters (2,743 feet). Visitors will need a car – and a guide – to face the four kilometers of paved road and 19 kilometers of dirt road, all poorly marked, that lead to the

monumental sandstone rock faces and quartz escarpments of **Cidade de Pedra**. Take this trip to the end of the afternoon: the rock faces, some more than 30 meters (98 feet) high, take on a red hue and flocks of scarlet macaws come back to roost for the night.

Park main building: Rodovia Emanuel Pinheiro (MT-251), Km 51 (11 km from the town of Chapada dos Guimarães), tel. (65) 3301-1133. Daily, 8am – 6pm.

OUR RECOMMENDATION

Solar do Inglês, the most charming guesthouse in Chapada dos Guimarães, has eight rooms with different décor and great attention to detail. The veranda, outfitted with wicker furniture, takes guests back to the days of the 19th-century explorers. The English owner, a former hunter named Richard Mason, serves guests personally. He'd lived in the Pantanal for over 30 years before he opened the guesthouse in 2002.

Additional information on page 462.

NOBRES

Walking through Duto do Quebó cave

Anyone planning to visit Nobres, 150 kilometers (93 miles) from Cuiabá, should know that tourist facilities are very limited – despite the region's many attractions, including many caves, waterfalls, and crystal-clear rivers. Visitors should take initiative and be willing to improvise. The only exception is Salobra River in the Recanto Ecológico *(tel. (65) 3376-1809)*. This spot supplies masks, flippers, life jackets, and snorkels, and it has specialized guides and a restaurant. Floating down the river takes 30 minutes. The river current carries visitors for 500 metros (almost half a mile) while they observe fish such as *piraputangas* (a type of small dorado), *piaus* (banded leporinus), and other species from the River Plate Basin. Nearby is the **Gruta do Lago Azul**, a cave that serves as the town's landmark site. It is often closed, however, so make sure to check before setting out. The village of Bom Jardim is 13 kilometers (eight miles) from the cave and 69 kilometers (43 miles) from the center of Nobres. It offers simple lodging and restaurant options. To visit other attractions in the region – such as the **Duto do Quebó**, a cavern that extends for 292 meters (958 feet) with a river running through it – hire a guide from the Nobres Tourism Department *(Secretaria de Turismo de Nobres: tel. (65) 3376-1809)*.

The crystal-clear waters of the Rio Salobra, in Nobres

SOUTHERN PANTANAL

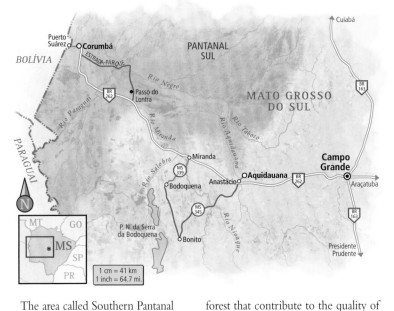

The area called Southern Pantanal encompasses part of the floodplains in the state of Mato Grosso do Sul. The paved Rodovia BR-262 highway divides the region from east to west. It connects the capital, Campo Grande, to Corumbá, a historic city near the Bolivian border. It sits on the banks of the Rio Paraguai and is very popular among fishing buffs. Pantanal's main tourist ranches are in the municipalities of Aquidauana and Miranda, both of which can be reached on Rodovia BR-262 highway. The Estrada Parque, an alternative to the BR-262, also goes to Corumbá. Its 120 kilometers (75 miles) of dirt road cross a region of surprising beauty, with good options for accommodations.

CAMPO GRANDE

The pleasant state capital of Mato Grosso do Sul is distinctive for its urban planning and wide, tree-lined avenues. It is almost flat, and it boasts well-kept parks and reserves of native forest that contribute to the quality of life of its more than 700,000 inhabitants. In the second half of the 19th century, the city flourished as a cattle-trading post; now, it serves as a base for the Southern Pantanal or Bonito, in the Serra da Bodoquena mountain range. Anyone who wants to try the local cuisine should head for the restaurant **Fogo Caipira**. The menu includes Pantanal fish and meat dishes such as *carne-de-sol na moranga* (shredded beef served in a pumpkin shell) *(Rua José Antônio Pereira, 145, Centro, tel. (67) 3324-1641; Tue – Fri, 11am – 2pm and 7pm – 11pm; Sat, 11am – midnight; Sun, 11am – 4pm).* To learn more about local culture and wildlife, visit the **Museu Dom Bosco**, a museum with about 5,000 indigenous pieces and more than a thousand stuffed Pantanal animals *(Avenida Afonso Pena, 7000, Parque das Nações Indígenas, tel. (67) 3326-9788; the museum is currently being renovated and is due to reopen in December 2008).*

Visitors help to herd cattle on Fazenda Santa Inês near Miranda

RANCHES IN THE PANTANAL

On the ranches recommended here, visitors can experience everyday Pantanal life, whether it's dealing with cattle, walking, horseback riding, going on fishing trips, or taking boat excursions to see the landscape and observe animals. Although some of the houses are very simple, accommodations are. Each property is totally integrated with the landscape around it. Tourists can also accompany the herd, a true Pantanal caravan, when cattlemen move thousands of animals from one property to another.

REFÚGIO ECOLÓGICO CAIMAN

This charming, comfortable property is in Miranda on the Fazenda da Caiman, a 53,000-hectare (130,966-acre) ranch that combines cattle husbandry with scientific research and ecological tourism. The refuge includes four guesthouses Baiazinha and Cordilheira deserve special mention: both of them are independent facilities set apart from the main house, amid lovely natural surroundings. Caiman employs a team of university-educated guides who are fluent English-speakers and know a lot about the local fauna and flora. Available trips include hiking trails, photo safaris, horseback riding, Canadian canoe excursions, and bird watching.

At the Miranda intersection, take the highway towards Agachi for two kilometers. From there, drive 36 kilometers on dirt road to the main house. There is a landing strip, code SSEX. Tel. (67) 3242-1450.

Fazenda Santa Inês

This ranch, 19 kilometers (12 miles) away from Miranda, offers horseback riding and cattle handling, as well as climbing on artificial walls and flying fox. The 1,200-hectare (2,965-acre) property does conservation work and is re-introducing animals into the wild from a rehabilitation center in Campo Grande. The small, cozy guesthouse has six rooms and also rents rooms on a daily basis.
Access on the dirt road from Miranda to the village of Lalima, Km 16, tel. (67) 9988-4082.

Pousada Recanto Barra Mansa

This guesthouse belongs to the Fazenda Barra Mansa, a thousand-hectare (2471-acre) ranch in a hard-to-reach part of the Pantanal on the right bank of the Negro River, 120 kilometers (75 miles) from the municipality of Aquidauana. It has six rooms and an intimate atmosphere. The ranch also organizes horseback-riding, bird-watching, and fishing trips, as well as canoe trips to observe giant otters, alligators, tapirs, capybaras, and even jaguars. Sandy white beaches that are good for swimming appear between July and November.
Land access from Aquidauana is possible only in 4×4 vehicles between July and November. Guides are recommended. The ranch has a landing strip. Tel. (67) 3325-6807, 9986-0494.

Pequi Pousada Pantaneira

Family service and typical Pantanal lifestyle are this guesthouse's main attractions. It offers just seven spacious rooms, all inside the early 20th-century farmhouse. The property has an area of 2,700 hectares (6,670 acres) and is 47 kilometers (29 miles) from

Aquidauana. Cattle farming for meat is its main vocation. A tour shows visitors around the ranch, including the corral, kitchen, cheese house, sugar cane mill, and butchering section. It also offers day-use packages.

From Aquidauana, drive five kilometers along the paved Rodovia BR-262 highway toward Corumbá. A dirt road with signs on the left leads to the guesthouse. From there, it is 42 kilometers to the entrance to Pequi. The ranch has a landing strip. Tel. (67) 3245-0949, 9986-0449, 9934-5781.

ESTRADA PARQUE DO PANTANAL

The course of the Estrada Parque do Pantanal highway corresponds to the route Cândido Mariano da Silva Rondon (1865-1958) opened for telegraph lines at the beginning of the 20th century. Until the opening of Rodovia BR-262 highway, this road was the only way to access Corumbá over land. After falling into complete disrepair, it was brought back as an ecological tourism route and gained the name by which it is known today. It stretches for 120 kilometers (75 miles) of dirt road connected by 87 treacherous wooden bridges, which are passable in the rainy season only in 4×4 vehicles. It spans a beautiful, wild section of the Pantanal, where travelers can spot many different animals, and the road is one of the few parts of the region where visitors can be independent. The first 50 kilometers (31 miles) from Corumbá (where drivers should fill up their tanks) lead to the Serra do Urucum mountain range. The reddish color of the massive rocks comes from their high concentration of iron. At the end of the range is Porto da Manga, a fishing village on the banks of the Paraguai River that has a ferry crossing *(daily, 6am – 6pm)*. The trip proceeds for 18 kilometers (11 miles) to the Curva do Leque crossroads. Turn right and continue on for 42 kilometers (26 miles) to reach Passo de Lontra. It is the most populated settlement in the region, offering a gas station and guesthouses for fishing enthusiasts. The highway ends at Km 664 on the Rodovia BR-262, in an area known as Buraco das Piranhas. The **Xaraés** guesthouse is the most pleasant lodging option along the highway *(access, 17 Km from Buraco das Piranhas. Tel. (67) 9906-9272).*

BONITO

Bonito, population 17,000, is an ecological tourism mecca in Brazil. Every year, about 100,000 visitors arrive at this town in southwest Mato Grosso do Sul, 285 kilometers (177 miles) from Campo Grande and 140 kilometers (87 miles) from the start of the Pantanal. In addition to the natural beauty that inspired the town's name – *bonito* means beautiful – the area's fame lies in the way these attractions are presented to visitors. About 40 rural properties are open to the public, and strict rules govern the way the waterfalls, rivers, trails, and caves can be visited. Attention is paid to promoting so-called minimum-impact tourism. Only small groups of visitors are allowed, and they must always be accompanied by guides. In the high season – January, February, and July – it's a good idea to buy tickets to the main

Floating on Bonito's Sucuri River: a thrilling spectacle

attractions in advance. Visitors will need a car and a guide to get around Bonito; vehicles can be hired at local tour agencies, which also supply vans for small groups. These agencies, like all local services, can be found in the town itself, which sustains itself from tourism. The town center's main street, Rua Coronel Pilad Rebuá, has guesthouses, restaurants, cyber cafés, and tour and diving agencies. At night, when visitors return from day-trips, the center gets crowded. Good restaurant options include **Sale e Pepe**, which serves piranha, dorado, and *piraputanga* sashimi *(Rua 29 de Maio, 971, Centro, tel. (67) 3255-1822; Tue – Sun, 6pm – 11pm)*; and **Cantinho do Peixe**, which also specializes in fish *(Rua 31 de Março, 1918, Centro, tel. (67) 3255-3381; low season, Mon – Sat, 11am – 3pm and 6pm – 11pm; high season, daily, 11am – 11pm)*. Although most hotels are located in and around the town center, some very nice guesthouses are situated near the rivers and forests, far from the town's hustle and bustle and more in line with the

spirit of the region. One example is **Santa Esmeralda**, 18 kilometers (11 miles) from Bonito near the Formoso River. Accommodations are in wooden bungalows *(Rodovia Bonito–Guia Lopes da Laguna, Km 17.5, tel. (67) 3255-2683). Contact: Agência Ar, tel. (67) 3255-1008; Ygarapé Tour, tel. (67) 3255-1733.*

FLOATING

Visitors don't have to be experienced divers to have fun "floating" on Bonito's rivers – just put on a life jacket and drift with the current. The underwater spectacle is thrilling. With a mask, visibility can reach a staggering 50 meters (164 feet). This phenomenon results from the concentration of lime, a natural filter that eliminates impurities and leaves the waters crystal clear. The profusion of aquatic life is impressive; about 80 species of large, colorful fish such as *piraputangas*, dorados, and *curimbatás* swim nonchalantly alongside visitors. The four recommended rivers for floating are **Rio Sucuri, Rio da**

Beauty lies 85 meters beneath the surface in Gruta do Lago Azul cave

Prata, Rio Baía Bonita, and **Rio Formoso.** Equipment can be rented and experienced guides can be hired at these spots.

Rio Sucuri: 17 km from Bonito. Access on the road to São Geraldo. Daily, 8am – 6pm.
Rio da Prata: 50 km from Bonito. Access on Rodovia BR-267 highway, Km 518, tel. (67) 3255-2108. Low season, daily 8am – 1:30pm; high season, daily, 8am – 3pm.
Rio Baía Bonita: 7 km from Bonito. Access on Rodovia BR-267 highway towards Jardim, tel. (67) 3255-1193. Daily, 8am – 4pm.
Rio Formoso: 6 km from Bonito. Access on the road to Guia Lopes da Laguna. Daily, 8am – 4pm.

Gruta do Lago Azul

Bonito's most famous attraction is one of the largest flooded caves in Brazil. It draws about 60,000 visitors a year and was declared a national heritage site in 1978. It can be reached by a short trail from the visitors' center, where visitors walk down 100 meters to a lookout point that offers a view of the 85-meter (279-foot) deep lake. From December to February, the sun's rays enter the cave and illuminate the water, making it even bluer than usual. In addition to the water, the stalactites and stalagmites are very impressive. Sneakers and a helmet are required to visit the cave. (The latter can be acquired on site.) Before going, it's worth knowing that although the trip is truly unforgettable, there isn't much time to look at the visual effects: the excursion lasts just over an hour, and visitors are only allowed inside the cave for 20 minutes. The rules are strictly enforced.
20 km from Bonito. Access by dirt road toward Campos dos Índios. Daily, 7am – 2pm.

Abismo Anhumas

This cave has a lake at the bottom, which can only be reached by rappelling down the 72-meter

(236-foot) abyss. Anyone who wants to make the long descent to the lake must pass a training course before trying it. At the bottom, visitors will find themselves on a floating platform in the middle of the lake, which is 80 meters (262 feet) deep and the size of an Olympic swimming pool. It sits in a chamber full of limestone formations. After the rappelling, visitors will take a short boat trip and swim in the lake. Qualified divers can go down to 18 meters (59 feet). After this comes the most difficult part: going back up to the surface using the ropes from the descent, a task that demands a very high level of physical fitness.

22 km from Bonito. Access on the road to Campos dos Índios. Daily, 7am – 1pm.

Rio do Peixe

A trip to the Peixe River is highly recommended for anyone staying in Bonito for a few days. Two trails on the **Fazenda Água Viva** pass no fewer than 11 waterfalls. The property's farmhouse serves typical local food cooked on a wood-burning stove and offers hammocks for napping. Owner Moacir Barbosa de Deus greets guests personally, telling stories about the region and showing his familiarity with the local macaws and capuchin monkeys, who eat out of his hand.

35 km from Bonito. Access by the road to Bodoquena. Daily, 9am – 4pm.

Buraco das Araras

When **Fazenda Alegria** was bought by a local at the end of the 1980s, the huge crater in the property's limestone rock was considered a liability because it reduced the amount of grazing land on the ranch. But the crater, which is 500 meters (1,640 feet) across and 100 (328 feet) meters deep, ended up as a major tourist attraction. Its walls serve as nesting sites for 40 species of birds. Flocks of scarlet macaws can be seen in the mornings and late afternoons. A 500-meter (1,640-foot) trail connects the reception area to lookout points that offer a view of the crater. This trip is organized exclusively by agencies in Bonito and Jardim, and it lasts 40 minutes. The site also offers rappelling facilities.

58 km from Bonito, with access from Rodovia BR-267 highway, Km 30, heading toward Porto Murtinho. Daily, 7:30am – 5pm. Tel. (67) 9995-2586.

Buraco das Araras, a nesting site for many species

Three Reports from the Pantanal

1) The Spawning Season

Brazil is far and away the world champion when it comes to freshwater fish. Annual floods make the Pantanal impassable (or else people would have destroyed it by now). The rivers – and the fish – survive, but less and less, unfortunately.

Anyone who has seen the *piracema* (spawning) never forgets it. It's wonderful to watch two *corimbas* mate in an aquarium. They use up so much energy – and joy – in laying the eggs (the female) and fertilizing them (the male) that, after the celebrations, they collapse, spent, sated, defenseless. Imagine this in a river where tens of thousands of pairs mate at the same time. The fish have their own song, and during the *piracema,* they sing all the time. The river teems with their anthem of love.

Old Pantanal fishermen knew each group of migrating fish by the noises they made on their way upstream to lay their eggs. They knew by the song if it was the *corimba*, the *jaú*, the *pintado*…

2) Wild Rice

I read once that wild rice grew in the Pantanal, which the Indians used to eat. I spent a good 15 years looking for information in an article before I got it in 2001. I followed tips from Dona Josefina, who lives in Corumbá today but is a real *Guató* Indian. With Dona Josefina as our guide and Doctor Yeda from the University of Mato Grosso do Sul as our botanist, the TV crew and I went to gather wild rice in Baía Uberaba, in the middle of the Paraguai River.

The rice was gathered, crushed (to remove the husks) and then cooked for us to try. What a thrill!

How much is a sack of regular rice? Twenty *reais* (approximately 12 dollars). They tell me that in Canada, wild rice is 20 dollars – a kilo. Isn't there some way of helping the *Guató* commercialize their wild rice?

3) Jaguars in Trees

Estelito from Poconé has two surnames, but he doesn't really need any. Is there another Estelito in this huge land of ours? There isn't in the Pantanal, at any rate. So, when you mention Estelito, it's understood that you're talking about the ranch handyman, leather craftsman, boatman, and jaguar hunter from Poconé.

Estelito has hunted more jaguars in the Pantanal than the number of years he's been alive (he's about 75). He learned from his own experience, or has heard from people in the know, every story about the Pantanal. He's been in the game since he was 14 and has found as many jaguars to kill (when it was legal) as he has strung up to be filmed or photographed. It was Estelito who put that jaguar in a tree for *Globo Rural* to film for its Jaguar Hunting program, which was popular in the 1990s. (That jaguar wasn't killed, just filmed.)

Anyway, one day I said to Estelito, "I've got a Pantanal story you've never told me, and I bet you don't know it. At least I'll get one over on you with this!"

Estelito's eyes lit up. I told him that in 1975, when I was doing an article on the construction of the Rodovia Transpantaneira highway for the magazine *Realidade* (the predecessor to the famous *Veja* magazine), I was taken to a ranch that the road was going to cut through. I was admiring a photo on the wall: two jaguars in a tree! One in a tree is rare enough in those parts, but two! And to think there was someone there with a camera to capture the scene!

Constantino, the rancher, stood up and looked out the window. "That's the tree over there – you can see it from here. Look, that's the tree from the photo!" And it really was. I was so excited by this story that I turned to Estelito and said, "So, champ, you didn't know that one, did ya?" Estelito gave a little chuckle, not wanting to seem too boastful.

"'Course I knew it," he said.

"How come you know a story about two jaguars in a tree on Constantino's ranch?"

"I know 'cause it was me who put them there."

Constantino had once asked Estelito to deal with a jaguar that had been eating calves. He went with Inácio Bororo, in the latter's small plane, together with all the gear, hunters, and hunting dogs. They got to the ranch in the afternoon, learned all they needed to know, and early the next day let the dogs loose.

"We killed the jaguar in half an hour, right there. We were just hanging around a bit after the hunt when suddenly the dogs picked up another scent. It was the second jaguar, over by the door, and we got him quick as a flash. Somebody suggested dragging the two dead jaguars back to the farm, then the idea to put them in the tree came up – to put each one on a branch and take a photo. So I went up the tree, hauled them jaguars up and nailed them there."

Estelito from Poconé, raised in the culture of killing ("killing jaguars, killing fish, killing monkeys") adapted easily and happily to the idea of preserving the Pantanal's wildlife. He wanted no more of hunters or guns. His weapon now is just a camera, to film, photograph, and record the sounds of the Pantanal.

José Hamilton Ribeiro,
a journalist, was born in Santa Rosa do Viterbo, which is in the state of São Paulo. He wrote, among other works, Pantanal, amor baguá *(2003), which was named "the best children's book of the year" by the São Paulo Association of Art Critics (APCA). He has won the Esso Journalism Prize six times.*

THE SOUTH

The South of Brazil is made up of three states: Paraná, Santa Catarina and Rio Grande do Sul, where winters can get very cold – in some places, it even snows. An enjoyable train trip can take visitors from the coastal region of Paraná to its pleasant, modern capital, Curitiba. Paraná also boasts Guartelá Canyon and the world-famous Iguaçu Falls. The Island of Santa Catarina is home to the state's capital, Florianópolis, and its 42 beaches. Beaches in the coastal regions of the state will suit all tastes. Porto Alegre, the capital of Rio Grande do Sul, serves as a departure point for charming mountain ranges that are home to vineyards and the canyons of Aparados da Serra National Park. In the pampas of Rio Grande do Sul, travelers can see the ruins of 17th- and 18th-century Jesuit missions.

PARANÁ

Apucarana

PR 092

Itapeva

1 cm = 30 km
1 inch = 47.4 mi.

SP

PR

RS   SC

Maringá

Jaguariaíva

Piraí do Sul

Tibaji   ■ P. E. do Guartelá

BR 376

Castro

Rio Iapó

PARANÁ

São Paulo

SÃO PAULO

PR 151

Ponta Grossa

Rio Capivari

BR 116

P. N. do Superaguí

Foz do Iguaçu

Rio Imbitava

Iguaçu

Curitiba

Antonina

Baía de Paranaguá

Morretes

Paranaguá

BR 277

GRACIOSA

BR 277

Lapa   Mandirituba

Rio Cubatão

P. N. Saint-Hilaire/Lange

Rio

BR 116

BR 476

BR 376

ATLANTIC OCEAN

Passo Fundo

Florianópolis

Porto Alegre

N

SANTA CATARINA

HIGHLIGHTS

- **Curitiba**'s parks and cultural circuit.
- **Curitiba-Paranaguá Railway**.
- Guartelá Canyon in **Tibaji**.
- Iguaçu Falls in **Foz do Iguaçu**.

WHEN TO GO

- In **autumn**, for mild temperatures and dry weather.
- In **March**, for the Festival de Teatro de Curitiba.
- During the **summer**, when the Iguaçu Falls are the most active.
- At the end of **summer**, for whitewater rafting on the Iapó River in Guartelá Canyon.

CURITIBA

HISTORICAL CENTER

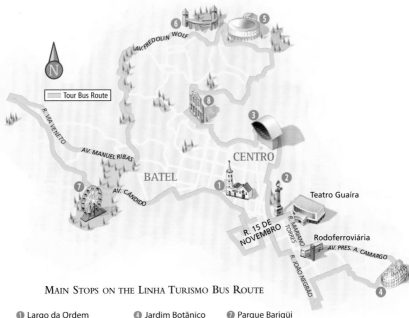

Tour Bus Route

AV. FREDOLIN WOLF

R. VIA VENETO

AV. MANUEL RIBAS

BATEL

AV. CÂNDIDO

CENTRO

Teatro Guaíra

R. 15 DE NOVEMBRO

R. MARIANO TORRES

Rodoferroviária

AV. PRES. A. CAMARGO

R. JOÃO NEGRÃO

MAIN STOPS ON THE LINHA TURISMO BUS ROUTE

- ❶ Largo da Ordem
- ❷ Rua das Flores
- ❸ Museu Oscar Niemeyer
- ❹ Jardim Botânico
- ❺ Ópera de Arame
- ❻ Parque Tanguá
- ❼ Parque Barigüi
- ❽ Bosque Alemão

With a population of little over 1.5 million, the capital of Paraná prides itself on its innovative approach to public transportation and its park system, both of which have revolutionized locals' quality of life in recent decades. Greenery is everywhere; the city boasts 30 parks and woods in addition to bike lanes, museums and important cultural events such as the **Festival de Teatro**, a theater festival that takes place every March and offers performances at several locations *(www.festivaldeteatro.com.br)*. When visiting Curitiba, make sure to pack a sweater and a raincoat, because it rains often. It is the coldest state capital in the country, and temperatures can be low even in the summer. The most practical way to explore the city is the **Linha Turismo**, a circular bus route with shuttles known as *jardineiras*, that stops at 25 tourist attractions. Tickets allow visitors to get on and off the line four times. Information is provided in Portuguese, Spanish and English *(tel. (41) 3352-8000)*.

❶ LARGO DA ORDEM AND ENVIRONS

This is the oldest group of buildings in the city. It includes the **Igreja da Ordem Terceira de São Francisco**, a church dating from 1737, and some fine examples of German architecture. The house of local historian **Romário Martins** – also from the 18th century

CULTURAL CIRCUIT

and reportedly the oldest house in Curitiba – is also located here. On Sundays, Largo da Ordem hosts a crafts fair with live music in the square from 9am to 2pm.

➋ RUA DAS FLORES
When it was closed to traffic in 1971 Rua Quinze de Novembro became the first pedestrian-only street in Brazil. Known locally as Rua das Flores (Street of Flowers), the avenue's old buildings house shops, bars and cafés. Children often gather here on Saturdays to paint and draw on the ground. Nearby is the "Cavalheiros da Boca Maldita" (Bad-mouthed Gentlemen), a men-only speaker's corner for discussing politics and criticizing others. In December, a children's choir sings Christmas carols from the windows of nearby **Palácio Avenida**, which houses a branch of HSBC bank.

➌ MUSEU OSCAR NIEMEYER
Oscar Niemeyer designed the two buildings of this museum, which was built in 2002. One building is a large rectangular structure that dates from the 1960s and once housed government offices. Next to it is the famous Olho (Eye), with its striking interior. The museum has a small permanent exhibition on Niemeyer and displays a range of temporary exhibitions.
Rua Marechal Hermes, 999, Centro Cívico, tel. (41) 3350-4400. Tue – Sun, 10am – 6pm.

➍ JARDIM BOTÂNICO
This Curitiba landmark is one of its most popular tourist attractions. Inside is the **Museu Botânico**, French-style gardens, a greenhouse built to mimic London's Crystal Palace, a stretch of native forest and a U-shaped gallery with a permanent

Bold architecture is the main attraction of the Museu Oscar Niemeyer in Curitiba

Parque Barigüi is Curitiba's largest park, covering 1.4 square kilometers

exhibit of sculptures by Frans Krajcberg. *Rua Engenheiro Ostoja Roguski, no #, Jardim Botânico, tel. (41) 3362-1800. Daily, 6am – 8pm (open until 9pm in summertime).*

➎ Ópera de Arame
Architecture is the biggest draw for this theater, which was built in an unused quarry. The music and drama program leaves much to be desired, and the acoustics are sub par. Lakes and waterfalls surround this tubular iron building, with glass walls and ceiling. Next door is the Pedreira Paulo Leminski, a former quarry that is now an enormous open-air amphitheater.
Rua João Gava, no #, Abranches, tel. (41) 3355-6071. Tue – Sun, 8am – 10pm.

➏ Parque Tanguá
Sitting in an abandoned quarry, Parque Tanguá is one of the city's most scenic parks. From its plateau, visitors can see a man-made waterfall that plunges 40 meters (131 feet) into a lake, as well as a huge expanse

of woods. The park also boasts a bike lane and jogging path. *Rua Nilo Peçanha, no #, Pilarzinho, tel. (41) 3352-7607. Daily, 24 hours.*

➐ Parque Barigüi
The city's biggest park covers 1.4 million square meters (346 acres) and boasts an amusement park and a car museum called the **Museu do Automóvel**. It is popular with sporty types and gets crowded on weekends. *Rodovia do Café (BR-277), Km 0, Santo Inácio, tel. (41) 3339-8975. Daily, 24 hours.*

➑ Bosque Alemão
These woods are dedicated to German immigrants. They are home to a concert hall and a lookout point that affords one of the best views of the city and the Serra do Mar mountain range. A trail for children has plaques telling the story of João and Maria (Hansel and Gretel), and there is also a children's library.
Rua Niccolo Paganini, no #, Jardim Schaffer. Daily, 24 hours.

The Serra do Mar by Train

It takes four hours for Brazil's most spectacular train ride to cover the 116 kilometers (72 miles) of the **Ferrovia Curitiba–Paranaguá**, a railway built at the end of the 19th century. The three-hour stretch between Curitiba and Morretes is the best part of the journey. Riders will be treated to breathtaking scenery on the descent through the Serra do Mar, by way of 13 tunnels and 30 bridges. Bilingual guides point out geographical features such as the **Véu de Noiva**, a waterfall with an 86-meter (282-foot) drop, the **Cânion do Ipiranga** and the **Serra do Cadeado** range. Try to reserve a seat on the left side of the train for a better view of the dizzying precipices plunging into the Atlantic Forest. Sports enthusiasts can disembark from the train at **Parque Estadual do Marumbi**, a spectacular mountain complex that is ideal for camping, trekking or climbing the Marumbi peak rock face, which reaches 1,539 meters (5,000 feet). A conventional train runs along the route daily. On weekends and holidays, visitors can take the Litorina, a single-carriage tram with panoramic windows and air conditioning. The train makes trips to the historical towns of **Morretes** and **Antonina**, which is in Paranaguá Bay. People with more time to spare can visit a lovely island, **Ilha do Mel**. Vans also run back to Curitiba, taking the winding road up the Serra da Graciosa range. Tickets and information can be obtained from **Serra Verde Express**, the company that operates the line *(tel. (41) 3323-4007 or www.serraverdeexpress.com.br).*

Our Recommendation

🍽 Make sure to try *barreado*, a typical dish from the Paraná coast, when visiting Morretes. The stew of shredded beef is cooked for about 12 hours, until it melts in your mouth. It comes accompanied by manioc flour and banana. Its name comes from the expression *barrear* (to seal). The region's first farmers developed the technique of sealing clay pots with a mixture of manioc flour and water to prevent the steam from escaping and the dish from drying out too quickly. Two good restaurants in town serve *barreado*: **Ponte Velha**, on the banks of the Rio Nhundiaquara *(Rua Almirante Frederico de Oliveira, 13, Centro, tel. (41) 3462-1674)*; and **Armazém Romanus**, which offers a lighter version with less fat *(Rua Visconde do Rio Branco, 141, Centro, tel. (41) 3462-1500).*

Additional information on page 462.

Atlantic forest encircles the railway

CURITIBA NIGHTLIFE

The bohemian neighborhood of Santa Felicidade has become a tourist attraction more for the size of its Italian restaurants than the quality of the food they serve. **Madalosso**, purportedly the second largest in the world, can seat 4,000 people and is part of the local culture for Curitiba families *(Avenida Manuel Ribas, 5852-5875,* *tel. (41) 3372-2121)*. **Cantinho do Eisbein,** in the Água Verde neighborhood, specializes in German food and serves an impressive dish of stuffed duck *(Avenida dos Estados, 863, tel. (41) 3329-5155)*. In the city center, **Schwarzwald** – also known as **bar do Alemão** – is rumored to have the best chope (draft beer) in Curitiba *(Rua Doutor Claudino dos Santos, 60, Largo da Ordem, tel. (41) 3223-2585)*. For live music, try **Hermes Bar**, where famous Brazilian artists perform *(Avenida Iguaçu, 2504, Água Verde, tel. (41) 3018-9320)*. Nightclubs are mostly in the Batel neighborhood and especially near the square, Pracinha do Batel.

GUARTELÁ

One of Brazil's best rivers for whitewater rafting can be found in the Paraná heartland, about 200 kilometers (124 miles) from Curitiba. The **Rio Iapó** cuts through the **Cânion Guartelá**, the sixth biggest canyon in the world, and extends for 32 kilometers (20 miles) in the **Parque Estadual do Guartelá** between Tibaji and Castro *(tel. (42) 3275-2269)*. This trip is recommended only for semi-experienced rafters. It lasts two days and includes an overnight stay in the canyon, and the outing is organized by **Canoar** in São Paulo *(tel. (11) 3871-2282)*. A less extreme option is rafting on the **Rio Tibaji**, which has gentler rapids. It's also possible to try sports such as trekking and rappelling in other parts of the park. Contact local agencies in Tibaji: **Ytayapé Ecoturismo & Aventuras** *(tel. (42) 3275-1766)* and **Cantinho das Águas Vivas** *(tel. (42) 3275-1357)*. The trails are safe and well marked. Try those that lead to **Cachoeira da Ponte de Pedra**, a waterfall with a drop of about 200 meters (656 feet), and the **Panelões do Sumidouro**, which has natural pools.

LAPA

The historical town of Lapa, 67 kilometers (42 miles) from Curitiba, has 14 blocks of well-preserved buildings that have been declared a national heritage site. Among these are the weapons museum, the **Museu de Armas** (1871); a church, the **Igreja de Santo Antônio** (1874); and the **Theatro São João** (1876), one of two theaters in Brazil that has a circular auditorium and boxes around the stage. (The other is in Sabará, in Minas Gerais.) Brazil's first spa, **Lar Lapeano de Saúde**, was built nearby in 1972. Also known as Lapinha, the spa operates on a 550-hectare (1,359-acre) farm, which grows the organic produce that stocks the vegetarian menu served to guests. The rooms are not equipped with TVs or telephones. The spa offers free transfers on Saturdays from Curitiba airport *(tel. (41) 3622-1044)*.

The Brazilian side offers the best view of the waterfalls in Parque Nacional do Iguaçu

FOZ DO IGUAÇU

One of the most famous Brazilian tourist attractions, Iguaçu Falls, straddles the border between Brazil and Argentina. It draws more than a million visitors every year. Although the image of the falls has very widely distributed, experiencing them in person outweighs any cliché. There are around 275 waterfalls – the number varies depending on the amount of rain at any given time – with an average height of 60 meters (197 feet) each. The falls produce an amazing volume of water and display impressive power. On the Brazilian side, the trails and walkways of the **Parque Nacional do Iguaçu**, the most popular and organized national park in Brazil, offer the best panoramic view of the whole falls. Visitors can also explore the area on boat or helicopter trips. On the Argentinean side, on the left bank of the Iguaçu River, visitors can closer to the falls and feel their brute force either on foot or by boat (on a trip that will soak people to their skin). Foz de Iguaçu is the city base for the falls' visitors. With a population of almost 300,000, the city lies 637 kilometers (396 miles) from Curitiba and is an unusual tourist town for Brazil. Everything runs smoothly, including the four tourist information centers, the bilingual road signs and the free information service in Portuguese, Spanish and English *(tel. 0800-451516)*. Most hotels line the Rodovia das Cataratas, the highway connecting Foz to the national park. Another attraction is the **Usina Hidrelétrica de Itaipu**, a hydroelectric plant that is one of the greatest engineering feats in the world. Foz do Iguaçu is also known for attractions just outside its borders: shopping in neighboring **Ciudad del Este** in Paraguay and the **Casinos** in **Puerto Iguazu**, Argentina.

PARQUE NACIONAL DO IGUAÇU

MS SP

PR

SC

RS

1 cm = 11 km
1 inch = 17.3 mi.

Guaíra

Curitiba

Santa Teresa
do Oeste

PARANÁ

Céu
Azul

Matelândia

Medianeira

São Miguel
do Iguaçu

Serranópolis
do Iguaçu

Parque
Nacional
do Iguaçu

Aurora do
Iguaçu

Santa Teresinha
de Itaipu

Assunção

Foz do
Iguaçu

Ciudad
del Este

Centro de
Visitantes

Rio Iguaçu

PARAGUAI

ARGENTINA

N

Cataratas
do Iguaçu

PR 495

BR 277

Rio Paraná

❶ Macuco Safári
❷ Helicopter flights
❸ Campo de Desafios

❹ Parque das Aves
❺ Usina Hidrelétrica de Itaipu
❻ Parque Nacional del Iguazu

The Parque Nacional do Iguaçu, a
national park of 185,262 hectares
(457,792 acres), was created in 1939.
The park's most exciting trip is the
Trilha das Cataratas, a trail that
includes lookout points with
excellent views of the falls. A
walkway over the falls ends with a
peek at their most impressive section:
Garganta do Diabo (Devil's Throat).
A food court waits at the end of the
trail. Cars are not allowed in the
park; visitors must use the double-
decker buses that leave from the
Visitor's Center, which has parking
spaces. In addition to the suggested
trips below, others such as **Trilha do
Poço Preto** and **Linha Martins**

combine walking trails and boat rides.
*Rodovia BR-469 (Rodovia das Cataratas),
Km 18, tel. (45) 3521-4400 or
www.cataratasdoiguacu.com.br. Daily, 9am
– 5pm (open until 6pm Nov – Feb).*

❶ MACUCO SAFÁRI

This tour is the national park's most
popular activity. An electric car with
trilingual guides follows a trail
of 3.5 kilometers (almost 2 miles)
through the forest and stops at the
beginning of a 600-meter trail.
Visitors who do not want to
continue on foot can keep going in
the car. The last part of the tour is a
boat trip up the Rio Iguaçu, getting
closer and closer to the falls until

they soak visitors with the spray from Cachoeira dos Mosqueteiros. You'll want a raincoat.
Information: tel. (45) 3574-4244.

❷ HELICOPTER FLIGHTS
A helicopter flight offers the most impressive view of the falls. Flights last for just 10 minutes, but they are unforgettable: the moment the pilot approaches the falls, hovers and inches the helicopter nose down will be remembered forever. Another option is a 35-minute flight passing over the Itaipu hydroelectric plant and the Marco Três Fronteiras, which

marks the spot where the borders of Paraguay, Brazil and Argentina meet.
Helisul, tel. (45) 3529-7327.

❸ CAMPO DE DESAFIOS
Inaugurated in 2003, this adventure park offers facilities, guides and safety equipment for extreme sports such as rappelling, whitewater rafting and rock climbing. Try canopy climbing, where adventurers can walk among the treetops at an average height of 12 meters (40 feet) before using a zip line to get back down to earth.
Consórcio Escalada Cânion Iguaçu, tel. (45) 3529-6040.

AROUND THE PARK

❹ PARQUE DAS AVES
This park, opened in 1994, is home to about 900 birds from 150 endangered species. The reserve's enormous aviaries are integrated with the forest and simulate the natural ecosystems of the birds

that live there. Visitors can walk through the aviaries, observe several reptile species and stop by the butterfly house.
Rodovia BR-469 (Rodovia das Cataratas), Km 17.1, tel. (45) 3529-8282. Daily, 8:30am – 5:30pm.

Boat trips on the Iguaçu River near the massive falls

⑤ Usina Hidrelétrica de Itaipu

Gather enough iron and steel to construct 380 Eiffel Towers and enough concrete for 210 Maracanã soccer stadiums. Add to this soil and rock equivalent of more than twice the volume of Sugarloaf Mountain, and the result is one of the greatest engineering feats in the world: Itaipu Hydroelectric Plant, which supplies energy to about 25 percent of Brazil and 90 percent of Paraguay. Guided visits at six different times between Monday and Saturday include a video and bus tour. The first stop is the floodgate where water gushes out when Itaipu Lake is above its normal level. The second stop at the central observation deck offers a panoramic view of the whole plant. Also on the premises are a museum, the **Ecomuseu**, and a nature reserve, the **Refúgio Biológico Bela Vista**. Make arrangements in advance to tour the inside of the plant. On Fridays and Saturdays at 8:30pm, take a trip to see the whole of Itaipu lit up.
Avenida Tancredo Neves, 6731, tel. (45) 3520-6999.

The Argentinean Side

⑥ Parque Nacional del Iguazu

The sheer magnitude of the view from the Brazilian side is amazing, but the Argentinean side really reveals the brute force of the falls up close. It can be reached by boat or by trails that starts as the visitors' center. The upper circuit is the shortest and easiest of the three trails. It extends for 650 meters, and there are no steps to climb. The river is visible several meters before it tumbles over the edge in giant waterfalls. The lower circuit, at 1.7 kilometers (just over a mile), has many steps and lookout points, and hikers can almost touch the falls. From that point, take a boat from the port to **Ilha San Martin**. Fit visitors can continue the walk on the island, which includes a steep climb to enjoy the view on a rail that takes five hours total. Boats that get very close to the falls also set out from the port. The third route is a walkway of approximately one kilometer that nears the high section of Garganta do Diabo (Devil's Throat). A train takes visitors to the beginning of the trail. Everyone, including children, needs a passport or original identity card to get into Parque Nacional del Iguazu.
Victoria Aguirre, 66, tel. (54-3757) 42-3252, 42-0722 or www.iguazuargentina.com. Daily, 8am – 6pm. Open until 7pm in spring and summer. Boat trips: Iguazu Jungle Explorer, tel. (54-3757) 42-1696.

Our Recommendation

On the Brazilian side of Iguaçu National Park, **Tropical das Cataratas Eco Resort**, a hotel built in Portuguese colonial style, sits in front of the falls. Eat breakfast at one of the highly coveted tables on the veranda and drink in the panoramic view. The only rooms with a similar view are the two presidential suites and the five luxury apartments *(Rodovia BR-469, Rodovia das Cataratas, Km 28, tel. (45) 2102-7000).*

Additional information on page 462.

SANTA CATARINA

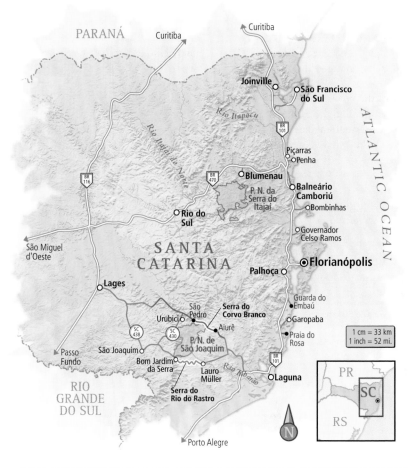

Curitiba

Curitiba

Porto Alegre

1 cm = 33 km
1 inch = 52 mi.

HIGHLIGHTS

- The beautiful beaches and lively Lagoa da Conceição in **Florianópolis**.
- Diving at the Reserva Biológica Marinha do Arvoredo in **Bombinhas**.
- Farol de Santa Marta in **Laguna**.
- Guarda do Embaú in **Palhoça**.

- Praia do Rosa in **Garopaba**.
- **Serra do Rio do Rastro** between Orleans and Bom Jardim da Serra.
- The Historic buildings in **São Francisco do Sul**.

WHEN TO GO

- In **summer** for visiting the fashionable beaches.
- In **autumn** to enjoy the sea in peace and quiet; it's still warm, but the beaches are less crowded than in the summer.
- In **winter** to see snow in São Joaquim.

- Between **August** and **March** for surfing (mullet-fishing season is between April and July, and surfing is forbidden).
- Between **July** and **November** to see the southern right whales on the southern coast.

Lagoinha do Leste beach, south of Florianópolis, is one of the island's most beautiful

FLORIANÓPOLIS

The capital of Santa Catarina sits on an island of 424,000 square kilometers (164,000 sq mi) – 40 percent of which is covered by thick Atlantic forest – and a small 12-square-kilometer chunk of mainland. The island's greenery and the beautiful

sea are the main reasons for the excellent reputation of "Floripa," as the city is affectionately known. The city, with a population of 370,000, maintains a provincial air and is surprisingly diverse, sporting places from built-up areas facing the mainland and on the mainland itself to simple fishing villages and wild beaches in the south of the island. Floripa officially has 42 beaches, but the number goes up to 100 if you count those that emerge from the rocks at low tide. Seasons are well defined in the city, with hot summers and cold winters. The dreaded south wind might kick up at any time of year, however, lowering the temperature by 10 degrees Celsius. In those conditions, find beaches that are protected from the wind.

GETTING AROUND

To tour Florianópolis' many beaches, stay in the central region to make it easy to access all the parts of the island. A car is almost required for a visit to the capital. Buses take a long time, because the island is relatively long: fifty-four kilometers (33 miles) from one end to the other. Taxis are expensive for the same reason. The most relaxing thing to do is choose one spot, explore the immediate surroundings and leave the rest of the island for another day.

THE NORTH COAST

This area boasts the calmest seas and most agreeable temperatures in Floripa, and it was the first spot to attract tourists – which is why it's very developed and has dozens of hotels and guesthouses. The north of the island is divided into "*mar de dentro*" and "*mar de fora*". Beaches on the northern part face the mainland northern part has beaches facing the mainland. They have calm, warm waters and include **Canasvieiras, Ponta das Canas**, and **Jurerê**, which has a shopping mall. On the other side, the beaches face the open sea and strong waves bring currents of cold water. They lower the overall temperature with the water on beaches such as **Praia dos Ingleses** and **Praia Brava**. Young people flock to Praia Brava, but the north coast tends to attract families. The good facilities on these beaches draw big crowds. **Daniela**, **Santinho**, and **Lagoinha do Norte** also merit a visit.

OUR RECOMMENDATION

Pousada da Vigia sits on the quiet beach of Lagoinha do Norte, on the northern part of the island. Roteiros de Charme, an association that rates hotels, recommends this guesthouse – the only one in Florianópolis to earn that distinction. The rooms have saunas, jacuzzis and entertainment centers *(Rua Cônego Valmor Castro, 291, Praia de Lagoinha de Ponta das Canas, tel. (48) 3284-1789).*

Additional information on page 462.

BEACHES IN THE EAST

Two ocean-facing beaches in the middle of the island attract a young crowd. **Praia da Joaquina** and **Praia Mole**, near Lagoa da Conceição, are known for good surfing. Too many tourists have hurt Joaquina, but the hills surrounding Mole protect it from the relentless building. Surfers also frequent unspoiled **Moçambique**.

THE SOUTH

The southern part of the island offers nearly untouched beaches where visitors can meet *Manezinhos*, as the locals are called. Don't forget: the ocean here is freezing. Beaches like **Praia de Pântano do Sul**, **Armação**, and **Matadeiro** still have authentic fishing villages. **Lagoinha do Leste**, the star of local ecotourism, is considered one of Floripa's most beautiful beaches. **Naufragados** and **Praia da Solidão** are also spectacular.

OUR RECOMMENDATION

Praia do Pântano do Sul's main attractions are the seafood and *cachaça* (white sugar-cane rum) served at **Bar do Arante**. Its walls are plastered with notes left by customers – a tradition from the 1960s *(Rua Abelardo Otacílio Gomes, 254, tel. (48) 3237-7022; daily, 11am–midnight).* Another restaurant worth a visit is **Pedacinho do Céu**. The owner, the famous Dona Zenaide, fishes in front of her house and makes what many consider to be the best *pirão* (sauce thickened with flour) *(Rua da Praia, 430, tel. (48) 3237-7280; high season: daily, 10am until the last customer leaves; low season: Fri and Sat, 10am – 11:30pm).*

Additional information on page 462.

BEACHES IN FLORIANÓPOLIS

❶ Daniela

Clear, warm waters make beach ideal for small children and a favorite among families. The Rio Ratones and the sea meet at the end of the beach to form a lagoon. Ilha Ratones island and its fort sit in front of the beach.

❷ Jurerê Internacional

A condo and houses for rent during high season are located on this beach, which also has calm waters and fine sand. A nature reserve protects the surrounding vegetation. Four restaurants also offer beach chairs and umbrellas. Next door is São José da Ponta Grossa Fort, located on Praia do Forte.

❸ Ponta das Canas

This beach sits at the end of the stretch of sand overlooking the mainland, which begins in Canasvieiras. The west-facing rocks afford a stunning view at sunset, and the beach has a few houses. A half-hour trail leads to Lagoinha do Norte.

❹ Lagoinha do Norte

Rocks on the right side of this beach are excellent for diving in the calm, clear waters. A 20-minute walk leads to Ponta do Rapa, the extreme north of Santa Catarina Island. A few bars and restaurants are located near the access road to a lagoon.

❺ Brava

Surfers are drawn to the strong waves breaking near the beach. The access road spans a hill overlooking the whole beach. Unfortunately, apartment buildings up to four stories high detract from the view

❻ Ingleses

As one of the most built-up beaches on the island, Ingleses offers facilities for huge numbers of tourists. It has the Museu do Naufrágio, a museum displaying parts of a Spanish vessel that sunk here in the 17th- century.

❼ Santinho

Rock inscriptions were found on this beach. Its huge waves attract surfers. A resort has taken over the entire right side of the beach, but dunes line the almost-deserted left-hand side.

❽ Moçambique

This long beach inside the Parque Florestal do Rio Vermelho reserve extends for 13 kilometers (8 miles). It is wild, and there are no kiosks serving drinks. It's not safe to walk on the beach at night.

❾ Barra da Lagoa

This fishing village has calmer seas than neighboring Moçambique, and its waves are perfect for beginning surfers. It offers several modest guesthouses, houses for rent in the high season, and simple restaurants. A suspension bridge leads to the rocks where visitors will find a lighthouse and natural pools ideal for diving.

❿ Galheta

Accessible by trails leading from Praia Mole or Praia de Barra da Lagoa, this beach is a conservation area with a section for nude sunbathing. The water is calmer and warmer than at Praia Mole. Ancient rock drawings grace the rock faces on the left.

⓫ Mole

Although the cold, rough ocean is dangerous for swimmers, this beach attracts surfers and young people. The island's gay meeting point is located at the end of the beach, before Galheta. Traffic often clogs the roads into Mole.

⓬ Joaquina

The waves on this beach are perfect for surf championships; its dunes are ideal for sand-boarding, a kind of snowboarding on sand. Tourist buses have started to visit Joaquina in recent years. They tend to cluster around the left-hand corner. Travelers looking for peace and quiet should go to the other side, where the beach is almost deserted. Campeche Village is at beach' southernmost point.

⓭ Armação

The name "armação" means "ship's tackle" and refers to the shipyard for fitting whaleboats in the 19th and 20th centuries. The waves attract surfers, who don't mind the freezing water. Visitors can rent boats for trips to Ilha do Campeche.

BR 101

BR 101

Porto Alegre

PR

SP

SC

RS

1 cm = 2.5 km
1 inch = 3.9 mi.

Ponta Grossa

Canasvieiras

Ilha Ratones
Grande

Ilha Ratones
Pequena

Santo Antônio
de Lisboa

Ratones

Vargem
Pequena

São João do
Rio Vermelho

Ingleses do
Rio Vermelho

Ilha das
Aranhas

Baía
Norte

SC
402

SC
403

SC
406

SC
401

Lagoa
da
Conceição

SC
404

Lagoa

Canto da
Lagoa

Ilha do
Xavier

Baía
Sul

Carianos

SC
406

Tapera
da Base

Aeroporto
Hercílio Luz

Ilha Maria
Francisca

Ribeirão
da Ilha

Campeche

SC
405

SC
405

Ilha do
Campeche

Lagoa
do
Peri

SC
401

SC
406

Tapera

Pântano do Sul

Caieiras da
Barra do Sul

Ilha Irmã
Pequena

Ilha Irmã
do Meio

Ilha Irmã
de Fora

Ilha
Moleques
do Sul

ATLANTIC OCEAN

⑭ Matadeiro

This beach is the only place on the island to rent a seafront house for a reasonable price. It is reachable by a 10-minute trail from Armação. Its rough seas attract surfers.

⑮ Lagoinha do Leste

Many people consider this untamed beach the most beautiful on the island. It is surrounded by native vegetation and boasts dunes, a river, and a lagoon, and it has rough seas and tube waves. The only way to reach it is by trail from Pântano do Sul or Matadeiro.

⑯ Da Solidão

This beach's name – "solitude" – says everything: this is a place for getting away from it all. Encircled by hills, it is accessible by car after a long, winding drive.

⑰ Naufragados

This beach is reachable only by trail or boat from Caieiras da Barra do Sul, but the heavenly scenery makes the effort worthwhile. Don't miss the view from the lighthouse. A fishing community is located here, as well as a campsite and houses to rent.

The Mercado Público occupies a 19th-century building

LAGOA AND THE CENTRAL REGION

LAGOA DA CONCEIÇÃO

No matter where visitors spend the day, anyone looking for fun at night heads for Lagoa da Conceição. Because it's in the center of the island, en route to the fashionable beaches of Joaquina and Mole, traffic is heavy and creates jams on weekends and holidays. Italian, Mexican, Portuguese, Japanese and pizza restaurants are clustered around the Centrinho area. All-you-can-eat shrimp and seafood restaurants are concentrated near the marina and on Avenida das Rendeiras. There are plenty of bars, too, lined up next to each other and blaring music. Try **Barracuda Grill**, a reliable spot to relish the city's traditional fare *(Avenida das Rendeiras, 30, tel. (48) 3232-5301; high season: daily, 11am until the last customer leaves; low season: Mon, Tue and Thu – Sat noon – midnight; Sun, 11am – 6pm)*. One place of particular interest is **Costa da Lagoa**, a village with a regular boat service from the marina in Lagoa. It can also be reached by a seven-kilometer (4.5-mile) trail. Fishermen and people looking for an alternative lifestyle live in the village, which also has reasonably priced restaurants.

CENTRO

The city center, 12 kilometers (7.5 miles) from Lagoa da Conceição, boasts bridge connecting the island to the mainland. At 819 meters (2,500 feet), the **Ponte Hercílio Luz** is one of the longest suspension bridges in the world. It's lit up at night and closed to traffic. Another attraction is the **Mercado Público**, a market operating out of a building dating from 1898 *(Avenida Paulo Fontes, no #, tel. (48) 3224-0189; Mon – Fri, 7am – 10pm; Sat, 8am – 1pm)*. The bar **Box 32** is always full of admirers of its delicious shrimp *pastel* (deep-fried pastry) accompanied by pepper sauce and the house *cachaça (tel. (48) 3224-5588; Mon – Fri, 10am – 10pm; Sat, 10am – 3pm)*. Next door is the equally interesting **Casa da Alfândega**, a building that dates from 1876 and now houses a gallery selling local arts and crafts, including *bilro* (bobbin) lace and miniature figures from folklore (*Rua Conselheiro Mafra, 141, tel. (48) 3028-8100, 3028-8102; Mon – Fri, 9am – 6pm; Sat, 9am –* *noon*). During a stroll around **Praça Quinze**, check out the Azorean-style semi-detached houses built with crushed seashells and whale oil.

A BOAT RIDE

If Santa Catarina Island doesn't satisfy the need for solitude, escape to the nearby islets. **Ilha do Campeche** has good water for diving and a nearly deserted beach. Trails lead to a cave with 150 cave drawings, which have made the spot a national heritage site. The attractions on **Ilha Anhatomirim** and **Ilha Ratones Grande** are the forts built by the Portuguese in the 18th century to protect the colony, although no shots were ever fired from them. The forts are mostly restored and open to visitors. Forte de Santa Cruz do Anhatomirim, dating from 1744 and situated on Anhatomirim, is the biggest and oldest fort in Florianópolis. Forte de Santo Antônio is on Ratones. After visiting the remains of the barracks and gunpowder stocks, explore the Atlantic forest trail.

Contact: Scuna Sul, tel. (48) 3225-1806.

AZOREAN HERITAGE

Overpopulation and natural disasters drove thousands of immigrants from their homes in the Azores Archipelago in the mid-18th century. More than 6,000 landed on the island of Santa Catarina between 1748 and 1756. These Azoreans first made their living hunting whales, fishing, and farming manioc. Signs of their heritage still remain in the local accent, crafts, and architecture. Azorean-style buildings can still be found in the immigrants' first villages, **Santo Antônio de Lisboa** and **Ribeirão da Ilha**. Waterfront restaurants in both villages serve mussels and local oysters. Another sign of Azorean heritage is the local version of *bumba-meu-boi*, seen at folk festivals and other events.

Deserted beaches and good diving spots dot Ilha do Campeche

The thermals at Lagoa da Conceição make for good kite-surfing

SPORTS

The combination of mountains, bays, beaches, and constant wind, makes Florianópolis an excellent place for adventure sports.

SURFING
Praia da Joaquina and **Praia Mole** are the main venues for surfing. Every year in October and November, Joaquina hosts stages of the WCT and WQS (the first and second divisions of the main world professional surfing circuit). **Praia Campeche**, **Praia da Armação**, **Praia do Matadeiro**, **Praia da Lagoinha do Leste**, and **Praia do Santinho** also have good waves. Surfing is not allowed on any of the island's beaches between April and July because it disrupts mullet fishing.

PARAGLIDING
Florianópolis offers countless locations with regular thermals that are ideal for paragliding. **Lagoa da Conceição** is the most popular. Beginners can try tandem flights.
Contact: Parapente Sul, tel. (48) 3232-0791.

WINDSURFING AND KITESURFING
Brave the strong winds on the **Joaquina**, **Mole**, and **Moçambique** beaches or sail on the calm waters of **Lagoa da Conceição**. Intensive courses are offered for beginners; experienced enthusiasts can simply rent the necessary equipment.
Courses and equipment rental: Openwinds, tel. (48) 3232-4443; Windcenter, tel. (48) 3232-2278.

SAND BOARDING
This sport – sliding down dunes on a wooden board – is very popular on **Praia de Joaquina**. Rent boards in front of Bar Dunas on the access road.

THE NORTH COAST

BOMBINHAS

This city deserves its glowing reputation for white beaches and clear water, but that fame has a price: big crowds in the summer. To enjoy the natural beauty of the spot, 60 kilometers (37 miles) north of Florianópolis, don't go in the high season. Lovers of the underwater world will enjoy **Ilha do Arvoredo**, the best diving spot in southern Brazil. It is a protected biological reserve, and with calm seas, visibility can reach 25 meters (82 feet). The **Parque Ambiental Família Schürmann** opened in 2005 on land owned by members of the Schürmann family, who spent 20 years sailing around the world on a yacht. Photographs of their voyage are displayed in the park, which also has small trails through Atlantic forest vegetation *(Avenida Vereador Manuel José dos Santos, 220, Praia do Ribeiro, tel. (47) 3369-3690; Dec – Feb: daily, 2pm – 8pm; other months: 2pm – 5pm)*. A boat ride from neighboring Porto Belo will take visitors to the island of the same name, to enjoy the beaches, trails, rock drawings, and museum.

OUR RECOMMENDATION

Charming **Ponta dos Ganchos Exclusive Resort**, in the town of Governador Celso Ramos next to Bombinhas, is a romantic, intimate resort offering bungalows with jacuzzis, saunas, and fireplaces. It also boasts a private beach and island. The resort does not accept guests under 18 *(Rua Eupídio Alves do Nascimento, 104, Praia de Gancho de Fora, tel. (48) 3262-5000, 3262-5024).*

Additional information on page 462.

A flying gurnard

A sea horse

BEACHES

Bombinhas sits on the tip of a peninsula, surrounded by sea. There are 29 beaches, although most are built-up and some are only accessible by forest trails. To request a guide, inquire at the **Casa do Turista** *(tel. (47) 3393-6000)*. For easy access to calm waters, try **Bombas**, **Bombinhas**, and **Zimbros**. A trail starts from Zimbros and leads to a string of five semi-deserted beaches and a small waterfall, all of which can also be reached by boat from Zimbros or Canto Grande de Dentro. The large beach at **Mariscal** and the cove at **Quatro Ilhas**, both face the open sea and have ideal conditions for surfing; both also offer good facilities and are easily reachable. **Canto Grande de Fora**, a continuation of Mariscal, has a pleasant trail called Trilha do Morro do Macaco that ends at a lookout point.

Another trail leads to tiny, isolated **Praia da Tainha**, which can also be reached by dirt road.

DIVING

The abundance of marine life near Ilha do Arvoredo led to the creation of the **Reserva Biológica Marinha**, a nature reserve that includes two neighboring islands, Ilha de Galé and Ilha Deserta. Visitors are not allowed on the islands. Diving is permitted only in the southwest section of Arvoredo, where several Bombinhas tour agencies organize trips for free diving or scuba diving. Take something to ward off seasickness before setting sail, because the trip to the reserve takes an hour on the open sea.

Contact: Patadacobra, tel. (47) 3369-2119; Submarine, tel. (47) 3369-2223, 3369-2473; Acquatrek, tel. (47) 3369-2137.

BALNEÁRIO CAMBORIÚ AND SURROUNDINGS

Balneário Camboriú, 81 kilometers (50 miles) from Florianópolis, is a quiet town that many retirees call home. In the summer, however, it turns into a hotspot for teenagers from the north coast of Santa Catarina, who cram the beaches. For those searching for excitement, the best accommodations can be found on the parallel streets Avenida Atlântica (also called Avenida Beira-Mar) and Avenida Brasil. Avoid traffic by taking the 24-hour tram that runs from one avenue to the other. Anyone looking for peace and quiet can find it to the north on **Praia dos Amores**, almost on the border with Itajaí, or to the south on beaches like **Taquaras**, **Estaleiro**, **Laranjeiras**, and **Praia do Pinho**, which can be reached by the Rodovia Interpraias highway. Praia do Pinho is a nude beach that is off-limits to clothed swimmers. Balneário Camboriú is popular with visitors to **Beto Carrero World**, the largest theme park in Latin America. It is located in nearby Penha, 36 kilometers (22 miles) away.

UNIPRAIAS CABLE CAR

A cable car provides spectacular views of Balneário Camboriú's shoreline from 1,600 meters (5,000 feet) in the air. The cars cross **Morro da**

Unipraias cable car affords the best view of the Barra do Sul coast

The Império das Águas ride at Beto Carrero World in Penha

Aguada and run from **Praia de Barra Sul** to **Praia de Laranjeiras**. Riders can stop halfway through at **Estação Mata Atlântica** for the lookout point and two canopy-climbing circuits, where walkways lead climbers through the treetops.
Avenida Atlântica, 6006, Barra Sul, tel. (47) 3367-0493. Wed – Sun, 9:30am – 6pm.

BETO CARRERO WORLD

This huge enterprise boasts 85 attractions divided into seven themed areas spread out over 2 million square meters (21 million square feet). The park opened in 1991 and draws around 600,000 visitors a year. The **Big Tower** ride drops passengers from a 100-meter (328-foot) tower that has a wonderful view of the ocean at 120 kilometers (75 miles) per hour. A circus has horse shows, magic shows, dance performances, and a mini-zoo with monkeys, tigers, giraffes, and camels, among other animals.
Rua Inácio Francisco de Sousa, 1597, Praia da Armação, tel. (47) 3261-2000; Mar – Jun and Aug – Oct: Thu – Sun, 9am – 7pm; Nov – Feb and July: daily, 9am – 7pm.

OKTOBERFEST IN BLUMENAU

Oktoberfest has brought fame to Blumenau, 65 kilometers (40 miles) inland from Balneário Camboriú. For 17 days every October, the city – which is home to a large German colony – turns into the beer capital of Brazil. It's a festival of dancing, music, fun, and ro- mance that young people espe- cially enjoy. The event was es- tablished in 1984 to raise funds after a flood. It was inspired by the festival of the same name in Munich, but Blumenau's event has grown far beyond its ori- gins. During the day, the *Bier- wagen* (beer truck) distributes free beer on Rua Quinze de Novembro, and nothing goes better with beer than German *bratwurst*. The merry-making continues at night in the Proeb Pavilion and Vila Germâni- ca, an arcade of snack bars and gift stores. Steer clear to avoid crowds of drunken teenagers.

SÃO FRANCISCO DO SUL

Residents of this charming town, 188 kilometers (117 miles) from Florianópolis, insist that Frenchman Binot Palmier de Gonneville in 1504 discovered the island on which the town sits. They even celebrated the town's 500th anniversary in 2004; however, São Francisco do Sul was officially founded in 1658. Collectively, its 150 or so buildings are a national heritage site that the Monumenta Program is restoring. A walk along Rua Babitonga shows off lovely examples of these buildings. Don't miss **Igreja Matriz Nossa Senhora da Graça**, a church begun in 1699 but not completed until the end of the 19th century. **Enseada**, **Ubatuba**, and **Prainha** beaches – all removed from the city center – offer the excitement not found in the town. **Itaguaçu** is calmer.

MUSEU NACIONAL DO MAR

The National Sea Museum's collection includes canoes, whaling boats, *jangada* rafts, and models from all over Brazil. One room is dedicated to Brazilian sailor Amyr Klink. Local fishing activity is commemorated with a replica of a fisherman's house.

Rua Quintino Bocaiúva, no #, tel. (47) 3444-1868, 3444-2612. Tue – Sun, 10am – 6pm.

OUR RECOMMENDATION

🍽 Some of the best seafood restaurants in the São Francisco region can be found in the fishing village of Glória. Cross Baía de Babitonga by boat to the famous **Jacizinho Batista** – the view alone is worth the trip *(Estrada Geral do Estaleiro, no #, tel. (47) 3449-5142; Mon – Sat, noon – 10pm; Sun, noon – 6pm).*

Additional information on page 462.

Museu Nacional do Mar in São Francisco do Sul: a collection of models and boats

Ilha do Papagaio, exclusively accessible to residents at the eponymous guesthouse

THE SOUTH COAST

GUARDA DO EMBAÚ

Guarda do Embaú combines the simplicity of a fishing village with the fun of a spot popular with surfers. Located 44 kilometers (27 miles) south of Florianópolis, the town lures visitors to its beautiful, wild beaches with strong waves. During high season, it attracts the largest concentration of young fun-seekers in the state of Santa Catarina. The beach itself – with powdery, white sand and a steep drop on the shoreline that causes its substantial waves – can be reached from the village by crossing the Rio da Madre by canoe or swimming, or walking for 10 minutes over a hill with a view of the entire region. One warning: Surfing is forbidden between April and July for mullet fishing, which is the locals' main livelihood. There are five more beaches in the neighborhood to please everyone from nudists to fans of the calm sea. **Gamboa** is the most deserted. Lodging and restaurant options in Guarda are limited, and many visitors rent houses for the summer. Located further inland, the **Parque Estadual da Serra do Tabuleiro** offers trails through native *restinga* and Atlantic forest vegetation, where visitors can see tapirs, capybaras, wild ducks, and rheas, among other animals *(Rodovia BR-101, Km 238, Baixada do Maciambu, Palhoça, (48) 3286-2624; Wed – Sun, 9am – 5pm).*

OUR RECOMMENDATION

Pousada Ilha do Papagaio is an exclusive hotel with just 20 chalets, all of which offer views of the sea. It sits on an island of the same name, which is completely covered in forest and accessible only to guests. The details make the difference: each room is outfitted with incense, chocolates and a bottle of sparkling wine. Members of the Sehn family own the guesthouse, live on the island, and greet guests personally. Activities include water-skiing, sailing, and diving *(tel. (48) 3286-1242).*

Additional information on page 462.

Praia de Garopaba, in the center of the town of the same name, with Siriú in the background

GAROPABA

Surfers and hippies from the neighboring state of Rio Grande do Sul discovered Garopaba in the 1970s. Located 96 kilometers (60 miles) from Florianópolis, the town retained the charm of a seaside village while developing good tourist facilities. Most visitors are surfers. All the beaches except Ferrugem are surrounded by hills, where many of the hotels are situated so that they can take advantage of the coastal views. Two unspoiled beaches, **Siriú** and **Gamboa**, are fairly far away from the town. Tiny **Praia de Garopaba** is right in the town center and popular with families. **Silveira** is favored by surfers, but young people gather on **Ferrugem**, where nightlife begins at 1 a.m. with no fixed end time. Ferrugem sports several guesthouses. It is a pretty beach, although the water is usually freezing.

WHALE WATCHING

Every year from July to November, the south of Santa Catarina becomes an open-air venue for whale-watching. Southern right whales migrate from Antarctica to reproduce and suckle their young in Brazilian waters. This species was hunted until 1973; since 2000, the whales have enjoyed shelter in a marine protection area of 140 kilometers (87 miles) called the Área de Proteção Ambiental (APA) da Baleia-Franca. Visitors can see the whales from the coast of Garopaba and other area, but biologist-led boat trips can take tourists very close to the whales.

Instituto Baleia-Franca: Rua Manuel Álvaro de Araújo, 200, Centro, tel. (48) 3254-4199.

Praia do Rosa

Considered one of the most beautiful beaches in southern Brazil, Praia do Rosa has two kilometers of sand surrounded by grassy hills, lagoons, and the sea. It is 18 kilometers (11 miles) from Garopaba, but it belongs to the municipality of Imbituba. Although this beach offers good food and sophisticated lodgings, it retains an air of simplicity. Its biggest fans are young people, especially surfers from Rio Grande do Sul. Argentineans also visit frequently, and some have settled here. The dirt access roads to the beach are in poor condition (made even worse when it rains) and do not have adequate signage. Park your car and go on foot, even though this means a lot of legwork on the hilly route. Make the most of the trails that lead to neighboring **Ibiraquera** and **Vermelha.** The main bars are in the southern corner of Praia do Rosa. Go to the other end of the beach for peace and quiet.

Our Recommendation

Pousada Quinta do Bucanero has rooms that are essentially observation decks with ocean views. A trail leads to the lagoon, where visitors can take boats to the beach. The Roteiros de Charme Hotel Association recommends the hotel *(Estrada Geral da Praia do Rosa, no #, tel. (48) 3355-6056).* The lovely **Pousada Caminho do Rei**, another hilltop guesthouse, has nine spacious, charming rooms that all overlook the sea *(Estrada do Alto do Morro, no #, tel. (48)3355-6062).*

Additional information on page 462.

Praia do Rosa, in Imbituba: sophisticated lodgings and haute cuisine in a rustic setting

LAGUNA

Laguna, founded in 1676, is the second oldest town in the state situated 118 kilometers (73 miles) south of Florianópolis. The thousands of visitors who flock to the town every year, however, are more interested in the beaches and lagoons – especially those in the **Farol de Santa Marta** region – than the rich architectural heritage. They are missing out: the 600 houses and buildings that make Laguna a national heritage site reveal a wealth of history. Highlights include the **Museu Anita Garibaldi**, which operates out of a building dating from 1747. During the War of Tatters, Giuseppe Garibaldi and his wife Anita, a native of Laguna, led the movement to proclaim the Juliana Republic in the house *(Praça da República Juliana, no #, tel. (48) 3644-4947; Mon, noon – 6pm; Tue – Sun, 9am – 6pm)*. Every year on July 22, an open-air performance with 300 actors re-enacts the revolutionaries capturing the town. The lively street carnival is famous throughout the state.

FAROL DE SANTA MARTA

The traditional fishing community of Farol de Santa Marta sits amid lagoons, dunes, and *restinga* vegetation. To get there, take a ferry across the Canal da Barra in Laguna and then travel by dirt road for 17 kilometers (10.5 miles). A working lighthouse overlooks the village of about 2,000 inhabitants. It offers good hotels and plenty of rental houses – generally belonging to locals who rent out their own places during the summer to supplement their income. Choose a hillside house for splendid ocean views. Although **Prainha** is centrally located, it is generally a fishing village and not particularly suitable for swimmers. Crossing the hill takes visitors to **Praia Grande**, a large, deserted beach surrounded by dunes. For a good walk, head from Praia Grande to **Galhetas**, a small village with an abandoned atmosphere that's been almost taken over by sand. Ask for directions to a beautiful, tiny beach hidden among the rocks.

MOUNTAIN RANGES

Snow falling in the winter is the biggest attraction in the mountains of Santa Catarina. The snow blankets the forests, freezes over small lakes and waterfalls, and creates a singular landscape for tropical Brazil. When snow is in the forecast, crowds flock to São Joaquim, 240 kilometers (150 miles) from Florianópolis. Because accommodations in hotels and guesthouses run out quickly, many locals in the town open their homes to visitors. Snow also falls in neighboring municipalities **Urubici** and **Bom Jardim da Serra**. From Urubici, visitors can take trips to waterfalls and cinematic mountain scenery. Remember that the water is freezing even in the summer, and it's better to be accompanied by a local guide *(Urubici Ecoturismo, tel. (49) 9125-7198)*. Bom Jardim da Serra offers comfortable lodgings at a high altitude in the **Rio do Rastro Eco Resort**, a hotel with sophisticated lakeside

Rio do Rastro Eco Resort, a hotel offering sophisticated chalets in the Santa Catarina mountains

chalets, on-site trails, and horseback riding *(Rodovia sc-438, Km 130, tel. (48) 3491-2610, 3491-2621)*. In Lages, 80 kilometers (50 miles) inland from São Joaquim, experience rural tourism with accommodations available on several farms.

Serra do Rio do Rastro

The stretch of winding road on the Rodovia sc-438 highway between Orleans and Bom Jardim da Serra is an unforgettable trip in itself. The 12-kilometer (7.5-mile) road climbs the huge rock face that separates the coast from the southern part of the plateau. The road alternates between asphalt and concrete amid the natural beauty of São Joaquim National Park. After the drive on one of Brazil's most beautiful highways, visitors emerge to see a view of the entire region: the winding road, the valley, and, on clear days, the ocean. Regular cars can climb the range with no

problem, but be careful behind the wheel, because snow can appear out of the blue at any time of year. In the winter, the ice forming on wet surfaces is the biggest potential danger. The transition from Atlantic forest on the plains and coastal hills to a landscape of araucaria pines and high-altitude woodland is evident all along the highway.

Adventure Park Snow Valley

This private park has 2.7 kilometers (two miles) of trails with giant ferns, araucaria pines, and an array of flowers, waterfalls, streams, and lakes. The trails range in difficulty from easy to medium, and some are appropriate for children. Specialist guides, a restaurant, craft store, camping area, and simple wooden cabins for overnight stays are all available *(Rodovia sc-438, 10 km from São Joaquim, going toward Bom Jardim da Serra, tel. (49) 3233-3447; Mon – Fri, 8am – 5pm; Sat and Sun, 7:30am – 7pm)*.

A winding road in the Serra do Rio do Rastro range

MORRO DA IGREJA AND SERRA DO CORVO BRANCO

The national record for cold temperatures – an incredible 17.86 degrees Celsius below zero – was recorded in 1996 at the top of Morro da Igreja, near the town of Urubici. The peak offers a wonderful view of the mountains, canyons, and the valley linking the range to the coast. Travelers can also see one of Santa Catarina's picture-postcard views: **Pedra Furada** a rock with the center worn away to leave a 30-meter (99-foot) hole. To get there from Urubuci, drive 10 kilometers of dirt road on Rodovia SC-439 highway, toward Grão-Pará, turning right at the sign. Then, a climb of approximately 15 kilometers (nine miles) begins on an asphalt road, with concrete on the steeper sections. Still heading toward Grão-Pará on Rodovia SC-439 highway, cross the beautiful Serra do Corvo Branco range. Some consider these mountains more beautiful than the Serra do Rio do Rastro. They are also extremely steep: three kilometers of dizzying bends and precipices link the high ground to the coastal plain. The asphalt and dirt roads demand drivers have dexterity and cool heads. Don't drive on this road when it's raining.

RURAL TOURISM IN LAGES

Lages is a pioneer of rural tourism, in which visitors stay in authentic farmhouses and experience the daily life on the farm. They watch milking chores and the daily tasks of cattle farming, and eat typical farm meals. At night, around the *fogo-de-chão* (a type of open fire), guests sip wine and *chimarrão* tea, munch on pine nuts, and chat. **Fazenda Pedras Brancas** was one of the first farms to try rural tourism activity. It offers rooms and cabins, sauna, a heated pool, and trails to the rocks that gave it its name *(Rodovia SC-438, Km 10, tel. (49) 3223-2073)*. **Fazenda do Barreiro** organizes horseback-riding trips that can last up to a week and pass through lovely woodland, araucaria pine forests, and crystal-clear rivers. The farm has a good historical museum, with documents and antiques. Their rooms are heated, and the larger ones have jacuzzis *(Rodovia SC-438, Km 43, tel. (49) 3222-3031)*. **Hotel Fazenda Boqueirão** offers good leisure facilities: a heated pool, sauna, gym, children's activities, and a group room. Typical farm activities are abundant, as well as trails and horseback riding through the countryside *(Rodovia BR-282, Km 225, tel. (49) 3221-9900)*.

RIO GRANDE DO SUL

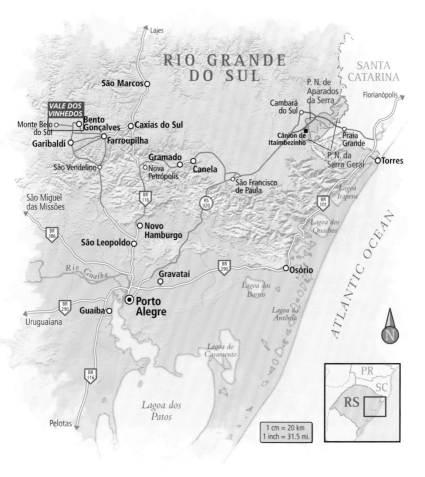

HIGHLIGHTS

- The **Porto Alegre** cultural circuit.
- **Gramado** and **Canela**, in the Serra Gaúcha region.
- The vineyards of **Bento Gonçalves**.
- The canyons of **Cambará do Sul**.
- The ruins of the São Miguel Arcanjo Jesuit Mission, in **São Miguel das Missões**.

WHEN TO GO

- **The first two weeks in August** for the Gramado Film Festival.
- Any time of year for the Caminho das Missões – **except September**, because of the risk of heavy rains.
- In **late October and early November** for the Porto Alegre Book Fair.
- From **January through March** for the grape harvest in the Garibaldi and Bento Gonçalves regions.

PORTO ALEGRE

CULTURAL CIRCUIT

① Memorial do Rio Grande do Sul
② MARGS
③ Mercado Público
④ Santander Cultural
⑤ Museu de Ciência e Tecnologia
⑥ Casa de Cultura Mário Quintana
⑦ Usina do Gasômetro
⑧ Theatro São Pedro
⑨ Parque Moinhos do Vento
⑩ Parque Farroupilha

Brazil's southernmost state capital, Porto Alegre, lies in a state famous for cherishing its traditions and keeping them alive. The city recently made international headlines for hosting events like the World Social Forum and the Mercosul Biennial art exhibit. With a population of almost 1.5 million and the country's highest per capita rate of both literacy and movie-going, "Porto (as locals call it) offers a wide variety of cultural centers and museums, as well as lively nightlife. The **Feira do Livro**, a book fair held in Praça da Alfândega since 1955, takes place in October and November. It offers books for sale, book release parties and talks by writers *(www.feiradolivro-poa.com.br)*. The city grew on the left bank of the Rio Guaíba river, close to its mouth at the estuarine Lagoa dos Patos lake, which looks like a large bay. The river is the ocean in this city; although it has no beaches for bathing, it does open the horizon and contribute to the region's high quality of life.

① MEMORIAL DO RIO GRANDE DO SUL

Much of the state's historical documentation is archived in the old post office and telegraph building, built in 1913. The memorial also displays panels with photographs of famous locals, such as and writer Érico Verissimo and singers Lupicínio Rodrigues and Elis Regina.
Rua 7 de Setembro, 1020, Centro, tel. (51) 3224-7210. Tue – Sat, 10am – 6pm.

② MUSEU DE ARTE DO RIO GRANDE DO SUL ADO MALAGOLI (MARGS)

This art museum in the Centro

neighborhood is one of several restored early 20th-century buildings. The museum houses the state's largest visual art collection, with works by Lasar Segall, Di Cavalcanti and Cândido Portinari. It also includes a bistro, café and a store selling decorative items, books and clothes. *Praça da Alfândega, no #, Centro, tel. (51) 3227-2311. Tue – Sun, 10am – 7pm.*

❸ MERCADO PÚBLICO

This building dates from 1869, and houses bars, restaurants and a market that sells food and other products. The most traditional restaurant is **Gambrinus**, which opened in 1889 and specializes in seafood and regional dishes *(tel. (51) 3226-6914)*. Bomba Royal – fruit salad served with ice cream and homemade cream – is the specialty at **Banca 40**, which is famous for its juices and ice cream *(tel. (51) 3226-3533)*. *Largo Glênio Peres, no #, Centro. Mon – Sat, 7:30am – 7pm.*

❹ SANTANDER CULTURAL

This neoclassical building contained a bank until 2001; now, it is home to a cultural center that offers a range of exhibits, lectures, shows and films. It also has a coin museum with a large collection of national coins and medals, a restaurant, bookstore, design store and a café installed in the old safety deposit room. *Rua 7 de Setembro, 1028, Centro, tel. (51) 3287-5500. Mon – Fri, 10am – 7pm; Sat, Sun, and holidays, 11am – 7pm.*

❺ MUSEU DE CIÊNCIA E TECNOLOGIA

Guides present more than 700 experiments at this science and technology museum. Although it's far away from other cultural attractions, the museum is a good destination for children and adolescents that adults will enjoy as well. *Avenida Ipiranga, 6681, Pontifícia Universidade Católica do Rio Grande do Sul (PUC-RS) campus, tel. (51) 3320-3521. Tue – Sun, 9am – 5pm.*

The Museu de Ciência e Tecnologia da PUC showcases various interactive experiments

⑥ Casa de Cultura Mário Quintana

For many years, renowned local poet Mário Quintana lived in a room in the old Hotel Majestic, where former presidents also used to stay. Now it is a lively cultural center with reading rooms, exhibit areas, libraries, theaters and centers for scenic and visual arts. The café on the top floor offers a lovely view of the Guaíba River.

Rua dos Andradas, 736, Centro, tel. (51) 3221-7147. Tue – Fri, 9am – 9pm; Sat, Sun and holidays, noon – 9pm.

⑦ Usina do Gasômetro

Built in 1928, this former thermal power plant was turned into a cultural center in 1989. Its location next to the Guaíba River makes it one of the best places to watch the sunset. It is also the departure point for boat trips on the river.

Avenida Presidente João Goulart, 551, Centro, tel. (51) 3212-5979. Tue – Sun, 9am – 9pm.

⑧ Theatro São Pedro

This neo-classical theater was built in 1858. It offers concerts, dance performances and plays from all over Brazil and abroad. Visits are guided. The charming foyer café has free live music on Thursdays at 8:30pm and serves lunch Monday through Friday.

Praça Marechal Deodoro no #, Centro, tel. (51) 3227-5300. Tue – Sun, from noon (except on show days). Café: Mon – Fri, 11:45am – 6:30pm; Sat, 4pm – 9pm; Sun, 4pm – 6pm.

⑨ Parque Moinhos de Vento

This 11.5-hectare (37-acre) park bordered by Rua Vinte e Quatro de Outubro, Rua Mostardeiro, Rua Comendado boasts tennis courts, a bowls area, a soccer field, ping-pong tables and a lake. The administrative headquarters are located inside a windmill. The park also serves as a meeting point for locals in the early evenings and on weekends.

Avenida Goethe, on the corner of Travessa

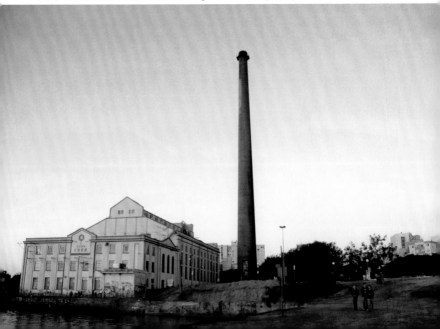

On the banks of the Guaíba River, Porto Alegre's old thermal power plant now houses a cultural center

The neoclassical Theatro São Pedro seats 700

Augusta, Moinhos de Vento, tel. (51) 3289-4868. Open 24 hours.

⑩ PARQUE FARROUPILHA
Better known as "Redenção," the park hosts a famous crafts fair with more than 300 stalls every Sunday.

The pleasant, lakeside **Café do Lago** is an excellent spot to enjoy live music in the evening *(tel. (51) 3212-4968; Mon – Fri, 2pm – 8pm; Sat and Sun, 10am – 8pm).*
Avenida João Pessoa, opposite # 1090, tel. (51) 3286-4458. Open 24 hours.

NIGHTLIFE

Cidade Baixa is the city's bohemian, alternative neighborhood. Try **Ossip**, which serves pizzas and snacks. Customers who can't find seats simply stand outside on the sidewalk *(Rua da República, 677, tel. (51) 3224-2422; daily, 7pm until the last customer leaves)*. The **Van Gogh** is famous for its soups and becomes a meeting spot at night *(Rua da República, 14, tel. (51) 3226-7480; daily, 5pm – 6am)*. Rua Fernando Gomes and Rua Padre Chagas – two interesting streets in the Moinhos de Vento neighborhood – are home to charming cafés, bars and restaurants. Young people meet at night at the Rua Fernando Gomes, nicknamed

calçada da fama (sidewalk of fame. In the summer, bars serve great food at outdoor tables. **Oficina Etílica Pub** offers a varied drinks menu, with accompaniments such as *carreteiro* (rice with beef jerky) served with bread, herbs and grated cheese *(Rua João Alfredo, 511, tel. (51) 3221-8542; Sun – Thu, 9pm – 4am; Fri and Sat, 9pm – 5am)*. Anyone looking for haute cuisine should try the French food from **Le Bistrot**. The house specialty is *linguado* (flounder) with a sesame crust with spinach and gorgonzola risotto *(Rua Fernando Gomes, 58, tel. (51) 3346-3812; Mon – Fri, 11:30am – 2:30pm and 7pm – midnight; Sat, Sun and holidays,*

noon – 4pm and 7pm – midnight). **Constantino Café**, which offers a wide menu, and couples might enjoy its back garden with discreet lighting *(Rua Fernando Gomes, 44, tel. (51) 3346-8589; Mon – Sat, 6pm – midnight)*. The classic **Ocidente**, a bar in the Bom Fim neighborhood, offers live music and parties with electronic music. An eclectic clientele frequents the bar, which serves vegetarian dishes during the day *(Avenida Osvaldo Aranha, 960, 1º floor, tel. (51) 3312-1347; Mon, 11:45am – 2:30pm; Tue and Thu, 11:45 – 2:30pm and 9:30pm – 3am; Fri, 11:45am – 2:30pm and 9:30pm – 6am; Sat, 11:45am – 3:30pm and 10pm – 6am)*.

Gramado offers gardens galore and Bavarian architecture

MOUNTAIN RANGES

GRAMADO AND CANELA

Located in the mountains, 131 kilometers (81 miles) north of Porto Alegre, Gramado is a traditional tourist destination – particularly during winter vacation season, when hotels are normally booked solid. This is particularly true during the first fortnight of August, when Gramado hosts Brazil's premiere film festival. Its attractions include Bavarian architecture and Swiss-style chalets; the town was originally colonized by the Germans. It also boasts chocolate factories, colonial furniture shops and restaurants serving trout and fondue. The town of Canela, 8 kilometers (5 miles) away, is quieter and offers nature activities in its parks. Don't forget to take warm clothing in winter, because temperatures can fall below zero.

BUDDHIST TEMPLE
The Chagdud Khadro, an unusual and very popular attraction, is a little piece of Tibet in the middle of the Serras Gaúchas region. It is located 20 kilometers (12 miles) from Gramado. Apprentice monks give tours of the temple and offer details on the richly decorated interior, replete with ornate altars, delicate sculptures and wall paintings depicting the life of Buddha. *Stupas* (large reliquaries) and statues surround the temple, all sheathed in silence. *Estrada Linha Águas Brancas, 1211, tel. (51) 3546-8200. Tue – Fri, 9am – noon and 1:30pm – 5pm; Sat and Sun, 9am – 5pm, except Buddhist holidays (call ahead to confirm).*

COLONIAL BREAKFAST IN NOVA PETRÓPOLIS

The best *café colonial* in the country is served in Nova Petrópolis, 34 kilometers (21 miles) from Gramado on Rodovia RS-235 highway. The tradition of this hearty meal began with the German immigrants and is kept alive in restaurants such as **Opa's Kaffehaus**, which offers a smorgasbord of 45 types of cakes, bread, cold cuts and typical German jellies *(Rua João Leão, 96, tel. (54) 3281-1273; Tue – Fri, 2pm – 8pm; Sat, 1pm – 8pm; Sun and holidays, midday – 8pm)*. **Colina Verde** serves Italian specialties like *capeletti* soup and local standards like stuffed beef ribs *(Rua Filipe Michaelsen, 160, exit at Km 185.5 on Rodovia BR-116, tel. (54) 3281-1388; Tue – Sun, 11:30am – 3pm)*.

FUN FOR THE KIDS

Children will especially enjoy Gramado's parks and lakes. Parque Knorr is home to **Aldeia do Papai Noel**, Santa's village. It includes a toy factory, a nativity scene and a museum of old toys *(Rua Bela Vista, 353, Centro, tel. (54) 3286-7332; Mon – Fri, 1:30pm – 8pm; Sat, 10:30am – 8pm; Sun, 10:30am – 7pm; winter: daily, 10:30am – 8pm)*. Another theme park, **Minimundo,** displays miniature replicas of Porto Alegre's port zone and Neuschwanstein Castle in Germany, among other sites *(Rua Horácio Cardoso,*

OUR RECOMMENDATION

🍽 **Restaurante Chez Pierre**, tucked away in the basement of a pottery shop, was the first restaurant in Gramado to serve fondue. But travelers who want to go beyond bread and cheese should try *pierrade*, pieces of meat grilled on a hot stone. Jazz is played in the background *(Avenida das Hortênsias, 1432, Centro, tel. (54) 3286-1477, 3286-2057; daily, 7pm – midnight)*.

Additional information on page 462.

291, Centro, tel. (54) 3286-4055, 3286-1334; Mon – Fri, 1pm – 5pm; Sat and Sun, 11am – 5pm).

CANELA'S NATURE RESERVES

Parque Estadual do Caracol is the main nature reserve of the six in Canela. Its 100 hectares (247 acres) offer trails, a train for children and the famous 131-meter (430-foot) Cascata do Caracol, accessible by a stairway of 927 steps *(Rodovia RS-466, Estrada do Caracol, 1, tel. (54) 3278-3035; Mon – Fri, 8:30am – 5:30pm; Sat, Sun, and holidays, 8:30am – 6pm)*. Lookout points in the **Parque da Ferradura**, a private reserve, offer a view of the Caí River Canyon. A two-hour trip into the canyon will take travelers to the river, past the **Cascata do Caçador**

waterfall *(Rodovia RS-466, Estrada do Caracol, no #, tel. (54) 3278-9000, 9972-8666; daily, 8:30am – 6pm)*.

OUR RECOMMENDATION

🏨 Surrounded by a hectare (2.5 acres) of greenery, the **Pousada Quinta dos Marques** boasts beautifully decorated suites. One has an antique cast-iron bathtub, and another has a jacuzzi and a fireplace. The leisure area has a Japanese-style *ofuro* bathtubs and massage service – and its amenities make up for its remote location *(Rua Gravataí, 200, Santa Teresinha, tel. (54) 3282-9812)*.

Additional information on page 462.

Cachoeira do Caracol, with a 131-meter drop, at the state park in Canela

VINEYARD TOURS IN
BENTO GONÇALVES AND GARIBALDI

Cabernets, merlots and tannats are the main grape varieties grown in the Vale dos Vinhedos (Vineyard Valley) in the rural region of Bento Gonçalves and Garibaldi. Wines from these vineyards complement tables laden with delicacies like *polenta*, *galeto* (spring chicken) and pasta. A trip to this region is a culinary tour with a warm welcome from hospitable, chatty locals. It's even better between January and March, when the trellises are heavy with grapes.

BENTO GONÇALVES

This is the biggest city in the region and the biggest grape and fine-wine producer in the country. With a population of 100,000, it offers good hotels but no big attractions. A trip on the **Maria-Fumaça** steam train takes an hour and a half to reach Carlos Barbosa and Garibaldi.
Giordani Turismo, tel. (54) 3452-6042.

PINTO BANDEIRA

The many vineyards in Pinto Bandeira, a charming part of Bento Gonçalves, warrant a visit. Check out **Vinha Cave de Amadeu**, which produces excellent sparkling wines *(Linha Jansen, no #, tel. (54) 3455-7461)*. Next door is **Pousada Don Giovanni**, which produces both sparkling and regular wine and offers accommodations in a colonial-style

1 cm = 6 km
1 inch = 9.5 mi.

❶ Maria-fumaça (Bento Gonçalves)
❷ Vinha Cave de Amadeu (Pinto Bandeira)
❸ Pousada Don Giovanni (Pinto Bandeira)
❹ Caminhos de Pedra
❺ Miolo
❻ Casa Valduga
❼ Don Laurindo
❽ Pousada Borguetto Sant'Anna
❾ Georges Aubert
❿ Chandon

house with a lovely garden and good food *(Linha Amadeu, Km 12, tel. (54) 3455-6294).*

CAMINHOS DE PEDRA

Pinto Bandeira's neighbor, Colônia de São Pedro, offers a seven-kilometer (four-mile) tour called the Caminhos de Pedra, which takes tourists past houses built from timber and stone. Several locals sell sheep's milk cheese, shawls, wine, hand-made woolen clothing, homemade pasta and yerba maté tea. **Giordani Turismo** organizes bus tours *(tel. (54) 3452-6042).* Private guides for people with their own transportation can be hired at **Opzionne Turismo** *(tel. (54) 3459-1813).*

VALE DOS VINHEDOS

Around 20 vineyards are strung along the Rodovia RS-444 highway, which runs through the valley that connects Bento Gonçalves to Monte Belo do Sul – the so-called Vale dos Vinhedos. The two most popular vineyards are **Miolo**, one of Brazil's major wine producers *(Rodovia RS-444, Km 21, Linha Leopoldina, tel. (54) 2102-1500),* and **Casa Valduga**, which gives tasting courses to guests staying at the adjoining guesthouse *(Linha Leopoldina, no #, tel. (54) 3453-1154).* **Don Laurindo** offers a more personal service: an enologist who explains all the details of the latest vintages and the quality of each variety at tasting sessions *(Estrada do Vinho, 8 km from Graciema, tel. (54) 3459-1600).* Sitting at the end of the valley, **Pousada Borghetto Sant'Anna** boasts five comfortable Italian-style chalets that overlook the vineyards *(Linha Leopoldina, tel. (54) 3453-2355).* Try the generous servings of *galeto* (spring chicken) at the classically Italian **Sbornea's** *(Rodovia RS-444, 19.8 km from Graciema, tel. (54) 3459-1224).*

The vineyard at Pousada Don Giovanni

SPARKLING WINES FROM GARIBALDI

More than half of Brazil's sparking wines are produced in Garibaldi, a tranquil town of 30,000 inhabitants located 16 kilometers (10 miles) from Bento Gonçalves. **Georges Aubert** receives its visitors in a small cultural center where they can watch a performance of *sabrage*, the top of a bottle being sliced off with a saber *(Avenida Independência, 1279, Centro, tel. (54) 3462-1155).* **Chandon**, the most popular vineyard, does not accept tours. It sells only to private individuals and only in six-bottle cases *(Rodovia RS-470, Km 224, Integração, tel. (54) 3462-2499).*

ESTRADA DO SABOR

Several farms around Garibaldi serve typical homemade meals to travelers along a route known as the Estrada do Sabor (Flavor Highway). They also host picnics, walks through valleys and vineyards and sampling sessions of wine, liqueur, salami and bread. *Information:* tel. (54) 3462-8235, 3464-0796.

Wandering in the Gaucho Mountains

Forget straight lines. Between the shore and the mountains, the shortest route between two points is a series of curves – at least along the stretch of coast where the Campos Gerais plateau hangs over the coastal plain. It looks like a basalt curtain slashed by canyons and threaded with roadways, where centuries ago, survey lines were traced by the hooves of mules. Following the muleteers' route, the visitors can swim in the ocean on a summer morning and relax in front of a fire at night; have fish for lunch and polenta for dinner; and contrast the fickle fashions of the beach with the austere figures of ranch hands clad in the traditional pants, hat and bandanna of Southern cowboys, as if they were rehearsing the roles of *gauchos* for TV.

The journey up the Serra do Mar extends for more than 100 kilometers and more than 1,000 meters in altitude. There are three main routes, but all of them share a style which is becoming increasingly rare in Brazil. It doesn't matter if visitors take the Rio do Rastro from Santa Catarina, whose smooth surface and nighttime illumination give it the appearance of an alpine highway, or the Corvo Branco, which offers more picturesque scenery and stretches of dirt road that are a real challenge for rental cars, or the Faxinal from Rio Grande do Sul, which resembles an off-road test track for four-wheel-drive vehicles during the rainy season.

Whichever path visitors choose, they will need a rapid course in driving etiquette to prepare for the standards of courtesy that await at the top. When a truck is having difficulty rounding a tight bend, all the other cars fall back as far as possible to help the maneuver. Overtaking is negotiated with almost diplomatic courtesy, and every shoulder that is a little wider than the norm is an unspoken invitation to park near a lookout point, where the sound of nearby waterfalls combined with the ocean view in the distance delights the senses.

It's sheer perfection – but this is just the beginning. Nineteenth-century naturalist Auguste de Saint-Hilaire described the scenery on the plateau bordering the canyons as paradise on Earth. In fact, he was gazing at a forest of Brazilian pine, a native tree whose noble lineage extends back 250 million years. The Brazilian pine lives surrounded by meadows of wild flowers and misunderstandings. Born in the era of the dinosaurs, it resisted climatic changes and geological upheavals only to fall prey to the teeth of the lumber-saws that transformed the Southern states into voracious timber exporters in the 20th century. It was almost extinguished by the sawmills' greed. Under siege, the pines changed both their appearance and their company, no longer clumping together in extensive forests but retreating into isolation along the edges of fences and the back of pastures. The strategy has been so successful that it seems it had been that way forever. Although the tree appears all over the country, it flourishes in the region's cold climate. It has become a fixture on postcards promoting the snowy winters, reinforcing the idea that the region is really a piece of Europe in the heart of the Serra Gaúcha.

But visitors who believe this have no idea what the travel agencies are hiding. There's nothing wrong with Gramado's Christmas Lights, Nova Petrópolis' *Frühlingsfest*, Flores da Cunha's *Mangiare di Polenta*, Vale Real's *Krönenthalfest*, Bom Princípio's strawberries, Bento Gonçalves' wine cellars and vineyards, Urussanga's *Ritorno Alle Origini*, São Vendelino's twice-weekly German masses, and everything else the German, Italian, Polish and Ukrainian immigrants brought. With a good deal of sweat and not a little feasting, they built one of Brazil's finest tourist destinations. But it doesn't hurt to remember that it is also a perfect place for anyone suffering from homesickness for the real Brazil.

And this Brazil is hard to find in other parts of the country – a Brazil that is organized and welcoming, typifying the "predominantly agricultural country" that used to fill the schoolbooks of not-so-long ago. In this Brazil, entire municipalities are interlaced with national parks and flourishing green pastures that cattle have wandered since the 16th century, and its rustic place names bear witness to its rural origins.

In São José dos Ausentes, the major tourist attraction is a waterfall called Cachoeirão dos Rodrigues. Leave the map in the glove compartment, though, because getting lost is the best way to explore side-roads with no signs or names and discover the carefully cultivated valleys, tree-covered hills, water wheels, clear rivers, cattle grazing behind fences, chickens running loose and houses with their windows wide open. If drivers take a wrong turn, it doesn't matter – they'll wind up in a similar place. This in itself is a major achievement in an era when the slightest detour in most other states can lead to unexpected encounters with huge potholes or shantytowns.

This side of the mountain has more inns than hotels; most of them are part of farms, some historical but all productive. They are normally decorated with family furniture and the outbuildings are filled to the rafters with agricultural implements that any decorator would love to have hanging in his or her living room. Sleeping in the main house, which is customary, on pillows with the scent of sun-bleached clothing, guests awaken before dawn to the smell of bread baking in the kitchen. Morning greetings from the host are accompanied by an outstretched hand holding a gourd cup full of yerba maté tea. The food, taken at the family table, usually nestled close to the fire, is made from time-honored recipes with home-grown ingredients, seasoned by the smoke of the wood stove, and it has a flavor that awakens the palate and unlocks the memory. The food couldn't be more Brazilian – so Brazilian, in fact, it fits perfectly with the universal definition that Gianni Brera from Milan gave the traditional mountain cuisine of northern Italy: "Simple fare prepared with a civility that is almost refined." It seems straightforward enough, but just try finding something similar anywhere else in Brazil.

Marcos Sá Corrêa,
journalist and photographer

THE SOUTHERN CANYONS

On the border between Santa Catarina and Rio Grande do Sul, a sequence of canyons forms the most spectacular spot in the mountain ranges of the South. The upper sections are in Rio Grande do Sul, and the lower sections are in Santa Catarina. The famous **Itaimbezinho** is 720 meters (2,362 feet) deep and almost six kilometers (3.5 miles) long. This canyon is located in the **Parque Nacional de Aparados da Serra**, a national park with a visitors' center that has a snack bar, models, maps and photos. It can be reached by a dirt road running between Praia Grande and Cambará do Sul. Two trails in the upper section, both of which start from the visitors' center, can be hiked without a guide. One of these takes 30 minutes there and back to reach the top of the canyon and a waterfall, Cachoeira das Andorinhas; the other takes two hours there and back and leads to a curve in the canyon. A guide is necessary for the **Trilha do Rio do Boi** in the lower section. Hikers must go through water for some stretches and can take seven hours total. Neighboring **Parque Nacional da Serra Geral**, a

The dramatic landscape of Malacara Canyon

OUR RECOMMENDATION

Refúgio Ecológico Pedra Afiada – located on the lower slopes of the range in Praia Grande, Santa Catarina – offers a view of Malacara Canyon. It has cozy rooms, and the hotel staff organizes walks, rappelling, horseback riding and *bóia-cross*, which involves floating downriver in an inner tube *(Estrada da Vila Rosa, no #, tel. (48) 3532-1059).*

Surrounded by lovely high mountain woodland in the municipality of Cambará do Sul, **Parador Casa da Montanha** offers thermal safari-style canvas bungalows. Some have a jacuzzi on the balcony and overlook the waterfalls of the Camarinhas River *(Estrada do Faxinal, no #, tel. (54) 3504-5302, 3295-7575).*

Additional information on page 462.

continuation of the Aparados da Serra National Park, is home to four canyons. The biggest is **Fortaleza**, extending for 8 kilometers (5 miles) and sinking to 900 meters (3,000 feet) at its deepest point. Visitors can get almost to the canyon's edge by car, driving 20 kilometers of dirt road from Cambará do Sul. From the edge, a one-hour trail leads to a lookout point. The coastline is visible on clear days. Walks through the canyon are only recommended for those with trekking experience. A seven-kilometer walk with a guide leads to the other two canyons, **Malacara** and **Churriado.** Beware: on some days, fog completely obscures views in the entire region. *Parque Nacional de Aparados da Serra, tel. (54) 3251-1277. Wed – Sun, 9am – 5pm. Parque Nacional da Serra Geral has free access but camping is not permitted. To hire a guide contact the **Tourist Information Center** (Centro de Informações Turísticas: tel. (54) 3251-1320); or the **Praia Grande Guide Association** (Associação Praia-Grandense de Condutores: tel. (48) 3532-1414).*

MISSÕES

Ruins in the Missions region, situated 500 kilometers (311 miles) west of Porto Alegre, serve as a reminder of one of the most important eras in the colonization of the Americas. In the 17th and 18th centuries, the kings of Spain and Portugal authorized Jesuit priests to settle in Brazil to convert the Guarani Indians to Catholicism. When this movement hit its peak in the mid-18th century, the indigenous population in the Jesuit-run missionary towns reached hundreds of thousands. In 1768, however, the Marquis de Pombal expelled the Jesuits from Brazil and the missions fell into decline. Almost 250 years later, the ruins of four of the seven Brazilian missions are still standing. (There are also eight in Paraguay and fifteen in Argentina.) On the Brazilian side, the most important and best preserved is **São Miguel Arcanjo**. It is in the municipality of São Miguel das Missões, 485 kilometers (301 miles) from Porto Alegre via Rodovia BR-386 highway to Carazinho, followed by the Rodovia BR-285 highway *(daily, 9am – midday and 2pm – 7:30pm; information: tel. (55) 3381-1294)*. A Unesco World Heritage Site, the mission contains the ruins of an old church dating from 1745. It also has the **Museu das Missões**, a museum designed by architect Lúcio Costa, whose collection is made up of about 100 religious statues carved from wood. The ruins are floodlit at night while a 50-minute multi-media presentation tells the history of the Missions *(in summer, 8pm; in winter, 7:30pm)*. An alternate means of exploring the region is to take the **Caminho das Missões**, a walking tour inspired by Spain's famous Santiago de Compostela pilgrimage. Trips of three, seven and 14 days are available; an average of 23 kilometers (14 miles) is covered per day. All the walks end at Santo Ângelo. Walkers take original trails, stay in local houses or hostels and visit the mission ruins. It's also possible to do the route by bicycle *(information: tel. (55) 3312-9632 or www.caminhodasmissoes.com.br)*.

Hotels, Restaurants, and Services

The information of the following pages is organized alphabetically by city or town Hotel prices are the daily rates for a double-occupancy room. Many hotels operate a day-use system, in which guests who don't need overnight accommodations can pay a reduced fee for daytime use of the facilities. Restaurant prices were calculated based on the price of the most popular dish, plus a 10% service charge, which is considered appropriate in Brazil. The dollar signs next to the name of each establishment indicate the price category (see the bottom of each page for a key to price ranges). Addresses, telephone numbers, hours, and prices were supplied by the establishments themselves and verified by our team of field researchers. Nevertheless, there may have been subsequent changes. Also, especially in smaller towns, tourist information services, restaurants, and tour operators may keep irregular hours in the low season. Throughout this chapter, the term "beach service" refers to beach-related services that many oceanside hotels provide, including lending guests towels, chairs, and shade umbrellas, and sometimes serving them drinks as well. The term "recreational team" (or "recreational staff") indicates that certain hotel employees can entertain guests' children (or, in some cases, adult guests themselves) by organizing games and other activities. When calling Brazil from abroad, please remember to dial "+55" before the telephone numbers listed in this guide.

Clockwise from the top left: Hotel Grand Hyatt in São Paulo; *vatapá* by the beach in the Northeast; café in the South; hotel-boat in the Pantanal wetlands

Abrolhos – Bahia (see Caravelas)

Andaraí – Bahia

AREA CODE 75 **POPULATION** 14,064 **DISTANCES** Salvador 414 kilometers (257 miles), Lençóis 101 kilometers (63 miles) **ACCESS** From Lençóis, drive 12 kilometers (7 miles) along the road to Highway BR-242. Follow the highway for another 12 kilometers (7 miles), then drive 52 kilometers (32 miles) on Highway BA-142 to Andaraí. Exit at Km 50 or 53

WHERE TO STAY

Pousada Ecológica $
The nice, airy rooms of this guesthouse lie virtually on the banks of the Paraguaçu River, which is a good place to fish, swim, stroll along the sand, and sunbathe. The restaurant serves tasty fried tucunaré fish. **ACCOMMODATIONS** 31; air-conditioning; minibar; TV. **FACILITIES AND SERVICES** bar; parking; stores; pool; playground; six-a-side soccer court; restaurant; river; conference room; games room; guided walking tours.
CREDIT CARDS MasterCard; Visa
Estrada Andaraí–Mucugê, Km 3, Vila da Passagem
TEL and **FAX** (75) 3335-2207

Pousada Sincorá $
One of the best places to stay in town, with an excellent breakfast. The owners are very knowledgeable about the Chapada Diamantina region and are excellent guides. **ACCOMMODATIONS** 8; air-conditioning; minibar; TV. **FACILITIES AND SERVICES** Internet access; library; parking; store; guided walking tours. **CREDIT CARDS** Diners; MasterCard; Visa
Avenida Paraguaçu, 120 (exit to Igatu/Mucugê)
TEL (75) 3335-2210 **FAX** (75) 3335-2486
www.sincora.com.br

SERVICES

Guides – Associação dos Condutores de Visitantes de Andaraí (ACVA)
Rua Dr. José Gonçalves Cincorá, no #
TEL (75) 3335-2022 **OPEN** High season: Mon – Fri, 8am – noon and 2pm – 5pm

Tourist Information – Secretaria de Turismo
Praça Aureliano Gondim, no #, Centro
TEL (75) 3335-2257 **OPEN** Mon – Fri, 8am – 2pm

Angra dos Reis – Rio de Janeiro

AREA CODE 24 **POPULATION** 148,476 **DISTANCE** Rio de Janeiro 150 kilometers (93 miles) **ACCESS** Highway BR-101 (Rodovia Rio–Santos) from Rio de Janeiro
www.angra.rj.gov.br

WHERE TO STAY

Blue Tree Park Angra dos Reis $$$$
This hotel has the most complete leisure facilities on the Rodovia Rio–Santos highway. Parents can relax at the spa while children have fun on the mini racetrack or the computer game network. **ACCOMMODATIONS** 318; air-conditioning; Internet access; minibar; pay TV; phone; private safe. **FACILITIES AND SERVICES** babysitter; bar; beachside service; beach-soccer facilities; beach-volleyball facilities; beauty parlor; boat; business center; canopy climbing; convenience store; fishing equipment; function room; games room; gym; Internet access; jogging track; kayaks; lifeguard; wine cellar; water skiing; 24-hour kitchen. **CREDIT CARDS** AmEx; Diners; MasterCard; Visa
Estrada Vereador Benedito Adelino, 8,413, Fazenda Tanguá
TEL (24) 3379-2800 **FAX** (24) 3379-2801
RESERVATIONS 0800-7037272 www.bluetree.com.br

Novo Frade $$$$
This large leisure complex offers opportunities to partake in multiple water sports (water skiing and motorboat outings), and outdoor activities such as horseback riding and rides in a horse-drawn carriage. **ACCOMMODATIONS** 178; air-conditioning; Internet access; pay TV; phone; private safe. **FACILITIES AND SERVICES** bar; beach volleyball facilities; beauty parlor; boat; business center; convenience store; function room; games room; golf course; gym; horses and carriage; jogging track; laundry; massage room; motorboat; parking; playground; pool; recreational teams for adults and children; restaurant; sauna; six-a-side soccer court; soccer field; water skiing. **CREDIT CARDS** AmEx; Diners; MasterCard; Visa
Praia do Frade, Rodovia BR-101, Km 513
TEL (24) 3369-9500 **FAX** (24) 3369-2254
www.hoteldofrade.com.br

Pestana Angra $$$$
One of the more sophisticated establishments in Angra dos Reis, this hotel is somewhat different from most large resorts. Its greenery-enveloped bungalows have ocean views and offer privacy in a romantic setting. **ACCOMMODATIONS** 27; air-conditioning; CD player; ceiling fan; DVD; jacuzzi (in 11 bungalows); minibar; pay TV; phone; private safe; sauna (in 11 bungalows). **FACILITIES AND SERVICES** bar; business center; fishing equipment; function room; games room; gym; heliport; Internet access; restaurant; sauna; spa; trails; TV room; valet service; beachside service; transport to airport and attractions; water skiing; 24-hour kitchen. **CREDIT CARDS** AmEx; Diners; MasterCard; Visa
Estrada Vereador Benedito Adelino, 3,700, Retiro
TEL and **FAX** (24) 3364-2005 **RESERVATIONS** 0800-266332
www.pestana.com

WHERE TO EAT

Chez Dominique $$
This restaurant offers delicious crevettes du chef (shrimp, mushrooms, herbs, white wine, and rice with palm heart) and more in a relaxed atmosphere with outdoor tables by the river. **CUISINE** French. **CREDIT CARDS** AmEx; Diners; MasterCard; Visa
Condomínio Porto Frade, Rodovia BR-101, Km 123 heading toward Paraty
TEL (24) 3369-5458, 3369-0142 **FAX** (24) 3369-5466. Mon – Thu, noon – midnight; Fri – Sun, noon – 1am (high season); Fri and Sat, noon – 1am; Sun, noon – midnight (low season).

SERVICES

Boat Hire – Associação dos Barqueiros de Angra dos Reis
Avenida Júlio Maria, no #, Centro
TEL (24) 3365-3165. Daily, 8am – 4pm

Tourist Information – Centro de Informações Turísticas
Avenida Ayrton Senna, 580, Praia do Anil
TEL (24) 3367-7826. Daily, 8am – 8pm

RESTAURANTS   **$** up to R$ 50   **$$** from R$ 51 up to R$ 100   **$$$** from R$ 101 up to R$ 150   **$$$$** above R$ 150

Tourist Information – Fundação de Turismo de Angra dos Reis (Turisangra)
Avenida Júlio Maria, 10 (two-story house), Centro
TEL (24) 3367-8718. Daily, 8am – 6pm

Alto Paraíso de Goiás – Goiás

AREA CODE 62 POPULATION 6,638 DISTANCE Brasília 230 kilometers (143 miles) ACCESS Highway GO-118 from Brasília

WHERE TO STAY

Casa Rosa Pousada das Cerejeiras $
This converted guesthouse is located in a beautiful spot and offers excellent service. There are spacious rooms and chalets, all with verandas and hammocks. ACCOMMODATIONS 22; fan; minibar; TV. FACILITIES AND SERVICES bar; barbecue facilities; Internet access; massage room; orchard; parking; pool; sauna; snack bar; video room; walking tours; woods. CREDIT CARDS Visa
Rua Gumercindo Barbosa, 233, Centro
TEL (62) 3446-1319, 3446-2065
www.pousadacasarosa.com.br

Pousada Portal da Chapada $
The spacious and comfortable wood chalets are near a waterfall and a suspended canopy-climbing circuit. ACCOMMODATIONS 14; fireplace (in 3 chalets); minibar; TV. FACILITIES AND SERVICES arts and crafts shop; bar; canopy-climbing circuit; games room; massage room; natural pool; orchard; parking; playground; restaurant; river; sauna; waterfall; woods. CREDIT CARDS Visa
Rodovia GO-327, Km 9
TEL (62) 3446-1820 www.portaldachapada.com.br

SERVICES

Ecological Trips – Alternativas
Avenida Ary Ribeiro Valadão Filho, 1,331, Centro
TEL (62) 3446-1000. Mon – Fri, 9am – 6pm; Sat, 9am – 2pm.

Ecological Trips – Eco Rotas
Rua das Nascentes, 129, Centro
TEL (62) 3446-1820. Mon – Fri, 8am – 8pm; Sat, 8am – 1pm.

Ecological Trips – Transchapada Turismo
Rua dos Cristais, 7, mezzanine Store # 1, Centro
TEL (62) 3446-1345. Daily, noon – 6pm.

Ecological Trips – Travessia
Avenida Ary Ribeiro Valadão Filho, 979, Centro
TEL (62) 3446-1595. Mon – Sat, 9am – 7pm; Sun, 9am – 2pm.

Tourist Information – Centro de Apoio ao Turista
Avenida Ary Ribeiro Valadão Filho, 1,100, Centro
TEL (62) 3446-1159. Daily, 8am – noon and 1pm – 5pm.

Aquidauana – Mato Grosso do Sul

AREA CODE 67 POPULATION 44,920 DISTANCE Campo Grande 130 kilometers (81 miles) ACCESS Highway BR-262 toward Corumbá

WHERE TO STAY

Pequi Pousada Pantaneira $$$
This guesthouse has spacious, comfortable rooms that sleep three or four people and chalets (in the fishing area). The rooms can also be hired for day-use as well as for overnight stays, and guests can choose from a range of guided trips. ACCOMMODATIONS 10; air-conditioning; mosquito-screens on windows; ceiling fan. FACILITIES AND SERVICES arts and crafts shop; bar; bilingual staff; environmental inspector; first-aid; Internet access; pool; restaurant; river; stores; transport to airport; video room. EXCURSIONS animal watching; boat trips; cattle handling; hiking; horseback riding; nocturnal wildlife spotting; river tour; safari. FISHING camping ground for fishing enthusiasts; lake. CREDIT CARDS MasterCard; Visa. ACCESS Highway BR-262, exit at AQN 4 and drive for 42 kilometers (26 miles) along a dirt road. During the rainy season, this road is accessible only to offroad motorcycles, buses or 4×4 vehicles. When it is dry, conventional automobiles and motorcycles can get through.
Rodovia BR-262, Km 54
TEL and RESERVATIONS (67) 3245-0949, 9986-0449, 9934-5781 www.pousadapequi.com.br

Pousada Recanto Barra Mansa $$
Well-located on the right bank of the Negro River, this guesthouse has simple, comfortable rooms and a chalet that can sleep up to eight people. Highlights here are the bird-watching and sport-fishing programs. Rooms can also be rented for day-use only. ACCOMMODATIONS 7; air-conditioning; ceiling fan. FACILITIES AND SERVICES bar; bilingual staff; convenience store; environmental inspector; first-aid; heliport; Internet access; lifeguard; restaurant; river; soccer field; stores; valet service; video room; walking tours. EXCURSIONS bird and animal watching; boat trips; canoeing; cattle handling; hiking; hiking; horseback riding; nocturnal wildlife spotting; scientific tourism. FISHING equipment; sport fishing; catch-and-release fishing. CREDIT CARDS AmEx; MasterCard; Visa. ACCESS From Aquidauana, take Estrada Aquidauana–Barra Mansa in a 4×4 vehicle or offroad motorbike. The 120 kilometers (75 miles) trip takes approximately 5 hours.
Estrada Aquidauana, no #
TEL (67) 9986-0494 FAX (67) 3383-5088
RESERVATIONS (67) 3325-6807
www.hotelbarramansa.com.br

SERVICES

Department of Tourism – Secretaria de Turismo
Rua Manoel Antônio Paes de Barros, 664 (old railway station)
TEL (67) 3241-7417. Mon – Fri 7am – noon

Aquiraz – Ceará

AREA CODE 85 POPULATION 67,264 DISTANCE Fortaleza 32 kilometers (20 miles) ACCESS From Fortaleza, on Highway CE-040 www.aquiraz.ce.gov.br

WHERE TO STAY

Beach Park Suítes Resort $$$
This resort is part of the Beach Park complex and has excellent leisure facilities, ideal for families with children. The suites, which sleep two or four, have ocean-facing verandas. ACCOMMODATIONS 182 suites; Internet access in some suites; air-conditioning; private safe; minibar; telephone; cable TV; veranda. FACILITIES AND SERVICES Internet access; bar; hairdresser; parking; tennis court; volleyball court; restaurant; conference room; gym; games room;

| PRICES | HOTELS (couple) | $ up to R$ 150 | $$ from R$ 151 up to R$ 300 | $$$ from R$ 301 up to R$500 | $$$$ above R$ 500 |

464 BRAZIL GUIDE

sauna; baby sitter; business center; 24-hour kitchen; valet parking; beach service. **CREDIT CARDS** AmEx; Diners; MasterCard; Visa

Rua Porto das Dunas, 2734, Praia Porto das Dunas
TEL (85) 4012-3084 **FAX** (85) 4012-3040
www.beachpark.com.br

Aracaju – Sergipe

AREA CODE 79 **POPULATION** 520,207 **DISTANCES** Maceió 290 kilometers (180 miles), Salvador 330 kilometers (205 miles) **ACCESS** From Maceió, on Highway BR-101. From Bahia, along Linha Verde Highway
www.aracaju.se.gov.br

WHERE TO STAY

Del Mar $$$
One of the biggest and most luxurious hotels in Aracaju, the Del Mar faces the sea on Atalaia Beach. The rooms with sea views are the best. **ACCOMMODATIONS** 113 (109 rooms, 4 suites); Internet access; air-conditioning; minibar; telephone; cable TV. **FACILITIES AND SERVICES** Internet access; bar; parking; snack bar; convenience store; pool; playground; tennis court; restaurant; conference room; games room; beauty parlor; sauna; gym; travel agency; business center; 24-hour kitchen; recreational team for adults and children (high season); valet parking. **CREDIT CARDS** AmEx; Diners; MasterCard; Visa
Avenida Santos Dumont, 1500, Praia de Atalaia
TEL (79) 2106-9100, 2106-9200 **FAX** (79) 2106-9292 **RESERVATIONS** (79) 2106-9142 www.delmarhotel.com.br

Hotel Parque dos Coqueiros $$
Well-located on Atalaia Beach, this hotel boasts extensive leisure facilities and is opposite the beach. It is ideal for family travel. **ACCOMMODATIONS** 114; Internet access; air-conditioning; private safe; minibar; telephone; cable TV. **FACILITIES AND SERVICES** bar; soccer field; parking; convenience store; pool; playground; beach; tennis court; beach volleyball arena; restaurant; conference room; gym; games room; beauty parlor; travel agency; business center; laundry; 24-hour room service. **CREDIT CARDS** AmEx; Diners; MasterCard; Visa
Rua Francisco Rabelo Leite Neto, 1075, Atalaia Velha
TEL (79) 2107-1511
www.hotelparquedoscoqueiros.com.br

Starfish Ilha de Santa Luzia $$$$
Located approximately 3 kilometers from Aracaju, it stands on the island of Santa Luzia. **ACCOMMODATIONS** 208 (179 rooms, 25 bungalows, 4 suites); air-conditioning; private safe; minibar; telephone; cable TV. **FACILITIES AND SERVICES** Internet access; bars; soccer field; parking; jacuzzi; kid's club; pool; pony; beach; tennis court; restaurants; convention, games room; workout, massage room; video room; beauty parlor; sauna; spa; travel agency; bilingual staff; business center; 24-hour kitchen; beach equipment; recreational team for adults and children; first aid service; lifeguard; pool and beach service; airport shuttle. **CREDIT CARDS** AmEx; Diners; MasterCard; Visa
Sítio Tingui, no #, Barra da Costa
TEL (79) 2104-8500 **RESERVATIONS** 0800-704-3210
www.superclubsbrasil.com.br

WHERE TO EAT

Cariri $
Adjoining a popular forró dance venue, the restaurant is open on all sides and has ocean views. Specialties include the camarão ao cariri (shrimp stewed in green coconut milk, crumbed shrimp, shrimp on sticks, rice and manioc flour) and the grilled goat. **CUISINE** Regional; fish and seafood. **CREDIT CARDS** AmEx; Diners; MasterCard; Visa
Avenida Santos Dumont, no #, Passarela do Caranguejo, Atalaia
TEL (79) 3243-1379 **RESERVATIONS** (79) 3243-5370 **OPEN** Daily, 10am until the last customer leaves.

O Miguel $
Famous for its excellent carne-de-sol (beef jerky), brought from inland Sergipe and prepared on site. The steak, seasoned only with salt, can be prepared on the hot plate and served with manteiga de garrafa (clarified butter), or over a fire, barbecue-style. **CUISINE** Regional. **CREDIT CARDS** MasterCard; Visa
Avenida Antônio Alves, 340 (intersects with Avenida Beira-mar), Atalaia Velha
TEL (79) 3243-1444 **RESERVATIONS** (79) 3243-4142 **OPEN** Mon, 11am – 4pm; Tue – Sun, 11am – 4pm and 6pm – 11:30pm

SERVICES

Airport – Aeroporto Santa Maria
Avenida Senador Júlio César Leite, no #, Atalaia Velha
TEL (79) 3212-8500, 3212-8557 **OPEN** Daily, 24 hours
www.infraero.gov.br

Bus Station – Rodoviária
Avenida Tancredo Neves, no #, Novo Paraíso
TEL (79) 3259-2848

Tourist Information – Bureau de Informações Turísticas
Praça Olímpio Campos, no #, Centro
TEL (79) 3214-8848 **OPEN** Daily, 8am – 1pm
www.turismosergipe.net

Travel Agency – Agência de Turismo Propagtur
Avenida Ermes Fontes, 1109, São José
TEL (79) 3234-4444, 3234-4434 **OPEN** Mon – Fri, 8am – 7pm; Sat, 8am – 1pm
Airport: **TEL** (79) 3179-4664 **OPEN** Daily, 5am – 8pm
www.propagtur.com.br

Arembepe – Bahia

AREA CODE 71 **DISTANCES** Salvador 40 kilometers (25 miles), Aracaju 220 kilometers (137 miles) **ACCESS** From Salvador, on Highway BA-099 (Estrada do Coco)

WHERE TO STAY

Aldeia de Arembepe Refúgio Ecológico $$
Located on a hill facing the sea, with its back to Arembepe Lake, this ecological refuge is near the Aldeia Hippie ('Hippie Village') and the Tamar turtle-conservation project. The bungalows sleep up to four. **ACCOMMODATIONS** 12 (11 bungalows and 1 chalet); min bar in half of the rooms; TV; ceiling fan. **FACILITIES AND SERVICES** swimming pool; playground; restaurant; bicycles; kayak; beach service; airport shuttle; transport to attractions. **CREDIT CARDS** AmEx; Diners; MasterCard; Visa
Estrada da Aldeia Hippie, no #, Projeto Tamar, lots 9 and 10, Arembepe Beach
TEL and **FAX** (71) 3624-1031
www.aldeiadearembepe.com.br

RESTAURANTS   **$** up to R$ 50   **$$** from R$ 51 up to R$ 100   **$$$** from R$ 101 up to R$ 150   **$$$$** above R$ 150

WHERE TO EAT

Mar Aberto $$

In a small house jutting towards the sea, this restaurant offers dishes such as grilled lobster for two, which comes with vegetables in butter, rice, and potato purée. **CUISINE** Regional; fish and seafood. **CREDIT CARDS** AmEx; Diners; MasterCard; Visa

Largo de São Francisco, 43, Arembepe Beach
TEL (71) 3624-1257 **RESERVATIONS** (71) 3624-1623 **OPEN** Mon – Thu, 11:30am –9:30pm; Fri and Sat, 11:30am – midnight; Sun, noon – 7pm

SERVICES

Bus Station – Rodoviária

Rua da Rodoviária, no #, Centro, Camaçari
TEL (71) 3621-5056

Tourist Information – Secretaria de Turismo

Rua da Alegria, 119, Centro
TEL (71) 3621-2499, 3621-2041 **OPEN** Mon – Fri, 8am – 6pm

Arraial d'Ajuda – Bahia

AREA CODE 73 **DISTANCES** Salvador 715 kilometers (444 miles), Porto Seguro 4 kilometers (2 miles), then another 10 minutes by ferry, Ilhéus 324 kilometers (201 miles) **ACCESS** From Porto Seguro, by car ferry, or take Highway BR-101 to Eunápolis, then BR-367 and BA-001

WHERE TO STAY

Arraial d'Ajuda Eco Resort $$$$

The biggest hotel in Arraial, the sophisticated Eco Resort stands between the sea and the Buranhém River, facing Porto Seguro. With rustic decor, it has good recreational facilities. **ACCOMMODATIONS** 160 (156 rooms, 4 suites); air-conditioning; private safe; minibar; jacuzzi in the master suites; telephone; cable TV; veranda with hammock and sea views (50% of the rooms) or over the Buranhém River; ceiling fan. **FACILITIES AND SERVICES** Internet access; bar; boat; nursery; kayaks; cinema; fishing equipment; parking; horse-riding; motorboat; convenience store; pool; jogging track; playground; tennis court; volleyball court; restaurant; river; conference room; gym; games room; exchange bureau; 24-hour kitchen; recreational team for adults and children; hiking guides; lifeguards; beach service; airport shuttle; transport to attractions. **CREDIT CARDS** AmEx; Diners; MasterCard; Visa

Ponta de Apaga-Fogo, 60, Centro
TEL (73) 3575-8500 **FAX** (73) 3575-1010
www.arraialresort.com.br

Canto d'Alvorada Hotel Pousada $$

This cozy, charming hotel, nestled in gardens overlooking the ocean, is popular among foreigners and families. The child-friendly beach has natural tide pools. **ACCOMMODATIONS** 21 (14 rooms, 7 chalets); air-conditioning; private safe; minibar; telephone; cable TV; veranda with hammock and garden views; ceiling fan. **FACILITIES AND SERVICES** Internet access; bar; kayaks; parking; pool; playground; beach volley facilities; restaurant; games room; TV room; sauna; exchange bureau; beach service; airport shuttle. **CREDIT CARDS** AmEx; Diners; MasterCard; Visa

Estrada do Arraial d'Ajuda, 1993, Praia do Araçaípe
TEL and **FAX** (73) 3575-1218
www.cantodalvorada.com.br

Casa Grande de São Vicente $$$$

Open since 2005, this hotel has only 6 suites, but all have seas views. The Portuguese owners have decorated it with artworks from their home country and Brazilian arts and crafts. Children under the age of 12 are not allowed. Breakfast is included. **ACCOMMODATIONS** 6 suites; Internet access; air-conditioning; minibar; telephone; cable TV; ceiling fan. **FACILITIES AND SERVICES** Internet access; wine cellar; parking; pool; restaurant; sitting room; massage room; TV room; poolside service; airport shuttle. **CREDIT CARDS** AmEx; Visa

Alameda Gustavo Carneiro, 2, Corais do Arraial
TEL (73) 3575-3249 **FAX** (73) 3575-3093
www.casagrandesaovicente.com.br

Hotel Pousada Caminho do Mar $$$

Decorated with wood and objects such as old cash registers and TV receivers, this guesthouse is where the action is, on the corner of Beco das Cores, which is brimming with stores and bars. It does not offer sea views. **ACCOMMODATIONS** 16; air-conditioning; private safe; minibar; telephone; TV; ceiling fan. **FACILITIES AND SERVICES** bar; parking; pool with hot tub; travel agency; beach service; airport shuttle. **CREDIT CARDS** AmEx; Diners; MasterCard; Visa

Estrada do Mucugê, 246
TEL and **FAX** (73) 3575-1099 www.caminhodomar.tur.br

Maitei $$$

Most of the rooms have ocean views, as well as jacuzzis and DVD players. There are comfortable deck chairs around the swimming pool on the terrace, with a view of the beach. Children under 14 are not allowed. **ACCOMMODATIONS** 17; Internet access; air-conditioning; private safe; DVD player; minibar; jacuzzi; telephone; cable TV; veranda with hammock. **FACILITIES AND SERVICES** Internet access; bar; parking; pool; restaurant; sitting room; gym; games room; massage room; beauty parlor; sauna; poolside service; airport shuttle; transport to attractions. **CREDIT CARDS** AmEx; Diners; MasterCard; Visa

Rua do Mucugê, 475, Centro
TEL (73) 3575-3877, 3575-3799 www.maitei.com.br

Saint-Tropez Praia Hotel $$$$

Facing Parracho Beach, this hotel is large by Arraial standards, with large rooms and good leisure facilities. **ACCOMMODATIONS** 55 (38 rooms, 12 suites, 5 chalets); Internet access; air-conditioning; private safe; DVD player; minibar; jacuzzi in the 2 master suites; veranda (with hammock only in the suites and chalets); telephone; cable TV. **FACILITIES AND SERVICES** bar; horses; parking; arts and crafts stores; costume jewelry store; pool; playground; tennis court; volleyball court; restaurant; magazine reading area; games room; massage room; sauna, video room; travel agency; recreational team for children; valet parking; airport shuttle. **CREDIT CARDS** AmEx; Diners; MasterCard; Visa

Estrada da Pitinga, 100, Praia do Parracho
TEL (73) 3288-7700 **RESERVATIONS** (73) 3288-7786
FAX (73) 3288-7785, 3288-7794
www.saint-tropez.com.brtropez.com.br

WHERE TO EAT

Boi nos Aires $

Specializing in Argentinean grilled meats, prepared on the parrilla. **CUISINE** Argentinean; meats. **CREDIT CARDS** Diners; MasterCard; Visa

Estrada do Mucugê, 200, Centro
TEL (73) 3575-2554 **OPEN** High season: daily, 5pm until the last customer leaves; low season: Mon – Sat, 5pm until the last customer leaves

PRICES	HOTELS (couple)	$ up to R$ 150	$$ from R$ 151 up to R$ 300	$$$ from R$ 301 up to R$500	$$$$ above R$ 500

Don Fabrizio $

The Sicilian Chef and owner, Fabrizio Abbate, comes from five generations of gourmets. There are ninety dishes on the Mediterranean menu. **CUISINE** Mediterranean; fish and seafood; pizza. **CREDIT CARDS** Diners; MasterCard; Visa
Estrada do Mucugê, 402, Centro
TEL (73) 3575-2407 **OPEN** High season: daily, 1:30pm – 11:30pm; low season: Wed – Sat and Mon, 4pm – 11:30pm; Sun, 1:30pm – 11:30pm

Rosa dos Ventos $$

The extensive menu has such items as fish baked in banana leaf, salads, crêpes, fowl, meats, and even suckling pig, as well as dishes for children. **CUISINE** Meats; fish; diverse. **CREDIT CARDS** Not accepted
Alameda dos Flamboyants, 24, Centro
TEL (73) 3575-1271 **OPEN** High season: daily, 4pm until the last customer leaves; low season: Thu – Sat, 4pm – midnight; Sun, 1pm – 10pm; Mon and Tue, 4pm – midnight

SERVICES

Diving Agency – Acqua Planet
Rua do Cais, 69, Centro (in Porto Seguro)
TEL (73) 3268-1499, 9993-1619, 9985-4996 **OPEN** Daily, 7am – 9pm

Ferry Crossing – Rio Buranhém Navegação
Praça dos Pataxós, no #, Centro, Porto Seguro
TEL (73) 3288-2516 **OPEN** Daily, 24 hours

Tourist Information – Centro de Informações Turísticas de Porto Seguro
Praça Manoel Ribeiro Coelho, 10, Centro (in Porto Seguro, near the ferry terminal)
TEL (73) 3268-1390 **OPEN** Mon – Sat, 9:30am – 11pm

Travel Agency – Brasil 2000 Turismo
Estrada do Mucugê, 165, Centro
TEL (73) 3575-1815, 3575-1627 **OPEN** High season: daily, 9am – midnight; low season: Mon – Sat, 9am – 10pm
www.brasil2000turismo.com.br

Travel Agency – Paraíso Turismo
Rua Via Veneto, 17, Estrada da Balsa, Arraial
TEL (73) 3575-2360, 9198-6283 **FAX** (73) 3575-1206 **OPEN** Mon – Fri, 9am – 6pm; Sat, 9am – noon; public holidays: call in advance www.paraisoturismo.com.br

Travel Agency – Selvagem Adventure
Estrada da Balsa, 1446, Araçaípe
TEL (73) 3575-3031, 9985-4675 **OPEN** Daily, 9am – 7pm
www.selvagemadventure.com.br

Arraial do Cabo – Rio de Janeiro

AREA CODE 22 **POPULATION** 25,248 **DISTANCE** Rio de Janeiro 158 kilometers (98 miles) **ACCESS** Highway BR-101 from Rio de Janeiro to Rio Bonito, followed by the RJ-124 (Via Lagos), RJ-106, and finally RJ-140
www.arraialdocabo-rj.com.br

WHERE TO STAY

Capitão n'Areia Pousada $$
Wood and light colors dominate the décor in this rustic beachside guesthouse. A boat "docked" inside the establishment functions as a bar. **ACCOMMODATIONS** 32; air-conditioning (in 25 rooms); ceiling fan; Internet access; jacuzzi (in 6 suites); pay TV; phone. **FACILITIES AND SERVICES** bar; beachside service; beauty parlor; boat; convenience store; function room; gym; Internet access; massage room; parking; pool; restaurant; sauna; trails; transport to airport and attractions; video room; walking tours; 24-hour kitchen. **CREDIT CARDS** Diners; MasterCard; Visa
Rua Santa Cruz, 7, Praia dos Anjos
TEL (22) 2622-2720 www.capitaopousada.com

Pousada Caminho do Sol $$
The interior garden makes this guesthouse, just 100 meters (110 yards) from the beach, especially charming. Many suites have a panoramic view of the city or a partial view of Grande Beach. **ACCOMMODATIONS** 25; air-conditioning; ceiling fan; jacuzzi (in 2 suites); minibar; pay TV; phone. **FACILITIES AND SERVICES** bar; internal garden; Internet access; parking; pool; restaurant; sauna. **CREDIT CARDS** AmEx; Diners; MasterCard; Visa
Rua do Sol, 50, Praia Grande
TEL and **FAX** (22) 2622-2029 **RESERVATIONS** (22) 2622-1347
www.caminhodosol.com.br

WHERE TO EAT

Saint Tropez $$
Local fishermen supply fresh fish to this restaurant each day, so its menu varies according to what's available. Enjoy the seafood moqueca (stew), with fish, shrimp, squid, and mussels, accompanied by rice and pirão (manioc-thickened gravy). **CUISINE** Fish and seafood. **CREDIT CARDS** Diners; MasterCard; Visa
Praça Daniel Barreto (Praça Cova da Onça), 2, Praia dos Anjos
TEL (22) 2622-1222. Mon and Tue, 6pm – midnight; Wed – Sun, noon – midnight. May – June: Mon – Thu, 6pm – midnight; Fri and Sat, noon – midnight; Sun, noon – 6pm

Viagem dos Sabores $
In a nautically themed setting, this restaurant serves up dishes with a Mediterranean touch. The Provençal shrimp (fried shrimp in cream, herbs, and cognac) is particularly popular. **CUISINE** Mediterranean; various. **CREDIT CARDS** Diners; MasterCard; Visa
Rua Santa Cruz, 12, Praia dos Anjos
TEL (22) 2622-2892. Tue – Sun, 1pm – 10:30pm

Balneário Camboriú – Santa Catarina

AREA CODE 47 **POPULATION** 94,344 **DISTANCE** Florianópolis 84 kilometers (52 miles) **ACCESS** Highway BR-101 from Florianópolis heading north

WHERE TO STAY

Pousada Felíssimo $$$
Far from the beach and busy parts of town, this is an ideal getaway for couples wanting some peace and quiet; children under 12 are not allowed. **ACCOMMODATIONS** 9; air-conditioning; CD player; DVD; Internet access; jacuzzi; minibar; pay TV; telephone. **FACILITIES AND SERVICES** bar; beach swimming; bicycles; Internet access; marina; ofuro tub; pool; restaurant; sauna; 24-hour kitchen. **CREDIT CARDS** AmEx; Diners; MasterCard; Visa
Rua Alles Blau, 201, Praia dos Amores
TEL (47) 3360-6291 **FAX** (47) 3360-8281
www.pousadafelissimo.com.br

RESTAURANTS $ up to R$ 50 $$ from R$ 51 up to R$ 100 $$$ from R$ 101 up to R$ 150 $$$$ above R$ 150

Recanto das Águas Hotel e Spa $$$$

This complete resort includes a private beach and a spa, and is only 5 minutes from the center. Guests can take golf carts around the property. **ACCOMMODATIONS** 118; air-conditioning; Internet access; jacuzzi (in the superluxo and master suites); minibar; pay TV; private safe; telephone. **FACILITIES AND SERVICES** bar; beachside service; function room; games room; gym; heated pool; Internet access; massage room; paddle-ball court; parking; playground; pool; recreational team for adults and children; restaurant; soccer field; spa; tennis court; transport to airport and attractions; video room; volleyball court. **CREDIT CARDS** AmEx; Diners; MasterCard; Visa
Estrada da Rainha, 800, Praia dos Amores
TEL (47) 3261-0300 **FAX** (47) 3261-0361
www.hotelrecantodasaguas.com.br

WHERE TO EAT

Vieira's $

This typical coastal-town seafood restaurant has an extensive menu, large servings, and simple facilities. The house specializes in grilled dishes, such as flounder and conger eel, accompanied by rice, pirão (manioc-thickened gravy) and vegetables. **CUISINE** Fish and seafood. **CREDIT CARDS** AmEx; Diners; MasterCard; Visa
Avenida Atlântica, 5,700, Barra Sul
TEL (47) 3361-0842. Dec – Feb: Mon – Fri, 11am – 4pm and 5:30pm – midnight; Sat and Sun, 11am – midnight

SERVICES

Tour Operator – CG Tour
Rua Osmar de Souza Nunes, 154,
Mezzanine Store # 1, Pioneiros
TEL (47) 3360-7950. Mon – Fri, 8am – noon and 1:30pm – 6:30pm; Sat, 8am – noon

Tourist Information – Posto de Informações Turísticas
Avenida do Estado, 5071, Centro
TEL (47) 3367-8005. Daily, 6am – midnight

Bananal – São Paulo

AREA CODE 12 **POPULATION** 10,233 **DISTANCE** São Paulo 330 kilometers (205 miles) **ACCESS** Highway BR-116 from São Paulo heading north to Queluz, then SP-068 (Rodovia dos Tropeiros), passing through São José do Barreiro and Arapeí www.bananal.sp.gov.br

WHERE TO STAY

Hotel Fazenda Boa Vista $$
Built in 1780, this farm has been used as a set for period TV dramas. The rooms are simple, and there are two chalets. **ACCOMMODATIONS** 21; air-conditioning (in 3 rooms); ceiling fan; phone; TV. **FACILITIES AND SERVICES** adult and children's pools; bar; fishing lake; heated adult and children's pools; horses; playground; recreational staff for adults and children; soccer field. **CREDIT CARDS** MasterCard; Visa
Rodovia dos Tropeiros, Km 327
(former Estrada Rio–São Paulo)
TEL (12) 3116-1539 www.hotelfazboavista.com.br

WHERE TO EAT

Dona Licéia $
Most of this eatery's ingredients are produced on the property's farm. We suggest the duck with orange and the free-range chicken. The dessert buffet has some thirty choices. Reservations are essential for dinner. **CUISINE** Brazilian. **CREDIT CARDS** Diners; MasterCard
Fazenda Caxambu, Rodovia dos Tropeiros,
Km 20, Arapeí
TEL (12) 3115-1412. Daily, 12:30 – 5pm

Barra de Cunhaú – Rio Grande do Norte (see Praia da Pipa)

Barra de Santo Antônio – Alagoas

AREA CODE 82 **POPULATION** 13,864 **DISTANCE** Maceió 44 kilometers (27 miles) **ACCESS** From Maceió, on Highway AL-101 (Rodovia Litorânea)

WHERE TO STAY

Hotel Pousada Arco-Íris $$
This two-story guesthouse has ocean views from the upper floor rooms. The décor combines paintings of European landscapes with elements of Northeastern culture. **ACCOMMODATIONS** 14 (12 rooms, 2 suites); air-conditioning; minibar; TV; veranda; ceiling fan. **FACILITIES AND SERVICES** Internet access; bar; bicycles and a kayak for rent; parking; pool; restaurant; windsurfing; laundry. **CREDIT CARDS** AmEx; Visa
Rua 10, 6, Loteamento Tabuba
TEL (82) 3291-1250 **FAX** (82) 3291-6000 www.tabuba.tk

SERVICES

Bus station – Rodoviária
Avenida Antônio Baltazar, no #
TEL (82) 3291-1166 (public phone)

Barra de São Miguel – Alagoas

AREA CODE 82 **POPULATION** 7,247 **DISTANCE** Maceió 34 kilometers (21 miles) **ACCESS** From Maceió, south on Highway AL-101 (Rodovia Litorânea)

WHERE TO STAY

Pousada Dunas de Marapé $
This all-inclusive guesthouse has simple, cozy rooms. Lunch is served on the other side of the Juquiá River, in the Dunas de Marapé leisure complex, which contains a restaurant, arts and craft shops, and a fishing shop. **ACCOMMODATIONS** 16 (12 rooms, 4 chalets); air-conditioning; minibar; TV; veranda with hammock. **FACILITIES AND SERVICES** boat; parking; stores; restaurant; river; travel agency; exchange bureau; 24-hour kitchen; recreational team for adults and children; guided walking tours; valet parking; lifeguards; beach service; airport shuttle; transport to attractions. **CREDIT CARDS** Not accepted
Barra de Jequiá da Praia (45 kilometers, 28 miles – from Barra de São Miguel)
TEL (82) 9308-2506 **FAX** (82) 3272-1188

Village Barra Hotel $$$
One of the best places to stay in town, this hotel stands on the sea front and has well-lit rooms offering panoramic views. **ACCOMMODATIONS** 74; air-conditioning; private safe; minibar; telephone; TV; veranda in the deluxe rooms. **FACILITIES AND SERVICES** bar; parking; pool; playground; six-a-side soccer court; volleyball court; restaurant; conference room; recreational team for chil-

---

PRICES | **HOTELS** (couple) | $ up to R$ 150 | $$ from R$ 151 up to R$ 300 | $$$ from R$ 301 up to R$500 | $$$$ above R$ 500

468
BRAZIL GUIDE

dren; catamaran tour; beach service; transport to attractions. **CREDIT CARDS** AmEx; Diners; MasterCard; Visa
Rua Senador Arnon de Mello, no #, Praia do Niquim
TEL and **FAX** (82) 3272-1000
www.villagebarrahotel.com.br

WHERE TO EAT

Bar and Restaurante do Tio $
The outdoor tables of this restaurant have a view of the quay. The house specialties are the peixada (fish stew), and the seafood selection, which includes peixada, shrimp, massunim (a small mussel), sururu (shellfish) omelet, pirão gravy and rice. **CUISINE** Fish and seafood; diverse. **CREDIT CARDS** Not accepted
Rua Manoel Eleutério da Silva, no #, Praça São Pedro
TEL (82) 9381-7670 **OPEN** High season: daily, 9am – 5pm; low season: Tue – Sun, 9am – 5pm

Sauaçuhy $
This air-conditioned restaurant operates a pay-by-the-pound buffet as well as an all-you-can-eat system where food is served at the table. **CUISINE** Fish and seafood; diverse. **CREDIT CARDS** Diners; MasterCard; Visa
Rodovia AL-101 Sul, Km 21.3
(in front of the São Francisco gas station)
TEL (82) 3272-1248 **OPEN** Daily, 11am – 5pm

Barra Grande – Bahia

AREA CODE 73 **DISTANCE** Salvador 330 kilometers (205 miles) by ferryboat to Bom Despacho, Itacaré 60 kilometers (37 miles), Ubaitaba 66 kilometers (41 miles) access By boat, which leaves every hour from the Camamu Port (1.5 hours by regular boat or 30 minutes by motorboat). In 4×4 vehicles, through Itacaré (take the car ferry across the Contas River and drive for another 50 kilometers, 31 miles), or through Ubaitaba (on Highway BR-030, along a stretch of potholed dirt road)

WHERE TO STAY

Kiaroa Eco-Luxury Resort $$$$
The rooms are decorated with tropical and maritime motifs and Asian touches. The bungalows have private swimming pools and DVD players. Bombaça Beach, in front of the resort, is practically exclusive. Children under 14 are not allowed. **ACCOMMODATIONS** 28 (14 rooms and 14 bungalows); air-conditioning; private safe; minibar; jacuzzi in 1 bungalow; telephone; cable TV; private veranda with hammock. **FACILITIES AND SERVICES** Internet access; bar; bicycles; parking; jacuzzi; stores; pool; tennis court; volleyball court; restaurant; conference room; gym; dry and wet saunas; spa; travel agency; exchange bureau; heliport; landing strip; lifeguards; transport into the village. **CREDIT CARDS** AmEx; Diners; MasterCard; Visa
Praia da Bombaça, Loteamento Barreta dos Três Coqueiros, Quadra 3, Maraú
TEL (73) 3258-6215, 3258-6213 **RESERVATIONS** and **FAX** (71) 3272-1320 www.kiaroa.com.br

Pousada Lagoa do Cassange $$
Situated on a narrow strip of land between the ocean and Cassange Lake, this is an alternative for those seeking peace and quiet. The comfortable chalets are decorated with local handicrafts, and those closer to the ocean have excellent views. **ACCOMMODATIONS** 15 chalets; CD player; air-conditioning; minibar; hammock; telephone; ceiling fan. **FACILITIES AND SERVICES** Internet access; bar; boat; kayaks; parking; fishing lake; motorboat; stores; vol-

leyball court; restaurant; reading and video room; hiking trails; travel agency; guided walking tours; beach service; airport shuttle; transport to attractions. **CREDIT CARDS** Diners; MasterCard; Visa
Praia do Cassange, no #, Península de Maraú
TEL and **FAX** (73) 3255-2348 **RESERVATIONS** (73) 3258-2166, 3258-2192 www.maris.com.br

WHERE TO EAT

Bar do Francês $
This casual beachside restaurant serves dishes such as fried agulhinha fish and the large shrimp known as camarão-pistola. **CUISINE** Fish and seafood. **CREDIT CARDS** Visa
Praia Bela, no #, Taipus de Fora
TEL (73) 3258-9036 **OPEN** Summer: daily, 7am – midnight; winter: daily, 7am – 5pm

Restaurante do Jorge $
This simple, family-run eatery offers dishes such as lagosta grelhada (grilled lobster) for two and octopus, lobster, crab, snapper, shrimp, snook, and grouper moquecas (stews). **CUISINE** Regional; fish and seafood. **CREDIT CARDS** Not accepted
Ilha do Sapinho (access by boat from the Barra Grande quay or from Camamu)
TEL (73) 8107-7312 **RESERVATIONS** (73) 3258-2309 (public phone) **OPEN** Daily, 10am – 6pm

Uai Bahia $
The owners of this restaurant are from Minas Gerais, and they have brought a touch of their native cuisine to the village of Barra Grande. There is also a sushi-bar in the same space. **CUISINE** Food from the state of Minas Gerais; fish and seafood. **CREDIT CARDS** Diners; MasterCard; Visa
Rua Desembargador Olny Silva, no #
TEL (73) 3258-6194 **OPEN** High season: daily, noon – midnight; low season: daily, 1pm – 10pm

SERVICES

Travel Agency – Camamu Adventure
Boat rental and crossing from Camamu to Barra Grande and back
Avenida Beira-mar, no #, Camamu
TEL (73) 3255-2138, 3258-6236 **OPEN** Daily, 7am – 6pm
www.camamuadventure.com.br

Travel Agency – Natur and Mar Turismo
Boat rental, crossing from Camamu to Barra Grande and back, motorboat and 4×4 trips
Avenida José Melo Pirajá, 35, Camamu
TEL (73) 3258-6361 **OPEN** Mon – Fri, 8am – 6pm; Sat, 8am – 5pm www.naturemar.tur.br

Barreirinhas – Maranhão

AREA CODE 98 **POPULATION** 44,869 **DISTANCES** São Luís 265 kilometers (165 miles); Parnaíba 441 kilometers (274 miles); Teresina 593 kilometers (368 miles) **ACCESS** From São Luís, on Highway MA-402 (Rodovia Translitorânea). By twin engine or single engine plane, about 50 minutes www.barreirinhas.ma.gov.br

WHERE TO STAY

Hotel Pousada do Buriti $$
This is the best option for those who want to stay in the center of Barreirinhas. The hotel has spacious rooms, and its breakfast is delicious. The tiny swimming pool

---

| **RESTAURANTS** | $ up to R$ 50 | $$ from R$ 51 up to R$ 100 | $$$ from R$ 101 up to R$ 150 | $$$$ above R$ 150 |

can be used at night. **ACCOMMODATIONS** 29; air-conditioning; minibar; telephone; TV; veranda with hammock. **FACILITIES AND SERVICES** bar; convenience store; pool; playground; restaurant; river; conference room; games room. **CREDIT CARDS** Diners; MasterCard; Visa
Rua Inácio Lins, no #, Centro
TEL and **FAX** (98) 3349-1338
www.pousadadoburiti.com.br

Porto Preguiças Resort $$$
One of the most comfortable and charming hotels in Barreirinhas, this resort is approximately 2 kilometers (1 mile) from the town center. The enormous swimming pool has a sandy bottom and contains water from the Preguiças River. **ACCOMMODATIONS** 30; air-conditioning; minibar; cable TV; ceiling fan. **FACILITIES AND SERVICES** Internet access; wine cellar; bar; nursery; bicycles; parking; stores; natural pool; playground; volleyball court; restaurant; river; games room; sauna; currency exchange bureau; trips; airport shuttle. **CREDIT CARDS** Diners; MasterCard; Visa
Estrada do Carnaubal, no #, right bank of the Preguiças River (a 2 kilometer off-road drive)
TEL (98) 3349-1220 **FAX** (98) 3349-0620
RESERVATIONS (98) 3349-1912
www.portopreguicas.com.br

Solare Lençóis Resort $$
Opened in 2005, this resort boasts better facilities than the other hotels in the region, with a swimming pool, restaurant, gym, and massage room. It also has a recreational team for children, which makes it ideal for families. **ACCOMMODATIONS** 242; air-conditioning; minibar; telephone; cable TV. **FACILITIES AND SERVICES** Internet access; bar; kid's club; marina; pool; restaurant; conference room; gym; massage room; sauna; business center. **CREDIT CARDS** AmEx; Diners; MasterCard; Visa
Estrada São Domingos, no #, Boa Vista
TEL (98) 3349-6000 www.gruposolare.com.br

WHERE TO EAT

Camarão da Luzia $
Shrimp, caught right here on Atins Beach, get prepared in this kiosk by Dona Luzia with salt, onion, garlic, and margarine. They're served with rice, beans, salad, and shrimp pie. **CUISINE** Seafood. **CREDIT CARDS** MasterCard
Canto do Atins, no #
TEL None

Paturi $
This highlight of this establishment is the moqueca de arraia (ray stew), which serves two. **CUISINE** Fish and seafood; regional. **CREDIT CARDS** MasterCard
Praia do Caburé, no #
TEL (98) 9608-3032, 9126-8602, 8129-7430
RESERVATIONS (98) 3246-7253 **OPEN** Daily, 6am until the last customer leaves

SERVICES

Tourist Information – Secretaria de Turismo
Avenida da Rodoviária, no #, Boa Fé
TEL None **OPEN** Mon – Fri, 8am – noon and 2pm – 6pm

Travel Agency – Eco-Dunas
Rua Inácio Lins, 164, Centro
TEL (98) 3349-0545 **OPEN** Daily, 7am – 7pm
www.ecodunas.com.br

Travel Agency – Rota das Trilhas
Avenida Joaquim Soeiro de Carvalho, 682-A, Centro
TEL (98) 3349-0372 **OPEN** Daily, 7:30am – 6pm

Travel Agency – Tropical Adventure
Rua Anacleto de Carvalho, 260, Cruzeiro (over the boat refueling station)
TEL (98) 3349-1987 **OPEN** Mon – Sat, 8am – noon and 2pm – 6pm www.tropical-adventure-expedicoes.com

Belém – Pará

AREA CODE 91 **POPULATION** 1,408,847 **DISTANCE** São Luís 803 kilometers (499 miles) **ACCESS** By car from São Luís on Highway BR-135 to Miranda do Norte, BR-222 to Bela Vista do Maranhão, then BR-316 to Presidente Médici, heading toward Belém www.belem.pa.gov.br

WHERE TO STAY

Hilton Belém $$$
Located in the city center, next to Theatro da Paz, this hotel has two floors just for executives. **ACCOMMODATIONS** 361; air-conditioning; Internet access; jacuzzi (in the presidential suite); minibar; pay TV; telephone. **FACILITIES AND SERVICES** bar; business center; conference room; gym; jogging track; massage room; pool; restaurant; sauna; 24-hour kitchen. **CREDIT CARDS** AmEx; Diners; MasterCard; Visa
Avenida Presidente Vargas, 882, Centro
TEL (91) 4006-7000 **FAX** (91) 3225-2942
RESERVATIONS 0800-7280888 www.belem.hilton.com

Hotel Regente $$
Next to the city's business and financial center, this hotel hosts a range of events. It caters to business travelers, and many of the guests are foreigners. **ACCOMMODATIONS** 219; air-conditioning; bathtub in the suites; clock-radio; Internet access; minibar; pay TV; telephone. **FACILITIES AND SERVICES** bar; business center; conference room; gym; Internet access; laundry; parking; pool; restaurant; sauna; travel agency; 24-hour room service. **CREDIT CARDS** AmEx; Diners; MasterCard; Visa
Avenida Governador José Malcher, 485, São Brás
TEL (91) 3181-5000 **FAX** (91) 3181-5005
www.hotelregente.com.br

WHERE TO EAT

Amazon Beer $
Located in Estação das Docas, one of Belém's tourist spots, this bar is always busy at happy hour. The brewery produces five types of beer and serves great food, such as fish fillet with risotto. **CUISINE** Brazilian. **CREDIT CARDS** AmEx; Diners; MasterCard; Visa
Avenida Boulevard Castilho França, no #, Armazém 1, Estação das Docas
TEL (91) 3212-5400. Mon – Wed, 5pm – 1am; Thu and Fri, 5pm – 3am; Sat, 11am – 3am; Sun and holidays, 11am – 1am

Lá em Casa $
This eatery serves regional food such as pato no tucupi (duck stew with manioc milk), maniçoba (beef jerky with manioc leaves, smoked pork and bacon), farofa de pirarucu (pirarucu fish with manioc meal) and grilled filhote (catfish). Adjoining the Lá em Casa are two more restaurants by the same owner: O Outro, which serves a delicious cordeiro de forno (baked lamb), and the Ver-o-pesinho, where guests serve themselves from a

PRICES | **HOTELS** (couple) $ up to R$ 150 $$ from R$ 151 up to R$ 300 $$$ from R$ 301 up to R$500 $$$$ above R$ 500

470   BRAZIL GUIDE

buffet, then pay for their food by its weight. **CUISINE** Regional. **CREDIT CARDS** AmEx; Diners; MasterCard; Visa
Avenida Dom Pedro I, 549, between Municipalidade and Senador Lemos
TEL (91) 3242-4222. Lá em Casa: Mon – Sat, noon – 3pm and 7pm – midnight; O Outro: Sun, noon – 4pm; Ver-o-pesinho: Mon – Sat, noon – 3pm. Branch of Lá em Casa: Avenida Bulevar Castilho França, no #, Centro, Estação das Docas, tel. (91) 3212-5588. Daily, noon – midnight

Manjar das Garças $

Standing in the beautiful Mangal das Garças Park, with a view of the Guamá River, this restaurant serves sophisticated dishes with regional ingredients, such as filhote (catfish) with spotflower sprouts and risotto. **CUISINE** Regional. **CREDIT CARDS** AmEx; Diners; MasterCard; Visa
Passagem Carneiro da Rocha, no #, Cidade Velha
TEL (91) 3242-1056. Tue – Sun, noon – midnight

SERVICES

Airport – Aeroporto Internacional de Belém

Avenida Júlio César, no #, Valdecans
TEL (91) 3210-6039

Tour Operator – Rumo Norte Expedições

Trips to Ilha dos Papagaios island in Hawaiian canoes.
Avenida Serzedelo Correa, 895, Vila Augusta, Casa 59, 2nd Floor
TEL (91) 3225-1697. Mon – Fri, 9am – 1pm and 2:30pm – 5pm

Tour Operator – Valeverde Turismo

Boat tours along the Belém coastline
Avenida Boulevard Castilho França, no #, Store # 7, Estação das Docas
TEL (91) 3212-3388. Tue – Sun, 10am – 10pm

Tourist Information – Posto de Informações Turísticas (Belemtur)

Avenida Júlio César, no #, Valdecans, Aeroporto Internacional de Belém
TEL (91) 3210-6268. Daily, 7am – 10pm

Tourist Police Station – Delegacia de Atendimento ao Turista

Avenida 28 de Setembro, 452, Comércio
TEL (91) 3222-0166. Mon – Fri, 7:30am – 2pm (administration). Daily, 24 hours

Belo Horizonte – Minas Gerais

AREA CODE 31 **POPULATION** 2,412,937 distâncias Rio de Janeiro 435 kilometers (270 miles); Brasilia 716 kilometers (445 miles); São Paulo 1,355 kilometers (842 miles) **ACESS** Highway BR-381 (Rodovia Fernão Dias) from São Paulo. Highway BR-040 (Rodovia Washington Luís) from Rio de Janeiro www.belohorizonte.mg.gov.br

WHERE TO STAY

Belo Horizonte Othon Palace $$$

In front of the municipal park and the arts and crafts fair on Avenida Afonso Pena, this hotel occupies a luxurious 25-story building. **ACCOMMODATIONS** 287; air-conditioning; Internet access; minibar; pay TV; phone. **FACILITIES AND SERVICES** beauty parlor; business center; convenience store; function room; gym; Internet access; massage room; pool; restaurant; sauna; secretary; valet serv-

ice; 24-hour kitchen. **CREDIT CARDS** AmEx; Diners; Master-Card; Visa
Avenida Afonso Pena, 1,050, Centro
TEL (31) 2126-0000 **FAX** (31) 2126-0061
RESERVATIONS 0800-7250505 www.othon.com.br

Hotel Mercure Belo Horizonte Lourdes $$

Great location, near the hubbub of the Savassi district. The rooms have broadband Internet and work. **ACCOMMODATIONS** 371; air-conditioning; Internet access; minibar; pay TV; private safe; 2 phones. **FACILITIES AND SERVICES** bar; business center; function room; gym; heated pool; Internet access; parking; pool; restaurant; sauna; transport to airport; valet service; 24-hour kitchen. **CREDIT CARDS** AmEx; Diners; MasterCard; Visa
Avenida do Contorno, 7,315, Lourdes
TEL (31) 3298-4100 **FAX** (31) 3298-4105
RESERVATIONS (31) 3298-4101 www.accorhotels.com.br

Ouro Minas Palace Hotel $$$$

The only five-star hotel in Belo Horizonte, the Ouro Minas Palace is located in Ipiranga, 8 kilometers (5 miles) from the city center. For guests with allergies, there are uncarpeted rooms stocked with hypoallergenic products. **ACCOMMODATIONS** 343; air-conditioning; Internet access; jacuzzi; minibar; phone; pay TV; private safe. **FACILITIES AND SERVICES** bar; beauty parlor; business center; convenience store; function room; games room; gym; heated pool; jacuzzi; lifeguard; parking; pool; recreation team for adults; restaurant; sauna; stores; travel agency; valet service; wine cellar. **CREDIT CARDS** AmEx; Diners; MasterCard; Visa
Avenida Cristiano Machado, 4,001, Ipiranga
TEL (31) 3429-4001 **FAX** (31) 3429-4002
RESERVATIONS (31) 3429-4000 www.ourominas.com.br

WHERE TO EAT

Aurora $$

One of the most highly praised restaurants in Belo Horizonte. The house fortes are the dishes involving jabuticaba fruits, such as lamb chops with a green chili and jabuticaba glaze and risotto. **CUISINE** Contemporary. **CREDIT CARDS** AmEx; Diners; MasterCard; Visa
Rua Expedicionário Mário Alves de Oliveira, 421, Pampulha
TEL (31) 3498-7567. Wed – Sat, 7pm until the last customer leaves; Sun, noon – until the last customer leaves

L'Osteria Casa Mattiazzi $

Seafood is a constant on the menu here. Highlight include the linguine with cockles and pesto, and the black tagliatelle with seafood and tomato sauce. **CUISINE** Italian. **CREDIT CARDS** MasterCard; Visa
Rua Soledade, 28, Santa Efigênia
TEL (31) 3483-3465. Tue – Thu, 6:30pm – midnight; Fri and Sat, 6:30pm – 1am; Sun, and holidays, noon – 5pm

Quintal Pampulha $

This restaurant specializes in exotic meats, such as capybara, boar, alligator, and frog. Bring a big party and try the leg of boar with crispy skin, served with garlic rice and honey and herb sauce, which serves 8 to 10. **CUISINE** Exotic meats. **CREDIT CARDS** Not accepted
Rua Sebastião Antônio Carlos, 350, Bandeirantes
TEL (31) 3443-5559. Thu and Fri, 6pm until the last customer leaves; Sun, 11am – 6pm

Taste Vin $

This restaurant is famous for its impeccable soufflés

RESTAURANTS	$ up to R$ 50	$$ from R$ 51 up to R$ 100	$$$ from R$ 101 up to R$ 150	$$$$ above R$ 150

(try the shrimp, gruyere cheese and champignon one), but the piece de resistance is the extensive wine list, which contains 600 labels. **CUISINE** French. **CREDIT CARDS** AmEx; Diners; MasterCard; Visa
Rua Curitiba, 2,105, Lourdes
TEL (31) 3292-5423. Mon – Thu, 7:30pm – midnight; Fri and Sat, 7:30pm – 1am

Xapuri $

Considered by many to be the best place in Belo Horizonte for regional food, this restaurant stands on a large property, surrounded by greenery. A highlight of the menu is the frango preguento do Bento: whole chicken stew with corn and served with rice, beans, chayote, okra and collard greens. **CUISINE** Regional. **CREDIT CARDS** Diners; MasterCard; Visa
Rua Mandacaru, 260, Trevo
TEL (31) 3496-6198. Tue and Wed, noon – 11pm; Thu, Fri and Sat, noon – 2am; Sun, noon – 6pm

SERVICES

Bus Station – Rodoviária
Praça Rio Branco, 100, Centro
TEL (31) 3271-3000

Tourist Information – BeloTur
Rua Pernambuco, 288, Funcionários
TEL (31) 3277-9777 **FAX** (31) 3277-9730. Mon – Fri, 8am – 6pm

Bento Gonçalves – Rio Grande do Sul

AREA CODE 54 **POPULATION** 100,643 **DISTANCES** Porto Alegre 120 kilometers (75 miles), Garibaldi 16 kilometers (10 miles) **ACCESS** Highway BR-116, RS-122, RS-446, and RS-470 from Porto Alegre www.bentogoncalves.rs.gov.br

WHERE TO STAY

Hotel Villa Michelon $$
Considered by many to be the most comfortable hotel in the Vale dos Vinhedos (Vineyard Valley), Villa Michelon has spacious rooms, good leisure facilities and a large convention center. **ACCOMMODATIONS** 50; air-conditioning; CD player; central heating; Internet access; jacuzzi (in 12 rooms); minibar; pay TV; private safe; telephone. **FACILITIES AND SERVICES** animal watching; bar; cultural space; function room; games room; gym; heated pool; jacuzzi; jogging track; mini farm; mini wine museum; natural pool; orchard. **CREDIT CARDS** AmEx; Diners; MasterCard; Visa
Rodovia RS-444, Km 18.9, Vale dos Vinhedos
TEL 0800-7033800 **FAX** (54) 3459-1807
RESERVATIONS (54) 3459-1800
www.villamichelon.com.br

Pousada Borghetto Sant'Anna $$
Just 5 minutes from the center of town, this guesthouse has comfortable suites and colonial Italian-style stone houses, with a view of the vineyards. Reservations are required. **ACCOMMODATIONS** 5; air-conditioning; digital sound system; fireplace; fully-equipped kitchen (in the houses); minibar; mini cellar; TV (in the houses). **CREDIT CARDS** Not accepted
Linha Leopoldina, 868, Vale dos Vinhedos
TEL (54) 3453-2355, 9147-3197 **FAX** (54) 3453-2355
www.borghettosantanna.com.br

Pousada Don Giovanni $$
This charming little guesthouse occupies a 1930s mansion on a large vineyard. It is decorated with rustic furniture and works of contemporary art. **ACCOMMODATIONS** 7; air-conditioning; ceiling fan; heating; minibar (in the suite); TV (in the suite). **FACILITIES AND SERVICES** bicycles; bowls; cellar; giant chess board; minibar; piano; pool; restaurant; sitting room; tour guides; TV; vineyard; visit to vineyard with wine tasting. **CREDIT CARDS** Visa
Linha Amadeu, Km 12
TEL/FAX (54) 3455-6293, 3455-6294
www.dongiovanni.com.br

Pousada Valduga $$
This is a complex of four guesthouses, all with simple rooms and a view of the grape arbors, which stand in the vineyard of the same name. **ACCOMMODATIONS** 20; ceiling fan (in 4 suites); heating; jacuzzi (in 1 suite); minibar; telephone; TV. **FACILITIES AND SERVICES** bar; cellar; games room; Internet access; parking; pool; restaurant; video room. **CREDIT CARDS** Diners; MasterCard; Visa
Linha Leopoldina, no #, Access from Rodovia RS-470, Vale dos Vinhedos
TEL (54) 3453-1154 www.casavalduga.com.br

WHERE TO EAT

Don Ziero $
The menu offers salads, pastas, and meat dishes. The house specialties are the lamb dishes, such as the crostata (lamb in an almond crust accompanied by aspargus risotto). **CUISINE** Italian; various. **CREDIT CARDS** AmEx; Diners; MasterCard; Visa
Rodovia RS-470, Km 219.75, Vinícola Cordelier
TEL (54) 3453-7593. Mon – Sat, noon – 3pm and 7pm – 10pm; Sun, noon – 3pm

Giuseppe $
Galeterias, which specialize in serving spring chicken, are a tradition in these mountains. At this particular eatery, you will find the best spring chicken in the region and excellent service. **CUISINE** Italian. **CREDIT CARDS** AmEx; Diners; MasterCard; Visa
Rodovia RS-470, Km 221.6, Garibaldina
TEL (54) 3463-8505, 3463-8138. Daily, 11:30am – 3pm

Sbornea's $
Hearty Italian food is served here. Waiters bring around different dishes for diners to choose from. The stuffed chicken is a specialty. Pancakes are served on Wednesday, Thursday, and Friday nights. **CUISINE** Italian. **CREDIT CARDS** MasterCard; Visa
Rodovia RS-444, Km 19.5, 8 da Graciema
TEL (54) 3459-1224. Mon and Tue, noon – 3pm; Wed – Sat, noon – 3pm and 8pm – 11pm; Sun, noon – 3pm

SERVICES

Tour Operator – Giordani Turismo
Rua Erni Hugo Dreher, 227, Planalto
TEL (54) 3452-6042, 3452-6455. Mon – Fri, 8am – 6:45pm; Sat, 8am – 5pm

Tour Operator – Opzionne Turismo
Rodovia RS-444, Km 18.9, Hotel Villa Michelon
TEL (54) 3459-1813. Mon – Sat, 8am – 5pm

Bezerros – Pernambuco

AREA CODE 81 **POPULATION** 60,652 **DISTANCE** Recife 107 kilometers (66 miles) **ACCESS** From Recife, on Highway BR-232 www.bezerros.pe.gov.br

---

PRICES | **HOTELS** (couple) | $ up to R$ 150 | $$ from R$ 151 up to R$ 300 | $$$ from R$ 301 up to R$500 | $$$$ above R$ 500

WHERE TO STAY

Brisa da Serra $

This establishment suits the needs of Bezerros, which receives an influx of tourists on festive occasions such as Carnival. At those times, the hotel is generally full. **ACCOMMODATIONS** 25; air-conditioning; minibar; telephone; TV. **FACILITIES AND SERVICES** Internet access; parking; store; pool; restaurant. **CREDIT CARDS** MasterCard; Visa
Avenida Major Aprígio da Fonseca, no #,
BR-232, Km 102
TEL and **FAX** (81) 3728-1232

WHERE TO EAT

Recanto das Colinas $

The restaurant decorated with carnival masks has several options involving steak, chicken and fish. The steak Parmegian and merluza empanada (battered hake) are the favorite items on the menu. At lunch the restaurant offers a buffet. **CUISINE** Varied; regional. **CREDIT CARDS** Mastercard; Visa
Avenida Major Aprígio da Fonseca, São Pedro
TEL (81) 3728 0519 **OPEN** Mon and Tue, 11am – 3pm and 6pm – midnight; Wed – Sat, 11am – midnight.

Bom Jardim da Serra – Santa Catarina

AREA CODE 48 **POPULATION** 4,214 **DISTANCE** Florianópolis 230 kilometers (143 miles) **ACCESS** From Florianópolis, take Highway BR-101 to Palhoça, then the BR-282 toward Santo Amaro da Imperatriz. At the entrance to Urubici and São Joaquim, take the SC-430 to the Bom Jardim da Serra exit on your left; from here it is another 30 kilometers (19 miles) to the town

WHERE TO STAY

Rio do Rastro Eco Resort $$$$

This sophisticated ecological resort, set against a backdrop of natural beauty, offers a range of recreational activities and a view of the lake. Guests sleep in chalets. **ACCOMMODATIONS** 18; central water heater; fireplace (in some chalets); heating; Internet access (wi-fi); jacuzzi (in some chalets); minibar; pay TV; telephone; towel heater; veranda. **FACILITIES AND SERVICES** bar; canoe; children's play shed; ecological trails; fishing equipment and lake; gym; heated pool; heliport; horses; Internet access (wi-fi, computer available); jacuzzi; library; massage room; playground; restaurant; river; sauna; spa; tour guides; transport to attractions; video library; video room; waterfalls. **CREDIT CARDS** Diners; MasterCard; Visa
Rodovia SC-438, Km 130
TEL (48) 3491-2610, 3491-2621 www.riodorastro.com.br

SERVICES

Ecological Tour Operator – Urubici Ecoturismo

Avenida Adolfo Konder, 351, Centro
TEL (49) 9125-7198. Mon – Fri, 9am – 6pm

Bombinhas – Santa Catarina

AREA CODE 47 **POPULATION** 12,456 **DISTANCE** Florianópolis 70 kilometers (44 miles) **ACCESS** From Florianópolis, take Highway BR-101 north to the turnoff to Porto Belo. From there, take SC-472 www.bombinhas.sc.gov.br

WHERE TO STAY

Morada do Mar Hotel $$$

This hotel on Bombas Beach caters to families and offers beach service and good leisure facilities for children. **ACCOMMODATIONS** 39; air-conditioning; ceiling fan; minibar; pay TV; safe; telephone. **FACILITIES AND SERVICES** bar; games room; Internet access; restaurant; room service; sitting room; tourist information; transport to airport and attractions; video room. **CREDIT CARDS** AmEx; Diners; MasterCard; Visa
Avenida Leopold Zarling, 1,221, Praia de Bombas
TEL (47) 3393-6090 www.moradadomar.com.br

Pousada Quintal do Mar $$

This guesthouse, a converted beach house, has only 4 suites, each decorated with local fruit and flower motifs. Children under 12 are not allowed. **ACCOMMODATIONS** 4; air-conditioning; CD player; Internet access (wi-fi); minibar; TV. **FACILITIES AND SERVICES** beach equipment and service; Internet access (wi-fi); sitting room with fireplace, TV and DVD; restaurant; veranda with hammocks. **CREDIT CARDS** MasterCard
Avenida Aroeira da Praia, 1,641, Praia do Mariscal
TEL (47) 3393-4389, 9980-2100
www.quintaldomar.com.br

Pousada Vila do Farol $$$

This spacious guesthouse resembles a village of colorful two-story houses. All rooms have fully-equipped kitchens. **ACCOMMODATIONS** 56; air-conditioning; coffee maker; Internet access; microwave oven; minibar; pay TV; private safe; toaster; telephone. **FACILITIES AND SERVICES** beachside service; function room; games room; Internet access; pool; pool bar; recreational team for children; restaurant; stores; transport to airport; video room; 24-hour kitchen. **CREDIT CARDS** AmEx; Diners; MasterCard; Visa
Avenida Vereador Manoel José dos Santos, 800, Centro
TEL (47) 3393-9000 **FAX** (47) 3393-9023
www.viladofarol.com.br

Pousada Villa Paradiso $$$$

This Balinese-style guesthouse is located on the side of a hill at the end of Bombinhas Beach. There are bungalows with high ceilings and outdoor decks with whirlpool tubs, pools, ofuro tubs and relaxation tents. **ACCOMMODATIONS** 25; air-conditioning; ceiling fan; fully equipped kitchen; Internet access; jacuzzi (in the rooms and 11 bungalows); minibar; pay TV; private safe; telephone. **FACILITIES AND SERVICES** bar; barbecue facilities; beach service; gazebo; hammocks; Internet access; jacuzzi; ofuro tub; pool; pool bar; pool service; transport to airport. **CREDIT CARDS** MasterCard; Visa
Avenida Garoupas, 5, Praia de Bombinhas
TEL (47) 3369-0005, 3369-0069
www.villaparadiso.com.br

WHERE TO EAT

Berro d'Água $

It is worth coming to this fishing village at Zimbros Beach, if only to taste this restaurant's Asian shrimp with soy sauce, bacon and mushrooms, or salmon with honey-mustard. **CUISINE** Fish and seafood. **CREDIT CARDS** AmEx; Diners; MasterCard; Visa
Rua Rio Juquiá, no #, Praia de Zimbros
TEL (47) 3393-3666. High season: daily, 10am – 11:30pm.

RESTAURANTS	$ up to R$ 50	$$ from R$ 51 up to R$ 100	$$$ from R$ 101 up to R$ 150	$$$$ above R$ 150

Low season: Fri and Sat, 11am – 4:30pm and 7:30pm – midnight; Sun, 11am – 5pm

Casa da Lagosta $$

This simple option in the town center specializes in seafood dishes, all of which come in with hearty servings. Despite the name (lagosta means "lobster" in Portuguese), the most popular dishes are the moqueca stews and shrimp dishes. CUISINE Fish and seafood. CREDIT CARDS Diners; MasterCard; Visa
Avenida Vereador Manoel José dos Santos, 987, Centro
TEL (47) 3369-2235. High season: daily, 10am – 11pm. Low season: Sun – Tue, 10am – 11pm

SERVICES

Adventure Sports and Tour Operator – Altura Climb
Rodovia SC-412 (access from BR-101 to Porto Belo)
TEL (47) 3369-4444, 8401-5701

Diving Operator – Acquatrek
Rua do Trapiche, 51, Centro
TEL (47) 3369-2137, 9973-0471. Tue – Sun, 9am – noon and 2pm – 6pm (closed in August)

Diving Operator – Patadacobra
Avenida Vereador Manoel José dos Santos, 215, Centro
TEL (47) 3369-2119. Daily, 8am – 6pm

Diving Operator – Submarine
Rua da Sardinha, 2, Centro
TEL (47) 3369-2223, 3369-2473, 3369-2867. Tue – Sun, 8:30am – noon and 1:30pm – 6pm

Tour Operator – Casa do Turista
Avenida Governador Celso Ramos, 2.460, store #5, Centro, Porto Belo
TEL (47) 3369-5030. Daily, 8am – 9pm
www.casadoturista.info

Tourist Information – Posto de Informações Turísticas/Prefeitura
Rua Baleia Jubarte, 322, José Amâncio
TEL (47) 3393-9500, Rua 522. Mon – Fri, 8am – noon and 1:30pm – 5:30pm

Bonito – Mato Grosso do Sul

AREA CODE 67 POPULATION 17,275 DISTANCES Campo Grande 299 kilometers (186 miles), São Paulo 1,201 kilometers (746 miles), Rio de Janeiro 1,753 kilometers (1,089 miles) ACCESS Highway BR-060 from Campo Grande www.bonito-ms.com.br

WHERE TO STAY

Zagaia Eco Resort $$$
Bonito's best hotel in terms of leisure facilities operates out of the old Hotel Zagaia, on a beautiful farm 3.5 kilometers (2 miles) out of town. The décor takes its inspiration from indigenous culture. ACCOMMODATIONS 100; air-conditioning; minibar; pay TV; private safe; telephone. FACILITIES AND SERVICES bar; bike path; bilingual staff; business center; conference room; convenience store; environmental inspector; first-aid; games room; gym; heated pool; heliport; Internet access; jacuzzi; jogging track; massage room; parking; playground; pool; recreational staff

for adults and children; restaurant; sauna; soccer field; stores; tennis court; trails. FISHING lake; fish-and-release. CREDIT CARDS AmEx; Diners; MasterCard; Visa
Rodovia Três Morros, Km 0 (exit to Campos dos Índios), 3.5 kilometers (2 miles) from the center of town
TEL (67) 3255-5500 FAX (67) 3255-1710
RESERVATIONS 0800 7904400 www.zagaia.com.br

Hotel Santa Esmeralda $$
This charming guesthouse is 18 kilometers (11 miles) out of town, on the farm of the same name. The rooms offer beautiful views of the region's forests. ACCOMMODATIONS 18; air-conditioning; hammock; minibar; TV; veranda. FACILITIES AND SERVICES bar; convention and video room; Internet access; kayaks; parking; restaurant; river; river floating; volleyball court; walking trails; waterfall. CREDIT CARDS Visa
Rodovia Bonito-Guia Lopes da Laguna, Km 17
TEL, FAX and RESERVATIONS (67) 3255-2683
www.hotelsantaesmeralda.com.br

WHERE TO EAT

Cantinho do Peixe $$
This restaurant is known for its fresh caldinho de piranha (piranha broth), and the delicious pintado ao urucum (catfish in palm fruit sauce), which comes with rice and pirão (manioc-thickened gravy) and serves two. CUISINE Regional. CREDIT CARDS AmEx; Diners; MasterCard; Visa
Rua 31 de Março, 1,918, Centro
TEL (67) 3255-3381. Daily, 11am – 11pm (high season); Mon – Sat, 11am – 3pm and 6pm – 11pm; Sun, 11am – 3pm (low season).

Sale e Pepe $$
This restaurant serves locally caught fish. There is also piranha and dorado sashimi, as well as other Japanese and Chinese dishes. CUISINE Chinese; Japanese; regional. CREDIT CARDS Diners
Rua 29 de Maio, 971, Centro
TEL (67) 3255-1822. Tue – Sun, 6pm – 11pm.

SERVICES

Diving operator – Bonito Scuba
Rua Filinto Muller, 656, Centro
TEL (67) 3255-3879. Daily, 7am – 9pm.

Ecological and regular tour guides – Agência Ar
Rua Coronel Pilad Rebuá, 1,184, Centro
TEL (67) 3255-1008. Daily, 24 hours.
www.agenciaar.com.br

Trips and tour guides – Ygarape Tour
Rua Coronel Pilad Rebuá, 1,956, Centro
TEL (67) 3255-1733. Daily, 7am – 10pm.
www.ygarape.com.br

Brasília – Distrito Federal

AREA CODE 61 POPULATION 2,405,903 DISTANCE Goiânia 209 kilometers (130 miles) ACCESS Highway BR-060 from Goiânia www.brasilia.df.gov.br

WHERE TO STAY

Blue Tree Park Brasilia $$$
Designed by Ruy Ohtake, this hotel is inside the Blue

| PRICES | HOTELS (couple) | $ up to R$ 150 | $$ from R$ 151 up to R$ 300 | $$$ from R$ 301 up to R$500 | $$$$ above R$ 500 |

474   BRAZIL GUIDE

Tree Alvorada complex, next to Alvorada Palace and facing Paranoá Lake. It has one of the largest convention centers in town, as well as an excellent leisure area. **ACCOMMODATIONS** 395; air-conditioning; Internet access; minibar; pay TV; private safe; telephone. **FACILITIES AND SERVICES** bars; beauty parlor; business center; conference room; convenience store; gym; Internet access; jogging track; laundry; motorboat; parking; pier; pool; recreational staff for adults and children (on weekends); restaurant; sailboat; sauna; spa; stores; tennis court; transport to airport and attractions; travel agency; valet service; 24-hour kitchen. **CREDIT CARDS** AmEx; Diners; MasterCard; Visa
Setor Hoteleiro Turístico Norte, Trecho 1, Conjunto 1B, Bloco C
TEL (61) 3424-7000 **FAX** (61) 3424-7001
RESERVATIONS 0800-150500 www.bluetree.com.br

Meliá Brasilia $$
This hotel offers good business and leisure facilities, but is mostly frequented by executives. **ACCOMMODATIONS** 334; air-conditioning; Internet access; jacuzzi (only in the presidential suites); minibar; pay TV; private safe; telephone. **FACILITIES AND SERVICES** bar; beauty parlor; business center; conference room; convenience store; gym; Internet access; parking; pool; restaurant; sauna; travel agency; valet service; wine cellar; 24-hour kitchen.
Setor Hoteleiro Sul, Quadra 6, Conjunto A, Bloco D, Asa Sul
TEL (61) 3218-4700 **FAX** (61) 3218-4705, 3218-4703
www.solmelia.com

Naoum Plaza Hotel $$$$
Famed for its friendly, efficient staff, this hotel receives a lot of executives and thus has good business facilities. **ACCOMMODATIONS** 186; air-conditioning; Internet access; minibar; pay TV; private safe; telephone. **FACILITIES AND SERVICES** bar; beauty parlor; business center; conference room; convenience store; gym; Internet access; jogging track; massage room; parking; pool; restaurant; sauna; travel agency; 24-hour kitchen. **CREDIT CARDS** AmEx; Diners; MasterCard; Visa
Setor Hoteleiro Sul, Quadra 5, Bloco H/I
TEL (61) 3322-4545 **FAX** (61) 3322-4949
RESERVATIONS 0800-614844 www.naoumplaza.com.br

WHERE TO EAT

Alice $$
This small restaurant has a homely, cozy ambience and few tables. Try the chicken dish galinha-d'angola aos cinco perfumes – seasoned with cinnamon, cloves, nutmeg, cardamom, and allspice. Reservations required. **CUISINE** French. **CREDIT CARDS** AmEx; Diners; MasterCard; Visa
QI 17, Comércio Local, Lago Sul, Edifício Fashion Park
TEL (61) 3248-7743. Tue – Sat, noon – 3pm and 8pm – midnight; Sun, noon – 4pm

Dudu Camargo $$$
Frequented by politicians and business executives, this is one of the most sophisticated restaurants in town. Try the robalo grelhado com crosta de baru (grilled snook with a tonka bean crust) or the risoto de pato (duck risotto). **CUISINE** Contemporary. **CREDIT CARDS** AmEx; Diners; MasterCard; Visa
Setor Comércio Local Sul, Quadra 303, Bloco A, Store #3
TEL (61) 3323-8082. Mon – Sat, noon – 3pm and 7pm – 1am; Sun, noon – 5pm

Lagash $
This Arabic restaurant serves family recipes. Try the apricot salad, a mixture of salad greens, honey, curd cheese and apricot, and the Moroccan lamb, which melts in the mouth. **CUISINE** Arabic. **CREDIT CARDS** AmEx; Diners; MasterCard; Visa
Setor Comércio Local Norte, 308, Bloco B, Store #11/17
TEL (61) 3273-0098. Mon – Sat, noon – 4pm and 7pm – midnight; Sun, noon – 4pm

Patu Anú $
The atmosphere is cozy, with a view over Paranoá Lake. The menu specializes in game and fish dishes, such as linguado yapuana – flounder with honey, orange and Brazilian peppers. Reservations required. **CUISINE** Contemporary. **CREDIT CARDS** AmEx; Diners; MasterCard; Visa
Setor de Mansões do Lago, Trecho 12, Conjunto 1, Casa 7
TEL (61) 3369-2788. Tue – Sat, 8:30pm – 1am; Sun, 1:30pm – 6pm

Universal Diner $$
In a relaxed atmosphere, chef Mara Alcamim serves contemporary dishes, such as tenderloin au poivre in green chili and rosemary sauce. **CUISINE** Contemporary. **CREDIT CARDS** AmEx; Diners; MasterCard; Visa
210 Sul, Bloco B, Store #30
TEL (61) 3443-2089. Mon, 7pm – midnight; Tue – Thu, noon – 3pm and 7pm – midnight; Fri and Sat, noon – 3pm and 7pm – 1:30am; Sun, noon – 3pm

SERVICES

Brasilia International Airport
Área especial do lago Sul, Aeroporto Internacional de Brasilia
TEL (61) 3364-9000

Department of Tourism – Secretaria de Turismo
Centro de Convenções Ulisses Guimarães, Ala Norte, 1st Floor
TEL (61) 3325-5215. Mon – Fri, 9am – 6pm.

Brotas – São Paulo

AREA CODE 14 **POPULATION** 20,996 **DISTANCE** São Paulo 245 kilometers (152 miles) **ACCESS** Highway SP-348 (Rodovia dos Bandeirantes) or SP-330 (Anhangüera) up to SP-310 (Rodovia Washington Luís). Then Highway SP-225 (Rodovia Engenheiro Paulo Nilo Romano)
www.brotas.tur.br

WHERE TO STAY

Pousada Sítio Recanto Alvorada $$
This farm-hotel, 12 kilometers (7 miles) from the center of town, is ideal for families with children – there are lots of activities and staff. Some rooms have a fireplace, while others overlook the lake. **ACCOMMODATIONS** 32; air-conditioning; ceiling fan; fireplace; phone; TV. **FACILITIES AND SERVICES** bar; boat; function room; games room; gym; horses; natural pool; playground; pool; recreational team for adults and children; restaurant; sauna; six-a-side court; soccer field; tennis court. **CREDIT CARDS** Not accepted
Rodovia SP-197 (Brotas–Torrinha), Km 12.5
TEL (14) 3656-6332 **FAX** (14) 3656-5082
www.recantoalvorada.com.br

Quinta da Cachoeira $

The rooms at this European-style inn are named after different European countries and decorated accordingly. **ACCOMMODATIONS** 16; air-conditioning; Internet access; jacuzzi (in 2 suites); minibar; phone; TV. **FACILITIES AND SERVICES** games room; pool. **CREDIT CARDS** Not accepted
Rua João Rebecca, 225, Parque dos Saltos, Centro
TEL (14) 3653-1854 **FAX** (14) 3653-4493
www.estalagembrotas.com.br

WHERE TO EAT

Malagueta $

This dimly lit restaurant serves grilled dishes and homemade pastas, such as the pasta bela, ravioli filled with buffalo cheese, tomato, and basil. **CUISINE** Various. **CREDIT CARDS** Diners; MasterCard
Avenida Mário Pinotti, 243, Centro
TEL (14) 3653-5491. Thu, 7pm – midnight; Fri, Sat and Sun, noon – midnight

SERVICES

Ecological tourism and Adventure sports – Alaya
Avenida Mário Pinotti, 230, Centro
TEL (14) 3653-5656. Daily, 8am – 6:30pm

Ecological tourism and Adventure sports – Brotas Aventura
Avenida Mário Pinotti, 113, Centro
TEL (14) 3653-4463. Mon, Wed and Fri, 8am – 6pm; Tue, Thu, Sat and Sun, 8am – 6:30pm

Ecological tourism and Adventure sports – EcoAção
Avenida Mário Pinotti, 205, Centro
TEL (14) 3653-8040. Mon – Fri, 8am – 7pm; Sat, 8am – 8pm

Tourist information – Diretoria de Turismo e Cultura
Rua Lourival Jaubert da Silva Braga, 101
TEL (14) 3653-5282, 3653-2288. Mon – Fri, 7:30am – 11:30am and 1pm – 5pm

Búzios (Armação dos Búzios) – Rio de Janeiro

AREA CODE 22 **POPULATION** 24,560 **DISTANCE** Rio de Janeiro 165 kilometers (102 miles) **ACCESS** Highway BR-101 from Rio de Janeiro to Rio Bonito, followed by RJ-124 (Via Lagos), RJ-106, and RJ-102

WHERE TO STAY

Colonna Park Hotel $$$

This hotel's design exploits its view of João Fernandes and João Fernandinho beaches. Ask for a room with a veranda facing the sea. **ACCOMMODATIONS** 63; air-conditioning; jacuzzi (in the suites); minibar; pay TV; phone; private safe. **FACILITIES AND SERVICES** bar; beachside service; bicycles; boat; business center; exchange service; fishing equipment; function room; games room; golf course; horses; Internet access; jet-ski; kayaks; massage room; motorboat; nursery; parking; playground; pool; restaurant; sauna; soccer field; transport to airport and attractions; travel agency; video room. **CREDIT CARDS** AmEx; Diners; MasterCard; Visa

Praia de João Fernandes, no #, Quadra J
TEL (22) 2623-2245 **FAX** (22) 2623-7102
www.colonna.com.br

Hotel Galápagos $$$

This inn is a favorite among celebrities, and many of their pictures are displayed on the walls. Almost all windows afford a view of the beautiful João Fernandinho Beach. **ACCOMMODATIONS** 37; air-conditioning; minibar; pay TV; phone; private safe. **FACILITIES AND SERVICES** bar; beachside service; boat; business center; function room; games room; gym; Internet access; jet-ski; kayaks; laundry; parking; playground; pool; restaurant; sauna; sitting room; transport to airport and attractions; valet service; water skiing. **CREDIT CARDS** AmEx; Diners; MasterCard; Visa
Praia de João Fernandinho, Lote 3, Quadra B
TEL and **FAX** (22) 2620-8800 www.galapagos.com.br

Pousada Pedra da Laguna $$

Located on Lagoinha Peninsula, this is one of the most charming guesthouses in town. **ACCOMMODATIONS** 25; air-conditioning; ceiling fan; jacuzzi (in the suite); minibar; pay TV; phone; private safe. **FACILITIES AND SERVICES** bar; beauty parlor; exchange service; function room; games room; gym; Internet access; massage room; parking; pool; restaurant; sauna; spa; stores; tennis court; tour guides; transport to airport and attractions; travel agency; valet service. **CREDIT CARDS** AmEx; Diners; MasterCard; Visa
Rua 6, Lote 6, Quadra F, Praia da Ferradura
TEL and **FAX** (22) 2623-1965
www.pedradalaguna.com.br

WHERE TO EAT

Capricciosa $

This pizza parlor faces the sea. It was the original store and has spawned a pizza chain that has become popular in Rio de Janeiro. **CUISINE** Pizza. **CREDIT CARDS** AmEx; Diners; MasterCard; Visa
Avenida José Bento Ribeiro Dantas, 500, Orla Bardot
TEL (22) 2623-2691. Wed – Mon, 6pm – 1am

Cigalon $$

With a beautiful sea view, this candle-lit bistro offers specialties such at lamb chops in peanut sauce with zucchini gratin. **CUISINE** French. **CREDIT CARDS** AmEx; Diners; MasterCard; Visa
Rua das Pedras, 199, Centro
TEL (22) 2623-0932 **FAX** (22) 2623-1249. Mon – Fri, 6pm – 1am; Sat and Sun, 1pm – 2am

Satyricon $$

This is the original Satyricon, the forerunner of the famous Rio restaurant. It offers top-quality fresh fish and lobsters kept in a special tank. **CUISINE** Pasta; fish and seafood. **CREDIT CARDS** AmEx; Diners; MasterCard; Visa
Avenida José Bento Ribeiro Dantas, 500, Orla Bardot
TEL (22) 2623-2691. Mon – Sat, 5pm – 1am; Sun, 1pm – 1am

Sawasdee $$

Highlights are the stir-fried shrimp in oyster sauce with slivers of mango and cashew nuts, and the grilled maigret of duck, marinated in spicy tamarind sauce and fried seaweed. **CUISINE** Thai. **CREDIT CARDS** AmEx; Diners; MasterCard; Visa

---

PRICES	**HOTELS** (couple)	**$** up to R$ 150	**$$** from R$ 151 up to R$ 300	**$$$** from R$ 301 up to R$500	**$$$$** above R$ 500

Avenida José Bento Ribeiro Dantas, 422,
Orla Bardot
TEL and **FAX** (22) 2623-4644. Daily, 6pm – 2am (closed on Wednesdays during the low season)

SERVICES

Boat hire and tours – Escuna Queen Lovy
Rua João Fernandes, 89, Ossos
TEL (22) 2623-1179, 2623-2286. Daily, 8am – 6pm

**Buggy hire and tours –
Oficina de Turismo**
Travessa de Santana, 58, Armação
TEL (22) 2623-8045. Daily, 9am – 8pm

**Tourist information –
Secretaria de Turismo**
Pórtico de Entrada (town gateway), no #
TEL (22) 2633-6200, 2633-3966. Mon – Fri, 8am – midnight

Cabo Frio – Rio de Janeiro

AREA CODE 22 **POPULATION** 162,229 **DISTANCE** Rio de Janeiro 148 kilometers (92 miles) **ACCESS** Highway BR-101, RJ-124, and RJ-140 from Rio de Janeiro
www.cabofrioturismo.rj.gov.br

WHERE TO STAY

La Plage Hotel $$
This well-located hotel faces the sands of Peró Beach, which lies north of Cabo Frio, on the way to Búzios. **ACCOMMODATIONS** 56; air-conditioning; ceiling fan; minibar; phone; private safe (in the luxury suites); TV. **FACILITIES AND SERVICES** bar; beachside service; function room; games room; gym; jacuzzi; Internet access; parking; playground; pool; restaurant; sauna; transport to airport and attractions; valet service; waterfall. **CREDIT CARDS** Not accepted
Rua dos Badejos, 40, Praia do Peró
TEL and **FAX** (22) 2647-1746 www.laplage.com.br

Pousada do Leandro $$$
Located on the busy Forte Beach, this rustic guesthouse is one of the most charming in Cabo Frio. **ACCOMMODATIONS** 17; air-conditioning; Internet access (in some suites); minibar; pay TV; phone; private safe. **FACILITIES AND SERVICES** bar; beachside service; games room; parking; pool with bar; reading room; restaurant; sauna; sitting room; stores; transport to airport and attractions; valet service; video room. **CREDIT CARDS** AmEx; Diners; MasterCard; Visa
Avenida Nilo Peçanha, 333, Centro
TEL (22) 2645-4658 **FAX** (22) 2647-5839
www.pousadaleandro.com.br

WHERE TO EAT

Hippocampus $
The menu changes frequently, but it always features fish and seafood dishes, such as the cherne grelhado (grilled grouper) served with rice and broccoli. **CUISINE** Fish and seafood. **CREDIT CARDS** AmEx; Diners; MasterCard; Visa
Rua Marechal Floriano, 285, São Bento
TEL (22) 2645-5757, 2645-6369. Daily, 11am – midnight

Zeppelin $
The menu's good options include the camarão gratinado (shrimp gratin) in catupiry cheese sauce. **CUISINE** Various **CREDIT CARDS** MasterCard, Visa
Rua Major Billgard, 525, Centro
TEL (22) 2645-6164. Daily, noon – midnight

SERVICES

Buggy hire – Casa do Buggy
Avenida Vereador Antônio Ferreira dos Santos, 836, Braga
TEL (22) 2645-3939, 8811-2131. Daily, 9am – 6pm

**Tourits information – Secretaria de
Turismo**
Praça Américo Vespúcio, no #, Algodoal
TEL (22) 2647-1689. Mon – Fri, 8:30am – 7pm; Sat and Sun, 9:30am – 7pm

Cáceres – Mato Grosso

AREA CODE 65 **POPULATION** 84,175 **DISTANCES** Cuiabá 215 kilometers (134 miles) **ACCESS** Highway BR-070 from Cuiabá. The highway's asphalt is in poor condition in the Serra das Araras range www.caceres.mt.gov.br

WHERE TO STAY

Barco-Hotel Babilônia $$$
This hotel-boat has a 15-horsepower engine and a river pilot on board. It can accommodate groups of up to 22 people and offers package deals for rooms that sleep up to four. From November to February, it is hired out for ecological tourism, so fishing isn't permitted then. **ACCOMMODATIONS** 6 cabins (4 of which sleep up to four people); air-conditioning; background music; bathroom. **FACILITIES AND SERVICES** cool room for fish; sport fishing (March to October); transport to airport; TV with DVD; 24-hour kitchen. **CREDIT CARDS** AmEx; Diners; MasterCard; Visa. **ACCESS** 200 kilometers (124 miles) from Cuiabá on Highway BR-174 heading toward Porto Velho. It berths on the left bank of the Paraguay River, before Ponte Marechal Rondon bridge.
Travessa dos Inervinos, 18, Jardim Ipanema
TEL (65) 9989-1896 **FAX** and **RESERVATIONS** (65) 3222-3489
www.barcobabilonia.com.br

Hotel Baiazinha $$$
This cozy hotel offers friendly service and sits on a small farm that breeds cattle, swine, and chickens. **ACCOMMODATIONS** 15; air-conditioning; minibar; mosquito-screens on windows; TV. **FACILITIES AND SERVICES** bar; bilingual staff; bird and animal watching; first-aid; games room; playground; pool; restaurant; river; soccer field; transport to airport, attractions and nearby towns; 24-hour kitchen. **EXCURSIONS** boat trips; hiking; horseback riding; motorboat; sport fishing. **CREDIT CARDS** MasterCard; Visa. **ACCESS** By boat along the river from Cáceres (2 hours by motorboat) or by air taxi (landing strip ID: SWWF). Driving here is not recommended, as the road is in poor repair.
Estrada do Barranco Vermelho, Km 60
TEL and **FAX** (65) 3291-1036
www.hotelbaiazinha.com.br

Hotel Porto Bello $
This is one of the most comfortable, best-kept hotels in Cáceres. **ACCOMMODATIONS** 40; air-conditioning; minibar; telephone; TV. **FACILITIES AND SERVICES** parking. **CREDIT CARDS** Diners; MasterCard; Visa. **ACCESS** by car or bus, on Highway BR-364, exit at Km 7

Avenida São Luís, 1,888, Jardim Cidade Nova
TEL, FAX and RESERVATIONS (65) 3224-1437

Pantanal 3 Rios Hotel $$$

Very popular among fishing enthusiasts, this hotel has good leisure facilities, including four pools, and is full fishing facilities. Rooms can also be hired for day-use only. ACCOMMODATIONS 64; air-conditioning; minibar; mosquito-screens on windows; telephone; TV. FACILITIES AND SERVICES bar; barbecue facilities; bilingual staff; bowls; conference room; convenience store; games room; gym; karaoke; playground; pools; restaurant; river; six-a-side soccer court; tennis court; transport to attractions and nearby towns. EXCURSIONS boat trips; ecological tours of the Paraguay River; horseriding; river tour. FISHING equipment; fish-and-release; motorboat; river pilot; sport fishing. CREDIT CARDS Not accepted. ACCESS By motorboat from Cáceres on the Paraguay River (50 min); by car for 60 kilometers (37 miles), 30 of which are paved and 30 on dirt road; or by air taxi
Fazenda Lucaisa, no #, Rio Paraguai, Zona Rural
TEL (65) 3223-9500 www.pantanal3rios.com.br

WHERE TO EAT

Kaskata Restaurante Flutuante $$

This traditional local restaurant is on a floating platform on the Paraguay River. The pintado fish is available in a range of recipes; the most popular is on a skewer. If you dine here at night, be sure to bring insect repellent. CUISINE Meat; fish. CREDIT CARDS AmEx; Diners; MasterCard; Visa
Rua Coronel José Dulce, no #, Beira Rio
TEL (65) 3223-2916, 3223-1107. Daily, 11am – 11pm

SERVICES

Travel Agency – Leão Tour

Rua Coronel José Dulce, 304, Centro
TEL (65) 3223-7357. Mon – Fri, 8am – 6pm; Sat, 8am – noon www.visitecaceres.com.br

Caldas Novas – Goiás
see Rio Quente – Goiás

Cabo de Santo Agostinho – Pernambuco

AREA CODE 81 POPULATION 169,229 DISTANCE Recife 37 kilometers (23 miles) ACCESS on highways BR-101 and PE-60 www.cabo.pe.gov.br

WHERE TO EAT

Bar do Artur $$

Located on Calhetas Beach and almost always full, this restaurant specializes in seafood. The peixada (fish stew) and the filé de lagosta (lobster steak) are the house suggestions. CUISINE Meats; fish and seafood. CREDIT CARDS AmEx; Diners; MasterCard; Visa
Rua dos Carneiros, 17, Praia de Calhetas
TEL (81) 3522-6382, 3512-0940 OPEN Daily, 8am – 6pm

SERVICES

Tourist Information – Secretaria de Turismo

Rua Júlio Alves de Souza, no #, Centro
TEL (81) 3522-2726 OPEN Mon – Fri, 8am – 5pm

Cachoeira – Bahia

AREA CODE 75 POPULATION 31,748 DISTANCES Salvador 116 kilometers (72 miles), São Félix 400 m (248 miles) ACCESS From Salvador, take the BR-234 to the Km 52 exit, where a viaduct provides access to Highway BA-420 (stay alert because the signs are often covered in vegetation). On Highway BR-101 there are two access points: at the junction to the town of Conceição de Feira (12 kilometers, 7 miles, of asphalted road) on the north–south stretch, or at the Muritiba junction.

WHERE TO STAY

Hotel Fazenda Villa Rial $$

This all-inclusive rural hotel offers participatory activities such as dairy farming and production. The rooms are smallish and stuffy. The special suites are better, and have air-conditioning and TV. ACCOMMODATIONS 41; air-conditioning and TV in the special suites; minibar; telephone; veranda; ceiling fan. FACILITIES AND SERVICES bar; waterfall; soccer field; horses; carriage; parking; lake and fishing equipment; snack bar; store; pool; playground; orchard; tennis court; volleyball court; restaurant; river; games room; massage room; video room; walking trails; recreational team for children (on request or for large groups); guided walking tours. CREDIT CARDS AmEx; Diners; MasterCard; Visa
Ladeira do Padre Inácio, no #, Murutuba
TEL and FAX (75) 3602-4600 www.villarial.com.br

WHERE TO EAT

A Confraria $

Inside Pousada do Convento, this restaurant has a small dining area and tables around the swimming pool. The kitchen turns out local fare such as the indigenous dish maniçoba (cooked manioc leaves with meat and seasonings) and the Afro-Brazilian xinxim de galinha (chicken cooked with palm oil, seasonings, dried shrimp, and nuts). CUISINE Regional; diverse. CREDIT CARDS Diners; MasterCard; Visa
Praça da Aclamação, no #, Centro
TEL (75) 3425-1716 OPEN Daily, 11am – 10pm

SERVICES

Tourist Information – Centro de Informações Turísticas

Rua Ana Nery, 7, Centro
TEL (75) 3425-1390, 3425-5225 (town hall) OPEN Mon – Sat, 9am – noon and 2pm – 5pm; Sun, 9am – noon

Camamu – Bahia
(see Barra Grande)

Cambará do Sul – Rio Grande do Sul

AREA CODE 54 POPULATION 6,959 DISTANCE Porto Alegre 180 kilometers (112 miles) ACCESS Highway BR-116 from Porto Alegre to the RS-239 exit, heading toward Taquara. From Taquara, take the RS-020, passing through São Francisco de Paula; the last few kilometers are unpaved

WHERE TO STAY

Parador Casa da Montanha $$$

This hotel looks like a luxury camping ground. Instead

PRICES	HOTELS (couple)	$ up to R$ 150	$$ from R$ 151 up to R$ 300	$$$ from R$ 301 up to R$500	$$$$ above R$ 500

478   BRAZIL GUIDE

of rooms or chalets, there are electrically heated tents with double beds, sinks, and toilets. **ACCOMMODATIONS** 12; ceiling fan; electric sheets; hammocks; heating; jacuzzi (in the 3 suites). **FACILITIES AND SERVICES** bicycles; fishing equipment and lake; horses; restaurant; river; trails; trips; walking tours. **CREDIT CARDS** AmEx; MasterCard; Visa
Estrada do Faxinal, no #, between Cambará do Sul and Itaimbezinho Canyon
TEL (54) 3504-5302, 9105-4624
FAX e **RESERVATIONS** (54) 3295-7575
www.paradorcasadamontanha.com.br

Refúgio Ecológico Pedra Afiada $$

This cozy hotel has a lovely view of Malacara Canyon, which it stands at the foot of. Set amid a 28-hectare (69-acre) area, just 20 kilometers (12 miles) from Aparados da Serra National Park, the hotel's leisure facilities are especially pleasing to adventure sports enthusiasts. **ACCOMMODATIONS** 11; balcony; ceiling fan; heating. **FACILITIES AND SERVICES** bar; children's canopy-climbing circuit; climbing wall; ecological tourism operator (floating downriver in tire tubes and rappel); fireplace; fruit and vegetable garden; games room; Internet access; pool; restaurant; river; sauna; waterfall. **CREDIT CARDS** MasterCard
Estrada da Vila Rosa, no #, Vila Rosa, Praia Grande (Santa Catarina)
TEL and **FAX** (48) 3532-1059 www.pedraafiada.com.br

SERVICES

Adventure Sports Operator – Atitude Ecologia e Turismo
Avenida Osvaldo Aranha, 391, mezzanine-level store # 16, Centro
TEL (54) 3282-6305. Daily, 8:30am – noon and 1:30pm – 6pm

Hiking and Walks – Canyon Turismo
Avenida Getúlio Vargas, 1,098, Centro
TEL (54) 3251-1027. Tue – Sat, 8am – noon and 1:30pm – 6pm

Tourist Information – Posto de Informações Turísticas
Rua Adail Valim, 39, Praça São José, Centro
TEL (54) 3251-1320. Daily, 8am – 6pm

Camocim – Ceará

AREA CODE 88 **POPULATION** 58,213 **DISTANCES** Fortaleza 370 kilometers (230 miles), Jericoacoara 87 kilometers (54 miles), Sobral 124 kilometers (77 miles) **ACCESS** From Fortaleza, on Highway BR-222 to Sobral, then take the CE-362 (through Massapê). Another option is Highway CE-085 (Estruturante) to Itapipoca, then BR-402. From Jericoacoara, you can take a dune buggy along the beach at low tide (approximately two hours, including three ferry crossings) www.camocim.ce.gov.br

WHERE TO STAY

Boa Vista Resort $$$

The only resort in Camocim, this hotel has large rooms with regional décor and sisal hammocks on the verandas. It has a large swimming pool in the center of its horseshoe-shaped footprint. **ACCOMMODATIONS** 123; air-conditioning; queen or king size bed; private safe; minibar; telephone; cable TV; veranda. **FACILITIES AND SERVICES** Internet access; bar; bicycles; nightclub; parking; kids' club; pool; playground; restaurant; river; conference room; gym; games room; beauty parlor; sauna; travel agency; recreational team for adults and children; guided walking tours; shuttle to and from Fortaleza. **CREDIT CARDS** AmEx; Diners; MasterCard; Visa
Avenida Beira-mar, no #, Praia das Barreiras, 2 kilometers (1mi) from the center of town
TEL (88) 3621-9888 **FAX** (88) 3621-9889
www.boavistaresort.com.br

WHERE TO EAT

Kiosks at Lagoa da Torta $$
The dishes, such as the robalo grelhado da Tatajuba (grilled snook), are simple and delicious. **CUISINE** Fish and seafood **CREDIT CARDS** Not accepted
Lagoa da Torta, Praia de Tatajuba
TEL None **OPEN** Irregular hours; some kiosk owners live on site

Leste Mar $
We suggest the cavala frita (fried mackerel), served with rice, beans, pasta, farofa (manioc flour) and salad. All very simple and tasty. **CUISINE** Home-style; fish and seafood. **CREDIT CARDS** Not accepted
Praia de Bitupitá, no #
TEL (88) 3623-3126 **OPEN** Daily, 10am – 8pm

SERVICES

Bus Station – Rodoviária
Praça Sinhá Trévia, no #, Centro
TEL (88) 3621-0028, 3621-0407 **OPEN** Daily, 6am – 10pm

Travel Agency – Jegue Tur
Rua Engenheiro Privat, 1927, Centro
TEL (88) 3621-7023 **OPEN** High season: Mon – Sat, 8am – 10pm; Sun, 8am – noon; low season: Mon – Sat, 8am – 6pm

Campina Grande – Paraíba

AREA CODE 83 **POPULATION** 376,132 **DISTANCE** João Pessoa 125 kilometers (78 miles) **ACCESS** From João Pessoa, Highway BR-232 (after Sapé the road is bad, with potholes and no signposting until Ingá)

WHERE TO STAY

Garden Hotel Campina Grande $
This is the best-equipped hotel in town, with a water park, sports facilities, recreation for kids, a convention center, and a business center. The rooms are comfortable and well equipped. **ACCOMMODATIONS** 192; Internet access; air-conditioning; private safe; minibar; telephone; cable TV. **FACILITIES AND SERVICES** Internet access; bar; soccer field; parking; stores; pool; multi-sports court; squash court; tennis court; restaurant; conference room; gym; games room; massage room; beauty parlor; sauna; business center; 24-hour kitchen; recreational team for adults and children; poolside service. **CREDIT CARDS** AmEx; Diners; MasterCard; Visa
Rua Engenheiro José Bezerra, 400, Mirante
TEL (83) 3310-4000 **FAX** (83) 3310-4001

Hotel Serrano $
The six-story hotel has been well maintained since it opened in 1977. The décor is somewhat bland, but inoffensive, and its downtown location is convenient. **ACCOMMODATIONS** 59; Internet access (in 8 rooms); air-conditioning; private safe; minibar; telephone; cable TV (in

10 rooms). **FACILITIES AND SERVICES** Internet access; bar; parking; pool; restaurant; conference room; games room; 24-hour kitchen; laundry; valet parking. **CREDIT CARDS** AmEx; Diners; MasterCard; Visa

Rua Tavares Cavalcanti, 27, Centro
TEL (83) 3341-3131 fax and **RESERVATIONS** (83) 3321-0635
www.hotelserranopb.com.br

Village $

These wide, well-designed buildings have a welcoming air about them. The décor is sober, with a predominance of brown and details in wood. **ACCOMMODATIONS** 63; Internet access; air-conditioning; private safe; minibar; telephone; cable TV. **FACILITIES AND SERVICES** Internet access; wine cellar; bar; parking; convenience store; pool; restaurant; conference room; gym; games room; business center; airport shuttle. **CREDIT CARDS** AmEx; Diners; MasterCard; Visa

Rua Otacílio Nepomuceno, 1285, Catolé
TEL (83) 3310-8000 **FAX** (83) 3310-8002
RESERVATIONS (83) 3310-8001 www.hoteisvillage.com.br

WHERE TO EAT

Manoel da Carne-de-Sol $

The place is reminiscent of a warehouse, with wooden tables and Formica chairs. The traditional and tasty carne-de-sol (beef jerky) is the highlight of the menu. **CUISINE** Brazilian; meats; regional. **CREDIT CARDS** Diners; MasterCard; Visa

Rua Félix Araújo, 263, Centro
TEL (83) 3221-2877 **OPEN** Daily, 11am – until the last customer leaves

Tábua de Carne $

Barbecued meats are served with boiled manioc, string beans, farofa (manioc flour) and vinaigrette. The portions are hearty – half a plate is enough for two people. **CUISINE** Meats; regional. **CREDIT CARDS** AmEx; Diners; MasterCard; Visa

Avenida Manoel Tavares, 1040, Alto Branco
TEL (83) 3341-1008, 3341-1647 **OPEN** Mon – Sat, 11am – 10pm; Sun, 11am – 4pm

SERVICES

Bus Station – Rodoviária
Rua Eutécia Ribeiro, no #, Catolé
TEL (83) 3337-3001, 3337-3028 **OPEN** Daily, 6am – 10pm

Tourist Information – Secretaria de Turismo
Rua 13 de Maio, 329, Centro
TEL (83) 3310-6100, 3310-6103 **OPEN** Mon – Fri, 8am – noon and 2pm – 6pm www.pmcg.pb.gov.br

Campo Grande – Mato Grosso do Sul

AREA CODE 67 **POPULATION** 724,524 **DISTANCES** Cuiabá 687 kilometers (427 miles), São Paulo 992 kilometers (616 miles), Brasília 1,088 kilometers (676 miles) **ACCESS** Highway BR-163, which connects the city with the South and North of Brazil, or BR-262, which connects it with the Southeast www.campogrande.ms.gov.br

WHERE TO STAY

Jandaia Hotel $$
This busy, luxurious hotel is located in the center of town, near the commercial district. The comfortable

rooms have large beds and spacious bathrooms, although some can be slightly musty. **ACCOMMODATIONS** 140; air-conditioning; Internet access; jacuzzi (in the master suites); minibar; pay TV; telephone. **FACILITIES AND SERVICES** bar; games room; gym; Internet access; parking; pool. **CREDIT CARDS** AmEx; Diners; MasterCard; Visa

Rua Barão do Rio Branco, 1,271, Centro
TEL and **RESERVATIONS** (67) 3316-7700
FAX (67) 3316-7777 www.jandaia.com.br

Novotel $$
Right in front of the Parque das Nações Indígenas, near the convention center and 10 minutes by car from the city center, this hotel has large rooms with subdued décor and a pleasant leisure area that's ideal for children. **ACCOMMODATIONS** 87; air-conditioning; Internet access; minibar; pay TV; private safe; telephone. **FACILITIES AND SERVICES** bar; barbecue facilities; bilingual staff; business center; conference room; convenience store; Internet access; paddle-ball court; parking; pool; restaurant; stores; tennis court; wine cellar; 24-hour kitchen. **CREDIT CARDS** AmEx; Diners; MasterCard; Visa

Avenida Mato Grosso, 5,555, Jardim Copacabana
TEL (67) 3326-1177 **RESERVATIONS** 0800-7037000
www.accorhotels.com.br

WHERE TO EAT

Fogo Caipira $
The moqueca de pintado (pintado fish stew) and the signature dish, pacu assado (baked pacu fish) stuffed with banana flour and pirão (manioc-thickened gravy), are hits in this simple, relaxed eatery. **CUISINE** Brazilian; regional. **CREDIT CARDS** AmEx; Diners; MasterCard; Visa

Rua José Antônio Pereira, 145, Centro
TEL (67) 3324-1641, 3382-0731. Tue – Fri, 11am – 2pm and 7pm – 11pm; Sat, 11am – midnight; Sun, 11am – 4pm

Lingüiça de Maracaju $
The specialty at this well-located restaurant is the homemade barbecued beef sausage. From Thursday to Sunday there are typical dance performances such as guarânia. **CUISINE** Meat; barbecue. **CREDIT CARDS** MasterCard; Visa

Rua Espírito Santo, 1,443 (corner of Rua Eduardo Santos Pereira), Vila Célia
TEL (67) 3029-1443. Wed – Sat, 6pm – midnight; Sun, 11am – 4pm

SERVICES

Department of Tourism – Secretaria de Turismo
Rua Bahia, 470, Jardim dos Estados
TEL (67) 3314 -3580. Daily, 7:30am – 11am and 1pm – 5:30pm

Campos do Jordão – São Paulo

AREA CODE 12 **POPULATION** 44,688 **DISTANCE** São Paulo 167 kilometers (104 miles) **ACCESS** SP-070 (Rodovia Ayrton Senna/Carvalho Pinto) or BR-116 (Rodovia Presidente Dutra) from São Paulo, followed by SP-123 (Rodovia Floriano Pinheiro)

WHERE TO STAY

Grande Hotel Campos do Jordão $$$$
Built in 1944, this hotel became a major hotel school in 1998, after extensive renovation. It is exquisitely deco-

PRICES | **HOTELS** (couple) $ up to R$ 150 $$ from R$ 151 up to R$ 300 $$$ from R$ 301 up to R$500 $$$$ above R$ 500

480   BRAZIL GUIDE

rated, with French clocks, Belgian tapestries, and art nouveau furniture. **ACCOMMODATIONS** 95; Internet access; jacuzzi; minibar; pay TV; phone. **FACILITIES AND SERVICES** bar; function room; games room; gym; heated pool; heliport; Internet access; massage room; playground; recreational team for adults and children; restaurants; sauna; tennis court; video room; 24-hour room service. **CREDIT CARDS** AmEx; Diners; MasterCard; Visa
Avenida Frei Orestes Girardi, 3549, Vila Capivari
TEL (12) 3668-6000 **FAX** (12) 3668-6100
RESERVATIONS 0800-7700790 www.sp.senac.br/hoteis

Park Hotel Toriba $$$$
One of the most traditional hotels in Campos do Jordão. The restaurant serves fondue. Bookings required. **ACCOMMODATIONS** 32; heater; minibar; pay TV; phone; private safe. **FACILITIES AND SERVICES** bar; function room; games room; gym; Internet access; jogging track; mini farm; playground; pool; reading room; recreational team for children (during school and public holidays); restaurant; sauna. **CREDIT CARDS** AmEx; Diners; MasterCard; Visa
Avenida Ernesto Diederichsen, 2,962, Toriba
TEL (12) 3668-5000 **FAX** (12) 3262-4211
RESERVATIONS 0800-178179 www.toriba.com.br

Pousada Villa Capivary $$$
Located in the main district of Campos do Jordão, this comfortable guesthouse has large rooms with balconies. **ACCOMMODATIONS** 15; individual and central heating; Internet access; jacuzzi (in the suites); minibar; pay TV; phone. **FACILITIES AND SERVICES** bar; games room; sitting room with fireplace. **CREDIT CARDS** AmEx; Diners; MasterCard; Visa
Avenida Vítor Godinho, 131, Vila Capivari
TEL (12) 3663-1736 **FAX** (12) 3663-1746
www.capivari.com.br

WHERE TO EAT

Harry Pisek $
Harry Pisek, a Brazilian of Austrian ancestry, has been producing his homemade array of frankfurters since 1997. He makes more than fifteen varieties, including white pepper and herbs, ementhal cheese, and pork or beef. **CUISINE** German. **CREDIT CARDS** Diners; MasterCard; Visa
Avenida Pedro Paulo, 857, on the way to Horto
TEL (12) 3663-4030. Mon – Fri, 10am – 5pm; Sat, 10am – 11pm; Sun, 10am – 6pm

Ludwig Restaurant $$
One of the best restaurants in town, the Ludwig specializes in dishes made with game meats, such as avestruz encabulado: ostrich steak with Parmesan tuiles in Camembert and raspberry sauces. The wine list has 120 labels. **CUISINE** French-Swiss. **CREDIT CARDS** AmEx; Diners; MasterCard; Visa
Rua Aristides de Souza Melo, 50, Vila Capivari
TEL (12) 3663-5111, 9771-5162. Mon – Fri, 6pm – 11pm; Sat and Sun, noon – 11pm

SERVICES

Ecological tourism – Verticália – Aventura no Rancho (canopy climbing)
Avenida Pedro Paulo, 7,997, on the way to Horto (park)
TEL (12) 3663-7400. Tue – Sun, 9am – 5pm

Ecological tourism – Altus Turismo Ecológico (hikes with rappelling)
Avenida Brasil, 108, Store #1, Centro
TEL (12) 3663-4122. Mon – Fri, 9am – 6pm

Tourist information – Portal da Cidade
Rodovia Floriano Rodrigues Pinheiro, Km 46
TEL (12) 3664-3525. Daily, 8am – 6pm

Canavieiras – Bahia

AREA CODE 73 **POPULATION** 36,765 **DISTANCES** Ilhéus 110 kilometers (68 miles), Salvador 560 kilometers (348 miles) access From Ilhéus, on Highway BA-001

WHERE TO STAY

Canes Porto Mar Hotel $$
Facing the kiosks on Costa Beach, this is the best option for those who like to be where it's all happening. The well-kept rooms have new appliances, but the leisure area leaves a little to be desired. **ACCOMMODATIONS** 47; air-conditioning; minibar; telephone; TV. **FACILITIES AND SERVICES** bar; parking; pool; playground. **CREDIT CARDS** Diners; MasterCard; Visa
Avenida Beira-mar, 601 – 631, Praia da Costa, Ilha de Atalaia, 2 kilometers (1 miles) from the center of town
TEL (73) 3284-1072 **FAX** (73) 3284-4994
www.canesportomar.com.br

WHERE TO EAT

Cantinho da Zezé $
Facing the quay, this eatery offers good food at a fair price. The dishes, like the place itself, are simple, but the food is tasty. The house fortes are seafood, such as arroz de polvo (octopus rice). **CUISINE** Regional; fish and seafood. **CREDIT CARDS** Not accepted
Avenida Felinto Melo, 18, Centro
TEL (73) 3284-2885 **OPEN** Daily, 11am – 1am

SERVICES

Boat Rental – Artmarina
Rua Felinto Melo, 70, Centro
TEL (73) 3284-1262 **OPEN** Daily, 8am – 6pm
www.artmarina.com.br

Boat Rental – Marina Canes
Alameda dos Periquitos, 13, Praia da Costa (first entry on the right after Ponte ACM bridge, on Ilha de Atalaia island)
TEL (73) 3284-3735 **OPEN** Daily, 6am – 6pm

Bus Station – Rodoviária
Avenida Professor Assis Gonçalves, no # (at the entrance to the city)
TEL (73) 3284-1399 **OPEN** Daily, 6am – 9pm

Tourist Information – Secretaria de Turismo
Praça da Bandeira, no #, Centro
TEL (73) 3284-1324, 3284-1893 **OPEN** Mon – Fri, 8am – 2pm

Canela – Rio Grande do Sul

AREA CODE 54 **POPULATION** 38,318 **DISTANCE** Porto Alegre 122 kilometers (76 miles) **ACCESS** Highway RS-020 from Porto Alegre www.canela.rs.gov.br

RESTAURANTS	$ up to R$ 50	$$ from R$ 51 up to R$ 100	$$$ from R$ 101 up to R$ 150	$$$$ above R$ 150

WHERE TO STAY

Pousada Cravo & Canela $$
This guesthouse occupies a 1950s Bavarian-style manor. Each room is uniquely decorated, with goose-feather eiderdowns and pillows and Egyptian-cotton towels. **ACCOMMODATIONS** 12; CD player; ceiling fan; DVD player; heating; Internet access; minibar; pay TV; telephone. **FACILITIES AND SERVICES** bar; business center; fireplaces; function room; games room; heated pool with whirlpool tub; Internet access; massage room; sauna; spa; transport to airport and attractions; video room. **CREDIT CARDS** AmEx; Diners; MasterCard; Visa
Rua Tenente Manoel Correia, 144, Centro
TEL and **FAX** (54) 3282-1120
www.pousadacravoecanela.com.br

Pousada Solar Don Ramón $$
Far from the center on the way to Caracol Park, this guesthouse has uniquely decorated rooms as well as 5 suites with fireplaces and DVD players. There are several massage and relaxation options to choose from. **ACCOMMODATIONS** 11; ceiling fan; DVD player (in 5 suites); fireplace (in 5 suites); heating; Internet access; minibar; telephone; TV. **FACILITIES AND SERVICES** bar; games room; Internet access; massage room; ofuro tub; pool; restaurant; TV room; winter garden with fireplace. **CREDIT CARDS** MasterCard
Rua José Pedro Piva, 745, Bosque Sinoserra
TEL (54) 3282-3306, 3282-3812 www.donramon.com.br

Quinta dos Marques $$$
This guesthouse occupies a remodeled 1930 manor far from the town center, set amid woods. The beds boast goose-feather eiderdowns and pillows, Egyptian-cotton sheets, and electrically heated sheets. **ACCOMMODATIONS** 13; DVD player; heating; Internet access; jacuzzi (in 1 suite); minibar; pay TV; telephone. **FACILITIES AND SERVICES** bar; function room; games room; heated pool; Internet access; massage room; ofuro tub; transport to airport and attractions; TV room; woods. **CREDIT CARDS** Dinners; MasterCard; Visa
Rua Gravataí, 200, Santa Teresinha
(Access from Rua Borges de Medeiros)
TEL (54) 3282-9812 www.quintadosmarques.com.br

SERVICES

Tour Operator – Brocker Turismo
Tours to the interior of Gramado and Canela.
Rua Borges de Medeiros, 747, Mezzanine Store #7, Centro
TEL (54) 3282-2668. Mon – Fri, 8:30am – 6:30pm; Sat, 9am – noon

Tourist Information – Central de Informações Turísticas
Largo da Fama, 227, Centro
TEL (54) 3282-2200. Daily, 8am – 7pm

Canoa Quebrada – Ceará

AREA CODE 88 **DISTANCE** Fortaleza 167 kilometers (104 miles) access From Fortaleza, on highways CE-040 and BR-304. After the bridge over the Jaguaribe River, the asphalt is in poor condition. Once you have passed the Posto BR gas station, drive another 2.5 kilometers (1.5 miles) and take the turnoff into Canoa Quebrada, on your left

WHERE TO STAY

Pousada Aruanã $
This rustic guesthouse receives mostly couples and families; children under 18 must be accompanied by adults. It has a large swimming pool with a view of the ocean. **ACCOMMODATIONS** 12; air-conditioning; private safe; minibar; cable TV; veranda with hammock. **FACILITIES AND SERVICES** Internet access; bar; parking; pool. **CREDIT CARDS** MasterCard; Visa
Rua dos Bugueiros, no #, Praia de Canoa Quebrada
TEL (88) 3421-7154 **FAX** (88) 3421-7081

Village Long Beach $$
This comfortable, charming hotel has large, two-story chalets with private terraces and hammocks. All of the rooms have king size beds and quality bed linens. There are English and Italian-speaking staff. **ACCOMMODATIONS** 42; air-conditioning; minibar; telephone; cable TV; ceiling fan. **FACILITIES AND SERVICES** Internet access; bar; parking; pool; restaurant and steakhouse; massage service. **CREDIT CARDS** Diners; MasterCard; Visa
Rua Quatro Ventos, no #
TEL (88) 3421-7404, 3421-7407
www.longbeachvillage.com.br

SERVICES

Bus Station – Rodoviária
Rua Coronel Alexandrino, no #
(at the entrance to the town), Aracati
TEL (88) 3421-6434 (public phone) **OPEN** Daily, 5am – 9pm

Tourist Information – Secretaria de Turismo
Rua Santos Dumont, 352, Centro, Aracati
TEL (88) 3446-2451 **OPEN** Mon – Fri, 8am – 2pm
www.aracati.ce.gov.br

Caraíva – Bahia

AREA CODE 73 **DISTANCES** Salvador 765 kilometers (475 miles), Porto Seguro 65 kilometers (40 miles) access From Trancoso, by motorboat. Or along Highway BR-101, with entry at Monte Pascoal, Km 753, with a 43-kilometer (27-mile) off-road stretch to the canoes that cross the Caraíva River

WHERE TO STAY

Pousada Lagoa $
Set amidst almost two acres of greenery, with trees, inlets, and a river running through it, this rustic, colorful guesthouse allows children and pets. **ACCOMMODATIONS** 7. **FACILITIES AND SERVICES** bar; heliport; inlet; restaurant; river; games room; currency exchange; laundry; boat trips; airport shuttle. **CREDIT CARDS** Not accepted
Beco da Lagoa, no #, Caraíva
TEL (73) 9985-6862 **FAX** and **RESERVATIONS** (31) 3225-5845
www.lagoacaraiva.com.br

Pousada Vila do Mar $$$
This well-equipped guesthouse has its own generator, solar heating, and leisure area. The charming rooms sleep up to three and have mosquito nets. **ACCOMMODATIONS** 7; air-conditioning; minibar; jacuzzi (in 2 rooms); cable TV; veranda (5 rooms); ceiling fan. **FACILITIES AND SERVICES** bar; private safe; motorboat (high season); pool;

PRICES | HOTELS (couple) | $ up to R$ 150 | $$ from R$ 151 up to R$ 300 | $$$ from R$ 301 up to R$500 | $$$$ above R$ 500

482 | BRAZIL GUIDE

restaurant; video room; guide recommendation; beach service (high season). **CREDIT CARDS** Not accepted
Rua da Praia, no #
TEL and **FAX** (73) 3668-5111
www.pousadaviladomar.com.br

WHERE TO EAT

Boteco do Pará $
The owner has his own fishing boat, which means there is always fresh fish. In addition to moquecas (fish stews) without the traditional dendê oil and coriander, they also serve delicious fried pastries. with a variety of fillings. **CUISINE** Regional; seafood; pastries. **CREDIT CARDS** Not accepted
Rua Beira-Rio, Ponto dos Mentirosos
(towards Barra)
TEL (73) 9112-1974 **OPEN** High season: daily, 11am until the last customer leaves; low season: daily, 11am – 8pm

SERVICES

Airport – Aeroporto Internacional Porto Seguro International
Estrada do Aeroporto, no #, Cidade Alta, Porto Seguro
TEL (73) 3288-1880, 3288-1877 **OPEN** Daily, 24 hours

Tourist Information – Centro de Informações Turísticas de Porto Seguro
Praça Manoel Ribeiro Coelho, 10, Centro, Porto Seguro (near the ferry terminal)
TEL (73) 3268-2853 **OPEN** Mon – Sat, 9am – 9pm

Caravelas – Bahia

AREA CODE 73 **POPULATION** 20,872 **DISTANCES** Salvador 886 kilometers (550 miles), Porto Seguro 210 kilometers (130 miles) access From Salvador, on Highway BR-101 and BA-290 to Alcobaça. From there, take BA-001 and BR-418 www.caravelas.ba.gov.br

WHERE TO STAY

Farol Abrolhos Hotel Iate Clube $
This hotel's advantages are its location facing the Caravelas River and the trips it offers to the Abrolhos Islands (with its own pier and boat). The small rooms are set around a garden. **ACCOMMODATIONS** 15; air-conditioning; minibar; TV. **FACILITIES AND SERVICES** bar; boat; bicycles; kayaks; parking; snack bar; stores; pool; volleyball court; restaurant; games room; video room; travel agency; laundry. **CREDIT CARDS** Visa
Estrada Caravelas-Barra, Km 1, Kitongos
TEL (73) 3297-1931, 3297-1173
www.farolabrolhos.com.br

Marina Porto Abrolhos $$
This hotel stands just 20 meters (66 feet) from Grauçá Beach, where the water, albeit a little dark, is clean and good for swimming. **ACCOMMODATIONS** 24; air-conditioning; minibar; cable TV; veranda with hammock in the rooms; ceiling fan. **FACILITIES AND SERVICES** bar; bicycles; golf and mini-golf courses; parking; convenience store; adult and kids' swimming pools; playground; volleyball court; restaurant; river; conference room; gym; games room; massage room; video room; sauna; 24-hour kitchen; beach service. **CREDIT CARDS** AmEx; Diners; MasterCard
Rua da Baleia, 333

TEL (73) 3674-1082, 3674-1059, 3674-1060
www.marinaportoabrolhos.com.br

WHERE TO EAT

Carinagem $
This simple eatery specializes in seafood, although it also serves meats and poultry. The most popular dishes are the moquecas de peixe (fish stews) and the sinfonia de peixe (snook, crab stew, oysters and prawns). **CUISINE** Regional; fish. **CREDIT CARDS** MasterCard; Visa
Avenida das Palmeiras, 210
TEL (73) 3297-1280 **RESERVATIONS** (73) 3297-1610 **OPEN** Daily, 10:30am until the last customer leaves

SERVICES

Boat Tours and Diving – Abrolhos Embarcações
Avenida Ministro Adalício Nogueira, 1294
TEL (73) 3297-1816, 3297-1172 **OPEN** Daily, 6:30am – 6pm
www.abrolhosembarcacoes.com.br

Boat Tours and Diving – Abrolhos Turismo
Praça Dr. Emílio Imbassahy, 8, Centro
TEL (73) 3297-1149, 3297-1332 **FAX** (73) 3297-1109 **OPEN** Mon – Sat, 7am – 7pm; Sun, 7am – 11:30am and 1pm – 7pm www.abrolhosturismo.com.br

Bus Station – Rodoviária
Praça Teófilo Otoni, no #, Centro
TEL (73) 3297-1422 (Viação Brasileira and Águia Branca) **OPEN** Daily, 6am – 10:30pm

Tourist Information – Secretaria de Turismo and Lazer
Praça Santo Antônio, 28, Centro
TEL (73) 3297-1404, 3297-1113 **OPEN** Mon – Fri, 8am – noon and 2pm – 5pm

Caruaru – Pernambuco

AREA CODE 81 **POPULATION** 278,655 **DISTANCES** Recife 134 kilometers (83 miles), Campina Grande 145 kilometers (90 miles) access From Recife, on Highway BR-232. From Campina Grande, take BR-104 www.caruaru.pe.gov.br

WHERE TO STAY

Caruaru Park Hotel $
The Caruaru Park stands on the edge of the highway and has a beautiful view of the hills around Caruaru. The rooms have verandas with hammocks and are located in colorful chalets that are basic but well kept. **ACCOMMODATIONS** 68; Internet access; air-conditioning; private safe; minibar (in all but the standard rooms); telephone; cable TV. **FACILITIES AND SERVICES** auditoriums; bar; parking; snack bar; pool; restaurant; airport shuttle; transport to attractions. **CREDIT CARDS** AmEx; Diners; MasterCard; Visa
Rodovia BR-232, Km 128
TEL and **FAX** (81) 3722-9191
www.caruaruparkhotelonline.com.br

Village $
This hotel is quiet, in spite of its proximity to the highway, and has comfortable rooms, a pleasant swimming pool and a hearty breakfast replete with regional dishes. **ACCOMMODATIONS** 61; Internet access; air-conditioning; private safe; minibar; telephone; cable TV. **FACILITIES AND SERVICES** Internet access; bar; parking; pool; playground;

| **RESTAURANTS** | **$** up to R$ 50 | **$$** from R$ 51 up to R$ 100 | **$$$** from R$ 101 up to R$ 150 | **$$$$** above R$ 150 |

restaurant; convention space, workout room, and games room; video room; sauna; business center; airport shuttle. **CREDIT CARDS** AmEx; Diners; MasterCard; Visa

**Rua Costa Carvalho, no #, Petrópolis
(BR-232, Km 135)**
TEL (81) 3722-5544 **FAX** (81) 3722-7033
www.hoteisvillage.com.br

WHERE TO EAT

Bode Assado do Luciano $

It serves all kinds of meats. Regional specialties include bode assado (roast goat) and carne de sol (beef jerky), always accompanied by cowpeas or broad beans, rice, farofa (manioc flour) and salad. **CUISINE** Regional. **CREDIT CARDS** AmEx; MasterCard; Visa

Rua Mestre Vitalino, 511, Alto do Moura
TEL (81) 3722-0413 **OPEN** Tue – Fri, 10am – 4pm; Sat and Sun, 10am – 6pm

SERVICES

Bus Station – Rodoviária

Rua do Terminal Rodoviário, 12, Pinheirópolis
TEL (81) 3721-3869 **OPEN** Daily, 6am – 7pm

Tourist Information – Secretaria de Turismo

Praça Coronel José de Vasconcelos, 100, Centro
TEL (81) 3722-2021, 3701-1533 **OPEN** Mon – Fri, 7:30am – 1pm www.caruaru.pe.gov.br/pontosturisticos.asp

Chapada Diamantina – Bahia
(see Andaraí, Lençóis, Mucugê,
and Vale do Capão [Caeté-Açu])

Chapada dos Guimarães – Mato Grosso

AREA CODE 65 **POPULATION** 17,377 **DISTANCE** Cuiabá 62 kilometers (39 miles) **ACCESS** Highway MT-251 from Cuiabá www.chapadadosguimaraes.mt.gov.br

WHERE TO STAY

Pousada Penhasco $$

This guesthouse is well located in verdant surroundings next to the chapada (plateau). Events are frequently held here, and rooms can be rented for day-use only. **ACCOMMODATIONS** 4; air-conditioning; ceiling fan; minibar; pay TV; private safe; telephone. **FACILITIES AND SERVICES** bar; conference room; games room; heated pool; karaoke; parking; playground; pool; restaurant; sauna; snack bar; soccer field; trail with lookout. **CREDIT CARDS** Diners; MasterCard; Visa. **ACCESS** On Highway Emanuel Pinheiro, exit at Km 65

Avenida Penhasco, no #, Bom Clima
TEL and **FAX** (65) 3301-1555 **RESERVATIONS** (65) 3624-1000 www.penhasco.com.br

Pousada Solar do Inglês $$

Perhaps the most pleasant accommodation option in the Chapada region, this small, charming guesthouse offers tastefully decorated rooms with verandas. **ACCOMMODATIONS** 8; air-conditioning; ceiling fan; minibar; mosquito-screens on windows; pay TV (in some rooms); private safe; telephone. **FACILITIES AND SERVICES** bar; gazebo with hammocks; lounge room with fireplace; parking;

pool; sauna. **CREDIT CARDS** Not accepted. **ACCESS** On Highway Emanuel Pinheiro exit at Km 65

Rua Cipriano Curvo, 142, Centro
TEL and **FAX** (65) 3301-1389 www.solardoingles.com.br

WHERE TO EAT

Estilo $$$

The menu offers many cod dishes, such as bacalhau à moda da casa (cod fillets with onion, potato, broccoli and rice). The wine list is also reasonable. **CUISINE** Portuguese. **CREDIT CARDS** Not accepted

Avenida do Penhasco, Lote 1, Quadra 42, Bom Clima
TEL (65) 3301-3430. Fri, 7pm – midnight; Sat, noon – 3pm and 7pm – midnight; Sun, noon – 3pm

Morro dos Ventos $$

Built in the shape of an Indian oca (hut) and thatched with babaçu palm, this eatery is located inside a private condominium. The menu offers good regional dishes, such as the galinhada (stewed chicken) prepared in an iron pot. **CUISINE** Fish; regional. **CREDIT CARDS** Not accepted

Estrada do Mirante, Km 1, Morro dos Ventos
TEL (65) 3301-1030, 9971-6464. Mon – Fri, 8am – 4pm; Sat and Sun, 8am – 6pm

SERVICES

Excursions – Ecoturismo Cultural

Praça Dom Wunibaldo, 464, Centro
TEL (65) 9952-1989. Daily, 8am – noon and 1pm – 5pm. www.chapadadosguimaraes.com.br

Excursions, horseriding, and adventure sports – Atmã Turismo Ecológico e Aventuras

Rua Cipriano Curvo, 655, Centro
TEL (65) 3301-3391. Mon – Sat, 8am – 11:30am and 2pm – 6pm; Sun, 8am – 11am. www.chapadaatma.com.br

Tourst Information – Centro de Atendimento ao Turista

Avenida Perimetral, no #, Bom Clima
TEL (65) 3301-3214. Daily, 8am – 6pm

Corumbá – Mato Grosso do Sul

AREA CODE 67 **POPULATION** 96,373 **DISTANCES** Campo Grande 403 kilometers (250 miles) **ACCESS** Highway BR-262 from Campo Grande www.corumba.ms.gov.br

WHERE TO STAY

Passo do Lontra Parque Hotel $$

Near the Estrada Parque highway, on the banks of the Miranda River, this hotel caters to fishing enthusiasts. Its wooden chalets stand on stilts, and its rooms have kitchens. **ACCOMMODATIONS** 28; air-conditioning; minibar; mosquito-screens on windows; telephone; TV; veranda with hammock. **FACILITIES AND SERVICES** bar; bilingual staff; camping ground; convenience store; environmental inspector; first-aid; lifeguard; parking; restaurant; river; snack bar; soccer field; transport to attractions and nearby towns; video room. **EXCURSIONS** animal watching; boat trips; canoeing; day and night river tours; horseback riding. **FISHING** equipment; fish-and-release; line fishing; sport fishing; troll fishing. **CREDIT CARDS** Visa. **ACCESS** On Highway BR-262 and MS-184 (Estrada Parque). You can also get there by plane

PRICES	HOTELS (couple)	$ up to R$ 150	$$ from R$ 151 up to R$ 300	$$$ from R$ 301 up to R$500	$$$$ above R$ 500

Estrada Parque, Km 7, Passo do Lontra
TEL and RESERVATIONS (67) 3231-6569, 9987-2523
FAX (67) 3231-6569 www.passodolontra.com.br

Pousada Xaraés $$$$

One of the most charming guesthouses in the Pantanal, the Xaraés draws mostly foreigners. It offers excellent trips around the Abobral River region. ACCOMMODATIONS 17; air-conditioning; ceiling fan; minibar; mosquito net; mosquito-screens on windows; telephone. FACILITIES AND SERVICES bar; bilingual staff; conference room; environmental inspector; first-aid; fish-and-release; games room; gym; hammocks; Internet access; jacuzzi; orchard; parking; pool; restaurant; river; soccer field; stores; tennis court; transport to attractions; video room; walking tours. EXCURSIONS bird and animal watching; boat trips; canoeing; hiking; horseback riding; nocturnal wildlife spotting; safari; scientific tours; ultra-light tours. CREDIT CARDS Visa. ACCESS On Highway BR-262 to Estrada Parque, exit near the Km 300 marker (Buraco das Piranhas); then drive another 17 kilometers (11 miles) to the entrance, and another 12 kilometers (7.5 miles) on the actual guesthouse property. During the rainy season, a boat can be arranged to pick up guests at the entrance (Ponte do Rio Abobral bridge). You can also get there by plane
Estrada Parque, Km 17
TEL and RESERVATIONS (67) 9906-9272
www.xaraes.com.br

WHERE TO EAT

Restaurante e Peixaria Ceará $

The highlights here are the pintado fish recipes, which comes either grilled or breaded, and is accompanied by rice, vegetables and pirão (manioc-thickened gravy). CUISINE Regional; fish. CREDIT CARDS MasterCard; Visa
Rua Albuquerque, 516, Bairro Universitário
TEL (67) 3231-1930. Tue – Sun, 11am – 2:30pm and 7pm – 11pm

SERVICES

Travel Agency – Joice Pesca e Tur
Ecological tourism and sport fishing.
Rua Manuel Cavassa, 1, Porto Geral
TEL (67) 3232-4048, 9912-0265. Mon – Sat, 7:30am – 7pm. www.joicetur.com.br

Travel Agency – Mutum Turismo
Boat tours and tours along the Estrada Parque highway.
Rua Frei Mariano, 17, Centro
TEL (67) 3231-1818 FAX (67) 3231-3027. Mon – Fri, 7am – 6:30pm; Sat, 7am – 1pm.
www.mutumturismo.com.br

Costa do Sauípe – Bahia

AREA CODE 71 DISTANCES Salvador 105 kilometers (65 miles), Praia do Forte 20 kilometers (12 miles) ACCESS From Salvador, take Highway BA-099 (Linha Verde)

WHERE TO STAY

Guests at all of the hotels and guesthouses in Costa do Sauípe have permission to use the local golf, sailing, horse riding, sports, and tennis centers, and the Marriot Renaissance Spa.

Costa do Sauípe Suítes $$$$

This is the smallest hotel in Costa do Sauípe, but also the coziest. The décor explores cacao as a theme and the reception area takes its inspiration from a manor house in the heyday of cacao production. ACCOMMODATIONS 198; Internet access; air-conditioning; private safe; minibar; jacuzzi in the master suites; telephone; cable TV. FACILITIES AND SERVICES Internet access; bar; parking; snack bar; pool; playground; restaurant; conference room; gym; games room; massage room; video room; beauty parlor; sauna; business center; 24-hour kitchen; recreational team for adults and children; valet parking. CREDIT CARDS AmEx; Diners; MasterCard; Visa
Rodovia BA-099, Km 76, Linha Verde
TEL (71) 2104-8000 RESERVATIONS (71) 2104-8080
www.costadosauipe.com.br

Marriott Resort & Spa $$$$

On the edge of the sea, this is the most formal of the hotels in the complex. The rooms are comfortable, spacious, and well equipped. Children under the age of 18 must be accompanied by their parents or have parental authorization. ACCOMMODATIONS 273; Internet access; air-conditioning; private safe; minibar; telephone; cable TV. FACILITIES AND SERVICES Internet access; bar; boat; parking; snack bar; stores; pool; playground; restaurant; conference room; gym; massage room; beauty parlor; sauna; spa; travel agency; business center; 24-hour kitchen; recreational team for adults and children; valet parking; lifeguards; beach service; airport shuttle; transport to attractions. CREDIT CARDS AmEx; Diners; MasterCard; Visa
Rodovia BA-99, Km 76, Linha Verde
TEL (71) 2104-7000 FAX and RESERVATIONS 0800-7031512
www.marriottbrasil.com

Pousadas $$

This complex has a series of thematic guesthouses that are the area's most affordable accommodation options. Pousada da Aldeia has colorful little houses imitating a fishing village and is the farthest away from the Vila Nova da Praia. Pousada do Agreste takes its inspiration from the Northeastern outlaw culture of the past and incorporates motifs from regional celebrations. The décor of Pousada Gabriela is reminiscent of the houses in Ilhéus during the cacao boom. Pousada Pelourinho is built in the style of the historical neighborhood of Pelourinho, in the city of Salvador, and is the closest to Vila Nova da Praia. CREDIT CARDS AmEx; Diners; MasterCard; Visa
Rodovia BA-99, Km 76, Linha Verde
TEL (71) 2104-8200 FAX (71) 2104-8239
RESERVATIONS (71) 2104-8241, 0800-7074004
www.costadosauipe.com.br

Renaissance Resort $$$$

The rooms of this Marriott-owned resort are identical to those at the neighboring Marriott. However, this resort is cheerier and its leisure facilities (water aerobics, dance, and aerobics classes) attract families with children. ACCOMMODATIONS 212; Internet access; air-conditioning; private safe; minibar; telephone; cable TV. FACILITIES AND SERVICES Internet access; bar; boat; parking; snack bar; stores; pool; playground; restaurant; conference room; gym; massage room; beauty parlor; sauna; spa (at the Marriott); travel agency; business center; 24-hour kitchen; recreational; lifeguards; beach service; airport shuttle; transport to attractions. CREDIT CARDS AmEx; Diners; MasterCard; Visa
Rodovia BA-99, Km 76, Linha Verde
TEL (71) 2104-7300 FAX (71) 2104-7301
RESERVATIONS 0800-7031512 www.marriottbrasil.com

RESTAURANTS	$ up to R$ 50	$$ from R$ 51 up to R$ 100	$$$ from R$ 101 up to R$ 150	$$$$ above R$ 150

Super Clubs Breezes Costa do Sauípe $$$$
At the liveliest hotel in the complex, the tariffs are all-inclusive, covering meals, leisure activities and drinks. The well-equipped rooms only differ in the views they offer (overlooking either the garden or the sea). **ACCOMMODATIONS** 324; air-conditioning; private safe; minibar; telephone; cable TV. **FACILITIES AND SERVICES** bar; nursery; bicycles; parking; snack bar; stores; pool; tennis court; restaurant; conference room; recreational team for children and adults; valet parking; bar service on the beach. **CREDIT CARDS** AmEx; Diners; MasterCard; Visa
Rodovia BA-099, Km 76
TEL (71) 2104-8888 **FAX** (71) 2104-8810
RESERVATIONS 0800-7043210 www.superclubs.com.br

SERVICES

Tourist Information – Casa da Cultura
Praça Amado Bahia, no # (Department of Culture and Tourism), Centro, Mata de São João
TEL (71) 3635-2409, 3635-2663 **OPEN** Mon – Fri, 8:30am – noon and 1pm – 4pm www.pmsj.ba.gov.br

Cuiabá– Mato Grosso

AREA CODE 65 **POPULATION** 526,830 **DISTANCE** Campo Grande 687 kilometers (427 miles) **ACCESS** Highway BR-163 from the Southeast, and BR-174 from Rondônia

WHERE TO STAY

Odara Hotel $$
One of the newest hotels in Cuiabá, the Odara is modern, with tasteful décor and pleasant rooms. **ACCOMMODATIONS** 105; air-conditioning; Internet access; minibar; pay TV; telephone. **FACILITIES AND SERVICES** bar; bilingual staff; business center; conference room; gym; Internet access; pool; restaurant; transport to airport; valet service. **CREDIT CARDS** AmEx; Diners; MasterCard; Visa
Avenida Fernando Correia da Costa, 93, Areão
TEL and **FAX** (65) 3616-3500 www.hotelodara.com.br

Taiamã Hotel $$
Of Cuiabá's big hotels, this is the best equipped for tourists. Rooms can also be rented for day-use only. **ACCOMMODATIONS** 125; air-conditioning; balcony (first-floor rooms); Internet access; jacuzzi (in the suites); minibar; pay TV; private safe; telephone. **FACILITIES AND SERVICES** art and craft store; bar; barbecue facilities; bilingual staff; business center; conference room; convenience store; exchange service; first-aid; gym; Internet access; lifeguard; parking; pool; restaurant; snack bar; valet service; 24-hour kitchen. **CREDIT CARDS** AmEx; Diners; MasterCard; Visa
Avenida Rubens Mendes de Mendonça, 1,184, Bosque da Saúde
TEL (65) 2121-1000 **FAX** (65) 3624-3384
www.hoteltaiama.com.br

WHERE TO EAT

Al Manzul $$$$
A ways out from the center of Cuiabá, this is one of the best restaurants in the region. For your main course, try the lamb stuffed with rice and almonds. Bookings are recommended. **CUISINE** Arabic. **CREDIT CARDS** Not accepted
Rua C, Casa 1, Loteamento Cachoeira das Garças, Coxipó (access via Avenida Arquimedes Pereira Lima)

TEL (65) 3663-2237. Thu and Fri, 6pm – 10:30pm; Sat, noon – 3pm and 6pm – 10:30pm; Sun, noon – 3pm

Peixaria Popular $$
This eatery boasts a cozy atmosphere and friendly service. The house specialty is the delicious fish dish ventrecha de pacu, hones to perfection through almost two decades of refinement and practice. **CUISINE** Fish. **CREDIT CARDS** Diners; MasterCard; Visa
Avenida São Sebastião, 2,324, Goiabeiras
TEL (65) 3322-5471. Mon – Sat, 11am – 4pm and 6pm until the last customer leaves; Sun, 11am – 4pm

SERVICES

Bird Watching Expeditions – Boute Expeditions
Rua Getúlio Vargas, 64 (Ipase), Várzea Grande
TEL (65) 3686-2231 www.boute-expeditions.com

Travel Agency – Kanzen Turismo
Package tours of the Pantanal, in Cuiabá and Chapada dos Guimarães.
Rua Desembargador Trigo de Loureiro, 602, Consil
TEL (65) 3642-1990, 3642-2224. Mon – Fri, 8am – 6pm; Sat, 8am – noon. www.kanzenturismo.com.br

Travel Agency – Pantanal Adventure
Package tours to the Pantanal and Bonito.
Rua Papa João XXIII, 72, Dom Aquino
TEL (65) 3624-4052. Mon – Fri, 8am – 6pm; Sat, 8am – noon. www.pantanaladventure.com.br

Cumuruxatiba – Bahia

AREA CODE 73 **DISTANCES** Salvador 844 kilometers (524 miles), Prado 42 kilometers (26 miles), Porto Seguro 70 kilometers (44 miles) **ACCESS** From Salvador, on Highway BR-101 to Itamaraju, then on the BA-489 to a left-hand turnoff onto a dirt road (watch the signs), and continue for another 18 kilometers (11 miles)

WHERE TO STAY

Pousada É $$
This guesthouse is set amidst a vast area of greenery. The Swiss owner, Hans Fritsch, has a collection of more than two hundred whiskies, which guests can taste. The food is international, and the highlight is the Thai cuisine. **ACCOMMODATIONS** 12; minibar; cable TV; ceiling fan. **FACILITIES AND SERVICES** Internet access; wine cellar; bar; library; bicycles; kayaks; parking; convenience store; pool; playground; volleyball court; restaurant; workout; games room; video room; recreational team for children (high season); beach service. **CREDIT CARDS** Diners; MasterCard
Alameda Roberto Pompeu, 8, Rio do Peixe Grande
TEL (73) 3573-1007 **FAX** (73) 3573-1160
www.portonet.com.br/pousadae

Pousada Mandala $$
Surrounded by a lot of greenery, this guesthouse has rustic décor. Opt for a ground floor room facing the garden – they have king size beds. A massage area facing the sea is open during the summer. **ACCOMMODATIONS** 9; air-conditioning; minibar; TV; ceiling fan. **FACILITIES AND SERVICES** Internet access; bar; nursery; library; bicycles; kayaks; parking; pool; restaurant; DVD room; reading room; massage room; beach service; airport shuttle. **CREDIT CARDS** Visa

| **PRICES** | **HOTELS** (couple) | $ up to R$ 150 | $$ from R$ 151 up to R$ 300 | $$$ from R$ 301 up to R$500 | $$$$ above R$ 500 |

486   BRAZIL GUIDE

Alameda Roberto Pompeu, 1, Praia do Rio do Peixe
TEL and FAX (73) 3573-1143, 3573-1145
www.pousadamandala.com.br

Pousada Rio do Peixe $

This family-friendly guesthouse stands on a large beachside property and its rooms have sea views, verandas, and hammocks. ACCOMMODATIONS 20; Internet access; air-conditioning; king size bed (in 4 rooms); minibar; telephone; cable TV. FACILITIES AND SERVICES Internet access; bar; parking; stores; pool; restaurant; games room; video room; beach service; airport shuttle. CREDIT CARDS AmEx; Diners; MasterCard; Visa
Alameda Roberto Pompeu, 26, Praia do Rio do Peixe
TEL and FAX (73) 3573-1213
www.pousadariodopeixe.com.br

WHERE TO EAT

Asa Branca $

Popular among people from Minas Gerais, this restaurant stands in the village center. Owner Dona Rosa's specialty is the carne-de-sol de picanha (beef jerky made with choice cuts), which serves two. CUISINE Meats; regional. CREDIT CARDS Not accepted
Avenida 13 de Maio, no #, Centro
TEL (73) 3573-1205 OPEN Mon – Sat, 10am – 6pm

Catamarã $

Perched atop a 45-meter cliff at the entrance to town, this eatery has a stunning view. Dishes include moqueca (traditional stew), octopus and octopus rice, meats, and pasta – as well as feijoada (black bean and pork stew) on Sundays. CUISINE Regional; meats; seafood; pasta. CREDIT CARDS Not accepted
Rua 1, Quadra 1, Areia Preta
TEL (73) 3573-1124 OPEN Daily, 8am – 9pm

Mama África $

In a relaxed seaside environment, diners can enjoy vegetarian dishes, seafood, fish and a good variety of cachaça liquors from Minas Gerais. CUISINE Bacalhau; diverse; vegetarian. CREDIT CARDS MasterCard; Visa (only in the high season)
Rua Santo Antônio, no #, Centro
TEL (73) 3573-1046, 8811-5284 OPEN Tue – Sun, 2pm – 10pm

Restaurante do Suíço $

The varied menu offers dishes such as picanha suína grelhada ao molho de ervas (grilled pork sirloin in herb sauce) and moqueca mista de peixe and camarão (fish and shrimp stew). CUISINE Diverse. CREDIT CARDS MasterCard
Alameda Roberto Pompeu, 8, Pousada É, Rio do Peixe Grande
TEL (73) 3573-1007 OPEN Daily, 1pm – 11pm

SERVICES

Boat Tours and Whale Watching – Aquamar Ecoturismo
Avenida Beira-Mar, 7, Centro
TEL and FAX (73) 3573-1360 OPEN High season: daily, 7am – 8pm; low season: daily, 7am – 6pm
www.aquamarba.com.br

Bus Station – Rodoviária
Avenida Itamaraju, no #, Centro
TEL (73) 3298-1273, 3298-1228

Tourist Information – Posto de Informações Turísticas
Rua Clarício Cardoso dos Santos, 100, Novo Prado
TEL (73) 3298-1047 OPEN Mon – Fri, 8am – 2pm
www.prado.ba.gov.br

Cunha – São Paulo

AREA CODE 12 POPULATION 22,951 DISTANCE São Paulo, 222 kilometers (138 miles) ACCESS Highway BR-116 (Rodovia Presidente Dutra) and SP-171 from São Paulo

WHERE TO STAY

Pousada Barra do Bié $$

This guesthouse stands on a 6-hectare (15-acre) property in a conservation area that protects a stand of Brazil's distinctive Atlantic forest. Chalets come in 35- to 60-square-meter (377- to 646-square-foot) dimensions, and all have fireplaces and king-size beds with box springs. ACCOMMODATIONS 6; bathtub (in 1 chalet); fireplace; jacuzzi (in 4 chalets); minibar; TV and DVD (in 3 chalets). FACILITIES AND SERVICES bar; gym; library; massage room; orchard; parking; pool; restaurant; river; sauna; TV room with DVD player. CREDIT CARDS Visa
Rodovia Cunha–Paraty (SP-171), Km 58, then another 6 kilometers (4 miles) on a dirt road; the guesthouse is 21 kilometers (13 miles) out of town
TEL and FAX (12) 3111-1477
www.pousadabarradobie.com.br

Pousada Candeias $$

This large property encompasses woods and a small waterfall. The chalets, which can sleep up to 4 people, are divided into a living room and bedrooms and have queen or king size beds. ACCOMMODATIONS 8; fireplace; minibar; veranda with hammock. FACILITIES AND SERVICES bar; fruit and vegetable garden; gazebo with hammocks; orchard; pool; restaurant; river; trails; waterfall; woods. CREDIT CARDS Not accepted
Estrada do Campo Alegre, no #, Aparição, exit at Km 58.5 on the SP-171 (Rodovia Cunha–Paraty), 12 kilometers (7 miles) from the center of town, including 1 on a dirt road
TEL (12) 3111-2775 www.pousadacandeias.com.br

Pousada Recanto das Girafas $$

Located near the center of Cunha, this guesthouse offers suites and chalets with king size beds, eiderdowns and goose-feather pillows. ACCOMMODATIONS 8; fan; minibar; TV. FACILITIES AND SERVICES bar; Internet access; pool; sauna; wine cellar. CREDIT CARDS Visa
Rua Professor Agenor de Araújo, 251, Vila Rica
TEL (12) 3111-1330, 3111-1965
www.recantodasgirafas.com.br

WHERE TO EAT

Ateliê e Restaurante Drão $

Located in the center of Cunha, this restaurant offers dishes with regional ingredients, such as trout and shiitake mushrooms. CUISINE Various. CREDIT CARDS Visa
Alameda dos Lavapés, 560, Vila Rica
TEL (12) 3111-1326. Thu – Sun, noon – midnight

Quebra-Cangalha $$

Perched above its surroundings, this restaurant offers a view of the mountains. Meats are the forte here: There

RESTAURANTS	$ up to R$ 50	$$ from R$ 51 up to R$ 100	$$$ from R$ 101 up to R$ 150	$$$$ above R$ 150

is a small but varied wine list. **CUISINE** Various. **CREDIT CARDS** Diners; MasterCard; Visa
Rua Manuel Prudente de Toledo, 540, Cajuru
TEL (12) 3111-2391. Daily, 11am until the last customer leaves (high season and holidays); Mon and Tue, 11am – 5pm; Wed – Sun, 11am until the last customer leaves (low season)

SERVICES

Tourist Information – Cunhatur
Praça Cônego Siqueira, 97, Centro
TEL (12) 3111-2634. Mon – Fri, 10am – 4pm; Sat and Sun, 9am – 6pm

Tourist Information – Portal da Cidade
Avenida Francisco da Cunha Meneses, no #, Rodeio
TEL (12) 3111-0283 (public phone). Wed – Sun, 8am – 6pm

Curitiba – Paraná

AREA CODE 41 **POPULATION** 1,797,408 **DISTANCES** Florianópolis 300 kilometers (186 miles), São Paulo 408 kilometers (254 miles) **ACCESS** Highway BR-101 from Florianópolis; Highway BR-116 from São Paulo www.curitiba.pr.gov.br

WHERE TO STAY

Four Points Sheraton $$
Catering mostly to executives, this hotel has subdued décor and several event spaces. Reservations required. **ACCOMMODATIONS** 165; air-conditioning; central heating; Internet access; jacuzzi (in 6 suites); minibar; pay TV; private safe; telephone. **FACILITIES AND SERVICES** bar; bilingual staff; business center; function room; gym; heated pool; Internet access; massage room; restaurant; saunas; transport to airport and attractions; 24-hour room service. **CREDIT CARDS** AmEx; Diners; MasterCard; Visa
Avenida 7 de Setembro, 4,211, Batel
TEL (41) 3340-4000 **FAX** (41) 3340-4001
www.fpsc.com.br

San Juan Charm $$
The place occupies a beautiful renovated building that housed the first hotel of Curitiba. Request one of the rooms in the front, which are more spacious and have wood floors. **ACCOMMODATIONS** 24; air-conditioning; Internet access; minibar; pay TV; private safe; telephone. **FACILITIES AND SERVICES** bar; business center; Internet access; parking; restaurant. **CREDIT CARDS** AmEx; Diners; MasterCard; Visa
Rua Barão do Rio Branco, 354, Centro
TEL (41) 3219-9900 **FAX** (41) 3219 9926
www.sanjuanhoteis.com.br

Slaviero Full Jazz $$$
The rooms spoil guests with touches such as goosefeather pillows. The bar has live music on Friday and Saturday nights. **ACCOMMODATIONS** 84; air-conditioning; DVD player; Internet access; jacuzzi (in 4 suites); minibar; private safe; telephone; work bench. **FACILITIES AND SERVICES** bar; business center; function room; gym; Internet access; parking; restaurant; transport to airport and attractions; 24-hour kitchen. **CREDIT CARDS** AmEx; Diners; MasterCard; Visa
Rua Silveira Peixoto, 1,297, Batel
TEL (41) 3312-7000 **RESERVATIONS** 0800-7043311
www.hotelfulljazz.com.br

Slaviero Rockfeller $$
This hotel occupies a 1940s-era building behind the Centro de Convenções Estação (convention center). Its wide hallways are lit with natural light, and the furniture and décor are reminiscent of New York in the 1920s. **ACCOMMODATIONS** 78; air-conditioning; Internet access; jacuzzi (in 18 suites); minibar; pay TV; private safe; telephone. **FACILITIES AND SERVICES** bar; business center; function room; gym; Internet access; massage room; restaurant; saunas; transport to airport; 24-hour kitchen; 24-hour room service. **CREDIT CARDS** AmEx; Diners; MasterCard; Visa
Rua Rockfeller, 11, Rebouças
TEL (41) 3023-2330 **RESERVATIONS** 0800-7042330
www.hotelslaviero.com.br

WHERE TO EAT

Boulevard $$
This restaurant has received many awards from specialized publications. The menu features contemporary dishes with French and Italian influences. The wine list has been awarded recognition by Wine Spectator. **CUISINE** Contemporary; French, Italian. **CREDIT CARDS** AmEx; Diners; MasterCard; Visa
Rua Voluntários da Pátria, 539, Centro
TEL (41) 3023-8244. Mon – Fri, noon – 2:30pm and 7:30pm – 11:30pm; Sat, 7:30pm – 11:30pm

Cantinho do Eisbein $
This simple restaurant, located far from the center, has a short menu that includes eisbein (pork knuckle), stuffed marreco (garganey) and kassler (smoked pork steak). **CUISINE** German. **CREDIT CARDS** AmEx; Diners; MasterCard; Visa
Avenida dos Estados, 863, Água Verde
TEL (41) 3329-5155, 3023-5155. Tue – Sat, 11:30am – 3pm and 7pm – 11:30pm; Sun, 11:30am – 3pm

Durski $
At this traditional restaurant, order the Slav banquet, a kind of tasting menu that includes specialties from Poland, Ukraine, and Russia. **CUISINE** Slavic. **CREDIT CARDS** AmEx; Diners; MasterCard; Visa
Avenida Jaime Reis, 254, São Francisco
TEL (41) 3225-7893. Tue – Fri, 11:30am – 2:30pm and 7:45pm – 11:30pm; Sat, noon – 3:30pm and 7:45pm – 11:30pm; Sun, noon – 3:30pm

Estrela da Terra $
The restaurant's lack of sophistication is offset by Curitiba's best barreado, a dish of seasoned, slow-cooked lean meat. **CUISINE** Regional. **CREDIT CARDS** Diners; MasterCard
Avenida Jaime Reis, 176, São Francisco
TEL (41) 3023-8007. Tue – Sun, 11:30am – 3pm

Schwarzwald $
This 1979 bar-restaurant is decorated like a German tavern. The menu offers typical German fare, such as eisbein (pork knuckle). **CUISINE** German. **CREDIT CARDS** AmEx; Diners; MasterCard; Visa
Rua Claudino dos Santos, 63, Largo da Ordem
TEL (41) 3223-2585. Mon – Sat, 11am – 2am; Sun, 10:30am – 2am

SERVICES

Airport – Aeroporto Internacional Afonso Pena
Avenida Rocha Pombo, no #, Afonso Pena
TEL (41) 3381-1515

PRICES	**HOTELS** (couple)	$ up to R$ 150	$$ from R$ 151 up to R$ 300	$$$ from R$ 301 up to R$500	$$$$ above R$ 500

Tour Operator – BWT
Train Rides from Curitiba to Morretes and Paranaguá
Avenida Presidente Afonso Camargo, 330, Centro
TEL (41) 3323-4007. Mon – Sat, 7am – 6:30pm; Sun, 7am
– noon

Tourist Information – Disque Turismo (Paraná Turismo)
Rua Deputado Mário de Barros, 1,290, 3rd Floor, Centro
TEL (41) 3313-3500. Mon – Fri, 8am – noon and 1:30pm
– 6pm

Travel Agency – AVS Câmbio e Turismo
Travel agency and currency exchange.
Avenida Marechal Deodoro, 630, Conjunto 504, Centro
TEL (41) 3223-2828. Mon – Fri, 9am – 6pm (travel agency). Mon – Fri, 10am – 5pm (currency exchange)

Travel Agency – Esatur
City Tours.
Rua Marechal Deodoro, 235, 1st Floor, Mezzanine Store #108, Centro
TEL (41) 3322-7667. Mon – Fri, 9am – 6pm

Travel Agency – Onetur
Night tour of city with dinner.
Rua Marechal Floriano Peixoto, 228, 11th Floor, Mezzanine Store #1,107, Centro
TEL (41) 3224-8509. Mon – Fri, 9am – 7pm

Delta do Parnaíba – Maranhão and Piauí (see Parnaíba)

Diamantina – Minas Gerais

AREA CODE 38 POPULATION 44,746 distâncias Belo Horizonte 298 kilometers (185 miles), Rio de Janeiro 732 kilometers (455 miles), São Paulo 884 kilometers (549 miles) ACCESS Highway BR-040 and BR-135 (in poor condition) from Belo Horizonte to Curvelo. The take BR-259 and BR-367, passing through Gouveia
www.diamantina.mg.gov.br

WHERE TO STAY

Hotel Tijuco $
Famed architect Oscar Niemeyer designed this charming Modernist building in the 1950s. The hotel is comfortable and most rooms look out over the town's historic center. ACCOMMODATIONS 27; minibar; phone; TV. FACILITIES AND SERVICES parking; TV room. CREDIT CARDS AmEx; Diners; MasterCard; Visa
Rua Macau do Meio, 211, Centro
TEL and FAX (38) 3531-1022 www.hoteltijuco.com.br

Pousada do Garimpo $
Some 600 meters (650 yards) from the historic center, this guesthouse offers comfortable rooms and good service. The rooms are divided into two blocks, and the more sophisticated rooms are in the second block. ACCOMMODATIONS 54; air-conditioning; ceiling fan; Internet access; jacuzzi (in 2 suites); minibar; phone; TV. FACILITIES AND SERVICES arts and crafts shop; badminton court; bar; function room; games room; Internet access; parking; pool; restaurant; sauna; TV room. CREDIT CARDS AmEx; Diners; MasterCard; Visa

Avenida da Saudade, 265, Centro
TEL (38) 3531-1044 FAX (38) 3531-2316
www.pousadadogarimpo.com.br

WHERE TO EAT

Armazém do Rosário $
The stone, adobe, and wood construction and indirect lighting give this restaurant an intimate atmosphere. The menu offers regional specialties from Minas Gerais, as well as crêpes and pastas. CUISINE Contemporary; Italian; regional. CREDIT CARDS MasterCard; Visa
Rua Caminho do Carro, 237 B, Centro
TEL (38) 3531-3862, 9954-7509. Wed and Thu, 6pm – midnight; Fri, 6pm – 2:30am; Sat, 11am – 3pm and 6pm – 2:30am; Sun, 11am – 7pm

O Garimpeiro $
This restaurant specializes in generously portioned regional dishes. The house specialty is the bambá do garimpo, a mixture of pork ribs, carioca beans, and collard greens, accompanied by angu mush and rice. CUISINE Regional; various. CREDIT CARDS AmEx; Diners; MasterCard; Visa
Avenida da Saudade, 265, Centro
TEL (38) 3531-1044. Mon – Thu, 6pm – 10pm; Fri – Sun, noon – 11pm

Trattoria La Dolce Vita $
You can't go wrong here with the pastas, some of which are made with ingredients such as souari nuts, jabuticaba berries, annatto, poppy seeds and saffron, accompanied by pork, lamb, or duck, among other meat choices. CUISINE Meats; Italian; regional. CREDIT CARDS Visa
Rua Vieira Couto, 232, Centro
TEL (38) 3531-8485, 9944-7597. Mon and Wed – Fri, 7pm until the last customer leaves; Sat and holidays, noon – 3pm and 7pm until the last customer leaves; Sun, noon – 3pm

SERVICES

Bus Station – Terminal Rodovia Geraldo Edson do Nascimento
Praça Dom João, 134, Dom João
TEL (38) 3531-9176

Domingos Martins – Espírito Santo

AREA CODE 27 POPULATION 31,175 DISTANCE Vitória 50 kilometers (31 miles) ACCESS Take the BR-262 from Vitória to Santa Isabel, followed by 3 kilometers (2 miles) to the turnoff to Domingos Martins
www.domingosmartins.es.gov.br

WHERE TO STAY

Aroso Paço Hotel $$
In contrast to the natural landscape around it, this huge building boasts incredible Roman columns and a sumptuous atmosphere. ACCOMMODATIONS 48; fireplace (in 13 suites); Internet access; jacuzzi (in 12 suites); minibar; pay TV; phone. FACILITIES AND SERVICES bar; function room; games room; heated pool; heliport; Internet access; massage room; multi-sports court; parking; playground; recreational staff for adults and children; restaurant; sauna; soccer field; tennis court; transport to attractions (weekends and holidays); TV room; walking tours. CREDIT CARDS Diners; MasterCard; Visa

RESTAURANTS	$ up to R$ 50	$$ from R$ 51 up to R$ 100	$$$ from R$ 101 up to R$ 150	$$$$ above R$ 150

Rodovia BR-262, Km 89, Aracê (54 kilometers, or 34 miles, from the center of Domingos Martins)
TEL (27) 3248-1147 **FAX** (27) 3248-1180
www.aroso.com.br

Pousada dos Pinhos $$

This guesthouse offers good amenities for families with children. The small farm where it is situated has a lake and trails, as well as a year-round recreation team and baby sitter. **ACCOMMODATIONS** 60; ceiling fan; jacuzzi and fireplace (in 4 chalets and 2 suites); minibar; pay TV; phone. **FACILITIES AND SERVICES** bar; fishing equipment and lake; function room; games room; gym; heated pool; horses; Internet access; massage room; multi-sports court; parking; playground; pool; restaurant; sauna; soccer field; tennis court; trails; TV room. **CREDIT CARDS** MasterCard; Visa
Rodovia BR-262, Km 90, Aracê (50 kilometers, or 31 miles, from the center of Domingos Martins)
TEL (27) 3248-1115   www.pousadadospinhos.com.br

Pousada Eco da Floresta $$

This guesthouse stands in a 10,000-hectare (25,000-acre) area covered in Atlantic forest, with a view of Pedra Azul. It has good leisure facilities for adults and children. **ACCOMMODATIONS** 82; air-conditioning; fireplace (in 6 chalets and 2 suites); jacuzzi (in 6 chalets and 3 suites); minibar; pay TV; phone. **FACILITIES AND SERVICES** bar; beauty parlor; function room; games room; gym; gymnasium; heated pool; horses; kayak; massage room; movie theater; multi-sports court; paddleboat; parking; playground; pool; rappel; recreational staff for adults and children; restaurant; sauna; soccer field; tennis court; trails. **CREDIT CARDS** Diners; MasterCard; Visa
Rodovia BR-262, Km 96, Aracê (62 kilometers, or 39 miles, from the center of Domingos Martins)
TEL (27) 3248-1196 **FAX** (27) 3248-1198
www.ecodafloresta.com.br

WHERE TO EAT

Italiano $

The pork-shank sausage is a popular appetizer. The restaurant also serves mouthwatering homemade pasta with organic sauces. **CUISINE** Italian. **CREDIT CARDS** MasterCard; Diners; Visa
Avenida Duque de Caxias, 16, Centro
TEL (27) 3268-1420. Mon – Thu, 11am – 3pm; Fri and Sat, 11am – midnight; Sun, 11am – 5pm

SERVICES

Local Tour Operators – Emoções Radicais (rappelling)

Rua do Lazer, 194 (Rua João Batista Wernersbach), Centro
TEL (27) 3268-2165. Tue – Sun, 8:30am – 6pm

Local Tour Operators – Rio da Montanha (rafting and rappelling)

Rua Jeferson Aguiar, 27, store #1, Centro
TEL (27) 3268-1765. Mon – Fri, 8:30am – noon and 1pm – 6pm; Sat, 10am – 8pm; Sun, 10am – 4pm
www.riodamontanha.com.br

Tourist information – Casa da Cultura

Avenida Presidente Vargas, 531, Centro
TEL (27) 3268-2550. Tue – Sun, 9am – noon and 1pm – 5pm

Fernando de Noronha – Pernambuco

AREA CODE 81 **POPULATION** 2,280 **DISTANCES** Recife 545 kilometers (339 miles), Natal 360 kilometers (224 miles) **ACCESS** Flights from Natal or Recife
www.noronha.pe.gov.br

WHERE TO STAY

Pousada Beco de Noronha $$$

This cozy guesthouse has wooden rooms with rustic décor, comfortable box beds, and bathrooms with solar-heated showers. **ACCOMMODATIONS** 3; air-conditioning; minibar; telephone; TV; ceiling fan. **FACILITIES AND SERVICES** garden; games room; music room; TV room; good guide hiring advice; buggy rental; trips; airport shuttle. **CREDIT CARDS** AmEx; MasterCard; Visa
Vila Floresta Nova, Quadra P., C. 3
TEL (81) 3619-1568, 3619-1569
www.becodenoronha.com.br

Pousada Maravilha $$$$

Designed by architect Sérgio Bernardes, this guesthouse was built with natural materials, such as wood, straw, and vines, to blend in with the landscape. **ACCOMMODATIONS** 8; air-conditioning; private safe; minibar; jacuzzi in the bungalows; telephone; cable TV. **FACILITIES AND SERVICES** Internet access; wine cellar; bar; bicycles; parking; pool; restaurant; magazine reading area; massage room; sauna; airport shuttle. **CREDIT CARDS** AmEx; Diners; MasterCard; Visa
Rodovia BR-363, no #, Sueste
TEL (81) 3619-0028 **FAX** (81) 3619-0162
RESERVATIONS (81) 3619-1290
www.pousadamaravilha.com.br

Pousada Solar dos Ventos $$$

This guesthouse is ideal for those seeking peace and quiet. The social area has a veranda with a view of the beautiful landscape. **ACCOMMODATIONS** 8 chalets; air-conditioning; minibar; TV; veranda with hammock. **FACILITIES AND SERVICES** Internet access; tour bookings; airport shuttle. **CREDIT CARDS** AmEx; Diners; MasterCard; Visa
Estrada do Sueste, no #, Sueste
TEL (81) 3619-1347 **FAX** (81) 3619-1253
www.pousadasolardosventos.com.br

Pousada Zé Maria $$$$

The apartments have a privileged view of Conceição Beach. There are three special bungalows with jacuzzis. **ACCOMMODATIONS** 15; air-conditioning; private safe; minibar; jacuzzi (in 3 bungalows); telephone; cable TV; veranda with hammock in the bungalows. **FACILITIES AND SERVICES** wine cellar; bar; boat; fishing equipment; parking; motorboat; stores; pool; orchard; restaurant; gym; massage room; sauna; guided walking tours; scooter, bicycle, buggy and diving equipment hire; trips; airport shuttle; transport to attractions. **CREDIT CARDS** AmEx; Diners; MasterCard; Visa
Rua Nice Cordeiro, 1, Floresta Velha
TEL and **FAX** (81) 3619-1258
www.pousadazemaria.com.br

WHERE TO EAT

Ecologiku's $$

The specialty is the moqueca stew, but options include octopus, mussels, and lobster. There is neither poultry

PRICES	**HOTELS** (couple)	$ up to R$ 150	$$ from R$ 151 up to R$ 300	$$$ from R$ 301 up to R$500	$$$$ above R$ 500

490   BRAZIL GUIDE

nor meat on the menu. **CUISINE** Fish and seafood. **CREDIT CARDS** AmEx; Diners; MasterCard; Visa
Estrada Velha do Sueste (behind the airport)
TEL (81) 3619-1807 **OPEN** Daily, 7pm – 10:30pm (lunch available with advanced arrangements)

Museu dos Tubarões $

The shark museum restaurant serves tubalhau (shark balls). A nice main course is the tubalhoada: layers of shark with tomato, onion, red peppers, parsley and potato. **CUISINE** Fish. **CREDIT CARDS** AmEx; Diners; MasterCard; Visa
Avenida Joaquim Ferreira Gomes, 40,
Vila do Porto de Santo Antônio
TEL (81) 3619-1365 **OPEN** Mon – Sat, 8:30am – 6:30pm; Sun, noon – 6:30pm

Restaurante da Pousada Maravilha $$

The menu offers seafood options, meats, and risottos, as well as regional specialties such as curd cheese and sweet tapioca. The involtini de cavala (mackerel involtini) with lemon risotto and pitanga fruit sauce is particularly good. **CUISINE** Contemporary; diverse. **CREDIT CARDS** AmEx; Diners; MasterCard; Visa
Rodovia BR-363, no #, Sueste
TEL (81) 3619-0028 **OPEN** Daily, noon – 3pm and 8pm – 11pm

Zé Maria $$

On Wednesdays and Saturdays, a 'food festival' offers up more than 50 options, including seafood, sushi, meat, and pasta, for a fixed price. Bookings are required on these days. **CUISINE** Japanese; fish and seafood; diverse. **CREDIT CARDS** AmEx; Diners; MasterCard; Visa
Rua Nice Cordeiro, 1, Floresta Velha
TEL (81) 3619-1258 **OPEN** Daily, noon – 11:30pm

SERVICES

Buggy and Boat Rental – Loc Buggy

Avenida Major Costa, no #, Vila do Trinta
TEL (81) 3619-1490, 3619-1284 **OPEN** Daily, 8am – 8pm
www.locbuggy.com.br

Buggy Rental – Mulungu Locadora

Estrada da Alamoa, 211, Praia da Conceição
TEL (81) 3619-1755, 3619-1539 **FAX** (81) 3619-1913 **OPEN** Daily, 24 hours

Buggy-Taxis – Nortax

Rua São Miguel, no #, Vila dos Remédios
(next to the post office)
TEL (81) 3619-1314, 3619-1669 **OPEN** Daily, 24 hours

Tourist Information – Posto de Informações Turísticas

Porto de Santo Antônio, Vila de Santo Antônio
TEL (81) 3619-1744 **OPEN** Mon – Sat, 8am – 5pm; Sun, 8am – 2pm (or 6pm when tourist ships are in port)

Tourist Information – Sede da Administração

Palácio São Miguel, no #, Vila dos Remédios
TEL (81) 3619-1378 **OPEN** Mon – Fri, 8am – noon and 2pm – 7pm www.noronha.pe.gov.br

Tourist Police Station – Delegacia de Turistas

Centro de Convivência, no #, Vila do Trinta
TEL (81) 3619-1179 **OPEN** Daily, 24 hours

Travel Agency – Agência Receptiva Atalaia Noronha

Rua Major Costa, 7, Vila do Trinta
TEL (81) 3619-1328, 3619-1991 **OPEN** Daily, 7:30am – 7:30pm www.atalaia-noronha.com.br

Travel Agency – Yourway Noronha

Floresta Velha, no #
TEL (81) 3619-1796, 9949-1087, 9978-0135 **OPEN** Mon – Fri, 8am – 8pm www.yourway.com.br

Florianópolis – Santa Catarina

AREA CODE 48 **POPULATION** 396,723 **DISTANCES** Curitiba 300 kilometers (186 miles), Porto Alegre 459 kilometers (285 miles) **ACCESS** Highway BR-101 from Curitiba. Highway BR-290 and BR-101 from Porto Alegre www.pmf.sc.gov.br

WHERE TO STAY

Costão do Santinho $$$$

This is one of Brazil's best resorts, with a spa, comprehensive leisure facilities, and a friendly recreation team for children. The standard rooms are located in villas with fully-equipped kitchens, while the Ala Internacional wing has newer rooms. **ACCOMMODATIONS** 695; air-conditioning; Internet access; jacuzzi (in the Ala Internacional); minibar; pay TV; private safe; telephone. **FACILITIES AND SERVICES** archery; bar; bird watching; business center; canopy climbing; movie theater; function room; games room; gym; heated pool; horses; kayaks; marina; massage room; nocturnal wildlife spotting; outdoor archeological museum; playground; pool; recreational team for adults and children; restaurant; sand board; sauna; six-a-side soccer court; soccer field; spa; tennis court; volleyball court. **CREDIT CARDS** AmEx; Diners; MasterCard; Visa
Estrada Vereador Onildo Lemos, 2,505,
Praia do Santinho
TEL (48) 3261-1000 **RESERVATIONS** 0800-481000
www.costao.com

Pousada da Vigia $$$

This hillside guesthouse has a beautiful view of the beach and sunset. **ACCOMMODATIONS** 10; air-conditioning; balcony; barbecue facilities; ceiling fan; DVD player; Internet access; jacuzzi and sauna (in the suites); minibar; pay TV; private safe; telephone; TV. **FACILITIES AND SERVICES** bar; beachside service; gym; heated pool; Internet access; jacuzzi; massage room; restaurant; sauna; transport to airport and attractions. **CREDIT CARDS** AmEx; Diners; MasterCard; Visa
Rua Con. Walmor Castro, 291, Praia de Lagoinha
TEL (48) 3284-1789 **FAX** (48) 3284-1108
www.pousadavigia.com.br

Pousada Pé na Areia $$

This seaside guesthouse opened in 2003 and has tastefully decorated rooms with large bathrooms. The owners themselves serve guests breakfast. **ACCOMMODATIONS** 12; air-conditioning (in some rooms); ceiling fan; DVD (in some rooms); jacuzzi (in some rooms); minibar; private safe; telephone; TV. **FACILITIES AND SERVICES** beachside service; bicycles; board games; DVD player; frescobol (beach tennis); indoor climbing wall; Internet access; kayaks; library; mezzanine with fireplace; pay TV; sailboat; transport to airport and attractions. **CREDIT CARDS** MasterCard; Visa

---

Rua Hermes Guedes da Fonseca, 207,
Praia da Armação
TEL (48) 3338-1616 FAX (48) 3338-7156
www.pousadapenareia.com.br

Majestic Palace Hotel $$$

This downtown hotel is far from the beaches but close to the nightlife. All of the suites have ocean views. ACCOMMODATIONS 259; air-conditioning; Internet access (broadband); jacuzzi (in the 14 suites); minibar; pay TV; private safe; telephone. FACILITIES AND SERVICES bar; bilingual staff; business center; café; function room; gym; heliport; Internet access (broadband; computer available); jacuzzi; massage room; pool; poolside service; restaurants; sauna; spa; stores; transport to airport and attractions; valet service; 24-hour kitchen; 24-hour room service. CREDIT CARDS AmEx; Diners; MasterCard; Visa
Avenida Beira Mar Norte, 2,746, Centro
TEL and RESERVATIONS (48) 3231-8000 FAX (48) 3231-8008
www.majesticpalace.com.br

Praia Mole Eco Village $$

This hotel has a great location on a 9-hectare (23-acre) property that stretches from Praia Mole beach to Lagoa da Conceição lake. ACCOMMODATIONS 93; air-conditioning; ceiling fan; minibar; mini kitchen in the cabanas; pay TV; telephone. FACILITIES AND SERVICES bar; diving; function room; games room; gym; heated pool; Internet access; massage room; pool; recreational team for adults and children (in summer); restaurant; sauna; soccer field; spa; tennis court; transport to airport and attractions. CREDIT CARDS AmEx; Diners; MasterCard; Visa
Rodovia Jornalista Manoel de Meneses, 2,001,
Praia Mole
TEL (48) 3239-7500 FAX (48) 3232-5482 RESERVATIONS (48) 3239-7506, 3239-7505 www.praiamole.com.br

WHERE TO EAT

Bistrô D'Acampora $$

Half restaurant, half art gallery, this sophisticated space has a menu that changes weekly; the house fortes are the fish and shrimp dishes. Bookings required. CUISINE Contemporary; international. CREDIT CARDS Diners; MasterCard; Visa
Rodovia SC-401, Km 10, Santo Antônio de Lisboa
TEL (48) 3235-1073. Tue – Sat, 8pm – midnight

Bistrô Isadora Duncan $$$

This charming bistro has a beautiful view of Lagoa da Conceição lake and is an ideal place for a romantic dinner. CUISINE Contemporary; various. CREDIT CARDS MasterCard; Visa
Rodovia Jornalista Manoel de Meneses, 2658,
Praia Mole
TEL (48) 3232-7210. Mon – Sat, 7pm – 1am

Creperia Degrau $

This crêperie operates out of a historical building, which offers a glimpse of Lagoa da Conceição lake. It serves over 40 kinds of crêpe, both sweet and savory. CUISINE Crêpes. CREDIT CARDS Diners; MasterCard; Visa
Rua João Pacheco da Costa, 595, Lagoa da Conceição
TEL (48) 3338-1416. Tue – Sun, 6:30pm – 1am

Ponta das Caranhas $$

One of the most beautiful spots around Lagoa da Conceição, this restaurant has an excellent seafood menu. We suggest the peixe à moda Caranha: conger eel

stuffed with shrimp and catupiry cheese, accompanied by rice and chip stix. There is a wine list with 150 choices. CUISINE Seafood; various. CREDIT CARDS AmEx; Diners; MasterCard; Visa
Rodovia Jornalista Manoel de Menezes, 2,377,
Barra da Lagoa
TEL (48) 3232-3076. Daily, 11am – midnight; Sun, 11am – 11pm

Um Lugar $

This modern, casual spot is ideal for people watching. The dishes, such as curry shrimp and tuna with sesame seeds, are beautifully presented. Bookings required. CUISINE Contemporary. CREDIT CARDS AmEx; MasterCard; Visa
Rua Manuel Severino de Oliveira, 371,
Lagoa da Conceição
TEL (48) 3232-2451. Mon – Sun, 8pm – midnight; closed on Mondays during winter.

SERVICES

Airport – Aeroporto Hercílio Luz

Avenida Deputado Diomício Freitas, 3,393,
Carianos
TEL (48) 3331-4000

Gliding School – Parapente Sul

Hang gliding school and tandem rides in paragliders.
Rua João Antônio da Silveira, 201,
Lagoa da Conceição
TEL (48) 3232-0791. Mon – Sat, 8am – 7pm

Tour Operator – Openwinds

Hikes, horse riding tours, Hawaiian canoe trips.
Avenida das Rendeiras, 1,672, Lagoa da Conceição
TEL (48) 3232-5004. Tue – Fri, noon – 6pm; Sat and Sun, 10am – 6pm

Tourist Information – Posto de Informações Turísticas

Start of Rodovia BR-282, in front of Avenida XIV de Julho
TEL (48) 3348-9439. Daily, 8am – 7pm

Tourist Police Station – Delegacia de Atendimento ao Turista

Avenida Paulo Fontes, 1,101, Terminal Rodoviário Rita Maria
TEL (48) 3333-2103. Daily, 24 hours

Fortaleza – Ceará

AREA CODE 85 POPULATION 2,374,944 DISTANCES Natal 552 kilometers (343 miles), Recife 806 kilometers (501 miles), Teresina 635 kilometers (395 miles) ACCESS From Recife, on Highway BR-101, passing through João Pessoa, to Natal. From Natal, take highways BR-304 and then BR-116. From Teresina, on highways BR-343 and then BR-222; the road is in poor conditions in the Serra da Tianguá range and between Patos and Ubamirim
www.fortaleza.ce.gov.br

WHERE TO STAY

Gran Marquise Hotel $$$

This hotel has been renovated but retains a beautiful classic décor. The carpeted rooms have king size beds and ocean views (front and side). ACCOMMODATIONS 235; Internet access; air-conditioning; bathtub; private safe; minibar; jacuzzi in the presidential suite; telephone; ca-

PRICES | HOTELS (couple) | $ up to R$ 150 | $$ from R$ 151 up to R$ 300 | $$$ from R$ 301 up to R$500 | $$$$ above R$ 500

492 | BRAZIL GUIDE

ble TV. **FACILITIES AND SERVICES** Internet access; bar; parking; jacuzzi; pool; restaurant; conference room; gym; massage room; sauna; business center; 24-hour kitchen; valet parking. **CREDIT CARDS** AmEx; Diners; MasterCard; Visa
Avenida Beira-mar, 3980, Praia do Mucuripe
TEL (85) 4006-5000 **FAX** (85) 4006-5207
RESERVATIONS (85) 4006-5222
www.granmarquise.com.br

Luzeiros $$

This hotel stands next to the beach promenade and the rooms, almost all of which have verandas (facing the sea or the side of the hotel), are well equipped. There are English, French, German, and Italian-speakers on staff. **ACCOMMODATIONS** 202; Internet access; air-conditioning; private safe; minibar; jacuzzi in the executive suite; telephone; cable TV. **FACILITIES AND SERVICES** Internet access; bar; parking; pool; restaurant; conference room; gym; massage room; sauna; business center; 24-hour kitchen; valet parking. **CREDIT CARDS** AmEx; Diners; MasterCard; Visa
Avenida Beira-mar, 2600, Meireles
TEL (85) 4006-8585 **FAX** (85) 4006-8587
RESERVATIONS (85) 4006-8586 www.hotelluzeiros.com.br

Marina Park $$

Tucked away in a 4-hectare (10-acre) area, this hotel is ideal for families because of its good recreational facilities, highlights of which are the swimming pools and marina. **ACCOMMODATIONS** 315; Internet access (in some rooms); air-conditioning; private safe; minibar; telephone; cable TV. **FACILITIES AND SERVICES** Internet access; bar; parking; stores; marina; children's space; pool; playground; six-a-side soccer court; tennis court; volleyball court; restaurant; magazine reading area; conference room; gym; games room; massage room; beauty parlor; sauna; business center. **CREDIT CARDS** AmEx; Diners; MasterCard; Visa
Avenida Presidente Castelo Branco, 400,
Praia de Iracema
TEL (85) 4006-9595 **FAX** (85) 3253-1803
www.marinapark.com.br

Orixás Art Hotel $$$$

Located in the municipality of Flecheira, 130 kilometers (81 miles) from Fortaleza, this hotel has spacious suites have private outdoor swimming pools with jacuzzis. An art workshop and gallery are open to guests. **ACCOMMODATIONS** 20; air-conditioning; private safe; DVD player; minibar; jacuzzi; telephone; cable TV. **FACILITIES AND SERVICES** Internet access; art workshop and gallery; bar; boat; horses; vegetable garden; kite surfing; arts and crafts store; pool; beach; restaurant; tennis court; conference room; gym; games room; massage room; sauna; spa; surfing; windsurfing; poolside and beach service; airport shuttle, transport by a third-party company to attractions and nearby towns. **CREDIT CARDS** Diners; MasterCard; Visa
Rua das Praias, 871, Flecheiras
TEL (85) 3351-3114 **FAX** (85) 3351-3039
www.orixasclub.com.br

Othon Palace Fortaleza $$$

Situated on the seaside avenue, this executive-oriented hotel opened in 2000 and has some floors that are exclusively non-smoking. **ACCOMMODATIONS** 83; Internet access; air-conditioning; private safe; minibar; jacuzzi in the suites; telephone; cable TV. **FACILITIES AND SERVICES** Internet access; bar; parking; pool; restaurant; conference room; gym; massage room; sauna; business center; 24-

hour kitchen; valet parking. **CREDIT CARDS** AmEx; Diners; MasterCard; Visa
Avenida Beira-mar, 3470, Meireles
TEL (85) 3466-5500 **FAX** (85) 3466-5566
RESERVATIONS (85) 3466-5595 www.othon.com.br

WHERE TO EAT

Cantinho do Faustino $

There is an emphasis on regional ingredients, herbs, and wines here. Try the shelled lobster grilled in bitter cashew-fruit wine (known as mocororó). For dessert, we suggest the flambéed banana with rapadura (brown sugar) or basil ice cream. **CUISINE** Contemporary; regional. **CREDIT CARDS** AmEx; Diners; MasterCard; Visa
Rua Delmiro Gouveia, 1520, Varjota
TEL (85) 3267-5348 **OPEN** Tue – Fri, noon – 3pm and 7pm – midnight; Sat, noon – midnight; Sun, noon – 4pm

Cemoara $

The fish and seafood are prepared with top quality ingredients. Some dishes have strong local flavors, such as the camarões ao molho aromático de cajá (shrimp in aromatic cajá fruit sauce). **CUISINE** Fish and seafood. **CREDIT CARDS** AmEx; Diners; MasterCard; Visa
Rua Joaquim Nabuco, 166, Meireles
TEL (85) 3263-5001 **OPEN** Mon – Thu, noon – 3pm and 7pm – midnight; Fri and Sat, noon – 3pm and 7pm – 1am; Sun, noon – 5pm and 7pm – midnight

Colher de Pau $

This traditional restaurant serves carne-de-sol (beef jerky) made with choice beef cuts as well as delights such as manioc fried in manteiga de garrafa (clarified butter), baião-de-dois (rice and bean mash) and fried banana. This restaurant has two locations. **CUISINE** Regional. **CREDIT CARDS** AmEx; Diners; MasterCard; Visa
Rua Frederico Borges, 206, Varjota
TEL (85) 3267-3773 **OPEN** Daily, 11am – midnight
Rua dos Tabajaras, 412, Iracema
TEL (85) 3219-3605 **OPEN** Daily, 6pm – 12:30am

Marcel $

A branch of the restaurant by the same name in São Paulo, the Marcel is inside the Holiday Inn. The house specialties are the various soufflés. There is also a full wine list. **CUISINE** French. **CREDIT CARDS** AmEx; Diners; MasterCard; Visa
Avenida Historiador Raimundo Girão, 800,
Praia de Iracema
TEL (85) 3219-6767 **RESERVATIONS** (85) 3219-7246 **OPEN** Mon – Fri, noon – 2:30pm and 7pm until the last customer leaves; Sat, 7pm until the last customer leaves

Nostradamus $

The contemporary French menu has dishes such as robalo grelhado (grilled snook) in a cashew nut crust, accompanied by Parmesan risotto. Bookings are recommended. Dressy casual attire required. **CUISINE** Contemporary; French. **CREDIT CARDS** AmEx; Diners; MasterCard; Visa
Rua Joaquim Nabuco, 166 (Parthenon Flat),
Meireles
TEL (85) 4006-5353 **OPEN** Mon – Sat, 7pm – midnight

SERVICES

Airport – Aeroporto Internacional Pinto Marins

Avenida Senador Carlos Jereissati, 3000, Serrinha

| **RESTAURANTS** | $ up to R$ 50 | $$ from R$ 51 up to R$ 100 | $$$ from R$ 101 up to R$ 150 | $$$$ above R$ 150 |

TEL (85) 3392-1200 **OPEN** Mon – Fri, 8am – noon and 1pm – 5pm (switchboard operator available until 9pm) www.infraero.gov.br

Tourist Information – Secretaria de Turismo

Rua Leonardo Mota, 2700, Dionísio Torres
TEL (85) 3252-1444 **OPEN** Mon – Fri, 8am – noon and 1pm – 5pm (switchboard operator available until 9pm) www.fortaleza.ce.gov.br

Buggy Rental – Cooperativa de Buggy de Fortaleza

Rua Joaquim Nabuco, 1505, Aldeota (the buggies are parked on Avenida Beira-Mar, in front of the Clube Náutico sailing club)
TEL (85) 9108-1504 **OPEN** Daily, 9am – 4:30pm
www.cbfor.com.br

Foz do Iguaçu – Paraná

AREA CODE 45 **POPULATION** 311,336 **DISTANCES** Curitiba 637 kilometers (396 miles), São Paulo 1,047 kilometers (651 miles) **ACCESS** Highway BR-277 from Curitiba to the Foz do Iguaçu turnoff www.fozdoiguacu.pr.gov.br

WHERE TO STAY

Bourbon Cataratas $$$

This 35-year-old hotel is in very good condition and has great leisure activity options for kids. The best rooms in the new wing, especially those overlooking the pool. **ACCOMMODATIONS** 311; air-conditioning; Internet access; minibar; pay TV; private safe; telephone. **FACILITIES AND SERVICES** archery; babysitter; bar; beauty parlor; business center; convenience stores; gym; heated pool; Internet access; jacuzzi; jogging track; laundry; massage room; mini zoo; multi-sports court; playground; pool; poolside service; recreational team for children; restaurant; sauna; snooker room; soccer field; stores; tennis court; trails; travel agency; woods. **CREDIT CARDS** AmEx; Diners; MasterCard; Visa
Rodovia das Cataratas, Km 2.5, Carimã
TEL (45) 3529-0123 **FAX** (45) 3529-0000
RESERVATIONS 080-451010 www.bourbon.com.br

Mabu Thermas & Resort $$$$

This is the only hotel in town with hot springs. Rooms overlook either the five pools, which range in temperature from 32º to 36º C (90º to 97º F), or the garden, or the woods. **ACCOMMODATIONS** 208; air-conditioning; Internet access; jacuzzi (in the suites); minibar; pay TV; private safe; telephone. **FACILITIES AND SERVICES** archery; bar; beach-volleyball court; beauty parlor; carriages; climbing wall; flying-fox; function room; games room; gym; Internet access; mini farm; multi-sports court; nursery; paintball; playground; ponies; pools fed by hot springs; recreational staff for adults and children; restaurant; sauna; soccer field; sport fishing; store; tennis court. **CREDIT CARDS** AmEx; Diners; MasterCard; Visa
Rodovia das Cataratas, 3,175, Vila Carimã
TEL (45) 3521-2000 **FAX** (41) 3523-3432
RESERVATIONS 0800-417040 www.hoteismabu.com.br

Tropical das Cataratas Eco Resort $$$$

This is the only hotel inside Iguaçu National Park. The falls can be seen from the veranda and some rooms. **ACCOMMODATIONS** 203; air-conditioning; minibar; pay TV; private safe; telephone. **FACILITIES AND SERVICES** archery; bar; barbecue facilities; beach sports court; business center; cards room; fireplace; function room; games room; Internet access; parking; playground; pool; restaurant; soccer field; stores; tennis court; trails; travel agency; walking tours; 24-hour room service. **CREDIT CARDS** AmEx; Diners; MasterCard; Visa
Rodovia das Cataratas, Km 28, Parque Nacional do Iguaçu
TEL (45) 2102-7000 **FAX** (45) 3522-1717
RESERVATIONS 0800-7012670 www.tropicalhotel.com.br

SERVICES

Airport – Aeroporto Internacional de Foz do Iguaçu

Entrance on Rodovia das Cataratas, Km 16.5
TEL (45) 3521-4200

Tour Operator – Macuco Safári

Trips in open utility vehicles (pick-ups) through the park forest and in inflatable motorboats up to the falls.
Avenida das Cataratas, Km 25, Parque Nacional do Iguaçu
TEL (45) 3574-4244, 3529-6262. Daily, 9am – 5:30pm

Tourist Information – Posto de Informações Turísticas

Assistance in Portuguese, English, and Spanish.
Praça Getúlio Vargas, 69, Centro
TEL 0800451516. Daily, 7am – 11pm

Tourist Police – Delegacia de Atendimento ao Turista

Avenida Brasil, 1,374, Centro
TEL (45) 3523-3036. Mon – Fri, 8:30am – noon and 1:30pm – 5:30pm

Galinhos – Rio Grande do Norte

AREA CODE 84 **POPULATION** 2082 **DISTANCE** Natal 175 kilometers (109 miles) **ACCESS** On Highway BR-406, then RN-402 (25 kilometers, 16 miles, of asphalted road in poor condition), and across the Pratagi River by boat

WHERE TO STAY

Pousada Brésil Aventure $

The rooms are very simple and most have direct beach access. Beautiful ocean views make up for the modest décor. **ACCOMMODATIONS** 13; minibar; TV; ceiling fan. **FACILITIES AND SERVICES** Internet access; parking; restaurant **CREDIT CARDS** Not accepted
Rua Senador Dinape Mariz, 123, Centro
TEL (84) 3552-0085 **FAX** (84) 3552-0120
www.bresil-aventure.com

SERVICES

Tourist Information – Secretaria Municipal de Turismo

Praça dos Três Poderes, 717, Centro
TEL (84) 3552-0070 **OPEN** Mon – Fri, 8am – noon and 2pm – 6pm

Garanhuns – Pernambuco

AREA CODE 87 **POPULATION** 126,776 **DISTANCES** Recife 230 kilometers (143 miles), Caruaru 120 kilometers (75 miles), Maceió 155 kilometers (96 miles) **ACCESS** From Recife, on Highway BR-232 to Km 150 (town of São Caetano), then take the BR-423 www.garanhuns.pe.gov.br

PRICES	HOTELS (couple)	$ up to R$ 150	$$ from R$ 151 up to R$ 300	$$$ from R$ 301 up to R$500	$$$$ above R$ 500

494 BRAZIL GUIDE

WHERE TO STAY

Sesc Garanhuns $
This is perhaps the best accommodation option for tourists. A spacious, tree-filled area and a well-tended garden offer numerous recreational options. ACCOMMODATIONS 60; air-conditioning in the luxury rooms, fan in the standard rooms; minibar; telephone; TV. FACILITIES AND SERVICES Internet access; bar; toy library; parking; snack bar; pool; heated pool; playground; volleyball court; restaurant; games room; video room; recreational team for adults and children. CREDIT CARDS Diners; MasterCard; Visa
Rua Manoel Clemente, 161, Centro
TEL (87) 3761-8300
RESERVATIONS (81) 3421-5054, 3421-2367
www.sesc-pe.com.br

WHERE TO EAT

Buchada do Gago $
This simple eatery has no menu, but proprietor Gago's gregariousness and his lightly spiced buchada (offal stew) draw an eclectic clientele. CUISINE Regional. CREDIT CARDS MasterCard
Rua Mariano Filho, 1, Vila do Quartel
(entry at Km 5 on Rodovia José Cardoso)
TEL (87) 3761-3894 OPEN Daily, 10am – 6pm

Chez Pascal $
This was once one of the most popular restaurants in Garanhuns, but its reputation as an expensive eatery has frightened off clients in recent times. Specializing in Swiss cuisine, it has cheese, meat, and shrimp fondues. CUISINE Fondue; Swiss. CREDIT CARDS MasterCard; Visa
Avenida Rui Barbosa, 891, Heliópolis
TEL (87) 3762-0070 OPEN Thu – Sun, noon – 3:30pm and 6pm until the last customer leaves

SERVICES

Bus Station – Rodoviária
Avenida Caruaru, no #, São José
TEL (87) 3761-3891, 3761-0237 (Viação Jotude bus company)

Tourist Information – Secretaria de Turismo
Rua Joaquim Távora, no #, Heliópolis
TEL (87) 3762-7095, 3762-7096 OPEN Mon – Fri, 8am – 2pm

Garibaldi – Rio Grande do Sul

AREA CODE 54 POPULATION 28,791 DISTANCES Porto Alegre 115 kilometers (71 miles), Bento Gonçalves 16 kilometers (10 miles) ACCESS Highways BR-116, RS-122, RS- 446 and RS-470 from Porto Alegre www.garibaldi.rs.gov.br

WHERE TO STAY

Hotel Casacurta $$
This very charming, traditional hotel has been in business for over five decades. The décor dates back to the 1950s and is in good condition, even in the oldest rooms. ACCOMMODATIONS 31; air-conditioning; ceiling fan; heating; minibar; telephone; TV. FACILITIES AND SERVICES function room; gym; games room; Internet access; park-ing; playground; reading room; restaurant. CREDIT CARDS AmEx; Diners; MasterCard; Visa
Rua Luís Rogério Casacurta, 510, Centro
TEL (54) 3462-2166 FAX (54) 3462-2354
www.hotelcasacurta.com.br

WHERE TO EAT

Hostaria Casacurta $
The best Italian restaurant in town, this place adjoins the eponymous hotel and makes its own pasta. CUISINE Italian. CREDIT CARDS AmEx; Diners; MasterCard; Visa
Rua Luís Rogério Casacurta, 510, Centro
TEL (54) 3462-2166. Mon – Sat, 7:30pm – 11:30pm

SERVICES

Tourist Information – Centro de Informações Turísticas
Rodovia RS-470 (1 kilometer, or 0.6 miles, out of town)
TEL (54) 3464-0796. Daily, 9am – 5pm

Garopaba – Santa Catarina

AREA CODE 48 POPULATION 16,399 DISTANCE Florianópolis, 96 kilometers (60 miles) ACCESS Highway BR-101 from Florianópolis heading south to the Araçatuba turnoff at Km 272. Here, take the SC-434 for another 15 kilometers (9 miles) www.garopaba.sc.gov.br

WHERE TO STAY

Morro da Silveira Eco Village $$
One of the newest hotels in Garopaba, this Balinese style establishment sits atop Morro da Silveira hill. ACCOMMODATIONS 22; ceiling fan; minibar; private safe; telephone; TV. FACILITIES AND SERVICES bar; beachside service; function room; games room; gym; heated pool; Internet access; jacuzzi; massage room; mini library; movie theater; pool; restaurant; sauna; surf school; tour guides; trails; whale watching (from July to October). CREDIT CARDS MasterCard; Visa
Rodovia GRP-454, 80, Praia da Silveira
TEL (48) 3354-1740 www.morrodasilveira.com

Pousada Basfak Praia $$
This Garopaba beach guesthouse caters to families and is open from December to March only. It is just one block from the main avenue and three blocks from the beach. ACCOMMODATIONS 31; air-conditioning; ceiling fan (in 7 suites); jacuzzi (in 2 suites); minibar; open kitchen (in 7 suites); telephone; TV. FACILITIES AND SERVICES bar; bar-becue facilities; bicycles; games room; lookout; parking; pool; restaurant; TV room. CREDIT CARDS Diners; MasterCard; Visa
Rua Santa Rita, 41, Praia de Garopaba
TEL (48) 3254-4507 www.pousadabasfak.com.br

SERVICES

Tour Operator – Ailton Coelho
Rua Francisco Pacheco de Sousa, 137, Centro
TEL (48) 3254-3259. Mon – Fri, 8am – noon and 1:30pm – 6pm; Sat, 9am – noon

Tour Operator – Irapuã Turismo
Rua Francisco Pacheco de Sousa, 184, Centro
TEL (48) 3254-3917, 8813-6953. Daily, 8am – 10pm

Tourist Information –
Centro de Atendimento ao Turista
Rodovia SC-434, Km 8, Encantada
TEL (48) 3254-2077, 3254-2078. Daily, 8:30am – 7pm

Goiânia – Goiás

AREA CODE 62 POPULATION 1,244,645 DISTANCES Brasilia 209
kilometers (130 miles), Belo Horizonte 906 kilometers
(563 miles), São Paulo 926 kilometers (575 miles) ACCESS
Highway BR-060 from Brasilia www.goiania.go.gov.br

WHERE TO STAY

Castro's Park Hotel $$$
This downtown hotel built in the 1980s is still Goiânia's
best option. ACCOMMODATIONS 176; air-conditioning; Internet access; jacuzzi (in 2 suites); minibar; pay TV; private
safe; telephone. FACILITIES AND SERVICES bar; business center; conference room; convenience store; games room;
gym; heated pool; Internet access; jacuzzi; massage
room; parking; play area with toys; recreational staff for
adults and children; sauna; stores; travel
agency; valet service; video room; 24-hour kitchen. CREDIT
CARDS AmEx; Diners; MasterCard; Visa
Avenida República do Líbano, 1,520, Setor Oeste
TEL (62) 3096-2000 FAX (62) 3096-2030
www.castrospark.com.br

WHERE TO EAT

Chão Nativo $
This self-service restaurant serves forty different hot
dishes baked in a wood-fired oven. Highlights are the
arroz com pequi (rice with souari nuts) and the empadão goiano (pastry turnover). CUISINE Regional. CREDIT
CARDS MasterCard; Visa
Avenida República do Líbano, 1,809, Setor Oeste
TEL (62) 3223-5396. Mon – Fri, 11am – 3:30pm; Sat, Sun,
and holidays, 11am – 4pm www.chaonativo1.com.br

SERVICES

Tourist Information – Agetur
Rua 30, no # (corner of Rua 4), 2nd floor, Centro
TEL (62) 3201-8100. Mon – Fri, 8am – 4pm.

Goiás – Goiás

AREA CODE 62 POPULATION 24,472 DISTANCE Goiânia 141
kilometers (88 miles), Brasilia 320 kilometers (199 miles)
ACCESS Highway BR-070 from Goiânia or Brasilia

WHERE TO STAY

Hotel Fazenda Manduzanzan $$
This quiet, well-located hotel is named after two of the
region's rivers, the Mandu and the Zanzan, and has a
fishing pond, cascade, and horseriding stable. ACCOM-
MODATIONS 10; air-conditioning; minibar; TV (in 9 of the
10 chalets). FACILITIES AND SERVICES bar; cascade; conference room; fishing equipment; fishing pond; games
room; horses; Internet access; natural pool; parking;
pool; restaurant; river; sauna; soccer field; trails; waterfall;
video room. CREDIT CARDS Not accepted
Rodovia Municipal do Assentamento
do Mosquito, Km 7
TEL (62) 9982-3373 www.manduzanzan.com.br

Pousada Dona Sinhá $
This 200-year-old house used to be the manor house of
a farm, but has been successfully converted into a 5-
bedroom guesthouse, now surrounded by greenery. It's
still furnished with 18th-century furniture. ACCOMMODA-
TIONS 8; air-conditioning (in 1 room); ceiling fan; minibar;
TV. FACILITIES AND SERVICES arts and crafts shop; babysitter;
bar; Internet access; library; parking; play area with toys;
pool; shuttlecock and volleyball court; snack bar; trails;
walking tours; woods. CREDIT CARDS Not accepted
Rua Padre Arnaldo, 13, Centro
TEL (62) 3371-1667 FAX (62) 3371-1667
www.pousadadonasinha.com.br

WHERE TO EAT

Goiás Pontocom $
For lunch, it serves only meat and salad dishes, the so-
called executive lunch. Dinner is à la carte, with dishes
such as filé mignon in wine sauce. CUISINE Contemporary; various. CREDIT CARDS Not accepted
Praça Dr. Tasso de Camargo (formerly Praça
do Coreto), 19, Centro
TEL (62) 3371-1691. Sun – Tue, 11:30am – 3pm; Thu – Sat,
11:30am – 3pm and 7:30pm – midnight

Paróchia $
A good option here is the conde d'arcos steak, with mus-
tard and caper sauce, and the filé de linguado (flounder)
with brie cheese sauce, both of which serve two. CUISINE
Contemporary. CREDIT CARDS Diners; MasterCard
Praça Dr. Tasso de Camargo (formerly Praça do
Coreto), 18, Centro
TEL (62) 3371-3291. Tue – Fri, 7:30pm – midnight; Sat,
noon – 4pm and 7:30pm – midnight; Sun, noon – 5pm

Governador Celso Ramos – Santa Catarina

AREA CODE 48 POPULATION 12,175 DISTANCE Florianópolis
49 kilometers (30 miles) ACCESS Highway BR-101 from
Florianópolis to the Governador Celso Ramos turnoff at
Km 180, followed by the SC-410

WHERE TO STAY

Ponta dos Ganchos Exclusive Resort $$$$
Located in the town next to Bombinhas, this Relais &
Chateux-chain resort offers spacious bungalows – some
with jacuzzis or pools on the veranda – with ocean
views. Guests under the age of 18 are not allowed.
ACCOMMODATIONS 20; air-conditioning; CD player; ceiling
fan; DVD player; fireplace; Internet access; jacuzzi, pool
and sauna (in some bungalows); minibar; pay TV; private
safe; telephone. FACILITIES AND SERVICES bar; beach equipment and service; billiards; business center; fishing lake;
fitness center; games room; kayaks; heated pool; Internet access; laundry; motorboat; movie theater; restaurant; sailboat; tennis court; trails; transport to airport and
attractions. CREDIT CARDS AmEx; Diners; MasterCard; Visa
Rua Eupídio Alves do Nascimento, 104,
Ganchos de Fora
TEL (48) 3262-5000, 3262-5024 FAX (48) 3262-5046
RESERVATIONS 0800-643-3346
www.pontadosganchos.com.br

Gramado – Rio Grande do Sul

AREA CODE 54 POPULATION 31,652 DISTANCE Porto Alegre
115 kilometers (71 miles) ACCESS Highway RS-020 from
Porto Alegre to Taquara, then RS-115

PRICES	HOTELS (couple)	$ up to R$ 150	$$ from R$ 151 up to R$ 300	$$$ from R$ 301 up to R$500	$$$$ above R$ 500

WHERE TO STAY

Kurotel Centro de Longevidade e Spa $$$$
This luxurious spa offers heath and beauty treatments, and a team of specialists is available to help guests schedule activities. The room rate includes breakfast, lunch, and dinner. **ACCOMMODATIONS** 35; air-conditioning; CD and DVD players (in some suites); electric fireplace in the suites; heating; Internet access (broadband); minibar; pay TV; private safe; telephone. **FACILITIES AND SERVICES** amphitheater; beauty center; bilingual staff; fruit and vegetable garden; games room; gym; health clinic; heated pool; heliport; Internet access; jacuzzi; massage room; museum; reading room; restaurant; store; tennis court. **CREDIT CARDS** AmEx; Diners; MasterCard; Visa
Rua Nações Unidas, 533, Bavária
TEL (54) 3295-9393 **RESERVATIONS** 0800-9098000
www.kurotel.com.br

Estalagem St. Hubertus $$$$
This lodge faces Negro Lake and sits in quiet surroundings, though not very far from the hustle and bustle. Tea and cakes are served at afternoon tea. **ACCOMMODATIONS** 27; air-conditioning; CD player; heating; Internet access; jacuzzi (in 7 rooms); minibar; pay TV; private safe; telephone. **FACILITIES AND SERVICES** bicycles; business center; games room; heated pool; Internet access; lake; massage room; sauna; sitting room with fireplace; trails; TV room. **CREDIT CARDS** AmEx; Diners; MasterCard; Visa
Rua da Carrière, 974, Planalto
TEL (54) 3286-1273 www.sthubertus.com

Hotel Ritta Höppner $$$
This Bavarian-style guesthouse is one of the oldest in town. Most of the chalets have private pools fed by thermal springs. **ACCOMMODATIONS** 29; air-conditioning; central heating; DVD player (in some rooms); Internet access; minibar; parking; pay TV; private thermal pool (in 10 chalets); telephone. **FACILITIES AND SERVICES** bar; function room; Internet access; pool; winter gardens. **CREDIT CARDS** Diners; MasterCard; Visa
Rua Pedro Candiago, 305, Planalto
TEL (54) 3286-1334 **FAX** (54) 3286-3129
www.rittahoppner.com.br

WHERE TO EAT

Casa da Velha Bruxa $
The Prawer chocolate factory cafeteria serves snacks, sandwiches, pizza, different types of coffee, and – of course – chocolates. **CUISINE** Snacks. **CREDIT CARDS** AmEx; Diners; MasterCard; Visa
Avenida Borges de Medeiros, 772, Centro
TEL (54) 3286-1551. Mon, 3pm – 10pm; Tue – Sun, 10:30am – 10pm

Belle du Vallais $
Amidst a French wine-cellar atmosphere and jazz music sound track, the Belle du Vallais serves typical Swiss dishes, the fortes being the different kinds of raclette and fondue. **CUISINE** Swiss. **CREDIT CARDS** Diners; MasterCard; Visa
Avenida das Hortênsias, 1,432, Centro
TEL (54) 3286-1744. Mon – Fri, 7:30pm – midnight; Sat and Sun, noon – 3pm and 7pm – midnight

Gasthof Edelweiss $
The wine cellar at this Germanic eatery has a wide variety of labels. If you find yourself admiring any of the objects on display, just ask about the price: the place is also an antique shop. **CUISINE** German; Swiss. **CREDIT CARDS** AmEx; Diners; MasterCard
Rua da Carrière, 1,119, Planalto
TEL (54) 3286-1861. Daily, noon – 3pm and 7pm – 11pm

La Caceria $$
This restaurant is inside Casa da Montanha Hotel and specializes in game meats. Only the deer is wild; the other animals are bred in captivity. Bookings required. **CUISINE** Game. **CREDIT CARDS** AmEx; Diners; MasterCard; Visa
Avenida Borges de Medeiros, 3,166, Centro
TEL (54) 3286-2544. Thu – Sun, 7pm – midnight

Le Petit Clos $$
A favorite among sweethearts, this romantic restaurant specializes in fondues and other Swiss delicacies. **CUISINE** Swiss. **CREDIT CARDS** Diners; MasterCard; Visa
Rua Demétrio Pereira dos Santos, 599, Planalto
TEL (54) 3286-1936. Daily, 7pm – midnight

SERVICES

Tour Operator – Terra Turismo
Avenida das Hortênsias, 804, Planalto
TEL (54) 3286-2087, 3295-9100. Mon – Fri, 9am – noon and 1:30pm – 6pm

Tour Operator – Turistur
Avenida Borges de Medeiros, 3,165, Mezzanine Store #2-A, Centro
TEL (54) 3286-3939. Mon – Fri, 9am – noon and 1:30pm – 6pm; Sat, 9am – noon and 1:30pm – 4:30pm

Tourist Information – Pórtico via Nova Petrópolis
Rodovia RS-235, Planalto
TEL (54) 3286-2803. Tue – Sun, 9am – 3pm

Tourist Information – Posto de Informações Turísticas
Avenida Borges de Medeiros, 1,647, Praça Major Nicoletti, Centro
TEL (54) 3286-1475. Mon – Fri, 9am – 7pm; Sat, 9am – 8pm; Sun, 9am – 7pm

Gravatá – Pernambuco

AREA CODE 81 **POPULATION** 70,899 **DISTANCE** Recife 80 kilometers (50 miles) **ACCESS** From Recife, on Highway BR-232 www.prefeituradegravata.com.br

WHERE TO STAY

Casa Grande $$$
This hotel has good facilities for leisure pursuits and conventions. **ACCOMMODATIONS** 119; air-conditioning; minibar; telephone; TV. **FACILITIES AND SERVICES** Internet access; bar; nightclub; woods; waterfall; parking; jacuzzi; fishing lake; snack bar; pool; thermal pool; playground; six-a-side soccer court; tennis court; volleyball court; restaurant; games room; sauna; business center; recreational team for children. **CREDIT CARDS** AmEx; Diners; MasterCard; Visa
Rodovia BR-232, Km 82
TEL (81) 3533-0812, 3533-0920
FAX and **RESERVATIONS** (81) 3465-3011
www.hotelcasagrandegravata.com.br

RESTAURANTS $ up to R$ 50 $$ from R$ 51 up to R$ 100 $$$ from R$ 101 up to R$ 150 $$$$ above R$ 150

WHERE TO EAT

Pinheiros $

Chef Geraldo José da Silva serves dishes such as costela no bafo (smoked ribs), his specialty, as well as fondue and cordeiro fatiado (sliced lamb). **CUISINE** Regional; diverse. **CREDIT CARDS** MasterCard; Visa
Avenida Cícero Batista de Oliveira, 1778
TEL (81) 3533-5217 **RESERVATIONS** (81) 3533-5297 **OPEN** Wed and Thu, 10am – 10pm; Fri – Sun, 10am – 1am

SERVICES

Bus Station – Rodoviária

Avenida Padre Cícero Batista de Oliveira, no # (BR-232)
TEL (81) 3533-2031 (public phone) **OPEN** Daily, 6am – 7pm

Tourist Information – Secretaria de Turismo

Rua Rui Barbosa, no #, Centro
TEL (81) 3563-9047 **OPEN** Mon – Fri, 7am – 1pm; special events, Sat and Sun, 7am – midnight www.prefeituradegravata.com.br

Guarapari – Espírito Santo

AREA CODE 27 **POPULATION** 98,073 **DISTANCE** Vitória 59 kilometers (37 miles) **ACCESS** Rodovia do Sol from Vitória www.guarapari.es.gov.br

WHERE TO STAY

Hotel Fazenda Flamboyant $$

This hotel is situated on a working farm and offers great leisure facilities. **ACCOMMODATIONS** 90; air-conditioning; jacuzzi (in one suite); minibar; phone; TV. **FACILITIES AND SERVICES** bar; canopy-climbing circuit; convenience store; function room; games room; gym; heated pool; horses; Internet access; kayaks; multi-sports court; parking; playground; pool; recreational teams for adults and children; restaurant; sauna; soccer field; tennis court; trails; valet service. **CREDIT CARDS** Diners; MasterCard; Visa
Fazenda Querência, no #, Amarelos
TEL and **FAX** (27) 3229-0066
www.hotelflamboyant.com.br

Hotel Porto do Sol $$

This hotel's prime location at the end of a beach affords a view of Morro and Muquiçaba beaches. **ACCOMMODATIONS** 88; air-conditioning; DVD (in 38 suites); Internet access (in 38 suites); jacuzzi (in 6 suites); minibar; pay TV; phone; private safe (in 38 suites); sauna (in 6 suites). **FACILITIES AND SERVICES** bar; business center; convenience store; function room; games room; gym; laundry; massage room; parking; playground; pool; restaurant; sauna; soccer field; tennis court; transport to airport and attractions; video room. **CREDIT CARDS** AmEx; Diners; MasterCard; Visa
Avenida Beira-mar, 1, Praia do Morro
TEL (27) 3361-1100, 3161-7100
RESERVATIONS (27) 3161-7101
www.hotelportodosol.com.br

WHERE TO EAT

Cantinho do Curuca $$

Moqueca stews, the house forte, are preceded by complementary fried shrimp and are accompanied by rice, pirão (manioc-thickened gravy) and moqueca de banana-da-terra (plantain). **CUISINE** Regional. **CREDIT CARDS** AmEx; Diners; MasterCard; Visa
Avenida Santana, 96, Praia de Meaípe
TEL (27) 3272-2009. Daily, 11am – 10pm

Gaeta $$

The locally devised moqueca de banana-da-terra, which accompanies the traditional seafood moquecas, is complementary. Other options include lobster gratin and, for dessert, a distinctive variation on coconut pie. **CUISINE** Regional. **CREDIT CARDS** Diners; MasterCard; Visa
Avenida Santana, 47, Praia de Meaípe
TEL (27) 3272-1202. Daily, 11am – 10pm

SERVICES

City tours – Praiatour Receptivo

Avenida José Ferreira Ferro, 99, store #1, Praia do Morro
TEL (27) 3361-5858, 3361-2097. Mon – Fri, 8am – 6pm; Sat, 9am – noon

Diving operators – Acquasub

Avenida Anísio Fernandes Coelho, 30, Store #1, Jardim da Penha (in Vitória)
TEL (27) 3325-0036. Mon – Fri, 9am – 8pm; Sat, 9am – 1pm

Diving operators – Atlantes

Rua José Barcellos de Matos, 341, Centro
TEL (27) 3361-0405. Mon – Sat, 9am – noon and 2pm – 6pm. www.atlantes.com.br

Tourist information – Secretaria de Turismo de Guarapari

Rua Paulo de Aguiar, no #, Centro
TEL (27) 3262-8759. Mon – Fri, 8am – 6pm

Ilha de Boipeba – Bahia

AREA CODE 75 **DISTANCE** Salvador 256 kilometers (159 miles), plus a 40-minute motorboat ride **ACCESS** From Salvador, by catamaran (2 hrs) or motorboat (2 hrs, 10 min) to Morro de São Paulo, plus a stretch in a 4×4 vehicle or by motorboat (1 hr) or on Highway BR-324 and BR-101 to Valença, plus a boat trip (3 hrs, 30 min) or by motorboat (40 min). You can also go by motorboat from the village of Torrinhas, in Cairu (30 min).

WHERE TO STAY

Pousada Maliale $

This guesthouse stands in the middle of São Miguel Island, in the Inferno River, facing Boipeba and the extreme south of Tinharé Island. There are two motorboats to take guests to Boipeba. **ACCOMMODATIONS** 16; air-conditioning; minibar; TV; ceiling fan. **FACILITIES AND SERVICES** bar; boat; waterfall; kayaks; deck; fishing equipment; water skiing; motorboat; snack bar; pool; restaurant; games room; beach service. **CREDIT CARDS** Diners; MasterCard
Ilha de São Miguel, beach
TEL (75) 3653-6134, 9981-3322
RESERVATIONS (11) 4794-7474
www.pousadamaliale.com.br

Pousada Tassimirim $

This simple guesthouse, almost at the end of Boca da Barra beach, exudes rustic charm. **ACCOMMODATIONS** 15;

PRICES | **HOTELS** (couple) | $ up to R$ 150 | $$ from R$ 151 up to R$ 300 | $$$ from R$ 301 up to R$500 | $$$$ above R$ 500

498   BRAZIL GUIDE

air-conditioning or ceiling fan. FACILITIES AND SERVICES Internet access; bar; boat; table games; restaurant; walking trails; TV; boat trips. CREDIT CARDS Diners; MasterCard; Visa
Praia Boca da Barra, no #, Vila Velha Boipeba
TEL and FAX (75) 3653-6030 RESERVATIONS (75) 9981-2378
www.ilhaboipeba.org.br/tassimirim.html

Pousada Vila Sereia $$

Among the most charming guesthouses in Boipeba, this one has only four wooden bungalows, which are spacious and airy, and enjoy sea views. ACCOMMODATIONS 4; minibar; veranda with hammock; ceiling fan. FACILITIES AND SERVICES garden with deck chairs. CREDIT CARDS MasterCard
Praia Boca da Barra, no #, Vila Velha Boipeba
TEL and FAX (75) 3653-6045 RESERVATIONS (75) 9967-2878
www.ilhaboipeba.org.br/vilasereia.html

WHERE TO EAT

Mar and Coco $

The house specialty at this simple but pleasant eatery is the moqueca de camarão (shrimp stew) with plantains. CUISINE Regional; fish and seafood. CREDIT CARDS Not accepted
Praia de Moreré, no #
TEL (75) 3653-6013 OPEN Daily, 10am – 5pm

Santa Clara $

An interesting option in the village of Boipeba, this eatery is run by American Mark Levitan, who prepares dishes based on which ingredients are available each day. CUISINE Regional; fish and seafood; diverse. CREDIT CARDS Visa
Praia Boca da Barra, 5
TEL (75) 3653-6085 OPEN Tue – Sun, 6pm – 10pm

Ilha de Marajó – Pará

AREA CODE 91 POPULATION 377,039 DISTANCE Belém 80 kilometers (50 miles) ACCESS By boat from the Belém port to the Câmara port or by ferryboat from Icoaraci

WHERE TO STAY

Marajó Park Resort $$$$

Accessible only by plane (a 50 minute flight from Belém), this well-equipped hotel occupies 38,000 hectares (94 acres) on Ilha Mexiana, an island 190 kilometers (118 miles) from Belém. ACCOMMODATIONS 80; air-conditioning; minibar. FACILITIES AND SERVICES bar; beach-side service; bike and boat hire; conference room; fishing lake; games room; landing strip; laundry; paddleboat hire; pool; restaurant; telephone; transport to airport; TV; 24-hour room service. CREDIT CARDS Visa
Ilha Mexiana
TEL (91) 3244-4613 (Fontur)
www.marajoparkresort.com.br

Pousada dos Guarás $

This guesthouse has a large natural area with direct access to Grande Beach. ACCOMMODATIONS 50; air-conditioning; minibar; telephone; TV. FACILITIES AND SERVICES bar; beachside service; conference room; games room; hiking and adventure sports instructors; horses; massage room; playground; pool; restaurant; soccer field; transport to airport; volleyball court. CREDIT CARDS AmEx; Diners; MasterCard; Visa
Avenida Beira-mar, no #, Salvaterra, Praia Grande (access at Km 24 on Rodovia PA-154)
TEL (91) 3765-1149 RESERVATIONS (91) 4005-5656
www.pousadadosguaras.com.br

Ilha Grande – Rio de Janeiro

AREA CODE 24 DISTANCE Rio de Janeiro 170 kilometers (106 miles) ACCESS Highway BR-101 (Rodovia Rio–Santos) from Rio de Janeiro to Angra dos Reis. From there, it is another hour and a half by boat

WHERE TO STAY

Pousada Sankay $$$

This waterfront guesthouse is surrounded by Atlantic forest and waterfalls and is a great place for diving. Close in June. ACCOMMODATIONS 12; air-conditioning; ceiling fan; minibar; private safe; TV. FACILITIES AND SERVICES bar; beach; boat; deck; exchange service; fishing equipment; games room; gym; kayaks; library; marina; motorboat; parking; playground; pool; restaurant; sauna; snack bar; store; trails; valet service; video room; walking tours; waterfall; woods. CREDIT CARDS Visa
Enseada do Bananal
TEL (24) 3365-1090 RESERVATIONS (24) 3365-4065
www.pousadasankay.com.br

Sítio do Lobo $$$

The rooms of this old seaside coffee plantation have ocean views. Also facing the sea is an inviting pool, a deck with tables, and a tent filled with cushions. The ACCOMMODATIONS 9; air-conditioning; minibar; private safe. FACILITIES AND SERVICES bar; boat; fishing equipment; games room; Internet access; jet-ski; kayaks; massage room; motorboat; pool; restaurant; sauna; trails; transport to Angra dos Reis and Rio de Janeiro; TV room; volleyball court; walking tours; water skiing.
Enseada das Estrelas, Ponta dos Lobos
TEL (24) 3361-4438, (21) 2267-7841, 2227-4139
www.sitiodolobo.com.br

WHERE TO EAT

Lua e Mar $

This unadorned restaurant serves one of the best shrimp moquecas on the island. The tables are set out under a large tree. CUISINE Fish and seafood. CREDIT CARDS Diners; MasterCard; Visa
Rua da Praia, no #, Praia do Abraão
TEL (24) 3361-5113. Thu – Tue, 10am – 10pm

Reis e Magos $$

This charming seaside restaurant and artist's studio is carefully decorated in a rustic style. The specialties are the shrimp and seafood moquecas and the paella. CUISINE Fish and seafood. CREDIT CARDS Not accepted
Entrada do Saco do Céu, no #,
Enseada das Estrelas
TEL (24) 3367-2812, 9979-0897, 9827-9142. Daily, 1pm – 6pm

SERVICES

Boat hire – Associação dos Barqueiros de Ilha Grande

Rua da Praia, no #, Abraão
TEL (24) 3361-5920. Daily, 8:30am – 11am and 4pm – 10pm

Tour operator – Sudoeste SW

Boat trips; hikes; canoeing excursions.
Rua da Praia, 647, Casa 5, Abraão
TEL (24) 3361-5516. Daily, 9am – 6pm

RESTAURANTS $ up to R$ 50 $$ from R$ 51 up to R$ 100 $$$ from R$ 101 up to R$ 150 $$$$ above R$ 150

Ilhabela – São Paulo

AREA CODE 12 **POPULATION** 23,886 **DISTANCE** São Paulo, 224 kilometers (139 miles) **ACCESS** Highway BR-116 (Rodovia Presidente Dutra) or SP-070 (Rodovia Ayrton Senna/ Carvalho Pinto) from São Paulo, followed by Highway SP-099 (Rodovia Tamoios) to São Sebastião, where you must take a ferry to the island (20 min.)

WHERE TO STAY

Porto Pacuíba Hotel $$
This environmentally friendly hotel was designed in such a way as to leave the existing trees untouched. Trash is separated for recycling, and there is a small water-treatment station. **ACCOMMODATIONS** 20; air-conditioning; ceiling fan; pay TV; phone. **FACILITIES AND SERVICES** bar; beachside service; games room; massage room; pool; restaurant; sauna; wine cellar. **CREDIT CARDS** AmEx; MasterCard; Visa
Avenida Leonardo Reale, 2,392, Viana
TEL and **FAX** (12) 3896-2466 www.portopacuiba.com.br

Pousada Canto da Praia $$$$
This guesthouse operates in a beautiful house with uniquely decorated rooms. Children under the age of 16 and pets are not allowed. **ACCOMMODATIONS** 8; air-conditioning; ceiling fan; pay TV (except in 2 rooms). **FACILITIES AND SERVICES** beachside service; bicycles; gym; kayaks; pool; reading room. **CREDIT CARDS** Not accepted
Avenida Força Expedicionária Brasileira, 793, Praia de Santa Teresa
TEL (12) 3896-1194 **FAX** (12) 3896-6415
www.cantodapraiailhabela.com.br

Pousada do Capitão $$
Located near the main village, this traditional guesthouse has comfortable rooms that look like a ship's cabins. **ACCOMMODATIONS** 21; air-conditioning; pay TV; phone. **FACILITIES AND SERVICES** bar; games room; gym; jacuzzi; pool; sauna; TV room. **CREDIT CARDS** AmEx; Diners; MasterCard; Visa
Rua Almirante Tamandaré, 272, Praia de Itaguaçu
TEL (12) 3896-1037 **FAX** (12) 3896-2253
www.pousadadocapitao.com.br

WHERE TO EAT

Deck $$$
This restaurant operates out of an airy two-story house that faces the beach. Try the camarão ilhabela, which is shrimp in manioc sauce and accompanied by tiny manioc fritters and grilled mango. **CUISINE** Seafood; pizza; various. **CREDIT CARDS** AmEx; Diners; MasterCard; Visa
Avenida Almirante Tamandaré, 805, Praia de Itaguaçu
TEL (12) 3896-1489. Daily, noon – until the last customer leaves (high season); Thu – Mon, noon – midnight (low season)

Ponto das Letras $
A cross between a bookstore and a cafeteria, this is the place for delicious banana pie, and chocolate mousse cake, as well as sandwiches, quiches, and pastry turnovers. **CUISINE** Coffee; sweets; savory snacks. **CREDIT CARDS** AmEx; Diners; MasterCard; Visa
Rua Dr. Carvalho, 146, Centro
TEL (12) 3896-2104. Daily, 9:30am – midnight (high season); Mon – Thu, 10am – 8pm; Fri, 10am – 11:30pm; Sat, 10am – midnight; Sun, 10am – 10:30pm

Viana $$$
This simple, bustling restaurant serves up delicious dishes that are worth waiting in the queues. Try the grilled shrimp with mango risotto. **CUISINE** Fish and seafood. **CREDIT CARDS** Not accepted
Avenida Leonardo Reale, 1,560, Praia do Viana
TEL (12) 3896-1089. Daily, 1pm – 11pm (high season); Mon – Thu, 1pm – 11pm (low season)

SERVICES

Ferry – Travessia de balsa
TEL (13) 3358-2741. The ferry functions day and night and typically leaves every 20 minutes, though on slow nights it doesn't run as often. The crossing lasts approximately 20 minutes. To avoid queues, you can book in advance on tel. (13) 3358-2743, 3358-3088, 3358-2277, although the ticket costs more.

Tourist information – Posto de Informações Turísticas
Rua Dr. Carvalho, no #, Centro (next to Píer Pizza)
TEL (12) 3896-3777. Daily, 9am – 10pm

Ilhéus – Bahia

AREA CODE 73 **POPULATION** 221,110 **DISTANCES** Salvador 462 kilometers (287 miles), Vitória da Conquista 270 kilometers (168 miles), Porto Seguro 318 kilometers (198 miles) **ACCESS** Highway BA-001

WHERE TO STAY

Cana Brava Resort $$$$
Located on a 17-square-hectare (42-acre) property on Canabrava Beach, this resort has good facilities. The resort's distance from town – 30-odd kilometers (19 miles) – may be inconvenient. **ACCOMMODATIONS** 170; air-conditioning; private safe; minibar; telephone; cable TV. **FACILITIES AND SERVICES** Internet access; bar; bicycles; kayaks; soccer field; parking; snack bar; convenience store; pool; tennis court; volleyball court; restaurant; river; conference room; gym; games room; massage room; beauty parlor; sauna; walking trails; travel agency; car rental; recreational teams for adults and children; guided walking tours; lifeguards; beach service; airport shuttle; transport to attractions. **CREDIT CARDS** AmEx; Diners; MasterCard; Visa
Rodovia Ilhéus–Canavieiras, kilometer 24
TEL (73) 3269-8000 www.canabravaresort.com.br

Hotel Fazenda da Lagoa $$$$
Between the sea and the Aliança River, next to mangrove swamps, this isolated hotel is sophisticated but not flashy. Its décor includes arts and crafts, antiques, and 19th-century furniture from Tiradentes, in the state of Minas Gerais. **ACCOMMODATIONS** 14; air-conditioning; private safe; minibar; telephone; cable TV. **FACILITIES AND SERVICES** bar; library; bicycles; kayaks; fishing lake; convenience store; pool; restaurant; massage room; games room; sauna; beach service; airport shuttle. **CREDIT CARDS** Visa
Rodovia Una–Ilhéus, Km 18, Região da Dependência
TEL (73) 3236-6046, 3236-6137
RESERVATIONS (21) 2259-8511
www.fazendadalagoa.com.br

Transamérica Ilha de Comandatuba $$$$
One of the best in Brazil, this resort stands on an enormous property with big gardens, mangrove swamps,

PRICES	HOTELS (couple)	$ up to R$ 150	$$ from R$ 151 up to R$ 300	$$$ from R$ 301 up to R$500	$$$$ above R$ 500

500

BRAZIL GUIDE

and impressive facilities, including those for sporting activities. It has rooms, suites, and bungalows. Beauty treatments are available at the L'Occitane spa. **ACCOMMODATIONS** 363; Internet access; air-conditioning; private safe; minibar; jacuzzi in the suites and luxury bungalows; telephone; cable TV. **FACILITIES AND SERVICES** Internet access; wine cellar; archery; bar; boat; bicycles; kayaks; soccer field; golf course; fishing equipment; water skiing; parking; jet-ski; motorboat; snack bar; stores; marina; ocean fishing; pool; playground; six-a-side soccer court; squash court; tennis court; volleyball court; restaurant; magazine reading area; river; conference room; gym; games room; massage room; video room; beauty parlor; sauna; spa; baby-sitter; business center; currency exchange bureau; 24-hour kitchen; recreational teams for adults and children; guided walking tours; beach service; airport shuttle. **CREDIT CARDS** AmEx; Diners; MasterCard; Visa
Ilha de Comandatuba, no #
TEL (73) 3686-1122 **FAX** (73) 3686-1457
RESERVATIONS 0800-126060   www.transamerica.com.br

WHERE TO EAT

Boca du Mar $
Facing Pontal Bay, this large, pleasant restaurant is a great place to try a badejo na chapa (hot-plate sizzled grouper) with vegetables, tasty arroz de polvo (octopus rice), or sushi and sashimi. **CUISINE** Fish and seafood. **CREDIT CARDS** AmEx; Diners; MasterCard; Visa
Avenida Lomanto Junior, 15, Pontal
TEL (73) 3231-2822 **OPEN** High season: Fri and Sat, 6pm – 2am; Sun, 11:30am – midnight; low season: Tue – Sun, noon – 2am

Cabana Gabriela $
House specialties include peixe à Gabriela (whole fried fish with shrimp in garlic and oil, served with farofa (manioc flour), fried potatoes, and salad) and moqueca de camarão (shrimp stew). **CUISINE** Fish and seafood. **CREDIT CARDS** AmEx; Diners; MasterCard; Visa
Rua Rui Penalva, 109, Centro
TEL (73) 3632-1836 **RESERVATIONS** (73) 3231-7373 **OPEN** Daily, 8am – 8pm

SERVICES

Airport – Aeroporto Jorge Amado
Rua Brigadeiro Eduardo Gomes, no #, Pontal
TEL (73) 3234-4000 **OPEN** Daily, 6am – 11pm

Travel Agency and Guides – NV Turismo
Avenida Lamant Junior, 1384, Pontal
TEL (73) 3634-4101, 3633-3331 **OPEN** Mon – Fri, 8:30am – 6pm; Sat, 8:30am – noon www.nvturismo.com.br

Tourist Information – Bahiatursa
Rua Eustáquio Bastos, 308, Centro
TEL (73) 3231-8679 **OPEN** Mon – Fri, 8am – noon and 2pm – 5pm

Tourist Information – Posto de Informações Turísticas
Praça da Catedral (booth)
TEL None **OPEN** Mon – Fri, 8am – 6pm

Itacaré – Bahia

AREA CODE 73 **POPULATION** 17,925 **DISTANCES** Salvador 440 kilometers (273 miles), Ilhéus 65 kilometers (40 miles) **ACCESS** From Ilhéus, on Highway BA-001 (Rodovia Ilhéus–

Itacaré/Estrada Parque). From Salvador, go south on Highway BR-101, then take the road to Uruçuca and Rodovia Ilhéus–Itacaré

WHERE TO STAY

Itacaré Eco Resort $$$$
This resort keeps a reserve with some animals, including capybaras and alligators. The rooms are all of the same design, with views of the mangrove swamp and Atlantic forest. **ACCOMMODATIONS** 25; air-conditioning; private safe; minibar; jacuzzi; telephone; cable TV; veranda. **FACILITIES AND SERVICES** Internet access; wine cellar; bar; woods; kayaks; soccer field; horses; parking; snack bar; stores; pool; natural pool; restaurant; river; conference room; gym; games room; massage room; video room; sauna; walking trails; travel agency; business center; lifeguards; beach service; airport shuttle; transport to attractions. **CREDIT CARDS** AmEx; Diners; MasterCard; Visa
Rodovia Ilhéus–Itacaré, BA-001, Km 65
TEL (73) 3251-2151 **FAX** and **RESERVATIONS** (73) 3251-3133
www.ier.com.br

Pousada Shambhala $$
On the banks of the Contas River, this new guesthouse is ideal for couples and is also popular among the LGBT crowd. The suites have four-poster beds, DVD players and views of the river. Breakfast, included in the room rate, is served until noon. **ACCOMMODATIONS** 7 (6 suites, 1 cabana); air-conditioning; DVD player; minibar; jacuzzi in one suite; telephone; cable TV; ceiling fan. **FACILITIES AND SERVICES** Internet access; bar; parking; pool; beauty parlor. **CREDIT CARDS** AmEx; Diners; MasterCard; Visa
Rua Magali, 102, Passagem
TEL (73) 3251-2541 www.itacaregls.com.br

Txai Resort $$$$
One of the best in Itacaré, this charming hotel occupies an old cacao farm that covers 100 hectares (nearly 250 acres). It has well decorated bungalows with privileged views. **ACCOMMODATIONS** 40; air-conditioning; CD player; private safe; minibar; jacuzzi in 4 bungalows; telephone. **FACILITIES AND SERVICES** Internet access; bar; bicycles; parking; stores; pool; tennis court; restaurant; games room; video room; sauna; spa; walking trails; travel agency; 24-hour kitchen; guided walking tours; lifeguards; beach service; airport shuttle; transport to attractions. **CREDIT CARDS** AmEx; Diners; MasterCard; Visa
Rodovia Itacaré–Ilhéus, BA-001, Km 48, Praia de Itacarezinho
TEL and **FAX** (73) 3634-6936 **RESERVATIONS** (73) 6858-7777
www.txai.com.br

Vila do Dengo $$
Inaugurated in 2006, this hotel has courteous service and is well located near the urban beaches and downtown Itacaré. All rooms have DVD players and verandas. **ACCOMMODATIONS** 22 (21 rooms, 1 master suite); air-conditioning; DVD player; minibar; cable TV; veranda. **FACILITIES AND SERVICES** Internet access; bar; parking; jacuzzi; pool; squash court; sauna. **CREDIT CARDS** MasterCard; Visa
Condomínio Conchas do Mar II, Quadra C, Lote 2, Nova Concha
TEL (73) 3251-3098, 3251-2750 **FAX** (73) 3251-3098
www.viladodengo.com.br

WHERE TO EAT

Boca de Forno $
Thin-crust pizzas are served on iron or rock platters. We

RESTAURANTS	$ up to R$ 50	$$ from R$ 51 up to R$ 100	$$$ from R$ 101 up to R$ 150	$$$$ above R$ 150

suggest the boca de forno (palm heart, Calabrese sausage, mozzarella, crunchy garlic, and sun-dried tomatoes). CUISINE Pizza. CREDIT CARDS AmEx; Diners; MasterCard; Visa
Rua Lodônio Almeida, 108, Centro
TEL (73) 3251-3121 OPEN Mon – Thu, 5pm – midnight; Fri – Sun, 5pm – 1am

Casa Sapucaia $

This cozy restaurant has modern dishes with an Asian touch. We suggest the camarão da ilha (grilled prawns on a skewer with caramelized ginger and lemon, served with sautéed vegetables and rice). CUISINE Asian; contemporary; Mediterranean. CREDIT CARDS Visa
Rua Lodônio Almeida, 84, Centro
TEL (73) 3251-3091 OPEN Mon – Sat, 6pm – 11:30pm

Dedo de Moça $

This well decorated restaurant with a terrace serves bobó de camarão (shrimp and manioc stew), peixe com castanha (fish with nuts) and medalhão ao vinho tinto (medallions in red wine). CUISINE Contemporary. CREDIT CARDS AmEx; Diners; MasterCard; Visa
Rua Plínio Soares, 26, Centro
TEL (73) 3251-3372 OPEN High season: daily, 4pm – midnight; low season: daily, 7pm – 11pm

Estrela do Mar $

This restaurant is airy and informal, with a view over Concha Beach. The menu includes dishes such as camarão com molho de maracujá (shrimp in passion fruit sauce) and filé de peixe (fish fillets) with tapioca and seafood. CUISINE Regional; fish and seafood; diverse. CREDIT CARDS Diners; MasterCard; Visa
Praia da Concha, no #, Aldeia do Mar Chalets
TEL (73) 3251-2230 OPEN Daily, 7am – 10pm

SERVICES

Bus Station – Rodoviária
Rua Joaquim Vieira, no #, Centro
TEL (73) 3251-2200 (public phone) OPEN Daily, 5am – 10pm

Surf School – Easy Drop Surf Camp
Rua João Coutinho, 140, Centro
TEL (73) 3251-3065 FAX (73) 3251-2078 OPEN Mon – Fri, 8am – noon and 2pm – 6pm; Sat; 8am – noon
www.easydrop.com

Travel Agency and Guides – Eco Trip Viagens and Turismo
Rua João Coutinho, 235, Centro
TEL (73) 3251-2191 OPEN Mon – Sat, 8am – noon and 4pm – 8pm; Sun, 8am – noon and 5pm – 9pm
www.ecotrip.tur.br

Travel Agency and Guides – Itacaré Ecoturismo
Rua Lodônio Almeida, 117, Centro
TEL (73) 3251-3666, 9996-1975 OPEN Mon – Sat, 8am – noon and 2pm – 9pm; Sun, 8am – 10am and 6pm – 9pm www.itacare.com.br

Travel Agency and Guides – NV Turismo
Rua Pedro Longo, 520-A, Pituba
TEL (73) 3251-2039, 9199-2227 OPEN Daily, 8am – 7pm
www.nvturismo.com.br

Itatiaia – Rio de Janeiro

AREA CODE 24 POPULATION 31,185 DISTANCES Rio de Janeiro 167 kilometers (104 miles), São Paulo 265 kilometers (165 miles) ACCESS Highway BR-116 (Rodovia Presidente Dutra) from Rio or São Paulo

WHERE TO STAY

Hotel Donati $$
Located inside Itatiaia National Park, the Donati offers chalets and a leisure area with two swimming pools (a covered heated one and one with unheated water). ACCOMMODATIONS 23; fireplace; jacuzzi (in 3 chalets); minibar; phone; private safe; TV. FACILITIES AND SERVICES bar; business center; function room; games room; Internet access; natural and thermal pools; parking; playground; reading room; recreational staff for adults and children (high season); restaurant; river; sauna; soccer field; trails; volleyball court; walking tours; waterfall; wine cellar; woods. CREDIT CARDS AmEx; Diners; MasterCard; Visa
Estrada do Parque Nacional, Km 9.5
TEL and FAX (24) 3352-1110, 3352-1509
www.hoteldonati.com.br

Hotel Pousada Esmeralda $$
Nestled in the national park, this hotel has four types of chalets. The deluxe ones have fireplaces, and the double deluxe ones face onto the lake. ACCOMMODATIONS 12; air-conditioning; ceiling fan; fireplace; minibar; phone; private safe; TV. FACILITIES AND SERVICES bar; fishing equipment and lake; games room; heated pool; horses; Internet access; natural pool; massage room; parking; playground; recreational team for children (during the holidays); restaurant; river; sauna; store. CREDIT CARDS AmEx; Diners; MasterCard; Visa
Estrada do Parque Nacional, Km 4
TEL (24) 3352-1643 FAX (24) 3352-1769
www.pousadaesmeralda.com.br

Itaúnas – Espírito Santo

AREA CODE 27 DISTANCE Vitória 273 kilometers (170 miles), Conceição da Barra 19 kilometers (12 miles) ACCESS Highway BR-101 from Vitória, heading north. After São Mateus, take Highway ES-421 toward Conceição da Barra. Drive for 14 kilometers (9 miles) to the turnoff for the ES-010 and go another 23 kilometers (14 miles) on dirt road to Itaúnas

WHERE TO STAY

Casarão Parque de Itaúnas $
This guesthouse enjoys a quiet location amidst trees and lawns. Guests can choose a large, basic room with either air-conditioning or a ceiling fan. ACCOMMODATIONS 12; air-conditioning; ceiling fan; minibar; TV; veranda with hammock. FACILITIES AND SERVICES barbecue facilities; parking; playground; pool; volleyball court. CREDIT CARDS MasterCard
Estrada de Itaúnas, Km 20
TEL and FAX (27) 3762-5000, 3762-1754
www.itaunas.com.br

Pousada Sol de Itaúnas $
The former Pousada do Coelho recently changed hands and underwent renovations. It still occupies a large, leafy-green area on the riverbank. ACCOMMODATIONS 10, air-conditioning; ceiling fan; minibar; TV. FACILITIES AND

| PRICES | HOTELS (couple) | $ up to R$ 150 | $$ from R$ 151 up to R$ 300 | $$$ from R$ 301 up to R$500 | $$$$ above R$ 500 |

502   BRAZIL GUIDE

SERVICES bar; barbecue facilities; pool. **CREDIT CARDS** Not accepted
Rua Projetada, no #
TEL (27) 3762-5216, 9966-3060 **FAX** (27) 3314-2537
www.solardeitaunas.com.br

SERVICES

Travel agency – Casinha de Aventuras
Avenida José Basílio, no # (formerly Bento Daher), Centro
TEL (27) 3762-5081. Daily, 9am – 8pm (Dec. – Feb., plus July and holidays) and 9am – noon (the rest of the year)

Jacumã – Paraíba

AREA CODE 83 **DISTANCES** João Pessoa 29 kilometers (18 miles), Recife 121 kilometers (75 miles) **ACCESS** From João Pessoa or Pitimbu, on Highway PB-008

WHERE TO STAY

Hotel Pousada Conchas $
This small, cozy guesthouse has simple rooms and chalets facing onto a swimming pool. The bar and restaurant are on a kind of deck that juts out over the beach, with a beautiful view. **ACCOMMODATIONS** 25; air-conditioning; minibar; TV. **FACILITIES AND SERVICES** Internet access; bar; parking; pool; playground; restaurant; games room; guided walking tours; beach service; airport shuttle; transport to attractions. **CREDIT CARDS** Visa
Rua Projetada, no #, Praia de Tabatinga
TEL (83) 3290-1303 www.conchashotel.com.br

WHERE TO EAT

Canyon do Coqueirinho $
This large, comfortable restaurant has tables on a spacious terrace overlooking the ocean. The moqueca de polvo (octopus stew) is light, and arrives at the table piping hot. **CUISINE** Fish and seafood. **CREDIT CARDS** MasterCard; Visa
Praia de Coqueirinho, no #
TEL (83) 9309-1990 **RESERVATIONS** (83) 9134-1414 **OPEN** Daily, 9am – 5pm

Terraço Tropical $
This rustic, seaside eatery is very welcoming. The Highlight is the filé de peixe terraço tropical (fish fillets with shrimp, grilled fruits, and white sauce). **CUISINE** Pasta; fish and seafood. **CREDIT CARDS** MasterCard
Praia de Carapibus, no # (just off Rodovia PB-008)
TEL (83) 9128-0404 **OPEN** Daily, 11am – 10pm

SERVICES

Bus Station – Rodoviária (João Pessoa)
Rua Francisco Londres, no #, Varadouro
TEL (83) 3221-9611 **OPEN** Mon – Fri, 8am – noon and 2pm – 6pm

Jalapão – Tocantins

AREA CODE 63 **DISTANCE** Palmas 250 kilometers (155 miles) **ACCESS** From Palmas to Ponte Alta do Tocantins on Highway TO-050 (toward Monte do Carmo) and TO-255, followed by dirt road with several areas of soft sand, which make a 4×4 vehicle necessary

WHERE TO STAY

Pousada Planalto $
This small guesthouse faces onto the main square of Ponte Alta do Tocantins, in front of the church. The busiest time of year is during July, when beaches appear along the rivers of Tocantins as the waters recede. **ACCOMMODATIONS** 13; air-conditioning; minibar; TV. **FACILITIES AND SERVICES** bar; Internet access; outings with guides; restaurant; transport to airport. **CREDIT CARDS** Not accepted
Praça Capitão Antônio Mascarenhas, 438, Centro, Ponte Alta do Tocantins
TEL (63) 3378-1141 **FAX** (63) 3378-1170

WHERE TO EAT

Panela de Ferro $
Located in Mateiros, this is a good option for homemade food. It serves only rice, beans salad, and meat. Bookings required. **CUISINE** Brazilian. **CREDIT CARDS** Not accepted
Avenida Tocantins, Quadra 7, Lote 15, Centro, Mateiros
TEL (63) 3534-1038. Daily, 11:30am – 2:30pm and 6:30pm – 9pm

SERVICES

Rafting expeditions – 4 Elementos
Rodovia das Cataratas, Km 27.5, Parque Nacional do Iguaçu (in Foz do Iguaçu, Paraná)
TEL (45) 3529-6040. Daily, 9am – 5:30pm.
www.4elementos.tur.br

Camping Expeditions in Jalapão – Korubo Expedições
Avenida 11 de Junho, 625, Apto 35, Vila Clementino (in São Paulo, São Paulo)
TEL (11) 3582-6968. Mon – Fri, 9:30am – 6pm.
www.korubo.com.br

Jericoacoara – Ceará

AREA CODE 88 **DISTANCE** Fortaleza 300 kilometers (186 miles) **ACCESS** Approximately 20 kilometers (12 miles) of rough road, by bus, buggy, or 4×4 vehicle from the neighboring town of Jijoca, which one gets to from Fortaleza, on Highway CE-085 (Rodovia Estruturante)

WHERE TO STAY

Mosquito Blue $$
The rooms are situated around a garden and a beautiful swimming pool with a deck, and they have direct access to the beach. The upstairs rooms are slightly more private and have better views. **ACCOMMODATIONS** 43; air-conditioning; private safe; minibar; telephone; cable TV. **FACILITIES AND SERVICES** Internet access; bar; jacuzzi; pool; restaurant; gym; games room; sauna; beach service. **CREDIT CARDS** AmEx; Diners; MasterCard; Visa
Rua Ismael, no # (the street where the pharmacy is)
TEL (88) 3669-2203 **FAX** (88) 3669-2204
www.mosquitoblue.com.br

Pousada Sítio Verde $$
This guesthouse is popular among nautical sports enthusiasts and has a place to store equipment. Luckily, it sits on the edge of Paraíso Lake, which is good for windsurfing. **ACCOMMODATIONS** 5; air-conditioning; minibar.

RESTAURANTS	**$** up to R$ 50	**$$** from R$ 51 up to R$ 100	**$$$** from R$ 101 up to R$ 150	**$$$$** above R$ 150

FACILITIES AND SERVICES wine cellar; bar; parking; volley-ball court; restaurant; gym; games room; beach service.
CREDIT CARDS Visa
Córrego do Urubu, no #, Lagoa do Paraíso
TEL (88) 3669-1151 www.jericoacoara.tur.br/sitioverde

Pousada Vento Leste $$$
The beach is half a kilometer (about 500 yards) away, but there is a large swimming pool and a gym on the premises. **ACCOMMODATIONS** 8; Internet access; air-conditioning; private safe; DVD player and jacuzzis in some suites; minibar; telephone; cable TV; ceiling fan. **FACILITIES AND SERVICES** Internet access; bar; jacuzzi; pool; restaurant; gym; games room; sauna; spa; pool service; airport shuttle. **CREDIT CARDS** MasterCard; Visa
Rua Nova Jeri, no #, Centro
TEL (88) 3669-2274 **FAX** (88) 3669-2178
www.pousadaventoleste.tur.br

Vila Kalango $$
The chic yet rustic style of this restaurant suits the Jeri atmosphere. The bungalows and rooms have beach access. There are mini-decks with hammocks, huge cushions, and mats. **ACCOMMODATIONS** 18; Internet access; minibar; ceiling fan. **FACILITIES AND SERVICES** bar; library; parking; pool; restaurant; games room; massage room; video room; beach service. **CREDIT CARDS** Diners; MasterCard; Visa
Rua das Dunas, 30, Centro
TEL (88) 3669-2290 **FAX** (88) 3669-2291
www.vilakalango.com.br

WHERE TO EAT

Azul do Mar $
Facing Jangadas Port, the most urban part of Preá Beach, this restaurant serves freshly caught fish. **CUISINE** Fish and seafood. **CREDIT CARDS** Not accepted
Avenida Beira-mar, no #, Vila Preá (municipality of Cruz, 12 kilometers (7 miles) from Jericoacoara)
TEL (88) 3660-3062 **OPEN** Daily, noon – 6pm

Carcará $$
This eatery is small and simple. Try the lagosta tropical (lobster done on a hotplate) with fresh fruit. **CUISINE** Seafood; regional; diverse. **CREDIT CARDS** Diners; MasterCard; Visa
Rua do Forró, no #, Centro
TEL (88) 3669-2013 **OPEN** Mon – Sat, noon – 11pm; Sun, 6pm – 11pm

Chocolate $
This beachside restaurant enjoys a beautiful view of the ocean. There are good risotto, pasta, and salad options. Booking required. **CUISINE** Diverse. **CREDIT CARDS** Diners; MasterCard; Visa
Rua do Forró, 213, Centro
TEL (88) 3669-2190 **RESERVATIONS** (88) 9611-2344 **OPEN** Daily, 4pm until the last customer leaves

SERVICES

Tourist Information –
Posto de Informações Turísticas
Avenida Manoel Marques, no #
TEL (88) 3669-1546, 9903-7522 **OPEN** Daily, 7:30am – 11:30am and 1:30pm – 5:30pm

Jijoca de Jericoacoara – Ceará
(see Jericoacoara)

João Pessoa – Paraíba
AREA CODE 83 **POPULATION** 660,798 **DISTANCES** Recife 120 kilometers (75 miles), Natal 180 kilometers (112 miles)
ACCESS From Recife or Natal, on Highway BR-101
www.joaopessoa.pb.gov.br

WHERE TO STAY

Hardman Praia $$
The rooms here were originally serviced flats. All have open kitchens and sober décor that includes bedspreads in pastel tones and furniture in light-colored wood. **ACCOMMODATIONS** 110; Internet access; air-conditioning; private safe; minibar; telephone; cable TV. **FACILITIES AND SERVICES** Internet access; bar; parking; pool; playground; restaurant; conference room; gym; games room; sauna; travel agency; business center; 24-hour kitchen; valet parking; beach service. **CREDIT CARDS** AmEx; Diners; MasterCard; Visa
Avenida João Maurício, 1341, Praia de Manaíra
TEL (83) 3246-8811 www.hotelhardman.com.br

Pouso das Águas $
The charm of this hotel is its simplicity. A framed drawing by world-renowned landscape artist Roberto Burle Marx welcomes visitors to the sitting room. **ACCOMMODATIONS** 24; air-conditioning; minibar; telephone; TV. **FACILITIES AND SERVICES** parking; pool; airport shuttle; transport to attractions. **CREDIT CARDS** AmEx; Diners; MasterCard; Visa
Avenida Cabo Branco, 2348, Cabo Branco
TEL (83) 3226-5103 www.pousodasaguas.com.br

Tropical Tambaú $$
This charming hotel built in 1971 has aged well. The doors to the rooms open onto inner patios, an oval swimming pool, and children's playgrounds. Some face the ocean. **ACCOMMODATIONS** 175; air-conditioning; private safe; minibar; jacuzzi in the suites; garden; telephone; cable TV. **FACILITIES AND SERVICES** Internet access; bar; parking; stores; pool; playground; tennis court; restaurant; conference room; gym; games room; massage room; video room; beauty parlor; sauna; travel agency; car rental; business center; 24-hour kitchen; recreational teams for adults and children; valet parking; beach service. **CREDIT CARDS** AmEx; Diners; MasterCard; Visa
Avenida Almirante Tamandaré, 229, Tambaú
TEL (83) 2107-1900 **FAX** (83) 3247-1070 **RESERVATIONS** 0800-7012670 www.tropicalhotel.com.br

WHERE TO EAT

Adega do Alfredo $
The house specialty, bacalhau com batatas ao murro (codfish with baked potatoes), speaks to this eatery's Portuguese influences. There are also Mediterranean dishes, such as paella. **CUISINE** Fish and seafood; diverse. **CREDIT CARDS** AmEx; Visa
Rua Coração de Jesus, no #, Tambaú
TEL (83) 3226-4346 **RESERVATIONS** (83) 3226-3354 **OPEN** Tue – Sun, noon – 4pm and 7pm – midnight; Mon, 7pm – midnight

Badionaldo $
Housed in a kind of warehouse, this eatery has been serving tasty peixada de cavala (mackerel stew) since the late 1950s. The short menu lists fish and seafood dishes made with finesse. **CUISINE** Fish and seafood. **CREDIT CARDS** Visa

PRICES	**HOTELS** (couple)	$ up to R$ 150	$$ from R$ 151 up to R$ 300	$$$ from R$ 301 up to R$500	$$$$ above R$ 500

Rua Vitorino Cardoso, no #, Praia do Poço, Cabedelo
TEL (83) 3250-1299 OPEN Mon, noon – 3pm; Tue – Sat, noon – 9:30pm; Sun, noon – 6pm

Casa do Bacalhau $

The house specialty here is the Portuguese bacalhau alto (thickly sliced barbecued cod, in olive oil, garlic and onion, accompanied by rice and baked potatoes). There is a good wine list. CUISINE Fish and seafood; Portuguese; diverse. CREDIT CARDS Diners; MasterCard; Visa
Avenida Franca Filho, 52, Monaíra
TEL (83) 3247-6775 OPEN Daily, noon – 3:30pm and 6pm – 11pm.

Mangai $

This backlands-style eatery serves over 70 dishes. The rubacão or baião-de-dois (rice and bean mush) and sovaco-de-cobra (ground beef jerky with corn) are tasty options. CUISINE Regional. CREDIT CARDS MasterCard; Visa
Avenida Edson Ramalho, 696, Manaíra
TEL (83) 3226-1615 fax (83) 3247-5840 OPEN Tue – Sun, 7am – 10pm

Porto Madero $

This restaurant serves seafood, poultry, meats (such as rack of lamb), and sushi and sashimi out of a beautiful house with a garden. CUISINE International; diverse. CREDIT CARDS AmEx; Diners; MasterCard; Visa
Rua Antônio Carlos Araújo, 60, Cabo Branco
TEL (83) 3247-1594 OPEN Tue – Fri, 11:30am – 4pm and 6:30pm – 1am; Sat, 6:30pm – 1am; Sun, 11:30am – 4pm

SERVICES

Airport – Aeroporto Internacional Presidente Castro Pinto

Aeroporto Internacional Presidente Castro Pinto, Bayeux
TEL (83) 3041-4200 OPEN Daily, 24 hours

Bus Station – Rodoviária

Rua Francisco Londres, no #, Varadouro
TEL (83) 3221-9611

Tourist Information – Posto de Informações Turísticas

Avenida Almirante Tamandaré, 100, Tambaú
TEL (83) 3214-8279, 3214-8270, 0800-2819229 OPEN Daily, 8am – 7pm www.paraiba.pb.gov.br/pbtur

Tourist Information – Posto de Informações Turísticas (Bus Station)

Rua Francisco Londres, no #, Varadouro
TEL (83) 3218-6655 OPEN Mon – Fri, 9am – noon and 2pm – 6pm; Sat, 2pm – 4:30pm

Tourist Police Station – Delegacia de Atendimento ao Turista

Avenida Almirante Tamandaré, 100, Tambaú
TEL (83) 3214-8022, 3214-8023 OPEN Daily, 24 hours

Juazeiro do Norte – Ceará

AREA CODE 88 POPULATION 236,296 DISTANCES Fortaleza 495 kilometers (308 miles), Petrolina 373 kilometers (232 miles), ACCESS From Fortaleza, on Highway BR-116 to Milagres

WHERE TO STAY

Verdes Vales $$

Opened in 1996, this resort is located on a huge farm away from the center of town. The highlight of its leisure options is the water park. ACCOMMODATIONS 97; Internet access; air-conditioning; minibar; telephone; TV. FACILITIES AND SERVICES Internet access; bar; parking; convenience store; water park; pool; playground; six-a-side soccer court; tennis court; volleyball court; restaurant; conference room; gym; games room; beauty parlor; sauna; walking trails; travel agency; business center; valet parking CREDIT CARDS AmEx; Diners; MasterCard; Visa
Avenida Plácido Aderaldo Castelo, no #, Lagoa Seca
TEL (88) 3566-2544 FAX (88) 3566-2500
www.hotelverdesvales.com.br

WHERE TO EAT

Giradouro $

In the middle of the roundabout that links Juazeiro, Crato, and Barbalha, this eatery is famous for its lasanha de frango (chicken lasagna). Another good bet is the peixada cearense (baked mackerel). CUISINE Regional; diverse. CREDIT CARDS Diners; MasterCard; Visa
Praça Feijó de Sá, no #, Triângulo
TEL (88) 3571-2181 RESERVATIONS (88) 9965-0341 OPEN Tue – Sat, 4pm – midnight; Sun, 11am – 11pm

Mão de Vaca $

The tasty regional fare comes in hearty servings. The mão-de-vaca, served only on Saturdays, is baked oxfoot accompanied by couscous, rice, salad, and pirão (gravy thickened with manioc flour). CUISINE Meats; regional. CREDIT CARDS MasterCard; Visa
Rua Rui Barbosa, 25, Santa Teresa
TEL (88) 3512-2543 OPEN Mon – Sat, 11am – 3pm and 5pm – midnight

SERVICES

Airport – Aeroporto Regional do Cariri

Avenida Senador Virgílio Távora, 4000 (6 kilometers, 4 miles, from the downtown area)
TEL (88) 3572-0700, 3572-2118 OPEN Daily, 5am – 11pm

Juréia – São Paulo
(see Peruíbe)

Mangaratiba – Rio de Janeiro

AREA CODE 21 POPULATION 29,253 DISTANCES Rio de Janeiro 100 kilometers (62 miles), Angra dos Reis 54 kilometers (34 miles) ACCESS Highway Rio–Santos (BR-101) from Rio de Janeiro

WHERE TO STAY

Club Med Rio das Pedras $$$

This luxurious resort, named after the beautiful river that crosses the estate, offers complete facilities. Guests can accompany biologists on walks in the adjacent Atlantic forest. ACCOMMODATIONS 324; air-conditioning; Internet access; minibar; phone; pay TV; private safe. FACILITIES AND SERVICES archery; bar; beachside service; beauty parlor; boat; business center; exchange service; function room; games room; gym; Internet access; kayaks; mas-

sage room; nursery; parking; playground; pool; recreational staff for adults and children; restaurant; river; sauna; six-a-side soccer court; spa; squash court; store; tennis court; theater; trails; volleyball court; water skiing; woods. **CREDIT CARDS** AmEx; Diners; MasterCard; Visa
Rodovia Rio–Santos (BR-101), Km 445.5
TEL (21) 2688-9191 **FAX** (21) 2688-3333
RESERVATIONS 0800-7073782 www.clubmed.com

Portobello Resort Safari $$$$
All rooms overlook the sea. The 36 "beach rooms" and 16 "beach suites" each have an exit onto the sands. **ACCOMMODATIONS** 152; air-conditioning; Internet access; minibar; pay TV; private safe; phone. **FACILITIES AND SERVICES** babysitter; bar; beach; beachside service; beach volleyball arena; beauty parlor; bicycles; boat; business center; fishing equipment and lake; function room; games room; gym; heated pool; horses and carriage; Internet access; jacuzzi; jet-ski; kayaks; lifeguard; marina; massage room; motorboat; natural pool; parking; pool; playground; pony; recreational staff for adults and children; restaurant; sauna; spa; soccer field; stores; tennis court; trails; transport to airport and attractions; valet service; video room; walking tours; waterfall; water skiing; wine cellar; woods; 24-hour kitchen. **CREDIT CARDS** AmEx; Diners; MasterCard; Visa
Rodovia Rio–Santos (BR-101), Km 438
TEL (21) 2789-8000 **FAX** (21) 2689-3011
RESERVATIONS 0800-2820868 www.portotel.com.br

Lages – Santa Catarina

AREA CODE 49 **POPULATION** 161,583 **DISTANCE** Florianópolis 250 kilometers (155 miles) **ACCESS** Highway BR-282 from Florianópolis www.lages.sc.gov.br

WHERE TO STAY

Fazenda Pedras Brancas $$$
On an 18-square-kilometer (7-square-mile) property, this farm-hotel offers rural tourism, as well as dance, music, and theater performances that emphasize regional culture. **ACCOMMODATIONS** 30; air-conditioning; central water heating; fireplace (in the cabanas); TV. **FACILITIES AND SERVICES** bar; fishing lake; function room; games room; gym; horses and carriage; laundry; mini farm; playground; ponies; pool; rappel; reading room; restaurant; sauna; stores; tour guides; trails; woods. **CREDIT CARDS** Not accepted
Rodovia SC-438, Km 10
TEL and **FAX** (49) 3223-2073
www.fazendapedrasbrancas.com.br

Fazenda do Barreiro $$
Located on a farm that dates back to 1782, this hotel has a museum with local artifacts over a hundred years old. **ACCOMMODATIONS** 19; ceiling fan; fireplace (in the 3 suites); heating; jacuzzi (in the 3 suites); minibar (in the 3 suites); pay TV. **FACILITIES AND SERVICES** bar; fishing lake; games room; heated pool; horses; mini train; playground; restaurant; sauna; soccer field; tour guides; volleyball court. **CREDIT CARDS** Not accepted
Rodovia SC-438, Km 43, municipality of Urupema
TEL and **FAX** (49) 3222-3031
www.fazendadobarreiro.com.br

Hotel Fazenda Boqueirão $$$
In an area of 7.5 square kilometers (2.9 square miles), visitors can enjoy the setting of a fully functioning farm and a variety of leisure options, ranging from massage to adventure sports. **ACCOMMODATIONS** 31; ceiling fan; heating; minibar; ofuro tubs (in the suites); TV. **FACILITIES AND SERVICES** artificial lake; bowls; fishing lake; flying-fox; function room; games room; gym; heated pool; horses and carriage; Internet access; jacuzzi; laundry; massage room; pool; rappel; reading room; recreational team for children; restaurant; sauna; sitting room with fireplace and TV; soccer field; trips; walking tours; waterfall. **CREDIT CARDS** Diners; MasterCard
Rodovia BR-282, Km 225 (exit to São José do Cerrito)
TEL and **FAX** (49) 3221-9900
www.fazendaboqueirao.com.br

Laguna – Santa Catarina

AREA CODE 48 **POPULATION** 50,179 **DISTANCE** Florianópolis 124 kilometers (77 miles) **ACCESS** Highway BR-101 from Florianópolis heading South. After the town of Ibituba, you will come to a turnoff with signs pointing the way to Laguna. www.laguna.sc.gov.br

WHERE TO EAT

Laguna Tourist Hotel $$
Standing atop a hill, this hotel offers a privileged view of the nearby beaches. The sparingly decorated rooms have verandas with views of Lagoa de Santo Antônio or the sea. **ACCOMMODATIONS** 96; air-conditioning; Internet access (broadband; wi-fi); jacuzzi (in the suites and "luxo máster" rooms); minibar; pay TV; private safe; telephone. **FACILITIES AND SERVICES** bar; bilingual staff; function room; games room; gym; Internet access (wi-fi; computer available); parking; pool; recreational team in the high season; restaurant; sauna; six-a-side soccer court; tennis court; volleyball court; 24-hour kitchen. **CREDIT CARDS** AmEx; Diners; MasterCard; Visa
Avenida Castelo Branco, no #, Praia do Gi
TEL (48) 3647-0022 **FAX** (48) 3647-0123
www.lagunatourist.com.br

SERVICES

Tourist Information – Portal Turístico
Avenida Calistrato Müller Salles, no #, Portinho
TEL (48) 3644-2441. Daily, 7:30am – 6pm

Lapa – Paraná

AREA CODE 41 **POPULATION** 41,679 **DISTANCES** Curitiba 69 kilometers (42 miles) **ACCESS** Highway BR-476 from Curitiba towards Araucária. The Lapa turnoff is approximately 20 kilometers (12 miles) after the town of Contenda. www.lapa.pr.gov.br

WHERE TO STAY

Lapinha Clínica Spa Naturista $$$$
Located on a farm that produces the organic foods served at meals, this spa has rooms with Spartan décor and no TV or phone. Guests must be in their rooms by 9pm. Children under the age of 15 are not allowed. Packages are for a minimum of 5 days. **ACCOMMODATIONS** 40; ceiling fan; heating. **FACILITIES AND SERVICES** art workshop; beauty center; beauty parlor; bicycles; bilingual staff; dance lessons; fireplace; fruit and vegetable garden; games room; gym; heated pool; Internet access; lake; laundry; library; massage room; recreation team for adults; restaurant; sauna; spa; store; tennis court; trails; TV room; woods. **CREDIT CARDS** AmEx; Diners; MasterCard; Visa

| PRICES | HOTELS (couple) | $ up to R$ 150 | $$ from R$ 151 up to R$ 300 | $$$ from R$ 301 up to R$500 | $$$$ above R$ 500 |

506

BRAZIL GUIDE

Fazenda Margarida, Estrada da Lapa–Campo do Tenente, Km 16
TEL (41) 3622-1044 RESERVATIONS 0800-6431090
www.lapinha.com.br

WHERE TO EAT

Lipski $
This simple restaurant offers a choice of 13 different dishes for a fixed price. Highlights are the regional dishes quirera lapeana (corn and fried spare ribs) and the virado de feijão (cooked beans, bacon, manioc meal, and seasonings). CUISINE Regional CREDIT CARDS AmEx; Diners; MasterCard; Visa
Avenida Manuel Pedro, 1,855, Centro
TEL (41) 3622-1202. Mon, 11am – 4:30pm; Tue – Fri, 11am – 2:30pm and 7pm – 9:30pm; Sat, 11am – 4:30pm and 7pm – 9:30pm; Sun, 11am – 4:30pm

SERVICES

Guide specialized in the Lapa historical center
TEL (41) 3622-1422 (Márcio)

Travel Agency and Guides – Sprintur
Rua Desembargador Westhphalen, 43, Centro
TEL (41) 3622-5989. Mon – Fri, 8am – noon and 1:30pm – 6pm; Sat, 9am – 11:30am

Lençóis – Bahia

AREA CODE 75 POPULATION 9741 DISTANCE Salvador 425 kilometers (264 miles) ACCESS By plane or car. From Salvador, on Highway BR-324 to Feira de Santana, then Highway BR-116 (Rio–Bahia) for 76 kilometers, on a stretch with heavy truck traffic, then Highway BR-242 until just after the airport turnoff – there are no signs at the turnoff to this road, so look for a right-hand exit near some gas stations

WHERE TO STAY

Canto das Águas $$$
This hotel offers peace and quiet on the banks of the Lençóis River. The swimming pool area is very pleasant, and the décor in the rooms is simple. ACCOMMODATIONS 44; air-conditioning; minibar; jacuzzi in the "superior" suite; telephone; TV; ceiling fan. FACILITIES AND SERVICES bar; waterfall; parking; pool; restaurant; river; games room; massage room; sauna. CREDIT CARDS AmEx; Diners; MasterCard; Visa
Avenida Senhor dos Passos, 1, Centro
TEL (75) 3334-1154 FAX (75) 3334-1279
www.lencois.com.br

Hotel de Lençóis $$
This lovely, well-equipped colonial-style hotel is surrounded by gardens on a 5.7-hectare (14-acre) estate. Most of the facilities are in an old mansion. ACCOMMODATIONS 50; air-conditioning (in some rooms); private safe; minibar; telephone; TV; ceiling fan. FACILITIES AND SERVICES Internet access; wine cellar; bar; woods; parking; pool; playground; restaurant; conference room; games room. CREDIT CARDS AmEx; Diners; MasterCard; Visa
Rua Altina Alves, 747, Centro
TEL (75) 3334-1102 FAX (75) 3334-1201 RESERVATIONS (71) 3369-5000 www.hoteldelencois.com

Portal Lençóis $$$
This classy hotel has views over the Lençóis River Canyon and the town of Lençóis. It has spacious rooms, chalets, and bungalows and handicapped facilities. ACCOMMODATIONS 84; air-conditioning; private safe; minibar; telephone; cable TV. FACILITIES AND SERVICES Internet access; bar; parking; store; pool; playground; restaurant; river; conference room; gym; games room; sauna; travel agency; 24-hour kitchen; transport into town. CREDIT CARDS AmEx; Diners; MasterCard; Visa
Rua Chácara Grota, no #, Altina Alves
TEL (75) 3334-1233 FAX and RESERVATIONS (71) 3450-7337, 3450-1090 www.portalhoteis.tur.br

WHERE TO EAT

La Pergola $
Camping grounds, guesthouse, and French restaurant are located in a tranquil setting with large trees. The filet mignon comes with a choice of sauces – green peppercorns, Dijon mustard, Roquefort, or wine. CUISINE French; fish. CREDIT CARDS Diners; MasterCard; Visa
Praça do Rosário, 70, Centro
TEL (75) 3334-1241 OPEN Daily, noon – 4pm and 6pm – 11pm

Neco's Bar $
Neco has been serving carne-de-sol (beef jerky), carneiro (lamb), galinha caipira (country chicken) and tucunaré fish at his popular restaurant for the better part of two decades. CUISINE Regional. CREDIT CARDS Not accepted
Praça Maestro Clarindo Pacheco, 15, Centro
TEL (75) 3334-1179 OPEN Daily, noon – 9pm

Roda d'Água Gourmet (Hotel de Lençóis) $
The most popular dish is the filet mignon with rice, manioc purée (seasoned with basil, nutmeg, and cooked garlic), and tomato stuffed with curd cheese. CUISINE Contemporary; diverse. CREDIT CARDS AmEx; MasterCard; Visa
Rua Altina Alves, 747, Centro
TEL (75) 3334-1102 OPEN Daily, noon – 3pm and 6pm – 10pm

SERVICES

Airport – Aeroporto Coronel Horácio de Matos
Rodovia BR-242, Km 209 (25 kilometers, 16 miles, from the center), Coronel Otaviano Alves
TEL (75) 3625-8100 OPEN Daily, 5:30am – 6pm

Bus Station – Rodoviária
Avenida Senhor dos Passos, no #, Centro
TEL (75) 3334-1185 (public phone), 3334-1112 (Viação Real Expresso bus company)

Guides – Associação dos Condutores de Visitantes de Lençóis (ACVL)
Rua 10 de Dezembro, 22, Centro
TEL (75) 3334-1425 OPEN High season: daily, 7:30am – 10pm; low season: 7:30am – noon and 2pm – 10pm

Travel Agency – ACVTL Turismo
Avenida Senhor dos Passos, 77, Centro
TEL (75) 3334-1436 OPEN Daily, 7:30am – 10pm

Travel Agency – Adrenalina
Rua das Pedras, 121, Centro
TEL (75) 3334-1019 OPEN Daily, 8am – 5pm

RESTAURANTS $ up to R$ 50 $$ from R$ 51 up to R$ 100 $$$ from R$ 101 up to R$ 150 $$$$ above R$ 150

Travel Agency – Cirtur
Rua da Baderna, 41, Centro
TEL (75) 3334-1133 OPEN Daily, 7:30am – 10pm

Travel Agency – Explorer Brasil
Praça Maestro Clarindo Pacheco, 5, Centro
TEL (75) 3334-1183, 9984-1661 OPEN Daily, 8am – 12 and
5pm – 8pm

Travel Agency – Lentur
Avenida 7 de Setembro, 10, Centro
TEL (75) 3334-1271, 3334-1117 OPEN Daily, 8am – 11am
and 5pm – 10pm www.lentur.com.br

Travel Agency – Marimbus Ecoturismo
Praça Otaviano Alves, 36, Centro
TEL (75) 3334-1292 OPEN Daily, 8am – 10pm

Travel Agency – Nativos da Chapada
Rua Miguel Calmon, 29, Centro
TEL (75) 3334-1314, 9966-0131 OPEN Daily, 8am – noon
and 2pm – 10pm

Travel Agency – Velozia Cicloturismo
Rua do Lagedo, 68, Centro
TEL (75) 3334-1700 OPEN Mon – Sat, 8am – noon and
2pm – 6pm www.ronybikes.com

Travel Agency – Zentur
Praça das Nagôs, 1, Centro
TEL (75) 3334-1397 OPEN Daily, 7:30am – 10pm
www.zentur.tur.br

Lençóis Maranhenses – Maranhão (see Barreirinhas)

Maceió – Alagoas

AREA CODE 82 POPULATION 903,463 DISTANCES Aracaju 290
kilometers (180 miles), Recife 255 kilometers (158
miles) ACCESS From Aracaju or Recife, on Highway BR-
101 and BR-104 www.maceio.al.gov.br

WHERE TO STAY

Hotel Brisa Tower $$
This newly opened boutique hotel on the Jatiúca
beachfront has lovely, cozy rooms, each decorated by a
different designer. ACCOMMODATIONS 108; Internet access;
air-conditioning; private safe; minibar; telephone; cable
TV. FACILITIES AND SERVICES Internet access; parking; store;
pool; beach; restaurant; conference room; bilingual staff;
business center; 24-hour kitchen; beach equipment;
pool service. CREDIT CARDS AmEx; MasterCard; Visa
Avenida Álvaro Otacílio, 4201, Jatiúca
TEL (82) 2122-4000 www.hotelbrisatower.com.br

Jatiúca Resort $$$
This resort swaying with coconut palms facing onto
Jatiúca Beach is a 6-hectare (15-acre) complex with four
apartment blocks, serviced flats, garden, lake, and
leisure area. ACCOMMODATIONS 179; Internet access; air-
conditioning; private safe; minibar; radio; telephone; cable TV. FACILITIES AND SERVICES Internet access; bars; kids'
club; parking; stores; pools; playground; six-a-side soccer
court; tennis court; volleyball court; restaurants; conference room; gym; games room; massage room; beauty
parlor; sauna; baby-sitter; room service; business center;

exchange bureau; 24-hour kitchen; recreational team
for adults and children; laundry; valet parking; lifeguards; beach service. CREDIT CARDS AmEx; Diners; MasterCard; Visa
Rua Dr. Mário Nunes Vieira, 220, Mangabeiras
TEL (82) 2122-2000 FAX (82) 2122-2020
RESERVATIONS (82) 2122-2050, 2122-2040
www.hoteljatiuca.com.br

Maceió Atlantic Suits $$$
Whatever this sophisticated beachside hotel might lack
in terms of personality is more than made up for by the
excellent service and facilities. These include three
swimming pools surrounded by coconut trees and the
view of the bay from some rooms. ACCOMMODATIONS 204;
Internet access; air-conditioning; private safe; minibar;
telephone; cable TV. FACILITIES AND SERVICES Internet access; bar; kids' club; parking; pharmacy; vehicle hire;
stores; pool; playground; tennis court; restaurants; magazine reading area; conference room; gym; games
room; massage room; beauty parlor; sauna; travel
agency; business center; exchange bureau; 24-hour
kitchen; recreational team for adults and children; valet
parking. CREDIT CARDS AmEx; Diners; MasterCard; Visa
Avenida Álvaro Otacílio, 4065, Praia de Jatiúca
TEL (82) 2121-5656 FAX (82) 2121-5757
www.maceioatlantic.com.br

Ritz Lagoa da Anta $$$
Each floor has a different décor: the more romantic Bali
floor is aimed at couples, while the Design floor is more
modern with contemporary furniture. ACCOMMODATIONS
196; air-conditioning; private safe; minibar; ofuro tub in
the Bali suites; telephone; cable TV. FACILITIES AND SER-
VICES Internet access; wine cellar; bar; parking; jacuzzi;
stores; pool; playground; tennis court; volleyball court;
restaurant; conference room; gym; games room; massage room; sauna; spa; business center; currency exchange bureau; 24-hour kitchen; recreational team for
adults and children; valet parking; laundry; beach service. CREDIT CARDS AmEx; Diners; MasterCard; Visa
Avenida Brigadeiro Eduardo Gomes, 546,
Praia da Lagoa da Anta
TEL (82) 2121-4000, 2121-4120, 2121-4121
FAX (82) 2121-4123 www.ritzlagoadaanta.com.br

Verde Mar $
This hotel is well located near an arts and craft fair and
the Pajuçara tide pools. The rooms facing the sea have
large windows. ACCOMMODATIONS 62; air-conditioning;
private safe; minibar; telephone; cable TV. FACILITIES AND
SERVICES bar; parking; convenience store; pool; restaurant; conference room; games room. CREDIT CARDS AmEx;
Diners; MasterCard; Visa
Avenida Dr. Antônio Gouveia, 81, Praia de Pajuçara
TEL (82) 2123-5700 FAX (82) 2123-5799
www.hotelverdemar.com.br

WHERE TO EAT

Canto da Boca $
This eatery may be simple, but the different moquecas
(try the shrimp with octopus) served in clay dishes are
worth the visit. CUISINE Fish and seafood; regional. CREDIT
CARDS AmEx; Diners; MasterCard; Visa
Rua Ferroviário Manoel Gonçalves Filho, 80,
Mangabeiras
TEL (82) 3325-7346 RESERVATIONS (82) 3325-7279 OPEN
Mon, Wed and Thu, noon – midnight; Fri and Sat, noon
– 1am; Sun, noon – 6pm

PRICES | HOTELS (couple) | $ up to R$ 150 | $$ from R$ 151 up to R$ 300 | $$$ from R$ 301 up to R$500 | $$$$ above R$ 500

508 | BRAZIL GUIDE

Divina Gula $

Chef André Generoso's menu has classics of Minas Gerais cuisine, such as tutu à mineira (bean, pork, and manioc mush, homemade sausage, shank steak, collard greens, crunchy bacon, banana fritters, and rice). **CUISINE** Regional. **CREDIT CARDS** AmEx; Diners; MasterCard; Visa
Rua Engenheiro Paulo Brandão Nogueira, 85, Jatiúca
TEL (82) 3235-1016 fax and **RESERVATIONS** (82) 3235-1262
OPEN Tue – Sun, noon – until the last customer leaves

Lua Cheia $

The kitchen turns out delicious dishes such as filé alto grelhado ao molho de roquefort (thick grilled steak in Roquefort sauce) and camarão ao creme de leite com ervas provençais (shrimp in cream sauce with Provençal herbs). **CUISINE** French-Brazilian. **CREDIT CARDS** AmEx; Diners; MasterCard
Rodovia AL-101, Km 14
TEL (82) 3355-1186 **OPEN** Wed – Fri, 4pm – midnight; Sat, noon – midnight; Sun, noon – 5pm

Recanto do Picuí $

This home-style restaurant is owned and run by a family from Paraíba, where beef jerky is the specialty. The gororoba (literally 'mishmash') contains onions, manioc purée, and grilled curd cheese. **CUISINE** Regional. **CREDIT CARDS** Diners; MasterCard; Visa
Avenida Álvaro Calheiros, 110, Mangabeiras
TEL (82) 3325-7537 **OPEN** Mon – Sat, 11:30am – 11pm

Wanchaco $

The specialties here are Peruvian and Japanese-Peruvian dishes. Try the ceviche (lime-marinated fish) or the peixe grelhado com camarões ao molho de gengibre agridoce (grilled fish with shrimp in sweet-and-sour ginger sauce). **CUISINE** Peruvian. **CREDIT CARDS** Diners; MasterCard; Visa
Rua São Francisco de Assis, 93, Jatiúca
TEL (82) 3377-6114 **RESERVATIONS** (82) 3377-6024 **OPEN** Mon – Thu, noon – 3pm and 7pm – 11:30pm; Fri, noon – 4pm and 7pm – 12:30am; Sat, 7pm – 2am

SERVICES

Airport – Aeroporto Internacional Zumbi dos Palmares
Rodovia BR-104, Km 91, Tabuleiro
TEL (82) 3036-5200 **OPEN** Daily, 24 hours

Bus Station – Rodoviária
Avenida Leste-Oeste, no #, Feitosa
TEL (82) 3221-4615

Tourist Information – Posto de Informações Turísticas
Aeroporto Internacional Zumbi dos Palmares
OPEN Mon – Sat, 10am – 10pm; Sun, 3pm – 10pm

Tourist Information – Posto de Informações Turísticas (Shopping Iguatemi)
Avenida Gustavo Paiva, 2990, Mangabeiras
TEL (82) 2126-1010 **OPEN** Mon – Sat, 10am – 10pm; Sun, 3pm – 10pm

Travel Agency – Edvantur
Trips to Mundaú and Manguaba estuarine lagoons in Maceió; 9 Ilhas (9 Islands) tour

Avenida Belmiro Amorim, 26, Bloco 1, Store #301 (mezzanine), Condomínio Galápagos, Santa Lúcia
TEL (82) 3351-9067, 8845-6327, 9976-2189 **OPEN** Daily, 8am – 7pm (but open anytime by appointment; call ahead)

Manaus – Amazonas

AREA CODE 92 **POPULATION** 1,646,602 **DISTANCE** Brasilia 3,490 kilometers (2,169 miles) **ACCESS** The best way to Manaus is by plane. www.pmm.am.gov.br

WHERE TO STAY

Tropical Manaus Eco Resort Experience $$$
This is one of the best-equipped, most luxurious hotels in the region. It is 16 kilometers (10 miles) out of the city center and has many attractions for guests, especially children. **ACCOMMODATIONS** 594; Internet access; air-conditioning; private safe; minibar; jacuzzi (in 27 suites); telephone; pay TV. **FACILITIES AND SERVICES** bar; beauty parlor; conference room; games room; Internet access; jogging track; massage room; playground; pool; recreational staff for adults and children; restaurant; sauna; soccer field; tennis court; 24-hour room service. **CREDIT CARDS** AmEx; Diners; MasterCard; Visa
Avenida Coronel Teixeira, 1,320, Ponta Negra
TEL (92) 2123-5000 **FAX** (92) 3658-5026
RESERVATIONS 0800-7012670 www.tropicalhotel.com.br

HOTELS IN THE FOREST

Ariaú Amazon Towers $$$$
Two hours by boat from Manaus, the Ariaú – the most famous jungle hotel in the Amazon – is built on suspended towers with 8 kilometers (5 miles) of suspended walkways at treetop level. There are two observation towers, each 41 meters (134 feet) high, where guests can enjoy views of the jungle. **ACCOMMODATIONS** 360; air-conditioning; Internet access; jacuzzi (in the "Tarzan" rooms and suites); minibar; telephone; TV (in the Tarzan rooms). **FACILITIES AND SERVICES** bar; conference room; games room; Internet access; massage room; pool; restaurant; soccer field; transport to airport; 24-hour kitchen. **CREDIT CARDS** AmEx; Diners; MasterCard; Visa
Lago do Ariaú, Iramduba
TEL (92) 2121-5000 **FAX** (92) 3233-5615
RESERVATIONS 0800-7025005 www.ariau.tur.br

Guanavenas Pousada Jungle Lodge $$$$
Located deep in the jungle, this hotel is five hours from Manaus – 350 kilometers (218 miles) – by bus and motorboat. It has good leisure facilities. The region is crisscrossed by narrow channels known as igarapés, which can be seen from a 30-meter (100-foot) tower. **ACCOMMODATIONS** 70; air-conditioning; minibar. **FACILITIES AND SERVICES** bar; conference room; games room; pool; restaurant; transport to airport; trips; TV room; volleyball court; walking tours. **CREDIT CARDS** Not accepted
Lago do Canaçari, Silves
RESERVATIONS (92) 3656-1500, 3656-3656
www.guanavenas.com.br

Pousada Uacari $$
Located in the largest protected floodplain in the Amazon, this guesthouse is run by the Mamirauá Institute for Sustainable Development. Guests can go animal watching, canoeing, visit local communities, and attend

talks about the Institute's research. **ACCOMMODATIONS** 10.
FACILITIES AND SERVICES bar; canoe trips; conference room;
library; natural pool; restaurant; sundeck; transport to
airport; video room. **CREDIT CARDS** MasterCard; Visa
**Canal do Lago Mamirauá, Margem Direita,
RDS Mamirauá, Uarini**
TEL (97) 3343-4160 **FAX** (97) 3343-2967
www.pousadauacari.com.br

Tiwa Amazonas Ecoresort $$$$
Facing across the Negro River toward Manaus, this hotel doesn't actually feel as if it's in the forest. Rooms can
be rented for day-use only. **ACCOMMODATIONS** 52; air-conditioning; minibar. **FACILITIES AND SERVICES** bar; conference
room; games room; Internet access; pool; restaurant;
soccer field; transport to airport; trips; video room; walking tours. **CREDIT CARDS** AmEx; Diners; MasterCard; Visa
Margem Direita do Rio Negro, no #, Iranduba
TEL (92) 9995-7892, 9982-3939 www.tiwa.com.br

WHERE TO EAT

Açaí e Cia $
A local institution, this relaxed restaurant boasts special-
ties such as tacacá (a typical Amazon soup with man-
ioc milk), caldeirada de tambaqui (a bouillabaisse made
with a local fish) and açaí fruit served with manioc meal.
CUISINE Fish and seafood; regional. **CREDIT CARDS** AmEx;
Diners; MasterCard; Visa
Rua Acre, 92, Conjunto Vieira Ives
TEL (92) 3584-0188. Mon – Thu, 10am – 11pm; Fri and
Sat, 10am – 2am; Sun, 4pm – 11:30pm

Bar do Armando $
This traditional bar in the nostalgic Largo de São Se-
bastião square is a favorite haunt of local artists and in-
tellectuals. Try a cold beer with a delicious pork snack.
CUISINE Snacks. **CREDIT CARDS** Not accepted
Rua 10 de Julho, 593, Centro
TEL (92) 3232-1195. Mon – Sat, 2pm until the last cus-
tomer leaves

Canto da Peixada $
On one of the tables you'll see a stuffed, 30-kg (66 lb)
tambaqui fish. This should inspire you to order the char-
coal-grilled tambaqui ribs is this informal eatery's delicious specialty. **CUISINE** Fish. **CREDIT CARDS** AmEx
Rua Emílio Moreira, 1,677, Praça 14
TEL (92) 3234-3021. Mon – Sat, 11:30am – 3:30pm and
7pm – 11pm

SERVICES

Airport – Aeroporto Internacional Eduardo Gomes
Avenida Santos Dumont, 1,350, Tarumã
TEL (92) 3652-1210

Tour Operator – Amazon Explorers
Trips to jungle hotels and jungle survival expeditions.
**Avenida Djalma Batista, 2,100, Mezzanine stores
#225 and 226, Chapada**
TEL (92) 3613-3558. Mon – Fri, 8am – 7pm; Sat, 8am –
1pm

Tour Operator – Amazonas Clipper
Boat trips through Jaú National Park.
Rua Sucupira, 249, Dom Pedro II
TEL (92) 3656-1246. Mon – Fri, 8am – 5pm; Sat, 8am – noon

Tour Operator – Fontur
Various trips, including visits to the Presidente Figueire-
do waterfalls.
Avenida Coronel Teixeira, no #, Ponta Negra
TEL (92) 3658-3052. Mon – Sat, 7am – 8pm; Sun, 7am –
3pm

Tourist Information – Centro de Atendimento ao Turista/Aeroporto Internacional Eduardo Gomes
Avenida Santos Dumont, 1,350, Tarumã
TEL (92) 3652-1120. Daily, 24 hours

Tourist Information – Centro de Atendimento ao Turista/Amazonas Shopping Centro
Avenida Djalma Batista, 482, Chapada
TEL (92) 3236-5154. Mon – Sat, 9am – 10pm; Sun, 2pm –
8pm

Tourist Information – Centro de Atendimento ao Turista Eduardo Ribeiro
Rua Tapajós, 180, Centro
TEL (92) 3622-0767. Mon – Fri, 8am – 5pm

Mangue Seco – Bahia

AREA CODE 75 **DISTANCES** Salvador 246 kilometers (153
miles), Sítio do Conde 77 kilometers (48 miles), Aracaju
100 kilometers (62 miles) **ACCESS** From Salvador, take the
Linha Verde highway to the border with Sergipe. From
there, take SE-318 to Indiaroba (15 kilometers, 9 miles),
followed by the dirt road (12 kilometers, 7 miles) to the
village of Pontal. Motorboats run from Pontal to
Mangue Seco (15 min.). From Aracaju, SE-438 to Porto
do Mato (73 kilometers, 45 miles), where you catch the
Mosqueiro-Caueira ferryboat. From the ferry drop-off,
it's another 25 min. by motorboat.

WHERE TO STAY

Pousada Asa Branca $
This two-story guesthouse facing the Real River is
shaped like a horseshoe, with a pool in the centre. The
upstairs rooms are the most pleasant and offer a fine
view of the river. **ACCOMMODATIONS** 20; air-conditioning
(in 15 rooms) or a fan; minibar; TV. **FACILITIES AND SERVICES**
Internet access; bar; buggy; motorboat; pool; restaurant;
river. **CREDIT CARDS** MasterCard; Visa
Rua da Frente, 4, Praia de Mangue Seco
TEL (75) 3445-9054 **FAX** (75) 3445-9053
www.infonet.com.br/asabranca

Pousada O Forte $
Simple and rustic in style, this guesthouse features 12
rooms and a garden, all facing Real River Beach. **ACCOM-
MODATIONS** 12; ceiling fan in 3 rooms, otherwise air-
conditioning; minibar; TV. **FACILITIES AND SERVICES** Inter-
net access; bar; kayaks; motorboat; pool; surfboards;
restaurant; ecological trips. **CREDIT CARDS** Diners; Master-
Card; Visa
Praia da Costa, no #
TEL and **FAX** (75) 3445-9039 www.pousadaoforte.com

WHERE TO EAT

Frutos do Mar $
A highlight of this simple restaurant is the aratu (a type
of crab), available fried, in a moqueca stew, or in catado
– stewed in a sauce of tomatoes, bell peppers, onions,

PRICES | **HOTELS** (couple) | $ up to R$ 150 | $$ from R$ 151 up to R$ 300 | $$$ from R$ 301 up to R$500 | $$$$ above R$ 500

510   BRAZIL GUIDE

and coriander. **CUISINE** Home-style; fish and seafood. **CREDIT CARDS** Diners; MasterCard
Praça Santa Cruz, 58, Centro
TEL (75) 3445-9049 **OPEN** Daily, 7am – 9pm

Maragogi – Alagoas

AREA CODE 82 **POPULATION** 25,233 **DISTANCES** Maceió 130 kilometers (81 miles), Recife 130 kilometers (81 miles) **ACCESS** From Maceió, take Rodovia Litorânea (AL-101)

WHERE TO STAY

Marrecas Hotel Fazenda $$
Dating from 1817, this farm is a major attraction in Maragogi, thanks to its lovely restored main building, with guest rooms where the old slave quarters used to be. **ACCOMMODATIONS** 25; air-conditioning; private safe; minibar; telephone; TV. **FACILITIES AND SERVICES** bar; horse and cart; parking; fishing lake; paddleboats; pool; restaurant; games room; sauna; walking trails; recreational team for adults and children; guided walking tours. **CREDIT CARDS** MasterCard; Visa
Rodovia AL-101, Km 130.9 (then follow a dirt road 4 kilometers to the farm)
TEL and **FAX** (82) 3666-1600 **RESERVATIONS** (81) 2123-5656
www.marrecas.com.br

Miramar Maragogi Eco Resort $$$$
Soon to open (as of mid-2008), this all-inclusive seaside resort will have an excellent leisure area. **ACCOMMODATIONS** 185; air-conditioning; private safe; minibar; telephone; cable TV. **FACILITIES AND SERVICES** Internet access; bar; bicycles; kayaks; parking; stores; diving instructors and equipment; pool; playground; beach; beach volleyball; restaurant; conference room; gym; games room; massage room; video room; beauty parlor; spa; travel agency; bilingual staff; business center; 24-hour kitchen. **CREDIT CARDS** AmEx; Diners; MasterCard; Visa
Rodovia AL-101 Norte, no #, Ponta de Mangue
TEL (82) 3296-3200 **RESERVATIONS** (82) 3296-9112
www.miramarmaragogiresort.com.br

Pousada do Alto $$
This guesthouse sits atop a hill, giving all of the rooms wonderful sea views. **ACCOMMODATIONS** 10; air-conditioning; DVD player in some rooms; minibar; TV. **FACILITIES AND SERVICES** Internet access; boats, bicycles and horses (outsourced service); parking; pool; restaurant. **CREDIT CARDS** Visa
Sítio Biquinha, no #, Centro, Japaratinga
TEL (82) 3297-1210 www.pousadadoalto.com.br

WHERE TO EAT

Restaurante do Mano $
This restaurant is on São Bento Beach, two kilometers from the centre of town. We suggest the lobster or aratu crab in coconut sauce. **CUISINE** Fish and seafood. **CREDIT CARDS** Visa
Rua Simeão Ribeiro de Albuquerque, no #, São Bento
TEL (82) 3296-7106 **OPEN** Daily, 8am – 9pm

Maraú – Bahia
(see Barra Grande)

Marechal Deodoro – Alagoas
(see Praia do Francês)

Mariana – Minas Gerais

AREA CODE 31 **POPULATION** 51,693 distâncias Belo Horizonte 115 kilometers (71 miles), Ouro Preto 12 kilometers (7 miles), São Paulo 709 kilometers (440 miles), Rio de Janeiro 795 kilometers (494 miles) **ACCESS** Highway BR-040 and Rodovia dos Inconfidentes (BR-356 and MG-262) from Belo Horizonte
www.mariana.mg.gov.br

WHERE TO STAY

Pousada da Chácara $
A 15-minute walk from the center of town and somewhat thus removed from the hustle and bustle, this simple guesthouse maintains new and refurbished rooms in a pleasant green area. **ACCOMMODATIONS** 15; ceiling fan; Internet access; minibar; phone; TV. **FACILITIES AND SERVICES** badminton court; laundry; lawn; pool. **CREDIT CARDS** Diners; MasterCard; Visa
Rua Amélia Alves, 77, Chácara
TEL and **RESERVATIONS** (31) 3557-2750, 3557-3497
www.pousadachacara.com

Pousada Solar dos Corrêa $
This traditional guesthouse operates out of an 18th century building near the downtown attractions. **ACCOMMODATIONS** 12; bathtub; ceiling fan; Internet access; minibar; phone; TV. **FACILITIES AND SERVICES** laundry; parking; TV room. **CREDIT CARDS** Diners; MasterCard; Visa
Rua Josafá Macedo, 70, Centro
TEL and **FAX** (31) 3557-2080
www.pousadasolardoscorrea.com.br

WHERE TO EAT

Bistrô $
This bistro serves a little bit of everything: pizza (very popular), pasta, meat, snacks, pastry turnovers, stuffed potatoes, and fish. **CUISINE** Regional; fish; pizza; various. **CREDIT CARDS** MasterCard; Visa
Rua Salomão Ibrahim, 61-A, Centro
TEL (31) 3557-4138. Mon – Sat, 6pm – 1am; Sun, 11:30am – 11pm

Pizzaria, Restaurante e Lanchonete Dom Silvério $
The pizzas here are made on a wood-fired oven and can be prepared with your selection of 48 toppings. The lasagnas (Bolognese, chicken, or four-cheese) are also a success. **CUISINE** Italian; pizza. **CREDIT CARDS** Diners; MasterCard; Visa
Praça Dr. Gomes Freire, 242, Centro
TEL (31) 3557-2475. Mon – Sat, 6pm – midnight; Sun, and holidays, 11:30am – midnight

SERVICES

Bus station – Rodoviária
Rodovia Rodrigo Mello Franco de Andrade, no #, Catete (exit to Mariana)
TEL (31) 3557-1215

Tourist information – Portal Turístico
Rodovia Rodrigo Mello Franco de Andrade, no #, Catete (bus station)
TEL (31) 3558-5455. Mon – Fri, 8am – 5pm

Tourist information – Secretaria Municipal de Cultura e Turismo
Rua Direita, 91-93, Centro

RESTAURANTS	**$** up to R$ 50	**$$** from R$ 51 up to R$ 100	**$$$** from R$ 101 up to R$ 150	**$$$$** above R$ 150

TEL (31) 3557-9088. Mon – Fri, 8am – 5pm; Sat and Sun, 9am – 5pm

Travel agency – Mariana Turismo
Rua Frei Durão, 114, Centro
TEL (31) 3557-3899, 3557-2233. Mon – Fri, 9am – 7pm; Sat, 9am – noon

Miranda – Mato Grosso do Sul

AREA CODE 67 POPULATION 23,965 DISTANCES Campo Grande 205 kilometers (127 miles) ACCESS Highway BR-262 from Campo Grande www.miranda.ms.gov.br

WHERE TO STAY

Fazenda Santa Inês Pousada e Turismo Rural $$$
Near Rodovia BR-262 highway, this guesthouse offers comfortable rooms and sporting activities. Rooms can also be rented for day-use only. ACCOMMODATIONS 6; air-conditioning; mosquito-screens on windows; TV. FACILITIES AND SERVICES bar; climbing wall; environmental inspector; first-aid; flying-fox; games room; pool; rappelling facilities; restaurant; river; six-a-side soccer court; video room; transport to attractions. EXCURSIONS animal watching; bicycles; boat trips; canoeing; cattle handling; hiking; horseback riding; nocturnal wildlife spotting; photography safari; tour through the Pantanal (together with guests from neighboring farms); walking tours. FISHING equipment; fishing lake; catch-and-release. CREDIT CARDS Visa. ACCESS From Miranda, on Estrada Miranda–Aldeia Lalima. After the signposted turnoff, drive for another 6 kilometers (4 miles) to the farm
Estrada Miranda–Aldeia Lalima, Km 16
TEL (67) 9988-4082, 9982-9514 FAX (67) 3324-2040 RESERVATIONS (67) 3326-9070 www.fazendasantaines.com.br

Refúgio Ecológico Caiman $$$$
The best is the Baiazinha, which is set apart from the others and in a beautiful setting. There is a good range of tours on offer. Rooms can also be hired for day-use only. ACCOMMODATIONS 11 in the main building, 6 in Baiazinha and 8 in Cordilheira; air-conditioning; ceiling fan; mosquito-screens on windows. FACILITIES AND SERVICES bar; bicycles; bilingual staff; conference room; environmental inspector; first-aid; Internet access; massage room; parking; pool; restaurant; river; soccer field; stores; transport to airport, attractions and neighboring town; video room. EXCURSIONS bird and animal watching; boat trips; canoeing; cattle handling; hiking; horseback riding; nocturnal wildlife spotting; walking tours. CREDIT CARDS MasterCard. ACCESS On Highway BR-262; exit at Miranda turnoff, then drive toward Agachi on asphalted road, followed by another 36 kilometers (22 miles) of dirt road to the main gate.
Rua Estância Caiman, no #, Zona Rural
TEL (67) 3242-1450 FAX (67) 3242-1102
RESERVATIONS (11) 3706-1800 www.caiman.com.br

WHERE TO EAT

Churrascaria Pioneiro $
This self-serve steakhouse on Rodovia BR-262 highway is one of the main pit stops for those driving to the Pantanal. The complex also includes a tire-repair shop, a snack bar, a travel agency, a guesthouse, and a gas station. CUISINE Grill. CREDIT CARDS Not accepted
BR-262, Km 535, Posto Pioneiro
TEL (67) 3242-1392. Daily, 5am – 11:30pm

SERVICES

Tour Operator – Águas do Pantanal Tour
Avenida Afonso Pena, 367, Centro
TEL (67) 3242-1242, 3242-1497. Daily, 24 hours.
www.aguasdopantanal.com.br

Tour Operator – Pioneiro Turismo
BR-262, Km 535
TEL (67) 3242-1392, 3258-1058. Daily, 6am – 11pm.
www.pioneirotour.com.br

Morro de São Paulo – Bahia

AREA CODE 75 DISTANCES Salvador 248 kilometers (154 miles) of driving, followed by 90 minutes by regular boat or 30 minutes by motorboat ACCESS By sea: motorboats and catamarans leave from the pier at Salvador's Mercado Modelo for the 2-hour crossing. By land and sea: from Salvador, take BA-001 to Valença; boats (90-minute trip) and speedboats (30-minute trip) depart for Morro from there. By air: two air-taxi services run flights from Salvador (20 min.)

WHERE TO STAY

Hotel Fazenda Vila Guaiamu $$
This laid-back, extremely pleasant hotel stands in a nature reserve that protects the guaiamum crab. The property sits at the spot where the hubbub of Terceira Praia beach gives way to peace and quiet. The rooms are simple, but airy and private. ACCOMMODATIONS 22; air-conditioning; private safe; minibar; TV; veranda with hammock. FACILITIES AND SERVICES bar; soccer field; restaurant; river; games room; massage room; video room; walking trails; beach service. CREDIT CARDS AmEx; MasterCard; Visa
Terceira Praia, no #
TEL and FAX (75) 3652-1073, 3652-1035
www.vilaguaiamu.com.br

Patachocas Eco-Resort $$$
The spacious bungalows of this eco-resort are scattered among the coconut palms near the rock pools of Quarta Praia beach. ACCOMMODATIONS 26; air-conditioning; private safe; minibar; telephone; TV. FACILITIES AND SERVICES Internet access; bar; bicycles; snack bar; convenience store; stores; pool; restaurant; outdoor massage space; travel agency; recreational team for adults; guided walking tours; beach service; airport shuttle; transport to attractions. CREDIT CARDS AmEx; Diners; MasterCard; Visa
Quarta Praia, no #
TEL (75) 3652-2134 fax and RESERVATIONS (75) 3652-2129
www.patachocas.com.br

Porto do Zimbo Small Resort $$$$
This charming hotel faces the rock pools of Quarta Praia beach; definitely ask for a room with a sea view. ACCOMMODATIONS 16; air-conditioning; private safe; minibar; jacuzzi in 7 rooms; telephone; cable TV; ceiling fan. FACILITIES AND SERVICES Internet access; bar; bicycles; kayaks; snack bar; pool with whirlpool tub; restaurant; games room; massage room; video room; spa; travel agency; airport shuttle; transport to attractions. CREDIT CARDS Diners; MasterCard; Visa
Quarta Praia, no #
TEL (75) 3652-2030 fax and RESERVATIONS (75) 3652-1278
www.hotelportodozimbo.com.br

Pousada Villa das Pedras $$$
This guesthouse faces onto the lively Segunda Praia and

PRICES	HOTELS (couple)	$ up to R$ 150	$$ from R$ 151 up to R$ 300	$$$ from R$ 301 up to R$500	$$$$ above R$ 500

is next door to a popular square with stores, snack bars, and a cachaça bar. **ACCOMMODATIONS** 24; air-conditioning; private safe; minibar; telephone; cable TV. **FACILITIES AND SERVICES** Internet access; bar; snack bar; stores; pool; restaurant; games room; massage room; video room; travel agency; beach service. **CREDIT CARDS** AmEx; Diners; MasterCard; Visa
Segunda Praia, no #
TEL (75) 3652-1075 **FAX** (75) 3652-1122
www.villadaspedras.com.br

WHERE TO EAT

Piscina $
The highlight is the shrimp and lobster stew with thick pirão gravy, rice, salad, beans, and seasoned manioc flour (serves two). **CUISINE** Regional; fish and seafood. **CREDIT CARDS** Diners; MasterCard; Visa
Quarta Praia, no #
TEL (75) 9985-1664 **OPEN** Daily, 8am – 10pm (winter); 8am – midnight (summer)

Via Brasil $
The atmosphere is relaxed, with live music almost every day. Though the menu is varied, the kitchen's forte is pizzas made in a wood-burning oven. **CUISINE** Pizza; diverse. **CREDIT CARDS** Diners; MasterCard; Visa
Praça Aureliano de Lima, 155
TEL (75) 3652-1443 **OPEN** Daily, 6pm – 11pm

SERVICES

Air-Taxi – Addey
Rua Caminho da Praia, no #
TEL (75) 3652-1242; in Salvador: (71) 3377-2451 **OPEN** Daily, 7am – 7pm www.addey.com.br

Air-Taxi – Aero Star
Rua Caminho da Praia, no #
TEL (75) 3652-1312 **OPEN** Daily, 8am – 10pm
www.aerostar.com.br

Diving Agency – Companhia do Mergulho
Primeira Praia, no # (Pousada Farol do Morro, ground floor)
TEL (75) 3652-1200, 3653-7127, 9981-2110 **OPEN** Daily, 9am – 9pm www.ciadomergulho.com.br

Flying Fox – Tirolesa do Morro
Primeira Praia, no #
TEL (75) 3652-1219, 8805-9796 **OPEN** Daily, 10am – 5pm
www.tirolesadomorro.com.br

Tourist Information – Centro de Informações Turísticas
Rua da Prainha, no #
TEL (75) 3652-1589 **OPEN** Daily, 8am – 6pm

Tour Guides and Trips – Itha do Mar
Rua da Prainha, no #
TEL (75) 3652-1104, 3652-1225 **OPEN** Daily, 8am – 9pm

Tour Guides and Trips – Madalena Tur
Segunda Praia, no #
TEL (75) 3652-1317, 9987-0177 **OPEN** High season: daily, 8am – midnight; low season: 8am – 10pm
www.madalenaturismo.com.br

Mucugê – Bahia

AREA CODE 75 **POPULATION** 15,780 **DISTANCES** Lençóis 150 kilometers (93 miles), Salvador 460 kilometers (286 miles) **ACCESS** From Lençóis, on highways BR-242 and BA-142

WHERE TO STAY

Alpina Resort $
This hilltop hotel (it isn't really a resort, despite the name) on the edge of Chapada Diamantina National Park offers magnificent panoramas. **ACCOMMODATIONS** 32; minibar; TV; ceiling fan. **FACILITIES AND SERVICES** Internet access; bar; horse and cart; parking; fireplace; stores; pool; six-a-side soccer court; volleyball court; restaurant; conference room; games room; video room. **CREDIT CARDS** Visa
Rodovia BA-142, Km 90, Alto do Capa-Bode
TEL (75) 3338-2150 fax and **RESERVATIONS** (71) 3451-4900
www.alpinamucuge.com.br

Pousada Mucugê $
The biggest and oldest guesthouse in town, the beautiful Pousada Mucugê is in the town center. **ACCOMMODATIONS** 30; minibar; telephone; TV; ceiling fan. **FACILITIES AND SERVICES** parking; pool; restaurant; video room. **CREDIT CARDS** Diners; MasterCard; Visa
Rua Dr. Rodrigues Lima, 30, Centro
TEL and **FAX** (75) 3338-2210
www.pousadamucuge.com.br

WHERE TO EAT

Dona Nena $
Try the prato feito (meal served on a single plate) or a regular meal, which is served on platters. This place is very informal and has no fixed operating hours. **CUISINE** Regional; home-style **CREDIT CARDS** Not accepted
Rua Direita do Comércio, 140
TEL (75) 3338-2123 **OPEN** Daily, from midday.

SERVICES

Guides – Associação dos Condutores de Visitantes de Mucugê (ACVM)
Praça Coronel Propércio, 88, Centro
TEL (75) 3338-2414 **OPEN** Daily, 8am – noon and 2pm – 9pm

Travel Agency – Km Viagens and Turismo
Car and motorcycle rental, guides, tourist information, carwash, Internet access, taxi
Praça Coronel Douca Medrado, 126, Centro
TEL (75) 3338-2152, 3338-2277 **OPEN** Daily, 8am – 8pm

Travel Agency – Terra Chapada
Guides and tourist information
Rua Dr. Rodrigues Lima, 10
TEL (75) 3338-2284 **OPEN** Daily, 3pm – 9pm
www.terrachapada.com.br

Natal – Rio Grande do Norte

AREA CODE 84 **POPULATION** 778,040 **DISTANCES** Fortaleza 552 kilometers (343 miles), João Pessoa 180 kilometers (112 miles) **ACCESS** From Fortaleza, on Highway BR-116 and BR-304. From João Pessoa, on Highway BR-101
www.natal.rn.gov.br

RESTAURANTS	$ up to R$ 50	$$ from R$ 51 up to R$ 100	$$$ from R$ 101 up to R$ 150	$$$$ above R$ 150

WHERE TO STAY

Escola de Turismo and Hotelaria Barreira Roxa $

The view is magnificent, but the rough sea is not suitable for swimming. In the halls, charming Brennand-tiled floors look like floral carpets. ACCOMMODATIONS 53; Internet access; air-conditioning; private safe; minibar; telephone; cable TV. FACILITIES AND SERVICES Internet access; wine cellar; bar; parking; stores; pool; restaurant; conference room; video room; business center; 24-hour kitchen. CREDIT CARDS AmEx; Diners; MasterCard; Visa

Avenida Senador Dinarte Mariv, 4020, Areias Pretas

TEL (84) 3209-4000 FAX (84) 3209-4001
www.barreiraroxa.com.br

Manary Praia $$$

The atmosphere here is rustic. The rooms have four-poster beds with cotton canopies, and treats like incense and candles. ACCOMMODATIONS 24; Internet access; air-conditioning; private safe; minibar; telephone; cable TV; veranda with hammock; ceiling fan. FACILITIES AND SERVICES Internet access; wine cellar; bar; parking; convenience store; pool; restaurant; magazine reading area; conference room; video room; business center; 24-hour kitchen; vehicle hire; surfboard and body board rental. CREDIT CARDS AmEx; Diners; MasterCard; Visa

Rua Francisco Gurgel, 9067, Ponta Negra

TEL (84) 3204-2900 FAX (84) 3204-2908
RESERVATIONS (84) 3204-2904 www.manary.com.br

Ocean Palace & Resort $$$$

This resort stands on a calm stretch of beach, and is like small village. The rooms have floral curtains and bedspreads. There are also bungalows. ACCOMMODATIONS 236; Internet access; air-conditioning; private safe; minibar; telephone; cable TV. FACILITIES AND SERVICES Internet access; wine cellar; bar; nursery; bicycles; parking; pool; jogging track; six-a-side soccer court; tennis court; volleyball court; restaurant; conference room; gym; games room; massage room; video room; beauty parlor; sauna; spa; travel agency; business center; exchange bureau; recreational team for adults and children; valet parking; beach service; airport shuttle. CREDIT CARDS AmEx; Diners; MasterCard; Visa

Via Costeira, Km 11, Ponta Negra

TEL (84) 3219-4144 FAX (84) 3219-3321
RESERVATIONS 0800-844144 www.oceanpalace.com.br

Pestana Natal Beach Resort $$$$

One of Natal's best hotels, Pestana Natal is popular among foreign tourists. ACCOMMODATIONS 184; Internet access; air-conditioning; private safe; minibar; telephone; cable TV. FACILITIES AND SERVICES Internet access; bar; bicycles; soccer field; parking; art gallery; jacuzzi; stores; pool; playground; restaurant; magazine reading area; conference room; gym; games room; massage room; sauna; business center; exchange bureau; 24-hour kitchen; recreational team for adults and children; guided walking tours; valet parking; lifeguards; beach service. CREDIT CARDS AmEx; Diners; MasterCard; Visa

Avenida Senador Dinarte Mariz (Via Costeira), 5525, Ponta Negra

TEL (84) 3220-8900 FAX (84) 3220-8901 RESERVATIONS (84) 3220-8923, 3220-8924 www.pestana.com

Sehrs Natal Grand Hotel $$$$

This luxury resort has rooms with jacuzzis and private pools. The extensive facilities include 4 bars and 4 restaurants, as well as pools and recreation activities for children. ACCOMMODATIONS 396 (327 rooms, 69 suites); Internet access; air-conditioning; private safe; minibar; jacuzzi and private pool in some suites; telephone; cable TV. FACILITIES AND SERVICES Internet access; bar; parking; Kid's Club; stores; jacuzzi; pool; beach; restaurant; conference room; gym; games room; massage room; sauna; spa; theater; multi-sports court; bilingual staff; business center; 24-hour kitchen; beach equipment; recreational team for adults and children; laundry; pool and beach service; airport shuttle; transport to attractions. CREDIT CARDS MasterCard; Visa

Avenida Senador Dinarte Mariz, 6045, Via Costeira

TEL (84) 4005-2000 FAX (84) 4005-2001
RESERVATIONS (84) 4005-2002
www.sehrsnatalgrandhotel.com

WHERE TO EAT

Abade $$

The fortes at this luxurious restaurant are the Norwegian cod dishes. CUISINE Portuguese; diverse. CREDIT CARDS AmEx; Diners; MasterCard; Visa

Rua Hélio Galvão, 8828, Via Costeira, Ponta Negra

TEL (84) 3219-4469 OPEN Mon – Fri, 11:30am – 3pm and 6pm until the last customer leaves; Sat, 6pm until the last customer leaves; Sun, 11am – 10pm

Camarões $

Offering generous portions at good prices, this is the place for shrimp lovers. CUISINE Fish and seafood. CREDIT CARDS AmEx; Diners; MasterCard; Visa

Avenida Engenheiro Roberto Freire, 2610, Ponta Negra

TEL (84) 3209-2425 OPEN Mon – Thu, 11:30am – 3:30pm and 6:30pm – midnight; Fri and Sat, 11:30am – 3:30pm and 6:30pm – 1am; Sun, 11:30am – 4pm and 6:30pm – 11pm

Mangai $

A great spot for breakfast and lunch, this restaurant serves great regional food, including carne-de-sol (beef jerky) with cream, goat leg, and tapioca. Alcohol isn't available. CUISINE Regional. CREDIT CARDS AmEx; MasterCard; Visa

Avenida Amintas Barros, 3300, Lagoa Nova

TEL (84) 3206-3344 OPEN Daily, 11am – 10pm

Paçoca de Pilão $

This restaurant is worth the 25-kilometer (16 mile) drive from Natal. It is simply decorated and very pleasant. Try the signature dish: beef jerky pounded with a mortar and pestle, accompanied by banana, rice, lima beans, manioc, and curd cheese. CUISINE Regional; fish and seafood. CREDIT CARDS Diners; MasterCard

Rua Deputado Márcio Marinho, 5708, Pirangi do Norte

TEL (84) 3238-2088 OPEN Sun – Thu, 11am – 8pm; Fri and Sat, 11am – 11pm

Peixada da Comadre $

Since 1931, this simple restaurant has been serving freshly caught fish. The highlight and most famous dish here is the mouthwatering Peixada da Comadre, or fish cutlet poached in stock with vegetables and accompanied by rice and pirão gravy. CUISINE Fish and seafood. CREDIT CARDS Diners; MasterCard; Visa

Avenida Praia da Ponta Negra, 1948, Ponta Negra

TEL (84) 3219-3016 RESERVATIONS (84) 3219-5711 OPEN Tue – Sat, 11:30am – 4pm and 6:30pm – 11pm; Sun, 11:30am – 5pm

PRICES	HOTELS (couple)	$ up to R$ 150	$$ from R$ 151 up to R$ 300	$$$ from R$ 301 up to R$500	$$$$ above R$ 500

SERVICES

Airport – Aeroporto Internacional Augusto Severo
Aeroporto Internacional Augusto Severo, no #, Emaús, Parnamirim
TEL (84) 3087-1200 OPEN Daily, 24 hours

Bus Station – Rodoviária
Avenida Capitão-Mor Gouveia, 1237, Cidade da Esperança
TEL (84) 3232-7311

Tourist Information – Posto de Informações Turísticas (Airport)
Aeroporto Internacional Augusto Severo, no #, Emaús, Parnamirim
TEL None OPEN Mon – Sat, 8am – noon and 1pm – 5pm

Tourist Information – Posto de Informações Turísticas (Praia Shopping)
Avenida Engenheiro Roberto Freire, no # (Central do Cidadão), Ponta Negra
TEL (84) 4008-0810 OPEN Mon – Fri, 10am – 10pm; Sat and Sun, 3pm – 9pm

Tourist Police Station – Delegacia do Turista
Avenida Engenheiro Roberto Freire, 8790, Ponta Negra
TEL (84) 3232-7404, 3232-7402 OPEN Daily, 24 hours

Travel Agency – Cariri Ecotours
Avenida Prudente de Morais, 4262, Store #3-B, Room #2 (mezzanine), Lagoa Nova
TEL (84) 3086-3601 FAX (84) 3206-4949 OPEN Mon – Fri, 8:30am – 6pm; Sat, 9am – noon
www.caririecotours.com.br

Niterói – Rio de Janeiro

AREA CODE 21 POPULATION 474,002 DISTANCE Rio de Janeiro 17 kilometers (11 miles) ACCESS Over the Ponte Rio–Niterói (bridge) from Rio de Janeiro
www.niteroiturismo.com.br

WHERE TO EAT

Caneco Gelado do Mário $$
Highlights of the menu are the moqueca stews, which serve 3 people, and the bolinho de bacalhau (cod fritters). CUISINE Fish and seafood; Portuguese. CREDIT CARDS Not accepted
Rua Visconde do Uruguai, 288, Store #5, Centro
TEL (21) 2620-6787. Mon – Fri, 9am – 10pm; Sat, 9am – 7pm

Nobres – Mato Grosso

AREA CODE 65 POPULATION 14,862 DISTANCE Cuiabá 142 kilometers (88 miles) ACCESS Highway BR-163 toward Santarém from Cuiabá to Jangada; from here, continue along the BR-364

WHERE TO STAY

Pousada Mangueiras $
The best accommodations option in town operates here out of a one-story building, and its rooms face on-

to a center area full of mango trees. ACCOMMODATIONS 30; air-conditioning; ceiling fan; minibar; TV. FACILITIES AND SERVICES parking. CREDIT CARDS Visa
Avenida Getúlio Vargas, 1,501, Centro
TEL and FAX (65) 3376-1345

WHERE TO EAT

Vitória $
This simple eatery has a self-serve buffet. Highlights are the ventrecha (fried pacu fish) and the ensopado de pintado (pintado fish soup), as well as the popular vaca atolada (beef, manioc, carrots, potatoes, and sweet potatoes). CUISINE Meats; fish; regional. CREDIT CARDS Not accepted
Rua Porto Quatro, no #, Centro
TEL (65) 9923-0507. Mon – Sat 10:30am – 2:30pm.

SERVICES

Tourist Information and Guides – Secretaria Municipal de Turismo, Cultura, Meio Ambiente e Agricultura
Avenida Juscelino Kubitschek, 757, Centro
TEL (65) 3376-1809. Mon – Fri, 8am – 11am and 1pm – 5pm.

Nova Petrópolis – Rio Grande do Sul

AREA CODE 54 POPULATION 17,747 DISTANCE Porto Alegre 100 kilometers (62 miles) ACCESS Highway BR-116 from Porto Alegre www.novapetropolis.rs.gov.br

WHERE TO EAT

Colina Verde $
This eatery serves German dishes, such as eisbein (pork knuckle), Italian fare such as capeletti soup, and regional specialties, such as matambre (stuffed flank steak) and bolinho de aipim (manioc fritters). CUISINE German; Italian; regional. CREDIT CARDS Diners; MasterCard
Rua Filipe Michaelsen, 160, Vila Olinda (50 meters from Rodovia BR-116, Km 185.5)
TEL (54) 3281-1388. Tue – Sun, 11:30am – 3pm

Opa's Kaffehaus $
This is the place for the most famous cafés coloniais (colonial tea) in the region. There are 45 options of cakes, bread rolls, cold cuts, and fruit conserves, and customers can eat until they are satisfied. CUISINE Café colonial. CREDIT CARDS MasterCard; Visa
Rua João Leão, 96, Centro
TEL (54) 3281-1273. Tue – Fri, 2pm – 8pm; Sat, 1pm – 8:30pm; Sun, noon – 8:30pm

SERVICES

Tourist Information – Pórtico
Avenida 15 de Novembro, 100, turnoff to Rodovia BR-116
TEL (54) 3281-1398. Sun – Thu, 9am – 6pm; Fri and Sat, 9am – 10pm

Olinda – Pernambuco

AREA CODE 81 POPULATION 384,510 DISTANCE Recife 7 kilometers (4 miles) ACCESS Less than 15 minutes north of Recife www.olinda.pe.gov.br

| RESTAURANTS | $ up to R$ 50 | $$ from R$ 51 up to R$ 100 | $$$ from R$ 101 up to R$ 150 | $$$$ above R$ 150 |

WHERE TO STAY

Pousada do Amparo $$$

This lovely guesthouse, decorated with works by local artists, occupies an old building on buzzing Rua do Amparo. ACCOMMODATIONS 11; Internet access; air-conditioning; private safe; minibar; telephone; TV FACILITIES AND SERVICES bar; parking; pool; restaurant. CREDIT CARDS AmEx; MasterCard; Visa

Rua do Amparo, 191/199, Carmo
TEL and FAX (81) 3439-1749
www.pousadadoamparo.com.br

Sete Colinas $

The rooms have tiled floors, large box-spring beds, and understated, rustic decor. The lovely garden is a highlight. ACCOMMODATIONS 39; Internet access; air-conditioning; private safe; minibar; telephone; cable TV; ceiling fan; veranda. FACILITIES AND SERVICES Internet access; parking; pool; museum; restaurant; sauna. CREDIT CARDS AmEx; Diners; MasterCard; Visa

Ladeira de São Francisco, 307, Carmo
TEL and FAX (81) 3439-6055 www.hotel7colinas.com.br

WHERE TO EAT

Kwetú $

With striking views of Olinda and the sea from outdoor tables, this restaurant serves predominantly French cuisine, with Moroccan, Thai, and Vietnamese influences. CUISINE French; international. CREDIT CARDS Diners; MasterCard; Visa

Avenida Manoel Borba, 338, Praça do Jacaré
TEL (81) 3439-8867 OPEN Mon, Wed, and Thu, 6pm – midnight; Fri – Sun, noon – 4pm and 6pm – midnight

Marim dos Caetés $

This cross between an artist's studio and restaurant is very romantic. The focus of the menu is fish and seafood and the signature dish is the papelote de peixe e camarão na folha de bananeira (fish and shrimp in banana leaves). CUISINE Contemporary; fish and seafood. CREDIT CARDS MasterCard; Visa

Rua do Amparo, 157
TEL (81) 3429-8762 OPEN Wed – Mon, noon – 11pm.

Oficina do Sabor $$

Pumpkin, the star of the menu, is stuffed with tantalizing fillings, such as shrimp in pitanga fruit or mango sauce. The view over Olinda and the background music add to the ambience. CUISINE Regional; fish and seafood. CREDIT CARDS AmEx; Diners; MasterCard; Visa

Rua do Amparo, 335, Cidade Alta
TEL (81) 3429-3331 OPEN Tue – Fri, noon – 4pm and 6pm – midnight; Sat, noon – 1am; Sun, noon – 5pm
www.oficinadosabor.com

SERVICES

Guides – Associação de Condutores Nativos de Olinda

Rua Prudente de Morais, no #, Quatro Cantos – Casa do Turista
TEL (81) 3053-5150, 3053-1051, 8811-8096 OPEN Daily, 7am – 8pm www.acno.com.br

Guides – Projeto Guia Mirim

Avenida da Liberdade, 100, Carmo
TEL (81) 3439-1988 OPEN Mon – Fri, 8am – 5pm
www.olinda.pe.gov.br

Ouro Preto – Minas Gerais

AREA CODE 31 POPULATION 67,048 DISTANCES Belo Horizonte 96 kilometers (60 miles), Santa Bárbara 85 kilometers (53 miles), Brasília 860 kilometers (534 miles) ACCESS Highway BR-040 and Highway Inconfidentes (BR-356 and MG-262) from Belo Horizonte

WHERE TO STAY

Grande Hotel de Ouro Preto $$

This no-frills hotel occupies a beautiful modernist construction, one of Oscar Niemeyer's early designs from the 1940s. The two-story building is a little run-down, but it offers wonderful panoramic views. ACCOMMODATIONS 35; blackout curtain; Internet access; minibar; phone; TV; veranda. FACILITIES AND SERVICES bar; convenience store; function room; Internet access; pool; restaurant; valet service. CREDIT CARDS AmEx; Diners; MasterCard; Visa

Rua Senador Rocha Alagoas, 164, Centro
TEL (31) 3551-1488 FAX (31) 3551-5028
www.hotelouropreto.com.br

Hotel Solar do Rosário $$

Housed in a three-story 19th-century building in the center of town, this hotel retains décor inspired by the era in which it was built. The rooms with balconies have views of the neighborhood's historic buildings, while the windows of the others open onto the inner part of the building. ACCOMMODATIONS 41; air-conditioning; central heating; Internet access; jacuzzi (in 5 suites); minibar; pay TV; phone; private safe. FACILITIES AND SERVICES bar; function room; gym; heated pool; Internet access; jacuzzi; parking; pool; restaurant; sauna. CREDIT CARDS AmEx; Diners; MasterCard; Visa

Rua Getúlio Vargas, 270, Largo do Rosário
TEL (31) 3551-5200 FAX (31) 3551-4288
www.hotelsolardorosario.com.br

Luxor Ouro Preto Pousada $$

This charming, well-located guesthouse operates out of an 18th-century manor. All of the rooms have panoramic views. The sitting room has a fireplace, board games, and reading corner. ACCOMMODATIONS 19; minibar; satellite dish; pay TV; phone. FACILITIES AND SERVICES games room; Internet access; magazine-reading area; nursery; parking; restaurant; transport to attractions; walking tours. CREDIT CARDS AmEx; Diners; MasterCard; Visa

Rua Dr. Alfredo Baeta, 16, Centro
TEL and FAX (31) 3551-2244 RESERVATIONS 0800-165322
www.luxor-hotels.com

Pousada do Mondego $$

This guesthouse operates in a restored 1747 manor, where some rooms have views of Itacolomi Peak. Pieces of 18th-century furniture from Minas Gerais and an important collection of Brazilian art remain. ACCOMMODATIONS 24; Internet access; minibar; pay TV; phone; private safe. FACILITIES AND SERVICES bar; convenience store; exchange service; function room; Internet access; parking; restaurant; stores; transport to attractions; travel agency; valet service. CREDIT CARDS Diners; MasterCard; Visa

Largo de Coimbra, 38, Centro
TEL (31) 3551-2040 FAX (31) 3551-3094
www.mondego.com.br

WHERE TO EAT

Casa dos Contos Restaurante $

This restaurant operates out of former slave quarters at

PRICES | HOTELS (couple) | $ up to R$ 150 | $$ from R$ 151 up to R$ 300 | $$$ from R$ 301 up to R$500 | $$$$ above R$ 500

516 BRAZIL GUIDE

the rear of an 18ᵗʰ-century manor. There is a regional-style buffet at lunch; dinner service is à la carte. The menu offers pasta, meat, and soup options, as well as snacks. **CUISINE** Meats; pasta; regional; various. **CREDIT CARDS** Visa
Rua Camilo de Brito, 21, Centro
TEL (31) 3551-5359 **FAX** (31) 3551-5358. Sun – Tue, noon – 4pm; Wed – Sat, noon – 10pm

Chafariz $

This restaurant opened in 1950. One of the best options in town for lunch, it serves a buffet of regional dishes from Minas Gerais, as well as homemade desserts, jabuticaba fruit liqueur and cachaça. **CUISINE** Regional. **CREDIT CARDS** MasterCard; Visa
Rua São José, 167, Centro
TEL (31) 3551-2828. Tue – Sun, 11am – 4pm

Bené da Flauta $$

Housed in a two-story manor next door to the beautiful São Francisco de Assis Church, this café-restaurant has a varied menu and charming décor that features the work of local artists. **CUISINE** Regional; various. **CREDIT CARDS** Diners; MasterCard; Visa
Rua São Francisco de Assis, 32, Centro
TEL (31) 3551-1036. Daily, noon – 1am

Perypatus $

This restaurant is located inside the Grande Hotel de Ouro Preto. The house specialty is the Argentinean picanha steak, accompanied by rice, manioc meal, and vinaigrette. **CUISINE** Meats; regional; various. **CREDIT CARDS** AmEx; Diners; MasterCard; Visa
Rua Senador Rocha Lagoa, 164, Centro
TEL (31) 3551-1488 **FAX** (31) 3551-5028. Mon – Thu, noon – 3pm and 7pm – 10pm; Fri and Sat, noon – 11pm; Sun, noon – 8pm. In July, daily, noon – 11pm

Piacere $

Try the mushroom risotto or the spaghetti with escalopes. The wine list offers a selection of about 30 labels. **CUISINE** Italian. **CREDIT CARDS** Diners; MasterCard; Visa
Rua Getúlio Vargas, 241, Rosário
TEL (31) 3551-4297. Tue – Sat, 7pm – midnight; Sun, and holidays, noon – 4:30pm

SERVICES

Bus station – Rodoviária

Praça Presidente Tancredo Neves, 661, Centro
TEL (31) 3559-3252

Guides and tours – Aliar Turismo e Cultura

Rua Paraná, 41, Store #2, Centro
TEL (31) 3552-2614. Mon – Fri, 9am – 6pm; Sat, 9am – 1pm

Guides and tours – GrandTour Ouro Preto

Praça Tiradentes, 52, Centro
TEL (31) 3552-1100, 9961-1220. Mon – Fri, 8am – 6pm; Sat, 8am – noon

Tourist information – Posto de Informações Turísticas

Praça Tiradentes, 41, Centro
TEL (31) 3559-3269. Daily, 8am – 6pm

Tourist information – Secretaria de Turismo

Rua Cláudio Manoel, 61, Centro
TEL (31) 3559-3287. Mon – Fri, 8am – 6pm

Palhoça – Santa Catarina

AREA CODE 48 **POPULATION** 122,471 **DISTANCE** Florianópolis 18 kilometers (11 miles) **ACCESS** Highway BR-101 from Florianópolis www.palhoca.sc.gov.br

WHERE TO STAY

Pousada Ilha do Papagaio $$$

This guesthouse, which stands on an island, can only be reached by motorboat, boat, or helicopter. Guests stay in chalets scattered throughout the rainforest. It closes in August. **ACCOMMODATIONS** 20; air-conditioning; CD player; DVD player; fireplace (in some chalets); Internet access; minibar; private safe; telephone; TV. **FACILITIES AND SERVICES** bar; beach equipment and service; boat; diving; function room; games room; gym; kayak; Internet access; massage room; motorboat; parking; pool; rafting; restaurant; trails; transport to airport and attractions; TV room (pay TV, with DVD); volleyball court; water skiing; whale watching. **CREDIT CARDS** AmEx; Diners; MasterCard; Visa
Ilha do Papagaio, no #, Praia do Sonho
TEL (48) 3286-1242 **FAX** (48) 3286-1342
www.papagaio.com.br

WHERE TO EAT

Seacoquille $

The owner's house becomes a restaurant from December to March. Shrimp with coconut and green mango headlines the menu. **CUISINE** Fish and seafood. **CREDIT CARDS** MasterCard
Rua da Antena, no #, Guarda do Embaú
TEL (48) 3283-2559. Dec – Mar: Tue – Sun, 1pm – midnight

SERVICES

Tourist Information – Portal do Lazer

Rodovia BR-101, Km 224, next to the Posto Cambirela gas station
Daily, 9am – noon and 1pm – 5pm

Palmas – Tocantins

AREA CODE 63 **POPULATION** 178,386 **DISTANCES** Brasilia 847 kilometers (526 miles), Belém 1,243 kilometers (772 miles) **ACCESS** From Brasilia, take Highway BR-060 to Anápolis, followed by the BR-153 (Belém–Brasilia) to Paraíso do Tocantins, then the TO-080
www.palmas.to.gov.br

WHERE TO STAY

Pousada dos Girassóis $

Located in the town center, this old guesthouse has friendly service and is an ideal place for a night's rest before heading to Jalapão. **ACCOMMODATIONS** 62; air-conditioning; Internet access; minibar; telephone; TV. **FACILITIES AND SERVICES** bar; conference room; Internet access; pool; restaurant; 24-hour room service. **CREDIT CARDS** AmEx; Diners; MasterCard; Visa
Quadra 103 Sul, Conjunto 3, Lote 44
TEL (63) 3219-4500 **FAX** (63) 3215-2321
www.pousadadosgirassois.com.br

WHERE TO EAT

Cabana do Lago $

One of the best restaurants in town, the Cabana serves typical regional fare, a favorite of which is the carne-

RESTAURANTS	**$** up to R$ 50	**$$** from R$ 51 up to R$ 100	**$$$** from R$ 101 up to R$ 150	**$$$$** above R$ 150

de-sol (beef jerky). **CUISINE** Regional. **CREDIT CARDS** AmEx;
Diners; MasterCard; Visa
Quadra 103 Sul, Rua SO, 9, Lote 5
TEL (63) 3215-4989. Daily, 11am – 11pm

SERVICES

Airport – Aeroporto de Palmas
Avenida Joaquim Teotônio Segurado, no #,
Aureny III (Expansão Sul)
TEL (63) 3219-3700

Tour Operator – Jalapão Tour
Car rental and guides to Jalapão.
804 Sul, Alameda 14, HM, Lote 6
TEL (63) 3214-6137, 9978-3695. Daily, 24 hours

Paraty – Rio de Janeiro

AREA CODE 24 **POPULATION** 32,838 **DISTANCES** Rio de Janeiro
248 kilometers (154 miles), São Paulo 350 kilometers
(218 miles) **ACCESS** Highway BR-101 (Rio–Santos) from
São Paulo or Rio de Janeiro

WHERE TO STAY

Pousada da Marquesa $$
Quiet and sophisticated, this 18th-century manor has
antique furniture and a pool. **ACCOMMODATIONS** 28; air-
conditioning; minibar; phone; private safe; TV. **FACILITIES
AND SERVICES** bar; Internet access; parking; pool; sitting
room; TV room; valet service. **CREDIT CARDS** AmEx; Diners;
MasterCard; Visa
Rua Dona Geralda, 99, Centro Histórico
TEL (24) 3371-1263 **FAX** (24) 3371-1299
www.pousadamarquesa.com.br

Pousada do Ouro $$
The very comfortable guesthouse is located in a colonial manor in the historic center, and its rooms are set
around a beautiful courtyard garden. **ACCOMMODATIONS**
26; air-conditioning; ceiling fan (in 2 rooms); minibar;
phone; private safe; TV. **FACILITIES AND SERVICES** bar; function room; games room; gym; Internet access; parking;
pool; sauna; valet service; video room. **CREDIT CARDS**
AmEx; Diners; MasterCard; Visa
Rua Dr. Pereira, 145 (Rua da Praia),
Centro Histórico
TEL (24) 3371-1378 **FAX** (24) 3371-1311
www.pousadaouro.com.br

Pousada Pardieiro $$$
Though in the historic center, this manor is far from the
busy areas. The rooms face onto a large garden. Children under 15 are not allowed. **ACCOMMODATIONS** 27; air-
conditioning; minibar; private safe. **FACILITIES AND SERVICES**
bar; function room; games room; Internet access; parking; pool; restaurant; sauna; store; video room. **CREDIT
CARDS** AmEx; Diners; MasterCard; Visa
Rua do Comércio, 74, Centro Histórico
TEL (24) 3371-1370 **FAX** (24) 3371-1139
www.pousadapardieiro.com.br

Santa Clara $$$
Located 10 kilometers (6 miles) out of town, this guesthouse is surrounded by mountains and Atlantic forest
and has beautiful ocean views. There is an ofuro tub in
the leisure area. **ACCOMMODATIONS** 35; air-conditioning;
jacuzzi (in 1 suite); minibar; pay TV; phone; private safe.
FACILITIES AND SERVICES bar; function room; games room;

Internet access; massage room; ofuro tub; parking; pool;
restaurant; sauna; valet service. **CREDIT CARDS** AmEx; Diners;
MasterCard; Visa
Rodovia Rio–Santos, Km 567
TEL (24) 3371-8900 **FAX** (24) 3371-8955
www.santaclarahotel.com.br

WHERE TO EAT

Banana da Terra $
This relaxed, traditional restaurant offers up tasty dishes
such as lambe-lambe (shellfish risotto). The drinks are
also creative. **CUISINE** Fish and seafood. **CREDIT CARDS**
AmEx; Diners; MasterCard
Rua Dr. Samuel Costa, no #, Centro Histórico
TEL (24) 3371-1725. Mon, Wed and Thu, 6pm – midnight;
Fri – Sun, noon – 4pm and 7pm – midnight

Hiltinho $$
This place serves the best camarões casadinhos in the
region: giant prawns stuffed with shrimp farofa (manioc
meal). The restaurant has a branch on Algodão Island
(open Fri – Sun and holidays, 11am – 5pm). **CUISINE** Fish
and seafood. **CREDIT CARDS** AmEx; Diners; MasterCard; Visa
Rua Marechal Deodoro, 233, Centro Histórico
TEL (24) 3371-1432, 3371-2155. Daily, 10am – midnight

Kontiki $$
This sophisticated restaurant has a boat to take cus-
tomers from the Paraty dock to the island (a 10 minute
trip). Try the seafood paella, which packs in prawns,
squid, octopus, and mussels. **CUISINE** Fish and seafood.
CREDIT CARDS MasterCard; Visa
Ilha Duas Irmãs
TEL (24) 3371-1666. Daily, noon – 5pm

Le Gite d'Indaiatiba $$
Hidden in the mountains beside a beautiful waterfall,
this restaurant is an hour from the town center. The crab
moqueca comes cooked in dende oil, with coconut
milk, onions and coriander, and is worth the visit. **CUISINE**
French; fish and seafood. **CREDIT CARDS** Visa
**Road to Graúna, Km 4, exit at Km 562 on Rodovia
Rio–Santos**
TEL (24) 3371-7174. Daily, 1:30pm – 9pm; closed in May

Merlin o Mago $$
Perfect for couples. Its French cuisine has Asian and
Brazilian influences, and lobster and shrimp dishes are
highlights of the menu. Try the sonho de Merlin: prawns
flambéed in cognac with aromatic herbs. **CUISINE** French.
CREDIT CARDS Diners; MasterCard; Visa
Rua do Comércio, 376, Centro Histórico
TEL (24) 3371-2157. Daily, 7pm – 1am, except Wednesday.

Refúgio $$
Very popular with couples, this restaurant has candle-
lit tables. The camarão à espanhola (shrimp cooked in
a clay pot with garlic and olive oil) is one of the best
items on the menu. **CUISINE** Fish and seafood. **CREDIT
CARDS** Diners; MasterCard; Visa
Praça do Porto, 1, Store #4, Centro
TEL (24) 3371-2447. Mon – Thu, 11am – 11pm; Fri – Sun,
11am – midnight

SERVICES

Tourist information –
Centro de Informações Turísticas
Avenida Roberto Silveira, 1, Centro
TEL (24) 3371-1897. Daily, 9am – 9pm

PRICES	**HOTELS** (couple)	**$** up to R$ 150	**$$** from R$ 151 up to R$ 300	**$$$** from R$ 301 up to R$500	**$$$$** above R$ 500

Parintins – Amazonas

AREA CODE 92 **POPULATION** 102,044 **DISTANCE** Manaus 325 kilometers (202 miles) by river **ACCESS** From Manaus, there are regular flights; alternatively, it's 4 hours by boat on the river. One can also take a yacht from Manaus

WHERE TO STAY

Amazon River Resort Hotel $$
The best accommodation option in Parintins, this hotel operates at full capacity during the Parintins Festival in June. **ACCOMMODATIONS** 61; air-conditioning; minibar; telephone; TV. **FACILITIES AND SERVICES** bar; convenience stores; hall for events; laundry; multi-sports court; pools; restaurant; 24-hour room service. **CREDIT CARDS** AmEx; MasterCard; Visa
Lagoa da Francesa, 697, Santa Rita
TEL (92) 3533-1342

Parque do Caraça – Minas Gerais
(see Santa Bárbara)

Penedo – Alagoas

AREA CODE 82 **POPULATION** 59,968 **DISTANCES** Maceió 173 kilometers (107 miles), Aracaju 165 kilometers (103 miles) **ACCESS** From Maceió, on Highway AL-101. From Aracaju, on Highway BR-101, for approximately 70 kilometers (44 miles) to the federal police station. There, take the right-hand turnoff to Neópolis, where the ferryboat departs for Penedo

WHERE TO STAY

Pousada Colonial $
This simple guesthouse occupies a 1754 building very near Nossa Senhora da Corrente Church. **ACCOMMODATIONS** 52; Internet access; air-conditioning in 10 rooms; minibar in 6 rooms; telephone; TV in 8 rooms; ceiling fan. **FACILITIES AND SERVICES** Internet access; bar; snack bar; restaurant; games room; TV room. **CREDIT CARDS** Not accepted
Praça 12 de Abril, 21, Centro
TEL (82) 3551-2355 **FAX** (82) 3551-6767

São Francisco $
Opened in 1963, this guesthouse has excellent views of the São Francisco River. **ACCOMMODATIONS** 32; Internet access; air-conditioning; minibar in some rooms; telephone; TV. **FACILITIES AND SERVICES** Internet access; parking; snack bar; pool; restaurant; conference room; games room. **CREDIT CARDS** AmEx; MasterCard; Visa
Avenida Floriano Peixoto, 237, Centro
TEL (82) 3551-2273 **FAX** (82) 3551-2274
www.hotelsaofrancisco.tur.br

WHERE TO EAT

Forte da Rocheira $
The specialty of this restaurant at the foot of Rocheira, on the banks of the São Francisco, is jacaré ao molho de coco (alligator in coconut sauce). **CUISINE** Meats; diverse. **CREDIT CARDS** Visa
Rua da Rocheira, 2, Santo Antônio
TEL (82) 3551-3273 **RESERVATIONS** (82) 3551-2578 **OPEN** Daily, 11am – 4pm and 6pm – 10pm

Penedo – Rio de Janeiro

AREA CODE 24 **DISTANCES** Rio de Janeiro 165 kilometers (102 miles), São Paulo 267 kilometers (166 miles) **ACCESS** Highway BR-116 from São Paulo or Rio de Janeiro

WHERE TO STAY

Pousada Serra da Índia $
Perched on a mountaintop 2 kilometers (1 mile) from the center, this guesthouse has a stunning view. Two chalets with whirlpool tubs and sound systems are ideal for couples. **ACCOMMODATIONS** 13; air-conditioning; DVD (in 2 chalets); fireplace; Internet access; jacuzzi (in 2 chalets); minibar; sound system (in 2 chalets); pay TV; phone. **FACILITIES AND SERVICES** games room; gym; Internet access; jacuzzi; massage room; parking; pool; sauna. **CREDIT CARDS** AmEx; Diners; MasterCard; Visa
Estrada Vale do Ermitão, no #, Vale do Ermitão
TEL (24) 3351-1185 **RESERVATIONS** (24) 3351-1804
www.serradaindia.com.br

WHERE TO EAT

Koskenkorva $
If you've never had Finnish food before, why not try it here in Brazil? The artist who owns the place has decorated the lush garden with his own sculptures. **CUISINE** Finnish. **CREDIT CARDS** Not accepted
Estrada das Três Cachoeiras, 3,955
TEL (24) 3351-2532. Daily, noon – midnight

Zur Sonne $
This German restaurant is 15 kilometers (9 miles) from Penedo, 4 of which are a dirt road. The seasonings are brought from Germany. The highlight here is the roast with red cabbage and apple puree. Children under 12 are not allowed. **CUISINE** German. **CREDIT CARDS** Not accepted
Estrada da Serrinha do Alambari, Km 4, Serrinha de Resende
TEL (24) 3381-7108, 9906-6320. Mon – Fri, noon – 3pm, reservations required for dinner; Sat, Sun, and holidays, noon – until the last customer leaves, but only with reservations

Penha – Santa Catarina

AREA CODE 47 **POPULATION** 20,868 **DISTANCE** Florianópolis 120 kilometers (75 miles) **ACCESS** Highway BR-101 from Florianópolis

WHERE TO STAY

Pousada Pedra da Ilha $$$
This guesthouse faces the beach and caters to families with small children. There are suites with whirlpool tubs and a room for disabled guests, and, for kids, swimming pools, a games room, and a playground. **ACCOMMODATIONS** 31; air-conditioning; ceiling fan; Internet access; jacuzzi (in the suites); minibar; telephone; TV. **FACILITIES AND SERVICES** bar; function room; games room; heated pool; Internet room; playground; pool; recreational team for children; restaurant; sauna; transport to airport and attractions; video room. **CREDIT CARDS** AmEx; Diners; MasterCard; Visa
Rua Abraão João Francisco, 46, Praia Alegre
TEL and **FAX** (47) 3345-0542 www.pedradailha.com.br

RESTAURANTS $ up to R$ 50 $$ from R$ 51 up to R$ 100 $$$ from R$ 101 up to R$ 150 $$$$ above R$ 150

WHERE TO EAT

Pirão d'Água $$
Chef Sarita Santos offers a range of Azorean dishes. The servings of fish and seafood are generous. CUISINE Regional. CREDIT CARDS Not accepted
Avenida São João, 954, Praia Armação do Itapocoroí
TEL (47) 3345-6742. Daily, 11:30am – 3:30pm and 7pm – midnight (high season); Thu and Fri, 6pm – 10:30pm; Sat, 11:30am – 3:30pm and 6pm – 10:30pm; Sun, 6:30pm – 10:30pm (low season)

Peruíbe – São Paulo

AREA CODE 13 POPULATION 54,457 DISTANCE São Paulo 128 kilometers (80 miles) ACCESS Take the Anchieta–Imigrantes highway system (SP-150/SP-160) from São Paulo. When you reach the SP-055 exit, head toward Mongaguá until you get to Peruíbe www.peruibe.sp.gov.br

WHERE TO STAY

Waldhaus Hotel $
The rooms are simple, but the view is stunning. The hotel has its own ecotourism agency, Eco Adventure. Remo, the German owner, can take you to neighboring Juréia. ACCOMMODATIONS 11; fan; minibar; TV. FACILITIES AND SERVICES bar; beachside service; function room; games room; massage room; parking; pool; restaurant. CREDIT CARDS MasterCard
Rua Gaivota, 1,201, Praia do Guaraú
TEL (13) 3457-9170 www.jureiaecoadventure.com.br

SERVICES

Tour operator – Eco Adventure
Canoeing, jeep rides and trekking.
Rua Gaivota, 1,201, Praia do Guaraú
TEL (13) 3457-9170, 3457-9390. Sat and Sun, 9am – 6pm; during the week, subject to prior booking

Tourist information – Ecotur
Jeep and jardineira (tractor-pulled wagon) rides to beaches and waterfalls.
TEL (13) 3455-8083. Daily, 24 hours

Petrolina – Pernambuco

AREA CODE 87 POPULATION 253,686 DISTANCES Recife 767 kilometers (477 miles), Salvador 517 kilometers (321 miles) ACCESS From Recife, take Highway BR-232 to Salgueiro, then the BR-116, BR-428 and BR-122. The safest route, however, is via Juazeiro (Bahia) on Highway BR-407 from Salvador. There are flights from Recife and São Paulo www.petrolina.pe.gov.br

WHERE TO STAY

Petrolina Palace $$
One of Petrolina's best hotels, Petrolina Palace is a historical three-story building offering views of the São Francisco River. ACCOMMODATIONS 52; air-conditioning; minibar; telephone; cable TV. FACILITIES AND SERVICES Internet access; bar; parking; snack bar; pool; restaurant; river; conference rooms; business center; 24-hour kitchen; transport to attractions. CREDIT CARDS AmEx; Diners; MasterCard; Visa
Avenida Cardoso de Sá, 845, Centro

TEL (87) 3866-3300 FAX (87) 3861-4858
www.petrolinapalace.com.br

WHERE TO EAT

Barretu's Grill $
Though this informal restaurant hosts lots of mosquitoes in the afternoon, the owner always has repellent on hand. Portions are generous. CUISINE Regional; diverse. CREDIT CARDS AmEx; Diners; MasterCard; Visa
Avenida Cardoso de Sá, 3, Orla
TEL (87) 3861-4277 OPEN Daily, 11am until the last customer leaves

Capivara $$
Meals are cooked to order in clay dishes. The house specialty is grilled surubim fish in caper or passion fruit sauce. CUISINE Regional; fish and seafood. CREDIT CARDS Diners; MasterCard; Visa
Avenida Cardoso de Sá, 429, Orla Velha
TEL (87) 3862-2585 RESERVATIONS (87) 3862-2715 OPEN Tue – Fri, noon – 3:30pm and 6:30pm – 11pm; Sat, noon – midnight; Sun, noon – 6pm

SERVICES

Airport – Aeroporto Senador Nilo Coelho
Rodovia BR-235, Km 11 (10 kilometers, 6 miles, from the centre)
TEL (87) 3863-3366 FAX (87) 3863-3699 OPEN Mon – Fri, 8am – noon and 1pm – 5pm (administration)
www.infraero.gov.br

Tourist Information – Associação Interestadual de Turismo
Travel agency and guides.
Avenida Tancredo Neves, no #, Centro de Convenções Senador Nilo Coelho
TEL (87) 3862-1616 OPEN Mon – Fri, 8am – noon and 2pm – 6pm www.valedosaofrancisco.tur.br

Tourist Information – Secretaria de Cultura and Turismo
Avenida 31 de Março, no #, Centro de Convenções Senador Nilo Coelho
TEL (87) 3862-9261 OPEN Mon – Fri, 7:30am – 1pm

Travel Agency – GTUR Guimarães Turismo
Avenida Dr. Fernando Góes, 87, Centro
TEL (87) 3861-0234 OPEN Mon – Fri, 8am – noon and 2pm – 6pm; Sat, 8am – noon

Petrópolis – Rio de Janeiro

AREA CODE 24 POPULATION 306,645 DISTANCES Rio de Janeiro, 65 kilometers (40 miles) ACCESS Highway BR-040 from Rio de Janeiro www.petropolis.rj.gov.br

WHERE TO STAY

Fazenda das Videiras $$$
This former farm has cozy chalets and rooms with whirlpool tubs. Grape and vine motifs are a feature of the decor. As well as having a large green area, the 19th-century guesthouse has a wine cellar and mini movie theater. ACCOMMODATIONS 8; air-conditioning (in 2 chalets); fireplace (in 2 chalets); jacuzzi (in 2 chalets); minibar; phone; private safe; TV. FACILITIES AND SERVICES bar; games room; gym; jacuzzi; mini movie theater with

| PRICES | HOTELS (couple) | $ up to R$ 150 | $$ from R$ 151 up to R$ 300 | $$$ from R$ 301 up to R$500 | $$$$ above R$ 500 |

pay TV; natural pool; parking; restaurant; sauna; trails; wine cellar. **CREDIT CARDS** Diners; MasterCard
Estrada Paulo Meira, 6,000, access from Estrada Araras–Vale das Videiras
TEL (24) 2225-8090 www.videiras.com.br

Hotel Solar do Império $$$
Opened in 2005, this national-heritage-listed hotel stands in the center of Petrópolis, in a lovely 1875 mansion surrounded by lakes and gardens. **ACCOMMODATIONS** 16; air-conditioning; Internet access; minibar; pay TV; phone; private safe. **FACILITIES AND SERVICES** bar; function room; gym; heated pool; Internet access; massage room; mini spa; ofuro tub; parking; pool; restaurant; sauna; snack bar; transport to airport and attractions. **CREDIT CARDS** AmEx; Diners; MasterCard; Visa
Avenida Koeler, 376, Centro
TEL (24) 2242-0034 **RESERVATIONS** (24) 2103-3000
www.solardoimperio.com.br

Locanda della Mimosa $$$
Six rooms are distributed between two buildings: three overlook a pool, two overlook a garden, and one gazes out on a fruit and vegetable garden. When guests return from dinner, they find chocolates on their pillows. The owner of this guesthouse is a famous chef who also owns a restaurant by the same name. **ACCOMMODATIONS** 6; air-conditioning; DVD player; heating; Internet access; minibar; phone; private safe; TV. **FACILITIES AND SERVICES** bar; fruit and vegetable garden; games room; gym; massage room; parking; pool; restaurant; sauna; trails; valet service. **CREDIT CARDS** Diners; MasterCard Diners;
Alameda das Mimosas, 30, Vale Florido, access from Rodovia BR-040 at Km 72
TEL (24) 2233-5405 www.locanda.com.br

Parador Santarém $$$
This complete leisure complex offers great options for young children. The cheeses and butter are homemade, and organic fruits and vegetables are grown on site. Fondue and wine tastings are served in the basement. **ACCOMMODATIONS** 19; air-conditioning; DVD Player; Internet access; minibar; pay TV; phone. **FACILITIES AND SERVICES** bar; business center; fishing equipment and lake; fruit and vegetable garden; function room; games room; gym; heliport; home theater; horses; Internet access; jacuzzi; jogging track; massage room; multi-sports court; orchard; parking; pitch and putt course; play area with toys; playground; pool; restaurant; sauna; tennis court; trails; transport to airport and attractions; wine cellar. **CREDIT CARDS** AmEx; Diners; MasterCard; Visa
Estrada Correia da Veiga, 96, Santa Mônica–Itaipava
TEL (24) 2222-9933 www.paradorsantarem.com.br

Pousada da Alcobaça $$$
Once the summer residence of the owner's grandfather, this home was later renovated and converted into a guesthouse. The air in the central heating is warmed by the main hall's fireplace, and beautiful gardens surround the building. **ACCOMMODATIONS** 11; air-conditioning; DVD player; heating; Internet access; pay TV; phone. **FACILITIES AND SERVICES** bar; fruit and vegetable garden; garden; massage service; parking; pool; restaurant; sauna; tennis court; trails; transport to airport and attractions; valet service; 24-hour kitchen. **CREDIT CARDS** AmEx; MasterCard; Visa
Rua Dr. Agostinho Goulão, 298, Correas
TEL (24) 2221-1240 **FAX** (24) 2221-3162
www.pousadadaalcobaca.com.br

Pousada das Araras $$$
This 15-hectare (37-acre) estate is at the foot of Maria Comprida Rock. Trails run through the Atlantic forest on the property, and two pools, one natural and one with treated water, are also on hand. The chalets are fitted with whirlpool tubs. **ACCOMMODATIONS** 29; fireplace (in the chalets); jacuzzi (in 19 chalets); minibar; phone; private safe; TV. **FACILITIES AND SERVICES** bar; function room; games room; heated pool; Internet access; massage room; multi-sports court; natural pool; parking; restaurant; sauna; store; trails. **CREDIT CARDS** MasterCard; Visa
Estrada Bernardo Coutinho, 4,570, access from Estrada Araras–Vale das Videiras
TEL (24) 2225-4000 www.pousadadasararas.com.br

Pousada Tambo los Incas $$$
Decorated with pre-Columbian pottery and Latin American handicrafts, this guesthouse has two suites fitted with whirlpool tubs and two with ofuro tubs. It also has a wine cellar with a stunning 400 labels. Children under 12 are not allowed. **ACCOMMODATIONS** 14; air-conditioning; DVD player; fireplace; Internet access; jacuzzi (in 2 suites); minibar; ofuro tub (in 2 suites); pay TV; phone. **FACILITIES AND SERVICES** bar; function room; games room; gym; heated pool; Internet access; jacuzzi; massage room; ofuro tub; parking; restaurant; TV room; sauna; spa; wine cellar. **CREDIT CARDS** AmEx; Diners; MasterCard; Visa
Estrada Ministro Salgado Filho, 2,761, Vale do Cuiabá
TEL (24) 2222-5666 **FAX** (24) 2222-5668
www.tambolosincas.com.br

WHERE TO EAT

Alvorada $
Spring chicken and delicious, crispy sun-dried meat with battered onions, pumpkin, and roasted banana are prepared on a wood-burning stove. A creek crosses the garden, giving the place a bucolic feel. **CUISINE** Various. **CREDIT CARDS** Diners; MasterCard
Estrada Bernardo Coutinho, 1,655, Araras
TEL (24) 2225-1118. Fri and Sat, 1pm – midnight; Sun, 1pm – 6pm

Artesão do Pão $
In operation for over a decade, this establishment offers a large array of bread, desserts, and savory snacks. Highlights are the traditional donuts called rosca de massa doce (with chocolate cream) and rosca mineira (with guava jam and white cheese). **CUISINE** Desserts; bread. **CREDIT CARDS** MasterCard; Visa.
Rua 31 de Março, 20, Centro
TEL (24) 2222-2890. Mon – Thu, 6am – 9pm; Fri and Sat, 6am – 10pm; Sun, 6:30am – 8pm

Casa D'Angelo $
Founded in 1914, this snack bar-restaurant-bakery is famous for its traditional tea, served with delicious Petrópolis-style toast. For lunch, we suggest the Portuguese cod, which comes with rice, collard greens, potato, hard-boiled eggs, carrots, onion, and olives. **CUISINE** Various. **CREDIT CARDS** AmEx; Diners; MasterCard; Visa
Rua do Imperador, 700, Centro
TEL (24) 2242-0888. Daily, 8am – midnight

Casa do Alemão $
This large eatery with German-style décor offers breads, croquettes, sandwiches, and sausages, as well as tasty

sweets. **CUISINE** German. **CREDIT CARDS** AmEx; Diners; MasterCard; Visa
Avenida Ayrton Senna, 927, Quitandinha
TEL (24) 2242-3442. Daily, 7am – 9:30pm

Chico Veríssimo $$
This restaurant serves trout, escargot, boar ribs, pâtés, and salads prepared by chef Christina Heilborn. The backdrop to this quality cuisine is the sound of a nearby waterfall and the gurgling of the river. **CUISINE** Contemporary; international. **CREDIT CARDS** AmEx; Diners; MasterCard; Visa
Rua Dr. Agostinho Goulão, 632, Correas
TEL (24) 2221-3049. Wed and Thu, 1pm – 10pm; Fri and Sat, 1pm – midnight; Sun, 1pm – 7pm

Churrascaria Majórica $
Operating in the historic town center for over four decades, this restaurant serves a wide variety of meat dishes. A great choice is the picanha nobre steak, which comes with rice, fried potato, soufflé, and manioc meal (serves 2). For dessert, try the profiteroles. **CUISINE** Meats. **CREDIT CARDS** AmEx; Diners; MasterCard; Visa
Rua do Imperador, 754, Centro
TEL (24) 2242-2498. Sun – Thu, 11:30am – 10pm; Fri and Sat, 11:30am – 11pm

Clube do Filé $
Housed in an old farm manor, surrounded by a beautiful garden with a fountain, this eatery serves a good selection of meats, chicken, and fish. The bottle-shop next door specializes in imported wines. **CUISINE** Meats. **CREDIT CARDS** Not accepted
Estrada União–Indústria, 9,153, Itaipava
TEL (24) 2232-1213. Thu, noon – 3pm; Fri and Sat, 1pm – midnight; Sun, 1pm – 6pm

Farfarello $
In a rustic setting, the Farfarello serves Italian food. Try the focaccia or burrata (white cheese filled with whipping cream and served with salad and toast) for starters and the fig and ricotta ravioli in cheese sauce for your main course. **CUISINE** Italian. **CREDIT CARDS** MasterCard; Visa
Estrada União–Indústria, 13,470, Itaipava
TEL (24) 2222-3120. Tue – Thu, noon – 11pm; Fri and Sat, noon – midnight; Sun, noon – 6:30pm

Fazenda das Videiras $$
This guesthouse has two dining rooms, one with a fireplace and the other with a beautiful view of the mountains. The house specialty is the canard confit (duck confit), served in a Parmesan cheese basket with grana padano risotto. The wine cellar has over 300 labels. Reservations required. **CUISINE** French. **CREDIT CARDS** Diners; MasterCard
Estrada Paulo Meira, 6,000, Vale das Videiras
TEL (24) 2225-8090. Fri, 8:30pm – 11pm; Sat, 1pm – 4pm and 8:30pm – 11pm; Sun, 1pm – 5pm

Locanda Della Mimosa $$
Award-winning Danio Braga is one of the most renowned chefs in Rio de Janeiro. His name draws many gourmands to the Locanda, which also has one of the best wine cellars in Brazil. The seasonings produced in Braga's private garden give his dishes a special touch. The menu changes weekly. **CUISINE** Contemporary; Italian. **CREDIT CARDS** Diners; MasterCard
Alameda das Mimosas, 30, Vale Florido, access from the Rodovia BR-040, Km 72
TEL (24) 2233-5405. Fri and Sat, noon – 4pm and 8pm – midnight

Massas Luigi $
In operation since 1979, this restaurant also has a separate pizza parlor and a store that sells homemade pasta made with imported flour. House specialties include lasagna bolognese. **CUISINE** Italian. **CREDIT CARDS** AmEx; Diners; MasterCard; Visa
Praça Rui Barbosa (Praça da Liberdade), 185, Centro
TEL (24) 2244-4444, 2244-4422. Daily, 11am – midnight

Mr. Paul of Petrópolis $
In the 1980s, the American owner, Paul, used to bake for his friends. He now has a factory that ships brownies and fruitcakes all over Brazil. In his store, visitors can also find chutney and 13 types of jelly, including flavors like mint, to serve with meats. **CUISINE** Confectionary. **CREDIT CARDS** Diners; MasterCard; Visa
Avenida Ayrton Senna, 179, Quitandinha
TEL (24) 2243-3641. Tue, Wed, and Thu, 10am – 7pm; Fri and Sat, 10am – 8pm

Parador Valencia $$
The Spanish cuisine here features spectacular paellas and squid filled with black rice. Chef Paquito lives in the house where the restaurant operates, and his paintings, sculptures and furniture decorate the place. **CUISINE** Spanish. **CREDIT CARDS** AmEx; Diners; MasterCard; Visa
Rua Celita de Oliveira Amaral, 189, Estrada União–Indústria, near #11,389
TEL (24) 2222-1250. Fri and Sat, noon – 11pm; Sun, noon – 6pm

Parrô do Valentim $$
This is the place to find Portuguese food in the mountains. Menu highlights are the toucinhos do céu (convent sweets), codfish, and charbroiled sardines, always accompanied by Portuguese wines. **CUISINE** Portuguese. **CREDIT CARDS** MasterCard; Visa
Estrada União–Indústria, 10,289, Itaipava
TEL (24) 2222-1281. Tue – Thu, and Sun, 11:30am – 10pm; Fri and Sat, 11:30am – midnight

Pousada da Alcobaça $$
Even non-overnighters are allowed to have the colonial-style breakfast at this guesthouse restaurant. The menu has French, Italian, and Portuguese influences, but this is also the place for a good Brazilian feijoada (black-bean and pork stew) on Saturdays. Reservations recommended. **CUISINE** Various. **CREDIT CARDS** Not accepted
Rua Dr. Agostinho Goulão, 298, Correas
TEL (24) 2221-1240. Daily, 8am – noon and 1:30pm – 10pm

Tamboatá $
The pizzas, which come with a variety of toppings, are baked in a wood-fired oven. In addition to two bars, there's a large hall with a dance floor, which often features live music. During the week, the Espaço Tamboatá offers lessons in singing, painting, theater, yoga, and the like. **CUISINE** Pizza. **CREDIT CARDS** Diners; MasterCard; Visa.
Estrada União–Indústria, 12,360, Itaipava
TEL (24) 2222-5007, 2222-5221. Fri and Sat, 10pm until the last customer leaves

SERVICES

Cultural Center –
Centro de Cultura Raul de Leoni
Praça Visconde de Mauá, 305, Centro
Mon – Fri, 9am – 6:30pm

PRICES	HOTELS (couple)	$ up to R$ 150	$$ from R$ 151 up to R$ 300	$$$ from R$ 301 up to R$500	$$$$ above R$ 500

Horse farm – Haras Analu

Estrada Ministro Salgado Filho, 5,230, Vale do Cuiabá, Itaipava
TEL (24) 2222-9666, 2527-1044. Daily, 10am – 5pm. Bookings required

Local tour operators – Campo de Aventuras Paraíso Açu

Estrada do Bonfim, 3,511, Correas
TEL (24) 2236-0003, 2236-0272, 8805-0004. Daily, 9am – 6pm. www.campodeaventurasparaisoacu.com.br

Local tour operators – Rios Brasileiros Rafting

Rua Silva Jardim, 514/104, Centro
TEL (24) 2243-4372. Daily, 10am – 7pm.
www.rbrafting.com.br

Tourist information – Disque Turismo

TEL (24) 2246-9377, 2246-9379, 0800-241516. Mon and Tue, 9am – 6:30pm; Wed – Sat, 9am – 8pm; Sun, 9am – 4pm

Tourist information – Pórtico da Quitandinha

Avenida Ayrton Senna, no #, Quitandinha
Mon – Fri, 8am – 6pm; Sat, 8am – 7pm; Sun, 8am – 5pm

Piaçabuçu – Alagoas

AREA CODE 82 POPULATION 16,688 DISTANCES Maceió 138 kilometers (86 miles), Penedo 26 kilometers (16 miles) ACCESS From Maceió, on Highway AL-101. The road from Penedo is asphalted and in good condition

WHERE TO STAY

Pousada Chez Julie $

This unpretentious, friendly guesthouse opened in 1998 and is run by Belgian-born Roeland Eniel, a naturalized Brazilian. The guesthouse is 18 kilometers (11 miles) from Piaçabuçu and accessible by car along the riverside beach. ACCOMMODATIONS 10; air-conditioning; TV FACILITIES AND SERVICES Internet access; bar; pool; restaurant; airport shuttle; transport to attractions CREDIT CARDS MasterCard; Visa
Avenida Beira-Mar, 53, Praia de Pontal do Peba
TEL (82) 3557-1217

WHERE TO EAT

Beira-Rio – Alô Alô $

On the banks of the São Francisco, this simple restaurant is the ideal place to enjoy peixada ao molho de camarão (fish in shrimp sauce). Carne-de-sol (beef jerky) and carne guisada (beef stew) are other highlights. CUISINE Fish and seafood; diverse. CREDIT CARDS Not accepted
Rua Tamandaré, 272, Centro
TEL (82) 3552-1837 OPEN Daily, 7am – 8pm

Piranhas – Alagoas

AREA CODE 82 POPULATION 23,483 DISTANCES Maceió 327 kilometers (203), Aracaju 215 kilometers (134 miles) ACCESS From Maceió, take Highway BR-316 to Pilar, then BR-101 to São Sebastião, AL-110 to Arapiraca, AL-220 to Olho d'Água do Casado, and finally AL-225. From Aracaju, take Highway BR-101, then SE-206

WHERE TO STAY

Guesthouses $

Piranhas has no hotels, only guesthouses. Some, like Lírio do Vale and Lampião, are simply family homes that rent out individual rooms. These guesthouses charge a high price for offering very little – the rooms are extremely simple and there are barely any facilities, although the tariff does include breakfast. The town is small, so visit all the guesthouses before making a decision. The guesthouses don't have addresses: if you can't find one, just ask a local.

Lampião TEL (82) 3686-3335

Lírio do Vale TEL (82) 3686-3145
Rua José Martiniano Vasco, no #

Maria Bonita TEL (82) 3686-1777
Rua Alto do Bonfim, no #

Marihá TEL (82) 3686-1326
Rua Pacatuba, 17

Nosso Lar TEL (82) 3686-3406
Rua Josélia Maria de Souza Rezende, 2

Remanso TEL (82) 3686-1157
Avenida Antonio Rodrigues Pereira, 53

Pousada da Trilha TEL (82) 3686-1172

WHERE TO EAT

Flor de Cáctus $

Atop a lookout point built at the end of the 19th-century, this restaurant offers views of the São Francisco River and the colorful houses of Piranhas. The restaurant has a bistro-like atmosphere, and the menu includes meat, fish, and soups. The delicious house specialty fish dishes such as surubim and tilapia are baked to order and brought whole to the table. CUISINE Meats; fish; diverse. CREDIT CARDS MasterCard; Visa
Mirante Secular, 1600, Centro
TEL (82) 3686-1365, 3686-1162 OPEN Mon – Sat, 8am – 10pm; Sun, 8am – 8pm

SERVICES

Travel Agency – Angico Tour

Trips through the São Francisco River Canyon
Rua Martiniano Vasco, 210, Centro
TEL (82) 3686-1782, 9965-1104 OPEN High season: daily, 8am – 10pm; low season: 8am – 6pm

Travel Agency – MS-Tur

Organizes boat tours around Xingó Dam
Avenida Ananias Fernandes, 1140, Centro, in Canindé de São Francisco (bordering Piranhas)
TEL (79) 9972-1320, (82) 9986-2038 FAX (79) 3346-1184
OPEN Mon – Fri, 8am – 5:30pm

Pirenópolis – Goiás

AREA CODE 62 POPULATION 20,460 DISTANCE Goiânia 125 kilometers (78 miles), Brasilia 140 kilometers (87 miles) ACCESS Highways BR-070, BR-414 and BR-225 from Brasilia. From Goiânia, Highway BR-060 to Anápolis, then

BR-414 and BR-225. Or take Highway BR-153 and GO-431 from Anápolis www.pirenopolis.go.gov.br

WHERE TO STAY

Pousada dos Pireneus Resort $$

This resort nests in a wooded area in the elevated area of town, so its restaurant boasts beautiful views. The site has good leisure facilities, including a children's water park. There are also rooms for disabled guests. **ACCOMMODATIONS** 111; air-conditioning; minibar; telephone; TV. **FACILITIES AND SERVICES** bar; beauty parlor; bicycles; conference room; convenience store; games room; gym; horses and carriage; horse-riding; Internet access; lifeguard; massage room; nursery; orchard; parking; playground; pool; recreational staff for adults and children; restaurant; river; sauna; six-a-side soccer court; snack bar; soccer field; spa; stores; tennis court; trails; transport to airport and attractions; travel agency; video room; volleyball court; walking tours; wine cellar; woods; 24-hour kitchen. **CREDIT CARDS** Diners; MasterCard; Visa
Chácara Mata do Sobrado, 80, Carmo
TEL (62) 3331-1345 **FAX** (62) 3331-1345
RESERVATIONS (61) 2101-7818
www.pousadadospireneus.com.br

WHERE TO EAT

Café & Tarsia Ristorante $

This restaurant specializes in contemporary and Mediterranean food and features live music on the weekends. The most popular dishes are the pastas, such as the gnocchi and lasagna. **CUISINE** Contemporary. **CREDIT CARDS** Visa
Rua do Rosário, 34, Centro
TEL (62) 3331-1274, 8414-5625. Tue – Sun, 7am – 9pm

Le Bistrô $

This candle-lit bistro serves the owner's favorite inventions, such as shitake risotto with chicken in orange, mint and tonka bean sauce, or Provençal steak with herb sauce. **CUISINE** Contemporary. **CREDIT CARDS** Diners; MasterCard; Visa
Rua do Rosário, 23, Casa 3, Centro
TEL (62) 3331-2150. Wed – Fri, 7pm – midnight; Sat, Sun, and holidays, 1pm – 5pm and 7pm – 1am

Pedreiras $

This airy restaurant offers a buffet of regional fare, including feijão tropeiro (seasoned beans thickened with manioc flour) and risoto do cerrado (Cerrado-style risotto), to the sound of live music. The property has a waterfall and natural pool that's good for swimming. **CUISINE** Regional. **CREDIT CARDS** Diners; MasterCard; Visa
Estrada dos Pireneus, Km 1.5
TEL (62) 3331-1853. Sat and Sun, noon – 5pm

Piripiri – Piauí

AREA CODE 86 **POPULATION** 61,965 **DISTANCES** Sete Cidades National Park 25 kilometers (16 miles), Teresina 183 kilometers (114 miles) **ACCESS** From Teresina, take Highway BR-343 towards Fortaleza

WHERE TO STAY

Parque Hotel Sete Cidades $

The high point of this hotel is its location inside the national park, in a beautiful setting with a lovely natural pool, just 2 kilometers (1 mile) from the park's visitors'

center. The rooms are very basic and the restaurant's home-style cooking is fine but unremarkable. Visitors who want to eat something different will have to travel 25 kilometers (16 miles) to Piripiri. **ACCOMMODATIONS** 12; air-conditioning; minibar. **FACILITIES AND SERVICES** parking; natural pool; restaurant; games room; video room; walking trails. **CREDIT CARDS** MasterCard
Parque Nacional de Sete Cidades (exit Km 63 on Rodovia BR-222 to Fortaleza)
TEL (86) 3223-3366, 9424-0024 **FAX** and **RESERVATIONS** (86) 3223-2423 www.hotelsetecidades.com.br

Poconé – Mato Grosso

AREA CODE 65 **POPULATION** 31,118 **DISTANCE** Cuiabá 96 kilometers (60 miles) **ACCESS** Highway BR-070 from Cuiabá toward Cáceres; turn left at the exit to Highway MT-060 www.pmpocone.com.br

WHERE TO STAY

Pousada Araras Eco Lodge $$$

This charming jungle hotel built was with woods harvested from the Pantanal and decorated with indigenous artifacts. The area is home to the beautiful blue hyacinth macaw, which accounts for the property's three lookouts for animal watching. The nearby highway can be busy during the fishing season. **ACCOMMODATIONS** 19; air-conditioning; ceiling fan; mosquito-screens on windows. **FACILITIES AND SERVICES** bar; bilingual staff; convenience store; first-aid; massage room; parking; pool; restaurant; snack bar; transport to airport and attractions; walking tours. **EXCURSIONS** boat; bicycles; bird and animal watching; buffalo, cattle, chicken and pig breeding; carriage ride; cattle handling; hiking; horseback riding; kayaks; lassoing; nocturnal wildlife spotting; sport fishing. **CREDIT CARDS** Diners; MasterCard; Visa. **ACCESS** From Cuiabá, on Highway BR-070, followed by 32 kilometers (20 miles) on a unpaved stretch of Highway MT-060 (Rodovia Transpantaneira).
Rodovia Transpantaneira, Km 32
TEL (65) 9603-0529 **FAX** (65) 3682-1260
RESERVATIONS (65) 3682-2800 www.araraslodge.com.br

Pousada Rio Claro $$

This friendly, well-kept guesthouse is located on a farm and surrounded by gardens. A deck overhanging the river is a good place to enjoy the sunset. Rooms can also be rented overnight or for day-use only. **ACCOMMODATIONS** 20; air-conditioning; ceiling fan; mosquito-screens on windows (in some rooms). **FACILITIES AND SERVICES** convenience store; parking; pool; restaurant; river; snack bar. **EXCURSIONS** bird and animal watching; boat trips; bicycles; fishing; hiking; horseback riding; nocturnal wildlife spotting; walking tours. **CREDIT CARDS** Visa. **ACCESS** From Cuiabá to Poconé take the Rodovia Transpantaneira; you will have to drive for 100 kilometers (62 miles) on asphalted road, followed by an unpaved stretch of 42 kilometers (26 miles) to the guesthouse
Rodovia Transpantaneira, Km 42
TEL (65) 3345-2449, 3345-1054
www.pousadarioclaro.com.br

Refúgio Ilha do Caracará $$$$

Twenty-five minutes by boat from Porto Jofre, this is the most sophisticated hotel in the region. The island ("ilha" in Portuguese) is formed when neighboring marshes fill with water. The rooms all face onto a lovely center garden, and there are fishing facilities on site. There is a so-called "boat-hotel" to take visitors on fish-

| PRICES | HOTELS (couple) | $ up to R$ 150 | $$ from R$ 151 up to R$ 300 | $$$ from R$ 301 up to R$500 | $$$$ above R$ 500 |

524

BRAZIL GUIDE

ing trips. Rooms can be rented overnight or for day-use only. **ACCOMMODATIONS** 20; air-conditioning; ceiling fan; jacuzzi (in 2 suites); minibar; mosquito-screens on windows. **FACILITIES AND SERVICES** bar; convenience store; first-aid; Internet access; pool; restaurant; river; soccer field; video room; 24-hour kitchen. **EXCURSIONS** bird and animal watching; boat trips; canoeing; hiking; horseback riding; nocturnal wildlife spotting; sport fishing; walking tours. **CREDIT CARDS** Visa. **ACCESS** At the end of the Rodovia Transpantaneira, in Porto Jofre, you must take a boat; the trip lasts 25 to 30 minutes. You can also get here by air taxi or private plane (landing-strip ID: SIYY)
Right bank of the São Lourenço River, no #, exit at Km 15 on Rodovia Transpantaneira, Porto Jofre, Zona Rural
FAX (31) 2126-5657 **RESERVATIONS** (31) 2126-5656
www.ilhadocaracara.com.br

SERVICES

Tourist Information – Secretaria de Turismo e Meio Ambiente
Praça da Matriz, no #, Centro
TEL (65) 3345-1952, 3345-1357. Mon – Fri, 7am – 1pm.

Ponta do Corumbau – Bahia

AREA CODE 73 **DISTANCES** Salvador 844 kilometers (524 miles), Porto Seguro 220 kilometers (137 miles) **ACCESS** Take the BR-101 to Itamaraju and BA-489 (15 kilometers, 9 miles), then drive 57 kilometers (35 miles) along a dirt road. By sea, take a motorboat or boat from Cumuruxatiba

WHERE TO STAY

Fazenda São Francisco $$$$
This seaside coconut plantation has an exclusive, sophisticated air and only 8 airy, well-decorated rooms and bungalows, each designed by Roberto Migotto. In addition to the plantation's 1,000 meters (3,300 feet) of private beach, there is also a river out back with mangroves and islands. Children are allowed, but only if accompanied by a full-time babysitter. **ACCOMMODATIONS** 8; air-conditioning; private safe; minibar; telephone; ceiling fan; veranda. **FACILITIES AND SERVICES** Internet access; bar; boat; bicycles; woods; horses; parking; pool; orchard; pony; restaurant; magazine reading area; river; games room; video room; walking trails; guided walking tours; helipad; beach service; airport shuttle; transport to attractions. **CREDIT CARDS** AmEx
Praia de Ponta do Corumbau, no #
TEL and **FAX** (73) 3294-2250 **RESERVATIONS** (11) 3078-4411
www.corumbau.com.br

Jocotoka Eco Resort $$$
With 700 meters (2,300 feet) of beach, a branch of the river out back, and several walking trails, this seaside coconut plantation is another charming option. It offers spacious, rustic chalets and excellent water-sports facilities. In the high season, dinner is included in the tariff. **ACCOMMODATIONS** 20; air-conditioning; private safe; minibar; ceiling fan. **FACILITIES AND SERVICES** Internet access; wine cellar; bar; boat; kayaks; horse and cart; fishing equipment; parking; motorboat; stores; pool; volleyball court; beach volleyball arena; restaurant; games room; massage room; video room; travel agency; exchange bureau; recreational team for adults and children; guided walking tours; beach service; airport shuttle; transport to attractions. **CREDIT CARDS** MasterCard

Praia de Ponta do Corumbau, no #
TEL (73) 3294-1244, 3288-2291 **FAX** (73) 3288-2540
www.jocotoka.com.br

Tauana Hotel $$$$
The all-inclusive luxury hotel, one of the newest in the region, is located on a farm. The manor house and cabanas have wattle-and-daub and adobe brick walls. Guests can swim and go canoeing in a small river. Children under the age of 12 are not allowed. **ACCOMMODATIONS** 9; air-conditioning; private safe; minibar; telephone. **FACILITIES AND SERVICES** Internet access; wine cellar; bicycles; woods; parking; stores; orchard; restaurant; river; walking trails; masseuse; beach service; airport shuttle. **CREDIT CARDS** Visa
Estrada Guarani–Corumbau
(Fazenda Riacho Grande)
TEL, FAX and **RESERVATIONS** (73) 3668-5172
www.tauana.com

Vila Naiá $$$$
This hotel stands on a private nature reserve with a river beach, native restinga vegetation, and mangroves. The rooms were built without nails by local artisans to imitate old local wooden dwellings. **ACCOMMODATIONS** 7; private safe; minibar; telephone; TV; ceiling fan. **FACILITIES AND SERVICES** Internet access; wine cellar; bar; boat; bicycles; woods; soccer field; kayaks; horses; parking; motorboat; convenience store; pool; restaurant; river; gym; massage room; video room; walking trails; recreational team for adults; guided walking tours; airport shuttle; transport to attractions; beach service. **CREDIT CARDS** AmEx; Diners; MasterCard; Visa
Estrada Guarani–Corumbau, no #,
Ponta do Corumbau
TEL and **FAX** (73) 3573-1006 **RESERVATIONS** (11) 3063-1872, 3063-2023 www.vilanaia.com.br

SERVICES

Travel Agency – Aquamar
Tourist information and trips
Avenida Beira-mar, 7, Centro, Cumuruxatiba
TEL and **FAX** (73) 3573-1360 **OPEN** High season: daily, 7am – 8pm; low season: daily, 7am – 6pm
www.aquamarba.com.br

Ponte Alta do Tocantins – Tocantins (see Jalapão)

Porto Alegre – Rio Grande do Sul

AREA CODE 51 **POPULATION** 1,420,667 **DISTANCE** Florianópolis 476 kilometers (296 miles) **ACCESS** Highway BR-101 and BR-290 from Florianópolis
www.portoalegre.rs.gov.br

WHERE TO STAY

Blue Tree Millenium Porto Alegre $$
This well-located serviced apartment building stands next to the Shopping Praia de Belas mall. The gym, swimming pool, and sauna are on the top floor: guests can exercise while watching the sun set over the Guaíba River. **ACCOMMODATIONS** 177; air-conditioning; Internet access; minibar; mini kitchen with microwave oven; pay TV; private safe; telephone. **FACILITIES AND SERVICES** bar; function room; gym; heated pool; Internet access;

| RESTAURANTS | $ up to R$ 50 | $$ from R$ 51 up to R$ 100 | $$$ from R$ 101 up to R$ 150 | $$$$ above R$ 150 |

restaurant; sauna; 24-hour business center; 24-hour kitchen. **CREDIT CARDS** AmEx; Diners; MasterCard; Visa
Avenida Borges de Medeiros, 3,120, Praia de Belas
TEL (51) 3026-2200 **FAX** (51) 3026-6704
RESERVATIONS 0800-150500 www.bluetree.com.br

Plaza São Rafael Hotel $$
This is one of the most traditional hotels in Porto Alegre. Shops in the lobby sell antiques and jewelry. The pool is in a building across the street. **ACCOMMODATIONS** 283; air-conditioning; Internet access; jacuzzi (in some suites); minibar; pay TV; telephone. **FACILITIES AND SERVICES** bar; beauty parlor; business center; function room; gym; pool; restaurant; stores; 24-hour kitchen. **CREDIT CARDS** AmEx; Diners; MasterCard; Visa
Avenida Alberto Bins, 514, Centro
TEL (51) 3220-7000 **FAX** (51) 3220-7001
RESERVATIONS (51) 3220-7259 www.plazahoteis.com.br

Sheraton Porto Alegre Hotel $$$$
In one of the fanciest districts, next to a shopping mall, this is the best hotel in town. There is a theme floor, where the room décor is reminiscent of places such as Tahiti and New York. **ACCOMMODATIONS** 171; air-conditioning; Internet access; jacuzzi (presidential suite); minibar; pay TV; telephone. **FACILITIES AND SERVICES** bar; business center; function room; gym; heated pool; Internet access; massage room; parking; restaurant; sauna; transport to airport and attractions; valet service; 24-hour kitchen. **CREDIT CARDS** AmEx; Diners; MasterCard; Visa
Rua Olavo Barreto Viana, 18, Moinhos de Vento
TEL (51) 2121-6000 **FAX** (51) 2121-6010
RESERVATIONS (51) 2121-6015
www.sheraton-poa.com.br

Quality Porto Alegre $$
This hotel is surrounded by the greenery of Moinhos de Vento Park. The best view of the park is from upper-floor rooms ending in 4 and 5. **ACCOMMODATIONS** 80; air-conditioning; Internet access; minibar; pay TV; telephone. **FACILITIES AND SERVICES** business center; function room; gym; massage room; restaurant; sauna; 24-hour kitchen. **CREDIT CARDS** AmEx; Diners; MasterCard; Visa
Rua Comendador Caminha, 42, Moinhos de Vento
TEL (51) 3323-9300 **FAX** (51) 3323-9301
www.atlanticahotels.com.br

WHERE TO EAT

Al Dente $$
This restaurant serves freshly prepared pasta in a refined atmosphere. It specializes in the cuisine of northern Italy. Try the involtini al dente, a dish of colorful balls of pasta stuffed with ricotta, walnuts, and sultanas in cream, cognac, and black truffle sauce, accompanied by scaloppini. **CUISINE** Italian. **CREDIT CARDS** Diners; MasterCard; Visa
Rua Mata Bacelar, 210, Auxiliadora
TEL (51) 3343-1841. Mon – Thu, 7:30pm – midnight; Fri and Sat, 7:30pm – 1am

Churrascaria Barranco $
One of the best steakhouses in town, this simple place stays busy. Service is à la carte. The picanha steak and pork loin with cheese are the most popular dishes. **CUISINE** Grill. **CREDIT CARDS** AmEx; Diners; MasterCard; Visa
Avenida Protásio Alves, 1,578, Petrópolis
TEL (51) 3331-6172. Daily, 11am – 2am

{A} Restaurante Copacabana $
Since 1939, this restaurant has been serving good Italian

food with homemade and imported Italian pasta. There are also great seafood and meat dishes to choose from, such as vitela assada (baked veal) with potatoes and onions. **CUISINE** Italian. **CREDIT CARDS** AmEx; Diners; MasterCard; Visa
Praça Garibaldi, 2, Cidade Baixa
TEL (51) 3221-4616. Tue – Sun, 11am – 3:30pm and 7pm – 1am

Koh Pee Pee $$$
The main kitchen is in the middle of the restaurant, imitating a Thai food kiosk. Fried rice with vegetables and shrimp, conger eel with curry sauce, and seafood pasta are the house fortes. **CUISINE** Thai. **CREDIT CARDS** AmEx; Diners; MasterCard; Visa
Rua Schiller, 83, Moinhos de Vento
TEL (51) 3333-5150. Mon – Sat, 7:30pm – 11:30pm

Mercado del Puerto $
This is the place for an Uruguayan barbecue. The meat is charcoal grilled without skewers. The abundant servings contain 350 grams (12 oz) of meat on average and are accompanied by condiments such as chimichurri sauce. **CUISINE** Uruguayan. **CREDIT CARDS** AmEx; Diners; MasterCard; Visa
Avenida Cairu, 1,487, São João
TEL (51) 3337-1066. Mon – Fri, 7pm – 2am; Sat, Sun and holidays, noon – 2am

Le Bateau Ivre $$
The excellent dishes by chef Gerard Durand make this one of the best French restaurants in town. Specialties include the magret de pato (maigret of duck) in red wine sauce and spices. A tasting menu can be prepared if requested in advance. **CUISINE** French. **CREDIT CARDS** AmEx; Visa
Rua Tito Lívio Zambecari, 805, Mont Serrat
TEL (51) 3330-7351. Tue – Sat, 8pm until the last customer leaves

SERVICES

Airport – Aeroporto Internacional Salgado Filho
Avenida Severo Duilius, 90,010, São João
TEL (51) 3358-2000

Boat Trips on the Guaíba River – Fellini Turismo
Rua General Bento Martins, 24, Conjunto 401, Centro
TEL (51) 3228-6388, 3227-5400. Mon – Fri, 9am – 6pm; Sat, 9am – noon

Tourist Information – Posto de Informações Turísticas (Mercado do Bom Fim)
Avenida Osvaldo Aranha, Store #12, Parque Farroupilha
TEL (51) 3333-1873. Daily, 9am – 6pm

Tourist Information – Serviço de Atendimento ao Turista
At several locations around the city.
TEL 0800-517686. Daily, 7:30am – 11:45pm

Porto de Galinhas – Pernambuco

AREA CODE 81 **DISTANCE** Recife 60 kilometers (37 miles)
ACCESS From Recife, take Highway BR-101 toward the

south coast. From there, take PE-060 to Ipojuca, then PE-038 to Nossa Senhora do Ó, and finally PE-09, which leads to the town

WHERE TO STAY

Enotel Resort & Spa $$$$

This resort, constructed as a boutique hotel and open since 2006, was the first investment of the Portuguese group Enotel. The spaces were designed by Nini Silva and ooze sophistication from the décor to the furniture. Facing Cupe Beach, which isn't good for swimming, is one of the resort's two enormous pools. Guests can choose between breakfast-only or full board room rates, although neither tariff covers laundry, Internet, babysitter, and massage services. Eight of the rooms face the sea. The spa has a covered pool and includes mineral salt baths, massages, and thalassotherapy. **ACCOMMODATIONS** 348 (4 have handicapped facilities); Internet access; air-conditioning; king size bed; private safe; minibar; jacuzzi in some rooms; telephone; cable TV; veranda. **FACILITIES AND SERVICES** Internet access; wine cellar; bars; nursery; bicycles; soccer fields; golf course; convention center; cycle path; nightclub; parking; jacuzzi; kid's club; stores; ofuro tub; jacuzzi; pools; jogging track; playground; six-a-side soccer court; multi-sports court; squash court; tennis court; beach volleyball arena; restaurant; conference room; gym; massage room; video room; beauty parlor; games room; sauna; spa; travel agency; bilingual staff; swimming lessons; squash lessons; beach volleyball lessons; dance classes; soccer lessons; water-aerobics classes; stretching classes; business center; exchange bureau; 24-hour kitchen; diving equipment; beach equipment; recreational team for adults and children; guides; walking tours; heliport; valet parking; lifeguards; beach service; poolside service; airport shuttle; transport to attractions; nightly shows. **CREDIT CARDS** AmEx; Diners; MasterCard; Visa
Rodovia PE-09, Gleba 6BA, Porto de Galinhas, Ipojuca
TEL (81) 3552-5555 **FAX** (81) 3552-5514
www.enotel.com.br

Marulhos Suítes Hotéis $$$

Located in a condo with residential apartments and a hotel structure, Marulhos Suítes is equipped with an array of leisure options, a highlight of which is the series of five pools. Breakfast is included. **ACCOMMODATIONS** 100; Internet access; air-conditioning; private safe; electric stove; minibar; microwave; telephone; cable TV **FACILITIES AND SERVICES** wine cellar; pool bar; nursery; parking; convenience store; mini golf course; pools; playground; beach; six-a-side soccer court; volleyball court; tennis court; restaurant; conference room; gym; games room; massage room; video room; beauty parlor; sauna; spa; bilingual staff; business center; beach equipment; recreational team for adults and children; pool and beach service; airport shuttle; transport to attractions and nearby towns. **CREDIT CARDS** Diners; MasterCard; Visa
Gleba 6B, Praia de Muro Alto, Ipojuca
TEL (81) 3117-6100 www.marulhossuites.com.br

Nannai Beach Resort $$$$

This charming resort on Muro Alto Beach is ideal for swimming, thanks to the protection afforded by the adjacent reef. Its understated Polynesian-style wooden bungalows, each with a private pool, DVD player, and 29" TV, are popular with honeymooners. The huge swimming pool in the communal area is 6,000 square meters (65,000 square feet). **ACCOMMODATIONS** 91; Internet access; air-conditioning; private safe; DVD player in the bungalows; minibar; jacuzzi in the master bungalow; telephone; cable TV. **FACILITIES AND SERVICES** Internet access; bar; parking; helipad; stores; pool; playground; six-a-side soccer court; tennis court; volleyball court; restaurant; gym; games room; massage room; beauty parlor; sauna; recreational team for adults and children; guided walking tours; valet parking; beach service; airport shuttle; transport to attractions. **CREDIT CARDS** AmEx; Diners; MasterCard; Visa
Rodovia PE-09, Km 3 (exit to Muro Alto)
TEL (81) 3552-0100 **FAX** (81) 3552-1474, 3552-5097
www.nannai.com.br

Pousada Tabajuba $$

On the seafront at Praia do Cupe, this sophisticated guesthouse is tastefully decorated with rustic furniture and local craftwork. The communal areas face the garden courtyard. Very popular with honeymooners, the guesthouse doesn't accept children under the age of 12. **ACCOMMODATIONS** 24; air-conditioning; minibar; telephone; TV; ceiling fan. **FACILITIES AND SERVICES** bar; parking; snack bar; stores; pool; restaurant; airport shuttle; transport to attractions. **CREDIT CARDS** AmEx; Diners; MasterCard; Visa
Praia do Cupe, Loteamento Merepe II, Quadra I, Lote 6 (exit Km 6.5, Rodovia PE-09)
TEL (81) 3552-1049 **FAX** (81) 3552-1006
www.tabajuba.com

Summerville Beach Resort $$$$

This resort offers a range of leisure activities for the entire family, including a large 2,300-square-meter (25,000-square foot) pool that stretches over a large part of the grounds. In the suites and bungalows, guests get to choose from more than 10 different kinds of pillows, each containing a unique blend of herbs. **ACCOMMODATIONS** 101; Internet access; air-conditioning; private safe; minibar; jacuzzi in 2 bungalows; telephone; cable TV. **FACILITIES AND SERVICES** Internet access; wine cellar; archery; bar; nursery; bicycles; kayaks; soccer field; water skiing; parking; jacuzzi; jet-ski; snack bar; stores; pool; playground; tennis court; volleyball court; restaurant; conference room; gym; games room; massage room; sauna; spa; travel agency; business center; exchange bureau; recreational team for adults and children; valet parking; lifeguards; beach service; airport shuttle; transport to attractions. **CREDIT CARDS** AmEx; Diners; MasterCard; Visa
Rodovia PE-09, Km 2 (exit to Muro Alto)
TEL (81) 3302-5555 **FAX** (81) 3302-5577
www.summervilleresort.com.br

WHERE TO EAT

Beijupirá $

This charming restaurant has several different dining areas. The kitchen prepares typical regional dishes, but adds its own twist with new ingredients. The maracatu imperial, for example, is shredded beef jerky cooked with butter, tabbouleh made with rice, cracked wheat, and Northeastern cuscuz, colored bell peppers and honey vinaigrette. **CUISINE** Fish and seafood; regional. **CREDIT CARDS** AmEx; Diners; MasterCard; Visa
Rua Beijupirá, no #
TEL (81) 3552-2354, 3552-2758 **OPEN** Daily, noon – midnight

Peixe na Telha $$

This restaurant has a sophisticated but casual beach style and serves delicious food. The tile-cooked fish in shrimp sauce arrives at the table piping hot and garnished with saffron rice and golden-brown potatoes.

CUISINE Fish and seafood; diverse. CREDIT CARDS AmEx; Diners; MasterCard; Visa
Avenida Beira-mar, 40-B
TEL (81) 3552-1323 RESERVATIONS (81) 3552-1851 OPEN Daily, 10am until the last customer leaves

Porto Seguro – Bahia

AREA CODE 73 POPULATION 133,976 DISTANCES Salvador 723 kilometers (449 miles), Itabuna 250 kilometers (155 miles), Vitória 600 kilometers (373 miles) ACCESS From Salvador or Vitória, take highways BR-101 and BR-367

WHERE TO STAY

Porto Seguro Praia $$
Set along 50,000 square meters (12 acres) of beautiful woods and gardens on the beach avenue, this hotel has spacious, well-equipped rooms, with understated décor and balconies. The suites have unparalleled sea views. ACCOMMODATIONS 150; air-conditioning; private safe; minibar; jacuzzi in the suites; telephone; cable TV; veranda. FACILITIES AND SERVICES Internet access; bar; beach tent; chapel; parking; stores; pool; playground; tennis court; volleyball court; restaurant; gym; games room; massage room; video room; sauna; business center; currency exchange bureau; 24-hour kitchen; recreational team for adults and children; valet parking. CREDIT CARDS Visa
Avenida Beira-mar, 1500, Praia de Curuípe
TEL (73) 3288-9393 FAX (73) 3288-2069
RESERVATIONS (73) 3288-9321 www.psph.com.br

Vela Branca Resort $$
This resort comprises 120,000 square meters (38 acres) of gardens and lawns in the upper city, next to the historical town centre. It offers a magnificent view of the coastline and excellent facilities and services. ACCOMMODATIONS 120; air-conditioning; private safe; minibar; telephone; cable TV. FACILITIES AND SERVICES Internet access; bar; soccer field; parking; convenience store; pool; tennis court; restaurant; gym; massage room; beauty parlor; sauna; business center; recreational team for children. CREDIT CARDS AmEx; Diners; MasterCard; Visa
Rua Antônio Ricaldi, 177, Cidade Histórica
TEL (73) 3288-2318 fax and RESERVATIONS (73) 3288-2316 www.velabranca.com.br

Villagio Arcobaleno $$
The high-quality services and facilities make this Beach Avenue Hotel one of the best places to stay in Porto Seguro. The hotel has spacious rooms and even its own kiosk. The main building stops the noise from nearby beach kiosk Axé Moi from reaching them. ACCOMMODATIONS 163; Internet access; air-conditioning; private safe; minibar; telephone; cable TV. FACILITIES AND SERVICES Internet access; bar; parking; jacuzzi; stores; pool; playground; tennis court; restaurant; conference room; gym; games room; massage room; video room; beauty parlor; sauna; 24-hour kitchen; recreational team for adults and children; airport shuttle. CREDIT CARDS AmEx; Diners; MasterCard; Visa
Rodovia BR-367, Km 67, Praia de Taperapuã
TEL (73) 2105-5050, 0800-2845222 www.hotelarcobaleno.tur.br

WHERE TO EAT

Bistrô da Helô $
Creative dishes, such as lambreta (a type of shellfish) gratin and fish carpaccio, are served in an informal setting. Located in the historical building, this eatery has a wine list and live music. CUISINE Fish and seafood; diverse. CREDIT CARDS MasterCard
Rua Marechal Deodoro, 172, Paquetá
TEL (73) 3288-3940 RESERVATIONS (73) 9141-4999 OPEN Mon – Sat, 7pm until the last customer leaves

Tia Nenzinha $
One of the first restaurants in Porto Seguro, Tia Nenzinha is housed in a historical building. It serves a wide variety of simple fish, lobster, and meat dishes. We recommend the fish moqueca with shrimp and the tile-cooked fish with rice, potato salad, and seasoned manioc flour. CUISINE Meats; fish and seafood; regional. CREDIT CARDS Visa
Avenida Portugal, 170 (Passarela do Álcool), Centro
TEL (73) 3288-1846 RESERVATIONS (73) 9141-9812 (ask for Fernanda) OPEN Daily, 11am – midnight

SERVICES

Airport – Aeroporto Internacional de Porto Seguro
Estrada do Aeroporto, no #, Cidade Alta
TEL (73) 3288-1877 OPEN Daily, 24 hours

Tourist Information – Centro de Informações Turísticas de Porto Seguro
Praça Manoel Ribeiro Coelho, 10, Centro, Porto Seguro (near the ferryboat)
TEL (73) 3268-2853 OPEN Mon – Sat, 9am – 9pm

Travel Agency – Brasil Travel
Avenida 22 de Abril, 186, Store #6
TEL (73) 3288-3513, 3288-4285 OPEN Mon – Fri, 9am – 6pm www.braziltravel.com.br

Travel Agency – Pataxó Turismo
Rua Oscar Oliveira, 4 (Passarela do Álcool), Centro
TEL (73) 3288-1256, 3288-2507, 9979-5597 (24 hours) OPEN High season: daily, 8am – 11:30pm; low season: Mon – Fri, 8am – 7pm www.pataxoturismo.com.br

Travel Agency – Yes Tour Receptivo
Travel agency; trips along the Discovery Coast and the Whale Coast.
Rua Rui Barbosa, 15, Store #4 (mezzanine), Centro
TEL (73) 3288-3363, 8114-7236 FAX (73) 3288-3664 OPEN Mon – Fri, 8am – 6pm www.yestours.tur.br

Praia da Pipa – Rio Grande do Norte

AREA CODE 84 DISTANCE Natal 82 kilometers (51 miles) ACCESS From Natal, take Highway BR-101 to Goianinha, then continue for another 16 kilometers (10 miles) on RN-003

WHERE TO STAY

Kilombo Villas & Spa $$$$
On Sibaúma Beach, some 8 kilometers (5 miles) from Pipa, this charming, brand-new hotel is absolutely exclusive. Guests are accommodated in tastefully-decorated houses, with hot tubs, jacuzzis, and even a private gym or mini-golf course in some cases. The almost deserted beach and ocean are good for water sports and watching turtles lay their eggs. ACCOMMODATIONS 5; gym in one house; Internet access; air-conditioning; private safe; kitchen; whirlpool tub; jacuzzi; mini-gold course at one

house; telephone; cable TV. **FACILITIES AND SERVICES** Internet access; boat; buggy; kayaks; horses; delicatessen; parking; ocean fishing; pool; restaurant; gym; spa; surfing; business center; guides for trips; heliport; airport shuttle; transport to attractions and neighboring towns. **CREDIT CARDS** MasterCard; Visa

Rua das Tartarugas, no #, Praia de Sibaúma
TEL (84) 3246-5534

Hotel Marinas Tibau do Sul $$$

Chalets with verandas face the place where the Guaraíras estuarine lagoon meets the sea. The rooms have rustic décor, wood ceilings, and clay floor tiles. **ACCOMMODATIONS** 33; wine cellar; air-conditioning; private safe; minibar; telephone; cable TV; ceiling fan **FACILITIES AND SERVICES** wine cellar; bar; boat; kayaks; horse and cart; parking; lake; fishing equipment; motorboat; snack bar; marina; pool; playground; tennis court; volleyball court; restaurant; magazine reading area; massage room; walking trails; beach service; airport shuttle; transport to attractions. **CREDIT CARDS** Diners; MasterCard; Visa

Rua Governador Aluísio Alves, 301, (beach street), Tibau do Sul
TEL (84) 3246-4111 **FAX** (84) 3246-4228
www.hotelmarinas.com.br

Ponta do Madeiro $$$

These secluded chalets, far from the noise, are scattered along a path with a view of Ponta do Madeiro. The décor incorporates regional materials, such as lampshades woven out of vines by a local artisan. The trip down to the sea requires negotiating almost 200 stairs, but it is worth it. **ACCOMMODATIONS** 26 rooms; air-conditioning; private safe; minibar; jacuzzi in the master chalet; telephone; cable TV. **FACILITIES AND SERVICES** wine cellar; bar; parking; pool; restaurant; 24-hour kitchen; airport shuttle. **CREDIT CARDS** AmEx; MasterCard; Visa

Rota do Sol, Km 3, Tibau do Sul
TEL (84) 3246-4220 **FAX** (84) 3502-2377
RESERVATIONS (84) 3246-4220, 3502-2377
www.pontadomadeiro.com.br

Toca da Coruja Pousada $$$

The chalets are scattered throughout well-kept gardens on a 2.5-hectare (6-acre) property. The night lighting is cozy and romantic. Fresh tapioca is served at breakfast. **ACCOMMODATIONS** 15; Internet access; air-conditioning; private safe; minibar; jacuzzi in the luxury chalets; telephone; cable TV; ceiling fan. **FACILITIES AND SERVICES** bar; boat; parking; stores; restaurant; gym; games room; sauna; airport shuttle. **CREDIT CARDS** AmEx; Diners; MasterCard; Visa

Avenida Baía dos Golfinhos, 464, Pipa
TEL and **FAX** (84) 3246-2226 www.tocadacoruja.com.br

WHERE TO EAT

Camamo $$$$

Chef and host Tadeu Lubambo receives customers, gives them a tour of his kitchen, and serves a menu of six dishes of his choice (he checks with customers in advance about any restrictions). He takes no more than four tables of two per night. Bookings are essential; book about a month in advance in the high season. **CUISINE** Contemporary. **CREDIT CARDS** Not accepted

Fazenda Pernambuquinho, no #, Pernambuquinho, Estrada Tibau–Goianinha
TEL (84) 3246-4195 **OPEN** Daily, 8pm until the last customer leaves

Solimar $

On the busy Barra do Cunhaú beachfront, this restaurant has several outdoor and indoor dining areas. Beautiful views make the area overlooking the sea is best. Try the delicious grilled shrimp. **CUISINE** Fish and seafood. **CREDIT CARDS** MasterCard, Visa

Rua Gilberto Rodrigues, no #, Barra do Cunhaú
TEL (84) 3241-4242 **OPEN** Daily, 10am – 5pm

SERVICES

Tourist Information – Posto de Informações Turísticas

Praia de Barra do Cunhaú, near the multi-sports court
TEL None **OPEN** Mon – Fri, 8am – 5pm (only in January and February)

Praia do Espelho and Curuípe – Bahia

AREA CODE 73 **DISTANCES** Salvador 790 kilometers (491 miles), Trancoso 25 kilometers (16 miles) **ACCESS** From Trancoso, on a battered dirt road, with access via a private condo. From Caraíva or Trancoso, by boat or motorboat

WHERE TO STAY

Fazenda Calá $$$

Potter João José Calazans Luz Filho set up this beachfront guesthouse. The airy chalets are a reasonable distance from one another, and have sea views, terraces with hammocks, king size beds, cotton linens, and feather pillows. **ACCOMMODATIONS** 8 suites. **FACILITIES AND SERVICES** bar; kayaks; horses; parking; games room; restaurant; video; guide hiring advice; beach service; shuttle service. **CREDIT CARDS** Not accepted

Estrada de Caraíva, no #, Praia do Espelho
TEL (73) 3668-5112 www.fazendacala.com.br

Pousada do Baiano $$$$

The rooms and bungalows of this guesthouse have super king size beds and enormous windows facing the sea. White is the predominant color of the décor. Guests can have a massage in the open air under the coconut palms and can decide what time they want lunch and dinner. **ACCOMMODATIONS** 18; private safe; minibar; ofuro tub; telephone; TV; ceiling fan. **FACILITIES AND SERVICES** bar; woods; parking; restaurant; horses; 24-hour kitchen; guided walking tours; beach service; airport shuttle. **CREDIT CARDS** MasterCard

Praia do Espelho da Maravilha, no #
TEL and **FAX** (73) 3668-5020
www.pousadadobaiano.com

Pousada Enseada do Espelho $$$

A full beach service operates out of this charming glass-and-wood guesthouse surrounded by coconut palms; even breakfast can be eaten right on the beach. The main suite has a jacuzzi and the best view of the sea. Other suites have partial views of the beach. There are no TVs and no leisure area. The restaurant specializes in seafood. **ACCOMMODATIONS** 7; central water heating; air-conditioning; king size bed; jacuzzi in 1 suite; telephone; veranda with hammock; ceiling fan. **FACILITIES AND SERVICES** bar; parking; restaurant; guides; trips; recommendation of airport shuttle; transport to attractions; beach service. **CREDIT CARDS** MasterCard; Visa

---

RESTAURANTS	$ up to R$ 50	$$ from R$ 51 up to R$ 100	$$$ from R$ 101 up to R$ 150	$$$$ above R$ 150

Praia de Curuípe (10 meters from the beach)
TEL (73) 3668-5091 **RESERVATIONS** (73) 9985-4608
www.enseadadoespelho.com.br

Pousada Porto Espelho $$$
This rustic yet sophisticated guesthouse has rooms with views of either the sea or the gardens. Attention to detail is evident in the silverware, linen bedclothes, and crystal glasses. There is also a day-use system that allows non-overnight guests to use the facilities. **ACCOMMODATIONS** 11; air-conditioning in 3 rooms; ceiling fan. **FACILITIES AND SERVICES** Internet access; wine cellar; bar; library; parking; restaurant; gym; beach service; airport shuttle. **CREDIT CARDS** MasterCard
Praia de Curuípe, no #
TEL and **FAX** (73) 3668-5031, 9985-4482, 9985-4709
www.portoespelho.com.br

WHERE TO EAT

Restaurante da Silvinha $
This charming little restaurant is ideal for those who want to spend the day on Espelho and Curuípe beaches. We recommend booking a table in advance. There is no menu. The owner simply suggests and then prepares delicious Thai dishes, such as smoked fish in spicy passionfruit sauce. **CUISINE** Thai. **CREDIT CARDS** Not accepted
Praia do Espelho, no # (22 kilometers, or 14 miles, from Trancoso)
TEL (73) 9985-4157 **OPEN** Mon – Sat, 1pm – 5pm

Restaurante do Baiano $$
The menu has options such as giant prawns, picanha steak, pasta, beef jerky, and isca de peixe (freshly prepared fish cakes). We suggest the fresh tomato bruschetta. **CUISINE** Regional; seafood; diverse. **CREDIT CARDS** Diners; MasterCard
Praia do Espelho da Maravilha, no #
TEL (73) 3668-5020 **OPEN** Daily, 9am – 9pm.

SERVICES (see Porto Seguro)

Praia do Forte – Bahia

AREA CODE 71 **DISTANCES** Salvador 91 kilometers (57 miles), Costa do Sauípe 20 kilometers (12 miles) **ACCESS** From Salvador, take Highway BA-099 (Estrada do Coco)

WHERE TO STAY

Iberostar Bahia $$$$
Opened in June 2006, this seaside luxury resort is the first of three resorts to be built in this region by the Spanish Iberostar group. Tariffs are all-inclusive (meals, alcoholic beverages, and leisure activities are included), although shuttle and laundry services are extra. The resort has five restaurants, serving Japanese, Mediterranean, Brazilian, and international cuisine. There are 77 suites with sea views. **ACCOMMODATIONS** 632; air-conditioning; bathtub; private safe; minibar; telephone; TV; veranda; ceiling fan. **FACILITIES AND SERVICES** Internet access; five bars; snack service; 18-hole golf course; soccer field; parking; jacuzzi; six stores; three beach massage kiosks; four pools; playground; basketball court; volleyball court; six-a-side soccer court; tennis court; five restaurants; gym; games room; conference room with a capacity for 800; target shooting with rifles; two travel agencies; bilingual staff; capoeira lessons; aerobics classes; dance classes; stretching classes; beach volley-

ball lessons; water basketball lessons; tennis lessons; business center; beach equipment; recreational team for adults and children; guides; walking tours; visits to Tamar Project headquarters; lifeguards; pool service; airport shuttle; transport to attractions. **CREDIT CARDS** AmEx; Diners; MasterCard; Visa
Rodovia BA-99, Km 56, Praia do Forte
TEL (71) 3676-4200 www.iberostar.com.br/bahia/

Praia do Forte Eco Resort & Thalasso Spa $$$$
This is one of the oldest resorts in Brazil. Though it is situated on one of the area's best beaches for swimming, some guests never make any farther than the excellent on-site pools. The relaxation spa, with seawater-based treatments, is the highlight of many a stay. **ACCOMMODATIONS** 252; Internet access; air-conditioning; private safe; minibar; telephone; cable TV; veranda. **FACILITIES AND SERVICES** Internet access; bar; soccer field; parking; jacuzzi; motorboat; stores; pool; jogging track; six-a-side soccer court; tennis court; volleyball court; restaurant; conference room; gym; games room; massage room; video room; beauty parlor; spa; business center; 24-hour kitchen; recreational team for children; beach service; airport shuttle; transport to attractions. **CREDIT CARDS** AmEx; Diners; MasterCard; Visa
Avenida do Farol, no #
TEL (71) 3676-4000 **RESERVATIONS** 0800-118-289
www.ecoresort.com.br

Vila Galé Marés $$$$
Standing between Guarajuba Lake and Guarajuba Beach, this resort, opened in 2006, has rustic, Polynesian-inspired décor. The large, well-equipped chalets have sound-proof windows, coffeemakers, and Thai-style roofs. Some have sea views. Tariffs are all-inclusive, but do not cover babysitting, laundry, and shuttle services or certain leisure activities. The hotel has a rock-climbing wall, a canopy climbing structure, and a nautical center. **ACCOMMODATIONS** 447; wi-fi Internet access; air-conditioning; private safe; DVD player in some chalets; telephone; pay TV. **FACILITIES AND SERVICES** Internet access; bicycles; business center; bar; 24-hour snack service; nursery; soccer field; parking; jacuzzi; diaper-changing area; stores; ofuro tub; jacuzzi; jogging track; playground; six-a-side soccer court; volleyball court; tennis court; gym; restaurant; conference room; games room; massage room; beauty parlor; sauna; spa; travel agency; bilingual staff; business center; exchange bureau; horse-riding; canoeing; DVD player; diving equipment; recreational team for adults and children; valet parking; whale watching; motorboat tour; fishing; first aid service; four-wheeler; lifeguards; pool service; airport shuttle; transport to attractions; parasailing. **CREDIT CARDS** AmEx; MasterCard; Visa
Rua Praia de Guarajuba, no #, Praia de Guarajuba
TEL and **FAX** (71) 3674-8300 www.vilagale.pt

WHERE TO EAT

Sabor da Vila $
Zequinha, a former carpenter, is the owner and operator of this restaurant. We suggest the moqueca mista (octopus, shrimp, and fish stew) and the badejo (grouper) in passionfruit sauce. All of the dishes serve two. **CUISINE** Regional; fish and seafood. **CREDIT CARDS** Diners; MasterCard; Visa
Avenida ACM, no #
TEL (71) 3676-1156 **OPEN** Daily, 10am – 11pm

PRICES	**HOTELS** (couple)	$ up to R$ 150	$$ from R$ 151 up to R$ 300	$$$ from R$ 301 up to R$500	$$$$ above R$ 500

Praia do Francês – Alagoas

AREA CODE 82 **DISTANCES** Maceió 20 kilometers (12 miles), Marechal Deodoro 8 kilometers (5 miles) **ACCESS** From Maceió, take Highway AL-101

WHERE TO STAY

Pousada Hotel Mahon-Mar $

Just 200 meters from the beach, this guesthouse has neat, cozy rooms with wooden furniture and maritime decorative motifs. The restaurant serves fish, meat, and snacks. **ACCOMMODATIONS** 30; air-conditioning; minibar; telephone; TV; veranda **FACILITIES AND SERVICES** bar; parking; snack bar; pool; playground; tennis court; volleyball court; restaurant; games room; laundry; beach. **CREDIT CARDS** AmEx; Diners; MasterCard; Visa
Avenida Caravela, no #, Praia do Francês
TEL (82) 3260-1223 **FAX** (82) 3260-1133
www.hotelmahonmar.com.br

WHERE TO EAT

Chez Patrick $

Decorated with paintings by local artists, this cozy restaurant has just ten tables and a varied wine list. Try the camarão à jangadeiro (shrimp in cheese sauce with rice). **CUISINE** French; seafood. **CREDIT CARDS** AmEx; MasterCard; Visa
Rua Maresia, 15
TEL (82) 3260-1377 **OPEN** Mon – Sat, noon – 10pm; Sun, noon – 5pm (high season); Tue – Sat, noon – 10pm; Sun, noon – 5pm (low season)

Parada de Taipas $

This simple, agreeable restaurant features wattle-and-daub walls in the kitchen and an open eating area. The owner, Wilson, claims to be the creator of chiclete de camarão (fried shrimp with garlic, bell pepper, tomato sauce, cream cheese, and mozzarella), a dish that is served throughout the region. **CUISINE** Fish and seafood. **CREDIT CARDS** Diners; MasterCard; Visa
Avenida Caravelas, no #
TEL (82) 3260-1609 **OPEN** Daily, noon – 10pm

Praia do Rosa – Santa Catarina

AREA CODE 48 **DISTANCE** Florianópolis 70 kilometers (44 miles) **ACCESS** Highway BR-101 from Florianópolis, to the Garopaba turnoff. There, turn right onto Estrada Geral do Rosa

WHERE TO STAY

Pousada Caminho do Rei $$

This hilltop guesthouse has a privileged view of Rosa Beach. Each of its rustic chalets and suites is built and decorated in a unique style. In the low season, the owners serve meals in their own home. **ACCOMMODATIONS** 8; CD player; ceiling fan; fireplace (in some); heating; Internet access; jacuzzi (in some); minibar; private safe; telephone; TV. **FACILITIES AND SERVICES** arts and crafts shop; cafeteria; games room; home theater room; Internet access; library; parking; pool; restaurant; sauna; transport to airport and attractions; veranda with hammock. **CREDIT CARDS** MasterCard; Visa
Caminho do Alto do Morro, no #, Praia do Rosa
TEL (48) 3355-6062 **RESERVATIONS** (48) 3355-6071
www.caminhodorei.com.br

Quinta do Bucanero $$$

The rooms of this sophisticated guesthouse have beautiful ocean views. The drawback is that the beach is down a trail, and you'll have to cross a lake by a small boat to get there. The guesthouse doesn't allow children under 14, and it's closed in July. **ACCOMMODATIONS** 10; air-conditioning; CD player; gas-heated shower; minibar; pay TV; private safe; telephone. **FACILITIES AND SERVICES** bar; boat; games room; gourmet space; gym; Internet access; jacuzzis (indoor and outdoor); massage room; pool; restaurant; sauna; trails; woods. **CREDIT CARDS** Diners; MasterCard; Visa
Estrada Geral do Rosa, no #, Ibiraquera
TEL (48) 3355-6056 www.bucanero.com.br

WHERE TO EAT

Bistrô Pedra da Vigia $

Located inside the Regina Guest House, this bistro has an open kitchen but an otherwise French atmosphere. The house specialties include flounder in ginger and honey sauce and salmão pedra da vigia – salmon with herb sauce, accompanied by sweet potato with coriander. **CUISINE** French. **CREDIT CARDS** MasterCard; Visa
Rua Caminho do Rei, no #, Ibiraquera
TEL (48) 3355-6247. Summer: Daily, 7pm – 12:30am; other months: Thu – Sat, 7pm – 11pm

Tigre Asiático $

This is one of the best Thai restaurants in Southern Brazil. The most popular choices are chicken with rice served in a pineapple, and shrimp and fish in coconut milk. There's also a sushi bar. **CUISINE** Japanese; Thai **CREDIT CARDS** Diners; MasterCard; Visa
Estrada Geral do Rosa, no #, Ibiraquera
TEL (48) 3355-7045. Daily, 7pm – midnight

Praia Grande – Santa Catarina
(see Cambará do Sul)

Recife – Pernambuco

AREA CODE 81 **POPULATION** 1,501,008 **DISTANCES** João Pessoa 100 kilometers (62 miles), Maceió 255 kilometers (158 miles) **ACCESS** Coming from the north or south, take Highway BR-101; from the east or west, take BR-232
www.recife.pe.gov.br

WHERE TO STAY

Blue Tree Towers $$

This modern, 20-story hotel facing Piedade Beach is well equipped and offers pleasant sea views from all of its luxury rooms and junior suites. Each room has a small veranda. **ACCOMMODATIONS** 125; Internet access in some rooms; air-conditioning; private safe; minibar; telephone; cable TV; veranda. **FACILITIES AND SERVICES** Internet access; bar; parking; convenience store; pool; restaurant; conference room; gym; massage room; sauna; business center; 24-hour kitchen; valet parking; beach service. **CREDIT CARDS** AmEx; Diners; MasterCard; Visa
Avenida Bernardo Vieira de Melo, 550, Piedade, Jaboatão dos Guararapes
TEL (81) 2123-4567 **FAX** (81) 2123-4550 **RESERVATIONS** (81) 2123-4568 www.bluetree.com.br

Boa Viagem Praia $

This hotel has both business and leisure facilities. All of the rooms have wooden furniture and sparse décor. To

get a sea view, ask for a "luxury" room. The suites are more spacious and can accommodate families. **ACCOMMODATIONS** 95; air-conditioning; private safe; minibar; telephone; cable TV. **FACILITIES AND SERVICES** Internet access; parking; convenience store; pool; conference room; gym; business center; laundry; room service; airport shuttle. **CREDIT CARDS** AmEx; Diners; MasterCard; Visa
Avenida Boa Viagem, 5576, Boa Viagem
TEL (81) 3462-6454 www.boaviagempraia.com.br

Dorisol Recife Grande Hotel $$
Right on the seafront, this is the former Sheraton Hotel.Excepting the luxury suites, most rooms have just an angled sea view. The understated décor features wicker furniture. The hotel provides a beach service with security guards. **ACCOMMODATIONS** 198; Internet access; air-conditioning; bathtub; private safe; minibar; telephone; cable TV. **FACILITIES AND SERVICES** Internet access; bar; parking; florist; convenience store; pool; playground; volleyball court; restaurant; conference room; gym; games room; massage room; video room; beauty parlor; sauna; business center; exchange bureau; 24-hour kitchen; recreational team for adults; guided walking tours; laundry; lifeguards; beach service; airport shuttle. **CREDIT CARDS** AmEx; Diners; MasterCard; Visa
Avenida Bernardo Vieira de Melo, 1624, Piedade, Jaboatão dos Guararapes
TEL and FAX (81) 2122-2700 **RESERVATIONS** (81) 2122-2712 www.dorisol.com.br

Mar Hotel $$$$
About 200 meters (660 feet) from fashionable Boa Viagem Beach, this hotel has good business and leisure facilities as well as a large pool. The property is spacious and open, and the water park was landscaped by noted designer Burle Marx. **ACCOMMODATIONS** 207 (175 rooms and 32 suites); Internet access in the executive rooms; air-conditioning; bathtub; private safe; minibar; telephone; cable TV; veranda. **FACILITIES AND SERVICES** Internet access; bar; parking; stores; pool; tennis court; restaurant; conference room; gym; games room; massage room; beauty parlor; sauna; travel agency; vehicle hire; baby-sitter; business center; infirmary; kids club; laundry; room service; airport shuttle. **CREDIT CARDS** AmEx; Diners; MasterCard; Visa
Rua Barão de Souza Leão, 451, Boa Viagem
TEL (81) 3302-4446 www.marhotel.com.br

WHERE TO EAT

O Buraquinho $
The highlights of this eatery are its informality, delicious regional cuisine, and the music played in the courtyard at night. The menu options are few but good: galinha de cabidela (chicken in blood-enriched sauce), beef jerky, and several kinds of omelets, including crab. **CUISINE** Regional. **CREDIT CARDS** Not accepted
Pátio de São Pedro, 28, São José
TEL (81) 3224-6431 **OPEN** Mon – Sat, 11am until the last customer leaves

Casa de Banhos $
Built on a dyke, Casa de Banhos (which means "bathhouse") used to be a popular bathing spot for the local elite, who frequented it from 1887 to the mid-1920s, believing the waters had medicinal properties. The high points of the simple menu are the caldinho (traditional Northeastern broth, made with sururu shellfish or mussels) and the peixada (a fish stew made with amberjack or white marlin). **CUISINE** Fish and seafood. **CREDIT CARDS** Diners; MasterCard; Visa

Arrecifes do Porto do Recife, Km 1, Brasília Teimosa
TEL (81) 3075-8776 **RESERVATIONS** (81) 3467-9951 **OPEN** Daily, 10am – 5pm

Casa dos Frios $
This refined restaurant is located inside a traditional delicatessen. The wine list is one of its greatest attractions, as are the cod-based dishes. There are good meat, pasta, and seafood options. **CUISINE** Contemporary; fish and seafood. **CREDIT CARDS** Diners; MasterCard; Visa
Avenida Engenheiro Domingos Ferreira, 1920A, Boa Viagem
TEL (81) 3327-0612 **OPEN** Tue and Wed, noon – 3pm and 6pm – 11pm; Thu – Sat, noon – 3:30pm and 6pm – midnight

Entre Amigos – O Bode $
Goat meat is the forte at this welcoming cross between restaurant and bar. The bode na chapa (grilled goat) is served with lima beans, rice, fried manioc, paçoca (fried beef jerky with manioc flour), cheese-thickened pirão sauce, manioc flour with butter and vinaigrette. **CUISINE** Regional. **CREDIT CARDS** AmEx; Diners; MasterCard; Visa
Rua Marquês de Valença, 50, Boa Viagem
TEL (81) 3466-2023, 3466-8282 for delivery **OPEN** Daily, 11am until the last customer leaves

La Cuisine Bistrô $
This restaurant serves classic French cuisine as well as simpler dishes such as salads and sandwiches. The steak in Roquefort sauce with peeled tomato and basil risotto is a dependable choice. For dessert, we suggest the delicious apple pie with caramel syrup and cinnamon ice cream. **CUISINE** French; snacks; diverse. **CREDIT CARDS** MasterCard; Visa
Avenida Boa Viagem, 560, Pina
TEL (81) 3327-4073 **RESERVATIONS** (81) 3466-0555 **OPEN** Mon – Wed, noon – 11pm; Thu, noon – midnight; Fri – Sun, noon – until the last customer leaves

Leite $
Open since 1882, this old restaurant has a menu with a strong Portuguese influence, though it also offers regional and international options. A highlight is the bacalhau à moda do chef (salted cod, grilled with onions, boiled potatoes, olives, olive oil, and garlic. For dessert, try the cartola (grilled banana and cream cheese, sprinkled with sugar and cinnamon). **CUISINE** Portuguese; diverse. **CREDIT CARDS** AmEx; Diners; MasterCard; Visa
Praça Joaquim Nabuco, 147, Centro
TEL (81) 3224-7977 **OPEN** Sun – Fri, 11:30am – 4pm

Parraxaxá $
The buffet here serves regional specialties, such as carne-de-sol (beef jerky, baião-de-dois (rice and bean mush), lasanha de macaxeira (manioc lasagna), cabrito (baby goat), galinha de capoeira (corn-fed chicken), and paçoca (ground beef jerky, clarified butter, flour, and onion). **CUISINE** Regional. **CREDIT CARDS** MasterCard; Visa
Rua Baltazar Pereira, 32, Boa Viagem
TEL (81) 3463-7874 **OPEN** Mon – Thu, 11:30am – 10pm; Fri, 11:30am – 11pm; Sat and Sun, 6am – 11pm

Portoferreiro $
This elegant restaurant boasts a wonderful menu, with Italian, French, and Portuguese influences, and wine list. The mignon de cordeiro (lamb filet) with mushroom risotto and fresh asparagus is very popular. A piano, flute, and violin trio plays through dinnertime from

PRICES	HOTELS (couple)	$ up to R$ 150	$$ from R$ 151 up to R$ 300	$$$ from R$ 301 up to R$500	$$$$ above R$ 500

Thursday to Saturday. **CUISINE** Diverse. **CREDIT CARDS** AmEx; Diners; MasterCard; Visa
Avenida Rui Barbosa, 458, Graças
TEL (81) 3423-2795 **RESERVATIONS** (81) 3423-0854 **OPEN** Mon – Thu, noon – 4pm and 6:30pm – midnight; Fri and Sat, noon – 2am; Sun, noon – 4pm

Restaurante da Mira $
This restaurant operates out of the house of its proprietors, a mother and her five children, and features dishes such as galinha ao molho pardo (chicken in blood-thickened sauce). To get to the tables, guests must pass through the kitchen, where Aldemira, now past her 65th year, allows them to watch her work. **CUISINE** Regional. **CREDIT CARDS** Not accepted
Rua Dr. Eurico Chaves, 916, Casa Amarela
TEL (81) 3268-6241 **RESERVATIONS** (81) 9973-3274 **OPEN** Daily, noon – 6pm

Tasca $
The big attraction here is the rare Norwegian codfish, also used in the restaurant's signature fish cakes. Also popular is the thick codfish cutlet, sprinkled with garlic and baked with onions, potatoes, Portuguese olives, parsley and olive oil. **CUISINE** Portuguese. **CREDIT CARDS** AmEx; Diners; MasterCard
Rua Dom José Lopes, 165, Boa Viagem
TEL (81) 3326-6309 **OPEN** Tue – Thu, 6:30pm – midnight; Fri and Sat, noon – 1am; Sun, noon – 4pm

Wiella Bistrô $
Chef Claudemir Barros' menu features international dishes that incorporate local ingredients. For starters, try the deep-fried pastéis with beef jerky, cream cheese, and pumpkin purée. We suggest the robalo com molho de uvas (snook in grape sauce) for a main course, and the crunchy cashew-nut pavê for dessert. **CUISINE** Contemporary. **CREDIT CARDS** AmEx; Diners; MasterCard; Visa
Avenida Domingos Ferreira, 1,274 (Shopping Decoração), Boa Viagem
TEL (81) 3463-3108 **OPEN** Tue – Thu, noon – midnight; Fri and Sat, noon – 1pm and 7pm until the last customer leaves

SERVICES

Airport – Aeroporto Internacional dos Guararapes
Praça Ministro Salgado Filho, no #, Imbiribeira
TEL (81) 3322-4188 **OPEN** Daily, 24 hours

Bus Station – Rodoviária
Rodovia BR-232, Km 15
TEL (81) 3452-1103 or 3452-2824 **OPEN** Daily, 24 hours

Tourist Information – Centro de Informações Turísticas (Airport)
Praça Ministro Salgado Filho, no #, Imbiribeira
TEL (81) 3232-3594 **OPEN** Daily, 24 hours

Tourist Information – Centro de Informações Turísticas (Bus Station)
Rodovia BR-232, Km 16
TEL (81) 3452-1892 **OPEN** Daily, 7am – 7pm

Rio de Janeiro – Rio de Janeiro

AREA CODE 21 **POPULATION** 6,093,472 **DISTANCES** São Paulo 429 kilometers (267 miles), Belo Horizonte 434 kilometers (270 miles), Vitória 521 kilometers (324 miles) **ACCESS**

Highway BR-116 (Rodovia Presidente Dutra) from São Paulo. BR-040 (Rodovia Washington Luís) from Belo Horizonte. BR-101 from Vitória www.rio.rj.gov.br

WHERE TO STAY

Caesar Park Ipanema Hotel $$$$
Considered the most luxurious hotel in Ipanema, the Caesar's prime location facing Posto 9 put it at the center of the action on this famous beach. It is also close to the best shops and restaurants. While most rooms have wonderful views of the beach, the view from the top floor and from the gym is especially breathtaking. **ACCOMMODATIONS** 222; air-conditioning; DVD player; Internet access; jacuzzi (in some suites); minibar; pay TV; phone; private safe. **FACILITIES AND SERVICES** bar; beach; beachside service; bicycles; bilingual staff; business center; diving equipment; exchange service; first-aid; gym; horse-riding; Internet access; lifeguard; massage room; motorboat; parking; pool; rafting; rappel; restaurant; sauna; transport to airport and attractions; travel agency; valet service; walking tours; 24-hour kitchen. **CREDIT CARDS** AmEx; Diners; MasterCard; Visa
Avenida Vieira Souto, 460, Ipanema
TEL (21) 2525-2525 **FAX** (21) 2521-6000
RESERVATIONS (21) 3906-8999
www.caesarpark-rio.com

Copacabana Palace $$$$
Open since 1923, this glamorous hotel has become a Rio icon. It has two restaurants, the Pérgula, next to the pool, and the famous Cipriani, with Northern Italian dishes. The leisure facilities include a semi-Olympic pool and a tennis court. The business center is well equipped. **ACCOMMODATIONS** 225; air-conditioning; DVD player; fax; Internet access; minibar; pay TV; phone; private safe. **FACILITIES AND SERVICES** bar; beachside service; beauty parlor; bilingual staff; business center; exchange service; first-aid; function room; gym; Internet access; laundry; lifeguard; massage room; parking; pool; restaurants; stores; tennis court; transport to airport and attractions; 24-hour kitchen. **CREDIT CARDS** AmEx; Diners; MasterCard; Visa
Avenida Atlântica, 1,702, Copacabana
TEL (21) 2548-7070 **FAX** (21) 2235-7330
www.copacabanapalace.com.br

Fasano Hotel e Restaurante $$$$
The Fasano Group, a hospitality brand connoting quality and sophistication, inaugurated its Ipanema hotel in August 2007. Designed by architect Philippe Starck, its décor is reminiscent of the 1950s and 1960s. **ACCOMMODATIONS** 91; air-conditioning; bathtub (only in the suites); CD Player (in some suites); DVD player; Internet access; minibar; pay TV; phone; private safe. **FACILITIES AND SERVICES** babysitter; bar; beachside service; bilingual staff; business center; butler; car hire; exchange service; function room; gym; Internet access; lifeguard; massage room; parking; pool; restaurant; sauna; spa; transport to airport and attractions; valet service; walking tours; 24-hour kitchen; 24-hour laundry. **CREDIT CARDS** AmEx; Diners; MasterCard; Visa
Avenida Vieira Souto, 80, Ipanema
TEL (21) 3202-4000 **FAX** (21) 3202-4010
www.fasanovieirasouto.com.br

Hotel Glória $$$
A symbol of Rio's luxury, this hotel was inaugurated with great pomp in 1922 by the then-president Epitácio Pessoa. The rooms are exquisitely decorated and some have views of Guanabara Bay. Persian carpets, antique

| **RESTAURANTS** | $ up to R$ 50 | $$ from R$ 51 up to R$ 100 | $$$ from R$ 101 up to R$ 150 | $$$$ above R$ 150 |

furniture, and works of art are scattered throughout the building. There are two pools, one of which is heated and offers a panoramic view. **ACCOMMODATIONS** 608; air-conditioning; Internet access; minibar; pay TV; phone; private safe. **FACILITIES AND SERVICES** bar; beauty parlor; bilingual staff; business center; exchange service; first-aid; function room; gardens; gym; heated pool; heliport; Internet access; jogging track; lifeguard; magazine-reading area; massage room; parking; playground; pool; restaurants; saunas; sports facilities; stores; theater; transport to airport and attractions; 24-hour kitchen and room service. **CREDIT CARDS** AmEx; Diners; MasterCard; Visa
Rua do Russel, 632, Glória
TEL (21) 2555-7272, 2555-7283 **FAX** (21) 2555-7283
www.hotelgloriario.com.br

JW Marriott Hotel Rio de Janeiro $$$$

Located near Posto 4 on Copacabana Beach, this hotel opened in 2001. Some rooms overlook the beautiful inner courtyard, while others have ocean views. There are two restaurants, one Mediterranean and the other Japanese. **ACCOMMODATIONS** 245; air-conditioning; CD player; Internet access; minibar; pay TV; phone; private safe. **FACILITIES AND SERVICES** bar; beachside service; bilingual staff; business center; convenience store; exchange service; function room; gym; Internet access; lifeguard; magazine-reading area; massage room; parking; pool; restaurant; sauna; spa; stores; transport to airport and attractions; valet service; 24-hour kitchen. **CREDIT CARDS** AmEx; Diners; MasterCard; Visa
Avenida Atlântica, 2,600, Copacabana
TEL (21) 2545-6500 **FAX** (21) 2545-6555
www.hoteis.marriott.com.br

La Maison $$$$

This hotel occupies a charming residence in Alto Gávea, facing Corcovado and its Christ statue, and is very popular among foreigners. Each of the five rooms is decorated in a different theme. In the garden, guests can watch tiny monkeys, toucans, and hummingbirds. **ACCOMMODATIONS** 5; air-conditioning (in 2 rooms); pay TV. **FACILITIES AND SERVICES** bar; garden; Internet access; library; massage room; parking; pool; sauna; sun deck; transport to airport and attractions. **CREDIT CARDS** Not accepted
Rua Sérgio Porto, 58, Gávea
TEL (21) 3205-3585 **FAX** (21) 2540-0554

Marina All Suítes $$$$

Located by Leblon Beach, this hotel offers ocean views and personalized service. Some suites have been decorated by famous interior designers and architects. The upstairs leisure area is lovely, and the bar stays busy. **ACCOMMODATIONS** 38; air-conditioning; bathtub (in some suites); DVD player (in some rooms); Internet access; minibar; mini-kitchen (in some suites); pay TV; phone; safe. **FACILITIES AND SERVICES** bar; beachside service; bilingual staff; business center; exchange service; first-aid; gym; Internet access; jogging track; lifeguard; lounge; massage room; meeting room; parking; pool; poolside service; restaurant; sauna; valet service; video room. **CREDIT CARDS** AmEx; Diners; MasterCard; Visa
Avenida Delfim Moreira, 696, Leblon
TEL (21) 2172-1100 **FAX** (21) 2172-1110
RESERVATIONS (21) 2172-1001
www.marinaallsuites.com.br

Sheraton Barra Hotel & Suites $$$$

This seafront hotel is the most luxurious in Barra da Tijuca. The rooms are well equipped and the leisure area and beach service excellent. The hotel provides free transport to the Barra Shopping mall and has event space available. **ACCOMMODATIONS** 292; DVD player (in some suites); Internet access; jacuzzi (in some suites); pay TV; phone. **FACILITIES AND SERVICES** bar; beach service; beauty parlor; bilingual staff; business center; convenience store; exchange service; first-aid; function room; garden; gym; Internet access; jacuzzi; lifeguard; magazine-reading area; massage room; ofuro tub; parking; playground; pool; restaurant; sauna; spa; squash court; stores; transport to airport and attractions; valet service; walking tours; wine cellar; 24-hour kitchen. **CREDIT CARDS** AmEx; Diners; MasterCard; Visa
Avenida Lúcio Costa, 3,150, Barra da Tijuca
TEL (21) 3139-8000 **FAX** (21) 3139-8085
www.sheraton-barra.com.br

Sheraton Rio Hotels & Towers $$$$

This enormous seaside hotel between Leblon and São Conrado has an excellent leisure area and suites with balconies and beautiful ocean views. Free transport is provided to the beaches of Leblon, Ipanema, and Copacabana, with a final stop at the Rio Sul shopping mall in Botafogo. **ACCOMMODATIONS** 559; air-conditioning; Internet access; minibar; pay TV; phone; private safe. **FACILITIES AND SERVICES** babysitter; bar; beachside service; bilingual staff; business center; butler; convenience store; exchange service; first-aid; function room; games room; gym; Internet access; lifeguard; lobby-bar; magazine-reading area; massage room; nursery; parking; pool; recreational team for children; restaurants; secretarial service; spa; stores; tennis court; transport to airport and attractions; valet service; 24-hour kitchen. **CREDIT CARDS** AmEx; Diners; MasterCard; Visa
Avenida Niemeyer, 121, Leblon
TEL (21) 2274-1122 **FAX** (21) 2239-5643
www.sheraton.com/rio

Sofitel Rio de Janeiro $$$$

Located between Copacabana and Ipanema beaches, this hotel has rooms with balconies and panoramic views of both Rio's waterfront and its other attractions, such as Sugarloaf Mountain. It has good facilities and access to a shopping mall. **ACCOMMODATIONS** 388; air-conditioning; Internet access; minibar; pay TV; phone; private safe. **FACILITIES AND SERVICES** babysitter; bar; beachside service; bicycles; bilingual staff; business center; convenience store; exchange service; first-aid; function room; gym; Internet access; jacuzzi; laundry; library; lifeguard; magazine-reading area; massage room; parking; pool; restaurant; sauna; valet service. **CREDIT CARDS** AmEx; Diners; MasterCard; Visa
Avenida Atlântica, 4,240, Copacabana
TEL (21) 2525-1232 **FAX** (21) 2525-1200
www.sofitelrio.com.br

WHERE TO EAT

Adega do Pimenta $

This rustically decorated restaurant faces the tram tracks in the bohemian district of Santa Teresa. The house forte is German food, including pork knuckle (eisbein) with sauerkraut. Book reservations ahead. **CUISINE** German. **CREDIT CARDS** Diners; MasterCard; Visa
Rua Almirante Alexandrino, 296, Santa Teresa
TEL (21) 2224-7554. Mon – Fri, noon – 10pm; Sat, noon – 8pm; Sun, noon – 6pm

Adega do Valentim $$

Dishes such as the famous cod dish bacalhau à lagareira are generously served and feed two. Imported Por-

| **PRICES** | **HOTELS** (couple) | $ up to R$ 150 | $$ from R$ 151 up to R$ 300 | $$$ from R$ 301 up to R$500 | $$$$ above R$ 500 |

534   BRAZIL GUIDE

tuguese products are for sale at the counter. **CUISINE** Portuguese. **CREDIT CARDS** AmEx; Diners; MasterCard; Visa
Rua da Passagem, 176, Botafogo
TEL (21) 2295-2748. Mon – Sat, noon – 1am; Sun, noon – midnight

Adegão Português $$
This traditional restaurant in Rio's North Zone takes cod fish very seriously, offering it up in a range of varieties and in generous servings. Roast suckling pig and other delicacies round out the menu. **CUISINE** Portuguese. **CREDIT CARDS** AmEx; Diners; MasterCard; Visa
Rua Campo de São Cristóvão, 212, São Cristóvão
TEL (21) 2580-7288, 2580-8689. Mon – Sat, 11am – 11pm; Sun, 11am – 8pm

Alda Maria Doces Portugueses $
Alda Maria bakes recipes she learned at home from her Portuguese grandmother. Highlights include the dom Rodrigo (a confection made with egg yolks and almonds) and the pudim de tâmara com amêndoas (date and almond pudding). **CUISINE** Portuguese sweets. **CREDIT CARDS** Not accepted
Rua Almirante Alexandrino, 1,116, Santa Teresa
TEL (21) 2232-1320. Tue – Sun, 1pm – 8pm

Alessandro & Frederico Café $
This eatery serves sandwiches made with home-baked bread, such as baguette with sesame seeds and ciabatta made with yoghurt. Try the Ana Paula (dried apricots and brie with Parma ham), and the cachorro-quente Cláudia (a hotdog made with a sausage and cheddar cheese in a baguette). **CUISINE** Sandwiches. **CREDIT CARDS** AmEx; Diners; MasterCard; Visa
Rua Garcia d'Ávila, 134, Ipanema
TEL (21) 2521-0828. Daily, 9am – 2am

Alfaia $$
The most famous item on the menu is the cod dish bacalhau à patuscada. For dessert, follow the lead of the local families that flock here and try the pastel de nata (Portuguese custard tart). **CUISINE** Portuguese. **CREDIT CARDS** AmEx; Diners; MasterCard; Visa
Rua Inhangá, 30, Store #B, Copacabana
TEL (21) 2236-1222 Mon – Fri, noon – midnight; Sun, noon – 11pm

Álvaro's $
Frequented by Rio's night owls, this place serves excellent pastéis (pastry turnovers). The polvo grelhado (grilled octopus) is one of the highlights of a varied menu that also includes cod and daily specials. **CUISINE** Snacks; various. **CREDIT CARDS** AmEx; Diners; MasterCard; Visa
Avenida Ataulfo de Paiva, 500, Leblon
TEL (21) 2294-2148. Daily, 11am – 2am

Amarelinho $
In operation since the 1920s, this bar is a Rio institution that's popular among night owls. It serves feijoada (black bean and pork stew) and a range of other dishes, but its history is its greatest draw card. **CUISINE** Brazilian; snacks. **CREDIT CARDS** AmEx; Diners; MasterCard; Visa
Praça Floriano, 55, Cinelândia
TEL (21) 2240-8434. Daily, 10am – 2am

Antiquarius $$$
Inaugurated in 1975, this is one of Rio's best restaurants. It specializes in Portuguese food, with a range of cod dishes to choose from, as well as the popular arroz de pato (duck rice) and excellent desserts. Its mezzanine serves as both a waiting room and an antique shop. **CUISINE** Portuguese. **CREDIT CARDS** Diners; MasterCard
Rua Aristides Espínola, 19, Leblon
TEL (21) 2294-1049, 2294-1496. Daily, noon – 2am

Bar Devassa $
The main attraction of this bar are the four varieties of chope (draft beer) brewed in-house: loura (blonde), ruiva (redhead), negra (black), and mulata (mulatta). The menu has meat, fish, and seafood options. **CUISINE** Snacks; various. **CREDIT CARDS** AmEx; Diners; MasterCard
Rua General San Martin, 1,241, Leblon
TEL (21) 2540-6087. Mon – Thu, 6pm – 1am; Fri, 6pm – 3am; Sat, 2pm – 4am; Sun, 2pm – 1am

Bar do Arnaudo $
This restaurant evolved out of an old bar and has become a benchmark in Brazilian Northeastern cuisine in Rio. Chef Arnaudo has run the kitchen ever since it opened, and the staff and facilities have been unchanged for decades. Try the carne-de-sol (beef jerky) with manioc, cowpeas, curd cheese, and pumpkin. **CUISINE** Northeastern. **CREDIT CARDS** MasterCard; Visa
Rua Almirante Alexandrino, 316-B, Santa Teresa
TEL (21) 2210-0817. Tue – Fri, noon – 11pm; Mon, noon – 6pm; Sat and Sun, noon – 9pm

Bar e Restaurante Urca $
This small, casual bar with nautical décor is the most traditional in Urca. It serves fresh-caught fish bought from local fishermen. Try the moqueca baiana stew or the lula espanhola (Spanish squid), each plentiful enough to serve two. **CUISINE** Fish and seafood. **CREDIT CARDS** Diners; MasterCard; Visa
Rua Cândido Gaffrée, 205, Urca
TEL (21) 2295-8744. Tue – Sat, 11am – 11pm; Sun, 11am – 7pm

Bar Lagoa $
The beautiful art deco styling of this high-ceiling bar dates back to the 1930s. The balcony offers a privileged view of Rodrigo de Freitas Lake. Famed for its chope (draft beer) and legendarily gruff waiters, it serves German fare and lighter options, such as grilled grouper with vegetables. **CUISINE** German; various. **CREDIT CARDS** AmEx; Diners; MasterCard; Visa
Avenida Epitácio Pessoa, 1,674, Lagoa
TEL (21) 2523-1135. Mon, 6pm – 2am; Tue – Sun, noon – 2am

Bar Luiz $
At almost 120 years of age, this is one of the famed, grand old establishments in Rio. It serves excellent chope (draft beer) and German food. Founded in 1887, it has been at its current address since 1927. **CUISINE** German. **CREDIT CARDS** AmEx; Diners; MasterCard; Visa
Rua da Carioca, 39, Centro
TEL (21) 2262-6900. Mon – Sat, 11am – 11:30pm

Barril 8000 $
The bar on the Barra beachfront has an excellent view and, at night, draws a younger crowd that gathers to play and listen to samba. To accompany a chope (draft beer), order the batata rostie (potato rösti), which come with various fillings, or the picanha na pedra (picanha steak cooked on a stone hotplate). **CUISINE** Snacks; various. **CREDIT CARDS** AmEx; Diners; MasterCard; Visa
Avenida Sernambetiba, 8,000, Barra da Tijuca
TEL (21) 2433-1730. Mon – Fri, 4pm – 3:30am; Sat, Sun, and holidays, 11am – 4:30am

Belmonte $

This simple tavern has been operating in the neighborhood of Flamengo since 1952. The house specialty is the pastel de carne-seca (pastry turnover filled with shredded beef). There is a selection of some 30 different cachaças from Minas Gerais. **CUISINE** Snacks; various. **CREDIT CARDS** Not accepted
Praia do Flamengo, 300, Flamengo
TEL (21) 2552-3349. Daily, 8am – 4am

Bip Bip $

It may be small, but this bar draws huge numbers thanks to the samba sessions with top-notch musicians on Sunday nights. Tuesday is chorinho music day, while Wednesday is the day for bossa nova. A serving of bolinho de bacalhau (cod croquettes) goes well with a cold beer. **CUISINE** Snacks; various. **CREDIT CARDS** Not accepted
Rua Almirante Gonçalves, 50-D, Copacabana
TEL (21) 2267-9696. Daily, 7pm – 1am

Bira $$

Far from the center, this restaurant has a lovely sea view. Its most popular dish is the snook with lime, served with prawn rice. Set aside plenty of time for dining here, as the service can be slow. **CUISINE** Fish and seafood. **CREDIT CARDS** Not accepted
Estrada da Vendinha, 68-A, Barra de Guaratiba
TEL (21) 2410-8304. Thu and Fri, noon – 6pm; Sat and Sun, noon – 8pm

Bracarense $

This 60-year-old spot is one of the busiest bars in Rio. The highlight is the icy-cold, well-poured chope (draft beer). Commendable snacks include the bolinho de bacalhau (cod croquettes) as well as the croquette made with manioc flour and filled with shrimp and catupiry cheese. **CUISINE** Snacks; various. **CREDIT CARDS** Not accepted
Rua José Linhares, 85 B, Leblon
TEL (21) 2294-3549. Mon – Sat, 7am – midnight; Sun, 9:30am – 10pm

Cais da Ribeira $$

Here, inside the Hotel Pestana Rio on Avenida Atlântica, chef Leonel Pereira has created a contemporary menu. Highlights include the arroz de pato (duck rice) and bacalhau (cod). **CUISINE** Portuguese. **CREDIT CARDS** AmEx; Diners; MasterCard; Visa
Avenida Atlântica, 2,964, Copacabana
TEL (21) 2548-6332. Daily, 6am – 10:30am; noon – 3pm; and 7:30pm – 11:30pm

Capricciosa $

São Paulo may have a better known tradition of excelling in Italian cuisine, but locals swear that the country's best pizzas are to be had here at the Capricciosa. There are over 30 options to choose from, such as marguerita and al pesto. The Ipanema branch is the busiest. **CUISINE** Pizza. **CREDIT CARDS** AmEx; Diners; MasterCard
Rua Vinícius de Moraes, 134, Ipanema
TEL (21) 2523-3394 Daily, 6pm – 2am

Carioca da Gema $

This eatery hosts daily samba and choro performances, with some big-name musicians, starting at 9pm. The menu offers a range of snacks, full meals, and caldinho de feijão (bean broth). There is also a pizza parlor here. **CUISINE** Brazilian; Pizza. **CREDIT CARDS** Not accepted
Avenida Mem de Sá, 79, Lapa

TEL (21) 2221-0043. Mon – Fri, 6pm – 2am; Sat, 9pm until the last customer leaves. Pizza parlor: Tue – Fri, 6pm until the last customer leaves; Sat and Sun, 7pm until the last customer leaves.

Carlota $$

The Rio branch of this famous São Paulo restaurant stands on one of Leblon's most charming streets. Try the Mandarin duck with tangerine. **CUISINE** Contemporary. **CREDIT CARDS** AmEx; Diners; MasterCard; Visa
Rua Dias Ferreira, 64, Leblon
TEL (21) 2540-6821. Tue – Thu, 7:30pm – midnight; Fri and Sat, 7:30pm – 12:30am; Sun, 1:30pm – 10:30pm

Casa Cavé $

Specialized in Portuguese desserts, this confectioner's is famous for its pastel de nata (custard tart). It has been making toucinhos do céu, dom-rodrigos, mil-folhas, and other sweet delights since 1860. **CUISINE** Confectionery.
CREDIT CARDS Not accepted
Rua 7 de Setembro, 137, Centro
TEL (21) 2221-0533, 2222-2358. Mon – Fri, 9am – 7pm; Sat, 9am – 1pm

Casa da Feijoada $

Since 1989, this restaurant has been serving one of Rio's most praised feijoadas. Bowls of black beans and meat are left on the tables, along with sliced orange, collard greens, and manioc meal. The waiters circulate between the tables offering other cuts of meat. Handmade cachaças wash it all down. **CUISINE** Brazilian. **CREDIT CARDS** AmEx; Diners; MasterCard; Visa
Rua Prudente de Moraes, 10-B, Ipanema
TEL (21) 2247-2776, 2523-4994. Daily, noon – midnight

Celeiro $

This eatery has soups, bread rolls, 30 varieties of salad and an extensive menu that includes meats, pasta, and quiches. Highlights are the chicken curry and the bolinho de cenoura (carrot croquettes), but the daily specials are surefire bets. **CUISINE** Salad. **CREDIT CARDS** Diners; MasterCard
Rua Dias Ferreira, 199, Store #ABC, Leblon
TEL (21) 2274-7843. Mon – Sat, 11:30am – 5pm. Bread counter: 10am – 6pm

Cervantes $

This establishment attracts night owls, who come for its famous sandwiches. In business for over half a century, Cervantes serves unusual combinations such as filet mignon with cheese and pineapple. **CUISINE** Sandwiches; various. **CREDIT CARDS** Visa
Avenida Prado Junior, 335, Store #B, Copacabana
TEL (21) 2275-6147. Tue – Thu, and Sun, noon – 4am; Fri and Sat, noon – 6am

Cipriani $$

Run by Venetian chef Francesco Carli, this sophisticated restaurant is located inside the Copacabana Palace. The menu changes every six months. For a main course, try the lamb chops with herbs and vegetable and saffron ravioli. **CUISINE** Italian. **CREDIT CARDS** AmEx; Diners; MasterCard; Visa
Avenida Atlântica, 1,702, Copacabana
TEL (21) 2545-8747. Mon – Thu, 12:30pm – 3pm and 7pm – midnight; Fri and Sat, 12:30pm – 3pm and 7pm – 1am

Confeitaria Colombo $

Since opening in 1894, this teahouse has become the most important icon of Rio's belle époque. It still has its

| PRICES | HOTELS (couple) | $ up to R$ 150 | $$ from R$ 151 up to R$ 300 | $$$ from R$ 301 up to R$500 | $$$$ above R$ 500 |

536   BRAZIL GUIDE

original Belgian mirrors, French stained-glass windows, Carrara marble, and Portuguese flooring. Its afternoon tea is an institution. CUISINE Sandwiches; various. CREDIT CARDS AmEx; Diners; MasterCard; Visa
Rua Gonçalves Dias, 32, Centro
TEL (21) 2232-2300. Mon – Fri, 9:30am – 8pm; Sat and holidays, 9:30am – 5pm

Copa Café $
Facing Copacabana Beach, this is one of the few friendly eateries along this stretch. The bistro serves eight types of hamburger, such as lamb with red-wine sauce, and fish. CUISINE Contemporary; hamburgers. CREDIT CARDS AmEx; MasterCard; Visa
Avenida Atlântica, 3,056, Store #B, Copacabana
TEL (21) 2235-2947. Mon – Thu, 7pm – 2am; Fri and Sat, 7pm until the last customer leaves

D'Amici $$
The four owners, all from the state of Ceará, take turns on the floor to ensure the efficient service that has earned this restaurant its good reputation. The wine cellar has 500 labels. Highlights of the menu are the baked dishes, such as the duck in green-pepper sauce served with an apple crêpe. CUISINE Italian. CREDIT CARDS AmEx; Diners; MasterCard; Visa
Rua Antônio Vieira, 18-B, Leme
TEL (21) 2541-4477, 2543-1303. Daily, noon – 1am

Degrau $
This casual eatery is great for hungry beach-goers coming straight from the sands. If you have no shirt, the establishment will provide you with one. How's that for service? This place is famed for its delicious pastry turnovers filled with cod and other fish. CUISINE Snacks; various. CREDIT CARDS AmEx; Diners; MasterCard; Visa
Avenida Ataulfo de Paiva, 517-B, Leblon
TEL (21) 2259-3648, 2259-2842. Daily, 11am – 1am

Escola do Pão $
This restaurant, which also functions as a bistro, serves one of the best breakfasts in Rio on Saturdays and Sundays. There is much to choose from, including sweet corn pudding, papaya cream with granola, bread rolls and hot drinks – and you can go back as often as you like. CUISINE French; Italian. CREDIT CARDS AmEx; Diners; MasterCard; Visa
Rua General Garzon, 10, Lagoa
TEL (21) 3205-7275. Tue – Fri, 5pm – midnight; Sat, Sun, and holidays, 9am – 1pm

Filé de Ouro $
This low-key bar serves top-notch food. The tenderloin and strip loin servings are generous and come with several side dishes. The Oswaldo Aranha tenderloin, with garlic, rice, beans, potatoes, and egg farofa (manioc meal with eggs and seasonings) is a good choice. CUISINE Brazilian; meats. CREDIT CARDS Not accepted
Rua Jardim Botânico, 731, Jardim Botânico
TEL (21) 2259-2396. Tue – Sat, noon – 11pm; Sun, noon – 7pm

Forneria $
A branch of the popular São Paulo Forneria, run by the Fasano Group, this restaurant serves great pasta and sandwiches. Try the asparagus, brie, and Parma ham sandwich served in pizza-bread. CUISINE Italian. CREDIT CARDS AmEx; Diners; MasterCard; Visa
Rua Aníbal de Mendonça, 112, Ipanema

TEL (21) 2540-8045. Mon – Sat, noon – 1am; Sun, noon – midnight

Garcia & Rodrigues $$
Chef Christophe Lidy has adapted his French dishes to the Brazilian climate, using a wider variety of olive oils and vegetables. One menu classic is the grouper baked over potatoes with olive oil. A pastry shop, a wine cellar, and a brasserie share the premises. CUISINE Various. CREDIT CARDS AmEx; Diners; MasterCard; Visa
Avenida Ataulfo de Paiva, 1,251, stores #A and B, Leblon
TEL (21) 3206-4120. Mon – Fri, 8am – midnight; Sat and Sun, 8am – 1am.

Gero $$
The São Paulo Fasano Group has won a huge clientele in Rio with this Ipanema branch of Gero. The breaded veal cutlets are especially popular. The wine list has 60 labels to choose from, and the place really gets hopping at night. CUISINE Italian. CREDIT CARDS AmEx; Diners; MasterCard; Visa
Rua Aníbal de Mendonça, 157, Ipanema
TEL (21) 2239-8158. Mon – Fri, noon – 4pm and 7pm – 1am; Sat and Sun, noon – midnight

Guimas $
This traditional Brazilian restaurant has been operating in the Baixo Gávea district for over 20 years and has added French touches to its dishes. Try the duck with honey and pear rice or the picadinho carioca (beef stew served with manioc meal, banana fritters, rice, beans, and boiled egg). The bolinho de bacalhau (cod croquettes) are a must. CUISINE Brazilian. CREDIT CARDS AmEx; Diners; MasterCard; Visa
Rua José Roberto Macedo Soares, 5, stores #D, E, I, F, Gávea
TEL (21) 2259-7996. Daily, noon – 1am

Gula Gula $
The standard menu offers salads and grilled meats, but there are also daily specials such as quiches and pasta. All meals are prepared to be light and wholesome – a hallmark of the chain. CUISINE Various. CREDIT CARDS AmEx; Diners; MasterCard; Visa
Rua Aníbal de Mendonça, 132, Ipanema
TEL (21) 2259-3084. Sun – Thu, noon – midnight; Fri and Sat, noon – 1am

Hipódromo $
A meeting point since 1937 for an eclectic clientele, this restaurant gets very busy, especially on Thursday and Sunday nights. The menu offers meat dishes such as charbroiled picanha steak for two. The Saturday feijoada is sublime. CUISINE Meats; pizza. CREDIT CARDS AmEx; Diners; MasterCard; Visa
Praça Santos Dumont, 108, Gávea
TEL (21) 2274-9720. Daily, 10h – 1am

Jobi $
This Leblon bar has been in business for half a century, and is a refuge for Rio's night owls, musicians, artists, and journalists. Its well-poured chope (draft beer) is a must. The menu has a selection ranging from pastry turnovers to carne-seca (seasoned shredded beef) with onion, manioc, and beans. CUISINE Brazilian; Portuguese. CREDIT CARDS AmEx
Rua Ataulfo de Paiva, 1,166, Leblon
TEL (21) 2274-0547, 2274-5055. Daily, 9am – 4am

RESTAURANTS	$ up to R$ 50	$$ from R$ 51 up to R$ 100	$$$ from R$ 101 up to R$ 150	$$$$ above R$ 150

Lamas $

In operation for over 130 years, and always open well into the small hours, this restaurant is famous for its filet mignon dishes, such as the filé à Oswaldo Aranha and the breaded bife à milanesa. **CUISINE** Brazilian; meats. **CREDIT CARDS** AmEx; Diners; MasterCard; Visa
Rua Marquês de Abrantes, 18, Flamengo
TEL (21) 2556-0799. Daily, 11am until the last customer leaves

Le Pré Catelan $$

Chef Roland Villard runs this French restaurant and changes its menu fortnightly. The salmon comes in five different variations. **CUISINE** French. **CREDIT CARDS** AmEx; Diners; MasterCard; Visa
Avenida Atlântica, 4,240 (Hotel Sofitel), Copacabana
TEL (21) 2525-1160. Mon – Sat, 7:30pm – 11:30pm

Majórica $

The picanha steak at this traditional à la carte grill is famous, but the excellent starter of sausage on a skewer leaves nothing to be desired. Accompaniments likes fries, manioc meal, and salads must be ordered separately. **CUISINE** Meats; seafood. **CREDIT CARDS** AmEx; Diners; MasterCard; Visa
Rua Senador Vergueiro, 11-15, Flamengo
TEL (21) 2205-6820. Mon – Thu, and Sun, noon – midnight; Fri and Sat, noon – 1am

Margutta $$

This cozy, typically Italian restaurant specializes in fish and seafood, such as the pescado al cartoccio (fish in a pouch) and the peixe ao sal grosso (fish in rock salt), served with spicy potatoes or grilled endives. **CUISINE** Italian. **CREDIT CARDS** AmEx; Diners; MasterCard; Visa
Avenida Henrique Dumont, 62, Ipanema
TEL (21) 2259-3718. Mon – Fri, 6pm – 1am; Sat and holidays, noon – 1am; Sun, noon – midnight

A Marisqueira $

In business for over half a century, this eatery serves cod dishes, caldeirada (seafood stew) for one or two people, and other seafood dishes. On Sundays, there are specials such as tripas à moda do Porto (a mixture of tripe, chorizo sausage, and pork cuts in a butter-bean stew). **CUISINE** Portuguese. **CREDIT CARDS** AmEx; Diners; MasterCard; Visa
Rua Barata Ribeiro, 232, Copacabana
TEL (21) 2547-3920. Daily, 11am – midnight

Mil Frutas Café $

This Ipanema shop is different to the other branches of the same chain. Here they serve not only ice cream, but also coffee, sandwiches, wraps, and salads. Try the guava and cheese ice cream. **CUISINE** Salads; sandwiches; ice cream. **CREDIT CARDS** Diners; MasterCard
Rua Garcia D'Ávila, 134, Store #A, Ipanema
TEL (21) 2521-1384, 2247-2148. Mon – Thu, 10:30am – midnight; Fri and Sat, 9:30am – 1:30am; Sun; 9:30am – 12:30am

Mr. Lam $

Chef Sik Chung Lam, or just Mr. Lam, who once ran the famous Mr. Chow in New York, is at the helm of this restaurant along with his nephew, Kin Li Lam. A highlight is the pato laqueado (Peking duck), and there's also a tasting menu. **CUISINE** Chinese. **CREDIT CARDS** AmEx; Diners; MasterCard; Visa

Rua Maria Angélica, 21, Lagoa
TEL (21) 2286-6661. Tue – Thu, 7pm – 12:30am; Fri, 7pm – 1am; Sat, 1pm – 1:30am; Sun, 1pm – 7pm

Oásis $

This steakhouse serves rotisserie meat. The highlight is the picanha steak prepared in the southern Brazilian tradition. The service is a cut above that of most steakhouses. **CUISINE** Meats. **CREDIT CARDS** AmEx; Diners; MasterCard; Visa
Rua Gonçalves Dias, 56, Mezanine Store, Centro
TEL (21) 2252-5521. Mon – Fri, 11am – 4pm

Olympe $$

Chef Claude Troisgros creates dishes that blend French techniques with Brazilian ingredients. The menu is refreshed every three months. Try the grilled scallops with palm heart salad in Madras curry and cream. **CUISINE** French. **CREDIT CARDS** MasterCard; Visa
Rua Custódio Serrão, 62, Jardim Botânico
TEL (21) 2539-4542. Mon – Thu, 7:30pm – 12:30am; Fri, 12:30pm – 4pm and 7:30pm – 12:30am; Sat, 7:30pm – 12:30am

Plataforma $$

This was the steakhouse to be seen at in the 1980s, thanks to celebrity clients such as Tom Jobim and Chico Buarque. It has undergone rather unfortunate renovations, which have done away with most of its charm. The meats, however, are still excellent. Try the picanha steak with potato soufflé or the lombo de badejo na brasa (charbroiled grouper), both of which serve two. **CUISINE** Meats; grill. **CREDIT CARDS** AmEx; Diners; MasterCard; Visa
Rua Adalberto Ferreira, 32, Leblon
TEL (21) 2274-4022. Mon – Thu, noon – midnight; Fri and Sat, noon – 1am

Porcão $$

With the most traditional rodízio (rotisserie meat) in Rio, this restaurant offers good choices for carnivores as well as an extensive salad buffet. It has become a brand name, with branches abroad as well. In Rio, the Enseada da Glória branch has a beautiful view of the Morro da Urca and Sugarloaf Mountain. **CUISINE** Meats; grill. **CREDIT CARDS** AmEx; Diners; MasterCard
Rua Barão da Torre, 218, Ipanema
TEL (21) 3202-9155, 3389-8989. Mon – Thu, noon – midnight; Fri and Sat, noon – 12:30am; Sun, noon – 11pm

Quinta da Boa Vista $

Since 1954, this restaurant has been operating out of an old chapel that once belonged to the imperial family. The Portuguese-inspired menu includes dishes such as caldeirada (seafood stew) and coelho à caçadora (rabbit stew). An exceptional rabada (ox stew) is served on Tuesdays. **CUISINE** Various. **CREDIT CARDS** AmEx; MasterCard; Visa
Parque da Quinta da Boa Vista, no #, São Cristóvão
TEL (21) 2589-6551, 2589-4279. Daily, 11am – 6pm

Rio Minho $

This local institution opened in 1884 and frequently served the Baron of Rio Branco and the famous linguist Antônio Houaiss. It is famous for its classic soup, the Leão Velloso, made with seafood, fish and shrimp stock, coriander, and leeks. **CUISINE** Seafood; snacks. **CREDIT CARDS** AmEx; Diners; MasterCard; Visa
Rua do Ouvidor, 10, Centro
TEL (21) 2509-2338. Mon – Fri, 11am – 4pm

PRICES	HOTELS (couple)	$ up to R$ 150	$$ from R$ 151 up to R$ 300	$$$ from R$ 301 up to R$500	$$$$ above R$ 500

Roberta Sudbrak $$$$

This restaurant belongs to the former chef of the Palácio do Planalto, seat of the Brazilian government. Brazilian recipes are served at two tables and a counter at lunchtime. Upstairs, Friday and Saturday night dinners are served at a communal table from the open kitchen. Reservations required. **CUISINE** Contemporary. **CREDIT CARDS** MasterCard
Rua Lineu de Paula Machado, 916,
Jardim Botânico
TEL (21) 3874-0139. Tue and Wed, 7:30pm – 10:30pm; Thu, noon – 3pm and 7:30pm – 10:30pm; Fri, noon – 3pm and 8:30pm – 2am; Sat, 9:30pm – 2am

Satyricon $$

This prestigious restaurant is a temple of seafood. Shrimp, oysters, crayfish, snapper, and lobsters are served, on occasion to celebrities such as Madonna or famous Spanish chef Ferran Adrià. **CUISINE** Italian; Mediterranean. **CREDIT CARDS** AmEx; Diners; MasterCard; Visa
Rua Barão da Torre, 192, Ipanema
TEL (21) 2521-0627. Daily, noon – 1am

Shirley $

This tiny, simple restaurant opened in 1952. Spanish food is its forte, and the paella is the house specialty. When it gets very busy, the food quality can drop. **CUISINE** Spanish. **CREDIT CARDS** Not accepted
Rua Gustavo Sampaio, 610, Store #A, Leme
TEL (21) 2275-1398. Daily, noon – 1am

Sobrenatural $

This Santa Teresa restaurant serves its own catch of fish. The monkfish moqueca, with shrimp sauce, rice, and pirão (manioc-thickened gravy) or yellow farofa (manioc meal), is very popular and serves two. Reservations are recommended on weekends. **CUISINE** Brazilian; seafood. **CREDIT CARDS** AmEx; Diners; MasterCard; Visa
Rua Almirante Alexandrino, 432, Santa Teresa
TEL (21) 2224-1003. Daily, noon – until the last customer leaves

Sushi Leblon $$

This Japanese restaurant has contemporary choices such as foie gras marinated in sweet sake, as well as a lovely sushi bar and sake menu. **CUISINE** Japanese **CREDIT CARDS** AmEx; MasterCard; Visa
Rua Dias Ferreira, 256, Leblon
TEL (21) 2512-7830. Mon – Fri, noon – 4pm and 7pm – 1:30am; Sat, noon – 1:30am; Sun, 1pm – midnight

Talho Capixaba $

Choose from more than 30 types of bread 20 different sandwich fillings – pasta, cheese, meat, and antipasto options. Then you just weight and pay – the price is set by the kilo. The breakfast here is an institution. **CUISINE** Bread; sandwiches. **CREDIT CARDS** AmEx; Diners; MasterCard; Visa
Avenida Ataulfo de Paiva, 1,022, Stores #A and B, Leblon
TEL (21) 2512-8760. Mon – Sat, 7am – 9pm; Sun, 8am – 9pm

Tia Palmira $$

This restaurant has been drawing locals to the distant Barra de Guaratiba for over 40 years, thanks to its home-style seafood. The trip is worth it: the vatapá, risottos, and moqueca stews are delicious. **CUISINE** Fish and seafood. **CREDIT CARDS** AmEx; Diners; MasterCard; Visa
Rua Caminho do Souza, 18, Barra de Guaratiba
TEL (21) 2410-8169. Tue – Fri, 11:30am – 5pm; Sat, Sun, and holidays, 11:30am – 6pm

Zuka $$$

Chef Ludmilla Soeiro changes the menu here every four months. Try the fresh foie gras steak with mini-pancakes, marmalade, and Grand Marnier. **CUISINE** Contemporary. **CREDIT CARDS** AmEx; MasterCard; Visa
Rua Dias Ferreira, 233, Leblon
TEL (21) 3205-7154. Mon, 7pm – 1am; Tue – Fri, noon – 4pm and 7pm – 1am; Sat, 1pm – 1am; Sun, 1pm – midnight

00 $

This establishment operates inside the city's Planetarium and is a cross between a bar, a restaurant, and a nightclub, with a varied cultural program, including theater and short films. It serves meat, salads, fish, and sandwiches. On weekends, DJs and bands get the place going at 10pm. **CUISINE** Contemporary; sushi bar. **CREDIT CARDS** AmEx; Diners; MasterCard; Visa
Avenida Padre Leonel Franca, 240, Gávea
TEL (21) 2540-8041. Daily, 8:30pm – 3am

SERVICES

Airports – Aeroporto Internacional do Rio de Janeiro – Galeão/Antônio Carlos Jobim
Avenida 20 de Janeiro, Ilha do Governador
TEL (21) 3398-5050, 3398-4106

Airports – Aeroporto Santos Dumont
Praça Senador Salgado Filho, Centro
TEL (21) 3814-7070

Bus station – Rodoviária
Avenida Francisco Bicalho, 1, Santo Cristo
TEL (21) 3213-1800

Hang Gliding, paragliding and sky diving – Hilton Fly Rio Hang Gliding Center
Avenida Prefeito Mendes de Moraes, no #, Praia do Pepino
TEL (21) 9964-2607, 7840-6325. Opens at 8am
www.hiltonflyrio.com

Paragliding– Just Fly
Rua Barão da Torre, 177, Ipanema
TEL (21) 2268-0565, 9985-7540, 7816-5004 (phone in advance). Daily, 9am – 3pm   www.justfly.com.br

Hang gliding and paragliding – Superfly
Estrada da Canoa, 722, Bloco 5, Apto. 109
TEL (21) 3322-2286, 9887-6084, 9982-5703. Daily, with prior bookings   www.riosuperfly.com.br

Skydive Rio
Avenida Ayrton Senna, 2,541, Barra da Tijuca (Jacarepaguá Airport, in front of the tower)
TEL (21) 3410-4599, 7845-7119. Daily, 8:30am – 6pm

Surfing lessons – Escola Pedro Muller
Avenida Sernambetiba, between Posto 5 and Posto 6, in front of building #4,000, Barra da Tijuca
TEL (21) 2428-2271, 9644-638. Tue and Thu, 7am, 8:30am and 3:30pm; Sat and Sun, 7am, 8:30am, 10am
www.escolapedromuller.com.br

| **RESTAURANTS** | $ up to R$ 50 | $$ from R$ 51 up to R$ 100 | $$$ from R$ 101 up to R$ 150 | $$$$ above R$ 150 |

Surfing lessons – Escola de Surf Rico de Souza
Avenida Sernambetiba, in front of Posto 4
TEL (21) 2438-1692, 2438-4096, 2438-1821. Tue and Thu, 9:30am – 11:30am and 3pm – 5pm; Sat and Sun, 9:30am – 11:30am www.ricosurf.com.br

Kitesurfing lessons – Frajola Kitesurf School (K-08)
Avenida do Pepê, Kiosk 8, in front of 1,070, Barra da Tijuca
TEL (21) 2494-4869, 9808-1548. Daily, 8am – 8pm
www.k08.com.br

Kitesurfing and surfing lessons – KS Naish – Kitecenter
Avenida Armando Lombardi, 663, Barra da Tijuca
TEL (21) 2494-2540, 9935-6247. Daily, 6am – 11pm; Sat, 8am – 2pm and 5pm – 8pm; Sun, 9am – 2pm

Windsurfing lessons – Rio Wind
Avenida Prefeito Dulcídio Cardoso, 400, Barra da Tijuca
TEL (21) 9106-1045 www.riowind.com.br

Local tour operators – Aribira
Adventure sports; kayaking; climbing; hikes.
Ladeira dos Tabajaras, 196/601, Copacabana
TEL (21) 2235-3716, 9221-8741. Daily, 8am – 7pm
www.aribira.com.br

Local tour operators – Be a Local
Favela tours; transport to matches at Maracanã Stadium; and funk dances.
TEL (21) 9643-0366, 7816-9581 www.bealocal.com

Local tour operators – Carioca Tropical Tour Operator
Trips to the Sambódromo, where the official carnival parades are held.
Avenida Nossa Senhora de Copacabana, 534, Mezzanine Store #304, Copacabana
TEL (21) 2547-6327. Mon – Fri, 9am – 6pm

Local tour operators – Favela Tour
Estrada das Canoas, 722, Bloco 2, Apto. 124-125, São Conrado
TEL (21) 3322-2727, 9989-0074, 9772-1133. Daily, 8am – 10pm www.favelatour.com.br

Local tour operators – Jeep Tour
Jeep tours through Rio's forests.
Rua João Ricardo, 24, Conrado
TEL (21) 2108-5800. Mon – Fri, 10am – 2pm (by phone, daily, 7am – 7pm) www.jeeptour.com.br

Local tour operators – Rio Hiking
Hikes; rock climbing; rafting; ocean kayaking; surf lessons; paragliding; cycling; horse riding; bird watching; sky diving; rafting.
Rua Coelho Neto, 70/401, Laranjeiras
TEL (21) 2552-9204, 9721-0594 (phone in advance). Daily, 9am – noon www.riohiking.com.br

Local tour operators – Trilharte
Photography courses and trips; hikes; rappelling; ocean kayaking.
Rua Almirante Tamandaré, 77/01, Flamengo
TEL (21) 2225-2426, 2205-0654. Mon – Fri, 9am – 6pm
www.trilharte.com.br

Local tour operators – Trilhas do Rio
Guided hikes; adventure sports.
Rua Francisca Sales, 645, Jacarepaguá
TEL (21) 2424-5455, 7823-2520, 9207-1360. Mon – Fri, 9am – 6pm www.trilhasdorio.com.br

Panoramic helicopter tours – Cruzeiro Táxi-Aéreo
Avenida Ayrton Senna, 2,541, Hangar 11, Aeroporto de Jacarepaguá
TEL (21) 3325-6500. Mon – Fri, 8am – 5pm
www.cruzeirotaxiaereo.com.br

Panoramic helicopter tours – Helisight
Avenida Borges de Medeiros, no #, Heliponto da Prefeitura
TEL (21) 2511-2141. Daily, 9am – 6pm
www.helisight.com.br

Rock climbing – Centro de Escalada Limite Vertical
Rua Bambina, 141 (out back), Botafogo
TEL (21) 2246-9059. Mon – Fri, 5pm – 11pm

Rock climbing – Cia. da Escalada
Rua Valparaíso, 81, Apto. 401, Tijuca
TEL (21) 2567-7105. Daily, 9am – 6pm
www.guiadaurca.com/companhia

Tourist information – Centro de Atendimento ao Turista
Avenida Princesa Isabel, 183, Copacabana
TEL (21) 2542-8004. Mon – Fri, 9am – 6pm

Tourist information – Riotur
Praça Pio 10, 119, 9° Floor, Centro.
TEL (21) 2271-7000, 0800-285-0555

Tourist police station – Delegacia de Atendimento ao Turista
Avenida Humberto Campos, 315, Leblon
TEL (21) 3399-7170. Daily, 24 hours

Rio Quente – Goiás

AREA CODE 64 POPULATION 2,959 DISTANCES Goiânia 165 kilometers (103 miles), Brasilia 295 kilometers (183 miles), Caldas Novas 30 kilometers (19 miles) ACCESS Highway BR-153 and GO-213 from Goiânia. After Morrinhos, it is approximately 47 kilometers (29 miles) to the Rio Quente exit, where you take the GO-207

WHERE TO STAY

Hotel Parque das Primaveras $$
Located in the municipality next to Caldas Novas, this hotel is surrounded by greenery and all the rooms have jacuzzis and verandas. In the leisure area, there are four natural pools fed by hot springs. ACCOMMODATIONS 29; air-conditioning (except in the chalet); ceiling fan (in the chalet); jacuzzi; minibar; private safe; telephone; TV. FACILITIES AND SERVICES bar; conference room; games room; Internet access; massage room; natural pools; parking; playground; restaurant; sauna; six-a-side soccer court; snack bar; woods. CREDIT CARDS Diners, Master-Card, Visa
Rua do Balneário, 1, Caldas Novas
TEL (64) 3453-1268, 3453-1355, 3453-1280
FAX (64) 3453-1294 www.hpprimaveras.com.br

Rio Quente Resorts $$$

This spa resort has three hotels and three managed apartments. There are two water parks, the Hot Park, and the Parque das Fontes. Stay at Hotel Turismo, which offers the best accommodation and gardens designed by world-famous landscape artist Burle Marx. ACCOMMODATIONS 122; air-conditioning; baby-sitter; beauty parlor; gym; Internet access; jacuzzi (in the suites); minibar; pay TV; private safe; telephone. FACILITIES AND SERVICES archery; bar; bicycles; business center; conference room; convenience store; fishing equipment; fishing lake; Internet access; jacuzzi; jogging track; lifeguard; massage room; mini-golf course; mini spa; parking; recreational staff for adults and children; restaurant; sauna; snack bar; soccer field; stores; tennis court; thermal water park; trails; transport to airport and attractions; valet service; video room; volleyball court; walking tours; waterfall; 24-hour kitchen. CREDIT CARDS AmEx; Diners; MasterCard; Visa
Fazenda Água Quente, no #
TEL (64) 3512-8000 FAX (64) 3512-8088
RESERVATIONS (64) 3512-8080
www.rioquenteresorts.com.br

Sabará – Minas Gerais

AREA CODE 31 POPULATION 120,770 distâncias Belo Horizonte 23 kilometers (14 miles) ACCESS Highway MG-262 from Belo Horizonte www.sabara.mg.gov.br

WHERE TO EAT

314 Sabarabuçu $

This restaurant has a buffet at lunch and barbecued foods on Saturdays and Sundays. There are also à la carte options for lunch and dinner, such as the delicious bean dish feijão-tropeiro, which comes with collard greens, pork loin, rice, bacon, sausage, and boiled egg. At night, diners choose among 20 types of pizza. CUISINE Meats; pasta; regional; pizza; various. CREDIT CARDS Diners; MasterCard; Visa
Rua Dom Pedro II, 279, Centro
TEL (31) 3671-2313. Mon – Thu, 11am – midnight; Fri and Sat, 11am – 2:30am; Sun, 11am – 1am

SERVICES

Tourist Information – Posto do Teatro Municipal de Sabará
Rua Dom Pedro II, no #, Centro
TEL (31) 3672-7728. Daily, 8am – 5pm

Salvador – Bahia

AREA CODE 71 POPULATION 2,673,560 DISTANCES Aracaju 337 kilometers (209 miles), Maceió 617 kilometers (383 miles), Rio de Janeiro 1726 kilometers (1072 miles), São Paulo 2025 kilometers (1258 miles) ACCESS On highways BR-101, BR-324, or BA-099 (the Linha Verde Highway) www.salvador.ba.gov.br

WHERE TO STAY

A Casa das Portas Velhas $$$

Five minutes from Pelourinho, this sophisticated hotel occupies a 230-year-old building. The individually decorated rooms offer numerous amenities including personal care items, sound equipment, and a DVD player. If you wish to have lunch, order one day in advance. ACCOMMODATIONS 15; Internet access; air-conditioning; private safe; minibar; telephone; cable TV; ceiling fan. FACILITIES AND SERVICES Internet access; bar; parking; jacuzzi; reading room; guide hiring advice; transport to attractions. CREDIT CARDS AmEx; Diners; MasterCard; Visa
Largo da Palma, 6, Santana
TEL (71) 3324-8400 FAX (71) 3321-5677
www.acasadasportasvelhas.com.br

Catharina Paraguaçu $$

Location is this hotel's forte: in the Rio Vermelho neighborhood, a short hop from the historical centre, it is situated near busy nightlife and only two blocks from the beach. This historical mansion is decorated with paintings by local artists and craftwork from Maragogipinho. The delicious breakfast includes tapioca cuscuz and an irresistible bolinho de estudante cake. ACCOMMODATIONS 32; air-conditioning; private safe; minibar; cable TV. FACILITIES AND SERVICES Internet access; parking; restaurant; kitchen. OPEN until 10:30pm. CREDIT CARDS AmEx; Diners; MasterCard; Visa
Rua João Gomes, 128, Rio Vermelho
TEL (71) 3334-0089 FAX and RESERVATIONS (71) 3334-0089, 3334-2414 www.hotelcatharinaparaguacu.com.br

Club Med Itaparica $$$

The oldest resort in Brazil, Club Med Itaparica stands on Itaparica Island, in the Salvador metropolitan area. Its highlight is its recreational team. Visitors can pay either all-inclusive (overnight) or day-use tariffs. The décor in the rooms is rustic, with dark wooden furniture and thatched piassava palm roofs. ACCOMMODATIONS 346; Internet access; air-conditioning; private safe; minibar; telephone; cable TV. FACILITIES AND SERVICES Internet access; bar; boat; soccer field; golf course; parking; horse-riding; stores; pool; jogging track; six-a-side soccer court; tennis court; volleyball court; restaurant; beauty parlor; conference room; gym; games room; massage room; sauna; business center; 24-hour infirmary; recreational team for adults and children; guided walking tours; massage; beauty parlor; beach service. CREDIT CARDS AmEx; Diners; MasterCard; Visa
Rodovia Bom Despacho, Km 13, Nazaré
TEL (71) 3681-8800 FAX (71) 3681-7380
RESERVATIONS 0800-7073782 www.clubmed.com

Convento do Carmo $$$$

One of the largest historic luxury hotels in Brazil, Convento do Carmo used to be a Carmelite Convent. Renovations have blended modern refinements with architectural features from the 17th and 18th centuries. The hotel is comprised of two cloisters with 79 suites. The larger cloister contains the restaurant, which specializes in Portuguese cuisine and is open to the public. The staff is well-trained and helpful. ACCOMMODATIONS 79; Internet access; air-conditioning; bathtub in 5 rooms; private safe; minibar; telephone; cable TV. FACILITIES AND SERVICES bar; jacuzzi; pool; restaurant; gym; massage room; sauna; spa; laundry; pillow menu; butler (master suite). CREDIT CARDS AmEx; Diners; MasterCard; Visa
Rua do Carmo, 1, Santo Antônio
TEL (71) 3327-8400 FAX (71) 3327-8401
RESERVATIONS (71) 3327-8410

Pousada do Boqueirão $$

Located in the upper part of the city in a tastefully decorated historic building, this guesthouse is popular among foreign travelers. Its leisure facilities are limited to a cable TV room and a bar with a beautiful view over Todos os Santos Bay. It has ten regular rooms and five dormitories that share a communal bathroom. ACCOM-

RESTAURANTS	$ up to R$ 50	$$ from R$ 51 up to R$ 100	$$$ from R$ 101 up to R$ 150	$$$$ above R$ 150

MODATIONS 10; Internet access, air-conditioning; private safe; minibar; telephone; ceiling fan. FACILITIES AND SERVICES bar; cable TV. CREDIT CARDS AmEx; MasterCard; Visa
Rua Direita de Santo Antônio, 48, Santo Antônio
TEL (71) 3241-2262 FAX (71) 3241-8064
www.pousadaboqueirao.com.br

Sofitel Salvador $$$

Standing on a hilltop with a wonderful view of the sea at Itapuã, on the way to the fashionable beaches of Stella Maris and Flamengo, this is an excellently located hotel for anyone wanting to enjoy the city's beaches. Elegant and luxurious, it offers impeccable service. ACCOMMODATIONS 206; Internet access; air-conditioning; private safe; minibar; cable TV. FACILITIES AND SERVICES Internet access; bar; soccer field; golf course; parking; arts and crafts store; pool; playground; six-a-side soccer court; tennis court; restaurant; conference room; gym; games room; massage room; exhibition space; sauna; 24-hour kitchen; recreational team for adults and children; guided walking tours; valet parking; beach service; airport shuttle. CREDIT CARDS AmEx; Diners; MasterCard; Visa
Rua da Pasárgada, no #, Itapuã
TEL (71) 3374-8500 FAX (71) 3374-6946
RESERVATIONS (71) 2106-8500 www.sofitel.com.br

Solar Santo Antônio $$

While this 3-story, 18th-century building has only two guest rooms, those staying here find themselves immersed in the culture of Bahia. The Moroccan-born owner, Dimitri, is passionate about the city and actively involved in its cultural life. ACCOMMODATIONS 2; minibar; ceiling fan; airport shuttle. CREDIT CARDS Not accepted
Rua Direita de Santo Antônio, 177, Santo Antônio
TEL (71) 3242-6455

Vila Galé Bahia $$

This hotel, opened in 2003, sits next to museums, the historical centre, and the hustle and bustle of Barra and Rio Vermelho. The highlight here is the exceptional view of the sea. ACCOMMODATIONS 224; Internet access; air-conditioning; private safe; minibar; telephone; cable TV. FACILITIES AND SERVICES Internet access; bar; parking; jacuzzi; convenience store; pool; playground; restaurant; conference room; gym; meeting room; sauna; travel agency; business center; 24-hour kitchen; laundry. CREDIT CARDS AmEx; Diners; MasterCard; Visa
Rua Morro do Escravo Miguel, 320, Ondina
TEL (71) 3263-8888 FAX (71) 3263-8800
RESERVATIONS 0800-2848818
www.vilagale.pt/hoteis/bahia/salvador

WHERE TO EAT

Agdá $

This reasonably priced restaurant has been serving generous helpings of well-seasoned fish and seafood for four-plus decades. The crab moqueca arrives bubbling at the table, exhaling a mouthwatering aroma. For the health-conscious, there's a version made with out dendê palm oil. CUISINE Regional. CREDIT CARDS AmEx; MasterCard; Visa
Rua Orlando Moscoso, 1, Praia dos Artistas, Boca do Rio
TEL (71) 3461-3375 OPEN Mon – Tue, 11:30am – 4pm; Wed – Sun, 11:30am – midnight

Amado $$

Chef Edinho Engel brings to Salvador the ingenuity and art he showed while in charge at the impeccable Manacá restaurant in Camburi, on the north coast of São Paulo. The menu consists of contemporary cuisine with an emphasis on Brazilian, especially Bahian, flavors. One of the most popular dishes is the prato dos pescadores (fishermen's dish), with shrimp, octopus, squid, mussels, and slices of grilled summer squash, eggplant, and tomato. CUISINE Contemporary. CREDIT CARDS AmEx; Diners; MasterCard; Visa
Avenida Lafaiete Coutinho, 660
TEL (71) 3322-3520 OPEN Mon – Thu; noon – 3:30pm and 7pm – midnight; Fri and Sat; 7pm – 1am

Bate-Boca $

This restaurant serves a traditional supper every Sunday starting at 6pm. This meal consists of two kinds of soup, pasta, and a wide variety of savory and sweet dishes, as well as hot drinks (chocolate, coffee, tea) and fresh juices. During the week, the restaurant offers an à la carte menu of simple dishes. CUISINE Regional; diverse. CREDIT CARDS Diners; MasterCard; Visa
Alameda Antunes, 56, Barra Avenida
TEL (71) 3264-3821 OPEN Thu – Sun, 11:30am – 3pm and 6pm – 10pm

Jardim das Delícias $

Operating out of a well-kept old building in Pelourinho, this restaurant serves up live music – chorinho and MPB at lunchtime and jazz and blues during dinner. The menu features dishes from the interior of the Northeast, with a contemporary touch. Try the carne-de-sol da Gabriela (beef jerky, grilled with a sprinkling of olive oil and sugar). CUISINE Regional; diverse. CREDIT CARDS AmEx; Diners, MasterCard; Visa
Rua João de Deus, 12, Pelourinho
TEL (71) 3321-1449 FAX and RESERVATIONS (71) 3322-7086 OPEN Daily, noon – 1am

Maria Mata Mouro $$

This charming restaurant offers refined, appetizing contemporary cuisine – and an excellent wine cellar. The menu features well-presented, delicately flavored dishes, such as fresh sea bass in caper sauce, served with potatoes. There are also good meat dishes and some regional cuisine. CUISINE Contemporary. CREDIT CARDS AmEx; Diners; MasterCard; Visa
Rua da Ordem Terceira de São Francisco (formerly Rua Inácio Acioly), 8, Pelourinho
TEL (71) 3321-3929 OPEN Daily, 11:50am until the last customer leaves

Mercado do Rio Vermelho $

This popular market known as Marcadão comprises a collection of 30 box-like kiosks to the left of Largo da Mariquita square. This market is the place to go after a long night of partying, generally for a plate of moqueca (seafood stew), feijoada (black bean and pork stew), or sarapatel (tripe stew) and a glass of beer.
Avenida Juracy Magalhães Junior, 1624, Rio Vermelho
TEL (71) 3452-1566 OPEN Mon – Sat, 7am – 6pm; Sun, 7am – noon

Mistura Fina $

This restaurant, housed in a pleasant old building near the Itapuã lighthouse, serves a menu of Mediterranean and regional Brazilian dishes. We recommend the seafood pasta dishes. A good buffet of antipasti and salads can be bought by the kilo. CUISINE Italian; regional; seafood. CREDIT CARDS Diners; MasterCard; Visa
Rua Sousa Brito, 41, Itapuã

PRICES	HOTELS (couple)	$ up to R$ 150	$$ from R$ 151 up to R$ 300	$$$ from R$ 301 up to R$500	$$$$ above R$ 500

TEL (71) 3375-2623 **RESERVATIONS** (71) 3285-0291 **OPEN** Mon – Thu, 11:30am – midnight; Fri – Sun, 11:30am – 1am

Paraíso Tropical $$
Here, at one of the best restaurants in Salvador, chef/owner Beto Pimentel cooks local food in a new fashion. Dendê palm oil, for example, is replaced with dendê fruit juice, and coconut pulp is used instead of coconut milk, resulting in a more delicate flavor. An abundant fruit basket accompanies most dishes. **CUISINE** Regional. **CREDIT CARDS** AmEx; Diners; MasterCard; Visa
Rua Edgar Loureiro, 98-B, Cabula
TEL (71) 3384-7464 **OPEN** Mon – Sat, noon – 11pm; Sun, noon – 10pm

Porto do Moreira $
In operation since the 1930s, this relaxed, traditional restaurant serves meat moqueca, made with beef, beef jerky, dried shrimp, eggs, and seasonings. Their sarapatel (stewed pig's tripe and liver enriched with thickened blood), served only on weekends, is a sensation, as are other offal recipes. Leave room for a homemade dessert. **CUISINE** Regional. **CREDIT CARDS** AmEx; Diners; MasterCard; Visa
Rua Carlos Gomes, 488, Centro
TEL (71) 3322-4112 **RESERVATIONS** (71) 3322-2814 **OPEN** Daily, 11am – 4pm

Soho $$
This is the best place in Salvador for Japanese food. Chefs prepare sushi and robatas at two counters, in view of customers. Local cuisine makes an appearance in some of the robatas, such as those made with beef jerky, and in some desserts, like banana roll with tapioca and coconut ice cream. **CUISINE** Japanese. **CREDIT CARDS** AmEx; Diners; MasterCard; Visa
Avenida Lafaiete Coutinho, 1010, Píer D, Bahia Marina, Comércio
TEL (71) 3322-4554 **RESERVATIONS** (71) 3322-8150 **OPEN** Daily; noon – 3pm and 7pm – midnight

Trapiche Adelaide $$
This highly professional restaurant has light, modern décor and a view of Todos os Santos Bay. The contemporary international menu, by Luciano Boseggia, balances meat dishes, pasta, fish, and seafood. **CUISINE** Contemporary; international. **CREDIT CARDS** MasterCard; Visa
Praça dos Tupinambás, 2 (Avenida do Contorno), Comércio
TEL (71) 3326-2211 **RESERVATIONS** (71) 3326-0443 **OPEN** Mon – Thu, noon – 4pm and 7pm – 1am; Fri and Sat, noon – 1am; Sun, noon – 5pm

Uauá $
This restaurant specializes in dishes from Brazil's Northeastern backlands, such as the delicious paçoca: beef jerky pounded in a mortar and then shredded, cooked with onion, coriander, parsley, and flour, then served with banana manioc flour and rice. The guisado de carneiro (mutton stew) with chayote and pumpkin is also excellent. **CUISINE** Regional; diverse. **CREDIT CARDS** AmEx; Diners; MasterCard; Visa
Rua Gregório de Matos, 36, 1ˢᵗ floor, Pelourinho
TEL (71) 3322-1778 **OPEN** Tue – Sun, 11am – 3pm and 7pm – 11pm

Yemanjá $
Overlooking Armação Beach, this is one of the city's most traditional restaurants. The 12 varieties of hearty moqueca stew are legendary in Salvador and can be prepared with olive oil and low-sodium salt for the health-conscious. **CUISINE** Regional. **CREDIT CARDS** AmEx; Diners; MasterCard; Visa
Avenida Otávio Mangabeira, 4655, Jardim Armação
TEL (71) 3461-9010 **OPEN** Sun – Thu, 11:30am – midnight; Fri and Sat, 11:30am – 1am

SERVICES

Airport – Aeroporto Internacional de Salvador Deputado Luís Eduardo Magalhães
Praça Gago Coutinho, no #, São Cristóvão
TEL (71) 3204-1010 **OPEN** Daily, 24 hours
www.infraero.com.br

Tourist Information – Bahiatursa
Rua das Laranjeiras, 12, Pelourinho
TEL (71) 3321-2133, 3321-2463, 3370-8694 (main office) **OPEN** Mon, Wed – Sat, 8:30am – 9pm; Tue and Sun, 8:30am – 8pm
Avenida Simon Bolívar, no #, Centro de Convenções
TEL (71) 3117-3000 **OPEN** Daily, 10am – 11pm
www.bahiatursa.ba.gov.br

Tourist Information – Emtursa
Elevador Lacerda, Praça Municipal, no #
TEL (71) 3321-2697, 3321-2598, 3176-4200 **OPEN** Mon – Fri, 8:30am – 7pm www.salvadordabahia.ba.gov.br

Tourist Police Station – Delegacia de Proteção ao Turista
Largo Cruzeiro de São Francisco, 14, Pelourinho
TEL (71) 3322-1188, 3322-7155 **OPEN** Daily, 24 hours

Santa Bárbara – Minas Gerais

AREA CODE 31 **POPULATION** 26,185 distâncias Belo Horizonte 99 kilometers (62 miles) **ACCESS** Highway BR-262 from Belo Horizonte, with some stretches of dirt road. If you only want to drive on paved stretches, take the BR-381 to the Barão de Cocais exit, where you take the BR-262 www.santabarbara.mg.gov.br

WHERE TO STAY

Hospedaria do Caraça $
Located in the Parque Natural do Caraça nature reserve, the rooms in this monastery – most of which sleep up to 5 – are very simple, small, and cold, especially in the old wing. The refurbished ones are reasonable, though, and the view outside is magnificent. Daily rates are for full board. **ACCOMMODATIONS** 59 (8 with outdoor bathroom); minibar (in 2 suites). **FACILITIES AND SERVICES** function room; games room; natural pool; parking; restaurant; river; soccer field; souvenir shop; trails; TV room; video room; walking tours; waterfall; wood. **CREDIT CARDS** MasterCard
Parque Natural do Caraça, Rodovia Padre Jerônimo (MG-436), access from Rodovia BR-381, between Barão de Cocais and Santa Bárbara
TEL and **FAX** (31) 3837-2698

Hotel Quadrado $
The most convenient accommodation option in Santa Bárbara is housed in a historic building. Simple but pleasant, it receives visitors to the Parque Natural do

| **RESTAURANTS** | $ up to R$ 50 | $$ from R$ 51 up to R$ 100 | $$$ from R$ 101 up to R$ 150 | $$$$ above R$ 150 |

Caraça with a modicum of comfort. **ACCOMMODATIONS** 15; air-conditioning; minibar; phone; TV. **FACILITIES AND SERVICES** bar; function room; parking; period furniture; TV room. **CREDIT CARDS** AmEx; Visa
Praça Cleves de Faria (Praça da Matriz), 136, Centro
TEL and **FAX** (31) 3832-3106, 3832-3879

SERVICES

Bus station – Rodoviária
Rua Antônio Pereira Rocha, no #, Centro
TEL (31) 3832-1434 (Viação Pássaro Verde)

Tourist information – Casa da Cultura
Avenida Petrina de Castro Chaves, 70, Centro
TEL (31) 3832-1616, 3832-2763. Mon – Fri, 7am – 11am and 1pm – 5pm

Santarém – Pará

AREA CODE 93 **POPULATION** 274,285 **DISTANCE** Belém 1,369 kilometers (851 miles) **ACCESS** The best way here is by boat or plane, from Manaus or Belém

WHERE TO STAY

Beloalter Hotel $$
The hotel is organized and clean, and offers access to the river beach Alter do Chão. Most impressively, the accommodations are surrounded by forest. A highlight is the Casa da Árvore suite, which has a tree inside it. **ACCOMMODATIONS** 26; air-conditioning; minibar; telephone; TV. **FACILITIES AND SERVICES** bar; beach service; conference room; Internet access; playground; pool; restaurant. **CREDIT CARDS** MasterCard; Visa
Rua Pedro Teixeira, no #, Caruari, Alter do Chão
TEL (93) 3527-1247, 3527-1230 **FAX** (93) 3527-1230
www.beloalter.com.br

SERVICES

Tour Operator – Santarém Tur
Expeditions to archeological sites in caves and hiking trails in Tapajós National Forest.
Avenida Adriano Pimentel, 44, Centro
TEL (93) 3522-4847. Mon – Fri, 7:30am – 6pm; Sat, 8am – noon www.santaremtur.com.br

Santo André – Bahia

AREA CODE 73 **DISTANCES** Salvador 660 kilometers (410 miles), Porto Seguro 30 kilometers (19 miles) **ACCESS** From Porto Seguro, take the Highway BR-367 to Santa Cruz Cabrália, plus 10 minutes by ferryboat

WHERE TO STAY

Costa Brasilis Resort $$$
This sea-front resort has lovely gardens and woods and spacious rooms with colonial touches. Bungalows are also available, and there's a spa, too. The leisure program, including many water sports, is a big attraction. **ACCOMMODATIONS** 122; Internet access; air-conditioning; private safe; minibar; jacuzzi in some rooms; telephone; cable TV; ceiling fan. **FACILITIES AND SERVICES** Internet access; bar; boat; bicycles; kayaks; fishing equipment; parking; motorboat; stores; pool; thermal pool; playground; six-a-side soccer court; tennis court; volleyball court; beach volleyball arena; restaurant; conference room;

gym; games room; massage room; beauty parlor; sauna; business center; 24-hour kitchen; recreational team for adults and children; guided walking tours; lifeguards; beach service; airport shuttle. **CREDIT CARDS** AmEx; Diners; MasterCard; Visa
Avenida Beira-mar, 2,000, Praia de Santo André
TEL (73) 3282-8200 **FAX** (73) 3282-8219 **RESERVATIONS** 0800-7038201, 0800-7011413
www.costabrasilis.com.br

Toca do Marlin $$$$
This hotel offers suites with sea views and adjustably positioned Swiss beds. Works of art and antiques featured in the décor. The bread and desserts are made in the hotel's own bakery. Full and half-board tariffs are available. **ACCOMMODATIONS** 11; Internet access; air-conditioning; position-control beds; private safe; minibar; telephone; cable TV. **FACILITIES AND SERVICES** Internet access; wine cellar; bar; boat; bicycles; kayaks; fishing equipment; water skiing; parking; horse-riding; motorboat; stores; pool; orchard; restaurant; river; conference room; gym; games room; massage room; currency exchange; 24-hour kitchen; recreational team for adults and children; valet parking; beach service; airport shuttle; transport to attractions. **CREDIT CARDS** AmEx; MasterCard
Rodovia BA-001, Km 40.5, Estrada Santo André–Belmonte
TEL (73) 3671-5009 www.tocadomarlin.com.br

Santo Antônio do Pinhal – São Paulo

AREA CODE 12 habitantes 6,560 **DISTANCE** São Paulo 177 kilometers (110 miles) **ACCESS** Highway BR-116 (Rodovia Presidente Dutra) or SP-070 (Rodovia Ayrton Senna–Carvalho Pinto) from São Paulo, then SP-123 (Rodovia Floriano Rodrigues Pinheiro) to the SP-046 exit

WHERE TO STAY

Pousada do Cedro $$$
Ideal for couples, since children under 12 are not allowed, this guesthouse stands on a 10-hectare (25-acre) property at an altitude of 1,300 meters (4265 feet) above sea level. Its spacious lofts have wooden sun decks, living rooms, and huge floor-to-ceiling windows on one side, yet they still offer plenty of privacy. **ACCOMMODATIONS** 10; DVD player; fireplace; minibar; ofuro tub (in 7 lofts); TV. **FACILITIES AND SERVICES** bar; bicycles; hiking trails; jacuzzi; living room; massage room; pool; restaurant; sauna; wine cellar. **CREDIT CARDS** AmEx
Estrada do Pico Agudo, Sertãozinho (4.5 kilometers, or 3 miles, from the center)
TEL (12) 3666-1873 **FAX** (12) 3666-1713
www.pousadadocedro.com.br

Pousada Quinta dos Pinhais $$$
This sophisticated guesthouse stands at 1,400 meters (nearly 4600 feet) above sea level, surrounded by greenery and looking out on a view of Pedra do Baú. Its 10 chalets have fireplaces and verandas with hammocks, and 2 of them have private heated pools and whirlpool tubs. The biggest, with an area of 130 square meters (1400 square feet), also has a sauna. **ACCOMMODATIONS** 10; fireplace; minibar; phone; private safe; TV; veranda with hammock. **FACILITIES AND SERVICES** archery; beach volleyball arena; deck with panoramic views; DVD room; gym; hiking trails; horses; karaoke room; lake; massage room; mini-golf course; orchard; pool; relaxation room; restaurant; sauna; soccer field. **CREDIT CARDS** Visa

| PRICES | HOTELS (couple) | $ up to R$ 150 | $$ from R$ 151 up to R$ 300 | $$$ from R$ 301 up to R$500 | $$$$ above R$ 500 |

544 BRAZIL GUIDE

Estrada do Pico Agudo, Sertãozinho (3.5 kilometers, or 2 miles, from the center)
TEL and **FAX** (12) 3666-2030
www.quintadospinhais.com.br

WHERE TO EAT

Picanha & Pasta $
Situated inside a shopping mall, this restaurant specializes in picanha steak. On Saturdays they serve feijoada (black-bean and pork stew). **CUISINE** Meats. **CREDIT CARDS** Diners; MasterCard; Visa
Avenida Antônio Joaquim de Oliveira, 345, Centro
TEL (12) 3666-1162. Mon – Thu, noon – 10pm; Fri and Sat, noon – midnight; Sun, noon – 8pm

SERVICES

Tourist information – Associação Comercial
Avenida Ministro Nélson Hungria, 44, Centro. Tue – Fri, 9am – 5pm; Sat and Sun, 10am – 5pm
TEL (12) 3666-1444.

Santos – São Paulo

AREA CODE 13 **POPULATION** 418,288 **DISTANCE** São Paulo 70 kilometers (44 miles) **ACCESS** The Anchieta–Imigrantes (SP-150/SP-160) highway system from São Paulo

WHERE TO STAY

Mendes Plaza $$
This hotel is located on a busy street next to a shopping mall and two blocks from the beach. The swimming pool on the roof has ocean views. The business-support facilities are good. **ACCOMMODATIONS** 104; air-conditioning; Internet access; minibar; pay TV; phone; private safe. **FACILITIES AND SERVICES** bar; beachside service; business center; function room; games room; gym; Internet access; parking; pool; recreational team for children (high season); restaurant; sauna; snack bar; transport to airport and attractions; travel agency; valet service; 24-hour kitchen. **CREDIT CARDS** AmEx; MasterCard; Visa
Avenida Marechal Floriano Peixoto, 42, Gonzaga
TEL (13) 3208-6500, (11) 5082-1530
www.mendesplaza.com.br

Parque Balneário $$
Among the most luxurious hotels in Santos, this place is just a stone's throw from the beach. The presidential and "balneária" suites have private gardens and pools. The rooftop pool, open to all other guests, has a lovely ocean view. **ACCOMMODATIONS** 119; air-conditioning; bathtub; Internet access; minibar; pay TV; phone; private safe. **FACILITIES AND SERVICES** bar; beachside service; business center; function room; games room; gym; heated pool; Internet access; jacuzzi; lifeguard; parking; pool; recreational staff for adults and children; restaurant; sauna; valet service; 24-hour kitchen. **CREDIT CARDS** Diners; MasterCard; Visa
Avenida Ana Costa, 555, Gonzaga
TEL (13) 3289-5700 www.parquebalneario.com.br

WHERE TO EAT

Paco Paquito $
A Spanish family has long tended this eatery. Although simple and not very close to the beach, it draws a good crowd thanks to its fresh seafood and paella. **CUISINE** Fish and seafood. **CREDIT CARDS** AmEx; MasterCard; Visa
Rua Constituição, 607, Encruzilhada
TEL (13) 3233-2594. Tue – Sat, 11am – midnight; Sun, 11am – 5pm

Tamariz $
Facing José Menino Beach, this traditional restaurant is more sophisticated than others of in its price range. It specializes in fish and seafood. The caldeirada (seafood stew) serves four. **CUISINE** Brazilian. **CREDIT CARDS** AmEx; Diners; MasterCard; Visa
Avenida Presidente Wilson, 88, Pompéia
TEL (13) 3237-6234. Daily, noon – midnight

Último Gole $$
Located on a narrow street by Gonzaga Beach, this traditional Portuguese eatery serves delicious bacalhoada (codfish stew) and the best bolinhos de bacalhau (cod croquettes) in town. **CUISINE** Portuguese. **CREDIT CARDS** AmEx; Diners; MasterCard; Visa
Rua Carlos Afonseca, 214, Gonzaga
TEL (13) 3284-0508. Daily, 11am – 1am

SERVICES

Tourist information – Centro de Informações Turísticas
Praça Paulo Viriato Corrêa da Costa, no # (formerly Ilha da Conveniência)
TEL 0800-173887. Daily, 8am – 8pm

São Francisco do Sul – Santa Catarina

AREA CODE 47 **POPULATION** 37,613 **DISTANCE** Florianópolis 226 kilometers (140 miles) **ACCESS** Highway BR-101 from Florianópolis heading north. After 200 kilometers (124 miles), get onto the BR-280 at the signposted turnoff to the town

WHERE TO STAY

Hotel Villa Real $$
This villa has good leisure facilities, especially for those with boats, since it has its own marina. Ask for a room on one of the upper floors, which have been remodeled recently. **ACCOMMODATIONS** 71; air-conditioning; Internet access; minibar; pay TV; private safe; telephone. **FACILITIES AND SERVICES** bar; business center; fishing equipment and lake; function room; games room; gym; heated pool; Internet access; laundry; marina; playground; pool; restaurant; schooner tours; snack bar; valet service. **CREDIT CARDS** AmEx; Diners; MasterCard; Visa
Rua Francisco Machado de Sousa, 1,135, Paulas
TEL (47) 3444-2010 www.villareal.com.br

WHERE TO EAT

Jacizinho Batista $
To enjoy this great all-you-can-eat seafood rodízio, you'll have to take a boat or ferryboat to the fishing village of Glória. While it takes half an hour to cross, the bay's stunning natural beauty will whet your appetite. **CUISINE** Fish and seafood. **CREDIT CARDS** Not accepted
Estrada Geral do Estaleiro, no #, Vila da Glória
TEL (47) 3449-5124, 9984-1073. Mon – Sat, 11am – 9pm; Sun, 11am – 7pm

RESTAURANTS	**$** up to R$ 50	**$$** from R$ 51 up to R$ 100	**$$$** from R$ 101 up to R$ 150	**$$$$** above R$ 150

SERVICES

Boat Hire – Marujo Amigo
Avenida Atlântica 1430, Enseada
TEL (47) 3449-0875, 9974-3986. Mon – Sat, 8am – noon and 2pm – 6pm

São João del-Rei – Minas Gerais

AREA CODE 32 POPULATION 81,918 distâncias Belo Horizonte 197 kilometers (122 miles), Ouro Preto 180 kilometers (112 miles) (on the Estrada Real) ACCESS Highway BR-040 and BR-383 from Belo Horizonte

WHERE TO STAY

Garden Hill Small Resort $$$
Rededicated as a resort and spa, this complex has a 9-hole golf course and practice driving range. A green fee is charged for the use of the course and lessons. The hotel is near the airport, and its rooms have views of the golf course. ACCOMMODATIONS 21; air-conditioning; jacuzzi; minibar; pay TV; phone. FACILITIES AND SERVICES bar; function room; games room; golf course; gym; heated pool; hike and tour guides; Internet access; laundry; massage room; parking; pool; recreational staff for adults and children; restaurant; sauna; soccer field; tennis court. CREDIT CARDS AmEx; Diners; MasterCard; Visa
Rodovia BR-383, Km 96, Colônia do Marçal
TEL and FAX (32) 3371-2551 www.gardenhillgolf.com.br

Pousada Beco do Bispo $
This charming, well-located guesthouse (next to São Francisco de Assis Church) has large, tastefully decorated rooms. Breakfast is a full colonial-style affair. ACCOMMODATIONS 13; air-conditioning; ceiling fan; fireplace; Internet access; minibar; pay TV; phone. FACILITIES AND SERVICES Internet access; minibar; pay TV; sitting room with fireplace. CREDIT CARDS AmEx; Diners; MasterCard; Visa
Rua Irmã Eugênia Luz Pinto, 93 (Beco do Bispo), Centro
TEL and FAX (32) 3371-8844 www.becodobispo.com.br

Villa Magnólia Pousada $$
This old building still has its 19th-century cellar, where guests have breakfast. Though in the historic town center, it's surrounded by a large patch of greenery. The windows offer views of the town's monuments. The five "luxury" suites are more spacious and have king size beds. ACCOMMODATIONS 13; air-conditioning (in 7 suites); Internet access (in 7 suites); minibar; phone; TV. FACILITIES AND SERVICES parking; pool. CREDIT CARDS AmEx; Visa
Rua Ribeiro Bastos, 2, Centro
TEL and FAX (32) 3373-5065
www.pousadavillamagnolia.com.br

WHERE TO EAT

L'Arlequin $
The menu has Belgian, Italian, and French influences. Suggestions include the bouef braisé, meat cooked in black beer and spices. CUISINE Various. CREDIT CARDS Not accepted
Travessa Américo Brighenti, 22, Colônia do Marçal
TEL (32) 3371-5246. Fri and Sat, 7pm – midnight; Sun, noon – 5pm; Mon – Thu, subject to bookings

Quinto do Ouro $
One house forte is the leitão pururuca (crispy roast suckling pig) with rice, collard greens, and torresmo

(crispy fried pork rinds) and either feijão-tropeiro or tutu de feijão (both regional bean dishes). Other typical regional dishes and a few meats complete the list of specialties. CUISINE Regional; various. CREDIT CARDS Diners; MasterCard; Visa
Praça Severiano de Resende, 4, Centro
TEL (32) 3371-7577, 3371-8555. Daily, 11am – 10pm

SERVICES

Bus station – Rodoviária
Rua Cristovão Colombo, no #, Bairro das Fábricas
TEL (32) 3373-4700

Tourist information – Secretaria de Cultura e Turismo
Praça Frei Orlando, 90, Centro
TEL (32) 3372-7338. Mon – Fri, 8am – 6pm; Sat and Sun, 8am – 11am and 1pm – 5pm

Travel agency – Tiradentes Turismo
Avenida Tiradentes, 600 A, Centro
TEL (32) 3371-9586. Mon – Fri, 8:30am – 6pm; Sat, 8am – noon

São Jorge – Goiás

AREA CODE 62 DISTANCE Brasilia 266 kilometers (165 miles) ACCESS Highway GO-118 from Brasilia to Alto Paraíso; then another 36 kilometers (22 miles) on GO-239

WHERE TO STAY

Pousada Casa das Flores $$
This charming hotel offers candle-lit rooms and breakfast on the veranda in rustic chalets and rooms. ACCOMMODATIONS 21; air-conditioning; ceiling fan; Internet access; minibar; private safe; telephone. FACILITIES AND SERVICES bar; business center; conference room; convenience store; heated pool; Internet access; jacuzzi; massage room; parking; pool; restaurant; sauna; store; trails; video room; walking tours; waterfall. CREDIT CARDS Not accepted
Rua 10, Quadra 2, Lote 14
TEL (62) 3455-1055 FAX (62) 3455-1049
www.pousadacasasdasflores.com.br

WHERE TO EAT

Rancho do Waldomiro $
If you want to taste matula, a dish typical of the Brazilian savannah, this simple eatery is the place to do it. We recommend stopping by the restaurant in the morning to place an early order, then going off to do some exploring before coming back to eat. CUISINE Regional. CREDIT CARDS Not accepted
Estrada Alto Paraíso–São Jorge, Km 18
TEL No #

São José do Barreiro – São Paulo

AREA CODE 12 POPULATION 4,278 DISTANCE São Paulo 270 kilometers (168 miles) ACCESS Highway BR-116 from São Paulo to Queluz, then SP-068 (Rodovia dos Tropeiros)

WHERE TO STAY

Hotel Porto da Bocaina $
Located by the Funil Dam, this hotel has a stunning view; spacious, comfortable rooms; and good amenities

---

PRICES	HOTELS (couple)	$ up to R$ 150	$$ from R$ 151 up to R$ 300	$$$ from R$ 301 up to R$500	$$$$ above R$ 500

for water sports. The spa offers programs for those wanting to get in shape or those who seek merely to relax. **ACCOMMODATIONS** 35; air-conditioning; ceiling fan; jacuzzi (in the suites); phone; TV. **FACILITIES AND SERVICES** bar; soccer field; horse; pool; tennis court; restaurant; function room; gym; games room; trails; recreation team for adults and children (during school and public holidays). **CREDIT CARDS** AmEx; Diners; MasterCard; Visa
Rodovia dos Tropeiros, Km 260, Represa do Funil
TEL (12) 3117-1221 **FAX** (12) 3117-1303
www.hoteisdabocaina.com.br

Refúgio Ecológico Vale dos Veados $$$
At an altitude of 1,800 meters (about 5900 feet), this 1926 farm manor was built of pine logs and stones. The place is lit with gas lighting or lanterns and there's one bathroom for every two rooms in the main house; the suites have private bathrooms. To get here, you have to travel 42 kilometers (26 miles) on a dirt road in a 4×4 vehicle. **ACCOMMODATIONS** 9; fireplace (in the suites). **FACILITIES AND SERVICES** fruit and vegetable garden; lake; ofuro tub; parking; restaurant; river; hiking trails and guides; valet service; waterfall; wood. **CREDIT CARDS** Diners; MasterCard; Visa
Estrada do Bocaina, Km 42, Parque Nacional da Serra do Bocaina
TEL and **FAX** (12) 3117-1221 **RESERVATIONS** (12) 3117-1192
www.hoteisdabocaina.com.br

SERVICES

Local tour operator – MW Trekking
Hikes to waterfalls and the Gold Trail.
Praça Coronel Cunha Lara, no #, Centro
TEL (12) 3117-1220. Mon – Sun, 9:30am – 4:45pm

São Luís – Maranhão

AREA CODE 98 **POPULATION** 978,824 **DISTANCES** Teresina 463 kilometers (288 miles), Belém 803 kilometers (499 miles) **ACCESS** Take Highway BR-135 www.saoluis.ma.gov.br

WHERE TO STAY

Grand São Luís $
Well-located in the historical town center, this is one of the most comfortable hotels in São Luiz. Its rooms have views of São Marcos Bay and the town's historic buildings. The hotel itself has good leisure facilities, and breakfast is included. **ACCOMMODATIONS** 208; Internet access; air-conditioning; minibar; cable TV. **FACILITIES AND SERVICES** Internet access; bar; parking; pool; playground; restaurant; conference room; gym; massage room; sauna; 24-hour room service. **CREDIT CARDS** AmEx; Diners; MasterCard; Visa
Praça Dom Pedro II, 299, Centro
TEL (98) 2109-3500 **RESERVATIONS** (98) 2109-3540
www.grandsaoluis.com.br

Pestana São Luís Resort Hotel $$$
One of the most luxurious hotels in town, the Pestana São Luís is close to Calhau Beach. The magnificent foyer has fountains that imitate the city's stone fountains. **ACCOMMODATIONS** 109; Internet access; air-conditioning; private safe; minibar; telephone; cable TV. **FACILITIES AND SERVICES** Internet access; bar; woods; soccer field; parking; convenience store; stores; pool; playground; tennis court; volleyball court; restaurant; conference room; gym; games room; sauna; travel agency; 24-hour kitchen;

massage; airport shuttle. **CREDIT CARDS** AmEx; Diners; MasterCard; Visa
Avenida Avicênia, no #, Praia do Calhau
TEL (98) 2106-0505 **FAX** (98) 3235-4921
www.pestana.com.br

Portas da Amazônia $
This guesthouse is in the historic centre, making it a good option near the main attractions. The restored, 1835 building has a cozy, charming atmosphere. **ACCOMMODATIONS** 28; air-conditioning; minibar; telephone; TV. **FACILITIES AND SERVICES** Internet access; bar; snack bar; travel agency; airport shuttle. **CREDIT CARDS** AmEx; MasterCard; Visa
Rua do Giz, 129, Centro
TEL (98) 3222-9937 **FAX** (98) 3221-4193
www.portasdaamazonia.com.br

Pousada do Francês $
One of the best places to stay in the city centre, this lovely three-story building has been completely restored. The best rooms are on the top floor: One weak point is the lighting, which is white and cold. **ACCOMMODATIONS** 29; Internet access; air-conditioning; minibar; telephone; TV. **FACILITIES AND SERVICES** Fish and seafood; period furniture; restaurant. **CREDIT CARDS** AmEx; Diners; MasterCard; Visa
Rua da Saavedra, 160, Centro
TEL (98) 3231-4844

WHERE TO EAT

Cabana do Sol $
This restaurant serves generous portions of excellent carne-de-sol (beef jerky), accompanied by a veritable banquet: baião-de-dois (rice and bean mush), lima beans, paçoca, boiled manioc, manioc purée, banana fritters, and clarified butter. **CUISINE** Regional; fish and seafood. **CREDIT CARDS** AmEx; Diners; MasterCard; Visa
Rua João Damasceno, 24-A, Farol de São Marcos
TEL (98) 3235-2586 **OPEN** Daily, 11am – midnight

Cheiro Verde $
This is among the best spots in town to enjoy fish and seafood. The grilled fish fillets with shrimp sauce are very nicely cooked with tomato and chopped onions, and they're served with vatapá (fish and shrimp with cashews in a chili and coconut sauce) and arroz de cuxá rice that doesn't disappoint. **CUISINE** Fish and seafood. **CREDIT CARDS** AmEx; Diners; MasterCard; Visa
Avenida São Luís Rei de França, 131, Olho d'Água
TEL (98) 3248-1641 **OPEN** Sun – Thu, 11am – 3pm and 6pm – midnight; Fri and Sat, 11am – 1:30am

A Diquinha $
At this simple restaurant, you can't avoid one of the most famous cuxás (sorrel leaves, dried shrimp, sesame seeds, and manioc flour) in Maranhão – it accompanies every dish. Try the delicious fried pescada amarela (sea trout) or the beef jerky, crab claws, and fried pig's tripe served as an appetizer. **CUISINE** Regional. **CREDIT CARDS** Not accepted
Rua João Luís, 62, Diamante
TEL (98) 3232-5655 **OPEN** Daily, 11am – 9pm

A Varanda $
The welcoming atmosphere and food – home-style fish and seafood dishes – make this place unforgettable. Leave room for a desert made from local fruits. **CUISINE** Regional; fish and seafood. **CREDIT CARDS** MasterCard; Visa
Rua Genésio Rego, 185, Monte Castelo

RESTAURANTS **$** up to R$ 50 **$$** from R$ 51 up to R$ 100 **$$$** from R$ 101 up to R$ 150 **$$$$** above R$ 150

TEL (98) 3232-8428 **RESERVATIONS** (98) 3232-7291 **OPEN** Mon – Sat, noon – until the last customer leaves

SERVICES

Airport – Aeroporto Marechal da Cunha Machado
Avenida dos Libaneses, no #, Tirirical
TEL (98) 3217-6133 **OPEN** Daily, 24 hours
www.infraero.gov.br

Boats to Alcântara
Terminal Hidroviário, no #, Rampa Campos Melo
TEL (98) 3322-6092 (public phone) **OPEN** Departures from São Luís at 7am, 9:30am, and 3pm; from Alcântara at 3pm and 5pm

Bus Station – Rodoviária
Avenida dos Franceses, no #, São Cristóvão
TEL (98) 3249-2488

Tourist Information – Central de Serviços Turísticos
Praça Benedito Leite, no #, Centro
TEL (98) 3212-6211 **OPEN** Mon – Fri, 8am – 7pm; Sat and Sun, 8am – 2pm

Tourist Police Station – Delegacia de Atendimento ao Turista
Rua da Estrela, 427, Centro
TEL (98) 3214-8682 **OPEN** Mon – Fri, 8am – 6pm

Travel Agency and Guides – Lótus Turismo and Aventura
Travessa Marcelino Almeida, 85, Centro
TEL (98) 3221-0942 **OPEN** Mon – Fri, 9am – 8pm; Sat, 9am – 1pm www.lotusturismo.com.br

Travel Agency and Guides – Maranhão Turismo
Avenida Avicênia, no # (Hotel São Luís Park), Calhau
TEL (98) 3227-2136 **OPEN** Mon – Fri, 8am – 6pm; Sat, 8am – noon www.maranhaoturismo.com.br

São Miguel do Gostoso – Rio Grande do Norte

AREA CODE 84 **POPULATION** 8,680 **DISTANCES** Natal 105 kilometers (65 miles) **ACCESS** From Natal, take Highway BR-101, then RN-221

WHERE TO STAY

Pousada Arraial do Marco $
This simple, but special guesthouse stands on a deserted stretch of Marco Beach. Fifteen white rooms face the sea and have space on the veranda for a hammock. **ACCOMMODATIONS** 15; air-conditioning; ceiling fan. **FACILITIES AND SERVICES** bar; horse and cart; parking; pool; playground; restaurant; games room; TV; guided walking tours; airport shuttle; transport to attractions. **CREDIT CARDS** Not accepted
Praia do Marco, no #
TEL (84) 9986-0176, 9972-9074 **FAX** (84) 3213-6065
www.pousadaarraialdomarco.com.br

Pousada dos Ponteiros $
This guesthouse offers spacious, colorful chalets, each with a bedroom and a small living room. **ACCOMMODA-**

TIONS 14; air-conditioning; minibar; cable TV; ceiling fan. **FACILITIES AND SERVICES** bar; library; bicycles; parking; arts and crafts store; ofuro tub; pool; restaurant; conference room; living room; games room; massage room; video room; spa; beach service; airport shuttle; transport to attractions. **CREDIT CARDS** MasterCard; Visa
Rua Enseada das Baleias, 1000, Centro
TEL (84) 3263-4007 **FAX** (84) 3263-4008
www.pousadadosponteiros.com.br

São Miguel dos Milagres – Alagoas

AREA CODE 82 **POPULATION** 6463 **DISTANCE** Maceió 100 kilometers (62 miles) **ACCESS** From Maceió, on Highway AL-101

WHERE TO STAY

Aldeia Beijupirá $$$
The good taste of the proprietors is evident in every detail of this hotel. **ACCOMMODATIONS** 9; air-conditioning; DVD player; minibar; jacuzzi in three chalets; telephone; TV. **FACILITIES AND SERVICES** bar; parking; pool; restaurant; airport shuttle; transport to attractions. **CREDIT CARDS** AmEx; MasterCard; Visa
Sítio Roteio, no #, Praia da Lage
TEL (82) 3298-6520 **FAX** and **RESERVATIONS** (82) 3298-6549
www.aldeiabeijupira.com.br

Pousada do Toque $$$
This guesthouse has a happy, fun atmosphere. The chalets are equipped with king size beds, flat-screen TVs, and CD and DVD. Reaching the guesthouse requires driving 2 kilometers (1 mile) down a dirt road. **ACCOMMODATIONS** 12; air-conditioning; private safe; minibar; jacuzzi; telephone; cable TV; ceiling fan. **FACILITIES AND SERVICES** Internet access; wine cellar; bar; bicycles; kayaks; parking; chlorine-free pool; tennis court; video room; restaurant; beach service; airport shuttle. **CREDIT CARDS** Not accepted
Sítio Santo Antônio de Trindade, Km 2, Praia do Toque (access via Rua Felisberto de Ataíde)
TEL and **FAX** (82) 3295-1127, 9119-1792

Pousada Um Milhão de Estrelas $$
This guesthouse receives many visitors from Portugal, the owners' country of origin. It has well-kept gardens and large, tasteful décor (in both the restaurant and other facilities), and chalets just a few meters from the beach. **ACCOMMODATIONS** 15; air-conditioning; DVD player; minibar; TV; ceiling fan. **FACILITIES AND SERVICES** Internet access; bar; boat; bicycles; kayaks; horses; parking; pool; restaurant; babysitter; beach service; airport shuttle. **CREDIT CARDS** AmEx; MasterCard; Visa
Praia de Tatuamunha, no #
TEL (82) 3298-6223 **FAX** (82) 3298-6239
RESERVATIONS (82) 3298-6223, 9987-1626
www.pousadaummilhaodeestrelas.com.br

WHERE TO EAT

Restaurante do Toque $
Located inside the guesthouse named Pousada do Toque, this restaurant specializes in fish and seafood dishes for one or two people. The calda de lagosta (lobster soup) with grilled fruits and vegetables and the peixe assado na folha de bananeira (fish baked in banana leaves) are always on the menu, but every six

---

PRICES | **HOTELS** (couple) $ up to R$ 150 $$ from R$ 151 up to R$ 300 $$$ from R$ 301 up to R$500 $$$$ above R$ 500

548   BRAZIL GUIDE

months chef Burgarelli revamps the menu with new creations. **CUISINE** Fish and seafood. **CREDIT CARDS** Diners; MasterCard; Visa
Sítio Santo Antônio de Trindade, Km 2, Praia do Toque (access via Rua Felisberto de Ataíde)
TEL (82) 3295-1127 **OPEN** Daily, noon – 9pm

São Paulo – São Paulo

AREA CODE 11 **INHABITANTS** 10,886,518 **DISTANCE** Curitiba 408 kilometers (254 miles), Rio de Janeiro 429 kilometers (267 miles) **ACCESS** Highway BR-116 (Rodovia Régis Bittencourt) from Curitiba. Then BR-116 (Rodovia Presidente Dutra) from Rio de Janeiro

WHERE TO STAY

Emiliano $$$$
This luxurious hotel offers impeccable service and has earned its membership in the Leading Hotels of the World association. Furniture designed by architect Arthur Casas decorates the foyer and guests are spoiled with Egyptian sheets and Hungarian goose-feather eiderdowns in the rooms. **ACCOMMODATIONS** 57; air-conditioning; DVD player; Internet access; minibar; pay TV; phone; private safe. **FACILITIES AND SERVICES** bar; bilingual staff; business center; first-aid; function room; gym; heliport; Internet access; massage room; ofuro tub; parking; restaurant; sauna; spa; transport to attractions; valet service; wine cellar; 24-hour kitchen. **CREDIT CARDS** AmEx; Diners; MasterCard; Visa
Rua Oscar Freire, 384, Cerqueira César
TEL (11) 3068-4399 **FAX** (11) 3068-4394
www.emiliano.com.br

George V $$$$
These luxurious, serviced apartments are good for those who want to feel more like they're at home and less in a hotel. The living rooms are large and tastefully furnished, and the kitchens are well equipped. **ACCOMMODATIONS** 23; air-conditioning; DVD player (ask for one at reception); Internet access; jacuzzi; kitchen; minibar; pay TV; phone; private safe. **FACILITIES AND SERVICES** bilingual staff; business center; gym; heated pool; Internet access; massage room; parking; restaurant; sauna; valet service; 24-hour kitchen. **CREDIT CARDS** AmEx; Diners; MasterCard; Visa
Rua José Maria Lisboa, 1,000, Jardim Paulista
TEL (11) 3088-9822 **FAX** (11) 3082-7431
www.georgev-etoile.com.br

Gran Meliá Mofarrej $$$
This luxury hotel belonging to the Sol Meliá chain has lovely, large windows in the lobby and rooms, which are exquisitely decorated. **ACCOMMODATIONS** 228; air-conditioning; DVD player (in the "diplomata" suite); Internet access; minibar; pay TV; phone; private safe. **FACILITIES AND SERVICES** bar; business center; first-aid; function room; gym; heated pool; heliport; Internet access; parking; pool; restaurant; sauna; spa; stores; transport to airport and attractions; valet service; 24-hour kitchen. **CREDIT CARDS** AmEx; Diners; MasterCard; Visa
Alameda Santos, 1,437, Cerqueira César
TEL (11) 3146-5900 **FAX** (11) 3289-8670
RESERVATIONS 0800 703 33 99 www.solmelia.com.br

Grand Hyatt São Paulo $$$$
This large, luxurious hotel is located in the business district of Berrini. Excellent service and three restaurants

(Italian, Japanese, and French) are distinguishing features. **ACCOMMODATIONS** 470; air-conditioning; coffee maker; Internet access; minibar; pay TV; phone; private safe. **FACILITIES AND SERVICES** bar; beauty parlor; bilingual staff; business center; concierge; convenience store; first-aid; function room; gym; heated pool (at the spa); heliport; Internet access; magazine-reading area; massage room; parking; pool; restaurant; sauna; spa; stores; transport to airports; valet service; wine cellar; 24-hour kitchen. **CREDIT CARDS** AmEx; Diners; MasterCard; Visa
Avenida das Nações Unidas, 13,301, Brooklin Paulista
TEL (11) 6838-1234 **FAX** (11) 6838-1235
www.hyatt.com.br

Hilton São Paulo Morumbi $$$
Located in the Avenida Berrini area, in the Centro Empresarial Nações Unidas, this sophisticated hotel is ideal for business travelers. The building has a striking, high-ceilinged lobby and glassed-in swimming pool. **ACCOMMODATIONS** 485; air-conditioning; DVD player (except in the standard rooms); Internet access; jacuzzi (in the suites); minibar; mosquito-screens on windows; pay TV; phone; private safe. **FACILITIES AND SERVICES** bar; bilingual staff; business center; first-aid; function room; gym; Internet access; jacuzzi; massage room; parking; pool; restaurant; sauna; spa; snack bar; transport to airport and attractions; valet service; video room (not available to guests in standard rooms); wine cellar; 24-hour kitchen. **CREDIT CARDS** AmEx; Diners; MasterCard; Visa
Avenida das Nações Unidas, 12,901, Brooklin Paulista
TEL (11) 6845-0000 **FAX** (11) 6845-0001
www.saopaulomorumbi.hilton.com

Hotel Fasano $$$$
This is one of São Paulo's most expensive, sophisticated, famous, and luxurious hotels. The elegant lobby has antique armchairs from France and England, while the rooms have lovely leather furniture. **ACCOMMODATIONS** 60; air-conditioning; DVD player; Internet access; jacuzzi; minibar; pay TV; phone; private safe. **FACILITIES AND SERVICES** bar; bilingual staff; business center; exchange service; first-aid; function room; gym; heated pool; Internet access; massage room; ofuro tub; parking; poolside service; restaurant; sauna; spa; transport to airport and attractions; valet service; wine cellar; 24-hour kitchen. **CREDIT CARDS** AmEx; MasterCard; Visa
Rua Vitório Fasano, 88, Cerqueira César
TEL (11) 3896-4067 **FAX** (11) 3896-4155
www.fasano.com.br

Hotel Unique $$$$
Near Ibirapuera Park, this enormous boutique hotel designed by Ruy Ohtake has airy rooms with modern, light-colored furniture. The roof is an attraction in itself, being the location of the Skye restaurant and a swimming pool, and offering one of the best views of the city. **ACCOMMODATIONS** 95; air-conditioning; DVD player; Internet access; jacuzzi; minibar; pay TV; phone; private safe. **FACILITIES AND SERVICES** bar; bilingual staff; exchange service; first-aid; function room; gym; heated pool; Internet access; library; parking; personal trainer; pool; restaurant; sauna; transport to airport and attractions; valet service; wine cellar; 24-hour kitchen. **CREDIT CARDS** AmEx; Diners; MasterCard; Visa
Avenida Brigadeiro Luís Antônio, 4,700, Jardim Paulista
TEL (11) 3055-4700 **FAX** (11) 3889-0005
www.hotelunique.com.br

RESTAURANTS	**$** up to R$ 50	**$$** from R$ 51 up to R$ 100	**$$$** from R$ 101 up to R$ 150	**$$$$** above R$ 150

L'Hotel São Paulo $$$$

Just a few meters from Avenida Paulista, this sophisticated hotel has a good Italian restaurant, the Trebbiano, and a piano bar. It belongs to the Leading Hotels of the World association. **ACCOMMODATIONS** 80; air-conditioning; DVD player (in the suites); Internet access; minibar; pay TV; phone; private safe. **FACILITIES AND SERVICES** bar; bilingual staff; business center; exchange service; first-aid; function room; gym; heated pool; Internet access; magazine-reading area; massage room; ofuro tub; parking; restaurant; sauna; transport to airports; valet service; wine cellar; 24-hour kitchen. **CREDIT CARDS** AmEx; Diners; MasterCard; Visa
Alameda Campinas, 266, Bela Vista
TEL (11) 2183-0500 **FAX** (11) 2183-0505
www.lhotel.com.br

Novotel Jaraguá São Paulo Conventions $$

This downtown hotel, run by the Accor chain, offers few services, but it's still one of the best options in the area because the noise-blocking windows in the rooms muffle most of the traffic sounds outside. It has a nice confectioner's shop. **ACCOMMODATIONS** 415; air-conditioning; Internet access; minibar; pay TV; phone; private safe. **FACILITIES AND SERVICES** bar; beauty parlor; bilingual staff; business center; function room; gym; Internet access; massage room; restaurant; stores; 24-hour kitchen. **CREDIT CARDS** AmEx; Diners; MasterCard; Visa
Rua Martins Fontes, 71, Centro
TEL and **FAX** (11) 3120-8000 www.novotel.com.br

Radisson Faria Lima $$

This hotel occupies a beautiful building close to Avenida Faria Lima, a bustling business district, and the Shopping Iguatemi mall. The rooms are tastefully decorated with dark wood furniture. **ACCOMMODATIONS** 216; air-conditioning; CD player; DVD player; Internet access; microwave oven; minibar; pay TV; phone; private safe. **FACILITIES AND SERVICES** bar; bilingual staff; business center; exchange service; first-aid; function room; gym; heated pool; Internet access; laundry; parking; restaurant; sauna; transport to airports; valet service; wine cellar; 24-hour kitchen. **CREDIT CARDS** AmEx; Diners; MasterCard; Visa
Avenida Cidade Jardim, 625, Itaim Bibi
TEL (11) 2133-5960 **FAX** (11) 2133-5969
www.atlanticahotels.com.br

Renaissance São Paulo Hotel $$$$

Just one block from Avenida Paulista, this elegant hotel belonging to the Marriott chain has cozy rooms with bathtubs. The service is formal, though not stuffy. **ACCOMMODATIONS** 445; air-conditioning; DVD player (except in the standard rooms); Internet access; minibar; pay TV; phone; private safe. **FACILITIES AND SERVICES** bar; bilingual staff; business center; exchange service; first-aid; function room; gym; heated pool; heliport; Internet access; jacuzzi; massage room; ofuro tub; parking; poolside service; restaurant; sauna; snack bar; spa; squash court; stores; transport to airport and attractions; valet service; video room; 24-hour kitchen. **CREDIT CARDS** AmEx; Diners; MasterCard; Visa
Alameda Santos, 2,233, Cerqueira César
TEL (11) 3069-2233 **FAX** (11) 3064-3344
www.marriott.com.br/saobr

Sofitel São Paulo $$$

The most elegant hotel of the Accor chain in the city, the Sofitel is next to Ibirapuera Park. There are French touches in the décor and the service is discreet and compe-tent. The comfortable suites have bathtubs and balconies with views of the park. **ACCOMMODATIONS** 219; air-conditioning; DVD player (in the suites); Internet access; jacuzzi (in the 19th floor suites); minibar; pay TV; phone; private safe. **FACILITIES AND SERVICES** bar; beauty parlor; bilingual staff; business center; convenience store; exchange service; first-aid; function room; gym; heliport; Internet access; massage room; parking; pool; restaurant; sauna; spa; stores; tennis court; transport to airport and attractions; valet service; wine cellar; 24-hour kitchen. **CREDIT CARDS** AmEx; Diners; MasterCard; Visa
Rua Sena Madureira, 1,355, Vila Clementino
TEL (11) 5087-0800 **FAX** (11) 5575-4544
www.sofitel.com.br

WHERE TO EAT

Acrópoles $

At São Paulo's most traditional Greek restaurant, founded in 1963, customers choose from the food displayed in cooking pots and a waiter then brings the order to the table. Menu highlights are the stews and roast dishes, such as lamb, the seafood options, and the traditional house moussaka. **CUISINE** Greek. **CREDIT CARDS** Diners; MasterCard; Visa
Rua da Graça, 364, Bom Retiro
TEL (11) 3223-4386. Daily, 6:30am – midnight

Alimentari di Sergio Arno $

Here in his own home, chef and restaurateur Sergio Arno serves dry pasta dishes with the customer's choice of sauce (try the pappardelle with lamb sauce). Among the meat dishes, a highlight is the grilled lamb cutlets with herb crust and garlic and olive-oil sauce. **CUISINE** Italian. **CREDIT CARDS** AmEx; Diners; MasterCard; Visa
Rua Pedroso Alvarenga, 545, Itaim Bibi
TEL (11) 3167-5667. Mon – Fri, noon – 11pm; Sat, noon – midnight; Sun, noon – 10pm

America $

This chain of fast-food restaurants serves basic pasta, salad, meat, poultry, fish, and sandwich options. **CUISINE** Fast food; various. **CREDIT CARDS** AmEx; Diners; MasterCard; Visa
Avenida 9 de Julho, 5,363, Jardim Europa
TEL (11) 3708-3620. Sun – Thu, 11:45am – midnight; Fri, 11:45am – 1am; Sat, 11:45am – 1:30am

Antiquarius $$$$

The excellent quality and competent service of the original Antiquarius in Rio is repeated at this branch, which serves painstakingly prepared Portuguese dishes. Try the impeccable bacalhau à lagareira (thick codfish cutlets pan-fried with garlic and onion) or the squid or octopus done in a traditional Portuguese cataplana clam cooker. **CUISINE** Portuguese. **CREDIT CARDS** Diners; MasterCard; Visa
Alameda Lorena, 1,884, Jardim Paulista
TEL (11) 3082-3015. Mon, 7pm – 1am; Tue – Thu, noon – 3pm and 7pm – 1am; Fri, noon – 3pm and 7pm – 2am; Sat, noon – 2am; Sun, noon – 6pm

Arábia $

One of the best Arabic restaurants in town. Moroccan couscous and vine leaf cigars are the house fortes, as well as delicious salads. **CUISINE** Arabic. **CREDIT CARDS** MasterCard; Visa
Rua Haddock Lobo, 1,397, Cerqueira César
TEL (11) 3061-2203. Sun – Thu, noon – midnight; Fri and Sat, noon – 1am

PRICES | **HOTELS** (couple) | $ up to R$ 150 | $$ from R$ 151 up to R$ 300 | $$$ from R$ 301 up to R$500 | $$$$ above R$ 500

550 BRAZIL GUIDE

Astor $

One of the most charming bars in São Paulo, the Astor has an extensive menu: Patrons can just snack or can choose from an infinity of meal options, accompanied by the excellent chope (draft beer). Try the file mignon picadinho or snacks such as bolinho de bacalhau (cod croquettes). **CUISINE** Brazilian; quick meals; snacks. **CREDIT CARDS** AmEx; Diners; MasterCard; Visa

Rua Delfina, 163, Vila Madalena

TEL (11) 3815-1364. Mon – Thu, 5pm – 3am; Fri and Sat, noon – 4am; Sun, noon – midnight

Baby-Beef Rubaiyat $$

The outstanding beef – for example picanha (rump cover) – is the specialty of this establishment, but the feijoada (various meats and sausage served with black beans and traditional accompaniments) served for lunch on Wednesdays and Saturdays is also highly recommended. **CUISINE** Meats; feijoada. **CREDIT CARDS** Visa

Alameda Santos, 86, Cerqueira César

TEL (11) 3141-1188. Mon – Fri, 11:30am – 3:30pm and 7pm – 12:30am; Sat, noon – 12:30am; Sun, noon – 6pm

Bar Brahma $

Standing on São Paulo's most famous street corner – the intersection of Avenida Ipiranga and Avenida São João – this bar, which opened in the late 1940s, is a local institution. The feijoada served on Saturdays, to the sound of authentic samba, is famous. **CUISINE** Quick meals; feijoada; snacks. **CREDIT CARDS** AmEx; Diners; MasterCard; Visa

Avenida São João, 677, Centro

TEL (11) 3333-0855. Mon, 11am – 1am; Tue and Wed, 11am – 2am; Thu – Sat, 11am – 3am; Sun, 11am – 11pm

Bar Léo $

Opened in 1940, this traditional downtown tavern is always packed in the early evenings. The reason for its success is its excellent Brahma chope (draft beer). To accompany it, chomp down on some bolinhos de bacalhau (cod croquettes) or acepipes (cold cut platter). There are also sandwiches and proper meals. **CUISINE** German; quick meals; snacks. **CREDIT CARDS** Diners; MasterCard; Visa

Rua Aurora, 100, Santa Ifigênia

TEL (11) 3221-0247. Mon – Fri, 11am – 8:30pm; Sat, 11am – 4pm

Barbacoa $$

Great all-you-can-eat barbecue with meat prepared on a gas barbecue grill. The cold cuts, cheese, and salad buffet also deserves a mention. The two São Paulo branches, the Barbacoa Grill and the Barbacoa Grill e Bier, also have an à la carte menu. **CUISINE** Grill. **CREDIT CARDS** AmEx; Diners; MasterCard; Visa

Rua Dr. Renato Paes de Barros, 65, Itaim Bibi

TEL (11) 3168-5522. Mon – Thu, noon – 3:30pm and 7pm – midnight; Fri, noon – 4pm and 7pm – midnight; Sat, noon – 5pm and 7pm – 12:30am; Sun, noon – midnight

Bassi $

This restaurant serves excellent meats. The different cuts come with classic accompaniments such as garlic rice, manioc meal, manioc, fried polenta, and deep-fried banana fritters. **CUISINE** Meats; grill. **CREDIT CARDS** AmEx; Diners; MasterCard; Visa

Rua 13 de Maio, 659 and 668, Bela Vista

TEL (11) 3251-1442, 3288-7045. Mon – Sat, noon – midnight; Sun, noon – 6pm

A Bela Sintra $$

Run by acclaimed chef Carlos Bettencourt, this lovely, modern restaurant serves excellent Portuguese food, including bacalhau do Porto: thick, oven-baked codfish cutlets with garlic and olive oil, accompanied by fried vegetables and seasoned and thinly sliced potatoes. **CUISINE** Portuguese. **CREDIT CARDS** AmEx; Diners; MasterCard; Visa

Rua Bela Cintra, 2,325, Cerqueira César

TEL (11) 3891-0740, 3891-1090. Mon – Thu, 11:30am – 3:30pm and 7pm – 1am; Fri, 11:30am – 3:30pm and 7pm – 2am; Sat, noon – 2am; Sun, noon – 11:30pm

Bráz $

Some of the best pizza in São Paulo is to be had here. The house pizza is made with tomato sauce and sliced pumpkin drizzled with olive oil, sprinkled with mozzarella and topped with grated Parmesan. **CUISINE** Pizza. **CREDIT CARDS** AmEx; Diners; MasterCard; Visa

Rua Vupabuçu, 271, Pinheiros

TEL (11) 3037-7975. Sun – Thu, 6:30pm – 12:30am; Fri and Sat, 6:30pm – 1am

Ca'd'Oro $$

Inside the Ca'd'Oro hotel, this restaurant is one of the most traditional in town, having served typical northern Italian dishes for over five decades. House fortes include the osso buco with saffron risotto and the picanha (rump cover) steak in red wine, garnished with gnocchi tossed in butter and sage. **CUISINE** Italian. **CREDIT CARDS** AmEx; Diners; MasterCard; Visa

Rua Augusta, 129 (Hotel Ca'd'Oro), Consolação

TEL (11) 3236-4300. Daily, 12:30pm – 3pm and 6:30pm – 11pm

Camelo $

In operation since 1957, this restaurant serves great pizzas with thin, crispy crusts, such as the "JK" (which has mozzarella, spicy sausage, basil and black olives) and the à moda da casa (diced ham, sliced olives, and mozzarella). **CUISINE** Pizza. **CREDIT CARDS** AmEx; Diners; MasterCard; Visa

Rua Pamplona, 1,873, Jardim Paulista

TEL (11) 3887-8764, 3887-6004. Mon – Wed, 6pm – midnight; Thu, 6pm – 12:30am; Fri and Sat, 6pm – 1am; Sun, 6pm – midnight

Capuano $

The photos displayed on the walls tell the story of this traditional cantina, open since the early 20th century. The menu offers generous portions of good Italian cooking: Try the fusilli ao sugo, roast kid goat, or the popular tripe Parmigiana. **CUISINE** Italian. **CREDIT CARDS** Diners; MasterCard; Visa

Rua Conselheiro Carrão, 416, Bela Vista

TEL (11) 3288-1460. Tue – Fri, 11:30am – 3pm and 7pm – 11pm; Sat, 11:30am – 4:30pm and 7pm – 12:30am; Sun, 11:30am – 5pm

Carlota $

The duck confit in tangerine sauce is commendable, as is the Scandinavian salmon with crunchy potato "meteorites" (a kind of chip stix) and a creamy mustard and dill sauce. **CUISINE** Contemporary. **CREDIT CARDS** AmEx; Diners; MasterCard; Visa

Rua Sergipe, 753, Higienópolis

TEL (11) 3661-8670. Mon, 7pm – midnight; Tue – Thu, noon – 4pm and 7pm – midnight; Sat, noon – 1am; Sun, noon – 6pm

---

| **RESTAURANTS** | $ up to R$ 50 | $$ from R$ 51 up to R$ 100 | $$$ from R$ 101 up to R$ 150 | $$$$ above R$ 150 |

Casa Búlgara $

This traditional Bulgarian restaurant is the place for bureka, flaky pastry rings with savory (cheese, beef, and chicken, among others) or sweet fillings (apricot, chocolate, banana, and apple). It also serves desserts such as apple and walnut strudel. **CUISINE** Bulgarian. **CREDIT CARDS** Not accepted
Rua Silva Pinto, 356, Bom Retiro
TEL (11) 3222-9849. Mon – Fri, 9am – 6:30pm; Sat, 9:30am – 2pm

Casa da Fazenda do Morumbi $$

This restaurant, located on the pleasant grounds of an old 19th-century farm, serves a range of dishes, including the house suggestion – fillet of flounder with gruyere gratin and shiitake mushrooms – and traditional Brazilian farmer's fare. **CUISINE** Brazilian; feijoada; various. **CREDIT CARDS** AmEx; Diners; MasterCard; Visa
Avenida Morumbi 5,594, Morumbi
TEL (11) 3742-2810. Tue – Fri, 11am – 1am; Sat, noon – 5pm and 8pm – 1am; Sun, noon – 5pm

Casa Garabed $

This simple restaurant in the city's north zone is famous for its traditional Arabic and Armenian food, all prepared in a wood-burning oven. Try the kofta with hummus, dry cheese curd, or baba ghanoush (eggplant paté), and bread. **CUISINE** Arabic; Armenian. **CREDIT CARDS** AmEx; Diners; MasterCard; Visa
Rua José Margarido, 216, Santana
TEL (11) 6976-2750. Tue – Sun, noon – 9pm

Castelões $

In operation since 1924, this is the oldest – and many consider it to be the best – pizza parlor in town. Try the pizza that carries the restaurant's name, with mozzarella and spicy sausage topping, or the romana, which comes with anchovies. **CUISINE** Italian; pizza. **CREDIT CARDS** Not accepted
Rua Jairo Góes, 126, Brás
TEL (11) 3229-0542. Mon – Fri, noon – 3pm and 6:30pm – midnight; Sat and Sun, noon – 4pm and 6:30pm – midnight

Cristal $

This establishment serves traditional thin-crust pizza, prepared in a wood-burning oven. For starters, try the tasty calabresinha (Calabrese sausage) with vinaigrette. Try the house pizza (Parmesan, basil and mushrooms). **CUISINE** Pizza; sandwiches; various. **CREDIT CARDS** AmEx; Diners; MasterCard; Visa
Rua Professor Artur Ramos, 551, Jardim Paulistano
TEL (11) 3031-0828. Sun – Thu, 7pm – 1am; Fri, 7pm – 1:30am; Sat, 7pm – 2am

DeliParis $

With delicious quiches, bread rolls, and mouth-watering sweets, this charming, French-influenced bakery is a great place for brunch or a late-afternoon snack. **CUISINE** Quick meals; desserts; bread; sandwiches. **CREDIT CARDS** Diners; MasterCard
Rua Harmonia, 484, Vila Madalena
TEL (11) 3816-5911. Mon – Sat, 7am – 10:30pm; Sun, 8am – 11pm

D.O.M. $$$$

Chef-owner Alex Atala combines haute cuisine, Brazilian ingredients, and creativity, for which the restaurant was voted one of the 50 best restaurants in the world

in 2007 by the English magazine Restaurant. Menu highlights include snook with tucupi (manioc juice) and tapioca, as well as a range of dishes that can be tried in two different tasting menus, accompanied by a good wine from the cellar. **CUISINE** Contemporary. **CREDIT CARDS** AmEx; Diners; MasterCard; Visa
Rua Barão de Capanema, 549, Jardim Paulista
TEL (11) 3088-0761. Mon – Thu, noon – 3pm and 7pm – midnight; Fri, noon – 3pm and 7pm – 1am; Sat, 7pm – 1am

Don Curro $$$

This very traditional restaurant serves the best and most famous paella in São Paulo. Lobster, kept on-site, arrives fresh at the table. The service is excellent. **CUISINE** Spanish; seafood. **CREDIT CARDS** AmEx; Diners; MasterCard
Rua Alves Guimarães, 230, Pinheiros
TEL (11) 3062-4712. Tue – Thu, noon – 4pm and 7pm – midnight; Fri, noon – 4pm and 7pm – 1am; Sat, noon – 1am; Sun, noon – 5pm

Due Cuochi Cucina $

Talented chef Paulo Barroso de Barros has designed an Italian menu with starters such as free-range-egg ravioloni tossed in butter and sage and perfumed with white truffle olive oil, and main dishes such as papardelle with rabbit ragu. The wine list is great. Reservations recommended. **CUISINE** Italian. **CREDIT CARDS** AmEx; Diners; MasterCard; Visa
Rua Manuel Guedes, 93, Itaim Bibi
TEL (11) 3078–8092. Mon – Thu, noon – 3pm and 7:30pm – midnight; Fri, noon – 3pm and 7:30pm – 1am; Sat, 7:30pm – 1am; Sun, noon – 5pm.

Estadão Bar & Lanches $

This traditional eatery is famous for its classic roast pork sandwich, served with onion, bell pepper and tomato sauce. Besides snacks, they serve a variety of hot dishes at good prices, as well as milkshakes, juices, and alcoholic beverages. **CUISINE** Sandwiches; various. **CREDIT CARDS** Diners; MasterCard; Visa
Viaduto 9 de Julho, 193, Centro
TEL (11) 3257-7121. Daily, 24 hours

Fasano $$$$

The flagship of the Fasano group, which owns several of the most sophisticated restaurants in the city, the Fasano has a menu by celebrity chef Salvatore Loi. Traditional dishes and tasting menus from different regions of Italy are all exquisitely presented. Sommelier Manoel Beato – one of Brazil's best – runs the wine cellar, which is brimming with great labels. **CUISINE** Italian. **CREDIT CARDS** AmEx; Diners; MasterCard; Visa
Rua Vitório Fasano, 88, Cerqueira César
TEL (11) 3062-4000. Mon – Sat, 7:30pm – 1am

Feijoada da Lana $

The feijoada buffet in this friendly restaurant is one of the most famous in town. The black beans and meats, including pork ribs and beef jerky, plus other traditional accompaniments (trotters, ears, tongues, and tails) are served in separate clay dishes. The owner, Lana Nowikow, is of Russian descent. **CUISINE** Brazilian; feijoada. **CREDIT CARDS** AmEx; Diners; MasterCard; Visa
Rua Aspicuelta, 421, Vila Madalena
TEL (11) 3814-9191. Mon – Fri, noon – 3:30pm; Sat and Sun, 12:30pm – 6pm

A Figueira Rubaiyat $$

This elegant restaurant is named after the big old fig tree

| PRICES | HOTELS (couple) | $ up to R$ 150 | $$ from R$ 151 up to R$ 300 | $$$ from R$ 301 up to R$500 | $$$$ above R$ 500 |

552

BRAZIL GUIDE

in the center of the first room (figueira is Portuguese for "fig tree"). The kitchen is run by chef Francisco Gamelera, who has been with the group led by the famous restaurateur Belarmino Iglesias for 16 years. One of the main courses served here is the caixote marinho (octopus, scallops, shrimp, squid, fish, and carnaroli rice). There is also a wide selection of meats and other dishes. The restaurant has one of the most acclaimed wine cellars in town. CUISINE Meats; seafood; various. CREDIT CARDS Visa
Rua Haddock Lobo, 1,738, Jardim Paulista
TEL (11) 3063-3888. Mon – Thu, noon – 12:30am; Fri and Sat, noon – 1am; Sun, noon – midnight

Filial $

This busy bar in the bohemian neighborhood of Vila Madalena serves great chope (draft beer) and snacks, like deep-fried pastries filled with artichoke and mozzarella. The bean broth, served with bread and pork crackling, is very popular. CUISINE Brazilian; quick meals; snacks. CREDIT CARDS AmEx; Diners; MasterCard; Visa
Rua Fidalga, 254, Vila Madalena
TEL (11) 3813-9226. Mon – Thu, 5pm – 3:30am; Fri, 5pm – 4:30am; Sat, noon – 4:30am; Sun, 4pm – 2am

Fogo de Chão $$

Considered by many to be the city's best "all-you-can-eat" barbecue restaurant, the Fogo de Chão has an extensive selection of good meats and cooks them to perfection. The generous buffet includes fresh salads and the wine cellar is well stocked with special labels. CUISINE Meats; barbecue. CREDIT CARDS AmEx; Diners; MasterCard; Visa
Avenida dos Bandeirantes, 538, Brooklin
TEL (11) 5505-0791. Mon – Fri, noon – 4pm and 6pm – midnight; Sat, noon – midnight; Sun, 12:30pm – 10:30pm

Forneria San Paolo $

This snack bar belongs to the Fasano group and flaunts a modern décor and atmosphere. Menu highlights include a steak tartar and rocket sandwich in crustless sliced bread and a hot dog served on pizza base or Portuguese pão de leite bread and covered in mozzarella. CUISINE Quick meals; sandwiches. CREDIT CARDS AmEx; Diners; MasterCard; Visa
Rua Amauri, 391, Jardim Europa
TEL (11) 3078-0099. Sun – Wed, noon – 2am; Thu, noon – 3am; Fri and Sat, noon – 4am

Frangó $

The popular Frangó has the most extensive and refined selection of beers in town, including imported brands. To accompany your beer, try their immensely popular crispy coxinha (chicken croquette) filled with Catupiry cream cheese. The charbroiled chicken with herbs is also very popular. CUISINE Snacks; quick meals. CREDIT CARDS AmEx; Diners; MasterCard; Visa
Largo da Matriz de Nossa Senhora do Ó, 168, Freguesia do Ó
TEL (11) 3932-4818. Tue – Thu, 11am – midnight; Fri and Sat, 11am – 2am; Sun, 11am – 11pm

Freddy $$$$

In operation since the 1930s, this classic French restaurant has an extensive menu of dishes beautifully prepared by chef Geraldo Rodrigues, who has worked here for over forty years. Game, such as rabbit, partridge, and pheasant, are the forte here. Don't fail to try the exceptional french fries. CUISINE French. CREDIT CARDS AmEx; Diners; MasterCard; Visa

Rua Pedroso Alvarenga, 1170, Itaim Bibi
TEL (11) 3167-0977. Mon – Fri, noon – 3pm and 7pm – midnight; Sat, 7pm – 1am; Sun, noon – 5pm

Frevo $

This establishment has retained its original décor since it opened in the 1950s. The delicious beirute sandwich comes in toasted Lebanese bread with roast beef, cheese, tomato, and oregano. There are cooked dishes such as beef fillet in mustard sauce and beef stroganoff. The chope (draft beer) is well poured. CUISINE Quick meals; snacks; sandwiches; various. CREDIT CARDS AmEx; Diners; MasterCard; Visa
Rua Oscar Freire, 603, Cerqueira César
TEL (11) 3082-3434. Sun – Wed, 10:30am – 1am; Thu and Fri, 10:30am – 2am; Sat, 10:30am – 3am

Galeria dos Pães $

This establishment houses a bakery, a confectioner's, a buffet section (breakfast, brunch, lunch, afternoon tea, and soup buffet), a convenience store, and a sandwich shop. CUISINE Bread; sandwiches; soup. CREDIT CARDS AmEx; Diners; MasterCard; Visa
Rua Estados Unidos, 1,645, Jardim América
TEL (11) 3064-5900. Daily, 24 hours

Gero $$

This classic Italian kitchen is true to the high quality of the Fasano group, to which the restaurant belongs. Try the fried zucchini for starters. Main course highlights include breaded veal ribs and traditional lasagna Bolognese, made with spinach pasta. CUISINE Italian. CREDIT CARDS AmEx; Diners; MasterCard; Visa
Rua Haddock Lobo, 1,629, Jardim Paulista
TEL (11) 3064-0005. Mon – Thu, noon – 3pm and 7pm – 1am; Fri and Sat, noon – 4:30pm and 7pm – 1:30am; Sun, noon – 4pm and 7pm – midnight

Hamburgueria Nacional $

Run by famous sushi master Jun Sakamoto, the high points of this house are the quality ingredients and the preparation techniques: the thick, juicy hamburger is grilled instead of fried, and the ice cream used in the milkshakes is homemade and free of trans fat. You also can't go wrong with the roast pork or barbecue sandwich on French bread. CUISINE Sandwiches. CREDIT CARDS AmEx; Diners; MasterCard; Visa
Rua Leopoldo Couto Magalhães Junior, 822, Itaim Bibi
TEL (11) 3073-0428. Sun – Thu and holidays, noon – midnight; Fri and Sat, noon – 2am

Jardim di Napoli $

Opened in the 1940s, this is one the city's classic cantinas, with excellent service. Don't miss the wonderful breaded polpettone (meatballs), filled with mozzarella, fried, and served in tomato sauce, topped with Parmesan. The pizzas are also yummy: ask for half garlic, half mozzarella. CUISINE Italian. CREDIT CARDS AmEx; MasterCard
Rua Dr. Martinico Prado, 463, Higienópolis
TEL (11) 3666-3022. Mon, noon – 3pm and 6:30pm – 11:30pm; Tue – Fri, noon – 3pm and 6:30pm – midnight; Sat, noon – 4pm and 6:30pm – midnight; Sun, noon – 4pm and 6:30pm – 11:30pm

Jun Sakamoto $$$$

The excellent food prepared by the sushi master who gave his name to the restaurant makes a meal here a true gourmet experience. While sitting at the counter,

customers can watch Sakamoto working with fresh, quality ingredients that he purchases daily. Go for the tasting menus, prepared to order (book in advance). The à la carte service at the tables is equally impeccable. Reservations required. **CUISINE** Japanese. **CREDIT CARDS** AmEx; MasterCard; Visa
Rua Lisboa, 55, Pinheiros
TEL (11) 3088-6019. Mon – Thu, 7pm – 12:30am; Fri and Sat, 7pm – 1am

Kinoshita $$

After three decades in the heavily Japanese district of Liberdade, this restaurant moved to Vila Nova Conceição in January 2008. In spite of the change of address, the Kinoshita is still run by the extroverted sushi master Tsuyoshi Murakami, better known as "Mura," who invents unusual combinations with quality ingredients. He produces secret menus for certain clients, if they make reservations. Don't miss the udons and teishokus. Reservations are recommended for all. **CUISINE** Japanese. **CREDIT CARDS** Diners; MasterCard
Rua Jacques Félix, 405, Vila Nova Conceição
TEL (11) 3849-6940. Mon – Sat, noon – 3pm and 7pm – midnight

Konstanz $

With some of the best German food in town, the Konstanz is both bar and restaurant. It serves traditional dishes such as pork knuckle and sausages cooked in steinhäger, draft beer, as well as excellent pastries and fondues. **CUISINE** German; Swiss. **CREDIT CARDS** AmEx; Diners; MasterCard; Visa
Avenida Aratãs, 713, Moema
TEL (11) 5543-4813. Mon – Sat, noon – 1am; Sun, noon – 6pm; dishes that serve 1 person only available at lunchtime, Mon – Fri, noon – 3pm

La Brasserie Erick Jacquin $

French chef Erick Jacquin's menu mixes classic dishes with more elaborate ones. The famous steak tartar and the simple filé-mignon au poivre deserve special mention. The french fries are very popular and there are also three vegetarian options on the menu. The place is relaxed and elegant, with a glass-ceilinged bar at the entrance. **CUISINE** French. **CREDIT CARDS** AmEx; Diners; MasterCard; Visa
Rua Bahia, 683, Higienópolis
TEL (11) 3826-5409. Mon – Thu, noon – midnight; Fri and Sat, noon – 1am; Sun, noon – 5pm

La Casserole $$$

This friendly, traditional bistrô faces the historic Mercado das Flores. Inaugurated in 1954, it is now run by Marie-France Henry, a member of the second generation of owners. Classic dishes include the roast leg of mutton with white beans and grilled rack of lamb with eggplant caviar and sultana couscous. Reservations recommended. **CUISINE** French. **CREDIT CARDS** AmEx; Diners; MasterCard; Visa
Largo do Arouche, 346, Centro
TEL (11) 3331-6283. Tue – Thu, noon – 3pm and 7pm – midnight; Fri, noon – 3pm and 7pm – 1am; Sat, 7pm – 1am; Sun, noon – 4pm and 7pm – 11pm

La Table O&CO $

Run by chef-owner Clo Dimet, this restaurant offers dishes from the south of France and houses an olive-oil boutique called Olivier's&CO. **CUISINE** Mediterranean; southern French. **CREDIT CARDS** AmEx; Diners; Marter-Card; Visa

Rua Bela Cintra, 2,023, Jardins
TEL 3063-4433. Mon – Sat, noon – 5pm and 7pm – midnight; Sun, noon – 5pm

La Vecchia Cucina $

Chef Sergio Arno frequently changes the menu, but the forte remains the distinctive pastas such as beefy-jerky ravioli and mascarpone in pumpkin and red curry sauce. **CUISINE** Italian. **CREDIT CARDS** AmEx; Diners; MasterCard; Visa
Rua Pedroso Alvarenga, 1,088 (Flat Transamérica), Itaim Bibi
TEL (11) 3167-2822, extension 1005. Mon – Thu, noon – 3pm and 7pm – midnight; Fri and Sat, noon – 3pm and 7pm – 1am; Sun, noon – 5pm

Le Vin Bistrô $$

Sharing ownership with the Lê Vin Pâtisserie and the L'ami Bistrô, this charming bistro serves dishes such as duck confit au poivre vert, served with sauté potatoes. A table with fresh oysters from Santa Catarina stands on the sidewalk outside. An attraction in itself, the oysters can be enjoyed with a glass of champagne or sparkling wine. Be warned: Smoking is allowed anywhere in the bistro. **CUISINE** French. **CREDIT CARDS** AmEx; Diners; MasterCard; Visa
Alameda Tietê, 184, Cerqueira César
TEL (11) 3668-7400. Mon – Thu, noon – midnight; Fri and Sat, noon – 1am; Sun, noon – 11pm

Martín Fierro $

This restaurant serves cuts of Argentinean beef under the supervision of owner Ana Maria Massochi. The meats are the big draw card here, and the barbecuer prepares them as customers look on. The chorizo warrants special mention. All meats are accompanied by fresh green salad, but don't neglect to try the typical empanadas (pastry turnovers). **CUISINE** Argentina; meats. **CREDIT CARDS** AmEx; Diners; MasterCard; Visa
Rua Aspicuelta, 683, Vila Madalena
TEL (11) 3814-6747. Mon – Fri, noon – 10:30pm; Sat and Sun, noon – 5:30pm

Massimo $$

This sophisticated, traditional restaurant is run by Massimo Ferrari. The menu includes a wide variety of tasty dishes, such as spaghetti with fresh tomatoes, basil, and aromatic herbs, seafood carpaccio, and grilled fish. **CUISINE** Italian. **CREDIT CARDS** Not accepted
Alameda Santos, 1,826, Cerqueira César
TEL (11) 3284-0311. Mon – Thu, noon – 3pm and 7:30pm – midnight; Fri, noon – 3pm and 7:30pm – 1am; Sat, noon – 4:30pm and 7:30pm – 1am; Sun, noon – 4:30pm and 7pm – 11pm

Mercearia do Conde $

Quiches, pies, sandwiches, and salads are all beautifully prepared here. The décor is quite unusual (handicraft-inspired with a splash of kitsch) and all items are for sale. **CUISINE** Contemporary; quick meals; sandwiches; various. **CREDIT CARDS** Diners; MasterCard; Visa
Rua Joaquim Antunes, 217, Jardim Paulistano
TEL (11) 3081-7204. Mon and Tue, noon – 4pm and 7pm – midnight; Wed and Thu, noon – midnight; Fri, noon – 1am; Sat, 1pm – 1am; Sun, 12:30 – midnight

Nagayama $$

The Nagayama family has been in the restaurant business since 1988, but this Itaim Bibi establishment opened only in 2006. Chef Quiang's menu excels in hot

| **PRICES** | **HOTELS** (couple) | $ up to R$ 150 | $$ from R$ 151 up to R$ 300 | $$$ from R$ 301 up to R$500 | $$$$ above R$ 500 |

554

BRAZIL GUIDE

dishes, such as the centolla à moda Quiang (Quiang's giant crab), one of the most popular. **CUISINE** Japanese. **CREDIT CARDS** AmEx; Visa
Rua Bandeira Paulista, 385, Itaim Bibi
TEL 3079-7553. Tue – Thu, 7:30pm – midnight; Fri and Sat, 7:30pm – 12:30am; Sun, 7pm – 11:30pm

Nam Thai $$

Inaugurated in 2005, the São Paulo branch of this Rio restaurant has a menu designed by the same chef, David Zisman. The décor is thematic, but not over the top, and the menu is authentically Thai. A highlight is the gaeng kua sapparod (shrimp with pineapple, coconut milk, and red curry). Lunch offers both a tasting menu and individual dishes, known as "executive" dishes. **CUISINE** Thai. **CREDIT CARDS** AmEx; Diners; MasterCard; Visa
Rua Manuel Guedes, 444, Itaim Bibi
TEL 3168-0662. Mon – Thu, noon – 3pm and 7pm – midnight; Fri, noon – 3pm and 7pm – 1am; Sat, 7pm – 1am; Sun, noon – 6pm

Padaria Barcelona $

This bakery has been pleasing a loyal Higienópolis clientele for thirty years, not to mention the visitors who drive across São Paulo for its delicious desserts and bread. It also serves mini bread rolls. **CUISINE** Cakes; desserts; sandwiches. **CREDIT CARDS** MasterCard; Visa
Rua Armando Penteado, 33, Higienópolis
TEL (11) 3826-4911. Daily, 6am – 10pm

Parigi $$

This excellent Fasano Group restaurant has two menus: one French, designed by chef Eric Berland, and one Italian, created by Salvatore Loi. If you can, get the cozido italiano (the famous bollito misto Italian stew), served only on Wednesdays and Sundays. **CUISINE** Franco-Italian. **CREDIT CARDS** MasterCard; Visa
Rua Amauri, 275, Jardim Europa
TEL (11) 3167-1575. Mon – Thu, noon – 3pm and 7pm – 1am; Fri, noon – 4pm and 7pm – 1:30am; Sat, 7pm – 1:30am; Sun, noon – 5pm

Pâtisserie Douce France $

All of the sweets here are the painstaking work of French confectioner Fabrice Lenud. They include classics such as mille feuilles (flaky pastry, confectioner's cream, and icing sugar) and macarons, made with almond meal and filled with raspberry, pistachio, coffee, and chocolate. **CUISINE** Desserts. **CREDIT CARDS** AmEx; Diners; MasterCard; Visa
Alameda Jaú, 554, Jardim Paulista
TEL (11) 3262-3542. Tue – Sun, 8am – 8pm

Pirajá $

This laid-back Rio-style bar serves well-poured Brahma chope (draft beer) and has a snack counter with finger food such as pumpkin patties stuffed with beef jerky, and polenta cakes with oxtail filling. **CUISINE** Snacks. **CREDIT CARDS** AmEx; Diners; MasterCard; Visa
Avenida Brigadeiro Faria Lima, 64, Pinheiros
TEL (11) 3815-6881. Mon – Thu, 5pm – 3am; Fri, 5pm – 4am; Sat, noon – 4am; Sun, noon – midnight

Piselli Vineria & Osteria $

Run by Juscelino Pereira, former sommelier and manager of the Fasano Group, this restaurant has a varied menu with traditional dishes from middle and northern Italy. The bracciola served as a starter will work up your appetite for main courses such as spaghetti à carbo-

nara, and tasty fish dishes. **CUISINE** Italian. **CREDIT CARDS** AmEx; Diners; MasterCard; Visa
Rua Padre João Manuel, 1,253, Jardim Paulista
TEL (11) 3081-6043. Mon – Thu, noon – 4pm and 7pm – 1am; Fri and Sat, noon – 2am; Sun, noon – midnight

Ponto Chic $

Dating back to 1922, this is the snack bar that invented the famous bauru sandwhich: French bread with roast beef, three cheeses, pickled cucumber and tomato. The cheese is melted in hot water to eliminate fat. **CUISINE** Sandwiches. **CREDIT CARDS** AmEx; Diners; MasterCard; Visa
Largo do Paiçandu, 27, Centro
TEL (11) 3222-6528. Mon – Sat, 7am – midnight

Porto Rubaiyat $$

Belonging to the same group as the prestigious Figueira and Baby-Beef Rubaiyat, this restaurant pride itself on the freshness of its ingredients; many of the fish served here are taken straight from the aquarium in the dining room. Highlights of the menu are the Spanish dishes, such as the typical Galician specialty polvo a feira ("fairgrounds octopus," seasoned with salt, olive oil, and spices). **CUISINE** Fish and seafood. **CREDIT CARDS** Visa
Rua Leopoldo Couto de Magalhães Junior, 1,142, Itaim Bibi
TEL 3077-1111. Mon – Fri, noon – 3pm and 7pm – midnight; Sat, noon – midnight; Sun, noon – 6pm

Rincón de Buenos Aires $

In a typically porteño atmosphere, the highlights are the imported meats such as ojo de bife (tender, center-cut entrecote) and the parrillada (mixed grill). There is usually a tango performance on Thursday nights. On Fridays it's Brazilian popular music and jazz. **CUISINE** Argentina; grill. **CREDIT CARDS** AmEx; Diners; MasterCard; Visa
Rua Santa Justina, 99, Vila Olímpia
TEL (11) 3849-0096. Mon – Fri, noon – 3:30pm and 7pm – midnight; Sat, noon – midnight; Sun, noon – 6pm

Ritz $$

This popular meeting place has young staff and varied background music. The bar makes special drinks, such as a lychee caipirinha. Try the pasta dishes, such as penne in cream sauce, with asparagus and raw ham, or the thick, juicy hamburger, cooked to perfection. **CUISINE** Various. **CREDIT CARDS** AmEx; Diners; MasterCard; Visa
Alameda Franca, 1,088, Jardim Paulista
TEL (11) 3088-6808, 3062-5830. Mon – Wed, noon – 3pm and 8pm – 1am; Thu and Fri, noon – 3pm and 8pm – 1:30am; Sat, 1pm – 1:30am; Sun, 1pm – 1am

Rodeio $$

One of the oldest carnivore-oriented restaurants in town, the Rodeio serves excellent ribs, traditional Argentinean bife ancho (sirloin) and chorizo steaks, and cupim (a prime cut taken from the zebu cattle hump), always à la carte. The house forte, however, is the sliced picanha (rump cover) steak. For starters try the irresistible manioc-flour bread and Minas cheese, griddled heart of palm, and sausage. **CUISINE** Meats. **CREDIT CARDS** AmEx; Diners; MasterCard; Visa
Rua Haddock Lobo, 1,498, Jardim Paulista
TEL (11) 3474-1333. Mon – Thu, 11:30am – 3:30pm and 6:30pm – 1am; Fri and Sat, 11:30am – 1am; Sun, 11:30am – midnight

Santo Grão $

This lovely café-come-restaurant offers dishes such as chicken with vegetables, spicy sauce, and jasmine rice.

| **RESTAURANTS** | **$** up to R$ 50 | **$$** from R$ 51 up to R$ 100 | **$$$** from R$ 101 up to R$ 150 | **$$$$** above R$ 150 |

But the real forte is the excellent house blend of coffee, while can also be bought to take home. **CUISINE** Contemporary. **CREDIT CARDS** AmEx; Diners; MasterCard; Visa
Rua Oscar Freire, 413, Jardim Paulistano
TEL (11) 3082-9969. Mon, noon – 1am; Tue – Sat, 9am – 2am; Sun, 9am – midnight

Speranza $

This traditional establishment, in operation since 1958 and decorated in the style of a cantina, adds to the Bexiga neighborhood's charm. Try the tortano (homemade bread with sausage) and the delicious pizzas. The most popular toppings are the Calabrese sausage and margarita. **CUISINE** Italian; pizza. **CREDIT CARDS** Diners; MasterCard; Visa
Rua 13 de Maio, 1,004, Bexiga
TEL (11) 3288-8502, 3288-3512. Mon – Fri, 6pm – 1:30am; Sat, 6pm – 2am; Sun, 6pm – 1am

Spot $$$

This popular modern restaurant takes on a bar-like atmosphere at night, with an emphasis on the drinks, such as dry martini. The menu offers starters such as marinated salmon in mustard and dill sauce, and main course such as flambéed fillet steak with cream and three-pepper sauce. **CUISINE** Various. **CREDIT CARDS** AmEx; Diners; MasterCard; Visa
Alameda Ministro Rocha Azevedo, 72, Cerqueira César
TEL (11) 3283-0946. Mon – Fri, 6pm – 1:30am; Sat, 6pm – 2am; Sun, 6pm – 1am

Suplicy Cafés Especiais $

With modern décor, this busy café's well-trained team of baristas serves up delicious espressos and espresso drinks. The top-quality coffee beans are their own, from Santa Izabel Farm, roasted in the simultaneously decorative and functional handsome coffee roaster. **CUISINE** Café. **CREDIT CARDS** AmEx; Diners; MasterCard; Visa
Alameda Lorena, 1,430, Jardim Paulista
TEL (11) 3061-0195. Mon – Thu, 8am – midnight; Fri and Sat, 8am – 1am; Sun, 8am – midnight

Sushi Yassu $$

This restaurant is traditional in terms of appearance and menu. It serves good sushi, always made with fresh fish and seafood, such as octopus, squid, snook, and mackerel. It also offers hot dishes such as grilled eel with sweetened sauce and rice. **CUISINE** Japanese. **CREDIT CARDS** AmEx; Diners; MasterCard; Visa
Rua Tomás Gonzaga, 98, Liberdade
TEL (11) 3209-6622. Tue – Thu, 11:30am – 3pm and 6pm – 11pm; Fri, 11:30am – 3pm and 6pm – 11:30pm; Sat, noon – 4pm and 6pm – midnight; Sun, noon – 10pm

348 Parrilla Porteña $

Argentinean steaks cooked to perfection. Try the classic cuts like the chorizo and ancho (sirloin). The house specialty is the vazio (flank). The salads are excellent, as is the Norteña beer. **CUISINE** Argentinean; meats. **CREDIT CARDS** AmEx; Diners; MasterCard; Visa
Rua Comandante Miguel Calfat, 348, Vila Olímpia
TEL (11) 3849-5839. Tue – Fri, noon – 3:30pm and 7pm – midnight; Sat, noon – midnight; Sun, noon – 6pm

Varanda Grill $

Excellent Argentinean, American and Brazilian cuts of meat, served à la carte and accompanied by tasty side dishes like roast heart of palm and farofa varanda (seasoned manioc meal). The owner, Silvio Lazzarinni, is the author of books on the subject and produces meat under his own label. **CUISINE** Meats. **CREDIT CARDS** Diners; MasterCard; Visa
Rua General Mena Barreto, 793, Jardim Paulista
TEL (11) 3887-8870. Mon – Thu, noon – 3pm and 7pm – 11:30pm; Fri, noon – 5pm and 7pm – 11pm; Sat, noon – midnight; Sun – 5:30pm

Vinheria Percussi $

The pastas, made in-house under the supervision of chef-proprietor Silvia Percussi, are delicious. Suggestions include the different lasagnas, mezzelune (fresh half-moon pasta shapes filled with brie and apricot, in prosecco and shiimeji sauce) and cod risotto with tomatoes, olives, and pine nuts. **CUISINE** Italian. **CREDIT CARDS** AmEx; Diners; MasterCard; Visa
Rua Cônego Eugênio Leite, 523, Jardim Paulista
TEL (11) 3088-4920. Tue – Thu, noon – 3pm and 7pm – 11:30pm; Fri, noon – 3pm and 7pm – 1am; Sat, noon – 4:30pm and 7pm – 1am; Sun, noon – 4:30pm

Z-Deli $

This delicatessen serves a wide variety of Jewish foods, including typical gefilte fish cakes. Customers can order at the counter, eat from the buffet (Monday through Saturday), or choose from the "executive" menu (individual meals). The sweets are delicious. Special takeout dishes can be ordered in advance for festive occasions. **CUISINE** Jewish. **CREDIT CARDS** AmEx; Diners; MasterCard; Visa
Alameda Lorena, 1,689, Cerqueira César
TEL (11) 3088-5644. Mon – Fri, 11:30am – 6pm; Sat, 9am – 4pm

SERVICES

Aiports – Aeroporto Internacional São Paulo/Guarulhos (Aeroporto Internacional de Cumbica)

Rodovia Hélio Smidt, no # (access from Rodovia Dutra, exit at Km 219-B; or Ayrton Senna, exit at Km 19)
TEL (11) 6445-2945 **FAX** (11) 6445-3173

Aiports – Aeroporto de Congonhas

Avenida Washington Luís, no #, Campo Belo
TEL (11) 5090-9000, 5090-9195 **FAX** (11) 5090-9039

Bus stations – Rodoviária (Barra Funda)

Avenida Mário de Andrade, 664, Barra Funda
TEL (11) 3235-0322

Bus stations – Rodoviária (Tietê)

Avenida Cruzeiro do Sul, 1,800, Carandiru
TEL (11) 3235-0322

Bus stations – Rodoviária (Jabaquara)

Rua dos Jequitibás, Jabaquara, no #
TEL (11) 3235-0322

Tourist information – Posto de Informação Turística

Avenida São João, 473, Galeria Olido, Centro
TEL (11) 3331-7786. Daily, 9am – 6pm
Avenida Paulista, 1578, Masp, Bela Vista
TEL None. Tue – Sun, 11am – 6pm

Tourist Police station – Delegacia de Atendimento ao Turista

Rua São Bento, 380, 5º Floor, Centro
TEL (11) 3107-5642, 3107-8721, extension 218. Mon – Fri, 9am – 8pm

PRICES	HOTELS (couple)	$ up to R$ 150	$$ from R$ 151 up to R$ 300	$$$ from R$ 301 up to R$500	$$$$ above R$ 500

Avenida São Luís, 91, República
TEL (11) 3120-3984. Mon – Fri, 8am – 8pm; Sat, Sun, and holidays, 1pm – 6pm

São Raimundo Nonato – Piauí

AREA CODE 89 POPULATION 28,993 DISTANCES Teresina 530 kilometers (329 miles), Picos 339 kilometers (210 miles) ACCESS From Teresina, on Highway BR-343, followed by PI-140

WHERE TO STAY

Serra da Capivara $
Doubling as the unofficial national park headquarters, this hotel is probably the best in São Raimundo Nonato. It has large rooms and extensive grounds, with a pool and lovely restaurant serving home-style dishes. ACCOMMODATIONS 19; air-conditioning; minibar; TV. FACILITIES AND SERVICES bar; parking; snack bar; restaurant; pool. CREDIT CARDS MasterCard; Visa
Rodovia PI-140, Km 0, Santa Luzia
TEL (89) 3582-1389 FAX (89) 3582-1798

WHERE TO EAT

Bode Assado do Tango $
This restaurant serves just griddled goat or mutton, accompanied by rice, feijão-tropeiro (spicy bean mush), tapioca, and fried manioc. It has open air and closed dining areas. CUISINE Meats; regional. CREDIT CARDS Not accepted
Rua Francisco Antunes de Macedo, 449, Santa Fé
TEL (89) 3582-2128 (public phone) RESERVATIONS (89) 9405-6347 OPEN Mon – Sat, 6pm until the last customer leaves; Sun, 10am until the last customer leaves

SERVICES

Travel Agency – Trilhas da Capivara
Trips through the national park
Rua Moisés de França, 22, Santa Luzia
TEL (89) 3582-1294 OPEN Daily, 8am – 6pm

São Sebastião – São Paulo

AREA CODE 12 INHABITANTS 67,348 DISTANCE São Paulo 220 kilometers (137 miles) ACCESS Highways Presidente Dutra (BR-116) or Ayrton Senna (SP-070) from São Paulo to Rodovia dos Tamoios (SP-099). Take the SP-099 to the Rodovia Rio–Santos (BR-101/SP-055). Another option for the beaches on the south coast is the Anchieta–Imigrantes highway system (SP-150/SP-160), followed by Rodovia Rio–Santos

WHERE TO STAY

Juquehy Praia $$$
Ideal for families, this place has an extensive leisure area surrounded by natural beauty, with a swimming pool right next to the beach. The rooms are large and comfortable, with simple décor. ACCOMMODATIONS 54; air-conditioning; ceiling fan; minibar; pay TV (regular TV only outside of the main building); phone; private safe. FACILITIES AND SERVICES bar; beach service; beauty parlor; children's play room; ecotourism agency; function room; gym; massage room; pool; restaurant; sauna; tennis court; video room. CREDIT CARDS AmEx; Diners; MasterCard; Visa
Avenida Mãe Bernarda, 3,221, Praia de Juqueí
TEL (12) 3891-1000 FAX (12) 3891-1063
www.juquehy.com.br

Maresias Beach $$$
The facilities of this comfortable hotel stretch down to the sand of Maresias Beach, the busiest in São Sebastião. The rooms have views of either the Serra do Mar range, the gardens, or the sea. Ideal for families as well as couples. ACCOMMODATIONS 93; air-conditioning; ceiling fan; jacuzzi (master suite); minibar; pay TV; phone; private safe. FACILITIES AND SERVICES bar; beach service; function room; games room; gym; playground; pool; recreational team for children; restaurant; sauna; tennis court. CREDIT CARDS Diners; MasterCard; Visa
Avenida Francisco Loup, 1,109, Praia de Maresias
TEL (12) 3891-7500 FAX (12) 3891-7509
www.maresiashotel.com.br

Sambaqui $$
Just 30 meters (100 feet) from the beach, the rooms of this rustic guesthouse vary in size and have views of either the sea or the Atlantic forest. ACCOMMODATIONS 16; air-conditioning; ceiling fan; Internet access; minibar; phone; TV; veranda. FACILITIES AND SERVICES bar; beach service; function room; gym; Internet access; library; pool; restaurant; sauna; TV room. CREDIT CARDS Diners; MasterCard
Rua Xavantes, 57, Praia da Juréia
TEL and FAX (12) 3867-1291
www.hotelsambaThucom.br

Villa Bebek $$$
This Thai-style guesthouse has rooms scattered around a pool that is long, narrow, and curvy, like a river. One room can be set up to accommodate disabled guests. ACCOMMODATIONS 28; air-conditioning; ceiling fan; DVD Player; minibar; phone; private safe; TV. FACILITIES AND SERVICES bar; beach service; gazebo; heated pool; massage room; pool; restaurant; sauna. CREDIT CARDS Diners; MasterCard; Visa
Rua do Zezito, 251, Camburizinho
TEL and FAX (12) 3865-2123 www.villabebek.com.br

WHERE TO EAT

Acqua $$$
This charming and sophisticated hilltop restaurant has a lovely view of Camburi Beach. It serves contemporary Italian-style seafood dishes. It serves risoto al Nero (squid risotto in its own ink, with broccoli) or the spaguetti di gamberi (shrimp spaghetti). CUISINE Italian. CREDIT CARDS AmEx; Diners; MasterCard; Visa
Estrada do Camburi, 2,000, Camburi
TEL (12) 3865-1866. Fri and Sat, 2pm – 1am; Sun, 1pm – 10pm; in summer, daily, 2pm – 1am

Manacá $$$
Run by renowned chef Edinho Engel, this is one of the best restaurants on the north coast of São Paulo. In gazebos on stilts, surrounded by greenery, it serves magical dishes such as the papillote de robalo (snook baked in a banana leaf), with shrimp farofa (manioc meal), banana, and capers. The wine cellar has a good range of labels. Bookings recommended. CUISINE Contemporary. CREDIT CARDS AmEx; Diners; MasterCard; Visa
Rua do Manacá, 102, Camburizinho
TEL (12) 3865-1566 Thu, 6pm – 11pm; Fri and Sat, 1pm – 11pm; Sun, 1pm – 9pm

Tiê Sahy $$$
Set back from the beach, this house's large windows look out over a beautiful swimming pool. It is a branch

---

of the Tiê de Camburi, with sophisticated touches. The combination of prawns flambéed in whisky, with stir-fried shiitake, shimeji, onion, and pear strips, is a good choice. **CUISINE** Contemporary. **CREDIT CARDS** AmEx; Diners; MasterCard; Visa
Avenida Adelino Tavares, 160, Barra do Sahy
TEL (12) 3863-6369 Fri – Sat, 1pm – midnight; Sun, 1pm – 9pm

SERVICES

Tourist information – Centro de Informações Turísticas
Rua Altino Arantes, 174, Centro
Mon – Thu, 10am – 7pm; Fri and Sun, 10am – 8pm; Sat, 10am – 9pm
TEL (12) 3892-2620, extension 23

Serra da Capivara (National Park) – Piauí
(see São Raimundo Nonato)

Serras Catarinenses – Santa Catarina
(see Bom Jardim da Serra)

Serro – Minas Gerais

AREA CODE 38 **INHABITANTS** 20,862 distâncias Belo Horizonte 330 kilometers (205 miles), Diamantina 90 kilometers (56 miles) **ACCESS** On highways BR-040 and BR-135 from Belo Horizonte to Curvelo, then BR-259

WHERE TO STAY

Pousada Serrana $
Having opened in 2003, this simple guesthouse has modern facilities and comfortable rooms. Noise is the biggest problem, as it's near the highway. The breakfast is yummy. **ACCOMMODATIONS** 14; minibar; portable fan; TV. **FACILITIES AND SERVICES** parking. **CREDIT CARDS** Not accepted
Travessa Magalhães, 55, Centro
TEL (38) 3541-1949

WHERE TO EAT

Restaurante Itacolomi $
This restaurant operates out of a colonial manor. On a wood-burning oven, guests can help themselves to beans, ribs with manioc, pasta, and other dishes. Typical dishes from Minas Gerais are served à la carte (the specialty is the bean dish feijão-tropeiro, with rice and pork loin), as well as pasta dishes, soups, pizza, and snacks. **CUISINE** Meats; regional. **CREDIT CARDS** AmEx; Diners; MasterCard
Praça João Pinheiro, 20, Centro
TEL (38) 3541-1227. Daily, 11am – 11pm

SERVICES

Bus Station – Rodoviária
Praça Ângelo Miranda, 26, Centro
TEL (38) 3541-1366

Tourist information – Informações Turísticas
Praça João Pinheiro, 154, Centro

TEL (38) 3541-2754. Mon – Fri, 8am – 6pm; Sat and Sun, 9am – noon and 1pm – 5pm

Tourist information – Secretaria de Turismo
They can arrange visits and recommend guides.
Praça João Pinheiro, 154, Centro
TEL (38) 3541-2754

Sete Cidades (National Park) – Piauí (see Piripiri)

Sítio do Conde – Bahia

AREA CODE 75 **DISTANCE** Salvador 202 kilometers (126 miles) **ACCESS** From Salvador, take the Estrada do Coco highway, then take Linha Verde to the Conde exit. Continue for 6 kilometers (4 miles)

WHERE TO STAY

Resort Itariri $$
The facilities may be old, but the rooms are spacious and comfortable, and the extras make this one of the best resorts in the region. The lake beside the hotel offers a lovely view of nearby Itariri Beach. During low season, the resort caters to business and school groups. If you're looking for privacy, choose a chalet. **ACCOMMODATIONS** 30; air-conditioning; minibar; radiotelephone; TV; fan in the chalets. **FACILITIES AND SERVICES** bar; boat; bicycles; kayaks; horse and cart; parking; fishing lake; paddleboat; pool; playground; volleyball court; restaurant; river; games room; flying fox; recreational team for adults and children; beach service in the high season. **CREDIT CARDS** MasterCard
Fazenda Ribeiro, no # (Km 131, Linha Verde), Barra do Itariri
TEL and **FAX** (75) 3449-1142 www.itariri-resort.com

Sobral – Ceará

AREA CODE 88 **POPULATION** 172,685 **DISTANCES** Fortaleza 235 kilometers (146 miles), Jericoacoara 152 kilometers (94 miles) **ACCESS** From Fortaleza or Teresina, take Highway BR-222. (Note: From Teresina, there is a stretch of road in the Tianguá Mountain Range that's in poor condition. From Fortaleza, there is a similar stretch between Ubamirim and Patos.) www.sobral.ce.gov.br

WHERE TO STAY

Visconde $
A good option for travelers who wish to stay in the heart of town and get around on foot. Rooms at Visconde get booked up quickly because good service and spotless rooms are a sure thing year-round. **ACCOMMODATIONS** 48 (36 rooms and 12 suites); air-conditioning; minibar; telephone; cable TV. **FACILITIES AND SERVICES** Internet access; parking; restaurant; conference room; video room. **CREDIT CARDS** AmEx; Diners; MasterCard; Visa
Avenida Lúcia Sabóia, 473, Centro
TEL (88) 3611-5800 **FAX** (88) 3613-1887

WHERE TO EAT

Aragão $
The most popular dish here is the generously portioned carne-de-sol (beef jerky), which owner Aragão has perfected over nearly two decades. Set just outside of the

| PRICES | HOTELS (couple) | $ up to R$ 150 | $$ from R$ 151 up to R$ 300 | $$$ from R$ 301 up to R$500 | $$$$ above R$ 500 |

558

BRAZIL GUIDE

center of town in a simple neighborhood, this restaurant is frequented by local politicians, tourists, and executives, all of whom dine against a backdrop of antique wall clocks. CUISINE Regional. CREDIT CARDS Not accepted
Rua Sousa Aguiar, 42, Sinhá Sabóia
TEL (88) 3614-4004 RESERVATIONS (88) 3614-4003 OPEN Daily, 11am – 11pm

SERVICES

Airport – Aeroporto Coronel Virgílio Távora
Avenida Geraldo Rangel, no #, Betânia
TEL (88) 3613-2552 (public phone) OPEN Daily, 24 hours

Bus Station – Rodoviária
Rua Deputado Emanoel Rodrigues, no #, Tamarino
TEL (88) 3611-1554

Tamandaré – Pernambuco

AREA CODE 81 POPULATION 18,831 DISTANCE Recife 89 kilometers (55 miles) ACCESS From Recife, take Highway BR-101, followed by PE-060

WHERE TO STAY

Fazenda Amaragi $$
This charming hotel has a wide variety of good leisure options, such as guided tours by horse and catamaran, as well as a pool. The rooms and bungalows are spartan: Most don't have TVs, and none has a minibar. The hotel kitchen, however, is open for guests night and day. Tariffs are basically all-inclusive, but a few itens are extra. ACCOMMODATIONS 29; air-conditioning; TV in 3 bungalows. FACILITIES AND SERVICES Internet access; banana-boat; bar; soccer field; horses; water skiing; jet-ski; motorboat; pool; pony; beach; restaurant; games room; massage room; TV room; sauna; beach equipment; pool service; beach service; airport shuttle; transport to attractions. CREDIT CARDS Not accepted
Fazenda Amaragi, no #, Rio Formoso
TEL (81) 3678-1227 FAX (81) 3678-1237
www.amaragi.com.br

Pontal dos Carneiros Beach Bungalows $$$$
These cozy bungalows sleep up to six people each. Just 60 meters (200 feet) from the beach, they are separated from one another by lawn and surrounded by hammocks, mats, and wicker sofas. Breakfast is served in the bungalows (as are other meals, on request). ACCOMMODATIONS 8; air-conditioning; private safe; kitchen; minibar; stereo; DVD player; telephone; TV; veranda with hammock. FACILITIES AND SERVICES Internet access; parking; playground; volleyball court; restaurant; games room; motorboat trips; jet-ski; waterskiing; beach service; airport shuttle; transport to attractions. CREDIT CARDS AmEx; Visa
Sítio dos Manguinhos (access via road to Carneiros, Km 5)
TEL (81) 3676-2365 www.pontaldoscarneiros.com.br

Resort Praia dos Carneiros $$
This resort offers fantastic hilltop views of the mouth of the Formoso River and its mangroves, as well as catamaran trips to Carneiros Beach, which are included in the daily rate. All of the rooms have exposed brick walls. ACCOMMODATIONS 32; air-conditioning; private safe; minibar; telephone; cable TV. FACILITIES AND SERVICES Internet

access; boat; horses; water skiing; parking; snack bar; stores; pool; playground; restaurant; recreational team for adults and children; valet parking; lifeguards; beach service; airport shuttle; transport to attractions. CREDIT CARDS Diners; MasterCard; Visa
Granja Havaí, no #, Zona Rural, Rio Formoso
TEL and FAX (81) 3678-1102/1170
www.hotelpraiadoscarneiros.com.br

WHERE TO EAT

Frente de Quintal $
The speciality of this restaurant, located on a quiet street about 700 meters (0.4 miles) from the center of Tamandaré, is arroz de polvo (octopus rice). We also recommend the generously portioned peixada (fish cooked in coconut milk, served with rice, pirão gravy and vegetables). CUISINE Fish. CREDIT CARDS Mastercard; Visa
Rua José Paulo Lins, no #
TEL (81) 3676-1863 OPEN Daily, 10am – 10pm

O Pescador $
Just 150 meters from the shoreline, this restaurant's fortes are the peixada (fish in coconut milk), arroz de polvo (octopus rice), and peixe ao molho de camarão (fish in shrimp sauce). Patrons can watch the cooks at work. A small bar inside the restaurant plays Brazilian pop (mpb) music. CUISINE Fish and seafood. CREDIT CARDS AmEx; Diners; MasterCard; Visa
Rua Raul de Pompéia, no #, Loteamento Brigite
TEL (81) 3676-1345 OPEN Daily, 7am – 10pm

Tambaba – Paraíba (see Jacumã)

Teresina – Piauí

AREA CODE 86 POPULATION 788,773 DISTANCES São Luís 463 kilometers (288 miles), Parnaíba 348 kilometers (216 miles), Fortaleza 634 kilometers (394 miles) ACCESS From Fortaleza, take Highway BR-222 (there is a stretch in poor conditions between Umirim and Patos), then BR-343. From Parnaíba, take Highway BR-343. From São Luís, take Highway BR-135 and then BR-316
www.teresina.pi.gov.br

WHERE TO STAY

Metropolitan Hotel $$$
One of Teresina's best hotels, the Metropolitan is well situated in the heart of the city. It has three bars; the one on the 10th floor offers an excellent view of the region. Even non-guests can and should go up to take in the view. ACCOMMODATIONS 129; Internet access; air-conditioning; private safe; minibar; jacuzzi in 2 suites; telephone; cable TV. FACILITIES AND SERVICES Internet access; bar; parking; pool; restaurant; conference room; gym; sauna; travel agency; business center; 24-hour kitchen; valet parking; VIP lounge at the airport. CREDIT CARDS AmEx; Diners; MasterCard; Visa
Avenida Frei Serafim, 1696, Centro
TEL and FAX (86) 3216-8000
www.metropolitanhotel.com.br

WHERE TO EAT

Longá $$$
Specializing in regional cuisine and popular among executives, this restaurant is an oasis of air-conditioning and comfortable chairs. Try the breaded guinea fowl or

mutton capote. **CUISINE** Regional. **CREDIT CARDS** Diners; MasterCard; Visa
Avenida Ininga, 1245, Fátima
TEL (86) 3232-6868. **OPEN** High season: daily, 10am until the last customer leaves; low season: Mon – Sat, 10am until the last customer leaves and Sun, 10am – 6pm

SERVICES

Airport – Aeroporto Senador Petrônio Portella
Avenida Centenário, no #, Aeroporto
TEL (86) 3133-6270 **OPEN** Daily, 24 hours

Bus Station – Rodoviária
Rodovia BR-343 (towards Campo Maior), Km 3, Redenção
TEL (86) 3218-2037, 3218-1514

Tourist Information – Piemtur (Piauí Turismo)
Rua Acre, no #, Centro de Convenções, Cabral
TEL (86) 3222-6254 **OPEN** Mon – Fri, 8am – 1:30pm

Teresópolis – Rio de Janeiro

AREA CODE 21 **INHABITANTS** 150,268 **DISTANCES** Rio de Janeiro 87 kilometers (54 miles), São Paulo 484 kilometers (301 miles), Belo Horizonte 405 kilometers (252 miles) **ACCESS** Highways BR-040 and BR-116 from Rio de Janeiro

WHERE TO STAY

Hotel Fazenda Rosa dos Ventos $$$
Situated between Teresópolis and Nova Friburgo, this hotel combines comfort and country life. There are plenty of leisure options and a wine cellar, which offers tasting and serves fondues. The spacious rooms have large beds. **ACCOMMODATIONS** 42; ceiling fan; fireplace (in 5 suites); Internet access; jacuzzi (in 1 suite); minibar; ofuro tub (in 1 suite); phone; pay TV; private safe. **FACILITIES AND SERVICES** bar; beauty parlor; boat; business center; convenience store; fishing equipment and lake; function room; games room; gym; heated pool; hiking trails and guides; horses; Internet access; massage room; multisports court; parking; pool; restaurant; sauna; valet service; video room; wine cellar. **CREDIT CARDS** AmEx; Diners; MasterCard; Visa
Estrada Teresópolis–Nova Friburgo, Km 22.5 Campanha
TEL (21) 2644-9900 **FAX** (21) 2240-8125
RESERVATIONS (21) 2532-1197
www.hotelrosadosventos.com.br

Pousada Urikana $$$
This guesthouse nests on a plateau in the Serra dos Órgãos mountains, 1000 meters (almost 3300 feet) above sea level, surrounded by private woods and hiking trails. Some chalets have whirlpool tubs. **ACCOMMODATIONS** 23; air-conditioning; ceiling fan; fireplace (in 13 chalets); jacuzzi (in 10 chalets); minibar; pay TV; phone; private safe. **FACILITIES AND SERVICES** bar; business center; convenience store; function room; games room; gym; jacuzzi; massage room; mini golf course; parking; pool; recreational staff for adults and children; restaurant; sauna; trails; transport to airport and attractions; valet service; video room; walking tours. **CREDIT CARDS** AmEx; Diners; MasterCard; Visa
Estrada Ibiporanga, 2,151, Parque do Imbuí
TEL (21) 2641-8991 www.pousadaurikana.com.br

Toca-Terê Pousada $$$
There are 12 chalets on this several-acre lot; 7 have whirlpool tubs, and all have views of the surrounding greenery. The guesthouse is built up on wooden decks, and the paths between the different areas are made of stone and cross hanging bridges. It stands inside Ingá Park, an environmental conservation area. **ACCOMMODATIONS** 12; air-conditioning (in 4 chalets); fireplace; Internet access; jacuzzi (in 7 chalets); minibar; pay TV; phone; private safe. **FACILITIES AND SERVICES** bar; convenience store; function room; games room; gym; heated pool; Internet access; jacuzzi; massage room; parking; restaurant; river; sauna; spa; trails; transport to airport; valet service; video room; waterfall; wine cellar. **CREDIT CARDS** AmEx; Diners; MasterCard; Visa
Praça dos Namorados, 257, Parque do Ingá
TEL (21) 2642-1100 **FAX** (21) 2642-3657
www.tocatere.com.br

WHERE TO EAT

Cremerie Genève $
This restaurant, on a goat farm, has ready access to some of the best goat cheese in the country. The menu features classic French recipes, such as magret de canard (duck magret) with cassis sauce, and, of course, a dozen varieties of goat cheese. Kids love visiting and feeding the goats. **CUISINE** French. **CREDIT CARDS** Diners; MasterCard
Estrada Teresópolis–Nova Friburgo, Km 16
TEL (21) 3643-6391. Fri and Sat, noon – 10pm; Sun, noon – 6pm

Dona Irene $$
Set two hours aside to enjoy this genuine Russian banquet. The meal begins with piroskis (meat turnovers) and herrings accompanied by homemade vodka. Then, Kiev chicken and beet soup, or the "real" stroganoff, among other delicacies. Reservations are recommended, and are required on Mondays. **CUISINE** Russain. **CREDIT CARDS** Not accepted
Rua Tenente Luiz Meirelles, 1,800, Bom Retiro
TEL (21) 2742-2901. Wed – Sat, noon – midnight; Sun, noon – 6pm; Mon, by reservation

Manjericão $
Located in the district of Alto, this is reputed to be the best pizza parlor in the region. The crust is thick yet light. The Parmesan cheese, cream and walnut topping is a great choice. **CUISINE** Pizza. **CREDIT CARDS** Diners; MasterCard
Rua Flávio Bertoluzzi de Souza, 314, Alto
TEL (21) 2642-4242. Thu, 6pm – 11pm; Fri, 6pm – midnight; Sat, noon – midnight; Sun, noon – 11pm

SERVICES

Tourist information – Secretaria de Turismo
Avenida Rotariana, no #, Town Gateway
TEL (21) 2742-3352. Mon – Fri, 9am – 6pm; Sat, 9am – 5pm; Sun, 9am – 1pm

Tibau do Sul – Rio Grande do Norte (see Praia da Pipa)

Tiradentes – Minas Gerais

AREA CODE 32 **INHABITANTS** 6,547 distâncias Belo Horizonte 190 kilometers (118 miles), Ouro Preto 260 kilo-

| PRICES | HOTELS (couple) | $ up to R$ 150 | $$ from R$ 151 up to R$ 300 | $$$ from R$ 301 up to R$500 | $$$$ above R$ 500 |

560

BRAZIL GUIDE

meters (162 miles), Rio de Janeiro 330 kilometers (205 miles), São Paulo 480 kilometers (293 miles) **ACCESS** Highway BR-040 from Belo Horizonte, followed by BR-383 and BR-265. Highway BR-381 (Rodovia Fernão Dias) from São Paulo to the Lavras turnoff, followed by BR-265. Highway BR-040 and BR-265 from Rio de Janeiro

WHERE TO STAY

Pousada dos Inconfidentes $$$$
Located on a large property inside a closed condominium complex, this guesthouse lies 1.5 kilometers (1 mile) from the town center. It has good leisure facilities, and the ground-floor suites have private gardens. Colonial-style tea is served daily at 5pm. Children under 14 are not allowed. Reservations recommended. **ACCOMMODATIONS** 12; fireplace; Internet access; minibar; pay TV; phone; private safe. **FACILITIES AND SERVICES** gym; home theater; Internet access; orchard; parking; pool bar; reading room; sauna; semi-Olympic pool; video room; wine cellar. **CREDIT CARDS** AmEx; Diners; MasterCard; Visa
Rua João Rodrigues Sobrinho, 91,
Condomínio Parque dos Bandeirantes
TEL and **FAX** (32) 3355-2135
www.pousadadosinconfidentes.com.br

Pousada Richard Rothe $$
This guesthouse operates out of a manor in the historic center of Tiradentes. The large rooms have distinctive décor composed of 18th-century furniture and art nouveau pieces. In high season, children under 12 are not allowed. **ACCOMMODATIONS** 12; heater; minibar; phone; TV. **FACILITIES AND SERVICES** parking; pay TV; pool; reading room with fireplace; sauna. **CREDIT CARDS** Not accepted
Rua Padre Toledo, 124, Centro
TEL and **FAX** (32) 3355-1333
www.pousadarichardrothe.com.br

Pousada Villa Paolucci $$$
Located in an Atlantic forest conservation area not far from the town center, this guesthouse is known for its restaurant's large kitchen – which makes it an important address during Semana de Gastronomia (Gastronomy Week), in August. Rooms are large and airy. In the high season, rooms are not available for less than two nights on the weekend. **ACCOMMODATIONS** 12; air-conditioning (in 9 rooms); fireplace; minibar; pay TV; phone. **FACILITIES AND SERVICES** bar; chapel; function room; parking; pool; restaurant; sauna; tennis court; wine cellar; 24-hour kitchen. **CREDIT CARDS** AmEx; MasterCard; Visa
Rua Francisco Cândido Barbosa, no #, Centro
TEL and **FAX** (32) 3355-1350, 9981-8003
www.villapaolucci.com.br

Pousada Xica da Silva $$$
Just 800 meters (a half mile) from the town center on a large property brimming with greenery, this is a great option for families with children. It is one of the few guesthouses that accepts them and has adequate amenities for them, including a baby-sitting service. There are rooms and chalets for up to four or five people. **ACCOMMODATIONS** 20; fireplace (in 5 rooms); minibar; pay TV; phone. **FACILITIES AND SERVICES** bar; barbecue facilities; bicycles; function room; games room; horses and carriage; Internet access; jacuzzi; library; mini farm; orchard; parking; piano-bar; playground; pool; pony; reading room; recreational team for children (in high season); restaurant; sauna; stores; transport to airport; walking tours; woods. **CREDIT CARDS** AmEx; Diners; MasterCard
Avenida Governador Israel Pinheiro, 400, Estação

TEL and **FAX** (32) 3355-1874/1461
www.xicadasilva.com.br

WHERE TO EAT

Estalagem do Sabor $
Of various dishes typical of Minas Gerais, one house specialty here is the abóbora real, pumpkin stuffed with beef jerky, queijo-do-reino cheese, onion, bacon, and sugar-cane syrup, which serves three. There is a wine list. **CUISINE** Regional. **CREDIT CARDS** Not accepted
Rua Ministro Gabriel Passos, 280, Centro
TEL (32) 3355-1144. Mon – Fri, 11am – 4pm and 7pm – 10pm; Sat, 11am – 10pm; Sun, 11am – 5pm

Quartier Latin $
The restaurant serves light, tasty meals, such as brie and jabuticaba ravioli with Parma ham, olives in balsamic caramel sauce and lime. For dessert, try the pineapple gratiné with zabaglione and Brazilian pepper, served with creme and basil ice cream. The wine list has some 200 labels. **CUISINE** Contemporary; French; Mediterranean. **CREDIT CARDS** AmEx; Diners; MasterCard; Visa
Rua São Francisco de Paula, 46, Centro
TEL (32) 3355-1552. Mon – Thu, 5pm – until the last customer leaves; Fri – Sun, and holidays, noon – until the last customer leaves

Theatro da Villa $$
The menu changes four times a year, but examples of the kinds of dishes produced by this contemporary kitchen are octopus carpaccio with soy sauce and strips of sweet, pickled ginger and filé mignon chateaubriand flambéed in cognac with green pepper sauce, accompanied by a baked potato stuffed with palm heart cream and green thyme. Reservations are recommended. **CUISINE** Contemporary. **CREDIT CARDS** AmEx; Diners; MasterCard; Visa
Rua Padre Toledo, 157, Centro
TEL (32) 3355-1275, 3355-1533. Tue, Wed, Thu and Sun, 8pm – midnight; Fri and Sat, 8pm – until the last customer leaves

Tragaluz $
Classic dishes include the beef dish picadinho cooked in the meat juices and wine, served with julienned vegetables and mushrooms, served with puree, honey banana, and carrot wrapped in kale. For dessert, try the goiabada (guava conserve) coated in crushed cashew and fried in butter, served on a layer of soft Catupiry cheese and accompanied by guava ice cream. **CUISINE** Contemporary. **CREDIT CARDS** AmEx; Diners; MasterCard; Visa
Rua Direita, 52, Centro
TEL (32) 3355-1424, 9968-4837. Mon and Wed – Fri, 7pm – 10:30pm; Sat and Sun, 12:30 – 4pm and 7:30pm – 12:30am

Trattoria Via Destra $
This is the best Italian restaurant in Tiradentes. We suggest the saffron and shrimp risotto and the bistecca alla fiorentina (Tuscan porterhouse) with rosemary potatoes. The wine list has 35 labels. Ask for a table in the back garden under the trellis. **CUISINE** Italian. **CREDIT CARDS** MasterCard; Visa
Rua Direita, 45, Centro
TEL (32) 3355-1906. Daily, noon – 5pm and 7pm until the last customer leaves (high season); Wed and Thu, 7pm until the last customer leaves; Fri, Sat and Sun, noon – 5pm and 7pm until the last customer leaves (low season)

| **RESTAURANTS** | $ up to R$ 50 | $$ from R$ 51 up to R$ 100 | $$$ from R$ 101 up to R$ 150 | $$$$ above R$ 150 |

Viradas do Largo $

This establishment specializes in mouthwatering regional fare, such as viradinho (rice, beans, egg, bacon, onion, serenada beef, collard greens, and pine nuts), which serves three. Next door, a small store sells arts and crafts, sweets, chilies, sausage, and other items. The restaurant has a wine list and an English menu and belongs to the Restaurantes da Boa Lembrança Association. **CUISINE** Regional. **CREDIT CARDS** AmEx; Diners; MasterCard; Visa

Rua do Moinho, 11, Prainha
TEL (32) 3355-1111, 3355-1110. Daily, noon – 10pm

SERVICES

Local tour operators –
Agência de Turismo Estrada Real

Tours of the historical towns of Minas Gerais.
Rua dos Inconfidentes, 218, Centro
TEL (32) 3355-1187. Daily, 8am – 7pm

Local tour operators – Tiradentes Brasil

Walks to the São José Range.
Rua Henrique Diniz, 119, Centro
TEL (32) 3355-2477. Mon – Fri, 8am – 5pm; Sat, 9am – 5pm; Sun, 9am – 2pm www.tiradentesbrasil.com

Tourist information – Posto de Informações Turísticas

Rua Resende Costa, 71, Centro
TEL (32) 3355-1212. Mon – Fri, 9am – 6pm; Sat and Sun, 9am – 7pm

Touros – Rio Grande do Norte

AREA CODE 84 **POPULATION** 32,052 **DISTANCES** Natal 88 kilometers (55 miles) **ACCESS** From Natal, take Highway BR-101

WHERE TO STAY

Pousada Sinos do Vento $$$

All the rooms and pools at this rustic, laid-back guesthouse afford views of the calm sea. The guests' rooms and communal areas are far apart. Horse are kept here, as are chickens, ensuring fresh eggs for breakfast. **ACCOMMODATIONS** 14; Internet access; air-conditioning; minibar; telephone; cable TV in the master suite **FACILITIES AND SERVICES** Internet access; wine cellar; bar; horse and cart; parking; convenience store; pool; playground; orchard; restaurant; magazine reading area; games room; massage room; valet parking; airport shuttle; transport to attractions. **CREDIT CARDS** AmEx; Diners; MasterCard; Visa

Praia das Graças, no #, Prainha
TEL (84) 3263-2353, 3263-2020 **FAX** (84) 3263-2021 www.sinosdovento.com.br

Siri Resort $$$

Refined, yet rustic, this resort is popular among European tourists. The cozy, wooden chalets open onto Perobas Beach. This is a great place for peace and quiet in the low season. **ACCOMMODATIONS** 23; Internet access; air-conditioning; minibar; TV; veranda. **FACILITIES AND SERVICES** bar; parking; pool; playground; restaurant; games room; massage; manicure; trips; beach service. **CREDIT CARDS** Visa

Estrada de Carnaubinha, no #, Praia de Perobas

TEL (84) 3693-3035, 3693-3036 **RESERVATIONS** (84) 3263-2353, 9953-0198

Trancoso – Bahia

AREA CODE 73 **DISTANCES** Salvador 735 kilometers (457 miles), Porto Seguro 25 kilometers (16 miles, by road and ferryboat) **ACCESS** From Porto Seguro, take a ferry to Arraial d'Ajuda, followed by a stretch of road to Trancoso, or go direct on the BA-001 (47 kilometers, 29 miles) which is hazardous in places

WHERE TO STAY

Club Med Trancoso $$$$

This cliff-top resort offers beautiful views. The multicolored blocks of spacious rooms recall the architecture of Trancoso's main square, the Quadrado. Guests can relax at the spa and try the beauty treatments on offer. **ACCOMMODATIONS** 250; air-conditioning; private safe; minibar; telephone; cable TV. **FACILITIES AND SERVICES** Internet access; wine cellar; archery; bar; boat; sailboat; kayaks; soccer field; golf course; horses; parking; jacuzzi; stores; kids' club (for children over 4); pool; playground; six-a-side soccer court; tennis court; volleyball court; restaurant; magazine reading area; river; conference room; gym; massage room; beauty parlor; sauna; spa; walking trails; travel agency; business center; exchange bureau; recreational team for adults and children; guided walking tours; valet parking; lifeguards; beach service; airport shuttle; transport to attractions. **CREDIT CARDS** AmEx; Diners; MasterCard; Visa

Fazenda Itaípe, no #, Estrada Arraial–Trancoso, Km 18
TEL (73) 3575-8400 **FAX** (73) 3575-8484
RESERVATIONS 0800-7073782 www.clubmed.com.br

Hotel da Praça $$

This charming guesthouse, about 700 meters (0.4 miles) from the beach, is set among spacious gardens dotted with sofas, tables, and deck chairs. Each room has its own color and ambiance. **ACCOMMODATIONS** 11; air-conditioning; private safe; minibar; telephone; cable TV. **FACILITIES AND SERVICES** wine cellar; bar; parking; restaurant; video room; airport shuttle. **CREDIT CARDS** Visa

Praça São João, 1, Quadrado
TEL and **FAX** (73) 3668-2121 www.hoteldapraca.com.br

Pousada Capim Santo $$

This guesthouse sits amid woods and gardens, with an outdoor ofuro tub and massage kiosk, 700 meters (0.4 miles) from the beach. The décor is rustic, but emphasizes comfort. While the small rooms are charming, the spacious suites have mezzanines. **ACCOMMODATIONS** 15; Internet access; air-conditioning; minibar; jacuzzi in 1 suite; telephone; TV. **FACILITIES AND SERVICES** wine cellar; bar; parking; ofuro tub; pool; restaurant; massage room; video room; babysitting; airport shuttle. **CREDIT CARDS** AmEx; MasterCard; Visa

Rua do Beco, 55, Quadrado
TEL and **FAX** (73) 3668-1122 www.capimsanto.com.br

Pousada Estrela d'Água $$$$

Once the home of singer Gal Costa, this rustic guesthouse faces the sea, which can be seen from the pools and charming communal areas. Guests can enjoy therapeutic massages, physical activities (Pilates, stretching, walks), and organic food. **ACCOMMODATIONS** 27; air-conditioning; private safe; minibar; jacuzzi in the master suites; private pool adjoining the master suites; tele-

| PRICES | HOTELS (couple) | $ up to R$ 150 | $$ from R$ 151 up to R$ 300 | $$$ from R$ 301 up to R$500 | $$$$ above R$ 500 |

562

BRAZIL GUIDE

phone; cable TV. **FACILITIES AND SERVICES** Internet access; bar; bicycles; horses; parking; motorboat; stores; pool; restaurant; gym; games room; massage room; video room; walking trails; currency exchange; guided walking tours; valet parking; beach service; transport to attractions. **CREDIT CARDS** AmEx; Diners; MasterCard; Visa
Estrada do Arraial, no #, Praia dos Nativos
TEL (73) 3668-1030 **FAX** (73) 3668-1485
www.estreladagua.com.br

WHERE TO EAT

O Cacau $$
This airy, simply decorated restaurant sits in the city's historic center . We suggest the camarão nativo (shrimp in coconut sauce, with coconut rice, toasted coconut shavings and pink peppercorns). There is a wine list, wine cellar, and outdoor tables. **CUISINE** Diverse. **CREDIT CARDS** MasterCard; Visa
Praça São João, 96, Quadrado
TEL (73) 3668-1266 **RESERVATIONS** (73) 3668-1144 **OPEN** Tue – Sun, 5:30pm until the last customer leaves

Capim Santo $$
Trancoso's first restaurant, Capim Santo has been so successful that it now has a branch in São Paulo. Its relaxed atmosphere emanates from the surrounding coconut palms and gardens. Highlights are the lobster gratin in pineapple, the grilled tuna in soy sauce, and the shrimp flambéed in vodka. **CUISINE** Contemporary; fish and seafood. **CREDIT CARDS** AmEx; MasterCard
Rua do Beco, 55, Quadrado
TEL (73) 3668-1122 **OPEN** Mon – Sat, 5pm – 11pm

El Gordo $$
Portuguese food is the speciality here. Two good picks are the bacalhau ao murro com natas (salted cod with potatoes) and the bacalhoada (cod baked with vegetables). But there are also Indian and Chinese dishes. Small outdoor tables offer sea views. **CUISINE** Chinese; Indian; Portuguese; diverse. **CREDIT CARDS** MasterCard; Visa
Praça São João, 7, Quadrado
TEL (73) 3668-1193, 3668-2041 **OPEN** Daily, 1pm – midnight

Maritaka $
Pizzas with a variety of toppings are this restaurant's forte – try one with asparagus and brie. Maritaka also serves sandwiches and rolos (rolled pizza filled with grilled meats). Large cushions and sofas complement the rustic décor. The restaurant stands at the entrance to the Quadrado. **CUISINE** Pizza; sandwiches. **CREDIT CARDS** Not accepted
Rua do Telégrafo, no #
TEL (73) 3668-1702 **RESERVATIONS** (73) 3668-1258 **OPEN** High season: Thu – Tue, 7pm until the last customer leaves; low season: 7pm – 11pm

SERVICES

Travel Agency – Brasil 2000 Turismo
Estrada do Mucugê, 165, Centro, Arraial
TEL (73) 3575-1815, 3575-1627 **OPEN** High season: daily, 9am – 11pm; low season: Mon – Sat, 9am – 9pm
www.brasil2000turismo.com.br

Travel Agency – Trancoso Receptivo
Rua Carlos Alberto Parracho, no #
TEL (73) 3668-1333, 3668-1183 **OPEN** High season: daily,

9am – 10pm; low season: Mon – Fri, 9am – 7:30pm; Sat, 9am – 1pm www.trancosoreceptivo.com

Triunfo – Pernambuco

AREA CODE 87 **POPULATION** 14,846 **DISTANCES** Recife 450 kilometers (280 miles) **ACCESS** From Recife, take Highway BR-232 to Serra Talhada, then PE-365 for another 31 kilometers (19 miles)

WHERE TO STAY

Pousada Baixa Verde $
Near the center of Triunfo, but nice and quiet. Some of the inn's spacious rooms overlook the pool and garden. The convenience store sells products from the Engenho São Pedro mill, including cachaças, other liquors, and rapadura (brown sugar candy). **ACCOMMODATIONS** 17; minibar; telephone; TV; fan. **FACILITIES AND SERVICES** Internet access; bar; waterfall; mill; parking; convenience store; pool; playground; skating rink; restaurant; conference room; guided walking tours. **CREDIT CARDS** AmEx; Diners; MasterCard; Visa
Rua Manoel Paiva dos Santos, 114, Centro
TEL (87) 3846-1103 **FAX** (87) 3846-1410
www.baixaverdetriunfo.hpg.ig.com.br

WHERE TO EAT

Baixa Verde $
The buffet's options include diced beef jerky, potato soufflé gratin, and the unusual goat fondue, which is prepared with meat from Serra Talhada. Some dishes, such as the pernil de cabrito (roast leg of goat), are made to order. **CUISINE** Regional. **CREDIT CARDS** Diners; MasterCard; Visa
Rua Manoel Paiva dos Santos, 114, Centro
TEL (87) 3846-1103 fax and **RESERVATIONS** (87) 3846-1410
OPEN Daily, 7am – 11pm

Ubatuba – São Paulo

AREA CODE 12 **INHABITANTS** 75,008 **DISTANCE** São Paulo 235 kilometers (146 miles) **ACCESS** Highway BR-116 (Rodovia Presidente Dutra) or SP-150 (Ayrton Senna) from São Paulo to the exit to Rodovia dos Tamoios (SP-099). Stay on the SP-099 until you reach the Rodovia Rio–Santos (BR-101/SP-055), which you take north

WHERE TO STAY

Recanto das Toninhas $$$$
This rustic guesthouse has spacious rooms with verandas. The kid's club offers activities for kids all day. Feijoada, served on Saturdays, is included in the daily rate. **ACCOMMODATIONS** 54; air-conditioning; Internet access; minibar; pay TV; phone; private safe; veranda. **FACILITIES AND SERVICES** bar; beach service; function room; games room; gym; heated pool; massage room; pool; recreational staff for adults and children (on school and public holidays); restaurant; sauna; tennis court. **CREDIT CARDS** AmEx; Diners; MasterCard; Visa
Rodovia SP-055, Km 55.5, Praia das Toninhas
TEL (12) 3842-1410 **FAX** (11) 3288-2260
RESERVATIONS 0800-177557 www.toninhas.com.br

Refúgio do Corsário $$
Frequented by families, this place is ideal for those who want peace and quiet while immersed in nature. Located right on the sea and next door to an Atlantic forest

---

RESTAURANTS $ up to R$ 50 $$ from R$ 51 up to R$ 100 $$$ from R$ 101 up to R$ 150 $$$$ above R$ 150

conservation area, it outsources diving and trail-hiking services. **ACCOMMODATIONS** 42; air-conditioning; TV. **FACILITIES AND SERVICES** beach service; games room; gym; pool; restaurant; TV room. **CREDIT CARDS** MasterCard; Visa
Trilha do Corsário, 10, Praia da Fortaleza
TEL and **FAX** (12) 3848-9229 www.corsario.com.br

Solar das Águas Cantantes $$

Tucked away between two beaches, this lovely and romantic hotel was built to imitate the simple Brazilian colonial style. Moquecas (seafood stews) are served by the poolside and next to a beautiful garden. When coming here, pay attention to the small signs that indicate the way on the bumpy, unpaved roads between the Lázaro and Sununga beaches. **ACCOMMODATIONS** 20; air-conditioning; ceiling fan; minibar; phone; TV. **FACILITIES AND SERVICES** bar; beach service; games room; pool; restaurant. **CREDIT CARDS** Diners; MasterCard; Visa
Estrada do Saco da Ribeira, 253, between Lázaro and Sununga beaches
TEL (12) 3842-0178 **FAX** and **RESERVATIONS** (12) 3842-0288
www.solardasaguascantantes.com.br

WHERE TO EAT

Bardolino $

Operating in a colonial building in the town's historical center, this cozy and sophisticated restaurant serves pasta dishes such as spaghettini with spicy lobster. **CUISINE** Mediterranean. **CREDIT CARDS** AmEx; Diners; MasterCard; Visa
Rua Dr. Esteves da Silva, 18, Centro
TEL (12) 3833-9725. Mon – Fri, 6pm until the last customer leaves; Sat, 11am until the last customer leaves; Sun, 11am – 10pm

Peixe com Banana $$

In a simple setting, this restaurant serves a delicious azul-marinho ("sea blue"): thick fillets of fish (such as grouper) and green dwarf banana cooked in an iron pot. The banana takes on a subtle blue color, hence the name of the dish. **CUISINE** Fish and seafood. **CREDIT CARDS** Diners; MasterCard; Visa
Rua Guarani, 255, Centro
TEL (12) 3832-1712. Daily, noon – 11pm

Solar das Águas Cantantes $

This restaurant, considered one of the best in the region, is inside the charming hotel of the same name (see separate listing above). The tasty grouper and shrimp moqueca stews, served by the pool, are the house specialties. Pay attention to the small signs that indicate the way on the bumpy, unpaved roads between the Lázaro and Sununga beaches. **CUISINE** Fish and seafood. **CREDIT CARDS** Diners; MasterCard
Estrada do Saco da Ribeira, 253, Praia do Lázaro
TEL (12) 3842-0178, 3842-0288. Mon – Fri, noon – 2pm and 6pm – 10pm; Sat and Sun, noon – 10pm

Terra Papagalli $

Located on a street corner in downtown Ubatuba, this restaurant is very romantic at night, with candles, candelabros, and sea views. The menu changes frequently, as they use the fish of the day, such as cambucu, snook, and dorado. The portions are generous and one dish usually serves two. The menu also has meat options. Reservations are recommended. **CUISINE** Fish and seafood. **CREDIT CARDS** AmEx; Diners; MasterCard
Rua Xavantes, 537-B, Itaguá

TEL (12) 3832-1488 Mon, Wed and Thu, 6pm – 11pm; Fri and Sat, noon – midnight; Sun, noon – 10pm

SERVICES

Local tour operators – Mykonos Turismo
Schooner trips.
Avenida Plínio França, no #, Saco da Ribeira
TEL (12) 3842-0329, 3842-1388. Daily, 8:30am – 5pm

Tourist information – Secretaria de Turismo
Avenida da Praia, 331, Centro
TEL (12) 3833-9123. Daily, 8am – 6pm

Vale do Capão (Caeté–Açu) – Bahia

AREA CODE 75 **DISTANCE** Lençóis 70 kilometers (44 miles)
ACCESS From Lençóis, take Highway BR-242 towards Seabra to the Palmeiras exit. From there, take Estrada Palmeiras–Capão (dirt road) to Caeté-Açu

WHERE TO STAY

Pousada Candombá $

with simple rooms, rustic Candombá is a pleasant, quiet spot. The hot-stone sauna operates out of a kind of candlelit igloo. Frenchman Claude Samuel grows most of the organic ingredients used in the restaurant. **ACCOMMODATIONS** 7; minibar in the luxury chalets; ceiling fan. **FACILITIES AND SERVICES** Internet access; wine cellar; parking; orchard; restaurant; sauna; walking trails. **CREDIT CARDS** MasterCard; Visa
Rua das Mangas, no #, Vale do Capão, Caeté-Açu
TEL and **FAX** (75) 3344-1102 www.infochapada.com

Pousada do Capão $

The second-floor rooms of this guesthouse have lovely views of the Morro Branco do Capão (Morrão) mountainside. The chalets are very private. There is also an indigenous-style hot-stone sauna. **ACCOMMODATIONS** 12; minibar; ceiling fan. **FACILITIES AND SERVICES** Internet access; bar; woods; parking; store; natural pool; orchard; restaurant; river; games room; reading room with fireplace; massage room; video room; sauna; walking trails. **CREDIT CARDS** Diners; MasterCard
Rua do Chamego, no #, Vale do Capão, Caeté-Açu
TEL and **FAX** (75) 3344-1034
www.pousadadocapao.com.br

WHERE TO EAT

Casa das Fadas $

This is one of the coziest and best-maintained eateries in Vale do Capão. Italian dishes are the house forte, and there are beautiful views of the surrounding mountain landscape. If you can, wait for sunset. The restaurant is just a few kilometers from the village and well signposted. **CUISINE** Italian. **CREDIT CARDS** MasterCard
Estrada Palmeiras–Capão, Km 12, Riachinho, Caeté–Açu
TEL (75) 3344-1166 **OPEN** Thu – Tue, 1pm – 9pm. Closed November 20 to December 20

Dona Beli $

Dona Beli serves tasty homemade food in her own home. There's no menu, just a list of daily dishes served with palma (prickly pear), banana godó (a thick broth),

PRICES	HOTELS (couple)	$ up to R$ 150	$$ from R$ 151 up to R$ 300	$$$ from R$ 301 up to R$500	$$$$ above R$ 500

or pepino de jaca (peeled, fried, and seasoned jackfruit) – all typical accompaniments in Chapada Diamantina. There is usually a wait for tables on public holidays and at the end of the year. CUISINE Regional; home-style. CREDIT CARDS Not accepted
Rua do Folga, no #, Vale do Capão, Caeté–Açu
TEL (75) 3344-1085 OPEN Daily, noon – 8pm

SERVICES

Guides – Associação dos Condutores de Visitantes do Vale do Capão (ACVVC)
Rua Campos, no # (on the way up to Fumaça Waterfall)
TEL (75) 3344-1087 OPEN Daily, 8am – 6pm
www.acvvc.com.br

Travel Agency – Pé no Mato
Tourist information and guides
Ladeira da Vila, no #, Centro
TEL (75) 3344-1105 OPEN Daily, 7am – 10pm
www.penomato.com

Travel Agency – Tatu na Trilha
Tourist information and guides
Rua da Vila, no #
TEL (75) 3344-1124 OPEN Mon – Fri, 8:30am – noon and 2pm – 6:30pm; Sat, 8:30am – noon (closed in May)
www.infochapada.com

Travel Agency – Terra Chapada
Tourist information and guides
Vila do Capão, no #
TEL (75) 3334-1428, 9977-7767 OPEN High season: daily, 8am – noon and 5pm – 10pm; low season: 8am – noon
www.terrachapada.com.br

Vassouras – Rio de Janeiro

AREA CODE 24 INHABITANTS 32,495 DISTANCE Rio de Janeiro, 111 kilometers (69 miles) ACCESS Highway BR-116 and RJ-127 from Rio de Janeiro

WHERE TO STAY

Hotel Fazenda Galo Vermelho $$$
This hotel has good leisure facilities for nature-oriented recreation, and more than 1000 acres to play in, nearly half of which are clad in Atlantic forest. There are hiking trails and a vacation resort for kids. In the low season, rooms can be hired for day-use only. ACCOMMODATIONS 14; air-conditioning; ceiling fan; Internet access; minibar; pay TV; phone. FACILITIES AND SERVICES archery; bar; canoes; climbing wall; function room; games room; horses; lake; massage room; multi-sports court; orchard; parking; playground; pool; recreational teams for adults and children; restaurant; sauna; soccer field; video room. CREDIT CARDS Not accepted
Estrada RJ-121, 6814
TEL (24) 2491- 9500 FAX (24) 2491-9505
www.hotelfazendagalovermelho.com.br

Mara Palace Hotel $
The unit in the center of Vassouras has simple amenities, but the country resort, 7 kilometers (4 miles) away, has a fishing lake, barbecue, and sauna, as well as sports courts, a playground, and trails. ACCOMMODATIONS 52; air-conditioning; Internet access; minibar; pay TV; phone; private safe. FACILITIES AND SERVICES bar; function room;

games room; gym; Internet access; massage room; parking; playground; restaurant; sauna; trails; video room; walking tours. CREDIT CARDS AmEx; Diners; MasterCard; Visa
Rua Chanceler Raul Fernandes, 121, Centro
TEL (24) 2471-1993 FAX (24) 2471-2524
RESERVATIONS 0800-7041994
www.marapalace.com.br

Vila Velha – Espírito Santo

AREA CODE 27 INHABITANTS 398,068 DISTANCE Vitória 9 kilometers (6 miles) ACCESS Highway ES-060 from Vitória.
www.vilavelha.es.gov.br

WHERE TO EAT

Atlântica $$
A traditional option on the seaside, this restaurant opened in the 1960s. Paintings by local artists, all for sale, decorate the simple facilities. Try the mixed moqueca (seafood stew), with fish, shrimp, lobster, and mussels, accompanied by rice, pirão (manioc-thickened gravy) and banana moquequinha. CUISINE Fish and seafood. CREDIT CARDS AmEx; Diners; MasterCard; Visa
Avenida Antônio Gil Veloso, 80, Praia da Costa
TEL (27) 3329-2341. Mon and Wed – Sat, 11:30am – midnight; Sun and Tue, 11am – 5pm

Café do Museu $
This café operates inside an old train car at Pedro Nolasco Station, next to the Museu Ferroviário (Railway Museum). The short menu features Italian dishes. We suggest the camarão VG (grilled shrimp in cognac), served with spaghetti in olive oil and garlic. CUISINE Italian; various. CREDIT CARDS Visa
Rua Vila Isabel, no #, Estação Pedro Nolasco, Argolas (Museu da Vale do Rio Doce)
TEL (27) 3326-8190. Tue, Wed, and Sun 10am – 6pm; Thu – Sat, 10am – 1am

SERVICES

Tourist iformation – Coordenação de Turismo
Avenida Presidente Lima, 516, Centro
TEL (27) 3139-9980. Mon – Fri, 9am – 6pm

Visconde de Mauá – Rio de Janeiro

AREA CODE 24 DISTANCES Rio de Janeiro 200 kilometers (124 miles), São Paulo 305 kilometers (190 miles) ACCESS Highway br-101 (Rodovia Presidente Dutra) from Rio de Janeiro to Km 304, followed by RJ-163. From São Paulo, take Highway BR-101 to Km 311

WHERE TO STAY

Fronteira Arte e Hotelaria $$$$
Far from the center, this hotel offers a stunning view of the mountains and large, well-decorated suites. Children under 14 are not allowed. ACCOMMODATIONS 10; CD player; DVD player; fireplace; jacuzzi; minibar; TV. FACILITIES AND SERVICES bar; gym; heliport; Internet access; natural pool; orchard; parking; restaurant; sauna; trails; wine cellar. CREDIT CARDS MasterCard
Estrada Mauá–Campo Alegre, Km 4
TEL (24) 3387-1219 www.hotelfronteira.com.br

RESTAURANTS $ up to R$ 50 $$ from R$ 51 up to R$ 100 $$$ from R$ 101 up to R$ 150 $$$$ above R$ 150

Hotel Bühler $$$

This is one of the few hotels in Visconde de Mauá that welcomes children, and even has a playground for them. Guests can choose between chalets with two rooms and suites. **ACCOMMODATIONS** 21; fireplace; jacuzzi (in 5 suites); minibar; pay TV; private safe. **FACILITIES AND SERVICES** bar; childcare (outsourced); fruit and vegetable garden; function room; games room; gym; heated pool; Internet access; jogging track; massage room; mini golf course; movie theater; multi-sports court; natural pool; orchard; parking; playground; pool; restaurant; sauna; soccer field; tennis court; trails; volleyball court. **CREDIT CARDS** AmEx; Diners; MasterCard; Visa

Praça Maringá, no #, Maringá
TEL (24) 3387-1204 FAX (24) 3387-1378
www.hotelbuhler.com.br

Jardins do Passaredo $$

The large, luxuriant garden here has hundreds of species of bromeliads, orchids, pine trees, and palms. The rooms have goose-feather pillows and quilts, and a shallow pond lies in front of each chalet. There is also a flat with a kitchen, cable TV, and CD player. Children under 12 are not allowed. **ACCOMMODATIONS** 8; fireplace; jacuzzi (in 1 chalet); minibar; pay TV (in 3 chalets). **FACILITIES AND SERVICES** natural pool; sauna; trails. **CREDIT CARDS** Not accepted

Estrada Maringá, Km 6
TEL (24) 3387-1190 www.jardinsdopassaredo.com.br

Mauá Brasil Hotelaria e Gastronomia $$$

This exclusive guesthouse is a good option for those seeking peace and quiet. The large chalets are scattered on top of a hill with a view of the mountain range. The rooms are nicely decorated and have fireplaces and whirlpool tubs with panoramic views. Children under 15 are not allowed. **ACCOMMODATIONS** 11; fireplace; jacuzzi; minibar; phone; TV. **FACILITIES AND SERVICES** bar; fruit and vegetable garden; horses; Internet access; massage service; parking; pool; restaurant; sauna; sitting room; tennis court; trails; walking tours; wine cellar. **CREDIT CARDS** Diners; MasterCard; Visa

Estrada Visconde de Mauá–Campo Alegre, Km 4
TEL (24) 3387-2077 www.mauabrasil.com.br

Pousada Terra da Luz $$$

In the heart of the village of Maringá, on the Minas Gerais side of the border, this pleasant guesthouse has a great restaurant, with live jazz performances on Saturdays. Children are not allowed. **ACCOMMODATIONS** 6; fireplace; jacuzzi (in 2 chalets); minibar; pay TV; phone. **FACILITIES AND SERVICES** bar; convenience stores; Internet access; massage rooms; ofuro tub; orchard; parking; pool; reading room; restaurant; river; sauna; trails; transport to airport and attractions; valet service; walking tours; wine cellar. **CREDIT CARDS** AmEx; Diners; MasterCard

Estrada Maringá-Minas, Km 6.5
TEL (24) 3387-1306 RESERVATIONS (24) 3387-1545
www.pousadaterradaluz.com.br

Verde Que Te Quero Ver-te $$$

Frequented mostly by couples, this guesthouse has spacious chalets, surrounded by plenty of green and a well-tended garden. Breakfast is served at all hours. **ACCOMMODATIONS** 7; CD Player; coffeemaker; fireplace; heating; jacuzzi (in the chalets); minibar; pay TV; phone. **FACILITIES AND SERVICES** bar; games room; gym; heated pool; Internet access; massage room; parking; restaurant; sauna; trails; wine cellar; woods. **CREDIT CARDS** AmEx; Diners; MasterCard; Visa

Estrada Maringá-Minas, Km 7.5
TEL (24) 3387-1322
www.verdequetequeroverte.com.br

WHERE TO EAT

Gosto com Gosto $

In a rustic setting, this restaurant serves several regional dishes from the state of Minas Gerais, including its own creations, such as the lombo ao molho de laranja (pork loin in orange sauce). There is a dessert buffet and 400 types of cachaça. **CUISINE** Regional. **CREDIT CARDS** AmEx; Diners; MasterCard; Visa

Rua Wenceslau Braz, 148
TEL (24) 3387-1382. Sun – Thu, noon – 6pm; Fri and Sat, noon – 8pm

Rosmarino Officinalis $$

Set among green mountains, this restaurant is surrounded by an enormous garden. The food is some of the most acclaimed in the region. Chef Julio Buschinelli prepares excellent pastas and seasons them with herbs from the garden. One of the most popular dishes is the veil ossobuco with creamy Italian polenta. **CUISINE** Various. **CREDIT CARDS** AmEx; Diners; MasterCard

Estrada Mauá–Maringá, Km 4
TEL (24) 3387-1550. Mon – Thu, 7pm – 10pm (plus 1pm – 3pm in July and January); Fri and Sat, 1pm – 5pm and 7pm – midnight; Sun, 1pm – 6pm

Terra da Luz $$

Located inside the guesthouse of the same name, this lively restaurant features jazz performances on Saturdays. Try the mushroom risotto with trout, the lamb with couscous or the cheese fondue. **CUISINE** Contemporary. **CREDIT CARDS** AmEx; Diners; MasterCard

Estrada Mauá-Maringá, Km 6.5
TEL (24) 3387-1306. Fri – Sun, 8pm – 1am

Vitória – Espírito Santo

AREA CODE 27 **INHABITANTS** 314,042 **DISTANCES** Rio de Janeiro 525 kilometers (326 miles); Belo Horizonte 526 kilometers (327 miles) **ACCESS** Highways BR-381 and BR-262 from Belo Horizonte. Highway BR-101 from Rio de Janeiro www.vitoria.es.gov.br

WHERE TO STAY

Hotel Ilha do Boi $$

This Senac hospitality-school hotel, located on top of a hill on Boi Island, has a view of Vitória Bay. A separate leisure area has a marina, tennis courts, and playground. The spacious rooms have discreet décor and balconies. **ACCOMMODATIONS** 95; air-conditioning; minibar; pay TV; phone; private safe. **FACILITIES AND SERVICES** bar; boat; function room; Internet access; parking; playground; pool; restaurant; sauna; tennis court; trails; valet service; video room; 24-hour room service. **CREDIT CARDS** AmEx; Diners; MasterCard; Visa

Rua Bráulio Macedo, 417, Ilha do Boi
TEL (27) 3345-0111 RESERVATIONS 0800-2839991
www.hotelilhadoboi.com.br

Novotel Vitória $$

Located on the beachfront avenue, this building has ample common areas and modern décor. With a busi-

| PRICES | HOTELS (couple) | $ up to R$ 150 | $$ from R$ 151 up to R$ 300 | $$$ from R$ 301 up to R$500 | $$$$ above R$ 500 |

566

BRAZIL GUIDE

ness center and a 24-hour cyber café, it's great for both executives and tourists looking for leisure and beaches. It offers towels, chairs, and beach umbrellas to beachgoers. **ACCOMMODATIONS** 162; air-conditioning; Internet access; minibar; pay TV; phone; private safe. **FACILITIES AND SERVICES** bar; business center; cyber café; function room; gym; Internet access; parking; pool; restaurant; sauna; travel agency; 24-hour kitchen. **CREDIT CARDS** AmEx; Diners; MasterCard; Visa
Avenida Saturnino de Brito, 1,327, Praia do Canto
TEL (27) 3183-2500 **FAX** (27) 3183-2555
www.accorhotels.com.br

WHERE TO EAT

Estação Primeira de Manguinhos $$
Located in Manguinhos, some 30 kilometers (19 miles) from Vitória, this restaurant has a seaside garden with tables arranged under thatched gazebos. The peixe à jardineira is a highlight: muttonfish, snapper, or grouper baked in olice oil with vegetables. It can take a while to prepare, so go out after you order and enjoy the beach. A train car next to the restaurant hosts cultural events. **CUISINE** Fish and seafood. **CREDIT CARDS** AmEx; Diners; MasterCard; Visa
Avenida Atapuã, no #, corner of Rua Piraquira, Praia Ponta dos Fachos, Balneário de Manguinhos
TEL (27) 3243-2687. Tue – Sun, 10am – 5pm. At night, only with reservations.

Lareira Portuguesa $$
This restaurant is quiet and elegant, with well-trained staff adept at recommending wine pairings. The menu has tasty charbroiled codfish (au gratin, with peppers and capers), and mariscada (a type of bouillabaisse, that includes codfish), among other offerings. **CUISINE** Portuguese. **CREDIT CARDS** AmEx; Visa
Rua Saturnino de Brito, 260, Praia do Canto
TEL (27) 3345-0329. Mon – Sat, 11:30am – 3pm and 6:30pm – midnight; Sun, 11:30am – 4:30pm

Oriundi $$
This small, congenial restaurant has efficient service. Chef-owner Juarez is usually visible in the glassed-in kitchen, where he prepares filé crosta (crusted fillet) with powdered mushrooms and shiitake risotto and penne gambere with shrimp and mushroom sauce. There's a wine cellar. **CUISINE** Italian. **CREDIT CARDS** MasterCard; Diners
Rua Elias Tomasi Sobrinho, 130, Santa Lúcia
TEL (27) 3227-6989. Mon, 11:30am – 2:30pm; Tue – Thu, 11:30am – 2:30pm and 7pm – 11:30pm; Fri and Sat, 11:30am – 2:30pm and 7pm – 1am; Sun, noon – 3:30pm

Pirão $$
Attention to detail and fresh ingredients earned this sophisticated restaurant its good name. It's famous for its moquecas (stews), salted grouper, and torta capixaba (seafood pie). The pastelzinho de Belém (cream puff) is the most popular dessert. **CUISINE** Regional. **CREDIT CARDS** MasterCard; Visa
Rua Joaquim Lírio, 753, Praia do Canto
TEL (27) 3227-1165. Mon – Fri, 11am – 4pm and 6pm – midnight; Sat and Sun, 11am – 5pm

SERVICES

Airport – Aeroporto de Vitória Eurico Sales
Avenida Fernando Ferrari, no #, Goiabeiras
TEL (27) 3235-6300

Boat hire – Dolphin Pesca Oceânica
Rua Paulo Miled, 63, Mezzanine Store #201, Barro Vermelho
TEL (27) 3345-9455, 9981-3699. Mon – Fri, 9am – 6pm

Boat hire – Iate Clube do Espírito Santo
Information on boat hire.
Praça do Iate, 200, Praia do Canto
TEL (27) 3225-0422. Mon – Fri, 8am – 6pm; Sat, 8am – noon

Diving operators – Acquasub
Rua Anísio Fernandes Coelho, 30, Store #1, Jardim da Penha
TEL (27) 3325-0036. Mon – Fri, 9am – 8pm; Sat, 9am – 1pm

Diving operators – Flamar
Rua Almirante Tamandaré, 255, Praia do Suá
TEL (27) 3227-9644. Mon – Fri, 9am – 7pm; Sat, 9am – noon

Local tour operators – Fomatur
Trips through the region and rafting.
Rua Adalberto Simon Nader, 985, República
TEL (27) 3200-3155, 9944-0685. Mon – Fri, 8am – 6pm

Local tour operators – Vitória Receptive
City tours.
Avenida Marechal Mascarenhas de Moraes, 1,627, Ilha de Montebelo
TEL (27) 3322-2247. Mon – Fri, 9am – 6pm; Sat, 9am – noon

Tourist Police station – Delegacia de Atendimento ao Turista
Avenida Américo Buaiz, 200 (Shopping Vitória)
TEL (27) 3137-9117. Mon – Fri, 10am – 10pm

RESTAURANTS	**$** up to R$ 50	**$$** from R$ 51 up to R$ 100	**$$$** from R$ 101 up to R$ 150	**$$$$** above R$ 150

USEFUL INFORMATION

Airports

Most of Brazil's airports have tourist information desks that provide useful listings such as accommodations options and telephone numbers for the city's tourist police. Most airports offer Internet access at cyber cafés or designated computer terminals. The addresses and telephone numbers of the airports mentioned in this guidebook are listed in the Hotel, Restaurant, and Services chapter.

AIRPORTS OF BRAZIL'S MAJOR CITIES

Aracaju – Sergipe
Aeroporto Santa Maria
TEL (79) 3212-8500, 3212-8557

Belo Horizonte – Minas Gerais
Aeroporto da Pampulha (Carlos Drummond de Andrade)
TEL (31) 3490-2001
Aeroporto Internacional Tancredo Neves (Confins)
TEL (31) 3689-2701, 3689-2702

Brasília – Distrito Federal
Aeroporto Internacional de Brasília Presidente Juscelino Kubitschek
TEL (61) 3364-9000

Campo Grande – Mato Grosso do Sul
Aeroporto Internacional de Campo Grande
TEL (67) 3368-6000

Cuiabá – Mato Grosso
Aeroporto Internacional Marechal Rondon
TEL (65) 3614-2500

Florianópolis – Santa Catarina
Aeroporto Internacional Hercílio Luz
TEL (48) 3331-4000

Fortaleza – Ceará
Aeroporto Internacional Pinto Martins
TEL (85) 3392-1030

João Pessoa – Paraíba
Aeroporto Internacional Presidente Castro Pinto
TEL (83) 3041-4200

Maceió – Alagoas
Aeroporto Internacional Zumbi dos Palmares
TEL (82) 3036-5200

Natal – Rio Grande do Norte
Aeroporto Internacional Augusto Severo
TEL (84) 3087-1200

Porto Alegre – Rio Grande do Sul
Aeroporto Internacional Salgado Filho
TEL (51) 3358-2000

Recife – Pernambuco
Aeroporto Internacional dos Guararapes/Gilberto Freyre
TEL (81) 3322-4353

Rio de Janeiro – Rio de Janeiro
Aeroporto Internacional do Rio de Janeiro/Galeão – Antônio Carlos Jobim
TEL (21) 3398-5050
Aeroporto Santos Dumont
TEL (21) 3814-7070

Salvador – Bahia
Aeroporto Internacional Deputado Luís Eduardo Magalhães
TEL (71) 3204-1555, 3204-1544

São Luís – Maranhão
Aeroporto Marechal Cunha Machado
TEL (98) 3217-6133

São Paulo – São Paulo
Aeroporto Internacional de Congonhas
TEL (11) 5090-9000, 5090-9195
Aeroporto Internacional São Paulo/Guarulhos
(Aeroporto Internacional de Cumbica)
TEL (11) 6445-2945

Teresina – Piauí
Aeroporto Senador Petrônio Portela
TEL (86) 3133-6270

Airline Companies

GOL – (11) 0800-7040465;
RESERVATIONS: 0300-1152121 www.voegol.com.br
OCEAN AIR – CALLING FROM MAJOR CAPITALS: (11) 4004-4040;
CALLING FROM OTHER LOCATIONS: 0300-7898160
www.oceanair.com.br
RICO – (92) 4009-8333 www.voerico.com.br
PANTANAL LINHAS AÉREAS – (11) 5044-8957, 0800-7025888
www.voepantanal.com.br
TAM – CALLING FROM ALL CAPITALS: (11) 4002-5700;
CALLING FROM OTHER LOCATIONS: 0800-5705700
www.tam.com.br
TRIP – (19) 3743-3100/0800-558747;
RESERVATIONS: 0300-7898747 www.voetrip.com.br

ESTIMATED FLIGHT TIME BETWEEN CAPITALS[*]

Brasília–Belo Horizonte	1hr10min	741 km (460 mi)
Brasília–Rio	1hr37min	1148 km (713 mi)
Brasília–São Paulo	1hr30min	1015 km (631 mi)
Curitiba–Florianópolis	45min	300 km (186 mi)
Curitiba–Porto Alegre	55min	711 km (442 mi)
Florianópolis–Porto Alegre	50min	476 km (296 mi)
Fortaleza–Salvador	1hr35min	1389 km (863 mi)
Manaus–Belém	3hr	5298 km (3292 mi)
Recife–Salvador	1hr10min	839 km (521 mi)
Recife–Fortaleza	1hr15min	800 km (497 mi)
Rio–Belo Horizonte	50min	434 km (270 mi)
Rio–Recife	2hr45min	2338 km (1453 mi)
Rio–Salvador	2hr	1649 km (1025 mi)
Salvador–Porto Seguro	50min	653 km (406 mi)
São Paulo–Belo Horizonte	1hr	586 km (364 mi)
São Paulo–Campo Grande	1hr40min	1014 km (630 mi)
São Paulo–Curitiba	50min	408 km (254 mi)
São Paulo–Florianópolis	1hr05min	705 km (438 mi)
São Paulo–Manaus	3hr30min	3971 km (2467 mi)
São Paulo–Porto Alegre	1hr30min	1109 km (689 mi)
São Paulo–Recife	3hr08min	2660 km (1653 mi)
São Paulo–Rio	45min	429 km (267 mi)
São Paulo–Salvador	2hr15min	1962 km (1219 mi)

*Sources: Airlines Departamento Nacional de Infra-estrutura de Transportes

Highways

Brazil has municipal, state, and federal highways. Some are run by private concessionaires that also offer services such as medical assistance, towing, rescue, and rest areas. The public and private toll highways are generally in a better state of repair. Before heading out on a road trip, contact the federal and state highway patrols about road conditions and maintenance updates along the highways you plan to travel. Consider asking about the appropriate type of car (4×4 or passenger), available services, and toll fees. In some regions there are few gas and service stations, so keep your tank topped up and take food and water with you. Much of this information can also be found on the websites of the Brazilian Road Association (Associação Brasileira das Concessionárias de Rodovias: www.abcr.org.br) and the National Department for Transport Infrastructure (Transport Departamento Nacional de Infra-estrutura de Transportes: www.dnit.gov.br).

STATE HIGHWAY PATROL
Alagoas – (82) 3231-8026, 3217-9200
Bahia – (71) 3301-9868, 3301-7590, 3301-9440
Ceará – (85) 3383-1674, 3383-2444
Distrito Federal – (61) 3367-6423, 3302-1133
Espírito Santo – (27) 3244-3742
Goiás – (62) 3295-3113, 3201-6311
Mato Grosso do Sul – (67) 3388-7700
Minas Gerais – (31) 2123-1900, 2123-1903, 2123-1926
Paraíba – (83) 3231-3366
Paraná – (41) 3273-6622
Pernambuco – (81) 3181-3620
Rio de Janeiro – (21) 3399-4857, 3399-4856
Rio Grande do Norte – (84) 3318-3440
Rio Grande do Sul – (51) 3339-6799
Santa Catarina – (48) 3271-2300
São Paulo – (11) 3327-2727
Sergipe – (79) 3179-3567
Tocantins – (63) 3215-7991

FEDERAL HIGHWAY PATROL
Alagoas – (82) 3324-1135
Amazonas – (92) 3216-5270
Bahia – (71) 2101-2201, 2101-2250
Ceará – (85) 3295-3591
Distrito Federal – (61) 3394-3420
Espírito Santo – (27) 3212-6900
Goiás – (62) 3901-3700
Maranhão – (98) 3244-5390
Mato Grosso – (65) 3322-0005
Mato Grosso do Sul – (67) 3320-3600
Minas Gerais – (31) 3064-5300
Pará – (91) 3242-1800
Paraíba – (83) 3231-7711, 3231-3366
Paraná – (41) 3361-8500
Pernambuco – (81) 3464-0707, 3464-0700
Piauí – (86) 3233-1414
Rio de Janeiro – (21) 3503-9000
Rio Grande do Norte – (84) 4009-1550, 4009-1555
Rio Grande do Sul – (51) 3374-0003
Santa Catarina – (48) 3389-8038, 3288-0250
São Paulo – (11) 2795-2300
Sergipe – (79) 2107-3999
Tocantins – (63) 3215-7991

Car Rental Companies
Avis – (11) 2155-2847, 0800-198456, 0800-7252847
www.avis.com.br
Hertz – (11) 2246-4200, 0800-7017300 www.hertz.com.br
Localiza – 0800-9792000 www.localiza.com
Mobility – (11) 5091-7771, 0800-160525
www.mobility.com.br

Taxis
Find taxis at official taxi stands or call the central office. When requesting the service, check if the company charges for the trip to pick up the passenger. Ride rates are fixed and generally consist of an initial fee plus a per-kilometer charge. If there has been a recent price adjustment and the meter has not been recalibrated, a new price table pasted on the window will show the corrected value in relation to the meter reading. Prices are approximately 20%

to 30% higher at night, in the early morning hours, and on Sundays and public holidays. There is a surcharge to use the trunk or boot. In some locations, taxis charge a fixed rate for a trip from the airport to the city's downtown area.

Safety
IN THE CITIES: Avoid flaunting valuables such as expensive jewelry and watches. Be careful about carrying cameras and laptops, and leave them in your hotel whenever practical. Stay clear of poorly lit, deserted streets, especially at night. Keep a firm hold on backpacks and handbags, and wear them across the front of your body if you can. Men should avoid putting wallets in their back pockets, and all travelers should keep important items like passports and plane tickets in concealed pouches underneath their clothing. Split up your money and keep it in different pockets so you aren't left penniless if a pickpocket strikes.
AT ATMS: Look for ATMs in busy places, like shopping centers. In some places, there is a limit to the amount that can be withdrawn between 10pm and 6am.
IN THE CAR: Avoid asking for or giving lifts. Never stay long in a parked car. In big cities, keep your windows up, even during the day. Keep doors locked and don't leave belongings in view.
AT THE BEACH: Only take the money you need for the day. Don't leave belongings on the sand while you go for a walk or swim. Don't hang handbags over the backs of chairs at kiosks, bars, and restaurants.
AT THE SOCCER STADIUM: To avoid encounters with rowdy fans, get numbered seats (some are even covered) as opposed to the stadium seating, where most local spectators go. Don't carry valuable belongings. Try to get to the stadium about 40 minutes before the match starts and leave after most of the crowd has gone. Don't wear team jerseys and avoid public transport to get to and from the stadium. Go by car or taxi, keep the windows rolled up, and be prepared for slow-moving traffic. Don't park on the street or in improvised locations.
AT THE HOTEL: Stow valuables and documents in the safe. Don't accept services you haven't requested.
ON PUBLIC TRANSPORT: Before you get on, set aside the money you need to pay the fare so you don't have to open your wallet in public. Avoid waiting alone at out-of-the-way bus stops, especially at night. In empty buses, sit near the driver, and avoid train carriages that have few passengers. When carrying handbags, backpacks, and briefcases, always try to keep them in front of your body.

TOURIST POLICE DIVISIONS
Several states offer special police divisions with officers trained to handle crimes involving tourists and foreigners. In locations that do not offer this service, complaints may be registered at regular police stations. For further information, consult the local civil police.

ALAGOAS (Maceió): Rua Abdom Assis, no #, Jatiúca, (82) 3327-6009
AMAZONAS (Manaus): Aeroporto Internacional Eduardo Gomes, Avenida Santos Dumont, 1350, Tarumã, Posto da Polícia Militar, (92) 3652-1197, 3652-1210
BAHIA (Salvador): Praça Anchieta, 14, Pelourinho, (71) 3116-6817
CEARÁ (Fortaleza): Avenida Almirante Barroso, 805, Praia de Iracema, (85) 3101-2488
DISTRITO FEDERAL (Brasília): Aeroporto Internacional de Brasília, Área Especial Lago Sul, Posto da Polícia Civil, (61) 3364-9461
ESPÍRITO SANTO (Vitória): Avenida Américo Buaiz, 200, Enseada do Suã (Shopping Vitória), (27) 3137-9117
GOIÁS (Goiânia): Aeroporto de Goiânia, Praça Capitão Frasão,

913, Setor Santa Genoveva, Posto da Polícia Civil, (62) 3201-2365

MARANHÃO (São Luís): Rua da Estrela, 427, Centro, (98) 3214-8682

MINAS GERAIS (Belo Horizonte): Aeroporto Internacional Tancredo Neves (Confins), Rodovia MG-010, Km 39, Confins, Grande Belo Horizonte, Posto da Polícia Civil, (31) 3689-2310, 3689-2315

PARÁ (Belém): Avenida Magalhães Barata, 209, Nazaré, (91) 4006-9000

PARAÍBA (João Pessoa): Avenida Tamandaré, 100, Store #1, Tambaú, (83) 3214-8022

PERNAMBUCO (Recife): Aeroporto dos Guararapes, no #, Imbiribeira, tel. (81) 3322-4867

PIAUÍ (Teresina): Rua Barroso, 241, Centro, (86) 3216-5212 Rio de Janeiro (Rio de Janeiro): Rua Humberto de Campos, 315, Leblon, (21) 3399-7170

RIO GRANDE DO NORTE (Natal): Avenida Engenheiro Roberto Freire, 8790, Praia Shopping, Ponta Negra, (84) 3232-7402

RIO GRANDE DO SUL (Porto Alegre): Aeroporto Internacional Salgado Filho, Avenida Severo Dulius, 90010, São João, Posto da Polícia Civil, (51) 3358-2255

SANTA CATARINA (Florianópolis): Avenida Paulo Fontes, 1101, Centro, tel. (48) 3333-2103

SÃO PAULO (São Paulo): Rua da Consolação, 247, Store #8, Consolação, (11) 3257-4475, 3151-4167, 3120-4417

SERGIPE (Aracaju): Avenida Santos Dumont, no #, Praia de Atalaia, (79) 3255-2155

TOCANTINS (Palmas): Avenida Juscelino Kubistchek, 164, Quadra 103 Sul, Plano Diretor Sul, (63) 3218-6874

POLICE REPORTS BY INTERNET

In some states a police report may be registered by Internet for the loss or theft of documents:

RIO DE JANEIRO (www.delegaciavirtual.rj.gov.br)

RIO GRANDE DO SUL (www.pc.rs.gov.br)

SANTA CATARINA (www.ssp.sc.gov.br)

SÃO PAULO (www.ssp.sp.gov.br)

Health

Yellow fever is a hazard in the North and Central-West regions, the states of Maranhão and Minas Gerais, the southwest of Piauí, the west of Bahia, the west of Paraná, the west of Santa Catarina, the northwest of Rio Grande do Sul, and the northwest of São Paulo. This infectious disease is transmitted by mosquito bites. Those planning to travel in these regions should get vaccinated 10 days before traveling. Vaccines are available at the ports, airports, and border posts. There is no vaccine for malaria, also transmitted by a mosquito bite, which is primarily a problem in the Amazon region. The best protection is to use repellents on all exposed skin, sleep in places protected by window screens and mosquito nets, wear long pants and long-sleeved shirts, preferably in light colors, and use insecticides in all rooms. In parks or forests, use repellents and avoid going out after 5pm. Diarrhea is very common among travelers. To prevent it, avoid eating raw vegetables and fruits from street stands or other locations with questionable hygiene standards. Steer clear of nonpasteurised milk. Safer bets include dry food like breads and crackers, peelable fruits, bottled or boiled water. Piping-hot cooked meals are fine, as long as hands, plates, and utensils are clean. Do not drink water from fountains even if it appears clear; also avoid ice. Sunscreens are essential throughout the country, due to the strong tropical sun.

MEDICAL ASSISTANCE FOR TRAVELERS

For those traveling internationally, vaccines are given at the airports and in specialized health clinics. If you are traveling within Brazil, they can also be taken at bus stations and public health clinics.

AMAZONAS (Manaus): Aeroporto Internacional Eduardo Gomes, (92) 3652-1498

BAHIA (Salvador): Aeroporto Internacional Luís Eduardo Magalhães, (71) 3377-3138

DISTRITO FEDERAL (Brasília): Aeroporto Internacional de Brasília, (61) 3364-9228, 3364-9220

RIO DE JANEIRO (Rio de Janeiro): Aeroporto Internacional do Rio de Janeiro/Galeão–Antônio Carlos Jobim, (21) 3398-2377

RIO GRANDE DO SUL (Porto Alegre): Aeroporto Internacional Salgado Filho, (51) 3358-2459

SÃO PAULO (São Paulo): Aeroporto Internacional de Congonhas, (11) 5093-6308; Aeroporto Internacional de Guarulhos, (11) 6445-2308

Public Restrooms

Public restrooms in Brazil are limited to airports, bus stations, malls, and locations with masses of people. In emergencies, find a hotel, bar, bakery, or restaurant that looks adequate. It is often not necessary to purchase anything to use the facilities.

Currency Exchange

Exchange rates are published daily in all major Brazilian newspapers and are announced on the evening TV news. Banks generally offer better rates than currency exchange agencies, but the process is usually more bureaucratic and there are additional fees. The exchange agencies located in the major cities accept travelers' checks issued by major international institutions.

Internet

Most small towns have access to the World Wide Web via computers in cyber cafés, hotels, libraries, malls, and post offices. Large centers have wireless and broadband access. Many hotels offer Internet access in the rooms.

Time Zones

Brazil has four time zones and most of the country is within the Brasilia time zone (3 hours behind GMT). Mato Grosso, Mato Grosso do Sul, Rondônia, Roraima, most of the Amazon, and half of Pará are one hour behind Brasilia; Acre and the southwestern portion of the Amazon are two hours behind Brasilia. Fernando de Noronha, east of Brasilia, is one hour ahead. The Southeast, South, and Central-West regions adjust their clocks for Daylight Savings between October and February, which puts them one hour ahead of their normal time relative to the rest of the country. If you are traveling close to the time change dates, verify the exact dates and check your flight times with the airline companies.

Climate

Brazil's tropical location makes for a hot climate that – whether it's humid or not – has minimal differences between minimum and maximum temperatures. Throughout most of Brazil, between December and February, the somewhat hotter summer season is usually rainy. A colder and drier winter prevails from June through August. The climactic differences of spring, from September to December, and autumn, from March to June, are less distinct. In the summer, the high relative humidity makes the atmosphere oppressive. In Rio de Janeiro the temperature at the beach may vary between 30°C and 40°C (86°F and 104°F) – away from the beach, the average summer temperature is 27° C (81° F). Porto Alegre, in Rio Grande do Sul, is cooler but even more humid and heavy-aired. The Northeastern coast is even hotter, although the humidity is lower and the constant ocean breeze alleviates discomfort. In the *sertão* (backlands), there are long periods of drought punctuated by torrential rains in the summer. In the Amazon, on the other hand, it rains all year long. In the South there is a more distinct difference between the four seasons, and the winter is much colder. In some parts of the mountains in Rio Grande do Sul, it even snows. In the Pantanal wetlands, the seasons can basically be divided into the rainy season (November to April) and the dry season (May to September).

Getting Around

Brazil doesn't have an extensive train network, although short train rides are sometimes offered for sightseeing purposes. The best way to travel between cities is by plane or coach.

Holidays

Brazil's national holidays include:

JANUARY 1st New Year's Day
FEBRUARY/MARCH Carnival (floating date)
MARCH/APRIL Easter (floating date)
APRIL 21st Tiradentes (in memory of the man who was hung for leading an independence movement in Brazil against the Portuguese crown)
MAY 1st Labor Day
MAY/JUNE Corpus Christi (floating date)
SEPTEMBER 7th Independence Day
OCTOBER 12th Our Lady Aparecida
NOVEMBER 2nd All Souls' Day
NOVEMBER 15th Proclamation of the Republic
DECEMBER 25th Christmas

Major Regional Events

ALAGOAS
Tradições Populares Festival (folk festival) and Bom Jesus de Penedo Procession, in Penedo – second weekend in January
São Sebastião Festival, in Barra de Santo Antônio – January
São João de Maceió, in Maceió – June
Maceió Fest, in Maceió – November

AMAZONAS
Parintins Folk Festival, in Parintins – last week of June

BAHIA
Nosso Senhor do Bonfim Festival, in Salvador – first Monday after Epiphany (January 6th)
São Sebastião Festival, in Trancoso – January 20th
Iemanjá Festival, in Salvador – February 2nd
Glorioso Espírito Santo Festival, on Ilha de Boipeba – early June (floating date)
Nossa Senhora da Boa Morte Festival, in Recôncavo Baiano – August 15th and 16th

CEARÁ
Processions in honor of Padre Cícero, in Juazeiro do Norte – September 15th; October 30th to November 2nd; January 30th to February 2nd
Fortal (off-season carnival), in Fortaleza – July

ESPÍRITO SANTO
Ticumbi and Alardo folk performances (in honor of Saint Benedict and Saint Sebastian, respectively), in Itaúnas – January 19th and 20th
Festival Nacional do Forró and Encontro Nacional de Forró Pé-de-Serra (*forró* dance festivals), in Itaúnas – July
Vital (off-season carnival), in Vitória – November

GOIÁS
Fogaréu (Procession of the Torches), in Goiás – Easter (floating date)

Divino Espírito Santo Festival, in Pirenópolis – May or June
International Film Festival (Fica), in Goiás – June

MARANHÃO
Divino Espírito Santo Festival, in Alcântara – May
Bumba-meu-boi (folk festival), in São Luís – June 23

MATO-GROSSO
International Fishing Festival, in Cáceres – second fortnight in September

MINAS GERAIS
Film Festival, in Tiradentes – January
Holy Week Processions in Ouro Preto – Holy Week
Harley Davidson Meet, in Tiradentes – June
International Culture and Cooking Festival, in Tiradentes – August
Jabuticaba Festival, in Sabará – October and November

PARÁ
Círio de Nazaré Festival, in Belém – second weekend in October

PARANÁ
Curitiba Theater Festival – March

PERNAMBUCO
The Passion of Christ, in Fazenda Nova – Easter (floating date)
Circuito do Frio (winter festival), in Garanhuns, Pesqueira, Triunfo, and Taquaritinga – August
Olinda, Arte em Toda Parte (art festival), in Olinda – November

RIO DE JANEIRO
Rio de Janeiro City Marathon – June
Festa Literária Internacional de Paraty (literary festival) – July
International Half Marathon of Rio de Janeiro, in Rio de Janeiro – second half of the year (floating date)

RIO GRANDE DO NORTE
Carnatal (off-season carnival), in Natal – beginning of December

RIO GRANDE DO SUL
Gramado Film Festival – first fortnight in August
Porto Alegre Book Fair – late October through early November

SANTA CATARINA
War of the Farrapos reenactment, in Laguna – July 22nd
Oktoberfest, in Blumenau – October

SÃO PAULO
São Paulo Fashion Week, in São Paulo – January and July
Divino Espírito Santo Festival, in São Luís do Paraitinga – May and June
Winter Festival, in Campos do Jordão – July
International Sailing Week, in Ilhabela – July
São Paulo Art Biennial, in São Paulo – October and November
São Silvestre International Race – December 31st
São Paulo International Marathon – floating date

SERGIPE
Encontro Cultural (cultural festival), in Laranjeiras – January
Forró Caju (*forró* dance festival), in Aracaju – June

Emergency Numbers

The telephone numbers for emergency and support services are standardized throughout the country. They are toll-free numbers and calls may be made from any public telephone.

Ambulance – 192
Civil Defense – 199
Civil Police – 197
Department of Sanitary Surveillance – 0800-61-1997
Department of Transport (DETRAN) – 154
Federal Highway Patrol – 191
Federal Police – 194
Fire Department – 193
IBAMA (Brazilian Institute for the Environment and Renewable Natural Resources) – 0800-61-8080
Military Police – 190

CONSULATES

ARGENTINA
Belo Horizonte – MG
Tel: (31) 3281-5288

Curitiba – PR
Tel: (41) 3222-0799

Florianópolis – SC
Tel: (48) 3024-3035, 3024-3036

Foz do Iguaçu – PR
Tel: (45) 3574-2969

Porto Alegre – RS
Tel: (51) 3321-1360

Recife – PE
Tel: (81) 3327-1451, 3327-1497

Rio de Janeiro – RJ
Tel: (21) 2553-1646

Salvador – BA
Tel: (71) 3241-4863

São Paulo – SP
Tel: (11) 3897-9522

AUSTRALIA
São Paulo – SP
Tel: (11) 2112-6200
www.cdasp.org.br

AUSTRIA
Rio de Janeiro – RJ
Tel: (21) 2102-0020

São Paulo – SP
Tel: (11) 3842-7500

BELGIUM
Rio de Janeiro – RJ
Tel: (21) 2543-8558
www.diplomatie.be/riodejaneiro

São Paulo – SP
Tel: (11) 3171-1599
www.diplomatie.be/saopaulo

BOLIVIA
Cuiabá – MT
Tel: (65) 3627-1343

Rio de Janeiro – RJ
Tel: (21) 2552-5490

São Paulo – SP
Tel: (11) 3289-0443

BULGARIA
Rio de Janeiro – RJ
Tel: (21) 2532-3912
www.bulgariario.org.br

CANADA
Rio de Janeiro – RJ
Tel: (21) 2543-3004

São Paulo – SP
Tel: (11) 5509-4321
www.brasil.gc.ca

CHILE
Porto Alegre – RS
Tel: (51) 3346-3970
www.congechile.com.br

Rio de Janeiro – RJ
Tel: (21) 2552-5349

São Paulo – SP
Tel: (11) 3284-2044
www.congechilesaopaulo.com.br

CHINA
Rio de Janeiro – RJ
Tel: (21) 2551-4578
http://riodejaneiro.china-consulate.org/pot/

São Paulo – SP
Tel: (11) 3082-9877
saopaulo.china-consulate.org

COLOMBIA
Manaus – AM
Tel: (92) 3234-6777

São Paulo – SP
Tel: (11) 3078-0322

COSTA RICA
São Paulo – SP
Tel: (11) 3875-2570, 3875-3430

CROATIA
São Paulo – SP
Tel: (11) 3815-4375

CUBA
São Paulo – SP
Tel: (11) 3873-2800

CZECH REPUBLIC
São Paulo – SP
Tel: (11) 3814-3728
www.mzv.cz/saopaulo

DENMARK
São Paulo – SP
Tel: (11) 3061-3625, 3068-9867

DOMINICAN REPUBLIC
São Paulo – SP
Tel: (11) 3868-2665

Rio de Janeiro – RJ
Tel: (21) 2553-3003

ECUADOR
São Paulo – SP
Tel: (11) 3031-7004
www.consulecuadorsp.com.br

FINLAND
São Paulo – SP
Tel: (11) 5087-9542
www.finlandia.org.br

FRANCE
Recife – PE
Tel: (81) 3465-3290

São Paulo – SP
Tel: (11) 3371-5400
www.consulfrance-saopaulo.org

Rio de Janeiro – RJ
Tel: (21) 3974-6699

GERMANY
Porto Alegre – RS
Tel: (51) 3224-9255
www.porto-alegre.diplo.de

Recife – PE
Tel: (81) 3463-5350
www.recife.diplo.de

Rio de Janeiro – RJ
Tel: (21) 2554-0004
www.rio-de-janeiro.diplo.de

São Paulo – SP
Tel: (11) 3097-6644
www.sao-paulo.diplo.de

GREECE
Rio de Janeiro – RJ
Tel: (21) 2552-6849

São Paulo – SP
Tel: (11) 3251-0675

GUATEMALA
Brasília – DF
Tel: (61) 3248-0573

GUYANA
Brasília – DF
Tel: (61) 3248-0874

HONDURAS
Rio de Janeiro – RJ
Tel: (21) 3813-5253

São Paulo – SP
Tel: (11) 3088-2993

HUNGARY
São Paulo – SP
Tel: (11) 5506-5011
www.hungria.org.br

ICELAND
Rio de Janeiro – RJ
Tel: (21) 2285-1795

INDIA
São Paulo – SP
Tel: (11) 3171-0340, 3171-0341
www.indiaconsulate.org.br

IRAN
Brasília – DF
Tel: (61) 3242-5733

IRELAND
São Paulo – SP
Tel: (11) 5506-8258

ISRAEL
Brasília – DF
Tel: (61) 2105-0500

ITALY
Belo Horizonte – MG
Tel: (31) 3281-4211, 3281-4224
www.consbelohorizonte.esteri.it

Curitiba – PR
Tel: (41) 3883-1750
www.conscuritiba.esteri.it

Porto Alegre – RS
Tel: (51) 3230-8200
www.consportoalegre.esteri.it

Recife – PE
Tel: (81) 3466-4200
www.consrecife.esteri.it

Rio de Janeiro – RJ
Tel: (21) 2282-1315
www.consriodejaneiro.esteri.it

São Paulo – SP
Tel: (11) 3549-5699
www.conssaopaulo.esteri.it

JAPAN
Belém – PA
Tel: (91) 3249-3344

Curitiba – PR
Tel: (41) 3322-4919

Manaus – AM
Tel: (92) 3232-2000

Porto Alegre – RS
Tel: (51) 3334-1299

Recife – PE
Tel: (81) 3465-9115

Rio de Janeiro – RJ
Tel: (21) 3461-9595
www.rio.br.emb-japan.go.jp

São Paulo – SP
Tel: (11) 3254-0100
www.sp.br.emb-japan.go.jp

LEBANON
Rio de Janeiro – RJ
Tel: (21) 2539-2125

São Paulo – SP
Tel: (11) 3262-0604

LIBYA
Brasília – DF
Tel: (61) 3248-6710

MALTA
Rio de Janeiro – RJ
Tel: (21) 2533-7274

MEXICO
Brasília – DF
Tel: (61) 3204-5200

Rio de Janeiro – RJ
Tel: (21) 3262-3200

São Paulo – SP
Tel: (11) 3081-4144

NETHERLANDS
Rio de Janeiro – RJ
Tel: (21) 2157-5400
www.mfa.nl/rio-pt

São Paulo – SP
Tel: (11) 3811-3300
www.mfa.nl/sao-pt

NEW ZEALAND
São Paulo – SP
Tel: (11) 3148-0616

NICARAGUA
São Paulo – SP
Tel: (11) 3283-0700

NORWAY
Rio de Janeiro – RJ
Tel: (21) 2541-7732

PANAMA
Rio de Janeiro – RJ
Tel: (21) 2255-9085

São Paulo – SP
Tel: (11) 3266-2923

PARAGUAY
Curitiba – PR
Tel: (41) 3222-9226

Rio de Janeiro – RJ
Tel: (21) 2553-2294

São Paulo – SP
Tel: (11) 3167-7793
www.paraguaysp.com.br

PERU
Rio de Janeiro – RJ
Tel: (21) 2551-4496

São Paulo – SP
Tel: (11) 3287-5555
www.consuladoperusp.com.br

POLAND
Rio de Janeiro – RJ
Tel: (21) 2551-8088

São Paulo – SP
Tel: (11) 3672-3778

PORTUGAL
Belém – PA
Tel: (91) 3241-6666
www.consportbelem.org.br

Belo Horizonte – MG
Tel: (31) 3291-8192

Brasília – DF
Tel: (61) 3032-9600

Curitiba – PR
Tel: (41) 3233-4211

Recife – PE
Tel: (81) 3327-2073, 3327-1514
www.secomunidades.pt/web/recife

Rio de Janeiro – RJ
Tel: (21) 3231-7250
http://www.consuladoportugalrj.
org.br/

Salvador – BA
Tel: (71) 3341-1499

São Paulo – SP
Tel: (11) 3084-1800
www.consuladoportugalsp.org.br

RUSSIA
Rio de Janeiro – RJ
Tel: (21) 2274-0097

São Paulo – SP
Tel: (11) 3814-4100

SAUDI ARABIA
Brasília – DF
Tel: (61) 3248-3525, 3248-2201

SLOVAKIA
São Paulo – SP
Tel: (11) 3255-9493
www.slovakiaconsulado.com.br

SOUTH AFRICA
São Paulo – SP
Tel: (11) 3265-0449
www.africadosul.org.br

SOUTH KOREA
São Paulo – SP
Tel: (11) 3141-1278

SPAIN
Porto Alegre – RS
Tel: (51) 3338-1300

Rio de Janeiro – RJ
Tel: (21) 2543-3200

Salvador – BA
Tel: (71) 3336-9055

São Paulo – SP
Tel: (11) 3059-1800
www.consuladoespanasp.org.br

SURINAME
Brasília – DF
Tel: (61) 3248-3595

SWEDEN
São Paulo – SP
Tel: (11) 5506-9994

SWITZERLAND
Brasília – DF
Tel: (61) 3443-5500

Rio de Janeiro – RJ
Tel: (21) 2221-1867

São Paulo – SP
Tel: (11) 3372-8200

SYRIA
São Paulo – SP
Tel: (11) 3285-5578

TURKEY
Brasília – DF
Tel: (61) 3226-1260, 3226-0970

Rio de Janeiro – RJ
Tel: (21) 2551-4673

UKRAINE
Curitiba – PR
Tel: (41) 3222-7773

Rio de Janeiro – RJ
Tel: (21) 2542-1704

UNITED ARAB EMIRATES
Brasilia – DF
Tel: (61) 3248-0717, 3248-0591

UNITED KINGDOM
Rio de Janeiro – RJ
Tel: (21) 2555-9600

São Paulo – SP
Tel: (11) 3094-2700

UNITED STATES
Rio de Janeiro – RJ
Tel: (21) 3823-2000

São Paulo – SP
Tel: (11) 5186-7000

URUGUAY
Belo Horizonte – MG
Tel: (31) 3296-7527

Brasília – DF
Tel: (61) 3322-1200

Florianópolis – SC
Tel: (48) 3222-3718

Porto Alegre – RS
Tel: (51) 3325-6198

Rio de Janeiro – RJ
Tel: (21) 2553-6015, 2553-6030

São Paulo – SP
Tel: (11) 3085-5941

VENEZUELA
Brasília – DF
Tel: (61) 3322-1011, 3322-9324

Rio de Janeiro – RJ
Tel: (21) 2551-5248
www.consuven.com.br

São Paulo – SP
Tel: (11) 3887-4583

EMBASSIES

MINISTRY OF FOREIGN RELATIONS
www.mre.gov.br
Tel: (61) 3411-6161, 3411-6456

EMBASSIES IN BRASÍLIA
Algeria
Tel: (61) 3248-4039

Angola
Tel: (61) 3248-4489

Argentina
www.brasil.embajada-argentina.gov.ar
Tel: (61) 3364-7600

Australia
www.brazil.embassy.gov.au
Tel: (61) 3226-3111

Austria
www.austria.org.br
Tel: (61) 3443-3111

Belgium
www.belgica.org.br
Tel: (61) 3443-1133

Bolivia
www.embolivia-brasil.org.br
Tel: (61) 3366-3432

Bulgaria
Tel: (61) 3223-6193, 3223-9849

Cameroon
www.embcameroun.org.br
Tel: (61) 3248-2400

Canada
www.canadainternational.gc.ca/brazil
Tel: (61) 3424-5400

Cape Verde
Tel: (61) 3364-3472

Chile
Tel: (61) 2103-5151

China
www.embchina.org.br
Tel: (61) 3346-4436

Colombia
www.embcol.org.br
Tel: (61) 3226-8997

Costa Rica
Tel: (61) 3328-2219, 3328-2485

Croatia
Tel: (61) 3248-0610

Cuba
www.embaixadacuba.org.br
Tel: (61) 3248-4710, 3248-4130

Czech Republic
www.mzv.cz/brasilia
Tel: (61) 3242-7785, 3242-7905

Democratic Republic of Congo
Tel: (61) 3365-4822

Denmark
Tel: (61) 3445-3443

Dominican Republic
Tel: (61) 3248-1405

Ecuador
www.embequador.org.br
Tel: (61) 3248-5360

Egypt
www.opengate.com.br/embegito
Tel: (61) 3323-8800

El Salvador
Tel: (61) 3364-4141

Finland
www.finlandia.org.br
Tel: (61) 3443-7151

France
www.ambafrance.org.br
Tel: (61) 3222-3999

Gabon
Tel: (61) 3248-3536, 3248-3533

Germany
www.brasilia.diplo.de
Tel: (61) 3442-7000

Ghana
Tel: (61) 3248-6047, 3248-6049

Greece
www.emb-grecia.org.br
Tel: (61) 3443-6573

Guatemala
Tel: (61) 3248-0573

Guyana
Tel: (61) 3248-0874

Haiti
Tel: (61) 3248-6860, 3248-1337

Honduras
Tel: (61) 3366-4082

Hungary
http://www.mfa.gov.hu/kulkepvis
elet/BR/HU
Tel: (61) 3443-0822

India
www.indianembassy.org.br
Tel: (61) 3248-4006

Indonesia
www.indonesia-brasil.org.br
Tel: (61) 3443-8800

Iran
www.webiran.org.br
Tel: (61) 3242-5733

Iraq
Tel: (61) 3346-2822

Ireland
Tel: (61) 3248-8800

Israel
brasilia.mfa.gov.il
Tel: (61) 2105-0500

Italy
www.ambbrasilia.esteri.it
Tel: (61) 3442-9900

Japan
http://www.br.emb-japan.go.jp/
Tel: (61) 3442-4200

Jordan
Tel: (61) 3248-5407, 3248-5414

Kuwait
Tel: (61) 3213-2333

Lebanon
www.libano.org.br
Tel: (61) 3443-3808

Libya
Tel: (61) 3248-6710, 3248-6716

Malaysia
Tel: (61) 3248-5008, 3248-6215

Malta
Tel: (61) 3272-0402

Mexico
www.mexico.org.br
Tel: (61) 3244-1011

Morocco
www.embmarrocos.org.br
Tel: (61) 3321-4487

Mozambique
Tel: (61) 3248-4222, 3248-5319

Namibia
Tel: (61) 3248-7621

Netherlands
www.mfa.nl/bra-pt
Tel: (61) 3961-3200

New Zealand
Tel: (61) 3248-9900

Nicaragua
Tel: (61) 3248-1115, 3248-7902

Nigeria
Tel: (61) 3226-1717, 3226-1870

North Korea
Tel: (61) 3367-1940

Norway
www.noruega.org.br
Tel: (61) 3443-8720

Pakistan
Tel: (61) 3364-1632

Panama
Tel: (61) 3248-7309

Paraguay
Tel: (61) 3242-3732

Peru
www.embperu.org.br
Tel: (61) 3242-9933, 3242-9435

Philippines
Tel: (61) 3224-8694

Poland
www.polonia.org.br
Tel: (61) 3212-8000

Portugal
www.embaixadadeportugal.org.br
Tel: (61) 3032-9600

Romania
Tel: (61) 3226-0746

Russia
www.brazil.mid.ru
Tel: (61) 3223-3094, 3223-4094

Saudi Arabia
Tel: (61) 3248-3525, 3248-2201

Senegal
Tel: (61) 3223-6110, 3223-5866

Serbia
Tel: (61) 3223-7272

Slovakia
Tel: (61) 3443-1263

South Africa
www.africadosul.org.br
Tel: (61) 3312-9500

South Korea
Tel: (61) 3321-2500, 3321-2506

Spain
Tel: (61) 3701-1600, 3701-1638

Sri Lanka
Tel: (61) 3248-2701

Syria
Tel: (61) 3226-1260, 3226-0970

Sudan
Tel: (61) 3248-4834, 3248-4835

Suriname
Tel: (61) 3248-3595, 3248-6706

Sweden
Tel: (61) 3442-5200

Switzerland
www.eda.admin.ch/brasilia
Tel: (61) 3443-5500

Thailand
www.thaiembassy.org/brasilia
Tel: (61) 3224-6943, 3224-6849

Trinidad and Tobago
Tel: (61) 3365-1132, 3365-3466

Tunisia
Tel: (61) 3248-7277, 3248-7366

Turkey
www.turquia.org.br
Tel: (61) 3242-4563

Ukraine
www.ucrania.org.br
Tel: (61) 3365-1457

United Arab Emirates
www.uae.org.br
Tel: (61) 3248-0717, 3248-0591

United Kingdom
www.uk.org.br
Tel: (61) 3329-2300

United States
www.embaixada-
americana.org.br
Tel: (61) 3312-7000

Uruguay
www.emburuguai.org.br
Tel: (61) 3322-1200

Vatican
Tel: (61) 3223-0794

Venezuela
Tel: (61) 3322-1011, 3322-9324

Vietnam
Tel: (61) 3364-5876, 3364-0694

Zimbabwe
Tel: (61) 3365-4801, 3365-4802

Acknowledgements

Ana Aveline, Aniko Santos, Berenice Abreu, Carla Joner, Carolina Spinola Montenegro, Cleide Pinheiro, Cristiano Mascaro, Debora Regina Dias de Almeida, Enrique A. Litman, Fernando Costa Barros, Jefferson Souza da Silva, Leonor Franco de Araujo, Lucas Richbitter, Marcelo Spinola Montenegro, Marcos Spinola Montenegro, Maria Helena Carneiro da Cunha, Maria Rossi Samora, Max Perlingeiro, Roberto Carneiro de Mendonça, and Tarsila do Amaral.

We would like to thank the following institutions

Biblioteca do Museu de Arte Moderna de São Paulo (MAM-SP) and Instituto Baleia Franca

Credits